Cambridge Handbook of Routine Dynamics

Over the last two decades, Routine Dynamics has emerged as an international research community that shares a particular approach to organizational phenomena. At the heart of this approach is an interest in examining the emergence, reproduction, replication, and change of routines as recognizable patterns of actions. In contrast to other research communities interested in those phenomena, Routine Dynamics studies are informed by a distinctive set of theories (especially practice theory and related process-informed theories). This Handbook offers both an accessible introduction to core concepts and approaches in Routine Dynamics, as well as a comprehensive and authoritative overview of research in different areas of Routine Dynamics. The chapters of this Handbook are structured around four core themes: (1) Theoretical resources for research on the dynamics of routines, (2) Methodological issues in studying the dynamics routines, (3) Themes in Routine Dynamics research and (4) Relation of Routine Dynamics to other communities of thought.

MARTHA S. FELDMAN is Professor of Urban Planning and Public Policy, Management, Political Science and Sociology and the Johnson Chair for Civic Governance and Public Management, University of California, Irvine.

BRIAN T. PENTLAND is the Main Street Capital Partners Endowed Professor in the Department of Accounting and Information Systems at Michigan State University.

LUCIANA D'ADDERIO is Chancellor's Fellow in Data Driven Innovation at the University of Edinburgh.

KATHARINA DITTRICH is Associate Professor of Organisation Studies in the Organisation and Human Resource Management (OHRM) Group at Warwick Business School.

CLAUS RERUP is Professor of Management at the Frankfurt School of Finance & Management.

DAVID SEIDL is Professor of Organization and Management at the University of Zurich.

Cambridge Handbook of Routine Dynamics

Edited by

MARTHA S. FELDMAN
University of California, Irvine

BRIAN T. PENTLAND
Michigan State University

LUCIANA D'ADDERIO
University of Edinburgh

KATHARINA DITTRICH
University of Warwick

CLAUS RERUP
Frankfurt School of Finance & Management

DAVID SEIDL
University of Zurich

CAMBRIDGE
UNIVERSITY PRESS

CAMBRIDGE
UNIVERSITY PRESS

University Printing House, Cambridge CB2 8BS, United Kingdom

One Liberty Plaza, 20th Floor, New York, NY 10006, USA

477 Williamstown Road, Port Melbourne, VIC 3207, Australia

314–321, 3rd Floor, Plot 3, Splendor Forum, Jasola District Centre, New Delhi – 110025, India

103 Penang Road, #05–06/07, Visioncrest Commercial, Singapore 238467

Cambridge University Press is part of the University of Cambridge.

It furthers the University's mission by disseminating knowledge in the pursuit of education, learning, and research at the highest international levels of excellence.

www.cambridge.org
Information on this title: www.cambridge.org/9781108834476
DOI: 10.1017/9781108993340

First published 2021

Printed in the United Kingdom by TJ Books Limited, Padstow Cornwall

A catalogue record for this publication is available from the British Library.

Library of Congress Cataloging-in-Publication Data
Names: Feldman, Martha S., 1953– editor.
Title: Cambridge handbook of routine dynamics / edited by Martha S. Feldman, University of California, Irvine, [and five others].
Description: Cambridge, United Kingdom : New York, NY : Cambridge University Press, 2021. | Includes bibliographical references and index.
Identifiers: LCCN 2021019406 (print) | LCCN 2021019407 (ebook) | ISBN 9781108834476 (hardback) | ISBN 9781108995092 (paperback) | ISBN 9781108993340 (epub)
Subjects: LCSH: Organizational behavior. | Organizational sociology. | Task analysis. | BISAC: BUSINESS & ECONOMICS / Organizational Behavior | BUSINESS & ECONOMICS / Organizational Behavior
Classification: LCC HD58.7 .C34337 2021 (print) | LCC HD58.7 (ebook) | DDC 302.3/5–dc23
LC record available at https://lccn.loc.gov/2021019406
LC ebook record available at https://lccn.loc.gov/2021019407

ISBN 978-1-108-83447-6 Hardback

Contents

Figures

Tables

Contributors

Simon Addyman
University College London

Giada Baldessarelli
Imperial College Business School

Hari Bapuji
University of Melbourne

Charlotte Blanche
HEC Montréal

Jan vom Brocke
University of Liechtenstein

Sergio Bulgacov
Getulio Vargas Foundation

Eugenia Cacciatori
Business School (formerly Cass), City, University of London

Marlys K. Christianson
University of Toronto

Patrick Cohendet
HEC Montréal

Luciana D'Adderio
The University of Edinburgh, Usher Institute

Anja Danner-Schröder
TU Kaiserslautern

Fleur Deken
Vrije Universiteit Amsterdam

Dionysios D. Dionysiou
ALBA Graduate Business School, The American College of Greece

Katharina Dittrich
University of Warwick

Martha S. Feldman
University of California, Irvine

Dehua Gao
Shandong Technology and Business University

Daniel Geiger
University of Hamburg

Vern L. Glaser
University of Alberta

Simon Grand
University of St. Gallen

Thomas Grisold
University of Liechtenstein

Benjamin Grossmann-Hensel
University of Zurich

Thorvald Hærem
BI Norwegian Business School

Timothy R. Hannigan
University of Alberta

Mathias Hansson
BI Norwegian Business School

Manpreet Hora
Georgia Institute of Technology

Jennifer Howard-Grenville
Cambridge Judge Business School

Paula Jarzabkowski
Business School (formerly Cass), City, University of London

Yooeun Jeong
BI Norwegian Business School

Emre Karali
Özyeğin University

Joanna Kho
The University of Queensland

Inkyu Kim
Michigan State University

Waldemar Kremser
Radboud University, Institute for Management Research

Nathalie Lazaric
Université Côte d'Azur

Curtis LeBaron
Brigham Young University

Huashan Li
University of Melbourne

Jan Lodge
Cambridge Judge Business School

Juan López-Cotarelo
University of Warwick

Christian A. Mahringer
University of Stuttgart

Jan Mendling
Vienna University of Economics and Business

Brian T. Pentland
Michigan State University

Andrea Prencipe
Luiss University

Claus Rerup
Frankfurt School of Finance & Management

Violina P. Rindova
University of Southern California

Rodrigo A. Rosa
Getulio Vargas Foundation

Mehdi Safavi
The University of Edinburgh Business School

Carlo Salvato
Bocconi University

David Seidl
University of Zurich

Kathrin Sele
Aalto University and Vrije Universiteit Amsterdam

Paul Spee
The University of Queensland

Bryan Spencer
Frankfurt School of Finance & Management

Jörg Sydow
Freie Universität Berlin

Haridimos Tsoukas
University of Cyprus and Warwick Business School

Scott F. Turner
University of South Carolina

Rodrigo Valadao
University of Alberta

Frithjof E. Wegener
Delft University of Technology

Bastian Wurm
Vienna University of Economics and Business

Jun Xiao
NEOMA Business School

Preface

At first glance, *Routine Dynamics* is a strange topic for a scholarly handbook because *Routine Dynamics* is an oxymoron. The word *routine* has a lot of connotations, but *dynamic* isn't usually one of them. From a distance, routines seem like habits: mindless, repetitive and notoriously hard to change. Routines seem *static*, so inquiring about routine *dynamics* seems like a waste of time. Yet here we are.

Routine Dynamics started with a simple but counterintuitive observation: If we look closely, the patterns of action we see are not as 'routine' as they seem from a distance (Feldman, 2000). From staging a ballet (Blanche and Cohendet, 2019) to drilling for oil (Bertels, Howard-Grenville and Pek, 2016), careful observation reveals patterns of action that are repetitive but also emergent, effortful and surprisingly dynamic. For instance, in a study of sequential patterns of action in a call centre, Pentland and Rueter (1994) initially found that the work was characterized by many exceptions, interruptions and deliberations, which led them to conclude that the work was non-routine. On closer inspection, however, they found that most of the interactions in the call centre followed a repetitive, functionally similar pattern, which made them conclude that the work was performed through routines. In this respect, Routine Dynamics embodies the same spirit of two-eyed inquiry that has led to progress in every empirical science. On the one hand, we see more clearly when we take a closer look. On the other hand, we also need to occasionally step back and see the big picture.

An important feature of Routine Dynamics is to see organizational routines as patterns of interdependent action (Feldman and Pentland, 2003). By looking at how actions unfold over time, we see how a single routine can embody a multiplicity of performances that (re)create the routine itself (Feldman, 2016). The actions follow patterns but, at the same time, the actions make the patterns. The emphasis on actions – situated actions and patterns of actions – is central to understanding why routines are inherently dynamic. A major goal of this Handbook is to introduce readers to this way of seeing, analysing and understanding patterns of action.

As this Handbook demonstrates, research on Routine Dynamics has begun to enjoy increased visibility in recent years. This is a remarkable accomplishment because, at its heart, the action-centric perspective is unorthodox. Traditional organizational theory and research revolves around actors (people, groups and organizations). Against this dogma, Routine Dynamics asks a heretical question: *What can we learn from the actions*? Putting actions in the foreground emphasizes the processual side of organizing (Langley and Tsoukas, 2017). Of course, there is no action without actors – foreground and background are needed for a complete picture – but emphasizing actions has been a distinctive feature of Routine Dynamics. This Handbook is focused on organizational routines, but the action-centric mindset translates to a broad range of social phenomena at different time scales and different levels of granularity. Whether action-centric thinking will have a transformative impact in Organization Theory and beyond remains to be seen, but the seeds have been sown.

By assembling this Handbook, we hope to help these seeds grow. The chapters provide grounds for engaging in deeper theoretical inquiries into organizational change and stability. Chapters also link to new topics and themes that have not been investigated from a Routine Dynamics perspective. In this way, the Handbook aims to create a big tent where there is room for exploration of new topics: new forms of organizing (e.g., holocracy); grand challenges (e.g., climate change); algorithms and artificial intelligence; and time and temporality.

Our goal is twofold. First, we take stock of how the field of Routine Dynamics has developed over the past twenty years, map where the field could be going and provide resources for scholars to invigorate and renew their scholarship and horizon on routines. More than a decade ago, Michael Cohen (2007: 774), reflecting on the history of research on organizational routines, wondered 'why it has proven so difficult to give really useful, research grounded answers to these questions about how routines arise, are maintained, change, or resist change'. After compiling this Handbook, we find ourselves on more solid ground and believe answers to these questions are starting to crystalize, and that we can put this knowledge to use to understand important topics in organizational research. Second, we want to help scholars from related areas (e.g., Strategy-as-Practice) and more distant communities (e.g., institutional theory, Dynamic Capabilities, social networks, behavioural strategy, Carnegie School) to join and enrich the conversation.

To encourage these connections, the Handbook is structured into four parts: (1) Theoretical Resources for Routine Dynamics Research, (2) Methodological Issues in Routine Dynamics Research, (3) Themes in Routine Dynamics Research and (4) Related Communities of Thought. We invited authors contributing to each of the four parts to answer the question: *What does someone need to know about this area to get started?* In the part on theoretical resources, topics as diverse as ethnomethodology, practice theory, process theorizing, socio-materiality, actor-network theory and pragmatism provide ideas to help scholars renew their approach to routines. The part on methodological issues expands the ways in which we can study Routine Dynamics by covering topics such as ethnography, sequence analysis, simulations, field experiments and video data. The most extensive part of the Handbook covers established and emerging themes in Routine Dynamics. The established themes range from ecologies of routines to truces while the emerging themes introduce ideas related to emotions, bodies, occupations and identities. Finally, the part on related communities plants ideas to create bridges between Routine Dynamics and Carnegie School learning, Dynamic Capabilities, Strategy-as-Practice, path dependence and Business Process Engineering.

The Handbook is a testament to the vibrant community that has emerged around Routine Dynamics. The community of scholars working on Routine Dynamics has grown over the past twenty years and has engaged in conscious community-building practices that have developed connections among scholars and promoted high-quality scholarship as well as camaraderie. By community, we mean not just people who publish in this field but also people who regularly gather to discuss their work, creating opportunities for collaboration and the development of new ideas. For years, members of the community have gathered regularly at the annual European Group for Organizational Studies (EGOS) conference, as well as other international venues. From 2005 to 2013, five EGOS subthemes related to what has become Routine Dynamics were held at various EGOS conferences and, from 2015 to 2020, Routine Dynamics has been an EGOS standing working group. As a standing working group, the community not only convened subthemes at the annual conference but also sponsored several Paper Development Workshops. These subthemes are attended not only by people presenting their own papers but also by people who consider themselves to be part of the community and want to participate in the ongoing conversation. At the same time, the community developed special issues in *Organization Science* in 2016 (Feldman et al., 2016) and Research in the Sociology of Organizations in 2019 (Feldman et al., 2019); produced an edited volume in the series Perspectives on Process Organization Studies (Howard-Grenville et al., 2016); and undertook the Handbook that this preface appears in. In 2018, the Routines.Research.Community began to meet quarterly and continues these quarterly meetings at the time of writing.

This volume would not have been possible without this community, including authors who agreed to write a chapter; the authors and reviewers of articles published in various journals on Routine Dynamics; participants in conferences such as EGOS and AOM; and Cambridge University Press. Thank you for your contributions to the community and to this Handbook.

References

Bertels, S., Howard-Grenville, J. and Pek, S. (2016). Cultural molding, shielding, and shoring at Oilco: The role of culture in the integration of routines. *Organization Science*, 27(3), 573–593.

Blanche, C. and Cohendet, P. (2019). Remounting a ballet in a different context: A complementary understanding of routines transfer theories. In M. Feldman, L. D'Adderio, P. Jarzabkowski and K. Dittrich, eds., *Routine Dynamics in Action: Replication and Transformation*. Research in the Sociology of Organizations, 61, Bingley: Emerald Publishing Limited, pp. 11–30.

Cohen, M. D. (2007). Reading Dewey: Reflections on the study of routine. *Organization Studies*, 28 (5), 773–786.

Feldman, M. S. (2000). Organizational routines as a source of continuous change. *Organization Science*, 11(6), 611–629.

Feldman, M. S. (2016). Routines as process: Past, present, and future. In J. A. Howard-Grenville, C. Rerup, A. Langley and H. Tsoukas, eds., *Organizational Routines: A Process Perspective*. Perspectives on Process Organization Studies. Oxford: Oxford University Press, pp. 23–46.

Feldman, M. S., D'Adderio, L., Jarzabkowski, P. and Dittrich, K., eds. (2019). *Routine Dynamics in Action: Replication and Transformation*. Research in the Sociology of Organizations, 61. Bingley: Emerald Publishing Limited.

Feldman, M. S. and Pentland, B. T. (2003). Reconceptualizing organizational routines as a source of flexibility and change. *Administrative Science Quarterly*, 48(1), 94–118.

Feldman, M. S., Pentland, B. T., D'Adderio, L. and Lazaric, N. (2016). Beyond routines as things: Introduction to the special issue on routine dynamics. *Organization Science*, 27(3), 505–513.

Howard-Grenville, J. A., Rerup, C., Langley, A. and Tsoukas, H., eds. (2016). *Organizational Routines: A Process Perspective*. Perspectives on Process Organization Studies. Oxford: Oxford University Press.

Langley, A. and Tsoukas, H., eds. (2017). *Perspectives on Process Organization Studies*. Oxford: Oxford University Press.

Pentland, B. T. and Rueter, H. H. (1994). Organizational routines as grammars of action. *Administrative Science Quarterly*, 39(3), 484–510.

CHAPTER 1

What Is Routine Dynamics?

MARTHA S. FELDMAN, BRIAN T. PENTLAND, LUCIANA D'ADDERIO, KATHARINA DITTRICH, CLAUS RERUP AND DAVID SEIDL

1.1 Introduction

Over the last two decades, Routine Dynamics has emerged as an international research community that shares a particular approach to organizational phenomena. At the heart of this approach is an interest in examining the emergence, reproduction, replication, and change of recognizable patterns of actions. In contrast to other research communities interested in those phenomena, Routine Dynamics studies are informed by a distinctive set of theories (e.g., practice theory and related process-informed theories) that directs researchers' attention to particular aspects of these phenomena (e.g., actions), yielding distinctive insights about them (e.g., routines are dynamic).

In this chapter, we offer an introduction to Routine Dynamics as a particular approach to studying organizational phenomena. For this purpose, we provide a brief description of the genealogy of research on routines; starting with the work of the management scholar Fredrick Taylor (1911) and the pragmatist philosopher John Dewey (1922) at the beginning of the last century, to the works of the Carnegie School on standard operating procedures around the middle of the last century, to the economics-based Capabilities approach and the practice-based approach of Routine Dynamics that emerged around the turn of the century. We also discuss the advantages of conceptualizing patterns of action as 'routines', as compared to 'practices', 'processes', 'activities' or 'institutions'. In particular, we highlight that the concept of routines directs the researcher's attention to certain features of action patterns, such as task orientation, sequentiality of actions, recurrence, and familiarity as well as attempts at reflexive regulation. We also introduce and explain the key concepts of the Routine Dynamics perspective and how they have developed over time. This chapter aims to provide the reader with a solid grasp of the Routine Dynamics approach as well with suggestions for further reading to deepen the understanding of particular aspects of this approach.

1.2 A Brief Genealogy of Research on Organizational Routines

To understand Routine Dynamics research, it is important to consider how research on routines has developed historically (see also Felin and Foss, 2009; Mahringer, 2019; Parmigiani and Howard-Grenville, 2011). Situated in a particular historical context, various scholars have developed the concept in response to specific questions at the time. One of the first to explore the role of routines in organizations was Frederick Taylor. Even though he did not use the term 'routine' his book *The Principles of Scientific Management*, published in 1911, laid the foundations for the standardization of work and thus the use of routines as a means for managerial control, supervision, and efficiency. Taylor applied scientific methods to identify the 'best' way to complete a task and encouraged managers to provide instructions and supervision to ensure that workers are using the most efficient way of working. A few years later, Stene (1940: 1129), who was interested in collective coordination in organizations, explicitly referred to routines as 'activities which ha[ve] become habitual because of repetition and which [are] followed regularly without specific directions or detailed supervision'.

In a different line of work, the concept of routines also appeared in the works of the pragmatist John Dewey (1922) (more on pragmatism can be found in Dionysiou [Chapter 5], this volume). Dewey was primarily interested in learning, both at the individual and collective level, and developed the notion of habit as reflective action. Dewey (1922) distinguished between intelligent habit and dead or mindless habit, highlighting that except for the pathological extreme (the dead routine), routines are lively, infused with emotions, reflection, and morality (Cohen, 2007; Winter, 2013). Even though Dewey and others suggest using the term 'routine' only for the pathological extreme of a dead routine, Routine Dynamics has instead chosen to keep the term 'routine' and show how it is lively, dynamic, and only in rare circumstances dead or mindless.

Between the mid-forties and mid-sixties, a distinctive view, known as the Carnegie School, developed, primarily as an effort to overcome the limitations of classical economic theory that was dominant at the time (see also Rerup and Spencer [Chapter 33], this volume). Simon's (1947) *Administrative Behavior*, March and Simon's (1958) *Organizations*, and Cyert and March's (1963) *Behavioral Theory of the Firm* were all concerned with opening up the black-box of the firm and developing theory on how firms behave as a result of lower-level processes, such as routines (see also Gavetti, Greve, Levinthal, and Ocasio, 2012). Simon (1947) was interested in decision-making of boundedly rational individuals and argued that routines, understood as simple rules, develop to save time and attention. March and Simon (1958) described routines as 'performance programs', that is, a fixed response to a defined stimulus that has been learned over time. Thus, in the case of a routine, search has been eliminated and choice simplified. In Cyert and March (1963), reliable, stable standard operating procedures (SOPs) are important because they allow firms to cope with uncertainty and enable effective decision-making. Overall, being concerned with bounded rationality, the Carnegie School foregrounded the cognitive dimension of routines and their ability to stabilize, and conserve resources (see also Lazaric [Chapter 18], this volume).

Another important milestone in the development of routines research was Nelson and Winter's (1982) *Evolutionary Theory of Economic Change*. The authors drew on evolutionary economics and the framework of variation, selection, and retention to counter traditional neoclassical assumptions of how firms develop and change over time. Defining routines as 'regular and predictable behavior patterns of firms' (Nelson and Winter, 1982: 14), Nelson and Winter defined three roles for routines: (1) Routines as genes: here, routines determine which firms are selected by the environment and thus survive. (2) Routines as organizational memory: organizations store knowledge in routinized activities and thus 'remember by doing' (Nelson and Winter, 1982: 99). (3) Routines as truces: because of the diverging interests of organizational members, routines serve as comprehensive truces that prevent intraorganizational conflict in repetitive activities (see also D'Adderio and Safavi [Chapter 15], this volume). In addition to outlining the role of routines, Nelson and Winter also identified the importance of organizational capabilities, broadly defined as 'the range of things a firm can do at any time' (Nelson and Winter, 1982: 52). Capabilities are seen as bundles of routines that give rise to a firm's competitive advantage (see also Salvato [Chapter 34], this volume).

Subsequently, two strands of research developed almost independently of each other: the Capabilities perspective and the Routine Dynamics perspective (Parmigiani and Howard-Grenville, 2011). The Capabilities perspective, grounded in organizational economics and drawing heavily on the work of Nelson and Winter, was primarily interested in understanding how capabilities as bundles of routines relate to firm performance (Dosi, Faillo, and Marengo, 2008; Dosi, Nelson, and Winter, 2000; Peng, Schroeder, and Shah, 2008). Authors working within this perspective thus 'black-boxed' routines and assumed that individuals execute routines as designed. From this perspective, organizational change was explained by so-called dynamic capabilities, that is, meta-routines that change operating routines (Winter, 2003).

In contrast, the Routine Dynamics perspective developed from an interest in what happens inside the routine. It 'altered the grain size or granularity of analysis and moved the unit of analysis from the firm and the routines that constitute them to the routine and the actions that constitute them' (Feldman, 2016: 27). It also moved the focus away from formal procedures and cognition to the actions taken by specific people in specific times and places. By drawing on different methods, in particular ethnographic observations, interviews, and archival data (see also Dittrich [Chapter 8], this volume), Routine Dynamics scholars started to challenge received wisdom about routines. For example, Pentland and Rueter (1994) found that there was more variety in performing routines than previous research acknowledged. And Feldman (2000) found that routines were sources of change over time – a finding that challenged the dominant view of routines as sources for stability and inertia.

In search of an alternative understanding of routines, one that accounts for human agency, variety, and change, scholars also started to draw on different theoretical resources. Even though the common saying is that Routine Dynamics is primarily informed by Giddens' (1984) structuration theory, in fact from the outset and in the ensuing years, the field has been influenced by a plethora of theories, a true latticework of ideas. For example, Martha Feldman (in Feldman and Orlikowski, 2011), reflecting on her early studies in Routine Dynamics, describes how she drew on various theories of practice (e.g., Bourdieu, 1977; 1990; Bourdieu and Wacquant, 1992; Giddens, 1976; 1979; 1984; for more see Feldman [Chapter 2], this volume), on phenomenology (Schutz, 1967; 1970), on ethnomethodology (Garfinkel, 1967; see Lopez-Cotarelo [Chapter 4], this volume), and on actor-network theory (ANT) (Latour, 1986, 2005; see Sele [Chapter 6], this volume) to theorize the findings from her fieldwork. All these theories are forms of process theorizing (Tsoukas [Chapter 3], this volume) that have enabled Routine Dynamics to shift towards a more processual focus of how routines are enacted and change over time. Subsequently, Routine Dynamics scholars also drew on pragmatism (Dionysiou [Chapter 5], this volume) and socio-materiality (D'Adderio [Chapter 7], this volume) to theorize the dynamics of routines.

This latticework or 'stew' (Feldman and Orlikowski, 2011: 1244) of ideas is important because the blending and mixing together of ideas produces new ways of thinking about routines. Often, different theories have more in common than we think, but in order to draw on them and combine them in generative ways, one needs to be familiar with them. Many works of Routine Dynamics can be understood in a deeper and more interesting way if understood with these theories in the background. We hope that the chapters contained in the first part of this Handbook provide the theoretical toolkit to better understand Routine Dynamics.

The new way of theorizing routines based on this latticework has shifted the focus from routines as 'entities' in early works to routines as being constituted of parts, that is, the ostensive and performative aspects of routines (Feldman and Pentland, 2003). It has also shifted the emphasis from routines as inherently static to routines as generative and dynamic (Howard-Grenville and Rerup, 2017; Parmigiani and Howard-Grenville, 2011). Theorizing the dynamic aspects of routines has helped to see that stability and change in routines are not opposites but that in fact they are mutually constituted (Farjoun, 2010; Tsoukas and Chia, 2002). This relation is captured in the 'paradox of the (n)ever-changing world' (Birnholtz, Cohen and Hoch, 2007: 316), that is, the assumptions that 'one does not step into the same river twice' and that 'there is no new thing under the sun' can coexist in routines. Routine dynamics has been progressively moving towards 'stronger process theorizing', and further progress has been achieved through the rhetorical shift from ostensive and performative to 'performing' and 'patterning' – or in other words 'the doing involved in the creating of both performative and ostensive aspects' (Feldman 2016: 39).

Overall, the conceptual development in research on routines over the last one hundred years has led to significant changes in the way we use the term 'routine'. In common language, the term 'routine' is primarily used as an adjective to describe the ordinary/mundane and the automatic/mindless and repetitious character of something. In the Carnegie School and evolutionary theory that sees routines as 'fixed things', the adjective and the noun 'routine' were the same thing, i.e., the automatic, mindless execution of a task. With Routine Dynamics, we moved 'beyond routines as things' (Feldman et al., 2016: 505). While we still use nouns to refer to routines, these nouns are no longer the same as the adjective 'routine' because we see routines as dynamic and generative. With an even stronger processual orientation, we are now moving from the noun to the verb, that is, from 'routines' to 'patterning' and 'performing' (the verb 'routinizing', however, is not what we mean here because 'routinizing' typically refers to managerial efforts to turn patterns of action into formalized, standardized, controllable and stable procedures). These changes in how the term 'routine' is used can be confusing at first, but once clarified this language can become very generative for understanding organizational phenomena. Before we discuss in more depth the key terminology used in Routine Dynamics research, we first turn to why it can be useful to call an empirical phenomenon a 'routine'.

1.3 What Is to Be Gained from Conceptualizing an Empirical Phenomenon as a 'Routine'?

Routine Dynamics scholars are not the only ones to examine recurrent patterns of interdependent actions (Parmigiani and Howard-Grenville, 2011). There are many other research communities who take an interest in action patterns, but they capture them with other concepts. For example, many practice scholars conceptualize action patterns as 'practices', such as when Reckwitz (2002: 249) defines practices as 'a routinized type of behaviour which consists of several elements, interconnected to one other: forms of bodily activities, forms of mental activities, "things" and their use, a background knowledge in the form of understanding, know-how, states of emotion and motivational knowledge'. Similarly Rasche and Chia (2009: 721) highlight that practices 'are first of all an observed patterned consistency of bodily activities; coherent clusters of activities that are condensed through repetition'. In business process management, such activity patterns are referred to as 'processes' (Weske, 2019). Benner and Tushman (2003: 240), for example, define processes as 'collections of activities that, taken together, produce outputs for customers'. Scholars concerned with activity systems conceptualize these action patterns as 'activities', where an activity is defined as 'a discrete economic process within the firm, such as delivering finished products to customers or training employees, that can be configured in a variety of ways' (Porter and Siggelkow, 2008: 34). Many institutional scholars, in turn, conceptualize these patterns as 'institutions'; highlighting that 'there is, and has been, a general understanding that institutions are ... patterns of action (behavior)' (Mayhew, 2008: 28) and defining institutions as 'stable, valued, recurring patterns of behavior' (Huntington, 1968: 9).

While it might seem irrelevant whether we *label* such action patterns 'routines', 'practices', 'processes', 'activities', 'institutions' or whatever else, these labels tend to be associated with different theoretical perspectives, which direct the researcher's attention to particular aspects of these patterns and away from others. This begs the question of what can be gained from studying action patterns as routines. This question is particularly acute when it comes to the concepts of routines and practices, as Routine Dynamics is explicitly based on a practice perspective (Feldman and Pentland, 2003).

The relation between the concept of routines and that of practices is somewhat complex, which has something to do with the fact that the concept of practices is defined differently in different practice theories. Most practice theorists, such as Giddens (1984) or Reckwitz (2002), would probably concur that 'while not all practices are routines, all routines are practices' (Feldman [Chapter 2], this volume). For example, the hiring routine can be considered a practice, while the practice of a handshake or gift-giving would not be considered a routine. Thus, from this perspective, routines are conceptualized as a sub-category of practices. Other practice theorists, such as Schatzki (2002), would at least agree that routines are an important element of practices, that is, they are a part of larger practices. In line with both interpretations, the Routine Dynamics perspective can be described as a practice perspective that sensitizes the researcher to certain specificities of particular action patterns; analogously to the way that organization theories tend to sensitize researchers better to the particularities of organizations than general social theories.

One aspect that characterizes routines as particular practices is the fact that routines are ostensibly directed at the accomplishment of particular tasks – even though routines do not always accomplish these tasks and not everyone involved in these routines necessarily wants the task accomplished. As Feldman (2016: 24) writes, 'organizational routines are enacted in order to do something in and for the organization'. For example, a hiring routine (Feldman, 2000; Rerup and Feldman, 2011) is directed at the task of hiring someone, a pricing routine (Zbaracki and Bergen, 2010) is directed at setting prices, a garbage collection routine (Turner and Rindova, 2012) is directed at the task of collecting garbage, a shipping routine (Dittrich et al., 2016) is directed at shipping something or a roadmapping routine (Howard-Grenville, 2005) is directed at developing and reviewing a roadmap. Because of this task orientation, routines are often associated with organizations or work contexts – i.e., accomplishing some subtasks of the organization. In contrast, some practices might lack a clear focus on specific tasks. For example, the practice of marriage (Whittington, 2007) is not directed at the accomplishment of a particular task; instead, practising the marriage is a purpose in itself. Similarly, the practice of horse betting (Schatzki, 2010) is not oriented at accomplishing a task which could then be measured as having been accomplished well or not. Thus, taking a routine lens directs the researcher's attention to the way that these tasks are accomplished and how orientation to the tasks affects the way the routines are enacted.

A second aspect that characterizes routines as particular practices is the significance of the particular *sequence*s in which actions are performed (see Mahringer and Pentland [Chapter 12], this volume). Some practice theorists such as Schatzki (2002: 2017) stress that the concept of practice does not focus on particular action *sequences*. As he writes, 'he doings and sayings that compose a practice need not be regular' (Schatzki, 2002: 73–74). The regular action sequences described by routines are then just a particular type of practice or even just an element of practices. For example, the practice of medicine can be said to contain many routines, such as particular treatment routines, diagnostic routines (Goh et al., 2011) or handoff routines (LeBaron et al., 2016), but as a whole this practice cannot be described as a regular sequence of actions. Thus, taking a routines lens directs the researcher's attention to the different patterns of action sequences and their variations, which can be described and visualized in the form of narrative networks (see Pentland and Kim [Chapter 13], this volume). In line with the emphasis on sequences of actions and how patterns of actions evolve over time, studies of Routine Dynamics are also process studies (Feldman, 2016; Howard-Grenville and Rerup, 2017).

A third aspect that characterizes routines as particular practices is the recurrent nature of the action pattern which results in some kind of familiarity with the routine. One would typically not speak of an organizational routine if an action pattern was just enacted once in the organization. This familiarity has important implications for the enactment of routines as the participants' earlier experiences with the routine provide them with particular competence and points of reference for the enactment (Birnholtz et al., 2007; Deken et al., 2016; Turner and Fern, 2012). In contrast, some practices, while recurring in wider society, might be enacted just once in the immediate context and thus be entirely novel to all participants. To be sure, this difference is just a matter of degree as all practices presuppose at least some rudimentary familiarity with the practice. Thus, by highlighting this repetitiveness and familiarity, a routine lens directs the researcher's attention to the participants' experiences with earlier enactments of the action pattern and how this affects future routine enactments.

A fourth aspect characterizing routines as particular practices are attempts at their reflective regulation. Because routines are directed at accomplishing particular tasks and tend to be repetitively enacted, we often find explicit attempts at 'managing' the action sequences of which the routines are made. We often find standard operating procedures or if-then statements providing instructions for the way routines are supposed to be enacted (Cyert and March, 1963). Managers and employees often also try to adapt routines (e.g., Salvato,

2009; Salvato and Rerup, 2018), design artifacts to change routines (e.g., Glaser, 2017; Pentland and Feldman, 2008) or switch between routines as a way of influencing the outcomes produced by those routines. In contrast, there are many practices where such attempts at reflective regulation would appear somewhat at odds. Practices such as marriage or dining are just taken for granted and attempts at reflectively regulating these practices would be rather unusual – even though not entirely impossible. Thus, taking a routines lens directs the researcher's attention to the role that explicit attempts at managing or influencing routines through artifacts, such as standard operating procedures or explicit rules, have on the enactment of routines as well as the co-evolution between those artifacts and actual routine performances.

1.4 Key Concepts of Routine Dynamics

In this section we review some of the key concepts used in Routine Dynamics, focusing on their origins and evolution over time. Many of the concepts were imported into Routine Dynamics from neighbouring theories, at times being reproduced faithfully, and at other times being modified or reinvented. We note that the vocabulary has grown substantially over time (we have a garden with old and new flowers) coming to form today an expressive, evolving language. One clear trend has been the progressive move towards a more deeply processual and performative language. This has allowed us to reveal the dynamics of routines and successively unravel the forces within Routine Dynamics. Next, we review some of the most common meanings that people in Routine Dynamics associate with this language.

Despite having identified some distinct trends in the Routine Dynamics vocabulary, we also acknowledge that part of the success behind the topic has been the lightness and flexibility with which we have so far held our terminology. It is true that there are some meanings that have more or less stabilized and gathered substantial consensus, as described in the previous section and in Feldman et al. (2016). At the same time, we are aware that there may be terms that change more rapidly or substantially and terms that extend, challenge or perhaps even replace established terminology. After two decades, the field may be stabilizing but it also remains open, both to retaining established meanings and interpretations and towards developing new vocabularies. In these changes we are guided by our questions and the world we explore.

In the following we discuss several terms that have grown to have specific meanings within Routine Dynamics and concepts that readers not already immersed in Routine Dynamics or related communities (like practice theory or relational sociology) might find confusing. While we describe these concepts here, they are best understood through the many detailed empirical accounts of Routine Dynamics where these concepts come to life. Moreover, there are many other concepts that are important to Routine Dynamics and used in Routine Dynamics studies that we do not discuss here. Temporality is a good example. Though clearly important to our understanding of routines and to the development of Routine Dynamics (see Turner and Rindova [Chapter 19], this volume), the Routine Dynamics community draws on ways of talking about time that one would readily understand without having read other Routine Dynamics studies.

1.4.1 Effortful and Emergent Accomplishments

That routines are both effortful and emergent has become a cornerstone of Routine Dynamics, in contrast with earlier understandings of routines as automatic or executed without explicit deliberation or effort (March and Simon 1958; Nelson and Winter 1982). Citing Giddens (who refers to both Goffman and Garfinkel), Pentland and Reuter note that 'routinized social activity is not mindless or automatic but, rather, an effortful accomplishment' and that '[e]ven some of the most routinized kinds of encounters, such as fast food service (Leidner, 1993) and buying stamps (Ventola, 1987), exhibit a considerable amount of variety and require effort on the part of the participants to accomplish successfully' (1994: 488). Picking up on the notion of effort, Feldman identified several kinds of effort that people make in the process of repeating routines,

> When actions do not produce the intended outcome, or produce an unintended and undesirable outcome, participants can respond by repairing the routine so that it will produce the intended and desired outcome. The result may be to restore the routine to a stable equilibrium and may not be associated with continued change. When the outcomes enable new opportunities, participants have the option of expanding. They can change the routine to take advantage of the new possibilities. Finally, when outcomes fall short of ideals, they can respond by striving. (Feldman, 2000: 620)

In identifying these types of effort, it also became clear that 'work practices such as organizational routines are not only effortful but also emergent accomplishments. They are often works in progress rather than finished products' (Feldman, 2000: 613). As a result, new patterns of action (change) may emerge through the gradual accretion of actions required to reproduce the same (i.e., stable) pattern of action. While expanding and striving are particularly oriented to change, even repairing may result in the emergence of new ways of accomplishing goals or tasks. Numerous studies in Routine Dynamics show that repetition and replication are not straightforward. Repetition introduces opportunities for changes that overcome minor or temporary obstacles but also introduces opportunities to do the routine differently or better. The result may be more or less effective communication (Bucher and Langley, 2016; LeBaron et al., 2016); better or worse products (Cohendet and Simon, 2016; Deken et al., 2016; Sele and Grand, 2016); or more or less efficient processes (for better or worse) (Aroles and McClean, 2016; Eberhard et al., 2019; Turner and Rindova, 2012).

The distinction between effortful and emergent can be used to orient us to the difference between variance in performance and change in practices and their results. In that case, effortful accomplishments often refer to variations in performance in order to do the same thing or produce stability, whereas emergent accomplishment refers to the effort involved in doing something different or producing change in routines or outcomes (Feldman et al., 2016). But this distinction is also often one that is in the eyes of the beholder. As Deken et al. (2016) showed in their study of three different kinds of 'routine work', what feels like a small change to one person may feel like a lot of change to another person. In practice, effortful and emergent accomplishments are entangled.

1.4.2 Performative and Ostensive Aspects and the Shift to Performing and Patterning

Another important set of concepts is the idea of performative and ostensive aspects. Compared to effortful and emergent accomplishments these concepts are less intuitive. The ostensive/performative distinction was initially introduced to the study of routines as a way of distinguishing an emic and etic orientation,

> Latour uses these terms in describing power, but the concepts apply as well to routines. An ostensive definition of a concept is one that exists in principle (Sevon 1996). It is created through the process of objectification as it is studied. A performative definition is one that is created through practice. 'Society is not the referent of an ostensive definition discovered by social scientists despite the ignorance of their informants. Rather it is performed through everyone's efforts to define it' (Latour 1986, p. 273). (Feldman, 2000: 622)

In this use – as in Latour's use – ostensive and performative are separable and there can be performative routines and ostensive routines. 'Ostensive routines may be devoid of active thinking, but routines enacted by people in organizations inevitably involve a range of actions, behaviors, thinking, and feeling' (Feldman, 2000: 622).

In Feldman and Pentland (2003), these terms were repurposed and integrated more completely with practice theory.

> We adopt language proposed by Latour (1986) in his analysis of power, in which he pointed out that power exists both in principle and in practice. He referred to the former as the ostensive aspect of power and the latter as the performative aspect. We propose that organizational routines also consist of ostensive and performative aspects, which are closely related to the concepts of structure and

> agency, as found in structuration theory (Giddens, 1984). We adopt specialized terminology because, in the domain of organizational routines, structure and agency are mediated by the repetitive collective, interdependent nature of the phenomenon. (Feldman and Pentland, 2003: 100)

The two terms were defined in the following way,

> The ostensive aspect is the ideal or schematic form of a routine. It is the abstract, generalized idea of the routine, or the routine in principle. The performative aspect of the routine consists of specific actions, by specific people, in specific places and times. It is the routine in practice. Both of these aspects are necessary for an organizational routine to exist. (Feldman and Pentland, 2003: 101)

That both aspects are necessary for an organizational routine to exist was an important statement that further moved the field by placing performative and ostensive aspects in a mutually constitutive relation to one another. '[W]e have emphasized that the ostensive and performative aspects of routines are mutually necessary. Without the ostensive aspect, we cannot name or even see our patterns of activity, much less reproduce them. Without the performative, nothing ever happens' (Feldman and Pentland, 2003: 115). Indeed, Feldman and Pentland (2003) connected the ostensive and performative not only to the duality of agency and structure highlighted by Giddens but also to the duality of subjective and objective emphasized in Bourdieu's work,

> The ostensive aspect of a routine enables us to create an apparently objective reality through the subjective acts of guiding, accounting, and referring. As practiced objective and subjective dimensions are mutually constitutive (Bourdieu, 1990). Objective and subjective aspects are inseparable because the objectified summaries of routines (the artifacts) are constructed from our subjective perceptions of them. Thus, ironically, routines exist as objects because of our subjective understandings of them. In a sense, our subjective understanding and interpretation is the glue that binds the actions into the patterns we recognize as the routine. (Feldman and Pentland, 2003: 109)

The emphasis in Routine Dynamics on both performative and ostensive aspects constitutes departures from previous ways of thinking about routines. First, an insistence on the performative aspect – on identifying specific actions in specific times and places – is a discipline that marks the empirical work in Routine Dynamics. Rather than describing dynamics in abstract terms, this discipline goes to the root of the organizational dynamics and enables scholars to see what others have missed. This discipline is very much influenced by the focus in actor-network theory on tracing actions and actants.

Second, as Feldman (2016: 27) writes, 'the introduction of the term "ostensive" drew attention to the relationality of performances and patterns and the constitutive nature of action in patterns. Similar to Wittgenstein's use of the term (2001), ostensive implies that patterns are constituted of specific instances that can be pointed to as a referent.' Take, for instance, the example of the pattern that makes up our everyday experience of a colour. 'While there is a scientific definition of blue (for example, a range of light wavelengths), on an everyday basis we know the color blue through the various blues (or objects coloured blue) that exemplify blue. In other words, there are things we can point to that make up the pattern that we recognize as blue' (Feldman, 2015: 321). Routine Dynamics makes a similar argument about performances and their associated patterns. Ostensive aspects of routines are always made up of performances that we can point to.

Latour has argued that the problem with ostensive definitions is that they become imbued with independence and mistaken as a cause of action – people mistake 'what is glued for the glue' (Latour, 1986: 276). The way Routine Dynamics has used the ostensive aspect militates against this mistake. While the ostensive aspect refers to the abstract patterns of routines, it is relationally entangled with performance. This allows Routine Dynamics to acknowledge the importance of abstract patterns without giving them priority over the actions that are integral to them. The notion of ostensive aspects that are enacted patterns, produced through action, moves Routine Dynamics away from a focus on patterns that are envisioned, intended or mandated.

As empirical work in Routine Dynamics gave meaning to the performative and ostensive aspects of routines by identifying the specific actions taken by specific people at specific times and places and the enacted patterns that emerged as a result of these specific actions, the processual ontology of routines also developed. For instance, in 2014, D'Adderio identified the effortful (Pentland and Rueter, 1994) and emergent (Feldman, 2000) '"patterning work" that is involved in the constantly challenged and never fully achieved (Tsoukas and Chia, 2002) pursuit of balance between competing goals' (1346). Danner-Schröder and Geiger (2016) draw on this idea of patterning work to 'understand the mechanisms that routine participants enact to create and recreate patterns, which they recognize as stable or changing' (656). Goh and Pentland (2019) 'conceptualize patterning as the formation of new paths and the dissolution of old paths in a narrative network (Pentland and Feldman, 2007) that describes a routine, (1901). There are different ways in which these patterns are created. For example, Turner and Rindova (2018) describe how time organizes patterning.

Feldman (2016) suggested performing and patterning as alternatives to the performative and ostensive aspects as a way to make action more focal in our study of routines, and particularly to emphasize the active nature of creating patterns. Routine Dynamics now offers both a weaker process ontology, based on the idea that routines consist of performative and ostensive aspects, and a stronger process ontology, based on the idea that routines are enacted through performing and patterning. The difference between the strong and weak process ontology has been defined by process theorists as 'different ontologies of the social world: one a world made of things in which processes represent change in things (grounded in a substantive metaphysics) and the other a world of processes, in which things are reifications of processes (Tsoukas and Chia, 2002) (grounded in process metaphysics)' (Langley et al., 2013: 4). Thus, 'according to a weak view, processes form part of the world under consideration, according to a strong view the world is process' (Hernes, 2008: 23).

1.4.3 Situated Action

The idea of situated action originated in anthropology/information systems (Suchman 2007; Lave, 1988) and acquired meaning in Suchman's distinction between 'plans' and 'situated action'.

> That term underscores the view that every course of action depends in essential ways on its material and social circumstances. Rather than attempt to abstract action away from its circumstances and represent it as a rational plan, the approach is to study how people use their circumstances to achieve intelligent action. Rather than build a theory of action out of a theory of plans, the aim is to investigate how people produce and find evidence for plans in the course of situated action. More generally, rather than subsume the details of action under the study of plans, plans are subsumed by the larger problem of situated action. (Suchman, 2007: 70)

One of the ways that the situated nature of action has informed Routine Dynamics is through the idea that practical consciousness (Giddens, 1984) or practical sense (Bourdieu, 1990; Boudieu and Wacquant, 1992) is important to how people enact routines because the actions required are too varied for rules to be able to determine action (Feldman and Pentland, 2003; Pentland and Feldman, 2005; Pentland and Reuter, 1994; Reynaud 2005). Suchman's (1983) study of filing in triplicate provided an early example of how an apparently simple routine with a sequence of seven clearly defined steps quickly becomes complicated when enacted in the real world. The routine participants have to draw on their practical sense to ensure that, in the end, it will look as if the sequence had been followed. The situated nature of action is thus twofold: actions are situated in specific material and social circumstances and they are situated in patterns (here, the pattern of filing in triplicate).

The development of a hiring routine in a Danish research lab provides a more complex example of situated action. The university that was the bureaucratic home for the research lab articulated rules for hiring, but the lab directors took action (based on their practical sense) to work around the rules so that they would be able to hire the kind of people they needed to realize the goals of the lab. As a result, actions taken in the hiring routine were situated in two different patterns: hiring in a university bureaucracy and hiring for a research lab. Although research on boundary objects has shown that it is possible to have action that is situated in different contexts and has different meanings in each of these contexts (Carlile, 2002; Star and Griesemer, 1989), in this particular case the effort to produce actions that were acceptable in both contexts ultimately provoked change in how the lab directors envisioned the work of the lab (Rerup and Feldman, 2011).

When Routine Dynamics scholars studied the situated nature of actions, they also noticed how the patterns of routines are themselves situated in a context. Howard-Grenville (2005) theorized the situatedness of routines as 'embeddedness' in a variety of structures (e.g., technology, coordination and culture). Embeddedness originally assumed that the context is separable from, though important to, the routine. An alternative way of theorizing the relation between situation and routine is to see them as inseparable and entangled. In this view, routines are 'enacted through' their situated socio-material context (D'Adderio 2014; Feldman et al., 2016; see also D'Adderio [Chapter 7], this volume). The latter definition highlights the constant entanglement and mutual shaping of routines and their context (see also Howard-Grenville and Lodge [Chapter 16], this volume).

1.4.4 Artifacts and Materiality

In reaction to a long-standing and persistent confusion in the study of routines that identified routines with artifacts, i.e., the written procedures or standard operating procedures (SOPs) describing routines, Pentland and Feldman initially described artifacts as important but exogenous to the generative system (Pentland and Feldman, 2005). This move allowed the focus to shift to actions and patterns (performative and ostensive aspects of routines). It, unfortunately, also gave some the impression that actions could be enacted and patterns could emerge without artifacts. This impression was rectified through later work. D'Adderio (2011) moved artifacts into the generative system, where they have remained. D'Adderio and other scholars have continued to develop our understanding of the centrality of artifacts, and materiality in general, through numerous empirical studies (Aroles and McLean, 2016; Boe-Lillegraven, 2019; Cohendet and Simon, 2016; D'Adderio, 2014; D'Adderio and Pollock, 2020; Glaser, 2017; Kiwan and Lazaric, 2019; Sele and Grand, 2016).

This work shows how, for instance, routines 'change dynamically as they are enacted through specific configurations of artifacts and communities which shape ostensive and action patterns leading to varying outcomes (i.e., alignment or improvement, replication or innovation)' (D'Adderio, 2014: 1347). The heterogeneous configurations shaping routines are referred to as socio-technical *agencements* (Callon, 1998; D'Adderio, 2008) or socio-material assemblages (D'Adderio, 2008; Orlikowski and Scott, 2008; Suchman, 2007). These are agentic arrangements which include a plethora of socio-material features (texts, bodies, objects, values, etc.) whose properties are always emergent. Assemblages are 'arrangements endowed with the capacity to act in different ways, depending on their configuration' (Callon and Çalışkan, 2010: 9), and different assemblage configurations bear different effects over routines. Thus for an SOP or rule to have an effect on performances, it has to generate an assemblage (including actors' intentions, emotions and actions, digital and physical artifacts, etc.), which together supports the assumptions, views and goals embedded in the SOP at design and/or usage stage. This suggests that the effect of a rule or SOP can only theoretically be 'fully descriptive (a passive, fixed representation of the actual [routine]) or fully prescriptive (univocally ordering and structuring the [routine], mostly they are performed' (D'Adderio, 2008: 786), meaning that they configure routines to various extents (e.g., weak vs. strong performativity). The notion of assemblage helps us move beyond the unhelpful ontological separation between actors and artifacts, physical and material, objects and subjects, solid and fluid, while also helping us theorize how emergent, heterogeneous socio-material configurations shape routines as they are performed within and across organizational locations, and over time (Blanche and Cohendet, 2019; D'Adderio, 2014; D'Adderio and Pollock, 2020).

This novel approach afforded by combining Routine Dynamics with ANT/STS (Science-and-Technology Studies)/Performativity Theory-related sensitivities has allowed us to shed new light on long-standing debates, including innovation, replication, truces and dynamic capabilities. As a result of its substantial potential to provide new insights into routines and organizations, the concept of materiality has been and continues to be central to the study of routine dynamics (see D'Adderio [Chapter 7], this volume). Detailed discussion of materiality, including the related concepts of artifacts, assemblage, performativity, affordance and inscription, is included in the Handbook chapters by D'Adderio on materiality (Chapter 7), by Sele on actor-network theory (Chapter 6), by Wegener and Glaser (Chapter 22) on design and by Glaser et al. on algorithms (Chapter 23).

1.4.5 Relationality

The concept of relationality goes beyond simply attention to relationships (whether relationships of people or things or people and things) and is in contrast to an orientation to substances or entities. In a relational framework, the 'dynamic, unfolding process, becomes the primary unit of analysis rather than the constituent elements themselves. Things are not assumed as independent existences present anterior to any relation, but ... gain their whole being ... first in and with the relations which are predicated of them' (Emirbayer, 1997: 287). In his *Manifesto for a Relational Sociology*, Emirbayer quoted Somers and Gibson (1994) to make a distinction between 'a social identity or categorical approach' that 'presumes internally stable concepts' versus a [relational, transactional] approach' that 'embeds the actor within relationships and stories that shift over time and space and thus precludes categorical stability in action' (1997: 286).

Routine Dynamics is fundamentally about going 'beyond routines as things' to understanding that routines are ongoing, unfolding processes. An analogy may be useful. We have tended to turn routines into things in much the same way that we speak of the wind as a thing. 'We say, "The wind is blowing," as if the wind were actually a thing at rest which, at a given point in time, begins to move and blow. We speak as if a wind could exist which did not blow' (Elias, 1978: 111–112, cited in Emirbayer, 1997: 283). Similarly, when we imagine that a routine is a thing rather than an unfolding process, we pretend that a routine could exist without being enacted. While descriptions of routines or formalized procedures (aka SOPs) can exist without being enacted, Routine Dynamics asserts that routines are ontologically processes rather than entities. Routines come into being (and continue coming into being) as people and artifacts enact them. As a result of this ontology, dynamism is intrinsic to routines.

Analytically, relationality refers to the inseparability of the analytical constructs that we use in Routine Dynamics. This relationality is fundamental to practice theory, which is an important theoretical base for Routine Dynamics (Feldman [Chapter 2], this volume).

> Relationality is central to the way practice theorists understand individuals and systems or structures. Separating individuals and structures lies at the heart of two dominant and competing explanations of social order. Reckwitz (2002) refers to these as homo economicus and homo sociologicus: 'The model of the homo economicus explains action by having recourse to individual purposes, intentions and interests; social order is then a product of the combination of single interests' (p. 245). Homo economicus is the foundation for theories of rational action and 'great man' theories. On the other hand, '[t]he model of the homo sociologicus explains action by pointing to collective norms and values, i.e. to rules which express a social "ought"; social order is then guaranteed by a normative consensus' (Reckwitz, 2002: 245). [...] As different as homo economicus and homo sociologicus theories are, they nonetheless share the fundamental assumptions that (1) individuals and structures are ontologically independent of one another and (2) either individual economic rational interests or social norms are the primary basis for social action. Breaking with these assumptions, the relationality of practice theory provides a third way to view social reality: that individual interests and social norms can only be separated analytically; in practice, they are always in relation to one another, a mutually constituted duality (Bourdieu, 1977; 1990; Giddens, 1979; 1984). (Feldman and Worline, 2016: 309)

Because dualities, such as stability and change, individual and institution, subjective and objective, are central to practice theory and, thus, to Routine Dynamics, discussions of the relationality of mutual constitution often concern dyadic relations. Mutuality, however, does not necessarily mean dyadic but does mean that the relationality cannot be one-sided. In Routine Dynamics, the initial focus was on a dyadic relationship – the performative and the ostensive aspects of routines – but before long, D'Adderio's (2011) work brought artifacts fully into this relationship and the dyad became a triad. In strengthening the process ontology of Routine Dynamics this triad becomes performing, patterning and materializing. Within Routine Dynamics theorizing, it has always been clear that these aspects of routines are not separable. The language of mutual constitution can, however, give the impression of things that are separable and that influence one another (Orlikowski, 2007). Thus, in further support of the stronger process ontology, it is also useful to discuss the relationality of aspects of routines as entangled.

1.4.6 Multiplicity

Multiplicity is another important concept for studying the dynamics of routines. Without multiplicity, there are no dynamics. Multiplicity makes possible the dynamics that produce stability and change. Initially, multiplicity meant simply that there are many – many people, many actions, many patterns, many artifacts, many routines. In more recent work (Pentland, Mahringer, Dittrich, Feldman and Ryan Wolf, 2020), the idea of multiplicity has expanded from a quantitative to a qualitative multiplicity (see Bergson, 1950) based on a relational rather than a substantive ontology (Emirbayer, 1997).

Multiplicity of the quantitative sort (numbers of things) is fundamental to the initial reconceptualization of routines that underlies the field of Routine Dynamics. Feldman and Pentland (2003: 95) distilled a core definition of organizational routine as 'a repetitive, recognizable pattern of interdependent actions, involving multiple actors'. Consistent with the work of previous organizational scholars, this definition 'emphasized the involvement of multiple individuals and the interdependence of their actions' (Feldman and Pentland, 2003: 96). The new conceptualization of routines, however, did not stop with this core definition, and multiplicity in Routine Dynamics does not stop with actors and actions but also includes patterns (ostensive aspects) and artifacts (materiality). While at times referring to both the performative aspect and the ostensive aspect in the singular, Feldman and Pentland specifically addressed the temptation to think of the ostensive aspect as a singular thing.

> It is tempting to conceptualize the ostensive aspect of the routine as a single, unified object, like a standard operating procedure. This would be a mistake, because the ostensive incorporates the subjective understandings of diverse participants. Like any socially distributed stock of knowledge, the ostensive aspect of a routine is usually not monolithic; it is likely to be distributed unevenly (Berger and Luckmann, 1966; Schutz, 1967). Each participant's understanding of a routine depends on his or her role and point of view. (2003: 101)

The multiplicity of artifacts in relation to routines was also important as this reconceptualization sought to distinguish routines from a unified rule or Standard Operating Procedure as noted in the previous quote. Indeed, Pentland and Feldman (2005: 797) note that, 'the range of artifacts that can constrain and enable routines is practically endless'.

Over time and through many empirical studies the focus of Routine Dynamics has expanded to include the multiplicity of routines and the dynamics that occur as multiple routines affect one another. As important as it is to see what happens within a routine, routines are enacted in relation to other routines. Thus, Routine Dynamics articles have explored ecologies of routines (Birnholtz et al., 2007; Sele and Grand, 2016), clusters of routines (Kremser and Schreyögg, 2016), intersecting routines (Spee, Jarzabkowski and Smets, 2016) and interdependent routines (Yi, Knudsen and Becker, 2016) to see how these multiplicities affect stability and change in organizations.

Recently, routine scholars have expanded the notion of multiplicity. to better understand stability and change. Both D'Adderio and Pollock (2020) and Pentland et al. (2020) theorize the multiplicity of processes, albeit in different ways. D'Adderio and Pollock (2020) refer to 'ontological multiplicity', while Pentland et al. (2020) theorize a specific notion of 'process multiplicity'.

D'Adderio and Pollock (2020) draw on the idea of ontological multiplicity developed by Mol (2002) that processes such as routines are not unified, singular 'objects' but are themselves multiplicities. Specifically, D'Adderio and Pollock (2020: 14) 'characterize routines as ontologically fluid and only coming together as "one routine" with great effort and as a temporary, challenged achievement'. Through a study of routines replication, they found that 'routines similarity and singularity did not consist in the complete absence of, but instead productively encompassed, difference and multiplicity' (D'Adderio and Pollock, 2020: 11). Similarity and singularity here emerge from the coordination of multiple versions of the routine across sites and over time (D'Adderio and Pollock, 2020).

Ontological multiplicity opens up new ways of studying routines and new questions for Routine Dynamics. As D'Adderio and Pollock note,

> studying routines as fluid patterns implies going a fundamental step further in unpacking routines dynamics. Now we can ask new questions such as: when is a routine the same routine? How much can a routine change before it becomes another routine? And if it does change that far, how can it be re-stabilized, or brought back into being the same routine? And through which agential devices or mechanisms? (D'Adderio and Pollock, 2020: 14)

The notion of process multiplicity in Pentland et al. (2020) defines processes as a duality of one and many in which the 'one' process or pattern or routine is always constituted of multiple paths (i.e., possible ways of performing a routine) that emerge from sequential relations among actions. The authors state that,

> [w]hile routine dynamics research has been very useful in showing how processes are generative systems in the interplay between the 'one' and actual performances, our conceptualization of process multiplicity takes this view one step further: it allows us to consider not only change in *actual* performances, but also changes in *possible* paths. Thus we can ask how does the space of possible paths change when organizational members change the idealized model? And what are the mechanisms that drive this change? (Pentland et al., 2020)

1.5 Conclusion: Where to Go from Here?

Routine Dynamics involves de-centring and dissolving conventional points of view. 'Routine' is a noun, but a routine is not a thing. Routines are repetitive, but not necessarily 'routine' (the adjective). Routines are *dynamic*. Each of the theoretical underpinnings of Routine Dynamics has this quality: ethnomethodology, pragmatism, practice theory, actor-network theory and socio-materiality have all been disruptive and decentring, each in its own way. Together, this latticework of theoretical perspectives has been generative.

In a way, decentring is a natural product of looking closely at the patterns of doings and sayings, along with the actors and artifacts that enact them. Rather than talking about routines in general, we have looked at routines in particular, but with a fresh lens. Dittrich (Chapter 8, this volume) counts 40+ ethnographies, plus many other works that have drawn on computational procedures, simulations and experiments. Through this work, we have developed a lively and continuously evolving vocabulary to describe the dynamics of routines.

So, the way forward is to begin addressing the implications of this way of seeing for important organizational and societal issues, including the grand challenges of society (George et al., 2016) and the little challenges of management. Each of the chapters contained in this volume charts several new areas for Routine Dynamics to explore. A common theme among these is that Routine Dynamics can do more to help solve real world problems. So far, Routine Dynamics research has been focused on theoretical development (which has been necessary and generative), but now is the time to put these new theoretical tools to work to better understand contemporary phenomena of societal concern, such as the rise of algorithms and automation and the gig economy; and ways to address inequality and racism, epidemics, natural disasters and climate change.

Moreover, more work could focus on exploring the role of routines in more thorny contexts, such as social injustice, fraud and organized crime. Only very recently, Routine Dynamics scholars have started to look at the dark sides of routines (e.g., Eberhard et al., 2019; den Nieuwenboer et al., 2017). A better understanding of the negative sides of the dynamics of routines will be useful in contributing to discussions and ideas about how to solve these problems.

We also very much welcome work that connects Routine Dynamics to other related fields of research, such as Strategy-as-Practice, institutional theory or dynamic capabilities. Moreover, Routine Dynamics can provide the basis for fields such as behavioural strategy (Levinthal, 2011) and practice-driven institutionalism (Smets, Aristidou and Whittington, 2017) that are looking for 'micro foundations'. Here, Routine Dynamics can provide micro-foundations that are grounded in the doings and sayings of people working in organizations (Powell and Rerup, 2017: 313–315; 329–331).

Lastly, we welcome enriching both our theoretical and methodological repertoire to explore routines. Routine Dynamics has started by using new methods and drawing on new theories and this development has been very generative. We hope that in future research new methods and theories will provide new ways of 'seeing' and overcoming conventional ways of thinking.

References

Aroles, J. and McLean, C. (2016). Rethinking stability and change in the study of organizational routines: Difference and repetition in a newspaper-printing factory. *Organization Science*, 27(3), 535–550.

Benner, M. J. and Tushman, M. L. (2003). Exploitation, exploration, and process management: The productivity dilemma revisited. *Academy of Management Review*, 28(2), 238–256.

Berger, P. L. and Luckmann, T. (1966). *The Social Construction of Reality: A Treatise in the Sociology of Knowledge*. Garden City, NY: Anchor Books.

Bergson, H. (1950). *Time and Free Will: An Essay on the Immediate Data of Consciousness*. London: George Allen & Unwin.

Bertels, S., Howard-Grenville, J. and Pek, S. (2016). Cultural molding, shielding, and shoring at Oilco: The role of culture in the integration of routines. *Organization Science*, 27(3), 573–593.

Birnholtz, J. P., Cohen, M. D. and Hoch, S. V. (2007). Organizational character: On the regeneration of Camp Poplar Grove. *Organization Science*, 18(2), 315–332.

Blanche, C. and Cohendet, P. (2019). Remounting a ballet in a different context: A complementary understanding of routines transfer theories. In M. Feldman, L. D'Adderio, P. Jarzabkowski and K. Dittrich, eds., *Routine Dynamics in Action: Replication and Transformation*. Research in the Sociology of Organizations, 61. Bingley: Emerald Publishing Limited, pp. 11–30.

Boe-Lillegraven, S. (2019). Transferring routines across multiple boundaries: A flexible approach. In M. Feldman, L. D'Adderio, P. Jarzabkowski, and K. Dittrich, eds., *Routine Dynamics in Action: Replication and Transformation*. Research in the Sociology of Organizations, 61. Bingley: Emerald Publishing Limited, pp. 31–53.

Bourdieu, P. (1977). *Outline of a Theory of Practice*. Cambridge: Cambridge University Press.

Bourdieu, P. (1984). *Distinction: A Social Critique of the Judgement of Taste*. Boston: Harvard University Press.

Bourdieu, P. (1990). *The Logic of Practice*. Stanford, CA: Stanford University Press.

Bourdieu, P. and Wacquant, L. J. (1992). *An Invitation to Reflexive Sociology*. Chicago: University of Chicago Press.

Bucher, S. and Langley, A. (2016). The interplay of reflective and experimental spaces in interrupting and reorienting routine dynamics. *Organization Science*, 27(3), 594–613.

Callon, M. (1998). An essay on framing and overflowing: Economic externalities revisited by sociology. In M. Callon, ed., *The Laws of the Markets*. Oxford: Blackwell, pp. 244–269.

Callon, M. and Caliskan, C. (2010). Economization, Part 2: A research programme on the Study Of Marketization. *Economy and Society*, 39(1), 1–32.

Carlile, P. R. (2002). A pragmatic view of knowledge and boundaries: Boundary objects in new product development. *Organization Science*, 13(4), 442–455.

Cohen, M. D. (2007). Reading Dewey: Reflections on the study of routine. *Organization Studies*, 28(5), 773–786.

Cohendet, P. S. and Simon, L. O. (2016). Always playable: Recombining routines for creative efficiency at Ubisoft Montreal's video game studio. *Organization Science*, 27(3), 614–632.

Cyert, R. M. and March, J. G. (1963). *A Behavioral Theory of the Firm*. Englewood Cliffs, NJ: Prentice-Hall.

D'Adderio, L. (2008). The performativity of routines: Theorising the influence of artefacts and distributed agencies on routines dynamics. *Research Policy*, 37(5), 769–789.

D'Adderio, L. (2011). Artifacts at the centre of routines: Performing the material. *Journal of Institutional Economics*, 7(2), 197–230.

D'Adderio, L. (2014). The replication dilemma unraveled: How organizations balance multiple goals in routines transfer. *Organization Science*, 25(5), 1325–1350.

D'Adderio, L. and Pollock, N. (2020). Making routines the same: Crafting similarity and singularity in routines transfer. *Research Policy*, 49(8), 104029.

Danner-Schröder, A. and Geiger, D. (2016). Unravelling the motor of patterning work: Toward an understanding of the microlevel dynamics of standardization and flexibility. *Organization Science*, 27(3), 633–658.

Deken, F., Carlile, P. R., Berends, H. and Lauche, K. (2016). Generating novelty through interdependent routines: A process model of routine work. *Organization Science*, 27(3), 659–677.

den Nieuwenboer, N. A., Cunha, J. V. d. and Treviño, L. K. (2017). Middle managers and corruptive routine translation: The social production of deceptive performance. *Organization Science*, 28(5), 781–803.

Dewey, J. (1922). *Human Nature and Conduct: An Introduction to Social Psychology*. New York: H. Holt & Company.

Dittrich, K., Guérard, S. and Seidl, D. (2016). Talking about routines: The role of reflective talk in routine change. *Organization Science*, 27(3), 678–697.

Dittrich, K. and Seidl, D. (2018). Emerging intentionality in routine dynamics: A pragmatist view. *Academy of Management Journal*, 61(1), 111–138.

Dosi, G., Faillo, M. and Marengo, L. (2008). Organizational capabilities, patterns of knowledge accumulation and governance structures in business firms: An introduction. *Organization Studies*, 29(8–9), 1165–1185.

Dosi, G. Nelson R. R. and Winter S. G., eds. (2000). *Nature & Dynamics of Organizational Capabilities*. Oxford: Oxford University Press.

Eberhard, J., Frost, A. and Rerup, C. (2019). The dark side of routine dynamics: Deceit and the work of Romeo Pimps. In M. Feldman, L. D'Adderio, P. Jarzabkowski and K. Dittrich, eds., *Routine Dynamics in Action: Replication and Transformation*. Research in the Sociology of Organizations, 61. Bingley: Emerald Publishing Limited, pp. 99–121.

Elias, N. (1978). *What Is Sociology?* Translated by Stephen Mennell and Grace Morrissey. New York: Columbia University Press.

Emirbayer, M. (1997). Manifesto for a relational sociology. *American Journal of Sociology*, 103(2), 281–317.

Farjoun, M. (2010). Beyond dualism: Stability and change as a duality. *Academy of Management Review*, 35(2), 202–225.

Feldman, M. S. (2000). Organizational routines as a source of continuous change. *Organization Science*, 11(6), 611–629.

Feldman, M. S. (2015). Theory of Routine Dynamics and connections to strategy as practice. In D. Golsorkhi, L. Rouleau, D. Seidl and E. Vaara, eds., *Cambridge Handbook of Strategy as Practice*, 2nd ed. Cambridge: Cambridge University Press, pp. 320–333.

Feldman, M. S. (2016). Routines as process: Past, present, and future. In J. A. Howard-Grenville, C. Rerup, A. Langley and H. Tsoukas, eds., *Organizational Routines: A Process Perspective*. Perspectives on Process Organization Studies. Oxford: Oxford University Press, pp. 23–46.

Feldman, M. and Orlikowski, W. J. (2011). Theorizing practice and practicing theory. *Organization Science*, 22(5), 1240–1253.

Feldman, M. S. and Pentland, B. T. (2003). Reconceptualizing organizational routines as a source of flexibility and change. *Administrative Science Quarterly*, 48(1), 94–118.

Feldman, M. S., Pentland, B. T., D'Adderio, L. and Lazaric, N. (2016). Beyond routines as things: Introduction to the special issue on routine dynamics. *Organization Science*, 27(3), 505–513.

Feldman, M. S. and Worline, M. (2016). The practicality of practice theory. *Academy of Management Learning & Education*, 15(2), 304–324.

Felin, T. and Foss, N. J. (2009). Organizational routines and capabilities: Historical drift and a course-correction toward microfoundations. *Scandinavian Journal of Management*, 25(2), 157–167.

Garfinkel, H. (1967). *Studies in Ethnomethodology*. Englewood Cliffs, NJ: Prentice-Hall.

Gavetti, G., Greve, H. R., Levinthal, D. A. and Ocasio, W. (2012). The behavioral theory of the firm: Assessment and prospects. *Academy of Management Annals*, 6(1), 1–40.

George, G., Howard-Grenville, J., Joshi, A. and Tihanyi, L. (2016). Understanding and tackling societal grand challenges through management research. *Academy of Management Journal*, 59(6), 1880–1895.

Giddens, A. (1976). *New Rules of Sociological Method: A Positive Critique of Interpretative Sociologies*, 1st ed. Oxford: Polity Press.

Giddens, A. (1979). *Central Problems in Social Theory: Action, Structure and Contradiction in Social Analysis*. Basingstoke: Macmillan.

Giddens, A. (1984). *The Constitution of Society*. Cambridge: Polity Press.

Glaser, V. L. (2017). Design performances: How organizations inscribe artifacts to change routines. *Academy of Management Journal*, 60(6), 2126–2154.

Goh, J. M., Gao, G. and Agarwal, R. (2011). Evolving work routines: Adaptive routinization of information technology in healthcare. *Information Systems Research*, 22(3), 565–585.

Goh, K. T. and Pentland, B. T. (2019). From actions to paths to patterning: Toward a dynamic theory of patterning in routines. *Academy of Management Journal*, 62(6), 1901–1929.

Hernes, T. (2008). *Theory for a Tangled World*. London: Routledge.

Howard-Grenville, J. (2005). The persistence of flexible organizational routines: The role of agency and organizational context. *Organization Science*, 16(6), 618–636.

Howard-Grenville, J. and Rerup, C. (2017). A process perspective on organizational routines. In A. Langley and H. Tsoukas, eds., *Sage Handbook of Process Organizational Studies*. London: Sage Publications, pp. 323–339.

Huntington, S. P. (1968). *Political Order in Changing Societies*. New Haven, CT: Yale University Press.

Kiwan, L. and Lazaric, N. (2019). Learning a new ecology of space and looking for new routines: Experimenting robotics in a surgical team. In M. Feldman, L. D'Adderio, P. Jarzabkowski and K. Dittrich, eds., *Routine Dynamics in Action: Replication and Transformation*. Research in the Sociology of Organizations, 61. Bingley: Emerald Publishing Limited, pp. 173–192.

Kremser, W. and Schreyögg, G. (2016). The dynamics of interrelated routines: Introducing the cluster level. *Organization Science*, 27(3), 698–721.

Langley, A. and Tsoukas, H, eds. (2017). *Perspectives on Process Organization Studies*. Oxford: Oxford University Press.

Langley, A., Smallman, C., Tsoukas, H. and Van de Ven, A. H. (2013). Process studies of change in organization and management: *Unveiling temporality, activity, and flow Academy of Management Journal*, 56(1), 1–13.

Latour, B. (1986). The powers of association. In J. Law, ed., *Power, Action and Belief: A New Sociology of Knowledge?* London: Routledge & Kegan Paul, pp. 261–277.

Latour, B. (1987). *Science in Action*. Boston: Harvard University Press.

Latour, B. (1992). Where are the missing masses? The sociology of a few mundane artifacts. In W. Bijker and J. Law, eds., *Shaping Technology/Building Society: Studies in Sociotechnical Change*. Cambridge, MA: MIT Press, pp. 225–258.

Latour, B. (2005). *Reassembling the Social: An Introduction to Actor-Network-Theory*. Oxford: Oxford University Press.

Lave, J. (1988). *Cognition in Practice: Mind, Mathematics and Culture in Everyday Life*. Cambridge: Cambridge University Press.

LeBaron, C., Christianson, M. K., Garrett, L. and Ilan, R. (2016). Coordinating flexible performance during everyday work: An ethnomethodological study of handoff routines. *Organization Science*, 27(3), 514–534.

Leidner, R. (1993). *Fast Food, Fast Talk: Service Work and the Routinization of Everyday Life*. Berkeley: University of California Press.

Levinthal, D. A. (2011). A behavioral approach to strategy: What's the alternative? *Strategic Management Journal*, 32(13), 1517–1523.

Mahringer, C. (2019). *Exploring Routine Ecologies: A Characterization and Integration of Different Perspectives on Routines*. PhD, Stuttgart: University of Stuttgart.

March, J. G. and Simon, H. (1958). *Organizations*. New York: Wiley.

Mayhew, A. (2008) Institutions, culture and values. In J. B. Davis and W. Dolfsma, eds., *The Elgar*

Companion to Social Economics. Cheltenham: Edward Elgar, pp. 28–43.
Mol, A. M. (2002). *The Body Multiple: Ontology in Medical Practice*. Oxford: Blackwell Publishing.
Nelson, P. R. and Winter, S. (1982). *An Evolutionary Theory of Economic Change*, Cambridge, MA: Harvard University Press.
Orlikowski, W. J. (2002). Knowing in practice: Enacting a collective capability in distributed organizing. *Organization Science*, 13(3), 249–273.
Orlikowski, W. J. (2007). Sociomaterial practices: Exploring technology at work. *Organization Studies*, 28(9), 1435–1448.
Orlikowski, W. J. and Scott, S. V. (2008). Sociomateriality: Challenging the separation of technology, work and organization. *Academy of Management Annals*, 2(1), 433–474.
Parmigiani, A. and Howard-Grenville, J. (2011). Routines revisited: Exploring the capabilities and practice perspectives. *Academy of Management Annals*, 5(1), 413–453.
Peng, D. X., Schroeder, R. G. and Shah, R. (2008). Linking routines to operations capabilities: A new perspective. *Journal of Operations Management*, 26(6), 730–748.
Pentland, B. T. and Feldman, M. S. (2005). Organizational routines as a unit of analysis. *Industrial and Corporate Change*, 14(5), 793–815.
Pentland, B. T. and Feldman, M. S. (2007). Narrative networks: Patterns of technology and organization. *Organization Science*, 18(5), 781–795.
Pentland, B. T. and Feldman, M. S. (2008). Designing routines: On the folly of designing artifacts, while hoping for patterns of action. *Information and Organization*, 18(4), 235–250.
Pentland, B. T., Mahringer, C., Dittrich, K., Feldman, M. S. and Ryan Wolf, J. (2020). Process multiplicity and process dynamics: Weaving the space of possible paths. Organization Theory. DOI: https://doi.org/10.1177/2631787720963138.
Pentland, B. T. and Rueter. H. H. (1994). Organizational routines as grammars of action. *Administrative Science Quarterly*, 39(3), 484–510.
Porter, M. and Siggelkow, N. (2008). Contextuality within activity systems and sustainability of competitive advantage. *Academy of Management Perspectives*, 22(2), 34–56.
Powell, W. W. and Rerup, C. (2017). Opening the black box: Microfoundations of institutions. In R. Greenwood et al., eds., *The SAGE Handbook of Organizational Institutionalism*, 2nd ed. London: Sage Publications, pp. 311–337.
Rasche, A. and Chia, R. (2009). Researching strategy practices: A genealogical social theory perspective. *Organization Studies*, 30(7), 713–734.
Reckwitz, A. (2002). Toward a theory of social practices: A development in culturalist theorizing. *European Journal of Social Theory*, 5(2), 243–263.
Rerup, C. and Feldman, M. (2011). Routines as a source of change in organizational schemata: The role of trial-and-error learning. *Academy of Management Journal*, 54(3), 577–610.
Reynaud, B. (2005). The void at the heart of rules: Routines in the context of rule-following. The case of the Paris Metro Workshop. *Industrial and Corporate Change*, 14(5), 847–871.
Salvato, C. (2009). Capabilities unveiled: The role of ordinary activities in the evolution of product development processes. *Organization Science*, 20(2), 384–409.
Salvato, C. and Rerup, C. (2018). Routine regulation: Balancing conflicting goals in organizational routines. *Administrative Science Quarterly*, 63(1), 170–209.
Schatzki, T. R. (2002). *The Site of the Social: A Philosophical Account of the Constitution of Social Life and Change*. University Park: Pennsylvania State University Press.
Schatzki, T. R. (2010). *The Timespace of Human Activity: On Performance, Society, and History as Indeterminate Teleological Events*. Lexington Books.
Schutz, A. (1967). *The Phenomenology of the Social World*. G. Walsh, F. Lehnert, trans. Evanston, IL: Northwestern University Press.
Schutz, A. (1970). *Reflections on the Problem of Relevance*, R. M. Zaner, ed., New Haven, CT: Yale University Press.
Sele, K. and Grand, S. (2016). Unpacking the dynamics of ecologies of routines: Mediators and their generative effects in routine interactions. *Organization Science*, 27(3), 722–738.
Sevon, G. (1996). Organizational imitation in identity transformation. In B. Czarniawska and G. Sevon, eds., *Translating Organizational Change*. New York: Walter de Gruyter.
Simon, H. A. (1947). *Administrative Behavior: A Study of Decision-Making Processes in Administrative Organization*. Basingstoke: MacMillan.

Smets, M., Aristidou, A. and Whittington, R. (2017). Towards a practice-driven institutionalism. In R. Greenwood et al., ed., *The SAGE Handbook of Organizational Institutionalism*, 2nd ed. London: Sage Publications, pp. 384–411.

Somers, M. R. and Gibson, G. D. (1994). Reclaiming the epistemological 'other': Narrative and the social constitution of identity. In C. Calhoun, (ed.), *Social Theory and Political Identity*. Oxford: Blackwell, pp. 37–99.

Spee, P., Jarzabkowski, P. and Smets, M. (2016). The influence of routine interdependence and skillful accomplishment on the coordination of standardizing and customizing. *Organization Science*, 27 (3), 759–781.

Star, S. L. and Griesemer, J. R. (1989). Institutional ecology, 'translations' and boundary objects: Amateurs and professionals in Berkeley's Museum of Vertebrate Zoology, 1907–39. *Social Studies of Science*, 19(3), 387–420.

Stene, E. O. (1940). An approach to a science of administration. *American Political Science Review*, 34(6), 1124–1137.

Suchman, L. A. (1983). Office procedure as practical action: Models of work and system design. *ACM Transactions on Information Systems (TOIS)*, 1 (4), 320–328.

Suchman, L. A. (2007). *Human-Machine Reconfigurations: Plans and Situated Actions*, 2nd ed. New York: Cambridge University Press.

Taylor, F. (1911). *The Principles of Scientific Management*. New York: Harper and Brothers.

Tsoukas, H. and Chia, R. (2002). On organizational becoming: Rethinking organizational change. *Organization Science*, 13(5), 567–582.

Turner, S. F. and Fern, M. J. (2012). Examining the stability and variability of routine performances: The effects of experience and context change. *Journal of Management Studies*, 49(8), 1407–1434.

Turner, S. F. and Rindova, V. P. (2012). A balancing act: How organizations pursue consistency in routine functioning in the face of ongoing change. *Organization Science*, 23(1), 24–46.

Turner, S. F. and Rindova, V. P. (2018). Watching the clock: Action timing, patterning, and routine performance. *Academy of Management Journal*, 61(4), 1253–1280.

Ventola, E. (1987). *The Structure of Social Interaction: A Systematic Approach to the Semiotics of Service Encounters*. London: Pinter.

Weske, M. (2019). *Business Process Management. Concepts, Languages, Architectures*, 3rd ed. Berlin; Heidelberg: Springer.

Whittington, R. (2007). Strategy practice and strategy process: Family differences and the sociological eye. *Organization Studies*, 28(10), 1575–1586.

Winter, S. G. (2003). Understanding dynamic capabilities. *Strategic Management Journal*, 24 (10), 991–995.

Winter, S. G. (2013). Habit, deliberation, and action: Strengthening the microfoundations of routines and capabilities. *Academy of Management Perspectives*, 27(2), 120–137.

Wittgenstein, L. (2001). *Philosophical Investigations*. Translated by G. M. Anscombe. London: Blackwell. [Orig. pub. 1953.]

Yi, S., Knudsen, T. and Becker, M. C. (2016). Inertia in routines: A hidden source of organizational variation. *Organization Science*, 27(3), 782–800.

Zbaracki, M. J. and Bergen, M. (2010). When truces collapse: A longitudinal study of price-adjustment routines. *Organization Science*, 21(5), 955–972.

PART I

Theoretical Resources for Routine Dynamics Research

CHAPTER 2 Practice Theory and Routine Dynamics

MARTHA S. FELDMAN

2.1 Introduction

This chapter deals with the role that practice theory has played and can play in developing the field of Routine Dynamics. Descriptions of what practice theory is are abundant (see, for example, Feldman and Orlikowski, 2011; Feldman and Worline, 2016; Gherardi, 2006; Nicolini, 2013; Ortner, 1984, Reckwitz, 2002). There is common agreement that practice theory is not a unified theory but 'a family of ideas which have been described as an approach (Gherardi, 2006; Nicolini et al., 2003; Ortner, 1984); a turn (Schatzki et al., 2001); a lens (Feldman and Orlikowski, 2011); or an idiom (Nicolini, 2013)' (Feldman and Worline, 2016: 308). The work of Pierre Bourdieu and Anthony Giddens forms the basis of practice theory and they have been described as 'the two leading exponents of practice theory' (Schatzki, 2012: 13). Documenting the role of this family of ideas in the development of Routine Dynamics is further complicated by its rhizome-like qualities,[1] producing shoots that may be relatively independent of one another and even of work by the leading exponents. In Section 2.2, I present some basics of practice theory. A comprehensive review of practice theory is beyond the scope of this chapter, and I heartily recommend that scholars interested in building on practice theory read both the original works of Bourdieu and Giddens as well as the work of scholars who have built on, interpreted and appropriated their work.

2.2 Some Basics of Practice Theory

A consistent feature of practice theory is that practice is the unit of analysis. This feature also distinguishes practice theory from pragmatism and Actor-Network Theory (ANT), which it nonetheless has much in common with. Practice is not only what people do; it is also the participation of that doing in the ongoing creation and recreation of institutions and social systems (Feldman and Orlikowski, 2011; Gherardi, 2006; Nicolini, 2013; Reckwitz, 2002). In other words, practice is not just about action or agency, though these are crucial to practice and practice theory does draw attention to the importance of action and agency. Practice is also not individual, though individuals do take action. Practice is collective and ongoing. Practice happens over time and through the actions of many.

Marriage is a good example of a practice. While one can point to particular moments – the 'I do' moment, signing the marriage license or signing divorce papers – as specific actions that make or unmake a marriage,[2] the practice of marriage involves the day-to-day realities of being married or not being married. And while I can talk about practices within my own marriage, my marriage is not the practice of marriage, though it does contribute to that practice in its own small way. The practice of marriage includes present, past and future marriages and marriages that are ongoing as well as marriages that are dissolving or have been dissolved. The practice of marriage changes over time. Divorce has

[1] '[A] **rhizome** . . . is a modified subterranean plant stem that sends out roots and shoots from its nodes' (Wikipedia: https://en.wikipedia.org/wiki/Rhizome, accessed May 4, 2020).

[2] Such 'speech acts' have been extensively analyzed by performativity scholars. See, for instance, Searle (1989).

become a more common part of the practice over time. More recently, same-sex marriages have become part of the practice of marriage. And while it may be expedient to define the practice of marriage by formal and state-sanctioned acts, what marriage is depends also on the partnerships that are not state-sanctioned and the ways in which these are both similar to and different from state-sanctioned marriages.

As a theoretical construct, practice transcends dualisms that have defined much of social science research, including agency/structure, individual/institutional, subjective/objective, mind/body, abstract/concrete, materiality/sociality. Indeed, Bourdieu suggests that the inability to transcend such dualisms – which he refers to as being 'locked in the usual antinomies ... of determinism and freedom, conditioning and creativity, consciousness and the unconscious, or the individual and society' (1990: 55) – is a major obstacle for understanding practice. Bourdieu begins his exposition of practice theory (1990) with an extended discussion of the objectivity/subjectivity antinomy, the transcendence of which animates his theorizing. Giddens (1984) is similarly animated by the transcendence of the agency/structure duality.

Taking practice as the unit of analysis is a way of transcending dualities. For instance, in taking practice as the unit of analysis, one is not focused on agents *instead of* institutions or institutions *instead of* agents but on the relationality of agents *and* institutions. Relationality is an important concept (see Feldman et al. [Chapter 1], this volume). Here, it refers to the inseparability of agents from institutions or of subjective from objective, stability from change, as well as the processual implications of orienting to dynamics rather than statics (Emirbayer, 1997; Feldman and Orlikowski, 2011; Feldman and Worline, 2016; Michel, 2014). While, of course, we can designate something as agent and something else as institution, one situation as stability and another as change, these are analytical distinctions. In *practice* these are not separable and they are not static. Institutions such as marriage, but also capitalism or racism and so forth, shape who we are and what we do. And who we are and what we do shape these institutions. Institutions and agents are mutually constituting or entangled. And this relationality occurs whether we are aware of it or not.

The issue of intention and awareness is an important one. Are we aware of our participation in the creation and recreation of institutions and social structures as we engage in actions? Mostly probably not. Our actions in relation to the practice of marriage, for instance, are seldom, if ever, in order to produce a social system. We marry or not, we divorce or not, for a vast array of reasons, but seldom to strengthen or weaken the practice of marriage. While we may, at times, realize that our actions do strengthen or weaken the practice of marriage, the collective nature of the practice makes it less likely that we will see our actions as consequential to the practice. The production and reproduction of social systems does not require our awareness or our intention, though we may be or become aware of the potential of our actions to contribute to the stability or change of the social system.

Does this general lack of awareness/intentionality mean that our actions are automatic, robotic or without reflection? This question relates to what some refer to as reflection in action or tacit knowledge (Polanyi, 1966; Schön, 1983; Shotter, 2006; Tsoukas [Chapter 3], this volume; Wegener and Glaser [Chapter 22], this volume). Bourdieu and Giddens use the terms 'practical sense' and 'practical consciousness', respectively. The following excerpt provides a succinct notion of practical consciousness:

> Human agents or actors – I use these terms interchangeably – have, as an inherent aspect of what they do, the capacity to understand what they do while they do it. The reflexive capacities of the human actor are characteristically involved in a continuous manner with the flow of day-to-day conduct in the contexts of social activity. But reflexivity operates only partly on a discursive level. Practical consciousness consists of all the things which actors know tacitly about how to 'go on' in the contexts of social life without being able to give them direct discursive expression (Giddens, 1984: xxii–xxiii).

While there is a great deal in common between practical consciousness and practical sense, Bourdieu's notion of practical sense extends

Giddens' notion of practical consciousness by emphasizing that practical sense is not the same as intellectual reflection. For Bourdieu, practice is 'the product of a *practical sense*, of a socially constituted "sense of the game"' (Bourdieu and Wacquant, 1992: 120–121). Bourdieu's focus is on the logic of practice, which is not the logic of an external observer who generalizes across practices. The logic of practice can only always be internal to a particular practice. Habitus as 'embodied history' (Bourdieu, 1990: 56) is central to the logic of practice as it is the basis for the sense of or feel for the game. Habitus is an internal sense of how to go on – what next steps can be taken and with what effect.

> The principle of this construction [habitus] is found in the socially constituted system of structured and structuring dispositions acquired in practice and constantly aimed at practical functions. … it emphasizes that this work [practice] has nothing in common with intellectual work, that it consists of an activity of practical construction, even of practical reflection, that ordinary notions of thought, consciousness, knowledge prevent us from adequately thinking (Bourdieu and Wacquant, 1992: 121).

With these underpinnings of practice theory in mind, the next section turns to the use of practice theory in Routine Dynamics.

2.3 Applying the Ideas of Practice Theory to Routines

Practice theory was foundational for the theorizing that has become the field of Routine Dynamics. Indeed, a fundamental move that created this field was to identify routines as practices. That the unit of analysis in practice theory is practice made it ideally suited to reconceptualizing organizational routines. If routines are practices, then we can use practice theory to think about the routine as the unit of analysis. Thinking about the routine as the unit of analysis invites a focus on how routines work rather than on, for instance, what they produce. Of course, what routines produce is still important, but the emphasis moves from *what* to *how*. What goes on in the routine or what is endogenous to the process of the routine comes into focus.

A common refrain among scholars of Routine Dynamics is that, while not all practices are routines, all routines are practices. The first chapter in this Handbook outlines several features of routines that make them a particular kind of practice (Feldman et al. [Chapter 1], this volume). Routines are task-oriented sequences of action that recur within a local context and where there is often an effort at reflective regulation or management. Practices do not necessarily have all of these qualities and some practices may have none of them. Marriage, for instance, is rarely task-oriented, could only be characterized with difficulty as a sequence of actions, may only be undertaken once in a lifetime and may or may not include conscious reflection. Thus, practices are not always routines. Routines, on the other hand, are always practices. Routines participate in the creation of social systems, they entail relationality and transcend dualisms and they engage a practical sense about how to go on. In the following section, we show how these features of routines formed the basis for the field of Routine Dynamics.

It is, of course, important to recognize that some people and even some organizational scholars speak about routines as if they were the written procedure, the checklist or the program. From a Routine Dynamics perspective, however, routines are enacted and it is these patterned actions that are the focus of the field and the reason that the conceptual apparatus of practice theory is so useful.

2.3.1 Practice Theory in the Foundational Articles of Routine Dynamics

Three papers are commonly seen as laying the foundation for Routine Dynamics: two empirical papers and one theory paper. The foundational empirical papers (Feldman, 2000; Pentland and Rueter, 1994) both introduce practice theory by citing Giddens (1984). Feldman (2000) also cites Giddens (1979, 1993) and Bourdieu (1977, 1990), as well as papers that engage and build on these theorists, including Brown and Duguid (1991), Lave (1988), Lave and Wenger (1991), Orlikowski (1992), Ortner (1984, 1989) and

Sewell (1992). The foundational theory article (Feldman and Pentland, 2003) draws on the same practice theorists, citing Giddens (1984) and Bourdieu (1977, 1990), as well as many scholars who draw on these works, including Barley (1986), Emirbayer and Mische (1998), Orlikowski (1992, 2000), Ortner (1989), Reynaud (1998) and Sewell (1992).

These papers engaged practice theory to help with some core theoretical issues that created a new way of thinking about routines. For Pentland and Rueter (1994), a key concern was to establish the effort involved in routine enactment and that rules and norms are resources for – but do not determine – actions. The notion of practical consciousness offered by Giddens was key to developing the idea that routines are *effortful accomplishments*. Pentland and Rueter note that

> Giddens (1984: 60) identified the concept of routinization, 'as grounded in practical consciousness,' as vital to the theory of structuration ... While Giddens did not offer an explicit definition of organizational routines per se, the critical insight here is that routinized social activity is not mindless or automatic but, rather, an effortful accomplishment (1994: 488).

The related contribution this article made and that the authors relied on Giddens, in part, to make was the idea that structures such as rules do not take the place of effort and practical consciousness. By proposing that we describe routines 'by grammars',[3] the authors did not intend to invoke the idea of a rigid set of rules or structures that determines action. As they note:

> A critical part of this conception of routines lies in the relationship between structure and agency. As Giddens (1984) and others have argued, rules, norms, schema, scripts, and other cognitive artifacts are 'resources' for action, but they cannot be understood as determining action. (1994: 491)

This point is reinforced in the conclusion:

> Finally, there is always the risk that describing patterns of social action with grammar will be misinterpreted as an attempt to objectify social life in a way that is inconsistent with our best understanding of the nature of the social world. Rules are resources for action, but they do not determine action (Zimmerman, 1970; Giddens, 1984) (1994: 507).

Feldman (2000) built on Pentland and Rueter's orientation to practice theoretic ideas and the idea of routines as effortful accomplishments and adds the idea of routines as *emergent accomplishments*. The central problem this article deals with is conceptualizing routines in a way that accommodated the simultaneity of stability and change. The initial focus of the study was finding mechanisms of stability, but after observing 'stable' routines over several years, it became clear that stability was only half of the story; the other half was change. This article relies on practice theory to support the contention that it is the *internal logic* of the routine that supports both stability and change. In the literature review, Feldman invokes the recursive relationship of action and structure present in Giddens' work and developed by scholars such as Barley, Orlikowski and Sewell as a way of thinking about routines that is consistent with the idea of organizing as an ongoing accomplishment:

> Theorists have suggested that structure consists of patterned actions (Manning 1977, 1982; Weick 1979) and of recursive relations between actions and the residue of past actions (Giddens 1979, 1984; Sewell 1992; Barley 1986, 1990; Orlikowski 1992). As we move toward a notion of organization (or organizing) as an ongoing accomplishment we need a notion of routine to match. (2000: 613)

The importance of practice theories for understanding both stability and change is further articulated in the methods section of the article:

> The third step [of the analysis] took place once I had found some theories that helped me to think about both change and stability in organizational routines. The theories I found most useful were structuration theory (Giddens 1979, 1984, 1993) and the theory of practice as developed by

[3] 'To the extent that organizational processes such as routines can be described as ordered sets of actions, they can also be described by grammars. By expressing the sequences of action observed in an organizational process using grammar, we can detect sequential structure and functionally similar patterns' (Pentland and Rueter, 1994: 489).

> Bourdieu (1977, 1990), Lave (1988) and Ortner (1984, 1989). As I read these theories, I used the concepts to organize my observations of the routines. This exercise led me to an appreciation of the relationship between action and structure through the medium of practice. This appreciation underlies much of what I understand about why and how organizational routines change (2000: 615).

These rather broad statements about how practice theory was helpful are somewhat more developed in the discussion following the findings where Feldman draws attention to 'the internal logic of systems' and cites the work of Giddens and Bourdieu (2000: 623). While, in future publications, Feldman comes to see the potential for change articulated in both Bourdieu's notion of practice as inherently improvisational and Giddens' ideas about the relevance of self-monitoring as a part of agency, in this early use of practice theory she has not yet seen the basis for change in the work of Giddens and Bourdieu. Instead, she turns to Sewell (1992), an article that draws on both Giddens and Bourdieu and argues that the basis for structural transformation is that,

> structures are 'multiple, contingent and fractured' (p. 16) rather than monolithic. Thus, he suggests several reasons for change: that structures are multiple and intersecting, that schemas are transposable, that resource accumulation is unpredictable, and that resources themselves have multiple meanings (Feldman, 2000: 623).

These two empirical pieces (Pentland and Rueter, 1994 and Feldman, 2000) formed the basis for the theoretical piece co-authored by Feldman and Pentland (2003). The influence of practice theory is more clearly acknowledged in this article,

> Our goal here is to create a new theory of organizational routines that retains the valuable insights of prior work while enabling us to account for the empirical observations that expose the limitations of this work. Beyond that, we strive for a conceptualization that enables us to see how stability and change in organizational routines are related. We offer a new ontology of organizational routines that adopts a perspective based on new understandings of the relation between structure and action (Bourdieu, 1977, 1990; Giddens, 1984; Ortner, 1989) and accounts for empirical findings about routines (2003: 100).

The role of practice theory is also much more fully developed. The authors rely on practice theory for several parts of the argument that were already at least partially developed in the earlier empirical articles, including that rules do not determine action (Feldman and Pentland, 2003: 101), that practical consciousness or self-monitoring is important to how people enact routines (2003: 102, 106, 108, 109) and that the duality of structure and agency helps to explain the conundrum of how routines can be both stable and changing (2003: 95, 100, 105). In addition, the authors situate change in the combination of Bourdieu's notion of practice as inherently improvisational and Giddens' ideas about the relevance of self-monitoring as a part of agency,

> In his theory of practice, Bourdieu (1977, 1990) argued that practice is inherently improvisational. Practices are carried out against a background of rules and expectations, but the particular courses of action we choose are always, to some extent, novel. Unreflective, habitual action is certainly possible, but even in highly constrained situations, participants engage in reflective self-monitoring in order to see what they are doing (Giddens, 1984) (2003: 102).

The authors also point to the importance of artifacts and the inseparability of artifacts from aspects of routines that are less material and may, therefore, be perceived as subjective,

> As practiced, objective and subjective dimensions are mutually constitutive (Bourdieu, 1990). Objective and subjective aspects are inseparable because the objectified summaries of routines (the artifacts) are constructed from our subjective perceptions of them. Thus, ironically, routines exist as objects because of our subjective understandings of them. In a sense, our subjective understanding and interpretation is the glue that binds the actions into the patterns we recognize as the routine (2003: 109).

Leaning heavily on the notion of a routine as a practice that therefore requires improvisation and a practical sense of how to go on that entails the mutually constituted relationship of actions and patterns (referred to as performative and ostensive aspects of routines), these articles launched the field of Routine Dynamics. Routines are theorized as ongoing, situated accomplishments that are both effortful and emergent. Consistent with Bourdieu's insistence on understanding the internal logic of practice (Bourdieu, 1990; Bourdieu and Wacquant, 1992), the internal dynamics of routines that entail stability and change and produce stability and change become focal (Feldman et al., 2016). These internal dynamics are attributed to the interaction and mutual constitution of the performative and ostensive aspects of routines. Though the terminology of ostensive and performative aspects was drawn from Latour (1986) via Sevon (1996) and carries with it some important features of that legacy (e.g., the notion that the ostensive aspect cannot be used as an explanation for the performative; see Sele [Chapter 6], this volume), the influence of practice theory can be seen in the recursive and mutually constituted relationship of performative and ostensive. While Bourdieu's habitus – an 'acquired system of generative schemes' (Bourdieu, 1990: 55) that are embodied and expressed through action – is useful for understanding the ostensive aspect, this connection remained in the background in these foundational papers.

2.3.2 *Practice Theory in the Developing Field of Routine Dynamics*

Routine Dynamics scholars have continued to rely on practice theory. Table 2.1 documents this reliance by analysing both the practice theoretic references and the way these references are used in two sets of articles, (1) articles written between 1994 and 2011 and (2) the articles in the 2016 *Organization Science* special issue on Routine Dynamics. The articles from 1994 to 2011 are from the formative stage of Routine Dynamics. These were years when there was a steady but small stream of Routine Dynamics articles.[4] Bibliometric research shows that by 2012 the number of Routine Dynamics articles had begun to increase sharply (Baldesarelli et al., 2020) and it is, thus, harder to review the post-2011 articles in the space of a handbook chapter. The articles in the 2016 *Organization Science* special issue on Routine Dynamics provide another snapshot from which we can see how practice theory has been engaged in Routine Dynamics articles.

2.3.2.1 References to Practice Theory (Second Column)

The analysis required many decisions. I only included published references and not conference papers, working papers or unpublished dissertations. Deciding what counts as a practice theory-oriented article is complicated. Some are obvious – Bourdieu, Gherardi, Giddens, Lave, Orlikowski, Ortner and Schatzki are all authors who have identified themselves as practice theorists. However, there are also many fuzzy boundaries and authors who straddle these. Ethnomethodologists such as Garfinkel or Suchman, ANT/STS scholars such as Callon or Latour, pragmatists such as Dewey or Mead, or performativity scholars such as MacKenzie all have much in common with practice theorists and for many purposes we would include them. In order to stick closely to the focus of this chapter – the influence of Practice Theory on Routine Dynamics – I did not include these scholars in the list of references, though often the point where the article references practice theorists is also a point at which these authors are cited, and sometimes the implication of the practice theoretic point can only be made through references to these authors.[5]

New practice theory references are in bold so that one can easily see the accretion of practice theory references. For the articles up to 2011, what is considered new is chronological, for the 2016 articles 'newness' is somewhat arbitrarily determined by the order of articles in the special issue. To keep the list of references manageable, when articles reference Routine Dynamics articles that are oriented to practice theory and are listed in the

[4] I have tried to be inclusive. I apologize if any articles that should be included were omitted.

[5] An instance of this is D'Adderio (2011), where the idea that materiality and practice are entangled draws on both practice theory and adjacent theories, but the point that artifacts have agency requires going beyond practice theory.

Table 2.1 Practice Theory in Routine Dynamics articles

Article	Practice theory works cited (first use in bold)	What did authors rely on practice theory to do? (new uses of practice theory in Routine Dynamics in bold)
Articles 1994–2011		
Pentland and Rueter (1994)	Giddens (1984)	**Routines as effortful accomplishments; Rules, norms are resources for but do not determine actions**
Feldman (2000)	Bourdieu (1977), (1990); **Brown and Duguid (1991)**; Giddens (1979), (1984), (1993); **Lave (1988)**; Manning (1977), (1982); **Orlikowski (1992); Ortner (1984)**, (1989); **Sewell (1992)**, cites previous RD article	**Routines as emergent accomplishments; Identifying internal dynamics of routines as source of change; Role of agency in routines**
Feldman and Rafaeli (2002)	Bourdieu (1990); Giddens (1984), cites previous RD articles	**Connections of micro and macro understandings in relation to stability, adaptability and power in routines**
Feldman (2003)	Bourdieu (1977), (1990); Giddens (1979), (1984), (1993); Orlikowski (1996), (2000); Sewell (1992), cites previous RD articles	**Agency, performance and power in stability and change**
Feldman and Pentland (2003)	Giddens (1984); Bourdieu (1977), (1990); **Barley (1986); Emirbayer and Mische (1998)**; Orlikowski (1992), (2000); Ortner (1989); Sewell (1992); **Reynaud (1998)**, cites previous RD articles	**Duality of structure and agency in routines; Stability and change engaged as duality rather than dualism**
D'Adderio (2003)	Brown and Duguid (2000); **Knorr-Cetina (1999)**; Lave and Wenger (1991); Orlikowski (1992); **Pickering (1995)**	**Distinction between configured knowledge and actionable knowledge**
Howard-Grenville (2005)	**Carlile (2002)**; Emirbayer and Mische (1998); Giddens (1984), (1993); Lave (1988) Orlikowski (1992), (2000); Sewell (1992), cites previous RD articles	**Unintended reproduction of structures**; Routines are recreated or revised with each instantiation; **Definition of power and resource**
Lazaric and Denis (2005)	cites previous RD articles	Routinization is not mindless or automatic, but effortful; Rules and representations are different from performance;
Reynaud (2005)	Bourdieu (1990), (2005), cites previous RD articles	**Routines because they entail habitus manage the incompleteness of rules – the void at the heart of rules; Routines as** effortful and emergent accomplishments and **capacity to learn**
Pentland and Feldman (2005)	Bourdieu (1977), (1990); Giddens (1984); Lave (1988); Orlikowski (1992), (1996), (2000); Ortner (1984); Sewell (1992), cites previous RD articles	**Routine/practice as unit of analysis;** Dualities and the choice of performative/ostensive as a duality that describes routines; Relationship between rules and action;
Levinthal and Rerup (2006)	Emirbayer and Mische (1998), cites previous RD articles	Engagement of past sequences of action is not mindless or automatic; Routinized behaviour as effortful and agentic
Pentland and Feldman (2007)	Barley (1986); Bourdieu (1990); Giddens (1984), (1989); Orlikowski (1992), (2000); **Orlikowski and Barley (2001); Orlikowski and Iacono (2001); DeSanctis and Poole (1994)**; Jones and Karsten (2003), cites previous RD articles	Organizational forms as emergent patterns of activity, **Duality of sociality and materiality, Technology in use is different from technology as a thing** Structures as enacted patterns of interaction and technology in practice **Recognizing involves misrecognizing**;

Table 2.1 (*cont.*)

Article	Practice theory works cited (first use in bold)	What did authors rely on practice theory to do? (new uses of practice theory in Routine Dynamics in bold)
Birnholtz, Cohen and Hoch (2007)	Lave and Wenger (1991); Orlikowski (2002), cites previous RD articles	To align their work with work that sees structure as created through action that takes place within structure; To distinguish their focus on disposition from the focus on practice
D'Adderio (2008)	Barley (1986); Bourdieu (1977); Brown and Duguid (1996); Lave and Wenger (1991); Orlikowski (1992), (2000), (2002); **Orr (1990)**; Pickering (1994); **Schatzki, Knorr Cetina and von Savigny (2001)**, cites previous RD articles	**Artifacts in routines as relating both to generative models of routines and to performativity;** Situates claims about performativity and artifacts as similar to practice-based research in rejecting the idea that rules determine behaviour, as distinct from practice-based research that suggests a large role for agency and discretion in rule interpretation
Pentland and Feldman (2008)	Emirbayer and Mische (1998); Orlikowski (1992), (2000), (2007); cites previous RD articles	Materiality enables and constrains action
Bruns (2009)	Gherardi, S. and Nicolini (2000), (2002); Gherardi, Nicolini and Odella (1998), cites previous RD articles	**Relationality of individual and collective action** as important to the production of safety; **Transfer in the form of concrete practices**
Hales and Tidd (2009)	Knorr-Cetina (2001), cites previous RD articles	**Innovation as a social accomplishment**; Artifacts as part of internal structure of routines; **Effects of rules often differs from intent of rule maker**
Salvato (2009)	cites previous RD articles	Heterogeneity in routine performances; Mundane details important for organizational outcomes
Pentland, Haerem, Hillison (2010)	Bourdieu (1990); Giddens (1984); Barley (1986); Desanctis and Poole (1994); Orlikowski (2000), cites previous RD articles	Reciprocal causation/duality Routines as duality of latent and expressed behaviours
Zbaracki and Bergen (2010)	cites previous RD articles	Routines as a source of endogenous change
D'Adderio (2011)	Bourdieu (1977), (2005); Giddens (1993); Lave (1988); Lave and Wenger (1991); Orlikowski (1992), (2000), (2002), (2010); Orlikowski and Iacono (2001); Schatzki et.al (2001)	Routines as generative systems that entail agency; **Materiality and practice are entangled;** Asymmetric power distribution
Rerup and Feldman (2011)	Bourdieu (1990); Giddens (1984); Ortner (1989); Sewell (1992), cites previous RD articles	Recursive relationship of performative and ostensive aspects of routines; **Same action constitutes multiple structures**
Salvato and Rerup (2011)	cites previous RD articles	Routines as generative systems
Articles in 2016 Organization Science special issue on Routine Dynamics		
Feldman, Pentland, D'Adderio, Lazaric (2016)	Bourdieu (1984); Bourdieu (1990); **D'Adderio (2014); Emirbayer (1997)**; **Feldman and Orlikowski (2011)**; **Gherardi (2006)**; Giddens (1984); **Michel (2014), Nicolini (2013);** Orlikowski (1992); **Orlikowski and Scott (2008),** cites previous RD articles	Practice/routines as effortful and emergent; Situated action/routines as unit of observation; **Relationality and how practices feel as they are practised**
LeBaron, Christianson, Garrett, Ilan (2016)	Orlikowski (2007); Orlikowski and Scott (2008), cites previous RD articles	Materiality and practice are entangled

Table 2.1 (*cont.*)

Article	Practice theory works cited (first use in bold)	What did authors rely on practice theory to do? (new uses of practice theory in Routine Dynamics in bold)
Aroles and McLean (2016)	D'Adderio (2014); **Orlikowski (2010)**; Orlikowski and Scott (2008), cites previous RD articles	Materiality and practice are entangled
Berente, Lyytinen, Yoo and King (2016)	Barley (1986); **DeSanctis and Poole (1994);** Orlikowski (1996); **Tyre and Orlikowski (1994)**, cites previous RD articles	**Misalignment (lack of coherence) as a challenge for practice**
Bertels, Howard-Grenville and Pek (2016)	D'Adderio (2014); Orlikowski and Scott (2008); Sewell (1992); **Swidler (2001)**; Tyre and Orlikowski (1994), cites previous RD articles	**Cultural context as embedded in/part of practice**
Bucher and Langley (2016)	D'Adderio (2014); Giddens (1984); **Jarzabkowski, Lê and Feldman (2012)**, cites previous RD articles	Recursive relation between performance and pattern and implications for change
Cohendet and Simon (2016)	D'Adderio (2014); Jarzabkowski, Le and Feldman (2012); **Schreyögg and Sydow (2010)**, cites previous RD articles	Routines entail efficiency-flexiblity/fluidity duality;
Danner-Schoeder and Geiger (2016)	Brown and Duguid, 1991, 2001; D'Adderio, 2014; **Feldman and Orlikowski (2011),** Gherardi (2000), (2006), (2009); Orlikowski (1992), (2002); Orlikowski and Scott (2008); **Reckwitz (2002)**; **Strati (2007),** cites previous RD articles	Relation of learning and knowing to practice and practising; **Knowing involves doing and is embodied**
Deken, Carlile, Berends and Lauche (2016)	Emirbayer (1997); Emirbayer and Mische (1998); Michel (2014); **Østerlund and Carlile (2005)**, cites previous RD articles	Relationality/mutual constitution as fundamental to practice and routines
Dittrich, Guerard, Seidl (2016)	Feldman and Orlikowski (2011); **Gherardi (2012)**; Orlikowski and Yates (1994), cites previous RD articles	Acts of communication as practice; Action in routines as based on reflection
Kremser and Scheyoegg (2016)	Feldman and Orlikowski (2011), cites previous RD articles	Routines as duality of practice and principle
Sele and Grand (2016)	D'Adderio (2014); Feldman and Orlikowski (2011); Nicolini (**2009**), (**2010**), (**2013**); Orlikowski and Scott (2008); Schatzki (2011), cites previous RD articles	Routine have mutually constituting parts; Practices/routines must be understood in relation to other practices/routines, that is, in use
Sonenshein (2016)	D'Adderio (2014); Michel (2014), cites previous RD articles	**Routines/practices can accomplish contradictory objectives;** Connection between practices or routines and identities;
Spee, Jarzabkowski and Smets (2016)	D'Adderio (2014); Feldman and Orlikowski (2011); Jarzabkowski, Le and Feldman (2012); Orlikowski (2002); **Parmigiani and Howard-Grenville (2011)**, cites previous RD articles	Duality of standardization and flexibility; Routines as generative systems
Yi, Knudsen, Becker (2016)	cites previous RD articles	Endogenous change in routines

table, I simply add the phrase 'cites previous RD articles'. Finally, I may have omitted some references to articles that are practice theory oriented through my own ignorance, though I did do my best to check[6] to see if references cited referred to practice theory.

Three trends emerge as one views the works cited. First, the work of Bourdieu and Giddens that constitutes the foundation of practice theory is cited in most but not all of the 1994–2011 articles and is cited in some but not most of the 2016 special issue articles. In the later articles, many of the practice theoretic points the authors rely on – such as the mutually constituted or entangled nature of various dualities – are made through the work of scholars who build on this foundational practice theory work. These scholars include but are certainly not limited to the authors of previous Routine Dynamics articles.

Second, previous Routine Dynamics articles are cited in nearly all of the articles in both the early and the later articles. While for the articles in the *Organization Science* special issue this is neither surprising nor particularly informative, it is notable that there is such a strong dependence from the beginning on the foundation that practice theory provided for Routine Dynamics. This pattern of referencing speaks to the development of a conversation among scholars that signifies the creation of a field.

Finally, the list of practice theoretic references expands and shifts over time. Some of this is because scholars continue to develop practice theory and many of the new references in the 2016 articles are recently published. The table also shows that Routine Dynamics scholars have consistently expanded the repertoire of practice theory scholarship that they have engaged. This suggests that practice theory continues to be a source of inspiration to Routine Dynamics scholars.

[6] I did search for signs of practice theory orientation in many, though not all, references unknown to me. My search criteria were use of the term practice theory and substantive use of work by Giddens, Bourdieu or Schatzki.

2.3.2.2 Themes Related to Practice Theory (Third Column)

I determined the entries in the third column by seeing how the authors used the references. In this process, it sometimes turned out that a reference that could be used to support practice theoretic points was instead used to make other points. In that case, I removed the reference. It is important, here, to note that this column does not necessarily capture what is the major contribution of the article, though sometimes the way practice theory is used is coincident with the contributions.

Given the breadth of references to practice theory scholarship, it is not surprising that Routine Dynamics scholars have used practice theory for a wide array of purposes. Here, I discuss a few key themes established by the foundational articles that continue to be relevant and are extended in various ways. These themes illustrate three different ways that practice theory has been integral to the growth of Routine Dynamics. The first theme shows how practice theory ideas have become taken for granted in Routine Dynamics research. The second theme shows how Routine Dynamics scholars have expanded the use of practice theorizing moves, allowing them to customize the move to the routines they are studying. The third theme shows how practice theory has opened possibilities for expanding to other theorizing.

That routines are effortful and emergent accomplishments, for instance, is a foundational theme that Routine Dynamics scholars used practice theory to establish. While practice theory was frequently used to support this foundation in the articles between 1994 and 2011, the connection between this point and practice theory is less evident in the later articles analysed here. Articles that do not specifically make this connection do often talk about the effort involved in enacting a routine and the ways that routines emerge or transform in the process of being enacted.

The taken-for-grantedness of the theoretical foundations of the idea that routines are effortful and emergent accomplishments is a good example of how developments within this field that initially required conscious and assiduous use of practice theory are now simply assumed. Being taken for granted has advantages and disadvantages. Clearly, a field cannot constantly be re-establishing its foundations. At the same time, if scholars become unaware of the ideas on which these foundations are built, they may lose touch with a generative source of questions that can continue to fuel the field. Have we plumbed the depths of understanding the internal logic of routines and how that internal logic produces stability and change? While several chapters of this handbook explore other sources of theory that have also been and continue to be generative, practice theory's focus on practice as the unit of analysis makes it unusually well-situated to help us understand the internal logic that is – in Bourdieu's words – 'in cahoots with the fuzzy and the vague' (Bourdieu, 1987: 96, cited in Bourdieu and Wacquant, 1992: 22).

Another common theme in the Routine Dynamics articles analyzed is the transcendence of dualisms. Feldman and Orlikowski (2011) identified rejecting dualisms 'as a way of theorizing' (2011: 1241) and instead recognizing 'the inherent relationship between elements that have often been treated dichotomously' (2011: 1242) as one of three generally accepted theorizing moves in practice theory. Routine Dynamics scholars have consistently made this move, starting with the idea that stability and change are, in practice, not opposites but implicated in one another. Indeed, how routines could be both stable and changing was an early animating conundrum for Routine Dynamics. This theorizing move underlies the somewhat controversial move to conceptualize performative and ostensive not as the opposing and separable constructs Latour introduced but as recursively related to one another (see Sele [Chapter 6], this volume). Much like the ideas of effortful and emergent accomplishment, turning dualisms into dualities has become one of the more consistent uses of practice theory in Routine Dynamics articles, extending beyond the stability/change, agency/structure or performative/ostensive dualities. More recently addressed dualities include latent/expressed, practice/principle, sociality/materiality, flexibility (fluidity)/efficiency and flexibility/standardization. These dualities show how authors can customize this move to understand the logic of routines in specific organizations and extend the impact of this practice theoretic move.

Exploring the relationship between rules and practice is another important theme. This theme has expanded over time. Although always seen as an important resource for action, an early concern was to establish that rules do not *determine* action. This concern followed from a history of routines research that largely mistook written rules and standard operating procedures for the routines and had, thus, produced an understanding of routines as static (Feldman et al. [Chapter 1], this volume). An additional concern related to the incompleteness of rules and the need for practice to fill in where the rules do not provide guidance about what actions to take. Gradually, the conceptualization of rules has emphasized the constraints on human agency as well as the agentic nature of rules. Though some of this work has relied on practice theory and Orlikowski's work in particular, some of the theorists whose work underlies the later moves in this area are not included here because they are in that category of theorists discussed earlier with close relations to practice theory but who have identified their work as other than practice theory. This theme, thus, shows how practice theory has provided a platform for Routine Dynamics scholars to connect to other theories in our expanding understanding of the dynamics that underlie stability and change in routines.

2.4 Future Avenues of Research

Practice theory so thoroughly undergirds Routine Dynamics that it is possible that there could be diminishing returns to further reliance on practice theory. Moreover, Routine Dynamics has gained much from the admixture of many ways of thinking about process and practice. That said, the use of practice theory in Routine Dynamics has been uneven and some features of the theory may yet be usefully engaged. Given the impossibility of an extended description of practice theory in this handbook chapter, I opted to emphasize several features. Some of these features, while central to practice theory, have not been as developed in

Routine Dynamics. In particular, the collective nature of practice and the role of practical sense or practical consciousness and, therefore, the embodied nature of practice, have more often been evident in the empirical representations of Routine Dynamics scholarship than in the theorizing (see Blanche and Feldman [Chapter 25], this volume).

The focus on routines in organizational settings has perhaps limited the focus on a broader sense of the collective nature of practice. In working on this Handbook, I have been surprised by claims that Routine Dynamics has focused on reflection on action rather than reflection in action (Tsoukas [Chapter 3], this volume; Wegener and Glaser [Chapter 22], this volume). Although the notion of the internal logic of practice animated the early work in Routine Dynamics, it has perhaps been replaced by a focus on the relationship between performative and ostensive aspects or performing and patterning (see Feldman et al. [Chapter 1], this volume). There is, however, an increasing interest in the connection between routines enacted in organizations and collective outcomes as indicated by the 2020 EGOS subtheme on Routine Dynamics and Grand Challenges. This interest may lead us to ask questions such as: How do collective practices reproduce collective benefits and harms such as privilege and discrimination? How does transformation occur in collective practices? What is the role of uncertainty and possibility in producing change in collective practices? Taking seriously how the logic of practice is 'consequential in the production of social life' (Feldman and Orlikowski, 2011: 1241) opens these and other questions.

Just as the practice of marriage described earlier in this chapter can promote privilege for some and inequality for others, so can the routines that we enact for teaching, for hiring, for allocating and distributing funds and so forth. Bourdieu claims that 'the logic of practice is logical up to the point where to be logical would cease being practical' (Bourdieu and Wacquant, 1992: 22–23). It is entirely consistent with practice theory to explore the logic of this practicality. What makes inequality practical? What is the practicality of denying same-sex partners the ability to engage in the practice of marriage? On what basis are criminal justice routines that lead to mass incarceration of black and brown men practical? What is practical about organizing college teaching in ways that assume students will be able to prioritize their school work over family responsibilities and that, thereby, make it difficult for many first-generation college students to complete their courses and graduate? Bourdieu notes that 'The simple possibility that things might proceed otherwise than as laid down by the "mechanical laws" of the "cycle of reciprocity" is sufficient to change the whole experience of practice and, by the same token its logic' (1990: 99). Unravelling the logic of specific practices, how that logic plays out for different people and what the possibilities are for acting otherwise is a challenge that practice theory can help us meet.

2.5 Conclusion

Routine Dynamics entails understanding routines as practices. Theories, in all their forms, that help us understand practice are relevant to Routine Dynamics. The foundational papers in Routine Dynamics relied heavily on practice theory as articulated by Bourdieu and Giddens to focus on the internal logic of routines and, particularly, the relationality of stability and change in routines. These ideas have been expanded and supplemented over time through engagement with empirical data as well as through more extensive use of practice theory and related theories. Practice theory has provided a firm basis for Routine Dynamics and still has much to offer.

References

Aroles, J. and McLean, C. (2016). Rethinking stability and change in the study of organizational routines: Difference and repetition in a newspaper-printing factory. *Organization Science*, 27(3), 535–550.

Barley, S. R. (1986). Technology as an occasion for structuring: Evidence from observations of CT scanners and the social order of radiology departments. *Administrative Science Quarterly*, 31, 78–108.

Berente, N., Lyytinen, K., Yoo, Y. and King, J. L. (2016). Routines as shock absorbers during organizational transformation: Integration, control, and NASA's Enterprise Information System. *Organization Science*, 27(3), 551–572.

Bertels, S., Howard-Grenville, J. and Pek, S. (2016). Cultural molding, shielding, and shoring at Oilco: The role of culture in the integration of routines. *Organization Science*, 27(3), 573–593.

Birnholtz, J., Cohen, M. D. and Hoch, S. (2007). Organizational character: On the regeneration of Camp Poplar Grove. *Organization Science*, 18(2), 315–332.

Bourdieu, P. (1977). *Outline of a Theory of Practice*. Cambridge: Cambridge University Press.

Bourdieu, P. (1984). *Distinction: A Social Critique of the Judgement of Taste*. Cambridge, MA: Harvard University Press.

Bourdieu, P. (1987). *Choses dites*. Paris: Editions de Minuit.

Bourdieu, P. (1990). *The Logic of Practice*. Stanford, CA: Stanford University Press.

Bourdieu, P. (2005). *The Social Structures of the Economy*. Cambridge: Polity Press.

Bourdieu, P. and Wacquant, L. (1992). *An Invitation to Reflexive Sociology*. Chicago: University of Chicago Press.

Brown, J. S. and Duguid, P. (1991). Organizational learning and communities-of-practice: Toward a unified view of working, learning and innovation. *Organization Science*, 2(1), 40–57.

Brown, J. S. and Duguid, P. (1996). Learning and communities-of-practice: Toward a unified view of working, learning, and innovation. In M. D. Cohen and L. S. Sproull, eds., *Organizational Learning*. London: Sage, pp. 59–82.

Brown, J. S. and Duguid, P. (2000). *The Social Life of Information*. Cambridge, MA: Harvard Business School Press.

Brown, J. S. and Duguid, P. (2001). Knowledge and organization: A social-practice perspective. *Organization Science*, 12(2), 198–213.

Bruns, H. (2009). Leveraging functionality in safety routines: Examining the divergence of rules and performance. *Human Relations*, 62(9), 1399–1426.

Bucher, S. and Langley, A. (2016). The Interplay of reflective and experimental spaces in interrupting and reorienting routine dynamics. *Organization Science*, 27(3), 594–613.

Carlile, P. R. (1997). Understanding knowledge transformation in product development: Making knowledge manifest through boundary objects. Unpublished doctoral dissertation, University of Michigan, Ann Arbor.

Carlile, P. R. (2002). *A Pragmatic View of Knowledge and Boundaries: Boundary Objects in New Product Development*. Providence, RI: Organization Science.

Cohendet, P. S. and Simon, L. O. (2016). Always playable: Recombining routines for creative efficiency at Ubisoft Montreal's Video Game Studio. *Organization Science*, 27(3), 614–632.

D'Adderio, L. D. (2003). Configuring software, reconfiguring memories: The influence of integrated systems on the reproduction of knowledge and routines. *Industrial and Corporate Change*, 12(2), 321–350.

D'Adderio, L. D. (2008). The performativity of routines: Theorising the influence of artifacts and distributed agencies on routines dynamics. *Research Policy*, 37, 769–789.

D'Adderio, L. D. (2011). Artifacts at the centre of routines: Performing the material turn in routines theory. *Journal of Institutional Economics*, 7(2), 197–230.

D'Adderio, L. D. (2014). Replication dilemma. *Organization Science*, 25(5), 1325–1350.

Danner-Schröder, A. and Geiger, D. (2016). Unravelling the motor of patterning work: Toward an understanding of the microlevel dynamics of standardization and flexibility. *Organization Science*, 27(3), 633–658.

Deken, F., Carlile, P. R., Berends, H. and Lauche, K. (2016). Generating novelty through interdependent routines: A process model of routine work. *Organization Science*, 27(3), 659–677.

DeSanctis, G. and Poole, M. S. (1994). Capturing the complexity in advanced technology use: Adaptive structuration theory. *Organization Science*, 5, 121–147.

Dionysiou, D. and Tsoukas, H. (2013). Understanding the creation and recreation of routines from within: A symbolic interactionist perspective. *Academy of Management Review*, 38, 181–205.

Dittrich, K., Guérard, S. and Seidl, D. (2016). Talking about routines: The role of reflective talk in routine change. *Organization Science*, 27(3), 678–697.

Emirbayer, M. (1997). Manifesto for a relational sociology. *American Journal of Sociology*, 103(2), 281–317.

Emirbayer, M. and Mische, A. (1998). What is agency? *American Journal of Sociology*, 103, 962–1023.

Feldman M. S. (2000). Organizational routines as a source of continuous change. *Organization Science*, 11(6), 611–629.

Feldman, M. S. (2003). A performative perspective on stability and change in organizational routines. *Industrial and Corporate Change*, 12(4), 727–752.

Feldman, M. S. and Orlikowski, W. J. (2011). Theorizing practice and practicing theory. *Organization Science*, 22(5), 1240–1253.

Feldman, M. S. and Pentland, B. T. (2003). Reconceptualizing organizational routines as a source of flexibility and change. *Administrative Science Quarterly*, 48, 94–118.

Feldman, M. S., Pentland, B. T., D' Adderio, L. and Lazaric, N. (2016). Beyond routines as things: Introduction to the Special Issue on routine dynamics. *Organization Science*, 27, 505–513.

Feldman, M. S. and Rafaeli, A. (2002). Organizational routines as sources of connections and understandings. *Journal of Management Studies*, 39(3), 309–331.

Feldman, M. S., and Worline, M. (2016). The practicality of practice theory. *Academy of Management Learning & Education*, 15(2), 304–324.

Gherardi, S. (2000). Practice-based theorizing on learning and knowing in organizations. *Organization*, 7(2), 211–223.

Gherardi, S. (2006). *Organizational Knowledge: The Texture of Workplace Learning*. Malden, MA: Blackwell Publishing.

Gherardi, S. (2009). Practice? It's a matter of taste. *Management Learning*, 40(5), 535–550.

Gherardi, S. (2012). *How to Conduct a Practice-Based Study: Problems and Methods*. Cheltenham: Edward Elgar Publishing.

Gherardi, S. and Nicolini, D. (2000). To transfer is to transform: The circulation of safety knowledge. *Organization*, 7, 329–348.

Gherardi, S. and Nicolini, D. (2002). Learning the trade: A culture of safety in practice. *Organization*, 9, 191–223.

Gherardi, S., Nicolini, D. and Odella, F. (1996). What do you mean by safety? Conflicting perspectives on accident causation and safety management in a construction firm. *Journal of Contingencies and Crisis Management*, 6, 202–213.

Giddens, A. (1979). *Central Problems in Social Theory: Action, Structure and Contradiction in Social Analysis*. Berkeley: University of California Press.

Giddens, A. (1984). *The Constitution of Society*. Cambridge: Polity Press.

Giddens, A. (1989). A reply to my critics. In D. Held and J. B. Thompson, eds., *Social Theory of Modern Societies: Anthony Giddens and His Critics*. New York: Press Syndicate of the University of Cambridge, pp. 248–301.

Giddens, A. (1993). *New Rules of Sociological Method*, 2nd ed. Stanford, CA: Stanford University Press.

Hales, M. and Tidd, J. (2009). The practice of routines and representations in design and development. *Industrial and Corporate Change*, 18(4), 551–574.

Howard-Grenville, J. A. (2005). The persistence of flexible organizational routines: The role of agency and organizational context. *Organization Science*, 16(6), 618–636.

Jarzabkowski, P., Lê, J. K. and Feldman, M. S. (2012). Toward a theory of coordinating: Creating coordinating mechanisms in practice. *Organization Science*, 23(4), 907–927.

Jones, M. R. and Karsten, H. (2003). Review: Structuration theory and information systems research. Working Paper 2003/11, Judge Institute of Management, Cambridge: Cambridge University.

Knorr-Cetina, K. (1999). *Epistemic Cultures: How the Sciences Make Knowledge*. Cambridge, MA: Harvard University Press.

Kremser, W. and Schreyögg, G. (2016). The dynamics of interrelated routines: Introducing the cluster level. *Organization Science*, 27(3), 698–721.

Latour, B. (1986). The powers of association. In J. Law, ed., *Power, Action and Belief: A New Sociology of Knowledge?* London: Routledge & Kegan Paul, pp. 264–280.

Lave, J. (1988). *Cognition in Practice: Mind, Mathematics and Culture in Everyday Life*. Cambridge: Cambridge University Press.

Lave, J. and Wenger, E. (1991). *Situated Learning: Legitimate Peripheral Participation*. Cambridge, MA: Cambridge University Press.

Lazaric, N. and Denis, B. (2005). Routinization and memorization of tasks in a workshop: The case of the introduction of ISO norms. *Industrial and Corporate Change*, 145, 872–896.

LeBaron, C., Christianson, M. K., Garrett, L. and Ilan, R. (2016). Coordinating flexible performance during everyday work: An ethnomethodological study of handoff routines. *Organization Science*, 27, 514–534.

Levinthal, D. and Rerup, C. (2006). Crossing an apparent chasm: Bridging mindful and less-mindful perspectives on organizational learning. *Organization Science*, 17(4), 502–513.

Manning, P. K. (1977). *Police Work: The Social Organization of Police Work*. Cambridge, MA: MIT Press.

Manning, P. K. (1982). Organizational work: Enstructuration of the environment. *British Journal of Sociology*, 33, 118–139.

Michel, A. A. (2014). The mutual constitution of persons and organizations: An ontological perspective on organizational change. *Organization Science*, 25(4), 1082–1110.

Nicolini, D. (2009). Zooming in and out: Studying practices by switching theoretical lenses and trailing connections. *Organization Studies*, 30 (12), 1391–1418.

Nicolini, D. (2010). Medical innovation as a process of translation: A case from the field of telemedicine. *British Journal of Management*, 21(4), 1011–1026.

Nicolini, D. (2013). *Practice Theory, Work, and Organization: An Introduction*. Oxford: Oxford University Press.

Nicolini, D., Gherardi, S. and Yanow, D., eds. (2003). *Knowing in Organizations: A Practice-Based Approach*. Armonk, NY: M.E. Sharpe.

Orlikowski, W. J. (1992). The duality of technology: Rethinking the concept of technology in organizations. *Organization Science*, 3(3), 398–427.

Orlikowski, W. J. (1996). Improvising organizational transformation over time: A situated change perspective. *Information Systems Research*, 7(1), 63–92.

Orlikowski, W. J. (2000). Using technology and constituting structures. *Organization Science*, 11(4), 404–428.

Orlikowski, W. J. (2002). Knowing in practice: Enacting a collective capability in distributed organizing. *Organization Science*, 13(3), 249–273.

Orlikowski, W. J. (2007). Sociomaterial practices: Exploring technology at work. *Organization Studies*, 28(9), 1435–1448.

Orlikowski, W. J. (2010). Practice in research: Phenomenon, perspective and philosophy. In D. Golsorkhi, L. Rouleau, D. Seidl and E. Vaare, eds., *Cambridge Handbook of Strategy as Practice*. Cambridge: Cambridge University Press, pp. 23–33.

Orlikowski, W. J. and Barley, S. R. (2001). Technology and institutions: What can research on information technology and research on organizations learn from each other? *MIS Quarterly*, 25(2), 145–165.

Orlikowski, W. J. and Iacono, C. S. (2001). Research commentary: Desperately seeking the IT in IT research – A call to theorizing the IT artifact. *Information Systems Research*, 12(2), 121–134.

Orlikowski, W. J. and Scott, S.V. (2008). Sociomateriality: Challenging the separation of technology, work and organization. *Academy of Management Annals*, 2(1), 433–474.

Orlikowski, W. J. and Yates, J. (1994). Genre repertoire: The structuring of communicative practices in organizations. *Administrative Science Quarterly*, 39(4), 541–574.

Orr, J. E. (1990). Sharing knowledge, celebrating identity: War stories and community memory in a service culture. In D. S. Middleton and D. Edwards, eds., *Collective Remembering: Memory in Society*. Beverley Hills, CA: Sage Publications.

Ortner, S. B. (1984). Theory in anthropology since the sixties. *Comparative Studies in Society and History*, 26(1), 126–166.

Ortner, S. B. (1989). *High Religion: A Cultural and Political History of Sherpa Buddhism*. Princeton, NJ: Princeton University Press.

Østerlund, C. and Carlile, P. R. (2005). Relations in practice: Sorting through practice theories on knowledge sharing in complex organizations. *The Information Society*, 21(2), 91–107.

Parmigiani, A. and Howard-Grenville, J. (2011). Routines revisited: Exploring the capabilities and practice perspectives. *Academy of Management Annals*, 5(1), 413–453.

Pentland, B. T. and Feldman, M. S. (2005). Organizational routines as a unit of analysis. *Industrial and Corporate Change*, 14(5), 793–815.

Pentland, B. T. and Feldman, M. S. (2007). Narrative Networks: Patterns of Technology and Organization. *Organization Science*, 18(5), 781–795.

Pentland, B. T. and Feldman, M. S. (2008). Designing routines: On the folly of designing artifacts, while hoping for patterns of action. *Information and Organization*, 18(2008), 235–250.

Pentland, B. T., Haerem, T. and Hillison, D. (2010). Comparing organizational routines as recurrent patterns of action. *Organization Studies*, 31(7), 917–940.

Pentland, B. T. and Rueter, H. H. (1994). Organizational routines as grammars of action. *Administrative Science Quarterly*, 39, 484–510.

Pickering, A. (1994). After representation: Science studies in the performative idiom. Proceedings of the Biennial Meeting of the PSA, (2), 413–419.

Pickering, A. (1995). *The Mangle of Practice: Time, Agency and Science*. Chicago: University of Chicago Press.

Polanyi, M. (1966). The logic of tacit inference. *Philosophy*, 41(155), 1–18.

Reckwitz, A. (2002). Towards a theory of social practices: A development in culturalist theorizing. *European Journal of Social Theory*, 5(2), 243–263.

Rerup, C. and Feldman, M. S. (2011). Routines as a source of change in organizational schemata: The role of trial-and-error learning. *Academy of Management of Journal*, 54(3), 577–610

Reynaud, B. (1998). Les propriétés des routines: Outils pragmatiques de decision et modes de co-ordination collective. *Sociologie du Travail*, 1998(4), 465–477.

Reynaud, B. (2005). The void at the heart of rules: Routines in the context of rule-following. The Case of the Paris Metro Workshop. *Industrial and Corporate Change*, 14(5), 847–871.

Salvato, C. (2009). Capabilities unveiled: The role of ordinary activities in the evolution of product development processes. *Organization Science*, 20(2), 384–409.

Salvato, C. and Rerup, C. (2011). Beyond collective entities: Multilevel research on organizational routines and capabilities. *Journal of Management*, 37(2), 468–490.

Schatzki, T. R. (2011). *Where the Action Is (on Large Social Phenomena Such as Sociotechnical Regimes)*. Sustainable Practices Research Group, Working Paper 1, University of Kentucky, Lexington.

Schatzki, T. R. (2012). A primer on practices: Theory and research. In J. Higgs, R. Barnett, S. Billett, M. Hutchings and F. Trede, eds., *Practice-Based Education: Perspectives and Strategies*. Rotterdam: Sense Publishers, pp. 13–26.

Schatzki, T. R., Knorr-Cetina, K. and von Savigny, E., eds. (2001). *The Practice Turn in Contemporary Theory*. London: Routledge.

Schön, D. A. (1983). *The Reflective Practitioner: How Professionals Think in Action*. New York: Basic Books.

Schreyögg, G. and Sydow, J. (2010). CROSSROADS – Organizing for fluidity? Dilemmas of new organizational forms. *Organization Science*, 21(6), 1251–1262.

Searle, J. R. (1989). How performatives work. *Linguistics and Philosophy*, 12(5), 535–558.

Sele, K. and Grand, S. (2016). Unpacking the dynamics of ecologies of routines: Mediators and their generative effects in routine interactions. *Organization Science*, 27(3), 722–738.

Sevon, G. (1996). Organizational imitation in identity transformation. In B. Czarniawska and G. Sevon, eds., *Translating Organizational Change*. New York: Walter de Gruyter.

Sewell, W. (1992). A theory of structure: Duality, agency and transformation. *American Journal of Sociology*, 98(1), 1–29.

Shotter, J. (2006). Understanding process from within: An argument for 'withness'-thinking. *Organization Studies*, 27(4), 585–604.

Sonenshein, S. (2016). Routines and creativity: From dualism to duality. *Organization Science*, 27(3), 739–758.

Spee, P., Jarzabkowski, P. and Smets, M. (2016). The influence of routine interdependence and skillful accomplishment on the coordination of standardizing and customizing. *Organization Science*, 27(3), 759–781.

Strati, A. (2007). Sensible knowledge and practice-based learning. *Management Learning*, 38(1), 61–77.

Swidler, A. (2001). *Talk of Love: How Culture Matters*. Chicago: University of Chicago Press.

Tyre, M. and Orlikowski, W. (1994). Windows of opportunity: Temporal patterns of technological adaptation in organizations. *Organization Science*, 5(1), 98–118.

Weick, K. E. (1979). *The Social Psychology of Organizing*, 2nd ed. Reading, MA: Addison Wesley.

Yi, S., Knudsen, T. and Becker, M. C. (2016). Inertia in routines: A hidden source of organizational variation. *Organization Science*, 27(3), 782–800.

Zbaracki, M. J. and Bergen, M. (2010). When truces collapse: A longitudinal study of price-adjustment routines. *Organization Science*, 21 (5), 955–972.

Zimmerman, D. H. (1970). The practicalities of rule use. In J. Douglas, ed., *Understanding Everyday Life: Toward the Reconstruction of Sociological Knowledge*. Chicago: Aldine, pp. 221–238.

CHAPTER 3

Process Theorizing and Routine Dynamics

The Case for Performative Phenomenology

HARIDIMOS TSOUKAS

3.1 Introduction

Organizations are filled with routines. Insofar as organizations are set up to handle recurring issues (from collecting garbage and hiring people to dispatching products and treating patients, etc.), they enact systematic ways of addressing them. Routines are repetitive patterns of interdependent action that are carried out to accomplish a recurring task (Feldman et al., 2016, 2019; Feldman and Pentland, 2003; Howard-Grenville et al., 2016; Howard-Grenville and Rerup, 2017; Parmigiani and Howard-Grenville, 2011). Given their centrality to organizational behaviour, conceptualizing routines has been a critical task in organization studies.

In contrast to the entitative view of routines – that is, the view that routines are stable entities, whose distinctive feature is 'uneventful' repetitiveness (Nelson and Winter, 1982: 97) – that had long been the staple approach in the field, the Routine Dynamics (hereafter: RD) perspective, increasingly influential since the early 2000s, takes a performative view of routines (D'Adderio, 2008; Dionysiou and Tsoukas, 2013; Feldman, 2016; Feldman et al., 2016). The performative approach has challenged what the entitative approach took for granted: the key question is not what routines do, as it was for Nelson and Winter (1982), but 'how routines are done' (Tsoukas, 2019: 4). Feldman et al. (2016:505) have playfully noted the difference between the two approaches as follows, 'where we used to say, "that work is routine", we can now say, "that routine is work"'. This pun aptly makes the point that the performance of routines requires *effort* by skilled agents. Routines do not apply themselves; they are applied.

The performative approach has furthered our understanding of routines. As Feldman et al. (2019: 1) have noted, by inserting agency to routines, RD researchers have methodologically highlighted the importance of focusing on actions and offered theoretical tools (such as practice theory) that have enabled researchers to overcome traditional dualisms and obtain new insights into the micro-foundations of routines (Dionysiou and Tsoukas, 2013; Feldman and Pentland, 2003; Felin et al., 2012). RD research has made visible the effort (or work) required for a repetitive pattern of action to come about: routinized action is not an automatic, identical response to an identical stimulus, as the entitative view would have it (Egidi, 2002: 109; March and Simon, 1953: 161), but an effortful accomplishment that simultaneously reproduces and modifies a pattern.

RD research has shown that routines have internal dynamics that makes them both stable and variable. Routines' internal dynamics are made visible by according *agency* a central place (Feldman, 2000, 2016; Feldman et al., 2016). Agency implies action-induced variability (Giddens, 1993:81), since the experience of agency changes the agent (Paul, 2014; Tsoukas and Chia, 2002) and the context in which agency is exercised is inherently 'fluctuating' (Cohen, 2007: 782), leading to variable performance. The very act of repeated performance carries in it the seed for a routine's endogenous change. *Re*production entails potential *re*vision.

The emphasis on exploring the *dynamics* of routines has made researchers particularly sensitive to process (Feldman, 2016). Traditionally, practice theory has been the main source of inspiration. Practice theory does incorporate process thinking and has usefully brought the unfolding of agency to the fore of our attention. In this chapter, I will argue that it can go still further by consistently adopting an even stronger conception of process. I will seek to demonstrate that blending practice theory with a 'strong process' view (Langley and Tsoukas, 2017: 4) will provide further insights into RD research.

Strong process theorizing underscores the importance of experience, heterogeneity and temporality (Langley and Tsoukas, 2017: 4; Tsoukas, 2019: 6). Specifically, the experience of action and its consequences changes the agent. Agents' experiences are singular (and, therefore, heterogeneous) each time they come about, since they are tied to context and temporal flow. Integrating practice theory with a strong process ontology will enable researchers to explore that 'how the past is drawn upon and made relevant to the present is not an atomistic or random exercise but crucially depends on the social practices in which actors are embedded' (Langley et al., 2013: 5). I call such an integrated practice-cum-process approach 'performative phenomenology' (Tsoukas, 2019: 10). In this chapter, I will employ it to explore how RD research may be further advanced. For this purpose, I will first revisit key tenets of RD research to take stock of its progress and note areas for further development, and then show how performative phenomenology may be drawn on to advance RD research.

3.2 Refining Routine Dynamics Theorizing

RD research has been prolific, impactful and enlightening. As a result of conducting several studies in diverse empirical contexts, we have obtained a better view of *how* routines contribute to stability and change; incorporate technology and artifacts in processes of organizational adaptation and innovation; transfer organizational knowledge across context and time; contribute to organizational replication, innovation and problem solving; intersect, interact and are integrated with other routines, etc. (Feldman et al., 2016, 2019). As Feldman et al. (2016: 506) have noted, three key conceptual principles have underlain RD research: (a) action is situated, (b) actors are knowledgeable and (c) stability is an accomplishment. In this section, I will focus on two main issues that need more refinement.

First, tacit knowledge and reflection-in-action have not been given the central place they ought to have in routine enactment. Actors are assumed to be 'knowledgeable and often reflective' (Feldman et al., 2016: 506). With a few exceptions (Blanche and Cohendet, 2019: 13; Danner-Schroder and Geiger, 2016: 655), empirical studies have taken knowledgeability to be mainly situated knowledge (i.e., knowledge 'about [actors'] local context', Feldman et al., 2016: 506) and/or discursive-cognitive in character (i.e., actors articulate in 'reflective talk' (Dittrich et al., 2016) what they know when enacting a routine). This, however, tends to underplay the tacit knowledge that is typically embedded in the 'body schemata' (Sandberg and Tsoukas, 2020) and the 'shared understandings' (Dionysiou and Tsoukas, 2013) that form the background to the disposition to act, which is at the core of human action involved in routines (Cohen, 2007: 777; Cohen and Bacdayan, 1994; Dreyfus, 2014, 2017; Hadjimichael and Tsoukas, 2019). Actors' knowledgeability is primordially non-deliberate (Dreyfus, 2014): actors are immersed in a background, which provides a tacit frame or, in Polanyi's (1962: 55) terms, the 'subsidiary particulars' that enable actors to focus on the tasks they engage in.

Moreover, in the formulation 'knowledgeable and often reflective', it needs to be clarified how reflectiveness is related to knowledgeability. It is well established that reflecting *on* one's action differs from reflecting-*in*-action (Schön, 1983; Yanow and Tsoukas, 2009), in terms of the type of knowledge and language used. Reflecting-in-action presupposes an actor absorbed in the task, tacitly integrating subsidiary particulars, whose use of language is primarily performative (Dreyfus, 2014, 2017). When absorbed in action, actors use language like all other kinds of equipment: to get things done (Cooren, 2007; Flores, 2012). When, for example, a firefighter crew chief shouts, in the middle of fighting a fire, 'Drop your tools' (Weick, 2001: 107), they are using language performatively

(Blattner, 2006: 103–108; Dreyfus, 2000: 317). When, however, actors' absorption in their tasks is interrupted, actors become aware of their activity and start thinking and talking *about* it deliberately: mental content arises, consisting of beliefs and propositional arguments. Language now points at the properties of distinct objects and situations. For example, when Susan, a pharmaceutical company employee who is involved in enacting a shipping routine, notices a problem with the lids to be shipped ('these are not the ones we usually ship') (Dittrich et al., 2016: 684), she points out a property of certain objects. While she is still involved in performing the routine, she makes statements about the task (Schatzki, 2000). To account for such subtle distinctions, we need an ontology that focuses on actors' modes of entwinement with the world (Sandberg and Tsoukas, 2011, 2020).

Second, when enacting a routine, actors do not merely do something: they act in the service of a collective goal – a *telos* – that underlies their practice. The modality of routine enactment does not involve merely situational knowledge plus occasional reflection, prompted by dialogue, but is critically shaped by a particular *ethos*, namely a morally oriented habit – a style of doing things that is 'drilled into habit' (Salvato, 2009: 400; see Cohen, 2007), driven by certain values. Thus, when the employees in the pharmaceutical company CellCo, in the context of enacting the shipping routine, reflect on how to solve a problem ('the fact that the plates are not yet packaged with the lids, which they normally are', Dittrich et al., 2016: 683); when employees of BoutiqueCo, a fast-growing retailer, act in the context of the merchandising routine to place the merchandise on a particular fixture (a table, a mannequin, etc.) and integrate it with the merchandise that is already on display, in order to 'create a visually compelling "look and feel" of the store' (Sonenshein, 2016: 744); or when hospital staff try to effect change in a surgical clinic's patient process involving the colon-resection routine (Bucher and Langley, 2016), what in all these cases occurs is not mere activity, in the sense of people undertaking situational action as part of a recurring routine, but *praxis*, that is, other-oriented and, therefore, morally laden action to normatively accomplish collective goals (Sayer, 2011: Tsoukas, 2018: 2–3). Such goals are necessarily suffused with values, that is, they articulate evaluative distinctions concerning what is good or acceptable (Sayer, 2011: 143; Tsoukas, 2018: 2).

Actors take part in a broader practice with its own 'internal goods' and 'standards of excellence' (MacIntyre, 1985; Moore, 2017; Tsoukas, 2018). The actions they undertake in pursuing a practice's goals disclose a 'certain kind of life' (MacIntyre, 1985: 190; see also Selznick, 2008: 89) that practitioners value and to the realization of which they contribute (Sayer, 2011: 144; Spinosa, et al., 1997: 20–26). In short, what participants in a routine strive to do is to act *well*. With few exceptions (see Eberhard et al., 2019), the moral dimension of routines performance has been understated in RD theorizing, although it has been implied by Feldman (2000: 620 and 622) with her concept of 'striving' (routine participants modifying their routine when outcomes fall short of ideals) and alluded to by Danner-Schroeder and Geiger (2016).

3.3 Theorizing Routine Dynamics Research through Performative Phenomenology

To help further advance RD theorizing, I will offer, in this section, a performative phenomenological vocabulary that integrates practice theory with a strong process ontology. I will illustrate my argument with several examples from RD research.

Practice worlds and tacit knowledge. Human agency is inextricably embedded in practice worlds. A practice world is a relational sociomaterial whole that is teleologically organized, in which embodied actors are immersed. A practice world normatively specifies a particular way of being, thinking and acting for its members (Sandberg and Tsoukas, 2020: 5; Schatzki, 2002; Spinosa, et al., 1997: 17–20). Actors do not encounter objects, tools and other people as stand-alone entities to which they, subsequently, attach meaning. Rather, bundles of materials and other humans become meaningful to actors only within a practice world – 'an intelligible ensemble of other meaningful things' (Sheehan, 2015: 117–118). To be involved in a practice world is to be immersed in a relational totality that is structured by tacit understandings, explicit rules and teleo-affective structures (Schatzki, 2002: 87).

For example, a BoutiqueCo employee, studied by Sonenshein (2016), is entwined with others and things in a meaningful socio-material practice world. The store she works for and, in particular, the merchandising routine she engages in, is not merely a collection of externally related objects available for contemplation, as it would perhaps be for a visitor, but a meaningful unified whole that is available for action (Merleau-Ponty, 1962/1945: 137). What the employee, others and objects (jewelry, mannequins, etc.) are depends on how they show up in the relational totality they are part of. The merchandising routine employee is driven by a certain *telos*, to 'create a visually compelling "look and feel" of the store' (Sonenshein, 2016: 744), the accomplishment of which *matters* to her (Dreyfus and Dreyfus, 2005). While she follows a visual merchandising manual (Sonenshein, 2016: 744), carrying out her tasks would be impossible without the tacit knowledge about how to creatively implement the manual, typically in coordination with her colleagues.

To enter a practice world – to become, say, a pharmaceutical company or retail employee – is to experience one's situation in terms of *already* constituted ends, meanings and acceptable emotions, articulated through the discourse that defines the practice world (Taylor, 1985a: 54–55). Members of a practice world engage in activities through which 'internal goods' (MacIntyre, 1985: 187) are realized, while aiming to achieve certain 'standards of excellence' (op. cit.). The already constituted evaluative distinctions of a practice world make up the 'inherited background' (Wittgenstein, 1979: §94), against which practitioners make focal sense of their particular tasks (Tsoukas, 2009: 943). Through their participation in a practice world, actors learn to relate to their tasks non-deliberately (i.e., spontaneously) (Dreyfus, 2014): to merchandise a store (Sonenshein, 2016), to pack and dispatch packages (Dittrich et al., 2016), to collect waste (Turner and Rindova, 2012), to treat or operate on patients (Buchner and Langley, 2016; Kiwan and Lazaric, 2019; LeBaron et al., 2016), etc. Thus, the world appears to actors as 'ready-to-hand' (Heidegger, 1962/1927), in which the most fundamental way of engaging with it is 'absorbed coping' (Dreyfus, 1991: 69; Sandberg and Tsoukas, 2011: 344). In absorbed coping, actors spontaneously respond to an evolving situation they are facing through using artifacts, tools and language. When, for example, a BoutiqueCo employee merchandises a store, she does not ordinarily stop to reflect on what is a mannequin or a jewelry table. Having grown familiar with them, she just does her job (see Cohen, 2007: 777).

Through their immersion in a practice world, actors acquire familiarity with it. Increased familiarity provides actors with a host of 'subsidiary particulars' (Polanyi, 1962: 55) that are necessary for skilled action to be accomplished. Once the use of tools (including language) and the roles of others have become familiar, the subsidiary particulars have been assimilated (or interiorized) by the actor, namely they have become *tacit* knowledge in which the actor dwells in order to *focus* on the task at hand. For example, a merchandising routine employee does not ordinarily need to think about what subsidiary particulars, such as an accessory table or a mannequin, are, namely what they are *for*. Unless she has interiorized what an artefact is for and how it should be used in the context of her practice world, she will not be able to create a proper display at a store (the focal task), just like a car driver cannot competently drive unless she has interiorized how to use the car instruments.

When absorbed in the execution of a task, actors may be interrupted by a disturbance, anomaly or breakdown (Sandberg and Tsoukas, 2011; see also Rerup and Feldman, 2011; Salvato and Rerup, 2018). Then, they seek to reflect on their tacit knowledge – the interiorized pattern of subsidiary particulars – in order to resume smooth action. If this happens while actors are still involved in a practical activity, the world becomes 'unready-to-hand' (Heidegger, 1962/1927), whereby actors shift from absorbed coping to 'involved thematic deliberation' (Sandberg and Tsoukas, 2011: 344). But when the breakdown is severe so that actors become detached from the practical situation at hand, viewing it from the 'outside', namely as an array of discrete objects with causally related properties, actors have then entered a situation of 'abstract detachment' (Tsoukas, 2015: 65). When in it, actors move from practical to quasi-theoretical understanding. In both cases, following a breakdown, actors engage in deliberative thinking – reflecting *on* action.

For example, when actors, in performing the shipping routine at CellCo, as studied by Dittrich et al. (2016: 683), find that the plates are not yet packaged with the lids, as would have normally been the case, routine participants face a mild breakdown: they shift from absorbed coping to involved thematic deliberation – they engage in 'reflective talk' (2016: 683) (e.g., 'we need to discuss how we do this', 2016: 684). On this occasion, reflective talk does not involve abstract reflection but is conducted in the context of practically addressing the problem: it 'takes place on the background of absorption in the world' (Dreyfus, 1991: 74). However, reflective talk marks the beginning of a potentially detached intentionality, through which actors may begin to form abstract representations of the task at hand (not in evidence in Dittrich et al., 2016). Whereas, in absorbed coping, the materials were immediately available to routine participants (the world was ready-to-hand), in involved thematic deliberation, the same materials become unavailable (the world is unready-to-hand).

Radial structure and reweaving. Through repeated performance, subsidiary particulars are not merely accumulated but form a pattern (Klein, 1998: 31–33; 2003: 21). This is important since patterns enable actors to recognize situations as *typical* and, thus, adopt relevant courses of action. This is particularly relevant for routines, since they derive from situated repetitiveness and, when performed, constitute patterns of actions. The knowledge of patterns is tacitly held: actors are subsidiarily aware of patterned experiences when carrying out particular tasks, just like a carpenter is subsidiarily aware of holding a hammer while driving a nail into a plank.

Patterns of subsidiary particulars stemming from past routine performances are *radially* structured: their structure is formed around a relatively stable core made up of prototypical (central) members that have been typically encountered in practice and an unstable part made up of non-prototypical (peripheral) members, radiating at various conceptual distances from the core (Johnson, 1993; Lakoff, 1987). The radial structure of practical experience is important since it enables actors to judge prototypicality. Insofar as the case at hand is close to the prototypical core, actors spontaneously undertake appropriate action (Klein, 1998: 149): focal awareness of a particular issue subsidiarily draws on familiar patterns in the spontaneous undertaking of action (Dreyfus, 2014, 2017).

When, however, absorbed coping is interrupted, either because participants have different understandings of the routine or the situation they face deviates from what is typically the case, or both, deliberate reflection in various degrees takes place. What was previously subsidiary now becomes focal. Through deliberating how to respond to a breakdown in the midst of action or reflecting on a pattern of actions ex post facto, actors reweave their beliefs to preserve a coherent sense of agency (Rorty, 1991). Such reweaving is a matter of degree (Rorty, 1991: 94).

For example, shipping routine participants tacitly know how to handle a prototypical case of plate shipment – they have done it countless times. When, however, the plates are not packaged with the lids, participants encounter non-prototypicality, calling for deliberation and, thus, the reweaving of beliefs – 'reflective talk' ensues (Dittrich et al., 2016). Similarly, a study of handoffs between intensive care unit physicians when they change shifts shows a pattern (LeBaron et al., 2016: 520). Its core (prototypical) component consists of five moves physicians have been trained, as well as experientially used, to expect in a handoff: patient identification, past events, current issues, future plans and family matters. Such a prototypical pattern furnishes physicians with shared understandings and body schemata (i.e., action dispositions), which they tacitly draw on (i.e., activate) when handling particular patients.

However, situational variability, namely patients' different circumstances, needs and understandings, creates various non-prototypical cases, which physicians flexibly handle by, for example, skipping, elaborating or modifying particular moves (LeBaron et al., 2016). As LeBaron et al. (2016) make clear, physicians' coordination of the joint task is actively sustained during handoffs by physicians rearranging their moves through verbal and bodily gestures, namely reweaving their patterns of understandings and actions *during* routine performance. Reweaving becomes more deliberate and radical, the more actors explicitly represent (as opposed to merely adapting to) the routine, namely the more they reflect on the patterns enacted. Dittrich et al. (2016: 685–686) provide an example of this when shipping routine participants at CellCo used particular breakdowns related to delays in delivering orders to both dispatch a particular order *and* reflect, more generally, on the desirability of hitherto dependence on a single shipping provider. In the latter case, reweaving of beliefs is more radical and the language used is representational (Sandberg and Tsoukas, 2020).

Performance, teleo-affectivity and virtuality. As argued earlier, routines are enacted in the service of a collective purpose – they are teleologically driven. Practice theory usefully underscores, among other things, the purposiveness of agency – its teleo-affective structure (Schatzki, 2002: 87). As Feldman (2000:614) perceptively noted, 'routines are performed by people who think and feel and care. [. . .] Their actions are motivated by will and intention'. Although, when absorbed in action, individual intentionality is subdued, the practice world is purposively organized (Chia and Holt, 2009; Dreyfus, 2014) – agents engage in action for the sake of accomplishing a collective goal, which drives the performance of related tasks (nursing, waste collection, hiring, etc.). Underlying the performance of a routine is the fulfilment of a 'justification' (Schauer, 1991: 53; Tsoukas, 2019: 415) that reflects the 'intrinsic goods' that a practice world is set to realize. A justification provides the *raison d'etre* of a routine (Rerup and Feldman, 2011: 581).

Even when explicitly formulated, a justification cannot be conveyed to actors in a propositional form (Tsoukas, 2019: 416). Justifications are part of subsidiary awareness: an actor subsidiarily relies on them for focally attending to something else (Tsoukas, 2011). If a justification were to be propositionally articulated, it would inevitably be based on a further justification, and so on ad infinitum. *Why* actors should enact a routine in a particular manner cannot be propositionally conveyed. As Wittgenstein (1958: §217) famously noted, 'if I have exhausted the justifications I have reached bedrock, and my spade is turned. Then I am inclined to say: "This is simply what I do"'. The justification is *virtual*, namely it constitutes a creative potential, which may be performed differently over time.

Specifically, a performance is a particular actualization of virtuality; what *is* is a manifestation of what can potentially be (Colebrook, 2005: 10). It is thanks to the virtual that repetition does not produce the same effects. An actual performance of a routine is governed by the contingencies, needs and interests of the present (Bertel et al., 2016: 587). However, the virtual is also part of reality – the power of reality to express itself in different actualities. Thus, any time a routine is performed, the justification that articulates its underlying *telos* is re-enacted; the actual performance contingently actualizes the potential – the virtual – that is captured by the justification. To re-enact a routine is to repeat the creative potential from which actual performances emerge (Colebrook, 2006: 82).

This is well illustrated by Feldman (2000) in her influential study of, among other things, the damage-assessment routine in student halls at a US university (i.e., building directors assessing any damage done in student halls of residence at the end of each academic year). Revisiting this study generates fresh insights. Specifically, routine participants are members of a practice world that has a teleo-affective structure – they are driven by a collective *purpose* about things that *matter* to them. The purpose of the building directors' practice world (what Feldman calls 'ideals') provides the justification of the routine, which, in this case, was holding room residents accountable for any damage caused in their rooms (Feldman, 2000: 616). This justification was tacitly upheld by building directors while focusing on their routine tasks – room inspection and assessment of fines. Justification constitutes a creative potential (i.e., it is virtual), which may be actualized differently over time. The contingent performance of the routine at the time – i.e., its situational enactment involving room assessment of fines after students had gone – showed that building directors had been turned into quasi-business managers rather than quasi-educators, which is how they saw themselves as a result of performing and, therefore, experiencing their jobs. Re-enacting the routine provided participants with the possibility of actualizing the routine's virtual aspect differently, thus leading to the modification of the routine. As Parr (2005: 223) notes, 'to repeat is to begin again'.

3.4 Discussion

Performative phenomenology enables RD research to move forward in interesting ways. The following new directions for future research are suggested.

First, studying tacit knowledge, which is at the core of routine performance, ought to receive greater attention in RD research, since tacit knowledge will provide a deeper understanding of what is entailed in patterning (i.e., interrelating stability and change in RD); add nuances to our understanding of endogenous change; and help account for the difficulties in changing routines exogenously. I briefly expand on them next.

Stability in routine performance stems, in part, from the embodied nature of human action and, in part, from the perceived prototypicality of practical experience. Insofar as human action depends on the development of body schemas, the latter take time to develop and change – they are a source of inertia (Sandberg and Tsoukas, 2020). Body schemas are a prime example of tacit knowledge that is developed through the habitual engagement of the body in action. One of the main effects of actors' immersion in a practice world is the training of the body, as well as equipping actors with relevant perceptual abilities and the use of language (Cohen, 2012: 1384). Future research can focus on how body schemas are developed through routine performance, and with what consequences.

Moreover, although RD research has done a lot to show that routine performance is an effortful accomplishment, what needs to be explored in more depth is the *effortlessness* of prototypical routine performance. Insofar as, during routine performance, participants handle cases that are close to the prototypical core, their action tends to be relatively stable and effortless in the sense that they spontaneously draw on subsidiary particulars (including body schemata) to engage in action. Endogenously induced change and novelty need not necessarily involve explicit 'agentic choice' (Sonenshein, 2016: 752), but may well be the outcome of spontaneous responsiveness to situational and agent-specific experiential variability. An overemphasis on 'interpretation' (Sonenshein, 2016: 752) and 'reflective talk' (Dittrich et al., 2016) risks missing the more subtle way (i.e., non-deliberate, non-discursive, non-cognitive) through which endogenous change emerges (Chia and Holt, 2009; Tsoukas and Chia, 2002; Yanow and Tsoukas, 2009).

Second, for all its emphasis on accounting for the internal dynamic of routines and the accompanying emphasis on non-deliberate change, RD research needs to explore in more depth how senior managers bring about deliberate change in routines. Research on organizational change has focused on language and cognition as both instruments and outcomes of change (Balogun et al., 2015). While this is important, further research can shed light on how language can bring about deliberate change in routines (Flores, 2012; Ford and Ford, 2009) by focusing on participants' mode of engagement with their practice world.

When, for example, deliberate change in a hospital's colon-resection routine involves the setting up of 'reflective spaces', in which participants 'intentionally develop new conceptions of routines' (Bucher and Langley, 2016: 608) through dialogue, participants can rethink the routine insofar as they step back from it to reflect explicitly *on* it. Thus, participants relate to the old routine through abstract detachment, whereby they point at properties of the routine from the 'outside' (Tsoukas, 2019). This representational use of language (i.e., pointing at abstract properties) contrasts with the moderately performative use of language, as shown by Dittrich et al. (2016), when actors enter involved thematic deliberation ('these lids are not the ones we usually ship'), which, in turn, is different from the strongly performative language actors use when engaged in routine through absorbed coping (e.g., 'Drop your tools', Weick, 2001: 107). Such distinctions need to be developed further through empirical research, focusing in particular on the different speech acts used in performative language (Flores, 2012; Ford and Ford, 2009; Searle, 1969).

However, there is more to deliberate routine change than the use of language. As mentioned, new body schemata are developed when actors strive to learn to *perform* a new routine. For example, Bucher and Langley (2016) have noted the importance of language and symbolic and temporal boundaries through the creation of 'experimental spaces' in intentional routine change. They allude to the importance of experimental spaces by noting how they enable 'new interactions' (2016: 609). Further research can unpack this by focusing on what it is that new interactions accomplish. Bucher and Langley rightly emphasize that what is distinctive in experimental spaces is the enabling of new *performances*. Further research may shed light on this by showing how new performances enable the development of new body schemata and fresh understandings without necessarily involving the full use of language (Dreyfus, 2014, 2017). In other words, an 'experimental space' carves out a new way of *doing* things, which enables participants to learn new skills.

Third, RD research needs to grapple with an under-researched topic, namely the *moral* dimension of routine enactment. Approaching this topic with the lens of performative phenomenology enables an understanding of routines as normatively bounded practices: not merely as what routine participants do but the *ethos* they are driven by to accomplish what they do (Selznick, 1992; Tsoukas, 2018). Such a perspective underscores the teleo-affective structures of even the most mundane or technical routines, along with the intrinsic goods that characterize and the standards of excellence that permeate their enactment.

For example, it is the *telos* of the colon-resection routine studied by Bucher and Langley (2016) – i.e., the improvement of patients' conditions – that propelled the nurses involved to want to 're-initialize' (i.e., re-energize) (2016: 604) the reflective space created for the enactment of the envisioned routine after experiencing 'blockages' in the 'experimental space' (2016: 603). Similarly, in their study of the network maintenance and trouble-fixing routines of an Italian cellular phone company, Narduzzo et al. (2000) noted the particular ethos of 'spontaneous re-engineering' (2000: 41) that underlay the performance of routines. The authors note that the particular mode of routine enactment manifests the distinctive normative way routine technicians work. 'Spontaneous re-engineering' does not merely arise from the technicians' need to adapt to situational uniqueness but, also, from the need to enact their routine in the service of their collective goal – the justification – of doing their job as responsibly and effectively as possible (Bertels et al., 2016). The collective goal reflects the intrinsic goods that are embedded in technicians' practice (Tsoukas, 2018).

Further research can explore how the intrinsic goods inform the enactment of routines as well as how the intrinsic goods change over time with experience, with what effects (Bertels, et al., 2016; Cohendet and Simon, 2016; LeBaron et al., 2016; Turner and Rindova, 2012). Focusing more explicitly on the moral dimension of routines (Eberhard et al., 2019), researchers may explore moral routines per se, namely routines that are explicitly set up to deal with ethical concerns, involving, for example, the allocation of scarce resources (Gkeredakis et al., 2014). Currently, whatever we know about this comes, mainly, from ethical decision-making (Trevino et al., 2014). RD could contribute further to the study of the latter by viewing it though the lens of Routine Dynamics, namely by focusing on moral routines' recurring enactment and how the intrinsic goods underlying routines are situationally accomplished.

3.5 Conclusions

In this chapter, I have sought to extend the hitherto valuable insights provided by RD research, by urging the adoption of a strong process-cum-practice perspective, which I have called performative phenomenology. I have argued that RD research will need to explore how tacit knowledge impacts on routine enactment; better understand exogenously originated deliberate change in routines; and take explicitly on board the moral dimension of routine enactment.

References

Balogun, J., Bartunek, J. M. and Do, B. (2015). Senior managers' sensemaking and responses to strategic change. *Organization Science*, 26, 960–979.

Bertels, S., Howard-Grenville, J. and Pek, S. (2016) Cultural molding, shielding, and shoring at Oilco: The role of culture in the integration of routines, *Organization Science*, 27, 573–593.

Blanche, C. and Cohendet, P. (2019) Remounting a ballet in a different context: A complementary understanding of routines transfer theories. In M. S. Feldman, L., D'Adderio, K. Dittrich and P. Jarzabkowski, eds., *Routine Dynamics in Action: Replication and Transformation (Research in the Sociology of Organizations)*, Vol. 61. Bingley: Emerald, pp. 11–30.

Blattner, W. (2006). *Heidegger's Being and Time*. London: Continuum.

Bucher, S. and Langley, A. (2016) The interplay of reflective and experimental spaces in interrupting and reorienting routine dynamics, *Organization Science*, 27, 594–613.

Chia, R. and Holt, R. (2009). *Strategy without Design*. Cambridge: Cambridge University Press.

Cohendet, P. S. and Simon, L. O. (2016). Always playable: Recombining routines for creative efficiency at Ubisoft Montreal's video game studio, *Organization Science*, 27, 614–632.

Cohen, M. D. (2007). Reading Dewey: reflections on the study of routine. *Organization. Studies*, 28, 773–786.

Cohen, M. D. (2012). Perceiving and remembering routine action: Fundamental micro-level origins, *Journal of Management Studies*, 49, 1383–1388.

Cohen, M. D. and Bacdayan, P. (1994). Organizational routines are stored as procedural memory: Evidence from a laboratory study. *Organization Science*, 5, 554–568.

Colebrook, C. (2005). Actuality. In A. Parr, ed., *The Deleuze Dictionary*. New York: Columbia University Press, pp. 9–11.

Colebrook, C. (2006). *Deleuze: A Guide for the Perplexed*. London: Continuum.

Cooren, F. (2007). *Interacting and Organizing*. Mahwah, NJ: Lawrence Erlbaum.

Danner-Schroder, A. and Geiger, D. (2016). Unravelling the motor of patterning work: Toward an understanding of the microlevel dynamics of standardization and flexibility. *Organization Science*, 27, 633–658.

D'Adderio, L. D. (2008). The performativity of routines: Theorising the influence of artifacts and distributed agencies on routines dynamics. *Research Policy*, 37, 769–789.

Dionysiou, D. and Tsoukas, H. (2013). Understanding the creation and recreation of routines from within: A symbolic interactionist perspective. *Academy of Management Review*, 38, 181–205.

Dittrich, K., Guerard, S. and Seidl, D. (2016). Talking about routines: The role of reflective talk in routine change. *Organization Science*, 27, 678–697.

Dreyfus, H. L. (1991). *Being-in-the-World: A Commentary on Heidegger's Being and Time, Division I*. Cambridge, MA: MIT Press.

Dreyfus, H. L. (2000). Responses. In M. Wrathall and J. Malpas, eds., *Heidegger, Coping, and Cognitive Science: Essays in Honor of Hubert L. Dreyfus*, 313–349. Cambridge, MA: MIT Press.

Dreyfus, H. L. (2014). *Skillful Coping: Essays on the Phenomenology of Everyday Perception and Action*. (M. A. Wrathall, ed.). Oxford: Oxford University Press.

Dreyfus, H. L. (2017). On Expertise and Embodiment: Insights from Maurice Merleau-Ponty and Samuel Todes. In J. Sandberg, L. Rouleau, A. Langley and H. Tsoukas, eds., *Skillful Performance: Enacting Capabilities, Knowledge, Competence and Expertise in Organizations*. Oxford: Oxford University Press, pp. 147–159.

Dreyfus, H. L. and Dreyfus, S. E. (2005). Expertise in real world contexts. *Organization Studies*, 26, 779–792.

Eberhard, J., Frost, A. and Rerup, C. (2019). The dark side of routine dynamics: Deceit and the work of Romeo pimps. In M. S. Feldman, L. D'Adderio, K. Dittrich and P. Jarzabkowski, eds., *Routine Dynamics in Action: Replication and Transformation (Research in the Sociology of Organizations)*, Vol. 61. Bingley: Emerald Publishing Limited, pp. 99–121.

Egidi, M. (2002) Biases in organizational behavior. In M. Augier and J. G. March, eds., *The Economics of Choice, Change and Organization*. Cheltenham: Edward Elgar, pp. 109–146.

Feldman M. S. (2000). Organizational routines as a source of continuous change. *Organization Science*, 11(6), 611–629.

Feldman, M. S. (2016). Routines as process: Past, present and future. In J. Howard-Grenville, C. Rerup, A. Langley and H. Tsoukas, eds.,

Organizational Routines: How They Are Created, Maintained, and Changed. Oxford: Oxford University Press, pp. 23–46.

Feldman, M. S., D'Adderio, L., Dittrich, K. and Jarzabkowski, P. (2019). Introduction: Routine dynamics in action. In M. S. Feldman, L. D'Adderio, K. Dittrich and P. Jarzabkowski, eds., *Routine Dynamics in Action: Replication and Transformation (Research in the Sociology of Organizations)*, Vol. 61. Bingley: Emerald Publishing Limited, pp. 1–10.

Feldman, M. S. and Pentland, B. T. (2003). Reconceptualizing organizational routines as a source of flexibility and change. *Administrative Science Quarterly*, 48, 94–118.

Feldman, M. S., Pentland, B. T., D' Adderio, L. and Lazaric, N. (2016). Beyond routines as things: Introduction to the Special Issue on routine dynamics, *Organization Science*, 27, 505–513.

Felin, T., Foss, N. J., Heimeriks, K. and Madsen, T. L. (2012). Microfoundations of routines and capabilities: Individuals, processes, and structures, *Journal of Management Studies*, 49, 1351–1374.

Flores, F. (2012). *Conversations for Action and Collected Essays* (ed. M. Flores Letelier). North Charleston, SC: CreateSpace Independent Publishing.

Ford, J. and Ford, L. (2009). *The Four Conversations*. San Francisco: Berrett-Koehler.

Giddens, A. (1993). *New Rules of Sociological Method*, Stanford, CA: Stanford University Press.

Gkeredakis, E., Nicolini, D. and Swan, J. (2014). Moral judgments as organizational accomplishments: Insights from a focused ethnography in the English healthcare sector. In F. Cooren, E. Vaara, A. Langley and H. Tsoukas, eds., *Language and Communication at Work: Discourse, Narrativity and Organizing*. Oxford: Oxford University Press, pp. 293–324.

Hadjimichael, D. and Tsoukas, H. (2019). Towards a better understanding of tacit knowledge in organizations: Taking stock and moving forward. *Academy of Management Annals*, 13(2), 672–703.

Heidegger, M. (1962/1927). *Being and Time* (J. Macquarrie and E. Robinson, Trans.). New York: SCM Press.

Howard-Grenville, J., Rerup, C., Langley, A. and Tsoukas, H. (eds.) (2016). *Organizational Routines: How They Are Created, Maintained, and Changed*. Oxford: Oxford University Press.

Howard-Grenville, J. and Rerup, C. (2017) A process perspective on organizational routines. In A. Langley and H. Tsoukas, eds., *The Sage Handbook of Process Organization Studies*. London: Sage, pp. 323–339.

Johnson, M. (1993). *Moral Imagination*. Chicago: The University of Chicago Press.

Kiwan, L. and Lazaric, N. (2019). Learning a new ecology of space and looking for new routines: Experimenting robotics in a surgical team. In M. S. Feldman, L.D'Adderio, K. Dittrich and P. Jarzabkowski, eds., *Routine Dynamics in Action: Replication and Transformation (Research in the Sociology of Organizations)*, Vol. 61. Bingley: Emerald Publishing Limited, pp. 173–189.

Klein, G. (1998). *Sources of Power: How People Make Decisions*. Cambridge, MA: MIT Press.

Klein, G. (2003). *The Power of Intuition*. New York: Currency/Doubleday.

Lakoff, G. (1987). *Women, Fire, and Dangerous Things*. Chicago: Chicago University Press.

Langley, A., Smallman, H., Tsoukas, H. and Van de Ven, A. (2013). Process studies of change in organization and management: Unveiling temporality, activity, and flow. *Academy of Management Journal*, 56, 1–13.

Langley, A. and Tsoukas, H. (2017). Introduction: Process thinking, process theorizing and process researching. In A. Langley and H. Tsoukas, eds., *The Sage Handbook of Process Organization Studies*. London: Sage, pp. 1–25.

LeBaron, C., Christianson, M. K., Garrett, L. and Ilan, R. (2016). Coordinating flexible performance during everyday work: An ethnomethodological study of handoff routines. *Organization Science*, 27, 514–534.

MacIntyre A. (1985). *After Virtue*. London: Duckworth, 2nd edition.

March, J. G. and Simon, H. A. (1953). *Organizations*. Cambridge, MA: Blackwell.

Merleau-Ponty, M. (1962/1945). *Phenomenology of Perception* (trans. C. Smith). London: Routledge & Kegan Paul.

Moore, G. (2017). *Virtue at Work*. Oxford: Oxford University Press.

Narduzzo, A., Rocco, E. and Warglien, M. (2000). Talking about routines in the field. In G. Dosi, R. R. Nelson and S. G. Winter, eds., *The Nature and Dynamics of Organizational Capabilities*. Oxford: Oxford University Press, pp. 27–50.

Nelson, R. R. and Winter, S. G. (1982). *An Evolutionary Theory of Economic Change*. Cambridge, MA: The Belknap Press of Harvard University Press.

Parmigiani, A. and Howard-Grenville, J. (2011). Routines revisited: Exploring the capabilities and practice perspectives. *The Academy of Management Annals*, 5, 413–453.

Parr, A. (2005). Repetition. In A. Parr, ed., *The Deleuze Dictionary*. New York: Columbia University Press, pp. 223–225.

Paul, L. A. (2014). *Transformative Experience*. Oxford: Oxford University Press.

Polanyi, M. (1962). *Personal Knowledge: Towards a Post-Critical Philosophy*. Chicago: University of Chicago Press.

Rerup, C. and Feldman, M. (2011). Routines as a source of change in organizational schemata: The role of trial-and-error learning. *Academy of Management Journal*, 54, 577–610.

Rorty, R. (1991). *Objectivity, Relativism, and Truth*. Cambridge: Cambridge University Press.

Salvato C. (2009). Capabilities unveiled: The role of ordinary activities in the evolution of product development processes. *Organization Science*, 20(2), 384–409.

Salvato, C. and Rerup, C. (2018). Routine regulation: Balancing conflicting goals in organizational routines. *Administrative Science Quarterly*, 63, 170–209.

Sandberg, J. and Tsoukas, H. (2011). Grasping the logic of practice: Theorizing through practical rationality. *Academy of Management Review*, 36, 338–360.

Sandberg, J. and Tsoukas, H. (2020). Sensemaking reconsidered: Towards a broader understanding through phenomenology. *Organization Theory*, 1, 1–34.

Sayer A. (2011). *Why Things Matter to People*. Cambridge: Cambridge University Press.

Schatzki, T. R. (2000). Coping with others with folk psychology. In M. Wrathall and J. Malpas, eds., *Heidegger, Coping, and Cognitive Science: Essays in Honor of Hubert L. Dreyfus*. Cambridge, MA: MIT Press, pp. 29–52.

Schatzki, T. R. (2002). *The Site of the Social: A Philosophical Account of the Constitution of Social Life and Change*. Pennsylvania: Pennsylvania State University Press.

Schauer, F. (1991). *Playing by the Rules*. Oxford: Clarendon.

Schön, D. A. (1983). *The Reflective Practitioner: How Professionals Think in Action*. New York: Basic Books.

Searle, J. (1969). *Speech acts*. Cambridge: Cambridge University Press.

Selznick P. (1992). *The Moral Commonwealth*. Berkeley: University of California Press.

Selznick P. (2008). *A Humanist Science*. Stanford, CA: Stanford University Press.

Sheehan, T. (2015). *Making Sense of Heidegger: A Paradigm Shift*. London: Rowman & Littlefield.

Sonenshein, S. (2016). Routines and creativity: From dualism to duality. *Organization Science*, 27, 739–758.

Spinosa, C., Flores, F. and Dreyfus H. L. (1997). *Disclosing New Worlds: Entrepreneurship, Democratic Action, and the Cultivation of Solidarity*. Cambridge, MA: MIT Press.

Taylor, C. (1985). *Human Agency and Language*, Vol. 1. Cambridge: Cambridge University Press.

Treviño, L. K., den Nieuwenboer, N. A. and Kish-Gephart, J. J. (2014). (Un)ethical behavior in organizations. *Annual Review of Psychology*, 65, 635–660.

Tsoukas, H. (2009). A dialogical approach to the creation of new knowledge in organizations. *Organization Science*, 20(6), 941–957.

Tsoukas, H. (2011). How should we understand tacit knowledge? A phenomenological view. In M. Easterby-Smith and M. Lyles, eds., *Handbook of Organizational Learning & Knowledge Management*. Chichester: Wiley, 2nd Edition, pp. 453–476.

Tsoukas, H. (2015). Making strategy: Meta-theoretical insights from Heideggerian phenomenology. In D. Golsorkhi, L. Rouleau, D. Seidl and E. Vaara, eds., *Cambridge Handbook of Strategy as Practice*. Cambridge: Cambridge University Press, 2nd Edition, pp. 58–77.

Tsoukas, H. (2018). Strategy and virtue: Developing strategy-as-practice through virtue ethics, *Strategic Organization*, 16, 323–351.

Tsoukas, H. (2019). *Philosophical Organization Theory*. Oxford: Oxford University Press.

Tsoukas, H. and Chia, R. (2002). On organizational becoming: Rethinking organizational change. *Organization Science*, 13, 567–582.

Turner, S. F. and Rindova, V. P. (2012). A balancing act: How organizations pursue consistency in routine functioning in the face of ongoing change. *Organization Science*, 23, 24–46.

Weick, K. E. (2001). The collapse of sensemaking in organizations. In K. E. Weick, ed., *Making Sense of the Organization*. Oxford: Blackwell, pp. 100–124.

Wittgenstein, L. (1958). *Philosophical Investigations* (G. E. M. Anscombe, Trans.). Oxford: Blackwell.

Wittgenstein, L. (1979). *On Certainty* (ed. G. E. Anscombe and G. H. von Wright, trans. D. Paul and E. M. Anscombe). Oxford: Blackwell.

Yanow, D. and Tsoukas, H. (2009). What is reflection-in-action? A phenomenological account. *Journal of Management Studies*, 46, 1339–1363.

CHAPTER 4

Ethnomethodology and Routine Dynamics

JUAN LÓPEZ-COTARELO

4.1 Introduction

Ethnomethodology (EM) is a distinctive approach to studying social phenomena, set forth by Harold Garfinkel (1917–2011) over a long and productive career spanning six decades.[1] His crucial insight is that social order is constructed from, and available in, the witnessable (visible, audible, etc.) details of each interaction. EM emphasizes elements such as agency, materiality, situatedness, relationality and processuality that have been central features in Routine Dynamics (RD) theorizing (Feldman, 2016; Parmigiani and Howard-Grenville, 2011). Indeed, scholars working within the EM tradition, such as Cicourel, Garfinkel, Heritage, Hutchins, Suchman, Schegloff and Zimmerman, have remained rich sources of conceptual inspiration for RD scholars (see e.g., D'Adderio, 2011; Feldman et al., 2016; Feldman and Pentland, 2003; Pentland and Rueter, 1994).

Over the past two decades, RD research has firmly established the elements just listed as constitutive of routines: performances of a routine are actions carried out by people in specific socio-material settings (Feldman, 2016). Far from being a mindless or automatic reproduction of structure, each performance is an 'effortful accomplishment' involving knowledgeable and reflective actors alongside a multitude of artifacts (Feldman et al., 2016).

In this chapter, I will argue that Ethnomethodology presents a unique basis for furthering RD research and theory, through its conceptualization of action as *situated*. Garfinkel (1967) argued that each instance of meaningful concerted action does not – indeed cannot – rely on a shared stock of abstract knowledge that pre-exists the interaction itself (Rawls, 2002). Instead, members of a social scene construct both meaning and action, at the same time and through the same means, in situ, through mutually recognizable sequential displays of orientation, attention and understanding.

Building on recent ethnomethodological studies in Routine Dynamics (LeBaron et al., 2016; Yamauchi and Hiramoto, 2016, 2021), my aim is to outline the implications of an ethnomethodological understanding of collective action for Routine Dynamics. I will argue that adopting such conceptualization of action offers the possibility of developing a more fully performative (Latour, 1986) understanding of organizational routines.

4.2 Theorizing Routine Dynamics

A distinctive feature of the Routine Dynamics literature is its focus on action and materiality as constitutive of routines (Feldman, 2016). Arguably, such focus has been achieved through three successive shifts. First, early RD scholars (Feldman, 2000; Feldman and Pentland, 2003; Pentland and Rueter, 1994) rescued action, actors and agency in routines, which researchers had often black-boxed and assumed automatic and mindless (Parmigiani and Howard-Grenville, 2011). Second, this refocusing on action set the ground for a fuller exploration of materiality in

[1] From early on, EM scholars have worked in close and very fruitful collaboration with Conversation-Analysis colleagues, giving rise to a largely hybrid field of EM-CA (Lynch, 2019; Mondada, 2019). In this chapter, I use the term Ethnomethodology to refer to research that acknowledges Garfinkel's work as a direct antecedent, irrespective of which group authors attach themselves to.

routine performances (D'Adderio, 2008, 2011; Pentland and Feldman, 2008). Finally, the latest shift affirms the processual nature of routines, and in particular rejects understandings of the ostensive as a structural cognitive entity that acts or exists at a higher level to action (Feldman, 2016; Feldman et al., 2016). I discuss these shifts in more detail in what follows.

4.2.1 First Shift: Bringing Action into Focus

The first shift pursued by Routine Dynamics scholars emphasized agency in routine performances. Researchers in the earlier capabilities perspective tended to consider action in routines as automatic and mindless by definition, driven by individuals' acquired habits and dispositions, or arising from their need to conserve limited cognitive capacity by repeating programmes of action adopted in the past (Parmigiani and Howard-Grenville, 2011). As a result, routines appeared as inherently stable patterns of action that needed an external force to change. Analytically, routines could be black-boxed and treated as entities.

By contrast, RD scholars pointed out that action in routines often requires actors to exercise judgment, deal with exceptions, deliberate, improvise solutions to unforeseen circumstances, and innovate improved ways of operating (Feldman, 2000; Pentland and Rueter, 1994). Once this is taken into account, performances of a routine appear as 'effortful accomplishments' rather than automatic responses (Pentland and Rueter, 1994) and routines can be a source of change as well as stability (Feldman, 2000, 2003).

These early advancements coalesced in the theoretical model proposed by Feldman and Pentland (2003). Drawing on theories of practice (e.g., Bourdieu, 1990; Giddens, 1984), their model posited a recursive relationship between distributed abstract understandings of a routine (ostensive aspects) and its specific performances (performative aspects). Ostensive and performative aspects have a recursive relationship in that they are mutually constitutive, and equally necessary to explain routines: actors enact the abstract idea of the routine in performances; while the actions performed create, maintain and modify the repetitive pattern than constitutes the ostensive aspects of the routine (Feldman and Pentland, 2003). This theoretical model of routines was decisive in bringing actions to the foreground, and in making the study of their relationship to observable patterns of such actions the focus of Routine Dynamics research (Feldman et al., 2016).

4.2.2 Second Shift: Turning to Materiality

Initial discussions of artifacts in Routine Dynamics aimed to challenge the view of SOPs and other 'artifactual representations of routines' as determining action, and therefore analytically interchangeable with the routine itself (D'Adderio, 2008; Pentland and Feldman, 2008). Such 'naïve top-downism' regarded actions in routines to be automatic and mindless, and therefore largely driven and constrained by the artifacts that managers design and put in place, precisely to that end. RD scholars, by contrast, emphasized the symbolic nature of many of the artifacts involved in routines, which participants interpret and use in various ways during performance of the routine (Pentland and Feldman, 2008).

Further, RD scholars have examined the process through which artifacts are created and how they impinge on subsequent action. D'Adderio (2008) described a process of articulation, codification and standardization whereby rules and procedures are 'disentangled' from local context and embedded in artifacts. The value of the resulting decontextualized artifactual representations of action stems from their being easier to 'describe, visualize, share, transfer and reproduce' across multiple organizational sites, where they can serve as common interpretative frames of reference which guide and constrain 'intentions, views and actions across the organization' (2008: 782). In this way, artifacts are central to the design, transfer and coordination of routines, as they mediate the relationship between ostensive and performative aspects of routines (D'Adderio, 2011).

4.2.3 Third Shift: From Ostensive Aspects to Patterning

RD scholars initially located the basis for repetitive organizational action in a socially distributed stock of knowledge about the routine in the abstract, the 'ostensive aspects' of the routine (Feldman and Pentland, 2003). However, Feldman (2016) laments that some researchers mistake the two aspects as 'separate entities', with the ostensive seen as a shared cognitive element operating at a different level from action. To avoid this pitfall, she calls for theorizing both performative and ostensive aspects as actions, and indeed recommends dropping the two-aspect terminology to speak of 'performing' and 'patterning' instead. In doing so, researchers should shift their attention to 'the work of recognizing and articulating or narrating these patterns' (Feldman, 2016: 40).

Several studies have examined the activities through which routine participants [re]create ostensive aspects through collective action and reflection. Rerup and Feldman (2011) found that ostensive aspects of routines emerge through trial-and-error experimentation. When organizational members confront problems, they try novel courses of action. If a set of actions repeatedly proves successful in addressing a class of problems, participants may interpret and justify that set of actions as appropriate, and individually held ostensive patterns of the routine thus emerge. Further, Dittrich, Guérard and Seidl (2016) found that talk enables routine participants to reflect collectively on both specific performances of the routine and the overall pattern of actions; and thereby work out new ways of enacting the routine. Similarly, Bucher and Langley (2016) found that routine participants establish social, physical, symbolic and temporal boundaries in order to set up reflective spaces where they develop new conceptualizations of the routine, and experimental spaces where they test these new concepts in provisional performances. Finally, Glaser (2017) examined the actions organizational members undertook to create artifacts intended to effect change on routine performances. Through iterative 'design performances', members produce assemblages of artifacts, theories, practices and actors that, in turn, produce changes in the routine's performances.

4.2.4 Next Move: Situating Routines

The developments just described constitute very significant progress in understanding the internal dynamics of routines, and have underpinned a remarkably rich body of empirical research. However, important conceptual difficulties remain in explaining how participants enact a specific performance as part of a pattern they can recognize – particularly if we wish to avoid conceptions of ostensive aspects and patterns as residing in the mind (Feldman et al., 2016).

Overcoming these difficulties, I argue, requires a fourth shift that furthers the recent emphasis by RD scholars (Feldman, 2016; Feldman et al., 2016) on studying routines as *situated actions* (Suchman, 2007). RD scholars have tended to view action as discrete steps, purposefully taken by individual actors in pursuit of particular ends – e.g. 'actions are simply doings and sayings' (Feldman, 2016: 30), 'by action we mean the things that actors do' (Pentland et al., 2012: 1484) or 'action refers to steps in a process of accomplishing an organizational task' (Pentland et al., 2012: 1484). The apparent simplicity of these definitions is in fact deceptive, in that they gloss over the social processes by which meaningful collective action is achieved in actual settings. Describing actions as 'doings and sayings' implies that a bodily movement *does something*, or an utterance *says something*, that is, that their consequence and meaning are inherent in the movement or the utterance, or in the intention with which the actor performed the movement or the utterance.

A situated action perspective grounded in ethnomethodology helps us realize that it is only when looking in retrospect at already accomplished events that action appears closed, planful and attributable to an individual actor, an enactment or realization of a pre-existing cognitive abstraction, 'a series of steps toward a foregone conclusion' (Rawls, 2002: 34). For EM scholars, action is always open-ended and tentative: its consequence and meaning are only established *collectively* in the sequence of movements and utterances that constitute the action in the first place (Streeck, Goodwin and LeBaron, 2011). Further, an EM perspective of action de-emphasizes the role of cognition as it is commonly understood in other traditions, as abstract conceptualizations existing and acting at a higher, more general level of reality than the concrete, contingent settings that actors inhabit. For EM scholars, action is processual and material: it has a durée; it is open-ended and emergent; and it involves bodies, utterances, objects and spatial arrangements that are visible and hearable in the world in front of us.

Thus, an EM approach affirms relationality, materiality, emergence, processuality and situatedness as constitutive features of action, not just of routines, performances or patterns. Crucially, it enables the empirical examination of the processes through which concerted action is constructed, in situ, by actors who do not interact with each other at a conceptual level, but through their bodies' movements and utterances as part of a material setting (Rawls, 2002). This fourth shift thus provides the opportunity to develop a more fully performative understanding of organizational routines in Latour's original usage of the term, that is, routines 'as a consequence *instead of* a cause of collective action' (Latour, 1986: 271, emphasis added; Yamauchi and Hiramoto, 2016). To paraphrase Latour's observation that 'as Garfinkel has taught us: it's practice all the way down'. (2005: 135), EM provides the theoretical scaffolding for an exploration of organizational routines as action all the way down.

4.3 Ethnomethodology

Since the beginnings of the RD literature, and throughout its subsequent development, ethnomethodology has been – along with related perspectives, practice theory and actor-network theory – a major source of ideas and vocabulary (Feldman et al., 2016). RD scholars have often cited EM authors when theorizing fundamental features of routines, such as relationality, materiality, emergence, processuality and situatedness, including Garfinkel (1967), Heritage (1984), Hutchins (1995), Suchman (2007) and Zimmerman (1970). However, the piecemeal adoption of EM concepts has meant that the full potential of a coherent EM approach to Routine Dynamics is yet to be realized. I suggest that adopting EM's understanding of *situated action* (Suchman, 2007) is central to such realization.

4.3.1 Situated Action

EM scholars have used the term 'situated action' to characterize their distinctive approach to the study of collective concerted action (Goodwin, 2000a; Mondada, 2019; Suchman, 2007). The key insight that Garfinkel pursued throughout his work is that mutually intelligible collective action can only be constructed from – and is therefore available in – the *witnessable* (visible, audible, etc.) details of each interaction (Rawls, 2002).

Similar to Wittgenstein's (1953: §201–202) thinking on rules and rule following, Garfinkel's (1967) stance is grounded in the principle that concerted action cannot result from individuals following or acting out a pre-existing shared abstraction (Rawls, 2002). His perspective, however, goes further than asserting the indeterminacy of abstract rules and the need for actors to 'know how to go on' (Wittgenstein, 1953: §154) in that ethnomethodology provides the means for empirical examination of just how actors do indeed manage to go on (Koschmann, 2011; Lynch, 2011; Rawls, 2011).

In this regard, Garfinkel insists that meaningful interaction can only be achieved through means that are public and accessible in the setting, 'just here, just now, with just what is at hand, with just who is here, in just the time that just this local gang of us have' (2002: 99n). Interactions are fundamentally embodied and material: actors can only interact through their bodies, by producing movements and utterances that are seeable and hearable by other participants in the interaction. Actors are thus members of a *social scene*, a public interactional space where they construct concerted action *and* shared meaning *at the same time and through the same means*, through sequences of witnessable bodily movements and utterances (Garfinkel, 1967; Rawls, 2002).

4.3.2 Accountability

Actors attempting to produce collective action need to ensure, first and foremost, that mutual intelligibility is achieved and sustained in their interaction (Rawls, 2008). For Garfinkel, such intelligibility, or common understanding of the unfolding interaction, does not rely on a pre-existing agreement between actors at a conceptual or abstract level, but on members' 'competent use of shared methods of organizing action' (Rawls, 2008: 702). EM takes as its phenomenon of interest these shared methods or systematic ways by which members create concerted action and common meaning, which Garfinkel (1967) calls *ethnomethods*.

Members of a social scene share a 'background of expectancies': they hold a mutual expectation that they will produce movements and utterances in ways that are recognizable to all competent members of the scene, against a set of shared taken-for-granted, common-sense, background expectancies as 'natural facts of life' (Garfinkel, 1967). They also expect others to see the meaning of their acts against the same common-sense expectancies, and expect others to expect the same of them.

Thus, members achieve mutual intelligibility by producing movements and utterances in ways that are recognizable to their peers, that is, by making their actions *account-able*. Accountable action is action prospectively produced to be patently recognizable in its details as coherent, consistent, rational, planful or methodical, as just the sort of action a competent member would produce (Garfinkel, 1967; Rawls, 2002, 2008). The accountability of action is embodied, not talked about; it is evident in the 'observable-and-reportable' features of members' visible and hearable practices, rather than in retrospective characterizations of their actions (Garfinkel, 1967). Likewise, accountable action is *instructable* action, that is, irreducible to a set of descriptive accounts and yet demonstrably reproducible, 'available to members as situated practices of looking-and-telling' (Garfinkel, 1967: 1).

4.3.3 Indexicality

An important concept to understand how members of a scene construct collective action and meaning in situ is *indexicality* or *orientation*. Objects, bodies, movements and utterances are oriented in the social scene, that is, they do not have meaning in themselves, but acquire their situational meaning from their spatial and temporal position relative to other elements of the social scene (Rawls, 2008).

Thus, members' bodies are not just *in* the setting; they are oriented to elements of the social scene (Mondada, 2016; Rawls, 2002): facing in one direction and turning its back on another, closer to some things and some actors' bodies and further from others, gazing at something or someone, adopting a particular posture as the result of a preceding action or in anticipation of an imminent one... Every movement and gesture of the body is similarly oriented to elements of the social scene: turning towards or away, approaching or leaving behind, following or anticipating, elements of the evolving social scene.

Utterances, likewise, are always indexical (Suchman, 2007). It is not only that the use of deictics such as 'I/you', 'this/that', 'now/then', 'here/there', which directly reference elements of the setting, is pervasive in speech. Rather, *every* expression is indexical, in the sense that it acquires its meaning by virtue of the specific space and time in which it is uttered, to whom it is addressed, to whom it may be audible, what was said before or might be said after, what else is going on in the scene and so on (Rawls, 2008).

Objects are not 'just there in front of us' (Rawls, 2008:713); they are temporally and spatially oriented, relative to elements of the scene including people's bodies and other objects. Moreover, members physically manipulate objects in order to alter their orientation, and use talk and bodily displays such as looking, pointing and so forth, to display their appreciation of the object. They also attend to each other's subsequent public display of orientation to ascertain the extent to which the other has 'found the object' (Hindmarsh and Heath, 2000). Through such sequences of talking, pointing, touching, holding, showing, etc., members construct in situ a common understanding of the relevance of features of the object to the specific interaction.

Finally, through their changing orientation to elements of the setting, members continually define and re-define the space and time that is relevant to the unfolding interaction. Members display, through their gaze, body position, posture, movements and utterances, a common orientation to elements whose discussion or manipulation is the joint focus of the interaction (Goodwin, 2000a). The social scene itself is therefore 'a practical interactional achievement' (Mondada, 2011a: 289), whose shape changes moment-by-moment through the oriented actions of its members (Suchman, 1996).

4.3.4 Reflexivity

The social scene is thus not just the setting in space and time occupied by members' bodies, but constitutes a public domain that members produce collectively in the interaction (Rawls, 2002). In this sense, actions are *reflexive*, that is, each movement or utterance develops and elaborates the social scene in a particular direction, casting new light on what came before, and/or extending the unfolding sequence of moves (Rawls, 2006). Through orienting objects, utterances and their own bodies, members collectively produce a social scene that is recognizably coherent (Rawls, 2002). The reflexive nature of actions and expressions thus forms the basis for the construction of intersubjective meaning that is not cognitive or abstract, but witnessable in the material details of the unfolding interaction (Mondada, 2011b; Rawls, 2006). In this sense, shared understandings have a situated, physical and material presence in the ordinary world – rather than being 'a transcendent "something"' inhabiting some other level of existence (Lynch, 2011: 555) – and are therefore discoverable in the observable detailed features of the unfolding interaction.

4.3.5 Multimodality

Members of a social scene have at their disposal a vast and diverse array of oriented elements that they can reference, manipulate, combine and juxtapose in situationally meaningful ways. Bodies, utterances, objects and spatial arrangements constitute *semiotic resources* that participants orient in order to produce shared meaning (Goodwin, 2000a; Streeck et al., 2011). In any interaction, members construct collective actions *and* meanings through the 'temporally unfolding juxtaposition' of multiple semiotic resources, such as talk, gaze, gestures, body posture, position and movement, objects, artifacts, tools, technologies documents, spatial arrangements and the material structure of the setting (Goodwin, 2000a).

The materiality of these semiotic resources is of importance here, as their physical properties enable different configurations of permanence, sequentiality and simultaneity (Goodwin, 2013; Mondada, 2014b). Human interactions can therefore be characterized as *multimodal* in that they typically combine semiotic resources with very different material properties, simultaneously or sequentially, in ways that mutually elaborate each other to create rich *contextures of action* that underpin broad repertoires of concerted action (Goodwin, 2011; Mondada, 2019).

4.3.6 Sequentiality

Human interactions are sequentially organized. The situational meaning of any movement or utterance is not intrinsic to its content or the intention of its actor, but is reflexively displayed in the response that it gets from other members of the interaction (Rawls, 2008). Thus, the construction of mutually meaningful action cannot be achieved in one move, but requires an organized series of turns where members talk, point, look, hold, touch, show, etc. in sequence (Mondada, 2014b).

Moreover, the sequence itself is built in the interaction, by members, through embodied practices of turn taking, turn construction and demonstrations of understanding (Mondada, 2016; Rawls, 2008). Members constantly monitor and respond to such public displays of orientation towards the developing sequence, and hold each other accountable for sustaining the unfolding sequential order (Rawls, 2008).

Sustaining the sequential production of the interaction constitutes for members an enforceable moral obligation to each other. When actors fail to display a commitment to producing recognizable actions in this way, the coherence and intelligibility of the interaction breaks down, producing 'bewilderment, consternation and confusion' (Garfinkel, 1967: 38). In this sense, human interactions are *co-operative* (Goodwin, 2011, 2018):

not necessarily characterized by harmony or solidarity, but demonstrably committed to building a mutually intelligible interaction 'as a morality' (Garfinkel, 1967: 53).

4.3.7 Instructed Action

Ethnomethodology takes a central interest in *instructed action*, that is, action performed in accordance to an instruction, a plan, a rule, a procedure, a precedent, a directive or any other abstract representation of action (Garfinkel, 2002; Lynch, 2015; Suchman, 2007). Instructions, plans and rules are always incomplete and ambiguous and, therefore, their relationship to the situated actions they prefigure can never be direct or causal (Mondada, 2011b; Suchman, 2007). However, the incomplete and ambiguous nature of instructions is not a shortcoming, but precisely what makes them effective and applicable to a diversity of settings, in a diversity of ways. Thus, the relationship between instructions and the action they prefigure is indexical: instructions acquire their sense and coherence in the achievement of the action they instruct (Garfinkel, 1967; Rawls, 2002).

The task of members attempting to 'follow' an instruction, plan or rule is to work out what can be done in the situation at hand, within the constraints of validity set by the instruction (Bittner, 1965; Rawls, 2002). The instruction constrains practices in this indirect way, but it is not constitutive of action as it unfolds: the correspondence between abstract representations and subsequent live actions is subject to demonstration of their praxeological validity, i.e., 'it must work, and must be seen to work by others' (Rawls, 2002: 41). In this sense, instructions are prospective accounts of the actions they instruct: if the action achieves its projected outcome, the instructions can retrospectively serve as 'an account of "what was done"' (Amerine and Bilmes, 1988: 329).

4.3.8 Institutional Orders

EM is well known – and, indeed, often pigeonholed and criticized – for its keen attention to local interaction orders; its relevance to explaining phenomena of institutional order that extend beyond local interactions is less often recognized (Rawls, 2008). In fact, for EM scholars, interaction orders are fundamental in explaining institutional orders (Rawls, 2002).

In EM terms, institutions can be described as 'contexts of accountability' that work by 'imposing accountability constraints on action' (Rawls, 2002, 2008). In many everyday settings, members are subject to multiple, overlapping contexts of accountability beyond the interaction unfolding at hand. In such settings, members attend to a combination of local and institutional accountabilities: they produce acts that are recognizable to members of the local ongoing interaction and, simultaneously, reportable according to institutional practices for accounting for actions as having followed institutionally sanctioned norms and rules (Rawls, 2002, 2008; Ueno, 2000). How participants to a local interaction become 'hooked' onto webs of institutional accountabilities becomes a focus of empirical inquiry for EM scholars (Smith, 2001, 2005).

In formal organizations, practices of accounting are largely mediated by *texts* (Anderson and Sharrock, 2018; Smith, 2001; Smith and Whalen, 1997). From an EM perspective, texts carry instructions for producing, recognizing, accounting and making sense of members' actions as *organizational* actions. Such instructions may come in the shape of plans, procedures, rules, model cases, examples, vocabularies, lists, visual aids, categories of participants, objects or events, and so on (Kameo and Whalen, 2015; Smith, 2001). Analytical emphasis is made on the *material presence* of the text – 'definite forms of words, numbers or images that exist in a materially replicable form' (Smith, 2001: 174) – as it enters the scenes of action and is variously taken up by members in the construction of their specific interaction. As instructions and prospective accounts of actions, the presence of a text makes the task of members to work out what can be done in the situation at hand, in a way that is demonstrably accountable to it (Bittner, 1965; Rawls, 2002). Across multiple sites and occasions, the continued, repeated presence of the text fosters the production of actions that share a common relationship of accountability to the same text (Smith, 2005).

Thus, the possibility, consistency and ease of replication of the text is key to the operation of formal organizations, as coordination rests on the presence of the *same form* of the text across multiple sites and occasions, and how it becomes part of local interactions in ways that give rise to recognizable patterns, across multiple settings, of actions accountable to a single text (Kameo and Whalen, 2015; Smith, 2001).

Moreover, although much EM research on institutional orders has highlighted the role of *written* texts on paper or electronic support, the argument has been extended to other resources that can be considered *oral*, *iconic* or *artifactual* 'texts' in that they exist in a more-or-less durable and/or replicable material form – such as diagrams, signs, tools, technologies, stories, vocabularies, phrases and sayings (Cooren, 2004; Goodwin, 2000b; Ueno, 2000). Indeed, it is typically by juxtaposing multiple 'texts' of different sorts that institutional, organizational and professional communities develop the specialized ways of accomplishing concerted activities that distinguish them as collective actors (Goodwin, 2000c, 2000a).

A final point of interest in how EM scholars have investigated institutional orders refers to the origin of many of the texts/resources that coordinate activities in formal organizations, where many of these resources are designed, authored and distributed by actors in centrally located settings (Smith, 2005; Smith and Whalen, 1997). These actors use textual technologies to establish 'accountability circuits' (Smith, 2005), whereby they organize activities across multiple settings, creating and maintaining an accountable relation between the institutional order represented in the texts and interactional orders achieved locally by actors (Suchman, 1997). This forms the basis for the ability of certain actors to influence the actions of others, which is arguably the essence of management as an activity (Anderson and Sharrock, 2018).

4.4 An Ethnomethodological Perspective of Routine Dynamics

Equipped with the concepts and vocabulary that underpin ethnomethodology's approach to social phenomena, we now turn to outlining an EM perspective of Routine Dynamics. In what follows, I first review recent ethnomethodological studies of routines (LeBaron et al., 2016; Yamauchi and Hiramoto, 2016, 2021) and then suggest possible avenues for extending this line of research.

4.4.1 EM Studies of Routine Dynamics

EM studies of Routine Dynamics have examined how action in routines is collectively constructed through sequences of oriented/indexical body movements and utterances.

LeBaron et al. (2016) examined end-of-shift handoffs at a hospital's intensive care unit. They recorded videos of handoff interactions between pairs of outgoing and incoming physicians as they discussed each of the patients in their care, and subsequently interviewed those physicians. Through their interviews, LeBaron et al. (2016) found that participants held 'strongly shared expectations' about how handoffs should be conducted, including specific steps and their sequence. Their video recordings, however, showed that instances of handoffs varied, so that steps were skipped or rearranged according to different circumstances. Moreover, even when a handoff followed the standard sequence of steps, participants devoted time and effort to signal to each other – through synchronized talk, body posture, gaze, movements and gestures – when individual steps were sufficient and when to move from one to the next. These observations allow the authors to reach two important conclusions. First, even in settings where actors strongly agree on the steps that should be followed to achieve an action, ongoing coordinating is needed to produce concerted action. Second, members used the 'sequential features' of their shared expectations as a resource to produce varied courses of action which, while suited to the specific circumstances of each interaction, remained recognizable as performances of the routine.

Yamauchi and Hiramoto (2016, 2021) studied service interactions in high-end sushi bars in Tokyo, where customers are often unfamiliar with deep traditions regarding the ordering of food and drink. Yamauchi and Hiramoto's (2016) analysis showed how participants presented their understandings of the ongoing action through their talk, body posture, movements and gaze; and how they responded to the understandings displayed by others in this same way. The authors conclude that prior shared understandings are not necessary for successful performance of routines: members achieve successful performances through a sequential process of exhibiting their understanding of the ongoing interaction and adjusting their performance to the understandings exhibited by others. Further, Yamauchi and Hiramoto (2021) revealed how participants make their actions recognizable as performances of a routine through the same sequential process, by which actors align their actions and assemble the materials necessary for the performance.

Together, these studies provide a critique of the view that coordination is enabled by overlaps in the pre-existing subjective understandings of individuals: a shared understanding is not necessary (Yamauchi and Hiramoto, 2016), nor is it sufficient (LeBaron et al., 2016), to achieve repetitive collective action. Rather, coordination in routines relies on the situational understandings that members construct and demonstrate *in situ*, through sequenced embodied displays of orientation to elements of the material setting and the unfolding interaction (Yamauchi and Hiramoto, 2021). It is through the sequence of turns of talk and action that participants construct an interaction that is meaningful to them and recognizable as a performance of a routine, independent of individuals' expressed or tacit understandings of that routine before or after the interaction.

4.4.2 Further Research

As exemplified by these works, EM studies of Routine Dynamics take a primary interest in members' methods for producing actions as part of a repetitive pattern, that is, the taken-for-granted yet systematic ways in which members produce actions that are accountably 'the same' across sites and occasions. In what follows, I propose a number of areas where this research programme may be developed further, and suggest examples of recent EM research that provide valuable insight.

First, an EM perspective could shed further light on how participants achieve situated performances of a routine: what displays of orientation they make to ensure their actions are recognizable as part of a pattern and what resources they orient to for that purpose. One class of resources of particular importance in the study of routines is formal procedure. LeBaron et al. (2016) have shown how physicians achieved handoffs flexibly by orienting to the sequential features of a standard set of steps. EM research provides further insight into how participants make such formalized sequences of steps relevant to the interaction at hand. For instance, Koschmann et al. (2011) describe *procedure work* as the work of 'locally producing the procedure as procedure'. They show how surgeons used deictics (e.g., 'now', 'here') to align the procedural account of the surgery with the action in progress, and then talked and manipulated the objects referred in the procedure into being part of the collective course of action. Through such work, members brought into relation their unfolding interaction with the prescriptive account contained in the procedure.

Another class of resources of interest to RD scholars is the various artifacts and material arrangements that constitute durable features of the settings in which a routine is performed. Yamauchi and Hiramoto (2021) showed that sushi bar chefs and customers relied on the material properties of spatial arrangements and their own oriented bodies to render their actions recognizable as performances of a routine. Other recent EM research has shown different ways in which participants made use of materiality in achieving repetition and variation in collective courses of action. For instance, cooking instructors spent time pre-arranging ingredients and utensils in ways that prefigured their use in a recipe, as a way to ensure that the recipe was then completed by the students in a consistent way (Mondada, 2014a). In another study, museum guides and guests collectively and continually produced the interactional space of a guided tour by orienting their talk, gaze and bodies – a process that was constitutive of each distinctive performance of the guided tour routine (Best and Hindmarsh, 2019). Finally, a study of fine art auctions found that a seemingly simple action involving an unsophisticated artifact, such as striking the gavel, could be variously articulated, through embodied multimodal displays, to accomplish different types of action (Heath and Luff, 2013).

Second, an EM perspective can provide useful insight into how action in routines is organized across multiple sites. One way of doing this would be to examine the overlapping, multi-layered accountabilities to which members orient in constructing their interactions. For instance, a study of a call centre found that sales representatives simultaneously oriented to the ongoing conversation with the customer, and to various documents available to them on paper and computer screens (Whalen et al., 2002). In this way, the reps' actions simultaneously enacted the local interactional order of the conversation with the customer, and the various trans-local institutional orders prefigured in the documents.

Alternatively, researchers could examine the means through which actors create and sustain routine-specific accountabilities for others, through different types of textual technologies (Anderson and Sharrock, 2018; Smith, 2005). For instance, Kameo and Whalen (2015) studied how emergency call takers produced standardized person descriptions from callers' 'vernacular accounts' and inputted them as part of a computerized incident record. The authors showed that call takers' work was part of talk-text-talk sequences that reified persons and events, and established courses of action as 'organizational'. The designed features of the computer form and other supplementary materials made the work of call takers accountable to an authorized standard. In another study, Moore, Whalen and Gathman (2010) examined the role of work-order paper forms in linking the activities of front-desk and back-office workers at a reprographics centre. They showed how standard forms were made to work as coordination devices through non-standard practices such as free-text notes, annotations and tagging. In this case, the flexibility afforded by the paper form to accommodate situationally relevant encoding practices ensured the reliable coordination of actions separated in time and space.

Third, an EM perspective could provide a useful framework for RD scholars to examine how participants become competent in the methods of interaction relevant to a routine. Such research may be particularly useful in providing insight into how actors achieve performances of a routine. For instance, Yamauchi and Hiramoto (2016) contrasted performances of the food ordering routine when inexperienced customers were involved to those where customers were regulars or sushi connoisseurs. Such research strategy helped highlight the taken-for-granted methods of interaction that may be harder to observe when actors are highly experienced.

Other EM research has examined how novices learn to engage in a broad array of organized activities in both formal and informal settings. For instance, Tulbert and Goodwin (2011) studied how children learn to brush their teeth in their family setting. They found that learning to brush your teeth entailed training the body to perform 'choreographies of movements' through the household's architectural space and the objects in it. Their analysis highlighted the role of architectural space in creating and sustaining patterns of family life. In a more formal – and professional – setting, Hindmarsh, Reynolds and Dunne (2011) studied dentist training. They found that instruction episodes progressed through sequences of modelled behaviour and online commentary on the part of instructors, and students' verbalized and embodied displays of understanding. These sequences provided insight into what understanding dental practice entails, not as a cognitive inner process, but as a 'public and witnessable doing' (2011: 501).

Finally, RD scholars could take an EM perspective to study how details of interactions in routines may lead to differential outcomes for organizations and individuals. For instance, Best and Hindmarsh's (2019) study of museum guided tours highlighted the importance of 'how bodies and spaces are marshalled' for fostering understanding and enjoyment in audiences – and, thereby, for the attainment of a museum's aims. Mondada (2011a: 313) found that the democratic and participatory character of town-hall meetings was 'practically and locally achieved through the way in which [space was] interactionally organized'. Finally,

Tulbert and Goodwin (2011) found that parents' embodied displays of either cooperation or domination in teaching their children activities such as brushing their teeth fostered differential socialization outcomes for those children.

4.5 Conclusion

This chapter has provided an overview of ethnomethodology's approach to the study of social phenomena, and has pointed to ways in which it could contribute to understanding routine dynamics. Researchers in the field should feel encouraged by the abundant opportunities that an EM perspective provides for empirical research on the methods that members use to produce action in routines, and the means for managing those actions. Additionally, the RD literature would benefit greatly from incorporating the findings of ethnomethodological studies of work, which over five decades have examined repetitive organizational actions in a huge variety of settings.

Adopting an EM view of action as situated should help the field move towards a more fully performative understanding of routines, and underpin an empirical research programme grounded in the observable material and embodied processes of interaction that constitute repetitive action patterns.

References

Amerine, R. and Bilmes, J. (1988). Following instructions. *Human Studies*, 327–339.

Anderson, R. J. and Sharrock, W. (2018). *Action at a Distance: Studies in the Practicalities of Executive Management*. New York: Routledge.

Best, K. and Hindmarsh, J. (2019). Embodied spatial practices and everyday organization: The work of tour guides and their audiences. *Human Relations*, 72(2), 248–271.

Bittner, E. (1965). The concept of organization. *Social Research*, 32(3), 239–255.

Bourdieu, P. (1990). *The Logic of Practice*. Stanford, CA: Stanford University Press.

Bucher, S. and Langley, A. (2016). The interplay of reflective and experimental spaces in interrupting and reorienting routine dynamics. *Organization Science*, 27(3), 594–613.

Cooren, F. (2004). Textual agency: How texts do things in organizational settings. *Organization*, 11(3), 373–393.

D'Adderio, L. (2008). The performativity of routines: Theorising the influence of artefacts and distributed agencies on routines dynamics. *Research Policy*, 37(5), 769–789.

D'Adderio, L. (2011). Artifacts at the centre of routines: Performing the material turn in routines theory. *Journal of Institutional Economics*, 7(2), 197–230.

Dittrich, K., Guérard, S. and Seidl, D. (2016). Talking about routines: The role of reflective talk in routine change. *Organization Science*, 27(3), 678–697.

Feldman, M. S. (2000). Organizational routines as a source of continuous change. *Organization Science*, 11(6), 611–629.

Feldman, M. S. (2003). A performative perspective on stability and change in organizational routines. *Industrial and Corporate Change*, 12(4), 727–752.

Feldman, M. S. (2016). Routines as process: Past, present, and future. In J. Howard-Grenville, C. Rerup, H. Tsoukas and A. Langley, eds., *Organizational Routines: How They Are Created, Maintained, and Changed*. Oxford: Oxford University Press, pp. 23–46.

Feldman, M. S. and Pentland, B. T. (2003). Reconceptualizing organizational routines as a source of flexibility and change. *Administrative Science Quarterly*, 48(1), 94–118.

Feldman, M. S., Pentland, B. T., D'Adderio, L. and Lazaric, N. (2016). Beyond routines as things: Introduction to the special issue on Routine Dynamics. *Organization Science*, 27(3), 505–513.

Garfinkel, H. (1967). *Studies in Ethnomethodology*. Englewood Cliffs, NJ: Prentice-Hall.

Garfinkel, H. (2002). *Ethnomethodology's Program: Working out Durkheim's Aphorism*. Lanham, MD: Rowman & Littlefield Publishers.

Giddens, A. (1984). *The Constitution Of Society: Outline of the Theory of Structuration*. Cambridge: Polity Press.

Glaser, V. L. (2017). Design performances: How organizations inscribe artifacts to change routines. *Academy of Management Journal*, 60(6), 2126–2154.

Goodwin, C. (2000a). Action and embodiment within situated human interaction. *Journal of Pragmatics*, 32(10), 1489–1522.

Goodwin, C. (2000b). Practices of color classification. *Mind, Culture, and Activity*, 7(1–2), 19–36.
Goodwin, C. (2000c). Vision and Inscription in Practice. *Mind, Culture, and Activity*, 7(1–2), 1–3.
Goodwin, C. (2011). Contextures of action. In J. Streeck, C. Goodwin and C. D. LeBaron, eds., *Embodied Interaction: Language and Body in the Material World*. New York: Cambridge University Press.
Goodwin, C. (2013). The co-operative, transformative organization of human action and knowledge. *Journal of Pragmatics*, 46(1), 8–23.
Goodwin, C. (2018). *Co-operative Action*. New York: Cambridge University Press.
Heath, C. and Luff, P. (2013). Embodied action and organisational interaction: Establishing contract on the strike of a hammer. *Journal of Pragmatics*, 46(1), 24–38.
Heritage, J. (1984). *Garfinkel and Ethnomethodology*. Cambridge; New York: Polity Press.
Hindmarsh, J. and Heath, C. (2000). Sharing the tools of the trade: The interactional constitution of workplace objects. *Journal of Contemporary Ethnography*, 29(5), 523–562.
Hindmarsh, J., Reynolds, P. and Dunne, S. (2011). Exhibiting understanding: The body in apprenticeship. *Journal of Pragmatics*, 43(2), 489–503.
Hutchins, E. (1995). *Cognition in the Wild*. Cambridge, MA: MIT Press.
Kameo, N. and Whalen, J. (2015). Organizing documents: Standard forms, person production and organizational action. *Qualitative Sociology*, 38(2), 205–229.
Koschmann, T. (2011). Understanding understanding in action. *Journal of Pragmatics*, 43(2), 435–437.
Koschmann, T., LeBaron, C., Goodwin, C. and Feltovich, P. (2011). 'Can you see the cystic artery yet?' A simple matter of trust. *Journal of Pragmatics*, 43(2), 521–541.
Latour, B. (1986). The powers of association. In J. Law, ed., *Power, Action, and Belief: A New Sociology of Knowledge?* London; Boston: Routledge & Kegan Paul.
Latour, B. (2005). *Reassembling the Social: An Introduction to Actor-Network-Theory*. Oxford; New York: Oxford University Press.
LeBaron, C., Christianson, M. K., Garrett, L. and Ilan, R. (2016). Coordinating flexible performance during everyday work: An ethnomethodological study of handoff routines. *Organization Science*, 27(3), 514–534.
Lynch, M. (2011). Commentary: On understanding understanding. *Journal of Pragmatics*, 43(2), 553–555.
Lynch, M. (2015). *Garfinkel's Studies of Work*. Ithaca, NY: Cornell University Press. Retrieved from ftp://ftp.ehess.fr/sg12/WebPro1516/Draft%20-%20Garf%20book.pdf.
Lynch, M. (2019). Garfinkel, Sacks and formal structures: Collaborative origins, divergences and the history of ethnomethodology and conversation analysis. *Human Studies*, 42(2), 183–198.
Mondada, L. (2011a). The interactional production of multiple spatialities within a participatory democracy meeting. *Social Semiotics*, 21(2), 289–316.
Mondada, L. (2011b). Understanding as an embodied, situated and sequential achievement in interaction. *Journal of Pragmatics*, 43(2), 542–552.
Mondada, L. (2014a). Cooking instructions and the shaping of things in the kitchen. In M. Nevile, P. Haddington, T. Heinemann and M. Rauniomaa, eds., *Interacting with Objects: Language, Materiality, and Social Activity*: Amsterdam: John Benjamins Publishing Company.
Mondada, L. (2014b). The local constitution of multimodal resources for social interaction. *Journal of Pragmatics*, 65, 137–156.
Mondada, L. (2016). Challenges of multimodality: Language and the body in social interaction. *Journal of Sociolinguistics*, 20(3), 336–366.
Mondada, L. (2019). Contemporary issues in conversation analysis: Embodiment and materiality, multimodality and multisensoriality in social interaction. *Journal of Pragmatics*, 145, 47–62.
Moore, R. J., Whalen, J. and Gathman, E. C. H. (2010). The work of the work order: Document practice in face-to-face service encounters. In N. Llewellyn and J. Hindmarsh, eds., *Organisation, Interaction and Practice: Studies in Ethnomethodology and Conversation Analysis*. Cambridge; New York: Cambridge University Press.
Parmigiani, A. and Howard-Grenville, J. (2011). Routines revisited: Exploring the capabilities and practice perspectives. *The Academy of Management Annals*, 5(1), 413–453.
Pentland, B. T. and Feldman, M. S. (2008). Designing routines: On the folly of designing artifacts, while hoping for patterns of action. *Information & Organization*, 18(4), 235–250.
Pentland, B. T., Feldman, M. S., Becker, M. C. and Liu, P. (2012). Dynamics of organizational

routines: A generative model. *Journal of Management Studies*, 49(8), 1484–1508.

Pentland, B. T. and Rueter, H. H. (1994). Organizational routines as grammars of action. *Administrative Science Quarterly*, 39(3), 484–510.

Rawls, A. W. (2002). Editor's introduction. In H. Garfinkel. *Ethnomethodology's Program: Working out Durkheim's Aphorism*. Lanham, MD: Rowman & Littlefield Publishers, pp. 1–64.

Rawls, A. W. (2006). Respecifying the study of social order: Garfinkel's transition from theoretical conceptualization to practices in details. In H. Garfinkel, ed., *Seeing Sociologically: The Routine Grounds of Social Action*. Boulder, CO: Paradigm Publishers, pp. 1–97. Rawls, A. W. (2008). Harold Garfinkel, ethnomethodology and workplace studies. *Organization Studies*, 29(5), 701–732.

Rawls, A. W. (2011). Harold Garfinkel. In G. Ritzer and J. Stepnisky, eds., *The Wiley-Blackwell Companion to Major Social Theorists. Vol. 2 Contemporary Social Theorists*. Malden: Wiley-Blackwell, pp. 89–124.

Rerup, C. and Feldman, M. S. (2011). Routines as a source of change in organizational schemata: The role of trial-and-error learning. *Academy of Management Journal*, 54(3), 577–610.

Smith, D. E. (2001). Texts and the ontology of organizations and institutions. *Studies in Cultures, Organizations & Societies*, 7(2), 159–198.

Smith, D. E. (2005). *Institutional Ethnography: A Sociology for People*. Walnut Creek, CA: AltaMira Press.

Smith, D. E. and Whalen, J. (1997). *Texts in Action*. Toronto: University of Toronto.

Streeck, J., Goodwin, C. and LeBaron, C. D. (2011). Embodied interaction in the material world: An introduction. In J. Streeck, C. Goodwin and C. D. LeBaron, eds., *Embodied Interaction: Language and Body in the Material World*. New York: Cambridge University Press.

Suchman, L. A. (1996). Constituting shared workspaces. In Y. Engeström and D. Middleton, eds., *Cognition and Communication at Work*. Cambridge; New York: Cambridge University Press.

Suchman, L. A. (1997). Centers of coordination: A case and some themes. In L. B. Resnick, R. Säljö, C. Pontecorvo and B. Burge, eds., *Discourse, Tools, and Reasoning: Essays on Situated Cognition*. Berlin; New York: Springer.

Suchman, L. A. (2007). *Human-Machine Reconfigurations: Plans and Situated Actions*. Cambridge; New York: Cambridge University Press.

Tulbert, E. and Goodwin, M. H. (2011). Choreographies of attention: Multimodality in a routine family activity. In J. Streeck, C. Goodwin and C. D. LeBaron, eds., *Embodied Interaction: Language and Body in the Material World*. New York: Cambridge University Press, pp. 79–92.

Ueno, N. (2000). Ecologies of inscription: Technologies of making the social organization of work and the mass production of machine parts visible in collaborative activity. *Mind, Culture, and Activity*, 7(1–2), 59–80.

Whalen, J., Whalen, M. and Henderson, K. (2002). Improvisational choreography in teleservice work. *The British Journal of Sociology*, 53(2), 239–258.

Wittgenstein, L. (1953/2010). *Philosophical Investigations*. Chichester: John Wiley & Sons.

Yamauchi, Y. and Hiramoto, T. (2016). Reflexivity of routines: An ethnomethodological investigation of initial service encounters at sushi bars in Tokyo. *Organization Studies*, 37(10), 1473–1499.

Yamauchi, Y. and Hiramoto, T. (2021). Performative achievement of routine recognizability: An analysis of order taking routines at sushi bars. *Journal of Management Studies*, 57(8), 1610–1642.

Zimmerman, D. H. (1970). The practicalities of rule use. In J. D. Douglas, ed., *Understanding Everyday Life: Toward the Reconstruction of Sociological Knowledge*. London: Routledge and Kegan Paul, pp. 221–238.

CHAPTER 5 Pragmatism and Routine Dynamics

DIONYSIOS D. DIONYSIOU

> . . . an attitude of orientation is what the pragmatic method means. The attitude of **looking away** from first things, principles, 'categories', supposed necessities; and of **looking towards** last things, fruits, consequences, facts. (James, 1907: 54–55 emphasis added)

5.1 Introduction

In this chapter, I explore the relevance of classical pragmatism to the study of Routine Dynamics. The two perspectives share a processual-relational view of the world, an emphasis on agency and situated action and reject all forms of dualism in the theorizing of social phenomena, suggesting that a rich common ground exists to allow cross-fertilization. While the influence of pragmatist ideas to the study of routines has so far been limited, pragmatism as a 'problem solving' philosophy holds great promise in advancing further our understanding of routine enactment in the face of increased novelty, contingency and potentiality, characteristics inherent to the nature of routines as processes.

Pragmatism, the 'most distinctive philosophical movement to emerge in the United States', emerged in the last quarter of the nineteenth century as a radical critique of Cartesianism and its principle of the self-certainty of the doubting ego as foundational for philosophy (e.g., Bernstein, 1992: 833; Lorino, 2018). This principle was responsible for a number of inescapable dualisms (e.g., mind/body, mental/physical, fact/value) that haunted modern philosophy and which pragmatists were determined to put aside, along with the traditional philosophical quest for absolute certainty.

The four major figures in the development of Classical Pragmatism were Charles Sanders Peirce, William James, John Dewey and George Herbert Mead (Bernstein, 2010; Joas 1996; Lorino, 2018). The founders of classical pragmatism drew on a variety of intellectual orientations (British empiricism, Kant, Hegel and Darwin) and there were sharp differences in their intellectual backgrounds, training and interests. Despite these differences, here I focus on the common themes that tied these thinkers together. For a more detailed exposition to classical pragmatism there are sources that interested readers may find useful (e.g., Bernstein, 2010; Lorino, 2018; Menand, 2002; Misak, 2013).

The chapter unfolds as follows. I discuss briefly the emergence of classical pragmatism and the common themes in the ideas of the four major figures. I also explore the commonalities between the key pragmatist ideas and the theoretical assumptions that underpin Routine Dynamics theorizing and trace their influence in the study of Routine Dynamics. Concluding, I suggest that a pragmatist perspective has much to offer to the study of routines as dynamic, processual phenomena, and discuss its implications and potential for research in Routine Dynamics.

5.2 Classical Pragmatism as a Philosophical Perspective: Key Figures and Common Themes

William James, 'the father of modern psychology and the face of American pragmatism' (Misak, 2013: 53), was the first to publicly introduce the term 'pragmatism' as a new philosophical position in 1898, in his address before the Philosophical Union of the University of California in Berkeley (Bernstein, 2010). James said that he heard the term some twenty years earlier from Peirce during the meetings of the Metaphysical Club, an informal discussion group who met in Cambridge, Massachusetts. Peirce, in his now famous 1878 paper *'How to make our ideas clear*', formulated what subsequently was referred to as the 'pragmatic principle' or 'maxim' (James, 1907: 47), namely, that our beliefs or ideas are rules for action and their meaning lies in their conceivable practical effects, the different modes of action to which they give rise. Peirce, therefore, called for a shift in our attention from the origins of ideas and beliefs to their consequences for conduct, from theoretical abstraction to lived experience and concrete practice (Emirbayer and Maynard, 2011). In this way, he established the inseparability of meaning and action in pragmatist thinking and of concrete experience (experienced practical consequences) as the ultimate test of our beliefs and ideas. His concept of 'inquiry' through which 'doubt' is resolved and new beliefs and habits of conduct are developed, and the key role he attributed to the community of inquirers in developing, testing and validating our hypotheses and theories, became central themes in pragmatist thinking (Peirce, 1992). However, the word 'pragmatism', 'caught on and spread like wildfire' when James published his Berkeley address (Bernstein, 2010: 3), and it is through his exposition that the world perceived and understood pragmatism (Misak, 2013).

James took Peirce's pragmatic principle and turned it to a philosophical orientation or 'attitude' (see James' opening statement), extending it to the problem of the nature of truth. He sought to help the public realize that philosophical debates are important because the beliefs they support lead to different ways of conduct (Dewey, 1981: 46). The insistence of both Peirce and James on the consequences and possibilities of action was 'almost revolutionary in its consequences' (Thayer 1982: 33); it suggested bringing the future into consideration and with it an evolutionary, processual view of the world filled with emergence, chance and contingency. Classical pragmatists abandoned the quest for certainty and embraced indeterminacy wholeheartedly; all our knowledge claims are fallible and open to potential criticism (Bernstein, 1992). Such a view leaves space for human agency, choice and creativity to shape the environment and the unfolding of events (Joas, 1993); reason, or thought, in its general sense, has a creative and constructive function (Mead, 1932). James believed that we play a role in creating our future,

> *I, for my part, cannot escape the consideration, forced upon me at every turn, that the knower is not simply a mirror floating with no foot-hold anywhere, and passively reflecting an order that he comes upon and finds simply existing. The knower is an actor, and co-efficient of the truth on one side, whilst on the other he registers the truth which he helps to create* (1878: 17, italics added).

This processual view of the world was shared by all classical pragmatists, including John Dewey and George H. Mead, who carried forward the pragmatic movement. The idea that permeates their thinking is that the social world consists of processes that 'connect all sorts of entities in relational and recursive ways' (Farjoun et al., 2015: 1789) (see also Tsoukas [Chapter 3], this volume). For Dewey, the distinction between the organism and its environment is a distinction between different phases of the same process of living; 'the organism is in and of the world' (Dewey, 1917: 15). He rejected the knower/known duality and viewed the problem of knowing as a problem of living and that thought and its object lie within the same experience. Individuals, society and environment are implicated in mutually constitutive relationships or 'transactions'; '[w]hat has been completely divided in philosophical discourse into man and the world, inner and outer, self and not-self, subject and object, individual and social, private and public, etc., are in actuality parties in life-transactions'. (Dewey and Bentley, 1949: 187). In other words, classical pragmatism is underpinned by a processual/relational ontology that is fundamentally anti-dualistic.

In his classic *Human Nature and Conduct* (1922), Dewey offered a comprehensive account of human nature and conduct and of intelligence as a process involving the creative solution of everyday problems and improving human life. Dewey's model of human conduct is characteristic of the 'pragmatist schema that anchors doubt in action' (Joas, 1996: 128). According to this model, we typically follow our well-exercised habits in a relatively thoughtless manner; nevertheless, our habits are frequently met with resistance from the world or conflict with each other, so that ongoing conduct is blocked (Dewey 1922: 173). This is when 'thought is excited by the irritation of doubt' (Peirce, 1992: 127), that is, we engage in deliberation, during which we thoughtfully experiment to find out 'what the various lines of possible action are really' (Dewey, 1922: 190). The outcome of this reconstruction of activity, if successful in dealing with the problem of action, is a creative accomplishment (Joas, 1996: 129). Following Peirce's work on inquiry, Dewey sought to develop a 'unified theory of inquiry' that would help us resolve problematic situations in everyday life (Dewey, 1938).

Dewey's lifelong friend and colleague at the University of Chicago, Mead, is recognized as the thinker who, next to Dewey, contributed most to the development of pragmatism (Reck, 1963). Mead, more than any other pragmatist thinker, developed a comprehensive and detailed social theory of action and language (Bernstein, 2010) and it is through his work that the relevance of pragmatism to sociology and social psychology became apparent (Joas and Knobl, 2009). Mead's work exemplifies pragmatist thinking, as, for instance, in developing his theory of the genesis of the self (Mead, 1934), he transcended many of the dualisms that still prevail in contemporary philosophy and science (Dionysiou, 2017). For Mead, the individual 'constitutes society as genuinely society constitutes the individual' (Mead 1935: 70). He maintained that 'the behavior of an individual can be understood only in terms of the behavior of the whole social group of which he is a member' (Mead, 1938: 6) and in this way he laid the foundation of a process theory of identity formation (Joas and Knobl, 2009). Mead, above all others, established the symbolic character of interaction (Stryker, 1980) and his work was foundational to Symbolic Interactionism as a distinct perspective in sociology (Blumer, 1969). Finally, his seminal theorization of temporality in *The Philosophy of the Present* (1932) has informed contemporary accounts of agency that capture more fully the complexity of agentic processes (Emirbayer and Miche, 1998).

5.3 Classical Pragmatism and Routine Dynamics

5.3.1 RD and Classical Pragmatism: Shared Assumptions

Pragmatism has never been completely absent from organizational studies (e.g., Selznick, 1957; Weick, 1979, 1995), but its influence has only recently reached research on organizational routines (e.g., Dionysiou and Tsoukas, 2013; Dittrich and Seidl, 2018). As Cohen (2007a) notes, due to its deep roots in modern organizational theory (Cyert and March, 1963; March and Simon, 1958), work on routines had traditionally promoted a rigid, static view of routines that emphasizes choice and considers 'action as less problematic, following more or less automatically from choice'. (Cohen, 2007b: 505). In this way, the so-called Carnegie School moved the pragmatists' emphasis on experience, action, habit and emotions to the background and brought back a number of dualisms that pragmatists abhorred (e.g., thought/action, fact/value, and means/ends).

Things started changing during the past decade, when Feldman (2000) and Feldman and Pentland (2003) challenged the traditional view by promoting a processual view of routines as emergent, ongoing accomplishments. Their work has been highly influential and gave rise to a new branch of research, 'Routine Dynamics', which is based on the idea that routines are practices with internal dynamics (Feldman et al., 2016). This radical shift in our understanding of the nature of routines brought the concept of routines much closer to key pragmatist ideas. How much closer becomes apparent when considering the key principles of practice theorizing (see also Feldman [Chapter 2], this volume) summarized by Feldman and Orlikowski (2011: 1241) – the consequentiality of situated actions in the production of social life; the rejection of dualisms as a way of theorizing; and the mutually constitutive nature of relationships, all consistent with pragmatist thinking. Table 5.1 summarizes the shared assumptions that underpin Routine Dynamics theorizing and classical pragmatism and suggests that there is sufficient

Table 5.1 Shared assumptions between Routine Dynamics and classical pragmatism

RD – Routines as practices (e.g., Feldman, 2000; Feldman and Pentland, 2003; Feldman and Orlikowski, 2011; Feldman et al., 2016)	Classical Pragmatism
Routines as processes, action transcends dualisms: (agency/structure, mind/body, etc.)	Rejects all dualisms as arbitrary conceptual 'cuts' made in the continuum of the life process to facilitate linguistic representation (e.g., Dewey, 1922; James, 1909: 285; Mead, 1934)
Action in routines is situated	Emphasis on concrete reality, facts, outcomes and their meaningful experience. Reality 'can be known adequately only by following its singularities from moment to moment as our experience grows' (James, 1911: 99).
Relationality of mutual constitution (e.g., the mutually constitutive relationship of performative and ostensive aspects)	The two parts of a dualism (e.g., subject/object, individual/ society, mind/body) are 'in actuality parties in life-transactions' (Dewey and Bentley, 1949:187). For instance, individuals, society and nature are mutually constituted (Dewey, 1922; Mead, 1934, 1938)
Stability is an accomplishment	For the pragmatists, what 'really exists is not things made but things in the making' (James, 1909: 263).
Individuals and their agency matter – actors are knowledgeable and often reflective	Individuals have an active role in creating the 'reality' they face (James, 1878). '[C]ognition, and thought as a part of the cognitive process, is reconstructive, because reconstruction is essential to the conduct of an intelligent being in the universe' (Mead, 1932: 37).

common ground for cross-fertilization between the two perspectives.

In the following, I examine how pragmatism has informed recent work in Routine Dynamics. As a number of routine scholars realized the affinity of Routine Dynamics theorizing with key pragmatist ideas, they sought to explore pragmatism's potential to advance our understanding of the dynamic nature of routines as processes.

5.3.2 The Influence of Classical Pragmatism in RD Research

The view of routines as flexible, emergent accomplishments (Feldman 2000; Feldman and Pentland 2003) gained rapid currency in the study of routines, so that when Cohen (2007a) argued first for the relevance of classical pragmatism to the study of routines, the field had already become more receptive to pragmatist ideas. In particular, Cohen (2007a) argued that Dewey's (1922) model of human nature and conduct, by accounting for the interactions between habits, cognitions and emotions, has great promise to illuminate the processes involved in routine adaptation to novel circumstances and the paradoxical nature of routines as '(n)ever changing' patterns of interaction. Dewey's model has also been suggested recently by Winter (2013: 121), albeit, this time as a useful orientation to 'strengthen the foundations and enhance the fruitfulness of theories of organizational routines and capabilities'. Both Cohen and Winter highlight the central role of habit in Dewey's work. Dewey suggested that habit should not be reduced to mindless automaticity and repetition, characteristics that pertain to a specific kind of habit that he called a '*routine*' or '*dead*' habit (1922: 71, 208). Instead, he emphasized the primacy of '*intelligent*' habit, which is 'infused with thought and feeling' (1922: 71) and 'grows more varied, more adaptable by practice and use' (1922: 72). Our habits filter 'all the material that reaches our perception and thought'. (1922: 32). Dewey's (1922) theorizing by seeing habit as fundamental to human action, along with its interplay with cognition and emotions, enables the 'unpacking' of human agency and action, thereby offering a richer and more realistic model of human conduct than that assumed by modern organization theory and economics (Cohen 2007b; Farjoun et al., 2015; Winter, 2013).

Simpson and Lorino (2016) focus on Dewey's concept of habit along with two interrelated pragmatist concepts, namely, inquiry and conversational transaction, suggesting that they may help strengthen the processual theorization of routines. They note that habits must be understood as social, acquired and continuously modified through experience (Dewey, 1922) and that they are mobilized and continuously adapted through the process of inquiry, which involves the transformation of an indeterminate or doubtful situation into one that is sufficiently unified so that a coherent course of action can be anticipated (Dewey, 1938). The mobilization of habits and inquiries is situated within social and temporal contexts, where agency plays a key role in the adjustment of conduct. Situating routine enactment into the temporal and relational contexts of the ongoing experience reveals that at every moment, 'the possibilities for action are manifold, the future is open, and even when uncertainty seems very low, options for action are still contingent' (Simpson and Lorino, 2016: 59). In particular, these authors emphasize the pragmatists' conception of agency as inherently relational and temporal (Emirbayer and Miche, 1998; Mead, 1932, 1934) and argue that agency arises within the conversational flow, which is 'a mutually constituting dynamic that engages the meanings of conversants' situations and conversants' selves'. (Simpson and Lorino, 2016: 62). This process is not a mere interaction among distinct entities, but a transaction (Dewey and Bentley, 1949), in which 'all entities participating in an inquiry are involved on an equal footing and that their very definition and delineation is completely contingent on the progress of the inquiry' (Simpson and Lorino, 2016: 62). Moreover, agency engages the past and the future as resources that provide actors with meaning and direction in the present moment. In this way, Simpson and Lorino (2016: 65) propose a framing of 'the social and temporal dimensions of ordinary everyday practice in terms of the mutually embedded and practically inseparable dynamics of habit, inquiry and conversational trans-action', which highlights the processual nature of routines.

Howard-Grenville's (2005) study of the road mapping routine in a high-tech manufacturing company contributes to the unpacking of agency in routines by showing that participants' temporal orientations – to the past, present or future – shape specific performances of the routine. To do so, she draws on Emirbayer and Miche's (1998) account of agency, who, in turn, relied heavily on Mead's (1932) theorizing of temporality. Her findings show that participants may choose to iterate on earlier performances (primary orientation to the past); apply elements of earlier performances pragmatically as they simultaneously pursue multiple ends (primary orientation to the present); or project elements of earlier performances to plan for or imagine future enactments of the routine (primary orientation to the future) (Howard-Grenville, 2005: 629), thereby influencing the stable or flexible performance of routines.

Tsoukas and I (Dionysiou and Tsoukas, 2013), in a theoretical paper, rely on Mead (1934, 1938), to propose a process model of routine (re)creation 'from within' and develop endogenous explanations of routine (re)creation grounded on the actions and understandings of mutually susceptible participants. In this article, we focus in particular on the process of the creation of the ostensive aspect from the situated interactions of participants (Feldman and Pentland, 2003). Mead's (1934) account of the process of emergence of the self is central to our work, as it helped us theorize the process through which routines emerge as collective, effortful phenomena, taking Mead's (1934) concept of 'role-taking' (i.e., taking fellow routine participants' roles into account to inform one's own actions) as the underlying mechanism. In particular, we propose that as participants in routines interact with reference to a common activity, they develop individual (routine-specific) selves and shared understandings and habits that become incorporated in the ostensive aspect of routines, which in turn facilitates the alignment of their actions to achieve coordination. The inherently social, relational nature of the self, advanced by Mead, helped us to clarify the construct of the ostensive aspect, in an effort to account for both its multiplicity and its capacity to introduce a level of stability or 'sameness' in routine performances over time. In particular, we argue that through repeated performances over time, individual understandings (schemata) and habits incorporated in the ostensive aspect of routines become 'shared' in the sense of becoming at minimum compatible or congruent (and therefore, not necessarily identical or overlapping). This minimum compatibility or congruence among individual cognitions and habits enables the 'patterning' (Feldman, 2016) of interactions by supplying participants with 'mutually consistent interpretations and evaluations of information, as well as with reciprocal expectations concerning what actions are appropriate for the situation they face' (Dionysiou and Tsoukas, 2013: 193), while it gives space for agentic intervention and the creative resolution of problems of action (Joas, 1996).

In a more recent work, Sutcliffe and I (Dionysiou and Sutcliffe, 2019) draw from both Dewey (1922) and Mead (1932) to propose a revised conceptualization of ostensive patterns or 'patterning' (Feldman, 2016), according to which 'patterning' refers to the process of enacting patterns of relations between participants' cognitions, habits and emotions to resolve emergent situations (unexpected events, breakdowns, opportunities, etc.). We suggest that as participants engage in ongoing repetitive interactions in the context of performing a routine, not only do their interactions become patterned or organized in a particular way but, as part of the same process of activity, so do their individual understandings, habits and emotions that relate to the enactment of a routine. This theorizing exemplifies pragmatist thinking by considering the individual and the collective levels as continuous – performing and patterning are implicated in a mutually constitutive process or 'transaction'.

Another important contribution in the field of Routine Dynamics is Dittrich and Seidl's (2018) empirical study of a start-up pharmaceutical company, who applied Dewey's (1922) notion of the means-ends relationship to explore the full spectrum of intentionality in routines. Dewey (1922: 223) argued that ends or goals are not fixed and set before action, but are 'ends-in-view' that 'arise and function within action'. As he remarked, an end-in-view, 'is the means by which an activity becomes adapted when otherwise it would be blind and disorderly, or by which it gets meaning when otherwise it would be mechanical. In a strict sense an end-in-view is a means in present action.' (1922: 226). By using this idea to interpret their findings, Dittrich and Seidl (2018) challenge the assumption, typically implicit in many routine studies, that participants pursue ends determined in advance of performing the routine. In particular, they show how routine participants, when faced with unfamiliar situations, develop new, emerging ends-in-view by 'foregrounding means within the concrete situation at hand'. (2018: 129). This emerging form of intentionality, in turn, can result in updating routines' goals. These findings suggest that we should understand intentionality in routines as a 'spectrum', 'ranging from ends-in-view that are primarily informed and aligned to any pre-established goals (*purposeful action*) to ends-in-view that are unrelated to any pre-established goals (*purposive action*)' (131, italics in the original).

As this brief review of extant work suggests, the influence of classical pragmatism in the study of Routine Dynamics is gaining momentum and scholars in the field have demonstrated the fertility of several key pragmatist ideas to the study of routines. In the following section, I suggest that there is still much that classical pragmatism could contribute to our understanding of Routine Dynamics.

5.3.3 Pragmatism and Routines Dynamics: Future Directions and Implications for Research

One of the most promising areas in which pragmatism may help advance our understanding of the nature of routines as processes is the role of participants' experience during the enactment of routines in time (Langley and Tsoukas 2017; Tsoukas [Chapter 3], this volume). Early research in Routine Dynamics promoted a rich conception of agency, according to which 'routines are performed by people who think and feel and care' (Feldman, 2000: 614) and agency 'involves the ability to remember the past, imagine the future, and respond to present circumstances' (Feldman and Pentland, 2003: 95). Routine Dynamics researchers, by relying mainly on ethnographic methods, have developed rich descriptions of routine performances in diverse settings; however, the lived experiences of participants, such as temporality and emotions, with few exceptions (e.g., Grodal et al., 2015; Howard-Grenville, 2005), have not been woven into theoretical accounts of Routine Dynamics. A pragmatist perspective prompts scholars of routines to ground their explanations to participants' experience, so that resulting theories will help us return to the field and shed more light on how these experiences shape the unfolding of routines – following James' (1908: 17) suggestion that theorizing 'begins with concreteness, and returns and ends with it'.

Dewey's (1922) model of human nature and conduct helps in disaggregating the concept of agency to focus researchers on how the interplay of habit, cognition and emotion shapes the agentic micro-processes involved in routine adaptation and flexibility, and has the promise to capture more fully participants' experiences of the unfolding of routines as processes. For example, emotions, such as doubt or worry, alert us that the situation demands our attention and motivate the process of inquiry (Dewey, 1922; Locke et al., 2008; Peirce, 1992;). As Dewey (1938: 70) noted, 'a problem must be felt before it can be stated'. Similarly, an intense emotional reaction to novel, unexpected events during routine enactment (e.g., intense surprise, anger or panic) may overwhelm routine participants' capacity to respond adaptively (Loewenstein and Lerner, 2003) and result in the breakdown of a routine or its re-direction in unpredictable paths (for a review of the role of emotions on routines, see Baldessarelli [Chapter 26], this volume).

Moreover, because human experience is inherently temporal (e.g., George and Jones, 2000; Langley and Tsoukas, 2017), capturing participants' experience of the relationship between past, present and future helps in revealing the nuances of the balancing between stability and change in routines and the indeterminate nature of routines as processes. Although the role of clock time and event time in the triggering and sequencing of actions in routines has received some attention from Routine Dynamics researchers (e.g., Turner and Fern, 2012; Turner and Rindova, 2012, 2018; see Turner and Rindova [Chapter 19], this volume), this has not been the case with participants' experience of temporality. Howard-Grenville's (2005) study discussed earlier makes a first step in this direction by showing that participants' temporal orientations (i.e., a primary focus on the past, present or future) influence the persistent or flexible enactment of specific routine performances. This contribution can be further extended by examining how participants experience the flow of time as they encounter unique circumstances and how this experience shapes the unfolding of routines, both of which are important to our understanding of the nature of routines as processes (Hernes, 2014; Langley and Tsoukas, 2017; Tsoukas [Chapter 3], this volume). Mead's (1932) theorizing of temporality is highly relevant here. As actors try to make sense of emergent situations, they integrate 'what has happened before' (i.e., the past) and what 'might happen next' (i.e., the future) (Feldman, 2016: 31) to create a meaningful experience of the present and decide what to do next. Participants select particular elements of the past to create new continuities between the past and the present, which in turn open up for them new possibilities for action. By attending to participants' evolving experience in time we are likely to develop a nuanced understanding of 'how things become the way they are in view of the multiple possibilities of becoming' (Hernes 2014: 3).

Dewey's and Mead's theorizing may also help illuminate the processes through which routine participants problem-solve in the face of dynamic, indeterminate situations. In particular, problem-solving from a pragmatist perspective highlights the continuously evolving, transactional relationship between habits and inquiry, means and ends, problems and solutions, as well as situations and actors, all of which become co-constituted throughout the process of inquiry (Dewey, 1922, 1938; Simpson and Lorino, 2016). Such a view promotes a more dynamic and exploratory approach to problem-solving and learning compared to traditional frameworks, which promote a separation between cognition and action (we think before we act) as well as means and ends (ends precede action and define the means) (Lorino, 2018). Instead, for pragmatists, problem-solving starts from a vague sense that 'there is something wrong' in a situation while the problem definition remains tentative and evolving during the process of inquiry. Learning is highly situated and provisional, fostered by the exploration of means–ends relations during problem-solving, and is subject to verification and revision based on new experiences. Learning outcomes are not necessarily explicit in nature but also become embodied in habits, which become revised and renewed through the process of inquiry (Dewey 1938: 104–110; Joas, 1996; Lorino, 2018: 106–108).

The application of pragmatist ideas has several methodological implications for the study of Routine Dynamics. Although the classical pragmatists did not develop an empirical programme for research[1] (Emirbayer and Maynard, 2011), research conducted in the tradition of ethnomethodology (e.g., Garfinkel, 1967; see also López-Cotarelo [Chapter 4], this volume), conversation analysis (e.g., Sacks, Schegloff and Jefferson, 1974), practice theory (e.g., Nicolini, 2009), as well as research employing ethnographic methods of research (particularly participant observation) (see also Dittrich [Chapter 8], this volume) are well-suited to put into practice many pragmatist ideas.

Pragmatism-inspired scholars of routines may also find Nicolini's (2009) ethnographic method useful, involving 'a recursive movement of zooming in and zooming out on the data and between data and theory' (2009: 120). By 'zooming in', scholars of routines may focus on the situated performances of routines, paying attention to how participants, immersed in the flow of activity, experience in a holistic manner (interplay of habits, emotions, cognition and temporality) the unfolding of routines, and tracing how participants' anticipations and retrospections contribute to the meaningful resolution of everyday problems of action and with what effects in the stability and change of routines. 'Zooming out' helps in exploring the 'thick texture of interconnections' (Nicolini, 2009: 128) or 'transactions', within which routines are immersed.

Moreover, as a 'problem solving philosophy' (Farjoun et al., 2015), pragmatism places great emphasis on how participants handle emergent situations (discrepancies from expectations, realizations of opportunities, surprise, etc.) that challenge the continuous unfolding of routines (Dionysiou and Tsoukas, 2013; Dittrich and Seidl, 2018). These situations represent 'turning points in activity' (Dewey, 1922: 223) that provide researchers with unique opportunities to uncover the 'logic' that is internal to routines as practices (e.g., Feldman and Worline, 2016; Howard-Grenville and Rerup, 2017) and explore the role of participants' 'experimenting intelligence' in the creative resolution of problems (Joas, 1993: 248). Similarly, Shotter (2010: 273) suggests that it is within such situations 'that we can find the uniquely new beginnings for genuinely innovative changes in organizations'. He proposes a 'withness' approach (Shotter, 2006), which requires the researcher to immerse himself or herself in the practices in question and, in 'dialogic interaction' with practitioners, contribute to identifying new possibilities for action. Wegener and Lorino (2020) operationalize the withness approach by embedding it within pragmatist inquiry and propose 'pragmatist withness inquiry' as a methodology for capturing the lived experiences of researchers and practitioners along with the changes in their beliefs and habits throughout the process of inquiry.

Finally, Sandberg and Tsoukas (2011: 348–349) discuss a number of techniques and methods well-suited for studying breakdowns in routine performance, and how scholars of routines may actively create a breakdown in a routine to uncover the 'relational whole' into which participants are

[1] It must be noted, however, that that research in the tradition of Symbolic Interaction has had a significant contribution in the generation of empirical knowledge by field research and is the disciplinary tradition that informed the development of grounded theory (Locke, 2001).

absorbed. Overall, scholars of routines have a large number of methods, tools and techniques available in order to pursue a pragmatism-inspired, empirical programme for research in Routine Dynamics.

5.4 Conclusion

As the ideas of the original Pragmatists are being rediscovered, scholars in diverse fields of study find that pragmatism offers useful resources in order to tackle problems in a world that becomes increasingly more complex, unpredictable and volatile. In the field of Routine Dynamics, the influence of pragmatist ideas has been limited so far but also indicative of the promise of pragmatism as a research programme to guide future research.

Pragmatism provides a rich and coherent conceptual framework to the study of routines as indeterminate social processes, always 'in the making' (James, 1909: 263). Pragmatism augments the tools scholars have for focusing on how people go about their everyday activities in a world filled with surprise, uncertainty and possibility, and for developing further our understanding of routines as emergent and effortful accomplishments and the dynamics of stability and change in routines. In particular, the pragmatist concepts of habit, emotion and cognition and their interplay in human conduct; of inquiry as a method to resolve everyday problems; and the role of temporality in the meaningful experience of present activities provide scholars of routines with a rich conceptual toolkit to theorize about the lived experiences of participants, which shape and are shaped by routine enactment (e.g., Hernes, 2014; Langely and Tsoukas, 2017). Pragmatism, therefore, prompts us to pay attention to concreteness and its meaningful experience, in order to weave into our theorizing what really matters to practitioners; only then will our theories lead us successfully 'back into sensible experience again' (James, 1909: 100).

I hope that this short exposition to classical pragmatism and its relevance to the study of routines will help spread the message that 'we can continue to draw inspiration from the pragmatic legacy and to develop it in creative ways'. (Bernstein, 1992: 840).

References

Bernstein, R. J. (1992). The resurgence of pragmatism. *Social Research*, 59(4), 813–840.

Bernstein, R. J. (2010). *The Pragmatic Turn*. Cambridge: Polity Press.

Blumer, H. (1969). *Symbolic Interactionism: Perspective and Method*. Berkeley: University of California Press.

Cohen M. D. (2007a). Reading Dewey: Reflections on the study of routine. *Organisation Studies*, 28 (5), 773–786.

Cohen, M. D. (2007b). Administrative behavior: Laying the foundations for Cyert and March. *Organization Science*, 18(3), 503–506.

Cyert, R. M. and March, J. G. (1963/1992). *A Behavioral Theory of the Firm*. Malden, MA: Blackwell Publishers.

D'Adderio, L. (2011). Artifacts at the centre of routines: Performing the material turn in routines theory. *Journal of Institutional Economics*, 7(2), 197–230.

Dewey, J. (1917). The Need for a Recovery of Philosophy. In J. Dewey, ed., *Creative Intelligence: Essays in the Pragmatic Attitude*. New York: Holt, pp. 3–69.

Dewey, J. (1922). *Human Nature and Conduct: An Introduction to Social Psychology*. New York: Random House/The Modern Library.

Dewey, J. (1938). *Logic: The Theory of Inquiry*. New York: Henry Holt and Company.

Dewey, J. (1981). *The Philosophy of John Dewey*. (J. J. McDermott, ed.). Chicago: University of Chicago Press.

Dewey J. and Bentley, A. (1949). *Knowing and the Known*. Boston: Beacon Press.

Dionysiou, D. D. (2017). Symbolic interactionism. In A. Langley and H. Tsoukas, eds., *The Sage Handbook of Process Organization Studies*. London: Sage Publications, pp. 144–159.

Dionysiou, D. D. and Sutcliffe, K. M. (2019). *Acting in a Dynamic World: Pragmatism and Routine Dynamics*. Paper presented at the Annual Meeting of the Academy of Management, 8–12 August 2019, Boston.

Dionysiou, D. D. and Tsoukas, H. (2013). Understanding the (re)creation of routines from within: a symbolic interactionist perspective. *Academy of Management Review*, 38(2), 189–205.

Dittrich, K. and Seidl, D. (2018). Emerging intentionality in routine dynamics: A pragmatist view.

Academy of Management Journal, 61(1), 111–138.

Emirbayer, M. and Maynard, D. W. (2011). Pragmatism and ethnomethodology. *Qualitative Sociology*, 34, 221–261.

Emirbayer, M. and Miche, A. (1998). What is agency? *American Journal of Sociology*, 103(4), 962–1023.

Farjoun, M., Ansell, C. and Boin, A. (2015). Pragmatism in organization studies: Meeting the challenges of a dynamic and complex world. *Organization Science*, 26(6), 1787–1804.

Feldman, M. S. (2000). Organizational routines as a source of continuous change. *Organization Science*, 11(6), 611–629.

Feldman, M. S. (2016). Routines as process: Past, present and future. In C. Rerup, J. Howard-Grenville, A. Langley and H. Tsoukas, eds., *Organizational Routines: How they are Created, Maintained, and Changed.* Perspectives on Process Organization Studies Series. Oxford: Oxford University Press, pp. 23–46.

Feldman, M. S. and Orlikowski, W. J. (2011). Theorizing practice and practicing theory. *Organization Science*, 22(5), 1240–1253.

Feldman, M. S. and Pentland, B. T. (2003). Reconceptualizing organizational routines as a source of flexibility and change. *Administrative Science Quarterly*, 48, 94–118.

Feldman, M. S., Pentland, B., D'Adderio L. and Lazaric N. (2016). Beyond routines as things: Introduction to the special issue on routine dynamics. *Organization Science*, 27(3), 505–513.

Feldman, M. S. and Worline, M. (2016). The practicality of practice theory *Academy of Management Learning and Education*, 15(2), 304–324.

Garfinkel, H. (1967). *Studies in Ethnomethodology*. Englewood Cliffs, NJ: Prentice-Hall.

George, J. M. and Jones, G. R. (2000). The role of time in theory and theory building. *Journal of Management*, 26(4), 657–684.

Grodal, S., Nelson, A. J. and Siimo, R. M. (2015). Help-seeking and help-giving as an organizational routine: Continual engagement in innovative work. *Academy of Management Journal*, 58(1), 136–168.

Hernes, T. (2014). *A Process Theory of Organization*. Oxford: Oxford University Press.

Hernes, T., Simpson, B. and Soderland, J. (2013). Managing and temporality. *Scandinavian Journal of Management*, 29, 1–6.

Howard-Grenville, J. A. (2005). The persistence of flexible organizational routines: The role of agency and organizational context. *Organization Science*, 16(6), 618–636.

Howard-Grenville, J. and Rerup, C. (2017). A process perspective on organizational routines. In A. Langley and H. Tsoukas, eds., *The Sage Handbook of Process Organization Studies*. London: SAGE Publications, pp. 323–339.

James, W. (1878). Remarks on Spencer's definition of mind as correspondence. *The Journal of Speculative Psychology*, 12(1), 1–18.

James, W. (1907). *Pragmatism: A New Name for Some Old Ways of Thinking*. New York: Longman, Green and Co.

James, W. (1908). The pragmatist theory of truth and its misunderstanders. *The Philosophical Review*, 17(1), 1–17.

James, W. (1909). *A Pluralistic Universe*. New York, Longman, Green and Co.

James, W. (1911). *Some Problems of Philosophy*. New York, Longman, Green and Co.

Joas, H. (1993). *Pragmatism and Social Theory*. Chicago: The University of Chicago Press.

Joas, H. (1996). *The Creativity of Action*. Chicago: The University of Chicago Press.

Joas, H. and Knobl, W. (2009). *Social Theory: Twenty Introduction Lectures*. New York: Cambridge University Press.

Langley, A. H. and Tsoukas, H. (2017). Introduction: Process thinking, process theorizing and process researching. In A. Langley and H. Tsoukas, eds., *The Sage Handbook of Process Organization Studies*. London: Sage Publications, pp. 1–25.

Locke, K. (2001). *Grounded Theory in Management Research*. London: Sage Publications Ltd.

Locke, K., Golden-Biddle, K. and Feldman, M. S. (2008). Making doubt generative: Rethinking the role of doubt in the research process. *Organization Science*, 19(6), 907–918.

Loewenstein, G. and Lerner, J. S. (2003). The role of affect in decision making. In R. J. Davidson, K. R. Scherer and H. H. Goldsmith, eds., *Handbook of Affective Sciences*. Oxford: Oxford University Press, pp. 619–642.

Lorino, P. (2018). *Pragmatism and Organization Studies*. Oxford: Oxford University Press.

March, J. H. and Simon, H. A. (1958). *Organizations*. New York: John Wiley.

Mead, G. H. (1932). *The Philosophy of the Present*. London: The Open Court Company.

Mead, G. H. (1934). *Mind, Self, and Society from the Standpoint of a Social Behaviorist*. London: The University of Chicago Press.

Mead, G. H. (1935). The philosophy of John Dewey. *International Journal of Ethics*, 46(1), 64–81.

Mead, G. H. (1938). *The Philosophy of the Act*. Chicago: University of Chicago Press.

Menand, L. (2002). *The Metaphysical Club*. London: Flamingo.

Misak, C. (2013). *The American Pragmatists*. Oxford: Oxford University Press.

Nicolini, D. (2009). Zooming in and zooming out: A package of method and theory to study work practices. In S. Ybema, D. Yanow, H. Wels and F. Kamsteeg, eds., *Organizational Ethnography: Studying the Complexities of Everyday Life*. London: SAGE Publications, pp. 120–138.

Peirce, C. S. (1992). *The Essential Peirce, Vol 1 (1867–1893)*. Bloomington: Indiana University Press.

Peirce, C. S. (1998). *The Essential Peirce, Vol 2 (1893–1913)*. Bloomington: Indiana University Press.

Pentland, B. T. and Feldman, M. S. (2005). Organizational routines as unit of analysis. *Industrial and Corporate Change*, 14(5), 793–815.

Reck, A. J. (1963). The philosophy of George Herbert Mead. In *Studies in Recent Philosophy*. Tulane Studies in Philosophy Series, Volume 12. Netherlands: Springer, pp. 5–51.

Sacks, H., Schegloff, E. A. and Jefferson, G. (1974). A simplest systematics for the organization of turn-taking for conversation. *Language*, 50, 696–735.

Sandberg, J. and Tsoukas, H. (2011). Grasping the logic of practice: Theorizing through practical rationality. *Academy of Management Review*, 36(2), 338–360.

Schatzki, T. R. (2001). Introduction: Practice theory. In T. R. Schatzki, K. Knorr-Cetina and E. V. Savigny, eds., *The Practice Turn in Contemporary Theory*. London and New York: Routledge, pp. 10–23.

Selznick, P. (1957). *Leadership in Administration: A Sociological Interpretation*. Berkeley: University of California Press.

Shotter, J. (2006). Understanding process from within: An argument for 'withness'-thinking. *Organization Studies*, 27 (4), 585–604.

Shotter, J. (2010). Situated dialogic action research: Disclosing 'beginnings' for innovative change in organizations. *Organizational Research Methods*, 13(2), 268–285.

Simpson, B. and Lorino P. (2016). Re-viewing routines through a pragmatist lens. In C. Rerup, J. Howard-Grenville, A. Langley and H. Tsoukas, eds., *Organizational Routines: How they are Created, Maintained, and Changed*. Perspectives on Process Organization Studies Series. Oxford: Oxford University Press, pp. 47–70.

Stryker, S. (1980). *Symbolic Interactionism*. New Jersey: The Blackburn Press.

Thayer, H. S. (1982). *Pragmatism: The Classic Writings*. Indianapolis: Hackett Publishing.

Turner, S. F. and Fern, M. J. (2012). Examining the stability and variability of routine performances: The effects of experience and context change. *Journal of Management Studies*, 49(8), 1407–1434.

Turner, S. F. and Rindova, V. (2012). A balancing act: How organizations pursue consistency in routine functioning in the face of ongoing change. *Organization Science*, 23(1), 24–46.

Turner, S. F. and Rindova, V. (2018). Watching the clock: Action timing, patterning, and routine performance. *Academy of Management Journal*, 61(4), 1253–1280.

Wegener, F. and Lorino, F. (2020). Capturing the experience of living forward from within the flow: Fusing 'withness' approach & pragmatist inquiry. In J. Reinecke, R. Suddaby, A. Langley and H. Tsoukas, eds., *Perspectives on Process Organization Studies Vol. 7: About Time: Temporality and History in Organization Studies*. Oxford: Oxford University Press, pp. 138–168.

Weick, K. E. (1979). *The Social Psychology of Organizing*, 2nd ed. Reading, MA: Addison-Westley.

Weick, K. E. (1995). *Sensemaking in Organizations*. Thousand Oaks, CA: Sage.

Weick, K. E. (2003). Theory and practice in the real world. In H. Tsoukas and C. Knudsen, eds., *The Oxford Handbook of Organization Theory*. Oxford: Oxford University Press, pp. 453–475.

Weick, K. E., Sutcliffe, K. M. and Obstfeld, D. (2005). Organizing and the process of sensemaking. *Organization Science*, 16(4), 409–421.

Winter, S. G. (2013). Habit, deliberation, and action: Strengthening the microfoundations of routines and capabilities. *Academy of Management Perspectives*, 27(2), 120–137.

CHAPTER 6

Actor-Network Theory and Routine Dynamics

KATHRIN SELE

6.1 Introduction

In this chapter, I aim to untangle the intimate relationship between routine dynamics research and the thinking underpinning actor-network theory (ANT). In summarizing ANT one can only fail. This is even truer if we consider reality to exist without us and out there. However, if we acknowledge that reality is multiple and fluid due to its constant enactment through practices (Mol, 2002), and we look at what we see from the inside (Latour, 1999b), the task at hand gets at least slightly easier.

I start out by providing a brief historical account of ANT, introducing some of its influential authors, its key terminology and their theoretical and empirical work. This first section will be followed by an overview of how routine dynamics researchers have appropriated ANT – ironically, often as an undercover actor 'in action' that remains invisible at first sight. Martha Feldman (2000) was the first in Routine Dynamics to make references to ANT when she called for an emic instead of an etic view on routines that would shift the attention away from external factors and towards internal dynamics (i.e., performative and ostensive aspects). Following this first mobilization, scholars have borrowed different ANT concepts to understand particular aspects of routines' dynamics. I introduce the most prominent ones – namely *translation, actants, inscriptions and multiplicity* – summarizing their original meaning in ANT and how they have advanced our understanding of organizational routines as generative and emergent systems. I will conclude by reflecting on how ANT can continue to be of use for advancing routine dynamics and related research by discussing its strengths and weaknesses as a theoretical and methodological perspective.

6.2 ANT: A Brief History and Overview

ANT was originally developed to understand the emergence and dominance of technological and scientific ideas. Born in science and technology studies (STS), the approach grew out of the anthropological project 'Laboratory Life: the Construction of Scientific Facts' by Bruno Latour and Steve Woolgar (1979) wherein they described science as happening 'in-the-making', as well as of Michel Callon's (1980) study of the unfolding of a public–private initiative to develop an electric vehicle in France. What unites these accounts is that what is being studied takes shape in and through actions (Latour, 1987). In 1981, Latour and Callon used their empirical insights and engaged in the task of unmasking what they call 'macro-actors'. They did so by questioning the 'givenness' of such actors that had up until then dominated and, in their eyes, misguided social studies. Using Hobbes' *Leviathan*, they argued that macro-actors are made up of many and that their form, which is neither defined 'a priori' nor in a 'definitive and lasting way', is the consequence of relations and performances that bring them into being. In their view, social scientists should engage in tracing how actors become and dissolve and, hence, grow or shrink in size and scope through a process of translation instead of presuming actors of different extents based on predefined features.

Following these first insights, Callon and Latour each published an influential chapter in the book *Power, Action and Belief*, edited by John Law (1986), in which they elaborated on some of the main features of ANT and particularly on the notion of *translation*. In his chapter, Callon (1986) reports on a failed research project by which French scientists aimed at bringing back to

France a method for breeding scallops they had learned about in Japan. He describes the effort of translation nurtured by the different actors, which he defines as the 'mechanism by which the social and natural worlds progressively take form' (Callon, 1986: 224), and how the scientists tried to engage the different actors (e.g., fishermen, scallops) by establishing themselves as an *obligatory passage point*. While the translation failed to succeed in the long term, Callon used this particular example to introduce a *sociology of translation* and its four characteristic moments: (1) the moment of problematization wherein translators attempt to define an issue by pulling together an initial set of actors; (2) the moment of interessement wherein translators determine and fix the interests of key actors, so that they become willing to partake in an emerging project; (3) the moment of enrolment wherein representatives of the main groups are assigned roles and are pulled together to build an alliance and (4) the moment of mobilization wherein the actor network is extended beyond the initial group. For Callon (1986: 196) this 'analytical framework [is] particularly well adapted to the study of the role played by science and technology in structuring power relations'.

Focusing on these relations, Latour (1986) introduces in his chapter what he calls a *sociology of associations*. He argues that we need to distinguish between things – in his case power – that are a mere possibility (i.e., *in potentia*) and those that are eventually established (i.e., *in situ*). This distinction 'allow[s] social scientists to understand power as a consequence and not as a cause of collective action' (1986: 269). Similar to Callon, he advocates for shifting from a model of diffusion to a model of translation. While diffusion builds on the idea that a 'token' (e.g., an order, claim, artefact) holds a particular force that triggers it to move on, translation assumes that for something to spread it needs people and their situated actions. In this view, power lies in the associations that are formed when actors interrelate. Taking the argument one step further, Latour calls for a second shift, namely the one from an *ostensive* definition of society to a *performative* one. For him the ostensive definition assumes properties and sees stability as the norm, while the performative definition assumes everything is made in practice and sees stability as the outlier (Latour, 2005: 34). Taking the concept of society as an example, he states that 'society is not what holds us together, it is what is held together. Social scientists have mistaken the effect for the cause, the passive for the active, what is glued for the glue' (Latour, 1986: 276). For the social scientist this means to stop assuming the existence of social aggregates and to trace the processes that nurture the *assembling* and *disassembling* of associations or, in other words, connections.

In parallel to these more theoretical accounts, empirical studies of particular innovation projects have strongly influenced ANT-driven research. For example, Latour (1996a) investigated an experimental personal rapid transit system developed in France. Written as a detective story wherein two researchers try to answer the question of 'who killed Aramis?', Latour traced the different actors of project Aramis, unravelling its up and downs and its ultimate failure. He literally hunted down what went wrong and why the desired convergence did not happen after all. By dropping a priori assumptions and explanations and focusing on the unfolding of the project he was able to open up the 'mysterious script' that lies in the middle between the start of a project and its ultimate success or failure (Akrich et al., 2002: 188). To find out and make sense of the failed Aramis project, you have to read the book yourself. In another project, Latour (1990) historically traced the mutual emergence of the Kodak camera and the mass market for amateur photographers. Of course, we know today that the 'macro-actor', Kodak, was only temporarily stable and disappeared in the wave of digital photography (Czarniawska, 2017).

In a similar manner, John Law studied a British military aircraft project (Law, 2002; Law and Callon, 1988) and the seventeenth-century Portuguese expansion (Law, 1987). He introduced the term *heterogenous engineering* to describe a process 'in which bits and pieces from the social, the technical, the conceptual and the textual are fitted together' (Law, 1992: 381). These bits and pieces should be considered and approached as *rhizomatic networks* (Law, 2002), whereby the *rhizome* stands in contrast to the tree metaphor that is a dominant model in Western thinking; while the latter favours a hierarchical interpretation (i.e., stemming from a single trunk), the former favours *multiple* explanations that emerge from different sources (Deleuze and Guattari, 1987). In that sense, Law's work is closely intertwined with the work of Annemarie Mol (2002), whose ethnography *The Body Multiple* is a detailed account of atherosclerosis, a common disease she studied at a Dutch university hospital. Through a continuous juxtaposing of the empirical material with theory-driven reflections she showed that the disease is multiple and only becomes a discrete entity when it is enacted in a singular way over time. Being multiple does not, however, imply that interpretation of the disease is fragmented; it is much more a way of showing how the disease is shaped through actions by many different actors (e.g., patients, doctors, procedures) instead of a unified set of actions.

When studying becoming and taking shape in action, Law refers to the theory of *performativity*, which has its origins among a group of Oxford philosophers, including Austin (1962), who introduced a new approach to language focused on performative utterances or 'How to Do Things with Words'. Whereas its initial focus was on making differences through discursive practices, performativity has since been 'subjected to multiple translations by social scientists and philosophers such as Derrida, Butler, Callon, Barad or Lyotard' (Gond and Cabantous, 2015: 508). Within ANT, the concept has been very influential in work on the performativity of markets and their role in constituting economic realities (Callon, 1998b; MacKenzie et al., 2007). Similar to Barad's (2003) concept of post-humanist performativity, Callon's (2007) work on socio-technical 'agencement' (Deleuze and Guattari, 1987) or 'assemblages' (Suchman, 2007) integrates materiality and refutes the idea that objects and humans can be separated in any meaningful way. His insights on 'performation' processes highlight the performativity of assemblages and, even more so, how assemblages are rendered performative in the first place (Yeow and Faraj, 2014).

While these studies (and many more) look at different processes, they all share some common features. First and foremost, they focus on how actors wax and wane in and through associations. Thereby, they reject distinctions made between human and non-human actors, between nature and culture, between mind and body, or between the micro and the macro. Advocating for a *symmetric approach*, these accounts adopt a position that is best paraphrased as anti-dualism. From an ANT perspective, the assumption that non-humans are passive is flawed, as every actor plays a role in social dynamics, not a priori but in its relationality with other actors (Emirbayer, 1997). Accordingly, an 'actor in ANT is a semiotic definition – an actant – that is something that acts or to which activity is granted by another [...] an actant can literally be anything provided it is granted to be the source of action' (Latour, 1996b: 373).

In rejecting a priori assumptions, proponents of ANT seek to open up black boxes and show, for example, what led to successes or failures. According to Latour (1996a: 78) this is necessary because 'if we say that a successful project existed from the beginning because it was well conceived and that a failed project went aground because it was badly conceived, we are saying nothing. We are only repeating the words "success" and "failure"'. A second important feature of ANT is that things take and lose form; nothing – be it a small or large actor – is ever fully accomplished but remains fluid. As described by de Laet and Mol (2000) in their account of the Zimbabwe Bush Pump, human as well as non-human actors hold a certain degree of *fluidity* in relation to their boundaries, which are not only vague but also moving as they are adapted and varied. The pump may provide water but also health; it may build communities but also an entire nation. However, what is needed for success and what success actually means is fluid in itself. The question we therefore have to ask is 'what is happening?' instead of 'who is doing what?'

Over the years, ANT has developed and become even more multiple than it used to be in its initial phase. It has spread into many different disciplines, ranging from anthropology and philosophy to geography and management and organizations studies. Despite this spread, it has been exposed to constant questioning from both within and outside (see e.g., Latour, 1999a; McLean and Hassard,

2004; Star, 1991; Whittle and Spicer, 2008). Without exaggeration, one can claim that everything in 'ANT' has been disassembled: the actor, the network, the theory and even the hyphen (Latour, 1996b). While some scholars see this disassembling process as indication for a failure of ANT, I suggest we see it – in the very spirit of ANT – as an opportunity to see multiples and provide insightful explanations for complex phenomena. Indeed, looking at ANT through an ANT lens, we can discern the emergence of a macro-actor that is multiple and is shaped in and through its associations (Callon and Latour, 1981).

6.3 ANT in Routine Dynamics: An Undercover Actant in Action

In the previous section, I briefly outlined the history of ANT, highlighting some of its central authors and their work. This historical tracing allowed me to highlight the main concepts of ANT that are of importance in unravelling how routine dynamics scholars have appropriated this perspective and how its use has shaped routine dynamics research.

6.3.1 First Appearances

ANT first appeared in Feldman's (2000: 611) foundational article in which she finds 'that organizational routines have a great potential for change even though they are often perceived, even defined, as unchanging'. Acknowledging these possibilities and shifting the attention to what is actually happening is closely related to Latour's (1986) distinction between things 'in potentia' and things 'in situ'. She hints at a rejection of the idea that routines are pre-defined; an assumption that drove early work on routines (Cyert and March, 1963; Nelson and Winter, 1982). Feldman specified that while the evolutionary view on routines was helpful in identifying routines, it was much less so in studying their participation in organizing. Feldman (2000: 613) states that in order to conceive of organizing as an ongoing accomplishment, 'we need a notion of routines that match[es]'.

In the discussion part of the paper, Feldman explicitly connects her conceptualization of performative routines to Latour's work, arguing for the importance of shifting to an emic approach – situated descriptions produced by researchers who immersed themselves in the specific culture. Moving to a performative model thus means that routines are 'flows'. Accordingly, we can no longer separate the routines from those who enact them, as routines are networks of actants (Feldman and Pentland, 2005). For Feldman (2000), the concepts of ostensive and performative are as much a theoretical tool as they are a methodological one. By following actors and actions one has direct access to an emic account of performances (Latour, 1987). It is for this reason that Routine Dynamics has relied on and learned so much from observational data (see Dittrich [Chapter 8], this volume).

The argument is further developed in Feldman and Pentland's joint 2003 article, wherein they propose a reconceptualization of organizational routines which has moved the field from an evolutionary approach that assumes shifts from one state to the next to a dynamic approach that captures relational and iterative processes of emergence (Feldman et al., 2016; Parmigiani and Howard-Grenville, 2011); a move that is equally important in ANT (Callon and Latour, 1981). Feldman and Pentland (2003: 99) criticize how 'the logic of evolutionary theory depends on the existence of some genealogical mechanism'; a reference that can be interpreted as an implicit statement about the need to move from the metaphor of the tree towards the metaphor of the *rhizome*. Instead of seeing routines and action patterns as vertical connections or causal relations with a clearly identifiable source, a rhizomatic approach does not assume beginnings or ends; rather, it is interested in the continuous establishment of connections and its generative power (Deleuze and Guattari, 1987). As already pointed out by Pentland and Rueter (1994: 491), 'an organizational routine is not a single pattern but, rather, a set of possible patterns'.

In line with this larger shift and advocating for a stronger focus on agency (i.e., actors and their actions or performances in practice), Feldman and

Pentland (2003) claim that by seeing and focusing on the relationality of ostensive and performative aspects, we can access their endogenous dynamics and we can understand the role routines play for stability and change. At this point, I shall mention that while their argument aligns with Latour's call to focus on the performative over the ostensive in order to reveal explanations for what we see and observe, Feldman and Pentland (2003) present the two parts on equal footing. They do so by replacing the notion of 'definition' by the notion of 'aspects'. This move turns out to be crucial as it points to the 'connectivity of performance and pattern in constituting what we see as a routine', and thus refutes the idea that the pattern is a stable entity that should be given priority over performance (Feldman, 2016: 27). An explanation for this can be found in the strong embedding of the reconceptualization of routines in a practice-theoretical perspective (see Feldman [Chapter 2], this volume); an approach that had already enriched adjunct fields such as the study of technologies (Orlikowski, 1992), learning and knowing (Gherardi, 2000) or strategy-as-practice research (Whittington, 1996).

What Feldman and Pentland (2005) did was to move organizational routines centre stage by portraying them as 'macro-actors' that needed explanation; or, in ANT jargon, actants that can no longer be taken for granted or seen as 'crucially important but relatively undifferentiated arrows connecting organizational inputs with organizational outputs within the economy of the firm' in organizational processes (Feldman, 2016: 25). In doing so, Routine Dynamics builds on one of the core arguments of ANT: stability is not the norm and we should not confound the routine as it has been designed with its performance (Pentland and Feldman, 2008). As Feldman stated on several occasions, 'While I searched for stability, I encountered change' – a puzzle that has been an inspiring force for many scholars over the past twenty years.

Opening up the black-box of routines has created a playing field that has advanced how we think about the role of routines for change and stability (Aroles and McLean, 2016; Bucher and Langley, 2016; Turner and Rindova, 2012) and how we conceive of routine interdependencies (Kremser and Schreyögg, 2016; Spee et al., 2016), their role for innovation and novelty (Deken et al., 2016; Sele and Grand, 2016) or processes of emergence (Bertels et al., 2016; Cohendet and Simon, 2016) to name just a few. Beyond the terms ostensive and performative and the idea that routines are processual, generative and emergent in a similar way as the laboratory routines described by Latour and Woolgar (1979), several ANT-concepts have been explicitly or implicitly mobilized by routine dynamics scholars. For the purpose of this chapter, I chose to discuss the appropriation of four concepts: (1) *translation*; (2) *actants*; (3) *inscriptions* and (4) *multiplicity*. One has to bear in mind, however, that these concepts are highly interconnected and separating them may seem artificial.

6.3.2 Main Concepts

Translation – A Hidden Gem. Despite the fact that the concept of translation is at the heart of ANT, its use in routine dynamics research is often implicit. Translation can be understood as 'displacement, drift, invention, mediation, the creation of a link that didn't exist before, [and that] . . . modifies two [or more] elements or agents' (Latour, 1994: 31). Accordingly, translation is the process through which connecting happens and connections are achieved (Callon, 1986). It has 'a geometric and a semiotic meaning' as it entails 'both the movement of an entity in space and time, as well as its translation from one context to another' (Gherardi and Nicolini, 2005: 287).

In Routine Dynamics, the concept of translation was introduced through D'Adderio's (2011, 2014) work on the wider phenomenon of routine replication and the dilemma that comes with the need of transferring routines within and across organizations. In these studies, she shows how organizational members face the issue of needing to replicate and innovate when enacting routines. Focusing on how people balance these pressures, she problematizes the notion of transfer and makes the important observation that translation needs to happen between formal rules, not to be mistaken for the routines, and the actual routines. In a recent study of the Grands Ballets Canadiens de Montréal, Blanche and Cohendet (2019) followed suit by showing the needs of translation in creatively reproducing an original choreography in a new context. Their case illustrates the importance of preserving the authentic character of the project's intent and shows how dialogue and a common artistic understanding supported the remounting of a ballet. Connected to the need of being innovative, Sele and Grand (2016) conceptualized routine interactions from a translational perspective, showing how 'translation is potentially achieved through the aggregation of generative connections' (2016: 723) as actants travel in ecologies of routines.

In her recent call for renaming performative and ostensive aspects as 'performing' and 'patterning', Feldman (2016) linked the process of patterning with the concept of translation, which is constituted by what Czarniawska (2014: 89) calls 'a collective act of creation'. The concept of translation builds on the idea that actions gain or lose power in their relations as connections are continuously (re)-created. Accordingly, it was influential in conceptualizing routines as dynamic and generative and to unravel the role routines play in organizational becoming (Feldman et al., 2016).

Actants – A Driving Force. Closely related to the notion of translation, ANT is strongly built on the idea that human and non-human actors – actants – are not only equally important but are also characterized by radical indeterminacy (Callon and Law, 1982) and fluidity (De Laet and Mol, 2000). Actants take form through performance and in relation with other actants, which means that characteristics have to be seen as effects that need to be understood (Law and Hassard, 1999).

Feldman and Pentland (2005) were the first to mention actants when they described routines as networks of actants. Later, D'Adderio (2008) paved the way for explicitly acknowledging the importance of materiality in routine dynamics research (see D'Adderio [Chapter 7], this volume). As she pointedly stated, the 'conscious effort to focus on the role of agency in shaping routines' (D'Adderio, 2011: 198) meant that artifacts and questions of materiality were for some time relegated to the back seat of routine dynamics research. Accordingly, artifacts were mostly viewed as 'fully deterministic' or 'largely inconsequential' (D'Adderio, 2011: 197). Mobilizing performativity theory, she showed how a symmetrical approach towards actors not only matches the dynamic and generative conceptualization of routines but makes them an inherent part of routines. Since then, several scholars studying routine dynamics have taken this approach, focusing, for example, on the role artifacts play for the interdependence and connectivity of routines (Jarzabkowski et al., 2016; Spee et al., 2016), the development of routines (Cacciatori, 2012) or the transformation of routines (Glaser, 2017; Lannacci, 2014). Sele and Grand (2016) with the notion of actants showed how their situated enactment makes them act as either intermediaries or mediators. Whereas intermediaries maintain connections, mediators modify connections (Latour, 2005). In connecting one routine with other routines, actants can have a more or less generative effect that ultimately influences the potential for novelty and innovation to emerge (see Deken and Sele [Chapter 21], this volume). Importantly, the impact of each actant is not pre-determined but emerges only as the network of routines is being performed.

Inscriptions – A Way of Patterning. A closely related ANT-term is the notion of inscriptions, which goes back to Latour and Woolgar's (1979) description of how laboratory work resulted in the inscribing of results into graphs, illustrations or maps which travel on, for example, becoming scientific propositions in journal articles or the basis of market applications. In case of a temporary stabilization or a certain endurance of scientific knowledge, we encounter what Latour has called 'immutable mobiles' (Latour, 1987); something movable and malleable but at the same time holding its shape. According to Callon (1991: 143), an inscription can be defined as 'the result of the translation of one's interest [and intentions] into material form', which Akrich et al. (2002) refer to as embodied patterns.

In Routine Dynamics, we see a first linkage to the concept of inscriptions in the mutual constitutions of performative and ostensive aspects (Feldman and Pentland, 2003), wherein the actual enactment of routines (i.e., performing) leads to their continuous and emergent inscribing into patterns (i.e., patterning). More explicitly and discussing the role artifacts play in guiding the performance of routines, D'Adderio (2008) explains how Standard Operating Procedures get inscribed into software and how that process creates linkages between rules and the actual performance of routines. Inscription happens when 'actors delegate knowledge and goals (i.e. innovation, replication) to artifacts during their design and usage stages' (D'Adderio, 2014: 1343). This underlines the idea that non-human actors are not neutral and that intentions or objectives are distributed due to what is inscribed into them and how that is being enacted. Inscriptions are also important in how transfer and replication happen in practice, as they are influential for the degree of variation in the actual performance of routines (D'Adderio, 2014). This aspect is further discussed by Aroles and McLean (2016) in their study of the increasing standardization of routines within a newspaper-printing factory. Relying on Deleuze's (1994) concept of repetition through difference and Latour's (2004) distinction between matters of fact and matters of concern, they show how scripts are more or less influential in the performance of the routine as well as in how it is being discussed and negotiated during meetings as well as evaluated in reports. For example, the script of reducing ink in the production process led to a continuous tension between conforming and deviating from what had been decided.

Multiplicity – Seeing Heterogeneity in the Black Box. It is this argument on variation that points to the idea of multiplicity prominently referred to in ANT. As outlined by Latour (2005: 116), 'multiplicity is a property of things, not of humans interpreting things'. Accordingly, things and networks of things are ontologically multiple and require us to let go of the idea that we can take things for granted and just apply different viewpoints on the same thing (Mol, 2002). Empirically, one needs to reveal the 'multiple realities' that shape what is happening (Law and Singleton, 2014).

This idea is strongly present in the notion that routines 'entail multiple actions (performative aspect), multiple patterns (ostensive aspect), and multiple human and nonhuman actants' (Feldman et al., 2016: 507). Neither ostensive nor performative aspects are singular (Feldman et al., 2016). Going back to Mol (2002), routines and, hence, organizations are multiple and moved by multiple actants. This does not mean that routines are not 'routine' anymore, but that they can be more or less 'routine'. The unexpectedness in these relations holds the potential for stability but simultaneously allows for change and novelty (Deken et al., 2016; Sele and Grand, 2016). For example, Turner and Rindova (2012) show in their study of waste collection routines that multiple ostensive aspects (or variations) are necessary for the routines to work in practice. D'Adderio (2014) as well as Salvato and Rerup (2018) focus on the constant need of balancing in pursuing multiple and in many cases conflicting goals. As argued by Pentland and Feldman (2005: 797), 'multiple and divergent understandings [are] probably more the norm than the exception'. Moving the focus from studying single routines and their dynamics to networks (see Rosa, Kremser and Bugacov [Chapter 17], this volume) and their dynamics 'multiplies the multiplicities' (Feldman et al., 2016: 507). Studying routine replication in complex settings, D'Adderio and Pollock (2020) recently raised the important question of 'how routines and their underlying patterns might be recreated (precisely) within a background of difference and multiplicity'. Building on insights from Mol (2002) and Law (2004), they identify repairing as well as distributing practices to show how the necessary similarity and singularity is produced over time and across organizational locations.

6.3.3 What Would We Have Missed?

Having discussed how routine dynamics scholars have more or less explicitly mobilized conceptual and methodological tools provided by ANT, we still need to address the question of what it adds to the study of routines. First, ANT has provided routine dynamic scholars with a unique vocabulary and a methodological approach that enabled important shifts: (1) from an evolutionary to a dynamic view; (2) from an etic to an emic approach and (3) from singularity to heterogeneity and multiplicity. In the words of Mol (2010: 265), '[ANT] has assembled a rich array of explorative and experimental ways of attuning to the world'. In that, ANT is as much method as theory or, as Gherardi and Nicolini (2005) called it, an 'open-ended sociology'.

Second, embracing the underlying assumption of ANT that there is no pre-defined social world but just 'patterned networks of heterogeneous materials' (Law, 1992: 381) offers crucial insights for theorizing stability and change (Steen et al., 2006) – a main focus in routine dynamics research since its beginnings (Feldman and Pentland, 2003). In particular, many advances were made by focusing on actors and actions and engaging in what Abbott (2004: 120) calls 'argument heuristics', meaning that we learn and see new aspects of phenomena by problematizing the obvious and making reversals. As Feldman and Pentland (2005: 107) put it, ANT has been influential in turning 'the traditional relationship between routines and stability on its head' and, hence, seeing variation as the norm and stability as what needs to be explained. An illustrative example of such a reversal is how routine dynamics scholars have re-thought the relationship between routines and innovation (Salvato, 2009; Sele and Grand, 2016).

Third, ANT builds on the idea that actions happen in connections and associations, not in an isolated manner (Latour, 1986). While this relational ontology is not unique to ANT, combining it with a radically flat ontology is. ANT makes obsolete the micro–macro distinction as well as the inside–outside divide (Seidl and Whittington, 2014) and has proven to be a unique approach to study ongoing achievements and explain the 'in-the-making' of phenomena (Callon, 1980; Latour and Woolgar, 1979). ANT enabled routine dynamics scholars to foreground generativity and the potential for transformation by focusing on the power of connecting within routines (Feldman and Pentland, 2003), within inter-organizational networks of routines (Sele and Grand, 2016) and within intra-organizational networks of routines (Mitzscherling, 2019).

6.4 The Future of ANT in Routine Dynamics Research

All of this said, what is it that ANT has to offer for the study of routines and organizational phenomena in the future? Routine dynamics scholars focus on untangling routines and their role in organizing by studying them from within. They have taken to heart what Latour (1999b: 13) once proclaimed, 'How is it possible to imagine an outside world? Has anyone seen such a bizarre oddity? No problem. We will make the world into a spectacle seen from inside.' And this is exactly how ANT can and should be a continuous theoretical as well as methodological force in this field of research; not alone but in combination with other theoretical lenses. Each perspective or theory enables us to see certain aspects while leaving others out. ANT enables us to trace networks and see movement. And while ANT never claimed to be a theory with a big T, ANT scholars have never been shy of speaking out to show the perspective's power in unravelling complex phenomena including grand challenges.

Latour himself recently and prominently entered the climate change debate and reminded us about the importance of unscrewing macro-actors 'in action'. As many of us are having difficulties understanding and dealing with what is happening around us, and why actors act the way they do, Latour (2018) engaged in dissecting the situation in his new book *Down to Earth: Politics in the New Climate Regime*. He identifies the different actors and presents their 'worlds' and how they do or do not relate. Thereby, he suggests that neither focusing on the local nor on the global discourse allows us to connect with today's realities. One of the main problems that he identifies is that planet Earth is becoming an increasingly political actant; it shows muscles and we do not know how to deal with its dynamic and unruly doings. Accordingly, we as social scientists have to become part of its unravelling.

As another example, we can think of the global spreading of coronavirus which has suddenly and dramatically changed the world we live in and with it our daily routines and how we organize. Even mundane, taken for granted activities such as going to work, shopping, organizing meetings, teaching classes or serving customers have changed in response to the pandemic. The pandemic disrupted, altered and enforced connections on an individual, group, organizational and societal level. To get a better understanding of the role organizations and their routines play in handling such a crisis, we need to focus on how routines are altered by the pandemic as well as on how routines influence how we respond and are able (or unable) to mitigate, in this case, the spreading of the virus and its socio-economic impact. As shown in this chapter, ANT is a very suitable approach to reveal complexities and contingencies as they happen and, hence, helps researchers to capture large societal phenomena such as a pandemic, climate change, financial markets or algorithmic work (see Glaser et al. [Chapter 23], this volume) that are becoming 'increasingly fluid, intricate and accelerated' (Baron and Gomez, 2016: 130).

For Routine Dynamics, two concepts seem particularly interesting for future studies. The first is what Mol and Law (1994) call fluid spaces. Unlike network spaces, wherein proximity and distance are dependent on the relations between its elements, fluid spaces are spatial relations that are constantly changing with coming and going boundaries. The idea of fluidity is particularly useful to study organizational phenomena that are driven by informal ties instead of formal structures and those that are moving and changing at a fast pace (Latour, 1996b). The notion of fluid spaces also addresses the fallacy of the network metaphor, which directs us to what is inside and thus reduces the researcher's ability to see 'otherness' in a meaningful way (Hetherington and Law, 2000).

The second concept that bears opportunities is what Callon (1998a) calls 'hot' and 'cold' situations. In his discussion of economic externalities, he shows that – no matter how hard we try to frame markets or other actors – there will always be overflow that cannot be contained. Establishing that such overflows are the norm, he distinguishes between cold situations, wherein we are able to identify actors, interests, etc., and hot situations, wherein we are confronted with uncertainty, controversies and many unknowns.

There are several reasons why fluid spaces and hot situations might be of help to Routine Dynamics. As we have moved from studying single routines to focusing on multiple routines and as organizations have become more permeable and fluid, focusing on spatial and temporal movements (Lefebvre, 2004) will allow us to see what orders without order and what role routines play in such ordering. Further, there is an increasing interest in organization studies to contribute to understanding social phenomena that matter and in particular grand challenges (George et al., 2016). Although such hot situations are tricky to grasp, Routine Dynamics' and ANT's joint interest in actors and actions enables one to start unravelling large and complex phenomena as it enables one to zoom in on the role that organizational routines have in manifold connections, how they are built and what consequences they have.

All of this said, I urge the reader to bear in mind that, by definition, ANT unfolds its strength in doing, and only thereafter in conceptualizing what one sees and experiences. Or as Latour (1999a: 20) once said: 'the ridiculous poverty of the ANT vocabulary – associations, translation, alliance, obligatory passage point, etc. – was a clear signal that none of these words could replace the rich vocabulary of the actor's practices'.

References

Abbott, A. D. (2004). *Methods of Discovery: Heuristics for the Social Sciences*. New York: Norton & Company.

Akrich, M., Callon, M. and Latour, B. (2002). The key to success in innovation part I: The art of interessement. *International Journal of Innovation Management*, 6(2), 187–206.

Aroles, J. and McLean, C. (2016). Rethinking stability and change in the study of organizational routines: Difference and repetition in a newspaper-printing factory. *Organization Science*, 27(3), 535–550.

Austin, J. L. (1962). *How to Do Things with Words*. Oxford: Oxford University Press.

Barad, K. (2003). Posthumanist performativity: Toward an understanding of how matter comes to matter. *Signs: Journal of Women in Culture and Society*, 28(3), 801–831.

Baron, L. F. and Gomez, R. (2016). The associations between technologies and societies: The utility of actor-network theory. *Science, Technology and Society*, 21(2), 129–148.

Bertels, S., Howard-Grenville, J. and Pek, S. (2016). Cultural molding, shielding, and shoring at Oilco: The role of culture in the integration of routines. *Organization Science*, 27(3), 573–593.

Blanche, C. and Cohendet, P. (2019). Remounting a ballet in a different context: A complementary understanding of routines transfer theories. In M. S. Feldman, L. D'Adderio, K. Dittrich and P. Jarzabkowksi, eds., *Routine Dynamics in Action: Replication and Transformation*. Bingley: Emerald Publishing, pp. 11–30.

Bucher, S. and Langley, A. (2016). The interplay of reflective and experimental spaces in interrupting and reorienting routine dynamics. *Organization Science*, 27(3), 594–613.

Cacciatori, E. (2012). Resolving conflict in problem-solving: Systems of artefacts in the development of new routines. *Journal of Management Studies*, 49(8), 1559–1585.

Callon, M. (1980). The state and technical innovation: A case study of the electrical vehicle in France. *Research Policy*, 9(4), 358–376.

Callon, M. (1986). Some elements of sociology of translation: Domestication of the scallops and the fishermen of St. Brieux Bay. In J. Law, ed., *Power, Action and Belief: A New Sociology of Knowledge?* London: Routledge & Kegan Paul, pp. 196–233.

Callon, M. (1991). Techno-economic networks and irreversibility. In J. Law, ed., *A Sociology of Monsters: Essays on Power, Technology and Domination*. London: Routledge, pp. 132–161.

Callon, M. (1998a). An essay on framing and overflowing: Economic externalities revisited by sociology. *The Sociological Review*, 46(S1), 244–269.

Callon, M., ed. (1998b). *The Laws of the Markets*. Oxford: Blackwell Publishers.

Callon, M. (2007). What does it mean to say that economics is performative? D. MacKenzie, F. Muniesa and L. Siu, eds., *Do Economists Make Markets? On the Performativity of Economics*. Princeton, NJ: Princeton University Press.

Callon, M. and Latour, B. (1981). Unscrewing the big Leviathan: How actors macro-structure reality and how sociologists help them to do so. In K. Knorr and A. Cicourel, eds., *Advances in Social Theory and Methodology: Toward an Integration of Micro-and Macro-Sociologies*. London: Routledge & Kegan Paul, pp. 277–303.

Callon, M. and Law, J. (1982). On interests and their transformation: Enrolment and counter-enrolment. *Social Studies of Science*, 12(4), 615–625.

Cohendet, P. S. and Simon, L. O. (2016). Always playable: Recombining routines for creative efficiency at Ubisoft Montreal's video game studio. *Organization Science*, 27(3), 614–632.

Cyert, R. M. and March, J. G. (1963). *A Behavioral Theory of the Firm*. Englewood Cliffs, NJ: Prentice-Hall.

Czarniawska, B. (2014). *A Theory of Organizing*. Cheltenham: Edward Elgar Publishing.

Czarniawska, B. (2017). Actor-network theory. In A. Langley and H. Tsoukas, eds., *The SAGE Handbook of Process Organization Studies*. Los Angeles: SAGE Publishing, 160–173.

D'Adderio, L. (2008). The performativity of routines: Theorising the influence of artefacts and distributed agencies on routine dynamics. *Research Policy*, 37(5), 769–789.

D'Adderio, L. (2011). Artifacts at the centre of routines: Performing the material turn in routines theory. *Journal of Institutional Economics*, 7(2), 197–230.

D'Adderio, L. (2014). The replication dilemma unravelled: How organizations enact multiple goals in routine transfer. *Organization Science*, 25(5), 1325–1350.

D'Adderio, L. and Pollock, N. (2020). Making routines the same: Crafting similarity and singularity in routines transfer. *Research Policy*, 49(8), 104029.

De Laet, M. and Mol, A. (2000). The Zimbabwe bush pump: Mechanics of a fluid technology. *Social Studies of Science*, 30(2), 225–263.

Deken, F., Carlile, P. R., Berends, H. and Lauche, K. (2016). Generating novelty through interdependent routines: A process model of routine work. *Organization Science*, 27(3), 659–677.

Deleuze, G. (1994). *Difference and Repetition*. New York: Columbia University Press.

Deleuze, G. and Guattari, F. (1987). *A Thousand Plateaus: Capitalism and Schizophrenia*. Minneapolis: University of Minnesota Press.

Emirbayer, M. (1997). Manifesto for a relational sociology. *American Journal of Sociology*, 103(2), 281–317.

Feldman, M. S. (2000). Organizational routines as a source of continuous change. *Organization Science*, 11(6), 611–629.

Feldman, M. S. (2016). Routines as process: Past, present and future. In C. Rerup and J. A. Howard-Grenville, eds., *Organizational Routines: How They Are Created, Maintained, and Changed*. Oxford: Oxford University Press, pp. 23–46.

Feldman, M. S. and Pentland, B. T. (2003). Reconceptualizing organizational routines as a source of flexibility and change. *Administrative Science Quarterly*, 48(1), 94–118.

Feldman, M. S. and Pentland, B. T. (2005). Organizational routines and the macro-actor. In B. Czarniawska and T. Hernes, eds., *Actor-Network Theory and Organizing*. Copenhagen: Liber, pp. 91–111.

Feldman, M. S., Pentland, B. T., D'Adderio, L. and Lazaric, N. (2016). Beyond routines as things: Introduction to the special issue on routine dynamics. *Organization Science*, 27(3), 505–513.

George, G., Howard-Grenville, J., Joshi, A. and Tihanyi, L. (2016). Understanding and tackling societal grand challenges through management research. *Academy of Management Journal*, 59(6), 1880–1895.

Gherardi, S. (2000). Practice-based theorizing on learning and knowing in organizations. *Organization*, 7(2), 211–223.

Gherardi, S. and Nicolini, D. (2005). Actor-networks: Ecology and entrepreneurs. In B. Czarniawska and T. Hernes, eds., *Actor-Network Theory and Organizing*. Copenhagen: Liber, pp. 285–306.

Glaser, V. L. (2017). Design performances: How organizations inscribe artifacts to change routines. *Academy of Management Journal*, 60(6), 2126–2154.

Gond, J.-P. and Cabantous, L. (2015). Performativity: Towards a performative turn in organizational studies. R. Mir, H. Willmott and M. Greenwood, eds., *The Routledge Companion to Philosophy in Organization Studies*. London: Routledge, pp. 508–516.

Hetherington, K. and Law, J. (2000). After networks. *Environment and Planning D: Society and Space*, 18, 127–132.

Jarzabkowski, P., Bednarek, R. and Spee, P. (2016). The role of artifacts in establishing connectivity within professional routines: A question of entanglement. In C. Rerup and J. Howard-Grenville, eds., *Organizational Routines: How They Are Created, Maintained, and Changed*. Oxford: Oxford University Press, pp. 117–131.

Kremser, W. and Schreyögg, G. (2016). The dynamics of interrelated routines: Introducing the cluster level. *Organization Science*, 27(3), 698–721.

Lannacci, F. (2014). Routines, artefacts and technological change: Investigating the transformation of criminal justice in England and Wales. *Journal of Information Technology*, 29(4), 294–311.

Latour, B. (1986). The powers of associations. In J. Law, ed., *Power, Action and Belief: A New Sociology of Knowledge?* London: Routledge & Kegan Paul, pp. 264–280.

Latour, B. (1987). *Science in Action: How to Follow Scientists and Engineers through Society*. Cambridge, MA, Harvard University Press.

Latour, B. (1990). Technology is society made durable. *The Sociological Review*, 38(1), 103–131.

Latour, B. (1994). On technical mediation. *Common Knowledge*, 3(2), 29–64.

Latour, B. (1996a). *Aramis, or, the Love of Technology*. Cambridge, MA: Harvard University Press.

Latour, B. (1996b). On actor-network theory: A few clarifications plus more than a few complications. *Soziale Welt*, 47(4), 369–381.

Latour, B. (1999a). On recalling ANT. In J. Law and J. Hassard, eds., *Actor Network Theory and After*. Oxford: Blackwell, pp. 15–25.

Latour, B. (1999b). *Pandora's Hope. Essays on the Reality of Science Studies*. Cambridge, MA: Harvard University Press.

Latour, B. (2004). Why has critique run out of steam? From matters of fact to matters of concern. *Critical Inquiry*, 30(2), 225–248.

Latour, B. (2005). *Reassembling the Social: An Introduction to Actor-Network-Theory*. Oxford: Oxford University Press.

Latour, B. (2018). *Down to Earth: Politics in the New Climatic Regime*. Cambridge: Polity Press.

Latour, B. and Woolgar, S. (1979). *Laboratory Life: The Social Construction of Scientific Facts*. Beverly Hills, CA: Sage Publications.

Law, J., ed. (1986). *Power, Action, and Belief: A New Sociology of Knowledge?* London: Routledge & Kegan Paul.

Law, J. (1987). Technology and heterogeneous engineering: The case of Portuguese expansion. In W. E. Bijker, T. P. Hughes and T. Pinch, eds., *The Social Construction of Technological Systems: New Directions in the Sociology and History of Technology*. Cambridge, MA: MIT Press, pp. 111–134.

Law, J. (1992). Notes on the theory of the actor-network: Ordering, strategy, and heterogeneity. *Systems Practice*, 5(4), 379–393.

Law, J. (2002). *Aircraft Stories: Decentering the Object in Technoscience*. Durham, NC: Duke University Press.

Law, J. (2004). *After Method: Mess in Social Science Research*. London: Routledge.

Law, J. and Callon, M. (1988). Engineering and sociology in a military aircraft project: A network analysis of technological change. *Social Problems*, 35(3), 284–297.

Law, J. and Hassard, J., eds. (1999). *Actor Network Theory and After*. Oxford: Blackwell.

Law, J. and Singleton, V. (2014). ANT, multiplicity and policy. *Critical Policy Studies*, 8(4), 379–396.

Lefebvre, H. (2004). *Rhythmanalysis: Space, Time and Everyday Life*. New York: Continuum Books.

MacKenzie, D. A., Muniesa, F. and Siu, L. (2007). *Do Economists Make Markets? On the Performativity of Economics*. Princeton, NJ: Princeton University Press.

McLean, C. and Hassard, J. (2004). Symmetrical absence/symmetrical absurdity: Critical notes on the production of actor-network accounts. *Journal of Management Studies*, 41(3), 493–519.

Mitzscherling, L. (2019). *Dynamiken und Entstehung von inter-organisationalen Routinen in Innovationsnetzwerken*. Dissertation Freie Universität Berlin.

Mol, A. (2002). *The Body Multiple: Ontology in Medical Practice*. Durham, NC: Duke University Press.

Mol, A. (2010). Actor-network theory: Sensitive terms and enduring tensions. *Kölner Zeitschrift für Soziologie und Sozialpsychologie. Sonderheft*, 50, 253–269.

Mol, A. and Law, J. (1994). Regions, networks and fluids: Anaemia and social topology. *Social Studies of Science*, 24(4), 641–671.

Nelson, R. R. and Winter, S. G. (1982). *An Evolutionary Theory of Economic Change*. Cambridge, MA: Harvard University Press.

Orlikowski, W. J. (1992). The duality of technology: Rethinking the concept of technology in organizations. *Organization Science*, 3(3), 398–427.

Parmigiani, A. and Howard-Grenville, J. A. (2011). Routines revisited: Exploring the capabilities and practice perspective. *The Academy of Management Annals*, **5**(1), 413–453.

Pentland, B. T. and Feldman, M. S. (2005). Organizational routines as a unit of analysis. *Industrial and Corporate Change*, 14(5), 793–815.

Pentland, B. T. and Feldman, M. S. (2008). Designing routines: On the folly of designing artifacts, while hoping for patterns of action. *Information and Organization*, 18(4), 235–250.

Pentland, B. T. and Rueter, H. H. (1994). Organizational routines as grammars of action. *Administrative Science Quarterly*, 39(3), 484–510.

Salvato, C. (2009). Capabilities unveiled: The role of ordinary activities in the evolution of product development processes. *Organization Science*, 20(2), 384–409.

Salvato, C. and Rerup, C. (2018). Routine regulation: Balancing conflicting goals in organizational routines. *Administrative Science Quarterly*, 63(1), 170–209.

Seidl, D. and Whittington, R. (2014). Enlarging the Strategy-as-Practice research agenda: Towards taller and flatter ontologies. *Organization Studies*, 35(10), 1407–1421.

Sele, K. and Grand, S. (2016). Unpacking the dynamics of ecologies of routines: Mediators and their generative effects in routine interactions. *Organization Science*, 27(3), 722–738.

Spee, P., Jarzabkowski, P. and Smets, M. (2016). The influence of routine interdependence and skillful accomplishment on the coordination of standardizing and customizing. *Organization Science*, 27(3), 759–781.

Star, S. L. (1991). Power, technology and the phenomenology of conventions: On being allergic to onions. In J. Law, ed., *A Sociology of Monster: Essays on Power, Technology and Domination*. London: Routledge, pp. 26–56.

Steen, J., Coopmans, C. and Whyte, J. (2006). Structure and agency? Actor-network theory and strategic organization. *Strategic Organization*, 4(3), 303–312.

Suchman, L. A. (2007). *Human-Machine Reconfigurations: Plans and Situated Actions*, 2nd ed. Cambridge: Cambridge University Press.

Turner, S. F. and Rindova, V. (2012). A balancing act: How organizations pursue consistency in routine functioning in the face of ongoing change. *Organization Science*, 23(1), 24–46.

Whittington, R. (1996). Strategy as practice. *Long Range Planning*, 29(5), 731–735.

Whittle, A. and Spicer, A. (2008). Is actor network theory critique? *Organization Studies*, 29(4), 611–629.

Yeow, A. and Faraj, S. (2014). Technology and sociomaterial performation. *Working Conference on Information Systems and Organizations*. Berlin; Heidelberg: Springer, 48–65.

CHAPTER 7

Materiality and Routine Dynamics

LUCIANA D'ADDERIO

7.1 Introduction

The research topics gathered under the headings of 'materiality' – and the related notions of 'artifacts' and 'technology'[1] – have witnessed a phenomenal surge of interest in the field of Routine Dynamics. Most likely in response to the increasing diffusion and influence of new advanced tools – such as digital technologies – into our work and everyday lives, routines scholars have progressively turned their attention to the study of how these changes impact individuals, teams, institutions, practices and organizations. The significant turn towards the study of materiality in organizations and organizing replaces at least two decades of partial neglect of the topic, not only by the Routines and Practices communities but also by Management and Organizational theorists more generally.

In their Annals piece, Orlikowski and Scott (2008), for example, highlight how, in the Management literature, 'technology is missing in action' (see also Latour, 1992), despite the fact that 'it is hard to think of any contemporary organization that does not, at some level, depend on some kind of technologies' (Orlikowski and Scott, 2008: 434). In their review of the management literature in the decade from January 1997 to December 2006 they find that 'over 95% of the articles [. . .] do not consider or take into account the role and influence of technology in organizational life'. A similar observation was raised in a contribution to the JOIE (Journal of Institutional Economics) special issue on Routines (D'Adderio, 2011), which pointed to the systemic lack of attention by Organizational and Routines scholars towards the role of artifacts and technology, despite the fact that 'it is [. . .] difficult, if not impossible, to envisage a routine that completes its course without involving any artifacts at all' (D'Adderio, 2011: 199). This contribution culminated in the call to 'take artifacts seriously' (2011: 214), which entailed 'perform[ing] a [. . .]"small Copernican revolution"' (2011: 198) to bring 'artifacts and materiality from the periphery to the very centre of routines and Routines Theory[2]' (2011: 197).

[1] Artifacts, technology and materiality are different but overlapping concepts that have been attributed many different meanings over time and across different domains of scholarship. Here I briefly define artifacts as 'objects created by man for a specific purpose' (D'Adderio, 2011). In rejecting the reductive but common definition of technology as the 'practical application of [scientific] knowledge' (Merriam-Webster, see Berg 1998 for a critique) I encourage readers to refer to Orlikowski and Scott (2008)'s discussion around the definition of technology as 'absent presence', 'exogeneous force', 'emergent process' and 'entanglement in practice'. The notion of materiality, and its variations including sociomateriality, capture various theoretical ways to explain the relationship between artifacts and human actors, or the effect of artifacts on practices and organizations. The ANT notion of socio-technical systems, and similarly 'heterogeneous engineering' (Law 1987), for example, refers to the inadequacy of analyses based on the separation of the social from the technical. The related notion of sociomateriality captures instead how characteristics are never predetermined but always emerge in a through their enactment in the context of practices. Despite the importance of definitions, in this chapter I ultimately align with D'Adderio's (2011), ANT-inspired observation that it may be more productive to focus on 'what artifacts do' rather than on their substance, as it directly acknowledges the primary importance of understanding their effects on routines, practices and organizations.

[2] Within Routines Theory we include both the early studies of routines (Behavioural and Evolutionary traditions) and the later and more recent Routine Dynamics stream (from Feldman, 2000 onwards).

This call for recognizing the central role of artifacts in routines was well-heeded by the Routines community. Today, ten years after the JOIE special issue's publication, we find a plethora of examples of papers in the field of Routine Dynamics which engage directly with the topics of technology, artifacts and materiality. In the Routine Dynamics Organization Science Special Issue (Feldman et al., 2016), for example, twelve out of fifteen articles – including the editorial – mention the word 'techn-ology' (-ogical, -ical) for a total of 53 times; ten mention the word 'artifact-s' (-ual) for a total of 205 times; and six 'material-ity' (-al, -als, socio-) for a total of 104 times. These statistics not only hold up but can be seen to rise significantly in the recent 2019 RSO Special Issue 'Routine Dynamics in Action: Transfer and Transformation', (Feldman et al., 2019). The 2016 and 2019 special issues represent only a relatively small – although indicative – subset of the overall percentage of publications in Routine Dynamics which mention the selected keywords. It thus appears that the 'small Copernican revolution' (D'Adderio, 2011: 198) has indeed taken place: artifacts, technology and materiality have moved from the role of peripheral accessories to human practices to being considered unquestionably central to routines, their performance and their outcomes. In fact, the trend appears to be moving on a substantial upwards trajectory, as also reflected by its sustained and escalating presence in this handbook.

While this is important from a theoretical perspective, it becomes even more relevant once we consider the seemingly exponential pace of digital technologies, especially those known as data-driven, algorithmic and self-learning and the increasing attention they are attracting from a variety of stakeholders (decision-makers and regulators; industrialists and industrial bodies; public sector practitioners and agencies; analysts and consultants; and, last but not least, academics). As automated and automating technologies become increasingly able to augment – or perhaps even replace – human actors and their agency, they promise to radically reshape practices, and routines, thus setting out a number of novel and steep challenges for organizational scholars. In this context, an important question that arises is what may be the opportunities for Routine Dynamics scholars to contribute to and influence these important debates and the governance thinking and actions stemming from them.

This chapter, which captures the progressive evolution of the notions of artifacts, technology and materiality in routines, analyses the way these topics have been treated over time in the study of Routines, including both the early Behavioural/Evolutionary approaches and the later Routine Dynamics work. In so doing, it highlights the successive theoretical steps which have taken the field from essentially ignoring the existence of artifacts and technology, to acknowledging the fundamental and central role of artifacts and materiality in routines, through performing the 'material turn' in routines research (D'Adderio, 2008, 2011). The chapter concludes by outlining some avenues for future research, while also touching on how the field of Routine Dynamics can help address some of the greatest – current and future – economic, technological and societal challenges.

7.2 Routines and Materiality: Behavioural and Evolutionary Traditions

The early debates in routines research were strongly influenced by developments in Computer Science, Machine Learning and Artificial Intelligence (Newell and Simon, 1976; Simon, 1945). The concept of 'routine' in Behavioural Theory, for instance, drew directly on the notion of computer program. According to Simon, there is a functional analogy between the human mind, the computer and organizations, where both the organization and its decision structure could be considered as being made up of a 'mosaic of programs' (Lazaric, 2000). Routines-as-programmes or 'executable procedure[s]' (Cohen et al., 1996: 660; Cyert and March, 1963; March and Simon, 1958/93), were defined as automated sequences of steps which could be performed by humans as much as computers and their algorithms (in other words, Turing machines). These formal rules helped organizations make decisions in the presence of complexity and 'bounded rationality' by providing automated responses to external stimuli.

The Evolutionary Theory-inspired notion of organizational routines (Nelson and Winter, 1982) shared with behavioural theorists the emphasis on automaticity, complexity and rule-following, albeit with a significant difference. They distinguished between two routine modalities: the 'abstract activity pattern' and the 'routine in operation at a particular site', the latter defined as 'a web of coordinating relationships connecting specific resources' (Winter, 1995: 149–150). This conceptualization was built on the biological distinction between genotype (where the routine's pattern-guidance is stored) and phenotype (which turns the genotype into a routinized expression). This early distinction between the representations of routines and their realization in practice was useful in providing insights into the difference between what the authors called 'real routines' (as patterns expressed in context) and standard operating procedures, or SOPs (the formalized representation of the routinized pattern), terms which had, until then, often been used interchangeably (Cohen et al., 1996: 674). According to Cohen et al. (1996), representations of routines could be written into artifacts such as computer programs and code which were then adopted at, and adapted to, various organizational sites with important consequences for work and organizations.

However, despite the significant progress achieved in characterizing routines, first through the simplified and stylized notions of formal rules and abstract patterns, and then as a dualism of representation-expression, no real attempt was made in early Routines Theory to theorize their relationship. Notwithstanding the awareness that 'real behavior diverges substantially from formalized SOPs' (673) and the subsequent recognition that 'the relation between the two levels [of routines], however defined, is a promising area of investigation' (1996: 674–675), we will have to wait for another branch of Organizational and Routines Theory to begin to bridge the apparent divide.

7.3 Materiality and Routine Dynamics

The stream of work developed under the heading of Routine Dynamics set out early on to address some of the limitations of the treatment of artifacts and materiality in early routines studies. When focusing on the theoretical and conceptual progression of materiality in Routine Dynamics we can identify a trajectory moving from artifacts as the routines' external context, to mutual constitution, and, finally to performativity and fluid ontology, the latter advances enabled by the theoretical move which placed artifacts at the centre of routines and Routine Dynamics.

7.3.1 Artifacts in Early Routine Dynamics

Starting from the early 2000s, the emerging work in what will be later known as the field of Routine Dynamics began to address the relationship between routines, on the one hand, and artifacts, technology and materiality, on the other. Here we identify two different work streams, one focusing on treating artifacts as external background to routines, and one which addressed the mutual production of routines and artifacts.

7.3.1.1 Artifacts as External Background

A new strand of Routines Theory took off in the early 00s, which drew from a sociological perspective grounded in the study of practice and informed by the work of Bourdieu, Giddens and Latour. This influential work (Feldman and Pentland, 2003; Pentland and Feldman, 2005), which was going to give birth to what is known today as Routine Dynamics, focused on the duality of the routine as comprising an abstract pattern, embodied in the actors performing the routines (the 'ostensive aspect') and an actual action pattern performed at a specific place and point in time (the 'performative aspect'). The ostensive–performative duality was intended to make up for the conflation in Behavioural Theory between the routine and its artifact (the SOP) highlighting that the artifact is not the routine (Pentland and Feldman, 2008). Drawing, among other theories, on Bourdieu's practice theory, Giddens' theory of structuration, and Feldman's (2000) analytical interpretation of Latour's (1986) discussion on power and society, these authors set out an agenda for theorizing 'routines as generative systems' (re)constituted through the internal dynamics of co-evolution between ostensive and performative patterns (Feldman and Pentland, 2003; Pentland and Feldman, 2005). In line with Structuration Theory, artifacts here are structures which frame actions, or, in other words, provide the contextual background which might constrain or enable emergent patterns of actions. For example, Pentland and Reuter define a routine as 'a set of possible patterns – enabled and constrained by a variety of organizational, social, physical and cognitive structures – from which organizational members enact particular performances' (491). Using the room inventory as part of a revised damage assessment routine that engaged students in understanding the cost of the damage they had inflicted on their rooms, thus, enabled building directors to act as educators rather than aggrieved landlords (Feldman, 2000). Technology is mentioned here as the bearer of external change, as opposed to the change induced by 'the internal dynamic of a routine' (2000: 613). We learn more about 'the range of artifacts that enable and constrain organizational routines' in Pentland and Feldman (2005: 797). Artifacts here can be '"enrolled" in the performance of a routine to varying degrees, at the discretion of the participants' (Pentland and Feldman, 2005). Particular emphasis is set on artifacts such as formal rules or standard operating procedures, which are considered important 'resources for action', which, however, 'do not determine performances' as contextual details always vary and it is impossible to specify behaviour (Pentland and Feldman, 2005, see also D'Adderio, 2008 for a discussion). As 'physical manifestations of the [...] routine' (Pentland and Feldman, 2005: 797), they can act as 'proxies for the ostensive aspect' and yet must not be confused for the ostensive, which is 'multiple and distributed in nature' (Pentland and Feldman, 2005). It follows that written rules or formal SOPs are 'poor representations of the ostensive aspect (routine in principle)' because they are unable to capture the different viewpoints which characterize the latter. In this framework, we learn how 'the abstract understandings, specific performances and artifacts are interrelated in complex ways' (2005: 794) but these dynamics are not as yet fully spelled out. Artifacts and materiality at this stage are introduced into the wider RD framework but remain external to the generative system of the ostensive and performative aspect, and 'not an essential part of the core [routines] definition' (Feldman and Pentland, 2003: 96).

In a related move, Howard-Grenville (2005) also addressed the role of artifacts and technology in routines. She develops the notion of 'embeddedness' (Granovetter, 1985) to capture how the enactment of a routine overlaps with that of other organizational structures, including technology. Technological structures emerge from the pre-existing physical properties of technical artifacts. Their role is to 'guide and constrain the actions of users or creators of the artifacts' (1985: 630). As one aspect of the wider organizational context, technological structures influence whether and how a routine can change over time. For example, technological artifacts, such as road mapping reports and SOPs, constrain road mapping performances through their inherent stability – achieved through repetition of prior performances. At the same time, artifacts are also enablers that 'cue representations or schemas that can guide action just as strongly as the concrete aspects of artifacts do'. In so doing, the theory argues, they do not determine routines but are intrinsically flexible and malleable (see also Hales and Tidd, 2009).

7.3.1.2 Interactions, Tensions and Mutual Constitution

Another strand of routines studies emerged at about the same time, which was influenced by neighbouring debates in Sociology, Practice Theory, Innovation Studies, Information Systems and Science and Technology Studies (STS)/ Actor-Network Theory (ANT) (D'Adderio 2001, 2003, 2008, 2011; see also chapters by Feldman and Sele [Chapters 2 and 6] in this volume). Contributions to this stream aimed to make up for the (earlier mentioned) lack of attention in earlier routines research towards the tensions and interactions, or 'mutual constitution' (Callon and Muniesa, 2005;

Leonard-Barton, 1988; Orlikowski and Scott, 2008; Pickering, 1993) – of routines and materiality. In being centrally about the relationship between routines and their artifacts, this debate was at the heart of the discussions about what is a routine and how does it differ from an SOP, or in other words, its ontological status.

The relationship between practices/routines and artifacts had been in fact at the forefront of a number of related debates (see D'Adderio, 2008 for a review) to the extent that one could find a variety of related notions in the literature which addressed the routine/artefact dilemma, with different nuances. Dualities used at the time to capture the distinction between actual routines and their artefacts included 'mental plans' and 'situated action' (Hutchins, 1991; Suchman, 1987), 'modus operandi' and 'opus operatum' (Bourdieu, 1977), 'espoused' and 'actual' practice (Orr, 1990), 'time-objective' and 'time-in-process', 'object-world' and 'process-world' (Bucciarelli, 1988), 'rules-as-represented' and 'rules- as-guides-in-practice' (Orr, 1996), 'canonical' and 'non-canonical' practice (Brown and Duguid, 1996), the 'map' and the 'terrain' (Berg, 1997), 'representations of work' and 'practical action' (Suchman, 1983).

The work of Lucy Suchman, who had been an in-house ethnographer at Xerox PARC in Palo Alto, was particularly useful to routines scholars (including this author) in theorizing the distance between rules (in Routine Dynamics language, formal routines or SOPs) and actual practice, through the development of the notion of 'articulation work' (Suchman, 1983 and 1987). The notion captured the continuous, ad hoc work conducted by computer scientists/programmers in their constant requirement to bridge the 'phronetic gap' (D'Adderio, 2008; Taylor, 1993) between the formula (or rule) and its enactment, the representation and the actual practice, office procedure and practical action (Suchman, 1983). This work influenced the routines debate in a direct and substantial way.

In her study of software implementation, for example, D'Adderio (2001) showed how routines, formalized and embedded in a digital product model, were appropriated at the local level by various organizational communities and functions through 'translation'. The study, inspired by contemporary insights from STS/ANT and Practice Theory, highlighted the socio-technical 'translations' (Callon, 1986) required to make formal, artifactual routines work across different organizational settings, by helping turn formal procedures into actual practice (and vice-versa). In so doing, the work emphasized the coordinating role of formal routines in mediating actions and knowledge across multiple (and potentially conflicting) organizational communities, their technologies and their cultures (see also D'Adderio and Safavi [Chapter 15], this volume). In its attempt to understand the effects of SOPs and other kinds of artifacts (i.e., the computer-embedded virtual product model) on actual routines, this work also drew on STS scholars Star and Griesemer (1989), and their theorization of the influence of standards – and standard objects – on practices. Building on this work, D'Adderio's (2001) study also showed how, when compared to informal hand sketches and clay prototypes, SOPs might fail to perform as 'boundary objects' due to their inherent rigidity, triggering the emergence of 'translation routines' to restore flexibility and support the work of local communities.

Building closely on Suchman's (1983), D'Adderio (2003)'s study of computer workflow and 'engineering product list' implementation captures the co-evolution of routines-as-plans (formal routines/representations) and situated action (actual routines/expressions). In relation to the workflow process, the study showed how engineers introduced flexible workarounds (D'Adderio, 2003, see also Bertels et al., 2016; Pentland and Haerem, 2015) in their effort to adapt formal routines to local ways of knowing and working. Similarly to the 'virtual product', standardized routines/SOPs were shown here to bring rigidities into the development process, causing human actors to act to restore flexibility through allowing for local interpretation and/or redesign. Similarly to the SOPs, the 'engineering list' acted as an intermediary and mediator (see also Bapuji et al., 2012), which was shown to be anything but a stable and opaque object which determined actions, as implicitly assumed in the early routines literatures. This theme was later picked up by Cacciatori (2012) who, in her study of 'project bidding routines', observed how effective problem-solving across different occupational groups required 'flexible representations that can be adapted to the needs of different specialists in local use, that are easy to manipulate, and that evolve in parallel with the problem-solving activity' (2012: 1563). In showing how occupational communities could gain influence by constructing boundary objects that sit at the junction of, and regulate access to, various areas of expertise, this study further contributed to theorizing the role of flexible and inflexible artifactual intermediaries in shaping routines. Similarly, Ewenstein and Whyte (2009) had distinguished between evolving 'epistemic objects' that leave opportunity in their structure for what is not yet known, and static 'boundary objects'. Building on D'Adderio (2001)'s notion of 'translating routines', they show how objects can facilitate the translation from physical into digital forms, and back.

The role of formal routines was later developed in a number of routine dynamics contributions, including Turner and Rindova (2012), who showed that different artifacts were designed to simultaneously support the enactment of standardized or flexible ostensive patterns in the 'garbage collection' routine. In adding to the literature which theorizes the role of artifacts in standardizing routine actions, they show how artifacts can also help in reorganizing routines under conditions of change in a way to preserve standard action sequences while also allowing discretion. D'Adderio (2014) built on this to theorize how artifacts were able to help organizations deal with conflicting goals through 'selective performance' (2014: 21), that is, by allowing at different times orienting routinized performances towards either standardizing (while holding improving in the background) or improving (while holding standardizing in the background). In so doing, she showed how standardized artifacts (such as the shared Computer Model) can be redesigned to support greater standardization or greater flexibility.

Further contributions later added to this fertile work stream. Danner-Schroeder and Geiger (2016) discussed the influence of SOPs on balancing organizational flexibility and standardization and, building on D'Adderio (2008, 2014), they articulate the mechanisms of selecting, recombining, aligning and prioritizing activities which underpin standardized or flexible routinized patterns. In their study of reinsurance, Spee et al. (2016) theorized the role of supplementary artifacts that inscribe the knowledge produced within an intersecting routine and make it accessible within a focal routine, thus explaining how intersects are enacted and amplify pressure towards different coexisting ostensive patterns of standardization and flexibility. Deken et al. (2016) also contribute to this work stream by comparing the espoused or documented version of the 'tree routine' with the actual routine. The 'tree routine' artifact here is instantiated in various, more or less formalized, versions including copies of the tree map printed from an Excel sheet and a digital version which was shared among managers by using a projector. Aroles and McLean (2016) highlighted how the emergence and coexistence of change and stability is related to the enactment of standard routines through a performative process of difference and repetition. Their ethnographic examination of the 'ink density usage' and the 'assessment of newspaper quality' routines within a newspaper-printing factory discusses the role of standard routines and procedures in the (re)creation of actual routines. Bapuji et al. (2019), in their experiment conducted on the towel changing routine at a hotel, show how routines redesign resulted in changes in the formal procedure that guided the performance of the routine, and in the physical artifacts that participants were drawing on while performing their roles.

7.3.2 The Material Turn in Routine Dynamics

7.3.2.1 Artifacts at the Centre of Routines

Despite the advances brought about by the 'interactions, tensions and mutual constitution' stream of work, much of the theoretical treatment of artifacts and materiality in Routine Dynamics at the beginning of the second decade of this century still displayed limitations which threatened to hinder progress in this important debate. To address this gap, a new stream of research in Routine Dynamics emerged at this point in time, which focused more firmly on the deeper influence of artifacts on a routine's internal dynamics. Building on Performativity Theory, this work stream shone a light on the central role of artifacts in routines, thus providing the basis for the 'material turn' in Routines Dynamics (D'Adderio, 2011).

Starting from the empirical observation that there can be no routines without artifacts, and that artifacts are fundamental to Routine Dynamics, this work sets out to make a theoretical move which placed artefacts and materiality at the centre of routines. Drawing on sensitivities residing in Performativity Theory and related framework (D'Adderio, 2008), the material turn in Routine Dynamics must be understood as a move to remedy the limited role ascribed to artifacts/rules until that point. In this work, D'Adderio (2008 and 2011) takes issue with the way artifacts had often been treated in Organizational Theory as passive and opaque features of a fixed and pre-existing context, whose agency remained at the discretion of human actors who could at any point in time decide whether to follow, or not to follow. In the structuration framework, for example, as seen earlier, human agency was privileged over technology defined as 'material artifacts that are socially defined and socially produced' (Orlikowski and Scott, 2008: 11). Technology was only relevant to the extent that actors engaged with it, and consciously decided to include it in their practices. In this view, the emphasis is on human actors at the expense of artifacts whose specific affordances (Hutchby, 2001) are mostly ignored or even depicted negatively. This was reflected in the negative emphasis given in Routine Dynamics to rules and SOPs, often referred to as 'dead routines' (Birnholz et al., 2007; Pentland and Feldman, 2008), a notion often invoked as a critique of the Carnegie approach. The notion of SOPs-as-dead-routines, however, tended to background the important role artifacts played in routine dynamics for two reasons: it appeared to perpetuate the notion that artifacts were passive objects, which could be involved in the performance of a routine only 'at the discretion of the participants' (Pentland and Feldman, 2008: 245); and second, in reiterating the 'importan(ce) of distinguish[ing the artefact] from the routine as a generative system' it reinforced the positioning of 'artifacts [. . .] outside of the routine itself' (Pentland and Feldman, 2005).

The significance of D'Adderio (2011)'s call for 'placing artifacts at the centre of routines and Routines Theory' must be understood in this respect. Situating artifacts as part of the routines' generative system allowed fully exploring their affordances and agency. It also allowed opening up the artifacts' proverbial 'black box' to theorize how artifacts might shape performances (and vice-versa). Such a shift, which called for a deeper, stronger and nuanced characterization of the coproduction of routines and materiality (D'Adderio, 2011: 208), involved focusing on four main advances.

First, recognizing that routinized knowledge and actions are not simply 'distributed between' but 'stretched across' actors and artifacts (D'Adderio, 2011). This means that the skills and capabilities of actors are mediated and fundamentally transformed by the capabilities of the tools and instruments that they use in their work (Latour, 2005), thus challenging the separation between humans and artifacts (Orlikowski and Scott, 2008). Second, placing artifacts at the centre afforded the investigation of how dominant interests or 'programs for action' may be 'inscribed' (Akrich, 1992; Latour, 1992) into, or delegated to, artifacts and technologies. This suggests that artifacts are not neutral but instead reflect the objectives, motivations, values and dispositions of the agencies that use/produce them, and that they encode knowledge that has been sifted, ordered and classified according to one or more assumptions, rationales or 'logics' (Bowker and Star, 1999). Third, placing artifacts at the centre meant surpassing the simple characterization of artifacts as merely 'guiding' and 'constraining' actions and action patterns to theorize their complex and relational affordances (Hutchby, 2001; Markus and Silver, 2011). This notion explains how artifacts, without being deterministic, may be able to influence actions even if the actors themselves are not aware of it (MacKenzie, 2006). And fourth, putting artifacts at the centre implied studying their full performative effects (Barad, 2007; Callon, 1998) as part of wider socio-material assemblages whose configurations shape routines and their outcomes in complex and emergent ways (D'Adderio and Pollock, 2020).

The call for placing artifacts at the centre of routines has been answered through a substantial number of contributions in Routine Dynamics. Feldman (2016), for example, draws on D'Adderio (2011) to discuss how artifacts have progressively made their way into Routine Dynamics. In so doing she concurs that, while the empirical work has always acknowledged the role of artifacts in routines, 'the early theorizing in routine dynamics separated artifacts from the performative and ostensive aspects [. . .] though such artifacts have important interactions with both' (2011: 27). Similarly, Danner-Schröder and Geiger (2016) acknowledge the role of ostensive (patterning), performative (performing) and material aspects (artifacts) as constitutive of routines and mediating routine dynamics. Berente et al. (2016) discuss how technological artifacts 'are important to the change and execution of routines and should rightfully belong at the centre of the study of routines' (3). Kiwan and Lazaric (2019) highlight how technology 'is at the centre of routines and needs to be theorized as such' (2019: 187).

7.3.2.2 Performativity Theory and Sociomaterial Assemblages

The present 'material turn' in Routine Dynamics relies on an advanced understanding of the relationship between human actors and technology built on the premises of Performativity Theory. Building on earlier contributions (D'Adderio, 2001, 2003), as well as drawing on contemporary debates within Economic Sociology and the Sociology of Financial Markets, D'Adderio (2008) introduces the 'performativity' construct (Austin, 1979; Barnes, 1982; Callon, 1998; MacKenzie, 2006) into the routines debate by proposing a theoretical framework that captures the mutual and dynamic adaptation between formal routines and rules, on one hand, and actual performances, on the other. According to this framework, the influence of formal rules/SOPs on routines is the outcome of iterative cycles of performation through which the SOP/rule frames the routine in practice, making performances more similar, or more compatible, to the SOP/rule; this generates overflows, which make performances less similar to, or compatible with, the SOP/rule, which may lead in turn to reframing of the performances by the SOP/rule. The 'performativity of routines' framework shows that, while possible, the extremes in which SOPs/rules fully prescribe performances (as in self-fulfilling prophecies) or merely describe performances (as in an 'automatically reproduced sequence of computer algorithms' (2008: 776) are rare, and that, in the case of routines distributed across complex settings and organizations, some level or degree of performativity is the norm.

Performativity (not to be confused with 'performance', which is more akin to enactment as in Goffman's [1959] notion of 'front stage', see Mol [2002] for a critique) affords a new understanding of materiality, or the effects of technology and artifacts on routines, which builds directly on the 'pragmatist turn' in STS/ANT (Callon, 2007). According to D'Adderio's (2008) take on this theory, formal artifacts or 'statements' (such as rules and SOPs), in order to shape performances, need to build their own '*agencement*' or 'assemblage' (D'Adderio, 2008). A socio-technical or sociomaterial assemblage (Callon, 1998; Suchman 2007) contains all the social and material elements required for the artifact/formula/rule/SOP to configure performances so that they may (directly or indirectly) support the rule. The notion of assemblage is based on an evolution of the STS notion of 'mixed ontology' which treats material artifacts and human actors as equally agentic and considers their agency impossible – and indeed unhelpful – to disentangle (see also Introna, 2007; Orlikowski and Scott, 2008; Suchman, 2007). In D'Adderio (2008) we can thus see how those artifacts which were able to exert their influence over routines did so by building an assemblage. Assemblages are heterogeneous ensembles, including actions, instruments, tools norms, values, bodies, emotions, etc. (D'Adderio, 2014, 2017; D'Adderio and Pollock, 2014, 2020; Glaser, 2017), which helped realize the goals, views, assumptions, intentions and 'programmes of action' progressively embedded in artifacts at design stage and throughout their life span. An artefact that is able to build a strong assemblage is relatively more likely to exert influence on practices or routines than one that isn't.

Recent developments in Routine Dynamics have since built on – and helped develop – the notion of sociomaterial assemblage in theorizing how routines emerge and evolve. D'Adderio (2014, 2017) and D'Adderio and Pollock (2014), for example, use the notion of assemblage to show how organizations learn to balance multiple, complementary and conflicting goals (see also Chapter 15 in this volume). The earlier mentioned paper by Aroles and McLean (2016) captures 'the assembling of different material and non-material forces (e.g. relating to the densitometer figures, reports, adverts, standards, ink levels) that underlie the process of routines repetition' (2016: 547). Glaser (2017) discusses how assemblages might support the efforts of organizational actors to intentionally change routines. In his study of the introduction of a policing algorithm at Metropol, he shows how design performances, to be effective, needed to produce not simply an artifact but a 'novel amalgamations of theories, artifacts, actors, and practices' (2017: 2127). D'Adderio and Pollock (2020) take the notion further by theorizing the role of assemblages in simultaneously performing different but overlapping versions of 'the same' routine. In so doing, they show how even slightly different sociomaterial assemblage configurations can generate very different effects on routines and organizations. Finally, Glaser et al. (2021) build on the concept of assemblage to discuss how algorithms may perform (influence) routines and organizations. Here they draw on the example of the 'credit scoring' algorithm to discuss how the assumptions inscribed (Akrich, 1992; Callon, 1998; D'Adderio, 2008) in an algorithm may 'travel' across sectors and organizations. In so doing, they illustrate the important consequences for routines and organizations of implementing an artifact whose encoded assumptions may or may not fit in with those of the new context in which they are introduced (on the issue of transfer, see also D'Adderio, 2014).

7.3.2.3 Multiplicity and Fluid Ontology

The previous discussion shows how the topics of artifacts and materiality have provided rich and fertile grounds for advancing Routine Dynamics. At this stage there is no sign of this stream reaching saturation. On the contrary, recent developments appear to indicate that the field of Routine Dynamics is preparing to turn towards the next move. This, according to D'Adderio and Pollock (2020), entails combining the theoretical affordances of the notion of sociomaterial assemblage with a novel ontological theorization of routines and Routine Dynamics based on Mol's realist philosophical notion of 'fluidity'. While even further highlighting the fundamental role of materiality in routines, this move, corresponding to a turn to 'fluid ontology', may equip the notion of Routine Dynamics with some important new affordances.

The first affordance builds on the notion of assemblage introduced earlier as one of the foundations of Performativity Theory. Drawing on Mol (2002) and Law (2004), D'Adderio and Pollock (2020) identify the sociomaterial assemblage as the main agentic unit (as opposed to simply human actors) in the emergence and persistence of routines (and therefore organizational stability and change). In so doing, they theorize an organizational routine as the constantly challenged, effortful, skilful and emergent outcome of multiple sociomaterial enactments or performations at different organizational 'sites' or 'locations'. Each site produces a different but overlapping version of the routine, and multiple routine versions need to be coordinated in order to come together as a single routine. A second affordance of this theory for routines is in showing how these are temporary and unstable achievements, constantly threatening to pull apart and dissolve in a multitude of patterns and performances to the extent that they can no longer be described as 'the same routine'. To protect routines from drifting, organizations devise a sophisticated range of sociomaterial practices aimed at effortfully and skilfully coordinating such disparate and dispersed enactments into a (temporarily singular) routine. For this purpose, the computing organization in D'Adderio and Pollock (2020) set up a range of 'repairing' and 'distributing' practices which help two different enactments of the routines converge towards similarity to the point that practitioners are able to treat it – and refer to it – as 'the same routine' (ontological singularity).

These new theoretical affordances based on ontological fluidity provide a highly dynamic theorization of routines which departs from previous contributions in Routine Dynamics by questioning the very assumption that we can easily point to something and identify it as being a (single, or 'the same') routine. A fluid ontology, inspired by contemporary advances in the philosophy of science and technology (Barad, 2007; Butler, 1990; de Laet and Mol, 2001; Mol, 2002), can thus advance Routine Dynamics by helping us move even further away from the original solid, static and objectified characterization of routines often found in early Routines and Capability Theory, to focus on the multiple enactments which may effortfully and temporarily become assembled into a routine (but might just as easily come apart). In so doing, this approach provides important new advances in terms of our ability to explore the effects and consequences of alternative sociomaterial routine configurations, as they emerge, evolve and transform across organizational sites, spaces or locations (Bucher and Langley, 2016; Nicolini, 2009; Schatzki, 2011), and over time. For example, the notion of routines fluidity combined with sociomaterial assemblages can help capture and theorize the 'dynamics of dynamic capabilities' (Wenzel et al., 2020), allowing – perhaps for the first time – reconciling of two until now incompatible streams of Routines Theory (Routines as Capabilities and Routine Dynamics) (D'Adderio and Pollock, 2020; see Parmigiani and Howard Grenville, 2011 for a discussion). Additionally, as argued in Glaser et al. (2021), these notions may allow us to further theorize new empirical phenomena such as the nature of algorithm-embedded routines by looking at the emergence and effects of different but overlapping configurations of algorithm-mediated actions and action patterns on routines, practices, institutions, organizations and beyond. This, for example, can be achieved by building on the notion of algorithms as 'nested assemblages' which differentially shape routines as they move across sites and over time as part of their unravelling 'biography' (Glaser et al., 2021).

7.4 Conclusions and Avenues for Future Research

This chapter has traced the evolution of the theorization of artifacts, technology and materiality in Routines Theory and Routine Dynamics. It has shown the progressive journey of materiality – and related constructs – from the periphery to the centre of routines. This has in turn encouraged a further turn to the sociomaterial assemblage (to replace the prevailing anthropomorphic theorization of routines) and a fluid ontology (which characterises routines as the emergent outcome of multiple, different and partially overlapping enactments).

As shown in Glaser et al. (2021), this novel theorization of routines lends itself to being productively applied to the study of important contemporary challenges and new material phenomena, including, for example, the increasingly important and pervasive role of artificial intelligence (AI), 'big data' and algorithmic technologies in routines and organizations and beyond. Starting, in contrast with some recent contributions (e.g., Murray et al., 2020), from the premise in ANT/Performativity Theory that artifacts and technologies have *always* been agentic, this perspective can help unravel the complex dynamics of co-performation of autonomous artifacts and routines. Recent technological developments, such as the rise of so-called learning algorithms in artificial intelligence, are increasingly delegating power to artifacts which behave in a subtle and obscure way, substantially affecting our ability – as human actors – to shape and control our work and our lives (Dourish, 2016; Introna, 2007). The increasing autonomous character of advanced algorithmic technologies, combined with their inscrutability and pervasiveness, is therefore raising new challenges. Included in these is the fact that the outcomes of increasingly complex algorithm-embedded routines are becoming ever more difficult to predict, identify and evaluate, thus imposing serious constraints on our ability to detect their effects and understand their implications (including organizational, economic and societal).

Building on the notion of sociomaterial assemblage and fluid ontology may provide new and important ways to assess the effects of different sociomaterial configurations on routines, organizations, institutions and beyond. This can help answer a number of key questions, such as, what are the effects of different sociomaterial assemblages on routines? How/when can the same assemblage perform different routines? And how/when can different assemblages perform the same routine? How/far is a routine changed as it travels across locations and over time? How far can a routine be changed before it becomes a different routine? When can we say that any two enactments can (or cannot) be considered the same routine?

The new performativity-inspired material ontology can also be particularly apt at theorizing unconventional and emergent organizational contexts where routines are particularly unstable and challenged. These include the context of new ventures (e.g., Blanche and Cohendet, 2019; Schmidt et al., 2019), where routines first begin to emerge and crystallize from a bundle of disconnected actions and action patterns into something more stable and durable; in the context of transfer and replication, where routines are recreated in new contexts which challenge their consistency and integrity; in the context of organizational acquisitions, where routines from different contexts are merged into new actions and action patterns; in the context of distance working (telework), where similar routines are performed every time in a new context; and in the context of new organizational forms such as digital platforms and block chains, where routines are distributed across a multitude of stakeholders exercising varying degrees of power and discretion over routines and their outcomes.

Table 7.1 Artifacts and materiality in Routines Theory: Papers and constructs

		Key concepts and constructs	Core papers
Behavioral Theory & Evol. Econ.	**Routines as artifacts and entities**	Routines as performance programmes Routines as genes Standard operating procedures	Simon (1945); Newell and Simon (1976); Cyert and March (1963); March and Simon (1958/93); Cohen et al. (1996); Winter (1995); Nelson and Winter (1982); Cohen et al. (1996); Becker et al. (2005)
Routine Dynamics	**Artifacts as external background**	Artifacts as structures external to the routine that enable or constrain action Artifacts as proxies for the ostensive aspect	Pentland and Reuter (1994); Pentland and Feldman (2005), (2008); Howard-Grenville (2005); Cohen (2007); Pentland and Feldman (2008)
	Interactions, tensions and mutual constitution	Representations and expressions Actual and artifactual routines Formal and informal routines Procedures and performances Flexible/inflexible routines and artifacts Standardised artifacts and boundary objects	D'Adderio (2001), (2003), (2008), (2011), (2014); Turner and Rindova (2012); Cacciatori (2012); Bapuji et al. (2012), (2019); Cohendet and Simon (2016); Spee et al. (2016); Sele and Grand (2016); Danner-Schroeder and Geiger (2016); Bucher and Langley (2016); Feldman (2016)
	Material turn in Routine Dynamics	Artifacts endogenous to routines Artifacts at the centre of routines Copernican revolution in Routines Theory Material turn in routines	D'Adderio (2008), (2011); Feldman et al. (2016); Berente et al. (2016); Blanche and Cohendet (2019); Kiwan and Lazaric (2019); Boe Lillegraven (2019); Glaser et al. in this volume; Blanche and Cohendet in this volume; Sele in this volume
	Performativity and ontological fluidity	Socio-material assemblage Socio-technical *agencement* Performativity Ontological multiplicity Ontological fluidity	D'Adderio (2008), (2011), (2014), (2017); D'Adderio and Pollock (2014), (2020); Aroles and McLean (2016); Feldman et al. (2016); Sele and Grand (2016); Glaser (2017); Feldman and Orlikowski (2011), Glaser et al. (2021); Glaser et al. in this volume; Wegener and Glaser in this volume; Sele in this volume.

References

Akrich, M. (1992). The description of technical objects. In W. E. Bijker and J. Law, eds., *Shaping Technology/Building Society: Studies in Sociotechnical Change*. Cambridge, MA: MIT Press, pp. 205–224.

Aroles, J. and McLean, C. (2016). Rethinking stability and change in the study of organizational routines: Difference and repetition in a newspaper-printing factory. *Organization Science*, 27(3), 535–550.

Austin, J. (1979). *Philosophical Papers*. Oxford: Oxford University Press.

Bapuji, H., Hora, M. and Saeed, A. M. (2012). Intentions, intermediaries, and interaction: Examining the emergence of routines. *Journal of Management Studies*, 49, 1586–1607.

Bapuji, H., Hora, M., Saeed, A. and Turner, S. F. (2019). How understanding-based redesign influences the pattern of actions and effectiveness of routines. *Journal of Management*, 45(5), 2132–2162.

Barad, K. (2007). *Meeting the Universe Halfway: Quantum Physics and the Entanglement of Matter and Meaning*. Durham, NC, and London: Duke University Press.

Barnes, B. (1982). *T.S. Kuhn and Social Science*. London and Basingstoke: Macmillan.

Bechky, B. A. (2003a). Sharing meaning across occupational communities: The transformation of understanding on a production floor. *Organization Science*, 14(3), 312–330.

Berente, N., Lyytinen, K., Yoo, Y. and King, J. L. (2016). Routines as shock absorbers during organizational transformation: Integration, control, and NASA's Enterprise Information System. *Organization Science*, 27(3), 551–572.

Berg, M. (1997). Of forms, containers, and the electronic medical record: Some tools for a sociology of the formal. *Science, Technology and Human Values*, 22(4), 403–433.

Berg, M. (1998). The politics of technology: On bringing social theory into technological design. *Science, Technology, & Human Values*, 23(4), 456–490.

Bertels, S., Howard-Grenville, J. and Pek, S. (2016). Cultural molding, shielding, and shoring at Oilco: The role of culture in the integration of routines. *Organization Science*, 27, 573–593.

Birnholtz, J. P., Cohen, M. D. and Hoch, S. V. (2007). Organizational character: On the regeneration of Camp Poplar Grove. *Organization Science*, 18(2), 315–332.

Blanche, C. and Cohendet, P. (2019). *Remounting a Ballet in a Different Context: A Complementary Understanding of Routines Transfer Theories. Routine Dynamics in Action: Replication and Transformation*. Research in the Sociology of Organizations, Volume 61. Bingley: Emerald Publishing Limited, 11–30.

Boe-Lillegraven, S. (2019). *Transferring Routines across Multiple Boundaries: A Flexible Approach. Routine Dynamics in Action: Replication and Transformation*. Research in the Sociology of Organizations, Volume 61. Bingley: Emerald Publishing Limited, 31–53.

Bourdieu, P. (1977). *Outline of a Theory of Practice*. Cambridge: Cambridge University Press.

Bowker, G. C. and Star, S. L. (1999). *Sorting Things Out: Classification and Its Consequences*. Cambridge, MA: MIT Press.

Brown, J. S. and Duguid, P. (1996). Learning and communities-of- practice: Toward a unified view of working, learning, and innovation. In M. D. Cohen and L. S. Sproull, eds., *Organizational Learning*. London: Sage, pp. 59–82.

Bucciarelli, L. L. (1988). Engineering design process. In F. A. Dubinskas, ed., *Making Time: Ethnographies of High-Technology Organisations*. Philadelphia: Temple University Press, pp. 92–122 (Chapter 3).

Bucher, S. and Langley, A. (2016). The interplay of reflective and experimental spaces in interrupting and reorienting routine dynamics. *Organization Science*, 27(3), 594–613.

Butler, J. (1990). *Gender Trouble: Feminism and the Subversion of Identity*. London: Routledge.

Cacciatori, E. (2012). Resolving conflict in problem-solving: Systems of artefacts in the development of new routines. *Journal of Management Studies*, 49(8), 1559–1585.

Callon, M. (1986). Some elements of a sociology of translation: Domestication of the scallops and the fishermen. In J. Law, ed., *Power, Action and Belief: A New Sociology of Knowledge*. London: Routledge & Kegan Paul, pp. 67–83.

Callon, M. (1998). An essay on framing and overflowing: Economic externalities revisited by sociology. In M. Callon, ed., *The Laws of the Markets*. London: Blackwell, pp. 244–269.

Callon, M. (2007). What does it mean to say that economics is performative? In D. MacKenzie,

F. Muniesa and L. Siu, eds., *Do Economists Make Markets? On the Performativity of Economics*. Oxford: Princeton University Press.

Callon, M. and Muniesa, F. (2005). Economic markets as calculative collective devices. *Organization Studies*, 26(8), 1229–1250.

Cohen, M. D., Burkhart, R., Dosi, G., Egidi, M., Marengo, L., War- glien, M. and Winter, S. (1996). Routines and other recurring patterns of organisations: contemporary research issues. IIASA Working Paper, March 1996.

Cohendet, P. S. and Simon, L. O. (2016). Always playable: Recombining routines for creative efficiency at Ubisoft Montreal's video game studio. *Organization Science*, 27(3), 614–632.

Cyert, R. M. and March, J. G. (1963). *A Behavioral Theory of the Firm*. Englewood Cliffs, NJ: Prentice Hall.

D'Adderio, L. (2001). Crafting the virtual prototype: How firms integrate knowledge and capabilities across organisational boundaries. *Research Policy*, 30(9), 1409–1424.

D'Adderio, L. (2003). Configuring software, reconfiguring memories: The influence of integrated systems on the reproduction of knowledge and routines. *Industrial and Corporate Change*, 12 (2), 321–350.

D'Adderio, L. (2008). The performativity of routines: Theorising the influence of artefacts and distributed agencies on routines dynamics. *Research Policy*, 37fs(5), 769–789.

D'Adderio, L. (2011). Artifacts at the centre of routines: Performing the material turn in routines theory. *Journal of Institutional Economics*, 7 (Special Issue 02), 197–230.

D'Adderio, L. (2014). The replication dilemma unravelled: How organizations enact multiple goals in routine transfer. *Organization Science*, 25(5), 1325–1350.

D'Adderio, L. (2017). *Performing the Innovation-Replication Dilemma in Routines Transfer. Companion Book on Innovation*. Northampton, MA: Edward Elgar.

D'Adderio, L., Glaser, V. and Pollock, N. (2019). Performing theories, transforming organizations: A reply to Marti and Gond. *Academy of Management Review*, 44(3), 676–679.

D'Adderio, L. and Pollock, N. (2014). Performing modularity: Competing rules, performative struggles and the effect of organizational theories on the organization. *Organization Studies*, 35(12), 1813–1843.

D'Adderio, L. and Pollock, N. (2020). Making routines the same: Crafting similarity and singularity in routines transfer. *Research Policy*, 49(8), 104029.

Danner-Schröder, A. and Geiger, D. (2016). Unravelling the motor of patterning work: Toward an understanding of the microlevel dynamics of standardization and flexibility. *Organization Science*, 27(3), 633–658.

Deken, F., Carlile, P. R., Berends, H. and Lauche, K. (2016). Generating novelty through interdependent routines: A process model of routine work. *Organization Science*, 27(3), 659–677.

De Laet, M. and Mol, A. (2000). The Zimbabwe bush pump: Mechanics of a fluid technology. *Social Studies of Science*, 30(2), 225–263.

Dittrich, K. and Seidl, D. (2018). Emerging intentionality in Routine Dynamics: A pragmatist view. *Academy of Management Journal*, 61(1), 111–138.

Dourish, P. (2016). Algorithms and their others: Algorithmic culture in context. *Big Data & Society*, 3(2). doi: 10.1177/2053951716665128.

Ewenstein, B. and Whyte, J. (2009). Knowledge practices in design: The role of visual representations 'epistemic objects'. *Organization Studies*, 30(1), 7–30.

Feldman, M. S. (2000). Organizational routines as a source of continuous change. *Organization Science*, 11(6), 611–629.

Feldman, M. S. (2016). Routines as process: Past, present, and future. In C. Rerup and J. Howard -Grenville, eds., *Organizational Routines and Process Organization Studies*. Oxford: Oxford University Press.

Feldman, M. S., D'Adderio, L., Dittrich, K. and Jarzabkowski, P. (2019). *Introduction. Routine Dynamics in Action: Replication and Transformation* (Research in the Sociology of Organizations, Volume 61). Bingley: Emerald Publishing Limited, 1–10.

Feldman, M. S. and Orlikowski, W. J. (2011). Theorizing Practice and Practicing theory. *Organization Science*, 22(5), 1240–1253.

Feldman, M. S. and Pentland, B. T. (2003). Reconceptualizing organizational routines as a source of flexibility and change. *Administrative Science Quarterly*, 48(1), 94–118.

Feldman, M. S., Pentland, B. T., D'Adderio, L. and Lazaric, N. (2016). Beyond routines as things: Introduction to the Special Issue on Routine Dynamics. *Organization Science*, 27(3), 505–513.

Glaser, V. L. (2017). Design performances: How organizations inscribe artifacts to change routines. *Academy of Management Journal*, 60(6), 2126–2154.

Glaser, V., Pollock, N. and D'Adderio, L. (2021). *The Biography of an Algorithm*. Working Paper. Organization Theory. doi: 10.1177/26317877211004609.

Goffman, E. (1959). *The Presentation of Self in Everyday Life*. Garden City, NY: Doubleday.

Granovetter, M. (1985). Economic action and social structure: The problem of embeddedness. *American Journal of Sociology*, 91(3), 481–510.

Hales, M. and Tidd, J. (2009). The practice of routines and representations in design and development. *Industrial and Corporate Change*, 18(4), 551–574.

Howard-Grenville, J. A. (2005). The persistence of flexible organizational routines: The role of agency and organizational context. *Organization Science*, 16(6), 618–636.

Hutchby, I. (2001). Technologies, texts and affordances. *Sociology*, 35(2), 441–456.

Hutchins, E. (1991). Organizing work by adaptation. *Organization Science*, 2 (1), 14–39.

Introna, L. D. (2007). *Towards a Post-Human Intra-Actional Account of Socio- Technical Agency (and Morality)*. Prepared for the Moral Agency and Technical Artifacts Scientific Workshop, NIAS, Hague, 22.

Jones, M. R. (2013). Untangling sociomateriality. In P. Carlile, D. Nicolini, D. Langley and H. Tsoukas, eds., *How Matter Matters: Objects, Artifacts and Materiality in Organization Studies*. Oxford: Oxford University Press, pp. 197–226.

Kho, J., Spee, A. P. and Gillespie, N. (2019). Enacting relational expertise to change professional routines in technology-mediated service settings. In M. S. Feldman, L. D'Adderio, K. Dittrich and P. Jarzabkowski, eds., *Routine Dynamics in Action: Replication and Transformation* (Research in the Sociology of Organizations, Vol. 61). Bingley: Emerald Publishing Limited, pp. 191–213.

Kiwan, L. and Lazaric, N. (2019). Learning a new ecology of space and looking for new routines: Experimenting robotics in a surgical team. In M. S. Feldman, L. D'Adderio, K. Dittrich and P. Jarzabkowski, eds., *Routine Dynamics in Action: Replication and Transformation* (Research in the Sociology of Organizations, Vol. 61). Bingley: Emerald Publishing Limited, pp. 191–213.

Latour, B. (1986). The powers of association. In J. Law, ed., *Power, Action and Belief*. London: Routledge and Kegan Paul.

Latour, B. (1992). Where are the missing masses? *The Sociology of a Few Mundane Artifacts*, 18, 151–180.

Latour, B. (2005). *Reassembling the Social: An Introduction to Actor Network Theory*. Oxford: Oxford University Press.

Lave, J. and Wenger, E. (1991). *Situated Learning: Legitimate Peripheral Participation*. Cambridge: Cambridge University Press.

Law, J. (1987). Technology, closure and heterogeneous engineering: The case of the Portuguese expansion. In W. E. Bijker, T. P. Hughes and T. J. Pinch, eds., *The Social Construction of Technological Systems, New Directions in the Sociology and History of Technology*. Cambridge, MA: MIT Press.

Law, J. (2004). *After Method: Mess in Social Science Research*. Psychology Press.

Leonard-Barton, D. (1988). Implementation as mutual adaptation of technology and organization. *Research Policy*, 17(5), 251–267.

Leonardi, P. M., Bailey, D. E. and Pierce, C. S. (2019). The coevolution of objects and boundaries over time: Materiality, affordances, and boundary salience. *Information Systems Research*, 30(2), 665–686.

MacKenzie, D. (2006). *An Engine, not a Camera: How Financial Models Shape Markets*. Cambridge, MA: MIT Press.

March, J. G. and Simon, H. A. (1958). *Organizations*. New York: Wiley.

Markus, M. L. and Silver, M. S. (2008). A foundation for the study of IT effects: A new look at DeSanctis and Poole's concepts of structural features and spirit. *Journal of the Association for Information Systems*, 9(10/11), 609–632.

Mol, A. (2002). *The Body Multiple: Ontology in Medical Practice*. Durham, NC: Duke University Press.

Murray, A., Rhymer, J. and Sirmon, D. G. (2020). Humans and technology: Forms of conjoined agency in organizations. *Academy of Management Review*.

Nelson, R. R. and Winter, S. G. (1982). *An Evolutionary Theory of Economic Change*. Cambridge, MA: Belknap Press of Harvard University Press.

Newell, A. and Simon, H. A. (1976). Computer science as empirical inquiry: Symbols and search. *Commun. ACM*, 19(3), 113–126.

Nicolini, D. (2009). Zooming in and out: Studying practices by switching theoretical lenses and

trailing connections. *Organization Studies*, 30(12), 1391–1418.
Orlikowski, W. and Scott, S. (2008). Sociomateriality: Challenging the separation of technology, work and organization, *The Academy of Management Annals*, 2(1), 433–474.
Orr, J. E. (1990). Sharing knowledge, celebrating identity: War stories and community memory in a service culture. In D. S. Middleton and D. Edwards, eds., *Collective Remembering: Memory in Society*. Beverley Hills, CA: Sage Publications.
Orr, J. (1996). *Talking about Machines: An Ethnography of a Modern Job*. Ithaca, NY: Cornell University Press.
Parmigiani, A. and Howard-Grenville, J. (2011). Routines revisited: Exploring the capabilities and practice perspectives. *Academy of Management Annals*, 5(1), 413–453.
Pentland, B. T. and Feldman, M. S. (2005). Organizational routines as a unit of analysis. *Industrial and Corporate Change*, 14(5), 793–815.
Pentland, B. T. and Feldman, M. S. (2008). Designing routines: On the folly of designing artifacts, while hoping for patterns of action. *Information and Organization*, 18(4), 235–250.
Pentland, B. T. and Hærem, T. (2015). Organizational routines as patterns of action: Implications for organizational behavior. *Annual Review of Organizational Psychology and Organizational Behavior*, 2, 465–487.
Pickering, A. (1993). The mangle of practice, agency and emergence in the sociology of science. *American Journal of Sociology*, 99(3), 559–589.
Pickering, A. (1995). *The Mangle of Practice, Time, Agency and Science*. Chicago: University of Chicago Press.
Schatzki, T. R. (2011). The spaces of practices and large social phenomena. Alexander von Humboldt Lecture Department of Philosophy, University of Kentucky Lexington, USA, Monday, September 12th.
Schmidt, T., Braun, T. and Sydow, J. (2019). Copying routines for new venture creation: How replication can support entrepreneurial innovation. In M. S. Feldman, L. D'Adderio, K. Dittrich and P. Jarzabkowski, eds., *Routine Dynamics in Action: Replication and Transformation* (Research in the Sociology of Organizations, Vol. 61). Bingley: Emerald Publishing Limited, pp. 55–78.
Sele, K. and Grand, S. (2016). Unpacking the dynamics of ecologies of routines: Mediators and their generative effects in routine interactions. *Organization Science*, 27(3), 722–738.
Simon, H. ([1945], 1976). *Administrative Behavior*, 3rd ed. Free Press: New York.
Simon, H. A. (1970). *The Sciences of the Artificial* (1st edition). Cambridge, MA: The MIT Press.
Sonenshein, S. (2016). Routines and creativity: From dualism to duality. *Organization Science*, 27(3), 739–758.
Spee, P., Jarzabkowski, P. and Smets, M. (2016). The influence of routine interdependence and skillful accomplishment on the coordination of standardizing and customizing. *Organization Science*, 27(3), 759–781.
Star, S. L. and Griesemer, J. R. (1989). Institutional ecology, translations and boundary objects: Amateurs and professionals in Berkeley's Museum of vertebrate zoology, 1907–39. *Social Studies of Science*, 19, 387–420.
Suchman, L. A. (1983). Office procedure as practical action: Models of work and system design. *ACM Transactions on Office Information Systems*, 1(4), 320–328.
Suchman, L. A. (1987). *Plans and Situated Action: The Problem of Human-Machine Communication*. Cambridge, MA: Cambridge University Press.
Suchman, L. A. (2007). *Human-Machine Reconfigurations: Plans and Situated Actions (2 edition)*. Cambridge; New York: Cambridge University Press.
Taylor, C. (1993). To follow a rule . . .. In C. Calhoun, E. LiPuma and M. Postone, eds., *Bourdieu: Critical Perspectives*. Cambridge: Polity Press, pp. 45–59.
Turner, S. F. and Rindova, V. (2012). A balancing act: How organizations pursue consistency in routine functioning in the face of ongoing change. *Organization Science*, 23(1), 24–46.
Wenzel, M., Danner-Schröder, A. and Spee, A. P. (2020). Dynamic capabilities? Unleashing their dynamics through a practice perspective on organizational routines. *Journal of Management Inquiry* (online 4 May 2020).
Winter, S. G. (1995). Four Rs of profitability: Rents Resources, Routines and Replication, unpublished working paper IIASA, WP-95-07.
Winter, S. G. and Szulanski, G. (2001). Replication as strategy. *Organization Science*, 12(6), 730–743.
Zuboff, S. (2019). *The Age of Surveillance Capitalism: The Fight for a Human Future at the New Frontier of Power* (1st edition). New York: Public Affairs.

PART II

Methodological Issues in Routine Dynamics Research

CHAPTER 8 Ethnography and Routine Dynamics

KATHARINA DITTRICH

8.1 Introduction

Ethnographic fieldwork has been essential in starting and developing the field of Routine Dynamics. Ethnography is not a research method but 'a way of writing about and analysing social life' (Watson, 2011: 202). It is the 'firsthand experience and exploration of a particular social or cultural setting on the basis of (though not exclusively by) participant observation' (Atkinson et al., 2007: 4). Studies of Routine Dynamics have explored a stunning variety of different settings, including student housing at universities, call centres, automotive, electronics and other kinds of manufacturers, children's summer camps, reinsurance firms, emergency relief agencies, artificial intelligence labs, video game companies, clothing stores, start-ups, hospitals, law enforcement agencies, consultancies, ballet productions, sushi bars, haut-couture producers and so forth. As this chapter highlights, the vast majority of studies of Routine Dynamics come from ethnographic fieldwork.

Ethnographic fieldwork has proven essential to the theorizing of Routine Dynamics for two reasons. First, ethnographies focus on the everyday actions and interactions of people working in organizations. Thereby, they 'altered the grain size or granularity of analysis and moved the unit of analysis from the firm and the routines that constitute them to the routine and the actions that constitute them' (Feldman, 2016: 27). As a result, what became visible are the efforts of people in performing routines. As Pentland and Rueter (1994: 489) describe, 'all the minor troubles and improvisations of daily life [became] apparent.' Ethnography helped to see 'what "actually happens"' (Watson, 2001: 204) when people perform routines.

Second, at the heart of ethnographic research is a logic of discovery (Locke, 2011). Ethnographers are open to surprises in the field and they work with these surprising observations to develop new ideas, concepts and/or explanations (Agar, 2010; Cunliffe, 2010). Feldman (2000: 611) describes her surprise as follows,

> I began my fieldwork in a student housing department of a large state university with the idea that organizational routines [. . .] do not change very much from one iteration to another. [. . . Instead,] I found that most of the routines I was studying were undergoing substantial change. [. . .] People have asked me how there can be such a thing as a routine that changes.

Working with a wide range of theories to explain the discrepancy between the concept of routine and her observations, Feldman (2000) came to theorize routines as emergent accomplishments, 'work in progress rather than finished products' (Feldman, 2000: 613). Ethnographic fieldwork has thus 'dissolved the illusion of sameness and simple repetition [of routines and . . .] it has also dissolved the illusions that routines are merely things' (Feldman, Pentland, D'Adderio and Lazaric, 2016: 505). To this day, ethnography continues to challenge 'received wisdom' about routines and their role in organizations.

For this chapter, I reviewed forty-five ethnographic studies. After describing some key characteristics of ethnography, I review the various ways in which Routine Dynamics studies have used this approach. I was intrigued by the variety of

I am very thankful for the guidance and support of the two editors, Martha S. Feldman and Brian T. Pentland, which have been very helpful in shaping this chapter. I also thank Christian A. Mahringer for his comments and suggestions on an early draft of this chapter.

evidentiary approaches that ethnographers used, the wide range of questions they grappled with and the nuances about routines that their work brought to light. With a very few exceptions (e.g., micro-ethnographies such as LeBaron, Christianson, Garrett and Ilan, 2016), ethnographers typically studied multiple routines, highlighting that a routine can seldom be studied in isolation. What also became evident is that one does not have to choose settings where routines are highly repetitive, stable and easily identifiable. Instead, ethnographers discovered interesting aspects of routine dynamics in settings such as disasters, start-ups, ballets or haute-couture.

The ethnographer's own experiences featured very little in the studies reviewed here. This provides an opportunity for future research, as Routine Dynamics scholars can explore more of the embodied and aesthetic dimensions of routines by writing about their own experiences. More innovative forms of ethnography, such as team, online or multi-sited ethnography, also provide opportunities for future work, especially as Routine Dynamics scholars are shifting to study 'bigger' phenomena, such as the grand challenges (George et al., 2016) of inequality or epidemics, and more complex phenomena, such as the gig economy and algorithms. I outline these directions for future research in the last section.

8.2 Some Key Characteristics of Ethnography

Ethnography has a long tradition in the social sciences, in particular in sociology and anthropology – a summary of its history in organization studies can be found in Yanow (2012) and Cunliffe (2010). Ethnography entails particular choices about the research site, how to carry out research, how to engage (or not) with respondents and what 'data' is (Cunliffe, 2015). Cunliffe (2010) identifies four key characteristics of ethnography. First, ethnography is concerned with culture, that is, 'the meanings and practices produced, sustained and altered through interactions [. . .] by particular people, in particular places, at particular times' (van Maanen, 2011: 221). Because ethnographers spend day in and day out with specific groups of people, they come to see the world from the 'native's point of view.' Traditionally, anthropologists studied culture per se, but in organization studies cultural meanings and practices often serve as the means through which to understand other aspects of organizational life, such as routines.

Second, ethnography captures context and temporality. Because ethnographers study people in their naturally occurring settings for a prolonged period of time (weeks, months and years), they are able to grasp both the local and broader context in which activities and interactions are embedded and how these things change over time. Third, ethnography is concerned with sociality. Ethnographers study how people live their lives; how they interact; the stories, symbols and language they use in their everyday interactions, and they pay attention to the relations between people, groups, things, context and culture. Fourth, ethnography employs thick descriptions (Geertz, 1973). In contrast to 'thin descriptions' that rely on generalized findings, and statistical data, thick descriptions provide detailed, rich insights into organizational life by describing micro interactions in the field in minute detail. The reader gets a sense of what it is like to be and work there.

Ethnographers employ a range of methods for getting close to their informants' work and life. The three most common methods include participant observations (see also Spradley, 1980), interviews and the collection of documents, though within each of these categories there are a variety of different approaches and styles. For example, participant observation typically implies being a full- or part-time member of the organization or community being studied and may involve participating in meetings, shadowing people, contributing to people's work, socializing in breaks and after-work events, and so forth. Interviewing ranges from very informal, ad-hoc interviews to more formal, structured or semi-structured interviews, interview to the double, life history interviews, and so forth. Ethnographers may also employ other methods suitable to capturing the phenomenon of interest, such as diaries, videos, photographs and others. While the researcher may make certain plans about the methods he/she would like to employ, in reality, it is 'the locals' [. . .] decision [. . .] as to what kind of participation and experience the fieldworker will be allowed' (van Maanen, 2011: 232).

The strength of ethnography in challenging taken-for-granted understandings comes from its logic of discovery (Locke, 2011). Ethnographers do not begin with a specific theory or plan, but rather with an interest in (a particular aspect of) organizational life. As they investigate the social processes at play, they often come across surprising observations of previously overlooked, ignored or taken-for-granted aspects. In search of explanations, the ethnographer employs an abductive style of reasoning (Locke et al., 2008; Tavory and Timmermans, 2014). In contrast to deduction (theory testing) and induction (generalizing from data to theory), abduction 'begins with an unmet expectation and works backward to invent a plausible world or a theory that would make the surprise meaningful' (van Maanen et al., 2007: 1149). It involves inventing a new way of understanding through the interplay of ethnographic experiences, theory and ideas (Cunliffe, 2015).

Ethnography poses a number of advantages and disadvantages that researchers need to consider. On the one hand, ethnography is often seen as 'subjective', depending on the perceptions, biases and theories of the researcher, and the context in which the research is carried out (Cunliffe, 2010; Yanow, 2012). It is also very time-consuming and requires a significant amount of emotional energy to deal with the anxieties, discomforts, misunderstandings and embarrassments that occur during fieldwork (van Maanen, 2011). Lastly, ethnographic research carries a range of risks, such as gaining access (for more details see Feldman et al., 2003; Hammersley and Atkinson, 2007). On the other hand, ethnography's main strengths lie in challenging received wisdom and current theory; looking at how things 'really' work, and grabbing the reader's attention with memorable details from the field. Beyond these objective aspects, becoming an ethnographer is often less of a choice but more of a calling. Those that already have an ethnographic sensibility sooner or later find their way to ethnography (see Kunda, 2013 for a compelling account).

8.3 How Ethnography Has Been Employed in Routine Dynamics

I identified forty-five studies that either describe themselves as ethnography or whose fieldwork practices exhibit the characteristics outlined earlier (i.e., observation, a prolonged engagement with the organization and a focus on culture and meaning-making). To organize my review, I draw on what van Maanen (2011) describes as the three main tasks of an ethnographer: fieldwork, headwork and textwork. Fieldwork refers to the work done to 'gather research materials by subjecting the self – body, belief, personality, emotions, cognitions – to a set of contingencies that play on others' (van Maanen, 2011: 219). Headwork refers to the conceptual work that informs fieldwork and provides the basis for writing ethnography. Textwork refers to the representational practices, the writing, that ethnographers use to convey their insights and findings to others. These three activities are constitutive and overlapping tasks that any ethnographer has to accomplish.

8.3.1 Fieldwork in Routine Dynamics

Similar to other ethnographic work (van Maanen, 2011; Watson, 2011), fieldwork practices in Routine Dynamics rely on a variety of evidentiary approaches (see Appendix 8.A1, columns 5–7). Studies ranged from a few months to several years and varied in intensity of participant observation. Some authors spent five days per week in the field (e.g., Kremser and Blagoev, 2021; Howard-Grenville, 2005), while others spent only a few days or hours every week, but extended this way of engaging with the organization over multiple years (e.g., Aroles and McLean, 2016; Feldman, 2000; Sele and Grand, 2016). Some authors attended a lot of meetings (e.g., Bucher and Langley, 2016; Deken et al., 2016), others engaged in many formal interviews (e.g., Sonenshein, 2016; Zbaracki and Bergen, 2010). Even though early studies in Routine Dynamics have primarily focused on the dynamics within routines, rather than across, it is evident from Appendix 8.A1, column 4 that ethnographers typically observed the performances of multiple routines. It was often in the data analysis and the writing up that authors started to focus on a single routine in order to analyse and depict the dynamics within a routine.

Most ethnographic fieldwork started with a question or interest related to the field site. For example, Sele and Grand's (2016: 726) study of an artificial intelligence lab was motivated by the question 'Why are organizations able to keep up their innovativeness over time and across contexts? [. . .and] how people do innovative work.' Yet, a few field studies were motivated already by questions about routines (e.g., Deken et al., 2016; Glaser, 2017; Rosales, 2018). For example, Feldman (in Feldman and Orlikowski, 2011: 1244) notes that she 'chose a research site that the participants assured me had routines of mind-numbing stability.' Independent of whether one starts with an interest in Routine Dynamics or not, the common denominator of all studies is an interest in how people accomplish work.

8.3.1.1 Unit of Observation Is Situated Action

The unit of observation in ethnographic studies of routines is situated actions (Suchman, 1987). Feldman and her colleagues (2016: 506; emphasis in original) clarify: 'Whereas other traditions that include a focus on specific actions focus on features of the actors' intent, motivation, or cognition (e.g., Michel 2014) [. . .] Routine Dynamics focuses on tracing *actions* and associations between *actions*.' This focus on situated actions is important for fieldwork practices. For example, Deken and her colleagues (2016: 664) note that 'we took actions as our main empirical focus [. . .] and collected detailed observational and interview data on how actions unfolded over time.' When shadowing nurses and physicians in an emergency department, Rosales (2018) had to remind herself that actions and not individuals were her unit of observation.

In turn, the unit of analysis is patterns of actions (Feldman et al., 2016), that is, the experienced regularities (i.e., patterns) that are created through repeated actions over time. These regularities can be identified from the participants' or the ethnographer's point of view (see more in Section 8.3.2.1) and can be captured through observations and interviews. For example, several authors note the importance of observing several iterations of a routine. For example, my co-author and I (Dittrich and Seidl, 2018: 116–117) note that we 'observed more than 80 performances of the assembling routine and more than 100 repetitions of the shipping routine over the course of our year-long study.' It is often not possible to observe all the actions of a routine performance in one piece because actions can be distributed across space and time. Howard-Grenville (2005: 622), for example, describes that she 'observed at least some aspects of the roadmapping routine being enacted at every one of the nine monthly Strategic Planning Council (SPC) meetings [she] had attended, and in most cases, had observed some steps of the routine enacted several times in the course of a single meeting.' Interviews are important in understanding the experienced regularities of participants, especially when these may differ from the experiences of the ethnographer. For example, Danner-Schroeder and Geiger (2016: 637) found that 'routine members described some routines as stable, whereas others were described as flexible [. . .] This contradicted our own observations indicating sequential variety in all routines.'

Routine Dynamics scholars pursued different strategies for anchoring their observations of situated actions and regularities (see Appendix 8.A1, column 3). The majority of studies (twenty-two out of forty-five) focused on a particular group of people (e.g., a work unit, an organization). For example, Howard-Grenville (2005) focused on EnviroTech, a new work unit established to improve environmental impact; Kremser and Blagoev (2021) studied a team of consultants; and Birnholtz and his colleagues (2007) focused on the overall organization of a children's summer camp. Typically, scholars first familiarized themselves with the variety of patterns of action being performed in the group and then identified the most important ones for more detailed data collection. For example, both Feldman (2000, 2003) and Schmidt and his colleagues (2019) used interviews to identify routines and then selected a few of them for further observations. Another strategy is to trace the unfolding of a project and how routines are enacted, adapted and changed through it. For example, D'Adderio (2003) observed a project to implement new software and how routine performances changed through this project. A third strategy is to focus on a particular process from the beginning. For example, Zbaracki and Bergen (2010) were invited to study the pricing process of a manufacturing company.

8.3.1.2 Tracing Situated Actions through Observations, Interviews and Documents

Routine Dynamics scholars typically relied on the three most common methods to capture situated actions (see also Appendix 8.A1, column 7). Observation, interviews and documents often worked in complementary ways, offering different vantage points for understanding situated actions. During observations, ethnographers took extensive and detailed field notes (see also Emerson et al., 1995; Spradley, 1979). Many also note how they rewrote and complemented these field notes at the end of each day. Rewriting field notes (or taking voice memos, see Kremser and Blagoev, 2021; Schmidt et al., 2019) is important because the ethnographer, as the main vehicle for collecting data, takes in much more than he or she can possibly write down during the observations. Several authors also used the opportunity of being with informants as they performed routines to conduct informal interviews. For example, Glaser (2017: 2131) describes that 'as part of this field work, natural opportunities emerged to interview employees [...] about the existing patrolling routines.'

Other studies supplemented their observations with more formal, semi-structured interviews. Deken and her colleagues (2016: 663) describe the kinds of questions Routine Dynamics scholars typically ask,

> we asked the interviewees to describe their actions (e.g., what they had been doing to progress the program), which other actors they had engaged with, and how they perceived the actions taken. Finally, we asked them to reflect on how actions diverged from or resembled performances they had engaged in or encountered in the past.

Interviews can also be useful to understand the reasons and motivations for particular actions, which might not be readily observable (Rosales, 2018). Moreover, discrepancies between interviews and observations can reveal differences between official, organizational objectives and the practical concerns in performing routines (e.g., Bruns, 2009).

All ethnographic studies also relied on the collection of documents and archival data. Documents can play various roles in studying Routine Dynamics: they can (1) provide important information about the context in which routines are performed; (2) be artifacts that are used in the performances of routines and (3) contain descriptions of the espoused, envisioned or scripted patterns of a routine. Comparing the latter kind of artifacts with enacted patterns can be useful for triangulating findings (e.g., Rosales, 2018) or for analysing in more detail the role of formalized representations in performing routines (e.g., D'Adderio, 2008; Hales and Tidd, 2009). Lastly, scholars have used archival data that traces sequences of actions, such as call records (Pentland and Rueter, 1994) or task sheets (Goh and Pentland, 2019), to extract and code grammars of actions. More details on sequence analysis can be found in Mahringer and Pentland (Chapter 12, this volume).

Beyond observations, interviews and documents, it may be necessary to employ other means of data collection to adequately capture situated actions. For example, several studies employed video methods to zoom into the moment-by-moment unfolding of verbal and embodied actions in the performance of a routine (e.g., LeBaron et al., 2016; Yamauchi and Hiramoto, 2016, 2020). Video recordings are useful to capture actions on a more fine-grained level than is possible through observations, but may pose greater challenges in gaining access. Similarly, my colleagues and I (Dittrich, Guérard and Seidl, 2016: 681) 'started to audio-record regular and unscheduled meetings as well as talk during specific enactments of the routines' because we noted the importance of verbal actions in performing routines. Grand (2016) and Blanche and Cohendet (2019) complemented their observations with photographs and other visual material because in their settings (e.g., ballet production, haute-couture) the visual dimension was crucial for capturing situated actions.

8.3.1.3 Forms of Participation and the Ethnographer's Relationships with Informants

Given the importance of immersing oneself in a setting, the form of participation of the ethnographer (Moeran, 2009) and the relationships with informants (Cunliffe and Karunanayake, 2013) are key to fieldwork. Most Routine Dynamics scholars took the role of an observer (thirty-three out of forty-five), a few shifted between being an observer and a more active participant (e.g., Feldman, 2000; Sonenshein, 2016) and seven mentioned taking an active role from the beginning (see Appendix 8.A1, column 6). Many reported having a desk at the organization and being able to move around freely. In some cases, this free access was enabled because organizational members had a university-related background and thus were more receptive to researchers than others (Dittrich et al., 2016; Schmidt et al., 2019; Sele and Grand, 2016). In other cases, scholars had long-standing relationships over several years with the respective organization (Addyman, 2019; Birnholtz et al., 2007; Cohendet and Simon, 2016; Grand, 2016). These relationships not only enabled access but were also useful for the 'co-production of knowledge between researchers and practitioners' (Grand, 2016: 117). Another way to gain deep insights is to develop relationships with key informants with whom the ethnographer can follow up informally, fill in gaps and clarify discrepancies arising from multiple sources (Deken et al., 2016; Dittrich et al., 2016; Howard-Grenville, 2005; Rosales, 2018). Key informants and long-term relationships are also useful to check emerging insights and results with participants (e.g., Birnholtz et al., 2007; Cohendet and Simon, 2016; Feldman, 2000, 2003).

Feldman (2000: 614) explains that shifting from an observer to an active participant in routine performances, 'deepens the understanding of what organizational members know and feel.' In some cases it may be useful to take on a more active role from the beginning in order to gain access (e.g., Danner-Schröder and Geiger, 2016; Glaser, 2017) or to study the processes by which a newcomer comes to understand and perform the patterns of action typical for the organization (Birnholtz et al., 2007). Addyman (2019, 2020) had the opportunity to conduct fieldwork in the setting that he was already working in.

Most Routine Dynamics scholars engaged in fieldwork on their own, while nine studies involved two or more researchers in the data collection (see Appendix 8.A1, column 6). Grand (2016: 71) describes that 'having two researchers enhanced our ability to develop multiple descriptions of the creation process [. . .], in the form of research diaries and short vignettes [. . .]. Empirical data was collected both jointly – especially the interview data and visual material – and in parallel, via research diaries [. . .] and workshop notes.'

Except for three studies (Danner-Schröder and Geiger, 2016; den Nieuwenboer et al., 2017; Eberhard, Frost and Rerup, 2019), ethical challenges featured very little in the studies reviewed here. However, depending on the phenomenon being investigated, ethnographers have to be very conscious of ethical risks (see also Fine, 1993; Murphy and Dingwall, 2007; Ybema et al., 2009).

8.3.2 Headwork in Routine Dynamics

8.3.2.1 Identifying and Analysing Patterns of Actions

Once the ethnographer has collected a significant amount of data about situated actions, the key question is 'what the actions add up to' (Feldman, 2015: 321), i.e., what patterns do they give rise to? Routine Dynamics studies report a significant amount of headwork to identify and analyse patterns of action. This is because situated actions can be interpreted or 'cut' (Strathern, 1996) in many different ways. As Feldman and her colleagues (2016: 506–507) point out, 'cuts are selective. For instance, a focus on how [. . .situated actions] enact efficiency can divert attention away from how [. . .these actions] enact creativity.' In this conceptual work, the ethnographer has to grapple with the multiplicity of actions and patterns.

In a first step, Routine Dynamics scholars tend to stick closely to the definition of routines as 'repetitive, recognizable patterns of interdependent actions, carried out by multiple actors' (Feldman and Pentland, 2003: 95). For example, Sonenshein (2016: 742) describes that the merchandising routine

> was broadly used (e.g., carried out by multiple actors such as store managers, full-time employees, and part-time employees), frequently used (e.g., a critical part of the organization's operations repeated weekly, sometimes daily), identifiable to employees (e.g., referred to explicitly in the data) [and] based on interdependent actions (e.g., the output of one action served as the input to another).

Sele and Grand (2016: 727)

> reviewed the patterns to eliminate those that were not in line with Feldman and Pentland's (2003, p. 95) definition of routines [...] For example, [they] eliminated the hiring of Ph.D. students or the management of project budgets from the list of action patterns because those tasks were performed by specific individuals rather than multiple actors and characterized by dispersed rather than interdependent practices.

In addition, it is helpful to identify the task that a routine accomplishes. As Feldman (2016: 24) writes, 'routines are enacted in order to do something in and for the organization.' Rerup and Feldman (2011: 586) note that 'defining organizational routines as task-specific was important to our ability to determine when participants' concerns were related to the recruitment routine and when they were related to an organizational schema.'

To identify enacted patterns, Routine Dynamics scholars often relied on multiple sources of data. For example, Bucher and Langley (2016: 599) explain how they 'drew on informants' accounts in interviews and during observations. Also, maps of the original and target patient processes served as proxies for assessing the ostensive aspects of patient routines.' Most studies tend to take an emic perspective, i.e., the perspective of participants, to identify patterns of actions. For example, in analysing customer service at sushi bars, Yamauchi and Hiramoto (2020: 8) note that 'the meal as a whole can be considered as a single routine, beginning with the entry to the establishment. In this study, we chose to treat activities such as order taking and food preparation as individual routines [... because] participants themselves orient[ed] to [them as] a patterned, repetitive activity.' However, sometimes it can also be useful to take an etic perspective, i.e., an outsider's perspective. For example, in her data analysis, Rosales (2018: 60–61) identified recurrent activities that neither her informants nor she saw while in the field, but that were important in sustaining routine performances. Similarly, Swan and her colleagues (2016: 213) also took an outsider perspective by 'identifying common, repeated patterns of actions' across several biotechnology firms in order to identify the ways in which these firms navigate the broader institutional environment.

To identify variations in performances and change in enacted patterns over time, ethnographers often relied on visual mapping strategies (Langley, 1999), depicting sequences of actions or a timeline of events. Some studies drew on narrative networks as developed by Feldman and Pentland (2007) to do so (e.g., Danner-Schröder and Geiger, 2016; Dittrich et al., 2016; Goh and Pentland, 2019; Pentland and Kim [Chapter 13], this volume). Others used computational methods to analyse sequences of actions (e.g., Goh and Pentland, 2019; Pentland and Rueter, 1994; for sequence analysis, see also Mahringer and Pentland [Chapter 12], this volume). In addition, Routine Dynamics scholars also frequently relied on detailed case descriptions and vignettes to contextualize and then analyse their observations of routine performances and patterns.

8.3.2.2 Discovery in Routine Dynamics

Discovery is at the heart of good ethnographies. Thus, surprises, puzzles and hunches should not be underestimated in the ethnographer's conceptual work (see also Appendix 8.A1, column 8). For example, Bertels and her colleagues (2016: 577) 'were struck by the degree to which informants regarded Oilco's culture as somewhat misaligned with the operational compliance routine, yet expressed great confidence that it, and the larger operational excellence effort, would become, in the words of one, "the dominant paradigm going forward".' Similarly, the conceptual work of Bucher and Langley (2016: 594) was driven by the 'puzzle of recursiveness.' Any ethnographer is well advised to ask 'What is interesting here?' while analysing their data (Davis, 1971).

The discovery process of developing new concepts or theories then involves iterating between various theories and the ethnographer's observations. Feldman (in Feldman and Orlikowski, 2011: 1244) describes her discovery process as follows:

> I was not able to understand what I was seeing using the theories I had available to me at the time. [. . .] Wanda Orlikowski suggested practice theory as an approach that might be useful. I spent a year reading [. . .], thinking about my data, and writing memos. I found the framework of structuration theory most immediately applicable, and most related to a foundation I already understood based on Schutz's (1967, 1970) phenomenology and Garfinkel's (1967) ethnomethodology (Heritage 1984). Bourdieu's relational framework and the concept of habitus were also intriguing and important for thinking about the way people enact routines on a day-to-day basis. Later, I incorporated some of Latour's (1986, 2005) ideas (Sevón 1996), or my interpretation of these ideas. This stew of theories provided a foundation for a new way of conceptualizing routines.

It is this kind of discovery process that has brought forth many of the rich insights of Routine Dynamics studies (see Appendix 8.A1, column 9).

8.3.3 Textwork in Routine Dynamics

The ways of depicting routine dynamics in writing are almost as varied as the empirical phenomena being studied. There is no 'one-size-fits-all' approach, but the ethnographer needs to skilfully craft the text in a way that it is convincing and compelling (see also Golden-Biddle and Locke, 1993; Hammersley and Atkinson, 2007). Some studies describe different ways of performing the same routine flexibly (e.g., Howard-Grenville, 2005), others describe different ways of how routines changed over time (e.g., Feldman, 2000). Some studies compare performances of the same routines that led to different outcomes (e.g., Sele and Grand, 2016) and some contrast how routines were performed before and after a major breakdown (e.g., Cohendet and Simon, 2016). In all cases, authors selected a particular strand from the fabric of everyday life to explain their findings. As Feldman (2000: 615) explains, authors 'must make decisions about what constitutes a 'strand' and about what surrounding fabric needs to be explained in order to make sense of the "strand."' As a result, scholars may decide to write two or more papers from the same ethnography, depicting different strands. For example, Yamauchi and Hiramoto use one paper to describe how a routine can be performed when participants have varied understandings of the routine (Yamauchi and Hiramoto, 2016) and another paper to analyse how recognizability of the routine is accomplished at its initiation (Yamauchi and Hiramoto, 2020).

An interesting way to depict routine performances is the composite narrative used by Spee and his colleagues (2016). The composite narrative brings together a range of different performances into one narrative and synthesizes what participants and the ethnographers experienced as 'typical' across performances (and in their case, firms as well). This approach might be useful in depicting the full breadth and depth of ethnographic data within a single, evocative story.

Since the majority of Routine Dynamics studies focus on the participants' situated actions and experiences, the researcher's own experiences were hardly visible in the texts reviewed here. Two exceptions are Howard-Grenville (2005: 622), who recounts how she was received by one of her informants after spending two months in the field, and Addyman (2019, 2020), who as an auto-ethnographer recounts the findings from his perspective. This absence of the ethnographer's own experiences presents an opportunity for future research that I will discuss next.

8.4 Future Research Directions: Extending Ethnographic Approaches in Routine Dynamics Research

Routine Dynamics research displays a great variety of approaches and methods. Yet, this variety tends to fall within the traditional bounds of ethnography. I identify three areas in which Routine Dynamics research can be extended to more novel and innovative forms of organizational ethnography. These extensions allow researchers to grasp and capture aspects of Routine Dynamics that have been neglected thus far (e.g., embodiment, emotions). Also, they enable us to bring the strengths of Routine Dynamics research to bear on new contemporary phenomena (e.g., the gig economy, algorithms) and/or that are of societal concern (e.g., inequality, epidemics).

In addition to these three extensions, ethnographers may want to consider how other research methods described in this volume may complement their insights. For example, Mahringer and Pentland (Chapter 12, this volume) describe how digital trace data can extend the temporal and spatial scope of the researcher, and LeBaron and Christianson (Chapter 9, this volume) describe how video can capture situated actions in more minute detail. Field experiments (Bapuji, Hora and Li, [Chapter 10] this volume), agent-based modelling (Gao, [Chapter 11] this volume) and narrative networks (Pentland and Kim, [Chapter 13] this volume) may equally complement an ethnographer's work. As researchers adopt these other methods, the ethnographic understanding still remains crucial. For example, Goh and Pentland (2019: 1906) note that when they coded the archival trace data into sequences, they iterated 'between the first author's familiarity with the context, field notes, and other archival documents to understand the intent of the task.'

8.4.1 From Observer to More Active Forms of Participation

As the majority of ethnographers took an observer role, Routine Dynamics research can take advantage of more active forms of participation. For example, in the 1950s, Roy undertook fieldwork by working 12 hours a day, 6 days a week in a garment factory, alongside other workers. He observes the physical challenges of this work: 'Before the end of the first day, Monotony was joined by his twin brother, Fatigue. I got tired. My legs ached, and my feet hurt.' (Roy, 1959: 160). This example reveals how actively participating in the work of others can help to gain more insights into the embodied dimensions of routines (see also Blanche and Feldman, [Chapter 25] this volume). Active forms of participation might also help us to explore the aesthetic qualities of routines (Feldman, 2016), i.e., whether patterns of actions feel familiar or repugnant, exciting or boring. Writing about these embodied and aesthetic dimensions of routines will require including the ethnographer's own experiences, as Roy (1959) did in the example just quoted.

Auto-ethnography (Addyman, 2019; Anteby, 2013; Doloriert and Sambrook, 2012), or at-home ethnography (Alvesson, 2009), is a particular form of ethnography whereby the researcher studies him/herself in a setting in which he/she is normally present. Routine Dynamics scholars participate in a variety of patterns of actions that might give us access to insights, without having to go somewhere else. I am writing this chapter in the midst of the coronavirus outbreak and notice how it feels when our regular patterns of going to work, going shopping and visiting family get disrupted. Auto-ethnographic accounts might also reveal the felt emotions in performing routines (see also Tallberg and her colleagues (2014); Baldessarelli, [Chapter 26] this volume).

Ethnographers can also work more directly and closely with informants so that research and practice mutually and synergistically inform each other. In action research (Kemmis, 2009; Kemmis et al., 2013), researchers and practitioners work closely together in problem diagnosis, action intervention and reflective learning. Para-ethnography (Islam, 2015: 231) takes advantage of the fact that in many settings there are 'informants [that] are themselves analysts and theorists of culture.' In recent process research, scholars (Fachin and Langley, 2018; John Shotter, 2006; Wegener and Lorino, 2020) have proposed a 'withness' approach that aims to capture the experience of living forward, i.e., how practitioners experience acting in an unknowable and unpredictable world, and to capture what *may be* rather than what *is*. These forms of ethnography may be particularly suitable when it comes to societal concerns that require deep and complex changes and where we as scholars are personally involved, such as changing teaching practices to address racism. They may also help to make Routine Dynamics research more practically relevant as scholars increasingly engage in conversations with practitioners about the dynamics of routines.

8.4.2 From the Lone Ethnographer to Team Ethnography

As most Routine Dynamics scholars engage in fieldwork alone, there is the potential to draw more on team ethnography. At least two avenues for future research stand out. First, by involving more than one ethnographer, the team is able to observe the same performances from different points of view and compare and contrast them. A team ethnographic approach may thus be useful to gain more insights into the multiplicity of actions and patterns and its consequences (Pentland et al., 2020). Second, as Jarzabkowski and her colleagues (Jarzabkowski et al., 2016; Spee et al., 2016) show, a team approach allows researchers to gather data on the same routine in multiple settings, e.g., in multiple groups, firms or geographic locations. This enables Routine Dynamics scholars to capture more complex, distributed phenomena (see also Section 8.4.3) and show the interconnectedness of patterns of action across large distances. Team ethnography poses a number of new challenges that an individual ethnographer does not face (for more insights see Jarzabkowski et al., 2015; Smets et al., 2014).

8.4.3 From Well-Bounded, Single Site Ethnography to Online, Mobile and Multi-Sited Ethnography

So far, Routine Dynamics scholars have studied primarily well-bounded, singular settings. However, as Feldman and Orlikowski (2011: 1240) point out, 'contemporary organizing is increasingly understood to be complex, dynamic, distributed, mobile, transient, and unprecedented, and as such needs approaches that will help us theorize these kinds of novel, indeterminant, and emergent phenomena.' For example, Uber driving is distributed across many different sites, ranging from Uber's corporate headquarters and its engineering labs to Uber drivers across the world, Uber users and the app on their phone, and Uber's secret computer algorithm. If one wants to study how the precarious situation of Uber drivers emerges, this raises new questions for ethnographic research (see also Rouleau, de Rond & Musca, 2014): How can we study situated actions and patterning when it is fragmented and dispersed across innumerable sites? What does it mean to 'be there' when phenomena unfold in the virtual, online world? How can we access the black box of an algorithm when it is hidden away? Extensions of traditional ethnographic methods by means of team ethnography or digital trace data as described earlier may be useful in capturing patterns of actions that are dispersed across numerous geographically distant sites. Similarly, new forms of online ethnography (Tunçalp and Lê, 2014), webnography (Puri, 2007) and network ethnography (Howard, 2002) can be useful for studying empirical phenomena that unfold online. Ethnographers also need to become more comfortable with using mobile approaches to collecting data, as they move from site to site, and 'scavenge' tactics (Seaver, 2017: 6) that draw on a disparate array of sources in an eclectic way. New methodological developments, such as the biographies of artifacts approach (Hyysalo et al., 2019) or networked field sites (Burrell, 2009), provide further inspiration for such approaches. Instead of anchoring the observation of situated actions and regularities in a particular group, project or process, ethnographers may trace an object as it travels across and is enacted in a variety of sites. New forms of fieldwork also raise new questions for the ethnographer's headwork: How can the situated actions that have been captured in various ways be knitted together? The promise of new methods is not only a better understanding of contemporary phenomena but also new ways of shaping social reality (Law, 2004), that is, making a difference through the theories we develop.

8.5 Conclusion

Due to its discovery-oriented nature, its ability to capture detail and its rich, contextualized insights, ethnography has been and will continue to be an important source of insights for Routine Dynamics research. This review has uncovered the variety of ethnographic practices employed and identified key issues to which ethnographers need pay attention when studying Routine Dynamics. Going forward, ethnographic approaches may need to be extended in various ways to capture new aspects of the dynamics of routines and to explore new contemporary phenomena. My hope is that this chapter provides useful, practical insights for novice ethnographers and inspiration for experienced ethnographers of Routine Dynamics.

References

Addyman, S. (2019). *The Timing of Patterning or the Patterning of Timing? Organisational Routines in Temporary Organisations*, The Bartlett School of Construction and Project Management, University College London, London.

Addyman, S., Pryke, S. and Davies, A. (2020). Re-creating organizational routines to transition through the project life cycle: A case study of the reconstruction of London's Bank Underground Station. *Project Management Journal*, 51(5), 522–537.

Agar, M. (2010). On the ethnographic part of the mix: A multi-genre tale of the field. *Organizational Research Methods*, 13(2), 286–303.

Aggerholm, H. K. and Asmuss, B. (2016). When 'good' is not good enough: Power dynamics and performative aspects of organizational routines. In J. Howard-Grenville, C. Rerup, A. Langley and H. Tsoukas, eds., *Organizational Routines. How They Are Created, Maintained, and Changed.* Series: Perspectives on Process Organization Studies. Oxford: Oxford University Press, pp. 140–178.

Alvesson, M. (2009). At-home ethnography: Struggling with closeness and closure. In S. Ybema, D. Yanow, H. Wels and F. H. Kamsteeg, eds., *Organizational Ethnography: Studying the Complexities of Everyday Life* Los Angeles: Sage, pp. 156–174.

Anteby, M. (2013). *Manufacturing Morals: The Values of Silence in Business School Education.* Chicago, London: University of Chicago Press.

Aroles, J. and McLean, C. (2016). Rethinking stability and change in the study of organizational routines: Difference and repetition in a newspaper-printing factory. *Organization Science*, 27(3), 573–593.

Atkinson, P., Coffey, A., Delamont, S., Lofland, J. and Lofland, L. eds. (2007). *Handbook of Ethnography*. London: Sage.

Baldessarelli, G. (2021). Emotions and routine dynamics. In L. D'Adderio, K. Dittrich, M. S. Feldman, B. T. Pentland, C. Rerup and D. Seidl, eds., *Cambridge Handbook of Routine Dynamics.* Cambridge: Cambridge University Press.

Bertels, S., Howard-Grenville, J. and Pek, S. (2016). Cultural molding, shielding, and shoring at Oilco: The role of culture in the integration of routines. *Organization Science*, 27(3), 573–593.

Birnholtz, J. P., Cohen, M. D. and Hoch, S. V. (2007). Organizational character: On the regeneration of Camp Poplar Grove. *Organization Science*, 18(2), 315–332.

Blanche, C. and Cohendet, P. (2019). Chapter 1, Remounting a ballet in a different context: A complementary understanding of routines transfer theories. In *Routine Dynamics in Action: Replication and Transformation.* Bingley: Emerald Publishing Limited, pp. 11–30.

Boe-Lillegraven, S. (2019). Chapter 2, Transferring routines across multiple boundaries: A flexible approach. In *Routine Dynamics in Action: Replication and Transformation.* Bingley: Emerald Publishing Limited, pp. 31–53.

Bruns, H. C. (2009). Leveraging functionality in safety routines: Examining the divergence of rules and performance. *Human Relations*, 62(9), 1399–1426.

Bucher, S. and Langley, A. (2016). The interplay of reflective and experimental spaces in interrupting and reorienting Routine Dynamics. *Organization Science*, 27(3), 594–613.

Burrell, J. (2009). The field site as a network: A strategy for locating ethnographic research. *Field Methods*, 21(2), 181–199.

Cohendet, P. S. and Simon, L. O. (2016). Always playable: Recombining routines for creative efficiency at Ubisoft Montreal's video game studio. *Organization Science*, 27(3), 614–632.

Cunliffe, A. L. (2010). Retelling tales of the field. *Organizational Research Methods*, 13(2), 224–239.

Cunliffe, A. L. (2015). Using ethnography in strategy as practice research. In D. Golsorkhi, L. Rouleau, D. Seidl and E. Vaara, eds., *Cambridge Handbook of Strategy as Practice*, 2nd ed. Cambridge: Cambridge University Press.

Cunliffe, A. L. and Karunanayake, G. (2013). Working within hyphen-spaces in ethnographic research: Implications for research identities and practice. *Organizational Research Methods*, 16 (3), 364–392.

D'Adderio, L. (2003). Configuring software, reconfiguring memories: The influence of integrated systems on the reproduction of knowledge and routines. *Industrial and Corporate Change*, 12 (2), 321–350.

D'Adderio, L. (2008). The performativity of routines: Theorising the influence of artefacts and distributed agencies on routines dynamics. *Research Policy*, 37(5), 769–789.

D'Adderio, L. (2014). The replication dilemma unravelled: How organizations enact multiple goals in routine transfer. *Organization Science*, 25(5), 1325-1350.

Danner-Schröder, A. and Geiger, D. (2016). Unravelling the motor of patterning work: Toward an understanding of the microlevel dynamics of standardization and flexibility. *Organization Science*, 27(3), 633–658.

Davis, M. S. (1971). That's interesting! Toward a phenomenology of sociology and a sociology of phenomenology. *Philosophy of the Social Sciences*, 1, 309–344.

Deken, F., Carlile, P. R., Berends, H. and Lauche, K. (2016). Generating novelty through interdependent routines: A process model of routine work. *Organization Science*, 27(3), 659–677.

den Nieuwenboer, N. A., Cunha, J. V. d. and Treviño, L. K. (2017). Middle managers and corruptive routine translation: The social production of deceptive performance. *Organization Science*, 28(5), 781–803.

Dittrich, K., Guérard, S. and Seidl, D. (2016). Talking about routines: The role of reflective talk in routine change. *Organization Science*, 27(3), 678–697.

Dittrich, K. and Seidl, D. (2018). Emerging intentionality in Routine Dynamics: A pragmatist view. *Academy of Management Journal*, 61(1), 111–138.

Doloriert, C. and Sambrook, S. (2012). Organisational autoethnography. *Journal of Organizational Ethnography*, 1(1), 83–95.

Eberhard, J., Frost, A. and Rerup, C. (2019). Chapter 5, The dark side of Routine Dynamics: Deceit and the work of romeo pimps. In *Routine Dynamics in Action: Replication and Transformation*. Bingley: Emerald Publishing Limited, pp. 99–121.

Emerson, R., Fretz, R. I. and Shaw, L. (1995). *Writing Ethnographic Fieldnotes 1995*. Chicago: The University of Chicago Press.

Fachin, F. F. and Langley, A. (2018). Researching organizational concepts processually: The case of identity. In L. Cassell, A. L. Cunliffe and G. Grandy, eds., *SAGE Handbook of Qualitative Business and Management Research Methods*. London: Sage Publications, pp. 308–327.

Feldman, M. S. (2000). Organizational routines as a source of continuous change. *Organization Science*, 11(6), 611–629.

Feldman, M. S. (2003). A performative perspective on stability and change in organizational routines. *Industrial and Corporate Change*, 12(4), 727–752.

Feldman, M. S. (2015). Theory of Routine Dynamics and connections to strategy as practice. In D. Golsorkhi, L. Rouleau, D. Seidl and E. Vaara, eds., *Cambridge Handbook of Strategy as Practice*, 2nd ed. Cambridge: Cambridge University Press, pp. 320–333.

Feldman, M. S. (2016). Routines as process: Past, present and future. In J. Howard-Grenville, C. Rerup, A. Langley and H. Tsoukas, eds., *Organizational Routines. How They Are Created, Maintained, and Changed*. Series: Perspectives on Process Organization Studies. Oxford: Oxford University Press, pp. 23–46.

Feldman, M. S., Bell, J. and Berger, M. T. (2003). *Gaining Access: A Practical Guide for Qualitative Researchers*. Lanham, MD; Oxford: AltaMira; Oxford Publicity Partnership.

Feldman, M. S. and Orlikowski, W. J. (2011). Practicing theory and theorizing practice. *Organization Science*, 22(5), 1240–1253.

Feldman, M. S. and Pentland, B. T. (2003). Reconceptualizing organizational routines as a source of flexibility and change. *Administrative Science Quarterly*, 48(1), 94–118.

Feldman, M. S., Pentland, B. T., D'Adderio, L. and Lazaric, N. (2016). Beyond routines as things: Introduction to the special issue on Routines Dynamics. *Organization Science*, 27(3), 505–513.

Fine, G. A. (1993). Ten lies of ethnography: Moral dilemmas of field research. *Journal of Contemporary Ethnography*, 22(3), 267–294.

Geertz, C. (1973). *The Interpretation of cultures: Selected Essays*. New York: Basic Books.

George, G., Howard-Grenville, J., Joshi, A. and Tihanyi, L. (2016). Understanding and tackling societal grand challenges through management research. *Academy of Management Journal*, 59 (6), 1880–1895.

Glaser, V. (2017). Design performances: How organizations inscribe artifacts to change routines. *Academy of Management Journal*, 60(6), 2126–2154.

Goh, K. and Pentland, B. T. (2019). From actions to paths to patterning: Toward a dynamic theory of patterning in routines. *Academy of Management Journal*, 62(6), 1901–1929.

Golden-Biddle, K. and Locke, K. (1993). Appealing work: An investigation of how ethnographic texts convince. *Organization Science*, 4(4), 595–616.

Grand, S. (2016). *Routines, Strategies and Management: Engaging for Recurrent Creation 'At The Edge'*. Cheltenham: Edward Elgar Publishing.

Hales, M. and Tidd, J. (2009). The practice of routines and representations in design and development. *Industrial and Corporate Change*, 18(4), 551–574.

Hammersley, M. and Atkinson, P. (2007). *Ethnography: Principles in Practice*, 3rd ed. London: Routledge.

Howard, P. N. (2002). Network ethnography and the hypermedia organization: New media, new organizations, new methods. *New Media & Society*, 4(4), 550–574.

Howard-Grenville, J. A. (2005). The persistence of flexible organizational routines: The role of agency and organizational context. *Organization Science*, 16(6), 618–636.

Hyysalo, S., Pollock, N. and Williams, R. A. (2019). Method matters in the social study of technology: Investigating the biographies of artifacts and practices. *Science & Technology Studies*, 32(3), 2–25.

Islam, G. (2015). Practitioners as theorists: Para-ethnography and the collaborative study of contemporary organizations. *Organizational Research Methods*, 18(2), 231–251.

Jarzabkowski, P. A., Bednarek, R. and Cabantous, L. (2015). Conducting global team-based ethnography: Methodological challenges and practical methods. *Human Relations*, 68(1), 3–33.

Jarzabkowski, P. A., Bednarek, R. and Spee, A. P. (2016). The role of artifacts in establishing connectivity within professional routines: A question of entanglement. In J. Howard-Grenville, C. Rerup, A. Langley and H. Tsoukas, eds., *Organizational Routines. How They Are Created, Maintained, and Changed.* Series: Perspectives on Process Organization Studies. Oxford: Oxford University Press, pp. 117–139.

Kemmis, S. (2009). Action research as a practice-based practice. *Educational Action Research*, 17(3), 463–474.

Kemmis, S., McTaggart, R. and Nixon, R. (2013). *The Action Research Planner: Doing Critical Participatory Action Research*. Heidelberg: Springer Science & Business Media.

Kho, J., Spee, A. P. and Gillespie, N. (2019). Chapter 9, Enacting relational expertise to change professional routines in technology-mediated service settings. In *Routine Dynamics in Action: Replication and Transformation*. Bingley: Emerald Publishing Limited, pp. 191–213.

Kiwan, L. and Lazaric, N. (2019). Chapter 8, Learning a new ecology of space and looking for new routines: Experimenting robotics in a surgical team. In *Routine Dynamics in Action: Replication and Transformation*. Bingley: Emerald Publishing Limited, pp. 173–189.

Kremser, W. and Blagoev, B. (2021). The dynamics of prioritizing: How actors temporally pattern complex role–routine ecologies. *Administrative Science Quarterly*, 66(2), 339–379.

Kunda, G. (2013). Reflections on becoming an ethnographer. *Journal of Organizational Ethnography*, 2(1), 4–22.

Langley, A. (1999). Strategies for theorizing from process data. *Academy of Management Review*, 24(4), 691–710.

Law, J. (2004). *After Method: Mess in Social Science Research*. International Library of Sociology. London: Routledge.

LeBaron, C., Christianson, M. K., Garrett, L. and Ilan, R. (2016). Coordinating flexible performance during everyday work: An ethnomethodological study of handoff routines. *Organization Science*, 27(3), 514–534.

Locke, K. (2011). Field research practice in management and organization studies: Reclaiming its tradition of discovery. *Academy of Management Annals*, 5(1), 613–652.

Locke, K., Golden-Biddle, K. and Feldman, M. S. (2008). Making doubt generative: Rethinking the role of doubt in the research process. *Organization Science*, 19(6), 907–918.

Mahringer, C. (2019). *Exploring Routine Ecologies – A Characterization and Integration of Different Perspectives on Routines*. PhD, University of Stuttgart, Stuttgart.

Moeran, B. (2009). From participant observation to observant participation. In S. Ybema, D. Yanow, H. Wels and F. H. Kamsteeg, eds., *Organizational Ethnography: Studying the Complexities of Everyday Life*. Los Angeles: Sage, pp. 139–155.

Murphy, E. and Dingwall, R. (2007). The ethics of ethnography. In P. Atkinson, S. Delamont, J. Lofland and L. Lofland, eds., *Handbook of Ethnography*. Los Angeles: Sage, pp. 339–351.

Pentland, B. T. and Feldman, M. S. (2007). Narrative networks: Patterns of technology and organization. *Organization Science*, 18(5), 781–795.

Pentland, B. T., Mahringer, C., Dittrich, K., Feldman, M. S. and Ryan Wolf, J. (2020). *Process Multiplicity and Process Dynamics: Weaving the Space of Possible Paths*. Working Paper.

Pentland, B. T. and Rueter, H. H. (1994). Organizational routines as grammars of action. *Administrative Science Quarterly*, 39(3), 484–510.

Puri, A. (2007). The web of insights: The art and practice of webnography. *International Journal of Market Research*, 49(3), 387–408.

Rerup, C. and Feldman, M. S. (2011). Routines as a source of change in organizational schemata: The role of trial-and-error learning. *Academy of Management Journal*, 54(3), 577–610.

Rosales, V. (2018). *The Interplay of Roles and Routines Situating, Patterning, and Performances in the Emergency Department: Studier i Företagsekonomi. Serie B*. Doctoral thesis, Umeå University, Umeå.

Rouleau, L., Rond, M. de and Musca, G. (2014). From the ethnographic turn to new forms of organizational ethnography. *Journal of Organizational Ethnography*, 3(1), 2–9.

Roy, D. F. (1959). 'Banana Time' Job satisfaction and informal interaction. *Human Organization*, 18(4), 158–168.

Schmidt, T., Braun, T. and Sydow, J. (2019). Chapter 3, Copying routines for new venture creation: How replication can support entrepreneurial innovation. In *Routine Dynamics in Action: Replication and Transformation*. Bingley: Emerald Publishing Limited, pp. 55–78.

Seaver, N. (2017). Algorithms as culture: Some tactics for the ethnography of algorithmic systems. *Big Data & Society*, 4(2), 1–12.

Sele, K. and Grand, S. (2016). Unpacking the dynamics of ecologies of routines: Mediators and their generative effects in routine interactions. *Organization Science*, 27(3), 722–738.

Shotter, J. (2006). Understanding process from within: An argument for 'withness'-thinking. *Organization Studies*, 27(4), 585–604.

Smets, M., Burke, G., Jarzabkowski, P. A. and Spee, P. (2014). Charting new territory for organizational ethnography. *Journal of Organizational Ethnography*, 3(1), 10–26.

Sonenshein, S. (2016). Routines and creativity: From dualism to duality. *Organization Science*, 27(3), 739–758.

Spee, P., Jarzabkowski, P. A. and Smets, M. (2016). The influence of routine interdependence and skillful accomplishment on the coordination of standardizing and customizing. *Organization Science*, 27(3), 759–781.

Spradley, J. P. (1979). *The Ethnographic Interview*. New York: Holt, Rinehart and Winston.

Spradley, J. P. (1980). *Participant Observation*. Long Grove, IL: Waveland Press.

Strathern, M. (1996). Cutting the network. *The Journal of the Royal Anthropological Institute*, 2(3), 517–535.

Suchman, L. (1987). *Plans and Situated Action*. Cambridge: Cambridge University Press.

Swan, J., Robertson, M. and Newell, S. (2016). Dynamic in-capabilities: The paradox of routines in the ecology of complex innovation. In J. Howard-Grenville, C. Rerup, A. Langley and H. Tsoukas, eds., *Organizational Routines. How They Are Created, Maintained, and Changed*. Series: Perspectives on Process Organization Studies. Oxford: Oxford University Press, pp. 203–229.

Tallberg, L., Jordan, P. and Boyle, M. (2014). The "Green Mile": Crystallization ethnography in an emotive context. *Journal of Organizational Ethnography*, 3(1), 80–95.

Tavory, I. and Timmermans, S. (2014). *Abductive Analysis: Theorizing Qualitative Research*. Chicago: University of Chicago Press.

Tunçalp, D. and Lê, L. P. (2014). (Re)Locating boundaries: A systematic review of online ethnography. *Journal of Organizational Ethnography*, 3(1), 59–79.

van Maanen, J. (2011). Ethnography as work: Some rules of engagement. *Journal of Management Studies*, 48(1), 218–234.

van Maanen, J., Sørensen, J. B. and Mitchell, T. R. (2007). Introduction to Special Topic Forum: The interplay between theory and method. *The Academy of Management Review*, 32(4), 1145–1154.

Watson, T. J. (2001). *In Search of Management: Culture, Chaos and Control in Managerial Work*. London: Cengage Learning EMEA.

Watson, T. J. (2011). Ethnography, reality, and truth: The vital need for studies of 'how things work' in organizations and management. *Journal of Management Studies*, 48(1), 202–217.

Wegener, F. E. and Lorino, P. (2021). Capturing the experience of living forward from within the flow: Fusing 'withness' approach & pragmatist inquiry. In J. Reinecke, R. Suddaby, A. Langley and H. Tsoukas, eds., *Perspectives on Process Organization Studies Vol. 7: About Time: Temporality and History in Organization Studies*. Oxford: Oxford University Press.

Yamauchi, Y. and Hiramoto, T. (2016). Reflexivity of routines: An ethnomethodological investigation of initial service encounters at sushi bars in Tokyo. *Organization Studies*, 37(10), 1473–1499.

Yamauchi, Y. and Hiramoto, T. (2020). Performative achievement of routine recognizability: An analysis of order taking routines at sushi bars. *Journal of Management Studies*, 57(8), 1610–1642.

Yanow, D. (2012). Organizational ethnography between toolbox and world-making. *Journal of Organizational Ethnography*, 1(1), 31–42.

Ybema, S., Yanow, D., Wels, H. and Kamsteeg, F. H., eds. (2009). *Organizational Ethnography: Studying the Complexities of Everyday Life*. Los Angeles: Sage.

Zbaracki, M. J. and Bergen, M. (2010). When truces collapse: A longitudinal study of price-adjustment routines. *Organization Science*, 21(5), 955–972.

Appendix 8.A1 Fieldwork Practices, Puzzles and Insights of Ethnographic Studies of Routine Dynamics

Please note: Papers are listed in chronological order. Where authors published several papers from the same ethnography these have been grouped together. These clustered papers might differ in terms of the subset of data that they draw on.

Study	Empirical context	Focus of fieldwork	Routines	Time of fieldwork	Role	Data Collection	Puzzle/ surprise	Insights
Pentland and Rueter (1994)	Software company	Group: customer support	Customer service	3 months	Observer - occasionally helped with simple tasks	5 days/ week full-time observations, archival data of 335 call records	How can apparently non-routine work display a high degree of regularity?	Members enact specific performances from among a constrained, but potentially large set of possibilities that can be described by a grammar, giving rise to the regular patterns of action we label routines.
Feldman (2000)	Large state university	Group: Student housing	Hiring, training, budgeting, moving-in and damage assessment	4 years	Observer, shifting to participant in last year	1,750h of observations (5 to 10h per week), 20 unstructured interviews at the beginning, multiple documents (e.g., agendas, emails)	How can there be such a thing as a routine that changes?	Routines change as participants respond to outcomes of previous iterations of a routine through repairing, expanding and striving. These internal dynamics promote continuous change.
Feldman (2003)	See above	See above	See above	See above	See above	See above	Why does the budgeting routine not change, even though managers were pushing for change and no one was against it?	Participants use what they understand about how the organization operates to guide their performances within the routine. This understanding may prevent them from enacting the requested changes.
D'Adderio (2003)	Automotive manufacturer	Project: Implementation of a new software in product development	Engineering workflow process	1,5 years	Observer	2 days/ week observations, semi-structured interviews and two additional case studies at other manufacturers	How are knowledge and routines reconfigured when they are embedded in software?	Knowledge and routines are restructured in the process of being codified in the software. Knowledge flows in performing routines are also fundamentally altered in this process.
D'Adderio (2008)		Project: complex vehicle development program of 18 months	Engineering freeze process	1,5 years	Observer	Observations, semi structured interviews and documents from company library, electronic archives, etc.	What are the dynamics between artefactual representations of routines (standard operating procedures, SOPs) and performances?	There is a mutual adaptation between SOPs/ rules and actual performances through iterative cycles of framing, overflowing and reframing of knowledge inputs and actions.

Howard-Grenville (2005)	Semiconductor manufacturer	Group: EnviroTech	Road mapping (in product development)	9 months	Participant (student intern)	Full-time observations (45+ hours/ week), several dozen semi-structured interviews and multiple documents (reports, minutes etc.)	How can a routine that is performed flexibly nonetheless persist over time?	Individuals and groups approach routines with different intentions and different temporal orientations, explaining the flexible use of the routine. Technological, coordination and cultural structures, while not restricting the flexible use of the routine, may constrain its change over time.
Birnholtz, Cohen and Hoch (2007)	Children's summer camp	Organization: the camp	Collective activities, e.g., gathering at flagpole	22 days/ 20 years	2 participants: Birnholtz worked for camp for 20 years; Hoch collected data as volunteer	22 days full-time observations (Hoch)	How can we regard the organization as the same entity over time?	Sameness stems from coherence and similarity of actions at the organizational level, referred to as organizational character. Several regenerative processes support the emergence of a mutually adapted ensemble of actions dispositions that leads members to regard an organization as the same entity over time.
Bruns (2009)	Biology lab	Group: Lab members	Safety	6 months	Observer	Observations, in particular shadowing lab employees, 15 semi-structured interviews and documents	Which factors in individuals and context cause performances of safety routines to differ?	The professional concern of individuals shapes how participants perform and vary safety routines. There is a divergence in performances when the professional concern (i.e., protecting experiments) differs from the organizational concern (i.e., protecting humans).

(*cont.*)

Study	Empirical context	Focus of fieldwork	Routines	Time of fieldwork	Role	Data Collection	Puzzle/ surprise	Insights
Hales and Tidd (2009)	Global company building plants for semiconductor manufacture	Project: A product development program	Product development process	24 weeks	Observer	2 days/ week, 15h of audio recording (e.g., meetings) and full access to project documentation	What is the role of various representations in the performance of routines?	Representations *of* routines (e.g., the central product development artefact) had limited impact on performances, but the representations *from* routines (e.g., PowerPoints, drawings) were highly significant. There is a dialectical and mediating relationship between routines and representations.
Zbaracki and Bergen (2010)	Manufacturing firm	Process: Pricing process	Adjusting prices	2 pricing seasons	Team of 5 observers from organization studies, marketing and economics	Observations during 1 pricing season, >50 interviews with 27 informants (45min to 7h) and various documents (price lists, emails, etc.)	How do truces in performing routines work?	Small price changes proceed through routines as truces that permit stable, but separate, market interpretations by sales and marketing. Large price changes put truces at risk, as latent conflict over information and interests becomes overt.
Rerup and Feldman (2011)	Learning Lab Denmark (LLD), new research venture sponsored	Organisation: LLD	Recruiting, mailing, producing a quarterly magazine, conference organizing, reimbursement, and hotel booking	3 years, with follow-ups 1 and 4 years later	Observer	Observed 50h of meetings; 109 semi structured interviews with 44 different informants, including 14 group interviews; 446 documents.	How is a new espoused organizational schemata enacted through routines?	Routines and organizational schemata are co-constituted through the actions people take in routines. Authors identify two kinds of trial-and-error learning processes: one to solve problems in routines and the other to resolve questions about schemata.
D'Adderio (2014)	Electronics manufacturer	Project: $30m transfer of a complex server from the US to the UK	Production meta-routine and related subroutines (assembly, testing and shipping)	3 years	Observer	2-year observations with 2.5-5h to full day almost daily, attending 120 meetings, 36 semi-structured interviews and multiple documents (emails, flowcharts, etc.)	How does an organization address the replication dilemma of copy exactly and innovate?	Organizational members harness artifacts and communities to establish two sets of ostensive patterns and performances, one supporting alignment (replication) and one improvement (innovation). They maintain a dynamic balance between replication and innovation by enacting them in different proportions.

Yamauchi and Hiramoto (2016)	3 sushi bars in Japan	Process: customer service	Order taking	N/A	Observer	Micro-ethnography: Videotaping of 24 customer visits, using multiple camcorders	How can a routine be performed when participants have varied understandings of the routine?	Reflexivity: An individual's own understanding of a routine is presented and used to organize the activities as a routine. Through this reflexivity routines can be performed without a priori shared understanding.
Yamauchi and Hiramoto (2020)	4 sushi bars in Japan	See above	See above	See above	See above	Micro-ethnography: Videotaping of 35 customer visits, using 4 to 8 camcorders and 6 to 10 voice recorders	How do participants achieve recognizability at the beginning of a routine performance?	Participants draw on performances of other routines and materiality, both of which are seemingly unrelated to the focal routine. Much material and embodied work is conducted in order to make the routine recognizable.
Deken et al. (2016)	Automotive firm	Project: A new business model around information-based services	Various routines in product development	21 months	Observer	Initially 1 to 5 days/ week; subsequent months 1 day per month; 68 meetings, 41 formal interviews, 57 informal interviews; documents	Participants considered some routine performances as more divergent than others and different participants evaluated performances differently.	Three types of routine work (stretching, flexing and inventing) generate increasingly novel actions and outcomes. Emerging consequences of such actions can lead to breakdowns and require iterative and cascading episodes of routine work.
Spee et al. (2016)	11 reinsurance firms globally	Process: Deal appraisal	Deal appraisal, broking, client meeting, modelling, business planning	N/A	Team of 3 researchers as observers	280 days of observations, each of them audio-recorded; interviews with underwriters, brokers, modellers and senior executives; documents	What are the implications of interdependent routines in coordinating the relationship between standardization and flexibility?	Performances of intersecting routines amplify the pressure towards either standardization or flexibility. Professionals skilfully orient/ re-orient toward either standardization or flexibility.

(cont.)

Study	Empirical context	Focus of fieldwork	Routines	Time of fieldwork	Role	Data Collection	Puzzle/ surprise	Insights
Jarzabkowski et al. (2016)	25 reinsurance firms globally	See above	See above	3 years	Team of 5 researchers as observers	935 observations in 25 organizations across 15 countries; 382 interviews	How can we theorize a professional routine (rather than an organizational) that stretches across several organizations and involves "tool-of-the-trade"?	Professional actors bring their expert knowledge to bear through the artefact in a way that is both consistent across the profession and yet varied with each localized enactment of the routine.
Bertels et al. (2016)	Major oil producer in Canada	Project: Introduction of operational excellence routine	Operational excellence	5 years	N/A	14 site visits between 1 and 4 days; 4 focus groups, 1 knowledge forum; 82 interviews between 45min and 2h; 17 reports and 6 newsletters	How is a coveted routine that is a poor fit with the organization's culture integrated?	Patterns to enact the coveted routine emerged through a process of cultural moulding (i.e., shaping artifacts and expectations through familiar cultural strategies), shielding (i.e., protecting workarounds) and shoring (i.e., protecting the integrity of the routine)
Danner-Schroeder and Geiger (2016)	High-reliability organization	Group: special unit for worldwide catastrophes	Setup of base operations, triage, marking, search, and rescue	19 months	Participant (volunteer)/ observer	>500h of observations; 12 formal and 45 informal interviews; 5,000 pages of guidelines, handbooks etc.	Routine members described some routines as stable, whereas others were described as flexible. This contradicted the ethnographer's observations indicating sequential variety in all routines.	Participants perceived patterns as stable when they carried out specific aligning and prioritizing activities that lock-stepped performances. They perceived patterns as flexible when they enacted specific selecting and recombining activities.
Sele and Grand (2016)	Artificial intelligence Lab	Group/ project: the lab and specific innovation projects	30 routines grouped into six core tasks: experimenting, funding, publishing, communicating, teaching and socializing	3 years	1 primary observer with the 2nd author joining in occasionally	0.5 to 5 days/ week; 19 semi-structured interviews; >1,500 documents	While the authors were looking for flexibility and change – factors that are commonly associated with innovation – they found recurring action patterns.	Routines can be more or less generative, depending on whether actants (human or non-human) traveling across routines maintain or modify connections between routines.

Cohendet and Simon (2016)	Video game company	Project: 'Always Playable'	Creation, conception and production routines in product development	Almost 20 years	2 researchers with long-term relationships in varying roles	3 data sets: interview-based case study (13 interviews) with 12 days of observation; ethnography of 22 months; 72 days of action research	How is creativity restored after a major disruption?	Restoring creativity entailed breaking, partitioning, and recombining aspects from different routines.
Sonenshein (2016)	Boutique retailer	Organization: the retailer	Merchandising routine	Several years	Observer/ participant	62,5h of observations; 60 interviews with corporate managers, regional managers and store employees; 151 documents	How can routines enact familiar patterns of action that nonetheless differ across space and time (i.e., familiar novelty)?	Personalizing and depersonalizing (i.e., to what extent participants intertwine their idiosyncratic self with the routine) produces patterns of familiar novelty. Creativity and routine are a duality, mutually constitutive of each other.
Dittrich, Guerard and Seidl (2016)	Pharmaceutical start-up	Group/ organization: production and operations	Six routines: producing cell tissues, assembling plates, shipping, warehousing, project management, laboratory organization and maintenance	1 year	Observer	2 to 3 full days/ week; 30 semi-structured interviews; 8,000 internal documents	Authors expected primarily nonverbal actions and found that people talked a lot about the routine, both while performing it and in other settings.	Talk enables routine participants to collectively reflect on the routine and work out new ways of enacting it through (1) naming and situating, (2) envisioning and exploring and (3) evaluating and questioning. Authors identify two types of reflective talk.
Dittrich and Seidl (2018)	See above	See above	See above	See above	See above	See above	How does using new means in performing routines lead to flexible performances and changes in a routine's pattern?	Participants foreground new means in performing routines, leading them to conceive of new ends-in-view in a specific performance. Relating these new actions to a routine's enacted pattern may lead to updating the goal of the routine and its associated patterns.

(cont.)

Study	Empirical context	Focus of fieldwork	Routines	Time of fieldwork	Role	Data Collection	Puzzle/ surprise	Insights
Aroles and McLean (2016)	Newspaper-printing factory	Organization: the factory	Ink density usage and assessment of newspaper quality	4 phases over 7 years	Observer	Several hundred hours of observations; interviews with managers and workers; documents	How can we go beyond early essentialist and black-boxed images of repetition, stability, and change to capture the complexity, difference, and heterogeneity underlying the repetition of routines in practice?	Stability and change in routines emerge and co-exist through a performative process of difference and repetition. Problems and solutions, facts and concerns, and ideas of good/bad practice emerge from the repetition of routines.
Bucher and Langley (2016)	Two teaching hospitals	Project: Initiatives aimed at changing patient processes	Patient routines, e.g., for colon-resurrection	20 and 36 months	Observer	8 days, shadowing professionals and following 1 patient; 42 meetings and workshops; 29 and 23 semi-structured interviews (45min to 2h); 150 documents	The puzzle of recursiveness: how can participants bring about change in performances when these are guided by pre-existing ideas on how to perform the routine?	Participants enact two types of spaces, reflective spaces that enable a novel conceptualization of a routine and experimental spaces that enable the integration of new actions into routine performances.
Grand (2016)	Haut-couture company (Jakob Schlaepfer) and entrepreneurial software engineering company (AdNovum)	Group: the creative studio at Jakob Schlaepfer and the management team at AdNovum	Creation routines at Jakob Schlaepfer (e.g., prototyping) and management routines at AdNovum (e.g., dynamic alignment)	Two 2-month time periods at Jakob Schlaepfer; three years with AdNovum	2 observers in long-term collaboration with both companies	Researchers split observations focusing on different aspects of routines; semi-structured interviews; variety of different documents (catalogues, magazines etc.)	How can companies invent new products on a regular basis? How are multiple managerial engagements routinized as recurrent patterns of action in the face of uncertainty?	At Jakob Schlaepfer, the enactment of six different creation routines and their complementary interplay contributes to recurrent creation 'at the edge.' At AdNovum, different processes of routinizing management actions contribute to the establishment of a new executive management.

Swan et al. (2016)	Biotechnology firms	Project: 11 innovation projects	Three strategic routines (protecting, evolving, and resourcing science) and three 'guesswork' routines (hedging, compressing and reprioritizing)	30 months	Team of two observers	Visiting 9 biotechnology companies four to five times each, attending formal and informal team meetings; minimum of 14 interviews per company; company reports, schedules etc.	How can actors develop routines that progress innovative activities while, at the same time, respond to institutionalized regulations that track a linear path to commercialization?	In the face of uncertainty, actors perform guesswork routines (hedging, compressing and re-prioritizing) to act as if things were predictable. These routines at the level of projects developed in response to strategic routines (protecting, evolving, and resourcing science) that reflect the concerns of the wider ecology of organizations.
Aggerholm and Asmuss (2016)	Two private organizations	Process: Performance appraisal interview	Performance appraisal interview	4 years	Observer	Micro-ethnography: 22h of video-recordings of 13 performance appraisal interviews; follow-up non-structured interviews with each participant	How does social interaction and negotiation of power in micro-level routines relate to the performance of larger routines?	Power serves as an interactional resource available to co-participants in the accomplishment and negotiation of micro-level routines. Traditional power relations between manager and employee can be reverted and changed by means of interactional negotiations.
LeBaron et al. (2016)	Large hospital	Process: Handoff in intensive care unit (ICU)	Handoff	N/A	Observer	Micro-ethnography: Video-recording of 262 handoffs within 27 sessions; semi structured interviews with 8 physicians; informal interactions in ICU	Flexible adaptation poses a coordination challenge: the performance must be flexible enough, but it must also remain mutually intelligible so that participants can move forward.	There is ongoing coordination: Physicians use the sequential features of the handoff routine – i.e., the expected moves and their expected sequence – to adapt each performance of the routine to the unique needs of each patient.

(cont.)

Study	Empirical context	Focus of fieldwork	Routines	Time of fieldwork	Role	Data Collection	Puzzle/ surprise	Insights
Glaser (2017)	Law enforcement agency	Project: Development of a game-theoretic tool to change patrolling routines	Counterterrorism patrolling; fare evasion patrolling	7 months	Participant (unpaid support staff)	10h of observations/ week; informal interviews; public documents, project emails and documents	How do the design activities associated with the creation of the artefact relate to existing theoretical constructs in routine dynamics research?	The author develops the notion of design performances, i.e., actions to create an artefact to intentionally change a routine. Through iterative design performances, participants develop a new socio-material assemblage that influences routine dynamics.
den Nieuwenboer et al. (2017)	Telecommunications firm	Group: desk sales unit	Performance routine	15 months	Observer	307 days of observations, primarily shadowing; 51 meetings; 104 semi-structured interviews with 121 interviewees; emails and formal reports	Employees raised concerns about the ethicality of their performance-related practices. How do middle managers induce and impose routine performances aimed at deceit?	Managers use routines as tools to induce widespread deceptive performance among their subordinates. Through corruptive translation, they deliberately created deviations from the higher-level prescriptions of upper management for the purpose of deceiving.
Rosales (2018)	University hospital	Group: Emergency department	Patient routines: arrival, triage, diagnosis, treatment, and discharge	4 years	Observer	25 visits (total of 136,5h); 3 meetings; 19 interviews; 28 documents	How do emergency departments that require reliable routines and roles enact routines as ongoing accomplishments? How do roles and routines come together in practice?	Both the ostensive aspect of routines and role expectations are 'enacted patterns' which are brought together in performances. Scripted and unscripted patterns of roles and routines provide organizations with stability and flexibility.
Mahringer (2019)	High-tech manufacturing company	Group: Software development team	Eight Scrum routines	1 year	Observer	2 to 3 full days/ week; 19 semi-structured interviews (between 29 and 105 minutes); 5,300 pages of documents; archival data from software	How can performing repetitive patterns of actions facilitate the unfolding of open-ended innovation processes?	Performing routines does not make the open-ended processes more predictable but instead orchestrates the process as it unfolds in action.

Blanche and Cohendet (2019)	Remounting of a ballet production	Group: the two artistic teams involved in replicating the ballet	Choreographic, musical, and design routines	8 months	Observer	Observations in dance studios, rehearsal rooms, and performance venues; 51 semi-directed formal interviews (45 minutes on average) and 42 informal interviews; 400 photographs and 80 short videos (2min. each)	How can participants replicate the show as accurately as possible in their local context while maintaining the artistic integrity of the performance?	A meta-routine that was embedded in a strong professional culture structured the transfer. To respect the choreographer's original intent, participants used innovation to achieve replication.
Boe-Lillegraven (2019)	Two large food multinationals	Project: transfer of a quality control system	Several quality control routines	2 years	Observer	Visiting production sites in Asia and Europe, observing training of quality inspectors, spending time with coordinators; shadowing; interviews; various documents	How can routines be transferred across multiple boundaries (e.g., organizational, geographical, cultural)?	The coordinators enacted a flexible, creative and pragmatic approach to transfer by splitting the transfer task into smaller chunks, focusing on artifacts, people and actions. As they blended the performances back into an overarching idea of what to transfer, they shifted away from a system for control to giving advice.
Schmidt et al. (2019)	A 'company builder' creating new ventures	Process: venture creation; prototyping	Set of routines used to build new ventures, focusing on prototyping and two accelerating routines	2 years	Observer	Two to three full days/ week over seven weeks (120 hours of observation); 38 semi-structured interviews; various documents (e.g., emails, web pages)	How can a new venture based on routine replication initiate innovation?	Replicating routines allows for innovating through performing accelerating routines that 'unburden' the innovation process and thereby unleash creative potential.

(cont.)

Study	Empirical context	Focus of fieldwork	Routines	Time of fieldwork	Role	Data Collection	Puzzle/ surprise	Insights
Kho et al. (2019)	Two residential aged care facilities	Process: Telehealth consultations	Telehealth routine and its three sub-patterns (selection, information-gathering and discussion)	15 months	Observer	1 day/ week for 10 to 15 weeks at each facility; 37 semi-structured interviews with 13 professionals	How does the introduction of new technologies influence the work practices of different professionals in interprofessional routine work?	The introduction of telehealth created a jurisdictional conflict over resident care. To overcome conflicts, the three professionals (GPs, nurses and geriatricians) developed and enacted selective and blending expertise.
Kiwan and Lazaric (2019)	Hospital	Group: Gastric bypass surgical team	Laparoscopic surgery vs robotic bariatric surgery	3 years	Observer	Micro-ethnography: Videotaping of 75h of surgery; observation of 90-min debriefing meetings	How does the introduction of a new technology influence the development of experimental and reflective spaces?	The new envisioned robotic surgery is put to test in experimental spaces; interactions are limited to problems and participants are only selectively involved. Reflective spaces are essential for debriefing and identifying new opportunities.
Eberhard et al. (2019)	Sex trafficking	Process: processes used by traffickers to lure women into sex work	Romeo pimp routine	2 years	Observer	3 ride along with police, 3 conferences, 20 public accounts of women and pimps, 27 interviews with police officers, social service workers and attorneys; other research reports	How do pimps use deceit to lure women into sex work?	A deceitful participant can use fraudulent role play and premeditated transitions between role sets to drive the phased emergence of a routine that eventually benefits the deceitful actor at the expense of the other participant.
Addyman (2019)	Construction projects	Project: Transition from the design stage to the construction stage	Transition routines, e.g., organising, governing, contracting, designing	1 year	Participant (autoethnography)	175h audio-recording from 130 meetings; 79 interviews; autoethnographic diary of 170,000 words	Despite the normative life cycle model for large projects, there is considerable newness and incompleteness in the transition between stages. How do project organizations manage this challenge?	The generative mechanisms involved in the (re)creation of organisational routines help to manage the incompleteness associated with transitioning from one life cycle stage to the next.

Addyman et al. (2019)	See above	See above	See above	See above	See above	See above	How are routines re-created through life cycle stage transitions in a project organization?	The authors develop a five-stage process model of transitioning, identify three generative mechanisms involved in re-creating patterns of action across predefined time boundaries and shed light on the relation between predefined time boundaries and available information.
Blagoev and Kremser (2020)	Consulting company	Group: Team of ten consultants	Seven routines	3 months	Participant (project intern)	Full-time observations (45+ hours/ week); 52 semi-structured interviews; internal documents and emails	How did the team manage to temporally coordinate multiple routines without being able to follow a pre-planned, formal schedule?	The dynamics of prioritizing based on person-roles and routines enabled actors to resolve their temporal coordination problem.
Goh and Pentland (2020)	Video game development studio	Project: Development of a new video game	Scrum routines	2 years	Observer	Observations of 50 meetings; 15 interviews; archival data: Scrum sheets with task records, other project documents	What drives a pattern of action to become more or less varied?	Action patterns change dramatically over time depending on project needs. Authors identify generic mechanisms that lead to more (or fewer) paths being enacted.
Geiger, Danner-Schroeder and Kremser (2020)	Fire brigade	Group: firefighters	Multiple routines, e.g., fire-extinguishing, dismantling, triage	N/A	2 observers	Twelve 24h shifts + post-reflection, 10 training days; 54 formal and informal interviews with instructors and firefighters; documents	How are routines coordinated under high levels of temporal uncertainty?	Firefighters gained temporal autonomy (capacity to temporally uncouple from the unfolding situation) by relying on rhythms they developed during training' and by opening up to the situation only when transitioning between routines.

CHAPTER 9

Video Methods and Routine Dynamics

CURTIS LEBARON AND MARLYS K. CHRISTIANSON

9.1 Definition

Video methods encompass a variety of qualitative and quantitative methodological approaches to collecting, analysing and presenting video data. Although video methods have long been used in other fields such as education, communication studies and anthropology, they are still rarely used in research on organizational behaviour (Christianson, 2018). However, recently this has begun to change. There is increasing awareness of the usefulness of video for studying Routine Dynamics (Salvato and Rerup, 2011; Wright, 2019).

Video has many features that make it well-suited to the study of situated action and interactions. Video recordings are a permanent record of what people said and did. Since much of people's activity is outside the scope of their own awareness, video can provide insight into actions or interactions that might have gone unreported. Video can be watched over and over again, which can help researchers deepen their theorizing and increase the accuracy of their findings. Video can be replayed, slowed down and/or zoomed in, which can help researchers notice small details they may not have appreciated on first viewing. Recordings can also be watched alongside other recordings of similar excerpts, which can help the researcher compare different enactments of the same routine. Video can be shared with others – researchers can have independent coders, co-authors or other peers review the video, which allows for additional evaluation of and feedback on the data. Excerpts of video recordings can also be presented to readers, allowing them to be in contact with primary data.

In this chapter, we argue that video methods are a powerful and largely untapped method for studying Routine Dynamics. First, video captures rich data about the performative aspect of routines – that is, actions carried out by specific people at specific times and locations. Second, video can also be analysed to shed light on the ostensive aspect of routines. By looking at a collection of instances of the same routine, researcher can examine the enacted patterns of routines and compare and contrast various performances. They can also see how participants create and account for variations in the routine performance. Last, video recordings enable a close examination of how people are using various modalities for communication such as speech, gaze and gesture (multimodality) and how people are interacting with each other, with objects, and with their environment (socio-materiality).

Our chapter is meant as a primer for routine scholars interested in using video methods – we review past research on video methods and Routine Dynamics; share practical examples and considerations for researchers interested in doing this kind of work; and suggest some generative ways forward.

9.2 Literature Review

Our literature review acknowledges the rich body of research using video in methodological traditions such as ethnomethodology and conversation analysis. While not invoking a Routine Dynamics framework, this research examines many things that Routine Dynamics scholars care about, such as the sequencing and ordering of action within a routine and the recurrent patterns of interaction that can be found across multiple instances of the same routine (e.g., C. Goodwin, 2018; M. H. Goodwin,

2008; Hindmarsh and Pilnick, 2007; Llewellyn and Hindmarsh, 2013; Luff et al., 2000; Mondada, 2014). However, this research has been largely siloed from the study of organizational routines, perhaps because the focus is often more on the pattern of actions and interactions than on the organizational context in which they occur. We touch on some of these studies, but a detailed review of this literature falls outside the scope of this chapter. Please refer to Lopez-Cotarelo (Chapter 4 in this volume) for more information on ethnomethodology.

Our literature review focuses on empirical work in the management and organizations literature where video was central to the research method. Since video data are used so infrequently, we also included research that used video to study organizational routines, even if the authors didn't invoke a Routine Dynamics lens. We began with a general search of the literature, both in Business Source Premier and Google Scholar, for the keyword combination[1]: 'video* + routines'. We used this same keyword combination to conduct a reverse citation search of Feldman and Pentland's (2003) foundational article on Routine Dynamics. This strategy served as a double-check for our initial literature review and is in keeping with past reviews of the Routine Dynamics literature (Howard-Grenville and Rerup, 2017).

The articles we identified in our literature review are summarized in Table 9.1.

Our review revealed four methodological approaches – ethnography, experiments, interaction pattern analysis (IPA) and microethnography – that used video data to study routines. In 40 per cent of the articles we identified, video alone was used to study routines. For the other 60 per cent, video was used in combination with other data in various ways to explore routines.

These approaches varied in the granularity of the analysis of the video data and the amount of video data that were included in the findings. Table 9.1 is organized such that the analysis of the video becomes increasingly detailed and central to the analysis. The presentation of findings in Table 9.1 is interesting not only for what is included but also for what is missing. There are methodological approaches such as discourse analysis or action research that have been used in conjunction with video to study other constructs and might be relevant to the study of Routine Dynamics but, to the best of our knowledge, have not yet been used to do so.

Ethnography. We identified two ethnographies on Routine Dynamics that used video data. Sele and Grand (2016) videotaped scientists building robots when they were studying the ecology of routines taking place in an artificial intelligence lab. Suarez and Montes (2019) video-recorded and photographed the mountaineering expedition team they were observing, as the team engaged in a challenging technical ascent up the Kangshung face of Mount Everest. However, despite this rich data, video was not presented as part of the findings. The role of video in these studies was to provide additional context for the analysis of other kinds of data. Suarez and Montes (2019) wrote, 'The video and photographs turned out to be important data sources because they allowed us to crosscheck information and compare the information obtained from members' diaries and interviews.' (2019: 577). Although video has significant potential for enriching ethnographic findings, video data remained in the background in these studies and did not directly shed light on routines or Routine Dynamics. While we understand the challenge that qualitative scholars face around the kind and amount of data to present from large datasets, video data can help bring the field to life, providing insight into how routines unfold over time and in context.

Experiments. We identified one experiment that used video to study routines. Cohen and Bacdayan (1994) devised an experiment involving pairs of subjects playing a card game to investigate the emergence of organizational routines. They video-recorded the subjects playing multiple trials of the game and used the video to create a precise measure of how long each move in the card game took. Combining this timing data with performance data, they were able to examine the reliability, speed and repetition of action sequences and found

[1] Note: using 'video*' ensures that we also identified words such as 'videos' or 'video-recordings'.

Table 9.1 Research using video data to study organizational Routine Dynamics

Authors	Year	Setting	Article title	Type of video	Other data	Method of analysis
Sele and Grand	2016	Field	Unpacking the dynamics of ecologies of routines: Mediators and their generative effects in routine interactions	Videotaped scientists building and testing robots	Interviews, observations, and archival data	Ethnography
Suarez and Montes	2019	Field	An integrative perspective of organizational responses: Routines, heuristics, and improvisations in a Mount Everest expedition	Videotaped team's ascent up Mount Everest	Interviews, observations, and archival data	Ethnography
Cohen and Bacdayan	1994	Lab	Organizational routines are stored as procedural memory: Evidence from a laboratory study.	Pairs of participants playing card game	None	Experiment
Stachowski, Kaplan and Waller	2009	Simulation lab	The benefits of flexible team interaction during crisis	14 intact nuclear power plant control teams participating in simulation	None	Interaction pattern analysis
Ziljstra, Waller and Phillips	2012	Simulation lab	Setting the tone: Early interaction patterns in swift-starting teams as a predictor of effectiveness	18 new pairs of commercial pilots participating in flight simulation	Expert ratings of performance from direct observation	Interaction pattern analysis
Aggerholm and Asmuß	2016	Field	Power dynamics and performative aspects of organizational routines	Video of 13 performance appraisal interviews	Observations and interviews	Microethnography
LeBaron et al.	2016	Field	Coordinating flexible performance during everyday work: An ethnomethodological study of handoff routines	Video of 262 patient handoffs between ICU physicians	Interviews	Microethnography
Yamauchi and Hiramoto	2016	Field	Reflexivity of routines: An ethnomethodological investigation of initial service encounters at sushi bars in Toyko	Video of customer service interaction between customers, chefs and their assistants at three sushi bars	None	Microethnography
Kiwan and Lazaric	2019	Field	Learning a new ecology of space and looking for new routines: Experimenting robotics in a surgical team	Video of 60 hours of GI surgery using robotics and 15 hours of laparoscopic surgery	Observations, interviews and debriefings using the video	Microethnography
Yamauchi and Hiramoto	2020	Field	Performative achievement of routine recognizability: An analysis of order taking routines at sushi bars	Video of customer service interaction between chefs and customers at four sushi bars	None	Microethnography

that participants' procedural memories contributed to the development of organizational routines. They argue that lab experiments are an underused resource for studying routines. In the lab, researchers can standardize the context and the task that participants face; they can randomize participants to help control for other variables; and they can run multiple trials of the same task – these features are particularly useful for studying how routines emerge or how learning occurs across a number of iterations of the same routine.

Interaction pattern analysis.[2] We identified two interaction pattern analysis (IPA) studies using video to study routines. This quantitative method analyses interaction patterns – recurring sequences of verbal and non-verbal actions – to compare enacted patterns across multiple groups of interdependent actors (often teams). Waller and colleagues have done much of the IPA-based research on routines and have developed a protocol of coding video in 10-second increments (see Waller and Kaplan, 2018, for more details). While the initial coding for IPA is done by coders who record what actor is taking what action at what time, the analysis is conducted by a pattern recognition software algorithm (Magnusson, 2000), which searches large volumes of data and can detect subtle recurring patterns. IPA abstracts up from details of individual performances and analyses the whole dataset for the frequency and characteristics of interaction patterns – for instance, the amount, complexity and timing of interaction patterns.

Although Waller and colleagues do not explicitly draw on a Routine Dynamics framework, they use video to study changes in organizational routines. For instance, Stachowski et al. (2009) analysed video of nuclear power plant crews as they responded to a simulated crisis to examine how patterns of team activity related to effectiveness and found that high-performing teams were more flexible during crisis, exhibiting fewer, shorter, and less complex interaction patterns, in contrast to average teams who continued to enact standardized protocols. Zijlstra et al. (2012) examined video of newly formed flight crews practicing on a flight simulator to investigate how patterns of team activity emerged in the first place. They found that effective teams were 'swift starting', quickly establishing stable and reciprocal patterns of interactions. Even though IPA is primarily situated in the team dynamics literature, it is well-suited for studying Routine Dynamics as well. We anticipate that this approach will gain more widespread use as researchers have increased access to 'big data' involving video and still want to conduct a fine-grained analysis of enacted patterns in routines.

Microethnography. We identified five microethnographic studies using video to study Routine Dynamics. Microethnography is a fine-grained, moment-by-moment analysis of what people say and do, evaluating how people, 'organize their conduct and make sense of each other's actions for the practical purposes at hand. This includes how verbal, bodily, and material resources are deployed in the coordination of work and organizational practice' (Llewellyn and Hindmarsh, 2013: 1403). Microethnography allows for the most detailed examination of what people say and do as they enact routines. Due to the richness of this approach, studies using this method tend to foreground specific aspects of Routine Dynamics for closer examination.

Yamauchi and Hiramoto (2016, 2020) focus on the performative aspect of Routine Dynamics. They studied video of the ordering routine at high-end sushi bars in Tokyo, a routine which is often unfamiliar to customers. Yamauchi and Hiramoto (2016) analysed this video to learn how people navigated differences in understandings about how the routine ought to be performed. They found that understanding was a reflexive part of the routine performance. Instead of relying on a pre-existing shared ostensive, understandings were presented and negotiated within the unfolding performance. Yamauchi and Hiramoto (2020) subsequently used video of customer interactions at sushi bars to study how routines become recognizable. Rather than finding that the ordering routine was a discrete performance, they found that the actions of this routine were entangled with a number of other ongoing (seemingly unrelated)

[2] This method is also known as temporal pattern or T-pattern analysis.

activities. Significant material and embodied work – often relying on factors that were not part of the focal routine – was required to make the initiation and the performance of the ordering routine recognizable.

LeBaron et al. (2016) and Aggerholm and Asmuß (2016) also examine the interactions between participants in their studies but considered both the ostensive and performative aspects of routines. LeBaron et al. (2016) examined video of ICU physician handoffs at shift change to understand the flexible performance of routines. They found that physicians used the sequential features of the routine – the expected moves and the sequence of those moves – to tailor individual performances of the routine to address the needs of specific patients. Yet, despite a strongly shared ostensive, they found significant work of coordination was required to ensure that these varied performances remained mutually intelligible. Aggerholm and Asmuß (2016) analysed video of performance appraisal interviews (PAI) to examine the enactment of power during the performance of routines. They found that the PAI was a negotiated and often contested process. Managers relied on the ostensive aspect of the routine to guide their performance. If employees pushed for more detailed feedback, managers could draw on their structural power to adhere to the routine's standardized assessments. However, employees could attempt to elicit non-standardized assessments through their relational power and the performative aspect of the routine. In both studies, we see that the ostensive and performative aspects of the routine served as interactional resources and that transitions between one 'move' to the next in the routine were important opportunities to ensure mutual intelligibility (LeBaron et al., 2016) or to exert power (Aggerholm and Asmuß, 2016).

Kiwan and Lazaric (2019) foregrounded issues of space and artifacts in their study. They analysed video of bariatric surgery teams as they adopted a new technology (robotic surgery). They found that the introduction of this artifact (robotic system) altered the roles of surgical team members and changed their physical configuration in relation to one another in the operating room (OR), resulting in a performative struggle to enact the bariatric surgery. As the team members adapted to their new roles and configuration, the performative and ostensive aspects of the routine were altered. This process of adaptation was facilitated by regular debriefing, where surgery team members could talk about issues they encountered.

Microethnography allows for the analysis of individual performances as well as enacted patterns over multiple performances. This method also pays particular attention to issues of multimodality and socio-materiality. Altogether, these factors make microethnography a powerful approach for examining Routine Dynamics.

9.3 How to Use Video Methods to Study Routine Dynamics

9.3.1 Research Design and Data Collection

The most fundamental decision that researchers must make is whether or not to use video data in their research project. Video data are not for everyone and not for every research project. While video can capture minute details of organizational activity – discursive, embodied and material – researchers may not want to study behaviour at such a granular level. While video recordings may capture subtleties of organizational activity that escape the conscious awareness of the participants themselves, researchers may want to focus on only the things that the participants 'know' and not what escapes their conscious awareness. Nonetheless, we maintain that video recordings provide an objective and verifiable representation of what 'really' happened. Having such data is not an obligation to use it, and sometimes video recordings become useful in ways that were not foreseen at the beginning of a research project.

Another basic issue of research design is: will researchers create video recordings themselves or will they tap an existing archive? Video technology and data are now popular and prevalent, relatively inexpensive to buy and rather easy to use, which gives researchers lots of options. Most people have mobile phones that include video technology for creating high-quality video recordings. But research projects may require a small cluster of recording devices that capture a variety of views for documenting a variety of phenomena. If researchers choose to create their own video recordings, they should be mindful about the issues and assumptions that accompany seemingly simple cinematic decisions (see Table 9.2). Many organizations are using video as a workplace tool, sometimes creating video archives that may be indefinitely stored and quickly accessed by researchers. When academic researchers use video data that were collected and archived by someone else, they may be exempt from some restrictions of Institutional Review Boards (IRB) – restrictions that can cause delay, increase costs and introduce complications.

Table 9.2 The practical and theoretical implications of cinematic decisions

Cinematic decisions	Commentary about things practical and theoretical
Get recording devices	Video data are only as good as the equipment used to capture them. Sometimes researchers need more than one video camera, such as when they are trying to record all members of a large group, or when the participants are in motion, or when the participants are spatially distributed. In some cases, a wide-angle lens may enable researchers to capture all of the participants with only one camera. The most common mistake is when researchers neglect their audio equipment and recordings, such as when a noisy air-conditioning unit ruins the recording. We recommend microphones that are external to the video camera, such as a boundary microphone located in the middle of a conference table.
Put the camera	When people work within organizations, they regularly come together physically or virtually, moving and talking in relation to each other, surrounded by objects, artifacts and tools within reach. An organizational routine may recur in the same place. Its recurrence in the same place may be part of what makes it a routine. To locate a camera is to make a decision or guess about where phenomena will most likely occur. Like people with bodies, cameras are always located, which affords a particular point of view.
Point the camera	Like the human body, cameras are always oriented or pointed in a particular direction. When people change their orientation, they change what they can see and hear. Orientation in a particular direction may also guide the orientation of others, who align their involvement through co-orientation. The human body may orient in more than one direction at a time (e.g., eyes or head turned to the side while the torso faces forward). Cameras may capture multiple orientations through PIP (picture-in-picture) windows or 360-degree views.
Adjust the camera's scope	Most video cameras have the ability to zoom in or zoom out. If possible, researchers should zoom out until they capture all of the participants within the camera's frame. When people engage in organizational activities and routines, they usually frame their activity by locating and orienting their bodies to show a focus of collective attention, always behaving relative to each other and their material environment. During an activity, participants should not be recorded in isolation from each other because who they are and what they do is inseparable from other people and things. When recording people, researchers should try to capture all body parts that are visible to the participants themselves. For example, if participants can see each other's gestures, then hands should be captured in the recording.
Start recording	The power button is an analytic tool. To turn a video camera on and to begin recording is to make an analytic decision that something is important and should be captured. When video recordings are combined with other methods, researchers need to be thoughtful about the sequence of their data collection. For example, ethnographic interviews may best be conducted after video recordings, because interview questions may disclose information about a research project that could influence a participant's subsequent behaviour.
Move the camera	When organizational routines are unfolding, people may begin moving. To conform to an evolving nexus of activity, researchers may need to move their cameras to capture what people are presenting to each other in the first place, and to researchers who are in the role of eavesdroppers.
Stop recording	When researchers stop the recording, they make an analytic decision that the current activity is no longer important, not worth capturing. We recommend that researchers start recording before anyone comes into the room and then stop recording only after everyone has departed. Sometimes called 'boundary moments' (LeBaron et al., 2009), the beginnings and endings of an organizational routine may be especially rich with information about the routine and its participants.

However, we caution researchers about using video data that were created by someone else, especially someone whose purposes are unknown. Cinematic decisions that may seem simple or straightforward on their face may involve ontological and epistemological assumptions about the nature of organizational activity and how people should be studied (see Table 9.2). Even after video recordings have been created, they can still be manipulated in a variety of ways that destroy their raw authenticity: portions may be deleted, added, rearranged, filtered, masked and so forth. Video taken from television shows and documentaries are usually heavily edited and thus problematic for researchers studying naturally occurring interactions, who should not thoughtlessly cede to others basic decisions about what is important.

As suggested by Table 9.2, video methods support both positivist and constructionist attitudes in research and scholarship. On the one hand, video methods may be used to discover and document 'reality' in the world, providing substantial answers to questions such as: What does an organizational routine look and sound like? What do Routine Dynamics look and sound like? How do people speak and move in relation to each other and their material environment when they are engaged in a dynamic routine? Answers to such questions may be located in the video recording and made available to all who want to watch and listen. On the other hand, video methods are only as good as the researchers who employ them. Researchers decide what to record and what to analyse, which makes them an author of any 'reality' they discover. On the one hand, video cameras are like vacuums that capture the details of an unfolding activity. On the other hand, video cameras are like a spray gun that paints a world of details through the user's attention to them. Through their use of video methods, researchers help to create the very objects of their study.

9.3.2 Data Analysis

When researchers are ready to analyse their video data they should proceed methodically. The volume and rich detail of video recordings can sometimes seem overwhelming. An analyst may watch an hour of their video data and have a feeling of panic that there is 'nothing there'. In our experience, there is always something there. First, we recommend that researchers log all of their video data. Especially if researchers were not in the room when their recording was created, they need to become familiar with what happened. They need to see the forest before they scrutinize the trees. We recommend that researchers watch their entire video recording from beginning to end while making rough notes with timestamps for moments that seem to jump out as interesting or relevant. Analysts may not know why a particular moment jumps out or seems especially relevant, but it is good to follow one's gut instinct when something seems important. The participants themselves may mark or signal the importance of a particular moment as they are enacting it. Certainly, if a fight breaks out and people start screaming or crying, that is noteworthy. In our own research, we have found important phenomena at the boundaries of organizational activity: the openings of meetings, the closings of telephone conversations, a subject's entrance into a room – these are sometimes called 'boundary moments' (LeBaron et al., 2009). Most of the information that an analyst logs will never be revisited. However, we have often gone back to something in our log that did not seem especially relevant initially, but later became relevant as our analysis matured.

After a video recording is logged, analysts may proceed in a few different ways. If they already have a sense of the phenomenon they wish to investigate, they can proceed *abductively*, which is to follow a 'hunch' and seek out a particular phenomenon and its recurrence through the entire video corpus. Working with their video data, researchers may identify the recurring patterns (audible and visible) that constitute a routine, then the differentiating features of Routine Dynamics. If analysts do not know what they are looking for, they may proceed *inductively* by looking for interesting phenomena and patterns in the data. The enactments of an organizational routine are both the same and different. They must be sufficiently the same for participants to recognize that they are engaged in a particular routine with its associated behaviours or requisite actions. Yet the enactments must be sufficiently different or dynamic so that they can be adapted to organizational needs of the moment. Video methods enable researchers to answer a couple of fundamental questions: What do organizational routines look and sound like, and how do these features change from one moment to another? If researchers already have research questions or hypotheses that they are looking to support, they may begin a process of coding and counting phenomena for the purpose of eventually making arguments based on the frequency of certain behaviours; this is a *deductive* process.

Video data are not self-explicating. Researchers need to present video findings and arguments in ways that enable audiences to recognize both the organizational routine and its dynamic variation. Most analysts begin with audible phenomena such as talk in conversation, creating transcriptions of spoken utterances they think are important for their study. Sometimes transcription systems are meticulously detailed in syntax, prose and timing, while other transcriptions are less meticulous and capture mainly the semantic meanings of words (e.g., Brown and Yule, 1983). Occasionally, analysts begin with visual images extracted from video recordings, and then turn their attention to the talk. During organizational activities, visible images usually include more than one person surrounded by objects, artifacts, tools, furniture and architecture, which altogether shape the activity.

9.3.3 Data Samples and Comments

A classic example of an organizational routine is the hiring routine (Feldman and Pentland, 2003). Typically, recruiters first identify and advertise a job opening; then collect and review applications for the position; interview select candidates; rank-order candidates; finally extend offers and negotiate terms. While this hiring routine may be easily recognized and deliberately standardized, it is always dynamic with 'endless variations on the appropriate way to go about hiring people for different kinds of jobs, in different departments, or at different times of the year' (Pentland and Feldman, 2005: 796).

In this section, we look at only a few excerpts from three different job interviews, which are part of a large video corpus of more than 100 interviews. We suppose that any part of the hiring routine is potentially interesting and worth recording, but we focus on job interviews for theoretical and practical reasons. First, the interview is both rich and consequential. The people who usually make hiring decisions come together for an extended and probing conversation that involves the body (e.g., facial expressions) and material artifacts (e.g., resumes). Second, the job interview is relatively accessible to us, occurring within a specified time and place, with relatively stationary participants who are easily captured within the scope of the camera's view. While space constraints prevent us from demonstrating video methods through a full-blown empirical study, we offer some simple observations and comments that relate to video methods. Our observations and comments are intended to demonstrate how video can shed light on Routine Dynamics. For more information about specific methodological approaches for analysing video, the resources listed at the end of this chapter provide more detail. We briefly show how interviews may be similar to and different from each other, providing instantiations of Routine Dynamics.

The four excerpts below represent an escalation of evidence and argument. Excerpt 1 has only one frame of video that some analysts might find meaningful. Excerpt 2 has three frames of video that sequentially depict (from left to right) unfolding interaction. Excerpt 3 has three frames from a different interview that are similar to the action pattern of Excerpt 2. Patterns of interaction that recur across organizational activities may be evidence of an organizational routine. Excerpt 4, which comes from yet another interview, shows a pattern of interaction that is both similar to and different from Excerpts 2 and 3 – potentially an instance of Routine Dynamics. Thus, analysts may need to examine multiple excerpts of video recording, first to establish the existence of an organizational routine, then to show dynamic patterns of audible and visible behaviour. Robust claims about Routine Dynamics must be supported by the empirical details of video recordings. Our excerpts include brief transcriptions of vocal utterance and drawings used to animate the still frames of video.

Excerpt 1: Some researchers may glean a lot of information from a single frame of video, such as ethnographers who work in the tradition of visual anthropology (Collier and Collier, 1986). Ethnographers do not search for natural law or cause-and-effect relationships. Rather, ethnographers look for meaning and meaning making within cultures that may include the researchers themselves (Geertz, 1973). For example, look at the single frame of video below (Figure 9.1), extracted from the opening seconds of a job interview. At a glance, we can see various features of this organizational activity – embodied, material and discursive (talk and/or text). Two people are located in a closed room, sitting at a table across from each other, positioned to make each other an object of attention. They are also oriented towards objects on the table in front of them, within reach, perhaps the residue of past acts of meaning. Their behaviour at this moment is contrasting: the person in white (the recruiter) is speaking and gesturing with one hand while taking notes with the other; the person in black (the applicant) holds her hands under the table, not touching the closed book in front of her where a pen is tucked away.

Figure 9.1 Video captures meaningful aspects of human interaction

What does a job interview look like? Figure 9.1 immediately helps to answer that question. Collectively, visual features contribute to a milieu of potential meaning about job interviews – particularly this job interview – interactively constituted by the participants in the first place and made available to analysts of the video recording. Ethnographic methods have long emphasized observation (Spradley, 1980), and video can help with that. The camera occupies a perspective that gives us and other analysts a 'seat at the table' of this organizational activity; and video recordings include empirical details (embodied, material, and discursive) that are fodder for making meaning. However, video runs at 29 frames per second, combining both visible and audible phenomena, going beyond the meanings that may be gleaned from a single frame.

Excerpt 2: Some research methods emphasize action more than meaning. Conversation analysis (e.g., Nofsinger, 1991), microethnography (e.g., Streeck and Mehus, 2005) and some kinds of discourse analysis (e.g., Mirivel, 2011) show how social action may be incrementally accomplished across spoken utterances and embodied behaviours captured on video. For example, in a study of strategy meetings, Gylfe et al. (2016) examined a social action they called 'bridging': managers made connections between people and ideas through (1) the onset, (2) the apex and (3) the conclusion of particular hand gestures at work. Each stage of the gestures provided for the recognition and interpretation of the other stages in an unfolding sequence of action. Organizational activity, such as a job interview, unfolds through time and space, and a particular audible or visible behaviour is made meaningful, as a form of action, through its temporal and spatial location within unfolding sequences of behaviour.

For example, consider the unfolding sequence of utterances in relation to the sequence of visible behaviour in Figure 9.2.

1	Recruiter:	Tell me a little about what (Figure 9.2a) got you interested in us here
2		at [company name] to come in and to interview (Figure 9.2b)
3	Applicant:	... I was the link between the client and the designing team
4	Recruiter:	Okay (Figure 9.2c)

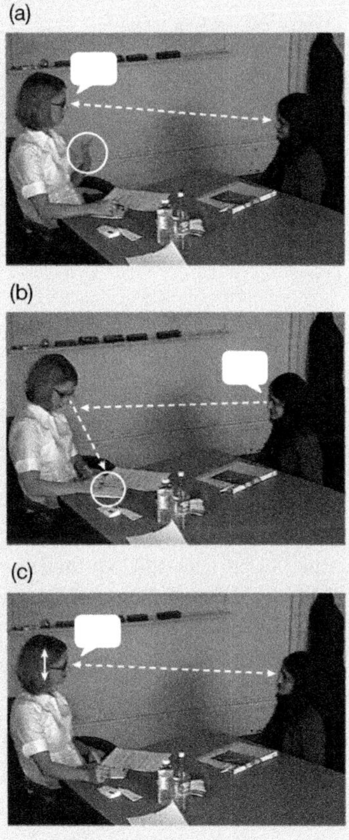

Figure 9.2 (a–c) Video captures unfolding social action

This brief excerpt shows a tri-part of social action. The first action is a 'tell me' question (Line 1), which the recruiter directs towards the applicant through bodily orientation, eye gaze and gesture (Figure 9.2a). The second action is a response or answer from the applicant, who talks (Line 2) and looks towards the recruiter as her audience (Figure 9.2b). The third action is a closing: eventually the applicant stops talking and the recruiter stops writing (Figure 9.2c), which jointly completes their question-answer sequence. The recruiter says 'Okay' (Line 3), which signals at least receipt, perhaps understanding, certainly a readiness to move on with next action (e.g., another question).

The tri-part action sequence in Excerpt 2 pervades our video corpus as a recurring feature of the hiring routine.[3] Each stage of the sequence consummates the immediately prior action and at the same time projects the next. Conversation analysts have shown convincingly that speech acts (Austin, 1962) are not necessarily performed by single utterances, but are instead accomplished across pairs or sets of utterances (Schegloff, 2007). For example, a question does not function as a question until it is answered; an invitation does not do inviting until it is accepted or rejected; a 'question' may become an insult, if that's how the next speaker responds; and so forth. In other words, the *doings* of utterances may largely depend on their location within and relationship to prior and subsequent utterances within unfolding strips of conversation. Moreover, visible behaviours are constantly present, providing for the interpretation of what participants are saying – just as vocal utterances provide for the interpretation of visible behaviour. By looking at each other, the participants may negotiate who speaks next. By taking notes when the applicant is talking, the recruiter *does* receipt or 'hearing'. Although visible behaviours are often silent, they are not secondary to talk and should not be overlooked by analysts.

Excerpt 3: Recurring patterns of visible and audible behaviour are a hallmark of organizational routines. Excerpt 2 and Excerpt 3 resemble each other, showing a strong family resemblance albeit across two different job interviews. Consider the question-answer-next pattern within the following transcription:

1	Recruiter:	I guess my question would be what did you find that you really enjoyed
2		(Figure 9.3a) and what did you find that you didn't enjoy
3	Applicant:	What I enjoyed the most I guess (Figure 9.3b), just for me personally . . .
4		I just think books are so important (Figure 9.3c)

[3] The question-answer-next action sequence in our data is similar to the IRE routine that has been observed in the field of education: teachers initiate (I), students respond (R) and teachers evaluate (E). See, for example, Mehan (1979).

(a)

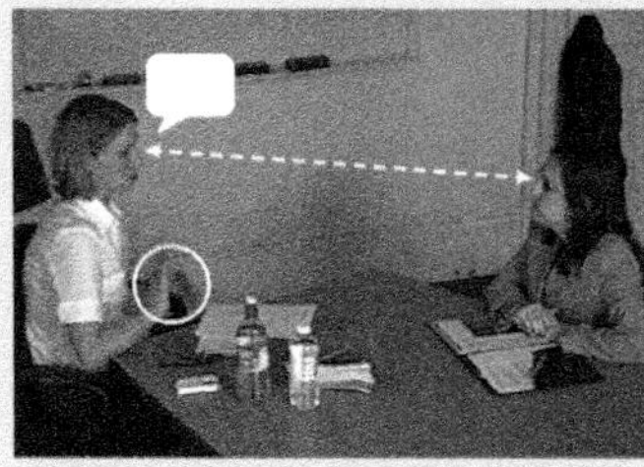

(b)

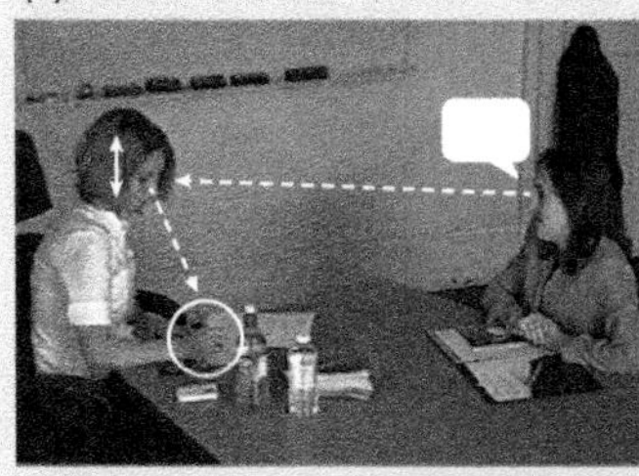

(c)

Figure 9.3 (a–c) Video captures recurring patterns in organizational routines

To begin, the recruiter looks and gestures towards the applicant (see Figures 9.2a and 9.3a) while asking a question about the applicant's past experience (Line 1 in Excerpts 2 and 3). As soon as the applicants begin to respond, the recruiter looks down and writes on the pad of paper in front of her (Figures 9.2b and 9.3b). Instead of saying 'Okay' (Excerpt 2, Line 3) as a turn towards next action, the recruiter repeatedly nods (Figure 9.3c), which at least signals receipt, perhaps understanding, certainly a readiness for next action. The question-answer-next action is an obvious feature of both Excerpts 2 and 3. The pattern of behaviour is audible and visible to both participants and analysts alike. The participants both conduct a hiring routine and signal to each other that a hiring routine is underway.

Excerpt 4: Changes in recurring patterns of visible and audible behaviour may be evidence of Routine Dynamics. Just as a recurring pattern of behaviour may signal or constitute an organizational routine, a deviation from pattern is evidence that the routine is dynamic, malleable or in flux. Sometimes people change their performance of a routine without comment – leaving other participants to recognize the change and its significance. Occasionally, participants explicitly acknowledge that they are changing a pattern of visible and audible behaviour and they may account for the change.

For example, consider the audible and visible features of Excerpt 4, taken from yet another job interview:

1 Recruiter: I guess I'd like to start by having you ask me questions
2 (Figure 9.4a) because I ask all the questions all the time
3 Applicant: In terms of questions, I want to get (Figure 9.4b) a sampling of
4 what's available for me (Figure 9.4c) what kind of things will I
5 be doing
6 Recruiter: Okay ...

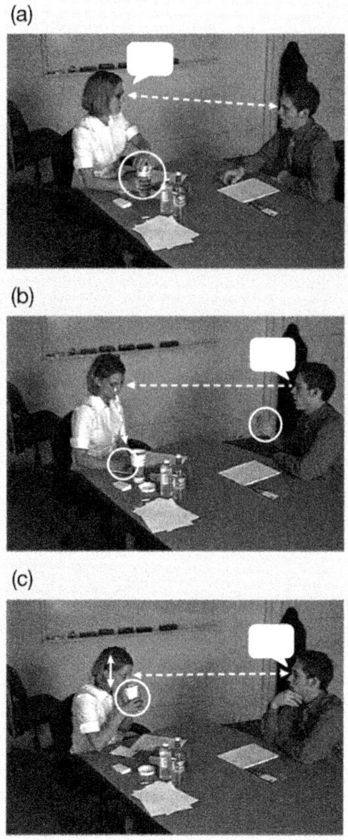

Figure 9.4 (a–c) Video captures Routine Dynamics

Excerpt 4 is both similar to and different from Excerpts 2 and 3. In all three interviews, the participants perform a tri-part sequence to launch their conversation. But Excerpt 4 is different. Instead of following the question-answer-next pattern, the recruiter asks the applicant to produce opening questions (Line 1). She explicitly acknowledges that her request is unusual and even accounts for her behaviour, suggesting that she is tired of asking all the questions (Line 2). Instead of holding her pen at the ready (Figures 9.2a and 9.3a), the recruiter fumbles with her coffee cup (Figure 9.4a), first working to remove the lid, then holding it up to drink (Figure 9.4c). Eventually, the recruiter writes down something (Figure 9.4b) while the applicant produces more questions, but the coffee cup continues to be an object of her attention (Figure 9.4c). When the conversational floor is a scarce resource, a re-allocation of speaking turns by the recruiter may disrupt her ability to get the information she needs. Certainly, her changes move the interview away from the pattern she has established in the prior interviews (Excerpts 1–3). Because organizational routines are sequences of action, changing something at the beginning of a routine can have downstream effects.

Minor deviations in an organizational routine (e.g., question-answer-next) may or may not have significant consequences. Sometimes small phenomena have a substantial outcome, sometimes not. Our purpose is to simply illustrate how video data, vocal and visible patterns of behaviour, can be used to locate and explicate Routine Dynamics. Video methods are useful for studying patterns of interaction and how people indicate recognition, breakdowns or variations from established patterns. These moments are key to understanding Routine Dynamics, which assume that routines have performative aspects (specific performance in specific times and places) and ostensive aspects (enacted patterns). This patterning allows participants to recognize when routines follow previously established patterns but also when they vary their specific performance, if the situation requires. Breakdowns in understanding may prevent people from enacting patterns and the performance of the routine may need to be repaired (Howard-Grenville and Rerup, 2017; LeBaron et al., 2016). Just as the people involved in the routine can make sense of what the other participants are saying and doing, the researcher has access to these same kinds of data through their video recordings.

Our four excerpts in this section are intentionally brief. Researchers who use video methods to study organizational routines and Routine Dynamics will likely want to gather an abundance of data, possibly hundreds of hours of video recording, which would give analysts plenty of instances to identify and explicate. Not only must analysts establish that a particular pattern of interaction constitutes an organizational routine but they must also show that changes to or deviations from the established pattern are nonetheless instances of the routine and not something else entirely. Our video database of job interviews involves dozens of recruiters meeting with dozens of applicants, which enables us to show recurring patterns of interaction, not behaviour that is idiosyncratic to a particular person or interview.

9.4 Guidelines for Methodological Approach and Future Directions

9.4.1 Guidelines

Video methods have great potential for studying organizational phenomena, especially Routine Dynamics. In each of the methods that we have reviewed, there is much more that could be done to leverage the advantages of video to gain insight into the ostensive and performative aspects of routines. Researchers could make better use of video in lab settings – whether experimental or simulation – to study factors that shape the emergence of routines or the evolution of routines over multiple iterations. Researchers could also make better use of video in the field. Despite a rich tradition of ethnographic studies that incorporate video recordings in anthropology (Jacknis, 1988) and sociology (Hindmarsh, 2009), video remains a largely untapped resource in organizational ethnographies.

Whatever methodological approach you use, it's important to follow best practices from that tradition around the collection, analysis and presentation of video data. Be deliberate about what kind of video you collect and how much; use the methodological approach that gives you the best insight into the phenomenon you are interested in; and be thoughtful about how you present video data. We expand on this last point next.

You may need to pay more attention to methodological rigour and transparency with video data than you do with other more established forms of data such as interviews or observations. Why?

Using video data to study organizational phenomena is still uncommon (Christianson, 2018). As with any new method moving into a field, early publications have to do ground-breaking work to explain what the method is and justify why it's useful to editors, reviewers and readers who may not be familiar with it. Early publications help set the stage for future research and may be used as examples by researchers who use video data that conform with one of these methodological applications.

Researchers need to carefully consider how to present video evidence. Video shouldn't be included because it is novel or interesting (LeBaron, 2017). Excerpts or other representations of video data (transcripts, screen captures, etc.) need to be thoughtfully selected and unpacked in the findings to bolster empirical claims. When presenting other kinds of data, researchers work hard to reduce the cognitive load for the reader and make it clear what they should pay attention to in the text – for instance, researchers may use interview pull quotes to precisely illustrate the point that they are making and select key ethnographic observations to complement the narrative they are constructing. This same philosophy of thoughtful data analysis and presentation should apply to video data as well. Any video data you include needs to do 'work' in your paper.

There are translational issues to consider. Standards for what counts as evidence and what counts as a theoretical contribution vary across fields. However, if anything, there are additional demands in our field – larger sample sizes, more comparison across time, etc. There is more consensus about how to analyse and present video data from a quantitative perspective (Waller and Kaplan, 2018), but how to present qualitative video data is still being negotiated in the field of organizational behaviour.

9.4.2 Future Directions

In the near future, the most important development would be for authors to use video methods more often and more robustly in organizational studies. Technological improvements have always been an impetus for new ways of doing research. Developments in video methods in other fields suggest that there are several key issues that are important for researchers to keep in mind going forward. First, advances in video recording technology mean that cameras are getting smaller and more kinds of video are being recorded (surveillance cameras, cell phone video, YouTube videos, etc.). Second, automated video analysis is improving quickly – for instance, facial recognition software is getting more sophisticated, and coding support technology (e.g., Transana or Noldus Observer XT) offers an increasing array of options for researchers. Third, advances in computational social sciences are opening new frontiers in the analysis of 'big data' related to video (Pilny and Poole, 2017). Methods such as ThreadNet (http://routines.broad.msu.edu/resources) which have been used on other kinds of data (i.e., workflow audit data) could also be used for fine-grained analysis of video data. Last, advances in artificial intelligence and Deepfake technology mean that researchers may need to interrogate the trustworthiness of video they did not collect, such as archival or 'found' video (Borel, 2018).

Appendix 9.A1 Methodological Resources for Video-Based Research

Special Issue on Video Methods

LeBaron, C., Jarzabkowski, P., Pratt, M. G. and Fetzer, G. (2018). An introduction to video methods in organizational research. *Organizational Research Methods*, 21(2), 239–260.

Video and Ethnography

Smets, M., Burke, G., Jarzabkowski, P. and Spee, P. (2014). Charting new territory for organizational ethnography: Insights from a team-based video ethnography. *Journal of Organizational Ethnography*, 3(1), 10–26.

Video and EMCA/Microethnography

Heath, C., Hindmarsh, J. and Luff, P. (2010). *Video in Qualitative Research: Analysing Social Interaction in Everyday Life*. Los Angeles: Sage Publications.

Streeck, J., Goodwin, C. and LeBaron, C. (2011). *Embodied Interaction: Language and Body in the Material World*. Cambridge: Cambridge University Press.

Video and Quantitative Methods

Congdon, E. L., Novack, M. A. and Goldin-Meadow, S. (2018). Gesture in experimental studies: How videotape technology can advance psychological theory. *Organizational Research Methods*, 21 (2), 489–499.

Waller, M. J. and Kaplan, S. A. (2018). Systematic behavioral observation for emergent team phenomena: Key considerations for quantitative video-based approaches. *Organizational Research Methods*, 21(2), 500–515.

References

Aggerholm, H. K. and Asmuß, B. (2016). When 'good' is not good enough: Power dynamics and performative aspects of organizational routines. In J. Howard-Grenville, C. Rerup, A. Langley ad H. Tsoukas, (eds.), *Organizational Routines: How They Are Created, Maintained, and Changed*. Oxford: Oxford University Press, Vol. 5, pp. 140–178.

Austin, J. L. (1962). *How to Do Things with Words*. Oxford: Oxford University Press.

Borel, B. (2018). Clicks, lies and videotape. *Scientific American*, 319(4), 38–43.

Brown, G. and Yule, G. (1983). *Cambridge Textbook in Linguistics: Discourse Analysis*. Cambridge: Cambridge University Press.

Christianson, M. K. (2018). Mapping the terrain: The use of video-based research in top-tier organizational journals. *Organizational Research Methods*, 21(2), 261–287.

Cohen, M. D. and Bacdayan, P. (1994). Organizational routines are stored as procedural memory: Evidence from a laboratory study. *Organization Science*, 5(4), 554–568.

Collier, J. and Collier, M. (1986). *Visual Anthropology: Photography as a Research Method*. Albuquerque: University of New Mexico Press.

Feldman, M. S. and Pentland, B. T. (2003). Reconceptualizing organizational routines as a source of flexibility and change. *Administrative Science Quarterly*, 48(1), 94–118.

Geertz, C. (1973). *The Interpretation of Cultures*. New York: Basic Books, Inc.

Goodwin, C. (2018). *Co-operative Action*. Cambridge: Cambridge University Press.

Goodwin, M. H. (2008). *The Hidden Life of Girls: Games of Stance, Status, and Exclusion*. Malden, MA: Blackwell.

Gylfe, P., Franck, H., LeBaron, C. and Mantere, S. (2016). Video methods in strategy research: Focusing on embodied cognition. *Strategic Management Journal*, 37(1), 133–148.

Hindmarsh, J. (2009). Work and the moving image: Past, present, and future. *Sociology*, 43(5), 990–996.

Hindmarsh, J. and Pilnick, A. (2007). Knowing bodies at work: Embodiment and ephemeral teamwork in anaesthesia. *Organization Studies*, 28(9), 1395–1416.

Howard-Grenville, J. and Rerup, C. (2017). A process perspective on organizational routines. In A. Langley and H. Tsoukas, eds., *The SAGE Handbook of Process Organization Studies*. London: Sage Publications, pp. 323–339.

Jacknis, I. (1988). Margaret Mead and Gregory Bateson in Bali: Their use of photography and film. *Cultural Anthropology*, 3(2), 160–177.

Kiwan, L. and Lazaric, N. (2019). Learning a new ecology of space and looking for new routines: Experimenting robotics in a surgical team. In M. S. Feldman, L. D'Adderio, K. Dittrich and P. Jarzabkowski, eds., *Routine Dynamics in Action: Replication and Transformation*, Research in the Sociology of Organizations, Vol 61. Bingley: Emerald Publishing Limited, pp. 173–189.

LeBaron, C. (2017). Leveraging new technologies to enrich and enable management research: AMD's media strategy. *Academy of Management Discoveries*, 3(1), 1–2.

LeBaron, C., Christianson, M. K., Garrett, L. and Ilan, R. (2016). Coordinating flexible performance during everyday work: An ethnomethodological study of handoff routines. *Organization Science*, 27(3), 514–534.

LeBaron, C., Glenn, P. and Thompson, M. P. (2009). Identity work during boundary moments: Managing positive identities through talk and embodied interaction. In L. M. Roberts and J. E. Dutton, (eds.), *Exploring Positive Identities and Organizations: Building Theoretical and Research Foundation*. New York: Routledge, pp. 119–215.

Llewellyn, N. and Hindmarsh, J. (2013). The order problem: Inference and interaction in interactive service work. *Human Relations*, 66(11), 1401–1426.

Luff, P., Hindmarsh, J. and Heath, C. (2000). *Workplace Studies: Recovering Work Practice and Informing System Design*. Cambridge: Cambridge University Press.

Magnusson, M. S. (2000). Discovering hidden time patterns in behavior: T-patterns and their detection. *Behavior Research Methods, Instruments, & Computers*, 32(1), 93–110.

Mehan, H. (1979). *Learning Lessons: Social Organization in the Classroom*. Cambridge, MA: Harvard University Press.

Mirivel, J. (2011). Embodied arguments: Verbal claims and bodily evidence In J. Streeck, C. Goodwin and C. LeBaron, (eds.), *Embodied Interaction: Language and Body in the Material World*. Cambridge: Cambridge University Press, pp. 254–263.

Mondada, L. (2014). The local constitution of multimodal resources for social interaction. *Journal of Pragmatics*, 65, 137–156.

Nofsinger, R. E. (1991). *Everyday Conversation*. London: Sage Publications, Inc.

Pentland, B. T. and Feldman, M. S. (2005). Organizational routines as a unit of analysis. *Industrial and Corporate Change*, 14(5), 793–815.

Pilny, A. and Poole, M. S. (2017). *Group Processes: Data-Driven Computational Approaches*. Berlin: Springer.

Salvato, C. and Rerup, C. (2011). Beyond collective entities: Multilevel research on organizational routines and capabilities. *Journal of Management*, 37(2), 468–490.

Schegloff, E. A. (2007). *Sequence Organization in Interaction: A Primer in Conversation Analysis (Vol. 1)*. Cambridge: Cambridge University Press.

Sele, K. and Grand, S. (2016). Unpacking the dynamics of ecologies of routines: Mediators and their generative effects in routine interactions. *Organization Science*, 27(3), 722–738.

Spradley, J. (1980). *Participant Observation*. New York: Holt, Rinehart, & Winston

Stachowski, A. A., Kaplan, S. A. and Waller, M. J. (2009). The benefits of flexible team interaction during crises. *Journal of Applied Psychology*, 94 (6), 1536–1543.

Streeck, J. and Mehus, S. (2005). Microethnography: The study of practices. In K. L. Fitch and R. E. Sanders, (eds.), *Handbook of Language and Social Interaction*. Mahwah, NJ: Erlbaum, pp. 381–406.

Suarez, F. F. and Montes, J. S. (2019). An integrative perspective of organizational responses: Routines, heuristics, and improvisations in a Mount Everest expedition. *Organization Science*, 30(3), 573–599.

Waller, M. J. and Kaplan, S. A. (2018). Systematic behavioral observation of dynamic phenomena: Key considerations for quantitative video-based approaches. *Organizational Research Methods*, 21(2), 500–516.

Wright, A. (2019). Embodied organizational routines: Explicating a practice understanding. *Journal of Management Inquiry*, 28(2), 153–165.

Yamauchi, Y. and Hiramoto, T. (2016). Reflexivity of routines: An ethnomethodological investigation of initial service encounters at sushi bars in Tokyo. *Organization Studies*, 37(10), 1473–1499.

Yamauchi, Y. and Hiramoto, T. (2020). Performative achievement of routine recognizability: An analysis of order taking routines at sushi bars. *Journal of Management Studies*, 57(8), 1610–1642.

Zijlstra, F. R. H., Waller, M. J. and Phillips, S. I. (2012). Setting the tone: Early interaction patterns in swift-starting teams as a predictor of effectiveness. *European Journal of Work & Organizational Psychology*, 21(5), 749–777.

CHAPTER 10

Field Experiments and Routine Dynamics

HARI BAPUJI, MANPREET HORA AND HUASHAN LI*

10.1 Introduction

Experiments are regarded as powerful techniques for establishing causal relationships and are considered a 'gold standard' for scientific research. Experiments have been widely used in social sciences due to their ability to verify causal relationships and to assure high internal validity (Colquitt, 2008; Lonati et al., 2018). Further, experiments have gained increasing popularity and wide acclaim as they can generate actionable insights for practice and policy. For example, the Nobel Memorial Prize in Economic Sciences was awarded twice in recent years to economists that have pioneered experiments: to Richard Thaler in 2017 for his contributions to behavioural economics based on experiments and to Abhijit Banerjee, Esther Duflo and Michael Kremer in 2019, for their experimental approaches to development economics. This stream of research is built on the work of Daniel Kahneman and Amos Tversky, which challenged well-established rationality assumptions then prevailing in economic theory (Kahneman and Smith, 2002).

Experimental approaches can range from field experiments to laboratory experiments, and from natural experiments to quasi-experiments. Within business and management, experimental research has been increasing in recent years (Podsakoff and Podsakoff, 2019). However, some experimental designs, especially laboratory experiments, have been criticized for artificial manipulation of the research setting and their lack of generalizability, which severely limits practical implications that can be derived from experiments. To address this issue, experimenters started to run experiments in the *field* and rely on natural settings to test their hypotheses (Shadish and Cook, 2009). Unlike researchers using a laboratory experiment design, researchers in field experiments do not have full control over their research settings. As a consequence, the research settings are operated in a *natural* way such that the research findings are valid and practically relevant. Thus, field experiments can leverage the high internal validity of experimental design through manipulation and randomization and achieve high external validity of field research through grounding the tests in a real world setting.

While field experiments can potentially combine the advantages of internal and external validity, they are not easy to adopt to study organizational problems because of issues with access to organizations and control over participants and their roles. Further, field experiments can be time and resource-intensive, which many researchers might not be able to afford. Despite these challenges, field experiments have been used to examine research topics related to Routine Dynamics, such as the emergence of routines (Bapuji et al., 2012), employee communication patterns after mergers (Schweiger and Denisi, 1991), knowledge sharing (Di Stefano, King and Verona, 2014), process transparency between customers and service providers (Buell et al., 2017), and understanding-based routine re-design (Bapuji et al., 2019). These studies reveal that field experiments, if designed well and executed properly, can shed new light on the study of Routine Dynamics. Accordingly, to help routines scholars familiarize themselves with field experiments and use them in

* All authors contributed equally and are listed in alphabetical order.

their studies, in this chapter, we will introduce field experiments and discuss their advantages and disadvantages. Further, we provide guidance on using field experiments to examine research questions related to Routine Dynamics.

10.2 Field Experiments: Advantages and Disadvantages

10.2.1 Field Studies, Experiments and Field Experiments

Empirical methods broadly include field studies and experimental studies, both of which have advantages and disadvantages regarding internal and external validities. Empirical studies that are grounded in real organizational contexts and use interactions with practitioners (i.e., field studies) offer external validity but may lack internal validity because of lack of effective control groups. Examples of such field-based studies are case study, action research, survey and archival data analysis. For example, action research is typically based on qualitative field data, and involves active and direct participation of researchers to help address organizational challenges. Action research studies often use an intervention and thus can generate insights relevant to practice. However, compared to field experiments, action research lacks rigour in execution due to the absence of a control group, which makes the findings vulnerable to alternative explanations.

Recent concerns on endogeneity issues have shown that quantitative field studies are prone to endogeneity issues caused by measurement error; selection bias; omitted variable bias; and simultaneous and dynamic relationship between dependent and independent variables (Ketokivi and McIntosh, 2017). In contrast, laboratory research studies that use randomized subject assignment and controlled research settings generally exhibit strong internal validity but lack external validity given that behaviour in the laboratory might not be representative of that in the real world, and that experiment participants might not be representative of the population of interest (Podsakoff and Podsakoff, 2019). Therefore, field experiments were created to minimize the issues of validity and to leverage the advantages of both field studies and experimental design.

Field experiments help establish causality within real organizational contexts and are defined as 'Studies that induce a change in a randomly selected subset of individuals (or teams, or units) within their natural organizational context, and compare outcomes to a randomly selected group for which the change was not introduced' (Hauser, 2017: 186). In field experiments, interventions are deliberately introduced to observe their effects. Experimenters establish a causal relationship between an independent variable x and a dependent variable y by manipulating x, and then observing the change in the dependent variable y at different levels of x. In experiments, researchers randomly assign participants to experimental conditions. To gauge the importance of the treatment effect, this random assignment of participants is one form to test the experimental conditions. The assignment is generally into two groups, a treatment group and a control group. The treatment group receives an intervention, e.g., changed lighting, redesigned job or changed instructions, while the control group operates as usual. The effects of the intervention are then measured by the difference in the outcome between treatment and control groups. Causality can be established if there is a significant difference between the treatment group and control group regarding the outcome variable, provided: (1) the assignment of participants to the treatment group and control group is random such that each participant has an equal likelihood of being assigned to the treatment group or the control group; (2) the manipulation is clean such that the treatment group and the control group differ only on the manipulated dimensions and not on any other dimension.

We present the advantages and disadvantages of field and experimental methods in Table 10.1 and discuss in the following paragraphs.

Table 10.1 Advantages and disadvantages of field and experimental methods

Research method	Advantages	Disadvantages
Field-based methods	• High external validity • Practically relevant	• Low internal validity
Lab experiments	• High internal validity	• Low external validity
Field experiments	• Balance between internal and external validity • Practically relevant	• Difficult to implement

10.2.2 Advantages of Field Experiments

10.2.2.1 Accounting for (Some) Sources of Endogeneity

While building models to posit and verify causal relationships is desirable in academic research, establishing such relationships requires accounting for several methodological concerns. To identify causally interpretable results, at least three conditions need to be accounted for. First, the independent variable and dependent variable should be correlated. Second, the occurrence of changes in the independent variable should precede the dependent variable. Third, alternative explanations should be ruled out such that changes in the dependent variable can be explained only by changes in the independent variable. In research methods such as survey and archival data analysis, researchers have been developing techniques to address endogeneity issues, but the most convincing solution for endogeneity remains randomized experiments (Lu et al., 2018).

In contrast to other research methods, such as survey studies and research based on secondary data, a field experiment design enables a ceteris paribus situation that helps researchers to isolate the effects of other variables. As participants are randomly assigned to treatment and control groups in a field experiment, the possibility of pre-existing conditions of the participants causing the change in the outcome variable is minimized. At the same time, clean manipulation ensures that the only difference between the treatment group and the control group is the level of intervention. Therefore, researchers can confirm that the change in the outcome variable has only been caused by the intervention.

10.2.2.2 Control over Measurement

Experiments enable researchers to eliminate alternative explanations, and thus increase the internal validity of the research. In contrast, in regression-based field research, the credibility of a causal test depends on the availability of control variables and the accuracy of measurements. However, many variables are not directly observable in routines research, and thus researchers have to rely on indirect measures to represent them. For example, performance is the dependent variable in many routine studies. However, performance itself is latent and thus researchers have to rely on indirect indicators to measure performance. In addition, performance is affected by multiple factors, many of which may not be observable and might vary simultaneously with independent variables. Relying on indirect measures might induce measurement errors and selection biases that raise doubts on the credibility of the results. To account for endogeneity, some studies use instrumental variables in their analyses. However, the choice and quality of instrumental variables depend on the availability of data, and low-quality instrumental variables may create more bias than fixing the endogeneity issues (Semadeni et al., 2014). Conversely, in field experiments, researchers can deliberately create an exogenous variable that captures the change in organizational practices. This allows researchers to design question-driven research instead of being constrained by existing observable variables. In addition, researchers can allow one factor to vary at a time and thus disentangle the forces that drive change in performance to eliminate alternative explanations (Chatterji et al., 2016).

10.2.2.3 Practically Relevant

In contrast to lab experiments, field experiments produce results that are more practically relevant. In laboratory experiments, the research settings are completely controlled by researchers, which also introduces artificiality and thus results may not be applicable to management practices. In contrast, in field experiments, participants are less aware of the research as field experiments are generally implemented by managers or employees within the organization; thus, subjects are less likely to change their behaviour due to observation by researchers. In addition, field experiments can capture factors that cannot be captured in lab experiments, such as the multifarious interactions between employees and managers, and changes in them. These factors make the results more applicable to practice. Further, field experiments examine the outcomes of actual responses rather than intended or imagined responses that might be captured by surveys and interviews. For example, to examine the effect of a redesigned bin on recycling behaviour of individuals, researchers can use a survey method that can capture either intentions to recycle (for a given redesigned bin presented to them in the survey) or recycling behaviour (after giving them a redesigned bin prior to the survey). Both these approaches are less accurate compared to observing their actual behaviour and comparing it to the behaviour of those who did not receive a redesigned bin (i.e., those who retained the old recycling bin). This is because intentions to recycle might not translate into actual action and reported recycling behaviour might be influenced by social desirability biases. Therefore, results based on field experiments can be more confidently used to provide actionable suggestions to change practices.

10.2.3 Disadvantages of Field Experiments

10.2.3.1 Internal Validity Concerns

Internal validity refers to the confidence that a researcher can have about the extent to which a change in the independent variable caused the change in the dependent variable (Podsakoff and Podsakoff, 2019). In experimental studies, internal validity issues arise when the treatment group and the control group differ on more than the intervened dimension. Further, internal validity of field experiments can be compromised by demand effects, unaccounted factors and lack of incentives.

Demand effect refers to 'change in behavior by experimental subjects due to cues about what constitutes appropriate behavior' (Zizzo, 2010: 75). These effects may arise when participants change their behaviours due to cues related to what constitutes proper behaviours and what behaviours are expected by experimenters (Zizzo, 2010). As the intervention differs between treatment and control groups, the cues for expected behaviours are also different. Therefore, the groups may differ not only on the intervention but also on the behavioural expectations that were cued to them; these demand effects might contribute differently to the outcomes in the two groups.

Controls are less precise in field experiments relative to laboratory experiments, as researchers in field experiments do not have control over the research setting, such as physical, psychological and social characteristics of the participants. These unaccounted factors might interact with the intervention to affect the outcome variable. As a result, the reported effects might not solely be caused by the treatment variable but by a combination of both the intervention and background factors (i.e., participant characteristics, physical setting and any unknown factors in the setting). Consequently, results based on field experiments may be prone to alternative explanations. For example, Gossling, Arana and Aguiar-Quintana (2019) found that other than the intervention, towel exchange behaviours in hotels are also affected by guest characteristics, such as nationality, age, length of stay and location of the hotel. In field experiments, it is difficult to have participants of similar profiles in both control and treatment groups. Thus, it is possible that participants in the treatment and control groups might differ in some unknown characteristics that might affect the outcome variable.

Finally, participants might not take the experiment seriously if there is no link between participant actions and consequences to them (Lonati et al., 2018). In other words, participant incentives – both extrinsic and intrinsic – might affect the effectiveness of an intervention. In routines research, a change in a routine might affect participant incentives, which might introduce covariates that might interact with the intervention. Therefore, researchers should pay attention to factors that might affect participant incentives in field experiments.

10.2.3.2 External Validity Concerns

External validity refers to the extent to which research findings in one research setting can be generalized across populations or contexts. Although external validity concerns are fewer for field experiments conducted in organizational settings, they are not completely absent because of the selection of research setting and participant interactions among themselves.

First, organizations that agreed to participate in a field experiment might be different in some dimensions from other organizations that did not participate. This issue is more salient when the selection of organizations is not random. Due to the difficulty in getting access to the research settings, many researchers rely on convenience (rather than random) criteria to select research setting. This might introduce extra variables that might affect the outcome variable, e.g., top management interest or other such signals that the research question is important to the organization. Second, within the research setting, social interactions among participants might interact with the interventions. This effect is particularly stronger for routines research as routines emerge as a consequence of interactions between actors (Bapuji et al., 2012).

10.2.3.3 Implementation Challenges

The implementation challenges in field experiments include difficulties in gaining access to and control over the organizational settings. Gaining access to appropriate research settings is difficult because organizations might be reluctant to participate in field experiments. This is understandable because the interventions might disrupt the daily operation of the organization and hinder the achievement of their performance goals. At the minimum, field experiments cause inconvenience to organizational members who participate in the treatment group and have to perform their roles in ways that are different than they have been accustomed to doing. Not surprisingly, field experiments occupy only a small portion of research articles in major management journals (Eden, 2017; Podsakoff and Podsakoff, 2019). Moreover, even when researchers gain access to a site, they cannot gain full control over it. Therefore, it is difficult to implement full factorial designs in field experiments that manipulate firms in multiple ways, just as researchers can do in laboratory experiments. Consequently, field experiments become more suitable for examining simpler and more direct research questions rather than complex ones.

10.3 Field Experiments to Study Routine Dynamics

10.3.1 Field Experiments in Routines Research

To understand how past research has used field experiments to study organizational routines, we conducted a topic search in the *Web of Science* for 'field experiments' in business and management categories. This resulted in several research studies that have referred to their studies as field experiments, but they did not follow the protocols of field experiments. For example, a study examining the effect of a new store display on consumer behaviour was presented as a field experiment, but it did not involve a control group. As such, it was difficult to identify true field experiments, particularly those that were conducted to study organizational routines. Therefore, we expanded our coverage to include studies that involved an intervention related to what can be considered a routine (e.g., changed instructions to perform a task) and included a treatment and control group. In other words, we focused on any field experiments that involved what one can identify as an organizational routine, irrespective of whether routines theory was used in the study.

As presented in Table 10.2, scholars have used field experiments to study organizational routines of various types, ranging from dining routines to towel changing routines. Also, field experiments were used to study job and office redesign and their consequences to employees. More broadly, field experiments have been predominantly conducted in service settings, such as hotels and restaurants. This is understandable because service sector organizations rely on routines to efficiently and effectively deliver services. It is also possible that these organizations were more willing to give

Table 10.2 Field experiments on organizational routines

Authors (year)	Research question	Research setting and intervention	Findings
Workman and Bommer (2004)	Effect of job redesign on job satisfaction, organizational commitment and performance	*Setting*: A computer technology call centre *Intervention*: Different types of work processes	High-involvement work processes increase job satisfaction, organizational commitment and job performance. Such increase is stronger in teams that have high preference for group work.
Goldstein, Cialdini and Griskevicius (2008)	Effect of message and social identity on towel reuse in hotels	*Setting*: Mid-sized, mid-priced hotel (190 rooms). *Intervention*: Different types of instructions.	Normative appeals (appeals employing descriptive norms) are more effective to evoke consumers' identities as environmentally concerned individuals, leading to increased reuse of towels in hotels.
McElroy and Morrow (2010)	Effect of office redesign on employee perceptions of culture and work-related attitudes	*Setting*: Financial services organization *Intervention*: treatment group assigned to smaller redesigned offices	Employees assigned to redesigned office have more favourable perceptions of culture and work-related attitudes.
Holman, Axtell, Sprigg, Totterdell and Wall (2010)	Effect of job characteristics on job redesign	*Setting*: Large UK healthcare company. *Intervention*: Job redesign with variations in job characteristics, such as job control, participation, skill utilization and feedback	The effect of job redesign intervention on employee wellbeing is mediated by the changes in job characteristics, such as job control, participation, skill utilization and feedback.
Bapuji et al. (2012)	Intermediaries and routine emergence	*Setting*: Small, independently operated hotel *Intervention*: Different procedures for towel changing	Routines emerge when interactions between routine participants are facilitated by intermediaries.
Buell et al. (2017)	Effect of visual transparency of service on customer perception and employee satisfaction.	*Setting*: A university food court *Intervention*: Treatment group with visual transparency of food preparation.	Visual transparency in service procedure increases both customer perceived service quality and service providers' job satisfaction.
Gössling, Araña and Aguiar-Quintana (2019)	Effect of message on towel reuse in hotels	*Setting*: Seven hotels in a large hotel chain *Intervention*: Different types of instructions for towel reuse.	Comprehensive messages that contain normative description of common identities and moral rewards are more effective to increase towel and linen reuse in hotels. This effect is contingent on guest demographics, such as nationality, age, length of stay and repeated visits.
Bapuji et al. (2019)	Effect of routine redesign on routine effectiveness	*Setting*: Small, independently operated hotel *Intervention*: Different procedures for towel changing	Understanding-based redesign that aligns with participants' understanding regarding how to perform their roles in a routine can improve the effectiveness of that routine.

access to their sites because any performance benefits due to interventions would be immediately visible to them.

Researchers have used field experiments for both theory development and theory testing in routines research. For example, Bapuji et al. (2012) used field experiments to examine how routines emerge within an organization. Specifically, by manipulating the towel exchange routine in a hotel, they found that routines emerge when interactions between routine participants are facilitated by intermediaries. Goldstein et al. (2008) examined effective communication strategies to consumers through field experiments in hotels. Their study shows that normative appeals (appeals employing descriptive norms), particularly those that describe how most people behave in a proximate setting, are more effective in evoking consumers' identities as environmentally concerned individuals, thus leading to the increase of towel reuse in hotels.

As field experiments have strong internal validity, they can also be used to test the causal relationships predicted by theories. For example, Buell et al. (2017) examined how visual transparency between service providers and consumers influences job satisfaction of service providers and quality perceptions of customers. Specifically, through two field experiments in food halls in two universities, they found that when customers observed the preparation of food by chefs and the chefs observed the customers, customer satisfaction with food was higher and so was the chefs' job satisfaction. In another study, Gössling et al. (2019) found that comprehensive messages that contain normative description of common identities and moral rewards were more effective in evoking resource conservation awareness in customers, leading to the increase of towel and linen reuse in hotels.

In short, even if field experiments have been few in number, they have made valuable contributions to routines research. Given that field experiments afford both internal and external validity and that they can be used to both develop theory and to test it, field experiments hold promise to further study Routine Dynamics. Accordingly, to help routines scholars use field experiments in their research, we present some guidelines in the following section.

10.3.2 Using Field Experiments

We present a few guidelines to design and conduct field experiments in Figure 10.1 and elaborate on them in the following paragraphs.

10.3.2.1 Research Question and Hypotheses

The first step in designing a field experiment is to clearly identify a research question and formulate hypotheses about relationships among the study variables. Field experiments can be used for different types of research questions. For example, Chatterji et al. (2016) categorized field experiments into two types: *strategy field experiments* that uncover a directional relationship between two variables; *process field experiments* that examine the mechanisms and mediators that link the independent and dependent variables. Similarly, Hauser, Linos and Rogers (2017) categorized field experiments into audit field experiments, procedural field experiments and innovation experiments. *Audit field experiments* aim to test the performance implications of existing processes, while *procedural field* experiments deal with how a changed process would affect outcomes and *innovation field experiments* explore new processes to solve an organizational problem. Contextualizing these to routines research, we suggest that field experiments can be used by routine researchers to examine the emergence of and changes in routines; theoretical mechanisms driving the emergence of and changes in routines; performance consequences of changes in a routine; and theoretical mechanisms driving the performance consequences of changes in a routine.

Although field experiments attempt to address both the external and internal validity concerns, these concerns are not completely eliminated. Therefore, to overcome the external validity challenges, it is suggested that researchers combine field experiments with other research methods; examine the mechanisms through which independent variables affect dependent variables; and use appropriate theoretical perspectives to speculate how background factors might affect the outcome variable (Podsakoff and Podsakoff, 2019).

To enhance the internal validity of the results, it is suggested to include mediating variables that examine the mechanism through which the independent variable affects the dependent variable. For example, following the use of field experiments to establish the relationship between process transparency and customer satisfaction, Buell et al. (2017) also used lab experiments to establish that 'process transparency increases the degree to which customers perceive employee effort, which in turn increases their appreciation of the

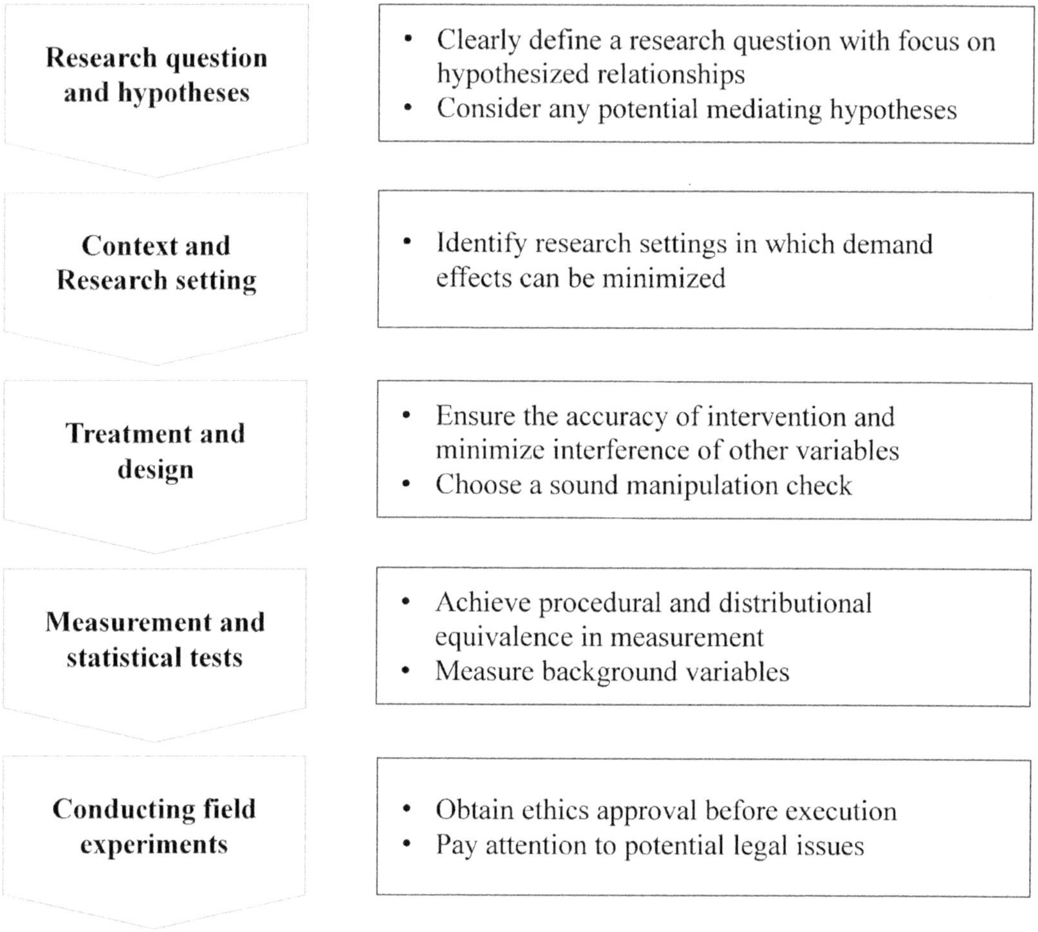

Figure 10.1 Designing and conducting field experiments

employee, leading to increased perceived value of the service' (2017: 1688). Efforts like this can help researchers to unravel the mechanisms driving the change and generalize the findings to other contexts. Similarly, Bapuji et al. (2019) used photo-elicitation interviews to identify the processes through which their redesigned routine worked through participant actions to enhance routine effectiveness: understanding of expected actions (through the processes of *interpreting* and *relating*); understanding of action outcomes (through *functioning* and *rendering* processes); and understanding of implications for interactions (through *communicating* and *facilitating* processes). In short, by clarifying the research question and hypotheses, researchers can choose an appropriate experiment design and also complement it with additional methods to improve both the internal and external validity of their findings.

10.3.2.2 Context and Research Setting

Choosing a proper research setting to test the hypotheses is a critical factor to ensure both internal and external validity. In routines research, a proper research setting is one where routines are widely prevalent, and the hypothesized variables can be easily and most frequently observed. For example, for the study of process transparency, Buell et al. (2017) chose the food preparation process as the research setting because process transparency is relevant and can also be manipulated in that setting.

Once a research setting is selected, the next step is to find an organization that provides access to that setting. Getting access to organizations for field experiments has become less difficult in recent years as managers are now more interested in evidence-based management and development of information technologies (Hauser et al., 2017). In recent years, both researchers and practitioners have become more interested in evidence-based interventions. In routines research, this is an advantage as managers are more interested in evidence of the outcomes of routines. In addition, when negotiating with managers for access to the organizational setting, researchers can specify the potential positive effects of field experiments on employee attitudes, perceptions and behaviours about the firm's commitment to the issue under question and to evidence-based management. Such positive effects can potentially increase employee commitment and improve their performance. In our own experience of conducting a field experiment on a towel-changing routine in a hotel, we highlighted reduced workload and improved efficiency due to the reuse of towels as potential benefits to the organization. In turn, the general manager of the hotel commented that it can also reduce the strain on the backs of housekeepers, which was enough incentive to find out, by allowing us to conduct the experiment, whether the intervention would work.

The development of information technology also offers new opportunities for field experiments. In recent years, firms have been focusing on data-driven decisions and thus track data regarding daily operations and performance. This can help researchers to minimize measurement errors and overcome the inference of other background factors as objective measures can induce less bias than subjective measurements (Hauser et al., 2017).

10.3.2.3 Treatment and Design

Once the research setting has been chosen, participants are then randomly assigned to treatment and control groups. However, randomization is hard to achieve sometimes, especially when the unit of analysis is employees in organizations. This is mainly because experimenters might not have the luxury to assign subjects to groups that they do not naturally reside in. For example, in organizations, tasks are completed by participants that are well fitted into organizational structures rather than randomly assigned by researchers. In such a situation, experimenters might have to adjust their research design or convince managers about the importance of random assignment.

The design of intervention is at the core of field experiments. To eliminate alternative explanations, it is important to make sure that the intervention is precise and interferences are minimal. In an ideal situation, the control group and treatment group should differ only in one dimension (i.e., the intervention). In designing an intervention, a fair comparison is important. A widely used example of unfair comparison in medical experiments is comparing the survival of a treatment group that takes a pill to cure a condition with a control group that takes a pill that may worsen the condition (rather than a placebo). This comparison is unfair because the treatment group and control group differed in more than one dimension, i.e., they took two different medicines, which makes it difficult to know what caused the observed difference.

To determine whether the intervention worked, experimenters use manipulation checks. However, manipulation checks can enhance the demand effect by cuing participants to expected behaviours. Therefore, experimenters should choose an appropriate timing for a manipulation check. Conducting a manipulation check before measuring the outcome variable might reveal the nature of the study and enhance the demand effect. However, conducting manipulation checks after the outcome measurement might incur bias as the effect might have dissipated. Therefore, manipulation checks can be done in the pilot test stage if the researchers include such a stage. If the manipulation check found that the intervention affected only the dependent variable without affecting other confounds, the intervention is effective (Perdue and Summers, 1986). In manipulation checks, researchers can also account for individual-level variables, such as age, gender and education to exclude alternative explanations.

10.3.2.4 Measurement and Statistical Tests

Depending on the research question, routines researchers should devise measures to capture (i) change in routine and (ii) routine outcomes. When measuring the outcome variable, it is important to achieve both procedural equivalence (different variables should be operationalized in an equivalent way) and distributional equivalence (variance should be equivalent within the population). Also, to mitigate external validity concerns, it is suggested to replicate the manipulation in different contexts and capture outcome variables using alternative measures. If the effect is robust across different research settings and measurements, then the generalizability of findings can be established. To eliminate alternative explanations for the change in a dependent variable, it is important to discuss how background factors might affect or interact with the treatment effect, measure some background factors and use them as control variables in analyses.

10.3.2.5 Conducting Field Experiments

Field experiments involve manipulating participants in a real world and thus, researchers should pay attention to potential ethical and legal issues. First, in field experiments, researchers directly manipulate human subjects, and therefore, experimenters should pay attention to risks this might pose to participation. For example, through changing the organizational processes, researchers might indirectly influence issues of importance to employees, such as performance, compensation and relationships with others. As a result, field experiments might affect employee wellbeing. Therefore, researchers designing and conducting field experiments should comply with the rules and regulations related to human ethics. Second, in many field experiments, participants are not aware that they are in an experiment. In other words, their participation is not voluntary but imposed, even if it is part of their job description. As researchers do not take consent from the participants, they should attempt to honour and follow ethics protocols to minimize any concerns. Further, researchers should also pay attention to potential legal issues arising out of experiment conduct or implications of experiment findings, when conducting field experiments.

In sum, to make an effective use of field experiments for research, routines scholars can take a number of steps to clarify the relationships, choose the research setting, design the experiment, select measures and conduct the field experiment. By taking these steps, routines scholars can study a range of important phenomena.

10.3.3 Potential Research Questions Suitable for Field Experiments

Although field experiments are challenging to implement, they also provide an exciting avenue to generate new insights on Routine Dynamics, i.e., the study of internal dynamics of routines (Feldman et al., 2016). According to Feldman et al. (2016), three core observations are intrinsic to research on Routine Dynamics: action in routines is situated; actors are knowledgeable and often reflective; and routines exhibit both stability and change. Therefore, field studies are useful to study routines so that the actions of actual participants can be observed to identify the action patterns that show both stability and change; surveys or interviews are less useful for the phenomenon. Similarly, laboratory experiments cannot reproduce routines because routines emerge from the actions of knowledgeable and reflective actors, not participants who respond to a stimulus. Field studies (e.g., ethnography or case studies) are, however, more prone to researcher biases and preferences, thus making it difficult to verify the explanations or replicate the findings.

Given this, field experiments are particularly suitable to study Routine Dynamics because they involve actual participants (i.e., both knowledgeable and reflective) who perform actions in their natural settings, which generates the pattern of interactions that exhibit both stability and variation. A number of questions related to routines can be empirically studied by using field experiments. However, we would like to discuss the potential of three types of contexts where field experiments are more amenable: fewer participant roles, prominence of artifacts and online or indirect settings.

First, to study Routine Dynamics that capture the richness of the effortful and emergent accomplishment, it is important to identify routines where participant roles are fewer. Please note that we are referring to participant roles (e.g., receptionist, customer service representative, waiter, nurse, doctor) rather than participant numbers. By limiting the participant roles, researchers can focus more on the interactions among the participants. Further, background factors that might interfere with the routine can also be minimized by limiting the participant roles. The importance of limiting participant roles for an effective field experiment is also evidenced by past field experiments. For example, the towel changing routine used only two participant roles: housekeepers and hotel guests (Bapuji et al., 2012; 2019; Goldstein et al., 2008; Gössling et al., 2019). Similarly, the dining routine involved only two roles, chef and diner (Buell et al., 2017).

Second, routines in which artifacts play a prominent role appear to be more suitable for field experiments. This is because implementing an intervention using artifacts is easy compared to using individuals, which might introduce idiosyncratic variation in the intervention. Further, managers are more likely to provide access to settings if the intervention involves mundane objects as opposed to intervening in the way knowledgeable and reflective employees act. Additionally, examining the interactions of 'lifeless' artifacts with lively actors is theoretically exciting, and can generate novel insights about participant actions in routines. Not surprisingly, field experiments in past research have used changes in artifacts such as signs and baskets (Bapuji et al., 2012, 2019; Goldstein et al., 2008; Gössling et al., 2019).

Third, given the increasing intertwining of the physical and virtual lives of individuals, online spaces provide a suitable avenue to conduct field experiments with limited interruptions to the natural functioning of organizations. By splitting participants into control and treatment groups and exposing them to different online content (e.g., a changed signature, an inspirational quote, a different webpage layout, a different image, a different duration of exposure), routines researchers can examine recipient actions and the subsequent emergence of action patterns.

In sum, field experiments are a fruitful research method to study Routine Dynamics and generate novel insights on the emergence and effectiveness of routines. While they are difficult to implement, field experiments can be particularly easy to do in settings that involve fewer participant roles, have prominent presence of artifacts and intertwine with online spaces.

10.4 Conclusion

In this chapter, we discussed the advantages and disadvantages of field experiments as well as how field experiments can be used in Routine Dynamics research. Although field experiments can address endogeneity issues, control measurement and generate practically relevant and actionable insights for practitioners, researchers relying on field experiments have to deal with internal and external validity challenges and implementation challenges. We recommend researchers to consider field experiments as an option for research questions related to Routine Dynamics in future research.

References

Bapuji, H., Hora, M. and Saeed, A. M. (2012). Intentions, intermediaries, and interaction: Examining the emergence of routines. *Journal of Management Studies*, 49(8), 1586–1607.

Bapuji, H., Hora, M., Saeed, A. and Turner, S. (2019). How understanding-based redesign influences the pattern of actions and effectiveness of routines. *Journal of Management*, 45(5), 2132–2162.

Buell, R. W., Kim, T. and Tsay, C.-J. (2017). Creating reciprocal value through operational transparency. *Management Science*, 63(6), 1673–1695.

Chatterji, A. K., Findley, M., Jensen, N. M., Meier, S. and Nielson, D. (2016). Field experiments in strategy research. *Strategic Management Journal*, 37(1), 116–132.

Colquitt, J. A. (2008). From the editors publishing laboratory research in AMJ: A question of when, not if. *Academy of Management Journal*, 51(4), 616–620.

Di Stefano, G., King, A. A. and Verona, G. (2014). Kitchen confidential? Norms for the use of transferred knowledge in gourmet cuisine. *Strategic Management Journal*, 35(11), 1645–1670.

Eden, D. (2017). Field experiments in organizations. *Annual Review of Organizational Psychology and Organizational Behavior*, 4, 91–122.

Feldman, M. S., Pentland, B. T., D'Adderio, L. and Lazaric, N. (2016). Beyond routines as things: Introduction to the special issue on routine dynamics. *Organization Science*, 27(3), 505–513.

Goldstein, N. J., Cialdini, R. B. and Griskevicius, V. (2008). A room with a viewpoint: Using social norms to motivate environmental conservation in hotels. *Journal of Consumer Research*, 35(3), 472–482.

Gossling, S., Arana, J. E. and Aguiar-Quintana, J. T. (2019). Towel reuse in hotels: Importance of normative appeal designs. *Tourism Management*, 70, 273–283.

Hauser, O. P., Linos, E. and Rogers, T. (2017). Innovation with field experiments: Studying organizational behaviors in actual organizations. In B. M. Staw and A. P. Brief, eds., *Research in Organizational Behavior: An Annual Series of Analytical Essays and Critical Reviews*, 37. Bingley: JAI Press, pp. 185–198.

Holman, D. J., Axtell, C. M., Sprigg, C. A., Totterdell, P. and Wall, T. D. (2010). The mediating role of job characteristics in job redesign interventions: A serendipitous quasi-experiment. *Journal of Organizational Behavior*, 31(1), 84–105.

Kahneman, D. and Smith, V. (2002). Foundations of behavioral and experimental economics. *Nobel Prize in Economics Documents*, 1(7).

Ketokivi, M. and McIntosh, C. N. (2017). Addressing the endogeneity dilemma in operations management research: Theoretical, empirical, and pragmatic considerations. *Journal of Operations Management*, 52, 1–14.

Lonati, S., Quiroga, B. F., Zehnder, C. and Antonakis, J. (2018). On doing relevant and rigorous experiments: Review and recommendations. *Journal of Operations Management*, 64, 19–40.

Lu, G., Ding, X. D., Peng, D. X. and Chuang, H. H.-C. (2018). Addressing endogeneity in operations management research: Recent developments, common problems, and directions for future research. *Journal of Operations Management*, 64, 53–64.

McElroy, J. C. and Morrow, P. C. (2010). Employee reactions to office redesign: A naturally occurring quasi-field experiment in a multi-generational setting. *Human Relations*, 63(5), 609–636.

Perdue, B. C. and Summers, J. O. (1986). Checking the success of manipulations in marketing experiments. *Journal of Marketing Research*, 23(4), 317–326.

Podsakoff, P. M. and Podsakoff, N. P. (2019). Experimental designs in management and leadership research: Strengths, limitations, and recommendations for improving publishability. *The Leadership Quarterly*, 30(1), 11–33.

Schweiger, D. M. and Denisi, A. S. (1991). Communication with employees following a merger: A longitudinal-field experiment. *Academy of Management Journal*, 34(1), 110–135.

Semadeni, M., Withers, M. C. and Certo, T. S. (2014). The perils of endogeneity and instrumental variables in strategy research: Understanding through simulations. *Strategic Management Journal*, 35(7), 1070–1079.

Shadish, W. R. and Cook, T. D. (2009). The renaissance of field experimentation in evaluating interventions. *Annual Review of Psychology*, 60, 607–629.

Workman, M. and Bommer, W. (2004). Redesigning computer call center work: A longitudinal field experiment. *Journal of Organizational Behavior*, 25(3), 317–337.

Zizzo, D. J. (2010). Experimenter demand effects in economic experiments. *Experimental Economics*, 13(1), 75–98.

CHAPTER 11 Agent-Based Modelling in Routine Dynamics

DEHUA GAO

11.1 Introduction

Agent-based modelling (ABM)[1] is a valuable methodology for advancing our understanding of organizational routines (Felin and Foss, 2009; Kahl and Meyer, 2016). ABM allows researchers to construct an artificial environment within which autonomous agents are distributed, meet and interact, and complex phenomena emerge at the system level. Through ABM, researchers can gain insights into the micro–macro link and observe the collective effects of agents' social interactions in a controlled manner (Bonabeau, 2002; Neumann and Secchi, 2016; Squazzoni et al., 2014). Therefore, ABM is an ideal or even unique means for organization scientists to conduct conceptual experiments (Fioretti, 2013). It provides opportunities for either generalizing empirical observations or conceiving new theories, and thus potentially brings important advances to Routine Dynamics research (Kahl and Meyer, 2016).

In this chapter, I review how the ABM methodology has been used in Routine Dynamics. An overview of ABM methodology and its use in organization studies is provided in Section 11.2. Then, based on an extensive literature search, a brief review of contemporary ABMs in Routine Dynamics is presented in Section 11.3. Next, some challenges and suggestions for future work in Routine Dynamics are summarized in Section 11.4.

11.2 What Is ABM?

11.2.1 ABM Methodology in Organization Research

ABM methodology can be traced to investigations into complex systems in fields ranging from engineering to economics and social science in the 1990s (Heath et al., 2009). Thereafter, ABM gained in popularity as a tool for exploring complex social and organizational phenomena (Axelrod, 1997; Bonabeau, 2002; Epstein and Axtell, 1996). By creating 'active' agents and their interactive rules that generate a target phenomenon at the macro-level, ABM aims to reproduce real-world actors in an artificial environment (Fioretti, 2013) and derive findings for the aggregate outcome from the agents' individual activities (Wall, 2016), enabling us to explain a variety of complex phenomena from the 'bottom-up'.

Miller (2015) and Neumann and Secchi (2016) highlighted that through making assumptions and relations explicit and clarifying the resulting dynamics, ABM can bridge the gap between qualitative and quantitative methods and advance methodology in organizational behaviours. That is, by combining with qualitative and/or quantitative empirical studies, ABM can replicate a certain quantitative set of data and then help to analyse

The research has been supported by Shandong Provincial Natural Science Foundation (No. ZR2020MG023 and ZR2016GB06), and Shandong Technology and Business University's (SDTBU) Doctoral Foundation (No. BS201606). The author also would like to thank editors Brian T. Pentland and Martha S. Feldman for their constructive comments on an earlier version of the manuscript.

[1] The phrase 'agent-based modelling' is often synonymous with agent-based models, agent-based simulation or agent-based modelling and simulation (Squazzoni, 2010). In this chapter, the abbreviation ABM is used for 'agent-based modelling' and 'agent-based model' under the condition of no ambiguity in context.

resulting emergent properties at the organizational-level (Janssen and Ostrom, 2006). Further, ABM can also be used to statistically test theoretical hypotheses that come out of qualitative data (Lee et al., 2015; Wall, 2016).

In addition, description and prediction are also often commonly expected from users of ABM research (Gómez-Cruz et al., 2017). ABMs, unlike equation-based models, provide description that closely resembles the system under study (Squazzoni, 2012). Moreover, 'prediction' means that ABM can explore the structural, dynamic and functional possibilities of complex organizational systems, and thus give us quantitative forecasting under case-specific scenarios (Gómez-Cruz et al., 2017; Sun et al., 2016).

To sum up, on the one hand, the 'bottom-up' way of ABM provides us a lens to unpack stability and change in routines as emerging results of individual interactive activities between human and non-human actants (Pentland et al., 2011). On the other hand, the simulation-based nature of ABM enables carrying out conceptual experiments regarding Routine Dynamics in a natural, flexible, cost-effective and low-risk way (Bonabeau, 2002) via extensive exploitation of computational power and tools (Chang and Harrington, 2006; Wall, 2016). This makes it extremely valuable when being used to reveal boundary conditions of empirical findings or to investigate the micro-dynamics underpinning the longitudinal patterns in routines that are often difficult or even impossible to study empirically because of the unavailability of data.

11.2.2 Guidelines on How to Use ABM

Fioretti (2013) and Wall (2016) showed that the ABM methodology can capture complex organizational structures and thus be fruitfully employed in specific domains of organizational research. However, ABM is not a panacea. The first task in using ABM should be to determine whether the research object involves interacting agents and shares some common features, including: (1) relations between agents are intricate so that the structure matters and cannot be ignored; (2) the overall behaviour arises out of interacting agents in a 'bottom-up' way and (3) equilibrium is not a concern – rather, researchers focused on 'out-of-equilibrium' dynamics that are relevant for their research programme (Fioretti, 2013: 233).

If these conditions are met, the next step is to clarify the model's scope and boundaries, and decide what level of detail to include or leave behind while addressing their purpose of modelling (Kasaie and Kelton, 2015). Then, both agents' attributes and their interaction rules need to be identified and conceptualized in a correct way. For doing this, the 'KISS' (i.e., Keep It Simple Stupid) principle favours making the model as simple as possible, given the objective of the research (Neumann and Secchi, 2016). In contrast, Edmonds and Moss (2004) proposed another principle called 'KIDS' (i.e., Keep It Descriptive Stupid), which favours making the model complicated and detailed enough to mimic the richness of target systems. However, neither the KISS nor the KIDS approach will always be best – it depends on the research question and intended use of the model (Bruch and Atwell, 2015).

Third, parameterization and calibration are also important points in developing simulation models (Railsback and Grimm, 2019). Here, the term 'parameterization' means to define a set of appropriate parameter values of the model based on knowledge gathered from the real system of interest. However, this is often difficult because of the uncertainty in, or lack of observational data in practice. In this case, calibration methods are needed to help modellers find reasonable parameter values that guarantee the model will reproduce patterns observed in the real system sufficiently well (Grimm et al., 2005; Thiele et al., 2014).

Fourth, when a model is designed and run, it challenges the modeller to express his/her confidence that 'the results of that model bear a direct relation to the system of interest' – which is often called 'validation' (Silverman, 2018). It is worth noting that only validated models have sufficient predictive capability and accuracy of explanation power regarding the targeted reality (Yilmaz, 2006). However, creating validated models is hard work (Kasaie and Kelton, 2015).

The last but not least step is the experimentation and output analysis. The fact is that ABMs in organizational research usually involve a multi-level structure with several parameters that have significant impact on different performance measures (Thiele et al., 2014). Thus, a systematic design of experiments (DOEs) is required to draw valid and objective conclusions in an efficient way (Lorscheid et al., 2012).

Moreover, we need to take care of three themes of currently used techniques in tackling the complexities of ABM output data analysis (Lee et al, 2015; Secchi and Seri, 2017), including

(1) ***Statistical issues in defining the number of appropriate simulation runs***. Given the stochastic nature of most ABMs, knowing how many times the program should be performed becomes extremely relevant information to control type I and type II errors in hypothesis testing of simulation results (Seri and Secchi, 2013). To cope with this problem, Secchi and Seri (2017) provided a 'smallest effect size of interest' (SESOI) approach based on statistical power analysis.
(2) ***Solution space exploration and sensitivity analysis***. By examining certain parameter settings and their corresponding output measures, parameter/input–output solution space exploration provides us additional insight into the ABM's behaviours. Further, sensitivity analysis, as a variation of solution space exploration, seeks to identify parameters for which small variations most impact the model's outputs (Lee et al., 2015). However, this is often challenging work due to the inherent nonlinearity and emergence properties of ABMs.

And **(3)**, ***processing ABM output data over temporal and spatial scales***. Most ABMs are capable of generating both time series data and spatial outputs (Hooten and Wikle, 2010; Lee et al., 2015). In this case, reporting and visualizing ABM results over time and space can not only improve the scientific value of ABM results but also help in gaining valuable insights.

11.2.3 Steps for Developing ABMs

Guidelines on how to use the ABM methodology in organization research are summarized in Section 11.2.2. However, the fact is that ABMs are often developed by steps and not by leaps, and that iterating through the modelling tasks several times is usually a necessity (Railsback and Grimm, 2019). According to the tutorial on ABM given by Macal and North (2010) and Railsback and Grimm's (2019) view of modelling as an 'iterative' circle, the author suggests the following six steps to develop an ABM, as shown in Figure 11.1.

(1) ***Formulate the question***. A clear and concise statement of the research question – e.g., either to zoom in or out on organizational routines – is often by itself a major task. If we do not first know what specific questions the model should answer, it is impossible to make any decisions about the model – i.e., what should and should not be included in it.
(2) ***Assemble hypotheses.*** We need to formulate hypotheses for what essential processes and structures are required to the research question or problem being addressed. Here, bear in mind that we usually begin with the simplest model

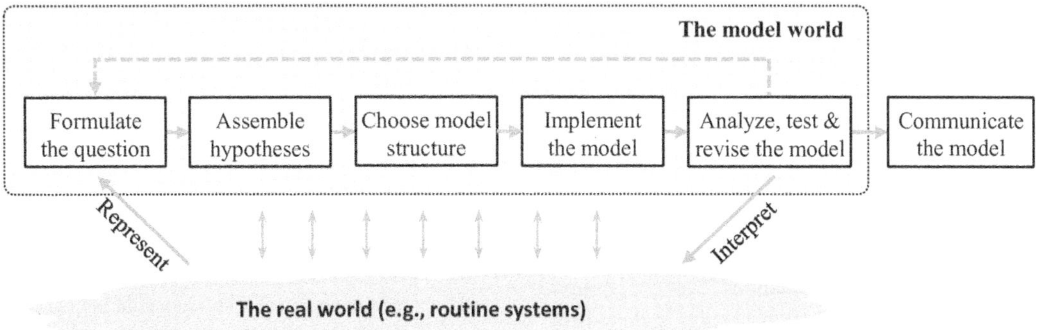

Figure 11.1 Six main steps for developing ABMs.
Source: Adapted from Railsback and Grimm (2019: 7–10)

possible – that is, to focus on the absolute minimum number of factors in the first model version, rather than too much detail.

(3) ***Choose model structure***. Once some hypotheses and simplifications are chosen to represent our system of interest, detailed design of the model should be explicitly stated and formulated, including: (a) choosing appropriate temporal and/or spatial scales which are often determined by the research question you define at the first step, (b) identifying entities and their state variables and (c) describing specific processes and parameters that portray the behaviour or dynamics of the model's entities. Eberlen et al. (2017) argued that these details of the model are necessary not only because there is a protocol such as the ODD mentioned earlier or a best-practice way to proceed, but for the implementation of the model itself.

(4) ***Implement the model***. In this step, we can translate our verbal model description into an 'animated' object using either general, all-purpose software or programming language such as Matlab, or some specially designed software and toolkits such as NetLogo and Repast. However, when considering issues such as usability, ease of learning and cross-platform compatibility etc., specialized software and toolkits often have more advantages than those general software and programming languages.

(5) ***Analyze, test and revise the model***. This is often the most time-consuming and demanding task in the modelling cycle. By testing we refer to 'checking whether a model or submodel is correctly implemented and does what it is supposed to do'; while analysing the model refers to 'trying to understand what a model or submodel system does under certain circumstances' (Railsback and Grimm, 2019: 281). Analysing and testing activities help us to improve – or in other words, revise – the model's implementation and design. Moreover, by analysing, testing and revising the model, we are pursuing the ultimate goal of modelling – i.e., to interpret not only the model system but also patterns in the real world.

(6) ***Communicate the model***. This step means to thoroughly document what we have done and to publish or transfer our findings to peer researchers, scientific readers, clients and even the public. This is beneficial not only for the 'cumulative science' (Axelrod, 1997), but also for getting feedback on what we should do next.

11.3 Contemporary ABMs in Routine Dynamics

11.3.1 An Overview

The literature on Routine Dynamics conceptualized routines as 'generative systems' (Feldman, 2000; Feldman and Pentland, 2003). This focuses attention on the internal structure, process and dynamics from which routines and capabilities emerge and evolve (D'Adderio et al., 2012; Feldman et al., 2016). Felin and Foss (2009) discussed the feasibility of using ABM as an ideal tool in delivering 'careful specifications' of the micro-foundations that lead to particular macro-outcomes like organizational routines or capabilities (Felin and Foss; 2009: 166). Kahl and Meyer (2016) conducted a thorough comparison of four specific agent-based models in organizational routines (Cohen et al., 2014; Gao, et al., 2014; Miller et al., 2012; Pentland et al., 2012). They affirmed that ABM can be used as a fitting and promising method to extend our understanding of organizational routines – and in particular, Routine Dynamics – as emerging results from 'bottom-up'.

In this chapter, I did an extensive search of literature by adopting a similar method[2] as Kahl and Meyer (2016). The time interval of literature

[2] I selected articles containing the word pairs 'routine' and 'agent-based' or 'routine' and 'multi-agent' in their titles, abstracts or keywords from databases including Web of Science, Science Direct, EBSCO, EconBiz, Jstor and SSRN. Further, the same word pairs were also searched in Springer and Google Scholar. In addition, while considering the equivalence between 'agent-based' and 'individual-based' in literature, articles containing the word pair 'routine', 'individual-' and 'models' were also selected and manually judged.

was limited between 2012 (i.e., the time when the first two models appeared) and February 2020. This resulted in a total of eleven contributions, as shown in Table 11.1.[3]

Table 11.1 shows that all the models explore organizational routines as an emerging phenomenon that originates from interactive activities between individual actors, actions and artifacts. Further, research questions in literature can be categorized into the following four types depending on the role ABM plays in people's pursuit of Routine Dynamics studies:

(1) *To mimic and visualize the formation of routines as emerging results from individual interactions.* For example, some scholars linked routines as some organizational outcomes to micro-level actions (Miller et al., 2012; Pentland et al., 2012) and habits (Cohen et al., 2014), while others addressed the interrelation between individual actors and specific kinds of artifacts that plays a fundamental role in Routine Dynamics (Gao et al., 2014, 2018a).
(2) *To observe detailed dynamics – e.g., patterns of action over time – and conduct virtual experiments with a well-controlled manner.* That is, by building up an ABM as the 'Artificial Lab', some manipulated experiments were conducted on the computer, and the role of many factors such as individual learning process (Aggarwal et al., 2017) and memory (Miller et al., 2014), intra-organizational network structure (Gao et al., 2015), cognitive artifacts (Gao et al., 2018a), etc. in Routine Dynamics. Moreover, Gao et al. (2018b) employed ABM in discussing dynamics – i.e., both stability and change – in the replication of routines.
(3) *To clone an 'in-silico' world of some empirical scenarios and examine micro-mechanisms underpinning both stability and change in routines.* Here, two empirically grounded cases are involved. One is the space shuttle Challenger accident in 1986 referred to by Shimazoe and Burton (2013). The other one is the classroom audio and video (AV) equipment management in colleges referred to by Gao et al. (2014).
(4) *To develop and refine theories regarding Routine Dynamics by replication of existing models.* Hauke et al. (2020) duplicated Miller et al.'s (2012) model while simultaneously following the ODD protocol and DOE principles. Then, they investigated some additional scenarios aiming at generalization and refinement of previous theoretical insights on how individuals' memory can affect the formation and performance of routines.

11.3.2 Comparison of the Models

In this section, I present a comparison of the eleven models using the following criteria, including:

(1) ***The purpose***, which determines what aspects of reality should and should not be considered (Grimm et al., 2006). Following the discussion in Section 11.2.1, the main purposes in ABM can be categorized as exploration, description and prediction, and hypothesis testing.
(2) ***Entities***, which is 'a distinct or separate object or actor that behaves as a unit and may interact with other entities or be affected by external environmental factors' (Grimm et al., 2010: 2763).

[3] It's worthy to note that the model by Pentland et al. (2012) is not a strictly agent-based model – as Kahl and Meyer (2016) pointed out that 'one cannot speak of heterogeneous agents in this model as actions represent its basic entities' (Kahl and Meyer, 2016: 92). However, it was nevertheless selected for comparison as it (1) concerns 'actions' in organizational routines and simulates the routines' emergence from mutual interaction between ostensive and performative aspects; (2) directly links micro-level actions to the macro-level dynamics of organizational routines; and (3) has profound influence on some of the following ABMs in routine studies (e.g., Gao et al., 2015, 2018a). But some models, such as Bai et al. (2016) and Yi et al. (2016),were excluded because they only formalize the effects of routines on either the formation and change in IT Capabilities or the process of organizational adaptation – but not focus on the internal structure and dynamics of routines.

Table 11.1 Summary of articles using ABM in Routine Dynamics

	Articles	Description of the model	Main findings
1	Pentland, Feldman, Becker and Liu (2012)	A general model that focused on 'actions' and directly linked individual actions to the macro-level outcome of organizational routines	Focusing on action provides a useful and parsimonious foundation for a theory of organizational routines and capabilities
2	Miller, Pentland and Choi (2012)	A model addressed the dynamic interplay between actions and memory in routines, and examined the role of many distinct forms of individual-level memory during the formation, efficiency and adaptability of organizational routines.	(1) Declarative memory built from past experience facilitates efficient routines in stable contexts. (2) Transactive memory enhances problem-solving efficiency and facilitates adaptation to novel problems. (3) Transactive memory serves as a bridge between individuals' skills and collective capabilities.
3	Miller, Choi and Pentland (2014)		
4	Shimazoe and Burton (2013)	A simulation model with an empirical background of the space shuttle Challenger accident in 1986 that discussed the impact of low-probability uncertainty – e.g., which they called 'near-misses' – in routine changes.	Uncertainty due to lack of requirements and data does not make a difference in frequencies and degrees of underestimation of known risks of near misses vis-à-vis overestimation of reliabilities of existing routines – i.e., justification shift.
5	Cohen, Levinthal and Warglien (2014)	The authors introduced a completely new terminology named 'collective performance' to substitute and encompass concepts involving organizational routines and practices, etc., and presented a comprehensive framework for modelling it based on individual habit systems or skills.	The framework provides a set of core principles and desirable model properties that can serve as a guide in the development of formal models of collective performance.
6	Gao, Deng and Bai (2014)	A model simulated the formation of some specific genuine routines regarding a case of managing the classroom audio and video (AV) equipment in colleges.	(1) Performance feedback loops underlying interactions between actants including both human actors and non-human artifacts are key factors underpinning the formation and dynamics of organizational routines. (2) Imitation by individual actors may accelerate the emergence of routines.
7	Gao, Deng, Zhao, Zhou and Bai (2015)	A model simulates the emergence of organizational routines on connection typologies including regular, random, small-world and scale-free networks, and then investigates the role of cognitive artifacts in Routine Dynamics.	(1) Network topologies among individual actors to some extent determine the dynamic characteristics of organizational routines. (2) The routine system on scale-free networks have a better performance and obtain a much higher coherency and routinization level of collective behaviours than that with other network typologies. (3) The two kinds of knowledge inherent in cognitive artifacts have different effects on Routine Dynamics and when they complement each other, routines are more efficacious.
8	Gao, Squazzoni and Deng (2018a)		
9	Aggarwal, Posen and Workiewicz (2017)	A model focuses on individual learning processes, and simulates the emergence of organizational routines and the role of these routines in influencing heterogeneous firm adaptation to various forms of technological changes.	Exploration policy in the formative period of routine development can influence a firm's capacity to adapt to change in maturity.

Table 11.1 ***(cont.)***

	Articles	Description of the model	Main findings
10	Gao, Squazzoni and Deng (2018b)	A model simulates the micro-process of routines' replication between units within a decentralized organization while simultaneously considering the embeddedness of two distinct kinds of network contexts – e.g., (1) the typology of multiple units in the organization and (2) the coupling relationship between different routines.	(1) With some appropriate level of absorptive capacity, an optimal parameter setting of both intra-organizational and routine networks existed that is beneficial to routine replicating practices and organization adaptation. (2) Variations of template-duplicating errors and innovative activities are instrumental to enhance organizational adaptive changes.
11	Hauke, Achter and Meyer (2020)	A replication of Miller et al.'s (2012) model, but with the ODD (Overview, Design concepts, and Details) protocol and DOE (design of experiments) principles being considered.	(1) Replication of ABMs can be used to develop and refine theory of routines. (2) Using standards such as ODD and DOE is beneficial for replicating simulation models.

There are three interdependent elements – e.g., individual actors, actions and artifacts – that are often conceived as fundamental entities constituting of organizational routines (Pentland et al., 2015).

(3) ***The empirical basis***: Is there any empirical data referred to in the model?
(4) ***Validation techniques*** as well as ***the software*** being used are also discussed due to the requirement that all models be completely validated and the necessity in helping to determine how modellers are creating their ABMs, respectively (Heath et al., 2009).

A comparison of all the models is shown in Table 11.2. First, it is obvious that the main purpose in eight of the eleven models is concentrated on exploration – i.e., by conducting computational experiments, ABMs enable us to probe the structural, procedural and dynamic possibilities of routines as 'generative systems'. Three of the models were used to describe micro-mechanisms underpinning the routines. But there is only one model regarding theoretical prediction (Pentland et al., 2012) and hypothesis testing (Gao et al., 2014), respectively.

Second, except Pentland et al. (2012), which conceives actions as its basic entities, all the remaining models conceive individual actors as the basic entities of their models. In addition, actions and artifacts are also considered as two different entities in Gao et al. (2015) and Gao et al. (2018a, b), respectively. However, there is no model that simultaneously involves all the three entities (e.g., actors, actions and artifacts) as yet, even though the triple relationship between them plays a fundamental role in Routine Dynamics (Pentland et al., 2015).

Third, there are just two articles that based their models on the empirical background (Gao et al., 2014; Shimazoe and Burton, 2013). For contrast, Cohen et al. (2014) provided a general framework for modelling the so-called collective performances, such as organizational routines. This model, together with the other seven, is purely theoretical with neither concrete organizational backgrounds nor empirical data being involved.

Fourth, validation of simulation models is often emphasized in ABM research to ensure that models are accurate representations of the real systems of interest (Heath et al., 2009). However, only five of the eleven models contain the crucial step of simulation validation. Two of them use operational validation (e.g., to validate simulation results against results from the real system) (Gao et al., 2014; Shimazoe and Burton, 2013), and another three use conceptual validation (e.g., to validate the conceptual model) (Gao et al., 2018a, b; Hauke et al., 2020).

Fifth, there are five different kinds of software and toolkits being used (the software is unspecified in Aggarwal et al. 2017). Some general, all-purpose programming languages such as Matlab and Mathematica are used in Pentland et al. (2012) and Miller et al. (2012, 2014), and in

Table 11.2 A comparison of ABMs in Routine Dynamics

	The models	The purpose(s)	Entities	The empirical basis		Validation techniques	Software and toolkits
				Background	Empirical data		
1	Pentland, Feldman, Becker and Liu (2012)	Description and prediction	Actions	Theoretical	None	None	Matlab
2	Miller, Pentland and Choi (2012)	Exploration	Actors	Theoretical	None	None	Matlab
3	Shimazoe and Burton (2013)	Explanation	Actors	Empirical	Qualitative	Non-statistical	Repast Simphony
4	Cohen, Levinthal and Warglien (2014)	Description	Actors	General	None	None	Mathematica
5	Gao, Deng and Bai (2014)	Explanation and Hypothesis testing	Actors/ Artifacts	Empirical	Qualitative/ Quantitative	Statistical	Swarm
6	Miller, Choi and Pentland (2014)	Explanation	Actors	Theoretical	None	None	Matlab
7	Gao, Deng, Zhao, Zhou and Bai (2015)	Exploration	Actors/ Actions	Theoretical	None	None	Swarm
8	Aggarwal, Posen and Workiewicz (2017)	Description	Actors	Theoretical	None	None	Unspecified
9	Gao, Squazzoni and Deng (2018a)	Exploration	Actors/ Artifacts	Theoretical	None	Statistical	Swarm
10	Gao, Squazzoni and Deng (2018b)	Exploration	Units[4]	Theoretical	None	Statistical	NetLogo
11	Hauke , Achter and Meyer (2020)	Exploration	Actors	Theoretical	None	Statistical	NetLogo

Shimazoe and Burton (2013), respectively. ABM-specific software and toolkits such as Repast Simphony (Shimazoe and Burton, 2013), Swarm (Gao et al., 2014, 2015, 2018a) and NetLogo (Gao et al., 2018b; Hauke et al., 2020) are used in the other studies.

Finally, Hauke et al. (2020) replicated the model of Miller et al. (2012) and employed it to develop and refine theory of organizational routines. In their model, standards such as the ODD (Overview, Design concepts and Details) protocol and DOE principles were also used to support the replication, evaluation and further analysis. Here, it is worth noting that even though standardization is believed beneficial for description, documentation as well as communication of ABMs, and the ODD protocol has existed for years and been used in many publications since Grimm et al. (2006; 2010), it still rarely appears in models of routines as shown in Tables 11.1 and 11.2. Nevertheless, the author believes Hauke et al. (2020) did a good job. Standardization using the ODD protocol and DOE principles to a large extent improves the transparency and rigour of models, which helps enhance the credibility of findings, and thus promotes the popularity of ABM among the community of routine researchers. In this sense, we hope

[4] In this model, the authors use the term 'unit' to represent an aggregation of actors and artifacts within an organization.

that the work by Hauke et al. (2020) will bring a fresh start on the journey of ABM in Routine Dynamics.

11.4 Challenges and Direction for Future Work

Using ABM in Routine Dynamics research has many obvious advantages. First, ABMs could help us to vividly depict the internal structure, processes and dynamics from which routines emerge and evolve in time and space. This, to some extent, is beneficial in advancing our understanding of organizational routines, and in particular, the dynamics of routines as a specific branch of research (Kahl and Meyer, 2016). Second, ABM captures the emergent characteristic of routines in a 'bottom-up' way, and provides insights into the micro–macro link (Neumann and Secchi, 2016) between individual actions and routines at the organizational level. Third, a simulation model provides an 'Artificial Laboratory' that enables researchers to conduct flexible, cost-effective and low-risk computational experiments (Bonabeau, 2002). This makes it possible to test theoretical hypotheses of Routine Dynamics that are otherwise difficult or even unrealistic to analyse empirically (Hauke et al., 2020; Silverman, 2018; Smaldino, 2015).

Nevertheless, there are also some huge challenges that impede further development of ABMs in Routine Dynamics research. First, with the practice perspective (Parmigiani and Howard-Grenville, 2011) being more popular in the area of organizational routines in the past few years, researchers have begun to focus on the performative aspect of routines and address the living implementation of specific routines within concrete contexts. This requires the simulation models to be realistic enough to capture the natural world (Edmonds and Moss, 2004), not just theoretical 'toy' models composed of typified agents following bundles of simple behavioural rules. In other words, the simulation models in Routine Dynamics should to some extent be constructed descriptively (i.e., KIDS), rather than simplistically (i.e., KISS). The degree of empirical realism desired in the models depends on its analytical and empirical goals (Bruch and Atwell, 2015). Nevertheless, increasing the descriptivity prerequisite in ABMs may require modellers to start with a relatively complex world, which may make simulation models too cumbersome and difficult to be understood.

The use of ABMs for research on Routine Dynamics entails both zooming in and out themes as two distinct directions of future work (Howard-Grenville et al., 2016). The former, by zooming in, is to peer deep into how the three fundamental elements – e.g., actors, actions and artifacts (Pentland et al., 2015) – interact with each other and together shape routine performance (see models in Aggarwal et al., 2017; Cohen et al., 2014; Gao et al., 2014, 2015, 2018a; Hauke et al., 2020; Miller et al., 2012, 2014; Pentland et al., 2012; Shimazoe and Burton, 2013). The latter, by zooming out, is to understand routines in larger contexts (Kremser and Schreyögg, 2016; Sele and Grand, 2016), concerning interactions between routines in a cluster or the so-called ecology and network of routines (see the model in Gao et al., 2018b). We must be aware that a universal framework for ABM in Routine Dynamics does not exist. Therefore, one needs to develop specific simulation models regarding either the distinct levels of analysis or concrete research questions with which one is confronted.

Next, despite the many advantages of ABMs in Routine Dynamics as mentioned previously, most of the simulation models from literature tend to be highly stylized and have had only limited impact on mainstream routines research. There is an absence of dialogue between ABM and empirical data-driven research within the discipline (Boero and Squazzoni, 2005; Bruch and Atwell, 2015). Even though all simulation models have been inspired by observation of routines in practice, it is still necessary to embed them in empirical data to rigorously test the findings and ensure that the simulation models are accurate representations of the real system of interest for a given set of objectives (Heath et al., 2009). Especially with the rapid development of digital technologies, more relevant empirical data – such as workflow event logs, video data, etc. – have become available in research of organizational routines (Feldman et al., 2016). This may provide a way to develop more empirically grounded ABMs.

11.5 Conclusion

This chapter provides an overview of the ABM methodology in Routine Dynamics research with a brief comparison of eleven contemporary ABMs that helps us to identify challenges and suggestions for future work. ABM captures emergent phenomena such as routines and enables a researcher to create, analyse and experiment with 'in-silico' models composed of agents that interact within an environment (Gao et al., 2014; Gilbert, 2008). The capacity of ABM in creating the link between micro- and macro- levels from 'bottom-up' meets the requirement of Routine Dynamics researchers well when they treat routines as 'generative systems' (Feldman and Pentland, 2003) and endeavour to understand the internal structure, process and dynamics from which routines and capabilities emerge and evolve (D'Adderio et al., 2012; Feldman et al., 2016). In this sense, we are confident that developing ABMs can provide a super opportunity to investigate the routines' internal structure and dynamics; to visualize their emerging processes; and to identify factors such as connection typology and memory of individual actors that affects both emerging and change in routines. Thus, we hope ABM offers an approach to enrich our understanding of Routine Dynamics – and further, organizational routines in general. It is not a substitute for, but a supplement to empirical methods. However, one needs to design ABMs in Routine Dynamics to account for both levels of analysis and the concrete research questions. Developing empirically grounded ABMs in Routine Dynamics is challenging, but worthwhile.

References

Aggarwal, V. A., Posen, H. E. and Workiewicz, M. (2017). Adaptive capacity to technological change: A microfoundational approach. *Strategic Management Journal*, 38(6), 1212–1231.

Axelrod, R. (1997). Advancing the art of simulation in the social sciences. *Complexity*, 3(2), 16–22.

Bai, B., Yoo, B., Deng, X., Kim, I. and Gao, D. (2016). Linking routines to the evolution of IT capability on agent-based modeling and simulation: A dynamic perspective. *Computational and Mathematical Organization Theory*, 22(2), 184–211.

Boero, R. and Squazzoni, F. (2005). Does empirical embeddedness matter? Methodological issues on agent-based models for analytical social science. *Journal of Artificial Societies and Social Simulation*, 8(4), 6 http://jasss.soc.surrey.ac.uk/8/4/6.html

Bonabeau, E. (2002). Agent-based modeling: Methods and techniques for simulating human systems. *Proceedings of the National Academy of Sciences*, 99(suppl 3), 7280–7287.

Bruch, E. and Atwell, J. (2015). Agent-based models in empirical social research. *Sociological Methods & Research*, 44(2), 186–221.

Chang, M. H. and Harrington, J. J. (2006). Agent-based models of organizations. In L. Tesfatsion and K. L. Judd, ed., *Handbook of Computational Economics* (volume 2). Oxford: Elsevier, pp. 1273–1337.

Cohen, M. D. and Bacdayan, P. (1994). Organizational routines are stored as procedural memory: Evidence from laboratory study. *Organization Science*, 5(4), 554–568.

Cohen, M. D., Levinthal, D. A. and Warglien, M. (2014). Collective performance: Modeling the interaction of habit-based actions. *Industrial and Corporate Change*, 23(2), 329–360.

D'Adderio, L., Feldman, M. S., Lazaric, N. and Pentland, B. T. (2012). Call for papers – Special issue on routine dynamics: Exploring sources of stability and change in Organizations. *Organization Science*, 23(6), 1782–1783.

Eberlen, J., Scholz, G. and Gagliolo, M. (2017). Simulate this! An introduction to agent-based models and their power to improve your research practice. *International Review of Social Psychology*, 30(1), 149–160.

Edmonds, B. and Moss, S. (2004). From KISS to KIDS – an 'anti-simplistic' modelling approach. In *International Workshop on Multi-Agent Systems and Agent-Based Simulation*. Berlin, Heidelberg: Springer, pp. 130–144.

Epstein, J. M. and Axtell, R. (1996). *Growing Artificial Societies: Social Science from the*

Bottom-up. Washington, DC: Brookings Institution Press.

Feldman, M. S. (2000). Organizational routines as a source of continuous change. *Organization Science*, 11(6), 611–629.

(2003). A performative perspective on stability and change in organizational routines. *Industrial and Corporate Change*, 12(4), 727–752.

(2016). Routines as process: Past, present, and future. In J. Howard-Grenville, C. Rerup, A. Langley and H. Tsoukas, eds., *Organizational routines: How They Are Created, Maintained, and Changed*. Oxford: Oxford University Press, pp. 23–46.

Feldman, M. S. and Pentland, B. T. (2003). Reconceptualizing organizational routines as a source of flexibility and change. *Administrative Science Quarterly*, 48(1), 94-118.

Feldman, M. S., Pentland, B. T., D'Adderio, L. and Lazaric, N. (2016). Beyond routines as things: Introduction to the special issue on routine dynamics. *Organization Science*, 27(3), 505–513.

Felin, T. and Foss, N. J. (2009). Organizational routines and capabilities: Historical drift and a course-correction toward microfoundations. *Scandinavian Journal of Management*, 25(2), 157–167.

Fioretti, G. (2013). Agent-based simulation models in organization science. *Organizational Research Methods*, 16(2), 227–242.

Gao, D., Deng, X. and Bai, B. (2014). The emergence of organizational routines from habitual behaviours of multiple actors: An agent-based simulation study. *Journal of Simulation*, 8(3), 215–230.

Gao, D., Deng, X., Zhao, Q., Zhou, H. and Bai, B. (2015). Multi-agent based simulation of organizational routines on complex networks. *Journal of Artificial Societies and Social Simulation*, 18(3), 17. http://jasss.soc.surrey.ac.uk/18/3/17.html

Gao, D., Squazzoni, F. and Deng, X. (2018a). The role of cognitive artifacts in the evolutionary dynamics of organizational routines: An agent-based model. *Computational and Mathematical Organization Theory*, 24(4), 473–499.

(2018b). The intertwining impact of intra-organizational and routine networks on routine replication dynamics: An agent-based model. *Complexity*, vol.2018, doi: https://doi.org/10.1155/2018/8496235

Geiger, D. and Schröder, A. (2014). Ever-changing routines? Toward a revised understanding of organizational routines between rule-following and rule-breaking. *Schmalenbach Business Review*, 66(2), 170–190.

Gilbert, G. N. (2008). *Agent-Based Models: Quantitative Applications in the Social Sciences*, vol 153. New York: Sage.

Gómez-Cruz, N. A., Loaiza Saa, I. and Ortega Hurtado, F. F. (2017). Agent-based simulation in management and organizational studies: A survey. *European Journal of Management and Business Economics*, 26(3), 313–328.

Grimm, V., Berger, U., DeAngelis D., Polhill, J., Giske, J. and Railsback, S. (2010). The ODD protocol: A review and first update. *Ecological Modeling*, 221, 2760–2768.

Grimm, V., Berger, U., Bastiansen, F., Eliassen, S., Ginot, V., Giske, J., Gross-Custar, J., Grand, T., Heinz, S., Rbbins, A., Robbins, M., Rossmanith, E., Rüger, N., Strand, E., Souissi S., Stillman, R., Vabø, R., Visser, U. and DAngelis, D. (2006). A standard protocol for describing individual-based and agent-based models. *Ecological Modeling*, 198, 115–126.

Grimm, V., Revilla, E., Berger, U., Jeltsch, F., Mooij, W. M., Railsback, S. F., Thulke, H.-H., Weiner, J., Weigand, T. and DeAngelis, D. (2005). Pattern-oriented modeling of agent-based complex systems: lessons from ecology. *Science*, 310(5750), 987–991.

Hauke, J., Achter, S. and Meyer, M. (2020). Theory development via replicated simulations and the added value of standards. *Journal of Artificial Societies and Social Simulation*, 23(1), 12, http://jasss.soc.surrey.ac.uk/23/1/12.html

Heath, B., Hill, R. and Ciarallo, F. (2009). A survey of agent-based modeling practices (January 1998 to July 2008). *Journal of Artificial Societies and Social Simulation*, 12(4), 9, http://jasss.soc.surrey.ac.uk/12/4/9.html

Hooten, M. B. and Wikle, C. K. (2010). Statistical agent-based models for discrete spatio-temporal systems. *Journal of the American Statistical Association*, 105(489), 236–248.

Howard-Grenville, J., Rerup, C., Langley, A. and Tsoukas, H. eds. (2016). *Organizational Routines: How They Are Created, Maintained, and Changed*. Oxford: Oxford University Press.

Janssen, M. and Ostrom, E. (2006). Empirically based, agent-based models. *Ecology and Society*, 11(2), 37, www.ecologyandsociety.org/vol11/iss2/art37/

Kahl, C. H. and Meyer, M. (2016). Constructing agent-based models of organizational routines. In D. Secchi and M. Neumann, eds., *Agent-Based Simulation of Organizational Behavior: New Frontiers of Social Science Research*. Cham: Springer, pp. 85–107.

Kasaie, P. and Kelton, W. D. (2015). Guidelines for design and analysis in agent-based simulation studies. In L. Yilmaz, W. K. V. Chan, I. Moon et al., eds., *Proceedings of the 2015 Winter Simulation Conference (WSC)*, pp. 183–193.

Kremser, W. and Schreyögg, G. (2016). The dynamics of interrelated routines: Introducing the cluster level. *Organization Science*, 27(3), 698–721.

Lee, J. S., Filatova, T., Ligmann-Zielinska, A., Hassani-Mahmooei, B., Stonedahl, F. et al. (2015). The complexities of agent-based modeling output analysis. *Journal of Artificial Societies and Social Simulation*, 18(4), 4. http://jasss.soc.surrey.ac.uk/18/4/4.html

Lorscheid, I., Heine, B. O. and Meyer, M. (2012). Opening the 'black box' of simulations: Increased transparency and effective communication through the systematic design of experiments. *Computational and Mathematical Organization·Theory*, 18(1), 22–62.

Macal, C. M. and North, M. J. (2010). Tutorial on agent-based modeling and simulation. *Journal of Simulation*, 4(3), 151–162.

Miller, K. D. (2015). Agent-based modeling and organization studies: A critical realist perspective. *Organization Studies*, 36(2), 175–196.

Miller, K. D., Choi, S. and Pentland, B. T. (2014). The role of transactive memory in the formation of organizational routines. *Strategic Organization*, 12(2), 109–133.

Miller, K. D., Pentland, B. T. and Choi, S. (2012). Dynamics of performing and remembering organizational routines. *Journal of Management Studies*, 49(8), 1536–1558.

Müller, B., Bohn, F., Dreßler, G., Groeneveld, J., Klassert, C., Martin, R. and Schwarz, N. (2013). Describing human decisions in agent-based models–ODD+ D, an extension of the ODD protocol. *Environmental Modelling & Software*, 48, 37–48.

Neumann, M. and Secchi, D. (2016). Exploring the new frontier: Computational studies of organizational behavior. In D. Secchi and M. Neumann, eds., *Agent-Based Simulation of Organizational Behavior: New Frontiers of Social Science Research*. Cham: Springer, pp. 1–16.

Parmigiani, A. and Howard-Grenville, J. (2011). Routines revisited: Exploring the capabilities and practice perspectives. *Academy of Management Annals*, 5(1), 413–453.

Pentland, B. T. and Feldman, M. S. (2005). Organizational routines as a unit of analysis. *Industrial and Corporate Change*, 14(5), 793–815.

Pentland, B. T., Feldman, M. S., Becker, M. C. and Liu, P. (2012). Dynamics of organizational routines: A generative model. *Journal of Management Studies*, 49(8), 1484–1508.

Pentland, B. T., Hærem, T. and Hillison, D. (2011). The (n) ever-changing world: Stability and change in organizational routines. *Organization Science*, 22(6), 1369–1383.

Pentland, B. T., Recker, J. and Wyner, G. (2015). A thermometer for interdependence: Exploring patterns of interdependence using networks of affordances. In *Proceedings of the 36th International Conference on Information Systems*. Association for Information Systems.

Pentland, B. T. and Rueter, H. H. (1994). Organizational routines as grammars of action. *Administrative Science Quarterly*, 39(3), 484–510.

Railsback, S. F. and Grimm, V. (2019). *Agent-Based and Individual-Based Modeling: A Practical Introduction*. Princeton, NJ: Princeton University Press.

Secchi, D. and Seri, R. (2017). Controlling for false negatives in agent-based models: A review of power analysis in organizational research. *Computational and Mathematical Organization Theory*, 23(1), 94–121.

Sele, K. and Grand, S. (2016). Unpacking the dynamics of ecologies of routines: Mediators and their generative effects in routine interactions. *Organization Science*, 27(3), 722–738.

Seri, R. and Secchi, D. (2013). How many times should one run a computational simulation? In B. Edmonds and R. Meyer, eds., *Simulating Social Complexity: A Handbook* (second edition). Cham: Springer International Publishing.

Shimazoe, J. and Burton, R. M. (2013). Justification shift and uncertainty: Why are low-probability near misses underrated against organizational routines? *Computational and Mathematical Organization Theory*, 19(1), 78–100.

Silverman, E. (2018). *Methodological Investigations in Agent-Based Modelling: With Applications for the Social Sciences*. Cham: Springer.

Smaldino, P. E., Calanchini, J. and Pickett, C. L. (2015). Theory development with agent-based models. *Organizational Psychology Review*, 5 (4), 300–317.

Squazzoni, F. (2010). The impact of agent-based models in the social sciences after 15 years of incursions. *History of Economic Ideas*, 18(2), 197–233.

(2012). *Agent-Based Computational Sociology*. Chichester: John Wiley & Sons, Ltd.

Squazzoni, F., Jager, W. and Edmonds, B. (2014). Social simulation in the social sciences: A brief overview. *Social Science Computer Review*, 32(3), 279–294.

Sun, Z., Lorscheid, I., Millington, J. D., Lauf, S., Magliocca, N. R. et al. (2016). Simple or complicated agent-based models? A complicated issue. *Environmental Modelling & Software*, 86, 56–67.

Thiele, J. C., Kurth, W. and Grimm, V. (2014). Facilitating parameter estimation and sensitivity analysis of agent-based models: A cookbook using NetLogo and R. *Journal of Artificial Societies and Social Simulation*, 17(3), 11. http://jasss.soc.surrey.ac.uk/17/3/11.html

Wall, F. (2016). Agent-based modeling in managerial science: An illustrative survey and study. *Review of Managerial Science*, 10(1), 135–193.

Yi, S., Knudsen, T. and Becker, M. C. (2016). Inertia in routines: A hidden source of organizational variation. *Organization Science*, 27(3), 782–800.

Yilmaz, L. (2006). Validation and verification of social processes within agent-based computational organization models. *Computational & Mathematical Organization Theory*, 12(4), 283–312.

CHAPTER 12

Sequence Analysis in Routine Dynamics

CHRISTIAN A. MAHRINGER AND BRIAN T. PENTLAND

12.1 Introduction

Sequence analysis can be defined as a family of methods that can be used to identify, describe, compare and visualize patterns in sequentially ordered data. The disciplinary origins of these methods include computer science (Sankoff and Kruskal, 1983), bioinformatics (Durbin et al., 1998), history (Griffin, 2007), life course sociology (Aisenbrey and Fasang, 2010), career research (Abbott and Hrycak, 1990), research on decision making (Levitt and Nass, 1989) and innovation research (Van de Ven et al., 1999). Sequence is essential to concepts such as progression, temporality and flow that are central to process organization studies (Langley and Tsoukas, 2017) and Routine Dynamics (Feldman et al., 2016).

In this chapter, we focus on sequence analysis as it applies to Routine Dynamics. The goal of this chapter is to help scholars use sequence analysis in their research on Routine Dynamics. We begin by considering the kinds of questions we can address with sequence analysis. We review prior Routine Dynamics research and show how it has used sequence analysis. Excellent resources are available for the mechanics of particular methods (e.g., Cornwell, 2015; Poole et al., 2017; Sankoff and Kruskal, 1983). Hence, rather than zooming in on particular sequence analysis methods (e.g., optimal string matching), we are zooming out to consider how sequence analysis can help ***identify***, ***describe***, ***visualize*** and ***compare*** routines and their dynamics. We show how scholars can get started with sequence analysis with any kind of sequential data (e.g., from ethnographic observation, interviews or digitized event logs). Finally, we suggest avenues for future research.

To illustrate our arguments, we draw on the example of Scrum software development routines in a medium-sized high-tech manufacturing company (Mahringer, 2019; Mahringer et al., 2019). Scrum is a software development framework which splits the software development process into phases of two to four weeks (i.e., sprints) (Schwaber and Beedle, 2002). The study includes ethnographic fieldwork of how the software development teams enacted the Scrum routines over a period of 12 months. The software development teams organized their work by using a software tool called Zoe (all names are pseudonyms) that recorded approximately 4,500 sequences and 90,000 events in a database. Sequence analysis can be used with any or all of this data.

12.2 How Does Sequence Analysis Help to Understand Routine Dynamics?

Abbott (1990: 375) identifies three kinds of questions where sequence analysis can be useful, '(1) questions about whether a typical sequence or sequences exist, (2) questions about why such patterns might exist and (3) questions about the consequences of such patterns.' Of these, he argues that the first question is most important. To the extent that an organizational routine contains recognizable patterns of action, we expect to find typical sequences in any routine. Sequence analysis can help us identify, describe, visualize and compare those sequences.

Abbott's (1990) questions are generic to any kind of sequential data, but there are more specific questions that are relevant to the analysis of organizational routines. By definition, routines are repetitive, so they generate multiple performances (Feldman and Pentland, 2003). To the extent that each performance of an organizational routine can be treated as a sequence of actions, we can ask the following kinds of questions (Salvato, 2009b),

- **What are the typical patterns of a routine?** Because routines are patterns in variety (Cohen, 2007) they can potentially generate a large number of different performances. Some of these performances occur more often and, hence, are more typical, while other performances are less typical. Abbott (1990: 378) refers to these as 'typical-sequence/families-of-sequences' questions; he argues that these are 'the central questions of the sequence area'.
- **How varied are the performances of a routine?** While the performances of some routines are more similar to each other, the performances of other routines differ tremendously. Pentland (2003a) offers metrics for measuring sequential variety.
- **How does sequence matter?** The sequential relations among actions of routine performances are essential (LeBaron et al., 2016). Sequence analysis can be used to unpack sequential relations between actions.
- **How does the pattern of a routine change?** Sequence analysis can also be used to show how the pattern of a routine changes over time. Dittrich, Guérard and Seidl (2016), for instance, analyse how the routine pattern changed, and identify reflective talk as a critical mechanism of routine change.
- **How do different action patterns influence performance outcomes?** Sequence analysis provides opportunities to better understand how different patterns influence performance outcomes. For example, first writing an exam and then learning the relevant content most likely results in a different performance outcome than the other way round.

While Abbott's (1990) primer provides a useful starting point, it has some important limitations, especially when applied to Routine Dynamics. First, Abbott treats events as objective, which undermines the idea that routine participants might interpret events in different ways. However, the significance of events for participants is central to the formation and dynamics of the routine (Sele and Grand, 2016). Therefore, sequence analysis of routines should include the notion of meaning and interpretation. An event, then, can be defined as an actual happening that sufficiently coheres to be experienced as similar, but which still incorporates different points of view (Hernes, 2014).

Second, Abbott (1990) treats patterns as stable or stationary. While Abbott's own research places history and temporality in the foreground (e.g., in the formation of professions), the methodologies he discusses in his primer are ahistorical. They focus on sequences of events, but not on how these sequences might change over time. In contrast, research on Routine Dynamics is explicitly concerned with change and temporality (Pentland et al., 2012).

Third, focusing on particular sequences tends to obscure the significance of multiplicity in routines. Routines are generative systems that can display a substantial number of different sequential patterns. Like other processual phenomena, routines are multiplicities (Pentland et al., 2020). Hence, when comparing routines or measuring change over time, we may need to compare whole action patterns, not just particular linear sequences.

12.3 Sequence Analysis in Prior Routine Dynamics Research

Sequence methods in Routine Dynamics research can be sorted into three different categories: whole sequence methods, pattern-mining methods and network methods. These methods can be differentiated according to the length of sequence that is considered in the analysis (Table 12.1).

12.3.1 Whole Sequence Methods

As the name implies, whole sequence methods operate on complete sequences of action (Salvato, 2009b). These methods build on the rationale that differences between empirically observable sequences yield meaningful insights. These methods treat whole performances of a routine as the unit of analysis. They derive from molecular biology and computer science (Sankoff and Kruskal, 1983). Abbott and Hrycak (1990) pioneered the use of these methods in career research.

Table 12.1 Three types of sequence analysis in Routine Dynamics

	Whole sequence methods	Pattern mining methods	Network methods
Sequence length	Variable, up to length of longest performance	Variable, typically three to five actions or events	Fixed, pairs of events
Typical applications	Identifying different types of patterns	Identifying a typical pattern of actions of a routine	Identifying handoffs between actions
Major drawbacks	Only considers differences between whole sequences, not within sequences	Size of the lexicon has a critical effect on the findings; limited applicability in comparing patterns	Only considers the immediate context (i.e., one action before and one after)
Exemplary references	Salvato (2009a, 2009b)	Pentland and Rueter (1994); Hansson, Pentland and Hærem (2017)	Pentland, Hærem and Hillison (2010); Goh and Pentland (2019)

Salvato (2009a), for instance, analyses new product development processes at Alessi over a period of 15 years. The author uses dossiers that report details about ninety new product development projects to identify the sequences of events for each project. He applies optimal matching (Abbott and Tsay, 2000) to identify clusters of similar sequences. To interpret the meaning of these clusters, the author went back to his raw data or asked participants. A similar approach is applied by Sabherwal and Robey (1993). These authors use optimal matching and cluster analysis to develop a taxonomy of implementation processes. Analysing fifty-three computer-based information system implementation processes, they identify six archetypes of these processes. Pentland (2003a) also uses whole sequence methods as one way to characterize variety in routines.

It is important to note that narrative analysis, based on ethnographic fieldwork, can also be considered a whole sequence method (Pentland, 1999a). When ethnographers describe the typical performance of a routine, from start to finish, they are engaging in sequence analysis. Constructing a narrative from field notes requires the same basic steps as a more formal, mathematical analysis: collecting the data, defining the lexicon, choosing a point of view, identifying the sequence and creating a representation.

12.3.2 Pattern Mining Methods

In contrast to whole sequence methods, pattern mining methods seek to identify common subsequences within performances of a routine. There is a broad class of algorithms and techniques for empirically identifying patterns (e.g., Fournier-Viger et al., 2014; Mabroukeh and Ezeife, 2010).

Hansson et al. (2017) investigate the application of these methods to organizational routines. They examine the use of regular expressions and inductive pattern mining. Regular expressions are a pattern matching tool that is available in nearly every modern computing language. Regular expressions provide a flexible tool for searching a corpus of sequence data (typically in the form of text) for particular combinations of letters and words. Hansson et al. (2017) refer to regular expressions as a deductive method because the search pattern must be defined in advance. In contrast, inductive pattern mining methods are algorithms that search through a corpus of text to find patterns that do not need to be defined in advance.

Keegan, Lev and Arazy (2016) analyse editorial events in Wikipedia articles. The authors use pattern mining to identify the most frequent sub-sequences of how articles are edited. The authors are interested in different contribution styles to Wikipedia articles, such as solo contributing or reactive contributing. They emphasize the opportunities that sequence analysis offers to better understand routines in online knowledge collaboration.

Pentland and Rueter (1994) apply a simple pattern mining approach to identify grammatical rules that could be used to describe organizational routines. The authors use a sample of 335 calls from a software support hotline. They define grammars (i.e., patterns) for the data set based on observations of the routine. Subsequently, they use the grammatical patterns to rewrite (i.e., substitute) the events in the actual sequences. This analysis led to the insight that a large number of performances could be described by a small number of patterns.

12.3.3 Network Methods

In contrast, network methods operate on adjacent pairs of actions or events within a sequence or set of sequences. Because they do not require whole sequences, network methods can be used where fragments of performances are observed, as often occurs in fieldwork (Pentland and Feldman, 2007). Network methods provide a convenient way to describe what Cohen (2007) referred to as the 'pattern-in-variety' of organizational routines. There are repetitive, recognizable patterns but there may also be a large number of variations.

Pentland and Feldman (2007) propose that sequences of events can be used to compute narrative networks, a special class of network in which nodes represent events and edges represent sequential relations between those events. 'A narrative network is an analytical device for describing, visualizing, and comparing these patterns.' (Pentland and Feldman, 2007: 782). This method has been used to visualize routine patterns from observational data (Danner-Schröder and Geiger, 2016; Dittrich et al., 2016) but it also offers the possibility to compute event networks from digitized digital trace data.

Pentland et al. (2010) analyse 4,781 invoice processing sequences in four Norwegian organizations. They aggregate those performances into an event network that represents the routines in each organization, and they compare those networks to determine whether the routines in these organizations are different. Note that this method is not comparing specific performances of the routine. Rather, it is comparing the relative frequency of sequential pairs of action in all observed performances of the routine. Pentland et al. (2011) extend these insights by showing that patterns change over time due to endogenous factors.

In summary, the network approach can be used to better understand the variability of routine patterns (Pentland, 2003b), complexity (Hærem et al., 2015; Hærem et al., this volume) and multiplicity of routines (Pentland et al., 2020).

12.4 A Guide to Sequence Analysis in Routine Dynamics Research

In this section we step-by-step show how to analyse sequential data based on the example of Scrum software development. As with any routine, in practice these steps may not follow a fixed, linear sequence. Rather, it may be necessary to jump back and forth.

12.4.1 Collecting the Data

As with any empirical work, sequence analysis starts with collecting data. The predominant empirical approach to understand Routine Dynamics is ethnographic fieldwork (Feldman et al., 2016). It should be evident from the prior review that sequence analysis can be applied to many different kinds of data, including observational data collected during fieldwork. Indeed, any source of data that includes temporal sequence can be used for sequence analysis. A major strength of ethnographic fieldwork is that it enables scholars to capture the mundane everyday actions and the meaning that actors associate with specific events (Dittrich, this volume). However, a drawback of ethnographic fieldwork is that it is limited to specific times and places.

Digital trace data is gaining popularity (Berente et al., 2019). It offers possibilities for extending ethnographic data in two important ways. First, digital trace data can extend the *temporal scope*, because these data oftentimes extend across several years or decades. This enables seeing patterns of stability and change over longer periods of time. For example, while the first author of this chapter spent twelve months observing the Scrum routines, the digital trace data covers a period of approximately four years. Taking earlier periods into consideration shows that the actors used different functions in Zoe than they used during the observation period.

Second, analysis of digital trace data can extend the *spatial scope*. Ethnographic fieldwork oftentimes focuses on local settings (Marcus, 1995). Digital trace data, however, particularly when provided by digital software tools that are used by actors in different locations, enable scholars to analyse sequences that extend across many locales. In the Scrum study, for instance, the Product Owner (i.e., the actor who was responsible for the software to be developed) typically spent some time in his private office space in the early morning to check the product backlog (i.e., a list of issues to be resolved). During this time he also clarified issues in Zoe and communicated with customers. These events are tracked in Zoe while they had not been directly observed.

By extending the spatial and temporal scope of research, digital trace data provides researchers with methods that can identify otherwise hidden patterns and dynamics. Computing a network of events from the Scrum sequences showed how events typically connected to each other. This network showed that the event 'PrioritizeIssue' (i.e., an event that signifies changes in the order of issues in the product backlog) took a central position in the network and connected with many other events. This made us reflect on the relevance of prioritizing issues.

12.4.2 Selecting Software Tools

Data in hand, the next step is to determine if any kind of software is needed to assist in the analysis. With a small amount of data, it is perfectly possible to identify, describe, visualize and compare patterns by hand (Barley, 1986; Pentland, 1999b). With larger amounts of data, and for specialized questions, it may be necessary to find a software tool that helps to analyse sequential data, such as TraMineR or ThreadNet.

TraMineR is a software package for R. After having installed R, the TraMineR package can be downloaded. TraMineR offers many different methods, including whole sequence analysis, pattern mining and network models. Gabadinho et al. (2011) offer a detailed user guide that explains the methods available.

ThreadNet is also a software package in R, available on GitHub (https://github.com/ThreadNet/ThreadNet). As the name implies, it converts threads (sequential data) into networks based on sequentially adjacent pairs of events. ThreadNet allows users to define events in a flexible manner, based on any combination of contextual factors. This allows users to quickly explore action patterns from different points of view (the actor, the location, etc.). ThreadNet itself is limited to visualization, but it can export network structures for analysis in TraMineR and other software packages. In analysing the Scrum data, for example, we started with ThreadNet and later extended to TraMineR when more specific functions were required.

We suggest the use of specialized tools rather than general qualitative analysis tools, like nVivio or Atlas/ti because sequence analysis poses some unique challenges. We are not just trying to sift and sort categories; we are looking for patterns of sequential relations between categories. The number of possible relations grows exponentially (as the square of the size of the lexicon). As a result, sequential relations can be difficult to keep track of without some kind of specialized, computerized help.

12.4.3 Identifying the Limitations of Your Data

All kinds of data have limitations. These limitations shape which kinds of questions can be answered and where additional inquiry is required. As we have discussed before, ethnographic data is limited in its temporal and spatial scope. Because ethnographic fieldwork requires the researcher to observe a setting in detail, the data typically covers a period of several months, and sometimes a few years, but rarely extends to a longer time horizon such as decades. The degree of detail of ethnographic fieldwork also requires researchers to make choices on what to observe and what not to observe (Van der Waal, 2009). Hereby, it is necessarily limited to a specific setting.

By contrast, digital trace data also face several limitations. First, trace data are *limited to events that are captured 'on-line'*, as part of the digital environment. Hence, they do not capture events that happened 'offline'. In the Scrum case, for instance, the daily standup was a routine which the developers enacted to synchronize their work. Even though this routine was an important part of software development, the developers did not use Zoe when performing it. Hence, the digital trace data did not contain information about the daily standup routine.

Second, trace data may not capture the *differences in meaning* associated with events. For instance, the same event in the digital trace data can have different meanings depending on the situation in which it is performed. A major feature of Zoe was the product backlog, which was an extensive list of issues to be resolved. When actors dragged an issue from the product backlog and dropped it to another position this resulted in an event which we called 'PrioritizeIssue'. The actors oftentimes coincidentally dragged and dropped an issue to another position when they were discussing the product backlog. In other cases, by contrast, actors intentionally dragged issues from the bottom of the product backlog to its top. Since issues at the top of the product backlog had the highest priority and were added to the next sprint, this was a significant event. Zoe, however, did not allow us to account for such differences. We noted that this event took a central position in the event network. We considered the possibility that coincidentally moving an issue could be an explanation for the central position of the event in the network. However, depending on the data it might also be possible to take account of such differences by considering additional data sources (e.g., fieldnotes).

Third, trace data may be limited in *capturing the duration of events*. The start of an event may be recorded with a specific time stamp, but the duration might not be recorded. This might be challenging if researchers try to interpret time lags between events, assuming that events do not have a specific duration. In the Scrum case, each issue in Zoe contained a description field. When an actor pushed the 'safe' button, Zoe created an event which included a specific time stamp. Whereas sometimes a description change was minor (e.g., correcting a spelling mistake), in other cases such an event could signify an extensive discussion about a complex issue. The duration of this discussion, however, was not captured in the event log data.

In summary, it is essential to identify the limitations of the data set. Ethnographic data might be limited to particular times and places. Digital trace data is limited to what happens online, might not capture meanings associated with events and is limited in capturing durations of events. Sometimes it may be possible to gather additional data that helps to resolve such limitations, but often it is not. This limits the kinds of questions that can be answered. Most likely, the list of limitations is continuously revised during the course of analysis, as new limitations are discovered and old limitations are resolved.

12.4.4 Defining the Lexicon of Events

Another critical step in sequential analysis is defining the lexicon of events (Berente et al., 2019). The lexicon is the set of event types that are used to depict the sequences. The key point is that there does not need to be a one-to-one correspondence between the raw data collected and the lexicon that is analysed. For example, some items in the raw data may be 'filler'. In the Scrum case, for instance, simultaneously adding multiple attachments to an issue in Zoe produced sequences of similar events in the event log data. Moreover, several different items in the raw data may be used as indicators of the same higher order category (Gioia, Corley and Hamilton, 2013). In general, the move from raw data to the lexicon of events is an essential part of making sense of your data (Abbott, 1990; Pentland and Liu, 2018).

The move from raw data to higher order constructs affects the granularity of the data. Selecting the granularity of events is a major challenge, because granularity can have a tremendous impact on the findings (Pentland, 2003a). Selecting a finer granularity (i.e., a larger lexicon) increases differences between sequences and makes it more difficult to identify patterns. Selecting a coarser granularity (i.e., a smaller lexicon) makes the sequences more similar, but might lead to the false assumption that there is only minor variation in routine performances. Hence, it is important to define granularity based on one's understanding of the setting and the phenomenon of interest. In the Scrum case, actors used different functions in

Zoe to indicate interdependencies. This resulted in different events in the raw data such as 'component', 'link' and 'epic link'. Since all of these events were used to indicate interdependencies, we aggregated them into the event 'AddInterdependency'.

12.4.5 Defining Sequences

The next step is to define according to which rationale events are sequenced. Similarly to ethnographers who have to make choices on 'what to follow' (Marcus, 1995), digital trace data may provide several ways of defining sequences, which could yield different insights into the phenomenon. For example, one could follow the Product Owner on a regular work day. From that point of view, one would see how the Product Owner interacts with customers, the developers and Zoe. Alternatively, one could follow an issue in Zoe (i.e., a bug to be resolved or a new feature to be developed in the software). From that point of view, one would see how a customer reports the issue in Zoe, how the Product Owner specifies the description of the issue and how the developers resolve it. Either point of view presents a partial view of the overall routine, which is why Feldman and Pentland (2003) emphasize that the ostensive and performative aspects of organizational routines are multiple.

In general, it is worthwhile to think about different ways of sequencing the data and which insights this could yield. In the Scrum case, we explored different ways of sequencing the data such as actors, weekdays and issues. Issues were promising because they described the sequences of events that were performed in order to implement new features in the software or resolve bugs.

12.4.6 Identifying, Describing, Comparing and Visualizing Patterns

Now that your data are ready, we can apply sequence methods. Three major questions are important for research on Routine Dynamics.

Identifying: Is there a sequential pattern? Whole sequence methods are useful to *identify* different types of sequences, but they cannot be used to identify common patterns of events across these sequences. Pattern mining is more useful to identify such patterns across sequences. The major challenge here is that the size of the lexicon influences the findings, because a larger lexicon makes the sequences more different. Hence, this approach has to trade-off pattern length and generalizability of patterns. The network approach overcomes this issue because it does not rely on pattern length, but on handoffs between events.

Describing and visualizing: What is the pattern? The most common method for describing sequential patterns in Routine Dynamics research is via narrative (i.e., texts, stories). Sequences of action have a natural narrative structure, and different characters or roles can enter and exit the story as needed. However, narrative tends to portray routines as having a specific, linear structure. It is difficult to capture the pattern-in-variety (Cohen, 2007) in narratives. Of course, one can describe exceptions and variations, but this quickly becomes tedious if the routine has a large number of variations.

Visualization is another common strategy for describing routines. However, as Feldman (2016) notes, most published visualizations are abstract simplifications. They may be easy to grasp, but they convey less information than a linear textual description. Visualizations based on detailed empirical data are starting to become available through software tools such as TraMineR and ThreadNet.

Comparing: How do patterns differ? Identifying a pattern of events is useful to gain an understanding of the routine, but it does not yield further insights. *Comparing* patterns across contexts can yield further insights into what influences these patterns. We could, for instance, ask whether the Scrum routines show more or less regularities in more or less institutionalized contexts. We could also look at whether differences in complexity and multiplicity (e.g., more or less complex software, more or less actors involved) shape the patterns of events.

More specifically, patterns can also be compared for different time periods. Because we are interested in change over time, Routine Dynamics creates an additional requirement for conventional sequence analysis. Where Abbott (1990) emphasized synchronic methods, Routine Dynamics suggests the need for diachronic analysis (De Saussure, 1916).

Diachronic analysis not only considers a pattern at a specific point in time, but takes its development over time into consideration (Barley, 1990; Berente et al., 2019).

All three methodological approaches could be used in the context of diachronic analysis. The whole sequence approach identifies differences between entire sequences. Comparing sequences across different time windows could help to understand that the sequences are changing over time. What is missing here is how the pattern changed. The network approach can be used to compare patterns for different time windows. Pattern mining methods face similar challenges, but could be suitable to understand whether routines become less or more patterned over time. The question whether patterns are changing over time requires iterating between synchronic and diachronic approaches (Berente et al., 2019).

12.4.7 *Interpreting*

Identifying, describing, comparing and visualizing patterns of action provides us with either numerical or visual results. However, we need to interpret these visualizations and numbers (Keegan et al., 2016). Interpreting results shows that we need an in-depth understanding of the context that we are analysing. We need to tell a story about the patterns. Even though this chapter presents interpreting as a discrete step in the analysis, we rather see it as a process that continuously unfolds during the analysis.

12.5 Implications and Agenda for Future Research

Clearly, sequence analysis has helped advance our understanding of Routine Dynamics and will continue to do so in the future. In the final section of this chapter, we offer some ideas for future research.

12.5.1 *Mutually Contextualizing Visualizations and Narratives*

The most common way to describe routines is through narrative (Feldman et al., 2016). Well written textual descriptions can be very detailed and compelling. Narrating is particularly valuable, because it strives to convey the researcher's experience of local meanings in the field (Yanow, 2012). However, narratives are limited as a way to describe processual phenomena (Mesle and Dibben, 2017), because it is difficult to portray variety, and the linear quality of narrative tends to lead to an understanding of routines as unitary sequences of action.

As our capability to analyse and visualize sequential data improves, we are beginning to have visualizations (and metrics) of action patterns, as well. Network methods, for instance, provide a particularly promising source of visualizations (Moody et al., 2005). A strength of visualizing lies in depicting multiplicity. Moreover, visualizing can help to structure and process complex data, which might reveal patterns that we did not see before. However, visualizations are impossible to interpret without some form of narrative explanation.

As shown in Figure 12.1, sequence analysis can provide narratives and visualizations (or metrics) of routines, both of which should contextualize each other. Many kinds of data can be used to create visualizations (or metrics) and narratives. These outputs mutually contextualize each other: visualizations add a sense of structure to narratives, and narratives help interpret visualizations. Sequence analysis informs both sides of this equation. It is the foundation for both the visualizations and the narratives.

In a sense, we are specifying Feldman et al.'s (2016: 511) statement that '[e]thnographic fieldwork will always be needed to interpret archival results, but digitized trace data provide a way to visualize and compare patterns of action that have not previously been available'. While Abbott (1992: 430) argues that '[t]here is nothing about thinking processually that requires interpretive attention to complexity of meaning', we argue that in Routine Dynamics, the opposite is usually true. Thus, we encourage future research on routines that embraces and integrates both approaches, since they are not mutually exclusive, but mutually contextualizing.

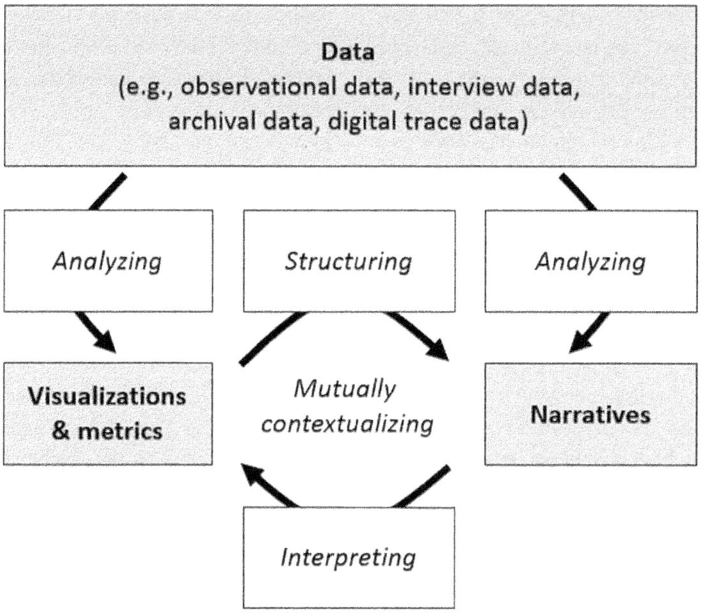

Figure 12.1 Mutually contextualizing visualizations and narratives generated by sequence analysis

12.5.2 Extending the Spatial and Temporal Scope

The rise of digital trace data provides new opportunities to further extend the spatial scope of research on Routine Dynamics. Dispersed settings such as platform collaboration and open source software development make it difficult to understand how people coordinate their work through ethnographic fieldwork (Marcus, 1995). Oftentimes, however, these new ways of working are supported by software tools that provide rich data. Lindberg et al. (2016) is an example of a study that has taken advantage of these kinds of data to better understand routines. Because these digitized contexts become more and more important we call for more empirical research in these contexts.

Moreover, we encourage Routine Dynamics scholars to extend the temporal scope of their analysis. Even though ethnographic fieldwork typically studies a considerable amount of time, sequence analysis also provides opportunities that show changes and patterns over several years or even decades (Salvato, 2009a). Hence, it might be fruitful to both zoom into the details of everyday work but also zoom out on longer time horizons to better understand routines.

12.5.3 Dynamics Implies Diachronic Analysis

Ferdinand De Saussure (1916) introduced the distinction between synchronic and diachronic analysis in linguistics. Synchronic analysis refers to studies of language structure or comparative language structure within a specific period of time. In contrast, diachronic analysis refers to changes in a language over time (De Saussure, 1916). Diachronic analysis attempts to describe and understand changes over time. Barley (1986, 1990) translated these concepts for use in organizational research.

Diachronic analysis is an obvious fit for Routine Dynamics because it provides a way to conceptualize change in a complex system of sequential relationships over time. Pentland et al. (2019) offer a methodology for applying diachronic analysis to organizational routines using sequence data. As an example of diachronic analysis based on fieldwork, consider Barley's (1986) classic study of the introduction of new technology in the radiology departments of two hospitals. As a participant observer,

Barley recorded the sequential interactions of radiologists, nurses and technicians over a one year period, pre- and post-implementation. Using this data, Barley was able to conduct a diachronic analysis of the roles and action patterns (see also Barley, 1990).

12.5.4 Moving from Singularity to Multiplicity

Sequence methods make it easy to measure similarity between sequences. However, routines are multiplicities, not singular sequences (Pentland et al., 2020). This ontological claim has methodological implications because we require approaches that operationalize multiplicity. Goh and Pentland (2019), for instance, introduce the notion of paths that could be used as an indicator of multiplicity of routines. More research is required to better understand multiplicity in and of routines.

12.5.5 Adopting Methodological Innovation

Business process management scholars have developed, and continue to develop, tools for analysing sequential data (Wurm et al., this volume). Research on Routine Dynamics research has just started to recognize the possibilities of adopting these methods. These include methods for analysing drift and variants, among other things. Research on machine learning is also providing a variety of tools for sequence analysis (Witten et al., 2016). There is a great deal of uncharted terrain that waits to be discovered and we hope that Routine Dynamic scholars will continue exploring.

References

Abbott, A. (1990). A primer on sequence methods. *Organization Science*, 1(4), 375–392.

Abbott, A. (1992). From causes to events: Notes on narrative positivism. *Sociological Methods & Research*, 20(4), 428–455.

Abbott, A. and Hrycak, A. (1990). Measuring resemblance in sequence data: An optimal matching analysis of musicians' careers. *American Journal of Sociology*, 96(1), 144–185.

Abbott, A. and Tsay, A. (2000). Sequence analysis and optimal matching methods in sociology: Review and prospect. *Sociological Methods & Research*, 29(1), 3–33.

Aisenbrey, S. and Fasang, A. E. (2010). New life for old ideas: The 'second wave' of sequence analysis bringing the 'course' back into the life course. *Sociological Methods & Research*, 38 (3), 420–462.

Barley, S. R. (1986). Technology as an occasion for structuring: Evidence from observations of CT scanners and the social order of radiology departments. *Administrative Science Quarterly*, 31(1), 78–108.

Barley, S. R. (1990). Images of imaging: Notes on doing longitudinal field work. *Organization Science*, 1(3), 220–247.

Berente, N., Seidel, S. and Safadi, H. (2019). Research commentary: Data-driven computationally intensive theory development. *Information Systems Research*, 30(1), 50–64.

Cohen, M. D. (2007). Reading Dewey: Reflections on the study of routine. *Organization Studies*, 28 (5), 773–786.

Cornwell, B. (2015). *Social Sequence Analysis: Methods and Applications*. New York: Cambridge University Press.

Danner-Schröder, A. and Geiger, D. (2016). Unravelling the motor of patterning work: Toward an understanding of the microlevel dynamics of standardization and flexibility. *Organization Science*, 27(3), 633–658.

De Saussure, F. (1916). *Cours de Linguistique Générale*. Paris: Payot.

Dittrich, K., Guérard, S. and Seidl, D. (2016). Talking about routines: The role of reflective talk in routine change. *Organization Science*, 27(3), 678–697.

Durbin, R., Eddy, S. R., Krogh, A. and Mitchison, G. (1998). *Biological Sequence Analysis: Probabilistic Models of Proteins and Nucleic Acids*. Cambridge: Cambridge University Press.

Feldman, M. S. (2016). Making process visible: Alternatives to boxes and arrows. In A. Langley and H. Tsoukas. eds., *The Sage Handbook of Process Organization Studies*. London: Sage, pp. 625–635.

Feldman, M. S. and Pentland, B. T. (2003). Reconceptualizing organizational routines as a source of flexibility and change. *Administrative Science Quarterly*, 48(1), 94–118.

Feldman, M. S., Pentland, B. T., D'Adderio, L. and Lazaric, N. (2016). Beyond routines as things: Introduction to the special issue on routine dynamics. *Organization Science*, 27(3), 505–513.

Fournier-Viger, P., Gomariz, A., Gueniche, T., Soltani, A., Wu, C.-W. and Tseng, V. S. (2014). SPMF: A java open-source pattern mining library. *The Journal of Machine Learning Research*, 15(1), 3389–3393.

Gabadinho, A., Ritschard, G., Studer, M. and Müller, N. S. (2011). *Mining Sequence Data in R with the TraMineR Package: A User's Guide*. Geneva: University of Geneva.

Gioia, D. A., Corley, K. G. and Hamilton, A. L. (2013). Seeking qualitative rigor in inductive research: Notes on the Gioia methodology. *Organizational Research Methods*, 16(1), 15–31.

Goh, K. and Pentland, B. T. (2019). From actions to paths to patterning: Toward a dynamic theory of patterning in routines. *Academy of Management Journal*, 62(6), 1901–1929.

Griffin, L. J. (2007). Historical sociology, narrative and event-structure analysis: Fifteen years later. *Sociologica*, 1(3), 1–17.

Hærem, T., Pentland, B. T. and Miller, K. D. (2015). Task complexity: Extending a core concept. *Academy of Management Review*, 40(3), 446–460.

Hansson, M., Pentland, B. T. and Hærem, T. (2017). Identifying mid-range patterns of action: Tools for the analysis of organizational routines. Academy of Management Proceedings.

Hernes, T. (2014). *A Process Theory of Organization*. Oxford: Oxford University Press.

Keegan, B. C., Lev, S. and Arazy, O. (2016). Analyzing organizational routines in online knowledge collaborations: A case for sequence analysis in CSCW. Proceedings of the 19th ACM Conference on Computer-Supported Cooperative Work & Social Computing, 1065–1079.

Langley, A. and Tsoukas, H. (2017). *The Sage Handbook of Process Organization Studies*. London: Sage.

LeBaron, C., Christianson, M. K., Garrett, L. and Ilan, R. (2016). Coordinating flexible performance during everyday work: An ethnomethodological study of handoff routines. *Organization Science*, 27(3), 514–534.

Levitt, B. and Nass, C. (1989). The lid on the garbage can: Institutional constraints on decision making in the technical core of college-text publishers. *Administrative Science Quarterly*, 34(2), 190–207.

Lindberg, A., Berente, N., Gaskin, J. and Lyytinen, K. (2016). Coordinating interdependencies in online communities: A study of an open source software project. *Information Systems Research*, 27(4), 751–772.

Mabroukeh, N. R. and Ezeife, C. I. (2010). A taxonomy of sequential pattern mining algorithms. *ACM Computing Surveys (CSUR)*, 43(1), 1–41.

Mahringer, C. A. (2019). *Exploring Routine Ecologies: A Characterization and Integration of Different Perspectives on Routines*. Dissertation, Stuttgart: University of Stuttgart.

Mahringer, C. A., Dittrich, K. and Renzl, B. (2019). Interdependent routines and innovation processes: An ethnographic study of Scrum teams. Academy of Management Proceedings.

Marcus, G. E. (1995). Ethnography in/of the world system: The emergence of multi-sited ethnography. *Annual Review of Anthropology*, 24(1), 95–117.

Mesle, C. R. and Dibben, M. R. (2017). Whitehead's process relational philosophy. In A. Langley and H. Tsoukas, eds., *The Sage Handbook of Process Organization Studies*. London: Sage, pp. 29–42.

Moody, J., McFarland, D. and Bender-deMoll, S. (2005). Dynamic network visualization. *American Journal of Sociology*, 110(4), 1206–1241.

Pentland, B. T. (1999a). Building process theory with narrative: From description to explanation. *Academy of Management Review*, 24(4), 711–724.

Pentland, B. T. (1999b). Organizations as networks of action. In J. Baum and B. McKelvey, eds., *Variations in Organization Science: In Honor of Donald T. Campbell*. Thousand Oaks, CA: Sage, pp. 237–253.

Pentland, B. T. (2003a). Conceptualizing and measuring variety in the execution of organizational work processes. *Management Science*, 49(7), 857–870.

Pentland, B. T. (2003b). Sequential variety in work processes. *Organization Science*, 14(5), 528–540.

Pentland, B. T. and Feldman, M. S. (2007). Narrative networks: Patterns of technology and organization. *Organization Science*, 18(5), 781–795.

Pentland, B. T., Feldman, M. S., Becker, M. C. and Liu, P. (2012). Dynamics of organizational routines: A generative model. *Journal of Management Studies*, 49(8), 1484–1508.

Pentland, B. T., Hærem, T. and Hillison, D. (2010). Comparing organizational routines as recurrent patterns of action. *Organization Studies*, 31(7), 917–940.

Pentland, B. T., Hærem, T. and Hillison, D. (2011). The (n)ever-changing world: Stability and change in organizational routines. *Organization Science*, 22(6), 1369–1383.

Pentland, B. T. and Liu, P. (2018). Network models of organizational routines: Tracing associations between actions. In R. Mir and S. Jain, eds., *The Routledge Companion to Qualitative Research in Organization Studies*. New York: Routledge, pp. 422–438.

Pentland, B. T., Mahringer, C. A., Dittrich, K., Feldman, M. S. and Ryan Wolf, J. (2020). Process multiplicity and process dynamics: Weaving the space of possible paths. *Organization Theory*, 1, 1–21.

Pentland, B. T. and Rueter, H. H. (1994). Organizational routines as grammars of action. *Administrative Science Quarterly*, 39(3), 484–510.

Pentland, B. T., Ryan, J. L., Xie, Y., Kim, I., Frank, K. and Pentland, A. P. (2019). Visualizing clinical routines: What can we see with digital trace data. 11th International Symposium on Process Organization Studies. Chania, Greece.

Poole, M. S., Lambert, N., Murase, T., Asencio, R. and McDonald, J. (2017). Sequential analysis of processes. In A. Langley and H. Tsoukas, eds., *The Sage Handbook of Process Organization Studies*. London: Sage, pp. 254–270.

Sabherwal, R. and Robey, D. (1993). An empirical taxonomy of implementation processes based on sequences of events in information system development. *Organization Science*, 4(4), 548–576.

Salvato, C. (2009a). Capabilities unveiled: The role of ordinary activities in the evolution of product development processes. *Organization Science*, 20(2), 384–409.

Salvato, C. (2009b). The contribution of event-sequence analysis to the study of organizational routines. In M. C. Becker and N. Lazaric, eds., *Organizational Routines: Advancing Empirical Research*. Northampton: Edward Elgar Publishing, pp. 68–102.

Sankoff, D. and Kruskal, J. B. (1983). *Time Warps, String Edits, and Macromolecules: The Theory and Practice of Sequence Comparison*. Reading, MA: Addison-Wesley Publishing.

Schwaber, K. and Beedle, M. (2002). *Agile Software Development with Scrum*. Upper Saddle River, NJ: Prentice Hall.

Sele, K. and Grand, S. (2016). Unpacking the dynamics of ecologies of routines: Mediators and their generative effects in routine interactions. *Organization Science*, 27(3), 722–738.

Van de Ven, A. H., Polley, D., Garud, R. and Venkatraman, S. (1999). *The Innovation Journey*. New York: Oxford University Press.

Van der Waal, K. (2009). Getting going: Organizing ethnographic fieldwork. In S. Ybema, D. Yanow, H. Wels and F. Kamsteeg, eds., *Organizational Ethnography: Studying the Complexities of Everyday Life*. London: Sage, pp. 23–39.

Witten, I. H., Frank, E., Hall, M. A. and Pal, C. J. (2016). *Data Mining: Practical Machine Learning Tools and Techniques*. Cambridge: Morgan Kaufmann.

Yanow, D. (2012). Organizational ethnography between toolbox and world-making. *Journal of Organizational Ethnography*, 1(1), 31–42.

CHAPTER 13

Narrative Networks in Routine Dynamics

BRIAN T. PENTLAND AND INKYU KIM

13.1 Introduction

Pentland and Feldman (2007) proposed narrative networks as a way to describe 'how technology and organization are intertwined' in organizational routines (781). Narrative networks also provide a way to summarize and compare the performances of routines. As Danner-Schröder and Geiger (2016: 633) explain: ' . . . studies have revealed that routines exhibit a high degree of performance variation; i.e., each iteration of the routine differs from the previous one'. This 'pattern-in-variety' (Cohen, 2007) makes it difficult to analyze stability and change in routines because even a stable routine can display a lot of variations. By summarizing patterns of action in a systematic way, narrative networks can help address a central problem in research on Routine Dynamics research: analyzing stability and change in routines.

In this chapter, our goal is to help readers get started using narrative networks for research on Routine Dynamics. We will introduce the basic idea of a narrative network and review existing literature that uses narrative networks as a way to represent routines and Routine Dynamics. We will discuss how to create a narrative network and suggest some possible applications to research on Routine Dynamics. A key point is that a single narrative network is a snapshot, frozen in time. To study dynamics, we need to capture a series of snapshots, such as a movie (Cloutier and Langley, 2020; Moody et al., 2005).

13.2 What Is a Narrative Network?

Narrative networks are a departure from social networks because the nodes are events, not people. The relations between the nodes indicate sequence (e.g., 'The patient checks in, then they go to the examination room, then they see the doctor'), not communication, affinity or kinship (Wasserman and Faust, 1994). As suggested by Feldman et al. (2016), the narrative network puts action in the foreground, but it does not just summarize actions: it summarizes *sequences* of action. Sequentially adjacent pairs of actions are the fundamental elements of a narrative network. Actions make the nodes, but sequential pairs of actions make the network.

Narrative networks have also been used for other kinds of sociological analysis. For example, Bearman and Stovel (2000) argued that 'by representing complex event sequences as networks, inducing "narrative networks", it is possible to observe and measure new structural features of narratives'. (69). To apply this idea to organizational routines, the key conceptual move is to consider the performances of a routine as a collection of narratives – sequences of events with beginning, middle and end – and then to analyse those narratives as a network.[1]

Figure 13.1 shows an example of a narrative network from Chao (2016). In the full study, Chao (2016) used a combination of interviews, observations and other techniques to gather data about changes in routines before and after the implementation of an electronic health record (EHR) system in the perinatal services department of a hospital in the United States in 2011. Figure 13.1 shows only the post-implementation network.

The left column of the figure is a flow diagram that shows a portion of the Admission Assessment routine as performed by a Registered Nurse (RN). The centre

[1] The term 'narrative network' has occasionally been used to refer to networks of actors within a piece of literature (e.g., Ahmad, 2013), but that usage seems to be rare.

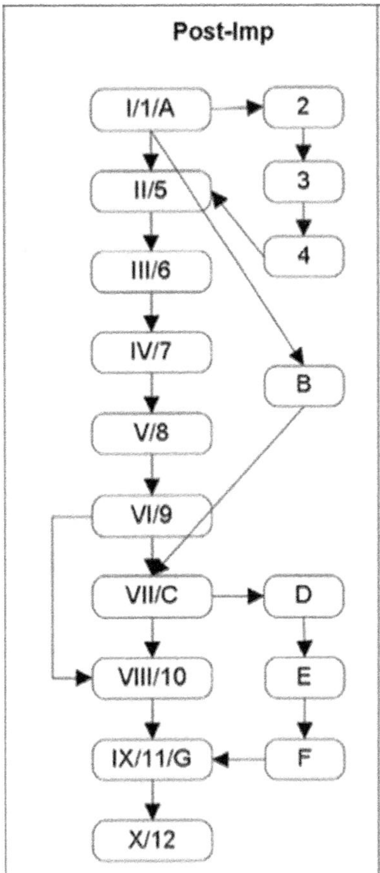

Post-EHR Admission Assessment in Room or on Medication Cart *

I. RN assesses patient
II. RN logs into EHR
III. RN documents assessment
IV. RN locate and merge patient prenatal records into EHR
V. RN prints assessment and prenatal records
VI. RN logs off EHR
VII. RN exits patient room
VIII. RN picks up printouts from printer
IX. RN inserts printouts in patient chart
X. RN notifies PP and Nursery new patient

Post-EHR Admission Assessment on Paper *

A. RN assesses patient
B. RN documents assessment on paper chart
C. RN exits patient room
D. RN collects/prints prenatal records
E. RN photocopies assessment and prenatal records for PP and Nursery
F. RN drops off photocopied records for pickup by PP and Nursery
G. RN inserts prenatal and assessment in patient chart

Post-EHR Admission Assessment at Nurses Station *

1. RN assesses patient
2. RN notes information in personal notes
3. RN exits patient room
4. RN finds a computer
5. RN logs into EHR
6. RN documents assessment
7. RN locate and merge patient prenatal records into EHR
8. RN prints assessment and prenatal records
9. RN logs off EHR
10. RN picks up printouts from printer
11. RN inserts printouts in patient chart
12. RN notifies PP and Nursery new patient

*For patient in triage room, recovery room, or surgical suite, nurse can choose to chart at nurses station, on medication cart, or on paper

Figure 13.1 Narrative network (from Chao, 2016)

and right columns of Figure 13.1 contain the labels (or annotations) for the nodes in the left column. We can use the example in Figure 13.1 to illustrate all of the basic concepts of a narrative network.

1. **Point of view.** Like any narrative, a narrative network incorporates a particular point of view. In this case, the network adopts the point of view of the Registered Nurse.

2. **Nodes are events.** The nodes in a narrative network are categories of action or functional events (Hendricks, 1972). A functional event can be any action or occurrence that advances a narrative. Functional events can be described by an action and any number of material, technological and contextual dimensions (Pentland et al., 2020). For example, in Figure 13.1, we see actions performed by the nurse using the EHR system, not just decontextualized actions.
3. **Events are sequentially related.** The edges (or arcs) in the network represent sequential relationships between the events. For example, the 'RN assesses patient' and then 'RN logs into EHR'.
4. **Snapshot.** The network provides a summary of the routine at one point in time. The network in Figure 13.1 is post-implementation.
5. **Choice of granularity/abstraction.** The lexicon of events in the network is chosen to include significant events, so it leaves out minor details. For example, Chao (2016) does not specify how the RN logs into the system.

This style of presentation (graph plus annotations) follows the example presented by Pentland and Feldman (2007). However, the underlying construct has a more formal definition: a narrative network is a weighted, directed graph where the nodes are categories of action and the edges (or ties or arcs) are sequential relations between those categories (Pentland et al., 2017). This definition paves the way for a rich set of tools for creating, visualizing, analysing and comparing networks. For example, the narrative network provides the foundation for an extended definition of task complexity that can be applied to organizational routines (see Haerem et al., Chapter 24, this handbook; Haerem et al., 2015). Narrative networks can show how frequently particular paths are followed and whether they are getting more or less frequent over time. By formalizing the definition, we lay the foundation for using narrative networks to analyse Routine Dynamics.

13.2.1 How to Create a Narrative Network

Narrative networks can be constructed from any corpus of data that contains coherent sequences of actions. Given a set of sequences generated by an organizational routine, creating a narrative network is straightforward.

Coherent sequential narratives. By *coherent*, we mean that there is a common thread that allows us to treat the sequences as a meaningful whole. Abbott (1990) refers to this property as colligation. The events in each sequence should be meaningfully related. Coherence comes from many sources (a common actor, location, topic, case, purpose, etc.). Rather than six people talking all at once, there may be three distinct conversations on three separate topics. If the goal is to understand conversations, these need to be treated separately. We refer to these as *threads*. In Figure 13.1, the common thread is the interaction between the patient and the RN.

Coding the events. The next step is to identify the set of actions that one wishes to include in the network. Berente et al. (2018) refer to this as determining the lexicon for the process. Researchers must decide which actions are relevant to their inquiry. For example, since Chao (2016) wanted to understand the difference between using the EHR and paper charts, actions like 'RN Logs into EHR' are quite salient. Once the lexicon is defined, each category of action in the lexicon becomes a node in the network.

The events in the threads need to be coded into a set of categories. As we discuss later, this may pose a significant challenge when events are fluid or have multiple interpretations, as events often do. The coding operation will do less violence to the data in situations where events are repetitive and readily recognizable. If coding seems excessively laborious or problematic, it raises questions about the suitability of the coding scheme or the suitability of narrative networks for the phenomenon in question.

Sequential pairs of events. Once the nodes have been defined, the next step is to identify the edges (or ties or arcs) in the network. To identify edges, we scan through the observed sequences and count each *sequentially adjacent pair of events*. Each pair of events becomes an edge in the network. The frequency of occurrence can be used as a weight for the edge. This is known as a 'directly follows graph' (DFG) (van der Aalst,

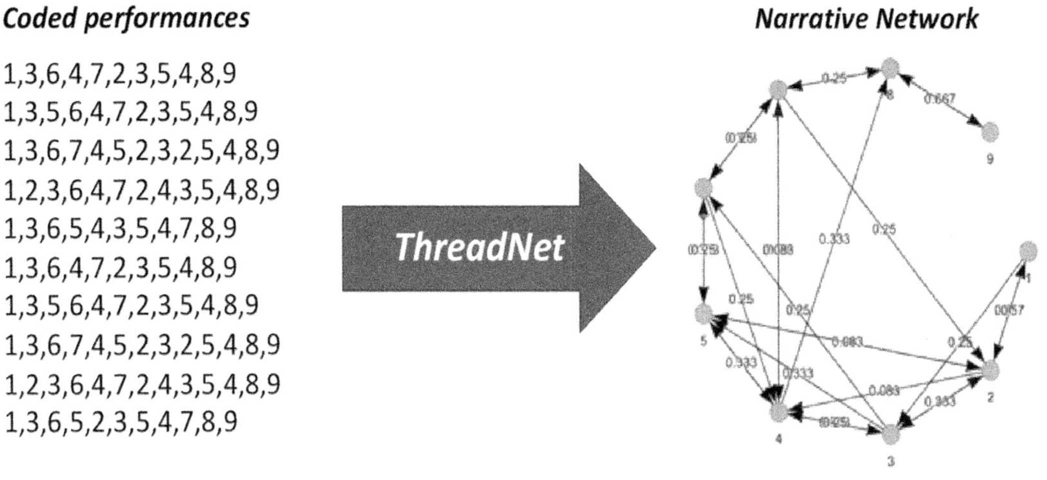

Figure 13.2 ThreadNet weaves threads into networks

2019) because it shows which action follows directly from other actions. Because the network summarizes an observed set of event sequences from a particular time window, it can be considered as a time-slice or aggregate network (Rossetti and Cazabet, 2018). Although they have limitations for some purposes, DFGs are used in commercial process mining and process management applications (van der Aalst, 2019).

It is important to note that the data to construct a narrative network can be collected using many different methods (e.g., interviews, observations, archival records, digital traces), as long as it contains coherent threads. With a small corpus of data and a little patience, the network can be constructed by hand. With a larger corpus of data, a computer is faster and more reliable. *ThreadNet* is an open source application written in R that performs this operation on sequences of actions.[2] The name is meant to suggest that it weaves *threads* into *networks*. *ThreadNet* implements what Pentland and Liu (2017) call the 'bottom-up' method for tracing associations between actions to create the network.

[2] *ThreadNet* was developed with support of the National Science Foundation (NSF SES-1734237, Antecedents of Complexity in Healthcare Routines). It is freely available on http://github.com/. Sample data and instructions for downloading, installing and using *ThreadNet* are available at http://routines.broad.msu.edu.

It is meant to provide qualitative researchers with a point-and-click tool for visualizing and exploring action patterns from different points of view.

Figure 13.2 provides a graphical illustration of the basic idea of what *ThreadNet* does. The left side consists of ten coded sequences. Each coded sequence could represent a visit to the perinatal services clinic in Chao (2016), where each digit (1–9) corresponds to an action by the registered nurse (RN). By scanning through these sequences, *ThreadNet* constructs the directed, weighted graph shown on the right-hand side of Figure 13.2.

13.2.2 Narrative Networks Incorporate Context

Unlike a social network, where the nodes are usually defined by individual persons, the nodes in a narrative network are defined by researcher choice. For example, Chao (2016) defined each node in terms of an action, an actor (the registered nurse) and the system being used (EHR or paper). This flexibility distinguishes narrative networks from any other class of network because it allows the researcher to bring context into the definition of the process (Hernes, 2007).

Context is usually treated as external (Avgerou, 2019), outside the process or routine. However, contextual specifics, such as who, what, when, where and why, are essential to the interpretation of human action, as suggested by this quote from Thomas Aquinas (1952), 'For in acts we must take note of who did it, by what aids or instruments he did it (with), what he did, where he did it, why he did it, how and when he did it.'

Adding context is what distinguishes a narrative network from an action-only network. Using a narrative network, we can bring contextual dimensions into the representation of a routine. This can include role (the RN), location (the clinic), technology (the EHR) and anything else that can be observed and coded. Adding or removing contextual features from the structure of the network provides a way to directly visualize how context affects the overall pattern of action.

Pentland, Recker, Wolf and Wyner (2020) provide an example based on twenty-five visits to a dermatology clinic, as shown in Figure 13.3. Each image in Figure 13.3 is based on the same data, but with the nodes defined by additional contextual dimensions. The images in Figure 13.3 are also produced by *ThreadNet*.

In the first row of Figure 13.3, nodes are defined only by actions (e.g., 'Check meds.'). In the second row, nodes are defined by actions and role (e.g., '*Physician* checks meds.'). In the third row, the specific workstation in the clinic is included (e.g., 'Physician checks meds *at the workstation in her office*.') The increasingly contextualized description of events results in a proliferation of categories (from N = 48 to N = 458), but it creates a graph that is much more readily interpreted. As we bring more context into the definition of the network, we can begin to see clusters in the network. These clusters correspond to groupings of activities by organizational role and by physical location in the clinic. In the same way that the physical layout of a clinic shapes the social network (Sailer and McCulloh, 2012), the workstations shape the narrative network. We can see how the process is entangled with context (Hernes, 2007).

Bringing in context renders a clearer, more precise picture of the routine. As in photography, an image with more pixels provides a clearer picture. Pentland et al. (2020) argue that a finer grained lexicon will result in a better visualization. The improvement is partly because of a finer grained image (more pixels), but most of the

Figure 13.3 One day in one clinic from different points of view

white space around the image grows as an exponential function of the number of events in the lexicon (white space ~ size of lexicon^2). Thus, when you increase the lexicon from 48 to 458 nodes, as in Figure 13.3, you increase the whitespace from 2,304 to 209,764. The whitespace around the network is important because it represents the sequential relations that did *not* occur in the data. Contrary to common practice in qualitative research, which recommends reducing the number of categories (Gioia et al., 2013), a narrative network will provide a more detailed visualization if you increase the number of categories. This can be accomplished by following the advice of Thomas Aquinas and including more context in the definition of the events in the network.

13.2.3 The Role of Time

Time and temporality are central issues in Routine Dynamics (see Turner and Rindova, Chapter 19, this handbook). For research on Routine Dynamics, we need a clear understanding of how time is (and is not) represented in narrative networks. Within a single thread, we use a sequence to determine the relation between events. If time stamps are present, they can be used to compute the speed (or duration) of events and transitions between events, but the basic structure is determined by sequence, not duration. In commercial applications, slow transitions can indicate bottlenecks in a process (van der Aalst, 2019).

As mentioned earlier, a narrative network represents a snapshot of an action pattern. Again, the metaphor of photography is useful. Imagine that data is collected by a camera that captures action while its shutter is open. If the shutter is open for too short a time, the image won't include enough information to render all the details of the pattern. If the shutter is open too long, the image will be blurry, especially if the pattern is changing. And of course, one can open and close the shutter repeatedly to create a series of images (a movie).

In photography, the choice of shutter speed depends on the subject, lighting and desired image; in other words, it depends. Similarly, there is no simple rule for capturing a good image of a narrative network. It is easy to understand some of the boundary conditions and trade-offs. At one extreme, if all performances of a routine conform to a single, fixed pattern, then a single performance is enough to get an accurate network. Of course, the 'shutter' needs to be open for at least one whole performance. This idealized case almost never occurs in practice.

At the other extreme, if the performances are highly variable, then data collection needs to include many performances. The exact number is a difficult and unsolved issue that depends on the kind of images you want to get and how you want to analyse them. For example, in our research on dermatology clinics, we use a time window of 'one day at one clinic' to capture clinical routines, as in Figure 13.3. One day typically consists of roughly 35–40 patient visits, which is too few to get a complete picture of all the ways that clinical routines are performed. However, clinic operations cease completely for roughly 16 hours/day and the clinical staff change on a daily basis (e.g., doctors and residents move between clinics). Thus, there is a rationale for treating each day separately.

In a situation where the routine is highly variable, one might be tempted to use a very wide window of observation. For example, one might aggregate a month or a year of clinic visits in order to get a better estimate of the true network. This strategy assumes that the wide variety of performances are coming from a perfectly stationary structure (Anderson and Goodman, 1957). However, if the subject is changing over time, as routines often do, this strategy will produce a misleading result with all the images blurred together. Thus, to capture Routine Dynamics with a narrative network, multiple distinct snapshots are desirable.

13.3 Empirical Research Using Narrative Networks

Table 13.1 summarizes applications of narrative networks in empirical research. In these studies, nodes are defined in various ways, but edges always represent sequential relations between actions. Most of the studies are descriptive or comparative; we are just beginning to see narrative networks applied to Routine Dynamics.

Most of the empirical examples in Table 13.1 examine a single time slice. We include them here for reference, but we will focus on the studies that use multiple time slices to examine stability and

Table 13.1 Empirical studies using narrative networks

Citation	Type of data	Nodes	Multiple time slices	Topic and finding
Pentland, Haerem and Hillison (2011)	Digital trace data	Action	No	Comparison of invoice processing routines; found that infrequent participants tend to increase the variety in action patterns.
Goh, Gao and Agarwal (2011)	Observation and interviews	Action, Actor	No	Introduction of electronic medical records; found 'virtuous' and 'vicious' cycles in the implementation of EMR technology.
Hayes et al. (2011)	Observation and interviews	Action, Actor	No	Information technology implementation in a hospital; used narrative network to explain why certain routines continue to exist, change or stop entirely.
Yeow and Faraj (2011)	Hypothetical	Action, Actor	No	Enterprise systems and organizational change; compares narrative network to other process modelling approaches
Weeks and Veltri (2013)	Archival	Action	No	Online communities and crowdsourcing; identifies factors that help or hinder knowledge creation.
Pentland, Recker and Wyner (2017)	Handwritten journals	Action, Actor, Artifact	No	Problem solving at Citibank Customer Service Center; found that handoffs between people are much less common that other kinds of handoffs (e.g., between activities and systems).
Sailer (2019)	Observations in two hospitals	Action, Actor, Location	No	Influence of spatial layout on organizational routines; found strong relationship between spatial layout and action patterns
Mahringer, Dittrich and Renzi (2019)	Observation and digital trace	Action, Role	No	SCRUM routines in software development; show how actors use routine patterns to orchestrate unpredictable innovation processes.
Pentland, Recker, Wolf and Wyner (2020)	Digital trace data	Action, Role, Location	No	Electronic health record keeping routines; found that adding context can result in exponential improvement in visualization
Chao (2016)	Interview and observation	Action, Actor	Yes	Effects of EHR utilization on organizational routines in hospitals; compares pre- and post-implementation networks.
Goh and Pentland (2019)	Observation and archival records	Action, Role	Yes	Dynamics of software development routines; found that complexity can change dramatically from sprint to sprint.
Pentland, Vaast and Wolf (2021)	Digital trace data	Action	Yes	Diachronic analysis of electronic health records; found that EHR recordkeeping routines can be quite stable except when there are exogenous shocks.

change over time. We have already mentioned Chao's (2016) study of EHR implementation. This was a classic pre-/post-implementation research design based on 18 months of data collection. The goal was to examine how EHR was changing work routines in the hospital.

Goh et al. (2011) also studied evolving hospital work routines. Their study identified the possibility of virtuous cycles (where technology and user action co-evolve in a positive way) and also vicious cycles, where the opposite is true. They used a narrative network perspective to analyse clinical routines. While they did not explicitly describe these changes in graph theoretic terms (changes to nodes and edges), the phenomena they observed could be interpreted this way.

In a study of agile video game development, Goh and Pentland (2019) identify a set of feedback loops that led the development team to change their goals and work patterns from sprint to sprint. In early sprints, the game developers want to make the game playable and engaging; in later sprints, they just need to finish. Goh and Pentland (2019) use narrative networks to explicitly visualize how these changes influence the work patterns in each sprint.

Pentland, Vaast and Wolf (2021) traced routines in dermatology clinics over a two-year period using data from electronic health records. The network model in this study was limited to actions. The data suggest that the basic clinical routines were quite stable, except when influenced by exogenous factors such as changes in hospital privacy policy or flu season. We discuss this example in more detail next.

13.4 Getting Started with Narrative Networks

From these examples, we can see that narrative networks provide a unique way to visualize Routine Dynamics and compare patterns of action over time. However, narrative networks can be a useful tool for just sketching out the basic pattern of a routine in any study of routines. Pentland and Liu (2017) identify two basic strategies: top-down and bottom-up, as outlined in Table 13.2.

Pentland and Liu (2017) provide a simple interview protocol for the top-down strategy that corresponds to the basic steps outlined earlier: (a) identify the lexicon and (b) identify sequential relations (e.g., 'What typically happens next? What else could happen?'). The process is iterative, because respondents may revise the lexicon as they talk. Nevertheless, this protocol makes it possible to get a narrative network in a single interview. The resulting network can be interpreted as an ostensive aspect of the routine, from the point of view of the interviewee. Different respondents may have different ideas of what is typical, so there may be multiple ostensive aspects. An interview-based network has some obvious limitations. For example, a given respondent may only see part of a routine, and it is not realistic to rely on interviews to establish the relative frequency of alternative paths. Nevertheless, the top-down approach can create a quick summary that can be compared to other perspectives on the routine.

Table 13.2 Strategies for creating narrative networks

	Top down	Bottom up
Sources of data	Interview	Observation Digital event logs
Example	Typical visits to a clinic	Actual visits to a clinic
What is captured?	Typical patterns (ostensive aspects)	Specific patterns (performative aspects)

In contrast, the bottom-up strategy starts from data about specific, situated performances. The bottom-up strategy aligns with the basic idea of process mining – using empirical observations to discover patterns of action (van der Aalst, 2011). For Routine Dynamics, there are several considerations:

1. **Collecting longitudinal data.** As discussed previously, each slice needs to cover a meaningful time period and you need multiple time slices. Across the entire corpus of data, you need to have coherent threads (e.g., visits to a clinic) and a relatively stable set of events. Even if you are working top-down, you will need multiple interviews (over time) to document that routines have changed or stayed the same.
2. **Coding the data.** The basic coding process is no different than any other coding process, except that you can use combinations of codes to define nodes in the network (roles, locations, etc.). Thus, you need to make decisions about how much context to include and make sure to capture and code the same set of contextual data factors for every event.
3. **Choosing the right temporal granularity.** The temporal granularity should be matched to the phenomenon. Fine-grained data (e.g., seconds or minutes) will reveal minor variations that will be invisible in coarse-grained data (days or weeks), but fine-grained data may be noisy, expensive to collect and difficult to work with.

4. **Sequencing and visualizing the networks.** Given a coherent set of coded threads, counting sequentially adjacent events is a simple, mechanical operation, as described earlier. You will need to make one network for each time slice. If you have a lot of data or a lot of time slices, it makes sense to use a computerized tool.

13.5 Routine Dynamics as Network Dynamics

Narrative networks provide a new set of tools for investigating Routine Dynamics. Rather than simply borrowing ideas from social network dynamics, we need to search for principles that are unique to the domain of narrative networks. In this way, we can develop theories of Routine Dynamics that are grounded in longitudinal, empirical observations. We envision three broad topics where narrative networks could be useful for research on Routine Dynamics.

13.5.1 Synchronic and Diachronic Analysis

Barley (1990) outlines the basic operations of synchronic and diachronic analysis as applied to organizational research. Barley examined how action patterns changed in two suburban hospitals after the introduction of new computerized tomography (CT) scanners. At any point in time, he could make a synchronic comparison between the two hospitals; over time, he could make a diachronic comparison within each hospital.

Diachronic analysis is fundamental to understanding Routine Dynamics and it can be facilitated by using narrative networks. Pentland, Vaast and Wolf (2021) used EHR data to visualize changes in recordkeeping routines over a two-year period in four dermatology clinics. The data include roughly 57,000 patient visits. Each visit includes an average of 133 time-stamped actions. Once the series of networks is constructed, they can be visualized and analysed in many ways, such as network movies (Handcock et al., 2008; Moody et al., 2005), where each network represents one day in one clinic. They generated a series of 1,767 such networks, each of which contains 300 possible actions. For simplicity, the nodes were defined by the actions only, as in the first row of Figure 13.3.

However, Figure 13.3 was based on one snapshot: one day in one clinic. By considering the full two years of data, the sequence of networks can reveal how the clinical routine changed over time. Pentland et al. visualized the change by comparing each clinic-day to a common reference (the first day in one of the clinics). Figure 13.4 shows the results of this analysis of the four dermatology clinics. The horizontal axis represents time, from January 2016 through December 2017, measured in days, without gaps for weekend or holidays. The vertical axis is cosine similarity for the list of edges, which provides a summary comparison of each network to the reference network (1 = same, 0 = different).

Figure 13.4 shows sudden and consistent changes in the pattern of action across all four clinics, as well as some ongoing variations. After some investigation, we discovered that these

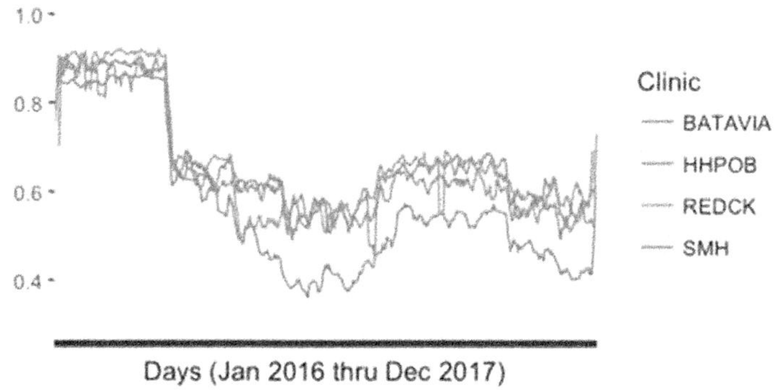

Figure 13.4 Changes in narrative networks in four clinics over two years

changes in the action pattern resulted from sources outside the process. The first change (June 2016) resulted from a change in management policy concerning privacy. The rest of the changes were due to flu season, which officially starts on 1 September and ends on 15 April each year. When flu season started, there was a significant shift in the process. When flu season ended, the process returned to normal.

13.5.2 Using Narrative Networks to Analyze Patterning

Narrative networks provide a method for analysing patterning in terms of network dynamics. Feldman (2016) introduced the concept of patterning as a way to highlight the processual core of Routine Dynamics (see also Danner-Schröder and Geiger, 2016; Turner and Rindova, 2018). Goh and Pentland (2019: 1901) offer an interpretation of patterning in network terms as 'the formation of new paths and the dissolution of old paths in the narrative network that describes the routine'. Pentland and Goh (2021) provide a visual metaphor for this process,

> A physical path across a grassy field makes a clear, precise analogy: we tend to follow paths where the grass is worn. We could cut across in a new direction, but the existing paths show where people have gone in the past and where they are likely to go in the future. Through paths, past performances influence but do not determine future performances. Paths are the metaphorical "ruts in the road" that describe routines (Cohen 2007). The metaphors of *path* and *rut* make sense because the word "routine" derives from the French word *route*, which means *road*.

Narrative networks provide a way to make the process patterning visible. By looking at successive time slices, we can observe paths that form and dissolve over time. Paths are a particularly relevant way to think about patterning because they correspond to ways of getting things done.

13.5.3 Small and Large Scale Patterns: Network Motifs and Communities

Using narrative networks makes it possible for research on Routine Dynamics to take advantage of conceptual and methodological innovations from other areas of network science. We mention two possibilities that seem particularly promising. One involves zooming in to analyse small patterns called network motifs (Milo et al., 2002) and the other involves zooming out to analyse larger patterns called network communities (Bedi and Sharma, 2016).

Motifs are micro-patterns which can be defined as 'recurring, significant patterns of interconnections' in a network (Milo et al., 2002: 824). Distinctive motifs can be identified in a wide variety of networks, including protein regulation, ecological food chains, neurons in the brain, links between pages on World Wide Web and more (Milo et al., 2002). Each type of network has distinctive motifs that reflect the generative principles of the larger network. For example, the basic motif in gift exchange is reciprocity. Researchers on team dynamics have started to use network motifs to identify typical interactions (Leenders et al., 2016). From social and organizational theory, we have many examples of generic action patterns, such as Weick's (1979) 'double interact'. Motifs provide a way to operationalize and study the role of these kinds of basic micro-patterns in narrative networks.

Larger network patterns appear as communities, which can be defined as densely connected regions in the network (Bedi and Sharma, 2016). Community detection is one of the most active areas in network science (Rosetti and Cazabet, 2018), but this concept has never been applied to patterns of action. Rosa et al. (Chapter 17, this handbook) describe a variety of relationships between routines (e.g., clusters, ecologies and bundles) that could be described as network communities. The conceptual vocabulary is in place to study networks of routines, and network community structure could provide the methodology.

13.6 Conclusion

Narrative networks provide a useful way to summarize the 'pattern in variety' that is typical of organizational routines (Cohen, 2007). They can be constructed using a single interview or through an elaborate computational scheme. Either way, narrative networks can help describe action patterns and how they change over time. For this reason, they provide a useful way to investigate Routine Dynamics.

References

Abbott, A. (1990). A primer on sequence methods. *Organization Science*, 1(4), 375–392.

Ahmad, M. A. (2013). *Towards the Analysis of Narrative Networks*. Retrieved from University of Minnesota.

Anderson, T. W. and Goodman, L. A. (1957). Statistical inference about Markov Chains. *The Annals of Mathematical Statistics*, 89–110..

Aquinas, T. (1952). *The Summa Theologica: Great Books of the Western World*. (F. o. t. E. D. Province, Trans. Vol. 19): Encyclopedia Britannica.

Avgerou, C. (2019). Contextual explanation: Alternative approaches and persistent challenges. *MIS Quarterly*, 43(3), 977–1006.

Barley, S. R. (1986). Technology as an occasion for structuring: Evidence from observations of CT scanners and the social order of radiology departments. *Administrative Science Quarterly*, 78–108.

Barley, S. R. (1990). Images of imaging: Notes on doing longitudinal field work. *Organization Science*, 1(3), 220–247.

Bearman, P. S. and Stovel, K. (2000). Becoming a Nazi: A model for narrative networks. *Poetics*, 27(2–3), 69–90.

Bedi, P. and Sharma, C. (2016). Community detection in social networks. *Wiley Interdisciplinary Reviews: Data Mining and Knowledge Discovery*, 6(3), 115–135.

Berente, N., Seidel, S. and Safadi, H. (2018). Research commentary: Data-driven computationally intensive theory development. *Information Systems Research*, 30(1), 50–64.

Burke, K. (1962). *A Grammar of Motives, and a Rhetoric of Motives*. Cleveland, OH: World Pub. Co.

Chao, C.-A. (2016). The impact of electronic health records on collaborative work routines: A narrative network analysis. *International Journal of Medical Informatics*, 94, 100–111.

Cloutier, C. and Langley, A. (2020). What makes a process theoretical contribution? *Organization Theory*, 1(1), 1–32.

Cohen, M. D. (2007). Reading Dewey: Reflections on the study of routine. *Organization Studies*, 28(5), 773–786.

Danner-Schröder, A. and Geiger, D. (2016). Unravelling the motor of patterning work: Toward an understanding of the microlevel dynamics of standardization and flexibility. *Organization science*, 27(3), 633–658.

Feldman, M. S. (2016). Routines as process: Past, present, and future. In J. Howard-Grenville, C. Rerup, A. Langley and H. Tsoukas, eds., *Organizational Routines: How They Are Created, Maintained, and Changed*. Oxford: Oxford University Press, pp. 23–46.

Feldman, M. S., Pentland, B. T., D'Adderio, L. and Lazaric, N. (2016). Beyond routines as things: Introduction to the Special Issue on Routine Dynamics. *Organization Science*, 27(3), 505–513.

Freelon, D. (2014). On the interpretation of digital trace data in communication and social computing research. *Journal of Broadcasting & Electronic Media*, 58(1), 59–75.

Gioia, D. A., Corley, K. G. and Hamilton, A. L. (2013). Seeking qualitative rigor in inductive research: Notes on the Gioia methodology. *Organizational Research Methods*, 16(1), 15–31.

Goh, J. M., Gao, G. and Agarwal, R. (2011). Evolving work routines: Adaptive routinization of information technology in healthcare. *Information Systems Research*, 22(3), 565–585.

Goh, K. T. and Pentland, B. T. (2019). From actions to paths to patterning: Toward a dynamic theory of patterning in routines. *Academy of Management Journal*, 62(6), 1901–1929.

Hærem, T., Pentland, B. T. and Miller, K. D. (2015). Task complexity: Extending a core concept. *Academy of Management Review*, 40(3), 446–460.

Handcock, M. S., Hunter, D. R., Butts, C. T., Goodreau, S. M. and Morris, M. (2008). Statnet: Software tools for the representation, visualization, analysis and simulation of network data. *Journal of Statistical Software*, 24(1), 1548.

Hayes, G. R., Lee, C. P. and Dourish, P. (2011). Organizational routines, innovation, and flexibility: The application of narrative networks to dynamic workflow. *International Journal of Medical Informatics*, 80(8), e161–e177.

Hendricks, W. O. (1972). The structural study of narration: Sample analyses. *Poetics*, 1(3), 100–123 (Reprinted in 1973, Essays on Semiolinguistics and Verbal Art. Mouton, The Hague, 1152–1174.).

Hernes, T. (2007). *Understanding Organization as Process: Theory for a Tangled World* (Vol. 2). London: Routledge.

Johns, G. (2006). The essential impact of context on organizational behavior. *Academy of Management Review*, 31(2), 386–408.

Leenders, R. T. A., Contractor, N. S. and DeChurch, L. A. (2016). Once upon a Time: Understanding team processes as relational event networks. *Organizational Psychology Review*, 6(1), 92–115.

Mahringer, C. A., Dittrich, K. and Renzl, B. E. (2019). *Interdependent Routines and Innovation Processes–An Ethnographic Study of Scrum Teams*. Paper presented at the Academy of Management Proceedings.

Milo, R., Shen-Orr, S., Itzkovitz, S., Kashtan, N., Chklovskii, D. and Alon, U. (2002). Network motifs: Simple building blocks of complex networks. *Science*, 298(5594), 824–827.

Moody, J., McFarland, D. and Bender-deMoll, S. (2005). Dynamic network visualization. *American Journal of Sociology*, 110(4), 1206–1241.

Pentland, B. T. and Feldman, M. S. (2007). Narrative networks: Patterns of technology and organization. *Organization Science*, 18(5), 781–795.

Pentland, B. T., and Goh, K. (2021). Organizational Routines and Organizational Change, In M, S. Poole and A. H. Van de Ven, eds., *Oxford Handbook of Organizational Change and Innovation*, 2nd Edition. Oxford: Oxford University Press, pp. 339–363.

Pentland, B. T., Hærem, T. and Hillison, D. (2010). Comparing organizational routines as recurrent patterns of action. *Organization Studies*, 31(7), 917–940.

Pentland, B. T., Hærem, T. and Hillison, D. (2011). The (N) ever-changing world: Stability and change in organizational routines. *Organization Science*, 22(6), 1369–1383.

Pentland, B. T. and Liu, P. (2017). Network models of organizational routines: Tracing associations between actions. In S. Jain and R. Mir, eds., *The Routledge Companion to Qualitative Research in Organization Studies*. London: Routledge, pp. 422–438.

Pentland, B. T., Recker, J., Wolf, J. R. and Wyner, G. (2020). Bringing context into the analysis of process with digital trace data. *The Journal of the Association for Information Systems (JAIS)*, 21(5), 1214–1236.

Pentland, B. T., Recker, J. and Wyner, G. (2017). Rediscovering handoffs. *Academy of Management Discoveries*, 3(3), 284–301.

Pentland, B. T., Vaast, E. and Wolf, J. R. (2021) Theorizing process dynamics with directed graphs: A diachronic analysis of digital trace data. *MIS Quarterly*, 45(2), 967–984.

Rossetti, G. and Cazabet, R. (2018). Community Discovery in dynamic networks: A survey. *ACM Computing Surveys (CSUR)*, 51(2), 1–37.

Sailer, K. (2019). *Action Network: Exploring Dynamic Organizational Routines in Outpatient Clinics*. Paper presented at the the 4th European Conference on Social Networks, Zurich.

Sailer, K. and McCulloh, I. (2012). Social networks and spatial configuration: How office layouts drive social interaction. *Social Networks*, 34(1), 47–58.

Turner, S. F. and Rindova, V. P. (2018). Watching the clock: Action timing, patterning, and routine performance. *Academy of Management Journal*, 61(4), 1253–1280.

van der Aalst, W. M. (2011). *Process Mining: Discovery, Conformance and Enhancement of Business Processes*. Heidelberg: Springer.

van der Aalst, W. M. (2019). A practitioner's guide to process mining: Limitations of the directly-follows graph. *Procedia Computer Science*, 164, 321–328.

Wasserman, S. and Faust, K. (1994). *Social Network Analysis: Methods and Applications* (Vol. 8). Cambridge: Cambridge University Press.

Weeks, M. R. and Veltri, N. F. (2013). Virtual communities as narrative networks: Developing a model of knowledge creation for crowdsourced environments. *International Journal of Knowledge Management (IJKM)*, 9(1), 21–41.

Weick, K. E. (1979). Cognitive processes in organizations. *Research in Organizational Behavior*, 1(1), 41–74.

Yeow, A. and Faraj, S. (2011). Using narrative networks to study enterprise systems and organizational change. *International Journal of Accounting Information Systems*, 12(2), 116–125.

CHAPTER 14

Bakhtin's Chronotope and Routine Dynamics

SIMON ADDYMAN

14.1 Introduction

Routine Dynamics scholars have invited us to explore more deeply the processual nature of routines, 'de-emphasizing the entity-like features and emphasizing more the continuity of becoming' (Feldman, 2016: 24). An action-centred focus to this process-oriented perspective invites further theorizing on *acting* and *patterning* (2016: 38) and, as the following quotation suggests, time and space are key features in this process, 'Organizational routines are dynamic because they exist through a process of (re)production, over time and space, through the ongoing effort of actants (people and things)' (Feldman et al., 2016: 505). From this process view, Howard-Grenville and Rerup (2017) have suggested that how we identify and interpret temporality and spatiality in understanding routines is 'an area ripe for further development ... ' (Howard-Grenville and Rerup, 2017: 334).

My aim in this chapter is to show how Mikhail Bakhtin's Dialogism (Holquist, 2002) could contribute to Routine Dynamics through widening our understanding of the interplay between temporal and spatial features of routines. In doing so, I connect Routine Dynamics with a growing body of work that explores the dialogical nature of organizing through the work of Bakhtin (Cunliffe et al., 2004; Lorino and Tricard, 2012; Shotter, 2008; Tsoukas, 2009). More specifically, I focus on applying Bakhtin's concept of the *chronotopes*, that is, time-space frameworks, which he developed originally in the context of literary analysis (Bemong et al., 2010). Bakhtin argued that each literary text exhibits a distinctive time-space framework that governs the way the plot unfolds.

In this chapter, I suggest Bakhtin's Dialogism can contribute to developing a better understanding of the interconnectedness of temporal and spatial features of actions (discursive and non-discursive, human and non-human) in the dynamics of routines. Through the chronotope, Bakhtin provides a way of engaging with the concrete lived experiences of individuals and how these are represented. I show how it can help us identify, analyse and represent the multiple configurations of time and space and their influence in the (re)creation of routines, thereby helping advance our understanding of the processual view.

The chapter is structured into three sections. In the first section I present the overlap between Dialogism and Routine Dynamics in understanding the spoken or written word as constituting both the performing and patterning of action. I then explore Bakhtin's concept of the chronotope and its application to the study of organizations and organizing processes. In the second section I illustrate how the chronotope can be applied to the analysis of routines by drawing on an autoethnographic study of routine change (Addyman, 2019). Methodologically, Dialogism draws specific attention to the role of the researcher in ethnographic work, their relationship with participants in exploring organizational phenomena and in writing their research findings (Cunliffe et al., 2014; Lorino et al., 2011).

I then look at two recent studies in Routine Dynamics, Dittrich et al. (2016) and LeBaron et al. (2016), who have identified the role of talk (dialogue) in routines. I seek to show how their work may be seen differently when using the chronotope as an analytical tool. I then conclude the chapter by summarizing and identifying opportunities for future research in the application of Dialogism to Routine Dynamics.

14.2 Bakhtin's Dialogism and the Chronotope

Mikhail Bakhtin (1895–1975) was a Russian philosopher and literary critic, whose work spanned many decades and made contributions to a range of different disciplines, including, for example, linguistics, theology and social theory (Cunliffe et al., 2014: 335). In his writings, Bakhtin was primarily concerned with the analysis of literary texts and the role of dialogue in the formation of social order (Clark and Holquist, 1984; Holquist, 2002). Although Bakhtin did not use the term himself, Holquist (2002) has brought this work together into what he has entitled Dialogism, which he defines as 'a pragmatically oriented theory of knowledge ... that seek[s] to grasp human behaviour through the use humans make of language' (2002: 15).

In organizational studies, Dialogism aligns with a process ontology of organizing and offers a way of understanding the multiplicity and relational aspects of organizing and how these might be represented (Cunliffe et al., 2014). A number of organizational scholars have applied Dialogism to such topics as novelty creation (Shotter, 2008); organizational knowledge (Tsoukas, 2009); inter-organizational cooperation (Lorino and Mourey, 2013); story telling (Haley and Boje, 2014); organizational change and identity (Jabri, 2004); and narratives (Cunliffe et al., 2004).

Bakhtin's primary concern was with the inseparability of language and speech and bridging the differential between them (Holquist, 1983: 310). Language – words, sentences, grammar, syntax – are dead until brought to life in actual speech acts through the *utterance*, the performed act of communication between *self* and *other*. These speech acts give meaning to language, where language is not cognitively a priori or detached in meaning creation from the consciousness of mind but is unified in acts of speech. As with Routine Dynamics, epistemologically it draws attention to the situated nature of action, becoming the place where different meanings are enacted within the performance of the routine through judgements made by routine participants when they engage in dialogue with other actors (human and non-human).

Utterance(s), as a *performance* of communication, can be understood as a form of action (Holquist, 1983: 59). Through observing situated action, the unit of analysis in Routine Dynamics is the performed pattern of action (Feldman et al., 2016: 506). In dialogism, the unit of analysis is the utterance. Through acts of speech (performative), language (ostensive) is enacted and so I suggest that utterances, as individual words or as bundles of words, either spoken or written, can be conceptualized as a place where both the *performing* and *patterning* of action takes place.

Utterances are not original abstract statements where the words have a common and agreed definition, but they ' ... emerge as an active expression of meaning. An utterance eventually generates another statement' (Jabri, 2004: 571). The utterance is not free of personal choice, but is laden with the values of the individual speaker in answering what has been said and authoring what is yet to come (Bakhtin, 1993; Shotter, 2008). As Tsoukas (2009) points out in his paper on dialogue and knowledge in organizations, 'an actor cannot know the meaning of his utterance until another actor has responded' (944). Utterances are a boundary between the said and the unsaid, where the words chosen have meaning within shared social settings and that meaning changes in different settings at different times (Holquist, 2002: 61).

Such a conception moves away from the assumption of means–end intentionality that Routine Dynamics seeks to challenge (Feldman, 2016: 30). By engaging with utterances as a way of conceptualizing the *performing* and *patterning* of action, we may be able to deepen our understanding of organizational routines as always unfinished and unfinalizable, always open to change but always in the process of being stabilized.

A key theme in Dialogism and the focus in this chapter is what Bakhtin termed the *chronotope*, a tool used to analyse the spatio-temporal characteristics of narratives (Bemong et al., 2010; Lorino and Tricard, 2012). Bakhtin introduced the chronotope for examining literary *genres*, which Bakhtin (1981) describes as follows, 'We will give the name *chronotope* [literally, "timespace"] to the intrinsic connectedness of temporal and spatial relationships that are artistically expressed in literature ... Time as it were, thickens, takes on flesh, becomes artistically visible, likewise, space becomes charged and responsive to the movements of time, plot and history' (1981: 84).

Bakhtin set out his thoughts and discusses a number of different generic chronotopes in his book *The Dialogic Imagination* (Bakhtin, 1981). Originally made up of nine chapters, Bakhtin later added a final tenth chapter entitled 'Concluding Remarks', which not only introduced additional major genres but also suggested that any one piece of literature or body of work by an author may include a number of dominant or recurring themes forming their own minor chronotopes (Bemong and Borghart, 2010: 6). It is in the final pages of this chapter that Bakhtin expresses the analytical significance of the chronotope, and I provide here an abbreviated but rather long quotation to highlight this.

> The chronotope is the place where the knots of narrative are tied and untied. It can be said without qualification that to them belongs the meaning that shapes narrative ... We cannot help but be strongly impressed by the *representational* importance of the chronotope. Time becomes, in effect, palpable and visible; the chronotope makes narrative events concrete, makes them take on flesh, causes blood to flow in their veins. An event can be communicated, it becomes information, one can give precise data on the place and time of its occurrence ... And this is so thanks precisely to the special increase in density and concreteness of time markers – the time of human life, of historical time – that occurs within well-delineated spatial areas. It is this that makes it possible to structure a representation of events in the chronotope (around the chronotope) ... Thus the chronotope, functioning as the primary means for materializing time in space, emerges as a center for concretizing representation, as a force giving body to the entire novel. All the novel's abstract elements – philosophical and social generalizations, ideas, analyses of cause and effect – gravitate toward the chronotope and through it take on flesh and blood, permitting the imaging power of art to do its work. Such is the representational significance of the chronotope (Bakhtin, 1981: 250, emphasis in original).

Applying the chronotope concept to organizational studies, Lorino and Tricard (2012) and Lorino (2010) show how it offers an opportunity around which to structure the narrative of the organizing inquiry. 'In organizational life, the chronotope of organizing processes is the presupposed time–space framework of organizing, which delineates the frontier between thinkable and unthinkable, and meaningful and meaningless practices' (Lorino and Tricard, 2012: 217). They suggest that, as Bakhtin has shown in literature (Bakhtin, 1981), organizations and organizing processes have generic chronotopes that make them distinguishable from each other. For example, manufacturing may have a more static spatial frame, the factory, with a more regulated temporal rhythm, the production line. Whereas construction has a new spatial frame each time it is executed and is temporally governed through predefined time boundaries.

Lorino analyses Bakhtin's work and in addition to time and space identifies eight categories of the organizing chronotope (Lorino, 2010), which I have adapted to apply to routines and summarized in Table 14.1.

Lorino and Tricard (2012) explain that 'the chronotope can be used, as it is in ethnological studies, to decipher organizing processes through their time-space frames and get access to deep, partly invisible values and representations. It then allows critical inquiries, making the tacit, presupposed and taken for granted chronotopes of organizing processes explicit and debatable' (2012: 229). These critical inquiries require us to identify openings in organizational practices that allow us to see beyond generic representational types and provide the boundaries of what is believable or unbelievable, intelligible or unintelligible within that given social context. Importantly, 'organisational chronotopes delineate the scope of conceivable futures, activities which are not carried out

Table 14.1 Categories of the chronotope

	The generic categories of the routine chronotope
Temporal frame	The inclusion of clock time (sequential and linear) and experienced time (past, present, future) involved in performing and patterning of the routine.
Spatial frame	The physical location(s) where action takes place and where actions reference other spaces. This is both within one routine and across multiple routines.
Meaning-making principles	Understanding and anticipations of future conditions, taken from present or past routine patterns and performances, in achieving the goals of the tasks associated with the routine.
Roles and characters	The variety of participants and their role in the routine. Their role as formally prescribed by the organization and its actual performance. Their role as interpreted by others.
Values	The personal and professional values that the participants express in their actions (doing and saying).
Crossing character	An action that contributes to the performance of more than one routine
Artifacts	The artifacts that are associated with the routine
Boundaries	The perceived and experienced boundaries of actions that constitute the repeatable and recognizable pattern of the routine.

Source: Adapted from Lorino and Tricard (2012).

today, but might emerge as part of organisational change . . . ' (2012: 215).

Methodologically, the chronotope moves beyond the codification and representation of organizational discourse (Cunliffe et al., 2014: 344). It is a move which captures the dynamic interplay between not just the multiplicity of voices (polyphony) but also what Bakhtin termed *heteroglossia* (Bakhtin, 1981: xix; Holquist, 2002: 69), where the fixed system of the participants' language (for example, an architect or a construction manager) comes to life through varied speech acts in a given context (Lorino et al., 2011: 779). For routines, it is not just that there are multiple participants, but the variety of dialogue (doing and saying) from and between participants that influences patterns of action.

Representing the temporal and spatial features of situated action requires the author to convey a degree of *imagination* between the dialogue captured as language and their interpretation of it as speech acts (Keunen, 2010). As Keunan states, 'A chronotope only becomes a chronotope when it shows something, when it brings to mind an image that can be observed by the mind's eye' (Keunan, 2010: 35). Keunan discusses how these images of action come to life not in the linear representations of time or the static representation of space, but by bringing to life the past, present and future, and multiplicity of spatial frames that are represented in dialogue. The categories of the chronotope help to identify, analyse and capture these frames of the action patterns in routines. Beyond presenting this in tabular format, writing and communicating the findings to the reader about the routine is an important aspect of articulating the temporal and spatial framework that governs how the routine is (re)created. (Cunliffe et al., 2014: 345; Czarniawska, 1999: 106).

In the following section I show how I applied this methodology in a study of routine (re)creation in a large construction project.

14.3 The Chronotope as an Analytical Tool for Examining Routine Dynamics

In this section I demonstrate how the concept of chronotope can be used as a tool for analysing organizational routines. The following example is based on a larger study examining the routines involved in a large underground railway construction project in the heart of the City of London (for details see Addyman, 2019 and Addyman et al., 2020). In this study, I used the categories of the chronotope to explore routines as they were (re)created over time and space. The study showed how participants' dialogue (re) aligned temporal and spatial configurations of their interdependent actions (intentionally or unintentionally), within and across multiple routines, to achieve a shared goal.

The first step in the process of using the chronotope is to analyse the collected ethnographic data and summarize it into the categories of the routine chronotope and present this in tabular format (Table 14.2). This first step allows the researcher to identify, capture and analyse the multiplicity of actants (human and non-human) and their actions involved in the performance of the routine. I illustrate this first step by analysing the consenting routine in Table 14.2. The consenting routine involves applying to the UK government for formal planning consent for a project and the granting of that formal consent. It entails the progression of the design, extensive stakeholder management and the preparation, collation and submission of a large suite of documentation. The routine is governed by predefined and emergent time and space boundaries (i.e., document submission and response times; different buildings and roads the project affects). These boundaries influence the actions taken in submitting the planning application and in discharging the conditions imposed on the project after the planning consent has been granted.

The second step of using the chronotope is to provide a polyphonic and heteroglossic narrative, bringing to life how participants' utterances recreate meaning through their different time and space frames. Next I analyse a piece of dialogue, which was primarily constituted in the consenting routine and came from a regular monthly senior team meeting. The meeting occurred just before consent was granted and at a time when the designers were progressing the detail of the design. Actions were constrained by the planning consent not yet being granted. The dialogue is situated in the office meeting room (space) and comes at the end (time) of the meeting as, '*any other business*', a dominant and recurring practice in the organization and as such in itself a minor chronotope within the consenting routine. It is centred on the

Table 14.2 Categories of the consenting routine chronotope

	Consenting routine chronotope
Temporal frame	Governed by predefined legislative timescales, the emergent date for granting the planning consent, and then applying statutory timescales to its enactment in practice once granted.
Spatial frame	Predominantly office based but stretching wide into the buildings that will be affected, including public spaces such as roads and pavements. The number of buildings being influenced emerges as the design develops in detail.
Meaning-making principles	The statutory planning consent process was new to the team and there was a reliance on external specialist support to be able to interpret the future enactment of the conditions as set out in the legal agreements with stakeholders
Roles and characters	Small internal staff numbers, a disparate number of specialist external consultants, multiple external stakeholders ranging from public, private, to non-governmental bodies.
Values	The project had been communicating with stakeholders over a number of years as the project developed and prior to formally commencing the time-bound consent process. Consistency in the project team that interfaced with stakeholders was seen as a strength in maintaining relationships.
Crossing character	Primarily actions that also constituted the construction, commercial, design and governance routine. Some interface with the organizing routine.
Artifacts	Predominantly the statutory planning documents, legal agreements between the client and stakeholders (predominantly building owners), contract between the client and suppliers, Stakeholder newsletter, temporary spreadsheets with financial information.
Boundaries	Started with error in understanding role and ended with highly integrated roles between teams.

Source: Addyman (2019).

engineering manager (EM), who needed permission to enter a building next to the construction site to undertake a survey of its condition. The EM highlights a potential breakdown of his own tasks and the project as a whole that must be resolved in order to progress the design.

L1: PD: OK, let's go around the table, XY, any other business?
L2: XY: No thank you
L3: EM: Viki, we have an issue on conditions, er, defects survey for A26, or Phoenix House?
L4: CM: Yes
L5: EM: You're aware of that?
L6: CM: Yes. We can't get access into the basement until the 26th.
L7: EM: So, I thought it was the 30th?
L8: CM: The 30th, yes.
L9: EM: Phoenix house is the one that is closest to the first building that we are going to demolish, so we cannot get access to ground floor and the basement until the 30th unless we use the powers?
L10: PM: When did we notify them?
L11: CM: A week ago.
L12: PM: That's why we ask for four weeks' notice in the contract . . ., exactly that reason.
L13: CM: yes, I get accept that.
L14: PM: . . . exactly for that reason.
L15: CM: We've got a really good relationship with them, it's just that the guy is not available with the keys to get into the basement until then and I don't really want to use entry powers and force him to come in on a day . . .
L16: PD: Okay, you've got to go away and talk about it and brief the project exec tomorrow what that means. If that slows down demolition or you're taking a risk, we need to know about that.
L17: PD: Anything else? XX?

The PD's opening statement of 'going round the table' and 'any other business' indicates the temporal frame of the dialogue itself as the participants' shared expectation of this being the final section of the meeting. In L3 the EM raises the issue of the condition survey for A26/Phoenix house (*Artifacts* – Phoenix House as a building and A26 as its reference on design drawings). In doing so, he informs the utterances that follow by extending the temporal and spatial frame (timely access to do the surveys; first building in the sequence of future actions, 6-L12) and the participants involved (*Roles and characters* – those in the meeting; external stakeholders), which draws attention to the time pressures involved in the routine, making them explicit and debatable.

As a material artifact, Phoenix House/A26 has a shared history from prior actions in the routine. It influences the variety in utterances from the participants, actions that constitute other routines, which bring to life the multiplicity of future temporal and spatial frames. For example (Line 15), CM had built up a good personal relationship (*time as experienced*) with stakeholders in Phoenix house (*values*), signalling that what can be achieved through formal process (entry powers) is balanced with the personal and professional values of CM. This indicates how reflecting on past patterns influences how future actions may unfold (*meaning making*) and how action *boundaries* emerge to stabilize the routine.

In turn, this triggers the project manager (PM) into a judgement to shift to a new spatial frame (office-based tasks) and temporal frame (4 weeks' notice – *clock time*), which connects with the contracting routine (*crossing character*) (L10–14) and indicates the pacing of actions within the routine, iterating between time as experienced and clock time. This subsequently triggers the project director (PD, L16) to bracket the bundle of utterances with a new temporal and spatial frame (brief the project executive tomorrow) that defines the immediate (*time*) imaginable future possibilities of the consenting routine (*boundary*).

What we learn from this small extract is that the temporal and spatial frame of the routine, as an organizational level pattern, is constituted by multiple configurations of time and space through the variety in interdependent utterances of participants. We can see that these different configurations emerge as the dialogue unfolds in sequence over time. This interplay of these actions emerges as participants understand the meaning of their utterances, and as the other participants respond in their effort to achieve the shared goals of the routine. This ongoing and dynamic iteration between different temporal and spatial frames shows how each utterance is incomplete in itself, becoming complete and recognizable (stabilizing) in its logical chronological sequence before it is moved on to a new spatial and temporal frame.

In the following section I look at how this methodology may be applied to look differently at other studies of routines.

14.4 Seeing Differently in Applying Bakhtin's Dialogism and the Chronotope

In this section, I juxtapose the above analysis with two recent studies that analyse the role of talk (dialogue) in routines, Dittrich et al. (2016) and LeBaron et al. (2016), to explore what we might see differently if the chronotope were applied to their work?

LeBaron et al. (2016) use Routine Dynamics to study how hospital physicians coordinate their actions when handing off patients at the change of a shift. They note the utterances' role in the shared understanding of sequential variation (2016: 523). They state that clinicians had 'strongly shared expectations about how handoff routines should be enacted, including particular moves in a particular sequence' (LeBaron et al., 2016: 515). They provide a rich narrative of the setting and the participants, showing how situated understandings deviate from shared expectations and that these deviations provide purpose and meaning for participants to be able to *move on* from the situation at hand (2016: 529). The authors propose *sufficiency of action* (2016: 531) as a way of understanding what it takes to *move on*. I propose that the organizing chronotope could be used to further our understanding of how *sufficiency of action* works,

Developing chronotopes for a number of handoff routines would enable us to identify different temporal and spatial frames for different instances of sufficiency/insufficiency of moves in the routine and how these emerge over time. For example, LeBaron et al. (2016) state that 'displays of sufficiency are both backward and forward looking in unfolding sequences of moves' (2016: 525–526). Backward and forward looking suggests different temporal and spatial frames and so following the methodology I presented earlier, we could complement their analysis by identifying the chronotope categories associated with these different frames (i.e., *artifacts* [different drugs], roles [different patients/physicians], *space* [patient in bed/moving around]). We may find and be able to compare and contrast the different chronotope categories for different physicians, different patients, different settings and different timings of the handoff routine, thereby showing how time and space influences the boundaries to action patterns in different instances of the handoff routine.

In the move between analysing speech acts into chronotope categories and writing the narrative, we may identify dominant or recurring themes, producing minor chronotopes within the routine that may help identify the generative mechanisms underlying the re-production of handoff routines. For example, whether different densities of time markers (i.e., how long the patient had been known to the physicians; age of the patient) influenced the extent of information search/exchange by different physicians and how these influenced the maintenance or modification of the routine. Or whether physicians' differing knowledge of different patient medical needs influenced the extent of information search/exchange and hence the temporal frame of the handoff (i.e., short or long in duration). This understanding may draw out dominant categories of the chronotope showing different orientations of participants to, for example, meaning making principles or values.

Similarly, the study by Dittrich et al. (2016) examines the role of reflective talk in routine change in a start-up company in the pharmaceutical industry and showed how talk influenced collective reflection. The authors identify three categories of reflective talk: naming and situating; envisaging and exploring; evaluating and questioning. They present two vignettes of reflective talk in changing the shipping routine, *adapting a specific performance* and *introducing changes to the routine's pattern*, and show differences in the three categories between the two vignettes (2016: 683). The chronotope can contribute to the analysis of these differences by providing the framework for understanding the interplay between different time and space configurations.

The focus in *adapting a specific performance* is oriented predominantly towards a present temporal frame (during the process of packaging) and centred on specific artifacts (the lids and the process router). While in the categories associated with *introducing changes to the routine's pattern*, there is an orientation towards a predominantly past and future temporal frame (problems of past and future supply) and routine participants (changing shipping providers). For example, in the *evaluating and questioning* category for *adapting a specific performance* they discuss repackaging the lids (*artifact*). In this instance, the configuration of present-day *time* constraints on *participants* in the building (*space*) provides the frame for imaginable future possibilities (*meaning making*) that avoid issues of quality (*values*). In the same category in *introducing changes to the routine's pattern*, the future (*time*) possible action of changing (*meaning making*) the shipping provider (*participant*) draws attention to different product shipments (*artifacts*) that have different time constraints (*time*) that will affect the performance of the routine (*value*). They make sense of this imaginable future situation by bringing to life past experiences (*time*) from a similar routine in a different organization (*space*).

I have limited my brief analysis here to a small section of one category. However, were we to extend this analysis we would find multiple instances within all categories of the chronotope for each of the three categories of reflective talk. As in my analysis of the consenting routine, identifying and representing these temporal and spatial markers as generative mechanisms would materialize itself in the writing of the routine chronotope. It will bring to life participants' different time and space configurations, showing the polyphonic and heteroglossic nature of the dialogue and its influence on the (re)creation of the shipping routine.

Theoretically, both studies are founded on Routine Dynamics' recognition of ostensive and performative aspects and both suggest that observing and analysing talk as action can help further theorize the interplay between these aspects. My interpretation of the utterance in Dialogism as a duality and its role in forming the routine chronotope epistemologically contributes to these studies by conceptualizing the inseparability of the ostensive (language) and performative (speech) aspects of the routine. In doing so, it highlights how temporal and spatial frames from different participants' utterances become constituted from within the dialogue itself.

14.5 Conclusion

In this chapter I have shown how Bakhtin's Dialogism and concept of the chronotope can be applied in the study of Routine Dynamics. In the following I propose three areas for further exploration of Dialogism and the chronotope.

First, how might we extend our understanding of the chronotope applied to Routine Dynamics? While I applied the chronotope at the level of the routine, there is opportunity to explore the chronotope of firm level configurations of routines (capabilities) or higher-level routines for adapting routines (dynamic capabilities) (see Salvato and Rerup, 2011: 471). This may help identify and explain how different temporal and spatial configurations from these levels influence the time and space configurations within the routine itself. Horizontally, we may find dominant or recurring themes across different professional roles and different organizational units involved in the same routine, thus producing minor chronotopes. We may use these minor chronotopes to understand differing motivations or dispositions to help inform, for example, our understanding of time and space in routines as truce (Salvato and Rerup, 2018; Zbracki and Bergen, 2010).

Second, the concept of the chronotope has not been used much in organizational theory and requires further development. Further identification of incidents within individual categories would allow us to see different densities of spatial and temporal frames within and between different routine chronotopes. This will help Routine Dynamic scholars develop a wider understanding of how the variety of temporal and spatial markers, and their configurations, influence routine change (Howard-Grenville and Rerup, 2017; Turner and Rindova, 2018).

Third, while I have shown how the concept of chronotope can be fruitfully applied to the study of Routine Dynamics, there are a range of other concepts in Bakhtin's work that might be of interest to Routine Dynamics scholars. Further research may explore Bakhtin's ideas on polyphony (Holquist, 2002: 34; Shotter, 2008: 509); heteroglossia (Holquist, 2002: 24; Jabri, 2004: 570;); addressivity and the excess of seeing (Holquist, 2002: 59); carnival and culture (Cunliffe et al., 2014: 9), to name but a few. Such an orientation may open up literary theory more generally to Routine Dynamics and help in understanding how we represent in our writing the dynamic and unfinalizable nature of routines and their (re)creation over time and space.

Organizing in today's world is becoming more dynamic and action patterns that constitute routines are dispersed across multiple temporal and spatial frames. While Bakhtin's Dialogism and his concept of chronotope is new to Routine Dynamics, I have illustrated in this chapter how its application can help further our understanding, through dialogue, of how different configurations of time and space influence the (re)creation of routines.

References

Addyman, S. (2019). The timing of patterning or the patterning of timing? Organisational routines in temporary organisations. PhD Thesis. http://discovery.ucl.ac.uk/10066709/

Addyman, S., Pryke, S. and Davies, A. (2020). Re-creating organizational routines to transition through the project life cycle: A case study of the reconstruction of London's Bank underground station. *Project Management Journal*, 51(5), 1–16.

Anderson, L. (2006). Analytic autoethnography. *Journal of Contemporary Ethnography*, 35(4), 373–395.

Bakhtin, M. M. (1981). *The Dialogic Imagination: Four Essays by M M Bakhtin* (ed. C. Emerson and M. Holquist, trans.). Texas: University of Texas Press Slavic Series.

Bakhtin, M. M. (1993). *Toward a Philosophy of the Act*. Texas: University of Texas Press.

Bakhtin, M. M., Holquist, M. and Liapunov, V. (1990). *Art and Answerability: Early Philosophical Essays* (Vol. 9). Texas: University of Texas Press.

Bemong, N., Borghart, P., De Dobbeleer, M., De Temmerman, K., Demoen, K. and Keunen, B. (2010). *Bakhtin's Theory of the Literary Chronotope: Reflections, Applications, Perspectives*. Ghent: Academia Press, pp. 1–227.

Bemong, N. and Borghart, P. (2010). Bakhtin's theory of the literary chronotope: Reflections, applications, perspectives. In N. Bemong, P. Borghart, M. De Dobbeleer, K. De Temmerman, K. Demoen and B. Keunen, eds., *Bakhtin's Theory of the Literary Chronotope: Reflections, Applications, Perspectives*. Gent: Academia Press, pp. 1–16.

Clark, K. and Holquist, M. (1984). *Mikhail Bakhtin*. Cambridge, MA: Harvard University Press.

Cunliffe, A. L., Helin, J. and Luhman, J. T. (2014). Mikhail Bakhtin (1895–1975). In J. Helin, T. Hernes, D. Hjorth and R. Holt, eds., *The Oxford Handbook of Process Philosophy and Organization Studies*. Oxford: Oxford University Press.

Cunliffe, A. L., Luhman, J. T. and Boje, D. M. (2004). Narrative temporality: Implications for organizational research. *Organization Studies*, 25(2), 261–286.

Czarniawska, B. (1999). *Writing Management: Organization Theory as a Literary Genre*. Oxford: Oxford University Press on Demand.

Dittrich, K., Guérard, S. and Seidl, D. (2016). Talking about routines: The role of reflective talk in routine change. *Organization Science*, 27(3), 678–697.

Feldman, M. S. (2016). Routines as process: Past, present, and future. In J. Howard-Grenville, C. Rerup, A. Langley and H. Tsoukas, eds., *Organizational Routines: How They Are Created, Maintained, and Changed*. Oxford: Oxford University Press, Chapter 2, pp. 23–46.

Feldman, M. S. and Pentland, B. T. (2003). Reconceptualizing organizational routines as a source of flexibility and change. *Administrative Science Quarterly*, 48(1), 94–118.

Feldman, M. S., Pentland, B. T., D'Adderio, L. and Lazaric, N. (2016). Beyond routines as things: Introduction to the special issue on routine dynamics. *Organization Science*, 27(3), 505–513.

Haley, U. C. and Boje, D. M. (2014). Storytelling the internationalization of the multinational enterprise. *Journal of International Business Studies*, 45(9), 1115–1132.

Holquist, M. (1983). Answering as authoring: Mikhail Bakhtin's trans-linguistics. *Critical Inquiry*, 10(2), 307–319.

Holquist, M. (2002). *Dialogism: Bakhtin and His World*. New York: Routledge.

Howard-Grenville, J., and Rerup, C. (2017). *A process perspective on organizational routines*. In A. Langley and H. Tsoukas, eds., *The Sage Handbook of Process Organization Studies*. Thousand Oaks, CA: Sage, Chapter 20, pp. 323–339.

Jones, S. H., Adams, T. E. and Ellis, C., eds. (2013). *Handbook of Autoethnography*. Walnut Creek, CA: Left Coast Press.

Keunen, B. (2010). The chronotopic imagination in literature and film. In N. Bemong, P. Borghart, M. De Dobbeleer, K. De Temmerman, K. Demoen and B. Keunen, eds., *Bakhtin's Theory of the Literary Chronotope: Reflections, Applications, Perspectives* Gent, Belgium: Academia Press, pp. 35–55.

LeBaron, C., Christianson, M. K., Garrett, L. and Ilan, R. (2016). Coordinating flexible performance during everyday work: An ethnomethodological study of handoff routines. *Organization Science*, 27(3), 514–534.

Lorino, P. (2010). The Bakhtinian theory of chronotope (spatial-temporal frame) applied to the organizing process. In Proceedings of International Symposium on Process Organization Studies. Theme: Constructing Identity in and around Organizations (pp. 11–13).

Lorino, P. and Mourey, D. (2013). The experience of time in the inter-organizing inquiry: A present thickened by dialog and situations. *Scandinavian Journal of Management*, 29(1), 48–62.

Lorino, P. and Tricard, B. (2012). The Bakhtinian theory of chronotope (time-space frame) applied to the organizing process. In M. Schultz, S. Maguire, A. Langley and H. Tsoukas, eds., *Constructing Identity in and Around Organizations* (Vol. 2). Oxford: Oxford University Press, Chapter 9, pp. 201–234.

Lorino, P., Tricard, B. and Clot, Y. (2011). Research methods for non-representational approaches to organizational complexity: The dialogical mediated inquiry. *Organization Studies*, 32(6), 769–801.

Salvato, C. and Rerup, C. (2011). Beyond collective entities: Multilevel research on organizational routines and capabilities. *Journal of Management*, 37(2), 468–490.

Salvato, C. and Rerup, C. (2018). Routine regulation: Balancing conflicting goals in organizational routines. *Administrative Science Quarterly*, 63(1), 170–209.

Shotter, J. (2006). Understanding process from within: An argument for 'withness'-thinking. *Organization Studies*, 27(4), 585–604.

Shotter, J. (2008). Dialogism and polyphony in organizing theorizing in organization studies: Action guiding anticipations and the continuous creation of novelty. *Organization Studies*, 29(4), 501–524.

Tsoukas, H. (2009). A dialogical approach to the creation of new knowledge in organizations. *Organization Science*, 20(6), 941–957.

Turner, S. F. and Rindova, V. P. (2018). Watching the clock: Action timing, patterning, and routine performance. *Academy of Management Journal*, 61(4), 1253–1280.

Zbracki, M. and Bergen, M. (2010). When truces collapse: A longitudinal study of price-adjustment routines. *Organization Science*, 21 (5), 955–959.

PART III

Themes in Routine Dynamics Research

CHAPTER 15 Truces and Routine Dynamics

LUCIANA D'ADDERIO AND MEHDI SAFAVI

15.1 Introduction

The notion of truce was originally introduced to capture the fundamentally important political and motivational side of organizational routines and has been carried forward in Routine Dynamics as a means of theorizing the influence of organizational tensions, conflicts and struggles on routines' emergence and persistence. The concept was initially formulated by Nelson and Winter (1982: 110), who discussed how '... routine operation involves a comprehensive truce in intraorganizational conflict'. The notion of truce builds on the assumption that conflict is a key feature of organizations, where different groups and sub-groups typically hold different goals and develop different procedures which reflect their particular interests (Cyert and March, 1963; March and Simon, 1958). The truce construct thus was initially established to help account for the divergence of goals and interests among organizational members (Cyert and March, 1963) and the implications of the ensuing territorial struggles for routines (Nelson and Winter, 1982).

Routines scholars (Becker et al., 2005; Cohen et al., 1996; Coriat and Dosi, 1999; Nelson and Winter, 1982; Zbaracki and Bergen, 2010) have highlighted how, despite the importance of truces for understanding routines, the topic has received surprisingly little attention in the literature since the early insights. A possible reason behind the lack of engagement with this core concept has been ascribed by these authors to the routines literature's early emphasis on the cognitive, as opposed to the motivational, side of routines. Yet another reason behind the neglect may be the fact that truces have been too often taken for granted, their character having been mostly associated with stability and the resolution of conflict (Salvato and Rerup, 2018; Zbaracki and Bergen, 2010). On closer inspection, however, these two assumptions appear to be relatively more relevant to the early routines literature than for the field of Routine Dynamics.

In this chapter we advance a third hypothesis, which is that the notion of truce has not so much been absent from the literature as much as developed under a range of neighbouring concepts. Therefore, if we look for Routine Dynamics papers which contain the term 'truce(s)' in both the title and the abstract, we find only Zbaracki and Bergen (2010). There are instead only four Routine Dynamics papers that contain 'truce(s)' in the abstract: Bertels et al. (2016); Cacciatori (2012); Salvato and Rerup (2018); and Zbaracki and Bergen (2010). If we look instead for Routine Dynamics papers where the term truce appears at least once, we come up with more than thirty papers. The number and variety of the contributions more or less closely related to the topic of truces suggests that this is a much more diverse – and intellectually lively – field than one might initially assume.

This suggests that the notion of truces is not so much a unified and consistent topic or clear-cut category but more of a doorway into some important routines/organizational dynamics. Therefore, on closer inspection, truces appear to operate as a concept aimed at capturing and directing our attention towards a range of organizational processes revolving around the wider notions of conflicts, tensions and struggles. We thus proceeded in our search by, first, looking for papers containing the words truce, conflicts, tensions and/or struggles, which – explicitly or implicitly (based on their citation in papers dealing explicitly with truces) – contributed to the scholarly conversation on truces; and, second, by identifying some distinctive emergent themes within the papers which contained those keywords.

Thus, in addition to *truces and truce dynamics* (theme one), the key processes emerging from our analysis of the literature include the conflicts, tensions and struggles among competing *interests, goals and motivations* (theme two); the related emergence and resolution of conflict, tensions and struggles among diverse *organizational cultures and communities* (theme three); and the processes by which conflict, tensions and struggles might be addressed by invoking and enacting a range of *material artifacts* (theme four).

Once, therefore, we move past the initial label to unpack the concept of truces, we find that the initial lack of interest in the motivational and political side of routines, and emphasis on truces as stable outcomes which has characterized the Carnegie School approach, has slowly but progressively been supplanted by a rich new stream of work in Routine Dynamics where scholars have begun to address the more complex and dynamic processes involved in truce (re)formation, maintenance and breakdown.

In addressing this emergent – albeit important – literature stream, we highlight the value of capturing and theorizing the dynamic aspects of truces, from now on simply 'truce dynamics' (Salvato and Rerup, 2018), which include the context-, agency- and time-dependent processes by which truces come together, fall apart and are reassembled. In our quest, we begin by outlining the notion of truce as originally conceived in the Carnegie and Evolutionary tradition. We then review the contributions to the (extended) truce debate in Routine Dynamics in their variety and diversity, by focusing on some of the salient topics (as identified by our keyword search outlined earlier). These include the notion of truce emergence and truce dynamics; the role of conflicting interests, goals and motivations; the ebbing and flowing of tensions and struggles between and across organizational communities and culture(s); and the role of artifacts and materiality in generating and mitigating conflict. We conclude by recommending some unexplored avenues for future research.

15.2 Truces in the Carnegie and Evolutionary Traditions

The relationship between routines and organizational conflict dates back to the Carnegie School's account of competing organizational goals and how these might be reconciled in an organization (Cyert and March, 1963; March and Simon, 1958; Lazaric [Chapter 18] in this handbook; Rerup and Spencer [Chapter 33)] in this handbook). Carnegie scholars here discuss how organizational members hold widely heterogeneous preferences and divergent interests while also addressing how organizations may be able to deal with differing, oftentimes opposing, views (Cyert and March, 1963; see also Ganz, 2018; Levinthal and Rerup, 2020 for related discussions). Conflict in this literature is considered an important aspect of organizational life as incompatible preferences, held by individuals or groups of organizational members, aggregate into competing organizational-level goals (Ethiraj and Levinthal, 2009) that lead to organizational clashes (March and Simon, 1958), often resulting in freezing the organization in favour of the status quo (Simon, 1955).

Despite the early interest in organizational conflict in the Carnegie literature (Cyert and March, 1963; March, 1962; March and Simon, 1958), it was Nelson and Winter (1982) who first connected the concept of organizational conflict with that of daily organizational routines by introducing the metaphor of 'routines as truces'. According to the authors, routines are not simply memory repositories for organizational knowledge; they also function as truces among intra-organizational conflicts. In highlighting the motivational aspects of the performances of organizational members ('whether they would actually choose to do what is "required" of them') in addition to the cognitive aspects ('whether they know what to do and how to do it') (1982: 98), Nelson and Winter proceeded to portray a new picture of routine operation in which 'some sort of stable accommodation between the requirements of organizational functioning and the motivations of all organization members is a necessary concomitant' (1982: 108).

Cohen and colleagues (1996) took a further step in explicating the dual nature of routines, both as 'problem-solving action patterns and as mechanisms of governance and control' (1996: 670). Building on March and Simon's (1958: 2) definition of organizations as 'systems of coordinated actions among individuals and groups whose preferences, informations, interests and knowledge differ', Cohen et al. (1996: 670) exposed the routine theory's primary concern with the cognitive side of routines at the expense of the governance aspects, thus 'miss[ing] the point that [routines] emerge and operate in a universe of (at least potential) conflict and diverging interests'.

The lack of attention towards the motivational side of routines was further reiterated by Coriat and Dosi (1999). They suggested that the double nature of routines 'as problem-solving skills and as mechanisms of governance appears with particular clarity when analyzing the emergence and establishment of new principles of management and work practices' (1999: 13). This led them to argue for the need to further delve into the truce aspects of routines. Mangolte (1997, 2000) and Lazaric and Mangolte (1998) similarly called for incorporating the governance (motivational) aspects in routine theory by (re)introducing the concept of truce as the outcome of the unseen peace-making processes in intra-organizational conflicts. In their opinion '[. . .] without the notion of "truce", one would have to explain how the different social relationships that permit the activation of the routine are themselves established in each period, and maintained over [. . .] time' (Mangolte, 1997; Becker 2004: 656).

The early 2000s witnessed the emergence of empirical studies touching on the disruption of established truces and the consequences for routine functioning (Burns, 2000; Lazaric and Denis; 2001; Lazaric et al., 2003). Lazaric and Denis (2001), for instance, showed how the process of codifying knowledge in an organization can result in organizational conflicts affecting both cognitive and governance aspects of routines and their recurrent activities. Their findings revealed that codifying the underlying knowledge bases of particular routines not only modifies the way routines are carried out but also changes the motivations of the routines' participants.

15.3 Truces in Routine Dynamics

Despite the occasional appearance of the notion of truces in early routines studies, however, the emphasis in this literature remained firmly on routines-as-truces as the outcomes of organizational conflict resolution. As cogently put by Nelson and Winter (1982), 'when one considers routine operation as involving a truce in intra-organizational conflict, one is led to expect routines to be patterned in ways that *reflect* features of the underlying problem of diverging individual member interests' (1982: 110–111, *emphasis added*).

In an even stronger statement, the view of truces as the embodiment of routines stability was highlighted in Cohen et al.'s (1996: 662) observation that,

> . . . once upon a time there was overt conflict, but in most cases it is largely over when the observer comes on the scene. What the observer sees is therefore the product of cognitive functioning constrained by sensitivity to the sources of conflict. However, the broader the temporal and geographical scale on which one seeks to address the motivational issues, the less of the problem is unlocked by the 'routine as truce' formulation.

Despite providing an important point of departure for addressing the fundamental motivational aspects of organizational routines, early accounts of routines-as-truces substantially missed out on the dynamic aspects of truce formation and breakdown, thus leaving scope for a new, rich and diverse stream of studies to emerge around the notion of 'truce dynamics'.

In the following sections, consistent with our inclusive and expansive approach, we set out to analyse this diverse stream which incorporates, but at the same time goes significantly beyond, what we might consider as 'core' truce dynamics contributions. This involves addressing not only those contributions which directly deal with the construct of truces and their dynamics but also those works for which truces might not be the central or exclusive focus but which nevertheless have significantly contributed to our understanding of truce dynamics through the lens of related concepts. As anticipated earlier, these topics include the influence of conflicting interests, goals and motivations; the emergence and resolution of tensions and struggles between and across organizational communities and culture (s); and the role of artifacts and materiality in addressing organizational conflict. Table 15.1

Table 15.1 Truces in Routine Dynamics literature

Themes	Articles	Research context	Key contributions	Key quotes
3.1 Routines and Truce Dynamics	D'Adderio (2008)	The introduction of software-embedded SOP creates conflict by reconfiguring the 'engineering freeze' routine in automotive manufacturing.	New artifact disrupts the engineering workflow resulting in breaking down the existing truce. Truce is reconstituted through introducing a workaround which supports the formal SOP while allowing for some local discretion.	'[...] notion of "truce" in its dynamic inception as a continuously challenged and emergent achievement' (787). '[...] here we can see clearly what the forces at play are that are responsible for stabilizing or destabilizing the routine' (ibid).
	Zbaracki and Bergen (2010)	Conflicts between functions over the pricing process at a manufacturing firm.	Truces break down and re-form in response to disputes over market forces. Call for a shift in our understanding of truces as resolutions of conflicts of interests to truces as adaptive and dynamic processes.	'Describing the routine as [stable] truce misses the conflict behind the truce; it reveals only the stable truce. Most of the conflict is latent' (956). 'When truces break, organizational members should fight for what they think the routine should be, thereby yielding evidence on the ostensive aspects of routines' (957).
	Cohendet and Simon (2016)	The introduction of a new creative project at a video game studio disrupts routines and triggers a radical reconfiguration of extant truces.	Organizations are able to switch between ostensive aspects in existing routines to support the emergence of a new truce.	' ... disruptions could lead to ... profound reformation of truces between actors in the organization, intense recombination between routines, and significant reconfiguration of the ways of resourcing and rebuilding parts of routines' (615).
	Salvato and Rerup (2018)	Rising tensions in the NPD department of an iconic design company are caused by the inclusion of mass-market, cheaper products.	Routines can be performed to address conflicting goals without breaking down. Process-based conceptualization of routines as truces where conflict is not suppressed or eliminated but is embraced.	'This process conceptualization offers a foundation for revisiting the assumption that routines as truces "show us how firms avoid conflict"' (202). 'The truce is actively built and expanded by routine participants engaging in effortful relating and regulatory actions' (ibid).
3.2 Truces and Conflicting Goals	Zbaracki and Bergen (2010)	Conflicts between sales and marketing departments over the pricing process at a manufacturing firm.	Truces break down and re-form in response to different interpretations of prices across different functions.	'Routines are not just stable entities, but adaptive performances that include conflict' (955). 'The ensuing battle shows how interests, information, and truces are intertwined in performing the routine' (ibid).

Table 15.1 ***(cont.)***

Themes	Articles	Research context	Key contributions	Key quotes
	Rerup and Feldman (2011)	Adoption of an 'espoused' change schema by a newly formed Danish research institution creates conflicts.	Tensions and conflicts among different functions emerge through the enactment of daily routine works.	'[...] trial-and-error processes can be a way of negotiating the various tensions and conflicts in organizations undergoing change' (605).
	Turner and Rindova (2012)	The waste collection routines of six waste management organizations undergoing change initiatives generate tensions between service providers and customers.	Truces emergence by balancing conflicting organizational goals across the organization-customer boundaries through simultaneously establishing and maintaining two different ostensive patterns.	'To maintain dual ostensive patterns that combine targeted consistency and enacted flexibility, organizational members leveraged artifacts and connections both in processes that standardize and stabilize behaviors and in processes that facilitate flexible and mindful responses.' (25).
	D'Adderio (2014)	Conflicting goals (replication and innovation) in routines transfer at a leading US computing manufacturer.	Organizations address multiple conflicting and coexisting goals by enacting routines selectively through a range of social and material features that favour one goal while relegating the other to the background.	[this study] 'generate[s] a framework that captures the dynamic, microlevel, and sociomaterial processes by which organizations unravel the replication dilemma by learning to simultaneously address contrasting goals and the ensuing tensions' (1345).
	D'Adderio and Pollock (2014)	Conflicts between modularity/efficiency and reliability at a high-end electronics manufacturing firm break an existing truce.	Multiple goals can shift over time from conflicting to complementary. Conflicts among complementary and contrasting goals design routines and organizational boundaries.	'[...] a more sophisticated temporary truce was required [...] between efficiency- and reliability-bearing strategies, two important (usually complementary, but in this particular case temporarily conflicting) sides of the lean production philosophy' (1835).
	Canales (2014)	Tensions at three Mexican microfinance institutions addressing flexibility and standardization simultaneously.	Conflicting goals can become generative in balancing simultaneous needs for standardization and local responsiveness.	'Branches that contain discretionary diversity ... perform best. This is because ... committees that contain discretionary diversity generate a productive tension that induces participants to justify decisions along broader organizational goals' (1526).

Table 15.1 (*cont.*)

Themes	Articles	Research context	Key contributions	Key quotes
	Bucher and Langley (2016)	Tensions between old and radically new ways of working in two change initiatives for surgical clinics' patients.	Experimental and reflective spaces produce opportunities for routine participants to engage in deliberate efforts which help prevent tensions and form new routines and underlying truces.	Experimental spaces helped redefine 'ostensive aspects of existing routines [which] inevitably conflicted with those of the envisioned routine' (609). 'A surgeon and subproject leader took responsibility for changing the configuration of the rounds [. . .] Earlier attempts to change it had failed because of [. . .] conflicting interests' (606).
	Cohendet and Simon (2016)	Conflicting goals (efficiency and flexibility) due to the introduction of a new creative project at a video game studio require radical reconfiguration of extant truces.	Restoring organizational creativity requires radical reconfiguration of existing routines, breaking down of exiting truces, and creation of new truces.	'Our aim [. . .] is thus to add to the literature on the dynamics of routines when organizations struggle to strike a balance between efficiency and flexibility' (618). 'A crisis in creativity triggered radical reconfiguration of routines and their artifacts in an effort to restore creativity by modifying the balance between efficiency and flexibility' (615).
	Spee et al. (2016)	Conflicting goals of flexibility and standardization in a professional service routine.	Actions by employees based on discretional knowledge manage the tensions between conflicting goals.	'There is professional skill in deciding what kind of impulse is salient at what stage in the process and enacting that salience by drawing upon knowledge inscribed in one or more of the interdependent routines available' (776).
	Salvato and Rerup (2018)	Rising tensions between design and efficiency at a design company.	Organizational members simultaneously accommodate conflicting goals without breaking the truce.	'Our study proposes a performative model of the routine as truce, in which actors [. . .] respond to problems by taking regulatory actions that create junctures between individuals supporting conflicting goals, thereby embracing conflict and keeping the truce balanced, flexible, and alive' (202).

Table 15.1 (*cont.*)

Themes	Articles	Research context	Key contributions	Key quotes
3.3 Truces, Culture(s) and Communities	Howard-Grenville (2005)	Cultural structures help create a stable truce among organizational members in the roadmapping routine of a high-tech manufacturing organization.	Embeddedness of routine performances in the cultural structures of an organizational context constrains change while allowing improvisation.	'[. . .] roadmapping functioned . . . as a form of organizational memory, as representative of organizational goals, and as a truce between the organization's members, three hallmarks of routines' (623).
	D'Adderio (2008)	The introduction of software-embedded SOP in automotive manufacturing clashes with extant professional cultures, objectives, incentives and views.	Performative struggles between competing cultures and their assemblages are resolved through 'workarounds' that support the formal SOP while allowing for some local discretion.	'The inflexibility of the software-embedded SOP whose philosophy clashed with the goals, views and resources that belonged to other functions [. . .] manifested as a deviation from the SOP. The deviation took the form of a workaround, which temporarily restored flexibility while preventing the freeze process from grinding to a halt' (782).
	Zbaracki and Bergen (2010)	Clashes caused by functional differences over big price adjustment at a manufacturing firm.	Differences in the interests of marketing and sales groups result in overt conflicts and breaking of the existing truce.	'Routines define organizational tasks and thereby aid in coordinating across different functions, but functional differences can create problems of individual incentives, vested interests, and influence' (955).
				'Functional differences may also lead to jurisdictional battles . . . as groups fight for control' (955).
	D'Adderio (2014)	Cultural clashes between UK and US engineering communities during routines transfer, due to the strictly enforced requirement that UK engineers copied exactly US engineers, even in areas where their expertise was deemed far superior.	The contrasting worldviews and objectives of copy-exactly (US) and innovation (UK) could be addressed by first building a truce around replication and then around innovation.	'[. . .] once we focus on conflict and instability rather than truce and stability, we can begin to see how any apparent balance between [contrasting worldviews] must always and necessarily be partial, temporary, and precarious' (1348).
	D'Adderio and Pollock (2014)	Performative struggles unfold between two coexisting cultures and related communities: a culture which supported efficiency and one which supported reliability.	The extant truce based around the culture/logic of efficiency was modified and augmented to incorporate the emerging culture/logic of reliability.	' . . . incorporating the errors and re-internalizing rework had the effect of temporarily restoring a truce between the two sides . . ., a truce which had been lost following the increasing emphasis on efficiency' (1839).

Table 15.1 (*cont.*)

Themes	Articles	Research context	Key contributions	Key quotes
	Bertels et al. (2016)	The integration of a coveted routine with low cultural fit at a major Canadian oil producer results in extra cultural work by organizational members.	Contrasting cultures can become generative when routine participants do not reject a routine with poor cultural fit at the outset but adjust it through a workaround.	'[. . .] an alternative understanding of routines as truces, moving away from the political and punctuated characterization of this construct and toward a more dynamic cultural conceptualization' (574). '[. . .] a cultural truce arises from the fact that culture dynamically accommodates ambiguity through its members' selective use of strategies of action' (590).
	Cohendet and Simon (2016)	Introduction of a new creative culture at a leading video game studio leads to clashes between 'creatives' and 'software developers', which requires establishing new truces.	Restoring organizational creativity requires the radical reconfiguration of existing routines by managers, tapping into cultural elements and shared values to maintain a truce/create a new truce.	'The "cultural routines" of the organization inspired by top management exhibit strong ostensive aspects that guide the organizational members to focus on the essence of their work, i.e., creativity . . . which] implied a drastic reconsideration of the power relations between the two main parties [. . .] in favor of the "creating side"' (626).
	Kho et al. (2019)	Cultural clashes between old and new ways of doing things in technology-mediated health and care services.	The development of relational expertise enables the telehealth professionals to make truces among them around 'overall patient well-being'.	'[Relational expertise] enriched the responses of health professionals and made truce-making possible among them' (191).
	Kiwan and Lazaric (2019)	Introduction of a new technology (robotics) in a surgical team brings about a new ecology of space that creates performative struggles across occupational roles.	Redefining roles and interactions helped avoid tensions, thus re-establishing a working truce to ease performative struggles in experimental and 'reflective' spaces.	'[. . .] reflective space enables practitioners through debriefings to discuss about the new patterns of interdependent actions [and] explore the different aspects of the performative struggle encountered with new artefacts and try to integrate new actions and to delineate the boundaries of this change during experimental performances' (173).

Table 15.1 ***(cont.)***

Themes	Articles	Research context	Key contributions	Key quotes
3.4 Truces, Artifacts and Materiality	D'Adderio (2008)	The introduction of software-embedded SOP reconfigures the 'engineering freeze' routine at an automotive manufacturer.	Formal procedures, or SOPs, are bridged through a workaround which helps restore flexibility and reconstituting the truce. Artefact-embedded rules tend to be more durable and difficult to change and bypass. They break down existing truces and make it more difficult to repair them.	'Framing by rules and SOPs [. . .] is never complete: there is always overflowing which opens up search spaces thus introducing scope for divergence, adaptation and change' (770). Divergence [from SOP] was contained '[. . .]by the prevailing management view that local drift would have offset the benefits of global coordination afforded by the SOP . . . it was the [rigid] SOP that was modified to resemble the actual process. This made the formal procedure more flexible than it had been initially' (783).
	Cacciatori (2012)	The development of a new bidding routine requires designing the system of artefacts to preserve extant truces among various functions in a design firm.	Artefacts are modified to address conflicts among the various groups and support a division of labour that preserves the extant truces through the creation of a new, acceptable truce.	' . . . The modified tool [artefact] becomes a boundary object because it is used to address interdependencies among the bodies of knowledge held by different groups . . . [the] new truce, may simply come to operate in parallel with existing ones . . . ' (1579).
	D'Adderio (2014)	Competing socio-material assemblages, and underlying dedicated artifacts, support the enactment of different routine patterns and different truces at different times.	A different configuration of people and artifact (assemblage) underpins different truces at different times. The artifact (computer model) itself is modified to first support a truce around replication (stage 1) and then one around innovation (stage 2).	'performing routines through selective configurations of artifacts and communities that alternatively supported one pattern or the other, by allowing specific knowledge, views, and actions to be foregrounded at the expense of others' (1345).
	D'Adderio and Pollock (2014)	Performative struggles unfold when assumptions/ logics built into the software database (supporting efficiency) clash with the new logic of reliability.	The extent to which practitioners were able to mobilize social and material features in support of one goal over another explains changes in organizational routines and boundaries, and establishment of new truces.	'In a context where multiple statements struggle to establish themselves, one at the expense of the other, the potential of a theory to gather strength and prevail is closely related to its ability to involve not only actors but also artifacts and material devices (i.e., texts, documents, technologies)' (1824).

Table 15.1 ***(cont.)***

Themes	Articles	Research context	Key contributions	Key quotes
	Aroles and McLean (2016)	The close analysis of two standardized routines at a large newspaper printing company shows how even the simplest of artifact incorporates tensions.	The microprocesses of routines repetition affect and are affected by complex socio-material assemblages that incorporate different stances of both stability and change in order to produce specific truces.	'We find that standard routines can be usefully theorized as ongoing assemblages of distributed actions, agencies, and creative forces that continually undergo a process of repetition, as they emerge and are repeated through specific events and different sociomaterial assemblages' (536).
	Cohendet and Simon (2016)	Introduction of a creative project at a leading video game studio radically reconfigures routines and their artifacts, and existing truces.	Restoring organizational creativity requires radical reconfiguration of routines' artifacts as they prevent flexibility and adaptation through 'excessive framing'.	'[. . .] excessive 'framing', which may lead to situations where the ostensive aspects "freeze" all the specific actions taken by actors of the routine and prevent any form of adaptation . . . Particular attention should be paid to artifacts that can influence the emergence and persistence of routines, both in destabilizing existing action patterns and by providing the glue that can hold patterns together' (630).
	Glaser (2017)	A US law enforcement organization introduces game theory to facilitate the random deployment of security resources in its patrolling routine.	Routine participants iteratively engage in design performances to envision new socio-material assemblages of actors, artifacts, theories and practices to enable constant changes in the routine and to establish dynamic truces around emergent political conflicts.	'The mechanisms produced by design performances may reduce political conflict by helping organizational actors overcome divergent interests and worldviews to develop assemblages that address common, overarching problems' (2146).
	Salvato and Rerup (2018)	Inclusion of mass-market, cheaper products generates new truce dynamics in the NPD department of an iconic design company and prompts the flexible use of artifacts.	With flexible use of artifacts, professionals repressed the need for autonomous work and decision-making and created a negotiated order and balanced interactions to work through their expert opinions while accommodating each other's viewpoint.	'[. . .] the specific actions and artifacts that enacted the NPD routine and balanced the conflicting goals of design and efficiency' (176). '[. . .] the various artifacts that actors mobilized to accomplish specific actions (e.g., product prototypes, items in the Alessi Museum, color samples)' (179).
	Kho et al. (2019)	The introduction of telehealth geriatric consultation routines creates new truce dynamics in professional health service settings.	While technology mediation broadens participation of health professionals, it also creates jurisdictional conflicts among them that requires new patterns of actions shaped by relational forms of professional expertise around 'overall patient well-being'	'Information and communication technologies broaden the participation of professionals with various specialist skills and expertise to accomplish work together' (191). '[. . .] professionals create new patterns of actions that are shaped by relational forms of professional expertise' (ibid).

provides a brief summary of the Routine Dynamics contributions cited in this chapter, articulated along the four themes.

15.3.1 Routines and Truce Dynamics

Among the first contributions to the truces debate from a dynamic perspective is the work of Zbaracki and Bergen (2010), where the authors call for the need to depart from the notion of truce as portrayed in Nelson and Winter (1982). While in fact Nelson and Winter's metaphor of routines as truces '[. . .] incorporates divergent information and interests [. . .]', the authors argue, 'it also shifts the focus away from the routine as adaptive process to the routine as solution, leaving us with an image of the routine as both structural and static' (Zbaracki and Bergen, 2010: 956). This was unconducive, the authors observe, as 'the most important dynamics may lie in the breach of that stability' (2010: 957). A similar limitation was shared by Cyert and March (1963), who had sought to introduce diverse interests in their theory of organizational routines but had also focused on the suppression, rather than the dynamics, of conflict. To appreciate the routine as truce, Zbaracki and Bergen (2010: 956–957) suggest, 'we need a process theory that addresses overt conflict and the dynamics of stability and change in routines as truces'. This includes investigating what happens when truces unravel, and how truces can be renegotiated.

In their paper, Zbaracki and Bergen (2010) show how truces break down and re-form in response to disputes over market forces. Building on the routine's ostensive/performative duality, they characterize truce breakdown as caused by the presence of two contrasting ostensive aspects which belonged to two separate organizational functions: 'a marketing group, [which] saw list price as the most important price, the end user as the customer, and the competition as other producers' and 'the sales force [which] saw the negotiated price as the most important price, the distributor as the customer, and competition as competing bids' (2010: 967). Conflict in this case was resolved through the intervention of authority, in the form of the vice-president who imposed his own solution while side-stepping the differences between the two teams. The VP's solution, we learn in this case, violated the assumptions of both groups, and yet each group supported it, choosing to ignore their differences, and agreeing to suspend the overt conflict, thus giving birth to a new truce.

In an earlier work, D'Adderio (2008) had examined the dynamics following the introduction of enterprise software that radically reconfigures organizational routines by enforcing the adoption of new, software-based, standard operating procedures. These disrupt the 'engineering freeze' routine, breaking down the existing truce among various product development functions. Conflict ensues, which is resolved through the creation of a workaround, with the modified workflow process indicating that a new truce has been reached (see Table 15.1). This early theorization of the dynamic aspects of truces highlights how routine participants are able to restore (temporary) stability to the routine, in the form of a new 'truce' in its '*dynamic* inception as a continuously challenged and emergent achievement' (D'Adderio, 2008: 787, emphasis added).

The more recent paper by Salvato and Rerup (2018) captures the internal dynamics of the New Product Development routine at the design company Alessi. Here the authors discuss how practitioners were able to assemble a truce by engaging in the 'regulatory' actions of splicing (e.g., through workshop briefings), activating (e.g., through joint panel evaluations) and repressing (e.g., through joint colour selection). In so doing, they add to the dynamic and processual theorization of routines-as-truces by showing how routines participants were able to take actions that dynamically accommodated tensions and problems between them through the enactment of 'zones of flexibility' (where actors take actions to create junctures and bridges between different groups of participants supporting different organizational goals). In this context they show how 'conflict is not suppressed or eliminated by the truce but is embraced, and the truce is actively built and expanded by routine participants engaging in effortful relating and regulatory actions', thus giving rise to a flexible truce (Salvato and Rerup, 2018: 202).

Among further studies which have contributed to identifying 'how' and 'why' truces break down is the paper by Cohendet and Simon (2016), which also adds to our understanding of truce dynamics by showing how restoring organizational creativity may involve the radical reconfiguration of existing routines, resulting in the breaking down of established truces and the creation of new ones. Their contribution here lies in showing how organizations may be able to switch ostensive aspects in existing routines, thus supporting the emergence of a new truce. Kho et al. 2019 (see also Kho and Spee [Chapter 28] in this volume) observe how, in the Routine Dynamics literature, there are two main ways in which conflict is resolved within truces: one is through collaboration (D'Adderio, 2008; Salvato and Rerup, 2018) and the other through recourse to a higher authority (Zbaracki and Bergen, 2010). The authors add to the debate by providing a third approach, which demonstrates how conflict can be managed through the enactment of 'selective' and 'blending' expertise (Kho et al., 2019) (see Table 15.1 for more details).

15.3.2 Truces and Conflicting Goals

Early accounts of 'routines as truces' incorporated occasional discussions of how routine performances may be used to provide resolutions to conflicting organizational goals (Nelson and Winter, 1982). However, these early accounts afforded only partial explanations for how organizations were able to deal with the conflict stemming from contrasting goals. Carnegie scholars (Cyert and March, 1963; March and Simon, 1958), for example, maintained that organizations were able to avoid the 'freezing-in' behaviour that would have otherwise followed the co-presence of conflicting goals by devising ad-hoc managerial strategies such as 'sequential attention' (Ethiraj and Levinthal, 2009). This selective attention-shifting strategy allowed organizational decision-makers to defer conflict by focusing on one goal at a time at the expense of the other(s). In turn, this rested on the assumption that there is a low 'probability [...] that [competing] demands are made simultaneously' (Cyert and March, 1963: 41), an assumption subsequently questioned by authors in the field of Routine Dynamics (D'Adderio, 2014; D'Adderio and Pollock, 2014; Salvato and Rerup, 2018) and beyond (see Gaba and Greve, 2019; Schad et al., 2016; Smets et al., 2015 for a wider discussion in the Organizational and Management Theory).

Salvato and Rerup (2018), for example, show how organizational members could simultaneously address conflicting goals of design and efficiency through a mechanism they name 'routines regulation'. Here organizational actors respond to tensions by taking regulatory actions that, without breaking the truce, 'create junctures between individuals supporting conflicting goals, thereby embracing conflict and keeping the truce balanced, flexible, and alive' (2018: 202). Their process-based conceptualization of truces contrasts with the former view that the notion of 'routines as truces show[s] us how firms avoid conflict' (the critique originally advanced by Zbaracki and Bergen, 2010: 957) to highlight how conflict is not suppressed but rather embraced by participants who take actions that dynamically accommodate tension and problems (Salvato and Rerup, 2018).

Similarly, in her study of routines transfer and replication at a leading US computing manufacturing organization, D'Adderio (2014) showed that the Carnegie assumption that organizations only need to deal with one set of demands at a time is severely challenged by the increasing organizational complexity and environmental uncertainty faced by contemporary organizations. Under these conditions, the author argues, 'the probability is not so low that competing demands are made concurrently, causing conflict to remain present and visible despite attempts to defer it by focusing on one goal at a time' (2014: 1327). In her quest to theorize how organizations may be able to manage the simultaneous but conflicting goals of innovation and replication, D'Adderio (2014) shows that organizational members are able to respond to simultaneous pressures through performing conflicting goals simultaneously but selectively, a device she names 'selective performance' (2014: 1346). This mechanism involves enacting routines through socio-material assemblages that support one goal, while relegating the conflicting goal(s) to the background (and vice-versa). The dynamic balance between foregrounded and backgrounded goals – and their associated truces – can shift over time, as different assemblages supporting alternative goals manage to prevail. Organizational goals, however, can at times lead to more complex truces, whereby more than one goal manages to configure routines at the same time. This is the case discussed in D'Adderio and Pollock (2014), who, building on Performativity Theory (Callon, 1998; MacKenzie, 2006), further challenge the notion of truce as 'static balance' of organizational conflicts by showing how goals themselves can shift over time from 'conflicting' to 'complementary' (see Table 15.1 for more details).

Other routines scholars joined the conversation by showing how organizational goals and their conflict can become generative in various contexts (see Table 15.1 for details). Canales (2014), for instance, explored the context of microfinances and found that branches with higher discretionary diversity in their communities perform better in balancing simultaneous needs for efficiency (standardization) and for local responsiveness (a theme further developed in Bertels et al., 2016). Building on Zbaracki and Bergen (2010) and Turner and Rindova (2012)'s argument that high magnitude change tends to surface latent conflicts, and thus pose different threats to routine stability, Cohendet and Simon (2016) explore how the gaming organization Ubisoft is able to address the conflict between different and coexisting ostensive aspects. Conflict in this case is between the goal of efficiency, driven by the formal stage-gating development process, and creativity, as supported by the introduction of the 'Always Playable' project. In similarly showing how conflicting ostensives may be dealt with simultaneously (D'Adderio, 2014), Cohendet and Simon (2016) add to the extant literature by theorizing how the imbalance across conflicting goals – and the resulting truce – can be dealt with through recombination of routines and routine aspects. Spee et al. (2016) studied the interconnection and interdependency of a professional service routine with other routines in the context of reinsurance. Here they showed how routine performances can dynamically settle tensions between standardization and flexibility – and the associated ostensive patterns – through exploiting routine interdependence. Interdependent routines are theorized as alternatively providing impulses which orient practitioners towards each ostensive pattern, thus coordinating them and turning conflict into complementarity.

Another means for organizations to address conflict is through experimentation. Rerup and Feldman (2011), for example, traced over several years the overt conflict between two organizations, Learning Lab Denmark (LLD) and the Danish University of Education. Here they show how the conflict between a more entrepreneurial and a more bureaucratic modus operandus prevented the hiring routine from being performed the way LLD wanted. Conflict in this case was addressed through experimenting with different ways of accomplishing the routine, leading to LLD changing its endeavour to match more closely DPU and the law. Another paper which shows how routine actors may take experimental actions to overcome conflict is Bucher and Langley's (2016) study of surgical clinics at two large teaching hospitals. In this context they show how routine participants were able to reconcile existing and envisioned routines by moving between experimental and reflective spaces.

15.3.3 Truces, Culture(s) and Communities

Another important theme in the truce dynamics literature is the relationship between truces and organizational communities and culture(s). In the early routines literature this fell under the heading of 'organizational politics', or 'the political relations among actors [that] shape cognitive and behavioral patterns' (Cohen et al., 1996: 15). Looking at the 'political side of truces' meant focusing on truces as the organizational means through which 'the underlying problem of diverging member interests' could settle (Nelson and Winter, 1982: 111). According to Nelson and Winter (1982: 111), 'the truce among organization members tends to give rise to a peculiar symbolic culture shared by the parties'. We learn that 'the terms [of a truce] become increasingly defined by a shared tradition arising out of the specific contingencies confronted and the responses of the parties to those contingencies. In the interpretive context of such a tradition, actions by individual members have connotations related to the terms of the truce'. In this context, the organizational culture, or 'the way things get done around here', might help avoid conflicts which could threaten the established truces by supporting the emergence of hard-to-change behaviours and inflexible routines. This explains how even 'adaptations that appear "obvious" and "easy" to an external observer may be foreclosed because they involve a perceived threat to internal political equilibrium' (Nelson and Winter, 1982).

This point was later taken up in Routine Dynamics, where authors highlighted the role of organizational culture in sustaining (in)flexible routines. In theory, organizational culture should make it easier, and therefore more likely, that some actions are taken which reinforce existing truces while making other actions harder and therefore less likely to happen as they engender overt conflicts (Feldman and Pentland, 2003; Howard-Grenville, 2005). Bertels et al. (2016) recently built on the notion of organizational culture as integrating mechanism in their investigation of the introduction of a new routine with poor cultural fit at a Canadian oil company. In this case, as the authors point out, practitioners did not appear to see latent or overt conflict, despite the fact that different individuals enacted the operational compliance routine in different ways. This was due to the ways in which ad-hoc 'cultural strategies', such as 'shielding' and 'shoring', were used to deal with deviations from the espoused routine by compensating for the mismatches between performances and the espoused routine.

In addition to those contributions that have highlighted the role of organizational culture in absorbing conflict there is another strand of Routine Dynamics which has focused on the multiplicity of organizational cultures and communities, and their role in supporting or obstructing the emergence of truces. According to this work stream, any but perhaps the simplest organizations are made up of a multiplicity of diverse cultures which often belong to different – at times collaborating, and at other times competing – organizational communities, including functions and teams, who speak idiosyncratic discipline- or task-specific languages and hold different worldviews (Barley, 1988; Carlile, 2004; D'Adderio, 2003; 2011; Dougherty, 1992; Galison, 1999).

D'Adderio (2008), for example, showed how the introduction of new software tools created strong tensions between organizational functions which up until that point had been collaborating harmoniously. In this case, the Production and Manufacturing functions, whose predilection for certainty and stability was supported by the software rules, clashed with the upstream Product Engineers function, whose ability to change designs and experiment was drastically curbed by the introduction of the new software. This led to a 'performative struggle' between those functions and the break-up of the established truce. This was followed by the construction of a new truce, whereby conflict was absorbed by the introduction of a workaround which allowed Engineering to modify their work beyond the official deadline, while at the same time giving Production the stability of a clear milestone (Table 15.1).

Similarly, differences in the interests of marketing and sales groups in Zbaracki and Bergen (2010) resulted in overt conflicts and the breaking of the existing truce around pricing. In their example, the two functions had different definitions of key variables such as price, competitor, product and customer. Here the marketing group saw list price as the most important price, the end user as the customer and the competition as other producers. The sales force saw instead the negotiated price as the most important price, the distributor as the customer and defined competition in terms of competing bids. A substantial change in pricing in this case made the underlying conflict between the functions overt, as the groups were not able to agree on the way to set future prices. The truce was reformed by the intervention of the vice-president, whose solution was implemented, despite the fact that it violated both groups' assumptions.

Relatedly, Kaplan (2015) studied the role of authority (in this case Citibank's CEO) in breaking and remaking truces in his attempt to modify the cognitive and motivational frames held by the organizational participants, i.e., what should be done and what gets rewarded or sanctioned. In so doing, she proposes that organizational routines are inertial because organizational participants find them to cohere to particular frames, while 'dissolution of the truce would be inconsistent' with those frames held by different communities within the organization, risking unleashing 'unmanageable conflict among interests in the organization' (Kaplan, 2015: 2).

More recently, in Routine Dynamics, Kho et al. (2019) added to the theorization of truces in relation to (jurisdictional or professional) communities in their study of the introduction of telehealth services in geriatric consultations. The new technology, they argue, created new interactions among the different professional groups which blurred existing professional boundaries, thus causing conflict among them. In so doing, they show how jurisdictional conflict over resident care was overcome by developing new, relational forms of expertise (including selective and blending expertise). The new kinds of expertise 'enriched the responses of health professionals and made truce-making possible among them' (2019: 191).

Other Routine Dynamics contributions further advanced the analysis of inter- and intra-organizational conflict by building on the notion of 'performative struggles' (D'Adderio, 2008; 2011). Thus, D'Adderio (2014) showed how the conflicts across two engineering communities during routines transfer escalated into a performative struggle (see Table 15.1). Here we can see how the truce shifted over time from a reliance on the US practitioners' practices and expertise (emphasis on a culture of 'replication') to a reliance on the UK practices and expertise (emphasis on 'innovation'). Relatedly, D'Adderio and Pollock (2014) theorized the struggle between two coexisting cultures, and their logics, and related communities: a culture which supported efficiency and one which supported reliability. In this case the extant truce based around the culture/logic of efficiency was modified and augmented to incorporate the emerging culture/logic of reliability. This particular outcome, the authors argue, suggested that 'a more sophisticated temporary truce was required at this point in time, in this particular organization, between efficiency- and reliability-bearing strategies' (2014: 1835), a finding, elsewhere described as a 'patchwork containing elements from competing worlds' (D'Adderio, 2008, cited in Kho and Spee [Chapter 28], this volume), which provides a deeper and more sophisticated theorization of truce dynamics.

In their study of the gaming company Ubisoft, Cohendet and Simon (2016) build directly on the notion of performative struggles to theorize truces. They similarly show how, instead of mobilizing an authority to resolve jurisdictional conflict, managers may 'exploit or tap into cultural elements, shared values and identities of the different parties to establish or maintain a truce' (Kho and Spee [Chapter 28], in this volume). Starting from the performative notion of 'framing and overflowing' (Callon, 1998; D'Adderio, 2008), they show how 'excess overflowing', in their case caused by the rigid implementation of the stage-gate meta-routine, brings on 'conflicts and struggles among competing agencies, which may preclude generative dynamics' (Cohendet and Simon, 2016: 616). The main competing 'communities of practice or epistemic communities' were in this case the writers, game designers and artists, on one hand, who supported a creative culture, and the programmers, sound designers and testers, on the other, who supported a more structured process (see Table 15.1).

Finally, Kiwan and Lazaric (2019) also add to the concept of performative struggles in their study of bariatric robotic surgery. The authors show how the new technology and associated practices produced 'experimental' and 'reflective' spaces in which both the ostensive and performative dimensions of routines were questioned and temporarily redesigned. The distance between the primary surgeon and his team, the authors argue, created new forms of interactions which were different from previous team rituals. This generated a performative struggle, as participants were attempting to identify a new surgical performance which could avoid any potential lack of fit. This involved redefining roles and interactions as scrub nurses started to anticipate the surgeon's actions. Role redesign in this case helped avoid tensions, and promote psychological safety within the team, thus re-establishing a working truce (see also Edmondson et al., 2001).

15.3.4 Truces, Artifacts and Materiality

The early organizational and routines literature has done little to analyse the role of artifacts and technology in truces formation and evolution (see also Chapter 7 in this volume). Failure to acknowledge the material side of routines, however, has resulted in overlooking some fundamental issues, including the role of artifacts and technology in mediating (e.g. creating, shaping, absorbing) the organizational tensions and conflicts that underpin a truce. Attention to materiality has been a major contribution of the field of Routine Dynamics, sensitized through a number of Actor Network Theory/Science and Technology Studies/Performativity notions which allowed positioning materiality more centrally in the routines literature (D'Adderio, 2011).

Routine Dynamics authors, for example, have discussed how occupational artifacts or tools may provoke and generate conflict during inter-occupational work with important implications for routines and truces (Kho et al., 2019). Glaser (2017) explored how design performances may help envisioning new socio-material assemblages to enable constant changes in the routine and therefore establish dynamic truces. In a study of a law enforcement organization introducing game theory for random deployment of security resources in its patrolling routine, he shows how routine participants iteratively engage in design performances to envision new socio-material assemblages to enable constant changes in the routine around emergent political conflicts (see also Table 15.1). Aroles and McLean (2016) explicate how the microprocesses of routines repetition shape and are shaped by complex socio-material assemblages that incorporate different stances of both stability and change in order to produce specific truces. Studying replication at a large newspaper printing company, the authors show how the introduction and use of the simplest artifacts (e.g., ink level scripts) may add tensions to the processes of routine repetition. In so doing, the authors explain how the microprocesses of routines repetition shape – and are shaped by – complex socio-material assemblages which underpin the (re)formation of old and new truces.

Cacciatori, (2012: 1579) discussed the role of 'systems of artifacts' in addressing conflict in the context of the creation of a new bidding routine. Here, she shows how artifacts such as costing models may spark conflict among different groups. They do so by characterizing idiosyncratically the way a problem is represented and constructed, and who will have a voice in solving it and at what stage, 'thereby providing "paths of least resistance" that funnel organizational action' (Cacciatori, 2012: 1563; see also D'Adderio, 2003). Costing models, for example, create clashes across different functions (e.g., quantity surveyors and facilities managers), as they depict maintenance costs differently from each other. In order to resolve the conflict, Cacciatori (2012) argues, actors intentionally (re)design the interactions between occupation-specific artifacts (e.g., the Excel Workbook used to estimate costs or technical drawings) and generic artifacts (e.g., bidding procedures). In so doing, they reconfigure positions of influence and power across routines participants, thus supporting the emergence of a new truce.

In earlier work, D'Adderio (2008) had theorized the effects of inflexible standard operating procedures (SOPs) in product development. She shows that these embedded assumptions, consistent with the IT and programme management objectives, clashed fundamentally with those of the downstream functions, thus generating conflict. A truce, in this case, was restored through the introduction of an informal workaround, including a set of additional screen annotations which were added to the official procedure and allowed practitioners to carry on with their work while at the same time coordinating their outputs with those of other functions (see Table 15.1 for more details).

More recent studies further contribute to investigating the role of artifacts as intermediaries and mediators in jurisdictional conflicts between organizational functions. In Salvato and Rerup (2018: 194), for example, professionals were able to use the 'color box' to repress the need for autonomous work and decision-making while creating a negotiated order and balanced interaction that allowed them to work through their expert opinions while also accommodating each other's point of view. A similar role was enacted by the notion of the 'overall patient well-being' in Kho et al. (2019: 210). Cohendet and Simon (2016) also add to the observation that some artifacts in certain contexts can provide stifling sources of rigidity. They show how excessively efficient and rigid stage-gating procedures implied a loss of flexibility which was restored in this case through the introduction of the tournament. This is viewed by the authors as 'a key artifact, which was not only a central mechanism for generating ideas within the team and for consolidating the new routines, but, more importantly, acted as an intermediary and mediator (D'Adderio, 2008; 2011) that facilitated the adoption and diffusion of the routines newly built by the team to the whole company' (Cohendet and Simon, 2016: 624–625). In so doing, the authors also add to the literature on routines that addresses cases of conflicts, 'in particular D'Adderio (2014), who explores the notion of conflict by showing how different ostensive aspects can be performed at the same time in different proportions across different sites (selective performance), or D'Adderio and Pollock (2014), who point out how organizations might deal with an imbalance between conflicting objectives (specifically efficiency and reliability)' (Cohendet and Simon, 2016: 629).

D'Adderio (2014) and D'Adderio and Pollock (2014) developed the notion of 'socio-material assemblage' to show how artifacts may be involved in enacting particular truces. D'Adderio (2014) showed how competing socio-material assemblages were able to support, at different times, the enactment of different routine patterns which shaped organizations, leading to two different truces (one around alignment and the other around improvement). D'Adderio and Pollock (2014) similarly show how socio-material assemblages mediated the conflict across different logics (in this case efficiency and reliability). They also show how different artifacts supporting different assumptions or logics might swing the assemblage – and thus its effects on routines and the organization – towards one truce or another. Importantly, we can see in this work not only how artifacts – as part of wider assemblages – may modify truces but also how they may be modified in turn (see Table 15.1 for further details).

15.4 Conclusions and Avenues for Future Research

In this chapter we have shown the substantial progress achieved within the Routine Dynamics literature in addressing the dynamics of truce emergence and demise. In so doing, we have shown how the literature has progressed from the foundational but early accounts of routines-as-truces, focusing on the resolution of conflict as an outcome, and the more recent accounts of truces as a dynamic process by which conflicts are managed and compromises are reached, often in the form of a new truce. The more recent, fine-grained and longitudinal empirical studies have captured the more complex dynamics by which conflicting interests and motivations may be woven into truces and may subsequently unravel or consolidate over time and across organizational settings. They have also theorized the role of organizational cultures and materiality in truce (re)formation. This progress has been enabled by a theoretical framework based on Routine Dynamics, supplemented by insights from the neighbouring fields of Practice Theory, Process Theory, Actor-Network Theory, Performativity Theory, Science and Technology Studies and Socio-materiality, underpinned by in-depth, often longitudinal empirical analyses based on ethnographic work.

There are a number of themes and topics emerging from these advances which deserve future attention. These include, for example, how truce dynamics might unravel across less traditional empirical settings. This would be, for example, the case of truce formation in new organizations including platforms and the gig economy; and in more dispersed organizational forms such as projects (see Chapter 30 in this handbook). Additional work is also needed to understand the role of culture in the formation and break down of truces in these new forms of organizing. An important new theme would be the study of truce dynamics in contexts affected by the introduction of new kinds of artifacts and technologies, such as artificial intelligence and learning algorithms. These are expected to reconfigure routines and their truces in relation to a number of fundamental organizational processes, ranging from problem-solving and decision-making to resource planning and allocations. And last but not least, the influence of time, timing and temporality on truce dynamics (Howard-Grenville and Rerup, 2017, Chapter 19 in this handbook) is an important issue which remains under-researched but which deserves further attention.

References

Aroles, J. and McLean, C. (2016). Rethinking stability and change in the study of organizational routines: Difference and repetition in a newspaper-printing factory. *Organization Science*, 27(3), 535–550.

Barley, S. R. (1988). Technology, power, and the social organization of work: Towards a pragmatic theory of skilling and deskilling. In N. DiTomaso and S. Bacharach, eds., *Research in the Sociology of Organizations: A Research Annual*, Vol. 7, Greenwich, CT: JAI Press, pp. 33–80.

Becker, M. C. (2004). Organizational routines: A review of the literature. *Industrial and Corporate Change*, 13(4), 643–677.

Becker, M. C., Lazaric, N., Nelson, R. R. and Winter, S. G. (2005). Applying organizational routines in understanding organizational change. *Industrial and Corporate Change*, 14(5), 775–791.

Bertels, S., Howard-Grenville, J. and Pek, S. (2016). Cultural molding, shielding, and shoring at Oilco: The role of culture in the integration of routines. *Organization Science*, 27(3), 573–593.

Bucher, S. and Langley, A. (2016). The interplay of reflective and experimental spaces in interrupting and reorienting routine dynamics. *Organization Science*, 27(3), 594–613.

Burns, J. (2000). The dynamics of accounting change: Interplay between new practices, routines, institutions, power and politics. *Accounting, Auditing & Accountability Journal*, 13, 566–586.

Cacciatori, E. (2012). Resolving conflict in problem-solving: Systems of artefacts in the development of new routines. *Journal of Management Studies*, 49(8), 1559–1585.

Callon, M. (1998). An essay on framing and overflowing: Economic externalities revisited by sociology. In M. Callon, ed., *The Laws of the Markets*. Oxford: Blackwell, pp. 244–269.

Canales, R. (2014). Weaving straw into gold: Managing organizational tensions between standardization and flexibility in microfinance. *Organization Science*, 25(1), 1–28.

Carlile, P. (2004). Transferring, translating, and transforming: An integrative framework for managing knowledge across boundaries. *Organization Science*, 15(5), 555–568.

Cohen, M. D., Burkhart, R., Dosi, G., Egidi, M., Marengo, L., Warglien, M. and Winter, S. G. (1996). Routines and other recurring patterns of organizations: Contemporary research issues. *Industrial and Corporate Change*, 5(3), 653–698.

Cohendet, P. S. and Simon, L. O. (2016). Always playable: Recombining routines for creative efficiency at Ubisoft Montreal's video game studio. *Organization Science*, 27(3), 614–632.

Coriat, B. and Dosi, G. (1999). Learning how to govern and learning how to solve problems: On the co-evolution of competences, conflicts and organizational routines. In A. D. Chandler, P. Hagstrom and Ö. Sölvell, eds., *The Dynamic Firm: The Role of Technology, Strategy, Organization, and Regions*. Oxford: Oxford University Press.

Cyert, R. M. and March, J. G. (1963). *A Behavioral Theory of the Firm*. Cambridge, MA: Blackwell.

D'Adderio, L. (2001). Crafting the virtual prototype: How firms integrate knowledge and capabilities across organisational boundaries. *Research Policy*, 30(9), 1409–1424.

D'Adderio, L. (2003). Configuring software, reconfiguring memories: The influence of integrated systems on the reproduction of knowledge and routines. *Industrial and Corporate Change*, 12(3), 321–350.

D'Adderio, L. (2008). The performativity of routines: Theorising the influence of artefacts and distributed agencies on routines dynamics. *Research Policy*, 37(5), 769–789.

D'Adderio, L. (2011). Artifacts at the centre of routines: Performing the material turn in routines theory. *Journal of Institutional Economics*, 7(2), 197–230.

D'Adderio, L. (2014). The replication dilemma unraveled: How organizations enact multiple goals in routines transfer. *Organization Science*, 25(5), 1325–1350.

D'Adderio, L. and Pollock, N. (2014). Performing modularity: Competing rules, performative struggles, and the effect of organizational theories on the organization. *Organization Studies*, 35(12), 1813–1843.

Dougherty, D. (1992). Interpretive barriers to successful product innovation in large firms. *Organization Science*, 3(2), 179–202.

Edmondson, A. C., Bohmer, R. M. and Pisano, G. P. (2001). Disrupted routines: Team learning and new technology implementation in hospitals. *Administrative Science Quarterly*, 46(4), 685–716.

Ethiraj, S. K. and Levinthal, D. (2009). Hoping for A to Z while rewarding only A: Complex organizations and multiple goals. *Organization Science*, 20(1), 4–21.

Feldman. M. S. (2000). Organizational routines as a source of continuous change. *Organization Science*, 11(6), 611–629.

Feldman, M. S. and Pentland, B. T. (2003). Reconceptualizing organizational routines as a source of flexibility and change. *Administrative Science Quarterly*, 48(1), 94–124.

Gaba, V. and Greve, H. R. (2019). Safe or profitable? The pursuit of conflicting goals. *Organization Science*, 30(4), 647–667.

Galison, P. (1999). Trading zone: Coordinating action and belief. In M. Biagioli, ed., *The Science Studies Reader*. New York: Routledge, pp. 137–160.

Ganz, S. C. (2018). Ignorant decision making and educated inertia: Some political pathologies of organizational learning. *Organization Science*, 29(1), 39–57.

Glaser, V. (2017). Design performances: How organizations inscribe artifacts to change routines. *Academy of Management Journal*, 60(6), 2126–2154.

Howard-Grenville, J. A. (2005). The persistence of flexible organizational routines: The role of agency and organizational context. *Organization Science*, 16(6), 618–636.

Howard-Grenville, J. and Rerup, C. (2017). A process perspective on organizational routines. In A. Langley and H. Tsoukas, eds., *The SAGE Handbook of Process Organization Studies*. London: SAGE Publications Ltd, pp. 323–337.

Kaplan, S. (2015). Truce breaking and remaking: The CEO's role in changing organizational routines. In G. Gavetti and W. Ocasio, eds., *Advances in Strategic Management*. Bingley: Emerald Insight, 32: pp. 1–45.

Kho, J., Spee, A. P. and Gillespie, N. (2019). Enacting relational expertise to change professional routines in technology-mediated service settings. In M. S. Feldman, L. D'Adderio, K. Dittrich and P. Jarzabkowski, eds., *Routine Dynamics in Action: Replication and Transformation* (Research in the Sociology of Organizations; Vol. 61). Bingley: Emerald, pp. 191–213.

Kiwan, L. and Lazaric, N. (2019). Learning a new ecology of space and looking for new routines: Experimenting robotics in a surgical team. In M. S. Feldman, L. D'Adderio, K. Dittrich and P. Jarzabkowski, eds., *Routine Dynamics in Action: Replication and Transformation* (Research in the Sociology of Organizations; Vol. 61). Bingley: Emerald, pp. 173–189.

Latour, B. (2005). *Reassembling the Social: An Introduction to Actor Network Theory*. Oxford: Oxford University Press.

Lazaric, N. and Denis, B. (2001). How and why routines change: Some lessons from the articulation of knowledge with ISO 9002 implementation in the food industry. *Economies et Sociétés*, 6, 585–612.

Lazaric, N. and Mangolte, P. A. (1998). Routines et mémoire organisationelle: un questionnement critique de la perspective cognitiviste. *Revue Internationale de Systémique*, 12, 27–49.

Lazaric, N., Mangolte, P. A. and Massué, M. L. (2003). Articulation and codification of know-how Organizational routines: A review of the literature in the steel industry: Some evidence from blast furnace control in France. *Research Policy*, 32, 1829–1847.

Levinthal, D. and Rerup, C. (2020). The plural of goal: Learning in a world of ambiguity. *Organization Science*, 32(3), 527–543.

MacKenzie, D. (2006). *An Engine, not a Camera: How Financial Models Shape Markets*. Cambridge, MA: MIT Press.

Mangolte, P. A. (1997). Le concept de 'routine organisationelle' entre cognition et institution. PhD Thesis, Université Paris-Nord, U.F.R. de Sciences Economiques et de Gestion, Centre de Recherche en Economie Industrielle.

Mangolte, P. A. (2000). Organisational learning and the organisational link: The problem of conflict, political equilibrium and truce. *European Journal of Economic and Social Systems*, 14, 173–190.

March, J. G. (1962). The business firm as a political coalition. *Journal of Politics*, 24(4), 662–678.

March, J. G. and Simon, H. A. (1958). *Organizations*. London: Wiley.

Nelson, R. R. and Winter, S. G. (1982). *An Evolutionary Theory of Economic Change*. Cambridge, MA: Harvard University Press.

Pentland, B. T. and Feldman, M. S. (2005). Organizational routines as a unit of analysis. *Industrial and Corporate Change*, 14(5), 793–815.

Rerup, C. and Feldman, M. S. (2011). Routines as a source of change in organizational schemata: The role of trial-and-error learning. *Organization Science*, 54(3), 577–610.

Simon, H. A. (1955). A behavioral model of rational choice. *The Quarterly Journal of Economics*, 69, 99–118.

Salvato, C. and Rerup, C. (2018). Routine regulation: Balancing conflicting goals in organizational routines. *Administrative Science Quarterly*, 63 (1), 170–209.

Schad, J., Lewis, M. W., Raisch, S. and Smith, W. K. (2016). Paradox research in management science: Looking back to move forward. *Academy of Management Annals*, 10(1), 5–64.

Smets, M., Jarzabkowski, P., Burke, G. T. and Spee, P. (2015). Reinsurance trading in Lloyd's of London: Balancing conflicting-yet-complementary logics in practice. *Academy of Management Journal*, 58(3), 932–970.

Spee, P., Jarzabkowski, P. and Smets, M. (2016). The influence of routine interdependence and skillful accomplishment on the coordination of standardizing and customizing. *Organization Science*, 27(3), 759–781.

Suchman, L. (2007). *Human-Machine Reconfigurations: Plans and Situated Actions*, 2nd ed. Cambridge: Cambridge University Press.

Turner, S. F. and Rindova, V. (2012). A balancing act: How organizations pursue consistency in routine functioning in the face of ongoing change. *Organization Science*, 23(1), 24–46.

Zbaracki, M. J. and Bergen, M. (2010). When truces collapse: A longitudinal study of price adjustment routines. *Organization Science*, 21(5), 955–972.

CHAPTER 16 Context, Embeddedness and Routine Dynamics

JENNIFER HOWARD-GRENVILLE AND JAN LODGE

16.1 Introduction

Organizational routines are never performed in a vacuum. Indeed, routine performances have long been recognized as enfolding and reflecting surrounding tasks, rules and organizational structures (Nelson and Winter, 1982; Pentland and Rueter, 1994), and individual and group habits and understandings (Gersick and Hackman, 1990). Acknowledging the relationship between routines and their organizational and broader contexts is important because the effectiveness of routine performances depends on the characteristics of surrounding organizations, people, tasks and technology (e.g., Dosi et al., 2000; Edmondson et al., 2001; Turner and Fern, 2012). Understanding how contexts shape routine performances is therefore important from both a practical and theoretical view.

Theoretically, the Routine Dynamics perspective, by drawing attention to routines as situated performances that are generative of emergent patterns of action (Feldman and Pentland, 2003), inherently invites inquiry into the ways in which routines are performed and evolve in relation to their contexts. However, as Parmigiani and Howard-Grenville (2011: 443) noted 'Perhaps somewhat ironically, [scholars]... are so concerned with situated action – the specific actions of specific people in specific organizations – that they sometimes ignore fundamental organizational attributes that exist above the level of the routine but nonetheless affect its performance.' There is more to be learned about how particular features of organizational contexts shape Routine Dynamics, including their effectiveness, outcomes and evolution. As Howard-Grenville, Rerup, Langley and Tsoukas (2016: 8) point out, 'Efforts to treat routines as entangled with their contexts (. . .) help us zoom out of the black box of the inner workings of routines and better situate them in the flow of organizing.' Further attention to context will shed light on how routines interact with other – also dynamic – aspects of organizing that are of interest to organizational scholars. For example, routine performances are shaped by organizational identity (Christianson et al., 2009), culture (Bertels et al., 2016), occupational norms (Bruns, 2009) and macro-cultural values (Essén, 2008). Better understanding of these interactions can advance Routine Dynamics theory, and also enable contributions to theories on organizational identity, culture, change, sense-making, learning and creativity (Howard-Grenville and Rerup, 2017).

Specific features of organizational contexts were explored explicitly in one of the chapter authors' earlier work (Howard-Grenville, 2005), through which she introduced the construct of 'routine embeddedness' to the Routine Dynamics literature. Our aim in this chapter is to revisit and explore routine embeddedness, identifying how it has been taken up and expanded on in more recent work, and reflecting on how it overlaps with related ideas in the literature. We end with articulating some ways in which future research on routine embeddedness and the role of context can advance our understanding of Routine Dynamics.

This research was supported by the Economic & Social Research Council (ESRC) through the University of Cambridge ESRC Doctoral Training Partnership.

16.2 What Is Routine Embeddedness?

Routine embeddedness captures 'the degree to which the use of a routine overlaps with the enactment of other organizational structures' (Howard-Grenville,

2005: 619). In her ethnographic study at a leading semiconductor manufacturing organization ('Chipco'), Howard-Grenville found that one of the reasons routines persist over time, despite being flexibly performed, was due to their being performed in relation to other social structures that guide organizational life. She characterized these as technological, cultural and coordination structures. For example, despite Chipco employees accommodating their routine performances to fit emergent situations, the physical properties of technological artifacts associated with semiconductor chip manufacturing entrained certain expectations about the timing and (lack of) flexibility of 'road-mapping,' a central planning routine. Further, Chipco's culture as a data-driven, highly disciplined decision-making environment led employees to rely repeatedly on the road-mapping routine, contributing to its persistence.

Howard-Grenville's paper was directly inspired by Martha Feldman's (2000) paper on how routines at a mid-western university changed continuously. Feldman documented changes to routines that emerged endogenously from situated performances. Studying budgeting, hiring, training, moving-in and closing-up routines in the university's student residence halls, Feldman observed surprising changes over the course of four years. She found that some changes emerged because people are self-reflective on how routines unfold in relation to their plans, and they may take steps to repair a routine that is not achieving its outcomes, or strive to produce a more appropriate outcome. Other changes emerged when outcomes presented new possibilities for action. In reading this work and thinking about her Chipco data, Howard-Grenville could relate to some aspects of Feldman's findings, including that situated performances of routines admitted a lot of variation. But in the Chipco context, these accommodations were rarely, if ever, perpetuated and taken up in subsequent performances. Her hunch was that the strong culture at Chipco and the nature of the work itself served to reign in endogenous change to the routines over time, even as specific routine performances were flexible. Through her subsequent analysis, the idea of routine embeddedness emerged as a boundary condition for the degree of endogenous change one might expect when routines are performed in a given organizational setting.[1]

While the language of 'structures' might give the construct of routine embeddedness an entitative feel, it was never intended to do so. In fact, Howard-Grenville (2005) drew on Sewell's (1992) work on structure and Giddens' (1984) structuration theory to develop the idea of embeddedness as inhering in the simultaneous enactment of multiple social structures. According to Sewell (1992: 27), structures are 'constituted by mutually sustaining cultural schemas and sets of resources that empower and constrain social action and tend to be reproduced by that action'. In other words, structures have a dual nature as they both shape and are shaped by human action – and are hence inseparable from it. Structures are therefore always emergent (Giddens, 1984) and inherently dynamic. Sewell (1992: 27) emphasizes that,

> Structure is dynamic, not static; it is the continually evolving outcome and matrix of a process of social interaction. Even the more or less perfect reproduction of structures is a profoundly temporal process that requires resourceful and innovative human conduct. But the same resourceful agency that sustains the reproduction of structures also makes possible their transformation – by means of transpositions of schemas and remobilizations of resources that make the new structures recognizable as transformations of the old. Structures, I suggest, are not reified categories we can invoke to explain the inevitable shape of social life.

Further, such social structures are never enacted in isolation. Structures often overlap and they may 'operate in harmony' or 'lead to sharply conflicting claims and empowerments' (Sewell, 1992: 16). Hence, as Howard-Grenville (2005: 630) argued,

> When we see routines as structures, that is, instantiated through ongoing practice, it becomes apparent that the practices that constitute routines also constitute other aspects of the organization.

[1] Howard-Grenville (2005) identified a second boundary condition on endogenous change of routines, which was individuals' agentic orientations towards performing the routine, namely their propensity to orient towards the past, present or future (Emirbayer and Mische, 1998).

> Routines ... are enacted simultaneously with other structures ... The artifacts and social expectations generated from enacting these other structures can overlap with and reinforce those that inform the enactment of routines.

Thus, Howard-Grenville (2005) asserted that routines could have differing degrees of overlap with, or embeddedness in, other organizational structures. The degree of embeddedness could produce different consequences for how persistent a routine is over time. She explained,

> The simultaneous enactment of multiple structures can contribute to the persistence of routines by generating multiple, often overlapping artifacts and expectations. I define the overlap between artifacts and expectations generated from routine performances and those generated from the enactment of other structures as a routine's embeddedness in other organizational structures (2005: 631).

The idea of routine embeddedness has been taken up in the subsequent literature on Routine Dynamics both directly and indirectly, the latter in the broader sense of authors attending to how organizational context 'matters'. Directly, scholars have shown how routines and organizational schema are 'coconstituted' through their interaction and enactment (Rerup and Feldman, 2011: 577); how artifacts and communities shape routines and are themselves transformed by routine performances (D'Adderio, 2014); and how routine performances also draw into use cultural strategies of action (Bertels et al., 2016). These works have further emphasized the dynamic nature of organizational structures, context and routine embeddedness. D'Adderio (2014: 1347) argues that her findings,

> highlight a crucial feature of embeddedness that has been so far insufficiently emphasized: rather than performing as a fixed background for routinized action that precedes action, context contributes to dynamically constituting and reconstituting routines. This implies that routines are not simply embedded in context, they are also enacted through context.

This signals a further refinement to the idea that routines are embedded in dynamic, emergent structures, as structurationalists would recognize, and suggests a different ontology, consistent with Actor Network Theory (ANT) (Callon, 1987; Latour, 1987) and sociomateriality (Orlikowski and Scott, 2008). These perspectives theorize the role of artifacts, alongside human agents, and highlight their co-construction (D'Adderio, 2011). They also draw attention to performativity, which explains how artifacts or models (e.g., rules, standard operating procedures) are not merely descriptions of what is going on, but perform – or actually alter – courses of action. Consistent with this perspective, D'Adderio (2014) finds in her study of routine transfer in a high tech company that 'artifacts and communities are transformed through being involved in routinized performances', and, further, that 'replication is not simply about the reproduction ... but also about the effortful recreation of a routine in and through a different context' (2014: 1347). Bertels et al. (2016) argue that routines and other generative structures that are enacted in organizational life, such as culture, could be regarded as entangled, borrowing this language from sociomaterial and ANT perspectives (Orlikowski and Scott, 2008), as they are inherently inseparable in practice. Simultaneously enacted social structures can therefore never be 'regarded as "in the background" to [one an]other' (Bertels et al., 2016: 591).

These more recent elaborations not only make routine embeddedness a more dynamic construct but also point out how it serves as more than a constraint or boundary condition on the change of routines. Indeed, the embeddedness or entanglement of routines with other social structures means that these might 'be dynamically enacted as resources to shape routines' (D'Adderio, 2014: 1347) and that 'the embeddedness of routines can at times be an *enabler* of change' (Bertels et al., 2016: 591; emphasis added) as employees skilfully draw on other social structures to direct routine performances.

In the following, we consider the ways in which routine embeddedness has been studied since Howard-Grenville's (2005) introduction of the construct, and, more broadly, explore how the idea of organizational context has been engaged in the Routine Dynamics literature. Specifically, we discuss how the three core aspects of structures as laid out in Howard-Grenville's (2005) initial study – technological, cultural and coordination – have been taken up, elaborated on and expanded in recent work on routine embeddedness and context. To do so, we undertook a systematic review of papers related to organizational routines and embeddedness across all major management journal outlets – including *ASQ, AMJ, AMR, Organization Science, JMS, Organization Studies* – and accompanied this with an additional Google Scholar search, using the term 'routine(s)' and coupling it with keywords such as 'embeddedness', 'context(s)', 'structure(s)', 'culture', 'ecologies' or 'entanglement'. This approach yielded an initial sample of forty-nine publications, covering the years 2005–2020, which we then narrowed down to twenty-six pieces of scholarly work that were most relevant to our aims (see Table 16.A1 in the Appendix).

16.3 How the Literature on Routine Embeddedness Has Evolved

Our review and analysis of papers that implicitly or explicitly investigated routine embeddedness revealed five aspects of routine embeddedness, three of which we classed as evolutions or extensions of the original three (technological, cultural and coordination), and two that had only recently been advanced (see Figure 16.1).

16.4 Shifts and Elaborations on Embeddedness in Technological Structures

Embeddedness in technological structures was originally defined as the extent to which routines were enacted simultaneously with 'technological structures result[ing] from the physical properties of technical artifacts, [which] guide and constrain ... actions' (Howard-Grenville, 2005: 630). For example, the technology to produce semiconductor chips relies on physically scaling the dimensions of features (i.e., transistors and connections) on the chip, to enable greater power and speed. These material properties generated among Chipco engineers an expectation that they were working to achieve Moore's Law, which predicated that features would shrink in size by

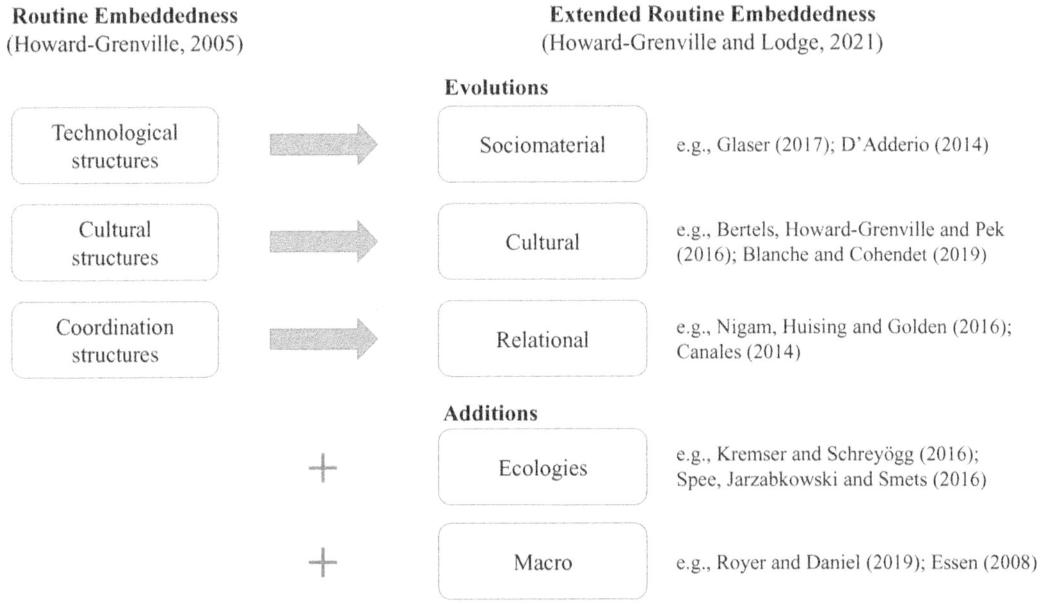

Figure 16.1 Overview of evolution of routine embeddedness aspects: 2005–2020

half every two years. Accordingly, performing the road-mapping (planning) routine at Chipco was guided by and reproduced these expectations of physical scaling (Howard-Grenville, 2005). The idea of how routines are embedded in technological structures has evolved alongside our understanding of the constraints and affordances posed by technologies and their properties. While earlier work highlighted how people's actions were guided and constrained by (largely) the material aspects of technologies (e.g., DeSanctis and Poole, 1994; Orlikowski, 1992), more recent work regards technologies as *sociomaterial* (Orlikowski and Scott, 2008). This perspective emphasizes the inherent inseparability of the social and material, and directs our attention to their ongoing interaction, which yields a processual as opposed to entitative understanding of technology.

The embeddedness of routines in technological structures, accordingly, has more recently focused on how routines performances are intertwined with the social and material aspects of technologies. For example, D'Adderio (2014), in studying how a routine is transferred from one geography to another through social and material features in an electronics organization, argues that routines are not only embedded within certain contexts but that routines are enacted through their contexts. She advances the idea that not only can routines change dynamically through certain configurations of communities and artifacts but that the context itself can evolve as communities and artifacts change through their enactment of routines. As such she concludes that 'rather than performing as a fixed background for routinized action which precedes action, context contributes to dynamically constituting and reconstituting routines' (D'Adderio, 2014: 1347). In doing so, D'Adderio provides nuance to the study of embeddedness by depicting how the social and the material context in which routines are enacted are mutually constituted with each other and with the evolving routine itself. Similarly, Pentland, Hærem and Hillison's (2011) study of invoice processing routines across four organizations demonstrates that the sociomaterial context is a crucial element in understanding (endogenous) change of organizational routines. Investigating both actors and the technology they rely on, their findings indicate how under some circumstances an 'increased automation can increase variation' (Pentland et al., 2011: 1369) and thus how routines can generate large amounts of varying patterns of action that evolve and change over time. An additional nuance to our understanding of technological embeddedness emerges from Glaser's (2017) study examining the design of newly automated patrol routines for a law enforcement agency. Focusing on how organizations consciously engage in designing artifacts to intentionally change routines, Glaser shows how material (including algorithmic) artifacts produced through design reflect various actors' assumptions and expectations, and also 'produce assemblages of actors, artifacts, theories, and practices that fundamentally influence future organizational actions' (2017: 2127). In sum, the original idea that routines are embedded in technological structures has been demonstrated in other settings, and has evolved to focus on a more nuanced conceptualization of technology, in line with concurrent development of a sociomaterial perspective on technology.

16.5 Shifts and Elaborations on Embeddedness in Cultural Structures

Howard-Grenville (2005) asserted that routines were also embedded in cultural structures, or those that 'reflect norms of appropriate behavior that enable and constrain particular types and sequences of action' (2005: 630). She referred specifically to organizational culture, although routines could certainly be embedded in other cultures – such as occupational or professional culture – of interest to organizational scholars. Our review of the literature revealed limited direct uptake of the cultural aspect of embeddedness at the level of organizational cultures per se. One paper that directly addressed and engaged in unpacking this aspect of embeddedness was co-authored by Bertels et al. (2016). These authors explored how the organizational culture of 'Oilco' shaped the integration and enactment of a routine that Oilco sought to copy from its peers.

The authors found that employees would often engage in extra efforts to navigate potential misfits between their organizational culture and a new routine they were aiming to implement. Even prior to the adoption of the routine by front-line workers, however, Bertels and colleagues found that Oilco's culture shaped their managers' intentions for and assumptions about the routine's design. Thus, culture can shape routines both before and during their specific performances. This study moves our understanding of embeddedness forward by suggesting that routines should be understood as 'mutually constituted with culture through their common grounding in actions' (Bertels et al., 2016: 574) and in doing so gives rise to the idea that cultural embeddedness can both be an enabler and an inhibitor to change.

In our review we discovered that, beyond Bertels et al.'s (2016) work, a number of studies, while not engaging with organizational culture in the context of Routine Dynamics explicitly, still provided relevant insights into routines' embeddedness in cultural structures. For example, Cohendet and Simon (2016) explored radical changes in routines that come about through organizational shocks. In particular, in the context of a video game company, the authors examined how the organization responded to a creativity crisis and how it worked to modify its project management routines to enable creativity to re-emerge and be maintained. They find that such re-emergence is closely linked to 'breaking existing rules and roles, rearranging existing patterns of interaction, and constant reshuffling and reconfiguring of the organizational structure' (2016: 615), in which organizational culture clearly played an important role without being front and centre of the paper. Other studies tend to focus on occupational communities or different cultural contexts rather than culture at the organizational level itself: D'Adderio (2011), for example, explores how new contexts and new settings in routine transfer can influence Routine Dynamics and bring routines 'to life' (2011: 19). In a different instance, Bruns (2009) examines the question of why and how the performance of routines in a biology laboratory may vary and relates this to differing interpretations of the routines based on different occupational norms and objectives (organizations vs. scientific) within the laboratory. Most recently, Blanche and Cohendet (2019) draw attention to how a ballet company managed to replicate a routine across different locations through the sharing of a professional culture. Overall, we thus find that cultural influences on routine performance and transfer have been explored even when organizational culture is not strongly explicit.

16.6 Shifts and Elaborations on Embeddedness in Coordination Structures

Embeddedness in coordination structures was originally described as the enactment of routines in relation to 'structures reflect(ing) the interdependence of action between multiple actors when accomplishing a complex task' (Howard-Grenville, 2005: 630). This aspect of routine embeddedness appears to have been significantly elaborated in recent years, with authors considering the embeddedness of routines in the relational fabric of organizing, and sometimes focusing specifically on coordination moves (e.g., LeBaron et al., 2016) or how organizational roles shape routine changes (e.g., Nigam et al., 2016). We regard these as elaborations on the idea of coordination structures, as they reflect and advance understanding of how interactions between people shape the change and stability of routines.

Advancing insights into how the relational fabric of organizations shapes routines' use, Canales' (2013) study of loan officers' different styles in a microfinance organization is telling. He found that some loan officers had a 'relational style' – i.e., they operated on the basis of embedded social ties – and hence exercised discretion in applying routines for loan decisions. Only in the presence of other loan officers who were 'rule-enforcers' did this style produce good branch performance. Canales attributes the effectiveness of diverse discretionary styles (i.e., some relational and some rule-following loan officers) to the fact that such diversity 'generate[s] a productive tension that induces participants to justify decisions along broader organizational goals, thus maintaining a productive balance between standardization and flexibility [of routines]' (2013:1). In sum, it is not only the formal coordination of tasks that shapes routine performance but the styles with which people performing the routines interact with routine participants, and each other, and the distribution of these styles within the organization. Further elaborating the idea that relational dynamics shape routine flexibility and persistence, LeBaron et al. (2016) show how physicians involved in handoff routines – i.e., passing a patient from one physician to another at the end of their shift – create mutually intelligible performances through their shared expectations of the routine and its sequencing, as they are able to use this knowledge to sometimes depart from or skip steps in the routine. Through a fine-grained video analysis of the handoff routine, these authors also show that coordinating is ongoing during the routine performance, further suggesting, as indicated in other work (Bertels et al., 2016; D'Adderio, 2014), that routines and other structures are mutually constituted in organizational life.

Other studies consider how routines are intentionally transformed due to participants' knowledge (and lack thereof) of coordinating structures and interaction patterns within their organizations. For example, Deken, Carlile, Berends and Lauche (2016) consider how people generated novel intended outcomes for a routine through ongoing 'routine work'. Routine work was demanded because interdependencies between routines and other tasks and expectations arose and cascaded as novel outcomes were sought. While not explicitly focusing on embeddedness, Deken et al.'s paper nonetheless reveals how routine change in a complex organization is conditioned by the relational structures at play, and by the interdependencies between people, expertise and tasks, as well as between routines themselves. Finally, in their study across seven hospitals, Nigam, Huising and Golden (2016) studied how occupational roles influenced which routines were selected to be changed in a planned change initiative. They asserted that because roles are crucial 'in defining people's authority, goals, and interpretive frames' (2016: 555), they are particularly important in explaining how people view routines – and which portions of them they view from their role-specific vantage point. This, in turn, influences interactions among diverse occupational leaders that can ultimately shape which routines get selected for attention. Nigam et al.'s (2016) emphasis on occupational roles – and their distribution and relative power within an organization – is a helpful addition to how we might think about the relational and coordinative fabric of organizations and its influence on routine performance and change.

Finally, a more nascent but still highly intriguing aspect of embeddedness emerged from our review, in which embeddedness was discussed in terms of spaces. In their paper, set in the context of two hospitals, Bucher and Langley (2016) investigate how spaces, which they define as 'bounded social settings in which interactions among actors are organized in distinctive ways' (2016: 594), can enable the deliberate altering of organizational routines. In particular, they engaged in a longitudinal investigation of change efforts in patient processes and tracked how core routine actors interacted in social spaces that were outside of the sphere of the routines to change them. They identified two different kinds of spaces related to routine change and argued that 'reflective' spaces allowed actors to interact with the aim of creating new concepts of a routine and 'experimental' spaces enabled 'their testing, appropriation, and modification in provisional performances guided by new concepts' (Bucher and Langley, 2016: 595). Although spaces have become an increasingly important research topic in other areas of management and organizational theory (e.g., Lawrence and Dover, 2015), the authors argue that the distinct and potentially novelty-inducing role of space has been underemphasized in the study of routine, and opportunities to change this abound. We group this study with others that we consider to have elaborated on the idea of embeddedness in structures of coordination because, while it foregrounds spaces, the potential for routine change lies in how people interact and relate within those.

16.7 New Themes Building on Embeddedness: Routine Ecologies and Macro Embeddedness

Two other themes related to routine embeddedness and context are evident in the recent literature. First, there is increasing attention to the idea that the enactment of routines is often influenced by the enactment of other routines within organizations. Regarding single routines as embedded in 'other' contexts might miss the important question of how routines are themselves interdependent and potentially mutually constitutive. For example, Kremser and Schreyögg (2016) focus on the interrelationship of routines and how routines interact with one another in distinct units, so called routine clusters, to achieve tasks. Exploring how a large photofinishing company's operations reacted and responded to the digital film revolution, the authors show how routines become grouped in clusters and in what manner 'complementarities between the specialized routines of a cluster will affect (their) evolution' (Kremser and Schreyögg, 2016: 505). Ultimately, the authors introduce a more nuanced understanding of how dynamics in singular routines and routine clusters may differ. Working in the context of professional service firms, Spee, Jarzabkowski and Smets (2016) show how interdependencies between multiple intersecting routines can be coordinated. Through their study, the authors highlight 'micromechanisms within which the overlaps that constitute embeddedness are enacted' (777). The study also draws attention to the idea that multiple routines do not interact in always predictable ways; different routines have different overlaps and touch points over time that can be both mandatory and discretionary. Finally, Sele and Grand (2016) study how human and non-human actors work to connect routines. They motivate their study by emphasizing the importance of learning more about how routine interactions specifically contribute to organizational goals and outcomes. In the context of a research laboratory, the authors highlight that the generative nature of routines does not only emerge from 'the recursive interactions between the ostensive and performative aspects of a single routine' but can also be garnered through 'continuous interactions between the routines' (Sele and Grand, 2016: 735).

A second theme that departs from how routine embeddedness was originally conceptualized is that focusing on how routine performances are shaped by larger macro-structures. We employ the term macro-structures to refer broadly to structures that are constituted and exist outside of formal organizations, such as institutions, national cultures or history. Both Royer and Daniel (2019), as well as Cajaiba, Cajaiba Santana and Lazaric (2015), for example, ask in broad terms how organizational routines are related to institutional-level characteristics. In the heavily regulated context of public nursing homes, the former pair of authors focus on the disciplinary sanction routine to examine how artifacts carrying the values of their institutionalized environments can impact routines. In particular, they show how routines are performed in 'institutionalized environment[s] designed to exert pressure to comply' (2015: 204) and thus contribute to our understanding of routine enactment in more coercive scenarios. Cajaiba et al. undertake an empirical study in the context of the bio-tech industry to explore how institutions impact the emergence of organizational routines. In particular, they analyse the micro-foundations of routine emergence through organizational practices that are kindled through institutional pressures. In doing so, the authors link external and internal developments to construct a more nuanced understanding of organizational routine emergence.

Essén (2008) also contributes to the idea of embeddedness within macro-structures but from a different angle. She theorizes how organizational routines are related to and influenced by the national cultures routine enactors embody. In the context of a home care setting for the elderly, the author argues that the enactment of routines can be heavily influenced by differing perceptions of national cultures. The author further highlights how values in society that are adopted by individuals who enact the routine can influence their routine performance. Similarly, Boe-Lillegraven (2019) expands on this by examining how routines are transferred across geographic boundaries. In the context of food companies in Europe and Asia, she illustrates the role national cultures play in routine transfers and the performative struggles that arise as a result.

A final type of embeddedness we identified that was related to macro-structures concerned a study by Mutch (2016). In an investigation in the context of church bodies, Mutch ventures to bring the idea of history into the study of organizational routines. He argues that much of the routines literature has to date focused extensively on the routine performance itself and has underemphasized the historical context in which these performances take place. Focusing on such historical context appears important as it shows how routine performances are 'shaped by factors which are beyond the immediate control or even knowledge' of the actors (Mutch, 2016: 1184). In addition, the author emphasizes that considering historical contexts in the study of routines draws attention to the fact that routines themselves do not just rapidly come to life but have a history, that is, they are connected to 'broader bodies of ideas and resources which shape their form' (Mutch, 2016: 1171).

In sum, our analysis of the current state of the literature on routine embeddedness, considering both those studies that speak about it explicitly and those that do so more implicitly, explores how the original three aspects proposed by Howard-Grenville (2005) – technological, cultural, coordination – have evolved over the years and have been expanded to develop an increasing awareness that routines are not performed in a vacuum but enacted and influenced by further factors, including other proximate routines and wider macro contexts.

16.8 Towards a Research Agenda of Routine Embeddedness

As our review of the literature on organizational routines reveals, studies relating to embeddedness have garnered substantial interest in the organizational routines community (and beyond) and have been taken up broadly since the initial conceptualization of this construct (Howard-Grenville, 2005). However, we believe that there is still ample space to contribute to this ongoing and valuable debate and thus propose three avenues for future exploration.

First, building on the last embeddedness aspect identified in our analysis – macro-structures – we encourage organizational and routines scholars to pay more attention to studying how routines link to and are influenced by occurrences and structures that lie beyond organizational boundaries. While there have been a few studies, mentioned earlier, that have recently taken such a perspective, we believe there is still a lot more that can be done. For example: How are routines influenced by – or how does their enactment influence – larger social, cultural or institutional structures? How might exogenous shocks or disruptions influence the change or stability of organizational routines? While the Routine Dynamics perspective sheds ample light on the endogenous change of routines, we need to situate such processes within the broader settings that might influence how they unfold (Parmigiani and Howard-Grenville, 2011). Linking the conversation of organizational Routine Dynamics to recent advances in grand challenges research (George et al., 2016) or social-symbolic work at the institutional level (Lawrence and Phillips, 2019; Phillips and Lawrence, 2012) may provide a fruitful avenue for future work.

Second, from an empirical perspective, many studies on organizational routines but particularly those that have focused on the topic of embeddedness seem to have been undertaken in settings that one might characterize as relatively 'low stakes' environments (e.g., garbage collecting; invoice processing). However, routines are not only found and enacted in these kinds of settings but also in contexts that are far more contested and emotionally draining, such as rape crisis centres, animal shelters or prisons (Claus et al., 2019; Rogers et al., 2017). We thus encourage routine scholars to actively engage in contexts, with actors, and with practices that are much more contested, controversial or even morally questionable (e.g., the lethal injection routine in the context of capital punishment). Taking such contested contexts more seriously in the study of organizational routines could also open up opportunities to study emotions or issues of morality in the enactment of routines in more detail.

Third, in discussion around embeddedness it appears that most research has paid attention to the active participants who enact or in some shape or form contribute to the routine performance. In organizational settings, however, we would suspect there to be a whole range of actors that are only passively involved in the context who, for example, receive or are impacted by the outcomes of the routines. Crucially, organizations can only control the performance and the consequences of routines to a certain extent. Learning more about these actors who appear as 'peripheral participants' or as 'bystanders' might help shine light on how broader stakeholder groups beyond the narrow focus of those who take part in the routine enactment are impacted by routines. Further, one could explore how these actors directly or indirectly shape contexts into which routines are embedded, ultimately shaping (or constraining) the routine performance itself. For example, Turner and Rindova (2018) investigate how peripheral actors – people putting out their garbage for curbside collection – contribute to the timing and to some degree the uncertainty of the garbage collection routine of waste management professionals. In a setting with more dramatic consequences for all, Lübcke, Steigenberger, Wilhelm and Maurer (2019) examine how peripheral participants are influenced and coordinated by the core enactors of routines. They show this through an ethnographic account of a rescue routine in the Aegean Sea during which refugees (peripheral participants) are transferred from overcrowded rubber boats to a rescue cruiser through specific practices of the rescue team (core participants). The authors develop the idea of 'meta actions' that core participants employ to coordinate the behaviours of peripheral participants and tie them into the routine. This is important, as, particularly with high stakes and time-sensitive routines, coordination of peripheral actors can be vital but often difficult to achieve given contextual pressures.

16.9 Concluding Thoughts

The idea that routine performances are shaped by the organizational contexts in which they are enacted remains important to understanding the conditions under which routines persist or change. In addition to being embedded in technological, cultural and coordination structures which rein in their tendency to change over time (Howard-Grenville, 2005), routines are increasingly regarded as entangled with (Bertels et al., 2016) and enacted through (D'Adderio, 2014) other generative structures. These can be sources of change as well as persistence. While considerable work has demonstrated the ways in which routine performances are shaped by and shape other aspects of organizational life, further work on routine embeddedness can expand our understanding of how organizational and macro contexts generate important outcomes – including the change and persistence of routines themselves – and what is at stake when they do so.

References

Anand, G., Gray, J. and Siemsen, E. (2012). Decay, shock, and renewal: Operational routines and process entropy in the pharmaceutical industry. *Organization Science*, 23(6), 1700–1716.

Bertels, S., Howard-Grenville, J. and Pek, S. (2016). Cultural molding, shielding, and shoring at Oilco: The role of culture in the integration of routines. *Organization Science*, 27(3), 573–593.

Blanche, C. and Cohendet, P. (2019). Remounting a ballet in a different context: A complementary understanding of routines transfer theories. In M. Feldman, L. D'Adderio, K. Dittrich and P. Jarzabkowski, eds., *Routine Dynamics in Action: Replication and Transformation* (Research in the Sociology of Organizations, Vol. 61). Bingley: Emerald Group Publishing, 11–30.

Boe-Lillegraven, S. (2019). Transferring routines across multiple boundaries: A flexible approach. In M. Feldman, L. D'Adderio, K. Dittrich and P. Jarzabkowski, eds., *Routine Dynamics in Action: Replication and Transformation* (Research in the Sociology of Organizations, Vol. 61). Bingley: Emerald Group Publishing, 31–53.

Bresman, H. (2013). Changing routines: A process model of vicarious group learning in pharmaceutical R&D. *Academy of Management Journal*, 56(1), 35–61.

Bruns, H. (2009). Leveraging functionality in safety routines: Examining the divergence of rules and performance. *Human Relations*, 62(9), 1399–1426.

Bucher, S. and Langley, A. (2016). The interplay of reflective and experimental spaces in interrupting and reorienting Routine Dynamics. *Organization Science*, 27(3), 505–800.

Cajaiba, A. P., Cajaiba Santana, G. and Lazaric, N. (2015). An institutional perspective on routine emergence: A case from the bio-tech industry. *Post-Print hal-01298030, HAL.*

Callon, M. (1987). Society in the making: the study of technology as a tool for sociological analysis. In W. Bijker, T. Hughes and T. Pinch, eds., *The Social Construction of Technological Systems*. Cambridge, MA: MIT Press.

Canales, R. (2013). Weaving straw into gold: Managing organizational tensions between standardization and flexibility in microfinance. *Organization Science*, 25(1), 1–28.

Christianson, M. K., Farkas, M. T., Sutcliffe, M. and Weick, K. E. (2009). Learning through rare events: Significant interruptions at the Baltimore & Ohio Railroad Museum. *Organization Science*, 20(5), 846–860.

Claus, L., de Rond, M., Howard-Grenville, J. and Lodge, J. (2019). When fieldwork hurts: On the lived experience of conducting research in unsettling contexts. In T. B. Zilber, J. M. Amis and J. Mair, eds., *The Production of Managerial Knowledge and Organizational Theory: New Approaches to Writing, Producing and Consuming Theory*. (Research in the Sociology of Organizations Series, Vol. 59). Bingley: Emerald Group Publishing, 157–172.

Cohendet, P. S. and Simon, L. O. (2016). Always playable: Recombining routines for creative efficiency at Ubisoft Montreal's video game studio. *Organization Science*, 27(3), 614–632.

D'Adderio, L. (2011). Artifacts at the centre of routines: Performing the material turn in routines theory. *Journal of Institutional Economics*, 7 (2), 197–230.

D'Adderio, L. (2014). The replication dilemma unravelled: How organizations enact multiple goals in routine transfer. *Organization Science*, 25(5), 1325–1350.

Deken, F., Carlile, P. R., Berends, H. and Lauche, K. (2016). Generating novelty through interdependent routines: A process model of routine work. *Organization Science*, 27(3), 659–677.

DeSanctis, G. and Poole, M. S. (1994). Capturing the complexity in advanced technology use: Adaptive structuration theory. *Organization Science*, 5(2), 121–147.

Dosi, G., Nelson, R. R. and Winter, S. G. (2000). *The Nature and Dynamics of Organizational Capabilities*. New York: Oxford University Press.

Edmondson, A. C., Bohmer, R. M. and Pisano, G. P. (2001). Disrupted routines: Team learning and new technology implementation in hospitals. *Administrative Science Quarterly*, 46(4), 685–716.

Emirbayer, M. and Mische, A. (1998). What is agency? *American Journal of Sociology*, 103 (4), 962–1023.

Essén, A. (2008). Variability as a source of stability: Studying routines in the elderly home care setting. *Human Relations*, 61(11), 1617–1644.

Feldman, M. S. (2000). Organizational routines as a source of continuous change. *Organization Science*, 11(6), 611–629.

Feldman, M. S. and Pentland, B. T. (2003). Reconceptualizing organizational routines as a source of flexibility and change. *Administrative Science Quarterly*, 48(1), 94–118.

George, G., Howard-Grenville, J., Joshi, A. and Tihanyi, L. (2016). Understanding and tackling societal grand challenges through management research. *Academy of Management Journal*, 59 (6), 1880–1895.

Gersick, C. J. and Hackman, J. R. (1990). Habitual routines in task-performing groups. *Organizational Behavior and Human Decision Processes*, 47(1), 65–97.

Giddens, A. (1984). *The Constitution of Society: Outline of the Theory of Structuration*. Oxford: Polity Press.

Glaser, V. (2017). Design performances: How organizations inscribe artifacts to change routines. *Academy of Management Journal*, 60(6), 2126–2154.

Howard-Grenville, J. (2005). The persistence of flexible organizational routines: The role of agency and organizational context. *Organization Science*, 16(6), 563–727.

Howard-Grenville, J. A. and Rerup, C. (2017). A process perspective on organizational routines. In A. Langley and H. Tsoukas, eds., *Handbook of Process Organizational Studies*. Thousand Oaks, CA: Sage, pp. 323–339.

Howard-Grenville, J., Rerup, C., Langley, A. and Tsoukas, H. (2016). Introduction. In J. Howard-Grenville, C. Rerup, A. Langley and H. Tsoukas, eds., *Organizational Routines: How They Are Created, Maintained, and*

Changed. Oxford: Oxford University Press, pp. 1–22.

Kremser, W. and Schreyögg, G. (2016). The dynamics of interrelated routines: Introducing the cluster level. *Organization Science*, 27(3), 698–721.

Latour, B. (1987). *Science in Action: How to Follow Scientists and Engineers Through Society*. Cambridge, MA: Harvard University Press.

Lawrence, T. B. and Dover, G. (2015). Place and institutional work: Creating housing for the hard-to-house. *Administrative Science Quarterly*, 60(3), 371–410.

Lawrence, T. B. and Phillips, N. (2019). *Constructing Organizational Life*. Oxford: Oxford University Press.

LeBaron, C., Christianson, M. K., Garrett, L. and Ilan, R. (2016). Coordinating flexible performance during everyday work: An ethnomethodological study of handoff routines. *Organization Science*, 27(3), 514–534.

Lübcke, T., Steigenberger, N., Wilhelm, H. and Maurer, I. (2019). How core actors coordinate distal actors in organizational routines. *Proceedings of the 79th Annual Meeting of the Academy of Management*. Boston.

Mutch, A. (2016). Bringing history into the study of routines: Contextualizing performance. *Organization Studies*, 37(8), 1171–1188.

Nelson, R. R. and Winter, S. G. (1982). *An Evolutionary Theory of Economic Change*. Cambridge, MA: The Belknap Press of Harvard University Press.

Nigam, A., Huising, R. and Golden, B. (2016). Explaining the selection of routines for change during organizational search. *Administrative Science Quarterly*, 61(4), 551–583.

Orlikowski, W. J. (1992). The duality of technology: Rethinking the concept of technology in organizations. *Organization Science*, 3(3), 398–427.

Orlikowski, W. J. and Scott, S. V. (2008). Sociomateriality: Challenging the separation of technology, work and organization. *Academy of Management Annals*, 2(1), 433–474.

Parmigiani, A. and Howard-Grenville, J. (2011). Routines revisited: Exploring the capabilities and practice perspectives. *Academy of Management Annals*, 5(1), 413–453.

Pentland, B. T., Hærem, T. and Hillison, D. (2011). The (n)ever-changing world: Stability and change in organizational routines. *Organization Science*, 22(6), 1369–1383.

Pentland, B. T. and Rueter, H. H. (1994). Organizational routines as grammars of action. *Administrative Science Quarterly*, 39(3), 484–510.

Phillips, N. and Lawrence, T. B. (2012). The turn to work in organization and management theory: Some implications for strategic organization. *Strategic Organization*, 10(3), 223–230.

Rerup, C. and Feldman, M. S. (2011). Routines as a source of change in organizational schemata: The role of trial-and-error learning. *Academy of Management Journal*, 54(3), 577–610.

Rogers, K. M., Corley, K. G. and Ashforth, B. E. (2017). Seeing more than orange: Organizational respect and positive identity transformation in a prison context. *Administrative Science Quarterly*, 62(2), 219–269.

Royer, I. and Daniel, A. (2019). Organizational routines and institutional maintenance: The influence of legal artifacts. *Journal of Management Inquiry*, 28(2), 204–224.

Sele, K. and Grand, S. (2016). Unpacking the dynamics of ecologies of routines: Mediators and their generative effects in routine interactions. *Organization Science*, 27(3), 722–738.

Sewell, W. (1992). A theory of structure: Duality, agency, and transformation. *American Journal of Sociology*, 98(1), 1–29.

Spee, P., Jarzabkowski, P. and Smets, M. (2016). The influence of routine interdependence and skillful accomplishment on the coordination of standardizing and customizing. *Organization Science*, 27 (3), 759–781.

Turner, S. F. and Fern, M. J. (2012). Examining the stability and variability of routine performances: The effects of experience and context change. *Journal of Management Studies*, 49(8), 1407–1434.

Turner, S. F. and Rindova, V. P. (2018). Watching the clock: Action timing, patterning, and routine performance. *Academy of Management Journal*, 61(4), 1253–1280.

Appendix

Table 16.A1 Overview of central works on routine embeddedness

#	Title	Authors	Year	Journal	Empirical context	Focus of paper	New embeddedness aspect
1	Organizational Routines and Institutional Maintenance: The Influence of Legal Artifacts	Royer and Daniel	2019	*JMI*	Public nursing home	Routines' relationship to institutions	Macro
2	Remounting a ballet in a different context: A complementary understanding of routines transfer theories	Blanche and Cohendet	2019	*RSO*	Ballet company	Routine replications through professional culture	Cultural
3	Transferring routines across multiple boundaries: A flexible approach	Boe-Lillegraven	2019	*RSO*	Food companies	Routine transfer across national and cultural boundaries	Cultural
4	Design Performance: How Organizations Inscribe Artifacts to Change Routines	Glaser	2017	*AMJ*	Law enforcement agency	Artifact design and influence on Routine Dynamics	Sociomaterial
5	Cultural Molding, Shielding, and Shoring at Oilco: The Role of Culture in the Integration of Routines	Bertels, Howard-Grenville and Pek	2016	*OrgScience*	Oil industry	Relationship of culture to the integration and enactment of routines	Cultural
6	Explaining the Selection of Routines for Change during Organizational Search	Nigam, Huising and Golden	2016	*ASQ*	Hospitals	Organizational roles' influence on which routines are chosen to be changed	Relational
7	The Dynamics of Interrelated Routines: Introducing the Cluster Level	Kremser and Schreyögg	2016	*OrgScience*	Photofinishing	Interrelationship of routines and routine clusters	Ecologies
8	Unpacking the Dynamics of Ecologies of Routines: Mediators and Their Generative Effects in Routine Interactions	Sele and Grand	2016	*OrgScience*	AI research laboratory	Human and non-human actors and how they connect routines	Ecologies
9	Generating Novelty through Interdependent Routines: A Process Model of Routine Work	Deken, Carlile, Berends and Lauche	2016	*OrgScience*	Automotive	How multiple actors accomplish interdependent routine performances directed at novel intended outcomes	Relational
10	The Influence of Routine Interdependence and Skilful Accomplishment on the Coordination of Standardizing and Customizing	Spee, Jarzabkowski and Smets	2016	*OrgScience*	Professional service firms	Coordination of interdependence between intersecting routines and the influence on the balancing of coexisting ostensive patterns	Ecologies

Table 16.A1 ***(cont.)***

#	Title	Authors	Year	Journal	Empirical context	Focus of paper	New embeddedness aspect
11	The Interplay of Reflective and Experimental Spaces in Interrupting and Reorienting Routine Dynamics	Bucher and Langley	2016	*OrgScience*	Hospitals	How spaces enable the deliberate altering of routines	Relational
12	Coordinating Flexible Performance During Everyday Work: An Ethnomethodological Study of Handoff Routines	LeBaron, Christianson, Garrett and Ilan	2016	*OrgScience*	Intensive care unit	Flexibility and ongoing coordination of routines	Relational
13	Always Playable: Recombining Routines for Creative Efficiency at Ubisoft Montreal's Video Game Studio	Cohendet and Simon	2016	*OrgScience*	Video games studio	Reconfiguration of routines after a crisis	Cultural
14	Bringing History into the Study of Routines: Contextualizing Performance	Mutch	2016	*JMS*	Church	Routines' relationship to history	Macro
15	An Institutional Perspective on Routine Emergence: A Case from the Bio-Tech Industry	Cajaiba, Cajaiba Santana and Lazaric	2015	*Working paper*	Biofuel	Routines' relationship to institutions	Macro
16	The Replication Dilemma Unravelled: How Organizations Enact Multiple Goals in Routines Transfer	D'Adderio	2014	*OrgScience*	Electronics	Routine enactment through social and material features	Sociomaterial
17	Weaving Straw into Gold: Managing Organizational Tensions between Standardization and Flexibility in Microfinance	Canales	2014	*OrgScience*	Microfinance	Routines and their relationship to rule enforcement and discretion	Relational
18	Changing Routines: A Process Model of Vicarious Group Learning in Pharmaceutical R&D	Bresman	2013	*AMJ*	Pharmaceuticals	How groups change based on prior experience of other groups	Relational
19	Decay, Shock, and Renewal: Operational Routines and Process Entropy in the Pharmaceutical Industry	Anand, Gray and Siemsen	2012	*OrgScience*	US FDA	Routines' relationship to external shocks and outsider examinations	Relational
20	Examining the Stability and Variability of Routine Performances: The Effects of Experience and Context Change	Turner and Fern	2012	*JMS*	Waste management	Experiences of routine actors and the relationship to routine performance	Relational

21	A Balancing Act: How Organizations Pursue Consistency in Routine Functioning in the Face of Ongoing Change	Turner and Rindova	2012	*OrgScience*	Waste management	Routine participants and how they view and balance pressures of consistency in the face of ongoing change	Relational
22	Artifacts at the Centre of Routines: Performing the Material Turn in Routines Theory	D'Adderio	2011	*J. of Instit. Econ.*	Standard operating procedures	Influence of artifacts and contexts on Routine Dynamics	Cultural
23	The (N)Ever-Changing World: Stability and Change Organizational Routines	Pentland, Hærem and Hillison	2011	*OrgScience*	Invoice processing	Endogenous change and sociomaterial context in understanding change in routines	Sociomaterial
24	Routines as a Source of Change in Organizational Schemata: The Role of Trial-and-Error Learning	Rerup and Feldman	2011	*AMJ*	Research institution	Routines' relationships to organizational schemata	Relational
25	Leveraging Functionality in Safety Routines: Examining the Divergence of Rules and Performance	Bruns	2009	*Human Relations*	Biology laboratory	How and why the performance of routines may vary	Cultural
26	Variability as a Source of Stability: Studying Routines in the Elderly Home Care Setting	Essen	2008	*Human Relations*	Community care	Routines' relationship to national culture	Macro

CHAPTER 17

Routine Interdependence

Intersections, Clusters, Ecologies and Bundles

RODRIGO A. ROSA, WALDEMAR KREMSER AND SERGIO BULGACOV

17.1 Introduction

Research on Routine Dynamics started with a focus on the dynamics within individual routines (Feldman and Pentland, 2003). In recent years, a number of scholars have begun to also examine the dynamics of coordination that arise among interdependent routines. Two (or more) routines can be said to be interdependent to the extent that performing one routine creates an enabling and/or constraining context for performing the other(s) (Kremser et al., 2019). In a small diner, for example, the (patterned) ways in which the cooking routine is performed (e.g., its average pace or the typical quality of the dishes) will both enable and constrain the performances of the serving routine (e.g., by creating waiting times or the necessity to deal with customer complaints), and vice versa. Defined as such, it becomes clear that routine interdependence is a prevalent feature of everyday life in all organizations because 'real routines occur in complex ecologies, nested hierarchies and networks' (Pentland, 2011: 290).

In this chapter, we show that Routine Dynamics scholars have started to analyse how routine interdependence is accomplished in organizational practice – in and through the situated actions of specific actors at specific times in specific places (Feldman and Orlikowski, 2011). In general, such an analysis has proven to be helpful in explaining how larger action patterns – organizational-level outcomes – emerge through accomplishing several smaller action patterns – routines – in a *coordinated* fashion (Feldman and Rafaeli, 2002; Feldman et al., 2016). The relevance of this nascent line of research is emphasized by empirical research showing that dynamics taking place among routines can differ markedly from those taking place within routines (Kremser and Schreyögg, 2016).

One purpose of this chapter is to clarify what kind of relations between routines we find in the current literature. More specifically, we group the literature around key concepts – Routine Boundaries and Intersections, Routine Clusters, Routine Ecologies and Routine Bundles – each corresponding to a specific lens or perspective on routine interdependence. Each lens helps us to unpack a different facet of the important observation 'that no routine is ever enacted in a vacuum of other routines' (Howard-Grenville et al., 2016: 12). Hence, we make an argument for leveraging the analytical differences of such concepts as cluster and ecologies, rather than treating them as synonyms. Another purpose of this chapter is to point out several avenues for future research.

17.2 Previous Research on Interdependence among Routines

Research on the dynamics that arise among interdependent routines resulted in several new concepts, such as boundaries, ecologies or clusters. Due to the relative newness of this line of research, however, the differences as well as the connections between these concepts are still largely implicit. In an effort to systematize the existing literature on interdependence among routines, we have grouped the different studies into four different lenses (see Table 17.1). Each is centred on a core concept

Table 17.1 Different lenses in research on routine interdependence

Core concepts	Boundaries and intersections	Clusters	Ecologies	Bundles
Analytical focus	Ad-hoc coordination through specific performances	Planned coordination through designed interfaces	Unplanned coordination through emergent couplings	Aggregate outcomes of multiple routines
Assumptions	Practice Perspective	Practice Perspective	Practice Perspective	Capabilities Perspective
Example Reference	Spee et al. (2016)	Kremser and Schreyögg (2016)	Birnholtz et al. (2007)	Prange et al. (2017)

which provides a distinct analytical focus (see also Hoekzema, 2020) and is embedded either in the practice or the capabilities approach, each with its own ontological and epistemological assumptions (Parmigiani and Howard-Grenville, 2011).

The first group of studies work with routine boundaries and routine intersections as their core concepts. The analytical focus of these studies is on the ad-hoc coordination of multiple routines in and through specific performances. This is different from research in the second group, which works with the concept of the routine cluster. These studies put an analytical focus on helping us to understand (the dynamic implications of) the planned aspects in the coordinating of multiple routines, which is accomplished through the designing of interfaces. The third group uses the concept of routine ecologies to refer to groupings of routines that are connected not through designed interfaces but rather emergent couplings, focusing the analysis on the dynamic implications of unplanned coordination. All studies of these groups are firmly based in a practice perspective on routines. Finally, we have subsumed research on routine interdependence that is embedded in a capabilities approach (see Salvato [Chapter 34], this volume) into a fourth group centred on routine bundles. These studies often background the dynamics of coordination, focusing on understanding the aggregate outcomes of multiple routines instead.

In what follows, we will review the most relevant empirical studies in each of these four lenses on routine interdependence. For each, we will first provide a general description, then elaborate on its analytical focus and, finally, provide a summary of the most important studies that have applied this lens in their research. All of the studies are also categorized and shortly summarized in our Table 17.2.

17.2.1 Routine Boundaries and Intersections

Studies in this group work on the more ad-hoc forms of coordination that will often take place among interdependent routines. The core concepts are boundary performances – signalling behaviours that established certain contextual cues as more or less important for the performance of a specific routine (Geiger et al., 2020; Kremser et al., 2019) – and routine intersections – where 'another routine provides an impulse that orients the performance of the focal routine' (Spee et al., 2016: 773). Observing intersections and boundaries between routines requires scholars to make detailed, ethnographic observations of a focal routine in order to understand how adjacent routines or practices affect specific performances of that focal routine. Concepts from other literatures such as 'junctures' (Quick and Feldman, 2014), 'boundaries' (Abbott, 1995), 'boundary objects' (Carlile, 2002), and 'boundary work' (Langley et al., 2019) provide a conceptual starting point for studies in this category.

The analytical focus of studies in this category is on the question of how a concrete performance of a focal routine is affected by or can be separated from other routines and practices. This perspective foregrounds the importance of socio-material artifacts in connecting one routine to another without

Table 17.2 Summary of most important studies

Author(s)	Type	Perspective	Context (Case)	Main method	Main insight research on interdependent routines
Birnholtz, Cohen and Hoch (2007)	Empirical	Ecology	Private Summer Camp (Camp Poplar Grove)	Participant Observation	Organization Character is regenerated as ecologies of action dispositions (ostensive aspects) are enacted in a mutually coherent way and remembered procedurally
Deken, Carlile, Berends and Lauche (2016)	Empirical	Cluster	International Automotive Firm (AutoCo)	Ethnographic	Routine Work (flexing, stretching, and inventing) enables actors to react to new and sometimes unexpected developments that flow from other, interdependent routines
Kremser and Schreyögg (2016)	Empirical	Cluster	European Market Leader in Photo-Finishing (CEWE)	Historical (embedded) Case Study	Interdependence relations between routines can be (per)formed through the programming or designing of interfaces. Over time, this can create dynamics on the cluster-level that follow a logic of complementarities
Sele and Grand (2016)	Empirical	Ecology	University of Zurich's AI Lab	Ethnographic	Innovative outcomes depend on the generative potential of relations between routines, which can either take the form of intermediaries or mediators
Spee, Jarzabkowski and Smets (2016)	Empirical	Intersections	Reinsurance Industry	Multiple Case Study	Coexisting ostensive patterns in a focal routine are coordinated as skilled professionals react to impulses coming from other, intersecting routines
Prange, Bruyaka and Marmenout (2017)	Empirical	Bundles	International Logistics Company (DPWN) and its subsidiary DHL	Longitudinal (in-depth) Case Study	Development of dynamics capabilities – acquisition-based and innovation-based – requires the transition and transformations of the underlying bundle of routines while preserving organizational path dependence
Davies et al. (2018)	Empirical	Bundles	England's Highways Agency (HA)	Case Study	Creation and replication of new routines across multiple sites are shaped by different organizational levels and capabilities through evolutionary cycles of variation and selective retention
Kremser, Pentland and Brunswicker (2019)	Empirical	Intersections	Transatlantic flight (Passenger Service)	Ethnographic	There is an empirically observable difference between interdependence within and between routines. Observing the performance of routine boundaries can help us to understand how routines are related to each other.
Hoekzema (2020)	Theoretical	Cluster and Ecology	–	–	Interdependence between routines is a complex phenomenon that depends on different modes and degrees of coordination.

Table 17.2 (*cont.*)

Author(s)	Type	Perspective	Context (Case)	Main method	Main insight research on interdependent routines
Geiger, Danner-Schröder and Kremser (2021)	Empirical	Intersections	Crisis Management Organizations (Hamburg Firefighters)	Case Study	Under temporal uncertainty, routine participants can temporally coordinate multiple routines by rhythmizing routine performances and performing temporal boundaries
Kremser and Blagoev (2021)	Empirical	Ecology	Agile Consulting Project (Best Advise)	Case Study	Routine participants can temporally coordinate multiple routines without a schedule by also enacting person-roles. Over time, this leads to the emergence of role-routine ecologies via role-routine coupling and temporal ripple effects.

fully conflating their patterns. Analysing how actors use these socio-material artifacts to send and receive 'impulses' (Spee et al., 2016) between routines has proven to be very helpful in understanding how routine intersections can be accomplished in practice. In this regard, a more nuanced understanding of routine boundaries as performative accomplishments also promises to be analytically fruitful (Kremser et al., 2019). This directs the researcher's attention to the signalling behaviours that actors engage in to direct attention towards a specific routine performance and, at the same time, away from everything else (Geiger et al., 2020).

To date, there are four Routine Dynamics studies falling into this category. The first study is that of Spee et al. (2016) on a group of eleven reinsurance firms. The authors theorized how actors coordinated by customizing and standardizing the performances of interdependent routines. They analysed a focal routine (called deal appraisal routine – DAR) and investigated the interdependencies with other intersecting routines. They illuminate how highly skilled professionals accomplish coordination between routines by selectively orienting the performance of the focal routine towards one of multiple ostensives based on impulses that come from intersecting routines. The second study comes from Dönmez, Grote and Brusoni (2016). The authors analyse how an agile software development team balanced the competing pressures between stability and change. In their analysis, Dönmez et al. (2016) elaborate on the role of routine links, which 'connect routines that are on the same hierarchical level and can exert mutual influence' (2016: 75). They show how this links can be established through the use of artifacts which 'permits asynchronous information exchange between routines without requiring their simultaneous performance' (2016: 75). In the third study, of this group, Kremser et al. (2019) use the illustrative example of a passenger service routine on a transatlantic flight to elaborate on how routine boundaries are performed through signalling behaviours that establish a (new) set of behavioural expectations. They also elaborate how an understanding of routine boundaries can help scholars to identify routines as units of analysis and to better understand interdependence within and between routines. Finally, Geiger et al. (2020), analyse a variety of deployments of the Hamburg firefighters, who have to perform their routines under temporal uncertainty. In their analysis, they find the firefighters were able to deal with temporal conditions that are different for every deployment and may change any time during each deployment also by performing temporal boundaries at the transition moments between routines. Through performing temporal boundaries, actors could energize pre-existing expectancy frameworks based on environmental cues that would help them to quickly and reliably adapt their action timing to new and unexpected situations.

17.2.2 Routine Clusters

A routine cluster 'consists of multiple, complementary routines, each contributing a partial result to the accomplishment of a common task' (Kremser and Schreyögg, 2016: 698). In describing and analysing work settings as routine clusters, scholars are often focusing on the planned forms of coordinating interdependent routines that are accomplished through the programming, or designing, of interfaces. Designing interfaces creates formal relations between routines by establishing a 'normative prescription of what can legitimately be expected of a complete performance of a routine by others – [. . .] the routine's "results"'. (Kremser and Schreyögg, 2016: 716; see also Glaser, 2017). The dynamics on the cluster level unfold over months or years, rather than within a few days or weeks, and emerge as past design performances influence the present (Kremser, 2017). Conceptually, the cluster-level perspective integrates a performative conception of routines (Feldman, 2000) with literature on organization design (Puranam et al., 2012; Simon, 1996) and the dynamic consequences of complementarities (Galunic and Weeks, 2005; Sydow et al., 2009).

The analytical focus of the cluster-level perspective is on the longer-term dynamics that take place when 'changes, triggered by whatever development, eventually "arrive" at a cluster in the form of new, envisioned routines pushing for integration' (Kremser and Schreyögg, 2016: 701). The main concern is to better understand how actions on the cluster-level – the designing of formal interfaces between routines – interact with the endogenous dynamics of multiple, complementary routines over longer periods of time. This brings the connections between different levels of analysis to the fore and helps us to understand how larger organizational outcomes are accomplished over longer observation intervals.

The exemplar paper from this perspective is the study of Kremser and Schreyögg (2016) which revealed that the dynamics that arise on the cluster-level – that is, between routines – can be markedly different from those that we typically observe within routines. More specifically, the authors show how routines can form routine clusters, 'partially autonomous behavioral units' (2016: 701), through the designing of interfaces. Designing of interfaces between routines can foster a self-reinforcing logic of complementarities that drives the evolution of the cluster in the longer term. Analysing the reaction of an (analogue) routine cluster of a firm in the photo-industry, this study demonstrates how routine clusters react differently to different types of innovation. New routines that amounted to an incremental innovation could be integrated since they fit the established pattern of integration and differentiation. Radical innovations, such as the routines for digital photofinishing, however, were rejected in the longer term. The misfit costs would have been too high. Deken et al. (2016), investigated a novel development programme in an international automotive organization (AutoCo). This programme was organized across several departments. The main contribution of this study is an elaboration of how routine work – 'actors' efforts through which they direct routine performances toward their intended outcomes and respond to emerging consequences of earlier routine work' (Deken et al., 2016: 660) – enables actors to react to new and sometimes unexpected developments that flow from other, interdependent routines. The authors identify three types of routine work across interdependencies (flexing, stretching and inventing) that generate novel actions and outcomes through directing the performances of interdependent routines.

17.2.3 Routine Ecologies

As with routine clusters, the notion of a routine ecology highlights the fact that routines will be interdependent with other routines and, therefore, can be expected to 'develop into a reasonably effective ensemble' (Birnholtz et al., 2007: 318). In contrast to research on clusters, the studies in this category generally foreground informal and emergent relations between routines which can result, for example, from (more or less) generative connections performed by (human and non-human) actants (Sele and Grand, 2016) or from ongoing negotiations of social order (Birnholtz et al., 2007; Kremser and Blagoev, 2021). To get at larger outcomes, research on routine ecologies also often takes a longer observation interval into account. In contrast to the cluster-perspective, this line of research takes a more bottom-up approach in defining its main unit of analysis – the routine ecology. To be able to account for informal and emergent relations, empirical studies in this category trace connections between routines (Birnholtz et al., 2007; Sele and Grand, 2016) or other patterns (Kremser and Blagoev, 2021) from the bottom-up by following actors' situated engagement in routine performances over time. Conceptually, these studies are often embedded in grander social theories such as, e.g., Actor-Network Theory (Latour, 2005) and relational sociology (Emirbayer, 1997) or the literature on negotiated order (Strauss et al., 1963).

The analytical focus of research in this group is usually on the emergence and dynamic consequences of unplanned forms of coordinating between routines. The bottom-up approach in identifying the ecology as a unit of analysis has proven to be specifically helpful in understanding processes that lead to the emergence of larger patterns out of several smaller patterns, such as technology adoption (Pentland, 2004), innovation (Sele and Grand, 2016), organizational character (Birnholtz et al., 2007) or a negotiated temporal order (Kremser and Blagoev, 2021).

In terms of empirical results, Birnholtz et al. (2007) used ethnographic research on the yearly resurrection of a Summer Camp to uncover how regenerative processes such as demonstration and guidance cascades can help explain 'organizational character'. Organizational character is defined as 'the ability of the participants to regenerate a coherent ecology of action patterns that are recognized as "the same" as the previous instances of the organization' (Birnholtz et al., 2007: 316). In another study, Sele and Grand (2016) analysed the interrelationship between several routines of an artificial intelligence laboratory at the University of Zurich. They find that 'how actants are engaged in routine performances impacts whether they become mediators or intermediaries, rendering the routine interaction more or less generative' (2016: 723). In addition, the authors identify several generative effects of mediating relationships between routines. Finally, Kremser and Blagoev (2021) leverage the notion of ecologies to show how routines can also develop emergent couplings to a different type of action pattern, that of person-roles. In analysing the case of an agile consulting project, this study illuminates how person-roles can become a principle of temporally coordinating routines through ongoing negotiations of temporal order.

17.2.4 Routine Bundles

In contrast to the studies in our other categories which all take a practice perspective on routines, research on routine bundles often takes a capabilities-based perspective (Helfat, 2018; Nelson and Winter, 1982; Teece et al., 1997). This generally backgrounds different forms of enacted relations between routines, instead (implicitly) assuming them to be under managerial control. Empirically, these studies often take a coarse-grained view on routines and their interdependencies, covering longer observation intervals. Oftentimes these studies use quantitative research designs to compare multiple cases with each other and rely on cross-sectional datasets (e.g., Peng et al., 2008). We have included these studies in our review to illustrate the contrast but also the potential for connections between Routine Dynamics – which usually zooms in on the practical accomplishment of coordination among routines – and other traditions in research on routines – which often tries to explain organizational outcomes.

The studies in this group usually put their analytical focus on understanding the basis of sustained competitive advantage. By summarizing these studies under the label routine bundle, we want to indicate that these studies usually do not focus on how coordination among routines is accomplished in organizational practice, but rather on how an aggregation of the results of multiple routines can generate a particular type of organizational-level outcome. Put differently, studies in this perspective are less interested in the product of routine interactions, as would be the case for Routine Dynamics studies, but focus more on explaining the aggregate result, that is, the sum of routine outcomes. Just like Routine Dynamics studies, therefore, they are concerned with analysing the structures and mechanisms that connect the micro- with the macro-level and enable organizational stability and change (Abell et al., 2008; Salvato, 2009). Dynamic capabilities play a specifically important role in this regard. 'Dynamic capabilities [. . .] are the organizational and strategic routines by which firms achieve new resource configurations as markets emerge, collide, split, evolve, and die' (Eisenhardt and Martin, 2000: 1107; see also Peteraf and Tsoukas, 2017).

Since the empirical results of research from this category has been extensively reviewed already (e.g., Barreto, 2010; Parmigiani and Howard-Grenville, 2011; Schilke et al., 2018), we only want to mention three examples that are explicitly concerned with the connection between routine bundles and capabilities. Salvato (2009) used historical data on the product development capability of Alessi, a famous Italian design company. This study zooms into a number of different product development processes in order to highlight the important role of 'the myriad intentional microactivities performed daily by organizational actors' (Salvato, 2009: 384–385). Prange et al. (2017) revealed from a qualitative and longitudinal case study of DHL the origin and development of dynamic capabilities through a bundle of routines. They showed how two types of dynamic capabilities – acquisition-based and innovation-based – were developed through changes of underlying bundles of routines. Another example is the paper of Davies et al. (2018). These authors made an effort to combine the practice and capabilities perspectives. This approach allowed them to show how different organizational levels (strategic and operational) shape the development of new routines and the different steps that involve the replication of a new routine across multiple sites.

17.2.5 Summary: The Multi-Facetted Morphology of Routine Networks

Looking across the four lenses, we can start to appreciate the multi-facetted nature of routine interdependence. It becomes clear that interdependence relations between routines are accomplished in different ways. Importantly, we would assume that all of these forms, while analytically different, will co-exist and maybe even co-evolve in most work settings. It seems difficult to imagine an organization in which only ad-hoc, or planned, or emergent interdependence relations exist between routines. Rather, we would expect all of them to be present, maybe in different times and at different places. And all these relations will usually contribute to some aggregate outcome. While it is important to recognize the analytical differences between the different lenses, it would be a mistake to believe that concepts such as cluster or ecology necessarily refer to different empirical phenomena. Instead, they should be understood as lenses that help us to foreground different facets of a more general empirical phenomenon which we want to label as routine networks – analytically useful groupings of interdependent routines. In what comes next, we highlight some directions for future research on the multi-facetted and dynamic nature of routine networks.

17.3 Future Directions

The study of the dynamics that arise in routine networks is an important but underexplored theme in Routine Dynamics research. Previous research has already highlighted different facets of how coordination between routines can be accomplished in organizational practice. Many of these studies also highlight in one way or another how routine interdependence leads to the emergence of larger patterns which can exhibit dynamics of their own and are important to understand organizational outcomes. Against this backdrop, a number of future research opportunities seem especially relevant.

Advancing and integrating existing perspectives. Research on interdependence among routines is just beginning. Therefore, there are opportunities for advances in all four perspectives just like there are opportunities to elaborate on connections and differences between these perspectives. For example, Hoekzema (2020) advances the debate on routine interdependence by discussing differences and linkages between research on clusters and ecologies. Building on these efforts, it would be especially worthwhile to think about plausible linkages between results from research on clusters and ecologies, which typically theorizes about dynamics that need months or years to unfold, and research on boundaries and intersections, which typically theorizes dynamics that unfold much quicker. Such differences in time scales are important to consider since they have tremendous impact on our theorizing (Zaheer et al., 1999).

Understanding the differences between dynamics within vs. among routines. It would also be worthwhile to investigate in more depth the differences and linkages between results from research on interdependence within versus among routines. First, empirical results indicate that dynamics of multiple, interdependent routines might differ in important respects from the dynamics that we can observe within individual routines (Kremser and Schreyögg, 2016). A more systematic investigation into the commonalities and differences between the dynamics of smaller and larger patterns promises important new insights on patterning, coordinating and the accomplishment of organizational outcomes.

Research on connections between the micro and macro levels. We believe that interdependence is central for understanding the relationships between the micro- and macro-level of analysis (Salvato and Rerup, 2011; Seidl and Whittington, 2014). Research that zooms in on the different forms of coordination between routines can be of tremendous help in understanding how smaller patterns, such as individual routines, become related into larger patterns, such as organizational innovation or structural inertia (see also Pentland et al., 2021). This kind of research would also open up opportunities for integrating the practice and the capabilities perspective on routines and routine interdependence (Davies et al., 2018; Parmigiani and Howard-Grenville, 2011).

Understanding the embeddedness of routine interdependence. Understanding how interdependence between routines is enacted differently under different conditions promises important insights as well. For example, first results indicate that the level of experienced uncertainty might be an important contingency factor in the accomplishment of routine interdependence (Geiger et al., 2020). Also, the embeddedness in different structures might help us understand how routine and boundary performances contribute to the stability and change of larger patterns (see also Howard-Grenville and Lodge [Chapter 16], this volume). For example, the introduction of new digital technologies can be expected to radically transform the dynamics we observe within and among routines (Pentland et al., 2021).

Leveraging new methods in research on routine interdependence. Most existing studies on routine interdependence have implemented single case-study designs based on ethnographic methods. Notwithstanding the important insights that come from such an approach, we believe that complexities involved in doing empirical research on multiple, interdependent routines makes it worthwhile to experiment with new methods of data collection and analysis. In this regard, the use of various forms of digital trace data to analyse 'routine as network of actions' seems to be a particularly promising avenue for analysing the dynamics of interdependent routines. Various software tools, such as ThreadNet (Pentland et al., 2015), for example, make it possible to analyse large amounts of fine-grained data on routines (e.g., Goh and Pentland, 2019). The large amounts of data one has to process in a study on multiple, interdependent routines makes the combination of human and machine pattern recognition an exciting new opportunity with enormous potential (Lindberg, 2020). Digital trace data might also make comparative research more feasible, which would be especially helpful to understand the embeddedness of routine interdependence. In this regards, experimental designs also open up exciting new possibilities to analyse interdependencies within and between routines (see e.g., Bapuji, Hora and Li [Chapter 10], this volume; Cohen and Bacdayan, 1994; Hansson et al., 2018.

17.4 Conclusion

In this chapter, we have identified four lenses or perspectives that routines scholars have taken in order to better understand the dynamics that emerge among interdependent routines. The perspectives presented are major avenues of research that reveal a rich variety of different insights on the dynamics of interdependent routines. Importantly, research on interdependent routines has just begun. Future research can leverage new methods and results in doing research on advancing and integrating existing perspectives, connections between the micro and macro levels, understanding the embeddedness of routine interdependence and by leveraging new methods in research on routine interdependence.

References

Abbott, A. (1995). Boundaries of social work or social work of boundaries? The social service review lecture. *Social Service Review*, 69(4), 545–562.

Abell, P., Felin, T. and Foss, N. (2008). Building micro-foundations for the routines, capabilities, and performance links. *Managerial and Decision Economics*, 29(6), 489–502.

Barreto, I. (2010). Dynamic capabilities: A review of past research and an agenda for the future. *Journal of Management*, 36(1), 256–280.

Birnholtz, J. P., Cohen, M. D. and Hoch, S. V. (2007). Organizational character: On the Regeneration of Camp Poplar Grove. *Organization Science*, 18(2), 315–332.

Carlile, P. R. (2002). A pragmatic view of knowledge and boundaries: Boundary objects in new product development. *Organization Science*, 13(4), 442–455.

Cohen, M. D. and Bacdayan, P. (1994). Organizational routines are stored as procedural memory: Evidence from a laboratory study. *Organization Science*, 5(4), 554–568.

Davies, A., Frederiksen, L., Cacciatori, E. and Hartmann, A. (2018). The long and winding road: Routine creation and replication in multi-site organizations. *Research Policy*, 47(8), 1403–1417.

Deken, F., Carlile, P. R., Berends, H. and Lauche, K. (2016). Generating novelty through interdependent routines: A process model of routine work. *Organization Science*, 27(3), 659–677.

Dönmez, D., Grote, G. and Brusoni, S. (2016). Routine interdependencies as a source of stability and flexibility: A study of agile software development teams. *Information and Organization*, 26(3), 63–83.

Eisenhardt, K. M. and Martin, J. A. (2000). Dynamic capabilities: What are they? *Strategic Management Journal*, 21, 1105–1121.

Emirbayer, M. (1997). Manifesto for a relational sociology. *American Journal of Sociology*, 103(2), 281–317.

Feldman, M. S. (2000). Organizational routines as a source of continuous change. *Organization Science*, 11(6), 611–629.

Feldman, M. S. and Orlikowski, W. J. (2011). Theorizing practice and practicing theory. *Organization Science*, 22(5), 1240–1253.

Feldman, M. S. and Pentland, B. T. (2003). Reconceptualizing organizational routines as a source of flexibility and change. *Administrative Science Quarterly*, 48(1), 94–118.

Feldman, M. S., Pentland, B. T., D'Adderio, L. and Lazaric, N. (2016). Beyond routines as things: Introduction to the special issue on routine dynamics. *Organization Studies*, 27(3), 505–513. Special Issue.

Feldman, M. S. and Rafaeli, A. (2002). Organizational routines as sources of connections and understandings. *Journal of Management Studies*, 39(3), 309–331.

Galunic, C. and Weeks, J. (2005). Intraorganizational ecology. In J. A. C. Baum, ed., *Blackwell Companion to Organizations*, 2nd ed. Malden, MA: Blackwell Publishers, pp. 75–98.

Geiger, D., Danner-Schröder, A. and Kremser, W. (2021). Getting ahead of time: Performing temporal boundaries to coordinate routines under temporal uncertainty. *Administrative Science Quarterly*, 66(1), 220–264. doi:10.1177/0001839220941010.

Glaser, V. L. (2017). Design performances: How organizations inscribe artifacts to change routines. *Academy of Management Journal*, 60(6), 2126–2154.

Goh, K. T. and Pentland, B. T. (2019). From actions to paths to patterning: Toward a dynamic theory of patterning in routines. *Academy of Management Journal*, 62(6), 1901–1929.

Hansson, M., Hærem, T. and Pentland, B. T. (2018). Repertoire, routinization, and enacted complexity in patterns of action. *Academy of Management Proceedings*, 2018(1), 10734.

Helfat, C. (2018). The behavior and capabilities of firms. In R. Nelson, G. Dosi, C. Helfat, A. Pyka, P. Saviotti and K. Lee, et al., eds., *Modern Evolutionary Economics: An Overview*. Cambridge: Cambridge University Press, pp. 85–103.

Hoekzema, J. (2020). Bridging the gap between ecologies and clusters: Towards an integrative framework of routine interdependence. *European Management Review*, 17(2), 559–571.

Howard-Grenville, J., Langley, A. and Tsoukas, H., eds. (2016). *Organizational Routines: How They Are Created, Maintained, and Changed* (vol. 5). Oxford: Oxford University Press.

Kremser, W. (2017). *Interdependente Routinen*. Wiesbaden: Springer.

Kremser, W. and Blagoev, B. (2021). The Dynamics of Prioritizing: How actors temporally pattern complex role-routine ecologies. *Administrative Science Quarterly*, 66(2), 339–379. doi:10.1177/0001839220948483.

Kremser, W., Pentland, B. and Brunswicker, S. (2019) Interdependence within and between routines: A performative perspective. In M. S. Feldman, L. D'Adderio, K. Dittrich and P. Jarzabkowski, eds., *Routine Dynamics in Action: Replication and Transformation*. Bingley: Emerald Publishing Limited.

Kremser, W. and Schreyögg, G. (2016). The dynamics of interrelated routines: Introducing the cluster level. *Organization Science*, 27(3), 698–721.

Langley, A., Lindberg, K., Mørk, B. E., Nicolini, D., Raviola, E. and Walter, L. (2019). Boundary work between groups, occupations, and organizations: From cartography to process. *Academy of Management Annals*, 13(2), 704–736.

Latour, B. (2005). *Reassembling the Social: An Introduction to Actor-Network-Theory*. Oxford: Oxford University Press.

Lindberg, A. (2020). Developing theory through integrating human and machine pattern recognition. *Journal of the Association for Information Systems*, 21(1), 90–116.

Nelson, R. and Winter, S. (1982). *An Evolutionary Theory of the Firm*. Cambridge, MA: Harvard, Belknap.

Parmigiani, A. and Howard-Grenville, J. (2011). Routines revisited: Exploring the capabilities and practice perspectives. *Academy of Management Annals*, 5(1), 413–453.

Peng, D. X., Schroeder, R. G. and Shah, R. (2008). Linking routines to operations capabilities: A new perspective. *Journal of Operations Management*, 26(6), 730–748.

Pentland, B. T. (2004). Towards an ecology of inter-organizational routines: A conceptual framework for the analysis of net-enabled organizations. In *System Sciences, 2004. Proceedings of the 37th Annual Hawaii International Conference* (pp. 264–271). IEEE.

Pentland, B. T. (2011). The foundation is solid, if you know where to look: Comment on Felin and Foss. *Journal of Institutional Economics*, 7(2), 279–293.

Pentland, B. T., Liu, P., Kremser, W. and Haerem, T. 2020. The dynamics of drift in digitized processes. *MIS Quarterly*, 44(1), 19–47.

Pentland, B.T., Liu, P., Kremser, W. and Hærem, T. (2021). Can small variations accumulate into big changes? In M. Lounsbury, D. Anderson and P. Spee, eds., *Research in the Sociology of Organizations Vol. 71. On Practice and Institution: New Empirical Directions*. Bingley: Emerald Publishing Limited, pp. 29–44.

Pentland, B. T., Recker, J. and Wyner, G. (2015). Conceptualizing and measuring interdependence between organizational routines. In *International Conference on Information Systems (ICIS 2016)*, December, Dublin, Ireland.

Peteraf, M. and Tsoukas, H. (2017). How differences in understanding the dynamic capabilities construct may be reconciled through process research. In Sandberg et al., eds., *Skillful Performance: Enacting Capabilities, Knowledge, Competence, and Expertise in Organizations*. Oxford: Oxford University.

Prange, C., Bruyaka, O. and Marmenout, K. (2017). Investigating the transformation and transition processes between dynamic capabilities: Evidence from DHL. *Organization Studies*, 1–27.

Puranam, P., Raveendran, M. and Knudsen, T. (2012). Organization design: The epistemic interdependence perspective. *Academy of Management Review*, 37(3), 419–440.

Quick, K. S. and Feldman, M. S. (2014). Boundaries as junctures: Collaborative boundary work for building efficient resilience. *Journal of Public Administration Research and Theory*, 24(3), 673–695.

Salvato, C. (2009). The contribution of event-sequence analysis to the study of organizational routines. In M. C. Becker and N. Lazaric, eds., *Organizational Routines*. Northampton, MA: Edward Elgar Publishing, pp. 68–102.

Salvato, C. and Rerup, C. (2011). Beyond collective entities: Multilevel research on organizational routines and capabilities. *Journal of Management*, 37(2), 468–490.

Schilke, O., Hu, S. and Helfat, C. E. (2018). Quo vadis, dynamic capabilities? A content-analytic review of the current state of knowledge and recommendations for future research. *Academy of Management Annals*, 12(1), 390–439.

Seidl, D. and Whittington, R. (2014). Enlarging the strategy-as-practice research agenda: Towards taller and flatter ontologies. *Organization Studies*, 35(10), 1407–1421.

Sele, K. and Grand, S. (2016). Unpacking the dynamics of ecologies of routines: Mediators and their generative effects in routine interactions. *Organization Science*, 27(3), 722–738.

Simon, H. A. (1996). *The Sciences of the Artificial*, 3rd ed. Cambridge, MA: MIT Press.

Spee, P., Jarzabkowski, P. and Smets, M. (2016). The influence of routine interdependence and skillful accomplishment on the coordination of standardizing and customizing. *Organization Science*, 27(3), 759–781.

Strauss, A. L., Schatzman, L., Ehrlich, D., Bucher, R. and Sabshin, M. (1963). *The Hospital and Its Negotiated Order*. New York: Free Press.

Sydow, J., Schreyögg, G. and Koch, J. (2009). Organizational path dependence: Opening the black box. *Academy of Management Review*, 34(4), 689–709.

Teece, D. J., Pisano, G. and Shuen, A. (1997). Dynamic capabilities and strategic management. *Strategic Management Journal*, 18(7), 509–533.

Zaheer, S., Albert, S. and Zaheer, A. (1999). Time scales and organizational theory. *Academy of Management Review*, 24(4), 725–741.

CHAPTER 18

Cognition and Routine Dynamics

NATHALIE LAZARIC

18.1 Introduction

The debate about cognition started with the Carnegie School, which put this notion at the centre of the routines' discussion (Cohen, 1991; Cyert and March, 1963; Nelson and Winter, 1982; Rerup and Spencer [Chapter 33], this handbook; Simon, 1991; Winter and Szulanski, 2001). More recently, the role of cognition in routines has been observed and researchers have started to scrutinize elements and parts of routines instead of regarding them as 'entities' (Howard-Grenville and Rerup, 2017). Within the context of Routine Dynamics, the original focus on cognition has moved to the background, but has not been ignored completely (Lazaric and Denis, 2005; Rerup and Feldman, 2011). Within the Routine Dynamics perspective, the notion of reflective action, thinking and debriefing about the content of the performance have been identified as critical for envisaging new and reconsidering current patterns of interdependent actions (Bucher and Langley, 2016; Dittrich et al., 2016; Kiwan and Lazaric, 2019). With a distinct but complementary frame, Archer (1995) defines the notion of self-talk as diverse 'modes of internal conversation' which can be helpful for understanding how the voice within routines might potentially (or might not) reframe existing patterns of routines and introduce new actions. Indeed, reflexivity and mindfulness, as has been demonstrated in prior works (Levinthal and Rerup, 2006; Salvato, 2009; Turner and Rindova, 2012), have the potential to shape both cognition and the representation of routines and provide different insights.

The aim of this chapter is to provide an overview of the role of cognition and to suggest an agenda for research into the role for cognition within the Routine Dynamics perspective. To this end, I will start with the treatment of cognition in classical studies on routines from the Carnegie School, I will show how and where cognition has been addressed in Routine Dynamics studies and I will propose and develop the notion of reflection as a way of returning cognition to the forefront of Routine Dynamics studies in a way that is compatible with the basic assumptions of the Routine Dynamics approach. The outline of this chapter is as follows.

In Section 18.2, I present the point of departure for the cognition in classical routines studies. In Section 18.3, I review the evidence and reveal what we know about cognition in Routine Dynamics and what remains to be investigated. In the following section, I argue that Archer's work should be reconsidered to understand how reflexivity and cognition are built through new patterns of actions. I show that Archer might be the starting point for a reinvestigation of the link between agency and structures, and that cognition should be reconsidered in the context of the enactment of actions and the different solutions to concrete and situated problems.

18.2 The Role of Cognition in Classical Routine Studies

Simon's (1955) vision of cognition is the classic frame for understanding the underlying assumptions related to cognition and problem solving. The notion of organizational docility is one of the main assumptions related to understanding this vision of routines and their foundation. Initially, the study of cognition was limited to the Carnegie School and Nelson and Winter's (1982) organizational knowledge, knowledge articulation and knowledge replication framework for building and diffusing routines (Becker et al., 2006; Gupta et al., 2015; Winter, 2013; Winter and Szulanski, 2001). More recently, this debate has been re-explored by the Routine Dynamics community.

18.2.1 Cognition, Problem-Solving and Routines

Simon's frame is focused on the process of decision-making and how people make decisions under conditions of limited computational and informational resources (Brette et al., 2017; Simon, 1955, 1959). In an attempt to get a better understanding of the human mind, Simon collaborated with Allen Newell and produced some decisive and pioneering work in cognitive psychology and artificial intelligence. The use of simulation tools produced some interesting results which can be considered a turning point in Simon's career and a departure from his early research (Brette et al., 2017). In 1958, Simon and James G. March published their famous book entitled *Organizations* and held the first RAND summer seminar on simulation techniques. These developments in the behavioural foundations of organizations and the exploration of the human mind resulted in important work on bounded rationality and a specific vision of problem solving.

In his view of the decision-making process, Simon underlines the implementation of cognitive mechanisms which to some extent are activated automatically. Simon further developed an opposition between habit and decision, and coined the terms 'routinized responses' *versus* 'problem-solving responses' (March and Simon, 1958). He argued that 'habit permits the conservation of mental effort by withdrawing from the area of conscious thought those aspects of the situation that are repetitive [...] and permits attention to be devoted to the novel aspects of a situation requiring decision' (Simon, 1947 [1976]: 88). In this classical frame, rationality required a conscious choice between diverse options, and a choice process in which habits support rationality in the sense that they enable cognitive resources to be devoted to novel and complex situations. However, habits are ambiguous in that they both support rationality and are an obstacle to its development. For Simon,

> In most cases, there seems to be a close relation [...] between the spheres of attention and of rationality. That is, docility is largely limited by (1) the span of attention, and (2) the area within which skills and other appropriate behaviors have become habitual. Hence to a considerable extent, the limits upon rationality [...] are resultants of the limits of the area of attention (Simon (1947 [1976]: 90).

18.2.2 Docility – An Important Prerequisite for Problem-Solving and Organizational Memory

The notion of docility was important for Simon in this process and refers to a situation in which '[the individual] observes the consequences of his movements and adjusts them to achieve the desired purpose'. Docility, then, is characterized by a stage of exploration and inquiry, followed by a stage of adaptation (Simon, 1947 [1976]: 85). In addition, Simon underlined the social nature of man: human beings are members of social groups, whether organizations or society, and this belongingness to a social order is not neutral for individuals (Simon, 1947 [1976]: 102).

This vision of 'framed' social interactions and docility towards organizational goals appears to be the solution to the limited cognitive resources of human beings. This epistemological foundation allowed Simon to focus on the decision-making process, and more specifically on the issue of problem solving (Newell and Simon, 1972; Sent, 2000). In this context,

> Habits and routines may not only serve their purposes effectively, but also conserve scarce and costly decision-making time and attention. For that reason, a very large part of an organization's activities (or a person's) is likely to proceed according to established rules and routines, which may be reviewed at shorter or longer intervals for possible revision (Simon, 1947 [1997]: 89).

Some dimensions of Simon's legacy related to organizational and administrative processes are reflected in Nelson and Winter's (1982) work where routines are the organizational memory allowing firms to accumulate knowledge and know-how to achieve coordination and cognitive efficiency. This legacy was revived by the introduction of the Schumpeterian vision of innovation and entrepreneurship, and an evolutionary perspective on the original Carnegie School framing. The notion of routines was closely linked to the expansion and replication of knowledge from an entrepreneurial perspective. Cognition was both a survival mechanism and a behavioural regularity in a competitive environment but not really a process of knowledge creation by individuals (Winter, 1964). The point of departure was important but not sufficient for explaining how individuals are acting to renew and to reconsider knowledge in their daily actions. According to this approach, notions of reflection and mindfulness were critical to reconsidering knowledge and cognition as something which is not inert but enacted and performed by actors (Lazaric and Denis, 2001, 2005; Levinthal and Rerup, 2006), and to go beyond the classic vision of routines as procedures that memorize knowledge and give some behavioural efficiency (Cohen, 1991; Cyert and March, 1963). In this classical vision of the firm, routines and cognition were designed as a fixed point that requires little change to gain cognitive efficiency. This vision has been reconsidered to some extent by Nelson and Winter (1982) but the main assumption remains that cognitive efficiency is essential for organizations to work smoothly. New empirical evidence has shown that a new frame for opening the black box of cognition should be built and this reconsideration of routines starts with mindfulness, individuals' voice and endogenous change (Feldman 2000; Pentland and Rueter, 1994).

18.3 What We Know about Cognition in RD

Feldman and Pentland (2003: 96) define routines as 'recognizable patterns of interdependent actions carried out by multiple actors' and highlight that the main outcome of this is a 'new understanding' about the relation between action and patterns as constituted by and through actions. For many years, the Routine Dynamics community gave cognition little attention, focusing rather on understanding the concept of routines and the potential for individual agency (Feldman, 2000; Feldman and Pentland, 2003; Feldman et al., 2016; Pentland and Rueter, 1994).

Making 'action' the essential building block of the micro-level dimension of routines allows us to study the creation of new routines from an agency perspective, as emerging from the 'relationship between specific actions and patterns of action' (Pentland et al., 2012: 1485), and opens a window to reconsider patterns of action and their cognitive roots. Along these lines, the following section reveals that the Routine Dynamics community has provided robust and significant empirical evidence on the role of artifacts, notably for guiding actions and patterns of actions, intentionality and reflection, and has provided new empirical evidence on cognition.

18.3.1 The Role of Artifacts in Cognition

Artifacts should not be ignored since they articulate knowledge and transform potential skills into future capabilities (Cacciatori, 2012; D'Adderio, 2008; Lazaric et al., 2003). It has been shown that artifacts are a source of memorization at the interface between the performative and ostensive aspects of routines (Cacciatori 2008, 2012; D'Adderio 2008, 2011). Much empirical evidence has accumulated about the critical role of artifacts as mediators and manifestations of cognition (see chapters by D'Adderio [Chapter 7], Sele [Chapter 6] and Glaser [Chapter 23] in this handbook). For instance, Orlikowski (1992) explains how human agency is mediated by manmade objects, while D'Adderio (2008) and Salvato (2009) discuss the criticality of how agents create and make use of artifacts in their practice to maintain or change routines and how artifacts serve to create external memories which are distributed among the actors. D'Adderio (2011: 197) highlights artifacts and acknowledges their importance as providers of ' ... the glue that can hold action patterns together'. Cacciatori (2012) suggests that rather than being considered individually, artifacts should be seen as systems of artifacts involved in the creation of routines. She demonstrates that the emergence of new routines is mediated by the development of systems of artifacts able to reproduce problem-solving structures at the heart of the routinization process. Furthermore, artifacts play a critical role in the building of 'standard operating procedures' (D'Adderio, 2008; Lazaric and Denis, 2005). They mediate routines and skills and transform experience into potential new patterns (Cacciatori, 2012), paying attention to the micro-processes 'through which patterns of actions are created and recreated from within' (Dionysios and Tsoukas, 2013: 184).

The role of actors in designing artifacts and routines by inscribing their vision of ways of doing things is also an important factor (Glaser, 2017). Artifacts encode knowledge and act as mediators between skills and routines (Cacciatori, 2012). They are rarely used in isolation; rather, they are used in systems which are important for stabilizing the firm structure. For instance, Lazaric and Denis (2005) show that handbooks describe ways of doing things, relying on subgroups of artifacts or subtasks such as the writing of procedures which convey and articulate knowledge at each step in the process. In short, systems of artifacts are arranged and are mutually reinforcing to stabilize existing performance and identify patterns that co-shape routines (Cacciatori, 2012). Some artifacts 'contain a visual representation of knowledge. They include procedure, manual, reports, technical drawings and virtual prototypes' (Cacciatori, 2012: 1362) and include the product and also the process representation, that is, the way things are done and how and why things are done in a certain way, and why they make sense to the actors. These cognitive tools are entangled at the heart of the performative and ostensive dimension of routines (D'Adderio, 2011). Relatedly, Parmentier Cajaiba et al. (2021) show for the biocontrol case (pesticides without chemical inputs) that the process of permanent adaptation is critical for artifacts involved in stabilizing the process. Further, the use of artifact-as-coordination tool enables progress towards an ideal future situation (developing a new activity in line with the firm's needs) and borrows from past situations (existing norms from the regulatory domain). Depending on the situation, the artifacts are viewed either as goals (ends-in-view) or as means (a spreadsheet, a database), showing that means and ends-in-view are not fixed but are rather 'fluid and flexible' (Dittrich and Seidl, 2018) because these elements are in the process of becoming (Tsoukas and Chia, 2002).

18.3.2 Replication and Emergence of New Routines

When organizations are faced with ill-structured problems and unstructured decision processes, building new routines may be more complicated (Obstfeld, 2012). In this case, the issue is not replicating the initial knowledge or resources but finding new patterns. Replication is complex and implies some degree of novelty for redesigning and adapting to the new context since knowledge cannot be replicated but must be discovered during this process (Becker et al., 2006; see chapter by Blanche and Cohendet [Chapter 20] in this handbook). Knowledge replication and codification are built through a process of knowledge transfer and transformation which generates negotiation of its core and adaptation of its scope (D'Adderio, 2014; Lazaric et al, 2003). D'Adderio (2014) shows precisely why agency is critical and that goals may differ in the process, leading to potential transformation of the template and a process of adjustment during knowledge replication.

Creating new routines is an effortful task since it involves the co-shaping of the ostensive and performative aspects of the routine. This duality represents a critical period of learning where the routines to be performed require the strong involvement of the actants through trial and error learning, experimentation and improvisation to reduce uncertainty while articulating and trying to codify some of the knowledge. More precisely, Rerup and Feldman (2011) highlight the combination of cognition and action for the emergence of new routines and the process of permanent adjustment that actors implement as they engage in trial and error learning. In short '[e]ach trial either replaced a specific performance in the (recruitment) routines with another specific performance or added a new performance to the existing set of performances' (Rerup and Feldman, 2011: 603), showing it is not a fixed but rather a heterogeneous process which leaves space for creativity when complex problems arise. These empirical findings show that in the context of difficult problems 'people are more like fire-fighters than they are like strategic decision makers' (Rerup and Feldman, 2011: 604).

18.3.3 Intentionality of Actors in the Building of New Patterns

Intentionality is important for solving problems and for cognition, but the vision of the intentionality is far from neutral. In that context, Dittrich and Seidl (2018), drawing on Dewey (1957), suggest that intentionality is not the product of the mind but is dynamically enacted in the performance of routines with ends in view. Ends in view are constitutive of action and help actors to experiment and to adjust their ends to the existing means. Thus 'ends-in-view' and means are mutually constitutive and 'this view allows us to appreciate intentionality not as something "of the mind"' (Chia and Holt, 2006: 648) but as something that is dynamically enacted in routine performances. Consequently, routine participants 'can develop a sense of purpose from action without consciously reflecting on action' (Dittrich and Seidl, 2018: 115). Thus, the construction of new patterns of actions is rooted in the practice itself rather than being the result of a pure process of reflection. This creates a sense of purpose from action without deliberating over the action. This new vision has some resonance with Cohen's (2007) vision of the interdependence between ends and means and the mutually constitutive vision of agency and structure (Emirbayer and Mische, 1998).

Along similar lines, Turner and Rindova (2012) show the need to maintain dual ostensive patterns to target diverse goals (targeted consistency or flexibility) which facilitate flexible and mindful responses within task coordination. They show a subtle combination of mindless and mindful behaviours according to goals and means during the performance of routines (Turner and Rindova, 2012). Here, cognition is linked directly to coordination, and modulated according to ends and means-in-view to provide flexible ostensive patterns which allow actors to handle task (in)consistency and challenges. This work echoes the vision of a continuum between mindful and less mindful behaviours rather than the separation between these two categories (Levinthal and Rerup, 2006).

18.3.4 Reflection as a Critical Step for Cognition

Talking about routines is a way of 'reflecting on what they are doing, and doing different things (or doing the same things differently) as a result of the reflection' (Feldman, 2000: 625). Feldman (2016: 14) shows there is no one single intentionality in routine creation but that actors perform and solve problems in relation to what others do. This relational view explains the interdependence between actors experimenting with actions. To resolve organizational problems, actors use 'collective discussions' to negotiate the content of the knowledge and their role in the implementation of new quality systems (Lazaric and Denis, 2005). Dittrich et al. (2016), in the case of a pharmaceutical start-up, highlight the role of 'reflective talk' in routine change and show how talking reveals diverse opportunities for routine changes.

Bucher and Langley (2016) discuss 'the role of collective reflection in routine change', where spaces and 'bounded social settings' influence the ostensive and performative aspects of routines (Bucher and Langley, 2016: 597). They consider two types of spaces in which actors 'engage in deliberate efforts to alter both performances and abstract aspects' (Bucher and Langley, 2016: 594). Experimental spaces enable the integration of new actions into a new routine formation while reflective spaces aim to conceptualize the routine. While reflective spaces can involve a set of distant actors involved in the original routine, experimental spaces are 'nested within the surrounding structure [. . .] cover subroutines, including actors who perform these subroutines but not others' (Bucher and Langley, 2016: 600). Experimental spaces involve testing concepts and challenging the coordinating mechanisms already in place. During experimentation by a surgical team using a robot, Kiwan and Lazaric (2019) show that actors try to build new ostensive and performative aspects of the surgical routine and talk about each of the sub-elements to find new ways of doings things. The experimental space helps the actors to solve the problem step by step while having the opportunity to stop the robotic surgery if the process becomes dangerous and discuss a safer option.

18.4 A Roadmap for the Coming Years

The notion of agency, which contrasts starkly with Carnegie School thinking, enables a new way of defining and naming routines with actors who are knowledgeable and often reflexive (Feldman et al., 2016). This provides a new vision of cognition for understanding the process and conditions allowing such reflexivity (Dittrich et al., 2016; Feldman, 2016). In order to study the role of cognition a step further, we might draw on the work of Archer (2003), who highlights diverse sources of human mental operation in a realist framework combining the notion of internal conversation with the concept of action. As such, she offers a nice entry to understanding the human mind in action and the limits to individual decision-making, allowing a potential renewed source of inspiration for Routine Dynamics.

18.4.1 Reflection without Neglecting the Role of Structures in Routine Dynamics

Archer (2003) illustrates how personal projects are formed and how they mediate the exercise of systemic constraints and enablements. Inspired by Roy Bhaskar's critical realism, she develops a theory of the emergence, reproduction and transformation of cultural systems and social structures and analyses how human beings develop their personal and social identities as they pursue their ultimate concerns in more or less coherent ways. By developing this argument she enters into the cognitive black box to understand human cognition and personal decision. She advances an alternative theory to give life to agency and structures that are interlinked and vibrant entities which can be observed when individuals struggle and face a problem. These diverse 'self- talk' and tensions during problem-solving show the difficulty of building patterns. Indeed 'patterns are constituted in and through action and emphasizing the constitutive nature of action in the process of patterning draws our attention to the work of recognizing and articulating or narrating these patterns' (Feldman, 2016: 40).

It has been argued that 'practice-based studies of routines have tended to give primacy to agency and have provided a less developed account of the role of structure in the dynamics of routines – partly as a reaction to a view of routines as rigid and automatic' (Turner and Cacciatori, 2016: 89). This opens the door to understand the place of structures when routines are observed as a process of performing and patterning and to scrutinize tensions within and through actions. There are many types of structures, of course, from institutions, to social norms, to technological paradigms (see chapter by Howard-Grenville and Lodge [Chapter 16] in this handbook). According to Dosi (1988), structures and scientific institutions contextually define the needs that are meant to be fulfilled, and the scientific principles and technology to be used in a given industry. Dosi (1988: 1127) defines a technological paradigm 'as an exemplar – an artifact that is to be developed and improved ... and a set of heuristics'. Heuristics support problem-solving and create shortcuts which allow individuals and organizations to operate in situations of uncertainty (Kahneman et al., 1982). Parmentier-Cajaiba et al. (2021), researching a start-up in the biocontrol industry, show how much effort was involved in creating new routines, as the company had to translate all the biological practices in reference to the old paradigm (based on chemical principles) and negotiate their validity and existence. I argue here that we need to investigate this evolutionary process in more depth, including the creation of new path-dependent patterns of actions to understand how new ostensive patterns are accepted, validated, built and re-built in a dynamic process. In this direction, Pentland and Ju Jung (2016) provide significant insights which need to be consolidated to get a better understanding of the weight of new heuristics in patterning and of the current heuristics performed by actors.

18.4.2 Diverse Levels of Reflexivity for Actors

Archer (2003) acknowledges diverse forms of 'self-talk' and provides a summary of diverse modes of mental operation across individual personality types. First, 'communicative reflexive' individuals distrust their own internal dialogues. Their decisions and cognition are co-shaped by 'similars and familiars' who maintain a 'micro-world' around them preventing them from exploiting opportunities, and thus maintaining some degree of social immobility (Archer, 2003: 166–167). Second, individuals may be 'autonomous reflexives' and show decisiveness in their actions. These groups of individuals weigh up the opportunities and constraints in the objective situations they face. They have past experience of contextual discontinuity in action and rely on their own judgement (Archer, 2003: 212). Third, 'meta reflexives', such as autonomous reflexives, also have experience of continual discontinuity and rely on their own judgements. However, 'meta reflexives' tend to have a strong idealized view of how they should be: their main concern is how to live in a context in which they can express certain ideals they hold (Archer, 2003: 258). Meta reflexives have a very critical orientation toward objective structures and situational constraints and try to maintain their ideal (their ostensive vision) and reject situations where the benefits are inconsistent with their ideals. This high vision of ideals implies difficulty related to their ambitions in practice. In this context, Archer refers to the 'fractured' reflexive', who engage in self-talk but are unable to form a plan or action or project and deal with it (Archer, 2003: 303–304).

These diverse categories of reflexivities are important for observing how an actor lacking mindfulness (or discursive awareness) performs habitual actions and acts on habitual beliefs, and how individuals can struggle to instantiate and enact their ostensive vision. Archer suggests that actors who are 'communicatively reflexive' rather than 'meta reflexive' have less faith in their ability to reach a decision based on their own self-talk. Exposure to a greater variety of objective contexts can produce situations where habitual actions are called into question, and habitual beliefs may be exposed to internal conversation (or not). 'Meta reflexive' actors are more oriented to 'treating its habitual beliefs as objects to be transformed into explicit "concerns" in a process of self-examination, and less oriented to using habitual beliefs and automatic judgment' (Fuller, 2013: 125). Huge uncertainties, such as those described in the literature of Grand Challenges (Ferraro et al., 2015), require that individuals and organizations must be 'active experimenters' and identify some actions while solving new problems (for instance, in agricultural practice, how to reduce mildew on vines using non-chemical treatments). The need to find new patterns and to handle Grand Challenges among other issues may create significant internal and external tensions during experimentation.

18.4.3 *Solving Problems Differently through and within Actions and Agency*

Archer's discussion of the diversity of levels of internal talk is important in the context of how actors question the ostensive level of routines, what their ideal vision of a routine should be and the degree of novelty in performative routines designed to change elements of their actions and practices. Some actors, identified by Archer as more inclined to engage in 'meta reflexive' talk, will be better able to reframe the ostensive and performative levels of routines because they are more prone to coping with discontinuity. Along similar lines, Pentland (1995) proposed 'grammars of action' to describe routines where grammars define the set of possibilities and variations related to a specific language, and the action is the routines required to achieve the task (Pentland, 1995; Pentland and Rueter, 1994). Indeed, 'an organizational routine is not a single pattern but rather a set of possible patterns' (Pentland and Rueter, 1994: 491).

This processual vision of routines is important for building cognition, actions and changes. Feldman (2000: 613) suggested that routines are not only 'effortful accomplishments' but also 'emergent accomplishments' and 'works in progress rather than finished products'. In other words, routines do not only involve mindful effort; they are enacted repeatedly, and each repetition provides stimuli for variation and change. Feldman and Pentland (2003) investigate the nature of the relation between action and patterns of routines and observe that the identification of ostensive aspects constituted of and by actions shows that enacted patterns may be more or less consistent with written or abstract patterns.

Thus, solving problems and ways of solving them opens diverse opportunities to challenge (or not) habitual beliefs and patterns of interdependent actions among actors.

Archer goes a step further and identifies the nature and context of this voice within routines, helping us to understand cognition and actions through patterning. For Archer, the human as a 'person' has an inner conversation not promoted by objective structures and related to his or her own causal powers (Archer, 1995, 2003; Fuller, 2013). Archer (2003) identifies diverse modes of 'self-talk' from her interviews and scrutinizes the place of diverse habitual beliefs and the relative autonomy of individuals in society, helping us to understand their ontological vision for acting and solving problems. Indeed, and in contrast to Simon's view of docility, individuals depend on but are not reducible to social structures.

18.5 Conclusion

Routine Dynamics provides new empirical evidence on cognition that deserves greater attention. The importance of artifacts, of intentionality and diverse levels of reflection provide new ways to reconsider this issue and to understand some degree of mindfulness at the ostensive and performative levels of routines. Cognition within the Routine Dynamics frame is built within and during action and is no longer considered as a product of the mind. These insights provide a new point of departure from the established classical studies of cognition. New patterns are built showing how cognition is dynamically rooted in the performance of action and brought into the action by actors. Reflection is one of the critical elements for linking action to the patterns of actions. Archer, among others, provides interesting insights that can be useful for responding to the question 'how do we do patterning' (Feldman, 2016: 39), and for understanding the construct of intersubjective meaning and the role taken by those actions in exploring the process of patterning (Dionysiou and Tsoukas, 2013). In short, despite significant empirical results, a lot of work remains to be done to scrutinize the impact of the mutual constitution of performative and ostensive aspects of routines as well as the impact of 'cognition in the wild' within the Routine Dynamics framework. Nevertheless, a great deal has already been achieved in this direction, showing the capacity of Routine Dynamics to renew its theoretical framework by integrating new elements of observations collected by researchers.

References

Archer, M. (1995). *Realist Social Theory: The Morphogenetic Approach*. Cambridge: Cambridge University Press.

Archer, M. (2003). *Structure, Agency and the Internal Conversation*. Cambridge: Cambridge University Press.

Archer, M. S. (2007). *Making Our Way through the World*. Cambridge: Cambridge University Press.

Becker, M. C., Knudsen, T. and March, J. G. (2006). Schumpeter, Winter, and the sources of novelty. *Industrial and Corporate Change*, 15, 353–371.

Bertels, S., Howard-Grenville, J. and Pek, S. (2016). Cultural molding, shielding, and shoring at Oilco: The role of culture in the integration of routines. *Organization Science*, 23, 573–593.

Brette, O., Lazaric, N. and de Vierera, V. (2017). Habit, decision making and rationality: Comparing Thorstein Veblen and early Herbert Simon, *Journal of Economic Issues*, 3, 567–587.

Bucher, S. and Langley, A. (2016). The interplay of reflective and experimental spaces in interrupting and reorienting routine dynamics. *Organization Science*, 27, 594–613.

Cacciatori, E. (2012). Resolving conflict in problem-solving: Systems of artefacts in the development of new routines. *Journal of Management Studies*, 49, 1559–1585.

Chia, R. and Holt, R. (2006). Strategy as practical coping : A Heideggerian perspective. *Organization Studies*, 27(5), 635–654.

Cohen, M. D. (1991). Individual learning and organizational routine: Emerging connections. *Organization Science*, 2(1), 135–139.

Cohen, M. D. (2007). Reading Dewey: Reflections on the study of routine. *Organization Studies*, 28 (5), 773–786.

Cyert, R. M. and March, J. G. (1963/1992). *A Behavioral Theory of the Firm*. Cambridge, MA: Blackwell Business.

D'Adderio, L. (2011) Artifacts at the centre of routines: Performing the material turn in routines theory. *Journal of Institutional Economy*, 7, 197–230.

D'Adderio, L. (2008). The performativity of routines: Theorising the influence of artefacts and distributed agencies on routines dynamics. *Research Policy*, 37, 769–789.

D'Adderio, L. (2014). The replication dilemma unravelled: How organizations enact multiple goals in routine transfer. *Organization Science*, 25, 1325–1350.

Deken, F., Carlile, P. R., Berends, H. and Lauche, K. (2016). Generating novelty through interdependent routines: A process model of routine work. *Organization Science*, 27, 659–677.

Dionysiou, D. D. and Tsoukas, H. (2013). Understanding the (re)creation of routines from within: A symbolic interactionalist perspective. *Academy of Management Review*, 38, 181–205.

Dittrich, K., Guerard, S. and Seidl, D. (2016). Talking about routines: The role of reflective talk in routine change. *Organization Science*, 27(3), 678–697.

Dittrich, K. and Seidl, D. (2018). Emerging intentionality in Routine Dynamics: A pragmatist view. *Academy of Management Journal*, 61, 111–138.

Dosi, G. (1982). Technological paradigms and technological trajectories. *Research Policy*, 11, 147–162.

Dosi, G. (1988). Sources, procedures, and microeconomic effects of innovation. *Journal of Economic Literature*, 26(3), 1120–1171.

Emirbayer, M. (1997). Manifesto for a relational sociology. *American Journal of Sociology*, 103, 281–317.

Emirbayer, M. and Mische, A. (1998). What is agency? *American Journal of Sociology*, 103 (4), 962–1023.

Feldman, M. S. (2000). Organizational routines as a source of continuous change. *Organization Science*, 11(6), 611–629.

Feldman, M. S. (2003). A performative perspective on stability and change in organizational routines. *Industrial and Corporate Change*, 12(4), 727–752.

Feldman, M. S. (2016). Routines as process: Past, present, and future. In J. Howard-Grenville, C. Rerup, A. Langley and H. Tsoukas, eds., *Organizational Routines: How They Are Created, Maintained, and Changed*. Oxford: Oxford University Press, pp. 23–46.

Feldman, M. S. and Orlikowski,. W. J. (2011). Theorizing practice and practicing theory. *Organization Science*, 22(5), 1240–1253.

Feldman, M. S. and Pentland, B. T. (2003). Reconceptualizing organizational routines as a source of flexibility and change. *Administrative Science Quarterly*, 48, 94–118.

Feldman, M. S., Pentland, B. T., D'Adderio, L. and Lazaric, N. (2016). Beyond routines as things: Introduction of the special issue on routine dynamics. *Organization Science*, 27(3), 505–513.

Feldman, M. S. and Rafaeli, A. (2002). Organizational routines as sources of connections and understandings. *Journal of Management Studies*, 39(3), 309–331.

Ferraro, F., Etzion, D. and Gehman, J. (2015). Tackling grand challenges pragmatically: Robust action revisited. *Organization Studies*, 36(3), 363–390.

Fuller, C. (2013). Reflexivity, relative autonomy and the embedded individual in economics. *Journal of Institutional Economics*, 9(1), 109–129.

Glaser, V. L. (2017). Design performances: How organizations inscribe artifacts to change routines. *Academy of Management Journal*, 60, 2126–2154.

Greve, H. R. (2008). Organizational routines and performance feedback. In M. C. Becker, ed., *Handbook of Organizational Routines*. Northampton: Edward Elgar Publishing Limited, pp. 187–204.

Gupta, A., Hoopes, D. G. and Knott, A. M. (2015). Redesigning routines for replication. *Strategic Management Journal*, 36, 851–871.

Howard-Grenville, J. A. (2005). The persistence of flexible organizational routines: The role of agency and organizational context. *Organization Science*, 16(6), 618–636.

Howard-Grenville, J. A. and Rerup, C. (2017). A process perspective on organizational routines. In A. Langley and H. Tsoukas, eds., *Sage Handbook of Process Organizational Studies*. London: Sage Publications, pp. 323–339.

Kahneman, D., Slovic, P. and Tversky, A., eds. (1982). *Judgment under Uncertainty: Heuristics and Biases*. Cambridge: Cambridge University Press.

Kiwan, L. and Lazaric, N. (2019). Learning a new ecology of space and looking for new routines: Experimenting robotics in a surgical team. In M. S. Feldman, L. D'Adderio, K. Dittrich, and P. Jarzabkowski, eds., *Routine Dynamics in Action: Replication and Transformation*. Bingley: Emerald Publishing, pp. 173–189.

Lazaric, N. (2008). Routines and routinization: An exploration of some micro-cognitive foundations. In M. C. Becker, ed., *Handbook of Organizational Routines*. Cheltenham: Edward Elgar, pp. 205–227.

Lazaric, N. (2011). Organizational routines and cognition: An introduction to empirical and analytical contributions. *Journal of Institutional Economics*, 7(2), 147–156.

Lazaric, N. and Denis, B. (2001). How and why routines change: Some lessons from the articulation of knowledge with ISO 9002 implementation in the food industry. *Economie et Sociétés*, 585–612.

Lazaric, N. and Denis, B. (2005). Routinization and memorization of tasks in a workshop: The case of the introduction of ISO norms. *Industrial and Corporate Change*, 14, 873–896.

Lazaric, N., Mangolte, P-A. and Massué, M-L. (2003). Articulation and codification of collective know-how in the steel industry: Evidence from blast furnace control in France. *Research Policy*, 32, 1829–1847.

Levinthal, D. A. and Rerup, C. (2006). Crossing an apparent chasm: Bridging mindful and less mindful perspectives on organizational learning. *Organization Science*, 17, 502–513.

March, J. and Simon H. (1958). *Organizations, NY: Wiley*, 2nd ed. Oxford: Blackwell Publishers.

Nelson, R. R. and Winter, S. G. (1982). *An Evolutionary Theory of Economic Change*. Cambridge, MA: Harvard University Press.

Newell, A. and Simon, H. A. (1972). *Human Problem Solving*. Englewood Cliffs, NJ: Prentice-Hall.

Obstfeld, D. (2012). Creative projects: A less routine approach toward getting new things done. *Organization Science*, 23(6), 1571–1592.

Orlikowski, W. J. (1992). The duality of technology: Rethinking the concept of technology in organizations. *Organization Science*, 3, 398–427.

Parmentier Cajaiba, A., Lazaric, N. and Cajaiba-Santana, G. (2021). The effortful process of routines emergence: The interplay of entrepreneurial actions and artefacts, *Journal of Evolutionary Economics*, 31(1), 33–63.

Parmigiani, A. and Howard-Grenville, J. (2011). Routines revisited: Exploring the capabilities and practice perspectives. *Academy of Management Annals*, 5(1), 413–453.

Pentland, B. T. (1992). Organizing moves in software support hot lines. *Administrative Science Quarterly*, 37, 527–548.

Pentland, B. T. (1995). Grammatical models of organizational processes. *Organization Science*, 6(5), 541–556.

Pentland, B. T. and Feldman, M.S. (2005). Organizational routines as a unit of analysis. *Industrial and Corporate Change*, 14(5), 793–815.

Pentland, B. T. and Feldman, M. S. (2008). Designing routines: On the folly of designing artifacts, while hoping for patterns of action. *Information and Organization*, 18(4), 235–250.

Pentland, B. T., Feldman, M. S., Becker, M. C. and Liu, P. (2012). Dynamics of organizational routines: A generative model. *Journal of Management Studies*, 49(8), 1484–1508.

Pentland, B. T. and Ju Jung, E. (2016). Evolutionary and revolutionary change in path-dependent patterns of action. In J. Howard-Grenville, C. Rerup, A. Langley and H. Tsoukas, eds., *Organizational Routines: How They Are Created, Maintained, and Changed*. Oxford: Oxford University Press, pp. 96–113.

Pentland, B. T. and Rueter, H.H. (1994). Organizational routines as grammars of action. *Administrative Science Quarterly*, 39, 484–510.

Possas, M. L, Salles-Filho, S. and Silveira, da J. M. (1996). An evolutionary approach to technological innovation in agriculture: Some preliminary remarks. *Research Policy*, 25, 933–945.

Rerup, C. and Feldman, M. S. (2011). Routines as a source of change in organizational schema: The role of trial-and-error learning. *Academy of Management Journal*, 54(3), 577–610.

Salvato, C. (2009). Capabilities unveiled: The role of ordinary activities in the evolution of product development processes. *Organization Science*, 20, 384–409.

Salvato, C. and Rerup, C. (2011). Beyond collective entities: Multilevel research on organizational routines and capabilities. *Journal of Management*, 37, 468–490.

Sent, E.-M. (2000). Herbert A. Simon as a Cyborg scientist. *Perspectives on Science*, 8(4), 380–406.

Simon, H. A. [1947] (1976). *Administrative Behavior*. New York: Free Press, 3rd edition.

Simon, H. A. [1947] (1997). *Administrative Behavior*. New York: Free Press, 4th edition.

Simon, H.A. (1955). A behavioral model of rational choice. *Quarterly Journal of Economics*, 69(1), 99–118.

Simon, H. A. (1956). Rational choice and the structure of the environment, *Psychological Review*, 63(2), 129–138.

Simon, H. A. (1957). *Models of Man: Social and Rational – Mathematical Essays on Rational Human Behavior in a Social Setting*. New York: Wiley.

Simon, H. A. (1959). Theories of decision-making in economics and behavioral science. *American Economic Review*, 49, 53–283.

Simon, H. A. (1991). Theories of bounded rationality. In C. B. McGuire and Roy Radner, eds., *Decision and Organization*. Amsterdam: North-Holland Publishing, pp. 161–176.

Simpson, B. and Lorino, P. (2016) Re-viewing routines through a Pragmatist lens. In J. Howard-Grenville, C. Rerup, A. Langley and H. Tsoukas, eds., *Organizational Routines: How They Are Created, Maintained, and Changed*. Oxford: Oxford University Press, pp. 47–70.

Tolman, E. C. (1932). *Purposive Behavior in Animals and Men*. New York: The Century Co,

Tsoukas, H. and Chia, R. (2002). On organizational becoming: Rethinking organizational change. *Organization Science*, 13, 567–582.

Turner, S. F. and Cacciatori, E. (2016). The multiplicity of habit: Implications for routines research. In J. Howard-Grenville, C. Rerup, A. Langley and H. Tsoukas, eds., *Organizational Routines: How They Are Created, Maintained, and Changed*. Oxford: Oxford University Press, pp. 71–95.

Turner, S. F. and Rindova, V. (2012). A balancing act: How organizations pursue consistency in routine functioning in the face of ongoing change. *Organization Science*, 23(1), 24–46.

Winter, S. G. (1964). Economic 'natural selection' and the theory of the firm. *Institute of Public Policy Studies, University of Michigan*, 4, 225–272.

Winter, S. G. (2013). Habit, deliberation, and action: Strengthening the microfoundations of routines and capabilities. *The Academy of Management Perspectives*, 27(2), 120–137.

Winter, S. G. and Szulanski, G. (2001). Replication as strategy. *Organization Science*, 12, 730–743.

CHAPTER 19

Time, Temporality and History in Routine Dynamics

SCOTT F. TURNER AND VIOLINA P. RINDOVA

19.1 Introduction

Temporality is a central issue in understanding the dynamics of routines, which are repetitive, recognizable patterns of interdependent actions (Feldman and Pentland, 2003). Scholars working from the Routine Dynamics perspective have developed an extensive body of research focused on the processes that generate both stability and change in routines, as well as in organizations. This work brings into focus the connectivity between performance (specific performances in specific places and times) and pattern (models of and for enacting the routine) in constituting routines (Feldman, 2016; Feldman et al., 2016; Howard-Grenville and Rerup, 2017; Pentland et al., 2012). Our review shows how temporality is integral to the dynamic, generative view of routines advanced by this perspective (Feldman et al., 2016; Langley and Tsoukas, 2017).

Given the growth of Routine Dynamics research, taking stock of the contributions made from this perspective has become increasingly important (e.g., Howard-Grenville and Rerup, 2017; Parmigiani and Howard-Grenville, 2011). Among the several important aspects of routines that the dynamic perspective has foregrounded, the issue of temporality is particularly novel and important. And yet, although time plays a vital role in understanding Routine Dynamics, research on the topic remains scant, providing an opportunity to both review extant research and offer an agenda for future work. Our review focuses on two aspects of routine temporality: (1) the effects of time – subjective, intersubjective and objective – on routine performance; and (2) the development and evolution of both specific routines and systems of interdependent routines over time. We then identify opportunities for advancing a number of core themes and questions in Routine Dynamics research (Feldman et al., 2016) through the lens of temporality, including: (1) how do routines interact?; (2) how do they emerge and change?; (3) how do they inhibit and promote creativity or novelty? and (4) how do they help organizations maintain pattern and variety?

19.2 How Time Affects the Performance of Routines

The question of how time affects the enactment of routines is of fundamental theoretical importance, as routines by their very nature are temporally constituted as unfolding sequences of actions. The theoretical importance of this question is further reinforced by the fact that time itself is theoretically complex, as evidenced in the distinction among subjective, intersubjective and objective time. These times represent 'a triad of complementary horizons of human experience' (Hernadi, 1992: 150), reflecting the nature of human beings 'as natural organisms, social role-players, and personal selves [who] exist at the intersections of objective, intersubjective, and subjective times' (1992: 147). Thus, a temporal lens on routines must take into account 'the individual or subjective, the social or intersubjective, and the natural or objective' time frames (Hernadi, 1992: 150).

A temporal lens must further consider the temporal structure of practices, as informed by the concepts of temporal orientation, temporal pattern and temporal conception (Ancona et al., 2001; Rowell et al., 2016). Bringing these ideas together provides an effective guide for examining how time affects the performance of routines in Routine Dynamics research. Figure 19.1 frames the ideas in the context of routines as performing and patterning (Feldman, 2016).

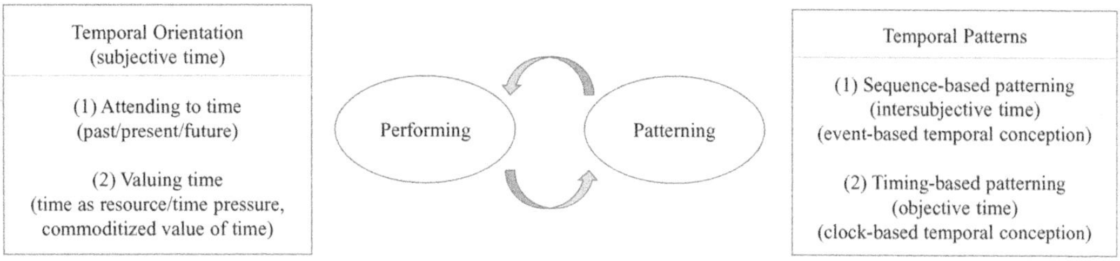

Figure 19.1 How time affects the performance of routines

19.2.1 Individuals and Subjective Time

Subjective time refers to subjective feeling of the passing of time or duration, and is also called experiential time or private time (Arstila and Lloyd, 2014). It aligns with the concept of temporal orientation (Bergmann, 1992; Howard-Grenville, 2005), which refers to the manner of attending to and valuing time in the enactment of a practice (Rowell et al., 2016). Much of the work on temporal orientation considers actors' focus of attention on the past, present or future (Bergmann, 1992; Emirbayer and Mische, 1998). Rowell et al. (2016) further emphasize orientation in terms of time as a resource and its valuation as a commodity (Zerubavel, 1981).

From the view of attending to the past, present or future, temporal orientation shapes the ways in which individuals perform practices. Howard-Grenville (2005) developed foundational theoretical ideas about how individuals' dominant temporal orientation affects the flexibility with which they perform a routine, and their willingness to introduce change in it. She showed that past orientation, evident in drawing on prior experience and iterating on past actions, reduces flexibility in routine performance, whereas present and future orientations, which focus on attending to the situation at hand and imagining new possibilities for the routine, increase flexibility.

Temporal orientation is also manifest in valuing time as a resource, and the associated time pressures (Rowell et al., 2016). For example, Turner and Fern (2012) found that participants perform a routine more flexibly, i.e., by diverging more from previous performance, in situations involving changes in time pressure – either increases or decreases. They further find that participants' prior experience with the routine amplified the effect of time pressure decreases, but they found no such effect on time pressure increases. They interpret these findings as evidence that experience provides greater understanding of the routine and context, and greater capacity to adapt in situations affording the time to do so. However, such experience-based agency cannot be exercised when time pressures increase.

19.2.2 Social Interactions and Intersubjective Time

Intersubjective time is a function of social engagement and shared temporal experiences and is constituted through the interactions among the members of a collective (Ballard and Seibold, 2006; Lin, 2013). Examining the influence of intersubjective time recognizes that 'approaching time only from the perspective of the individual subject ignores a fundamental condition of human beings – our temporal existence is intertwined with the temporal existence of other individuals' (Lin, 2013: 78). Intersubjective time plays an important role in establishing temporal patterns, which are observable temporal structures of practices (Rowell et al., 2016).

In Routine Dynamics research, intersubjective time is expressed in sequence-based patterns based on the temporal conception[1] of event time (Turner and Rindova, 2018; Zerubavel, 1981). Consistent with the idea of constructing intersubjective time

[1] Temporal conception refers to the properties that are ascribed to time that allow it to be comprehended and acted upon, e.g., event-based vs. clock-based (Ancona et al., 2001; Rowell et al., 2016).

through shared experiences (Lin, 2013), scholars have shown that participants establish routines as sequential patterns of actions through their interactions. These sequential patterns develop as routine participants take actions that stimulate or respond to those of other participants (Kremser et al., 2019; Pentland, 1992; Pentland and Rueter, 1994), and as they observe the actions that precede and follow their own (Dionysiou and Tsoukas, 2013). Participants develop understanding of patterns based on sequential order, recognizing a given action serves as a signal that it is time for performing subsequent ones (LeBaron et al., 2016; Pentland, 1992). Further, participants develop shared understandings of patterns – including variations in them – through interactions with others (Danner-Schröder and Geiger, 2016; Turner and Rindova, 2012), joint reflection (Dittrich et al., 2016; Kiwan and Lazaric, 2019) and the use of artifacts to represent action sequences (D'Adderio, 2011). Given the meaning often associated with the order of actions (Feldman et al., 2016), sequential patterns play an important role in guiding the performance of routines, as participants attend to the action-based cues provided by others.

19.2.3 Standard Measure and Objective Time

Closely associated with the temporal conception of clock time, objective time provides a standard external frame of reference, based on a linear continuum that is divisible into quantifiable units that are homogenous, uniform and measurable (Ancona et al., 2001; Bluedorn and Denhardt, 1988; McTaggart, 1908; Urry, 1996). Objective time represents an important basis for temporal patterns, particularly in modern, industrial and western societies (Rowell et al., 2016; Urry, 1996), where such time has been 'at the heart of the progressive rationalization of society' (Reinecke and Ansari, 2017: 404).

In Routine Dynamics research, objective time is expressed in timing-based patterns (Turner and Rindova, 2018), which affect routine performance based on clock time as a signal for action. Such patterns may arise from espoused patterns (Rerup and Feldman, 2011), as organizations seek to establish standard recurring interactions, often involving the design of complementary artifacts such as schedules (Dittrich et al., 2016; Yakura, 2002). For example, organizations may establish regular times for meetings, where clocks cue their beginning and end (Bucher and Langley, 2016). Alternatively, timing-based patterns may arise unexpectedly, as a consequence of how routines are performed. For example, Turner and Rindova (2012) found that customer participants in waste collection routines tended to recognize and develop timing-based patterns, based on relatively consistent collection timing by waste collection crews. In turn, this new 'unofficial' pattern led to service delivery problems, as collection crews were frequently unable to arrive at the same time on each service day, resulting in misalignment between when customers put their trash out and when crews were there to collect it. In related work, Turner and Rindova (2018) found that such emergent timing-based patterns were more likely when the historical consistency in routine performances was high, and when customers could observe the recurrent performance.[2] These findings suggest that objective time can play an influential role in the enactment of routines through timing-based patterns and consequent action cueing.

19.3 How Routines Evolve and Change Over Time

In considering the evolution of routines, the Routine Dynamics perspective emphasizes that routines exhibit aspects of path dependence and path creation (Pentland et al., 2012). In this sense, present and future performances build on past performances, which can have stabilizing and constraining effects along the lines of path dependence (Sydow et al., 2009). Participants, however, also have the ability to shape unfolding routines, consistent with the notion of path creation (Garud et al., 2010). In this section,

[2] Surprisingly, Turner and Rindova (2018) also found that prior bureaucratic experience, in the form of government employment, reduces this timing-based patterning that displaces the stipulated waste collection rules.

we consider how individual routines evolve over time through endogenous change; how they are transformed through intentional change; and how their dynamics are shaped by interdependence with other routines.

19.3.1 Evolutionary Change in Routines

Routine Dynamics scholars describe the evolution of routines through the recursive relationship between performances and patterns. When performing routines, participants may reproduce past performances, or they may depart from them. Participants may reproduce past performances for a variety of reasons. For example, they might be relying on the ongoing guidance of an extant pattern or an artifact (Cacciatori, 2012; D'Adderio, 2011; Feldman and Pentland, 2003); they could be seeking learning- or coordination-based efficiencies (Lazaric, 2008; Turner and Rindova, 2012); they may be maintaining an established truce (Kho et al., 2019; Salvato and Rerup, 2018; Zbaracki and Bergen, 2010); or they might be following temporal orientations directed towards the past (Howard-Grenville, 2005). They may also be striving for legitimacy and alignment with broader organizational practices and structures (Feldman, 2003; Howard-Grenville, 2005; Mutch, 2016).

Participants may deviate from patterns and past performances for a variety of reasons as well. Such reasons can include heterogeneity in the task (Danner-Schröder and Geiger, 2016; Spee et al., 2016) and/or in the conditions for performing it (Grodal et al., 2015; Turner and Fern, 2012). Change-oriented present and future temporal orientations (Howard-Grenville, 2005), the presence of competing goals (D'Adderio, 2014; Salvato and Rerup, 2018), and problems and opportunities that surfaced during past performances (Feldman, 2000; Kiwan and Lazaric, 2019; Rerup and Feldman, 2011; Salvato, 2009) can also play a role.

As participants enact the routine in ways that are similar to past performances, they establish and re-establish the routine as recognizable pattern through the history of performances (Feldman and Pentland, 2003), consistent with the idea of path dependence. Alternatively, when participants perform the routine in novel ways (Feldman, 2000) or reflectively explore and consider alternative patterns (Dittrich et al., 2016), they alter the performance repertoire, which can reshape the patterns constituting the routine, aligning with the idea of path creation (Garud et al., 2010). Such flexibility and multiplicity in performances (actual and envisioned) do not necessarily result in change in the routine. For example, change is unlikely for strongly embedded routines, even though flexibility can be likely (Howard-Grenville, 2005; Mutch, 2016), or in conditions when participants view novel performances as one-off situational responses, and do not consider them as a basis for endogenous change (Dittrich et al., 2016); in addition, change may not occur when support from higher levels in the organizational hierarchy is lacking (Salvato, 2009).

Further, changes in the routine can occur in the form of displacements, when preferred patterns replace existing ones, as well as extensions that result in greater multiplicity in the pattern reflecting different variants for different conditions (Feldman and Pentland, 2003; van Mierlo et al., 2019). In the latter case, examples include different patterns for developing new products, e.g., design vs. efficiency (Salvato and Rerup, 2018), or collecting garbage under typical vs. hazardous conditions (Turner and Rindova, 2012).

19.3.2 Change by Design

While the study of Routine Dynamics has predominantly employed evolutionary change models based on selective retention of performance variations (e.g., random, improvised), recent work has begun to examine intentional change through routine redesign. Such change arises from top-down initiatives led by senior organizational leaders (Bucher and Langley, 2016; Kaplan, 2015), as well as bottom-up ones led by those closer to the action (Bresman, 2013; Cohendet and Simon, 2016); and in some cases, researchers themselves are the source (Bapuji et al., 2019). From a practice perspective, a key puzzle associated with intentional change is how change can happen while the existing patterns are still being enacted and reproduced by participants' performances. In addressing this puzzle, scholars have frequently emphasized the importance of temporality.

While the decision to intentionally change a routine can reflect anticipatory search (Bresman, 2013), in many instances, it follows from problemistic search (Cyert and March, 1963), stimulated by crisis (Cohendet and Simon, 2016), infractions (Bertels et al., 2016), or environmental/organizational changes (D'Adderio, 2014; Zbaracki and Bergen, 2010). In some work, scholars have shown how intentional change efforts can be successful when they are preceded by crisis in the organization (Cohendet and Simon, 2016; Kaplan, 2015). This sequence-based pattern (i.e., change follows crisis) suggests that such changes may be effective when a priori patterns are inhibited, and greater motivation among participants to make needed changes can be elicited.[3] Along similar lines, scholars have identified timing-based patterns of intentional change (i.e., changes occurring at particular times). For example, Turner and Rindova (2012) found that waste collection organizations frequently time intentional changes in their collection routines to occur when customers are likely to expect changes or disruption (e.g., reorganizing routines at the start of a new fiscal year).

Bucher and Langley (2016) expand the focus of the study of intentional change to include spatial solutions, such as the use of reflective and experimental spaces. Reflective spaces are set apart by a range of boundaries (including timing-based ones) and oriented to developing new patterns; experimental spaces establish boundaries to signal the trial nature of the experimental performances, and to enable the new actions to be integrated into the original routine. For instance, with experimental spaces, Bucher and Langley (2016) found that participants set a specific duration for the experiments (e.g., four months), after which time the experiment would either end, undergo further adjustment or replace the original routine.

Other important factors for intentional change include how the change initiative fits with participants' understandings of the organization and its culture. For example, in the setting of university housing, Feldman (2003) found that a top-down intentional change initiative was not implemented by routine participants because they perceived the change to run counter to their understanding of how the organization operates. In another case, Bertels et al. (2016) found that efforts to integrate a routine that has a poor fit with the organizational culture resulted in change, but not the change intended. Specifically, they observed the establishment of action patterns that resembled but departed from the espoused routine, with participants doing additional cultural work as they performed the routine, while trying to reduce perceptions of mismatch between their actions and the espoused routine.

19.3.3 *Interdependence among Routines and Constraining/Enabling Change over Time*

In a number of Routine Dynamics studies, scholars have found that interdependence among routines tends to constrain change over time in the routines. For example, Howard-Grenville (2005) found that while flexibility could be observed in the performance of routines that are weakly or strongly embedded, change in routines is only likely for those routines that are weakly embedded in surrounding structures and routines, with strongly embedded routines tending to persist over time due to constraints on their ongoing adaptation. Similarly, Turner and Rindova (2012) found that organizational leaders emphasize the difficulties associated with changing their routines, when those routines have become tightly coupled with customer household routines. And more recently, Kremser and Schreyögg (2016) found evidence of constraints on routine change in clusters of interdependent routines, arguing that over time the scope of viable changes for routines narrows due to the development of complementarities across routines.

At the same time, these studies do suggest some paths for change in such routines. For example, Turner and Rindova (2012) found that organizations plan for intentional changes in routines to occur at particular points in time, e.g., the start of a new fiscal year, as other changes are taking place

[3] As another sequence-based example, D'Adderio (2014) found a pattern of change following replication in the context of routine transfer.

in the broader structures, such that there is a weakening in the constraints on change that are based in expectations for stability. Kremser and Schreyögg (2016) argue that routines in clusters will continue to change over time, but only along an emergent trajectory, as changes occurring along that trajectory avoid or limit complementarity disruption for the cluster as a whole.

While many studies examining interdependence among routines emphasize constraining effects that limit change in the routines over time, some studies point to enabling/generative effects. For example, Deken et al. (2016) put forward an alternative view of temporal trajectories of change across interdependent routines. Rather than change being inhibited by interdependencies (Kremser and Schreyögg, 2016), Deken et al. (2016) found that participants in the routines proceed along a trajectory, whereby they initially perform routine work to generate novel outcomes, and then engage in subsequent routine work to respond and re-stabilize in the face of breakdowns arising from extant interdependencies. In another case, Sele and Grand (2016) found evidence of generativity in routine interactions when actants are mediators (i.e., modify when performing routine connections), rather than intermediaries (i.e., merely maintain connections between routines).

19.4 Future Directions for Research on Temporality in Routine Dynamics

In identifying opportunities for future research, we focus on two central concepts identified in our review – temporal orientation and temporal patterns – and concentrate on four core themes and questions in Routine Dynamics scholarship, as identified in Feldman et al. (2016).

First, consider the fundamental question of how routines emerge and change, which has attracted a great deal of research attention, as our review illustrates. Whereas much of the work so far has focused on social interactions and context, and the related intersubjective and objective time, we see an opportunity for future research to build on Howard-Grenville's (2005) pioneering work by examining further how temporal orientation – and subjective time more broadly – shapes the flexibility of performances and change in routines. In extant work, process scholars have suggested that focusing on temporal orientation in terms of past, present or future alone may be too limiting, as it does not account for time experienced as flow, i.e., the 'flowing forth of time as experienced by a conscious being whereby different temporal orientations are knit together – the past is brought forward to the present in anticipation of the future' (Langley and Tsoukas, 2017). In related work focusing on subjective time, Shipp, Edwards and Lambert (2009) found that a majority of surveyed individuals simultaneously direct attention to multiple times among the past, present and future, and that a notable minority indicate low orientation to all three time periods (i.e., 'atemporal'). Moreover, as Rowell et al. (2016) indicate, the concept of temporal orientation incorporates both how time is attended to (i.e., past, present, future) and how it is valued (i.e., time as commoditized resource). In collective, this suggests that considering the role of subjective time through a richer conception of temporal orientation offers opportunities to advance our understanding of how routines emerge and change – in terms of shaping the flexibility of routine performances (Howard-Grenville, 2005), reflective consideration of alternative patterns (Dittrich et al., 2016) and change in routines, whether endogenously (Feldman, 2000) or via intentional redesign efforts (Bapuji et al., 2019; Cohendet and Simon, 2016).

As another direction, our understanding of the emergence and change in routines can benefit from greater research attention to the interrelations of temporal orientations and patterning. In Routine Dynamics research to date, scholars have primarily focused on the role of subjective time in terms of how temporal orientation affects agency and the performance of routines (Howard-Grenville, 2005). In related work focusing on institutions and the temporal structure of practices, Rowell et al. (2016) emphasize that there are strong interrelations among temporal patterns and temporal orientations. From this perspective, our understanding of the emergence of and change in routines might be advanced by considering the role of temporal orientation in patterning, and in efforts to change patterns; similarly, we may extend understanding of how patterns shape performances by taking into account the ways in which patterns shape and reshape the temporal orientation of routine participants. For example, orientations to the past versus future may shape to what extent participants engage in patterning, as well as the types of patterns they recognize; and conversely, the process of recognizing patterns may generate task-based reference points that influence the orienting capacity (e.g., towards the past) of participants.

Second, a temporal perspective can open up new avenues for understanding how routines inhibit and promote creativity or novelty. This question recognizes that many organizations require novelty and creativity to accomplish their missions and/or be competitive in the marketplace. While there has been a fair amount of scholarly attention directed to the role of routines in structuring creative and innovative tasks (Becker and Zirpoli, 2009; Hargadon and Sutton, 1997), researchers are just beginning to delve into the generative nature of routines centring on such tasks (e.g., Grand, 2016; Sele and Grand, 2016). To advance this line of work, we encourage future research on the effects of subjective, intersubjective and objective time on the generative nature of routines. For example, one type of subjective time experience identified in creativity research is the notion of flow (Csikszentmihalyi, 1997). The concept of flow may be of particular interest to routines researchers, as the experience of time stopping associated with it may alter the effects of time pressures that have been found to affect flexibility in routine performances (Turner and Fern, 2012). Future research could also examine different contexts where flow experiences occur and how they affect the performance of routines by the focal actors experiencing flow, as well as other routine participants. This work may build on expanded conceptualizations of temporal orientation to include time experienced as flow (Langley and Tsoukas, 2017), as well as recent work on cross-temporal sense-making, showing different patterns in which organizational members connect the past, present and future in different ways (Ravasi et al., 2019).

We also encourage greater attention on how different patterns affect the pursuit and outcomes of creative and novel tasks. For example, researchers have focused attention on sequence-based patterns for such routines (e.g., Deken et al., 2016; Salvato and Rerup, 2018), as well as timing-based ones (e.g., Brown and Eisenhardt, 1997; Goh and Rerup, 2018). In contrast, little attention has been directed to the implications of these patterns on the nature of task pursuit and outcomes (e.g., degree of creativity in a single new product, versus across a series of new products). This may be an important issue in research studying the effect of routines on innovation, as prior research suggests that certain patterns may reliably produce incremental innovations, while simultaneously crowding out radical innovations (Benner and Tushman, 2002).

Third, developing deeper understanding of routine temporality provides an opportunity to advance understanding of how routines help organizations maintain both pattern and variety. It is well understood that routines exhibit pattern in variety (Cohen, 2007), and that some organizations are particularly dependent on accomplishing the balance between pattern and variety, e.g., balancing among competing goals for consistency and change. In this research, scholars have tended to focus on the role of making and remaking truces when participant views diverge due to competing goals (e.g., Salvato and Rerup, 2018; Zbaracki and Bergen, 2010). Researchers have also studied the mechanisms and processes through which participants balance competing goals they agree about, such as valuing both consistency and flexibility (D'Adderio, 2014; Spee et al., 2016; Turner and Rindova, 2012). In terms of future research, we encourage scholars to examine how temporal orientation – particularly its multiplicity and dynamics – influence routine participants' understanding of the means for balancing among goals for consistency and change. For example, Ravasi et al. (2019) show how three different temporal sense-making patterns address issues of consistency and change in different ways in relating organizational history to future-oriented actions.

We also see fruitful opportunities for research exploring the role of patterns in accomplishing balance among competing goals, as well as the role of patterns for accomplishing such balance. In terms of the former, future work can delve into how the interrelations of temporal patterns (i.e., sequence-based, timing-based) affect balancing among goals for consistency and change. For example, with innovation in the semiconductor and computing industries, considerable emphasis has been placed on introducing innovations in accordance with Moore's Law (i.e., maintaining timing-based pattern for releasing new products), while affording flexibility in the sequence of underlying actions that might be needed to fulfil Moore's Law. In terms of the latter, we also see opportunities for advancing this research with greater attention to the role of patterns for balancing among competing goals. In extant research, scholars have placed more emphasis on mechanisms (e.g., artifacts, connections, communities) that enable the balancing act, with less attention directed to the temporal patterns by which participants simultaneously maintain pattern and variety. An exception is recent work by Spee et al. (2016), which emphasizes a sequence-based pattern of dynamic balancing, whereby participants enact a cycle of orienting towards one pattern that aligns with a given goal, followed by reorienting to an alternative pattern aligning with a competing goal, then reorienting back to the original pattern, etc. Alternatively, Routine Dynamics research is also suggestive of timing-based patterns for balancing; for example, Turner and Rindova (2012) highlight how waste organizations seek to maintain consistency in their waste collection routines throughout the year, and introduce intentional changes at specific times, when customers may be more likely to expect or accept disruption, such as reorganizing routes at the start of a new fiscal year.

Fourth, a temporal perspective may enable important advances in understanding how Routine Dynamics are shaped by interactions among routines. While Routine Dynamics research has tended to focus on individual routines, scholars have recently begun to explore interdependence among routines (Kremser et al., 2019), recognizing that the capacity for organizing is often based in systems/sets of interdependent routines. In extant research, scholars have tended to emphasize that interactions among routines produce constraints on the likelihood and scope of change due to embeddedness (Howard-Grenville, 2005), co-organizing/coupling effects (Turner and Rindova, 2012) and complementarities and path dependence (Kremser and Schreyögg, 2016). In recent work, scholars have highlighted that interactions among routines are not necessarily constraining, finding evidence that participants can pursue novel outcomes while dealing with the difficulties/breakdowns that arise due to interdependencies (Deken et al., 2016), and that routine interactions can even be generative when actants among routines serve as mediators (Sele and Grand, 2016).

Overall, we see considerable opportunity for advancing our understanding of Routine Dynamics by exploring further under what conditions interactions among routines may facilitate as well as constrain change. For one, we encourage future research to explore the role of temporal orientation, as the ways in which routine participants value and attend to time are likely to shape the constraining vs. enabling effects of routine interdependencies. Specifically, we expect that temporal orientation may play an important role in understanding when participants are likely to accept change constraints produced by interdependencies among routines, versus confront the present challenges/breakdowns arising from interdependencies in order to produce novel outcomes in the future. We also encourage future research to focus on the role of the patterns themselves, in terms of whether the interactions among routines involve patterns that are recognized in terms of sequence-based or timing-based patterning. For example, with timing-based patterning, the actions are positioned on an external, fixed, objective timeline, which may have more constraining effects for interactions with other interdependent routines; by contrast, with sequence-based patterning, the actions are based on an order reflecting internal, intersubjective time, which may be more amenable to flexibility and change. Last, we would encourage closer attention to how patterns of interactions among routines are situated in time. Recognizing the importance of such patterning for understanding the internal dynamics of individual routines, we see greater insight into the temporal pattern of interactions among routines playing an important role in understanding the dynamics of interdependent routines.

References

Ancona, D. G., Okhuysen, G. A. and Perlow, L. A. (2001). Taking time to integrate temporal research. *Academy of Management Review*, 26 (4), 512–529.

Arstila, V. and Lloyd, D. (2014). *Subjective Time: The Philosophy, Psychology, and Neuroscience of Temporality*. Cambridge, MA: The MIT Press.

Ballard, D. I. and Seibold, D. R. (2006). The experience of time at work: Relationship to communication load, job satisfaction, and interdepartmental communication. *Communication Studies*, 57(3), 317–340.

Bapuji, H., Hora, M., Saeed, A. and Turner, S. (2019). How understanding-based redesign influences the pattern of actions and effectiveness of routines. *Journal of Management*, 45(5), 2132–2162.

Becker, M. C. and Zirpoli, F. (2009). Innovation routines: Exploring the role of procedures and stable behaviour patterns in innovation. In M. C. Becker and N. Lazaric, eds., *Organizational Routines: Advancing Empirical Research*. Cheltenham: Edward Elgar, pp. 303–339.

Benner, M. J. and Tushman, M. (2002). Process management and technological innovation: A longitudinal study of the photography and paint industries. *Administrative Science Quarterly*, 47(4), 676–706.

Bergmann, W. (1992). The problem of time in sociology: An overview of the literature on the state of theory and research on the 'Sociology of Time', 1900–82. *Time & Society*, 1(1), 81–134.

Bertels, S., Howard-Grenville, J. and Pek, S. (2016). Cultural molding, shielding, and shoring at Oilco: The role of culture in the integration of routines. *Organization Science*, 27(3), 573–593.

Bluedorn, A. C. and Denhardt, R. B. (1988). Time and organizations. *Journal of Management*, 14(2), 299–320.

Bresman, H. (2013). Changing routines: A process model of vicarious group learning in pharmaceutical R&D. *Academy of Management Journal*, 56(1), 35–61.

Brown, S. L. and Eisenhardt, K. M. (1997). The art of continuous change: Linking complexity theory and time-paced evolution in relentlessly shifting organizations. *Administrative Science Quarterly*, 42(1), 1–34.

Bucher, S. and Langley, A. (2016). The interplay of reflective and experimental spaces in interrupting and reorienting routine dynamics. *Organization Science*, 27(3), 594–613.

Cacciatori, E. (2012). Resolving conflict in problem-solving: Systems of artefacts in the development of new routines. *Journal of Management Studies*, 49(8), 1559–1585.

Cohen, M. D. (2007). Reading Dewey: Reflections on the study of routine. *Organization Studies*, 28 (5), 773–786.

Cohendet, P. S. and Simon, L. O. (2016). Always playable: Recombining routines for creative efficiency at Ubisoft Montreal's video game studio. *Organization Science*, 27(3), 614–632.

Csikszentmihalyi, M. (1997). *Flow and the Psychology of Discovery and Invention*. New York: HarperPerennial.

Cyert, R. M. and March, J. G. (1963/1992). *A Behavioral Theory of the Firm*. Cambridge, MA: Blackwell Business.

D'Adderio, L. (2011). Artifacts at the centre of routines: Performing the material turn in routines theory. *Journal of Institutional Economics*, 7(2), 197–230.

D'Adderio, L. (2014). The replication dilemma unravelled: How organizations enact multiple goals in routine transfer. *Organization Science*, 25(5), 1325–1350.

Danner-Schröder, A. and Geiger, D. (2016). Unravelling the motor of patterning work: Toward an understanding of the microlevel dynamics of standardization and flexibility. *Organization Science*, 27(3), 633–658.

Deken, F., Carlile, P. R., Berends, H. and Lauche, K. (2016). Generating novelty through interdependent routines: A process model of routine work. *Organization Science*, 27(3), 659–677.

Dionysiou, D. D. and Tsoukas, H. (2013). Understanding the (re)creation of routines from within: A symbolic interactionalist perspective. *Academy of Management Review*, 38(2), 181–205.

Dittrich, K., Guerard, S. and Seidl, D. (2016). Talking about routines: The role of reflective talk in routine change. *Organization Science*, 27(3), 678–697.

Emirbayer, M. and Mische, A. (1998). What is agency? *American Journal of Sociology*, 103(4), 962–1023.

Feldman, M. S. (2000). Organizational routines as a source of continuous change. *Organization Science*, 11(6), 611–629.

Feldman, M. S. (2003). A performative perspective on stability and change in organizational routines. *Industrial and Corporate Change*, 12(4), 727–752.

Feldman, M. S. (2016). Routines as process: Past, present, and future. In J. Howard-Grenville, C. Rerup, A. Langley and H. Tsoukas, eds., *Organizational Routines: How They Are Created, Maintained, and Changed*. Oxford: Oxford University Press, pp. 23–46.

Feldman, M. S. and Pentland, B. T. (2003). Reconceptualizing organizational routines as a source of flexibility and change. *Administrative Science Quarterly*, 48(1), 94–118.

Feldman, M. S., Pentland, B. T., D'Adderio, L. and Lazaric, N. (2016). Beyond routines as things: Introduction of the special issue on routine dynamics. *Organization Science*, 27(3), 505–513.

Garud, R., Kumaraswamy, A. and Karnoe, P. (2010). Path dependence or path creation? *Journal of Management Studies*, 47(4), 760–774.

Goh, K. T. and Rerup, C. (2018). The role of space and time in balancing conflicting pressures through routine dynamics. *Academy of Management Proceedings*. Published online.

Grand, S. (2016). *Routines, Strategies and Management: Engaging for Recurrent Creation 'at the Edge'*. Cheltenham: Edward Elgar Publishing.

Grodal, S., Nelson, A. J. and Siino, R. M. (2015). Help-seeking and help-giving as an organizational routine: Engagement in innovative work. *Academy of Management Journal*, 58(1), 136–168.

Hargadon, A. and Sutton, R. I. (1997). Technology brokering and innovation in a product development firm. *Administrative Science Quarterly*, 42(4), 716–749.

Hernadi, P. (1992). Objective, subjective, intersubjective times: Guest editor's introduction. *Time & Society*, 1(2), 147–158.

Howard-Grenville, J. A. (2005). The persistence of flexible organizational routines: The role of agency and organizational context. *Organization Science*, 16(6), 618–636.

Howard-Grenville, J. and Rerup, C. (2017). A process perspective on organizational routines. In A. Langley and H. Tsoukas, eds., *The SAGE Handbook of Process Organization Studies*. London: Oxford University Press, pp. 323–337.

Kaplan, S. (2015). Truce breaking and remaking: The CEO's role in changing organizational routines. In G. Gavetti and W. Ocasio, eds., *Cognition and Strategy*. Bingley: Emerald Group Publishing, pp. 1–45.

Kho, J., Spee, A. P. and Gillespie, N. (2019). Enacting relational expertise to change professional routines in technology-mediated service settings. In M. S. Feldman, L. D'Adderio, K. Dittrich and P. Jarzabkowski, eds., *Routine Dynamics in Action: Replication and Transformation*. Bingley: Emerald Publishing, pp. 191–213.

Kiwan, L. and Lazaric, N. (2019). Learning a new ecology of space and looking for new routines: Experimenting robotics in a surgical team. In M. S. Feldman, L. D'Adderio, K. Dittrich and P. Jarzabkowski, eds., *Routine Dynamics in Action: Replication and Transformation*. Bingley: Emerald Publishing, pp. 173–189.

Kremser, W., Pentland, B. T. and Brunswicker, S. (2019). Interdependence within and between routines: A performative perspective. In M. S. Feldman, L. D'Adderio, K. Dittrich and P. Jarzabkowski, eds., *Routine Dynamics in Action: Replication and Transformation*. Bingley: Emerald Publishing, pp. 79–98.

Kremser, W. and Schreyögg, G. (2016). The dynamics of interrelated routines: Introducing the cluster level. *Organization Science*, 27(3), 698–721.

Langley, A. and Tsoukas, H. (2017). Introduction: Process thinking, process theorizing and process researching. In A. Langley and H. Tsoukas, eds., *The SAGE Handbook of Process Organization Studies*. Thousand Oaks, CA: Sage Publications, pp. 1–25.

Lazaric, N. (2008). Routines and routinization: An exploration of some micro-cognitive foundations. In M. C. Becker, ed., *Handbook of Organizational Routines*. Cheltenham: Edward Elgar, pp. 205–227.

LeBaron, C., Christianson, M. K., Garrett, L. and Ilan, R. (2016). Coordinating flexible performance during everyday work: An ethnomethodological study of handoff routines. *Organization Science*, 27(3), 514–534.

Lin, Y. (2013). *The Intersubjectivity of Time: Levinas and Infinite Responsibility*. Pittsburgh, PA: Duquesne University Press.

McTaggart, J. E. (1908). The unreality of time. *Mind: A Quarterly Review of Psychology and Philosophy*, 17(68), 457–474.

Mutch, A. (2016). Bringing history into the study of routines: Contextualizing performance. *Organization Studies*, 37(8), 1171–1188.

Parmigiani, A. and Howard-Grenville, J. (2011). Routines revisited: Exploring the capabilities and practice perspectives. *Academy of Management Annals*, 5(1), 413–453.

Pentland, B. T. (1992). Organizing moves in software support hot lines. *Administrative Science Quarterly*, 37(4), 527–548.

Pentland, B. T., Feldman, M. S., Becker, M. C. and Liu, P. (2012). Dynamics of organizational routines: A generative model. *Journal of Management Studies*, 49(8), 1484–1508.

Pentland, B. T. and Reuter, H. H. (1994). Organizational routines as grammars of action. *Administrative Science Quarterly*, 39, 484–510.

Ravasi, D., Rindova, V. and Stigliani, I. (2019). The stuff of legend: History, memory and the temporality of organizational identity construction. *Academy of Management Journal*, 62(5), 1523–1555.

Reinecke, J. and Ansari, S. (2017). Time, temporality, and process studies. In A. Langley and H. Tsoukas, eds., *The SAGE Handbook of Process Organization Studies*. Thousand Oaks, CA: Sage Publications, pp. 402–416.

Rerup, C. and Feldman, M. S. (2011). Routines as a source of change in organizational schema: The role of trial-and-error learning. *Academy of Management Journal*, 54(3), 577–610.

Rowell, C., Gustafsson, R. and Clemente, M. (2016). How institutions matter 'in time': The temporal structure of practices and their effects on practice reproduction. In J. Gehman, M. Lounsbury and R. Greenwood, eds., *How Institutions Matter*, Vol. 48A, Bingley: Emerald Group Publishing, pp. 305–330.

Salvato, C. (2009). Capabilities unveiled: The role of ordinary activities in the evolution of product development processes. *Organization Science*, 20(2), 384–409.

Salvato, C. and Rerup, C. (2018). Routine regulation: Balancing conflicting goals in organizational routines. *Administrative Science Quarterly*, 63(1), 170–209.

Sele, K. and Grand, S. (2016). Unpacking the dynamics of ecologies of routines: Mediators and their generative effects in routine interactions. *Organization Science*, 27(3), 722–738.

Shipp, A. J., Edwards, J. R. and Lambert, L. S. (2009). Conceptualization and measurement of temporal focus: The subjective experience of the past, present, and future. *Organizational Behavior and Human Decision Processes*, 110(1), 1–22.

Spee, P., Jarzabkowski, P. and Smets, M. (2016). The influence of routine interdependence and skillful accomplishment on the coordination of standardizing and customizing. *Organization Science*, 23(3), 759–781.

Sydow, J., Schreyögg, G. and Koch, J. (2009). Organizational path dependence: Opening up the black box. *Academy of Management Review*, 34(4), 689–709.

Turner, S. F. and Fern, M. J. (2012). Examining the stability and variability of routine performances: The effects of experience and context change. *Journal of Management Studies*, 49(8), 1407–1434.

Turner, S. F. and Rindova, V. (2012). A balancing act: How organizations pursue consistency in routine functioning in the face of ongoing change. *Organization Science*, 23(1), 24–46.

Turner, S. F. and Rindova, V. P. (2018). Watching the clock: Action timing, patterning, and routine performance. *Academy of Management Journal*, 61(4), 1253–1280.

Urry, J. (1996). Sociology of time and space. In B. S. Turner, ed., *The Blackwell Companion to Social Theory*. Oxford: Blackwell, pp. 369–395.

van Mierlo, J., Loohuis, R. and Bondarouk, T. (2019). The role of multiple points of view in non-envisioned routine creation: Taking initiative, creating connections, and coping with misalignments. In M. S. Feldman, L. D'Adderio, K. Dittrich and P. Jarzabkowski, eds., *Routine Dynamics in Action: Replication and Transformation*. Bingley: Emerald Publishing, pp. 153–172.

Yakura, E. K. (2002). Charting time: Timelines as temporal boundary objects. *Academy of Management Journal*, 45(5), 956–970.

Zbaracki, M. J. and Bergen, M. (2010). When truces collapse: A longitudinal study of price-adjustment routines. *Organization Science*, 21(5), 955–972.

Zerubavel, E. (1981). *Hidden Rhythms: Schedules and Calendars in Social Life*. Chicago: University of Chicago Press.

CHAPTER 20 Replication and Routine Dynamics

CHARLOTTE BLANCHE AND PATRICK COHENDET*

20.1 Introduction

Routines replication is an important topic in the management of organizations. Turning a small success into a big one is in fact a key competence for organizations that want to grow or stay profitable. Many industries (retail, catering, hotel, banking, financial services, etc.) have grown by replicating a successful idea, making franchise systems a dominant organizational form. How to best replicate routines in multiple organizational locations – often referred to as the 'McDonalds approach' – (Winter and Szulanski, 2001) thus became of central interest for researchers (Winter and Szulanski, 2001).

In order to understand the current notion of transfer and routines replication,[1] we draw on D'Adderio and Pollock's (2020) distinction between two streams of research: transfer as replication (drawing on the capabilities perspective on routines in Parmigiani and Howard-Grenville, 2011); and transfer as transformation or re-creation (drawing on the practice perspective on routines, ibid.). While both streams look at replication as 'the creation of another routine that is similar to the original routine in significant respects' (Szulanski and Jensen, 2004: 349), they are embedded in different theoretical traditions, methodologies and research fields.

The first research stream, transfer as replication, grounded in Evolutionary Economics, emphasized the 'what' or 'why' of replication and understood the routine as a stable phenomenon (Parmigiani and Howard-Grenville, 2011: 417). The focus was on how existing routines could be reproduced efficiently and accurately across the various sites of a given organization. This high-level perspective treated routines as black boxes which could be straightforwardly replicated across sites (Winter and Szulanski, 2001, Winter et al., 2012). The second, and more recent, research stream, grounded in sociology and practice theory, focuses instead on the internal dynamics of routines. This perspective on replication outlines the processes through which routines can be made similar (D'Adderio, 2014; D'Adderio and Pollock, 2020).

In analyzing these two streams of work, this chapter will place particular emphasis on how the Routine Dynamics approach and replication as re-creation perspective have enriched the understanding of routine replication and complemented the earlier literature.

20.2 Replication from a Capability Perspective: Transfer as Replication

Organizational routines initially appeared as an academic concept in the work of Stene (1940), but the Carnegie School (Cyert and March, 1963; March and Simon, 1958) and Nelson and Winter (1982) were the first to formalize it as a subject of inquiry. According to Nelson and Winter (1982), in order to achieve competitive advantage, firms had to manage their routines portfolio.

In the historico-economic context of global competition, turning a small success into a big one was the key competence for organizations that wanted to grow or stay profitable. The franchise system became the dominant organizational form

* The authors would like to express their deepest gratitude to Luciana D'Adderio and Katharina Dittrich for their time, insightful comments and unwavering support throughout this chapter project.

[1] Transfer refers to the general process of transferring a routine or a set of routines from one context to another. Replication is a specific kind of transfer where similarity between routines at the origin and the destination matters (see D'Adderio and Pollock, 2020).

in many industries (retail, catering, hotel, banking, financial services, etc.), rendering the study of replication of utmost importance. Reproducing an organizational set of routines in multiple locations thus became of central interest for researchers (Winter and Szulanski, 2001).

20.2.1 Qualifying the Routine to Be Transferred: Arrow Core, Templates and Principles

According to Winter and Szulanski (2001: 731), reliable routines are those which embody the 'Arrow Core'. The Arrow Core essentially represents the full and correct specification of the fundamental replicable features of a business model or formula as well as its ideal target applications. It ascertains '*which attributes of the formula are replicable and worth replicating*' to ensure success (Winter and Szulanski, 2001: 731). The Arrow Core is composed of tacit knowledge that is embedded within interdependent routines. Thus, the Arrow Core content cannot be precisely determined in advance but must be discovered and acquired through learning and adjusted through experimentation. The Arrow Core may lead to a specific replication instance (e.g., a franchise's outlet) to be identified as a concrete 'template' for further replication, or the template may be understood more abstractly in terms of a specification of preferred location choices, standard operating procedures, the products to be offered, etc., that is, a 'formula'. The template is a working example of a process in use. Within a growth strategy, and in order to create a competitive advantage (Jensen and Szulanski, 2007; Szulanski and Jensen, 2008; Winter and Szulanski, 2001) a successful replication has to be guided by a template: a well-documented business format (Szulanski and Jensen, 2004; Winter and Szulanski, 2001). Templates provide as this explicit identification and capture the information that contributes to the success of the replicated routine (Winter and Szulanski, 2001).

If one means of achieving the transfer of the Arrow Core is through the use of templates, however, the template should not be misunderstood or confused with the Arrow Core. Authors, in fact, caution that concepts need to be validated before using a template in a large-scale replication. This is because, while the template may be considered a repository of process knowledge, it cannot capture 'all the knowledge' in codified form (Baden-Fuller and Winter, 2005). Replicating organizational routines is therefore difficult because the embedded tacit knowledge, which cannot be articulated and arises from a specific context, must still be transferred to a new context. In addition to the tacit character of this knowledge (Collins, 2005, 2007), the process of determining which knowledge should be contained in the template is a political process (Szulanski, 1996).

As routines are opaque, complex and causally ambiguous, it is generally considered risky to bypass the use of a template (Jensen and Szulanski, 2007; Szulanski and Jensen, 2008; Winter and Szulanski, 2001). Authors instead suggested that organizations copy the template exactly, to avoid any unanticipated problems in new settings, before any attempts at local adjustment or modification. Findings suggested that deviating from a template increased the risk of replication failure.

Winter and Szulanski (2001), on this basis, presented an organizational strategy of replication that consisted of two phases. In the first phase, 'exploration', the business model is created and refined until the complex set of interdependent routines are understood and articulated. The goal at this stage is to uncover the Arrow Core described earlier. This initial important phase requires a precise explanation of the component routines, including guidance and diagnostic tools. This is followed by a second phase, 'exploitation', that is characterized by the use of the business model for large-scale replication. At this stage the final business format is stabilized within the local unit of the replicatee.

In replicating routines, practitioners face a dilemma or trade-off between the benefits of reproducing the template exactly (replication) or adapting the template to the new context by consequential learning (innovation) (Winter and Szulanski, 2001). The perceived value of the original template depends on it being replicated exactly at the new site, whereas local factors demand adaptation, which, however, must not occur until later when the transferred routines have stabilized. This is because of the interdependence across the complex network of routines which make the template causally ambiguous and prone to be disrupted by early adaptation when transferred routines are still unstable.

Although 'replication by template' is the dominant approach, an alternative also exists in the shape of 'replication by principles'. This approach involves identifying the objectives as well as the reasoning underlying the intended transfer outcome (Baden-Fuller and Winter, 2005). It requires an understanding of the history and the reasons why certain choices were made over others at a given time and in a specific context, so that the design of the routine to be replicated is understood as a solution to a specific problem. Once the principles are understood, so this approach goes, the replicatee will be able to find their own way to successfully implement the routines which does not entail copying precisely. Birnholtz et al. (2007), for example, have shown in their study of the regeneration of a children's summer camp that the principles underpinning the routines were embodied in artifacts, such as the salad table and the flagpole, as well as in the memories of key actors who revived the routines that made up the organizational character. Baden-Fuller and Winter's (2005) central thesis is that often 'organizations adopt some combination of two contrasting ["Principles" and "Templates"] strategies or approaches' (Baden-Fuller and Winter, 2005: 4).

20.2.2 Synthesis

Researchers drawing on the capability perspective on routines replication have developed a number of concrete theoretical concepts, covering the main steps and pitfalls typically involved in a transfer project. While this perspective is generally regarded as a useful approach, some of its basic assumptions have been subsequently criticized by authors in the stream of Routines Dynamics.

A first critique has been that the research has tended to focus mostly on organizations with simple business model formats (such as food franchises) that are not driven by rapid or sustained innovation (D'Adderio, 2014). Second, the focus of the capability perspective on the high-level aspects of transfer, and the reduction of routines to opaque black boxes, has meant that the roles of social (e.g., actors) and material (e.g., artifacts) features of replication have been left in the background (D'Adderio, 2014). We therefore conclude that, while the work of Nelson and Winter (1982), and the authors around them, has provided an abstract, general understanding of the main aspects of replication, this displayed limitations. In more recent years, a new perspective has emerged which responds to these concerns by bringing a micro-level and dynamic understanding of routines replication which complements the capability-oriented approach.

20.3 Replication from a Practice Perspective: Transfer as Re-Creation

The shift to a dynamic understanding of routines was pioneered in a transformative article by Feldman and Pentland (2003) published in *Administrative Science Quarterly*. This approach adopts an entirely different set of methodologies (namely the ethnographic methodology based on studying of the observable practice of actors, see chapter by Dittrich [Chapter 8], this volume), as well as different theoretical tools (namely, the theories of practices – see chapters by Feldman [Chapter 2] and Sele [Chapter 6], this volume).

Authors in the field of Routine Dynamics have focused on the socio-material (see chapter by D'Adderio [Chapter 7], this volume) and micro-dynamic aspects through which routines are performed and replicated (D'Adderio, 2014, 2017; D'Adderio and Pollock, 2020). They demonstrate that transferring routines involves the effortful enactment of the complex socio-material entanglement which underpins a routine. By focusing on the 'how', these authors theorize replication as a form of dynamic re-creation, rather than straightforward transfer of routines, as assumed in the capability perspective.

While building on and adding to the previous foundational strands of replication studies, D'Adderio (2014) is able to shed light on the replication dilemma by drawing on the lens of Routine Dynamics (Feldman and Pentland, 2003). Combining interests in ethnography and in practice theory, her work is influenced by Latour's 'model of translation' and his observation '*it is not difference across routines that needs to be explained but sameness (Latour, 1986)*' (D'Adderio and Pollock, 2020: 2).

The work of Luciana D'Adderio (2011, 2014, 2017) is a cornerstone in this new way of approaching routine replication. The article 'The replication dilemma unraveled: How organizations enact multiple goals in routine transfer', published in *Organization Science* in 2014, examines the exact replication of a complex computer server product and the related manufacturing capabilities. As compared to earlier approaches, D'Adderio's research analyzes a different type of setting characterized by complexity and uncertainty where innovation is important, but where copying exactly remains central, at least in the short term (D'Adderio, 2014). Her research shows how organizations address the 'replication dilemma' by invoking communities and artifacts that simultaneously and selectively enact the two contrasting organizational goals of alignment/replication and innovation/adaptation (D'Adderio, 2014).

D'Adderio's work proposes that socio-material features of context play an active roles in replication: artifacts evolve and change during the course of replication as a consequence of their involvement in performative struggles among contrasting organizational goals (innovation and replication). Thus, for D'Adderio (2017), physical or digital artifacts are no longer simple intermediaries (see Latour, 2005 for distinction) within the transfer but have roles more similar to mediators. This means that material features, rather than being passive representations, can directly influence replication and contribute to shaping and reshaping routines in far more fundamental ways than scholars have previously acknowledged (D'Adderio, 2017). D'Adderio's work, finally, enabled us to account for the combined influence of actors and artifacts, rather than simply invoking the role of human agency in replicating routines (D'Adderio, 2017). This understanding captures the more complex, micro-level Routine Dynamics, and advances the characterization of routines transfer as an effortful and distributed replication process (D'Adderio, 2014; Pentland and Rueter, 1994).

D'Adderio opens the opaque black box of routine replication by integrating socio-materiality into Routine Dynamics, and paves the way for other scholars to capture and recognize the role of ingenuity, know-how, tools and instruments in the replication process (Table 20.1). Mobilizing D'Adderio's shift and drawing on the Routine Dynamics lens, these authors explore how routine replication is performed in various socio-material contexts, providing additional evidence of the effortful character of replication and the dynamic and emergent nature of routines re-creation. Table 20.1 summarizes these articles while explaining how they address replication in different settings through different enactments.

By focusing on the micro level dynamics and the 'how' of replication, scholars inspired by Routine Dynamics favour deep and extended empirical investigations which add subtlety and nuance to the first phase of replication studies (Winter and Szulanski, 2001; Winter et al., 2012). In particular, the in-depth analysis of replication based on the study of routines and practices has highlighted the fundamental importance of actors and their efforts involved in re-creating routines; of the role of context in re-creating routines; the cultural aspects of transfer; and different strategies for re-creating routines.

20.3.1 The Role of Actors and Their Efforts in Re-Creating Routines

By taking a closer look at routines transfer, Routine Dynamics scholars have uncovered the important role of actors in performing the replicated routines and related micro-practices. The transfer process itself continues to be of interest, but a key emphasis is now on the actor's capacity for action, such as the role of steering teams during the transfer. Routine Dynamics studies have shown that there are many roles and mandates for those who are in charge of coordinating transfer. In the studies of D'Adderio (2014) and Bertels et al. (2016), for example, coordinating actors and communities can steer routine participants towards innovation or replication, or both but to different extents

Table 20.1 Spectrum of research on replication strategies

Authors	Research settings and highlights	Routines replication strategy
D'Adderio (2014)	Analysis of a supercomputer replication to the UK branch of a US high-end electronics world-leading innovator. Focusing on the 'how', the article highlights the effortful and creative aspect of routine replication, demonstrating the entanglement of artifacts and organizational communities embedded in routines to be replicated.	Routine replication participants address the competing pressures toward innovation and replication by enacting different goals, at different times and in different proportions ('selective performance': 1345). Heterogeneous configurations of artifacts and people (assemblages) support one pattern or another.
Aroles and McLean (2016)	Analysis of a printing factory where two industry standard organizational routines are introduced and replicated in order to standardize and reduce ink usage while assessing the quality of the copies published. Focus is on repeatability in practice, showing that there are socio-material or sociotechnical mediations underlying the process of repetition.	Empirical findings show mixed reactions to the changes introduced as they challenge roles, understandings of purpose and professional autonomy and integrity recognition. Repeatability requires the assembling of 'intensive forces, the shaping of extensive forms, the performance of different scripts, practices of simplifications and amplification, matters of fact and matters of concern' (544).
Bertels et al. (2016)	Analysis of the integration of an operational compliance routine used by oil industry peers. Focus on routine replication in a company where the organizational culture is poorly aligned with the discipline required for operational compliance.	The authors describe the workarounds devised by routines participants and show that deviations from the espoused routine are accompanied by additional patterns of action. Through the concept of cultural shielding (582), the authors depict actions aimed at cultural protection, a process by which employees use a cultural strategy to hide and protect their successful solutions even though they are not aligned with the routine to be adopted.
Bucher and Langley (2016)	Analysis of the large-scale change initiative to implement new patient routines from the beginning to the end of a hospital treatment process in pluralistic settings. Highlights the concept of spaces while introducing a new routine on a pre-existing conception of how to perform it.	Actors create two types of 'spaces' in which they deliberately engage in order to modify both their previous and new/expected performances (performative aspect) as well as the abstract understandings (ostensive aspect) that are attached to the new routine. Reflection spaces are aimed at developing new conceptualizations of a routine. Experimental spaces support the integration of new actions into routine performances by situating them in the original routine. These two spaces contribute to change in a complementary way and must be implemented iteratively in relation to each other.
Danner-Schröder and Geiger (2016)	Analysis of training processes for rescuers in a catastrophe management organization. Focus on the training practice developed to assure on site replication of effective rescuing routines despite chaotic conditions that rescuers will have to face once on site.	Authors show which mechanisms are enacted to maintain patterning work. Rescuers carry out aligning and prioritizing activities when they perceive the routine as stable and enact selecting and recombining activities when they perceive the routine as flexible. Authors point out the role of training and knowing in the re-creation of the base camp set up routines.
Blanche and Cohendet (2019)	Analysis of a ballet remounting seen as a replication of interrelated routines (dance, music and set design) focusing on the choreographer's intent. Highlights the roles of trades culture, memories and experiential knowledge carried by the actors involved in the routine to be replicated and the routine transfer itself.	Authors describe the existence of a professional meta-routine that imposes common temporality and key milestones on each of the trades sub-routines, thus enabling the transfer. The artistic team's reliance on its embodied memories and experiential knowledge of the work enables the transfer of tacit parts and guides adjustments imposed by the local context. The replication dilemma is solved by letting local teams be innovative in order to recreate routines on site.

Table 20.1 ***(cont.)***

Authors	Research settings and highlights	Routines replication strategy
Boe-Lillegraven (2019)	Analysis of the transfer of multiple related framing routines in a highly complex environment, where both replicator and replicatee present strong national and organizational structure and cultural differences. Highlights a work process, which involves splitting the transfer task into smaller chunks in order to adapt the transfer as it progresses.	Author shows how actors, engaged in the transfer process, adopt a pragmatic and flexible approach. Coordinating actors conceive new ideas on how to accomplish the transfer as they realize and respond to multiple stakeholders' interests engaged in the transfer. They gradually shift from transfer understood as exact replication to transfer as adaptation.
Kiwan and Lazaric (2019)	Analysis of the introduction of robotic bariatric surgery routines mediated by a new technological artifact. Highlights how the local team creates practices to adapt and recreate routines coordination in order to perform the interdependent actions of a surgery.	Authors show that to re-create a routinized socio-material ensemble the creation of two types of space are required: one experimental space and one reflective space in which both the ostensive and performative dimensions of routines are going to be questioned and temporarily redesigned.
Schmidt et al. (2019)	Analysis of a prototyping routine from an incubator that has been replicated across different ventures in order to generate novelty. Highlights how routines replication can support innovation.	Authors present two types of routines: • Innovation routines as a central process for finding new products, services or business models. • Acceleration routines support and free the basic innovation process from hindering activities. The interaction between innovation and acceleration routines during replication allows rapid (inter-) organizational scale-up as well as rapid exploration of new products, services or business models.
Sonenshein (2016)	Analysis of replication at branches of a midsize retail organization. Highlights replicating the outcome over the strict replication of specific routines in order to attain a desired and recognizable shop ambiance on an ongoing basis.	Author shows how participants are enabled to replicate outcomes that allow an organization to achieve recognizable creativity on an ongoing basis. Actors are asked to skilfully integrate their idiosyncratic backgrounds and experiences into the routine performances. Artifacts, auxiliary routines, external comparisons, as well as personalizing and depersonalizing, enable them to accomplish familiar novelty.
D'Adderio and Pollock (2020)	Analysis of the exact transfer of a supercomputer at a contemporary high technology organization within a world leading innovation company. Highlights how similarity and singularity involve the coordination of multiple socio-material enactments within and across 'sites.'	Authors show that in a highly demanding context where similarity matters, but uncertainty and complexity are substantial and pervasive, organizations enact two sets of 'repairing practices' and 'distributing practices' in order to recreate routines.

(D'Adderio, 2014). In Boe-Lillegraven (2019) coordinators abandon their initial focus on exact routine replication as they struggle to proceed with the transfer project. As they learn about the characteristics of their new environment, they decide to shift strategy from a transfer-as-replication to a transfer-as-adaptation. In Blanche and Cohendet (2019) the steering team, composed of individuals representing the trades that constitute a ballet, acted as the guarantor of the spirit of the routine to be replicated and, helped validate what was proposed by the local teams.

Authors from across the replication spectrum also converge around the finding that re-creation involves substantial effort by actors, in all but the simplest transfer conditions (D'Adderio and Pollock, 2020). Since routines coordinate actions and support truces among routines participants, routine replicas must be adapted to achieve similar coordination and efficiency. Spaces for experimentation and for reflection support the efforts of participants in re-creating and sustaining similarity (Blanche and Cohendet, 2019; Bucher and Langley, 2019; Kiwan and Lazaric, 2019). Meaning is recreated through shared stories and experiences ensuring the re-creation of cohesion among participants while performing a routine (Bucher and Langley, 2019; D'Adderio and Pollock, 2020; Kiwan and Lazaric, 2019).

20.3.2 The Role of Context in Transferring Routines

The contributions listed in Table 20.1 capture a range of empirical creative and pragmatic approaches to transfer as enacted in different contexts. The fact that routines are not simply 'embedded in' but are 'enacted through' context (D'Adderio, 2014: 1347) has prompted scholars to focus on the dynamics features of context, including human and material agencies. Researchers find that actors and artifacts, as part of wider socio-material assemblages (D'Adderio, 2014, 2017), help create or recreate the fit between the routine and its new context, by acting on the context and/or on the routine itself. For example, articles detail how actors help ensure that the local context is ready to enact the transferred routine. The authors in Table 20.1, for example, mention the introduction of training to acquire technical and practical knowledge (Boe-Lillegraven, 2019) or to prepare their bodies for action (Blanche and Cohendet, 2019; Danner-Schröder and Geiger, 2016). Artifacts can be adopted or designed to enable replicatees to understand the elements for recreating familiarity (Sonenshein, 2016) or communicate specific features of the original context (Blanche and Cohendet, 2019; Boe-Lillegraven, 2019). They enable replicatees to create an ideal context for the transfered routine to be performed. This work can be done prior to the transfer (Danner-Schröder and Geiger, 2016) and/or afterwards, as and when incompatibilities between contexts are discovered (Blanche and Cohendet, 2019; Boe-Lillegraven, 2019).

20.3.3 Cultural Aspects of Routine Transfer

Special attention has also been paid to the cultural aspects of replication, or how local communities and cultures (D'Adderio, 2014), organizational culture (Aroles and McLean, 2016; Bertels et al., 2016) and national culture (Boe-Lillegraven, 2019) can influence the re-creation of routines. When unconsciously pursuing different goals, actors may be influenced by different cultures. Bertels et al. (2016), for example, reported that replicating a routine can lead to more complex performances of action patterns than originally intended. In the process of recreating the routine, routine participants do additional work as they try to accommodate the misalignment between their culture and that embedded in the replicated routine (Howard-Grenville and Lodge [Chapter 16], in this handbook). Organizational members therefore rely on cultural action strategies when integrating a routine that is not aligned with the new context.

In addition, authors have shown that the introduction of a new routine has an impact on a whole series of hidden symbolic and pragmatic aspects that revolve around the performance itself (Aroles and McLean, 2016; Kiwan and Lazaric, 2019). In Aroles and McLean, for instance, the introduction of a routine that met industry standards provoked mixed reactions since it questioned the very meaning of the work of those performing it.

20.3.4 Strategies for Re-Creating Routines

A closer look at the work being done to replicate routines also reveales that actors might employ a variety of strategies for re-creating routines in different contexts. Both Boe-Lillegraven (2019) and Blanche and Cohendet (2019) identify how actors split the transfer task into subtasks or subroutines and later integrate these different aspects back together. Boe-Lillegraven (2019) describes how the coordinating actors split their work into smaller chunks based on artifacts, people and actions. In Blanche and Cohendet (2019), similarly, the steering team separated the transfer of a ballet into subroutines drawing on organizational subcultures such as music, dance and production.

Studies have also shown that, in some cases, a routine may be subject to modification while still being transferred. When the emphasis is mainly on the abstract principles underlying replication, for instance, some routines may be allowed to change early on in the replication process. For example, choreographic patterns in Blanche and Cohendet (2019) were allowed to change, provided they respected the choreographer's intent. In this case, change involves trusting the local actor's judgement. Similarly, in Sonenshein (2016), participants in the merchandising routine were allowed to introduce novelty based on their idiosyncratic backgrounds as long as they adhered to certain guidelines that ensure familiarity across all replicatees.

More recently, some authors have theorized the micro-level, sociomaterial practices that organizations develop in order to achieve 'sameness' across routines (D'Adderio and Pollock, 2020: 5). Practices that help achieve 'sameness' include '*repairing*' practices, which encompass all the activities enacted by practitioners to reduce any differences between the origin and destination routine; and '*distributing*' practices, which acknowledge but embrace and control any differences between origin and destination. These practices are necessary to support routines replication, as the performance of a routine in a new context is unknown and similarity can only ever be an emergent and challenged outcome (D'Adderio and Pollock, 2020).

20.3.5 Synthesis

Adopting a Routine Dynamics lens and a perspective based on socio-material enactment allows researchers to highlight how actors and artifacts can alter both the context and the routine being replicated. This perspective tells us that routines re-creation (as in the practice perspective), more than straightforward replication (as in the capability perspective), is taking place. No matter where replication is positioned on the spectrum going from very simple to very complex, it involves embracing difference. Accepting and incorporating dissimilarity, while counterintuitive, is in fact intrinsic to successful replication (D'Adderio and Pollock, 2020).

20.4 Conclusion and Avenues for Future Research

The aim of this chapter has been to outline the contribution of Routines Dynamics to the topic of replication. We have first described the view of replication theorizing inspired by a capabilities approach which viewed transfer from an elevated perspective. We then looked at a second view, influenced by Routines Dynamics, where a closer look at practice is enabling researchers to identify how routines may be re-created across various contexts. These studies have suggested (in contrast with Nelson and Winter, 1982; Szulanski and Winter, 2002; Winter and Szulanski, 2001) that some extent of 're-creation' always underpins replication, even in the most demanding contexts. The work of recreating similarity, being in tune with the context and embracing its diversity in ways that leave sufficient scope for – or indeed actively support similarity as in D'Adderio and Pollock (2020) – are key processes which require further investigation, thus opening many research avenues.

One main avenue could explore in depth the influence of materiality and human actors in shaping replication, understood as an emergent achievement, produced by heterogeneous configurations of actors and artifacts. While the role of actors has traditionally been framed, in the capability view of replication, from a primarily abstract perspective, in the practice perspective we can ask questions about the experiences of these actors, including: how do routine participants experience re-creation emotionally and physically? What do they get from engaging in an act of routine replication? How can we explore the sensorimotor and neuro-cognitive mechanisms that animate routine participants? How can the symbolic disruption experienced by participants in the new routine be anticipated? How are performative phenomenology and tacit knowledge involved in replication? Does characterizing the position of the actors in the replication of the routine (i.e., those who plan it and/or those who perform it) and their room to manoeuvre in the re-creation process have an impact on the outcome of the replication? Concerning the artifacts, what are the concrete impacts on the practice of replication of technological artifacts that blur the boundaries between body and object? What role does artificial intelligence play in the replication of organizational routines?

A second avenue for future research concerns the implication of new environments on the re-creation of routines in a dynamic perspective. In this chapter we have emphasized the role of culture and the specific role of actors, but there are many additional dimensions that require further investigation. In particular, recreating routines can be viewed as a distributed phenomenon, especially in contexts of replication and re-creation of socially dispersed routines. For instance, how to replicate routines in times of uncertainty, when the context is no longer comprehensible as we are experiencing in the COVID-19 crisis? In all previous approaches, the transfer of routines is assumed to be centrally coordinated, but increasingly in distributed social contexts, separate sets of actors in different locations try to establish very similar types of routines and draw from each other's experiences as a form of distributed phenomenon. For example, in the context of the recent pandemic, different groups and communities of citizens in different locations of the same country have experienced new practices of teleworking; new practices to help and protect elderly people; or new virtual ways to conduct family gatherings.

A third main avenue is to better understand the core social issues that animate the replication and re-creation of routines. The initial interest in routine replication which characterized the early replication studies had been conceived in an economic context marked by growth and the advent of global competition. This was based on the hypothesis that resources would be made available. However, recent years have seen the emergence of an ecological crisis (George et al., 2016; Howard-Grenville et al., 2019) followed by the recognition that resources need to be used sustainably. Routine Dynamics so far has not questioned the purpose of the replication. A historical analysis of the literature and the replication construct can afford us critical reflexivity and the theoretical possibility to extend the scope of the conceivable and the feasible, thus opening up avenues for future research that are relevant to the future of our planet and our communities. It seems appropriate, for example, to consider the new paradigm marked by the ecological crisis and to anticipate how this new situation could influence theorization of routines transfer and replication. What and why are we replicating? Is replication possible in a highly uncertain context characterized by the game-changing consciousness of new ecology conditions and the recent upheavals faced by organizations? Researching these and other questions calls for philosophical openness and interdisciplinary efforts to rethink replication as anchored in a theoretical context that is not only organizational or industrial but also socio-historical and eco-biological.

References

Aroles, J. and McLean, C. (2016). Rethinking stability and change in the study of organizational routines: Difference and repetition in a newspaper-printing factory. *Organization Science*, 27(3), 535–550.

Baden-Fuller, C. and Winter, S. G. (2005). Replicating organizational knowledge: rinciples or templates? (No. 0515). Papers on Economics and Evolution.

Bertels, S., Howard-Grenville, J. and Pek, S. (2016). Cultural molding, shielding, and shoring at Oilco: The role of culture in the integration of routines. *Organization Science*, 27(3), 573–593.

Birnholtz, J. P., Cohen, M. D. and Hoch, S. V. (2007). Organizational character: On the Regeneration of Camp Poplar Grove. *Organization Science*, 18(2), 315–332.

Blanche, C. and Cohendet, P. (2019). *Remounting a Ballet in a Different Context: A Complementary Understanding of Routines Transfer Theories. Routine Dynamics in Action: Replication and Transformation* (Research in the Sociology of Organizations, Volume 61). Bingley: Emerald Publishing Limited, pp. 11–30.

Boe-Lillegraven, S. (2019). *Transferring Routines across Multiple Boundaries: A Flexible Approach. Routine Dynamics in Action: Replication and Transformation* (Research in the Sociology of Organizations, Volume 61). Bingley: Emerald Publishing Limited, pp. 31–53.

Bucher, S. and Langley, A. (2016). The interplay of reflective and experimental spaces in interrupting and reorienting routine dynamics. *Organization Science*, 27(3), 594–613.

Collins, H. M. (2005). What is tacit knowledge? In *The Practice Turn in Contemporary Theory*. Oxford: Routledge, pp. 115–128.

Collins, H. (2007). Bicycling on the moon: Collective tacit knowledge and somatic-limit tacit knowledge. *Organization Studies*, 28(2), 257–262.

Cyert, R. M. and March, J. G. (1963). *A Behavioral Theory of the Firm*. Engelwood Cliffs, NJ: Prentice-Hall.

D'Adderio, L. (2008). The performativity of routines: Theorising the influence of artefacts and distributed agencies on routines dynamics. *Research Policy*, 37(5), 769–789.

D'Adderio, L. (2011). Artifacts at the centre of routines: Performing the material turn in routines theory. *Journal of Institutional Economics*, 7 (2), 197–230.

D'Adderio, L. (2014). The replication dilemma unravelled: How organizations enact multiple goals in routine transfer. *Organization Science*, 25(5), 1325–1350.

D'Adderio, L. (2017). Performativity and the innovation–replication dilemma. In *The Elgar Companion to Innovation and Knowledge Creation*. Cheltenham: Edward Elgar Publishing.

D'Adderio, L. and Pollock, N. (2020). Making routines the same: Crafting similarity and singularity in routines transfer. *Research Policy*, 49(8), 104029.

Danner-Schröder, A. and Geiger, D. (2016). Unravelling the motor of patterning work: Toward an understanding of the microlevel dynamics of standardization and flexibility. *Organization Science*, 27(3), 633–658.

Feldman, M. S. and Pentland, B. T. (2003). Reconceptualizing organizational routines as a source of flexibility and change. *Administrative Science Quarterly*, 48(1), 94–118.

George, G., Howard-Grenville, J., Joshi, A. and Tihanyi, L. (2016). Understanding and tackling societal grand challenges through management research. *Academy of Management Journal*, 59(6), 1880–1895. DOI: 10.5465/amj.2016.4007.

Howard-Grenville, J., Davis, G. F., Dyllick, T., Miller, C. C., Thau, S. and Tsui, A. S. (2019). Sustainable development for a better world: Contributions of leadership, management, and organizations. *Academy of Management Discoveries*, 5(4), 355–366. DOI: 10.5465/amd.2019.0275.

Jensen, R. J. and Szulanski, G. (2007). Template use and the effectiveness of knowledge transfer. *Management Science*, 53(11), 1716–1730.

Kiwan, L. and Lazaric, N. (2019). Learning a new ecology of space and looking for new routines: Experimenting robotics in a surgical team. In *Routine Dynamics in Action: Replication and Transformation*. Bingley: Emerald Publishing Limited.

Latour, B. (2005). *Reassembling the Social: An Introduction to Actor Network Theory*. Oxford: Oxford University Press.

March, J. S. and Simon, H. A. (1958). *HA (1958) Organizations*. New York: Wiley.

Nelson, R. R. and Sidney, G. (2005). *Winter 1982: An Evolutionary Theory of Economic Change*. Cambridge, MA: Belknap Press of Harvard University Press.

Nelson, R. R. and Winter S. G. (1982). *An Evolutionary Theory of Economic Change*. Cambridge, MA: Harvard University Press.

Parmigiani, A. and Howard-Grenville, J. (2011). Routines revisited: Exploring the capabilities and practice perspectives. *Academy of Management Annals*, 5(1), 413–453.

Pentland, B. T. and Rueter, H. H. (1994). Organizational routines as grammars of action. *Administrative Science Quarterly*, 484–510.

Schmidt, T., Braun, T. and Sydow, J. (2019). Copying routines for new venture creation: How replication can support entrepreneurial innovation. *Research in Sociology of Organizations*,(61), 55–78.

Sonenshein, S. (2016). Routines and creativity: From dualism to duality. *Organization Science*, 27(3), 739–758.

Stene, E. O. 1940. An approach to a science of administration. *American Political Science Review*, 34(6), 1124–1137.

Szulanski, G. (1996). Exploring internal stickiness: Impediments to the transfer of best practice within the firm. *Strategic Management Journal*, 17(S2), 27–43.

Szulanski, G. and Jensen, R. J. (2004). Overcoming stickiness: An empirical investigation of the role of the template in the replication of organizational routines. *Managerial and Decision Economics*, 25(6–7), 347–363.

Szulanski, G. and Jensen, R. J. (2008). Growing through copying: The negative consequences of innovation on franchise network growth. *Research Policy*, 37(10), 1732–1741.

Szulanski, G. and Winter, S. (2002). Getting it right the second time. *Harvard Business Review*, 80 (1), 62–69.

Winter, S. G. and Szulanski, G. (2001). Replication as strategy. *Organization Science*, 12(6), 730–743.

Winter, S. G., Szulanski, G., Ringov, D. and Jensen, R. J. (2012). Reproducing knowledge: Inaccurate replication and failure in franchise organizations. *Organization Science*, 23(3), 672–685.

CHAPTER 21

Innovation Work and Routine Dynamics

FLEUR DEKEN AND KATHRIN SELE

Innovation work refers to the process of developing new outcomes, including technologies, products, and services (Garud, Tuertscher and Van de Ven, 2013). As organizations face pressures to innovate their core offerings at an ever faster pace, many organizations attempt to routinize innovation work (see e.g., Hargadon, 2005). In this chapter, we focus on organizational routines for doing innovation work rather than innovation and change within routines. In what follows, we first discuss why routines and innovation are often considered an unlikely couple. We then conceptualize innovation work and provide a brief overview of the unique characteristics and current debates within this stream of literature, before we review studies of innovation work that adopted a Routine Dynamics perspective. Following this overview, we show how Routine Dynamics scholars have benefited from studying innovation processes and how innovation scholars have benefited from adopting a Routine Dynamics perspective. We conclude by identifying opportunities for future research.

21.1 Innovation and Routines: An Unlikely Couple?

Scholars and practitioners alike have often assumed a sharp distinction between 'routine' and 'innovation' tasks (e.g., Burns and Stalker, 1961; Obstfeld, 2012; Tushman and OReilly, 1996), suggesting that routines are the antithesis of innovation (Amabile, 1997; Ford and Gioia, 2000). This dichotomous view is in line with how organizational scholars have traditionally conceptualized firm behaviour, such as by separating exploitation and exploration (March, 1991); stability and change (Farjoun, 2010); and efficiency and flexibility (Adler, Goldoftas and Levine, 1999). The same distinction has been made for routines and innovation (Becker, 2004) based on the conviction that the flexibility required for innovation is undermined by routinization (Bartunek et al., 2007) – and maybe also because the word 'routine' connotes inertia (Hannan and Freeman, 1984) and mindlessness (Ashforth and Fried, 1988). Thus, how organizations 'get routine things done' is often juxtaposed with 'how [organizations] pursue markedly new things through creative projects' (Obstfeld, 2012: 1571).

Pointing to the importance of engaging with the relationship of 'routine behavior and innovation', Nelson and Winter (1982: 129) suggested that firms can develop meta-routines (i.e., heuristics and strategies) to enable innovation and renewal. Such meta-routines change and direct other routines, which enhances the overall performance of innovation tasks (Adler et al., 1999: 43), as routinization may free up the cognitive space and provide the stability necessary for innovation work (Becker and Zirpoli, 2009; Ohly et al., 2006). Building on these ideas, several scholars have identified specific standardized processes and procedures for innovation, or what Pavitt (2002) refers to as 'innovation routines', that are meant to systematize innovation work and creative processes. For example, studies in innovation management have reported on specific rules and standard operating procedures (SOPs) that enable firms to effectively develop product and service innovations (e.g., Cooper, 2008; Griffin, 1997).

This line of research has pointed at a more nuanced relationship between routines and innovation, according to which the routinization and systematization of innovation work facilitates, rather than inhibits, the development of innovations. However, we still lack important insight into the inner workings of such routines, because many scholars have treated innovation routines as stable entities – seeing them as univocal and persistent – in their efforts to investigate antecedents of innovation routines and overall effects on innovation tasks. This assumption is challenged by detailed empirical studies on innovation work. For example, Christiansen and Varnes (2009) found that the translation of pre-defined SOPs and rules into daily practices happens in a much more flexible way than previously assumed, and may involve alterations, modifications and even the abandoning of rules and SOPs altogether.

Whereas many organizational routines are oriented at generating consistency in outcomes, innovation routines enable generating novel outcomes time and again. To enable a deeper understanding of how innovation routines enable novel outcomes, we do not only need more research that takes a processual perspective on innovation work in general (e.g., Burgelman, 1983; Garud et al., 2011; Garud and Rappa, 1994; Van de Ven et al., 1999) but also research that accounts for the internal dynamics of routines (Feldman et al., 2016). Routine Dynamics is uniquely suited for this purpose as it provides the conceptual resources for uncovering the inner workings of innovation routines; for studying the interplay of interdependencies between actors and actions over time (Deken et al., 2016; Sele and Grand, 2016); and for disentangling formal SOPs from actual routines (D'Adderio, 2008). By distinguishing the artifact that represents a routine from the actual enactment of that routine (D'Adderio, 2011), we are able to see the interplay between the performative qualities of SOPs; i.e., how SOPs shape enactments of the routine and the agency involved in such enactments. In this sense, SOPs are blueprints for action, but do not equal such actions. A useful analogy is to consider a SOP as a sourdough starter: it is a key ingredient for the act of baking bread and, therefore, it does not fully encapsulate the practice (Pentland and Feldman, 2005) nor is it separate from it (D'Adderio, 2008).

21.2 Characterizing Innovations-in-the-Making

Innovation has often been conceptualized as a particular outcome such as a novel product, process, service or technology. Instead, we adopt a process view of innovation that focuses on the actions taken to support 'the invention, development, and implementation of new ideas' in organizations (Garud et al., 2013), which emphasizes that innovation work is characterized by emergence, dispersed collaboration between heterogeneous actors and novelty (e.g., Dougherty, 1992; Jelinek and Schoonhoven, 1990).

21.2.1 Emergence

Innovation work is characterized by emergence because the 'object of innovation' – the novel service, product, process or technology – remains 'in-the-making' for sustained periods and only gradually becomes manifest over time. Over the course of the innovation process, multiple 'intermediate outcomes' are produced that remain incomplete, underspecified and ambiguous (Bijker, 1995; Garud et al., 1997). However, through such intermediate outcomes (e.g., sketches, scenarios, prototypes or simulations) the innovation-in-the-making increasingly materializes (D'Adderio, 2001; Deken and Lauche, 2014; Van de Ven et al., 1999).

The emergent characteristics of innovation-in-the-making can explain why innovation scholars have taken a central role in the development of processual approaches in the field of organization studies (Garud et al., 2013; Van de Ven et al., 1999; Van de Ven and Poole, 1990) and contributed to the broader shift from studying 'outcomes' to 'processes' (chapter by Tsoukas [Chapter 3], this volume). Innovation process scholars have shown how innovations emerge through sequences of actions and events and found that innovation work progresses in multiple emergent paths and often involves false-starts and dead ends (Van de Ven et al., 1999). Particularly in earlier stages, the envisioned innovation is likely to change multiple times and often even radically so. Process studies on innovation have thus emphasized the innovators' intentional efforts that are needed to ensure that an early, ill-defined idea materializes and is eventually implemented (Akrich et al., 2002). Because the properties and structure of innovations are not known in advance, actors need to adapt their course of action over time (Simon, 1973) and rely on experimentation and learning along the way (D'Adderio, 2001; Rerup and Feldman, 2011; Thomke, 1998).

21.2.2 Dispersed Collaboration between Heterogeneous Actors

Innovation work is typically performed by various heterogeneous actors who come from different knowledge, functional backgrounds, communities or thought worlds (Adler, 1995; Barley, 1986; Dougherty, 1992). The diversity inherent in such dispersed collaborations provides a fertile ground for making creative recombinations and sparking new ideas for innovation (e.g., Hargadon and Sutton, 1997; Woodman et al., 1993). Moreover, as various aspects have to be considered for the development process of new products, diverse knowledge from functions such as manufacturing, sales, marketing and engineering is required (Wheelwright and Clark, 1992).

The involvement of heterogeneous actors, however, implies that different thought worlds and practices come into play that may complicate collaboration (Carlile, 2002, 2004; Dougherty, 1992; Harvey, 2013). Actors will have different perceptions of the innovation and all of them will hold an incomplete view of it (Deken and Lauche, 2014; Van de Ven, 1986). Any source of difference between actors may become – often unexpectedly – consequential for performing the innovation work and may result in breakdowns of the collaboration (Carlile, 2002, 2004). Innovation scholars who adopt a practice perspective (see chapter by Feldman [Chapter 2], this volume) have shown the intricate complexities of collaborating across boundaries and the resulting need for translation work (Bechky, 2003; Brown and Duguid, 1991; Carlile, 2002, 2004; Dougherty, 1992; Nicolini, 2010; Nicolini et al., 2012). In such collaborations, routines play a central part in coordinating the involvement of diverse actors; for example, by providing a shared means to engage over and strive for (Adler, 1995; Jarzabkowski et al., 2012; Okhuysen and Bechky, 2009; Salvato and Rerup, 2018).

21.2.3 Novelty

The novelty associated with innovation-in-the-making often renders innovation work illegitimate (Dougherty and Heller, 1994; Kannan-Narasimhan, 2014; Van Dijk et al., 2011). Actors' intentional efforts are needed to resolve and push the innovation-in-the-making from an early, ill-defined idea to becoming materialized and accepted by internal and external audiences (Hargadon and Douglas, 2001; Kannan-Narasimhan and Lawrence, 2018). For that reason, Bartel and Garud (2009) stress the importance of communicative actions in creating legitimacy for what is considered new.

To address the challenges associated with these characteristics of innovation work, many firms have developed extensive SOPs that are meant to coordinate innovation work (Cooper, 2008; Griffin, 1997; Kahn et al., 2013). These SOPs have been identified as important capabilities for firms that enable innovation over time (e.g., Cooper, 1996; Eisenhardt and Martin, 2000). SOPs have become widespread, as exemplified by various generations of gated development processes (Cohendet and Simon, 2016; Cooper, 2008) and are often seen as codified 'best' practices for organizing innovation work (D'Adderio, 2008). The extent to which SOPs are important for successful innovation and whether the level of detail in SOPs and the rigidness of application hampers or facilitates coordinating innovation work have been subject to debate in the innovation management literature (Cooper and Kleinschmidt, 1991; Griffin, 1997; Shaw et al., 2001).

21.3 A Routine Dynamics Perspective on Innovation Work

Routine Dynamics has provided fertile ground to study the relationship between routines and innovation work. With the reconceptualization of routines as endogenously dynamic, Feldman and Pentland (2003) not only opened the space to consider the possibility of change but also of innovation. This possibility emerges from the notion of multiplicity, which implies that routines not only 'occur in multiples' (i.e., in networks) but they 'entail multiple actions (performative

Table 21.1 Key differences between evolutionary economics and Routine Dynamics studies on innovation routines

	Evolutionary Econ perspective (Nelson and Winter, 1982)	Routine Dynamics perspective (Feldman and Pentland, 2003)
Main interest	Which routines lead to innovation outcomes and how to best design innovation routines	How routines facilitate innovating
Focal level of analysis	Innovation outcomes	Innovation-in-the-making (processes and practices)
Empirical attention to	Differences between routines (e.g., routine tasks vs. creative tasks)	Routines enactments
Assumptions on routines for innovation	Only specific routines (i.e., meta-routines) implicated in innovation work Routines free space for innovation tasks and might get into the way of flexibility/ creativity	Routines performed in networks enable innovation to occur, mundaneness not in contradiction with innovation/creativity Routines as integral part of innovation work, inseparable from the actions
Relationship between innovation and routines	Seen as dichotomous Innovation work and creative processes can be systematized, routinization through stable SOPs	Seen as two sides of the same coin Creating potentialities for action through an emerging repertoire of patterns
Nature of SOPs and relationship with routines	Innovation routines as stable and persistent entities Prescriptive tools for action	Dynamic and generative with different degrees of performativity Mutual adaptation between SOPs and routines
Key references	Adler et al. (1999) Bartunek et al. (2007) Becker and Zirpoli (2009) Obstfeld (2012) Ohly et al. (2006) Pavitt (2002)	D'Adderio (2008, 2011) Deken et al. (2016) Cohendet and Simon (2016) Salvato (2009) Sele and Grand (2016) Sonenshein (2016)

Source: Adapted from Parmigiani and Howard-Grenville (2011: 418).

aspect), multiple patterns (ostensive aspect), and multiple human and non-human actants' (Feldman et al., 2016: 507). In Table 21.1 we summarize the key differences between studies on innovation routines rooted in Routine Dynamics (Feldman and Pentland, 2003) and those building on an evolutionary economics perspective (Nelson and Winter, 1982). Whereas the exemplar references of the latter are introduced in Section 21.1, the Routine Dynamics studies will be summarized in Section 21.3.1.

21.3.1 Empirical Studies of Innovation Routines

A growing body of Routine Dynamics research dealing with innovation routines has emerged since. D'Adderio's (2001, 2008) work has been influential in launching and shaping research on innovation work within Routine Dynamics. Her studies squarely focus on innovation work and address its central aspects, including the role of technology, artifacts, and SOPs to organize the involvement of heterogeneous actors in innovation work. Several other Routine Dynamics scholars followed suit in studying the role of routines in innovation work. Salvato (2009) conducted a longitudinal study of the Italian design company Alessi and how their innovation capability in terms of its new product development process is adaptively renewed over time. He emphasized the role that everyday individual actions and local experimentation play in the continuous strategic renewal of the company. Cohendet and Simon (2016) studied the video game company Ubisoft and how a creativity crisis led them to overturn their traditional innovation process by recombining existing routines. Similarly, in their study of digital innovation in an automotive company, Deken et al. (2016) investigated how the development of a radical innovation shaped the performances of traditional innovation routines and studied consequences of alterations for downstream routine performances. Sele and Grand (2016) studied an AI and robotics laboratory at the University of Zurich, Switzerland, and showed how the situated enactments of routine networks (i.e., routine interactions) led to more or less innovative outcomes. Their findings suggest that interactions between human and non-human actors and, hence, the internal dynamics of networks are an important source for generativity. Finally, in their study on new venture creation, Schmidt et al. (2019) looked at the relationship between routine replication and entrepreneurial innovation and showed how the recursive process of 'unburdening' acts as a key mechanism between innovating routines (e.g., prototyping) and accelerating routines (e.g., legal setup).

These studies not only share a common focus on innovation work but they also reveal the strong routinization of it. Importantly, they point to the important role of mundane actions – as opposed to grand creative acts – in driving the development of innovations-in-the-making. As Sele and Grand (2016: 726) put it when describing their own analytical approach, 'while we were looking for flexibility and change – factors that are commonly attributed to an organization's capacity to innovate – we found recurring action patterns'. Indeed, many of the recurrent actions in innovation are mundane and might even seem irrelevant at first sight. This is an impression shared by many scholars who research innovation. Important recurring actions in and for innovation work include, for example, mundane actions such as freezing the so-called Bill of Materials (D'Adderio, 2008), contacting internal and external designers (Salvato, 2009), ranking partners (Deken et al., 2016), presenting to senior management (Cohendet and Simon, 2016), creating displays for merchandise in fashion stores (Sonenshein, 2016) or drinking beer (Sele and Grand, 2016).

These activities seem, at first sight, unrelated to the often considered highly creative process of innovating but nevertheless are a generative motor behind innovation work. While mundane routines are important drivers of innovation, they are so in their connecting, as actants travel from one routine to another (Sele and Grand, 2016). Depending on how the actants (e.g., research proposals, robots, visitors) are mobilized as the routine is performed, novelty may emerge. Thus, adopting a Routine Dynamics perspective helps to overcome the clear-cut distinction between 'routine' versus 'innovation' activities and helps explain the generativity of such mundane actions; an aspect which is underdeveloped in research focusing on creativity and innovation (Rahman and Barley, 2017).

21.3.2 Understanding Innovation through Actors and Their Actions

Various Routine Dynamics scholars have studied innovation work by focusing on the formalized structures for coordinating innovation work in organizations, or, in other words, the roles of SOPs for innovation. Such formalized innovation routines enable connections between actions performed by dispersed and heterogeneous actors across innovation settings (i.e., from different departments and functional backgrounds).

D'Adderio (2001, 2008) showed how 'the SOP [innovation routine] can provide a common reference point to coordinate heterogeneous knowledge and views across different communities' (2008: 782) and that adaptations are a source of conflict between communities. Her 2001 study unpacks how different organizational communities shape 'the co-evolution between different aspects of routines' (2008: 781) and that changes introduced in any action are likely to have unexpected consequences for other actions. For example, she showed that introducing new technologies in innovation SOPs had far-reaching consequences for up- and downstream actions. It required creating new routines to effectively translate physical into digital prototypes (and vice-versa). The implementation of a new technology surfaced the sometimes conflicting interests of routine participants (i.e., designers, engineers).

Zooming in on the generative properties of routines, D'Adderio (2008) showed that even in innovation SOPs that feature strong control mechanisms, performances of innovation processes often varied. In her study of a complex set of vehicle development projects, she found that the actual performances of the 'Bill of Materials (BoM) freeze' deviated from the associated SOP. For example, some actions that were usually part of the freezing routine were delayed, thereby bypassing the rule codified in the SOP (D'Adderio, 2008). This provides a more nuanced view on the relation between SOPs and actual performances which emphasizes that SOPs and formal rules do not determine actual performances of innovation routines but do often shape performances. Particularly when SOPs and formal rules are embedded in artifacts, such as software tools, they become more difficult to deviate from. These insights clarified the complex relation between formal SOPs and actual routines which D'Adderio (2008) outlined in her degrees of performativity framework. Based on MacKenzie's (2006) work, this framework maps the strength of the interrelation between SOPs and routines. At the extreme ends of the spectrum, SOPs can be seen as mere descriptions or complete prescriptions of routines; but the extremes are rare and most often, instead, SOPs are performative in that they shape enactments ranging from low to strong influence.

Salvato (2009) furthered our understanding of the evolution of product innovation routines over a longer time period. Through a historical analysis of event sequences, he studied ninety performances of NPD processes. His study showed that variations were introduced through the mundane, daily activities of individuals engaged in the product development routine. Of the ninety NPD performances, some 40 per cent closely resembled the prescribed SOP. However, about one-third of the performances were adapted by internal or external people through everyday actions, and about one-fourth of the variations were driven by managers' intentional attempts to adapt routine performances. This concerned especially projects that could be considered as more 'novel', i.e., different from past product development projects, such as projects that involved new collaboration partners or regarded new topics. Based on his findings, Salvato suggested that more radical product innovations are associated with performances that diverge more from the SOP. Adaptations introduced also increased the need for coordination between actors, specifically in the form of ad hoc approval. Finally, Salvato observed how managers shaped the retention of specific routine variations over time. Therefore, his findings help explain how some variations introduced in performances become retained over time and shed light on the process of how routines are being renewed over time.

Cohendet and Simon (2016) further unravelled the role of routines as sources of connections between different actors in the organization. Particularly, they studied the role of innovation routines in connecting senior management and innovation project teams at Ubisoft within the process of renewing innovation routines and uncovered that the divergent interests of different groups of actors involved in innovation work resurfaced during this reconfiguration process. The Ubisoft senior managers focused on efficiency in their gated development process, whereas game designers were mostly focused on the creativity that poured into their games-in-the-making. The reconfiguration process broke the truce between senior managers and game designers and had to be restored in the novel routines. The study shows the skilful manoeuvring of a game producer to restore the truce, which involved both appealing to existing ostensive patterns and introducing a broad range of novel performative actions.

Deken et al. (2016) studied the development of data-driven services, which were radically novel for the focal organization, by analysing how heterogeneous actors from various departments performed interdependent routines to generate such novel outcomes. The novelty associated with the innovation-in-the-making required innovators to adapt their enactments of the standardized innovation processes at the firm. However, such adapted enactments were often not recognized by other actors in the organization as legitimate, which triggered coordination breakdowns in the innovation work. The authors identified three practices (flexing, stretching and inventing) that innovators engaged in to simultaneously realize novelty while ensuring that innovation work across boundaries between heterogeneous actors in the organizations did not break down. Even seemingly straightforward changes in actions within the innovation routines could significantly affect downstream actions due to existing interdependencies with other SOPs. Accordingly, the likelihood of breakdowns increased.

Picking up on the role of artifacts and non-human actors in innovation work, D'Adderio (2011) called for a turn to artifacts and materiality within the study of Routine Dynamics (see chapter by D'Adderio [Chapter 7] in this volume). She highlighted that artifacts had been portrayed as too simplistic and deterministic, and that scholars had mainly focused on human agency. Arguing for a post-constructivist approach, she introduced socio-materiality (e.g., Orlikowski and Scott, 2008) and actor-network theory (e.g., Latour, 2005) as meaningful perspectives to study the relational, emergent and distributed nature of routine performance equally involving human and non-human actors.

This insight is taken up by Sonenshein (2016) in his study of the continuous recreation of 'familiar novelty' within fashion retail stores. He shows how routines and creativity are mutually endemic. Artifacts in the studied 'merchandising routine' were driving forces for store managers who continually tried producing novelty for their customers. Not only did the visual merchandising manual provide room for interpretation but also different fixtures, such as mannequins, tables and other displays, allowed for personal creativity. The inherent openness and flexibility of these artifacts enabled creative outcomes.

Sele and Grand (2016), in their study of a research laboratory, focus on the importance of routines for their ability to continuously innovate. By comparing different research projects, they showed how the same actants may act as intermediaries or mediators depending on the way they are enacted in the same routine, but in different projects. Focusing on the connecting of routines through travelling actants, they neither distinguish between human and non-human actors nor conceptualize actants as pre-defined entities. As suggested by actor-network theory (see chapter by Sele [Chapter 6] in this volume), the power of human and material agency lies in performance and not in their inherent characteristics (Latour, 2005). Particularly, how actants are appropriated created the necessary generative dynamics for novelty to emerge.

21.4 Towards a Research Agenda

As the summary of empirical research showed, studies from a Routine Dynamics perspective have begun to unpack how innovation work takes place through everyday actions. These studies looked at the generative dynamics of routines and how these enable or constrain the performance of innovation work in organizations. Taken together, they have established the central role of innovation routines for connecting heterogeneous and dispersed actors involved in innovation work – contributing to our understanding of routines for coordinating (Adler et al., 1999; Jarzabkowski et al., 2012) – and have emphasized the importance of studying both human and non-human actors (i.e., actants).

We hope this chapter will inspire future research to study innovation work from a Routine Dynamics perspective, as this stream of research is still in its infancy. Indeed, there is a wide range of routines that may be implicated in innovation work in various empirical settings that may be fruitfully studied from a Routine Dynamics perspective. Given the strategic importance of innovation for the longevity of established organizations and the birth of new ventures, Routine Dynamics studies of innovation work are an important topic in organization studies. And as most research has focused on operational work (e.g., routines for hiring, garbage collection, technical customer support), there is ample opportunity for Routine Dynamics scholars to develop new theoretical insight by studying innovation work. In what follows, we provide a number of specific suggestions for future Routine Dynamics research on innovation work that we feel would provide opportunities for theoretical development. We conclude with suggestions on how innovation scholars may mobilize Routine Dynamics to address important questions in the field of innovation management.

We see ample opportunities for developing new insights that advance a relational perspective on routine dynamics. Relationality has been a core aspect of a practice perspective (Feldman and Orlikowski, 2011; see Feldman's chapter [Chapter 2] in this volume). Routine Dynamics scholars have stressed that the connections between actors made through routines enable developing shared understanding of *what* actions to take and *why* such actions are appropriate in particular situations, facilitating the coordinating work between actors (Dionysiou and Tsoukas, 2013; Feldman and Rafaeli, 2002). Studies have shown that shared understanding may help in stabilizing performances as a form of 'balancing act' (Turner and Rindova, 2012). More research is needed, however, to understand how shared understanding is maintained in the context of innovation work and how this informs ostensive patterns. We thus echo Dionysiou and Tsoukas' (2013) call for research on how shared understanding develops in contexts where a large number of actors collaborate and where performances extend over longer time periods, such as in innovation work. Because innovation work is often highly dispersed across different organizational communities (e.g., marketing, engineering, product development, sales, manufacturing, senior management), it provides an excellent context for studying the development of shared understanding (Bechky, 2003).

Such research could also deepen our understanding of how truces between various groups in organizations are formed (Nelson and Winter, 1982; Salvato and Rerup, 2018). The involvement of heterogeneous actors means that innovation work is often associated with breakdowns (Carlile, 2002, 2004) and conflicts (Harvey, 2013), but simultaneously enables creativity and recombination. Such an empirical context is fruitful for studying how truces are dynamically enacted over time as part of the innovation process and how this shapes innovation outcomes. Moreover, since innovation work is oriented at ill-defined, highly novel tasks, it provides interesting opportunities for furthering our understanding of how shared intentionality develops over time. In the absence of a clear-cut starting point for joint action, innovation work provides an extreme setting where actors' ability to develop joint understanding is limited and needs to be seen as a constantly moving target. Such research could thus draw on insights from studies on emerging intentionality through routine performances (Dittrich and Seidl, 2018).

Second, we advocate for more research on the generative properties of routines in the context of innovation work in order to better understand why and how some interactions between routines break down while others facilitate renewal. Past studies have shed light on the different processes through which SOPs become renewed or reconfigured over time (e.g., Cohendet and Simon, 2016; Salvato, 2009), which contributed to our understanding of capability evolution (see chapter by Salvato [Chapter 34] in this volume). However, studies on dynamic capabilities and other meta-routines oriented towards flexibility still have a very static understanding of their dynamism (Wenzel et al., 2020). Because innovation work is oriented at generating novel outcomes, variation and flexibility in the enactment of routines is likely needed. Both managerial agency (Salvato, 2009) and the agentic orientations of routine participants (Howard-Grenville, 2005) play a role in the flexible performance of innovation routines.

When it comes to interdependencies between routines (see chapter by Rosa, Kremser and Bulgacov [Chapter 17] in this volume), scholars have focused on different aspects of interdependency (Hoekzema, 2020). Some studies on innovation work have emphasized generative properties of interrelated routines, suggesting that novelty emerges from recombining (Cohendet and Simon, 2016) and through their interacting (Sele and Grand, 2016), whereas others have pointed at the increased potential of breakdowns caused by interdependencies with other routine enactments (D'Adderio, 2008; Deken et al., 2016). This suggests a need to better understand when and why routine interdependencies enable and constrain generating novelty.

Finally, we see potential in further developing insights on materiality and the interplay between human and non-human actors in innovation work. Several Routine Dynamics studies have prepared the ground to see human and material agency on equal footing (D'Adderio, 2008, 2011; Sele and

Grand, 2016). These studies have not only provided the necessary empirical evidence for the role of socio-material assemblages in enacting routines but have also engaged in introducing the necessary theoretical armour to allow for this shift. Seeing the current rise of search algorithms and robotics in organizations and their everyday functioning, we believe that post-constructivist approaches are helpful tools in understanding such emerging phenomena (see also D'Adderio, 2011). A Routine Dynamics perspective is well-suited, as with these digital tools the design and enactment of routines is becoming increasingly conflated (refer to Chapter 23 by Glaser, Valadao and Hannigan).

For innovation management scholars, a Routine Dynamics perspective can enable conceptualizing routines not as monolithic 'things' but as a generative system within which interactive parts drive both stability and change in actual performances. The limitations of equalling routines such as SOPs are increasingly voiced in the literature on innovation management (e.g., Christiansen and Varnes, 2009) but not yet taken on in empirical studies in this domain.

Literature on innovation work has been studying the consequences of rigid and flexible implementation of innovation SOPs. Work by D'Adderio (2008), Pentland and Feldman (2008), Cacciatori (2012) and Jazabkowski et al., (2012) provide a useful starting point for exploring this relation. D'Adderio (2008) showed that when the SOP is inscribed in software, it shielded actors from conflicting interests of other organizational groups (in her case, by preventing excessive changes in the design of vehicles while preparing manufacturing). However, she also showed that *even* when SOPs are inscribed in rigid software, deviations are possible or even prevalent. Knowing that the emphasis of strict rules will inevitably result in innovators breaking these rules as they seek the flexibility required for innovation work is an important insight for managers responsible for SOPs. Yet, software-inscribed SOPs can make workarounds visible and therefore facilitate enforcing specific action patterns. In this context, Routine Dynamics could enable studying and tracing wider effects of workarounds and local deviations from formally described SOPs. As D'Adderio (2008: 780) showed, although a workaround 'may be feasible, it always entails a degree of disruption', which 'will generate confusion later in the process' and go against the logic underlying the design of the SOP and its purpose.

Routine Dynamics provides the conceptual apparatus to improve our understanding of the process of designing innovation routines, which has been a key theme in innovation management research. Pentland and Feldman (2008) unravel the complex relation between routines and SOPs, asserting that no SOP – no matter how carefully designed – will guarantee a particular action pattern. Because actors' understanding and experiences are invoked in enactments of innovation processes and because actors always have the opportunity to perform novel actions, SOPs are, at best, guiding actual action patterns.

Any attempt to implement a new or to alter an existing SOP for innovation will require extensive interactions between the actors involved in the day-to-day enactments so to develop the shared understandings needed to perform the routine together (Pentland and Feldman, 2008). Existing studies provide promising starting points for such research. For example, both Jazabkowski et al. (2012) and Cohendet and Simon (2016) show that actors who aim to change SOPs may benefit from first disrupting existing patterns to then start the process of creating new action patterns. The process of enacting new patterns was studied by Deken et al. (2016), who found that consequences of performing new action patterns significantly affected downstream actions, suggesting that such interdependencies should be considered when designing new innovation routines. Moreover, Cacciatori (2012) points to the need to connect new tools to the existing artifacts that actors use in routine enactments, based on her study of the development of a new bidding routine in a design company. She also nuances our understanding of different kinds of artifacts, suggesting that some kinds are better attuned to bring the 'flexibility needed for problem-solving' or the 'rigidity necessary to funnel action' (2012: 1575). Overall, such studies suggest that designing SOPs requires a more systemic view on how innovation processes interrelate with other SOPs in an organization (e.g., routines at manufacturing, purchasing, marketing). Innovation scholars could benefit from the detailed analyses of the consequences of adaptations – as is typically done in Routine Dynamics – to elaborate specific sub-SOPs that allow for more predictable variations (e.g., Cooper and Sommer, 2016), and to better understand in which artifacts SOPs should be embedded.

References

Adler, P. S. (1995). Interdepartmental interdependence and coordination: The case of the design/manufacturing interface. *Organization Science*, 6(2), 147–167.

Adler, P. S., Goldoftas, B. and Levine, D. I. (1999). Flexibility versus efficiency? A case study of model changeovers in the Toyota production system. *Organization Science*, 10(1), 43–68.

Akrich, M., Callon, M. and Latour, B. (2002). The key to success in innovation part I: The art of interessement. *International Journal of Innovation Management*, 6(2), 187–206.

Amabile, T. M. (1997). Motivating creativity in organizations: On doing what you love and loving what you do. *California Management Review*, 40(1), 39–58.

Ashforth, B. E. and Fried, Y. (1988). The mindlessness of organizational behaviors. *Human Relations*, 41(4), 305–329.

Barley, S. R. (1986). Technology as an occasion for structuring: Evidence from observations of CT scanners and the social-order of radiology departments. *Administrative Science Quarterly*, 31(1), 78–108.

Bartel, C. A. and Garud, R. (2009). The role of narratives in sustaining organizational innovation. *Organization Science*, 20(1), 107–117.

Bartunek, J. M., Trullen, J., Immediato, S. and Schneider, F. (2007). Front and backstages of the diminished routinization of innovations: What innovation research makes public and organizational research finds behind the scenes. *Strategic Entrepreneurship Journal*, 1(3–4), 295–314.

Bechky, B. A. (2003). Sharing meaning across occupational communities: The transformation of understanding on a production floor. *Organization Science*, 14(3), 312–330.

Becker, M. C. (2004). Organizational routines: A review of the literature. *Industrial and Corporate Change*, 13(4), 643–677.

Becker, M. C. and Zirpoli, F. (2009). Innovation routines: Exploring the role of procedures and stable behaviour patterns in innovation. In M. C. Becker and N. Lazaric, eds., *Organizational Routines: Advances in Empirical Research*. Cheltenham: Edward Elgar Publishing, pp. 303–339.

Bijker, W. E. (1995). *Of Bicycles, Bakelites, and Bulbs: Toward a Theory of Sociotechnical Change*. Cambridge, MA: MIT Press.

Brown, J. S. and Duguid, P. (1991). Organizational learning and communities-of-practice: Toward a unified view of working, learning, and innovation. *Organization Science*, 2(1), 40–57.

Burgelman, R. A. (1983). A process model of internal corporate venturing in the diversified major firm. *Administrative Science Quarterly*, 28(2), 223–244.

Burns, T. and Stalker, G. (1961). *The Management of Innovation*. London: Tavistock.

Cacciatori, E. (2012). Resolving conflict in problem-solving: Systems of artefacts in the development of new routines. *Journal of Management Studies*, 49(8), 1559–1585.

Carlile, P. R. (2002). A pragmatic view of knowledge and boundaries: Boundary objects in new product development. *Organization Science*, 13(4), 442–455.

Carlile, P. R. (2004). Transferring, translating, and transforming: An integrative framework for managing knowledge across boundaries. *Organization Science*, 15(5), 555–568.

Christiansen, J. K. and Varnes, C. J. (2009). Formal rules in product development: Sensemaking of structured approaches. *Journal of Product Innovation Management*, 26(5), 502–519.

Cohendet, P. S. and Simon, L. O. (2016). Always playable: Recombining routines for creative efficiency at Ubisoft Montreal's video game studio. *Organization Science*, 27(3), 614–632.

Cooper, R. G. (1996). Overhauling the new product process. *Industrial Marketing Management*, 25 (6), 465–482.

Cooper, R. G. (2008). Perspective: The stage-gate idea-to-launch process update, what's new, and nexgen systems. *Journal of Product Innovation Management*, 25(3), 213–232.

Cooper, R. G. and Kleinschmidt, E. J. (1991). New product processes at leading industrial firms.

Industrial Marketing Management, 20(2), 137–147.
Cooper, R. G. and Sommer, A. F. (2016). The Agile–Stage-Gate hybrid model: A promising new approach and a new research opportunity. *Journal of Product Innovation Management*, 33(5), 513–526.
D'Adderio, L. (2001). Crafting the virtual prototype: How firms integrate knowledge and capabilities across organizational boundaries. *Research Policy*, 30(9), 1409–1424.
D'Adderio, L. (2008). The performativity of routines: Theorising the influence of artefacts and distributed agencies on routine dynamics. *Research Policy*, 37(5), 769–789.
D'Adderio, L. (2011). Artifacts at the centre of routines: Performing the material turn in routines theory. *Journal of Institutional Economics*, 7(2), 197–230.
Deken, F., Carlile, P. R., Berends, H. and Lauche, K. (2016). Generating novelty through interdependent routines: A process model of routine work. *Organization Science*, 27(3), 659–677.
Deken, F. and Lauche, K. (2014). Coordinating through the development of a shared object: An approach to study interorganizational innovation. *International Journal of Innovation and Technology Management*, 11(1).
Dionysiou, D. D. and Tsoukas, H. (2013). Understanding the (re) creation of routines from within: A symbolic interactionist perspective. *Academy of Management Review*, 38(2), 181–205.
Dittrich, K. and Seidl, D. (2018). Emerging intentionality in routine dynamics: A pragmatist view. *Academy of Management Journal*, 61(1), 111–138.
Dougherty, D. (1992). Interpretive barriers to successful product innovation in large firms. *Organization Science*, 3(2), 179–202.
Dougherty, D. and Heller, T. (1994). The illegitimacy of successful product innovation in established firms. *Organization Science*, 5(2), 200–218.
Eisenhardt, K. M. and Martin, J. A. (2000). Dynamic capabilities: What are they? *Strategic Management Journal*, 21(10–11), 1105–1121.
Farjoun, M. (2010). Beyond dualism: Stability and change as duality. *Academy of Management Review*, 35(2), 202–225.
Feldman, M. S. and Orlikowski, W. J. (2011). Theorizing practice and practicing theory. *Organization Science*, 22(5), 1240–1253.
Feldman, M. S. and Pentland, B. T. (2003). Reconceptualizing organizational routines as a source of flexibility and change. *Administrative Science Quarterly*, 48(1), 94–118.
Feldman, M. S., Pentland, B. T., D'Adderio, L. and Lazaric, N. (2016). Beyond routines as things: Introduction to the special issue on routine dynamics. *Organization Science*, 27(3), 505–513.
Feldman, M. S. and Rafaeli, A. (2002). Organizational routines as sources of connections and understandings. *Journal of Management Studies*, 39(3), 309–331.
Ford, C. M. and Gioia, D. A. (2000). Factors influencing creativity in the domain of managerial decision making. *Journal of Management*, 26 (4), 705–732.
Garud, R., Gehman, J. and Kumaraswamy, A. (2011). Complexity arrangements for sustained innovation: Lessons from 3M Corporation. *Organization Studies*, 32(6), 737–767.
Garud, R., Nayyar, P. R. and Shapira, Z. B., eds. (1997). *Technological Innovation: Oversights and Foresights*. Cambridge: Cambridge University Press.
Garud, R. and Rappa, M. A. (1994). A sociocognitive model of technology evolution: The case of cochlear implants. *Organization Science*, 5(3), 344–362.
Garud, R., Tuertscher, P. and Van de Ven, A. H. (2013). Perspectives on innovation processes. *The Academy of Management Annals*, 7(1), 775–819.
Griffin, A. (1997). PDMA research on new product development practices: Updating trends and benchmarking best practices. *Journal of Product Innovation Management*, 14(6), 429–458.
Hannan, M. T. and Freeman, J. R. (1984). Structural inertia and organizational change. *American Sociological Review*, 49(2), 149–164.
Hargadon, A. (2005). Technology brokering and innovation: Linking strategy, practice, and people. *Strategy and Leadership*, 33(1), 32–36.
Hargadon, A. and Sutton, R. I. (1997). Technology brokering and innovation in a product development firm. *Administrative Science Quarterly*, 42(4), 716–749.
Hargadon, A. B. and Douglas, Y. (2001). When innovations meet institutions: Edison and the design of the electric light. *Administrative Science Quarterly*, 46(3), 476–501.
Harvey, S. (2013). A different perspective: The multiple effects of deep level diversity on group

creativity. *Journal of Experimental Social Psychology*, 49(5), 822–832.

Hoekzema, J. (2020). Bridging the gap between ecologies and clusters: Towards an integrative framework of routine interdependence. *European Management Review*. https://onlinelibrary.wiley.com/doi/full/10.1111/emre.12391

Howard-Grenville, J. A. (2005). The persistence of flexible organizational routines: The role of agency and organizational context. *Organization Science*, 16(6), 618–636.

Jarzabkowski, P. A., Lê, J. K. and Feldman, M. S. (2012). Toward a theory of coordinating: Creating coordinating mechanisms in practice. *Organization Science*, 23(4), 907–927.

Jelinek, M. and Schoonhoven, C. B. (1990). *The Innovation Marathon: Lessons from High Technology Firms*. San Francisco: Jossey-Bass Publishers.

Kahn, K. B., Kay, S. E., Slotegraaf, R. and Uban, S. (2013). *The PDMA Handbook of New Product Development*, 3rd ed. Hoboken, NJ: John Wiley & Sons.

Kannan-Narasimhan, R. (2014). Organizational ingenuity in nascent innovations: Gaining resources and legitimacy through unconventional actions. *Organization Studies*, 35(4), 483–509.

Kannan-Narasimhan, R. and Lawrence, B. S. (2018). How innovators reframe resources in the strategy-making process to gain innovation adoption. *Strategic Management Journal*, 39(3), 720–758.

Latour, B. (2005). *Reassembling the Social: An Introduction to Actor-Network-Theory*. Oxford: Oxford University Press.

MacKenzie, D. (2006). Is economics performative? Option theory and the construction of derivatives markets. *Journal of the History of Economic Thought*, 28(1), 29–55.

March, J. G. (1991). Exploration and exploitation in organizational learning. *Organization Science*, 2(1), 71–87.

Nelson, R. R. and Winter, S. G. (1982). *An Evolutionary Theory of Economic Change*. Cambridge, MA: Harvard University Press.

Nicolini, D. (2010). Medical innovation as a process of translation: A case from the field of telemedicine. *British Journal of Management*, 21, 1011–1026.

Nicolini, D., Mengis, J. and Swan, J. (2012). Understanding the role of objects in cross-disciplinary collaboration. *Organization Science*, 23(3), 612–629.

Obstfeld, D. (2012). Creative projects: A less routine approach toward getting new things done. *Organization Science*, 23(6), 1571–1592.

Ohly, S., Sonnentag, S. and Pluntke, F. (2006). Routinization, work characteristics and their relationships with creative and proactive behaviors. *Journal of Organizational Behavior*, 27(3), 257–279.

Okhuysen, G. A. and Bechky, B. A. (2009). Coordination in organizations: An integrative perspective. *The Academy of Management Annals*, 3(1), 463–502.

Orlikowski, W. J. and Scott, S. V. (2008). Sociomateriality: Challenging the separation of technology, work and organization. *Academy of Management Annals*, 2, 433–474.

Parmigiani, A. and Howard-Grenville, J. A. (2011). Routines revisited: Exploring the capabilities and practice perspective. *Academy of Management Annals*, 5(1), 413–453.

Pavitt, K. (2002). Innovating routines in the business firm: What corporate tasks should they be accomplishing? *Industrial and Corporate Change*, 11(1), 117–133.

Pentland, B. T. and Feldman, M. S. (2005). Designing routines: Artifacts in support of generative systems. *Presented in Sofia Antipolis, France, January 21–22*.

Pentland, B. T. and Feldman, M. S. (2008). Designing routines: On the folly of designing artifacts, while hoping for patterns of action. *Information and Organization*, 18(4), 235–250.

Rahman, H. A. and Barley, S. R. (2017). Situated redesign in creative occupations: An ethnography of architects. *Academy of Management Discoveries*, 3(4), 404–424.

Rerup, C. and Feldman, M. S. (2011). Routines as a source of change in organizational schemata: The role of trial-and-error learning. *Academy of Management Journal*, 54(3), 577–610.

Salvato, C. (2009). Capabilities unveiled: The role of ordinary activities in the evolution of product development processes. *Organization Science*, 20(2), 384–409.

Salvato, C. and Rerup, C. (2018). Routine regulation: Balancing conflicting goals in organizational routines. *Administrative Science Quarterly*, 63(1), 170–209.

Schmidt, T., Braun, T. and Sydow, J. (2019). Copying routines for new venture creation:

How replication can support entrepreneurial innovation. *Research in Sociology of Organizations*, 55–78.

Sele, K. and Grand, S. (2016). Unpacking the dynamics of ecologies of routines: Mediators and their generative effects in routine interactions. *Organization Science*, 27(3), 722–738.

Shaw, N., Burgess, T., Hwarng, H. and De Mattos, C. (2001). Revitalising new process development in the UK fine chemicals industry. *International Journal of Operations & Production Management*, 21(8), 1133–1151.

Simon, H. A. (1973). The structure of ill-structured problems. *Artificial Ingelligence*, 4, 181–201.

Sonenshein, S. (2016). Routines and creativity: From dualism to duality. *Organization Science*, 27(3), 739–758.

Thomke, S. H. (1998). Managing experimentation in the design of new products. *Management Science*, 44(6), 743–762.

Turner, S. F. and Rindova, V. (2012). A balancing act: How organizations pursue consistency in routine functioning in the face of ongoing change. *Organization Science*, 23(1), 24–46.

Tushman, M. L. and OReilly, C. A. (1996). Ambidextrous organizations: Managing evolutionary and revolutionary change. *California Management Review*, 38(4), 8–32.

Van de Ven, A. H. (1986). Central problems in the management of innovation. *Management Science*, 32(5), 590–607.

Van de Ven, A. H., Polley, D., Garud, R. and Venkataraman, S. (1999). *The Innovation Journey*. New York: Oxford University Press.

Van de Ven, A. H. and Poole, M. S. (1990). Methods for studying innovation development in the Minnesota Innovation Research Program. *Organization Science*, 1(3), 313–335.

Van Dijk, S., Berends, H., Jelinek, M., Romme, A. G. L. and Weggeman, M. (2011). Micro-institutional affordances and strategies of radical innovation. *Organization Studies*, 32(11), 1485–1513.

Wenzel, M., Danner-Schröder, A. and Spee, A. P. (2020). Dynamic capabilities? Unleashing their dynamic through a practice perspective on organizational routines. *Journal of Management Inquiry*, forthcoming.

Wheelwright, S. C. and Clark, K. B. (1992). *Revolutionizing Product Development: Quantum Leaps in Speed, Efficiency, and Quality*. New York: Free Press.

Woodman, R. W., Sawyer, J. E. and Griffin, R. W. (1993). Toward a theory of organizational creativity. *Academy of Management Review*, 18(2), 293–321.

CHAPTER 22

Design and Routine Dynamics

FRITHJOF E. WEGENER AND VERN L. GLASER

22.1 Introduction

Routine Dynamics research seeks to explain how organizational routines change. Often, organizational actors intentionally try to 'influence, design or manage [routines]' to achieve organizational goals (Pentland, 2005: 793). Organizational actors may import routine 'templates' from other organizations to deal with challenges (e.g., Bertels et al., 2016); create new artifacts to change routine performances (e.g., Bapuji et al., 2012, 2018; Glaser, 2017); and/or use different types of experiments to fundamentally change processes (e.g., Bucher and Langley, 2016). In this chapter, we suggest that such change initiatives can be understood using the label *routine design*, which we define as *intentional efforts to change one or more aspects of a routine to create a preferred situation.*[1] Such actions associated with the design and redesign of organizational routines are consequential to Routine Dynamics – even if these efforts to architect changes often stimulate unintended consequences that deviate from a designer's initial intent (Pentland and Feldman, 2008).

We begin by reviewing Routine Dynamics research on intentional change. Early routines researchers (e.g., Nelson and Winter, 1982) adopted a cognitive perspective on change that conceptualized routines as entities and suggested that intentional change involves planning the transfer of abstract knowledge about the routine from one context to another. With the introduction of the Routine Dynamics perspective, scholars (e.g., Feldman and Pentland, 2003) critiqued this entitative notion, and conceptualized routines as generative systems with ostensive, performative and artifactual aspects. They observed not only that routines change endogenously, but that planned changes often stimulate unintended consequences. Recently, Routine Dynamics scholars have adopted a stronger process perspective (e.g., Feldman, 2016; Feldman et al., 2016; Howard-Grenville and Rerup, 2016), highlighting the emergent nature of intentionality in routine change. Our review of the Routine Dynamics literature regarding routine design is structured around these three perspectives on routines that highlight specific elements of the design process and neglect others.

Following the review, we introduce two perspectives that draw on design studies and may enhance our understanding of the relationship between design and Routine Dynamics. Inspired by Simon's (1969) scientific perspective on design, we suggest that routines scholars can advance their understanding of Routine Dynamics by studying the effects and implications of designing artifacts – particularly the effects engendered by the actions taken to develop representations during the construction of these artifacts. Inspired by Schön's (1983) reflective practice perspective on design, we suggest that routines scholars can examine how actors define the problem's setting, and engage in (re)framing,

---

We thank the editors Katharina Dittrich and Martha Feldman for their insightful comments, which have propelled this chapter forward. We want to thank Barbara Simpson, Emilio Marti and Yan Feng for their reviews and feedback on earlier versions of this paper, helping us refine where to take this chapter. Next to these, earlier versions of this paper were presented in a brown-bag seminar of the Design, Organization and Strategy Department of the Industrial Design Engineering Faculty, TU Delft and the EGOS PDW for this handbook. We also want to thank those participants for their feedback. The authors would like to acknowledge that this research has been supported in part by funding from Canada's Social Sciences and Humanities Research Council.

[1] Our definition is inspired by Simon's (1969: 129) observation that 'to design is to devise courses of action aimed at changing existing situations into preferred ones'.

reflection-in-action and reflective conversation with the situation in routine design. In summary, we believe that these design studies perspectives offer routines scholars opportunities to better understand efforts to intentionally change routines.

22.2 Review of Design in Routine Dynamics

22.2.1 Cognitive Perspective

The cognitive perspective on routines builds on the Carnegie School's cognitive and information processing perspective of organizations (e.g., Cyert and March, 1963; March and Simon, 1958; Simon, 1947). Specifically, Nelson and Winter (1982) suggested that routines are a key unit of analysis in studying organizational behavior. They conceptualized routines as the 'genes' of an organization and theorized that routines reflect tacit organizational knowledge. Although Nelson and Winter (1982) acknowledge that some variations in routines can occur through slippage, laxity and rule-breaking from within the routine, more substantial change in routines has to come from the outside: substantial change requires deeper ad hoc problem-solving, thereby inspiring our interest in applying a design perspective to routines and their dynamics.

Because routines are conceptualized in terms of knowledge, intentional routine change involves identifying and implementing tacit knowledge of best practices for routine enactment (Szulanski, 1996, 2000). According to this research, tacit knowledge is inherently sticky and difficult to articulate due to challenges associated with the characteristics of knowledge, organizational actors and the context of the routine. Consequently, intentionally changing a routine involves identifying its fundamental aspects – the 'arrow core' (Winter and Szulanski, 2001: 731). New routines can be designed by finding and copying templates from elsewhere (e.g., Gupta et al., 2015), or by engaging in a process of vicarious learning (e.g., Bresman, 2012).

Gupta et al. (2015) illustrated the 'find and copy' approach to intentional routine change, describing an eight-step process to help remove cognitive and motivational roadblocks, including finding a template to copy; decomposing the routine into elements; solving for the elements; and resolving conflicts between stakeholders and with existing routines by determining decision rights. Gupta et al. (2015) described three key problems underlying routine redesign efforts: information, incentives and compatibility between existing routines and the redesigned routine, with corresponding solutions of aligning incentives with system-wide profits, codifying knowledge to make trade-offs and investigating interdependencies.

Bresman's (2012) study of vicarious group learning in a pharmaceutical organization provides an example of ad hoc learning (Nelson and Winter, 1982) in intentional routine change. The first step of the learning process is to identify a routine to learn from by engaging in an anticipatory and 'broadcast' search, rather than a structured search driven by a simple, pre-defined problem. Learning continues through a process of extensive translation, whereby the seeker and source of the new routine engage in intense discussions to learn about the original routine and adapt it to the new context. This translation is followed by an adoption process with a variety of modalities depending on contextual differences, whereby knowledge from the original routine is embedded in the changed routine. Vicarious learning culminates in a process of continuation, whereby actors decide whether to continue to use the changed routine or not. This decision is not only affected by the seeker's experience with the routine but also the source's experience with outcomes of the routine. Bresman (2012) thus suggested that the learning process underlying change is less 'copy and paste' and more a process of learning from others.

Overall, the cognitive perspective on routines suggests that the core problem of routine change is the tacit nature of knowledge and the effort required to explicitly represent it. From this perspective, actors can change routines through searching for alternative templates outside the existing routine by either (a) replicating an existing routine (e.g., Gupta et al., 2015), or (b) engaging in vicarious or ad hoc learning processes (Bresman, 2012). The change process then unfolds as planned and intended. The cognitive perspective thus assumes that once tacit knowledge has been articulated, implementing planned changes unfolds unproblematically. Put simply, in this perspective, the designers of routines assume that actors change the routine according to their pre-established plans and perform the routine in a manner specified by the template.

22.2.2 Practice Theory Perspective on Routine Dynamics

By introducing a practice perspective, Feldman and Pentland (2003) opened the black box of routines and suggested that changes in routines are attributable to unplanned, 'endogenous' actions generated from interactions between their ostensive, performative and artifactual aspects. This approach differs significantly from the cognitive approach to routines, where intentional change revolves around the search for alternatives outside of the routine and unfolds according to exogenously pre-established plans. From a Routine Dynamics perspective, 'knowledge' needs to be enacted within the routine (D'Adderio, 2003), but does not represent the 'true' routine. Intentional changes are envisioned, but not conceptualized in terms of an idealized routine such as the arrow core. Instead, an intention might be instantiated in an artifact such as a standard operating procedure (e.g., Lazaric and Denis, 2005) or a broad envisioning of a new cultural approach on organizing (e.g., Rerup and Feldman, 2011). By unpacking the black box of the routine, this practice-based perspective generates several insights about intentional routine change.

For instance, Feldman's (2000) ground-breaking study on routines around student housing at a US university shows how routine participants intentionally change the routine from within. One routine involved how building directors assessed student damages to the facilities to calculate reparations. On the surface, this routine did not need to be changed: assessed damages were collected by the university. However, the building directors were dissatisfied with the routine because students were not confronted with the damage they had done, and consequently never received a valuable learning opportunity. To address this issue, 'one of the building directors developed a system for checking people out of their rooms that resolved this problem' (Feldman, 2000: 616–617). This substantive change was not planned by a strategic manager, but initiated by actors who sought to redress outcomes that fell short of their ideal by exploring other ways to enact the routine.

Based on a study of a Danish government organization's strategic efforts to enact a new organizational schema, Rerup and Feldman (2011) similarly show how the actions taken by participants to enact the newly designed schema are crucial to how change unfolds. A new research organization, Learning Lab Denmark (LLD), was mandated 'to produc[e] cutting-edge, action-oriented research'. The challenge of enacting this new schema while continuing to operate within the existing bureaucratic environment became most apparent in the recruitment routine, as the salaries of applicants with the desired qualifications were not in line with the existing compensation structure. A trial and error process revealed flaws in the routine, such as the rejection of employment contracts because high salaries violated existing regulations. The LLD secretariat 'generated several new performances to solve the problems with the recruiting routine' (Rerup and Feldman, 2011: 594), including a different contract structure. As a result of this trial and error process, the organizational schema adapted over time. Thus, a key mechanism for endogenous change to a routine is not only dissatisfaction with outcomes (e.g., Feldman, 2000) but also the action-based learning inherent in trying new performances and adopting those that are successful.

The practice perspective has also been used to analyse the effects of planned changes to routines. Research has shown that attempts to change a routine by incorporating outside practices often generate unintended consequences (Pentland and Feldman, 2008). For instance, Lazaric and Denis (2005) revealed how an organization attempted to introduce ISO norms, but certain actors chose to not implement the designed change. Importantly, they showed that ISO norms were an artifact that played a role in the routine, but did not constitute it (see also D'Adderio, 2008). By showing that routines have different components, it became clear that a designed change does not automatically transfer from the intent of a designer into practice (see also Reynaud, 2005).

Similarly, by studying a new product design and development routine in a high technology company, Hales and Tidd (2009) showed that formal visualizations play a 'dialectic' and 'mediating' role rather than a representational one. D'Adderio (2008) theorized that because situated action can never be pre-specified (e.g., Suchman, 2007), formal representations frame a routine, but overflows occur when artifacts fail to account for the emergence of diverse contextual situations during routine enactment.

In contrast with the cognitive perspective, research in the Routine Dynamics tradition (Feldman and Pentland, 2003) has shown that intentional change not only unfolds as a process of searching for alternatives but can occur without planning. Planned efforts to change routines often lead to unintentional outcomes, because intentions or plans cannot fully account for the exigencies of situated action (Pentland and Feldman, 2008). Notably, formal representations of routines created for routine change purposes often fail and generate unintended consequences due to the inability to plan for all the contingencies that arise as routines are performed (Bertels et al., 2016; D'Adderio, 2008; Hales and Tidd, 2009; Lazaric and Denis, 2005). Instead, Routine Dynamics research shows that routines can change endogenously without premeditation.

22.2.3 Ontological Process Perspective on Routine Dynamics

Although process has always been part of the Routine Dynamics literature, we have observed a recent shift from an epistemological to an ontological process perspective driven by an increased focus on the relational (Emirbayer, 1997), processual (Tsoukas and Chia, 2002) and performative (see Feldman, 2016; Simpson and Lorino, 2016) nature of routines, most clearly observed as an increased focus on performing and patterning (Feldman, 2016). Reflecting the Routine Dynamics perspective post-2016, the processual perspective highlights the destabilization of routine ontologies (D'Adderio and Pollock, 2020). Going beyond the black box of action to study processual dynamics, routines researchers have highlighted the creativity of action itself (Feldman, 2016; Joas, 1996) and brought temporality to the fore (Emirbayer and Mische, 1998; Simpson and Lorino, 2016).

Feldman (2016) played a crucial role in strengthening the process perspective in the routines literature by introducing patterning as a complementary dynamic to performing. Drawing on 'the creativity of action' theorized by Joas (1996), who drew on the pragmatism of Mead and Dewey, Feldman (2016, p. 32) highlighted that 'action – not as an imagined construct but as enacted in time and space – tends to display a spectrum of intentionality, control over the body, and social autonomy'. She argued that an increased focus on action was a way forward to increase our understanding of Routine Dynamics. Routine Dynamics scholars have highlighted the situated nature of action, depicting the roles of reflective talk (Dittrich et al., 2016) and reflective spaces (Bucher and Langley, 2016) for actors who intend to reorient Routine Dynamics. Dittrich and Seidl (2018) likewise drew on the creativity of action (Joas, 1996), highlighting that Routine Dynamics emerge from dynamics associated with situated action.

While previous perspectives on routine designs have emphasized the pre-established existence of goals, intentions and purposes at the outset of routine design, more recent work from a process perspective highlights how new goals, intentions and ideas emerge during routine performances and require organizational actors to adapt goals and intentions during design activities. For example, drawing on Dewey's (1922) notion of inquiry, Dittrich and Seidl (2018) introduced the concepts of ends-in-view, emergent intentionality and the creativity of action (Joas, 1996) into Routine Dynamics. They showed how actors learn about new ends in light of existing means and how intentionality emerges during the inquiry process. According to Dittrich and Seidl (2018), actors foreground ends and means in action, thereby 'develop[ing] a "purposive" sense of what they ought to do . . . through the flow of action itself' (2018: 47), because 'every action-situation presents an opportunity for discovering new ends-in-view' (2018: 134). This research suggests that routines scholars should focus less on describing reflection-*on*-action and more on describing performance (see also Dionysiou [Chapter 5], this volume) and reflection-*in*-action (see also Tsoukas [Chapter 3], this volume).

For instance, Cohendet and Simon (2016) studied a crisis around creativity at a game developer that raised doubts about routines around the stage-gating process. The project manager of a previously successful game development team chose to stop his current project in light of growing frustrations. This moment was cathartic, as in the ensuing debate, the editorial team chose to give the project manager extra time to explore 'what could or should be done to avoid such traps in the future' (2016: 622). The project manager created new principles to redesign routines: 'fail faster' and 'follow the fun' (2016: 622). Rather than planning changes to routines and implementing them, the experience of the team and other employees became central. For example, 'no idea would be integrated in the work packages without being concretely experimented with and demonstrated' (2016: 623); playable prototyping occurred where 'some employees would play, some would just watch and discuss, and some would comment live on what was happening on the screens' (2016: 623). In turn, the game developers 'would do their own synthesis and get back to work on Monday with very clear goals and orientations' (2016: 623).

Cohendet and Simon (2016) highlighted three central moves in this process: questioning existing routines, repurposing existing routines at the core of the organization's culture and opening up this process to others in the organization (i.e., through organizational tournaments). The authors described how the game developer shifted from a stage-gate process to the redesigned 'always playable' process by combining and experimenting with aspects of different existing routines. An important aspect of design seems to be the ability to deliberately recombine existing routines (Pentland and Jung, 2016). Similarly, Bucher and Langley (2016) revealed how establishing reflective and experimental spaces can help make design efforts more impactful.

Deken et al. (2016) also unpacked how actors intentionally change their routines by studying how routine interdependencies at an automotive firm affected efforts to develop novel information-based services which constituted a radical departure from the firm's existing hardware products. Deken et al. (2016) identified that actors approached routine design through *flexing*, *stretching* and *inventing*. Flexing is used when the routine itself is not novel, but its instantiation is. Stretching is used to extend a routine beyond its usual context to actors who may be unfamiliar with it. Inventing is used to develop novel routines. Thus, novelty increases from flexing to stretching to inventing. Different actors can have different perspectives on routine design depending on how they perceive the novelty associated with the new performances. In addition, the authors' framework highlights how routine work generates consequences and surfaces differences that require more routine work, generating a cascading effect. A challenge for actors is to anticipate the consequences of routine work and address them proactively. This highlights the interplay of change and stability as complementary and sequential. Thus, the contribution of Deken et al. (2016) is two-fold: They show that, on the one hand, design processes need to be sensitive to the perspectives of people taking new actions and, on the other hand, that due to unanticipated consequences, design is an ongoing and continuous process (see also Garud et al., 2008).

In summary, researchers who adopted the practice perspective of Routine Dynamics highlighted that designing routines often leads to unintended consequences due to interactions between their artifactual, ostensive and performative aspects. That is, 'managers design artifacts, not routines. When the participants actually start producing performances, it is not necessarily what the designers had in mind' (Pentland and Feldman, 2008: 249). More recent Routine Dynamics research destabilized the routine and action itself by highlighting the interplay of patterning and performing in routines. By considering relationality, becoming and the emergent nature of intentionality, the work highlights how out of performances new goals and intentions emerge; how through that the preferred situation also keeps changing; and that this leads to a continuous design process where emerging consequences require additional design efforts.

22.3 Design Studies Insights to Advance Research on Design and Routines

We now draw on the design studies literature to highlight important insights that can inform future research on Routine Dynamics. Design studies offer generative inspiration for the study of Routine Dynamics because they focus on intentional change. An important difference between Routine Dynamics and design studies is the unit of analysis. Whereas in Routine Dynamics the unit of analysis is the routine, in design studies the core unit of analysis is the design process. Thus, while Routine Dynamics research highlights routine actions, design studies research highlights design actions. For example, *Design Studies*, the leading journal, is 'focused on developing understanding of *design processes*' (emphasis in original).[2]

We suggest that two traditions in design studies offer intriguing ideas for future research on Routine Dynamics: the scientific perspective advocated by Simon (1969), which highlights design as a process of addressing clearly defined problems and discovering optimal solutions; and the reflective perspective advocated by Schön (1983), which highlights the reflective nature of design processes. These two perspectives offer a starkly different look at design (see for a comparison Dorst and Dijkhuis, 1995). Simon (1969) highlighted the procedural rationality of design, as a positivist perspective on design. Fourteen years later, Schön (1983) offered a perspective on design that highlighted situated problem-solving as reflection-in-action, with constructivist phenomenological influences (see e.g., Dorst and Dijkhuis, 1995; Yanow and Tsoukas, 2009) and pragmatist influences (see e.g. Schön, 1992, 1995). Instead of choosing one perspective, we reinterpret both perspectives on design from an overarching pragmatist design perspective, as pragmatism offers a unique approach to design (Garud et al., 2008; Romme, 2003) and the study of routines (see, e.g., Dionysiou and Tsoukas, 2013; Dionysiou [Chapter 5], this volume; Dittrich and Seidl, 2018; Simpson and Lorino, 2016) in the spirit of Schön's calls for a pragmatist epistemology for design (see Schön, 1983, 1992, 1995). Such a pragmatic approach to design would build on the inherent strength of pragmatism to deal with complex, dynamic and interrelated phenomena (Farjoun et al., 2015).

22.3.1 The Scientific Perspective on Design

Simon (1969) described design as a science distinct from natural or social sciences, which are inherently interested in what nature and the social are. In contrast, design science is not about describing *what is*, but *what may be* through the design of something man-made and new (i.e., 'artificial'). Simon suggested that any human's intent to design something involves the design of an artifact (which may imitate natural objects, but is still human-made) that can be used to create a preferred situation. Although Simon has been viewed as providing a cognitive, representational perspective on design (e.g., Suchman, 2007), we suggest that Simon's description of artificial design provides Routine Dynamics scholars with a helpful orientation towards three different types of actions involved in design initiatives (for an analogous application of Simon's perspective on design in the entrepreneurship literature, see Berglund, Bousfiha and Mansoori, 2021). We highlight three key insights from Simon's work on design that we think would be helpful for Routine Dynamics scholars: (a) a focus on designing actions to create preferred situations (Simon, 1969); (b) the creation of artefacts (e.g., Glaser, 2017); and (c) the role of representing the environment.

First, Simon's definition of design highlights the designing of actions to create preferred situations as central to design. These actions to be designed are situated and intended to change the situation.

[2] www.journals.elsevier.com/design-studies

A consequence from this is that studies of Routine Dynamics need to broaden their scope, by including design actions outside of the routine, to understanding the dynamics of routines (see also Glaser, 2017).

Second, Simon (1969) highlights that designing often involves the creation of artifacts. Although actors often strive to create a preferred situation, to do so, they often need to design an artifact. For instance, to control the performances of a routine, a standard operating procedure might be created. Creating these artifacts – although they do not fully control an outcome, as the early routines dynamics research shows – engenders a variety of actions that may influence Routine Dynamics. Put simply, Simon's observation that actors attempt to control their environment by designing artifacts highlights important varieties of action that scholars can investigate to enhance an understanding of Routine Dynamics.

Third, Simon (1969) calls for a variety of representations that have to be created in order to create artifacts. Specifically, creating artifacts requires a designing process to occur that forces designing actors to establish goals, identify organizational resources, specify potential courses of action, represent possible environment circumstances and evaluate which courses of action are preferable (Simon, 1969). The process of creating these representations does not define future action (Suchman, 2007) but does result in the creation of something that frames future actions in a way that influences Routine Dynamics (D'Adderio, 2008).

To illustrate the potential of studying the types of designing actions Simon highlights, Glaser (2014) shows how actions of modelling and mapping take place when a law enforcement agency intentionally tries to randomize patrolling routines by creating a game-theoretic artifact. Specifically, they had to represent the types of security resources that existed and their capabilities such as plain clothes officers, officers armed with automatic weapons or canine patrol units. For this, the actors had to represent the importance of possible patrolling locations by identifying the number of people who might be visiting a location or qualitatively assess the importance of a particular target. The design also used a game-theoretic algorithm to evaluate which possible patrol routine would generate the best outcome according to Bayesian-Stackelberg game theory. Glaser (2017) connects these activities to Routine Dynamics by showing how these designing actions cause organizational actors to expose underlying assumptions; redistribute agency between actants in a routine; and re-examine measures used to evaluate the performance of a routine.

To sum up, although practice perspectives have highlighted that artefacts fail to exert the type of direct cognitive control over organizational actors in the way that the cognitive perspective might suggest, using a scientific perspective of design can be helpful for routines scholars to identify and understand the actions associated with design. These actions stimulate other actions, and we believe that paying attention to the processes of designing artifacts may provide additional insights into studies of routine change, such as the interplay of design and routine actions or the role of representations during design.

22.3.2 The Reflective Practice Perspective on Design

Schön (1983) criticized Simon's (1969) perspective on design and the cognitive perspective underlying the work and teaching of design professionals at that time (for a comparison of Schön and Simon, see Dorst and Dijkhuis, 1995). Studying professional practices, Schön observed that rather than cognitively navigating problems, design professionals engage in reflective practice. This critique of cognitivism and focus on actual practices aligns with the practice theory inherent to Routine Dynamics, albeit that practice theory as such was coined by Ortner (1984) the following year. We highlight three key insights from Schön's work on design that we think would be helpful for Routine Dynamics scholars: (a) shifting from reflection-*on*-action to reflection-*in*-action (see also Tsoukas [Chapter 3], this volume; Dittrich and Seidl, 2018); (b) shifting from framing design as situated action to 'conversation with the situation'; and (c) shifting from defining *problems* to *problem setting*, thereby framing problems, situations and possible solutions (Rein and Schön, 1977, 1996).

First, Schön (1983: 68) highlighted that the designer 'does not keep means and ends separate, but defines them interactively as [s/]he frames the problematic situation. [S/]he does not separate thinking from doing, ratiocinating [her/]his way to the decision which [s/]he must later convert to action.' This was to point out that beyond reflection-on-action, reflection can take place in the midst of action as reflection-in-action, thereby enabling new ends to emerge. Thus, design itself is an emergent process, whereby problems and solutions co-evolve (Dorst and Cross, 2001). Teleological assumptions about design can be problematic, because 'design processes are inherently ill-defined, and as such possess poorly specified initial conditions, allowable operations and goals' (Eckersley, 1988: 87; Joas and Beckert, 2002). These insights enable a better understanding of the creativity of action (Joas, 1996) by highlighting how intentions emerge and change through the routine design process.

Second, situated action (Suchman, 2007) has been a central concept to Routine Dynamics. Schön (1983) highlighted the relational nature of situation and action, where action itself changes the situation in a quasi-dialogical manner as a 'reflective conversation with the materials of the design situation' (Schön, 1992: 131). Schön observed professionals engaged in actions, particularly 'experts' teaching students. While not explicitly addressing the processual nature of design, Schön highlighted the unfolding of the design process through actions that generate a deeper understanding of the situation, and in turn lead to new actions. These insights highlight how actors engage with an unclear situation and begin to develop a better understanding through action. This is important for Routine Dynamics, as a situated action perspective can presuppose that actors already have an understanding of the situation. In contrast, Schön highlighted that actors engage in a type of dialogue with the situation, where new insights and intentions emerge on the spot as reflection-in-action (see also Yanow and Tsoukas, 2009). A consequence for future research is that Routine Dynamics scholars might consider designers' understandings of situations, and how those understandings change through action.

Third, Schön (1983) highlighted that rather than predefining problems as Simon (1969) advocated, actors need to take action before they are able to define the problem. A key insight here is that it is important to consider the framing of the situation and the underlying problem. Whereas Simon assumed pre-defined and structured problems, Schön realized that all too often problems cannot be neatly defined. In these situations, a designer could move ahead by hypothesizing a frame for the situation and testing it through experimentation (Schön, 1984a, 1984b). This might explain why Routine Dynamics scholars have shown how intentionality often fails to change routines. This finding is best understood by recognizing the intentionality that emerges through design actions (Joas, 1996; Joas and Beckert, 2002). The consequence of this is that Routine Dynamics scholars need to study framing, the role of problem-solution co-evolution (Dorst and Cross, 2001), how intentions interact with (understandings of) the situation (Paton and Dorst, 2011), and the role of experimentation in testing frames and potential solutions. For example, Dankfort (2018), Van Kuijk (2019) and Wegener et al. (2019) explored the role that design experiments can play in routine design by focusing on the role of reflective and experimental spaces (Bucher and Langley, 2016) and how one might create spaces for collective reflection-in-action (Yanow and Tsoukas, 2009). These studies suggest that we can better understand Routine Dynamics by carefully examining the actions and assemblages involved in routine design and the role of experiments therein.

In summary, when competent actors engage in praxis, they draw on their existing habits and improvise on the spot (i.e., engage in reflection-in-action) when 'the situation talks back' (Schön, 1983), which enables a new understanding for researchers of not only the potential solution in the form of a routine change but also the underlying design process. Intention emerges out of dialogue with the situation (Schön, 1983). Defining the problem setting is an important element of the design process, as are the frames that designers use. The designer acts to change the situation until a preferred situation is created.

22.4 Future Research

We propose adopting a more processual perspective on routine design in future research, in line with the focus on the design process in design studies. As of yet, such an ontological process perspective has not been adopted in research focused on the design process (Wegener and Cash, 2020) and therefore also not for routine design. Based on our review of both the routines literature and the design studies literature, we propose an agenda for future research.

A first step towards understanding routine design is to view the design process as the unit of analysis, in line with design studies perspectives offered by both Simon and Schön. For Routine Dynamics, this means going beyond the focus on routine actions to include design actions aimed at patterning a routine – both in terms of actions specifically associated with designing routine interfaces (e.g., Kremser and Schreyögg, 2016) and artifacts to control routines (e.g., extending research from Bucher and Langley, 2016 or Glaser, 2017, see also Glaser, Valadao and Hannigan [Chapter 23], this volume and D'Adderio [Chapter 7], this volume) and emergent actions that unfold during the enactment of a routine (e.g., extending research from Dittrich and Seidl, 2018). A potential research question could thus be: *How does the routine design process unfold along design actions and routine actions?*

Building on the analysis of design processes, future research could explore the performativity (D'Adderio et al., 2019) of design theories. Different theories of design, such as Simon's positivistic perspective highlighting planned approaches to design, Schön's constructivist perspective highlighting situated problem solving (Dorst and Dijkhuis, 1995) and the emergent perspective around pragmatist theory of design (see, e.g., Garud et al., 2008; Romme, 2003; Schön 1983, 1992, 1995), are likely to have a different impact on how participants enact the design process. Of specific interest here would be the theories-in-use of actors when they design situated actions. A potential research question could thus be: *How are performing and patterning of routines influenced by design theories-in-use?*

Researchers also should acknowledge the important role of emotions in design. Emotions such as surprise or doubt may instigate an inquiry (Cohen, 2007; Winter, 2013); emotional responses to characteristics such as aesthetics may guide an inquiry; and the elation of finding a preferable situation may end an inquiry (Baldessarelli [Chapter 26], this volume). Considering the role of emotions requires understanding the teleological and affective perspective (see Baldessarelli [Chapter 26], this volume; Dewey, 1934; Tsoukas [Chapter 3], this volume), such as how surprises guide the design process (Schön, 1983). A potential research question could be: *How do emotions trigger, guide and end the routine design process?*

Based on Schön's understanding of design as a conversation with the situation, we also need to understand the role of deliberation, both as an individual process and as a collective process of considering what actions to take next. The closer a researcher can get to actors' understandings of situations, problems, framings and solutions, and how these change over time, the more we can develop a nuanced understanding of the creativity of action, (collective) reflection-in-action and the role of experimentation. Potential research questions could be: *How does collective reflection-in-action unfold during routine design processes, particularly in contexts of innovation (see Deken and Sele [Chapter 21], this volume)? How do deliberations inform experiments and how do experiments inform deliberations during routine design?*

Investigating these research questions also requires some methodological adaptations. Considering the role of emotions, actors' understanding of situations, problems, frames and solutions, as well as reflection-in-action requires routine scholars to get closer to actors' lived experiences. Although ethnography is well-suited to this task (see Dittrich [Chapter 8], this volume), it can be challenging to keep the prospective nature of the participants' lived experiences alive (Weick, 1999). One way here would be to bring more of the ethnographer's own lived experiences into the theorizing, which so far few studies have done (Dittrich [Chapter 8], this volume). Another way would be research approaches that build on a process ontology, thereby enabling researchers to get close to the lived experiences of actors and incorporate these lived experiences into written outputs (see e.g., Wegener and Lorino, 2021). A potential research question could be: *How can researchers shift from reflection-on-action to reflection-in-action to accurately convey the lived experiences of actors engaged in routine design?*

22.5 Conclusion

In this chapter, we have aimed to elucidate the role of design in Routine Dynamics. Design is an empirically important consideration when studying routines, and routines research and design studies have yielded key insights into the relationship between the two. By studying the entire routine design process (including the role of emotions in inquiry), considering emergent intentionality, exploring experiments as design-in-use and exploring new methodological avenues to get closer to actors' lived experiences through reflection-in-action, scholars can generate new insights regarding how routines change and stay the same.

With these insights, our understanding of the definition of routine design is enriched. Complexifying the notion of intentionality as emergent highlights a move away from 'planned change' towards situated problem-solving. Including a change in a routine aspect highlights the importance of design as redesign of existing routines, not just completely new routines. And the notion of the preferred situation acknowledges the important role of emotions, purposes and goals, while realizing that in the end design is not just about artefacts, but about transforming situations.

With these insights, we argue that an enhanced theoretical understanding of routine design would be supported by entwining existing strands of pragmatism in organization studies (Farjoun et al., 2015; Lorino, 2018; Simpson, 2009, 2017), design studies (Dalsgaard, 2014; Dixon, 2020; Schön, 1983) and specifically routine design. This would support the establishment of 'live' routines (Cohen, 2007), explorations of more 'pragmatist' theories of design (Garud et al., 2008; Lorino, 2018) and ultimately, the design of 'healthier' organizations (Glaser, 2017). We hope that we have inspired scholars who study organizations to explore routine (re)design; likewise, we hope that design scholars welcome these insights on (designing) organizational processes from the organizational studies perspective.

References

Baldessarelli, G. (2021). Emotions & Routine Dynamics. In L. D'Adderio, K. Dittrich, M. S. Feldman, B. T. Pentland, C. Rerup and D. Seidl, eds., *Cambridge Handbook of Routine Dynamics*. Cambridge: Cambridge University Press.

Bapuji, H., Hora, M. and Saeed, A. M. (2012). Intentions, intermediaries, and interaction: Examining the emergence of routines. *Journal of Management Studies*, 49(8), 1586–1607.

Bapuji, H., Hora, M., Saeed, A. and Turner, S. (2018). How understanding-based redesign influences the pattern of actions and effectiveness of routines. *Journal of Management*, 45(5), 2132–2162. http://doi.org/10.1177/0149206317744251.

Becker, M. C. (2004). Organizational routines: A review of the literature. *Industrial and Corporate Change*, 13(4), 643–678.

Berglund, H., Bousfiha, M. and Mansoori, Y. (2020). Opportunities as artifacts and entrepreneurship as design. *Academy of Management Review*, 45 (4), 825–846.

Bertels, S., Howard-Grenville, J. and Pek, S. (2016). Cultural molding, shielding, and shoring at Oilco: The role of culture in the integration of routines. *Organization Science*, 27(3), 573–593.

Bresman, H. (2012). Changing routines: A process model of vicarious group learning in pharmaceutical R&D. *Academy of Management Journal*, 56(1), 35–61. http://doi.org/10.5465/amj.2010.0725.

Bucher, S. and Langley, A. (2016). The interplay of reflective and experimental spaces in interrupting and reorienting Routine Dynamics. *Organization Science*, 27(3), 594–613.

Cohen, M. D. (2007). Reading Dewey: Reflections on the study of routine. *Organization Studies*, 28(5), 773–786.

Cohendet, P. S. and Simon, L. O. (2016). Always playable: Recombining routines for creative efficiency at Ubisoft Montreal's video game studio. *Organization Science*, 27(3), 614–632.

Cyert, R. and March, J. G. (1963). *A Behavioral Theory of the Firm.* Malden, MA: Wiley-Blackwell.

D'Adderio, L. (2003). Configuring software, reconfiguring memories: The influence of integrated systems on the reproduction of knowledge and routines. *Industrial and Corporate Change*, 12(2), 321–350.

D'Adderio, L. (2008). The performativity of routines: Theorising the influence of artefacts and distributed agencies on routines dynamics. *Research Policy*, 37(5), 769–789. http://doi.org/10.1016/j.respol.2007.12.012.

D'Adderio, L. (2010). Artifacts at the centre of routines: Performing the material turn in routines theory. *Journal of Institutional Economics*, 7(2), 197–230.

D'Adderio, L. (2014). The replication dilemma unravelled: How organizations enact multiple goals in routine transfer. *Organization Science*, 25(5), 1325–1350.

D'Adderio, L., Glaser, V. L. and Pollock, N. (2019). Performing theories, transforming organizations: A reply to Marti and Gond. *Academy of Management Review*, 44(3), 676–679.

D'Adderio, L. and Pollock, N. (2014). Performing modularity: Competing rules, performative struggles and the effect of organizational theories on the organization. *Organization Studies*, 35(12), 1813–1843.

D'Adderio, L. and Pollock, N. (2020). Making routines the same: Crafting similarity and singularity in routines transfer. *Research Policy*, 49(8), 104029. http://doi.org/10.1016/j.respol.2020.104029.

Dalsgaard, P. (2014). Pragmatism and design thinking. *International Journal of Design*, 8, 143–155.

Dankfort, Z. (2018, December 4). *The Visual Storytelling Toolkit: A Way to Engage Employees with their Organization's Vision.* (M. Guerreiro Goncalves and F. Wegener, eds.). Delft.

Deken, F., Carlile, P. R., Berends, H. and Lauche, K. (2016). Generating novelty through interdependent routines: A process model of routine work. *Organization Science*, 27(3), 659–677.

Dewey, J. (1922). *Human Nature and Conduct.* New York: Henry Holt and Co.

Dewey, J. (1933/1998). *How We Think: A Restatement of the Relation of Reflective Thinking to the Educative Process.* Boston: Houghton Mifflin.

Dewey, J. (1934). *Art as Experience.* Minton: Balch.

Dewey, J. (1938). *Logic: The Theory Of Inquiry* (pp. 1–550). New York: Henry Holt & Company.

Dionysiou, D. (2021). Pragmatism & Routine Dynamics. In L. D'Adderio, K. Dittrich, M. S. Feldman, B. T. Pentland, C. Rerup and D. Seidl, eds., *Cambridge Handbook of Routine Dynamics.* Cambridge: Cambridge University Press.

Dionysiou, D. D. and Tsoukas, H. (2013). Understanding the (re)creation of routines from within: A symbolic interactionist perspective. *Academy of Management Review*, 38(2), 181–205.

Dittrich, K., Guérard, S. and Seidl, D. (2016). Talking about routines: The role of reflective talk in routine change. *Organization Science*, 27(3), 678–697.

Dittrich, K. and Seidl, D. (2018). Emerging intentionality in Routine Dynamics: A pragmatist view. *Academy of Management Journal*, 61(1), 111–138.

Dixon, B. S. (2020). *Dewey and Design: A Pragmatist Perspective for Design Research* (pp. 1–208). Cham: Springer International Publishing.

Dorst, K. and Cross, N. (2001). Creativity in the design process: Co-evolution of problem–solution. *Design Studies*, 1–13.

Dorst, K. and Dijkhuis, J. (1995). Comparing paradigms for describing design activity. *Design Studies*, 16(2), 261–274.

Eckersley, M. (1988). The form of design processes: A protocol analysis study. *Design Studies*, 9(2), 86–94.

Emirbayer, M. (1997). Manifesto for a relational sociology. *American Journal of Sociology*, 103(2), 281–317.

Emirbayer, M. and Mische, A. (1998). What is agency? *American Journal of Sociology*, 103(4), 962–1023.

Farjoun, M., Ansell, C. K. and Boin, A. (2015). PERSPECTIVE – pragmatism in organization studies: Meeting the challenges of a dynamic and complex world. *Organization Science*, 26(6), 1787–1804. http://doi.org/10.1287/orsc.2015.1016.

Feldman, M. S. (2000). Organizational routines as a source of continuous change. *Organization Science*, 11(6), 611–629.

Feldman, M. S. (2016). Routines as process: Past, present, future. In J. A. Howard-Grenville, C. Rerup, A. Langley and H. Tsoukas, eds., *Perspectives on*

Process Organization Studies: Organizational Routines. Oxford: Oxford University Press, pp. 23–46.

Feldman, M. S. and Orlikowski, W. J. (2011). Theorizing practice and practicing theory. *Organization Science*, 22(5), 1240–1253.

Feldman, M. S. and Pentland, B. T. (2003). Reconceptualizing organizational routines as a source of flexibility and change. *Administrative Science Quarterly*, 48(1), 94.

Feldman, M. S., Pentland, B. T., D'Adderio, L. and Lazaric, N. (2016). Beyond routines as things: Introduction to the special issue on Routine Dynamics. *Organization Science*, 27(3), 505–513.

Garud, R., Jain, S. and Tuertscher, P. (2008). Incomplete by design and designing for incompleteness. *Organization Studies*, 29(3), 351–371.

Glaser, V. L. (2014). Enchanted Algorithms: The Quantification of Organizational Decision-Making. *Dissertation, Marshall School of Business*.

Glaser, V. L. (2017). Design performances: How organizations inscribe artifacts to change routines. *Academy of Management Journal*, 60(6), 2126–2154.

Gupta, A., Hoopes, D. G. and Knott, A. M. (2015). Redesigning routines for replication. *Strategic Management Journal*, 36(6), 851–871.

Hales, M. and Tidd, J. (2009). The practice of routines and representations in design and development. *Industrial and Corporate Change*, 18(4), 551–574.

Howard-Grenville, J. A. (2005). The persistence of flexible organizational routines: The role of agency and organizational context. *Organization Science*, 16(6), 618–636.

Howard-Grenville, J. A., Rerup, C., Langley, A. and Tsoukas, H. (2016). *Organizational Routines*. Oxford: Oxford University Press.

James, W. (1909/1996). *A Pluralistic Universe: Hibbert Lectures at Manchester College on the Present Situation in Philosophy*. Lincoln: University of Nebraska Press.

Joas, H. (1996). *The Creativity of Action*. Chicago: University of Chicago Press.

Joas, H. and Beckert, J. (2002). A theory of action: Pragmatism and the creativity of action. *Transactional Viewpoints*, 1(4), 1–4.

Kremser, W. and Schreyögg, G. (2016). The dynamics of interrelated Routines: Introducing the cluster level. *Organization Science*, 27(3), 698–721.

Lazaric, N. and Denis, B. (2005). Routinization and memorization of tasks in a workshop: The case of the introduction of ISO norms. *Industrial and Corporate Change*, 14(5), 873–896.

Leutenegger, C., Tuckermann, H., Gutzan, S. and Ruegg-Sturm, J. (2018). Organizational routine design in a hospital: A narrative-based study of ostensive routine dimensions in the making. Presented at the *International Symposium on Process Organization Studies*, Halkidiki, Greece.

Locke, K., Golden-Biddle, K. and Feldman, M. S. (2008). Perspective – Making doubt generative: Rethinking the role of doubt in the research process. *Organization Science*, 19(6), 907–918.

Lorino, P. (2018). *Pragmatism and Organization Studies*. Oxford: Oxford University Press.

Lorino, P. and Mourey, D., (2013). The experience of time in the inter-organizing inquiry: A present thickened by dialog and situations, *Scandinavian Journal of Management*, 29(1), 48–62.

Lorino, P., Tricard, B. and Clot, Y. (2011). Research methods for non-representational approaches to organizational complexity: The dialogical mediated inquiry. *Organization Studies*, 32(6), 769–801.

March, J. G. and Simon, H. A. (1958). *Organizations*. Oxford: Wiley.

Nelson, R. R. and Winter, S. G. (1982). *An Evolutionary Theory of Economic Change*. Cambridge, MA: Belknap Press of Harvard University Press.

Nicolini, D. and Monteiro, P. (2016). The practice approach: For a praxeology of organisational and management studies. In *The SAGE Handbook of Process Organization Studies*. London: SAGE Publications Ltd, pp. 1–27.

Ortner, S. B. (1984). Theory in anthropology since the sixties. *Comparative Studies in Society and History*, 26, 126–166.

Parmigiani, A. and Howard-Grenville, J. (2011). Routines revisited: Exploring the capabilities and practice perspectives. *The Academy of Management Annals*, 5(1), 413–453.

Paton, B. and Dorst, K. (2011). Briefing and reframing: A situated practice. *Design Studies*, 32(6), 573–587.

Pentland, B. T. and Feldman, M. S. (2005). Organizational routines as a unit of analysis. *Industrial and Corporate Change*, 14(5), 793–815.

Pentland, B. T. and Feldman, M. S. (2008). Designing routines: On the folly of designing artifacts, while hoping for patterns of action. *Information and Organization*, 18(4), 235–250.

Pentland, B. T. and Hærem, T. (2015). Organizational routines as patterns of action: Implications for organizational behavior. *Annual Review of Organizational Psychology and Organizational Behavior*, 2(1), 465–487.

Pentland, B. T. and Jung, E. J. (2016). Evolutionary and revolutionary change in path-dependent patterns of action. In *Organizational Routines*. Oxford University Press, pp. 96–113.

Pentland, B. T., Recker, J. and Wyner, G. (2015) A thermometer for interdependence: Exploring patterns of interdependence using networks of affordances. In T. Carte, A. Heinzl and C. Urquahart, eds., *Proceedings of the 36th International Conference on Information Systems*. Association for Information Systems (AIS), http://aisel.aisnet.org/, pp. 1–11.

Peirce, C. S. (1998). *The Essential Peirce*. Bloomington: Indiana University Press.

Rein, M. and Schön, D. A. (1977). Problem setting in policy research. In C. H. Weiss, ed., *Using Social Research in Public Policy Making*. Lexington, MA: Lexington Books, pp. 235–251.

Rein, M. and Schön, D. A. (1996). Frame-critical policy analysis and frame-reflective policy practice. *Knowledge and Policy*, 9(1), 85–104.

Rerup, C. and Feldman, M. S. (2011). Routines as a source of change in organizational schemata: The role of trial-and-error learning. *Academy of Management Journal*, 54(3), 577–610.

Reynaud, B. (2005). The void at the heart of rules: Routines in the context of rule-following. The case of the Paris Metro Workshop. *Industrial and Corporate Change*, 14(5), 847–871. http://doi.org/10.1093/icc/dth073.

Romme, A. G. L. (2003). Making a difference: Organization as design. *Organization Science*, 14(5), 558–573.

Salvato, C. and Rerup, C. (2010). Beyond collective entities: Multilevel research on organizational routines and capabilities. *Journal of Management*, 37(2), 468–490.

Schön, D. A. (1983). *Reflective Practitioner: How Professionals Think in Action*. New York: BasicBooks.

Schön, D. A. (1984a). Design: A process of enquiry, experimentation and research. *Design Studies*, 5(3), 130–131.

Schön, D. A. (1984b). Problems, frames and perspectives on designing. *Design Studies*, 5(3), 132–136.

Schön, D. A. (1992). Designing as reflective conversation with the materials of a design situation. *Research in Engineering Design*, 3(3), 131–147.

Schön, D. A. (1995). Knowing-in-action: The new scholarship requires a new epistemology. *Change*, 27(6), 26–34. Retrieved from www.jstor.org/stable/40165285.

Simon, H. A. (1947). *Administrative Behavior: A Study of Decision-Making Processes in Administrative Organization*. London: Macmillan.

Simon, H. A. (1969). *The Sciences of the Artificial* (1st edition). Cambridge, MA: The MIT Press.

Simon, H. A. (1988). The science of design: Creating the artificial. *Design Issues*, 4(1/2), 67–82.

Simpson, B. (2009). Pragmatism, Mead and the practice turn. *Organization Studies*, 30(12), 1329–1347.

Simpson, B. (2017). Pragmatism: A philosophy of practice. In *The SAGE Handbook of Qualitative Business and Management Research Methods*. London: SAGE Publications Ltd, pp. 54–68.

Simpson, B. and Lorino, P. (2016). Re-viewing routines through a pragmatist lens. In J. A. Howard-Grenville, C. Rerup, A. Langley and H. Tsoukas, eds., *Perspectives on Process Organization Studies: Organizational Routines*. Oxford: Oxford University Press, pp. 47–70.

Suchman, L. (2007). *Human-Machine Reconfigurations: Plans and Situated Actions* (2nd edition). Cambridge; New York: Cambridge University Press.

Szulanski, G. (1996). Exploring internal stickiness: Impediments to the transfer of best practice within the firm. *Strategic Management Journal*, 17, 27–43. http://doi.org/10.2307/2486989.

Szulanski, G. (2000). The process of knowledge transfer: A diachronic analysis of stickiness. *Organizational Behavior and Human Decision Processes*, 82(1), 9–27. http://doi.org/10.1006/obhd.2000.2884.

Tsoukas, H. (2021). How to make Routine Dynamics research more dynamic: Advancing theorizing through performative phenomenology. In L. D'Adderio, K. Dittrich, M. S. Feldman, B. T. Pentland, C. Rerup and D. Seidl, eds.,

Cambridge Handbook of Routine Dynamics. Cambridge: Cambridge University Press.

Tsoukas, H. and Chia, R. C. H. (2002). On organizational becoming: Rethinking organizational change. *Organization Science*, 13(5), 567–582. http://doi.org/10.1287/orsc.13.5.567.7810.

Turner, S. F. and Rindova, V. P. (2012). A balancing act: How organizations pursue consistency in routine functioning in the face of ongoing change. *Organization Science*, 23(1), 24–46.

van der Bijl-Brouwer, M. (2019). Problem framing expertise in public and social innovation. *She Ji: The Journal of Design, Economics, and Innovation*, 5(1), 29–43.

van Hulst, M. and Yanow, D. (2015). From policy 'frames' to 'framing'. *The American Review of Public Administration*, 46(1), 92–112.

van Kuijk, K. (2019, October 18). *Designing a Live Routine*. (E. A. Hende and F. E. Wegener, eds.). Delft University of Technology.

Wegener, F. (2019). When designing routines: Dealing with the challenges of interdependency and affordances through design experiments. Presented at 11th *International Process Symposium Organization in the Digital Age: Understanding the Dynamics of Work, Innovation, and Collective Action* (pp. 1–8).

Wegener, F. and Cash, P. (2020). The future of design process research? Exploring process theory and methodology. *Proceedings of the Design Research Society Conference 2020*.

Wegener, F., Guerreiro Goncalves, M. and Dankfort, Z. (2019). Reflection-in-action when designing organizational processes: Prototyping workshops for collective reflection-in-action. *Proceedings of the Design Society: International Conference on Engineering Design*, 1(1), 1255–1264.

Wegener, F. and Lorino P, (2021). Capturing the experience of living forward through 'withness'. In J. Reinecke, R. Suddaby, A. Langley and H. Tsoukas, eds., *Perspectives on Process Organization Studies Vol. 7: About Time: Temporality and History in Organization Studies*. Oxford: Oxford University Press.

Weick, K. E. (1999). That's moving: Theories that matter. *Journal of Management Inquiry*, 8(2), 134–142.

Winter, S. G. (2013). Habit, deliberation, and action: Strengthening the microfoundations of routines and capabilities. *Academy of Management Perspectives*, 27(2), 120–137.

Winter, S. G. and Szulanski, G. (2001). Replication as strategy. *Organization Science*, 12(6), 730–743. http://doi.org/10.1287/orsc.12.6.730.10084.

Yanow, D. and Tsoukas, H. (2009). What is reflection-in-action? A phenomenological account. *Journal of Management Studies*, 46(8), 1339–1364.

CHAPTER 23

Algorithms and Routine Dynamics

VERN L. GLASER, RODRIGO VALADAO AND TIMOTHY R. HANNIGAN

23.1 Introduction

Increasingly, algorithms – 'abstract, formalized description[s] of computational procedure[s]' (Dourish, 2016: 3) –are becoming core components of organizational routines. For example, law enforcement agencies deploy algorithms within patrolling routines to predict the locations of future crimes (Brayne, 2017) and efficiently allocate security resources (Glaser, 2017); financial institutions use algorithms to calculate credit scores for individuals, which are used to determine credit amounts and terms of access to capital (Pasquale, 2015; see also Fourcade and Healy, 2017); internet companies use algorithms to classify text based on automated content analysis (MacCormick, 2012; Rieder, 2017); journalists use algorithmic metrics to shape their editorial and publishing activities (Christin, 2020); and academic organizations use algorithms to routinize the detection of plagiarism (Introna, 2007). Broadly speaking, many management scholars have suggested that using algorithms to handle 'traditional business processes operated by workers, managers, process engineers, supervisors, or customer service representatives' (Iansiti and Lakhani, 2020: 60) creates opportunities for organizations to develop new capabilities and generate value (e.g., Davenport, 2018; Mayer-Schonberger and Cukier, 2013; Schildt, 2020).

Recently, however, scholars have begun to explore the dark side of algorithms by suggesting that incorporating algorithms into organizational routines influences professional power dynamics (e.g., Curchod et al., 2020; Kellogg et al., 2020) and favours rational decision-making processes over more value-oriented decision-making processes (e.g., Lindebaum et al., 2019), which may in turn produce negative or unintended societal outcomes. With continued use, the power dynamics undergirding the use of algorithms may fade into the organizational background (D'Adderio, 2008) as concerns regarding the 'disempowered user' are superseded by the complexity of algorithmic systems (Burke, 2019: 12). Put simply, it is extremely difficult to effectively build accountability into algorithms (Buhmann et al., 2019; Martin, 2019). Although algorithms are becoming an increasingly important component of modern organizational life, Routine Dynamics scholars have only just begun to explore algorithms as a topic in its own right.

In this chapter, our objective is to review existing literature in Routine Dynamics that contributes to our understanding of algorithmic phenomena, and to stimulate routines-oriented research about algorithms. We start by defining what an algorithm is, highlighting that routines theory about the role of artifacts (D'Adderio, 2008) can be applied to explain the relationship between algorithms and Routine Dynamics. We then observe how routines scholars have studied algorithms in prior work, showing, (i) how algorithms can function as an actant that can make specific decisions in a routine or program a sequence of actions; (ii) that algorithms encode designer intent; (iii) that algorithms are entangled in broader assemblages of theories, artifacts, actors and practices; and (iv) the performativity of algorithms. We subsequently provide further methodological guidance by articulating five different analytical approaches that scholars can use in studying algorithms and Routine Dynamics.

We would like to acknowledge the insightful comments and guidance provided by editors Luciana D'Adderio and Katharina Dittrich, which have been invaluable in shaping this chapter. The authors would also like to acknowledge that this research has been supported in part by funding from Canada's Social Sciences and Humanities Research Council.

We close our chapter by suggesting potential avenues for future research on algorithms, highlighting specific opportunities for Routine Dynamics scholars to explore not only how understanding algorithms can advance our comprehension of Routine Dynamics but also how Routine Dynamics can help advance our broader understanding of algorithms in management research.

23.2 What Is an Algorithm?

In current social discourse, the 'algorithm' concept is used in a variety of ways, ranging from a simple 'recipe composed in programmable steps' (Gillespie, 2016: 19) to mystical 'boxes' that evoke 'feelings of a technological sublime' (Ames, 2018: 2). Cultural perspectives on algorithms emphasize the opacity of algorithms in practice, and highlight the importance of recognizing that algorithms are embedded in broader systems of activities (Seaver, 2017: 418–419). For the purposes of studying the role of algorithms in routines, we focus on the more tangible, practical definition of an algorithm as an 'abstract, formalized description of a computational procedure' (Dourish, 2016: 3). Algorithms are often depicted as mathematical models (Fei et al., 2017) that represent a problem in numerical or categorical terms that can be analysed to optimize a response to that problem. For instance, in an optimization algorithm, the algorithm designer optimizes performance with respect to a goal by choosing from among a 'set of given alternatives of action' that can be selected within an environment that is itself represented by 'a set of parameters, which may be known with certainty or only in terms of a probability distribution' (Simon, 1996: 115).

Although algorithms are computational procedures, they are often embedded in software as functions that operate based on data structures and produce outputs that can influence organizational activities (Dourish, 2016). This decision-making role of algorithmic artifacts was described in detail in a recent article in *Harvard Business Review*,

> At the core of the new firm is a decision factory – what we call the 'AI factory.' Its software runs the millions of daily ad auctions at Google and Baidu. Its algorithms decide which cars offer rides on Didi, Grab, Lyft, and Uber. It sets the prices of headphones and polo shirts on Amazon and runs the robots that clean floors in some Walmart locations. It enables customer service bots at Fidelity and interprets X-rays at Zebra Medical. In each case the AI factory treats decision-making as a science. Analytics systematically convert internal and external data into predictions, insights, and choices, which in turn guide and automate operational workflows (Iansiti and Lakhani, 2020: 61).

Thus, algorithms can be thought of as computational procedures embedded in broader networks of activities.

In research on algorithms in organizations, and in social science research more broadly, algorithms tend to be viewed from 'a narrow technical perspective' that conceptualizes them as artifacts that are 'self-standing, autonomous, and black-boxed entities' (Glaser et al., 2021: 4). For instance, Kellogg et al. (2020: 50) conceptualized algorithmic systems in organizational settings as entities that offer affordances that recommend or restrict human action – that is, an algorithm is an entity that organizational leaders use to control less powerful actors. Similarly, Curchod et al. (2020: 5) suggested that algorithms are 'instruments for the regulation of social relationships'. In general, management scholars conceptualize algorithms as tools that can be used by humans to exercise agency and dominion over a set of tasks conceptualized by a designer, such as by assisting, augmenting, arresting or automating organizational activity (e.g., Murray et al., forthcoming). However, other research in management has built out a more nuanced approach for conceptualizing algorithms in organizational life. For instance, Glaser et al.'s (2021) introduction of a performative, socio-material perspective on algorithms – which accounts for the relational, temporal and spatial dynamics that have been overlooked in these previous organizational studies – relies on two principles: algorithmic assemblages and biographical moments. In this chapter, we argue that this latter conceptualization of algorithms represents a more promising path for Routine Dynamics studies.

23.3 Artifacts, Algorithms and Routine Dynamics

While much of what has been discussed in management research regards algorithms as simple tools, as discussed earlier, we contend that algorithms are embedded in the fabric of organizations as ongoing social performances and therefore should not be framed as hermetically sealed objects with fixed characteristics. Given that routines research relies on a performative understanding of artifacts that resists conceptualizing artifacts as independent black-boxed entities (D'Adderio, 2008), this holds promise for the potential of a focused research programme in Routine Dynamics considering how algorithms are analysed in the context of their relational connections with other artifacts, actors, practices and theories (D'Adderio, 2011). In reviewing work in routines research on algorithms, we demonstrate the coherence of this emerging perspective.

Existing routines research has yielded several insights that provide us with a basic understanding of algorithms and their relationship to Routine Dynamics. First, algorithms are artifacts that function as actants to make specific decisions or to program sequences of actions (e.g., Callon 1980, 1986, 2017; Latour, 1986, 1996, 2005; Latour and Woolgar, 1979; Sele and Grand, 2016; see also D'Adderio [Chapter 7] and Sele [Chapter 6], this volume). Second, designers create algorithms to realize intended goals. Third, these algorithms are embedded in broader assemblages of actors, artifacts, theories and practices. Finally, algorithms influence routines through performative dynamics associated with algorithmic assemblages. It is important to recognize that an algorithm is a type of artifact, and that generalized routine theory about artifacts applies to algorithms (D'Adderio, 2008).

23.3.1 *Algorithms as Artifacts*

Routines scholars have shown that algorithms function as artifacts that automate decisions traditionally made by humans. For instance, Glaser (2017) described how a law enforcement agency used a game-theoretic algorithm to automatically generate randomized patrol schedules. Law enforcement agencies seek to deploy police officers to specific locations at specific times to best reduce or interdict crime. Traditionally, human schedulers have made these decisions. However, Glaser showed how game theoretic algorithms helped a law enforcement agency automate these decisions, thereby reducing human effort and increasing the randomness of patrol assignments to better achieve the goal of reducing crime. In another example, D'Adderio (2001) showed how organizational actors use algorithms to translate tacit knowledge automatically. Specifically, she studied the routines by which organizational actors created a digital model or virtual prototype. To convert the digital to the physical, and the physical to the digital, organizational actors used a series of algorithms to translate the tacit knowledge of designers into numeric parameters and algorithmic calculations. D'Adderio's (2001) study thus shows how organizations use algorithms to convert tacit knowledge into materialized decisions.

Studies in the routines literature also show that algorithms can automate sequences of actions. For example, D'Adderio and Pollock (2014: 1825) showed how an organization used a process called 'Autoswap': 'every time a faulty board was returned for a vendor to repair, this would immediately issue a new board and ship it to the integrator'. This algorithmic approach to addressing board failures resulted in the development of a recurring sequence of actions as the organization chose to handle defects by using the algorithmic Autoswap process as opposed to repairing faulty boards. Algorithms have also been shown to direct patterns of routine activity in agriculture (Labatut et al., 2012) and the credit industry (Kiviat, 2019; Pasquale, 2015). In the technology industry, algorithms automate not only human-operated routines but also patterns of action that did not exist previously, such as search engine indexing, page ranking or cryptography (MacCormick, 2012), indicating that algorithms also have the potential to autonomously create new routines.

Work has also shown how algorithms can be used to control the relationships between routines in organizations. One thread in this research stream has shown that programmed interfaces determine where one routine stops and another begins in routine clusters (Kremser and Schreyögg, 2016). For instance, Berente, Lyytinen, Yoo and King (2016) studied a software implementation project at NASA and found that algorithms can be used to control the interfaces between routines. Additionally, as another empirical example, financial institutions use fraud detection algorithms to initiate routines whereby humans verify the legitimacy of financial transactions. In summary, routines research has shown that algorithms are artifacts that can be used to replace individual decisions that are central to routines; to establish sequences of actions within routines or new routines; or to program interfaces between different routines.

23.3.2 Algorithm Design

Another important insight from routines research shows how an algorithm is an artifact that encodes the intent of a designer (Pentland and Hærem, 2015). Put simply, an algorithm's computational procedure must be specified a priori by a designer (Simon, 1970; see also, Wegener and Glaser [Chapter 22], this volume) who must construct a rational sequence of actions whereby a decision is contextualized, quantified and calculated (Cabantous et al., 2010). Algorithms therefore function as material artifacts or tools that carry this rationality (Cabantous and Gond, 2011). The process of creating and/or contextualizing an algorithm for a particular routine carries some important implications.

First, creating an algorithm requires organizational actors to project a future state of affairs (Wenzel et al., 2020). Simon (1970) observed that creating an artifact such as an algorithm requires a designer to construct a view of how things should be, as opposed to merely describing how things are. A designed artifact has a goal and is structured to take actions that enable it to adapt to a changing environment. Designers must model the environment based on a set of parameters, establish the set of actions available to the artifact and define a goal that will be used to evaluate the different potential courses of action (Simon, 1970: 115). Glaser (2014) showed how this unfolds by describing how organizational actors who design algorithms model organizational problems by establishing numerical parameters, selecting computational models and constructing evaluative measures for selecting a particular course of action.

Second, different actors attempt to embed different points of view into algorithms during the design process. For instance, Cacciatori (2012) observed that some artifacts instantiate formal representations of specific occupational knowledge. Occupational members inscribe their interests into algorithms during the design process (D'Adderio, 2008, 2011, 2014) by influencing how data are selected and constructed, and/or how algorithmic outputs are produced and interpreted. In summary, algorithms are artifacts that are designed and inscribed with particular points of view.

23.3.3 The Algorithmic Assemblage

Routines scholars have highlighted that artifacts such as algorithms are best understood and studied as being entangled within broader assemblages of theories, artifacts, actors and practices (D'Adderio et al., 2019; D'Adderio and Pollock, 2020). As a computational procedure, an algorithm is an artifact in and of itself but can only be understood relative to the theories, actors, other artifacts and practices involved in a routine's enactment.

Algorithms typically rely on a theory – a causal understanding that relates concepts (e.g., Marti and Gond, 2018) – to generate a computational procedure. For example, Glaser (2017) showed how algorithms used to generate law enforcement patrolling schedules relied on insights from game theory, specifically Bayesian Stackleberg games. Similarly, D'Adderio and Pollock (2014) showed how modularity theory informed the design of a swapping algorithm used in a routine to deal with circuit board failures. Theories are particularly important in the study of algorithms and routines, because they provide a conceptual infrastructure for generating the abstractions necessary to represent the environment parametrically (Cabantous and Gond, 2011).

Algorithms are also embedded in systems of artifacts that interact with each other (Cacciatori,

2012). For instance, Glaser (2017) described how a game theoretic algorithm uses a computational formula to generate patrolling recommendations; however, this formula requires data inputs which also generate visualized outputs in the form of Excel spreadsheets. Typically, algorithms are embedded in systems of other artifacts, such as software systems that capture different types of digital data, and visualization devices that help actors interpret and deploy outputs in routines.

23.3.4 The Performativity of Algorithms

Routines researchers have also developed theories about how artifacts such as algorithms influence Routine Dynamics by describing how they interact with the performative and ostensive aspects of routines (D'Adderio, 2011). Specifically, artifacts play a 'framing' role by providing organizational actors with important inputs and parameters that can shape routine performance (D'Adderio, 2008). To illustrate, during the enactment of a particular routine, situational factors may require actors to deviate from the standard operating procedure (e.g., a customer might begin to say something that was not envisioned in the artifact). When the specific performance of a routine is not accounted for by an artifact such as a standard operating procedure, the framing is not complete and an 'overflow' occurs. Under these circumstances, actors must integrate or account for these overflows in order to perform the routine. Consequently, the artifact frames the action by providing the actors who perform a routine with a resource that they may or may not use (Hales and Tidd, 2009); such overflows influence future routine performances if they change the artifacts or if actors respond by adjusting their understandings of ostensive aspects of the routine.

It is important to note that an algorithm can be seen as a particular type of artifact that differs significantly from other types of artifacts, such as physically written standard operating procedures in terms of the flexibility of the algorithmic assemblage. Whereas artifacts such as standard operating procedures often function as guidelines (e.g., hiring instructions outlined in the manual of the human resources department of a private company) that actors can readily ignore, algorithms can compute decisions by following rules designed prior to the routine's performance that are materially embedded in the algorithmic assemblage (e.g., operational procedures encoded in an enterprise resource planning software, such as SAP or Oracle). In other words, once rules and procedures are algorithmically embedded in a software, they become 'locked doors in that they truly constrain action' (Pentland and Feldman, 2008: 242) – even though actors that are part of the assemblage might always decide to look for alternative, unlocked doors elsewhere (e.g., D'Adderio, 2008).

This is crucial insight, because deploying algorithmic artifacts in a routine involves several prerequisites. First, algorithm designers must generate a representation of the environment (Simon, 1970). Although this abstraction does not completely represent the environment, it ultimately frames actions in a particular way. For example, an optimization algorithm might analyse a variable called 'customer importance'. Such a variable might be modelled categorically (e.g., 'high', 'medium' and 'low' levels of importance, or a 1–5 scale) and be used by the algorithm to calculate decisions. These inputs are embedded in software and thus less malleable and more 'durable' than the loose guidelines set up in a standard operating procedure (D'Adderio, 2008: 773). Put another way, 'artifacts are front-loaded with the habits, intentions, and rationales held by the agencies by which they have been created, adopted, and adapted' (D'Adderio, 2011: 207). Algorithms may be more deeply embedded in the material infrastructure of a routine than other types of artifacts because in most organizational settings, the assumptions and calculations of an algorithm might not be easily modified after deployment.

23.4 Methodological Precepts for Studying Algorithms and Routines

Studying algorithms can be challenging due to how they are embedded in complex systems (e.g., Gillespie, 2014; Seaver, 2017) and are often opaque and difficult to observe (Dourish, 2016; Pasquale, 2015) – necessitating careful methodological consideration by scholars interested in understanding the relationship between algorithms and Routine Dynamics. Put simply, Seaver (2017) observes that these unique characteristics of algorithms require the modification and customization of traditional ethnographic techniques (see Dittrich [Chapter 8], this volume). Routines scholars who adopt a practice perspective (Feldman and Orlikowski, 2011) recognize that the elements of an assemblage (i.e., actors, artifacts, theories and practices) are mutually constituted. This means that the differentiation between such elements is analytical rather than ontological, and that researchers are advised to study them not in terms of dualistic distinctions (such as the classic agency-structure dichotomy), but to acknowledge their entangled nature at the outset (see Glaser et al., 2021). There has been 'ongoing, shifting, and open-ended work to delimit and define the social and the material and the relationship between them' (Mazmanian et al., 2014: 832); the methodology deployed to study algorithms and routines must capture these dynamic relationships that constitute and reconfigure socio-material assemblages on an ongoing basis.

To capture such dynamism, the methodological perspective advanced here follows existing routines research in advocating for a highly action-focused approach (Feldman, 2016; Feldman and Orlikowski, 2011), but differentiates from studies that have considered algorithms as entities in and of themselves (e.g., Kellogg et al., 2019). In a nutshell, the perspective we advocate here is that algorithms should be studied as embedded in action, and more specifically, that researchers should follow the actions associated with algorithms. Although practical challenges may arise when deploying this approach because some algorithmic actions might be hidden and embedded in software (D'Adderio, 2008), recent work has unveiled promising avenues for ethnographic studies of algorithmic systems. For example, building on the concept of polymorphous engagement whereby the researcher interacts personally and virtually with informants across dispersed sites to collect eclectic data from unorthodox sources (Gusterson, 1997), Seaver (2017) advanced 'scavenging' tactics to study computational codes as heterogeneous and diffuse sociotechnical systems, proposing that algorithms manifest across sites in different ways. We suggest that the socio-material assemblage perspective (Glaser et al., 2021) articulated here can inform a set of analytical approaches that can be used to investigate algorithms from a Routine Dynamics perspective.

First, because algorithms are artifacts, researchers who study them must pay close attention to their materiality (see D'Adderio [Chapter 7] and Sele [Chapter 6], this volume). It is important to understand the computational procedures involved in the algorithm (Dourish, 2016). Key questions concern the decision and how it is computed. For example, the computation can be based on different types of evaluation criteria (i.e., optimization or satisficing). What are the steps involved in the computation? It is also important to understand how data are used within the computation. For example, which parameters are used in the computation, and how are they updated when the environment changes? Finally, it is important to understand how the algorithm is embedded in a broader software package. Paying attention to the material composition of the algorithm is particularly important when studying its relationship with Routine Dynamics (D'Adderio, 2008, 2011).

Second, to understand the relationship between algorithms and Routine Dynamics, we suggest it is important to analyse both the design and use of algorithms (see Wegener and Glaser [Chapter 22], this volume). One theme in practice-based research is to challenge the degree of control exercised by the designers of artifacts (e.g., algorithms) over the situated actions taken by actors who use them to perform routines (e.g., Pentland and Feldman, 2008; Suchman, 2007). Although research along these lines has demonstrated that intentional changes implemented by strategic leaders often lead to unintended outcomes due to actors' decisions during routine performances (Rerup and Feldman, 2011), we suggest that understanding Routine Dynamics requires particular care to be paid to understanding how emergent intentions influence action (Dittrich and Seidl, 2018). Specifically, although plans and intentions may not control future actions, the specific actions involved in artifact design can substantively influence Routine Dynamics (Glaser, 2017). This is likely to be of particular importance for artifacts such as algorithms that function as actants in a routine.

Third, in examining the role of algorithms in Routine Dynamics, it is particularly important to consider the underlying theories that inform computational decisions (D'Adderio et al., 2019; see also Pollock and Williams, 2016). An algorithm inherently reflects a model based on a theoretical understanding of the world that connects inputs with outputs in a particular way. Although algorithms can be conceptually unreflexive, they often rely on complex academic theories that function as instantiations of professional knowledge. More abstract, theoretical knowledge often generates political power (Zbaracki and Bergen, 2010); therefore, understanding how different communities of practice embed theoretical knowledge into artifacts such as algorithms is an important way to connect algorithms to Routine Dynamics (Cacciatori, 2012; D'Adderio, 2014; see also D'Adderio and Pollock, 2014) and may connect to our understanding of the political aspects of Routine Dynamics (see D'Adderio and Safavi [Chapter 15], this volume).

Fourth, it is also important to understand how an algorithm fits within the actions of both the routine itself and the broader cluster of routines (Kremser and Schreyögg, 2016). Because an algorithm typically makes one particular decision, the researcher must understand how the algorithm fits into the broader actions associated with the routine. How is the algorithm actually applied in a routine's enactment? The (in)flexibility of the artifact's algorithm can be differentially designed and used (D'Adderio, 2008), and is an important characteristic to analyse. Algorithms might also be used to stimulate new routines in contexts such as police work (Brayne, 2017).

Finally, researchers should pay attention to the temporal issues associated with algorithmic assemblages (D'Adderio et al., 2019; Garud and Gehman, 2019). Drawing on biographical approaches to software (Hyysalo et al., 2019; Pollock and Williams, 2009), Glaser, Pollock and D'Adderio (2020) noted the importance of recognizing that algorithmic assemblages differ at different moments in time. Specifically, they highlighted that in addition to the normal enactment of an algorithmic routine, there are other biographical moments in the life of an algorithm such as the inscribing and layering of programs of action; performative struggles between different algorithmic assemblages; and translating an algorithm from one context to another (Glaser et al., 2021).

To sum up, understanding how algorithms relate to Routine Dynamics requires paying careful attention to the methods involved in the design and use of algorithms. Routines research involves following actions (Feldman, 2016), and studying algorithms requires the researcher to take a somewhat broader perspective on those actions. We suggest that dynamic and thoughtful consideration of algorithmic assemblages will help researchers develop appropriate practice-theoretic perspectives on this topic.

23.5 Future Research Directions

Adopting a Routine Dynamics perspective that leverages the assemblage concept reveals several directions for future research that could provide opportunities to develop novel and important theory about algorithms and about Routine Dynamics. With that in mind, in this section we explore three specific avenues in which a cross-fertilization between Routine Dynamics and algorithmic perspectives and conceptualizations seems particularly promising.

23.5.1 Algorithms, Routine Dynamics and Replication

First, algorithms are likely to play an important role in our understanding of a central topic in routines and strategy research: routine replication. Management scholars have long acknowledged that transferring or replicating successful routines is critical for organizations that want to scale up, and that there is a tension between copying the template of a routine and innovating by modifying it (Winter and Szulanski, 2001); this tension is called the 'replication dilemma'. In practical terms, the digital character of algorithms enables both their exact replication and transposition with minimal effort, which introduces complexities that deserve further attention.

For example, an organization might implement the exact copy of a hiring algorithm that had been successfully deployed as part of the hiring routine of another organization. However, due to dynamics associated with other elements of the assemblage, such as theories, artifacts, actors and practices, efforts at replicating an algorithm exactly are likely to result in unexpected outcomes. Despite the relevance of the theme, to date, research examining routine replication has been limited in at least two significant dimensions. First, many researchers have focused on organizations with reduced dynamism when it comes to incentives to innovate (e.g., food franchise chains; see Winter et al., 2011). Second, when studying more complex settings, researchers have tended to focus on artifacts that articulate the pattern of a routine (e.g., standard operating procedures, models, rules) (see D'Adderio, 2014; D'Adderio and Pollock, 2020). Studying the effects of algorithmic artifacts in routine transfer processes constitutes a promising path to address both limitations.

Examining how an electronics organization dealt with competing pressures to replicate and innovate during routine transfer processes, D'Adderio (2014) found that representational artifacts could be harnessed to support both stability and change. Two artifactual mechanisms were highlighted as being associated with a routine's deviation from a template. The first mechanism, inscription (Latour, 1992), is the process whereby designers delegate knowledge and goals to artifacts. The second mechanism, affordances, corresponds to perceptual and negotiated possibilities of use that artifacts enable (Gibson, 1979; Hutchby, 2001; Leonardi et al., 2019). Building on these findings, we suggest that scholars should specifically investigate the interplay between inscription and affordances of algorithmic artifacts at the core of routine transfer processes. Often, as underlined here, designers of algorithms are not directly engaged in the routines they are attempting to address, and little is known about the micro-processes through which the inscription of such algorithmic artifacts might affect routine transfer. Additionally, and in the same vein, although representational artifacts might enable a wide range of affordances via relational negotiations among users, considerably more studies are necessary to understand how algorithmic inscriptions of artifacts might affect their range of affordances, which ultimately would affect the variance observed in routine transfer processes.

23.5.2 Algorithms, Routine Dynamics and Power

Second, there is an opportunity for routines scholars to study the political and power dynamics associated with algorithms. In the past decade, discussions have proliferated about how powerful actors such as Google are using algorithmic routines to exploit people (Zuboff, 2019). However, there are also means of resistance, as actors can deploy algorithms to fight back (Kiviat, 2019). Routines scholars can provide a nuanced view by examining how different occupational groups exert authority through algorithms (e.g., Curchod et al., 2019; Kellogg et al., 2019) or by exploring how algorithms affect the dynamic imbalance of routines as organizational truces (see D'Adderio and Safavi [Chapter 15], this volume). Moreover, they can cast more light on the specific mechanisms through which the actors who use algorithms resist, such as the ways that police officers resist their controllers (Brayne, 2017); the ways that journalists respond to algorithmic measurements (Christin, 2020); or drivers respond to algorithms that seek to control their job performance (Cameron, 2020).

Routines research provides a fairly straightforward account of the relationship between routines and power. Specifically, Nelson and Winter (1982) highlighted that routines play three fundamental coordinating roles in organizational life by providing, (i) a cognitive means to coordinate actors by functioning as a type of organizational memory, (ii) a motivational means of ensuring that people work together to achieve organizational goals, and (iii) targets for routine performance. They suggested that routine performance becomes a way for organizational actors to deal with conflict in a manner that minimizes its potential to create organizational dysfunction. Thus, by limiting conflict to 'largely predictable paths', routines can help build a 'comprehensive truce in organizational conflict'

(Nelson and Winter, 1982). For instance, Zbaracki and Bergen (2010) showed how sales and marketing departments enacted conflict over a price adjustment routine. Their empirical account shows how performative aspects of the routine were able to deal with smaller breakdowns but that ostensive aspects of the routine ended up dominating the actions associated with resolving a major breakdown in the routine truce. Routines are thus an important mechanism through which organizations stabilize inherent conflict between competing internal interests.

We suggest that studying algorithms can help scholars more effectively unpack power dynamics in routines. For example, researchers have shown that algorithms can be used by powerful actors to impose their will on organizations (Curchod et al., 2019; Kellogg et al., 2019). By adopting the methodological perspective we discussed earlier, scholars can theorize these dynamics more effectively. For example, examining the 'theory' component of the algorithmic assemblage can help explain how powerful actors envision a future organization. Similarly, understanding the materiality of the algorithm can help explain the amount of latitude held by those who perform the routine to either deviate or conform to the underlying vision. Moreover, understanding the design performances of a routine (Glaser, 2017) can help scholars understand how the powerful actually go about imposing their will on the less powerful (Clegg, 1989).

The methods outlined in this chapter also can be applied to understand how less powerful actors can resist more powerful actors (e.g., Brayne, 2017; Cameron, 2020). The algorithmic assemblage reveals how the material nature of the algorithm leads to cycles of framing and overflowing. Observing how actors who perform routines resist the visions cast by organizational leaders could help scholars expand theory that explains how visions of leadership can be subverted by trial and error (e.g., Rerup and Feldman, 2011) by revealing more active mechanisms of subversion.

Research on algorithms and Routine Dynamics can also address several questions that are relevant to organizational studies: How do powerful actors in organizations attempt to use materiality to increase their control over the less powerful? How do powerful actors use theories to increase their control over organizations? How do theories interact with the materiality of algorithms in this process? Although we have learned how actors involved in the performance of a routine resist the will of the powerful through actions, can they resist through other means such as materiality, or by developing alternative theories? In conclusion, we suggest that viewing algorithms as assemblages can help routines scholars better understand how power might influence Routine Dynamics, thereby enabling them to contribute to broader organizational discussions about power and politics (Clegg et al., 2006).

23.5.3 Algorithms, Routine Dynamics and Innovation

Third, routines scholars should explore how algorithms and routines are used creatively to foster innovation (e.g., Cohendet and Simon, 2016; Sele and Grand, 2016; Sonenshein, 2016). Creativity entails having organizational actors coming up with ideas for modifying products, services and processes, as a manner to better achieve organizational objectives (Amabile et al., 2005). As discussed by Deken and Sele ([Chapter 21], this volume), many organizations strive to channel creativity in an attempt to routinize organizational innovation (see Hargadon, 2005). For example, Cohendet and Simon (2016: 615) highlighted that when organizations face a "'creativity crisis' (i.e., inability to obtain novelty as the expected outcome of routines for doing innovation), changes to routines may be necessary that 'entail breaking existing rules and roles' and 'reshuffling and reconfiguring' the organizational structure. At the same time, Sonenshein (2016) revealed a different dimension in the relationship between routines and innovation by showing how organizational actors use the familiar artifacts of a routine to stimulate additional creativity. Sele and Grand (2016) argued that innovation is facilitated by routines that are more generative when actors or artifacts function as mediators who modify connections, rather than as intermediaries who maintain connections. These studies suggest that interactions among artifacts, actors and practices play an important role in explaining innovation.

We suggest that understanding the mediating role of algorithms in the creative process is becoming increasingly important to understand innovation, as actors begin to use algorithms and big data in creative processes, even in areas such as art and literature (e.g., Elgammal, 2018). Much of the existing work on algorithms highlights how they can be used to automate decision-making processes and deskill workers (Kellogg et al., 2019), or to remove bias from decision-making (Mayer-Schonberger and Cukier, 2013). In future work, researchers could also examine the links between algorithms and their manifestations, such as visualizations, which are central artifacts used by organizational actors to induce novel insights from data.

Finally, there is an opportunity in the area of machine learning[1] and artificial intelligence. As mentioned herein, the intersection between algorithms and Routine Dynamics is an area that remains underexplored. Although we have conceptualized algorithms as artifacts intertwined with other elements such as actors, practices and theories in dynamic socio-material assemblages that can have substantial effects on organizational routines, machine learning introduces another layer of complexity. Scholars from science and technology studies (Grint and Woolgar, 1997; Hutchby, 2001; Kling, 1991, 1992) have long debated about how technological artifacts enable different affordances (i.e., possibilities of use). Put simply, machine learning engenders affordances which entail algorithms creating subsequent algorithms through a process that often challenges the comprehension of more traditional designers (e.g., programmers, data analysts) and users. Consequently, we believe that a Routine Dynamics perspective can help scholars and practitioners better explain dynamics associated with artificial intelligence and machine learning. Such elements are at the core of what professional data scientists do. In this sense, investigating how the range of affordances of machine learning algorithms affect organizational routines constitutes an open and promising avenue for future research.

[1] Despite divergent uses among practitioners, in computing science, the term machine learning refers specifically to a branch of artificial intelligence that enables computers to learn from data without human assistance – or with minimum human intervention – to power ubiquitous applications such as spam filters for e-mail (Géron, 2017).

23.6 Conclusion

In this chapter, we have reviewed prior work on routines and algorithms and suggested that studying algorithms offers a fruitful opportunity for routines scholars to develop new theory about Routine Dynamics. Additionally, we believe that scholars can use the theoretical and methodological infrastructure provided by a routines lens to develop theory to move beyond management research that conceptualizes algorithms in an entitative manner (e.g., Curchod et al., 2020; Kellogg et al., 2020), and that this research has the potential to contribute unique insights to the broader social conversation around big data, predictive analytics, machine learning and artificial intelligence. By viewing algorithms as an integral part of the assemblage of a routine, scholars can see new connections that can help us better understand the relationships among algorithms, routines and important organizational outcomes such as routine replication, organizational power and innovation.

References

Amabile, T. M., Barsade, S. G., Mueller, J. S. and Staw, B. M. (2005). Affect and creativity at work. *Administrative Science Quarterly*, 50(3), 367–403.

Ames, M. G. (2018). Deconstructing the algorithmic sublime. *Big Data & Society*, 5(1), https://doi.org/10.1177/2053951718779194.

Berente, N., Lyytinen, K., Yoo, Y. and King, J. L. (2016). Routines as shock absorbers during organizational transformation: Integration, control, and NASA's Enterprise Information System. *Organization Science*, 27(3), 551–572.

Brayne, S. (2017). Big data surveillance: The case of policing. *American Sociological Review*, 82(5), 977–1008.

Buhmann, A., Paßmann, J. and Fieseler, C. (2019). managing algorithmic accountability: Balancing reputational concerns, engagement strategies, and the potential of rational discourse. *Journal of Business Ethics*. https://doi.org/10.1007/s10551-019-04226-4.

Burke, A. (2019). Occluded algorithms. *Big Data & Society*, 6(2), 1–15.

Cabantous, L. and Gond, J.-P. (2011). Rational decision making as performative praxis: Explaining rationality's éternel retour. *Organization Science*, 22(3), 573–586.

Cabantous, L., Gond, J.-P. and Johnson-Cramer, M. (2010). Decision theory as practice: Crafting rationality in organizations. *Organization Studies*, 31(11), 1531–1566.

Cacciatori, E. (2012). Resolving conflict in problem-solving: Systems of artefacts in the development of new routines. *Journal of Management Studies*, 49(8), 1559–1585.

Callon, M. (1980). Struggles and negotiations to define what is problematic and what is not. In K. D. Knorr, R. Krohn and R. Whitley, eds., *The Social Process of Scientific Investigation: Sociology of the Sciences, a Yearbook*. Dordrecht: Springer Netherlands, pp. 197–219. https://doi.org/10.1007/978-94-009-9109-5_8

Callon, M. (1986). The sociology of an actor-network: The case of the electric vehicle. In M. Callon, J. Law and A. Rip, eds., *Mapping the Dynamics of Science and Technology: Sociology of Science in the Real World*. London: Palgrave Macmillan UK, pp. 19–34.

Callon, M. (2017). Markets, marketization and innovation. In H. Bathelt, P. Cohendet, S. Henn and L. Simon, eds., *The Elgar Companion to Innovation and Knowledge Creation*. Northampton, MA: Edward Elgar Publishing. www.elgaronline.com/view/edcoll/9781782548515/9781782548515.00048.xml

Cameron, L. (2020). The Rise of Algorithmic Work: Implications for Organizational Control and Worker Autonomy. Dissertation, University of Michigan.

Christin, A. (2020). *Metrics at Work: Journalism and the Contested Meaning of Algorithms*. Princeton, NJ: Princeton University Press.

Clegg, S. (1989). *Frameworks of Power*. London: Sage.

Clegg, S. R., Courpasson, D. and Phillips, N. (2006). *Power and Organizations*. London: SAGE.

Cohendet, P. S. and Simon, L. O. (2016). Always playable: Recombining routines for creative efficiency at Ubisoft Montreal's video game studio. *Organization Science*, 27(3), 614–632.

Curchod, C., Patriotta, G., Cohen, L. and Neysen, N. (2020). Working for an algorithm: Power asymmetries and agency in online work settings. *Administrative Science Quarterly*, 65(3), 644–676.

D'Adderio, L. (2001). Crafting the virtual prototype: How firms integrate knowledge and capabilities across organisational boundaries. *Research Policy*, 30(9), 1409–1424.

D'Adderio, L. (2008). The performativity of routines: Theorising the influence of artefacts and distributed agencies on Routines Dynamics. *Research Policy*, 37(5), 769–789.

D'Adderio, L. (2011). Artifacts at the centre of routines: Performing the material turn in routines theory. *Journal of Institutional Economics*, 7 (Special Issue 02), 197–230.

D'Adderio, L. (2014). The replication dilemma unravelled: How organizations enact multiple goals in routine transfer. *Organization Science*, 25(5), 1325–1350.

D'Adderio, L., Glaser, V. and Pollock, N. (2019). Performing theories, transforming organizations: A reply to Marti and Gond. *Academy of Management Review*, 44(3), 676–679.

D'Adderio, L. and Pollock, N. (2020). Making routines the same: Crafting similarity and singularity in routines transfer. *Research Policy*, 49(8), 104029.

D'Adderio, L. and Pollock, N. (2014). Performing modularity: Competing rules, performative struggles and the effect of organizational theories on the organization. *Organization Studies*, 35 (12), 1813–1843.

Davenport, T. H. (2018). *The AI Advantage: How to Put the Artificial Intelligence Revolution to Work*, 1st edition. Cambridge, MA: The MIT Press.

Dittrich, K. and Seidl, D. (2018). Emerging intentionality in Routine Dynamics: A pragmatist view. *Academy of Management Journal*, 61(1), 111–138.

Dourish, P. (2016). Algorithms and their others: Algorithmic culture in context. *Big Data & Society*, 3(2), 1–11.

Elgammal, A. (2018, December 6). AI is blurring the definition of artist. *American Scientist*. www.americanscientist.org/article/ai-is-blurring-the-definition-of-artist.

Fei, H., Li, Q. and Sun, D. (2017). A survey of recent research on optimization models and algorithms for operations management from the process view. *Scientific Programming*. https://doi.org/10.1155/2017/7219656.

Feldman, M. S. (2016) Routines as process: past, present, and future. In C. Rerup and J. Howard-Grenville, eds., *Organizational Routines and Process Organization Studies*. Oxford: Oxford University Press.

Feldman, M. S. and Orlikowski, W. J. (2011). Theorizing practice and practicing theory. *Organization Science*, 22(5), 1240–1253.

Fourcade, M. and Healy, K. (2017). Seeing like a market. *Socio-Economic Review*, 15(1), 9–29.

Garud, R. and Gehman, J. (2019). Performativity: Not a destination but an ongoing journey. *Academy of Management Review*, 44(3), 679–684.

Géron, A. (2017). *Hands-On Machine Learning with Scikit-Learn and TensorFlow: Concepts, Tools, and Techniques to Build Intelligent Systems*, 1st edition. Beijing; Boston; Farnham; Sebastopol; Tokyo: O'Reilly Media.

Gibson, J. J. (1979). *The Ecological Approach to Visual Perception*, 1st edition. New York; London: Routledge.

Gillespie, T. (2014). *The Relevance of Algorithms*. Cambridge, MA: The MIT Press. https://mitpress.universitypressscholarship.com/view/10.7551/mitpress/9780262525374.001.0001/upso-9780262525374-chapter-9.

Gillespie, T. (2016). Algorithm. In B. Peters, ed., *Digital Keywords: A Vocabulary of Information Society and Culture*. Princeton, NJ: Princeton University Press, pp. 18–30.

Glaser, V. L. (2014). Enchanted Algorithms: The Quantification of Organizational Decision-Making. *Dissertation, Marshall School of Business*.

Glaser, V. L. (2017). Design performances: How organizations inscribe artifacts to change routines. *Academy of Management Journal*, 60(6), 2126–2154.

Glaser, V. L., Pollock, N. and D'Adderio, L. (2021). The biography of an algorithm: Performing algorithmic technologies in organizations. *Organization Theory*, 2, 1–27.

Grint, K. and Woolgar, S. (1997). *The Machine at Work: Technology, Work and Organization*. Cambridge, UK; Malden, MA: Blackwell Publishers; Polity Press.

Gusterson, H. (1997). Studying up revisited. *Studying Up Revisited*, 20(1), 114–119.

Hales, M. and Tidd, J. (2009). The practice of routines and representations in design and development. *Industrial and Corporate Change*, 18(4), 551–574.

Hargadon, A. (2005). Technology brokering and innovation: Linking strategy, practice, and people. (D. Knight and R. M. Randall, eds.) *Strategy & Leadership*, 33(1), 32–36.

Hutchby, I. (2001). Technologies, texts and affordances. *Sociology*, 35(2), 441–456.

Hyysalo, S., Pollock, N. and Williams, R. A. (2019). Method matters in the social study of technology: Investigating the biographies of artifacts and practices. *Science & Technology Studies*, 32(3), 2–25.

Iansiti, M. and Lakhani, K. R. (2020, January 1). Competing in the Age of AI. *Harvard Business Review*, (January–February 2020). https://hbr.org/2020/01/competing-in-the-age-of-ai.

Introna, L. D. (2007). Towards a post-human intra-actional account of socio- technical agency (and morality). *Prepared for the Moral Agency and Technical Artifacts Scientific Workshop, NIAS, Hague*, 22.

Kellogg, K., Valentine, M. and Christin, A. (2020). Algorithms at work: The new contested terrain of control. *Academy of Management Annals*, 14 (1), 366–410. https://doi.org/10.5465/annals.2018.0174.

Kiviat, B. (2019). The moral limits of predictive practices: The case of credit-based insurance scores. *American Sociological Review*, 84(6), 1134–1158.

Kling, R. (1991). Computerization and social transformations. *Science, Technology, & Human Values*, 16(3), 342–367.

Kling, R. (1992). Audiences, narratives, and human values in social studies of technology. *Science, Technology, & Human Values*, 17(3), 349–365.

Kremser, W. and Schreyögg, G. (2016). The dynamics of interrelated routines: Introducing the cluster level. *Organization Science*. https://doi.org/10.1287/orsc.2015.1042.

Labatut, J., Aggeri, F. and Girard, N. (2012). Discipline and change: How technologies and organizational routines interact in new practice creation. *Organization Studies*, 33(1), 39.

Latour, B. (1986). Visualisation and cognition: Drawing things together. In H. Kuklick, ed., *Knowledge and Society Studies in the Sociology of Culture Past and Present*. Bingley: JAI Press, 1–40.

Latour, B. (1992). Where are the missing masses? The sociology of a few mundane artifacts. In *Shaping Technology/Building Society: Studies in Sociotechnical Change*. Cambridge, MA: MIT Press, pp. 225–258.

Latour, B. (1996). On actor-network theory: A few clarifications. *Soziale Welt*, 47(4), 369–381.

Latour, B. (2005). *Reassembling the Social*. Oxford: Oxford University Press.

Latour, B. and Woolgar, S. (1979). *Laboratory Life*. Princeton, NJ: Princeton University Press.

Leonardi, P. M., Bailey, D. E. and Pierce, C. S. (2019). The coevolution of objects and boundaries over time: Materiality, affordances, and boundary salience. *Information Systems Research*, 30(2), 665–686.

Lindebaum, D., Vesa, M. and den Hond, F. (2019). Insights from the machine stops to better understand rational assumptions in algorithmic decision-making and its implications for organizations. *Academy of Management Review*. https://doi.org/10.5465/amr.2018.0181.

MacCormick, J. (2012). *Nine Algorithms That Changed the Future: The Ingenious Ideas That Drive Today's Computers* (2nd edition). Princeton, NJ: Princeton University Press.

Marti, E. and Gond, J.-P. (2018). When do theories become self-fulfilling? Exploring the boundary conditions of performativity. *Academy of Management Review*, 43(3), 487–508.

Martin, K. (2019). Ethical implications and accountability of algorithms. *Journal of Business Ethics*, 160(4), 835–850.

Mayer-Schonberger, V. and Cukier, K. (2013). *Big Data: A Revolution That Will Transform How We Live, Work, and Think*, 1st ed. London: Eamon Dolan/Houghton Mifflin Harcourt.

Mazmanian, M., Cohn, M. and Dourish, P. (2014). Dynamic reconfiguration in planetary exploration: A sociomaterial ethnography. *Management Information Systems Quarterly*, 38(3), 831–848.

Murray, A., Rhymer, J. and Sirmon, D. forthcoming. Humans and Technology: Forms of Conjoined Agency in Organizational Routines. *Academy of Management Review*.

Nelson, R. R. and Winter, S. G. (1982). *An Evolutionary Theory of Economic Change*. Cambridge, MA: Belknap Press of Harvard University Press.

Pasquale, F. (2015). *The Black Box Society* (Reprint edition). Cambridge, MA: Harvard University Press.

Pentland, B. T. and Feldman, M. S. (2008). Designing routines: On the folly of designing artifacts, while hoping for patterns of action. *Information and Organization*, 18(4), 235–250.

Pentland, B. T. and Hærem, T. (2015). Organizational routines as patterns of action: Implications for organizational behavior. *Annual Review of Organizational Psychology and Organizational Behavior*, 2, 465–487.

Pollock, N. and Williams, R. (2009). *Software and Organisations: The Biography of the Enterprise-Wide System or How SAP Conquered the World*. Abingdon: Routledge.

Pollock, N. and Williams, R. (2016). *How Industry Analysts Shape the Digital Future*. Oxford: Oxford University Press.

Rerup, C. and Feldman, M. S. (2011). Routines as a source of change in organizational schemata: The role of trial-and-error learning. *Academy of Management Journal*, 54(3), 577–610.

Rieder, B. (2017). Scrutinizing an algorithmic technique: The Bayes classifier as interested reading of reality. *Information, Communication & Society*, 20(1), 100–117.

Schildt, H. (2020). *The Data Imperative: How Digitalization Is Reshaping Management, Organizing, and Work*. Oxford: Oxford University Press.

Seaver, N. (2017). Algorithms as culture: Some tactics for the ethnography of algorithmic systems. *Big Data & Society*, 4(2), 1–12.

Sele, K. and Grand, S. (2016). Unpacking the dynamics of ecologies of routines: Mediators and their generative effects in routine interactions. *Organization Science*, 27(3), 722–738.

Simon, H. A. (1970). *The Sciences of the Artificial*, 1st edition. Cambridge, MA: The MIT Press.

Simon, H. A. (1996). *The Sciences of the Artificial*, 3rd edition. Cambridge, MA: The MIT Press.

Sonenshein, S. (2016). Routines and creativity: From dualism to duality. *Organization Science*, 27(3), 739–758.

Suchman, L. (2007). *Human-Machine Reconfigurations: Plans and Situated Actions*, 2nd edition. Cambridge; New York: Cambridge University Press.

Wenzel, M., Krämer, H., Koch, J. and Reckwitz, A. (2020). Future and Organization Studies: On the rediscovery of a problematic temporal category in organizations. *Organization Studies*.

Winter, S. G. and Szulanski, G. (2001). Replication as strategy. *Organization Science*, 12(6), 730–743.

Winter, S. G., Szulanski, G., Ringov, D. and Jensen, R. J. (2011). Reproducing knowledge: Inaccurate replication and failure in franchise organizations. *Organization Science*, 23(3), 672–685.

Zbaracki, M. J. and Bergen, M. (2010). When truces collapse: A longitudinal study of price-adjustment routines. *Organization Science*, 21(5), 955–972.

Zuboff, S. (2019). *The Age of Surveillance Capitalism: The Fight for a Human Future at the New Frontier of Power*, 1st edition. New York: PublicAffairs.

CHAPTER 24

Complexity in Routine Dynamics

THORVALD HÆREM, YOOEUN JEONG AND MATHIAS HANSSON

24.1 Introduction

The Routine Dynamics perspective enables us to look beyond the stereotypical view of routines as sameness and simplicity. While diverse themes are being researched in the literature on Routine Dynamics, the common underlying question is that of the processes that create the 'dynamics' of routines. Significant attention has been directed to, for example, how routines emerge, how they are performed and transformed over time (Feldman et al., 2016), and the dynamics between stability and change (Farjoun, 2010; Pentland et al., 2011).

To study dynamics is to study the mechanisms by which a system is changed and stabilized, or 'the forces that produce movement' as defined in the Cambridge Dictionary. Complexity[1] can be understood as a characteristic of the sources of such a force. Intuitively, one might think that in the simplest routine, there are only a few sources that can trigger changes, and stability is easy to maintain; as the complexity of the routine increases, so does the number of sources that can produce changes, and therefore stability may be more difficult to maintain. Gell-Mann (1994), a former Nobel Prize winner in physics, wondered late in his career about a similar issue, but arrived at the opposite conclusion. He suggested that more complex ecosystems, such as tropical forests, are more resilient; they have more capacity to absorb disturbances and changes without qualitatively changing the behaviour of the system, compared to relatively simpler systems such as a forest of oaks. This tension between stability and change has long been of interest to researchers in organizational routines (Farjoun, 2010; Pentland et al., 2011); however, the role of complexity in Routine Dynamics is still largely ignored.

Historically, organizational routines have been conceived of as a tool for stabilizing and simplifying work and search processes (Cyert and March, 1963; March and Simon, 1958). The Routine Dynamics perspective suggests that actors performing an organizational routine have agency. That is, actors have a repertoire of action patterns from which they choose their responses to meet situational demands (Feldman and Pentland, 2003; Hansson et al., 2018; Pentland and Rueter, 1994). Therefore, enactments of even a simple routine can entail dynamics and variations in patterns of actions, which can result in shifting levels of complexity (Pentland et al., 2020). Pentland et al. (2011) provided empirical support for the concept of ongoing endogenous change in routines by studying the variability of action sequences in a routine (Feldman, 2000; Feldman and Pentland, 2003; Tsoukas and Chia, 2002).

Although complexity has long been a key construct in organization theory, it is often used relatively arbitrarily to characterize anything humans find difficult to understand. In fact, the meaning of complexity in organization theory has often been used interchangeably with concepts such as difficulty, degree of analysability, routineness, uncertainty, ambiguity, equivocality and interdependence (e.g., Daft and Macintosh, 1981; Fields, 2002; Galbraith, 1973; Van de Ven and Delbecq, 1974; Van de Ven et al., 1976; Withey et al., 1983).

Even though, over the last 50 years, there has been a continuous effort directed at developing a more precise meaning of complexity, this effort has yet to influence the understanding of complexity in Routine Dynamics – such that

[1] We do not review the literature on complexity from the perspectives of system dynamics and chaos theory (e.g., Forrester, 1997; Senge, 2006; Stacey, 1996), since we see these perspectives as self-sustained and less integrated in the literature of organizational routines and organizational theory, and organizational psychology.

non-routine does not necessarily mean complex, and routine does not necessarily mean simple. One of the beauties of organizing is that the performance of complex tasks can be organized so that it is simple. But is it then still a complex task? With more clearly defined concepts, we can develop clearer distinctions. This chapter contributes to a clearer understanding of key terms related to complexity that are often arbitrarily used in Routine Dynamics research. To this end, our review identifies existing conceptualizations of complexity used to study routines and discusses the assumptions, merits and limitations of these. Moreover, we suggest directions for future research to improve the understanding of the role of complexity in Routine Dynamics research.

24.2 Review of Studies of Complexity in Routines

In extant research on routines, the concept of task complexity has often been used to characterize complexity of routines. Therefore, before we review and discuss complexity in routines, we need to develop the distinction between the complexity of routines and the complexity of tasks. The latter is a well-established field of research, while the former is not. Parallels between tasks and routines can be drawn by considering tasks as referring to those performed in organizations, and the task resolution processes as the setting for the situated actions (Hackman, 1969). Typically, organizations try to routinize performances of tasks by economizing search and standardizing task resolutions (March and Simon, 1958; Nelson and Winter, 1982), resulting in recognizable, repeated patterns of actions (Feldman and Pentland, 2003). In the research literature, task complexity has generally been conceptualized at the individual level. Performance of a routine, however, involves several individuals participating in the resolution of the tasks within the routine and only rarely does one person complete the whole task in isolation. Thus, when we use the term routine, we refer to the tasks jointly enacted by several actors. Routine complexity is, therefore, different from task complexity in that it pertains specifically to the subset of task resolutions that are solved jointly by several actors (human and non-human), repeatedly, and with recognizable, interdependent patterns of actions.

For our selective review of the use of the complexity construct in the literature on organizational routines, we conducted a broad search on Google Scholar. Our search words included 'complexity', 'complex' and 'routine(s)', as well as broader terms related to complexity and organizational routines such as 'routineness' and 'routinization'. The terms 'organization(s)' and 'organizational' were also added to exclude the search results not relevant to studies of organizations (e.g., clinical science and computer science). Moreover, we searched for the forward citations of comprehensive reviews of the task complexity construct (Campbell, 1988; Hærem et al., 2015; Wood, 1986) and identified the studies in which organizational routines were discussed.

We excluded from our review the studies that did not mention the terms complexity and routine, thereby excluding the studies concerning tasks carried out by single actors, or those that did not use the terms as referring to central constructs studied (e.g., studies speaking about the complexity of studying organizational routines). Additionally, we excluded the studies where the relationship between complexity and routines or related constructs is not explored. Studies using concepts such as job complexity or role complexity (e.g., Ohly et al., 2006) were also excluded, as a job and a role encapsulates the portfolio of tasks that the person in the job or the role should perform, and therefore, can entail participation in many different routines. Moreover, these descriptions would be static within a considerable time window, while routines vary significantly across performances (Pentland et al., 2010).

Therefore, our review in this chapter only included empirical studies that explicitly operationalized complexity in routines. The studies that fit our criteria are presented in Table 24.1. As seen in Table 24.1, we distinguish the studies adopting the traditional view on organizational routines from those adopting the Routine Dynamics approach (Parmigiani and Howard-Grenville, 2011). In the traditional view, organizational

Table 24.1 Examples of empirical studies (including simulations) on organizational routines and Routine Dynamics using different conceptualizations of complexity

	Perceptual	Idealized	Enacted
Organizational routines	Galbraith (1973); Van de Ven and Delbecq (1974); Van de Ven, Delbecq and Koenig (1976); Tushman and Nadler (1978); Van de Ven and Ferry (1980); Daft and Macintosh (1981); Withey, Daft and Cooper (1983); Daft and Lengel (1984); Daft and Lengel (1986)	N/A	N/A
Routine Dynamics	N/A	Gao, Deng, Zhao, Zhou and Bai (2015); Gao, Squazzoni and Deng (2018)	Goh and Pentland (2019); Hansson, Hærem and Pentland (2018); Pentland, Vaast and Wolf (2021)

routines are often likened to organizational DNA (Nelson and Winter, 1982), and a standardized method for solving tasks (March and Simon, 1958; Perrow, 1967). Albeit crucially important, routines are seen as a relatively invariant mechanism that connects organizational inputs and outputs (Feldman, 2016a). The Routine Dynamics perspective goes beyond this view on routines as entities (Feldman et al., 2016) and emphasizes the processual nature of routines (Howard-Grenville and Rerup, 2017). Research in the Routine Dynamics literature focuses on the actions and the patterns generated through enactments, and the internal dynamics created by the mutual constitution of performative and ostensive aspects of routines (Feldman, 2016a). Even though this conceptualization opens up an opportunity to discuss the complexity of enacted patterns of actions in a routine, perhaps surprisingly, we find that very little research attention has been directed at studying complexity in the Routine Dynamics literature.

Based on Hackman's (1969) and Campbell's (1988) discussion of alternative approaches to conceptualize tasks and a qualitative judgement of the available studies, we categorized the studies of routine complexity into three different approaches, or conceptualizations of complexity: that is, complexity as (a) a perceptual characteristic of routines, (b) a function of idealized characteristics of routines and (c) a function of enactments. Below, we review how these three approaches to complexity have been applied in empirical studies on organizational routines and Routine Dynamics. We discuss the merits, limitations and the underlying assumptions of each approach. Finally, we outline directions for future investigations of the complexity of routines.

24.3 Three Conceptualizations of Routine Complexity: Examples of Applications in the Literature

The empty cells in Table 24.1 reflect the historical change in the studies of organizational routines: From mainly considering routines as a concrete phenomenon that can be described by perceptions, to studies of the factors contributing to the dynamics of organizational routines where the phenomenon is not necessarily concrete and directly observable. In the Routine Dynamics literature, the processual nature of routines is emphasized (Feldman et al., 2016).

These empty cells also reflect the changes over time in the methodologies applied. The historical change can both be seen in the move from organizational routines to Routine Dynamics and in the movement from the perceptual approach to the enacted approach. The first wave of studies of organizational routines assessed complexity based mainly on individuals' perceptions reported in questionnaires. More recent studies in organizational routines and Routine Dynamics use other methodologies such as quantitative methods that enable the exploration of digital trace data. As described later, such methodologies were particularly prominent in the studies adopting the enacted approach to complexity. On the other hand, we have identified that simulations were used in the studies using the idealized approach to complexity. The absence of qualitative methods in studying complexity is striking, as qualitative methods are frequently used to study Routine Dynamics (e.g. Feldman et al., 2016).

24.3.1 Routine Complexity as a Perceptual Characteristic

This approach emphasizes the subjective perception of actors to the routines they are performing, rather than the more perception-independent characteristics of the tasks involved in routines. This approach was prominent in early research adopting the traditional view on organizational routines as described in March and Simon (1958) and Perrow (1967). Although operating on different assumptions, these studies building on March and Simon's (1958) and Perrow's (1967) conceptualizations of routines represent seminal studies in the history of current research on Routine Dynamics.

In this view, analysable tasks with few exceptions were considered routine, whereas the presence of a large number of exceptions and difficulty of analysing the exceptions would mark a task as non-routine (Perrow, 1967). Moreover, the term complexity was used interchangeably with concepts such as difficulty, variability, analysability and degree of routinization (Fields, 2002). The interchangeable use of these concepts indicates that the lack of clarity in the conceptual definitions in this tradition has persisted after Weick (1965) and Hackman (1969) first pointed out the problem.

24.3.1.1 Examples of Applications in Research on Organizational Routines

Examples of seminal studies from this tradition are Van de Ven and Delbecq (1974), Withey et al. (1983), Van de Ven and Ferry (1980), Daft and Macintosh (1981). In this research stream, the term 'routineness' denoted the complexity of a task – simple tasks were seen as routine tasks, whereas complex tasks were invariably classified as non-routine tasks (e.g., Galbraith, 1973; Tushman and Nadler, 1978; Van de Ven et al., 1976). The underlying idea is that the complexity of the task is a function of the information processing requirements of the task (Daft and Lengel, 1986; Galbraith, 1973; Tushman and Nadler, 1978): the more complex a task is, the larger the amount of information that needs to be processed.

These studies found empirical support for much of what March and Simon (1958) had proposed 20 years earlier; organizations routinize task resolution to reduce the information processing requirements of the task. Other influential articles studied similar relations; for example, Daft and Macintosh (1981) assessed the relationship between information processing requirements and self-reported measures of the routineness of the task. They found that whereas high task variety was related to the increased amount of information processing, high task analysability was associated with smaller amounts of information processing.

Many of these studies, therefore, focused on the effect of routineness on organizational variables such as coordination modes (Van de Ven et al., 1976), use of communication media (Daft and Lengel, 1984) and organization structure (Daft and Lengel, 1986). Although the empirical findings with these perceptual measures rendered general support for March and Simon's (1958) and Perrow's (1967) propositions, several results incompatible with the theory indicated that the relation between routineness and organizational variables suffered from confounding the routine and perceptions of the routine (Becker and Zirpoli, 2008; Hærem and Rau, 2007; Miller et al., 1991; Pentland, 2003).

Variation in action sequences can make a crucial difference in a routine; it matters whether you switch on the parking brake before or after driving the car. Variability is one characteristic of the structure of a process. Sequential variation may be an important source of Routine Dynamics, but it is not related to the perceptual complexity of routines in obvious ways. Pentland (2003) compared two quantitative measures of sequential variations in routine processes (measures based on string matching and Markov models) with three perceptual measures of the complexity of the routine (operationalized by questionnaires about perceived variability). The sequential variation measures differed consistently from the perceptual measures. Pentland (2003) suggested that this mismatch was due to differences in experience or the degree of proceduralization of the work among the respondents in the study. Such a difference in perceptions of variability and more objective measures of work have gained support from experimental research on perceptual differences between experts and novices (e.g., Hærem and Rau, 2007). The attempt to conceptualize routine complexity based on an idealized version of a routine introduced in the next section can be seen as a reaction to these limitations of the subjectivity inherent in the perceptual measures of routine complexity.

24.3.2 Routine Complexity as a Function of Idealized Characteristics

As a response to concerns regarding the problems of confounding the perceptions of a task with the task itself (e.g., Weick, 1965), Hackman (1969) proposed a framework for analysing tasks that can better accommodate an understanding of characteristics such as complexity. Subsequently, Wood (1986), presented a 'general theoretical model of tasks', and defined task complexity in terms of the 'task-as-such (task qua task)', separating the task itself from the task-doers' perceptions of it. Wood's concept of task complexity can be calculated as a linear combination of three dimensions of complexity: component, coordinative and dynamic. Component complexity refers to the number of non-redundant actions and information cues required to accomplish a task, whereas coordinative complexity is based on the interdependencies between the required actions to solve the task. Dynamic complexity is defined in terms of the changes over time in the other two dimensions. Importantly, Wood's conceptualization of complexity reflects the complexity of an 'idealized' version of a routine and therefore does not represent the variation in individual performances. The goal of the task qua task framework is to keep the task performers and the performances separate from the task-as-such in order to avoid confounding the task with individual performances. Still, defining routine complexity independent of the individual performances might provide researchers with a characteristic of the routine which is stable over a given time window.

As demonstrated by Hærem et al. (2015), Wood's (1986) task complexity construct can be extended to analyse tasks involving several actors and applied to organizational routines. However, most of the extant research based on the task qua task framework are focused on individual-level phenomena (the effectiveness of decision-making, employee performance, etc.), rather than on the investigations of collective phenomena such as organizational routines (Hærem et al., 2015). The mapping of acts and cues required to do the calculation of Wood's (1986) three dimensions of complexity may have deferred researchers from applying the measures more accurately. In the Routine Dynamics literature, the library of actions is often the starting point in analysing the Routine Dynamics (Pentland et al., 2010, 2011; Pentland and Hærem, 2015). The library of actions can be defined so that the component complexity is just the size of the library, and the coordinative complexity may be analysed using the transition matrix of action sequences. These measures are constants across performances of the routine – until the library of action changes. Although these measures do not reflect the dynamics in the routine, they may be important variables to control for, because the dynamics in routines may differ significantly across, for example, levels of component complexity – i.e., the size of the library of actions.

24.3.2.1 Examples of Applications in the Routine Dynamics Literature

In the Routine Dynamics literature, Wood's (1986) conceptualization of task complexity has been used in simulation studies to study how the shifting levels of component complexity influence the dynamics of routines. For example, in a multi–agent-based simulation study, Gao, Deng, Zhao, Zhou and Bai (2015) assessed the impact of the connections among individual actors on the formation of organizational routines. Their model manipulates two levels of component complexity of the organizational routine to study the dynamics arising from interacting factors, such as shifting network topologies and different levels of the memory capacity of the actors. Their results indicated that the level of component complexity of an organizational routine could play an important role in the formation of organizational routines. When confronted with routines with lower component complexity, the total number of actors searching for alternative actions can reduce quickly, thus stabilizing the routine. On the other hand, they found that high component complexity influences the total numbers of actors searching for alternative courses of action to fluctuate with time, maintaining the dynamic stability of routine systems. In a subsequent simulation study expanding on Gao et al.'s (2015) model, Gao, Squazzoni and Deng (2018) included cognitive artifacts as another important factor that influences the formation and change of organizational routines. Woods' (1986) component complexity, operationalized as the size of the library of actions, was incorporated as a parameter defining the actor agents' behaviours.

Both simulation studies suggest that there may be value in distinguishing a 'complex' routine from a less complex routine, by demonstrating that the dynamics of routines play out differently depending on the size of the library of actions available in a routine (Gao et al., 2015; 2018). Hackman (1969) and Weick's (1965) original recommendation to control task variation was based on just the assumption that the psychological variables would play out differently across levels of complexity.

Still, the view of complexity as an invariable characteristic of idealized tasks has several limitations, especially when applied to a setting where tasks are emergent and carried out by multiple actors, as is the case with organizational routines. The processual ontology, and the corresponding focus on repeated patterns of actions in routine research (e.g., Feldman and Pentland, 2003), stimulated a shift in the conceptualization of task complexity away from analysing the task as an idealized entity independent of the task-doer, towards analysing the task as enacted sequences of actions (Pentland et al., 2010, 2011). Much of the interest in the Routine Dynamics literature is about recognizing and analysing the dynamics within and between action patterns. For this purpose, another approach to complexity provides additional insights. Hackman (1969) referred to this approach as 'tasks as behavioral descriptions'. We view this approach to routine complexity as the enacted complexity approach.

24.3.3 Routine Complexity as a Function of Enactments

As Weick (1979) observed, actions, rather than actors, are central in organizational phenomena – tasks are not given, but enacted. In line with this processual ontology, Hærem et al. (2015) reformulated the concept of task complexity to capture the enactments performed while completing the task. 'Task as behavioral descriptions' was rejected by Hackman (1969) because he saw this as confounding the task and the responses to the task. Hærem et al. (2015) suggested that capturing the exact performances would disentangle the actions from the actor and the task-as-such, because the enactments as such can be analysed independently of the actor. The increasing availability of digital trace data makes this approach more useful than what one could anticipate in 1969. Moreover, it opens the opportunity to study Routine Dynamics as task performances, both as an independent and dependent variable. This enables researchers to study the sources of Routine Dynamics and their effect on enactments and enacted complexity in particular.

In the enacted task complexity framework, task complexity is defined as the number of paths in the network of enacted actions that lead to the attainment of the task outcomes (Hærem et al., 2015). When there are few paths to the desired end, the complexity is low; conversely, when there are many possible paths, the complexity is high. Tasks are represented as a network of actions where the nodes represent events or actions, and the edges represent sequential relations between these actions. Some of these sequences of actions make up the patterns that can be recognized, and by tracing these patterns as they constitute a path, we can begin to link the actions with the patterns of these actions and analyse the characteristics of routines in more detail. Further characterizing these patterns of actions and mapping the complexity of the routine can facilitate our understanding of the processes of both endogenous and exogenous dynamics in routines.

Defining complexity as a function of enactments, which can be mapped by a network structure, suggests that adding (or removing) nodes and edges will tend to increase (or decrease) the complexity. For any given number of actions, adding more paths increases complexity exponentially (Hærem et al., 2015). Rather than focusing on the number of required actions, this conceptualization of complexity emphasizes the sequential combinations of actions or paths during the performance of a task. Moreover, compared to the two other conceptualizations of complexity, the enacted complexity construct allows complexity to be calculated and analysed in a routine involving several actors across several units. The aggregation across actors and subtasks demonstrates the exponential property of complexity in task resolution processes (Hærem et al., 2015). Tasks in routines are seen as inseparable from performances and defined as actions performed by some actors at some moment in time. As such, enacted task complexity is in line with the basic idea in the Routine Dynamics research that routines are relations between actions carried out by multiple actors (e.g., Feldman and Pentland, 2003), and can be a useful tool for analysing the patterning of these interdependent actions.

Conceptualizing routine complexity in this way allows us to distinguish routine complexity from the concept of routinization. Feldman and Pentland's (2003: 96) definition of routines as 'a repetitive, recognizable pattern of interdependent actions, involving multiple actors' implies that a single, big pattern of actions constitutes a routine. On the other hand, recent empirical studies have documented traces of multiple patterns of smaller sequences of actions in the same routine (e.g., Goh and Pentland, 2019; Pentland et al., 2010; 2011). Based on this evidence, Hansson et al. (2018) put forward the notion that routines consist of a repertoire of small action patterns, rather than a single, big pattern. By disaggregating the single pattern into smaller patterns, they helped clarify the distinction between the concepts of repertoire of routines and routinization. Whereas repertoire refers to the number of distinct, recognizable patterns within a sequence of actions, routinization denotes the extent to which a sequence of actions follows recognizable patterns (Hansson et al., 2018).

By delineating these concepts, Hansson et al. (2018) depicted how repertoire, routinization and enacted complexity are distinguishable from one another. Whereas the degree of routinization is determined by the proportion of behaviours that is made up of recognized patterns, enacted complexity is defined by how many possible paths there are to the solution (i.e., in how many different ways a task can be/are resolved). For a path to be recognized, it has to be repeated a sufficient number of times. Since many paths may only be performed rarely and therefore are not recognized, routinization and enacted complexity do not necessarily co-vary (Hansson et al., 2018). In a directed graph of actions, one path can consist of many smaller sequences or patterns, and a set of patterns can be combined to enact multiple different paths (Pentland and Rueter, 1994). Even when the size of the repertoire (i.e., the number of unique patterns that are used to enact paths) is minimal, decreasing the degree of routinization (i.e., the percentage of behaviour that matches the repertoire) can add to the number of possible pathways and increase the enacted complexity. On the other hand, in a setting where routinization is perfect (i.e., all actions conform to the recognized patterns), increasing the size of the repertoire will tend to add more possible paths. That is, a few small patterns can generate a large number of ways in which a task can be completed. Therefore, contrary to the conventional view in the perceptual perspective on complexity, it is possible to have high routinization and high complexity, and vice versa.

24.3.3.1 Examples of Applications in the Routine Dynamics Literature

By showing how the concepts of repertoire, routinization and enacted complexity can be distinguished, Hansson et al. (2018) challenged the assumption prevalent in early organizational studies that routinized tasks are invariably simple, and complex tasks should be considered non-routine. They also demonstrated that the degree of routinization and the size of the action repertoire are important determinants of task performance. In two settings representing the extremes of task programmability – crisis management and invoice management – they found that a larger repertoire and a lower degree of routinization led to the complexification of enactments. While this was associated with higher performance in the crisis management setting, the opposite was true in invoice processing. Moreover, the effect of repertoire and routinization on routine performance was mediated by enacted complexity in both settings.

While the extant process studies on Routine Dynamics have predominantly adopted qualitative approaches (Howard-Grenville and Rerup, 2017), we find that the concept of enacted complexity is slowly but increasingly being adopted in empirical studies in the Routine Dynamics literature. Recently, Goh and Pentland (2019) examined a video game development project to investigate the mechanisms that drive a pattern of action to become more or less varied. They used the enacted complexity framework to trace the paths between patterns of actions in a network, where the enacted complexity index represents the variability of an action pattern. Focusing on the factors that contribute to the addition or removal of actions and paths and thus the enacted complexity of the process, Goh and Pentland (2019) identified six different mechanisms that impact the complexity of routines throughout the performance of the video game development project: reinforcement loop, performance loop, revision loop, delay loop, cut-back loop and motivation loop.

24.4 Discussion and Implications for Routine Dynamics Research

We have presented three approaches to define and analyse routine complexity as an extension of the task complexity concept. While Hackman (1969) and Wood (1986) recommended selecting one particular approach to analyse the complexity of tasks, we find that each approach, the perceptual, the idealized and the enacted, provides distinct insights. They enable us to identify and analyse unique aspects of the factors making up the complexity of routines. We have discussed how these factors can be understood as driving stability and change in Routine Dynamics. In this section, we discuss the underlying theoretical assumptions and methodological principles of each perspective and the implications they present for Routine Dynamics research.

24.4.1 Complexity as a Perceptual Characteristic of Routines

Studies of routinization based on perceptual measures have yielded strong support for the hypothesized relations when used with other perceptual measures, but often yielded little support for the hypothesized relations to variables more independent of perceptions (Becker and Zirpoli, 2008; Hærem and Rau, 2007; Miller et al., 1991; Pentland, 2003). Naylor, Pritchard and Ilgen (1980) were early to criticize this tendency to use perceptions of the task as characteristics of the task. Perceptual measures are associated with the same general limitations as perceptions: they are subjective and often systematically biased (e.g., Kahneman, 2011).

Another limitation of perceptual measures of complexity concerns the level of analysis. The perceptions of routinization of work are typically measured at an individual level, referring to the task each individual performs. Usually, these perceptions are aggregated to the work-unit level, thereby referring to the joint work performed in a unit. The psychometric aggregation of the individuals' perceptions of complexity to the work-unit level would usually refer to the average of individuals' perceptions, and at the aggregated level the routine may be very different from what is perceived by one individual. For example, perceptual measures would miss the often-exponential property of the complexity of the routine (Hærem et al., 2015).

The fact that perceptions confound the perceiver and the perceived object does not mean that the average and the variation in perceptions are irrelevant, but it does mean that we should not mistake the perceptions of routine complexity for the idealized or the enacted complexity of the routine. As can be seen in Table 24.1, perceptual measures have not been a popular methodology in the studies of Routine Dynamics. This may be a missed opportunity for research on Routine Dynamics since it matters how humans perceive the world.

24.4.2 *Complexity as a Function of Idealized Characteristics of Routines*

Underlying the measurement of the complexity of an idealized task is the assumption that the task is well understood, and it is possible to identify the required acts, information cues, the sequences of acts required to complete the task and any changes over time (e.g., Wood, 1986). By definition, these measures are constructed to be independent of each performance of the task, and thus do not reflect the variation occurring from each subjective performance. Therefore, the idealized complexity of a routine is not a variable – it is a constant for the routine in question.

Hackman's (1969) and Weick's (1965) original recommendation of the task qua task view of complexity was to control task variation to isolate the effect of psychological variables on behaviour. They believed the psychological variables would play out differently across levels of complexity. Even though the measure of idealized complexity does not reflect the dynamics in the routine, it may still be relevant for research in Routine Dynamics. As the simulation studies reported earlier demonstrate (Gao et al., 2015; 2018), the idealized complexity of a routine may be an important variable to control for, since the dynamics in routines may differ significantly across, for example, the levels of component complexity (i.e., the size of the library of actions). In other words, routine complexity conceptualized in this way can distinguish among idealized (ostensive) routines of different levels of complexity. We can, for example, hypothesize that routines with low idealized complexity have fewer sources of Routine Dynamics than routines with higher idealized complexity.

24.4.3 *Complexity as Function of Enactments*

The enacted complexity framework (Hærem et al., 2015) can be particularly useful in Routine Dynamics research that aims at disentangling the sources of stability and change. Readily observable behaviours of human and non-human actants serve as the basis for operationalizing complexity in this approach, thus making it possible to analyse stability, variation and change in routines over time. By modelling tasks as networks of enacted actions, it allows researchers to trace paths of actions and visualize the interdependencies between them. Therefore, this path-based approach offers an effective way of analysing Routine Dynamics – it allows us to understand how the paths are formed and dissolved over time, and how the patterns of actions in a routine change. The researchers' data are also less subject to the biases that influence perceptual measures (e.g., Hærem and Rau, 2007). Whereas conceptualizing complexity as an idealized characteristic of a task depicts the complexity of a routine as fixed, viewing complexity as enacted patterns of actions renders the complexity of a routine a dynamic characteristic, which changes, varies and evolves.

The distinction between simple and routinized is also clarified using the methodology and logic following from the enacted complexity approach. A routine that is highly routinized tends to be perceived as simple by the individuals performing it. The perceptual approach uses the concept of simple and routinized synonymously. Still, the performance of a task perceived to be simple might not really be simple. The enacted complexity approach demonstrates that the distinction between routinization and enacted complexity is important, and answers the question of how individuals performing a complex task can perceive it as simple: Due to a large repertoire of action patterns, a skilled organization can adapt its task resolution to a large set of environmental requirements – while the actors still use only recognized patterns to solve it – and therefore perceive it as simple.

The enacted complexity framework brings several methodological opportunities in studying the dynamics of routines. It can be applied at any level of analysis – individual, group and organizational – and the events can be defined for any kind of actor – humans, machines, organizational units or even entire organizations (Hærem et al., 2015). Viewing complexity as a network of enacted actions also allows a researcher to analyse patterns of actions by graph theory and thereby compute a wide set of specific characteristics of the patterns and structure properties of the network. For example, network properties, such as density and centralization, can be calculated and compared between patterns (Pentland et al., 2010). These measures can be used to analyse the consequences of increasing or decreasing complexity by forming or dissolving paths. The average distance measure, combined with multidimensional scaling (Kruskal and Wish, 1978), can be used to measure the extent to which a pattern in an organizational routine is atypical or exceptional (Pentland et al., 2011). The action network representation of sequences of actions in routines can also provide useful visualizations that are particularly valuable in analysing processual phenomena (Feldman, 2016b; Langley, 1999; Pentland et al., 2009).

24.4.4 Summary

Key points from the prior discussion are summarized in Table 24.2.

Each of the three approaches adds to the richness in the understanding of routine complexity, and, although one of the approaches may fit a certain problem better, none of the three approaches is without merits. On the other hand, routine complexity based on the enacted approach amends the fundamental problems that the two other approaches pose: In accordance with the assumptions in the Routine Dynamics literature that the sequences of actions vary across performances, enacted complexity captures variation both within and across time windows and the complexity as enacted by several actors. Perhaps more importantly, the enacted approach to routine complexity allows the researcher to identify finer nuances in the relations among characteristics of enactments and between enactments and other phenomena. For example, as mentioned previously, the perceptual approach to routine complexity has treated routinization and complexity as the same phenomenon. The enacted approach enables us to define and operationalize the degree of routinization more precisely. Therefore, we can measure the degree of routinization and complexity, and empirically investigate the connection between, as well as the antecedents and the consequences of, the two constructs.

Table 24.2 Assumptions of three approaches to routine complexity

	Approach to routine complexity		
Assumptions about ...	**Perceptual**	**Idealized**	**Enacted**
Task environment	Individuals' perceptions reflect the task accurately	It is possible to perfectly identify all the acts, information cues and their interactions required to solve the task	It is possible to observe what actors did when they performed the routine
Number of actors	Capture average perceptions of several actors	Originally for a single actor	From one to many actors
Location	Capture average perception across locations	Usually one location	Several locations
Variability	Assumes that variability is constant	Assumes variability is constant	Sensitive to variability across actors, actions, locations and time
Change	Assumes no change – measure average perception	Assumes change is at a constant rate	Sensitive to change across actors, actions, locations and time
Ability to discriminate between related constructs	Can easily be confounded with related perceptual phenomena such as difficulty, analysability and routineness	Confound individual variation in performances with the idealized version of performances	Discriminate across the variables considered in this chapter

24.5 Future Research Directions

Each of the three approaches provides directions for future studies, and combinations of these approaches may provide an interesting research avenue for even further directions. For example, several studies show that individuals' perceptions of change do not coincide with the changes that can be traced in the data (e.g., Hærem and Rau, 2007; Pentland 2003; Pentland, Vaast and Wolf, 2021). Therefore, a future line of research may explore the relations between the changes that are perceived and those that are not perceived. By combining the enacted complexity approach and the perceived complexity approach, researchers would be able to identify specific changes in trace data. Identifying the occasions where these changes are perceived might be important in managing stability and change in organizations. More specifically, investigations in this direction could investigate whether higher levels of enacted complexity are related to a lower probability of perceiving the exceptions in the process, or how many exceptions are needed for an actor to detect the changes in the routine process. Moreover, combining trace data and perceptions would allow researchers to more systematically study, for example, the process of normalization of deviance (e.g., Vaughan, 1996). The enacted complexity approach will allow us to study questions such as: Will the probability for detection of exceptions be moderated by the level of complexity? What is the stronger moderator – the level of idealized complexity, the degree of enacted complexity or the variation in enacted complexity?

The action network approach allows us to describe the enactments more concretely. At the same time, the mapping of paths enables us to infer possible alternative pathways through which a routine can be carried out. Some of these paths may never be acted on because they may be considered impractical or inefficient. However, it is this space of opportunities that contain rich possibilities for future research. In previous management research, the emphasis was often on reducing or simplifying this space. By the notion of bounded rationality (Simon, 1957), the key to solving a task effectively was seen as reducing the space that must be explored to achieve a desirable outcome (e.g., Newell and Simon, 1972). In the performance of routines, the habitual process of adhering to the same paths and repeating the same pattern of actions can lead to the rigidity of routines, resulting in path dependency and lock-ins (Sydow et al., 2009). On the other hand, in the literature on creativity, complexity is discussed as a key mechanism through which problem solvers can find creative solutions (e.g., Kaufmann, 1988). The action network perspective is useful for illustrating how the enactment of different paths can influence the possible paths in a routine. Small changes in the nodes and edges can change the entire set of possible pathways – just like changing the method of commuting from a bus to a bike can open up a number of new possible paths one can take to work.

In a more complex action network, there are more paths to a desired end. This allows for greater opportunities for an actor to take an alternative course of action, which in turn can open up new pathways. The importance of creating and maintaining such possibilities on emergent exploratory activities such as innovation and change has begun to be discussed in recent studies of organizations (e.g., Archer, 2010; Goh and Pentland, 2019). The enacted complexity framework enables us to analyse the accumulation of historical action patterns and how actors develop these patterns. By facilitating the analysis of how different actors in a routine consider 'local' opportunities in the set of previously performed acts, it can provide researchers with a useful tool in investigating how entrenchment and inertia, as well as change and innovation, are influenced by reducing and maintaining the variety of pathways.

24.6 Conclusion

Even though Feldman and Pentland's (2003) conceptualization of organizational routines as patterns of actions paved the way for discussing the complexity of routines, our review revealed that complexity has yet to become a core research topic in the Routine Dynamics literature. In this chapter, we outlined how characterizing the complexity of patterns of actions can illuminate the core mechanisms that generate the dynamics in routines. We reviewed three different approaches to the concept of complexity that have been applied in empirical research of routines, (a) complexity as a perceptual characteristic of routines; (b) complexity as a function of idealized characteristics of routines; and (c) complexity as function of enactments. Our selective review showed that early studies of routines have predominantly treated task complexity as a perceptual phenomenon, and in only a few studies has complexity been conceived of as an idealized characteristic of routines. More recently, in line with the practice-turn in routine research, a stream of research has begun to capture the complexity of routines as an enacted phenomenon and seems to fit especially well with the research agendas in the Routine Dynamics literature.

References

Archer, M. S. (2010). Morphogenesis versus structuration: On combining structure and action. *The British Journal of Sociology*, 61, 225–252.

Becker, M. C. and Zirpoli, F. (2008). Applying organizational routines in analyzing the behavior of organizations. *Journal of Economic Behavior & Organization*, 66(1), 128–148.

Campbell, D. J. (1988). Task complexity: A review and analysis. *Academy of Management Review*, 13(1), 40–52.

Cardoso, J., Mendling, J., Neumann, G. and Reijers, H. A. (2006). A discourse on complexity of process models. In J. Eder and S. Dustdar, eds., *Business Process Management Workshops. BPM 2006: Lecture Notes in Computer Science*, vol 4103. Berlin; Heidelberg: Springer, pp. 115–126.

Cyert, R. M. and March, J. G. (1963). *A Behavioral Theory of the Firm*. Englewood Cliffs, NJ: Prentice-Hall.

Daft, R. L. and Lengel, R. H. (1984). Information richness: A new approach to managerial information processing. *Research in Organizational Behavior*, 6, 191–233.

Daft, R. L. and Lengel, R. H. (1986). Organizational information requirements, media richness and structural design. *Management Science*, 32(5), 554–571.

Daft, R. L. and Macintosh, N. B. (1981). A tentative exploration into the amount and equivocality of information processing in organizational work units. *Administrative Science Quarterly*, 26(2), 207–224.

Farjoun, M. (2010). Beyond dualism: Stability and change as a duality. *Academy of Management Review*, 35(2), 202–225.

Feldman, M. S. (2000). Organizational routines as a source of continuous change. *Organization Science*, 11(6), 611–629.

Feldman, M. S. (2016a). Routines as process: Past, present, and future. In J. Howard-Grenville, C. Rerup, A. Langley and H. Tsoukas, eds., *Organizational Routines: A Process Perspective*. Oxford: Oxford University Press, pp. 23–46.

Feldman, M. S. (2016b). Making process visible: Alternatives to boxes and arrows. In A. Langley and H. Tsoukas, eds., *The Sage Handbook of Process Organization Studies*. London: Sage, 625–635.

Feldman, M. S. and Pentland, B. T. (2003). Reconceptualizing organizational routines as a source of flexibility and change. *Administrative Science Quarterly*, 48(1), 94–118.

Feldman, M. S., Pentland, B. T., D'Adderio, L. and Lazaric, N. (2016). Beyond routines as things: Introduction to the special issue on routine dynamics. *Organization Science*, 27(3), 505–513.

Fields, D. L. (2002). *Taking the Measure of Work: A Guide to Validated Scales for Organizational Research and Diagnosis*. London: Sage Publications.

Forrester, J. W. (1997). Industrial dynamics. *Journal of the Operational Research Society*, 48(10), 1037–1041.

Galbraith, J. R. (1973). *Designing Complex Organizations*. Reading, MA: Addison-Wesley Longman Publishing Co., Inc.

Gao, D., Deng, X., Zhao, Q., Zhou, H. and Bai, B. (2015). Multi-agent based simulation of organizational routines on complex networks. *Journal of Artificial Societies and Social Simulation*, 18 (3), 17.

Gao, D., Squazzoni, F. and Deng, X. (2018). The role of cognitive artifacts in organizational routine dynamics: An agent-based model. *Computational and Mathematical Organization Theory*, 24(4), 473–499.

Gell-Mann, M. (1994). *The Quark and the Jaguar: Adventures in the Simple and the Complex*. New York: W. H. Freeman & Co.

Goh, K. T. and Pentland, B. T. (2019). From actions to paths to patterning: Toward a dynamic theory of patterning in routines. *Academy of Management Journal*, 62(6), 1901–1929.

Hackman, J. R. (1969). Toward understanding the role of tasks in behavioral research. *Acta Psychologica*, 31, 97–128.

Hansson, M., Pentland, B. T. and Hærem, T. (2018, June). Identifying and describing characteristics of organizational routines as repertoires of action patterns, degree of routinization, and enacted complexity. *Academy of Management Global Proceedings*. https://journals.aom.org/doi/10.5465/amgblproc.surrey.2018.0037.abs

Howard-Grenville, J. and Rerup, C. (2017). A process perspective on organizational routines. In A. Langley and H. Tsoukas, eds., *The SAGE Handbook of Process Organization Studies*. London: SAGE Publications Ltd, pp. 323–339.

Hærem, T., Pentland, B. T. and Miller, K. D. (2015). Task complexity: Extending a core concept. *Academy of Management Review*, 40(3), 446–460.

Hærem, T. and Rau, D. (2007). The influence of degree of expertise and objective task complexity on perceived task complexity and performance. *Journal of Applied Psychology*, 92(5), 1320–1331.

Kahneman, D. (2011). *Thinking, Fast and Slow*. New York: Farrar, Straus and Giroux.

Kaufmann, G. (1988). Problem solving and creativity. In K. Grønhaug and G. Kaufmann, eds., *Innovation: A Cross-disciplinary Perspective*. Norway: Norwegian University Press, pp. 87–137.

Kruskal, J. B. and Wish, M. (1978). *Multidimensional Scaling* (Vol. 11). London: Sage.

Langley, A. (1999). Strategies for theorizing from process data. *Academy of Management Review*, 24(4), 691–710.

March, J. G. and Simon, H. A. (1958). *Organizations*. New York: Wiley.

Miller, C. C., Glick, W. H., Wang, Y. D. and Huber, G. P. (1991). Understanding technology-structure relationships: Theory development and meta-analytic theory testing. *Academy of Management Journal*, 34(2), 370–399.

Naylor, J. C., Pritchard, R. D. and Ilgen, D. R. (1980). *A Theory of Behavior in Organizations*. New York: Academic Press.

Nelson, C. R. and Winter, S. (1982). *An Evolutionary Theory of Economic Change*. Cambridge, MA: Harvard University Press.

Newell, A. and Simon, H. A. (1972). *Human Problem Solving*. Englewood Cliffs, NJ: Prentice-Hall.

Ohly, S., Sonnentag, S. and Pluntke, F. (2006). Routinization, work characteristics and their relationships with creative and proactive behaviors. *Journal of Organizational Behavior*, 27, 257–279.

Parmigiani, A. and Howard-Grenville, J. (2011). Routines revisited: Exploring the capabilities and practice perspectives. *Academy of Management Annals*, 5(1), 413–453.

Perrow, C. (1967). A framework for the comparative analysis of organizations. *American Sociological Review*, 32(2), 194–208.

Pentland, B. T. (2003). Sequential variety in work processes. *Organization Science*, 14(5), 528–540.

Pentland, B. T. and Hærem, T. (2015). Organizational routines as patterns of action: Implications for organizational behavior. *Annual Review of Organizational Psychology and Organizational Behavior*, 2(1), 465–487.

Pentland, B. T., Hærem, T. and Hillison, D. W. (2009). Using workflow data to explore the structure of an organizational routine. In M. C. Becker and N. Lazaric, eds., *Organizational Routines: Advancing Empirical Research*. Cheltenham: Edward Elgar, pp. 47–67.

Pentland, B. T., Hærem, T. and Hillison, D. (2010). Comparing organizational routines as recurrent patterns of action. *Organization Studies*, 31(7), 917–940.

Pentland, B. T., Hærem, T. and Hillison, D. (2011). The (n)ever-changing world: Stability and change in organizational routines. *Organization Science*, 22(6), 1369–1383.

Pentland, B. T., Liu, P., Kremser, W. and Hærem, T. (2020). The dynamics of drift in digitized processes. *MIS Quarterly*, 44(1), 19–47.

Pentland, B. T. and Rueter, H. H. (1994). Organizational routines as grammars of action. *Administrative Science Quarterly*, 39(3), 484–510.

Pentland, B. T., Vaast, E. and Wolf, J. R. (2021). Theorizing process dynamics with directed graphs: A Diachronic analysis of digital trace data. *MIS Quarterly*, 45(2), 967–984.

Senge, P. M. (2006). *The Fifth Discipline: The Art & Practice of The Learning Organization*. New York: Bantam Books.

Simon, H. A. (1957). *Models of Man: Social and Rational*. NewYork: Wiley.

Stacey, R. D. (1996). *Complexity and Creativity in Organizations.* San Francisco: Berrett-Koehler Publishers.

Sydow, J., Schreyögg, G. and Koch, J. (2009). Organizational path dependence: Opening the black box. *Academy of Management Review*, 34(4), 689–709.

Tsoukas, H. and Chia, R. (2002). On organizational becoming: Rethinking organizational change. *Organization Science*, 13(5), 567–582.

Tushman, M. L. and Nadler, D. A. (1978). Information processing as an integrating concept in organizational design. *Academy of Management Review*, 3(3), 613–624.

Van de Ven, A. H. and Delbecq, A. L. (1974). A task contingent model of work-unit structure. *Administrative Science Quarterly*, 19(2), 183–197.

Van de Ven, A. H., Delbecq, A. L. and Koenig Jr, R. (1976). Determinants of coordination modes within organizations. *American Sociological Review*, 41(2), 322–338.

Van de Ven, A. H. and Ferry, D. L. (1980). *Measuring and Assessing Organizations.* New York: Wiley.

Vaughan, D. (1996). *The Challenger Launch Decision: Risky Technology, Culture, and Deviance at NASA.* Chicago: University of Chicago Press.

Weick, K. E. (1965). Laboratory experimentation with organizations. In J. G. March, ed., *Handbook of Organizations.* Chicago: Rand McNally, pp. 194–260.

Weick, K. E. (1979). *The Social Psychology of Organizing.* Reading, MA: Addison-Wesley.

Withey, M., Daft, R. L. and Cooper, W. H. (1983). Measures of Perrow's work unit technology: An empirical assessment and a new scale. *Academy of Management Journal*, 26(1), 45–63.

Wood, R. E. (1986). Task complexity: Definition of the construct. *Organizational Behavior and Human Decision Processes*, 37(1), 60–82.

CHAPTER 25

Bodies and Routine Dynamics

CHARLOTTE BLANCHE AND MARTHA S. FELDMAN

The mechanism of walking remains the same for everyone, but each person walks differently and that's the expression. Merce Cunningham

I'm not so interested in how they move as in what moves them. Pina Bauch

25.1 Introduction

Organizational routines entail use of the human body. The body is central to the perceiving, feeling, communicating, judging, reflecting and moving that takes place as participants carry out routines. The importance of the body to work routines was identified early. For instance, Frederick Taylor's studies of coal shovelling and brick laying note the importance of matching the tool (shovel size or brick palettes) with what the body needs to do with the tool (Taylor, 1911). Despite the necessity of bodies in routines and this long recognition of their importance, theorizing about routines has only recently opened space for including the body specifically in how we understand what a routine is and what it takes to accomplish routines. Routine Dynamics opened this space by identifying 'specific actions, by specific people in specific places and times' (Feldman and Pentland, 2003: 101) as an essential aspect in our understanding of routines. As noted by Feldman (2000), 'When we do not separate the people who are doing the routines from the routine, we can see routines as a richer phenomenon. Routines are performed by people who think and feel and care' (2000: 613–614).

In this chapter, we illustrate the work of the body through several reference articles. We recognize the entangled nature of mind and body and that the distinction between mind and body is an analytical distinction that does not well serve fields of study that focus on action and agency (Joas, 1996: 145ff). Nonetheless, in the material we analyse we emphasize the physical or somatic aspects of action rather than the semiotic or cognitive ones in order to highlight aspects of the corporeal contribution that have been underappreciated and to illustrate and articulate the corporeal contribution to accomplishing stability and change. Because the somatic aspects of embodiment have not been the dominant focus of theorizing in Routine Dynamics, we bring forward the body as it is revealed in the findings sections of the reference articles in order to focus on the body's contribution to action and the concomitant effect on patterns.

25.2 Embodiment within Prior Research in Organization Theory

The organizational research on embodiment is vast, with contributions from numerous disciplines. The embodiment perspective explores broadly an understanding of action by emphasizing the tacit, sensitive and aesthetic aspects of knowledge (Collins, 2010; Ewenstein and Whyte, 2007; Polanyi 1966; Strati, 2007; Tsoukas [Chapter 3], this volume). Scholars of organization have explored the role of the body in knowing (Gherardi et al., 2007), learning (Strati, 2007; Yakhlef, 2010), sense-making (De Rond et al., 2019; Sandberg and Tsoukas, 2020) and communication (Ashcraft et al., 2009) among others. They have explored how practical knowledge and professional expertise are embodied (Dreyfus, 2017; Gherardi et al., 2013) and how members of teams share inter-corporeal knowledge enabling mutual understandings and coordination (D'Adderio, 2001; Hindmarsh and Pilnick 2007; Sergeeva et al., 2020). These studies have relied on a variety of philosophical bases, including phenomenology (Tsoukas [Chapter 3], this volume), pragmatism, (Dionysiou [Chapter 5], this volume) and practice theory (Feldman[Chapter 2], this volume).

While each of these philosophical traditions overlap to some extent, they each also make specific contributions to our understanding of the body's participation in organizational work. Phenomenology, for instance, draws our attention to conceiving the sensory apparatus as a means to know reality and access the world (Merleau-Ponty, 1962, 1964, 1968). Pragmatism draws our attention to embodied cognition through the link to action. Under the 'principle of continuity' articulated by Dewey, for instance, it is not possible to separate in action the experiences of perceiving, feeling and thinking (Johnson and Rohrer, 2007). Practice theory, similarly, draws attention to the specific practices our bodies engage in (Bourdieu, 1990; Bourdieu and Wacquant, 1992; Wacquant, 2015). The concept of habitus, which Bourdieu (1990) refers to as 'embodied history' (1990: 56), in particular, is an embodied disposition that makes it 'possible to respond instantaneously to all the uncertain and ambiguous situations of practice' (1990: 103–104). Each of these approaches reject any form of dualism including, as is particularly relevant here, the Cartesian separation of body and mind.

Routine Dynamics research has begun to include studies that theorize embodiment as related to routines and routine enactment. We identify two theoretical routes these studies have taken. One consists in perception and draws on pragmatism via symbolic interactionism. Dionysiou and Tsoukas (2013), for instance, place repetitive joint action at the core of routines. They draw on the work of Mead (1934, 1938, 2002/1932) to provide a process model for routine (re)creation. Another route consists in communication and focuses attention on practices as understood through practice theory and ethnomethodology (LeBaron et al. 2016; Wright, 2019; Yamauchi and Hiramoto, 2016). From observations of embodied acts of communication, these authors show how organizational routines are continually produced and reproduced through these acts.

While theorizing the body has just begun in Routine Dynamics, the body is ever present empirically. Indeed, there are more examples of bodies in routines than we could possibly portray in the space of a handbook chapter. Thus, to illustrate the empirical ubiquity of the body in Routine Dynamics, we focus on the thirteen articles based on observations of people enacting routines in the *Organization Science* Special Issue on Routine Dynamics (Feldman et al. 2016). Having previously read these articles, we had a sense that bodies were commonly portrayed in Routine Dynamics. What we did not know was whether these bodies related primarily to only some aspects of Routine Dynamics. In order to explore this question, we used established Routine Dynamics categories: performative/performing, ostensive/patterning and artefact/materializing (D'Adderio, 2011; Feldman and Pentland, 2003; see also Editors Introduction [Chapter 1], this volume). As articulated in Routine Dynamics theorizing, these three are separable only analytically and not in practice. Analysing bodies as they appeared in relation to each of these categories, nonetheless, helped us to see not only that embodiment is a significant presence in Routine Dynamics articles but also that embodiment is a significant part of each of these aspects of routines.

In Table 25.1, we provide excerpts from these articles that illustrate the presence of bodies as related to each of the Routine Dynamics categories of performance, pattern and materiality. Inspired by the work of Shotter (2006), who enjoins us to think from within process rather than to think about process, we conceptualize the body implication within routine as having directionality in relation to these categories. Shotter (2006) articulates a 'relationally-responsive form of understanding (or a withness-understanding)' (2006: 590). Drawing on the work of Bakhtin, he argues that relations within a living process are essentially dialogical, moving back and forth between action and situation in a manner that he likens to binocular vision, where two points of view create depth because they are combined but not merged. He refers to this as 'relational unity'.

> In other words, as we move around in such a landscape, in the orchestrated interplay occurring between our own outgoing, anticipation-shaped movements (toward the 'invitations' offered us by our surroundings) and the incoming 'resistances'-shaped responses arising from them as a result, we experience a continuously updated practical understanding of an 'action guiding' kind of how to 'go on' in our movements (Shotter, 2006: 596).

Table 23.1 Selected excerpts providing clear indications of the body explicitly expressed by the authors

	Embodied orientation		
	to/from performing	to/from situation/materiality	to/from pattern
LeBaron, Christianson, Garrett and Ilan (2016)	**To/from performing** **Embodied display of real time coordination** Coordinating included displays of sufficiency – such as agreeing, nodding, continuing writing – which audibly or visibly showed that the handoff was mutually intelligible and that the participants were ready to continue. Coordinating also included displays of insufficiency – such as questioning, repairing, stopping writing – which showed that something was wrong and needed to be changed before the handoff could go on. (520)	**From materiality** **Artefact handling orients performance** By looking toward their list, the physicians collaborated in a silent bid to close; the list is where they always looked before starting a new handoff because that's where they found the next patient's name. (527)	**To/from pattern** **Shared expectations rooted in embodied experiences of routine** Thus, the expectations that physicians brought to the table provided a backdrop for the mutual intelligibility of their flexible performance. (. . .) Their shared expectations were not officially mandated or standardized, but were rather rooted in past experiences, such as their shared history of coordinating while flexibly performing handoffs. (520)
Aroles and McLean (2016)	**To/from performance** **New way to perform reorients (and makes invisible) an embodied practice** Many printers raised this [the lack of discussion or opportunity to explain] as a matter of concern and stated that certain individual explanations and experiences could be 'lost' from these accounts when not presented within the simplified figures of management reports. This was also seen as a particular problem in meetings where people in the room were not from the factory floor and may not fully understand the complexity of these issues. (542)	**From materiality** **Embodied feedback from artefacts** For Roger, the copy 'was of really good quality with only light defects that you have to report, but nothing serious and nothing that people would notice when picking up the newspapers on the street.' (543)	**From pattern** **Embodied experience of desired outcome** Sam argued that he needed the flexibility to judge the appropriate level of ink for the run on a case-by-case basis, rather than being restricted by routinized and standardized procedures. The comments made by Sam resonated with discussions with other printers who expressed concerns about how certain routines and simplified forms of measurement can sometimes go against their feelings of professional integrity and autonomy. (542)
Berente, Lyytinen, Yoo and King (2016)	**To performance** **Actions are driven by feelings/ emotions** However, many project managers at Glenn felt that the ERP system did not meet their needs. Active resistance increased (e.g., project managers walked out of training) (562)		**To pattern** **Emotional reaction to envisioned pattern** They killed the system. They turned the systems off. When IFMP came live with SAP and even BW [Business Warehouse] wasn't live when they cut over, it was SAP or nothing. You had no alternative. (. . .) They pulled the rug out from everybody and nobody felt comfortable. (Project Manager C, transcript 2-12-04) (563)
Bertels, Howard-Grenville and Pek (2016)	**To performance** **Embodied culture orients performance** One respondent spoke at length about 'our culture of starting things and never really finishing them', and another affirmed: 'Oh yeah. You hear lots of colorful wording around that, you know, "fly by the seat of the pants," "firefighting." It's a very heroic culture. [We know that] we might have unanticipated problems, but we will be able to rise to the occasion.' (579)	**From materiality** **Being in contact with other beings reorients the performance** Hindered performance occurs when employees, making use of a cultural strategy of action aligned with the espoused routine, are unable to fully perform a step in the routine because their own performance relies on others who continue to draw on a misaligned strategy of action.(582)	

Table 25.1 (*cont.*)

	Embodied orientation		
	to/from performing	to/from situation/materiality	to/from pattern
Bucher and Langley (2016)	**To/From performance** **Experiencing new ways of performing influence own performance** Seeing patients leaving the Danish hospital after major operations within only three days and in good shape, the team returned very impressed and fully convinced of the need to introduce FTS in their clinic. (. . .) It was a quite extraordinary experience which will change my clinical behavior for the rest of my life (project surgeon, email). (602)	**From materiality** **Artifact reorients an embodied practice** The project team had instructed the hospital's outpatient center to mark the medical records of FTS patients with a colored dot in addition to the indication "FTS" to clearly indicate that the practice for treating these patients needed to be different from conventional ones across the overall routine (. . .) it came with the need to "unlearn old practices" and to "learn security anew" (nurse, informal conversation) (603)	**To pattern** **Emotional reaction to envisioned pattern** You know, FTS was not something we could just copy directly. We did not want to force the patient to leave the hospital after only three days, as in Denmark. (Project surgeon, interview) (602)
Cohendet and Simon (2016)	**To performance** **Actions are driven by feelings/emotions** You have this feeling of jumping in: we're making the game, we're not only talking about it anymore. . . . It's very exciting, but then again, even if we have a stronger feeling of progress and fulfillment through what we're producing, the integration is still a huge issue, and so is validation. (622)	**From materiality** **Embodied experience of the artefact identifies pattern essential to performance** Games, including video games, are supposed to be fun to play and generate a general sense of fun along with a challenging and rewarding experience. "Fun" is the core element of the value, and the main reason why gamers play. (. . .) You can't really assess the fun value of a feature and its contribution to the whole game play by talking about it or sketching it (623)	**To pattern** **Embodied expertise gives a sense of pattern** My people – a talented crew of artists and programmers – were still sharing a common background of hands-on expertise that should be defining what we do: years and years of playing video games, thinking about video games, dreaming about them and talking about them with great critical accuracy and sound judgment . . . (622)
Danner-Schröder and Geiger (2016)	**To performance** **Resisting emotions to perform effectively** John and Marc went around the warehouse, already hearing victims crying from inside. However, at this stage neither of them made any attempt to help; (. . .) Of course it is difficult to send victims away since we are called in in the first place to help them. But we have to get ready ourselves before we can help, otherwise we produce even more chaos., (648)	**From materiality** **Being in tune with other beings helps people take appropriate action** While he was searching for victims in a building, his dog (search dog) was running out of the building. First he was not sure why that happened, but then he realized that the dog must have recognized something. So he crawled under a table, and seconds later an aftershock started. Barry, standing next to that group, confirmed that animals have a good sense. He said that he always watched the ravens. As soon as they flew away he knew an aftershock would come. (647)	**From pattern** **Patterns to curb emotions and orient action** In the beginning, when you arrive it looks totally chaotic and overwhelming. We roll out our routines and start operating in the trained and prescribed way. This way we cope with chaos and focus on the most important aspects first . . . We cannot start experimenting here but have to rely on our standards. (639)

Deken, Carlile, Berends and Lauche (2016)	**To performance** **Performing according to its embodied knowledge** The examples in Narrative 1 illustrate how the different types of routine work differ in terms of the relative familiarity of the actors involved (ranging from all actors familiar with the routine in flexing work, to some of the actors in stretching work, to none of the actors in inventing work). (667)	**From materiality** **Contact with other people creates awareness of dependencies in routine** Dependencies may, however, not always be anticipated; sometimes dependencies are only identified when other people become involved or as people are confronted with the consequences of novel actions and outcomes in downstream actions. (668)	**To pattern** **Past experience provides sense of interdependency** Actors' past experiences with routine performances are central in anticipating (inter)dependencies between actions.(668)
Dittrich, Guérard and Seidl (2016)	**To performance** **Talking to adapt the performance** In this vignette, talk enables the routine participants to solve the problem of the lids and adapt the performance by facilitating collective reflection. Three aspects of talk support the enactment of collective reflection: (1) naming and situating the actions from different perspectives, (2) envisaging and exploring alternative ways of performing the routine and (3) evaluating and questioning the suggestions. (683)	**From materiality** **Objects support embodied notion of time/speeches** Chris: [glancing at the agenda in front of him] 'And then we have [customer X]. Last week, we sent them a shipment that did not work 100% on several levels . . . It seems that the box was first transferred to ShipCo's hub in [country Y], which is normal because it's their hub, and then it went to [country Z]. From there, back to ShipCo's hub and then again to [country Z] and, as a result, it arrived not on Thursday but on Friday. (686)	**To pattern** **Talking enables collective sense of how to adapt pattern** Indeed, almost half of the shipments involved some kind of flexible adaptation. In these instances, CellCo employees often engaged in talk, reflecting on the situated actions (i.e., the performative aspect) against the pattern of the routine (i.e., the ostensive aspect) . . . talk enables the routine participants to solve the problem . . . and adapt the performance by facilitating collective reflection. (683)
Kremser and Schreyögg (2016)	**From performance** **Feelings are reactions to failed actions** as the CTO of this time reports, the resistance against digital photofinishing was more subtle, 'Yes, those are critical questions, and, to speak frankly, there was hidden glee when something went wrong. The thinking was pretty much: "Didn't I tell you this isn't gonna work?" [. . .] They were less concerned with trying to find solutions than describing the problems (Interview SM4_2). (715)	**From materiality** **Artifact orients embodied practice** Film development starts upon the arrival of a trolley (. . .). Some cues, representing the program's trigger, help operators to quickly recognize the relevant specifics of the batch (i.e., the orders to be processed within one complete performance of the routine). The easily visible colour codes on the boxes enable prioritizing of time-critical orders. (705)	**To/From pattern** **Embodied adjustments needed to enact pattern and bodily alertness needed to enact desired pattern** Often, the actors performing this routine had to make small adjustments and improvise to keep the process reliable and results expectable for subsequent units. During film development, for example, the operators had to be specifically alert to the danger of film losses and actively had to monitor the chemical process for any unexpected disruptions. (706) **To pattern** **Enacting pattern requires stubbornness** Luckily for CEWE, however, top management was stubborn. They cancelled integration, but they did not give up on digital photofinishing altogether. (715)

Table 25.1 ***(cont.)***

	Embodied orientation		
	to/from performing	to/from situation/materiality	to/from pattern
Sele and Grand (2016)	**To performance** **Bodily engagement provides ideas for performance** The initial idea for the ALP emerged when a newly hired postdoc began weight lifting at the gym with a Ph.D. student. While doing the leg press, the two researchers discussed 'how what we knew from our research on sensory-motor tasks was not applied in training machines' (postdoc). Back at the lab, they continued to reflect on the idea that there must be ways to achieve smoother and less mechanical body movements. (p. 729)	**From materiality** **Engaging with artefact leads to new activities** Engaging with the commercial robot kits led one of the Ph.D. students to transform an existing theoretical seminar on AI into a practical teaching module within which students built their own robots using one of these kits. (729)	**To pattern** **Engaging bodies to identify patterns/arguments** They let the visitors test the prototype – a practice that allowed them to spot problems and to build up a repertoire of selling arguments that became very useful later when writing a business plan and communicating with potential investors. (729)
Sonenshein (2016)	**To performance** **Performing embodied style** I kind of use a little bit of my style with what I think the store style is, whether to put a big necklace with a blouse or dress. I kinda just use my own personal – what I think would look good, and then I always add just a little bit more, because I think that they want the mannequins to look more flashy and to show off what they have, so where I probably would wear a scarf with something, I would always put a scarf on the mannequin just because I think that's more of the BoutiqueCo style. (748)	**From materiality** **Artefact orients the feeling of the performance/pattern/routine** In discussing the use of the visual merchandising manual instead of a planogram: When you go into a lot of retailers . . . they have this table . . . this color. That color. So everything is mapped out for them exactly. So here we don't have that. We have more of in terms of the consistency pieces, more of like the aesthetics of the feel. . . . Making sure that the merchandise is color storied. The jewelry. Having the right jewelry neck cart. But we don't tell you what has to be on the jewelry carts. (747)	**From pattern** **Orienting embodied actions to coherence of pattern** The goal is to create a visually compelling 'look and feel' of the store. In this sense, even when employees merchandise at a particular time by themselves, they coordinate with other employees to create a coherent look and feel of the store. (744)
Spee, Jarzabkowski and Smets (2016)	**To performance** **Body is engaged while performing** The submission starts John's DAR. He quickly scans the cover email (Table 1, row B). He moves his cursor over the screen, briefly hovering over the 'key facts' and 'year-on-year changes' . . . to check any changes from last year that would ring alarm bells or give him a steer on how to customize his approach to this deal (769)	**From materiality** **Sensing pattern through artefact** He mumbles to himself as his fingers trace the color-coded zones on the map: '[tracing the green zone] 1% wind and hail deductibles, [tracing purple] 2% wind and hail deductibles, [tracing yellow and orange] all this business that they write has got no wind or hail . . ., [tracing red] looks like they managed to get off that most exposed zone all together except a few policies' (Vb. Obs.). In tracing these outlines, John refreshes his knowledge of the specific parameters of this deal, including the type of commercial. and residential property InsureCo insures in each zone. (771)	**To/From pattern** **Sensing the right deal** He looks at them for a few minutes, comparing the 11 curves of reinsurance deals in Louisiana, then mumbles: 'this one comes out on top of A [InsureCo's competitor A], but below B [InsureCo's competitor B], but I like the bottom layer of C too [InsureCo's competitor C]' (Vb. Obs.). John decides that he will make an offer on InsureCo as well as these other three deals, but discard the others. However, to be consistent, he will marginally lift the rate on Layers 1 and 2, because he thinks InsureCo needs to pay a bit more to align with the other deals. (773)

We attempt to capture this binocular vision by identifying the back and forth between body and routine as 'to' and 'from' within the studies that we analyse. 'To' thus includes a bodily inclination toward taking action, engaging materiality or enacting/referring to patterns. Whereas 'from' includes the information we receive from the performed action, the used materiality or guiding pattern.

Following Table 25.1, we discuss what we find in each column as a way of summarizing and further illustrating the presence of bodies in routines and how this bi-directionality shows up within each of the Routine Dynamics categories across the studied articles. After discussing what we see within categories across all thirteen articles, we explore how the body shows up across the categories in one article. This latter analysis allows us to see how making corporality central allows us to bring to light a living understanding of stability and change in routines.

25.3 Embodied Orientations and Routines

Our analysis of the thirteen articles shows the ubiquity of bodies in Routine Dynamics articles. By noting how bodies are involved in the accounts of organizational routines in these articles, we found that these categories helped us to see and to show various ways that the body participates in Routine Dynamics.

25.3.1 *Embodied Orientation to/from Performative/Performing*

These articles clearly show that performing is embodied. Embodied orientation 'to' performance aims to refer to the way bodies are deployed to take action in a routine. People have to have bodies to take action. Their bodies do things (hold film (Kremser and Schreyögg, 2016), create displays (Sonenshein, 2016), go on site visits (Bucher and Langley, 2016), gesture to indicate agreement or disagreement (LeBaron et al., 2016), talk (Dittrich et al., 2016), etc.). Bodies are also the source of emotions that propel people to take action (or to resist taking action) when they 'jump in' with excitement in making the game (Cohendet and Simon, 2016) or when they walk out of a training in frustration (Berente et al., 2016).

Embodied orientation 'from' the performance aims at referring to all the sensory input gathered by the body while taking action. Through embodied expertise and experience, their bodies provide them with a feel for what is an appropriate and acceptable action and what is an action that communicates assent or dissent. As we read the empirical material in these articles, most of the examples of bodies in relation to performance entailed the body informing performance (rather than performance informing the body). Sensations, for instance, are often the reason for people taking action in a routine. People sense that something needs to be done while taking action. The article by Kremser and Schreyögg (2016) provides an example of the body being informed by performance, when people reacted emotionally (with glee) to a failure in performance of the routine. Such embodied reactions from the performances in a routine must surely happen often. The relative lack of such examples in our reading of the thirteen articles may simply be a function of the focus of the authors as well as our search for excerpts that provide clear indications of the body.

25.3.2 *Embodied Orientation to/from Artefact/Materializing*

These articles show that bodies are essential for engaging with materiality (D'Adderio [Chapter 7], this volume). The materiality takes many forms – in some cases it is the physical product, (e.g., a game, a contract, a healed patient, a robot kit), in some cases it is another being or entity (human or nonhuman), a part of the situation like a wall or a map or a guideline or instrument for measuring alignment with a guideline. An embodied orientation 'to' materiality testifies to the implicit assumption made in every article that artefacts come into play through bodies; they are grasped, used and modified. An embodied orientation 'from' materiality tends to refer to the performative character of the artefact as well as the information we can gather from the situation we are in. Most of the examples we found in these articles that provided clear indications of the body entailed the body experiencing materiality, rather than the effect of the body on materiality. Materiality may affect practice through both performance (as when checklists orient hospital handoffs (LeBaron et al., 2016) or managers' reports orient the use of printer's ink (Arole and McLean, 2016) and through pattern (as when the experience of game helps to orient video game developers to the flow of fun (Cohendet and Simon, 2016) or when a map helps an underwriter sense the right combination of features in a contract (Spee et al., 2016)). Bodies also sense things (e.g., Deken et al., 2016) and see qualities (Aroles and McLean, 2016) thanks to past experience and the recognition that the world they engage in is informative. In some examples the described action does not present a bodily experience 'to' or 'from' an artefact but rather both to and from simultaneously. In those cases, the artefacts are understood as an extension of the body: tools for rescuers (Danner-Schröder and Geiger, 2016), computer mice to scroll documents (Spee et al., 2016).

25.3.3 Embodied Orientation to/from Ostensive/Patterning

Embodied experience relates to patterns through the same relationship. What we refer to as an embodied orientation 'to' pattern aims at highlighting the reference made to a guiding pattern, or the prospective summons of what has to be done. Bodies participate in creating and recreating these patterns through somatic reactions such as comfort and discomfort, stubbornness, confidence and anticipation. Patterns can come in the form of expectations. Other examples indicate that the body affects patterns. Having experienced gaming or health care, for instance, is important to how people enact the patterns entailed in creating games and producing specific health care protocols. An embodied orientation 'from' pattern refers to pattern's guiding force, and body movements being guided by taken for granted norms, outcomes or interdependencies that affect the routine. While most patterns are enacted (what a good video game feels like (Cohendet and Simon, 2016), whether a hand-off is satisfying (LeBaron et al., 2016), whether a publication looks right (Aroles and McLean, 2016), some patterns are in the process of becoming enacted (e.g., the FTS system for health care discussed by Bucher and Langley (2016) or a new software purchasing system discussed by Berente et al., (2016)), and one study draws our attention to patterns that are being avoided (Danner- Schröder and Geiger, 2016). Routines (i.e., enacted patterns) often take advantage of bodily reactions, but they may also curb bodily reactions as described by Danner- Schröder and Geiger (2016) who show how rescue routines help rescuers deal with their embodied sense of urgency about providing help to victims of disaster.

Our table includes many examples of the embodied reactions (both positive and negative) to either an envisioned or an enacted pattern. There are also some excellent examples of the recursive relation between bodies and patterns. For instance, the excerpts from LeBaron et al. (2016) and from Spee et al. (2016) show that when doctors engage in handoffs or contractors put together a refinance deal they both draw on and produce their embodied experience of handoffs and deals.

25.3.4 Bodies in Routine Dynamics Articles

We chose these thirteen articles as a way of exploring our intuition that the body was ubiquitous in the empirical work of Routine Dynamics articles. While not representative of all the ways that the body can be present in routines, these articles do capture a developed state of Routine Dynamics theorizing as applied to a broad range of research questions and, thus, provide a basis for our claims about the ubiquity of bodies in Routine Dynamics articles. Our analysis of these thirteen articles shows that the body shows up persistently in relation to each of three theoretical concepts often used in Routine Dynamics.

We do not suggest that these articles portray the full scope of embodied engagement in routines. Indeed, two articles come immediately to mind as additional examples of how the body is engaged in routines. One is by Eberhard, Frost and Rerup

(2019) about how the routines of Romeo pimps exploit the bodily needs for love and support to entrap women into sex trafficking. Another is by Yamauchi and Hiramoto (2016) about how hi-end sushi chefs use talk and gesture to figure out what their customers know about the sushi routine and to create a smooth flow of engagement with them. Our exploration of these thirteen *Organization Science* special issue articles convinced us that all you need to do is look for bodies and you will see them. For now, we conclude this section with the observation that bodies and routines are thoroughly and pervasively entangled.

25.4 Bodies and Dynamism

Looking at the many ways the body shows up in routines suggests that there is a lot of material for theorizing the role of the body in Routine Dynamics. In developing this theorizing, we seek to view the world of routines 'as a living, dynamic, indivisible world of events that is still coming into being' (Shotter, 2008: 501). Bodies are central to this dynamic view. As an apparatus enabling simultaneous articulation of an inner and an outer sphere, bodies provide the basis for understanding this indivisibility of a world constantly coming into being. The inner sphere encompasses embodied tacit knowledge that furnishes the routine participants with a 'bodily readiness' (Sandberg and Tsoukas, 2020) to anticipate important features of the routine in which they are immersed. The outer sphere includes perception and sensation through contact with the outside world (Strati, 2007). As a medium that engages both the inner and outer spheres, the body provides routine participants a way of engaging in responsive action (Yakhlef and Essén, 2013). This is important to the study of routines because bodies enable routine participants to perceive, think and act simultaneously as they enact stability and change in the routine. Figure 25.1 depicts the entangled connections among performance, materiality and pattern as bodies enact the movement between outer and inner sphere.

We turn to exploring and illustrating the potential for this theorizing by looking across the columns of one article in Table 25.1 to see how the body is invested in the dynamics of the routines

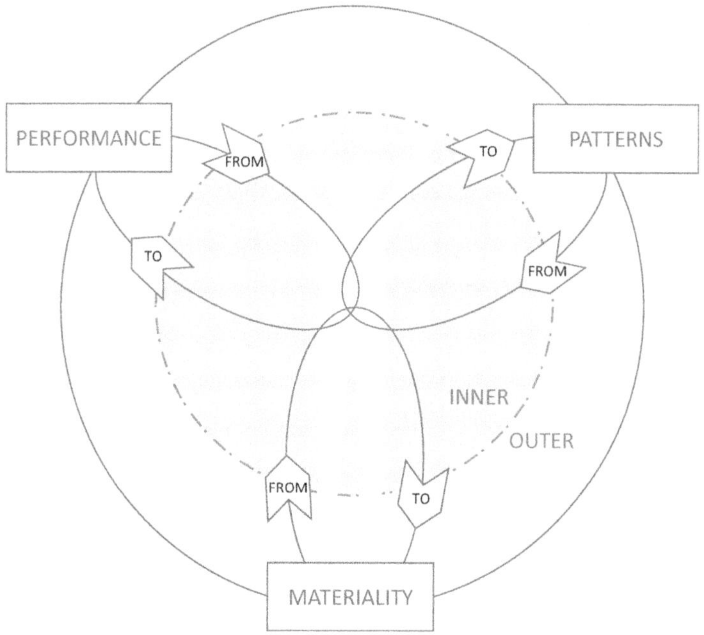

Figure 25.1 Embodied orientation to/from patterns, performance and materiality

discussed in this article. For this purpose, we analyse Danner-Schröder and Geiger's (2016) article because of the extensive and explicit presentation of bodily involvement in the dynamics of the routines. The study is about rescue workers. The authors present an embodied orientation 'from' pattern through the example of rescuers' bodies that are conditioned through training allowing them to develop habitual body movements. The authors show that achieving 'what (they) want and this is to rescue people' (2016: 638) requires that routine participants orient to an embodied knowledge of the general workflow.

Training plays an important role in achieving this embodied orientation, and we focus on this element in order to show the importance of paying attention to bodies while theorizing. Guided by a trained inner sphere and the embodied 'feeling of tendency' (Shotter, 2008), rescuers are enabled to anticipate their next move and orient their engagement 'to' the performance in spite of the difficulties encountered. In the outer sphere they experienced, the rescuers are confronted by people who may be hungry, dehydrated or bleeding and who are pleading for help for themselves and for others. Yet, engaging in direct assistance before properly setting up can endanger their mission. 'Normal human behavior would be to give her the water. But if I would do that, I would endanger the woman and the team because all other 1,500 people would bear down on her and on us to get water to survive' (Danner-Schröder and Geiger, 2016: 647). Thus, despite a powerful inner bodily urge to engage directly 'to' a performance of helping, rescuers have nonetheless to force their focal awareness 'to' the pattern of displaying and erecting tent camps before they are able to help anyone.

The rescuers' bodies are supported in their efforts to stay focused on what the authors refer to as standardization (e.g., setting up the camp before engaging in direct rescuing actions) by training that focuses not only on telling people what needs to be done and why but also on enacting scenes that the rescuers are likely to experience. 'I encountered exactly the same situation in a simulation in Hamburg where I gave a woman water and this [large numbers of people bore down on them to get water] happened. So I learned from this' (Danner-Schröder and Geiger, 2016). Training even goes so far as to familiarize the rescuers with the embodied experience of being in the place where they will be working. Being in contact with the external and responsive world of the new location, rescuers can be overwhelmed by the situation they are confronted with. 'During a simulation the coaches played the resounding calls of a muezzin at sunrise to wake us up. In that moment you think, oh my god, the simulation does not need to be so realistic. But, when you are lying in your tent in Indonesia and you wake up at 5 a.m., you think that is familiar' (Danner-Schröder and Geiger, 2016). This familiarity helps rescuers deal with the chaos they inevitably confront and to resist the urge to take immediate actions rather than to set things up in an orderly fashion that ultimately allows them to accomplish what they came to do. Thus a focal awareness-informed 'from pattern' enables them to get an inner sense of calm and focus despite the situation they may encounter.

Our analysis of this article shows how conceiving the human body as a site of experience and sensible action (Strati, 2007) deployed as routines are enacted can help Routine Dynamics scholars recognize and articulate how people accomplish the efforts that produce the dynamics of routines. In the next section, we briefly explore three research avenues related to embodiment.

25.5 Research Avenues

A focus on bodies (in their plurality and diversity) allows us to see routines from the perspective of the people enacting the routine and their experience of the process of enacting. Corporality plays a central role in fuelling the dynamics of stability and change that are fundamental to Routine Dynamics. Integrating the body more explicitly in our theorizing helps us show the innate aliveness of routines and could help scholars and practitioners alike to understand more about how that aliveness plays out in everyday action. It enriches our appreciation of routines as effortful and skilful accomplishments (D'Adderio, 2011; Feldman, 2000; Pentland and Rueter, 1994). It also highlights one of the driving forces behind the 'patterning' and 'performing' work in organization (Feldman, 2016). As a result, it strengthens our understanding of the relationship between routines, routine participants and action (Feldman et al., 2016).

An embodied perspective on the dynamics of routines enriches the emic perspective that has been so productive in Routine Dynamics (see Dittrich [Chapter 8], this volume) and opens up many research avenues. In the following we discuss three of these avenues: Purpose and intentionality; Diversity of routine participants; and Methodological issues.

25.5.1 Purpose and Intentionality

An embodied perspective on Routine Dynamics brings up the aim that participants bring into their actions. As Dittrich and Seidl (2018) have shown, intentionality not only informs routines but also emerges through routines. Thus, questions of the intentionality and purpose of the action cannot be approached from the outside. An embodied understanding of routines based in Shotter's (2006) concept of 'from within' would help Routine Dynamics scholars explore the purpose and meaning of action. Future researchers could explore what it means for a routine to 'make sense'. For whom or from what perspective is this routine sensible (see also Rerup and Spencer [Chapter 33], this volume)? What comprises the attraction or repulsion of specific patterns (e.g., Bourdieu, 1984) for certain routine participants, even though it doesn't make sense to an outsider? Is 'making sense' for the participant necessary to generate engagement? Is this engagement the result of a manipulated body (Eberhard at al., 2019; Michel, 2011)?

25.5.2 Diversity of Routine Participants

We showed how an embodiment lens allowed us to grasp an understanding on how groups are enabled to function within a routine in the first place. The example used emphasizes the training as a means to condition rescuers' bodies and the need for them to stay focused on the goal of the project. However, the suggested bodies were generic routine participant's bodies. But there is no such body. There are bodies, from different genders, shapes, ethnicities and mobilities. If our bodies shape the very way of being in the world (Shotter, 2008), what are the impacts of those specificities while performing or being involved in routines? Future research could explore the entanglement of bodies and systemic discriminations (racism, sexism, homophobia, etc.) as grounded in organizational routinized embodied experience.

25.5.3 Methodology

The thirteen articles we analysed for this chapter were all based on ethnographic data. Ethnographic data and the thick descriptions they afford have been central to the development of Routine Dynamics (Feldman et al. 2016; Dittrich [Chapter 8], this volume). Our review of the empirical material in the thirteen articles convinced us that authors with ethnographic data are likely to have sufficient data related to embodiment to be able to theorize the embodied aspect of routines. We do note, however, that the article that gave us the most material to work with on body involvement was conducted by authors that have not only observed but also participated in and experienced the training programme under investigation. Such extensive and intensive engagement with field sites may be particularly helpful in producing data about the body's importance to the creation, enactment and modification of routines.

Shotter (2008) claims that in order to see something we need to have developed a way of touching, hearing, smelling and looking at it. Future researchers could reflect on how to capture the intimacy of what constitutes action. What could we learn about organizational routines by exploring methodologies that mobilize our sensory apparatus differently? For example, what type of data could be collected through the use of the sense of smell to approach an organizational routine? We, thus, encourage authors to use their data or to approach Routine Dynamics through this lens in order to account for or complement the embodied dynamics we have described and participate in the issues and avenues of research that we foresee.

25.6 Conclusion

In this chapter, we shed light on bodies in the dynamics of routines. An embodied lens enables us to draw attention to the body in action; allowing us to conceive Routine Dynamics from within (Shotter, 2006) as a lived experience. Though theorizing the body has just begun to appear in current Routine Dynamics articles, the body is, nonetheless, pervasive. We have argued that it is useful to integrate it more explicitly in our theorization since it adds aliveness and helps to explain the processual mechanisms of routine dynamics. Focusing on the bodies involved in routines enables us to gain an understanding of the internal experience of enacting a routine and to demonstrate how routine participants organize their conduct in the course of their action. By shifting the locus of study to the embodied agent embedded in practices, we support the view that routines are not things frozen in time that can be explained fully to and by an outsider and we provide an orientation to investigating routines and their effects that opens new avenues of research.

As we introduce with our choreographer quotes at the beginning of the chapter, beyond the mechanism, listening to the bodies is hearing their expression. Through attending to bodies, we create opportunities for our theorizing to attend to expressions – to see beauty, be moved, touched, feel the collective bond, engage in meaningful actions, etc. – that are central to how people engage in routines and to the connection or lack of connections between effective organizational patterns and human aspirations.

References

Aroles, J. and McLean, C. (2016). Rethinking stability and change in the study of organizational routines: Difference and repetition in a newspaper-printing factory. *Organization Science*, 27(3), 535–550.

Ashcraft, K. L., Kuhn, T. R. and Cooren, F. (2009). Constitutional amendments: "Materializing" organizational communication. *Academy of Management Annals*, 3(1), 1–64.

Berente, N., Lyytinen, K., Yoo, Y. and King, J. L. (2016). Routines as shock absorbers during organizational transformation: Integration, control, and NASA's enterprise information system. *Organization Science*, 27(3), 551–572.

Bertels, S., Howard-Grenville, J. and Pek, S. (2016). Cultural molding, shielding, and shoring at Oilco: The role of culture in the integration of routines. *Organization Science*, 27(3), 573–593.

Bourdieu, P. (1984) *Distinction: A Social Critique of the Judgement of Taste*. Cambridge, MA: Harvard University Press.

Bourdieu, P. (1990) *The Logic of Practice*. Stanford, CA: Stanford University Press.

Bourdieu, P. and Wacquant, L. J. (1992). *An Invitation to Reflexive Sociology*. Chicago: University of Chicago press.

Bucher, S. and Langley, A. (2016). The interplay of reflective and experimental spaces in interrupting and reorienting routine dynamics. *Organization Science*, 27(3), 594–613.

Cohendet, P. and Simon, L. (2016). Always playable: Recombining routines for creative efficiency at Ubisoft Montreal's video game studio. *Organization Science*, 27(3), 614–632.

Collins, H. (2010). *Tacit and Explicit Knowledge*. Chicago: University of Chicago Press.

D'Adderio, L. (2001). Crafting the virtual prototype: How firms integrate knowledge and capabilities across organisational boundaries. *Research Policy*, 30(9), 1409–1424.

D'Adderio, L. (2011). Artifacts at the centre of routines: Performing the material turn in routines theory. *Journal of Institutional Economics*, 7(2), 197–230.

Danner-Schröder, A. and Geiger, D. (2016). Unravelling the motor of patterning work: Toward an understanding of the microlevel dynamics of standardization and flexibility. *Organization Science*, 27(3), 633–658.

Deken, F., Carlile, P. R., Berends, H. and Lauche, K. (2016). Generating novelty through interdependent routines: A process model of routine work. *Organization Science*, 27(3), 659–677.

de Rond, M., Holeman, I. and Howard-Grenville, J. (2019). Sensemaking from the body: An enactive ethnography of rowing the Amazon. *Academy of Management Journal*, 62(6), 1961–1988.

Dittrich, K., Guérard, S. and Seidl, D. (2016). Talking about routines: The role of reflective talk in routine change. *Organization Science*, 27(3), 678–697.

Dionysiou, D. D. and Tsoukas, H. (2013). Understanding the (re) creation of routines from within: A symbolic interactionist perspective. *Academy of Management Review*, 38(2), 181–205.

Dreyfus, H. L. (2017). On expertise and embodiment: Insights from Maurice Merleau-Ponty and Samuel Todes. In J. Sandberg, L. Rouleau, A. Langley and H. Tsoukas, eds., *Skillful Performance: Enacting Capabilities, Knowledge, Competence and Expertise in Organizations*. Oxford: Oxford University Press, pp. 147–159.

Eberhard, J., Frost, A. and Rerup. C. (2019). The dark side of routine dynamics: Deceit and the work of Romeo pimps. *Routine Dynamics in Action: Replication and Transformation. Research in the Sociology of Organizations*, 61, 99–121.

Ewenstein, B. and Whyte, J. (2007). Beyond words: Aesthetic knowledge and knowing in organizations. *Organization Studies*, 28(5), 689–708.

Feldman, M. S. (2000). Organizational routines as a source of continuous change. *Organization Science*, 11(6), 611–629.

Feldman, M. S. (2016). Routines as process: Past, present, and future. In J. Howard-Grenville, C. Rerup, A. Langley and H. Tsoukas, eds., *Organizational Routines: How They Are Created, Maintained, and Changed, Perspectives on Process Organization Studies*. Oxford: Oxford University Press, pp. 23–46.

Feldman, M. S. and Pentland, B. T. (2003). Reconceptualizing organizational routines as a source of flexibility and change. *Administrative Science Quarterly*, 48(1), 94–118.

Feldman, M. S., Pentland, B. T., D'Adderio, L. and Lazaric, N. (2016). Beyond routines as things: Introduction to the special issue on routine dynamics. *Organization Science*, 27(3), 505–513.

Gherardi, S., Merilainen, S., Strati, A. and Valtonen, A. (2013), Editors' introduction: A practice-based view on the body, senses and knowing in organization. *Scandinavian Journal of Management*, 4(29), 333–337.

Gherardi, S., Nicolini, D. and Strati, A. (2007). The passion for knowing. *Organization*, 14(3), 315–329.

Hindmarsh, J. and Pilnick, A. (2007). Knowing bodies at work: Embodiment and ephemeral teamwork in anaesthesia. *Organization Studies*, 28(9), 1395–1416.

Joas, H. (1996). *The Creativity of Action*. Chicago: University of Chicago Press.

Johnson, M. and Rohrer, T. (2007). We are live creatures: Embodiment, American Pragmatism, and the cognitive organism. In J. Zlatev, T. Ziemke, R. Frank and R. Dirven, eds., *Body, Language, and Mind*, vol. 1. Berlin: Mouton de Gruyter, pp. 17–54.

Kremser, W. and Schreyögg, G. (2016). The dynamics of interrelated routines: Introducing the cluster level. *Organization Science*, 27(3), 698–721.

LeBaron, C., Christianson, M. K., Garrett, L. and Ilan, R. (2016). Coordinating flexible performance during everyday work: An ethnomethodological study of handoff routines. *Organization Science*, 27(3), 514–534.

Mead, G. H. 1934. *Mind, Self, and Society from the Standpoint of a Social Behaviorist*. Chicago: University of Chicago Press.

Mead, G. H. 1938. *The Philosophy of the Act*. Chicago: University of Chicago Press.

Mead, G. H. 2002. (First published in 1932.) *The Philosophy of the Present*. Chicago: University of Chicago Press.

Merleau-Ponty, M. (1962/1945). *Phenomenology of Perception* (trans. C. Smith.). London: Routledge & Kegan Paul.

Merleau-Ponty, M. (1964) *The Primacy of Perception*, J. Edie, ed. Evanston, IL: Northwestern University Press.

Merleau-Ponty, M. (1968). *The Visible and the Invisible: Followed by Working Notes*. Evanston, IL: Northwestern University Press.

Pentland, B. T. and Rueter, H. H. (1994). Organizational routines as grammars of action. *Administrative Science Quarterly*, (39), 484–510.

Polanyi, M. (1966). The logic of tacit inference. *Philosophy*, 41(155), 1–18.

Sandberg, J. and Tsoukas, H. (2020). Sensemaking reconsidered: Towards a broader understanding through phenomenology. *Organization Theory*, 1(1), 1–34.

Sele, K. and Grand, S. (2016). Unpacking the dynamics of ecologies of routines: Mediators and their generative effects in routine interactions. *Organization Science*, 27(3), 722–738.

Sergeeva, A. V., Faraj, S. and Huysman, M. (2020). Losing touch: An embodiment perspective on coordination in robotic surgery. *Organization Science*, 1–24.

Shotter, J. (2006). Understanding process from within: An argument for 'withness'-thinking. *Organization Studies*, 27(4), 585–604.

Shotter, J. (2008). Dialogism and polyphony in organizing theorizing in organization studies: Action guiding anticipations and the continuous creation of novelty. *Organization Studies*, 29(4), 501–524.

Sonenshein, S. (2016). Routines and creativity: From dualism to duality. *Organization Science*, 27(3), 739–758.

Spee, P., Jarzabkowski, P. and Smets, M. (2016). The influence of routine interdependence and skillful accomplishment on the coordination of standardizing and customizing. *Organization Science*, 27(3), 759–781.

Strati, A. (2007). Sensible knowledge and practice-based learning. *Management Learning*, 38(1), 61–77.

Taylor, F. W. (1911). *Scientific Management*. Oxford: Routledge.

Wachsmuth, I., Lenzen, M. and Knoblich, G., eds. (2008). *Embodied Communication in Humans and Machines*. Oxford: Oxford University Press.

Wacquant, L. (2015). For a sociology of flesh and blood. *Qualitative Sociology*, 38(1), 1–11.

Wright, A. (2019). Embodied organizational routines: Explicating a practice understanding. *Journal of Management Inquiry*, 28(2), 153–165.

Yakhlef, A. (2010). The corporeality of practice-based learning. *Organization Studies*, 31(4), 409–430.

Yakhlef, A. and Essén, A. (2013). Practice innovation as bodily skills: The example of elderly home care service delivery. *Organization*, 20(6), 881–903.

Yamauchi, Y. and Hiramoto, T. (2016). Reflexivity of routines: An ethnomethodological investigation of initial service encounters at sushi bars in Tokyo. *Organization Studies*, 37(10), 1473–1499.

CHAPTER 26 Emotions and Routine Dynamics

GIADA BALDESSARELLI

26.1 Introduction

Emotions emerge as people respond subjectively to a *stimulus*, such as another person, an artifact, or an event (Elfenbein, 2007). Emotions are intimately connected with social reality and are an integral part of organizational processes (Ashforth and Humphrey, 1995; Zietsma et al., 2019). These include organizational routines (Salvato and Rerup, 2011) that, as interdependent patterns of actions, involve people with their feelings and sensations (Feldman, 2000). As such, emotions can emerge during routine performance and impact their situated enactment and the process of patterning.

Research on Routine Dynamics has provided empirical evidence that emotions affect routines. Studies have reported a range of emotions triggered during routine performance, including pleasant emotions, such as satisfaction and excitement (e.g., Grodal et al., 2015), and unpleasant ones, such as anger and frustration (e.g., Aroles and McLean, 2016; Feldman, 2000). Other studies have hinted at a possible relationship between emotions and the process of patterning, suggesting that emotions may encourage the emergence and change of patterns (e.g., Christianson et al., 2009; Salvato and Rerup, 2018) and that patterns may imbue performances with emotions (e.g., Danner-Schröder and Geiger, 2016). However, despite growing empirical evidence, we still lack a systematic understanding of how affective events are intertwined with routine performing and patterning. Emotions are essential aspects of our everyday lives because we feel and care about people, issues and events (Zietsma and Toubiana, 2018). For this reason, we cannot overlook them in the study of lived experiences and human actions that constitute routines. Although the field of Routine Dynamics has yet to fully explore the role of emotions, this perspective holds substantial potential to address the work of emotions in organizations. Specifically, the centrality of situated actions brought to the fore by Routine Dynamics opens up numerous avenues to explore how performing and patterning produce affective events and how the latter, in turn, influence routines.

In this chapter, I adopt a sociological approach to the study of emotions that recognizes feelings and sensations as situated and social events (Stets and Turner, 2014; Zietsma et al., 2019), and I introduce a framework to review the empirical evidence on how emotional dynamics are entangled with the processes of performing and patterning. This chapter illustrates how emotions emerge and influence organizational routines, emphasizing how affective events can arise during routine performance and impact their enactment, emergence, maintenance and change. Finally, this chapter provides opportunities for future research that embraces the performative role of emotions, and it outlines methodological considerations for the study of feelings and sensations in organizations.

26.2 Background

26.2.1 Emotions in Organization Studies and beyond

Emotions have been defined in many ways and because they 'operate at many different levels of reality – biological and neurological, behavioral, cultural, structural, and situational' (J. H. Turner, 2009: 2), scholars have yet to provide a cohesive definition of what emotions are. Nevertheless, most studies identify emotions as pleasant or unpleasant responses to stimuli of the environment (i.e., people, artifacts or events) that individuals appraise and register (Elfenbein, 2007; Kemper,

1987; Lawler and Thye, 1999; Thoits, 1989) and that stimulate or change their 'action readiness' (Frijda, 2004). Emotions can, therefore, be understood as 'lived, believed-in, situated, temporally embodied experience[s]' (Denzin, 1985: 66). Emotions include joy, frustration, anger, sadness, satisfaction, love and respect, among others (for a review, see Stets and Turner, 2014). Some emotions are short-lived (e.g., anger), while others are persistent (e.g., love) (Jasper, 1998). Emotions also vary in intensity. So, serenity and irritation are low-intensity emotions, while elation and outrage are high-intensity emotions (Stets and Turner, 2014). Regardless of their duration and intensity, however, all emotions involve a subjective response to a stimulus that can direct and change people's behaviour.

Emotions have long been of interest for scholars of sociology that have incorporated feelings and sensations into the analysis of many sociological arenas (for reviews see J. H. Turner, 2009; J. H. Turner and Stets, 2005, 2006) and explored the origin and nature of emotions (e.g., Lazarus, 1984; Zajonc, 1984), how many and what types of emotions exist (e.g., Kemper, 1987; J. H. Turner, 2009) and the expression and management of emotions (e.g., Hallett, 2003; Hochschild, 1983 [2012]). Altogether, sociological research has emphasized that emotions are the 'glue' of society and collective achievements and has brought to the fore the connection between emotions and situated actions (Collins, 1990; Stets and Turner, 2014; J. H. Turner and Stets, 2005, 2006).

In the past two decades, the study of emotions has become increasingly popular also among organizational scholars that have theorized emotions as inherently social and observed their emergence and work in organizational contexts (Zietsma and Toubiana, 2018; Zietsma et al., 2019). Given the focus on the situated and experiential nature of emotions, researchers have taken a sociological approach that is 'sensitive to the idea that emotions are experienced bodily by individuals ... in interaction with the social world' (Zietsma et al., 2019: 2). These scholars have acknowledged that 'emotions are an integral and inseparable part of everyday organizational life' (Ashforth and Humphrey, 1995: 98) and that they have a 'structural impact' on organizational processes (Zietsma et al., 2019). As a result, researchers have begun to unravel the dynamics of emotions in organizations (Elfenbein, 2007; Fineman, 2000, 2003)[1]. Studies have illustrated that emotions are an essential part of many organizational processes, such as strategizing (Liu and Maitlis, 2014), institutionalization (Voronov and Vince, 2012), sense-making (Cornelissen et al., 2014; Rafaeli and Vilnai-Yavetz, 2004; Schabram and Maitlis, 2017) and creativity and innovation (Adler and Obstfeld, 2007; Amabile et al., 2005; Metiu and Rothbard, 2013; Vuori and Huy, 2016), among others. These and other studies illuminate the performative role of emotions and emphasize how they may support or hinder organizational outcomes.

26.2.2 Emotions in Routine Dynamics

Like other organizational processes, organizational routines entail emotions (Salvato and Rerup, 2011). Routines are collective repetitive patterns of actions involving people, their thoughts and their feelings (Feldman, 2000).

Dewey (1922) was among the first to recognize the role of emotions in his book '*Human Nature and Conduct*', published in 1922. The book emphasized the role of 'impulse' (i.e., emotions) as a critical component of human behaviour, alongside cognition and habit (Cohen, 2007b; Dewey, 1922; Winter, 2013). In the decades that followed, however, scholars focused almost exclusively on the cognitive and behavioural aspects of organizational routines, prompted by the growth of the Carnegie school. Specifically, although Simon (1947 [2013]) acknowledged the role of emotions in the allocation of attention during decision-making processes (1947: 90), he fell short of recognizing the widespread influence of emotions and

[1] Scholarly effort has intensified in the past years, culminating with two special issues published in two leading management journals: one published on the *Academy of Management Review* in 2017, titled 'Integrating Emotions and Affect in Theories of Management', and one on Organization Studies in 2018, titled 'The Valuable, the Constitutive, and the Energetic: Exploring the impact and importance of studying emotions and institutions.'

placed them 'to the periphery of the organizational story' (Cohen, 2007a: 506).

The years that followed were marked by a 'long decline' of the concept of emotion in the scholarly work on organizational routines in particular (Cohen, 2007a) and on organizational theory in general. As Zietsma and colleagues (2019) argue, '[i]n much of organization theory, emotions, if considered at all, have been treated implicitly, or considered secondary to cognitive dynamics' (Zietsma et al., 2019: 1). Early research on organizational routines is no exception. Early studies mostly referred to routines as 'behavioral and cognitive regularities' (Howard-Grenville and Rerup, 2017: 325) and largely ignored the emotional side of their enactment (Salvato and Rerup, 2011).

With the emergence and growth of Routine Dynamics, however, actors and their actions have been brought to the forefront of organizational routines. Studies of Routine Dynamics have provided empirical evidence that actors' emotions are involved in routine performance (e.g., Feldman, 2000; Howard-Grenville, 2005), even though only a limited number of studies explore their role explicitly. Researchers have recently recognized this shortcoming and called for more research that explores the connection between emotions and Routine Dynamics. Howard-Grenville and colleagues (2016) write, 'Past work perhaps overly emphasized the importance of cognition (deliberation) in performing routines, but building on the work of John Dewey calls have been made also to include emotions or "impulse"' (Howard-Grenville et al., 2016: 13). Feldman (2016) and Salvato and Rerup (2011) make similar claims by inviting scholars to explore the emotional side of routines.

A few noteworthy exceptions to this trend should, nonetheless, be mentioned. Grodal et al.'s (2015) study shows how emotional mechanisms intervene in the performance of the help-seeking and help-giving routine and explains that emotions experienced by participants during interactions facilitate routine performance. A recent study by Eberhard et al. (2019) that explores the 'dark side of routine dynamics' illustrates how routine participants use deceiving talks of love to exploit others and drive the emergence of routines. Other recent studies also show the emotional side of Routine Dynamics, linking emotions and artifacts employed during routine performance. For example, Baldessarelli (2018) finds that emotions triggered by artifacts enable communication and understanding during routine performance in creative settings. In a study of software development processes, Mahringer (2019) finds that team members engage in 'emotional balancing' to counterbalance negative emotions that emerge vis-à-vis the artifacts.

Aside from these studies, other research has mentioned affective events and suggested that emotions may emerge during routine performance (e.g., Feldman, 2000; Zbaracki and Bergen, 2010) and influence patterning (e.g., Christianson et al., 2009). For example, Feldman (2000: 617) indicates that, before its change, the move-in routine at a US university caused long waits and traffic jams that resulted in 'angry parents and students'. Christianson et al. (2009) find that emotions were put into use to create narratives that supported the reconstruction of organizational routines after the collapse of a museum's roof. Finally, other scholars recognize the possible underlying contribution of emotions in routine performance, but leave its analysis unexplored (e.g., Birnholtz et al., 2007; Laureiro-Martinez, 2014; Sonenshein, 2016).

26.3 A Review of the Role of Emotions in Routine Dynamics

The theoretical foundations of Routine Dynamics provide fertile ground for integrating emotions in the study of organizational routines and contributing to a better understanding of the emotional dimension of organizing. Because routines are action patterns and affective events emerge from and impact actions, emotions shape and are shaped by the processes of performing and patterning.

In this chapter, I propose a framework for synthesizing the role of emotions in Routine Dynamics (Feldman, 2004; Feldman and Worline, 2011). Figure 26.1 illustrates such a framework, illuminating the relationship between emotions and patterning and performing (each arrow represents processes of emergence and/or presence and/or use of emotions).

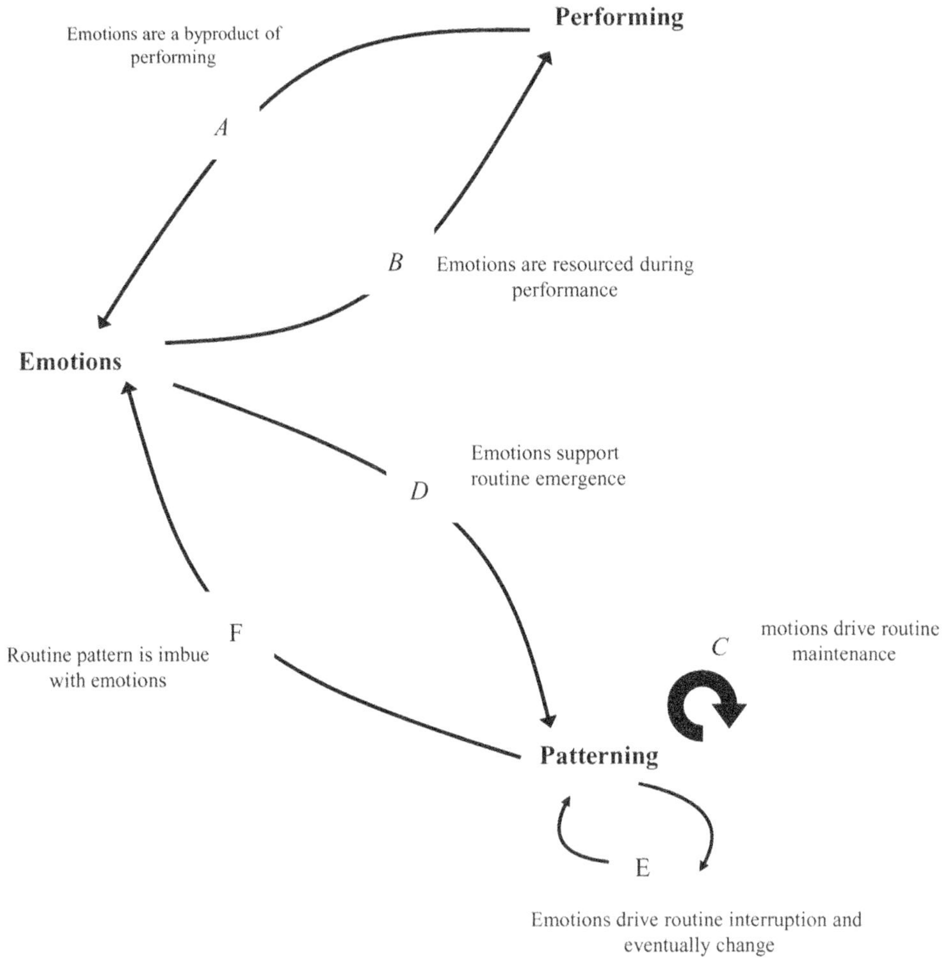

Figure 26.1 Emotions in Routine Dynamics

The framework illustrates that emotional responses emerge as routine participants carry out interdependent actions and that these responses can affect both the situated performance as well as the emergence, change, and maintenance of routine patterns. Also, the framework illustrates how emotions may purposefully arise as an intended consequence of patterning work or as a part of performing. Put simply, the framework outlines how emotions 'involve some change in action readiness' (Frijda, 1988, 2004) that leads to the repeated enactment of specific actions and the change or interruption of others.

Next, I provide a detailed explanation of the dynamics illustrated in the framework (i.e., each arrow) to clarify how emotions are entangled with the processes of performing and patterning. See also Table 26.1 for a summary of the relationship between organizational routines and emotions.

26.3.1 Emotions and Performing

Routine performance entails situated actions that involve people's emotions (Feldman, 2000). As participants carry out the routine, they interact with others, with artifacts and with events that may elicit emotional responses. Interactions may lead people to 'feel angry, frustrated, proud or joyful and these different reactions have different behavioral

Table 26.1 Emotions in Routine Dynamics: Empirical evidence and future research

RD	Mechanism	Examples	Future research
Performing	***Emotions emerge as a byproduct of routine performance (Arrow A)***	Aroles and McLean (2016) Deken et al. (2016) Feldman (2000) Howard-Grenville (2005) Mahringer (2019) Rerup and Feldman (2011) Sele and Grand (2016) Turner and Rindova (2012) Zbaracki and Bergen (2010)	**Under what conditions does the expression of emotions matter for routine performance?** Do positive and negative emotions have a different (distinct, complementary, obstructing) impact on routine performance? And how does it matter for performing? To what extent does the intensity of felt emotions matter in routine performance?
	Emotions are 'resourced' during routine performance (Arrow B)	Baldessarelli (2018) Grodal et al. (2015) Mahringer (2019) Obstfeld (2012)	And how does emotional contagion among routine participants influence situated performance? How does the context shape the expression of emotions during routine performance? And, in turn, to what extent does the expression of emotions influence the context?
Patterning	***Emotions maintain routines (Arrow C)***	Grodal et al. (2015) Karali (2018)	**Under what conditions do emotions influence routine patterning?**
	Emotions enable the emergence of routines (Arrow D)	Christianson et al. (2009) Turner and Rindova (2012)	How do emotions influence which routines are retained and which are abandoned? How do positive emotions influence the emergence and maintenance of routines?
	Emotions push towards the interruption and change of routines (Arrow E)	Berente et al. (2016) Salvato and Rerup (2018) Turner and Rindova (2012)	Under what conditions do they push towards routine change? How do negative emotions influence routine patterning?
	Routine pattern imbues performance with emotions (Arrow F)	Baldessarelli (2018) Danner-Schröder and Geiger (2016) Eberhard et al. (2019) Parker and Hackett (2012)	Can routines in which the expression of emotions is expected produce unforeseen consequences that generate change? And how so?

implications' (Weiss and Cropanzano, 1996: 11). Because affective events impact people's behaviour, interactions in routine performance act as stimuli that elicit emotional responses and influence participants' enactment of the action pattern. Hence, emotions can emerge as a by-product of routine performance and can simultaneously be 'resourced', to perform the routine (Feldman and Worline, 2011; Quinn and Worline, 2008).

First, emotional responses emerge as participants enact a routine and interact with others; engage with or develop material artifacts; and interact with the surrounding work environment (arrow A in Figure 26.1). For example, Turner and Rindova (2012) explain that customers' satisfaction and goodwill were unintended consequences of the consistent arrival time in the waste collection routine. Zbaracki and Bergen (2010) report that the conflicts between sales and marketing departments became an 'emotional issue' and escalated almost to the point of throwing punches. Rerup and Feldman (2011) report that participants were upset when they could not complete the routine or the outcomes were unsatisfactory. Sele and Grand (2016) illustrate that positive emotions emerged as the audience interacted with the prototypes at a university lab. Finally, Deken et al. (2016) report that participants experienced frustration when faced with different understandings of the novelty of a routine. All these studies provide clues that situated actions and performance outcomes can trigger positive or negative emotional responses.

Second, elicited emotions can also be used as a resource during the performance of the routine (arrow B in Figure 26.1). Pleasant sensations generate motivation that contributes to orient participants' attention to actions (Frijda, 1988, 2004). Seo et al. (2004) suggest that behaviour always involves some degree of improvisation that requires affect to give direction and intensity to participants' actions. In line with this argument, Grodal et al. (2015) describe a series of emotional moves used during the help-seeking and -giving routine that contributed to generate and reinforce participants' mutual focus of attention during repeated performances. Emotional moves, such as the display of humour or excitement, 'propelled the routine forward by maintaining continual engagement' (2015: 149).

In addition, organization studies have recognized that not only positive emotions encourage action. In some circumstances, emotions commonly regarded as negative or unpleasant, such as anger or frustration, can be motivational forces that push people to take action. For example, Barberá-Tomás et al. (2019) show how moral outrage elicited by visual images led people to enact social causes. Feldman and Quick (2009) find that the community's anger elicited by the city managers' budgeting process pushed managers to reengage with the community. Obstfeld (2012) illustrates how routine participants used the anger triggered by wayward participants, who tried to change the routine trajectory, to enforce routine performance. Negative emotions, therefore, can have a positive effect if they drive engagement and routine performance.

26.3.2 Emotions and Patterning

Since 'patterns are constituted in and through action' (Feldman, 2016: 40), affective events that emerge in action are connected to the process of patterning. Emotions are responsible for participants' motivation that allocates and preserves attention towards specific actions and moves it away from others (Dewey, 1922; Simon, 1947 [2013]). In other words, emotions affect the willingness and focus towards the repeated performance of some actions (and the avoidance of others) contributing to the emergence and maintenance of routines (and the interruption or change of others).

First, emotions can contribute to the maintenance of routines when they result in pleasant affective events (arrow C in Figure 26.1). Put differently, routines that produce positive emotions are likely to be maintained. Grodal et al. (2015) suggest that positive emotions generated during the enactment of the help-seeking and -giving routine could 'lead to a virtuous cycle', propelling future performances and, therefore, contributing to the maintenance of the routine. Simultaneously, positive emotions may be resourced to maintain routines. For example, Karali (2018) finds that hospital nurses engage in empathic behaviour towards patients to guarantee the quality of the patient diagnosis routine during peak moments, thus sustaining the routine pattern.

Second, emotions can lead to the emergence of routines (arrows D in Figure 26.1). When interactions generate positive emotions, actors will seek those same interactions in the future to rekindle and eventually intensify pleasant emotions (Collins, 2004; Furnari, 2014; Gray et al., 2015; Hallett, 2003). Therefore, affect can be the 'motivational energy' (Winter, 2013) that fosters repeated performances and makes the sequence of interdependent actions recognizable. For example, in Turner and Rindova's (2012) study of the waste collection routine, customers were pleased with the consistent pick-up time and co-organized their actions around it.

Third, a negative emotional appraisal may cause participants to withdraw from the routine or change it (arrow E in Figure 26.1). Interactions that do not generate positive emotions will be avoided or contested (Collins, 2004; Furnari, 2014). Again, in the study of the waste collection routine, Turner and Rindova (2012) illustrate that when the routine changed to allow for flexible performances, customers displayed disappointment for the unpredictable arrival time and neglected the new routine pattern. In the study of the implementation of a NASA information system, Berente et al. (2016) illustrate that dissatisfaction for the new system resulted in 'active resistance' that forced changes in the implementation. In their study of a new product development routine, Salvato and Rerup (2018) find that designers became increasingly unhappy with the company's 'Efficiency Factory pattern' to the point of causing a breakdown in the routine that necessitated a pattern update.

Finally, some routines are designed with the specific goal to elicit participants' emotions (arrow F in Figure 26.1) (Menges and Kilduff, 2015). In such circumstances, emotions are not a by-product of routine performance, but they are predicted and hoped for in the routine pattern or purposefully used by participants. Denzin (1985) refers to everyday routines, such as eating, cooking or watching a movie, as embodied patterns of actions that elicit and structure participants' emotions. Baker and Dutton (2007) present a series of organizational practices, including the selection and hiring routine, that create and sustain 'high-quality connections' characterized by positive emotions and reciprocity. In a study of the routines at a high-reliability organization, Danner-Schröder and Geiger (2016) explain that performance simulations intended to trigger emotions to prepare routine participants for future real-life situations, thus helping them to learn and embody the routine pattern. In a recent paper, Eberhard et al. (2019) show how Romeo pimps used love as a deceiving tool to drive the emergence and enactment of the 'Romeo pimp routine'. In this case, a feeling such as love – usually appraised as positive – was instrumentally used to achieve some participants' goals by coercing others. Finally, Rafaeli and Sutton (1991) find that criminal investigators and bill collectors routinely used emotional contrast strategies to perform their daily work. Nevertheless, it should be noted that while affective events may be desired and expected, they cannot be fully predicted. Because emotions are subjective responses to stimuli, differences in participants' experiences, roles and histories may result in different emotions. So, for example, Parker and Hackett (2012) find that, although organizers of the 'island time' – periodic meetings held on remote islands – intended for it to be an occasion to generate emotional commitment, the attendees experienced scepticism on some occasions that proved challenging to manage.

In summary, empirical evidence suggests that emotions emerge from routine performance and have the potential to affect how participants enact patterns of actions. Studies also indicate that emotions play an essential role in the processes of emergence, change and interruption of routines.

26.4 Opportunities for Future Research

There are many opportunities for future research that explores the relationship between organizational routines and emotions. Even if studies on routines have yet to systematically explore the role of emotions, they have provided clues that affective events permeate routines. By systematically integrating emotions into the study of Routine Dynamics, scholars can provide more nuanced theoretical insights into the dynamics that underpin the processes of performing and patterning. Figure 26.1 illustrates how emotions can be integrated into the research of Routine Dynamics, and each arrow provides opportunities for future studies. Overall, we miss an understanding of the conditions under which emotions matter in Routine Dynamics in terms of how they affect situated performances and how they contribute to the emergence, maintenance, change or interruption of routines (see Table 26.1 for a summary of future research directions).

First, we do not know under what conditions emotions emerge as a by-product of routine performance and whether they matter for routine enactment. In this regard, an interesting research direction is the emergence and interplay of positive and negative emotions during routine performance: How do they emerge? Do they play a different and complementary role? Or do they hinder each other? Mahringer (2019) provides some initial suggestions on the balancing role of positive emotions used to counteract negative emotions that emerge during routine performance. Barberá-Tomás et al. (2019) show how negative emotions transform into positive feelings that drive the enactment of social causes. We also lack an understanding of whether the intensity of expressed emotions matters for routine performance. Seo et al. (2004) theorize that affective events can influence actors' behaviour through three mechanisms, i.e., intensity, direction and persistence. These three mechanisms can affect the emergence and maintenance of routines differently, and future research could explore their underlying dynamics. Emotions that have high intensity may have a more prominent and persistent effect on routine enactment. It is also possible that emotions expressed through gestures and loud utterances have a contagion effect that influences the collective performance of routines.

We also need more research on the role of organizational contexts in promoting or suppressing the expression of emotions. For example, when routines involve the assessment of products or services, customers' spontaneous emotional reactions are expected and even encouraged (Baldessarelli, 2018; Rindova and Petkova, 2007). Yet, in the same context, employees' expression of emotions involves norms that establish appropriate emotional responses (Hochschild, 1983 [2012]; Rafaeli and Sutton, 1989). So, we can ask: How does the context shape participants' expression of emotions during routine performance? And, in turn, to what extent does the expression of emotions influence the context?

Second, we are still missing an understanding of when and how emotions may foster or constrain patterning work. For instance, it would be interesting to explore how emotions influence which routines are retained and which are instead abandoned. Karali (2018) provides preliminary evidence that empathic behaviour is instrumental in maintaining the quality of the routine during peak situations. Future research could explore whether and how pleasant emotions contribute to the emergence of routines or their change. Another promising area of research is the role of negative emotions in the process of patterning. It would be beneficial to understand whether and how anger, anxiety, frustration or dissatisfaction drive participants to shun routines or push toward the emergence of new routines. Finally, scholars could explore whether and how routines in which the expression of emotions is expected or desired produce unforeseen and emergent consequences that generate change.

26.5 Methodological Considerations

Many different approaches are available to measure and analyse emotions, from neural and psychological approaches (e.g., functional MRI) to observational and retrospective methods (e.g., self-reported surveys) (for a review, see Rogers and Robinson, 2014). Given the focus on the situated and experiential nature of emotions in organizational studies, approaches best suited to explore emotions in routines are those that capture them 'on the fly'. Because emotions are often short-lived but have structural effects on people's behaviour (Zietsma et al., 2019), research must aim to register emotions emerging in action and to understand their relationship with actions themselves. Suitable approaches would ideally encourage a close look at the discursive, embodied and situational expression of emotions and longitudinal analyses of the 'how', 'what' and 'when' emotions emerge and affect patterning and performing. One way to do so is through ethnographic and micro-ethnographic studies (Streeck and Mehus, 2005; Van Maanen, 1979) that rely on the direct observation of participants' interactions (e.g., Grodal et al., 2015; Liu and Maitlis, 2014) and/or video recordings of actions and interactions (for more on video methods in Routine Dynamics studies see LeBaron and Christianson [Chapter 9], in this volume; LeBaron et al., 2016). Another way is through experimental approaches, such as field experiments or lab experiments (for more on experiments in Routine Dynamics see Bapuji, Hora and Li [Chapter 10], in this volume; Bapuji et al., 2012), designed to capture participants' behaviour and emotions over time (e.g., Amabile et al., 2005; Barsade, 2002).

Regardless of the chosen methodology, scholars that wish to capture the emotional side of routines should employ tools to register both participants' verbal expressions and bodily expressions of emotions (i.e., facial expressions, gestures and movements) (Ekman, 1993). In practical terms, this would require using instruments such as video ethnography (LeBaron and Christianson [Chapter 9], in this volume) to capture and enhance the 'personalized seeing, hearing, and experiencing' of affective events (Van Maanen, 2011: 222). Other complementary tools for data collection may be necessary, such as retrospective surveys or diaries that register experiences and emotions (Rogers and Robinson, 2014; Wood et al., 2002). Complementary tools are especially relevant in circumstances when participants do not express felt sensations. In some situations, individuals experience emotions that they are not allowed to express, leading to a process of inhibition aimed to render expressed emotions 'appropriate' to the situation (Hochschild, 1979). The display of expected emotions, known as emotional labour (Ashforth and Humphrey, 1993; Hochschild, 1983 [2012]), is often seen during service encounters. '[F]light attendants are expected to feel cheerful and friendly, funeral directors are expected to feel somber and reserved, and nurses are expected to feel empathetic and supportive' (Ashforth and Humphrey, 1993: 89). As a result, service agents are often required to express certain emotions while repressing others. From a research design viewpoint, this means asking whether displayed emotions are the same as felt emotions and whether felt emotions that are not expressed matter for the enactment and patterning of routines.

Finally, considerations about the researcher's own emotions during data collection should be mentioned. During field studies, researchers experience emotions, and those emotions inform the understanding of the field. Hence, affective events are not only an integral part of organizational processes but also of the research process (Davies and Spencer, 2010; Hubbard et al., 2001). The researcher immerses himself or herself in the field, allowing 'to be imbued by sense experience' of the participants (Gagliardi, 1999) and his or her 'emotional response to a respondent's experiences can be used to interpret data' (Hubbard et al., 2001: 131) and may be a necessary part of the research process. This means documenting and reflecting not only on participants' emotions but also researchers' felt sensations. To do so, scholars should rely on auto-ethnographic methods that capture the researcher's behaviour, thoughts and felt sensations during fieldwork (for more on auto-ethnography see Dittrich [Chapter 8], in this volume).

26.6 Conclusion

Emotions are an integral part of organizational life (Ashforth and Humphrey, 1995; Fineman, 2000). Yet, research on Routine Dynamics has paid limited attention to date to the emotional component of performing and patterning (Howard-Grenville et al., 2016; Salvato and Rerup, 2011). This chapter lays the foundations for integrating emotions into the study of Routine Dynamics. Specifically, it illustrates how emotions are intertwined with the processes of performing and patterning and how scholars can move forward to explore the affective dimension of organizational routines.

References

Adler, P. S. and Obstfeld, D. (2007). The role of affect in creative projects and exploratory search. *Industrial and Corporate Change*, 16(1), 19–50.

Amabile, T. M., Barsade, S. G., Mueller, J. S. and Staw, B. M. (2005). Affect and creativity at work. *Administrative Science Quarterly*, 50(3), 367–403.

Aroles, J. and McLean, C. (2016). Rethinking stability and change in the study of organizational routines: Difference and repetition in a newspaper-printing factory. *Organization Science*, 27(3), 535–550.

Ashforth, B. E. and Humphrey, R. H. (1993). Emotional labor in service roles: The influence of identity. *Academy of Management Review*, 18 (1), 88–115.

Ashforth, B. E. and Humphrey, R. H. (1995). Emotion in the workplace: A reappraisal. *Human Relations*, 48(2), 97–125.

Baker, W. and Dutton, J. E. (2007). Enabling positive social capital in organizations. In J. E. Dutton and B. Ragins, eds., *Exploring Positive Relationships at Work: Building a Theoretical and Research Foundation*. Mahwah, NJ: Lawrence Erlbaum Associates, pp. 325–345.

Baldessarelli, G. (2018). *The Role of Emotions toward Artifacts in Interorganizational Routines*. Paper presented at the Academy of Management Proceedings.

Bapuji, H., Hora, M. and Saeed, A. M. (2012). Intentions, intermediaries, and interaction: Examining the emergence of routines. *Journal of Management Studies*, 49(8), 1586–1607.

Barberá-Tomás, D., Castello, I., de Bakker, F. G. and Zietsma, C. (2019). Energizing through visuals: How social entrepreneurs use emotion-symbolic work for social change. *Academy of Management Journal*, 62(6), 1789–1817.

Barsade, S. G. (2002). The ripple effect: Emotional contagion and its influence on group behavior. *Administrative Science Quarterly*, 47(4), 644–675.

Berente, N., Lyytinen, K., Yoo, Y. and King, J. L. (2016). Routines as shock absorbers during organizational transformation: Integration, control, and NASA's enterprise information system. *Organization Science*, 27(3), 551–572.

Birnholtz, J. P., Cohen, M. D. and Hoch, S. V. (2007). Organizational character: On the regeneration of camp poplar grove. *Organization Science*, 18(2), 315–332.

Christianson, M. K., Farkas, M. T., Sutcliffe, K. M. and Weick, K. E. (2009). Learning through rare events: Significant interruptions at the Baltimore & Ohio Railroad Museum. *Organization Science*, 20(5), 846–860.

Cohen, M. D. (2007a). Perspective – Administrative behavior: Laying the foundations for Cyert and March. *Organization Science*, 18(3), 503–506.

Cohen, M. D. (2007b). Reading Dewey: Reflections on the study of routine. *Organization Studies*, 28(5), 773–786.

Collins, R. (1990). Stratification, emotional energy, and the transient emotions. In T. D. Kemper, ed., *Research Agendas in the Sociology of Emotions*. Albany: State University of New York Press, pp. 27–57.

Collins, R. (2004). *Interaction Ritual Chains*. Princeton, NJ: Princeton University Press.

Cornelissen, J. P., Mantere, S. and Vaara, E. (2014). The contraction of meaning: The combined effect of communication, emotions, and materiality on sensemaking in the Stockwell shooting. *Journal of Management Studies*, 51(5), 699–736.

Danner-Schröder, A. and Geiger, D. (2016). Unravelling the motor of patterning work: Toward an understanding of the microlevel dynamics of standardization and flexibility. *Organization Science*, 27(3), 633–658.

Davies, J. and Spencer, D. (2010). *Emotions in the Field: The Psychology and Anthropology of Fieldwork Experience*. Stanford, CA: Stanford University Press.

Deken, F., Carlile, P. R., Berends, H. and Lauche, K. (2016). Generating novelty through interdependent routines: A process model of routine work. *Organization Science*, 27(3), 659–677.

Denzin, N. K. (1985). Emotion as lived experience. *Symbolic Interaction*, 8(2), 223–240.

Dewey, J. (1922). *Human Nature and Conduct*. New York: Modern Library.

Eberhard, J., Frost, A. and Rerup, C. (2019). The dark side of routine dynamics: Deceit and the work of Romeo pimps. In M. S. Feldman, L. D'Adderio, K. Dittrich and P. Jarzabkowski, eds., *Routine Dynamics in Action: Replication and Transformation*. Bingley: Emerald, pp. 99–121.

Ekman, P. (1993). Facial expression and emotion. *American Psychologist*, 48(4), 384.

Elfenbein, H. A. (2007). 7 Emotion in organizations: a review and theoretical integration. *Academy of Management Annals*, 1(1), 315–386.

Feldman, M. S. (2000). Organizational routines as a source of continuous change. *Organization Science*, 11(6), 611–629.

Feldman, M. S. (2004). Resources in emerging structures and processes of change. *Organization Science*, 15(3), 295–309.

Feldman, M. S. (2016). Past, present, and future. In J. Howard-Grenville, C. Rerup, A. Langley and H. Tsoukas, eds., *Organizational Routines: How They Are Created, Maintained, and Changed*. Oxford: Oxford University Press, pp. 23–46.

Feldman, M. S. and Quick, K. S. (2009). Generating resources and energizing frameworks through inclusive public management. *International Public Management Journal*, 12(2), 137–171.

Feldman, M. S. and Worline, M. (2011). Resources, resourcing, and ampliative cycles in organizations. In G. Spreitzer and K. Cameron, eds., *The Oxford Handbook of Positive Organizational Scholarship*. Oxford: Oxford Press.

Fineman, S. (2000). *Emotion in Organizations* (2nd edition) Thousand Oaks, CA: Sage Publications.

Fineman, S. (2003). Emotion and organizing. In S. R. Clegg, C. Hardy and W. R. Nord, eds., *The SAGE Handbook of Organization Studies*. Thousand Oaks, CA: SAGE Publications, pp. 543–565.

Frijda, N. H. (1988). The laws of emotion. *American Psychologist*, 43(5), 349.

Frijda, N. H. (2004). *Emotions and Action*. Paper presented at the Feelings and Emotions: The Amsterdam Symposium.

Furnari, S. (2014). Interstitial spaces: Microinteraction settings and the genesis of new practices between institutional fields. *Academy of Management Review*, 39(4), 439–462.

Gagliardi, P. (1999). Exploring the aesthetic side of organizational life. *Studying Organization: Theory & Method,* 169–184.

Gray, B., Purdy, J. M. and Ansari, S. (2015). From interactions to institutions: Microprocesses of framing and mechanisms for the structuring of institutional fields. *Academy of Management Review*, 40(1), 115–143.

Grodal, S., Nelson, A. J. and Siino, R. M. (2015). Help-seeking and help-giving as an organizational routine: Continual engagement in innovative work. *Academy of Management Journal*, 58(1), 136–168.

Hallett, T. (2003). Emotional feedback and amplification in social interaction. *The Sociological Quarterly*, 44(4), 705–726.

Hochschild, A. R. (1979). Emotion work, feeling rules, and social structure. *American Journal of Sociology*, 85(3), 551–575.

Hochschild, A. R. (1983 [2012]). *The Managed Heart: Commercialization of Human Feeling.* Oakland: University of California Press.

Howard-Grenville, J. (2005). The persistence of flexible organizational routines: The role of agency and organizational context. *Organization Science*, 16(6), 618–636.

Howard-Grenville, J. and Rerup, C. (2017). A process perspective on organizational routines. In A. Langley and H. Tsoukas, eds., *The SAGE Handbook of Organization Process Studies.* Thousand Oaks, CA: Sage Publications, pp. 323–337.

Howard-Grenville, J., Rerup, C., Langley, A. and Tsoukas, H. (2016). Introduction: Advancing a process perspective on routines by zooming out and zooming. In J. Howard-Grenville, C. Rerup, A. Langley and H. Tsoukas, eds., *Organizational Routines: How They Are Created, Maintained, and Changed.* Oxford: Oxford University Press, pp. 1–22.

Hubbard, G., Backett-Milburn, K. and Kemmer, D. (2001). Working with emotion: Issues for the researcher in fieldwork and teamwork. *International Journal of Social Research Methodology*, 4(2), 119–137.

Jasper, J. M. (1998). The emotions of protest: Affective and reactive emotions in and around social movements. *Sociological Forum*, 13, 397–424.

Karali, E. (2018). *Investigating Routines and Dynamic Capabilities for Change and Innovation.* Rotterdam School of Management, Unpublished dissertation.

Kemper, T. D. (1987). How many emotions are there? Wedding the social and the autonomic components. *American Journal of Sociology*, 93(2), 263–289.

Laureiro-Martinez, D. (2014). Cognitive control capabilities, routinization propensity, and decision-making performance. *Organization Science*, 25 (4), 1111–1133.

Lawler, E. J. and Thye, S. R. (1999). Bringing emotions into social exchange theory. *Annual Review of Sociology*, 25(1), 217–244.

Lazarus, R. S. (1984). On the primacy of cognition. *American Psychologist*, 39(2), 124–129.

LeBaron, C., Christianson, M. K., Garrett, L. and Ilan, R. (2016). Coordinating flexible performance during everyday work: An ethnomethodological study of handoff routines. *Organization Science*, 27(3), 514–534.

Liu, F. and Maitlis, S. (2014). Emotional dynamics and strategizing processes: A study of strategic conversations in top team meetings. *Journal of Management Studies*, 51(2), 202–234.

Mahringer, C. (2019). *Exploring Routine Ecologies – A Characterization and Integration of Different Perspectives on Routines.* Universität Stuttgart, Unpublished dissertation.

Menges, J. I. and Kilduff, M. (2015). Group emotions: Cutting the Gordian knots concerning terms, levels of analysis, and processes. *Academy of Management Annals*, 9(1), 845–928.

Metiu, A. and Rothbard, N. P. (2013). Task bubbles, artifacts, shared emotion, and mutual focus of attention: A comparative study of the microprocesses of group engagement. *Organization Science*, 24(2), 455–475.

Obstfeld, D. (2012). Creative projects: A less routine approach toward getting new things done. *Organization Science*, 23(6), 1571–1592.

Parker, J. N. and Hackett, E. J. (2012). Hot spots and hot moments in scientific collaborations and social movements. *American Sociological Review*, 77(1), 21–44.

Quinn, R. W. and Worline, M. C. (2008). Enabling courageous collective action: Conversations from United Airlines flight 93. *Organization Science*, 19(4), 497–516.

Rafaeli, A. and Sutton, R. I. (1989). The expression of emotion in organizational life. *Research in Organizational Behavior*, 11(1), 1–42.

Rafaeli, A. and Sutton, R. I. (1991). Emotional contrast strategies as means of social influence: Lessons from criminal interrogators and bill collectors. *Academy of Management Journal*, 34(4), 749–775.

Rafaeli, A. and Vilnai-Yavetz, I. (2004). Emotion as a connection of physical artifacts and organizations. *Organization Science*, 15(6), 671–686.

Rerup, C. and Feldman, M. S. (2011). Routines as a source of change in organizational schemata: The role of trial-and-error learning. *Academy of Management Journal*, 54(3), 577–610.

Rindova, V. P. and Petkova, A. P. (2007). When is a new thing a good thing? Technological change, product form design, and perceptions of value for product innovations. *Organization Science*, 18(2), 217–232.

Rogers, K. B. and Robinson, D. T. (2014). Measuring affect and emotions. In *Handbook of the Sociology of Emotions: Volume II*. Berlin: Springer, pp. 283–303.

Salvato, C. and Rerup, C. (2011). Beyond collective entities: Multilevel research on organizational routines and capabilities. *Journal of Management*, 37(2), 468–490.

Salvato, C. and Rerup, C. (2018). Routine regulation: Balancing conflicting goals in organizational routines. *Administrative Science Quarterly*, 63(1), 170–209.

Schabram, K. and Maitlis, S. (2017). Negotiating the challenges of a calling: Emotion and enacted sensemaking in animal shelter work. *Academy of Management Journal*, 60(2), 584–609.

Sele, K. and Grand, S. (2016). Unpacking the dynamics of ecologies of routines: Mediators and their generative effects in routine interactions. *Organization Science*, 27(3), 722–738.

Seo, M.-G., Barrett, L. F. and Bartunek, J. M. (2004). The role of affective experience in work motivation. *Academy of Management Review*, 29(3), 423–439.

Simon, H. A. (1947 [2013]). *Administrative Behavior*. New York: Free Press.

Sonenshein, S. (2016). Routines and creativity: From dualism to duality. *Organization Science*, 27(3), 739–758.

Stets, J. E. and Turner, J. H. (2014). *Handbook of the Sociology of Emotions* (Vol. 2). Berlin: Springer.

Streeck, J. and Mehus, S. (2005). Microethnography: The study of practices. In K. Fitch and R. Sanders, eds., *Handbook of Language and Social Interaction*. Mahwah, NJ: Lawrence Erlbaum Associates Publishers, pp. 381–404.

Thoits, P. A. (1989). The sociology of emotions. *Annual Review of Sociology*, 15(1), 317–342.

Turner, J. H. (2009). The sociology of emotions: Basic theoretical arguments. *Emotion Review*, 1(4), 340–354.

Turner, J. H. and Stets, J. E. (2005). *The Sociology of Emotions*: Cambridge: Cambridge University Press.

Turner, J. H. and Stets, J. E. (2006). Sociological theories of human emotions. *Annual Review of Sociology*, 32, 25–52.

Turner, S. F. and Rindova, V. P. (2012). A balancing act: How organizations pursue consistency in routine functioning in the face of ongoing change. *Organization Science*, 23(1), 24–46.

Van Maanen, J. (1979). The fact of fiction in organizational ethnography. *Administrative Science Quarterly*, 24(4), 539–550.

Van Maanen, J. (2011). Ethnography as work: Some rules of engagement. *Journal of Management Studies*, 48(1), 218–234.

Voronov, M. and Vince, R. (2012). Integrating emotions into the analysis of institutional work. *Academy of Management Review*, 37(1), 58–81.

Vuori, T. O. and Huy, Q. N. (2016). Distributed attention and shared emotions in the innovation process: How Nokia lost the smartphone battle. *Administrative Science Quarterly*, 61(1), 9–51.

Weiss, H. M. and Cropanzano, R. (1996). Affective events theory: A theoretical discussion of the structure, causes and consequences of affective experiences at work. In B. M. Staw and L. L. Cummings, eds., *Research in Organization Behavior* (Vol. 19). Greenwich, CT: JAI Press, pp. 1–74.

Winter, S. G. (2013). Habit, deliberation, and action: Strengthening the microfoundations of routines and capabilities. *Academy of Management Perspectives*, 27(2), 120–137.

Wood, W., Quinn, J. M. and Kashy, D. A. (2002). Habits in everyday life: Thought, emotion, and action. *Journal of Personality and Social Psychology*, 83(6), 1281.

Zajonc, R. B. (1984). On the primacy of affect. *American Psychologist*, 39(2), 117–123.

Zbaracki, M. J. and Bergen, M. (2010). When truces collapse: A longitudinal study of price-adjustment routines. *Organization Science*, 21(5), 955–972.

Zietsma, C. and Toubiana, M. (2018). The valuable, the constitutive, and the energetic: Exploring the impact and importance of studying emotions and institutions. *Organization Studies*, 39(4), 427–443.

Zietsma, C., Toubiana, M., Voronov, M. and Roberts, A. (2019). *Emotions in Organization Theory*. Cambridge: Cambridge University Press.

CHAPTER 27

Professional Identity and Routine Dynamics

EMRE KARALI

27.1 Introduction

Social identity theory (Abrams and Hogg, 1990; Tajfel and Turner, 1979; Turner, 1991) can enhance our understanding of Routine Dynamics. Routines are repetitive, recognizable patterns of interdependent actions, carried out by multiple actors (Feldman and Pentland, 2003). Routine Dynamics scholars have shown how the knowledgeable and skilful nature of routine participants is integral to stability and change in routines (Feldman et al., 2016). Whereas reflection sometimes occurs through explicit spaces (Bucher and Langley, 2016), it is often inherent to our interaction (Dittrich et al., 2016). In many occupations, reflection is integral to, and intertwined with, professional identity, and that is why it is important to connect professional identity to Routine Dynamics.

A professional identity concerns an individual's identification with a professional role and accompanying attributes, beliefs, values, motives and experiences (Ibarra, 1999). The Routine Dynamics literature takes on a social practice theoretical approach to routines (Feldman and Pentland, 2003). Within this approach, actors and actions are inseparable (Bourdieu, 1990; Giddens 1984). This focus necessitates considering how individuals enact routines as well as the contexts in which routines are enacted. Social practice theory centres on actions as 'consequential' in that action produces and reproduces structures which in turn shape action (Feldman and Orlikowski, 2011).

When routine participants exercise agency as part of their routine enactment, they do so contingent on their professional identity and in relation to others' (Feldman and Rafaeli, 2002: Kosmala, 2005). As a result, routine participants' professional identity can sometimes be under threat due to social pressures, such as negative perceptions by colleagues towards one's non-work identity, e.g., a mothering identity (Ladge et al., 2012). When such pressures cause change in routine participants' professional identity, such change is likely to alter how a routine is enacted.

Routine enactment is situated in professional identity. Similarly, professional identity is shaped through routine enactment. Hence, routine enactment and professional identity are entangled and mutually constitutive (Bradbury and Lichtenstein, 2000; Feldman and Pentland, 2003; Ibarra, 1999: Pratt et al., 2006). Despite the apparent relationality between professional identity and Routine Dynamics, few studies have been carried out at the intersection of the professional identity and Routine Dynamics literatures. The purpose of this chapter is to address this theoretical whitespace by explaining how both literatures are intertwined and why research at their intersection is needed to further enhance our knowledge on each literature separately.

In the following sections, I clarify what a professional identity is; how professional identity is related to Routine Dynamics; what research has been carried out; and what new research opportunities lie ahead.

27.2 Professional Identity, Behaviour and Agency

27.2.1 *What Is Professional Identity?*

A professional identity is 'the relatively stable and enduring constellation of attributes, beliefs, values, motives, and experiences in terms of which people define themselves in a professional role' (Ibarra, 1999: 764–765). Professions are subsets of occupations, rely on credentials (Freidson, 1988) and have convinced audiences that are characterized by

'(1) abstract, specialized knowledge, (2) autonomy, (3) authority over clients and subordinate occupational groups, and (4) a certain degree of altruism' (Hodson and Sullivan, 2012: 260). Research on professional identities often explore characteristic professions such as journalism, nursing and teaching (Deuze, 2005; Hoeve et al., 2014; O'Connor, 2008). Key aspects of journalists', nurses' and teachers' professional identities would be respectively objectivity, emotion and care.

27.2.2 Professional Identity Guides Behaviour

Identities in general and professional identities in particular are essential to how we make sense of our environment and enact our work (Weick, 1995; Zikic and Richardson, 2016). Professional identities are formed over the course of time, as an individual learns through experience and feedback (Ibarra, 1999; Pratt et al., 2006). Professional identities are thus relational, in the sense that an identity emerges and is shaped based on action and interaction, and thus is not independent of others' identities, actions and responses (Bradbury and Lichtenstein, 2000; Emirbayer, 1997). A professional identity guides behaviour, yet allows ample room for exercising agency (Kosmala, 2005). In a conceptual study of how teachers acquire professional identities, Coldron and Smith (1999) found that when teachers encounter conflicting demands from a wide array of institutions, empowered teachers choose and judge based on the professional self. In a conceptual study of journalism as an occupational ideology, Deuze (2005) explains that agency is a means through which journalists cope with varying external interpretations of how the journalism professional identity should be enacted. Vähäsantanen (2015) even writes that teachers' professional identities are resources for enacting their agency.

27.2.3 Professional Identity Is Shaped by Agency

It is not that professional identity just provides room for, or is the root of, the exercise of agency. Rather, professional identity is shaped by agency. Professional identities have relatively stable and unstable aspects. The unstable aspects are a manifestation of agents' daily quest of constructing and sustaining a relatively stable identity (Day et al., 2006). In a conceptual article of teachers' professional identity development, Coldron and Smith (1999) suggested that a professional teaching identity develops as teachers actively participate in educational traditions. In a conceptual study of identity formation and maintenance, Goldie (2012) argued that medical students can develop identity styles based on their engagement with medical practice. Hence, their identity as prospective physician is shaped by their agency. In a qualitative study of a global consulting firm, Reid (2015) writes that individuals can simply choose to deviate from a professional identity that's expected by their organizations, to enact what they believe in and prefer themselves to be, which is called the experienced professional identity. Such deviations can potentially shape professional identity. In a qualitative meta-study, Vähäsantanen (2015) found that teachers teach differently and are to different extents involved in educational reforms. These differences manifest in different professional identities among agents within the same profession.

27.2.4 Discourse, Personal Identity and Context Are Important in Shaping Professional Identity

Scholars have shown that discourse is an important mechanism through which agency allows individuals to shape their professional identities. In a qualitative study of professional service firms, Kosmala and Herrbach (2006), for example, found that auditors identify themselves with the firm to maintain performance that is congruent with what the organization expects and also purposefully engage in non-professional discourse to avoid a sense of failure and discontent with respect to the ideals that comprise their professional identity. In a qualitative study of teachers in multi-agency teams, Robinson et al. (2005) show how discourse among teachers during team activities led to the discovery of disagreements through knowledge exchange, which then led to the (re)negotiation of professional identities.

Another mechanism for professional identity change is the change in personal identity. An agent can enact multiple professional and personal identities at the same time. Ladge et al. (2012) show that a personal identity, such as that of a mother, can cause change to or a temporary distancing from a professional identity when there is incongruence between the agent's interpretation of a personal role such as motherhood and work.

Finally, the context has also been found to be imperative for shaping professional identity. As professional identities change under institutional strain, professional identities influence the way people from different professions interact with each other (Fitzgerald and Teal, 2004). In a qualitative study of a university, Smagorinsky et al. (2004) write that professional identity is interwoven with the context in which it is enacted, arguing that one's professional identity 'is not simply the emergence of internal traits and dispositions but their development through engagement with others in cultural practice' (21). The authors describe how the teacher who was analysed in the article was facilitated and restricted in terms of her professional identity by the authorities and institutions that were part of her education and training. Flores and Day (2006) write that there is a strong effect of positive and negative workplace culture and leadership on how teachers' professional identities are shaped. Finally, Kyratsis et al. (2017) describe how institutional logic change can bring about identity threats. They describe that physicians experienced the threats of professional value conflict, status loss and social identity conflict as a consequence of a shift in how their profession was organized and perceived.

Another important reason for professional identities to change might be inter-professional conflict as part of an identity threat. McNeil et al. (2013) write that such threats can arise because of differential treatment; the possession of different values; an unmet expectation of assimilation; facing insults and humiliation; or even simple contact in the face of anxiety.

Professional identities are, thus, provisionally constituted as they go through iterations of identity development, construction, deconstruction, reconstruction, threat, distancing, identification and negotiation. The reason why identities undergo change is that not only do the agents' dispositions matter in professional identity enactment, but so does their (interaction with their) environment. Professional identities are in flux.

27.3 Professional Identity as a Source of Dynamics in Routines

The Routine Dynamics literature builds on the principle that the individuals enacting routines are more or less mindful and reflective (Feldman and Pentland, 2003; Feldman et al., 2016; Levinthal and Rerup, 2006). As a consequence, routines vary across repetitions and change due to the agency that routine participants exercise in response to others and the environment (Emirbayer, 1997). Feldman and Orlikowski (2011) posit that social orders, such as routines, cannot be comprehended without understanding the agency that produces them, and vice versa. Such agency, however, is partly determined, and partly influenced, by those participants' professional identities (Kosmala, 2005; Vähäsantanen, 2015). In a conceptual study, Feldman and Rafaeli (2002) state that the interaction between people lays at the heart of routine enactment, as this interaction facilitates the transfer of information. They write that whereas the abstract routine pattern is likely to be similar across iterations, the actual enactment varies with the people involved and the understandings developed. Similarly, scholars have suggested that our professional identities are shaped through our interactions with others and our environment in general, for example, because our professional identity affects our sense-making (Zikic and Richardson, 2016). Underscoring the importance of individuals' dispositions, such as one's professional identity, Pentland and Feldman (2005) write in a conceptual paper that individual-level factors shape organizational routines. For example, differences in the hierarchical positions of the involved routine participants can shape a routine's abstract pattern. Similarly, routine participants can use power to affect a routine's enactment to motivate people to alter their behaviour.

27.3.1 *Current Research at the Intersection of Routine Dynamics and Professional Identity*

Using Ibarra's definition of professional identity as 'the relatively stable and enduring constellation of attributes, beliefs, values, motives, and experiences in terms of which people define themselves in a professional role' (Ibarra, 1999: 764–765), Table 27.1 presents a selective overview of articles at the intersection of Routine Dynamics and professional identity. I have included in this section only Routine Dynamics articles that explicitly describe how professional identity is intertwined with Routine Dynamics, which required both literatures to be explicitly named and brought together in the articles at hand.

Two studies have explicitly pointed to the importance of research at the intersection of the professional identity and Routine Dynamics literatures. Greenhalgh (2008) reviewed the work on organizational routines to understand how work routines not only hamper but also facilitate collaborative work in healthcare organizations. She argued that our professional identity is part of who we are and hence drives our enactment of routines. When our identity does not fit with what routine performance is envisioned by administrators, we may choose a different performance than envisioned. Essentially, routine participants' sense-making is contingent on their professional identities. Our professional identity also affects how we learn, hence the variation and change that routines will display across repetitions. In a case study of a law firm, Brown and Lewis (2011) showed that lawyers' talk about routines affected routine enactment, while lawyers' routine enactment shaped how they talked about routines. For instance, when lawyers talk to each other about how they enact billing practices, they adjust their practices based on the opinions of others, such as regarding putting down too much billable time. On the other hand, lawyers' experiences with billing practices shape the way they talk with others about these, such as lawyers' discontent with the IT system. Talk about how a routine was conceived to be performed influenced their norms and worldviews, thus shaping their professional identities. The importance of talk for Routine Dynamics as a means of reflection also comes forward particularly in work by Bucher and Langley (2016) and Dittrich et al. (2016). These studies show how routine enactment and talk about routine enactment are mutually constitutive.

27.3.2 *The Implicit Presence of Professional Identity in Routine Dynamics Studies*

In addition to studies that explicitly address the relationship between professional identity and

Table 27.1 Routine Dynamics studies at the intersection of the professional identity literature

	Way of bridging Routine Dynamics and professional identity		How professional identity affects Routine Dynamics, and vice versa, in the study at hand			
RD study	**Explicit**	**Implicit**	**Cognition**	**Emotion**	**Experience**	**Generative conflict**
Greenhalgh (2008)	X		X			X
Brown and Lewis (2011)	X		X		X	X
Howard-Grenville (2005)		X	X		X	
Danner-Schröder and Geiger (2016)		X	X	X	X	
LeBaron (2016)		X	X		X	
Eberhard et al. (2019)		X		X		
Feldman (2000)		X	X			X
Rerup and Feldman (2011)		X	X			X
Zbaracki and Bergen (2010)		X				X

routines, Table 27.1 shows that several studies implicitly address this relationship. In these studies, professional identity particularly helps us to better understand the stability and change that routines may display, without the professional identity literature being explicitly named and applied. Cognition, emotion, experience and generative conflict come forward as particularly important. Cognition and experience are important for routine participants' interpretation of and reflection on others' actions and the environment. Emotion feeds into how routine participants behave based on their sense-making. Conflict is important because the dynamics of routines are sometimes generated through routine participants' efforts to cope or deal with, or resolve conflict through their actions.

27.3.2.1 Professional Identity Affects Routine Dynamics through Cognition, Emotion and Experience

In a qualitative study of a semiconductor organization, Howard-Grenville (2005) found that routine change is contingent on agents' orientations towards the past, present and future of a routine. An orientation towards the past may cause agents to resist change as they hang on to how a routine was performed in the past, whereas an orientation towards the future may spur routine change as routine participants are more inclined to let go of the past in favour of improving how a routine is enacted. As the professional identity literature brings forward, the source of resistance to change can be the professional identities that underlie orientations.

By drawing on a case study of a German agency for technical relief, Danner-Schröder and Geiger (2016) show how flexible patterns of routine enactment can stem from the 'knowing' of routine participants what tasks constituting a routine to select and recombine. Knowing, the authors write, is different from knowledge in that it is not only cognitive but also comprises 'emotions, bodily expressions, and feelings' (2016: 655) and is inseparable from action. Similarly, professional identity comprises emotion, feeling and bodily expressions, and is mutually constitutive of behaviour, because they stem from one's attributes, beliefs and values (Ibarra, 1999; O'Connor, 2008; Vähäsantanen, 2015). The authors explain how identification as team members was important for knowing, because such a shared professional identity facilitated exchange of cognitive and emotional experience that shaped the knowing of routine participants.

Drawing on a qualitative study of hand-off routines in hospitals, LeBaron et al. (2016) describe how physicians developed shared expectations about the practice of handing off a patient to another physician at the end of a shift as they gained experience over the course of time. Such shared expectations led to congruence in physicians' experienced professional identities, and this became a source of stability in enacting the handoff routine. The physician's professional identity became a resource for enacting this stability and for responding when the need for flexibility arose. In another example, Eberhard et al. (2019) demonstrate in their coverage of Romeo pimps' deceit that the pimps' professional identities display a certain set of attributes, such as abuse, attentiveness, brutality, coerciveness, comforting, generosity and persuasiveness. These attributes manifest differently according to which of two roles these pimps enact: that of a caring and loving boyfriend or that of a pimp. When the pimp enacts a professional identity of a loving boyfriend, he, for example, displays more attentiveness, whereas the pimp displays more abuse when he enacts a professional identity of a pimp. The role-taking of Romeo pimps and the accompanying juggling with professional identity attributes ensures that the deceit routine's performance can be upheld.

27.3.2.2 Generative Conflict as a Source of Routine Dynamics

In a qualitative article by Feldman (2000) of a housing organization, the author shows that central administrators and building directors diverged in their interpretations of how hiring and training processes could be improved. The building directors' orientation was to the specific building where they worked and the staff who worked for them, whereas the central administrators were oriented to the entire residential housing system. This difference in professional orientation and, thus, professional identity lies at the root of their divergence in behaviour, because both groups acted differently 'on their interpretation of the outcome of uniformly qualified staff members in their successive actions' (622). Similarly, Rerup and Feldman (2011) show how the professionals in an entrepreneurial research organization (LLD) interpreted rules differently from the professionals in the organization (DPU) that exercised oversight over LLD. These differences were worked out through routines such as the hiring routine that both organizations participated in and ultimately had to coordinate their performances. As routine performances iterate, differences become clear through both actions taken and communication about these actions. In a case study of a Midwestern manufacturing company, Zbaracki and Bergen (2010) show how different convictions of the marketing group and sales force caused a rupture in the truce that enabled the routine's enactment. Amid an effort of the manufacturing company to enhance its sales, the marketing group believed that aggressive cuts in the list price to the distributor would lead to lower consumer prices and thus more sales, whereas the sales group disagreed as it was sceptical about whether such list price cuts would make it to the end customer. Essentially, we see here how the marketing professional identity, shared by the actors within the marketing group, assumed a list price cut to automatically lead to end price cuts, whereas the sales professional identity, shared by the actors within the sales group, caused scepticism towards this and also caused resistance to any compromise.

27.4 Suggestions for Future Research

While the studies reviewed help us see the relationship between professional identity and Routine Dynamics, there is ample room for research at the intersection of these two streams. Routine Dynamics scholars have predominantly focused on better understanding the actions that constitute or shape routines, independent from individual characteristics. In this section, I provide suggestions for future research, focusing on how scholars could shed light on how stability and change in routines may stem from stability and change in professional identity, and vice versa.

27.4.1 Professional Identity Change as a Source of Routine Dynamics and Vice Versa

One theme that requires future research concerns how variation in professional identity affects Routine Dynamics and vice versa. Scholars have shown that professional identities may change over the course of time (Ibarra, 1999), as a consequence of an identity threat (Ladge et al., 2012) or as part of an identity negotiation process (Robinson et al., 2005). Agents interact with others, learn from encounters and reflect on themselves.

As the behaviour of professionals is rooted in their professional identity (Vähäsantanen (2015), and as such behaviour manifests in the actions that constitute routines, change in professional identities probably is a source of change in how routines are enacted. If the professional identity of routine participant X changes, the routine enactment of this person will change. An exciting avenue for future research is the study of how routine participants may intentionally or unintentionally try to translate changes in their professional identity to the enacted routine. Such changes can be instances of distancing from and identifying with a professional identity (Kosmala and Herbach, 2006; Ladge et al., 2012), or of responding to a professional identity threat (McNeill et al., 2013). Other kinds of change may also be important. For instance, do all changes in professional identity cause a change in person X's routine enactment? Also, does it matter from where a change in routine enactment stems? So, does a change in routine enactment have different consequences to Routine Dynamics when it originates in professional identity change?

A change in the routine enactment of person X as a consequence of that person's professional identity change may also cause change in the routine enactment of participant Y. Person Y is reflective of person X's behaviour (Feldman et al., 2016) and may be convinced (Salvato and Rerup, 2018) or influenced (Eberhard et al., 2019) by it. This, in turn, could trigger a professional identity change in participant Y as professional identity and routine enactment are mutually constitutive. For example, Salvato and Rerup (2018), in a historical study of truce dynamics within an Italian design company, explain that because the interaction between routine participants is essential for maintaining conflicting goals, the company they investigated enhanced the connections between these participants through regulatory actions, by setting up points or moments at which bonds between routine participants could be deepened. The authors found that not only agency but also specific actors are essential for how conflicting goals are managed. Whereas the authors did not delve into how actors' professions guided differences in behaviour, the fact that actors varied in how they managed conflicting goals reinforces the argument that differences across professional identity can be a source of different routine enactment and hence offers ample room for future research.

Similarly, as professional identity and Routine Dynamics are mutually constitutive, the enactment of a routine can cause input for a process of professional identity reinterpretation. I suggest research on the circumstances in which routine variation and change may lead to distancing from and identifying with a professional identity, and which circumstances may lead to a professional identity change. Investigating situations in which a routine varies and changes, yet a professional identity remains relatively unchanged, would also be informative. One may think of a routine that changes due to the introduction of an artifact (Glaser, 2017). Because identities change relatively slowly, it is likely that routines in organizations may change faster than routine participants' professional identities. Scholars have suggested that a professional identity can be a resource to cope with change (Grubenmann and Meckel, 2017). Future research could focus on whether routine participants will try to align their professional identities with the changed routine, or whether they will try to change the routine to preserve their professional identity. The choice may very well be situational. Under certain circumstances, routine participants may choose to preserve their professional identity rather than align it with the changed routine, and vice versa. It is also possible that both dynamics will occur.

27.4.2 Professional Identity as a Source of Routine Stability

Professional identities may be difficult to change because they are intertwined with institutional fields and because they are deeply rooted in values (Ibarra, 1999; Kyratsis et al., 2007). Whereas there are instances in which professional identities change, plenty of occasions exist in which professional identities do not change (Day et al., 2006). Routine participants may simply resist threats to their professional identity (Ladge et al., 2012; O'Connor, 2008). When changes in routines present threats to professional identity, people may resist changing routines. In a conceptual study of identity threats, Petriglieri (2011) describes how individuals may enact identity-protecting responses, such as discrediting the validity of the threat's source, concealing their professional identity or enhancing others' perception on the threatened professional identity. As professional identities are important resources for behaviour, it would be useful to research whether resistance to professional identity change would also hamper Routine Dynamics. To what extent can routines vary and change without a change in routine participants' professional identities? Studies have shown that managers can be important in resolving conflict with respect to routine enactment (Zbaracki and Bergen, 2010). Hence, when routine participants' resistance to professional identity change prevents the enacted routine from changing, management may intervene to overcome such resistance and, hence, enable routine change. How could elements of resistance to professional identity change be targeted by managers so as to facilitate Routine Dynamics?

27.4.3 Routine Stability as a Source of Professional Identity Change

Routines comprise connections through the interaction of routine participants, and in this way facilitate shared understandings (Feldman and Rafaeli, 2002). One way in which such shared understandings manifest is in the form of truces (Kaplan, 2015; Salvato and Rerup, 2018; Zbaracki and Bergen, 2010). Even in the absence of a shared understanding (Zbaracki and Bergen, 2010) or when truces are counterproductive to an organization's functioning (Kaplan, 2015), routines can be relatively stable. The routines literature has shown that managers may intervene in both cases (Kaplan, 2015; Zbaracki and Bergen, 2010). However, we don't know what such an intervention would mean for the professional identities of those enacting the truce that was intervened with. Do professional identities change as a consequence of such interventions with routine change?

A lack of a shared understanding among routine participants with respect to a routine, or a counter-productive truce, does not always have to be resolved through an intervention. The generative force of routines may lead to the resolution of conflict among routine participants, as routine participants will reflect on the past. They may interact with other routine participants and eventually alter their subsequent actions. The professional identity literature may shed light on how this could be possible. For example, how do routines generate shared understandings, or resolve counter-productive truces? In a conceptual paper linking symbolic interactionism with Routine Dynamics, Dionysiou and Tsoukas (2013) write how routine participants engage in role taking to generate a shared understanding that will ensure performing a routine as a joint activity. Do, routine participants use their professional identities as a resource for (re-)negotiating shared understandings? Additionally, when they engage in role taking to generate a shared understanding with respect to the routine at hand, do routine participants distance themselves from their professional identity, or even change it, so as to uphold or facilitate a truce?

27.5 Conclusion

The professional identity and Routine Dynamics literatures are inherently related and mutually constitutive, because agency lies at the core of both. Despite this similarity, scholars have insufficiently carried out research at the intersection of both literatures. In this chapter, I have outlined the greater understanding that can be achieved in both literatures by carrying out research on Routine Dynamics from the perspective of professional identity, and vice versa.

First, I reviewed Routine Dynamics studies that had already adopted a professional identity lens. This review brought forward that little explicit research has been carried out at the intersection of Routine Dynamics and professional identity, despite great potential in at least the areas of cognition, experience and generative conflict. Second, I showed that at least seven key Routine Dynamics studies have implicitly drawn from the professional identity perspective in interpreting their results. The findings in these studies underscore behaviours that are rooted in features of routine participants' professional identity, such as emotion, and factors that are essential to professional identity dynamics and Routine Dynamics, such as cognition, experience and generative conflict. Finally, I outlined three potential avenues for future research at the intersection of both literatures.

References

Abrams, D. and Hogg, M. A., eds. (1990). *Social identity Theory: Constructive and Critical Advances*. Berlin: Springer-Verlag Publishing.

Beijaard, D., Meijer, P. C. and Verloop, N. (2004). Reconsidering research on teachers' professional identity. *Teaching and Teacher Education*, 20. 107–128.

Bourdieu, P. (1990). *The Logic of Practice*. Palo Alto, CA: Stanford University Press.

Bradbury, H. and Lichtenstein, B. M. B. (2000). Relationality in organizational research: Exploring the space between. *Organization Science*, 11(5), 551–564.

Brown, A. D. and Lewis, M. A. (2011). Identities, discipline and routines. *Organization Studies*, 32, 871–895.

Bucher, S. and Langley, A. (2016). The interplay of reflective and experimental spaces in interrupting and reorienting routine dynamics. *Organization Science*, 27(3), 594–613.

Coldron, J. and Smith, R. (1999). Active location in teachers' construction of their professional identities. *Journal of Curriculum Studies*, 31, 711–726.

Danner-Schröder, A. and Geiger, D. (2016). Unravelling the motor of patterning work: Toward an understanding of the microlevel dynamics of standardization and flexibility. *Organization Science*, 27, 633–658.

Day, C., Kingston, A., Stobart, G. and Sammons, P. (2006). The personal and professional selves of teachers: Stable and unstable identities. *British Educational Research Journal*, 32, 601–616.

Deuze, M. (2005). What is journalism? Professional identity and ideology of journalists reconsidered. *Journalism*, 6(4), 442–464.

Dionysiou, D. D. and Tsoukas, H. (2013). Understanding the (re)creation from within: a symbolic interactionist perspective. *Academy of Management Review*, 38(2), 181–205.

Dittrich, K., Guérard, S. and Seidl, D. (2016). Talking about routines: The role of reflective talk in routine change. *Organization Science*, 27(3), 678–697.

Eberhard, J., Frost, A. and Rerup, C. (2019). The dark side of Routine Dynamics: Deceit and the work of Romeo pimps. In M. Feldman, L. D'Aderio, K. Dittrich and P. Jarzabkowski, eds., *Routine Dynamics in Action: Replication and Transformation* (Research in the Sociology of Organizations, Vol. 61). Bingley: Emerald Publishing Limited, pp. 99–121.

Emirbayer. M. (1997). Manifesto for a relational sociology. *American Journal of Sociology*, 103(2), 281–317.

Feldman, M. S. (2000). Organizational routines as a source of continuous change. *Organization Science*, 11, 611–629.

Feldman, M. S. and Orlikowski, W. J. (2011). Theorizing practice and practicing theory. *Organization Science*, 22, 1240–1253.

Feldman, M. S. and Pentland, B. T. (2003). Reconceptualizing organizational routines as a source of flexibility and change. *Administrative Science Quarterly*, 48, 94–118.

Feldman, M. S., Pentland, P. T., d'Adderio, L. and Lazaric, N. (2016). Beyond routines as things: Introduction to The Special Issue on Routine Dynamics. *Organization Science*, 27, 505–513.

Feldman, M. S. and Rafaeli, A. (2002). Organizational routines as sources of connections and understandings. *Journal of Management Studies*, 39, 309–331.

Fitzgerald, A. and Teal, G. (2004). Health reform, professional identity and occupational subcultures: The changing interprofessional relations between doctors and nurses, *Contemporary Nurse*, 16, 71–79.

Flores, M. A. and Day, C. (2006). Contexts which shape and reshape new teachers' identities: A multi-perspective study. *Teaching and Teacher Education*, 22, 219–232.

Freidson, E. (1988). *Professional Powers: A Study of the Institutionalization of Formal Knowledge*. Chicago: University of Chicago Press.

Giddens, A. (1984). *The Constitution of Society*. Berkeley: University of California Press.

Glaser, V. L. (2017). Design performances: How organizations inscribe artifacts to change routines. *Academy of Management Journal*, 60, 2126–2154.

Goldie, J. (2012). The formation of professional identity in medical students: Considerations for educators. *Medical Teacher*, 34, e641–e648.

Greenhalgh, T. (2008). Role of routines in collaborative work in healthcare organisations. *British Medical Journal*, 337, 1269–1271.

Grubenmann, S. and Meckel, Miriam. (2017). Journalists' professional identity. *Journalism Studies*, 18(6), 732–748.

Hodson, R. and Sullivan, T. A. (2012). *The Social Organization of Work*. Belmont, CA: Wadsworth, Cengage Learning.

Hoeve, Y ten., Jansen, G. and Roodbol, P. (2014). The nursing profession: Public image, self-concept and professional identity. A discussion paper. *Journal of Advance Nursing*, 70(2), 295–309.

Howard-Grenville, J. A. (2005). The persistence of flexible organizational routines: The role of agency and organizational context. *Organization Science*, 16, 618–638.

Ibarra, H. (1999). Provisional selves: Experimenting with image and identity in professional adaptation. *Administrative Science Quarterly*, 44, 764–791.

Kaplan, S. (2015). Truce breaking and remaking: The CEO's role in changing organizational routines. In G. Gavetti and W. Ocasio, eds., *Advances in Strategic Management, 32*. Bingley: Emerald Insight, pp. 1–45.

Kosmala, K. (2005). Insights from Ricoeur's hermeneutics on best practice in professional service firms: On perpetual myth creation? *Qualitative Sociology Review*, 1, 31–50.

Kosmala, K. and Herrbach, O. (2006). The ambivalence of professional identity: On cynicism and jouissance in audit firms. *Human Relations*, 59(10), 1393–1428.

Kyratsis, Y., Atun, R., Phillips, N., Tracey, P. and George, G. (2017). Health systems in transition: Professional identity work in the context of shifting institutional logics. *Academy of Management Journal*, 60(2), 610–641.

Ladge, J. J., Clair, J. A. and Greenberg, D. (2012). Cross-domain identity transition during liminal periods: Constructing multiple selves as professional and mother during pregnancy. *Academy of Management Journal*, 55, 1449–1471.

LeBaron, C., Christianson, M. K., Garrett, L. and Ilan, R. (2016). Coordinating flexible performance during everyday work: An ethnomethodological study of handoff routines. *Organization Science*, 27, 514–534.

Levinthal, D. and Rerup, C. (2006). Crossing an apparent chasm: Bridging mindful and less-mindful perspectives on organizational learning. *Organization Science*, 17(4), 502–513.

McNeil, K. A., Mitchell, R. J. and Parker, V. (2013). Interprofessional practice and professional identity threat. *Health Sociology Review*, 22, 291–307.

Mitchell, R. J., Parker, V. and Giles, M. (2011). When do interprofessional teams succeed? Investigating the moderating roles of team and professional identity in interprofessional effectiveness. *Human Relations*, 64, 1321–1343

O'Connor, K. E. (2008). "You choose to care": Teachers, emotions and professional identity. *Teaching and Teacher Education*, 24, 117–126.

Pentland, B. T. and Feldman, M. S. (2005). Organizational routines as a unit of analysis. *Industrial and Corporate Change*, 14, 793–815

Pentland, B. T. and Feldman, M. S. (2008). Designing routines: On the folly of designing artifacts, while hoping for patterns of action. *Information and Organization*, 18, 235–250.

Pentland, B. T., Haerem, T. and Hillison, D. (2011). The (N)ever-changing world: Stability and change in organizational routines. *Organization Science*, 22, 1369–1383.

Petriglieri, J. L. (2011). Under threat: Responses to and the consequences of threats to individuals' identities. *Academy of Management Review*, 36, 641–662.

Pratt, M. G., Rockmann, K. W. and Kaufmann, J. B. (2006). Constructing professional identity: The role of work and identity learning cycles in the customization of identity among medical residents. *Academy of Management Journal*, 49, 235–262.

Reid, E. (2015). Embracing, passing, revealing, and the ideal worker image: How people navigate expected and experienced professional identities. *Organization Science*, 26, 997–1017.

Rerup, C. and Feldman, M. S. (2011). Routines as a source of change in organizational schemata: The role of trial-and-error learning. *Academy of Management Journal*, 54, 577–610.

Robinson, M., Anning, A. and Frost, N. (2005). 'When is a teacher not a teacher?': Knowledge creation and the professional identity of teachers within multi-agency teams. *Studies in Continuing Education*, 27, 175–191.

Salvato, C. and Rerup, C. (2018). Routine regulation: Balancing conflicting goals in organizational routines. *Administrative Science Quarterly*, 63, 170–209.

Smagorinsky, P., Cook, L. S., Moore, C., Jackson, A. Y. and Fry, P. G. (2004). Tensions in learning to teach: Accommodation and the development of a teaching identity. *Journal of Teacher Education*, 55, 8–24.

Spee, P., Jarzabkowski, P. and Smets, M. (2016). The influence of routine interdependence and skillful accomplishment on the coordination of standardizing and customizing. *Organization Science*, 27, 759–781.

Tajfel, H., and Turner, J. C. (1979). An integrative theory of intergroup conflict. In W. G. Austin and S. Worchel, eds., *The Social Psychology of Intergroup Relations*. Monterey, CA: Brooks-Cole, pp. 33–47.

Turner, J. C. (1991). *Social Influence*. Milton Keynes: Open University Press.

Vähäsantanen, K. (2015). Professional agency in the stream of change: Understanding educational change and teachers' professional identities. *Teaching and Teacher Education*, 47, 1–12.

Weick, K. E. (1995). *Sensemaking in Organizations*. Thousand Oaks, CA: Sage.

Zbaracki, M. J. and Bergen, M. (2010). When truces collapse: A longitudinal study of price-adjustment routines. *Organization Science*, 21, 955–972.

Zikic, J. and Richardson, J. (2016). What happens when you can't be who you are: Professional identity at the institutional periphery. *Human Relations*, 69, 139–168.

CHAPTER 28

Occupations, Professions and Routine Dynamics

JOANNA KHO AND PAUL SPEE

28.1 Introduction

While studies on Routine Dynamics focus on 'tracing actions and associations between actions' (Feldman et al., 2016: 506), it is the engagement of individuals that makes patterns of action possible (D'Adderio, 2011; Sele and Grand, 2016). Rather than proclaiming a focus on individuals, we draw attention to individuals' embeddedness in *occupations* and *professions* which shapes the accomplishment of routines.

An occupation refers to a category of work – understood by the actors themselves or others – with a distinct structural and cultural system (Abbott, 1988; Anteby et al., 2016). A profession, on the other hand, is a distinct occupational category characterized by members with autonomy in decision-making vested in their role, such as a consultant, teacher or doctor. The autonomy is based on abstract, specialized and often theoretical knowledge which professionals apply as deemed appropriate in a given situation (Hodson and Sullivan, 2012). Professionals' (i.e., the members/actors) affiliation may be stronger to the profession than the organization (Denis et al., 1996). Henceforth, we use the term 'occupations' to refer to occupational groups in a general sense, and 'professions' and 'professionals' more selectively.

The impact of occupations on routines is already recognized in Routine Dynamics with studies pointing to individuals' skills and expertise to accomplish patterns of stability and change (D'Adderio, 2008, 2014; Bresman, 2013; Danner-Schröder and Geiger, 2016; Spee et al., 2016; Zbaracki and Bergen, 2010). In this chapter, we draw on the literature on occupations and professions (e.g., Abbott, 1988; Anteby et al., 2016) to explore theoretical and empirical intersections with a focus on routines. Based on a thorough review of the literature on Routine Dynamics, we identified characteristics of occupations that come to the fore in research themes on skilful accomplishment, interdependence and truces, among other foci within Routine Dynamics. To strengthen the emphasis on occupations, we point to several promising avenues for future research into Routine Dynamics.

28.2 Facets of Occupations and Professions

We turned to the literature on occupations and professions to generate insights for the study of Routine Dynamics. Occupations and professions have long been central topics in organization studies (Abbott, 1988; Macdonald, 1995; Muzio et al., 2013). Occupations and professions are socially constructed entities (Anteby et al., 2016), which have sustained membership through 'institutions, associations, unions, friendly societies, licensing boards, and so on' (Abbott, 2005: 322). We introduce facets of occupations and professions based on three scholarly lenses – becoming, doing and relating (Anteby et al., 2016). The becoming, doing and relating lenses offer an analytical framework to unravel the characteristics of occupations/professions, honing in on how occupational members learn to be part of the collective (becoming lens), what activities they engage in (doing lens) and how they relate to others outside their group (relating lens). While each lens is compatible with the stream of research advancing Routine Dynamics, thus far the research shares particular affinities with the 'doing lens' and 'relational lens' on occupations and professions.

The *becoming* lens focuses on the worldviews of members in a given occupation by studying how individuals become occupational members through a process of socialization into a specific occupational group (Lave and Wenger, 1991). Studies examine how occupational members become controlled as they relinquish part of their autonomy to the collective and provide insights into the unequal distributions of workers or occupational segregation that occur within the occupations (e.g., Abbott, 1988; Becker et al., 1961; Lave and Wenger, 1991). The becoming lens typically focuses exclusively on the members of the studied occupational group during their entry period but tends to neglect the broader environment and how it impacts on the socialization process (Anteby et al., 2016). While acknowledging change and transformation in individuals entering an occupation, the becoming lens tends to assume stability within the occupational groups.

The *doing* lens places an emphasis on *how tasks are performed* by a particular occupation in understanding the implications for individual and group outcomes and in the emergence of a particular occupation (Anteby et al., 2016). Therefore, the route to understanding how occupations operate often lies in the knowledge and the expertise they enact through their actions and practices. However, one of the challenges faced by organizational researchers is to understand what constitutes professional expertise and how this is enacted (Sandberg et al., 2017). As Eyal (2013: 871) pointed out, 'this complex make-up of expertise is typically much more evident when it is still "in the making" and alternative devices, actors, concepts, and arrangements are still viable candidates for formulating the problem or addressing it.' The skills and knowledge of a professional seem to be veiled in mystery, as once a form of expertise has been developed, its complex make-up is obscured by a process of 'black boxing' and standardizing, as expertise is embodied in the expert (Cambrosio et al., 1992) or becomes embedded in artifacts (D'Adderio, 2008, 2011). Furthermore, when studying the skilful execution of particular tasks, the issues and actors alone tend to be foregrounded, while other aspects such as the tools used in the performance of the task, contributions made by other experts, front-line workers or lay people, as well as the mechanisms by which their cooperation have been secured, are often concealed from view (Eyal, 2013; Sandberg and Pinnington, 2009).

The doing lens not only shows how occupations engage in certain work activities but illustrates how they compete for the exclusive claim to perform those activities (Abbott, 1988). At this point, the difference between occupation and profession becomes most salient. Specific problems often fall within a particular *professional jurisdiction* in which professionals claim to classify a problem (e.g., a doctor diagnoses a patient), to reason about it (e.g., to infer from the diagnosis) and to take action on it (e.g., to treat a patient) (Abbott, 1988). 'Jurisdiction', according to Abbott, 'is the link between a profession and its work' (1988: 20). In some instances, jurisdictional claims determine, for example, who can legally operate on a patient, diagnose a mental state, etc. While the control of certain tasks is often associated with the professions, occupational groups in a broader sense can also experience jurisdictional struggles over certain tasks around the content of their work to which they lay claim. As a number of organizational studies have observed, occupational groups are often faced with jurisdictional battles (e.g., Bechky, 2003a; Lefsrud and Meyer, 2012; Salvato and Rerup, 2018; Zbaracki and Bergen, 2010; see also D'Adderio and Safavi [Chapter 15], this handbook) in an effort 'to assert their expertise over certain, unique tasks' (Anteby et al., 2016: 205). Such conflicts hold great importance for organizational outcomes, as well as societal issues (Anteby et al., 2016).

The *relating* lens, as described by Anteby and colleagues (2016), 'focuses attention on understanding when and *how occupational groups collaborate with other groups* to perform interdependent work or collectively expand their social influence' (2016: 212). Hence, different from the becoming lens, the relational lens emphasizes a more agentic view of actors placing action and relations of occupational members and its broader field centre stage (Anteby et al., 2016). It focuses on collaborative relations, which may include a web of stakeholders, to achieve shared or common goals. This facet goes beyond intra- and inter-occupational dynamics and focuses on 'generative relations between occupations and an entire ecosystem of stakeholders including clients, lay persons, organizations, and technology, in addition to other occupational groups' (Anteby et al., 2016: 212). As Adler and colleagues (2008) argue, professionals increasingly work in organizations and with collegial communities rather than in solo practices. This suggests that, in part, professionalism includes 'an image of collegial work relations of mutual assistance and support rather than hierarchical competitive or managerialist control' (Evetts, 2003: 407). Furthermore, collaborative relations also offer important insights for knowledge creation and diffusion (Adler et al., 2008), as well as the sharing of knowledge, both theoretical and practical, among communities (Adler, 2006; Lave and Wenger, 1991; Wenger and Snyder, 2000), and reveal how common ground can be created by different occupational communities in organizations (Bechky, 2003a). Often, organizational scholars start by observing jurisdictional battles between and among occupational groups and then show how these conflicts are resolved through collaborations, which may involve negotiating differences in their status, authority and dependency (e.g., Bechky, 2003a, 2003b, 2006; Kho et al., 2019). The ways in which occupations relate to their work and interact with other members to develop shared patterns of thought and action proves essential to understanding the interactive and relational nature of occupations.

28.3 The Salience of Occupations and Professions in Routine Dynamics

The salience of occupations and professions in Routine Dynamics is multifaceted. For instance, the salience is recognized in central ideas such as depicting routines as enacted through skilful accomplishment (e.g., D'Adderio, 2014; Pentland and Rueter, 1994) and has a bearing on the tensions described in many empirical studies, such as dynamics impeding the coordination of interdependent tasks (e.g., Cacciatori, 2012; Cohendet and Simon, 2016). To illuminate this salience, we focus on three research themes within Routine Dynamics that seem particularly important: *skilful accomplishment* (i.e., how actors perform tasks), *interdependence* (i.e., how actors collaborate to accomplish tasks) and *truces* (i.e., how actors compete for an exclusive claim to perform certain activities). Table 28.1 provides an overview of studies engaging with each research theme, albeit showing variation in the prevalence and extent of engagement. While some studies hone in on a particular occupational group (e.g., Dönmez et al., 2016; Kho et al., 2019; Spee et al., 2016), others demonstrate the dynamic unfolding as members of several occupational groups come together to accomplish routines (e.g., D'Adderio, 2008, 2014; Cacciatori, 2012; Salvato and Rerup, 2018; Zbaracki and Bergen, 2010).

28.3.1 Occupations and Professions: Expanding the Scope of Skilfully Accomplishing Routines

A central tenet of Routine Dynamics rests on the conceptualization of routines as an accomplishment, rather than static entities mindlessly reproduced (Feldman, 2000; Levinthal and Rerup, 2006). Such accomplishment is effortful (Pentland and Rueter, 1994), demanding skills and expertise from individuals to perform tasks. This conceptualization has been advanced by research illuminating the skilful accomplishment of routines as actors orient their performances by skilfully selecting when and how they should direct their actions depending on the situation at hand (e.g. D'Adderio, 2014; Davies et al., 2018; Spee et al., 2016).

Tasked with a transfer of a complex server product and related manufacturing capability to another site, D'Adderio (2014) uncovered the dynamics of engineers and managers who oriented their performances to either replicate or change particular aspects of routines. Managers and engineers employed their professional experience to modify or enact specific artifacts (rules, models, lists, etc.), enrolling communities or other people to support the alignment of routines. Davies and colleagues (2018) analysed the creation and replication of an entirely new routine

Table 28.1 An overview of the salience of occupations and professions in Routine Dynamics (listed in alphabetical order)

Study	Context and research focus	Professions and occupations	Theme in Routine Dynamics
Bucher and Langley (2016)	Research setting: Patient process routines in two hospitals Research focus: how organizational members intentionally change and reorient Routine Dynamics	Health care professionals involved in coordinating change involving the patient process routine.	*Interdependence*: Combining the insights of different professions is crucial when integrating changes requiring interdependent actions by different occupational groups at different points of the routine. Changing routines can be facilitated by organized interactions involving: (1) *reflective spaces*, which allows interactions geared toward evaluating the original routine, developing new concepts of routines and coordinating the change process and; (2) *experimental spaces*, which enables testing, appropriation and modification in provisional performances guided by new concepts of a routine.
Cacciatori (2012)	Research setting: Bidding process (routine) in response to new integrated procurement routes in an engineering design firm Research focus: the role of systems of artifacts in the development of new routines	Cross-disciplinary groups such as architects, engineers and quantity surveyors, contractors and facilities managers	*Truces*: The development of routines is mediated by the development of systems of artifacts (i.e., boundary objects), which within their own structures and relationships reproduce the structures of problem-solving and intra-organizational conflict. Artifacts can form the basis to sustain interaction patterns in which a truce among occupations could be preserved. *Interdependence*: Coordinated actions and cross-disciplinary collaboration are facilitated by interdependent artifacts, working as boundary objects (whose development is the objective of collaboration). Artifacts are created to facilitate the connections between different professional groups that shape patterns of interdependencies among bodies of knowledge held by different groups and communication among roles that make up routines. *Skilful accomplishment*: Artifacts, which embody occupational knowledge and assumptions and the expertise of those developing them, mediate and regulate the type and timing of expertise exploited for problem-solving.
Cohendet and Simon (2016)	Research setting: Creative process (sets of routines) at a video games development office Research focus: How routines are modified during times of disruption (i.e., lack of originality and strategic product differentiation) to allow creativity by reconfiguring routines	Cross-disciplinary teams such as project team and editorial team	*Truces*: Rebuilding routines may call for the redistribution of roles and positions, modifications in power relations and truces between parties. New truces can be established or reconstructed by leveraging shared values and shared elements of the identities of parties. *Skilful accomplishment*: Conflicting goals (i.e., efficiency vs. creativity) can be dealt with simultaneously and through the recombination of routines and routine aspects.

Table 28.1 (*cont.*)

Study	Context and research focus	Professions and occupations	Theme in Routine Dynamics
D'Adderio (2003)	Research setting: Implementation process of Product Data Manager (PDM) software at an automotive organization Research focus: How knowledge and routines are embedded in software and how they can be reproduced	Inter-organizational groups and departments such as engineering, production	*Truces*: New configurations produce conflict and incompatibilities between inter-organizational groups due to differences in function-specific languages, cultures and knowledge bases, which remain latent until there are attempts to impose standardized representations (through the introduction of software) across heterogeneous domains. *Interdependence*: Coordinating workflow effectively (through a PDM) calls for the interdependence of tasks but tight controls (i.e., the system does not allow the next task to start before the previous one) may cause rigidities or restrict potential for innovation and cooperation or informal exchanges across functions/disciplines. *Skilful accomplishment*: Organizational coherence and shared meaning may depend on the ability to achieve balance between forces of heterogeneity and standardization (i.e., overcoming incompatibilities between different functional groups)
D'Adderio (2008)	Research setting: Engineering freeze process (routine) at an automotive organization Research focus: The interaction and dynamics between formal routines (i.e., standard operating procedures, rules) and actual performances, their mutual adaptation and the role of artifacts in mediating these interactions	Inter-organizational members such as programme managers, directors, product and engineering administrators, design and manufacturing engineers, industrial designers, marketing, sales and accounting personnel	*Truces*: Conflict arising from varying views, aims and assumptions; about routines can be resolved through compromise by various organizational groups, where different professionals exert some influence based on their interest and expertise over the overall process.
D'Adderio (2014)	Research setting: Routine transfer in a manufacturing organization Research focus: How organizations address the replication dilemma and respond to coexisting and contrasting pressures for innovation and replication	Inter-organizational members belonging to functional groups such as project management, product engineering, production, manufacturing and information technology	*Skilful accomplishment*: Professionals balance the pressures to align (replicate) and improve (innovate) by drawing on artifacts (e.g., rules, models, lists) and engaging in communities (meetings, forums, etc.)
Danner-Schroder and Geiger (2016)	Research setting: Search and rescue routines during simulations and training in a federal agency that provides nationwide civil and catastrophe protection Research focus: Explores the mechanisms routine participants enact to create patterns that they recognize as stable or changing	Inter-organizational members belonging to functional groups, such as team/group/squad leaders, trainers, logistics officers and medics	*Skilful accomplishment*: Professionals deal with the tension between enacting stable performances while being able to adjust their performances in dynamic and changing settings by knowing how to align workflow, how to prioritize tasks and how to select and recombine actions.

Table 28.1 ***(cont.)***

Study	Context and research focus	Professions and occupations	Theme in Routine Dynamics
Davies et al. (2018)	Research setting: Road maintenance routines in England's Highways Agency Research focus: How new routines are intentionally created and reproduced with some degree of consistency and uniformity across multiple sites	Inter-organizational members belonging to operational and strategic units	*Truces*: Routines can be interpreted and performed in different ways by actors at different levels of the organizational hierarchy. Opposing cognitive and behavioural rationalities may contribute to a breakdown in communication, conflict and tension between different inter-organizational units, leading to failures in exchanging knowledge. *Skilful accomplishment*: Tension between standardizing and remaining flexible can be managed through trial-and-error learning and sharing of knowledge.
Deken et al. (2016)	Research setting: Programme development routines (i.e., toll gate and partner selection routines) in an automotive firm that manufactures vehicles and vehicle hardware Research focus: How multiple actors accomplish interdependent routine performances directed at novel intended outcomes and how this affects Routine Dynamics over time	Sub-departments involving marketing, sales, product development and purchasing	*Truces*: The performances in routine work create emerging consequences for other actions across routines due to interdependent actions by more than one actor with divergent interpretations, preferences and understandings that could lead to breakdowns, which can be resolved through iterative episodes of routine work (i.e., flexing, stretching and inventing work). *Interdependence*: Interdependence among professionals can produce novel outcomes in routine performance by engaging in *flexing* (adapting existing interdependent actions in a routine that actors are familiar with), *stretching* (adapting actions to stretch the application of an existing routine that actors are not familiar with) and *inventing* (building a new routine without drawing on a particular existing routine) routine performances.
Dönmez et al. (2016)	Research setting: Product development routines (agile software) in five different companies (i.e., telecommunications, financial services and software development) Research focus: How product development teams balance stability and flexibility when outcomes are not clearly defined nor certain; and how multiple routines are employed, maintained, changed and disestablished	Product development teams consisting of five or more members	*Skilful accomplishment and interdependence*: Stability and flexibility can be achieved by providing routine participants with various skill levels with sufficient autonomy to either protect or modify routines (i.e., processes and content of routines); and by employing and modifying different interdependent routines that trigger and feed into each other to provide mutual input.
Jarzabkowski et al. (2016)	Research setting: Financial deal appraisal routine in a reinsurance company Research focus: The role of artifacts in professional routines; how professional work is performed in routines through an entanglement of professionals and artifacts	Underwriters	*Interdependence*: The entanglement of artifacts and professionals is central to coordinating actions of dispersed inter-organizational actors within a profession, as well as to sustain collective work. *Skilful accomplishment*: The accomplishment of professional routines involves the entanglement of professional actors, who bring their expert knowledge to bear through artifacts in a way that is both consistent across the profession yet varied with each localized enactment of the routine.

Table 28.1 ***(cont.)***

Study	Context and research focus	Professions and occupations	Theme in Routine Dynamics
Kuiper (2018)	Research setting: Surgical teams in a Dutch hospital and how they use team checklists Research focus: How multiple professionals work with (or against) connective artifacts (i.e., checklists) and whether and how they connect the work of different professionals.	Surgeons	*Interdependence*: Communication and collaboration between professionals are not automatic outcomes of artifacts but considered effortful accomplishments and a requisite to make artifacts (like checklists) work in practice. Individuals in high-ranked positions play a key role in establishing connections and have the ability to help or hinder the process.
Kho et al. (2019)	Research setting: Telehealth consultation routines delivered in residential aged care settings Research focus: How professional/relational expertise is enacted and created to accomplish routines in the context of technology-mediated work	Geriatricians, general practitioners and nurses	*Truces*: Jurisdictional conflict can be managed through the enactment and creation of selective and blended expertise, which brings about a negotiated order to the way various professionals make decisions together *Interdependence*: The creation of relational expertise is conditional on the interpersonal actions that create and draw on it as a resource to accomplish collaborative practices of joint action. Relational expertise (i.e., selective and blending expertise) allows professionals to accommodate the relational demands of interdependent work. *Skilful accomplishment*: Adaptation to inter-professional routine work can redefine professional expertise and can be resourcefully harnessed by changing professional practices to overcome jurisdictional conflict and accomplish collaborative work.
LeBaron et al. (2016)	Research setting: Handoff routines in a hospital's ICU unit Research focus: how people coordinate actions during handoffs to create, maintain and repair flexible performance	Intensive care unit physicians	*Interdependence*: Ongoing work of coordination among participants occurs despite strongly shared ostensive patterns (schemata) to develop joint situated understandings and aligned actions. Strongly shared expectations about a sequence of a routine can facilitate sufficiency.
Salvato and Rerup (2018)	Research setting: new product development routines in a design company Research focus: how organizational routines serve as a source for balancing conflicting organizational goals of design and efficiency	Cross-functional groups of designers and manufacturing engineers	*Truces*: A truce is a process of actions performed by individuals. Conflicting goals can be worked through by engaging in collaborative activities and regulatory actions of splicing (e.g., through workshop briefings), activating (e.g., through joint panel evaluations) and repressing (e.g., through joint colour selection), which allows professionals to establish a dynamic truce, resulting in mutually agreed outcomes.
Sele and Grand (2016)	Research setting: Innovation routines in a research AI laboratory Research focus: how mediators can render routine interactions and ecologies of routines more or less generative	A networked organization involving academics and researchers from diverse fields of computer sciences, material sciences, biology, arts and psychology, as well as other external stakeholders	*Interdependence*: Actants (human and nonhuman) can become intermediaries or mediators through their engagement in performing routine connections. They have the potential for generative agency, meaning that they are able to modify routine performances to trigger new routines or innovative outcomes, depending on whether or not the actant is able to transform and translate through its engagement and become a mediator.

Table 28.1 ***(cont.)***

Study	Context and research focus	Professions and occupations	Theme in Routine Dynamics
Sonenshein (2016)	Research setting: Merchandising routines in running or managing retail boutiques	Various occupational groups such as retail employees, previous employees and managers	*Interdependence*: External routine patterns from other organizations, as well from previous employees, inform or shape routine performances in the focal organization, highlighting the other relations in the broader field of professional groups. *Skilful accomplishment*: Recognizable creative outcomes are produced from complex patterning and corresponding performances that depend on the actor intentionally personalizing (i.e., explicit intertwinement of the self with the routine) and depersonalizing (agentic choice not to explicitly intertwine the self with the routine) routines through interacting artifacts, auxiliary routines and external comparisons.
Spee et al. (2016)	Research setting: Deal appraisal routine and other intersecting routines (brokering, client meeting, modelling and business planning) in a reinsurance company Research focus: how routine interdependence is implicated in coordinating competing demands for standardization and flexibility	Reinsurance professionals (underwriters), brokers and clients	*Interdependence*: Interdependence between the focal routine and a number of intersecting routines coordinated by various skilled professional actors is required when balancing the competing demands for standardization and flexibility in the context of professional service routines *Skilful accomplishment*: Professionals are able to balance their performances (i.e., competing task demands) by orienting to either one ostensive pattern that ensures consistency (i.e., standardization) or to another ostensive pattern that promotes flexibility (i.e., customization).
Zbaracki and Bergen (2010)	Research setting: Pricing process (routine) of a manufacturing firm that sells products to warehouse distributors Research focus: How truces function and are intertwined in performing routines	Cross-disciplinary teams such as marketing and sales teams	*Truces*: Truces collapsed because of jurisdictional disputes, differing interests, professional views about the idea of a routine and how future performances should proceed. Truces can be reformed through shared beliefs on authority (e.g., decision made by the vice president) and needing to make a process work.

developed by a government executive agency responsible for managing the construction, maintenance and operations of England's road network. The study showed how occupational groups skilfully managed the tension between simultaneous pressures to standardize (i.e., consistent and uniform application of new road maintenance routines) and to remain flexible (i.e., remain flexible in the face of the needs of the local context). Such pressure was managed through trial-and-error learning and by sharing knowledge among different organizational units. Similarly, Spee et al. (2016) demonstrated how reinsurance professionals (i.e., professionals dealing with the insurance of insurance companies) drew on professional skills and judgement to skilfully balance their performances (i.e., competing task demands) by orienting to either patterns of consistency (i.e., standardization) or flexibility (i.e., customization). Sonenshein (2016) showed how professionals working in retail were able to skilfully integrate and draw on their experiences and various backgrounds to balance contradictory aspects of familiarity and novelty in managing boutiques. Danner-Schröder and Geiger (2016) illustrated how search and rescue workers skilfully handled the tension between enacting stable patterns while being able to adjust their performances to deal with dynamic and changing settings. Their study emphasized how actors' 'knowing' was enacted as rescue workers aligned their workflow to specific standards, e.g., to prioritize the rescue of victims.

The focus on the skilful accomplishment of routines shares affinities with that of the doing lens on occupations and professions. The doing lens offers a particular emphasis on professionals' knowledge, competencies, expertise and capabilities to accomplish organizational goals and outcomes (Sandberg et al., 2017). Organizational work demands considerable effort by occupational members, who are often depicted as experts skilfully manipulating their environment. According to Collins and Evans (2007), the highest level of proficiency is contributory expertise: 'to do an activity with competence' (2007: 140). A competent professional not only needs skills and knowledge to diagnose or solve a problem but must also be able to apply their expertise to tasks in an endeavour to accomplish work. Such focus contributes to the understanding of routines which 'are grounded in the expertise and knowledge of the profession' (Jarzabkowski et al., 2016: 118).

A focus on skilful accomplishment within Routine Dynamics and a doing lens also points to the essential role of artifacts intertwined with the performance of routines or tasks (Bechky, 2003a, 2003b; D'Adderio, 2008; Glaser, 2017; Sandberg and Pinnington, 2009; Spee et al., 2016). Artifacts contribute to the skilful accomplishment of routines as they orient their actions based on the work at hand. For example, Davies and colleagues (2018) showed how artifacts such as contracts and new guidebooks were used to articulate the rules and procedures to support the consistent and uniform application of new road maintenance routines across the local operating units to guide performance. Spee and colleagues (2016) provided numerous accounts of how artifacts such as the rating sheet are used in reinsurance deals, which was found to be integral to the way underwriters enact their expertise and orient their performances when doing deal appraisals.

Yet, the literature on occupations and professions reminds us that the work – in this case routines – also enacts and thus sustains an occupation or profession (e.g., Abbott, 1988). For instance, the performance of a patient diagnosis does not only achieve an organizational outcome (a billable consultation) but also sustains the profession of a doctor (e.g., a general practitioner). A closer consideration of the dynamics of occupations and profession in the performance of routines expands the conceptualization of routines, differentiating between *organizational routines* and *routines wedded to an occupation or profession*. To date, extant research has focused on organizational routines, honing in on patterns of actions typically observed in a single firm or setting. Looking at professions as a sub-category of occupations, Jarzabkowski et al. (2016) conceptualized 'professional routines' as supra-organizational, 'stretching across organizational boundaries because they are grounded in expertise and knowledge of the profession' (2016: 118). We do not suggest there is an empirical distinction between organizational routines and routines wedded to an occupation/profession. However, we suggest an analytical distinction offers avenues for future research to place dynamics and influences of occupations in the foreground. For example, it provides for (i) the investigation into the influence of standards, norms and moral codes of an occupation, shaping patterns of actions within an organization, and (ii) the demonstration of similarities and differences of 'seemingly similar' routines (e.g., surgery routine, or underwriting of reinsurance deals) across organizations (Edmondson et al., 2001). In addition, it may also provide an avenue for exploring the role of associations and other institutions in shaping the evolution of routines.

28.3.2 Interdependent Actions (aka Routines) Requiring Collaboration between Members of Multiple Occupational and/or Professional Groups

Another central tenet of Routine Dynamics rests on the conceptualization of routines as interdependent patterns of action (Feldman and Pentland, 2003). Integral to such an approach is the recognition that 'participants in an organizational routine must adjust to each other's actions' (Feldman and Pentland 2003: 104). Such *interdependence* is central to coordination and the generative nature of routines (Feldman, 2000; Feldman and Pentland, 2003) and has attracted a lot of attention, unravelling (i) how inter-occupational work creates new routines, actions and interactions to support organizational initiatives; (ii) how a functioning network of a web of stakeholders becomes part of work outcomes, acting as connections and intermediaries through their engagement in routine performances and; (iii) the entanglement of artifacts and how it facilitates collective work.

Studies have demonstrated that interdependence, often depicted as inter-occupational work, requires collaborative relations to accomplish routines; for instance, to develop new processes or initiatives (e.g. Bucher and Langley, 2016; D'Adderio, 2003; Kho et al., 2019; Salvato and Rerup, 2018; Sele and Grand, 2016). For example, Sele and Grand (2016) explored different collaborative practices involving various stakeholders which characterized innovation processes at an AI Lab focused on developing an exercise machine. The AI Lab comprised a networked organization that employed academics and researchers from diverse fields of computer sciences, material sciences, biology, the arts and psychology. The study illustrated how visitors to the AI Lab (e.g., athletes and coaches of the Swiss Olympic team) became mediators between researchers from diverse fields by providing valuable insights and feedback about the functionality of an exercise machine prototype (i.e., a leg press machine with AI capability). The athletes and coaches were able to gain access to and use the prototype for training purposes and, at the same time, researchers were able to record the training data and use it to improve the software and hardware of the machine. This fruitful collaboration thus accelerated the commercialization process of the exercise machine, which led to the emergence of a new routine involving the creation of a business plan.

Kho and colleagues (2019) showed how telehealth service routines triggered the creation of new interactions between nurses, geriatricians and general practitioners. Through their study of interdependent actions, the authors show how the health professionals created and drew on relational expertise to accomplish collaborative practices of joint action related to the shared goal of resident care. In another health care setting, Bucher and Langley (2016) examined routines involving the implementation of new patient processes in hospitals and showed how various health care professionals intentionally changed and reoriented their routines by creating two different spaces of organized interactions. The creation of temporary spaces for reflection (e.g., meetings) and experimentation (i.e., testing the new routines) facilitated the different occupational groups in combining their insights to facilitate routine changes in new patient processes.

A focus on interdependence corresponds with the relating lens (Anteby et al., 2016). It recognizes that occupational groups not only interact and compete with one another but also relate to other groups such as clients and managers. Thus far, a focus on non-occupational groups only partly features in routine studies, for example, on customers (e.g. Bapuji et al., 2012) or residents (Turner and Rindova, 2012). Relatedly, in a study about a deal appraisal routine in a reinsurance company (i.e., insurance of insurance companies), Spee and colleagues (2016) analysed a set of intersecting routines, such as the brokering, client meetings, modelling and business planning routines, revealing the work performances of underwriters or reinsurance professionals including their immediate managers, underwriting assistants, as well as the brokers and clients. The authors showed how certain stakeholders play a role in informing routine performances of standardizing and customizing within deal appraisals. For example, clients offered additional information about particular processes and/or developments during meetings, which consequently informed the underwriter to contextualize and customize modelled outputs. Furthermore, the authors also shed light on how brokers, who act as intermediaries, connect the underwriter and the client to help accomplish interdependent work. As Anteby and colleagues (2016: 218) note when describing 'relating as brokering', 'instead of competing with other groups for control over tasks, they [brokers] share and coordinate them ... rather than erect boundaries, they bridge them ... rather than concern themselves with their own occupational group's advancement, they connect people and tasks to benefit the entire network . . . ' In short, brokers can be viewed as an occupational intermediary group that provide links within a complex web of interactions and processes. Spee and colleagues (2016) also showed the ways in which the underwriter, broker and client collectively co-create or coproduce a reinsurance service by sharing data and accountability among themselves, underpinning the underwriter's professionalism and status.

Likewise, Sonenshein's (2016) study of a retail organization captured the different perspectives of various employees and managers at different stores and offices regarding running or managing boutiques. He examined a wider routine ecosystem of artifacts and auxiliary routines that extended beyond the traditional boundaries of a firm (i.e., employees and managers at different levels) to include external routine patterns from other organizations in the focal firm's industry, as well as from previous employers. Sonenshein (2016) found that these external routine patterns inform or shape routine performances in the focal organization, highlighting the other relations in the broader field of occupational groups.

Studies of interdependent routines also highlight the role of artifacts in collaborative work. For instance, Cacciatori's (2012) study illustrated the collaborative processes involved in producing a bid for a school project requiring the group effort and coordination of four organizational units consisting of investors, a group of architects and engineers, a facilities management division and the cost consulting division of a group of quantity surveyors. Coordinated actions were facilitated by interdependent artifacts, working as boundary objects to support cross-disciplinary work. Kuiper (2018) studied the routines of surgical teams in a Dutch hospital and focused on how they used team checklists as specific artifacts. Her study demonstrated collaborations between surgical team members were not outcomes of artifacts per se. Rather, medical professionals established connections which facilitated the successful use of artifacts such as standards and checklists.

Drawing on empirical insights from studies on Routine Dynamics, we suggest going beyond a rather 'neutral' conceptualization of 'individuals' or 'participants' in Routine Dynamics. Instead, we call for future research to recognize actors (i.e., individuals) as members of occupations. Such conceptualization goes beyond the initial conception of 'situated action', which remained wedded primarily to an organization (Feldman, 2000; Feldman and Pentland, 2003). Such a focus may provide an additional dimension to the notion of embeddedness (Howard-Grenville, 2005, see also Howard-Grenville and Lodge [Chapter 16], this handbook).

28.3.3 Truces at the Intersection of Occupations and Professions

A focus on interdependence, however, points to challenges such as conflicting interest among routine participants arising from routines requiring inter-occupational coordination (D'Adderio and Safavi [Chapter 16], this handbook). A *truce* is a prominent concept within Routine Dynamics to characterize 'an agreement to cease fighting or disputing for a period of time'. (Salvato and Rerup, 2018: 2). Since the development of early conceptualizations of routines, truces have been recognized as essential elements in the coordination of economic action (Nelson and Winter, 1982). Studies have demonstrated that once truces are established, they are embedded in organizational structures and are maintained or (re)formed by organizational members to promote a balance of stability and flexibility (Cohendet and Simon, 2016). Other scholarly work identified 'how' and 'why' truces break down (D'Adderio, 2014; Feldman and Pentland, 2003; Kho et al., 2019; Salvato and Rerup, 2018; Zbaracki and Bergen, 2010), pointing to processes that reveal how occupational groups are able to work through diverging interests to accomplish outcomes.

Some studies point to the different goals, information, values, incentives and perspectives that different occupational groups carry with them and bring to the processes of inter-occupational work as sources of jurisdictional conflict (e.g., D'Adderio, 2008; Salvato and Rerup, 2018). Importantly, these studies show how collaborative activities and forms of compromise resolve jurisdictional struggles to achieve mutually satisfactory outcomes. For example, Salvato and Rerup (2018) examined how designers and engineers from Alessi performed tasks related to new product development (NPD), each pursuing conflicting goals – one related to design (i.e., valued by the designers) and the other to efficiency (i.e., valued by the engineers). By examining the internal dynamics of the NPD routine, the authors observed how these two groups fostered a dynamic truce by engaging in regulatory actions of splicing (e.g., through workshop briefings), activating (e.g., through joint panel evaluations) and repressing (e.g., through joint colour selection from a colour box) to accomplish two conflicting goals. Similarly, D'Adderio's (2008) study at an automotive manufacturer showed how different professional groups (i.e., program and IT management and manufacturing) with varying views, aims and assumptions resolve conflicting interests about the process of 'engineering freeze'. Interestingly, D'Adderio (2008) pointed out that in addition to varying views of the freeze routine, these inter-occupational groups also worked towards different incentives and success criteria related to the routine that they were accomplishing. This conflict and jurisdictional struggle was resolved through compromise, which resulted in parts of each other's programme informing the development process, described by the author as a 'patchwork containing elements from competing worlds' (D'Adderio, 2008: 785), where different individuals exert some influence over the overall process based on their interest and expertise.

Other studies illustrate how truces can be negotiated or re-formed not by collaborative means but through a person of higher authority, who mediated diverging interests between occupational groups. For example, Zbaracki and Bergen (2010), who examined price-adjustment routines in a manufacturing firm, observed how conflict related to differences of professional opinion among a task force consisting of a marketing group and sales group led to a collapse of a truce impeding decision-making on major price changes. Each group demonstrated their own sets of experience, knowledge and expertise in either marketing or sales when deciding how to change prices, causing disputes in jurisdiction. Having produced two sets of decisions – from a sales perspective and marketing perspective – regarding price reduction, the vice president (VP) side-stepped their differences and decided how price adjustment should proceed. While the solution proposed by the VP violated the assumptions of both groups, their acceptance of the VP's authority to decide, as well as their shared belief of needing to make a process work, facilitated the restoration of the truce and suspended overt conflict. Instead of mobilizing an authority to resolve jurisdictional conflict, other studies show how managers can exploit or tap into cultural elements, shared values and identities of the different parties to establish or maintain a truce (Cohendet and Simon, 2016).

Studies on Routine Dynamics also illuminate how new interdependent tasks or actions and interactions play a role in how professional jurisdictions change. For example, Kho and colleagues (2019) observed how geriatric consultations delivered through ICTs (i.e., telehealth services) broadened the participation of residential aged care facility (RACF) professional staff and general practitioners to include geriatric specialists. As a result of telehealth services, interactions and interdependent actions among the different professional groups were created, blurring existing professional boundaries where jurisdictional claims over tasks, decisions and problems caused discord among the different professional groups. By analysing the interdependent actions and interactional patterns, the authors identified the development of relational forms of expertise (i.e., selective and blending expertise) as ways in which jurisdictional conflict over resident care was overcome and how truces were maintained to carry on with inter-professional work. In this study, they showed how jurisdictional claims emerge over task boundaries, provoking conflicts over jurisdictional control.

The artifacts or tools of an occupation have also been shown to provoke and generate conflict during inter-occupational work (Bechky, 2003b; Cacciatori, 2012; D'Adderio, 2003). For example, Cacciatori (2012) observed how different groups problem-solved and engaged in jurisdictional conflict during the development of a new bidding routine (i.e., relating to the procurement process of a finance initiative) involving several occupational groups (i.e., architects, engineers and quantity surveyors, contractors and facilities managers). In her study of boundary objects, she shows how an Excel Workbook used as a cost estimating tool sparked conflict among the groups (i.e., quantity surveyors and facilities managers) when they depicted maintenance costs differently from each other.

The focus on truces within Routine Dynamics resonates with insights from the 'doing lens', especially when it comes to jurisdictional claims (Anteby et al., 2016). Accomplishing tasks jointly is often seen as problematic, as individuals from different occupations approach the task based on principles grounded by their own (occupation-based) understanding of work, which may lead to conflict or jurisdictional struggles (Bechky, 2003a). The notion of 'jurisdictional claim' recognizes the sources of competing claims vested in roles, responsibilities and tasks vested in distinct occupational groups. Thus, we suggest jurisdictional claims are a precursor to, or co-constitute a breakdown of, a truce. A focus on the sources of jurisdictional claims may provide a stronger analytical focus for uncovering the dynamics resulting in a breakdown of truces, and to further understanding of the dynamics required to restore a truce.

Competing jurisdictional claims to and control over certain tasks become more apparent when two or more occupations intersect with each other and engage in inter-occupational action (Anteby et al., 2016). The distinction between occupation and profession is particularly relevant at this point. The autonomy of decision-making vested in some professions creates dispositions when accomplishing a routine. Bechky's (2003a) study is a case in point. It demonstrated the authority of engineers determining the shape and design of prototypes, although technicians and assembly line workers struggled to act on them. While many studies identified expertise – rooted in occupations/professions – as a source of conflict (Salvato and Rerup, 2018; Zbaracki and Bergen, 2010), Kho et al. (2019) demonstrated how specialist expertise provided a resource for establishing a truce. Their study introduced the notion of relational expertise, illustrating how geriatricians foregrounded aspects of interpersonal relationships, thus reducing their autonomy characterized by their role as a medical professional with specialist expertise.

28.4 Future Research Agenda

The salience of occupations on routines has been recognized in extant research on Routine Dynamics, as outlined in some of the prominent research themes on skilful accomplishment, interdependence and truce. However, considerations of occupations remain largely scattered within the literature on Routine Dynamics. In this chapter, we point to the role of occupations in extant work on Routine Dynamics, which opens up several opportunities for future research to advance understanding of Routine Dynamics.

First, a stronger recognition of occupations would expand the conception of routines. While existing studies have tended to assume or attribute a largely neutral status to 'actors', we propose future work to recognize individuals for the skills and expertise involved in performing interdependent actions. Indeed, it is a fine balance to retain the focus on 'routines' as a main unit of analysis instead of on the individual per se. However, a rather 'neutral' notion of the coordination of work, as often depicted in the literature, falls short of the dynamics observed and reported in empirical studies (e.g., Cohendet and Simon, 2016; Zbaracki and Bergen, 2010). Thus, we encourage future work to pay closer attention to the skills and expertise of 'actors' wedded to distinct occupations, for instance, by drawing on concepts such as 'skilful performance' (Sandberg et al., 2017), which shares onto-epistemological similarities with the notion of 'skill accomplishment' within Routine Dynamics. Also, the notion of jurisdictional claims provides a fruitful avenue in which to extend insights on the research themes of interdependence and truces, as well as other concepts such as routine embeddedness (Howard-Grenville, 2005; Howard-Grenville and Lodge [Chapter 16], this handbook). For instance, how do overlapping layers of authority (e.g., organizational and occupational) among the different occupational groups create sources of jurisdictional conflict, shaping decisions and promoting or impeding inter-occupational collaboration?

Second, we propose research that considers and interrogates the relation of routines as a constitutive element of occupations and professions, extending a line of inquiry suggested by Jarzabkowski et al. (2016). This line of enquiry recognizes that the expertise of individuals is mediated and fundamentally transformed by the capabilities of the tools and instruments deemed appropriate to use in their occupations (Latour, 2005; Mol, 2002). Several opportunities present themselves for pursuing new lines of inquiry. For instance, the work of particular occupations and professions continues to be subject to change, such as the increasing trend of the 'hybridization of jobs' (e.g., marketing and statistical analysis or design and programming) or the integration of automated systems and artificial intelligence (AI) technologies (Susskind and Susskind, 2015). These transformations raise questions relating to how certain skills and knowledge are combined and enacted to form 'new' routines? In addition, a focus on routines as constitutive of occupations offers an avenue for exploring how individuals develop skills and expertise to perform routines, which aligns with the becoming lens on occupations (Anteby et al., 2016). To date, research on Routine Dynamics has largely assumed and taken for granted that individuals possess particular expertise to accomplish work such as underwriting (e.g., Spee et al., 2016) or server operations (D'Adderio, 2014). Future studies may explore the role of associations such as accrediting bodies and other professional bodies involved in shaping 'professional routines' (Jarzabkowski et al., 2016). For example, what is the relationship between professional bodies or standards and how are these carried out by participating members of occupational groups through the daily work routines that they enact?

Third, and potentially a more radical suggestion, we propose drawing a distinction between organizational and professional routines, as this offers several opportunities for new lines of research, despite posing some challenges. A focus on professional routines, a supra-organizational routine (Jarzabkowski et al., 2016), provides the basis for expanding the scope of theorizing within Routine Dynamics. It shifts attention to the dimensions of routines that ensure consistency of a routine as accomplished across organizations, for example, those that adhere to professional standards. Spee et al.'s (2016) study of the deal appraisal routine performed by reinsurance underwriters offers some insights into a professional routine and its performance across several firms. A shift to foreground professional routines over organizational routines affords researchers the opportunity to explore the consistency and flexibility of routines beyond a particular organization. It presents opportunities for identifying how a seemingly 'identical' routine is performed across different 'contexts'. For example, researchers might consider how a robotic surgery routine is performed in different hospitals within the same medical district, or even across districts or countries. A focus on professional routines, however, offers some challenges. On the one hand, the distinction between organizational and professional routines is primarily of an analytical rather than a conceptual character. In terms of empirical research, a researcher may characterize and identify similar routines, yet the explanatory focus goes beyond one organization. It also raises a methodological challenge as it requires research designs to conduct research across multiple organizations (Edmondson et al., 2001; Jarzabkowski et al., 2016; Spee et al., 2016).

In conclusion, we encourage scholars to consider these potential research avenues by emphasizing occupations and professions that provide us with a prospect of further theorizing Routine Dynamics.

References

Abbott, A. (1988). *The System of Professions*. Chicago: University of Chicago Press.

Abbott, A. (2005). Sociology of work and occupations. In N. J. Smelser and R. Swedberg, eds., *Handbook of Economic Sociology*. Princeton, NJ: Princeton University Press. 2nd ed., pp. 307–330.

Adler, P. S. (2006). Beyond hacker idiocy: A new community in software development. In *The Firm as a Collaborative Community: Reconstructing Trust in the Knowledge Economy*. Oxford: Oxford University Press, pp. 198–259.

Adler, P. S., Kwon, S.-W. and Heckscher, C. (2008). Perspective – professional work: The emergence of collaborative community. *Organization Science*, 19(2), 359–376.

Anteby, M., Chan, C. K. and DiBenigno, J. (2016). Three lenses on occupations and professions in organizations: Becoming, doing, and relating. *The Academy of Management Annals*, 10(1), 183–244.

Bapuji, H., Hora, M. and Saeed, A. M. (2012). Intentions, intermediaries, and interaction: Examining the emergence of routines. *Journal of Management Studies*, 49(8), 1586–1607.

Bechky, B. A. (2003a). Sharing meaning across occupational communities: The transformation of understanding on a production floor. *Organization Science*, 14(3), 312–330.

Bechky, B. A. (2003b). Object lessons: Workplace artifacts as representations of occupational jurisdiction. *American Journal of Sociology*, 109(3), 720–752.

Bechky, B. A. (2006). Talking about machines, thick description, and knowledge work. *Organization Studies*, 27(12), 1757–1768.

Becker, H. S., Geer, B., Hughes, E. C. and Strauss, A. L. (1961). *Boys in White: Student Culture in Medical School*. Chicago: University of Chicago Press.

Bresman, H. (2013). Changing routines: A process model of vicarious group learning in pharmaceutical R&D. *Academy of Management Journal*, 56(1), 35–61.

Bucher, S. and Langley, A. (2016). The interplay of reflective and experimental spaces in interrupting and reorienting routine dynamics. *Organization Science*, 27(3), 594–613.

Cacciatori, E. (2012). Resolving conflict in problem-solving: Systems of artifacts in the development of new routines. *Journal of Management Studies*, 49(8), 1559–1585.

Cambrosio, A., Limoges, C. and Hoffman, E. (1992). Expertise as a network: A case study of the controversies over the environmental release of genetically engineered organisms. In N. Stehr and R. V. Ericson, eds., *The Culture and Power of Knowledge*. Berlin and New York: De Gruyter, pp. 341-361.

Cohendet, P. S. and Simon, L. O. (2016). Always playable: Recombining routines for creative efficiency at Ubisoft Montreal's video game studio. *Organization Science*, 27(3), 614–632

Collins, H. and Evans, R. (2008). *Rethinking Expertise*. Chicago: University of Chicago Press.

D'Adderio, L. (2003). Configuring software, reconfiguring memories: The influence of integrated systems on the reproduction of knowledge and routines. *Industrial and Corporate Change*, 12, 321–350.

D'Adderio, L. (2008). The performativity of routines: Theorising the influence of artefacts and distributed agencies on routines dynamics. *Research Policy*, 37(5), 769–789.

D'Adderio, L. (2011). Artifacts at the centre of routines: Performing the material turn in routines theory. *Journal of Institutional Economics*, 7 (2), 197–230.

D'Adderio, L. (2014). The replication dilemma unravelled: How organizations enact multiple goals in routine transfer. *Organization Science*, 25(5), 1325–1350.

Danner-Schröder, A. and Geiger, D. (2016). Unravelling the motor of patterning work: Toward an understanding of the microlevel dynamics of standardization and flexibility. *Organization Science*, 27(3), 633–658.

Davies, A., Frederiksen, L., Cacciatori, E. and Hartmann, A. (2018). The long and winding road: Routine creation and replication in multisite organizations. *Research Policy*, 47(8), 1403–1417.

Deken, F., Carlile, P. R., Berends, H. and Lauche, K. (2016). Generating novelty through interdependent routines: A process model of routine work. *Organization Science*, 27(3), 659–677.

Denis, J.-L., Cazale, L. and Langley, A. (1996). Leadership and strategic change under ambiguity. *Organization Studies*, 17(4), 673–699.

Dönmez, D., Grote, G. and Brusoni, S. (2016). Routine interdependencies as a source of stability and flexibility: A study of agile software development teams. *Information and Organization*, 26(3), 63–83.

Edmondson, A. C., Bohmer, R. M. and Pisano, G. P. (2001). Disrupted routines: Team learning and new technology implementation in hospitals. *Administrative Science Quarterly*, 46(4), 685–716.

Evetts, J. (2003). The sociological analysis of professionalism: Occupational change in the modern world. *International Sociology*, 18(2), 395–415.

Eyal, G. (2013). For a sociology of expertise: The social origins of the autism epidemic. *American Journal of Sociology*, 118(4), 863–907.

Feldman, M. S. (2000). Organizational routines as a source of continuous change. *Organization Science*, 11(6), 611–629.

Feldman, M. S. and Pentland, B. T. (2003). Reconceptualizing organizational routines as a source of flexibility and change. *Administrative Science Quarterly*, 48(1), 94–118.

Feldman, M. S. and Pentland, B. T. (2008). Routine dynamics. In D. Harry and H. Hansen, eds., *The SAGE Handbook of New Approaches in Management and Organization*. London: SAGE Publications Ltd, pp. 302–315.

Feldman, M. S., Pentland, B. T., D'Adderio, L. and Lazaric, N. (2016). Beyond routines as things: Introduction to the Special Issue on Routine Dynamics. *Organization Science*, 27(3), 505–513.

Felin, T., Foss, N. J., Heimeriks, K. H. and Madsen, T. L. (2012). Microfoundations of routines and capabilities: Individuals, processes, and structure. *Journal of Management Studies*, 49(8), 1351–1374.

Glaser, V. L. (2017). Design performances: How organizations inscribe artifacts to change routines. *Academy of Management Journal*, 60(6), 2126–2154.

Hodson, R. and Sullivan, T. A. (2012). *The Social Organization of Work*. Belmont, CA: Wadsworth, Cengage Learning.

Howard-Grenville, J. (2005). The persistence of flexible organizational routines: The role of agency and organizational context. *Organization Science*, 16(6), 618–636.

Jarzabkowski, P., Bednarek, R. and Spee, A. P. (2016). The role of artifacts in establishing connectivity within professional routines: A question of entanglement. In J. A. Howard-Grenville, C. Rerup, A. Langley and H. Tsoukas, eds., *Organizational Routines: How They Are Created, Maintained, and Changed*, Oxford: Oxford University Press, pp. 117–139.

Kho, J., Spee, A. P. and Gillespie, N. (2019). Chapter 9: Enacting relational expertise to change professional routines in technology-mediated service settings. In *Routine Dynamics in Action: Replication and Transformation* (Vol. 61. Bingley: Emerald Publishing Limited, pp. 191–213.

Kuiper, M. (2018). Connective routines: How medical professionals work with safety checklists. *Professions and Professionalism*, 8(1), e2251–e2251.

Latour, B. (2005), *Reassembling the Social: An Introduction to Actor Network Theory*. Oxford: Oxford University Press.

Lave, J. and Wenger, E. (1991). *Situated Learning: Legitimate Peripheral Participation*. Cambridge: Cambridge University Press.

LeBaron, C., Christianson, M. K., Garrett, L. and Ilan, R. (2016). Coordinating flexible performance during everyday work: An ethnomethodological study of handoff routines. *Organization Science*, 27(3), 514–534.

Lefsrud, L. M. and Meyer, R. E. (2012). Science or science fiction? Professionals' discursive construction of climate change. *Organization Studies*, 33, 1477–1506.

Levinthal, D. and Rerup, C. (2006). Crossing an apparent chasm: Bridging mindful and less-mindful perspectives on organizational learning. *Organization Science*, 17(4), 502–513.

Macdonald, K. M. (1995). *The Sociology of the Professions*. London: Sage.

Mol, A. (2002). *The Body Multiple: Ontology in Medical Practice*. Durham, NC: Duke University Press.

Muzio, D., Brock, D. M. and Suddaby, R. (2013). Professions and institutional change: Towards an institutionalist sociology of the professions. *Journal of Management Studies*, 50(5), 699–721.

Nelson, R. R. and Winter, S. G. (1982). *An Evolutionary Theory of Economic Change*. Cambridge, MA: Belknap Press/Harvard University Press.

Parmigiani, A. and Howard-Grenville, J. (2011). Routines revisited: Exploring the capabilities and practice perspectives. *Academy of Management Annals*, 5(1), 413–453.

Pentland, B. T. and Rueter, H. H. (1994). Organizational routines as grammars of action. *Administrative Science Quarterly*, 39(3), 484–510.

Salvato, C. and Rerup, C. (2018). Routine regulation: Balancing conflicting goals in organizational routines. *Administrative Science Quarterly*, 63(1), 170–209.

Sandberg, J. and Pinnington, A. H. (2009). Professional competence as ways of being: An existential ontological perspective. *Journal of Management Studies*, 46(7), 1138–1170.

Sandberg, J., Rouleau, L., Langley, A. and Tsoukas, H., eds. (2017). *Introduction: Skillful Performance: Enacting Capabilities, Knowledge and Expertise in Organizations*. Oxford: Oxford University Press.

Sele, K. and Grand, S. (2016). Unpacking the dynamics of ecologies of routines: Mediators and their generative effects in routine interactions. *Organization Science*, 27(3), 722–738.

Sonenshein, S. (2016). Routines and creativity: From dualism to duality. *Organization Science*, 27(3), 739–758.

Spee, P., Jarzabkowski, P. and Smets, M. (2016). The influence of routine interdependence and skillful accomplishment on the coordination of standardizing and customizing. *Organization Science*, 27(3), 759–781.

Susskind, R. E. and Susskind, D. (2015). *The Future of the Professions: How Technology Will Transform the Work of Human Experts*. New York: Oxford University Press.

Turner, S. F. and Rindova, V. (2012). A balancing act: How organizations pursue consistency in routine functioning in the face of ongoing change. *Organization Science*, 23(1), 24–46.

Wenger, E. C. and Snyder, W. M. (2000). Communities of practice: The organizational frontier. *Harvard Business Review*, 78(1), 139–146.

Zbaracki, M. J. and Bergen, M. (2010). When truces collapse: A longitudinal study of price-adjustment routines. *Organization Science*, 21(5), 955–972.

CHAPTER 29

Routine Dynamics and Management Practice

SIMON GRAND

29.1 Introduction

In the last two decades, we have seen the emergence of Routine Dynamics as an important research programme, which suggests studying routines from a practice perspective (Feldman and Orlikowski, 2011; Parmigiani and Howard-Grenville, 2011; Salvato and Rerup, 2011). In this perspective, routines are described as *recurrent* patterns of actions, performed by *multiple* actors, across *multiple* sites as well as *over time* (Feldman and Pentland, 2003). This allows scholars to empirically describe the importance of routines as particular patterns of action for organizations, and to explain the agency and dynamics inherent in the performance of routines on a sound theoretical foundation (Feldman, 2000, 2003; Feldman et al., 2016, 2019; Howard-Grenville and Rerup, 2016).

Conceptualizing routines as inherently dynamic phenomena has important consequences for the way we conceptualize management. Management can no longer be seen as defining and guiding organizational processes from outside, but as intimately entangled with organizational routines and their situated performances (Feldman, 2015). Furthermore, Routine Dynamics is a central focus for management practice to enact and shape change and stability in organizations. Finally, this makes it possible to advance research on management in the perspective of Routine Dynamics (Grand, 2016), with a particular emphasis on management routines as important for managerial agency (Grand and Bartl, 2019). In this chapter, I provide an overview of the ways that studies in Routine Dynamics have conceptualized the role of management and will outline directions for future research on the role of management in Routine Dynamics.

The rest of this chapter is structured into three sections. The next section introduces a practice perspective on management, which I see as an important conceptual precondition to relate management practice and Routine Dynamics on a coherent theoretical foundation. The following section will provide an overview of how empirical studies in Routine Dynamics have addressed and incorporated managerial activities and management practice. In the final section, research opportunities for future research on the role of management in Routine Dynamics, as well as on management practice itself, are identified.

29.2 A Practice-Based Perspective on Management

In order to discuss the role of management in Routine Dynamics one needs a concept of management that fits the practice-based conceptualization of routines. Hence, this section will introduce a practice perspective on management before discussing the role of management in Routine Dynamics to follow in Section 29.3. While there are various definitions of management in the literature, based on heterogeneous theoretical perspectives (Cunliffe, 2009), we see more recently a growing interest in approaching *management as a specific practice in organizations* (Korica et al., 2017). Thereby, management is specific insofar as it does not primarily focus on performing organizational tasks, but on *enabling others to perform their tasks*, often in relation to how they contribute to current and future organizational value creation on different scales, as well as to how the organization works and develops (Tengblad, 2012).

For the purpose of this chapter, I focus on a practice perspective (Schatzki et al., 2002), which sees Routine Dynamics as the primary focus of managerial activities, in order to enact how organizations work and develop, and in particular to how this contributes to stability and change (Feldman and Orlikowski, 2011; Feldman et al., 2016). In the practice perspective, management is seen as *intimately entangled with routine performances, while reflecting and shaping* these performances. A practice perspective allows scholars to gain a more detailed understanding of how managers gain agency and impact through the situated engagement in Routine Dynamics, as well as through the mobilization, enactment and performance of organization-specific repertoires of management practices (Korica et al., 2017; Tengblad, 2012), which eventually develop into management routines (Grand and Bartl, 2019).

In a practice perspective, the focus is on better understanding the social embeddedness of managing (Nicolini and Monteiro, 2017; Noordegraaf and Stewart, 2000), as well as how managers mobilize, enact and change specific management practices. Management is seen as proactive and creative, but always also as indirect (Jullien, 2005); as intervening as well as contained (Chia and Holt, 2009); as immanent in organizational processes and at the same time transcending them (Grand, 2016; Tsoukas and Chia, 2002). A practice perspective provides the theoretical foundation to addressing these different facets as intimately related.

For this chapter, I briefly introduce five aspects of a practice perspective, which are particularly important for the study of management practices in Routine Dynamics:

- Management practices gain impact and relevance through the *mundane everyday enactment of these practices* by managers, in multiple activities and interactions, across multiple situations and sites, as well as over time (Mintzberg, 1971, 2009). Managerial activities are characterized by high fragmentation, hectic work pace, an inherently processual dynamic, collective accomplishments and informal interactions among others (Mintzberg, 1994; Tengblad, 2012).
- Management practices *bundle managerial activities to coherent action patterns*, which can be observed across these multiple activities, interactions, situations and sites; they emerge, stabilize and change *in the entanglement of activities, artifacts, language and specific settings, which are* enacted in and across sites, temporally and spatially situated. Thereby, management practices are *often collective*, embedded in manager communities, which can be seen as communities-of-practice or -meaning in their own right (Brown and Duguid, 1991; Wenger, 1998).
- Individual management practices are embedded in *configurations of other practices*, which are addressed as 'knots, networks, nexuses, assemblages, textures underlying agency (Czarniawska, 2008; Gherardi, 2006; Latour, 2005; Nicolini, 2009; 2012)' (Nicolini and Monteiro, 2017: 4) and form organization-specific ecosystems. Management practices *differ in scope and spread* of the contexts, settings and sites in which they are mobilized, the communities enacting them, as well as their impact on the organization (Thévenot, 2001).
- Management practices are *meaningful action patterns, related to specific ends*; this is addressed when we discuss the 'management of … ' innovation, change or strategy, thus *favouring certain courses of action* (Reckwitz, 2002). It is not the individual intentions of autonomous managers as authors of their actions that define a practice, but the implied action patterns that allow for agency, impact and creativity. Thereby, managerial engagement can be indirect, and outcomes can emerge unintendedly and beyond dedicated purposes (Chia and Holt, 2009).
- Management practices are *normative, referring to values, intentions, expectations and interests* (Thévenot, 2006). By mobilizing management practices, managers mobilize specific valuations, which are enacted in a practice (Boltanski and Thévenot, 1991; Grand, 2016), and which turn them into 'meaning-making, identity-forming and order-producing activities' (Korica et al., 2017: 165). Individual preferences and organizational expectations come together in the situated enactment of these practices, and might be confirmed, reflected, adapted or challenged in the further course of action.

Based on this understanding of management practice, I discuss in the next section how existing research in the Routine Dynamics research programme addresses management, and in particular the role of management in enacting routine performance as a way of shaping how organizations work and change; in creating and establishing new routines; or in governing and orchestrating an organization's repertoire of routines.

29.3 Managing Routine Dynamics

With the practice perspective on Routine Dynamics and management comes a specific understanding of how managers enact and shape Routine Dynamics, as well as a critical view on alternative approaches that underestimate the generative, dynamic nature of routines. In this section, we discuss how the Routine Dynamics research programme allows scholars to critically reflect taken-for-granted understandings of management and routines (Section 29.3.1), as a context to cluster four important research areas that a practice perspective can inform: by addressing how managers engage in Routine Dynamics (Section 29.3.2); how managers reflect on Routine Dynamics (Section 29.3.3); how managers mobilize specific settings to enact Routine Dynamics (Section 29.3.4); and how managers mobilize, enact and change management routines in their practice (Section 29.3.5).

29.3.1 Managers Are Trying to Design Routines 'from Outside'

An important line of argumentation in Routine Dynamics research states that managers often try to design routines 'from outside', but fail to realize that the designed routine is different from the enacted routine (Feldman, 2003). Or managers try to change routines by re-designing them as if they were 'objects', but do not succeed (Pentland and Feldman, 2008). To address routines as inherently dynamic and not as given entities, and to understand management as engaging in Routine Dynamics rather than designing routines as objects from outside is at the core of the Routine Dynamics research programme and its view on management. Hence, routines are seen as collective accomplishments (Feldman et al., 2016).

Pentland and Feldman (2008) show in their study on a failed software implementation that routines cannot be treated as objects that can be designed 'from outside'. As the authors discuss, this view from outside leads managers to mistake explicit rules and designed artifacts for routines themselves. But organizational routines are not fixed programmes. Rather, they are generative systems that can produce patterns of action, and are based on local judgement and situative improvisation by the actors involved. Managers do not gain direct impact on Routine Dynamics by designing routines and prescribing how routines have to be performed because the people who enact the routines do not necessarily enact what managers as designers have in mind.

It is rather the situated enactment of a routine by multiple actors across many situations and sites that specifies the action patterns comprised in the ostensive aspect, and indicates whether and how a routine is performed, stabilized or changed. In addition, we learn from Feldman's (2003) study on a budgeting routine of a large state university that the situated performances of the routine by the multiple participants involved are informed by their understandings of how the organization operates. These understandings include the performances of managers interpreted by the actors and mindfully created and re-created in the actual enactment of the routine, often outside any direct guidance by management itself.

A practice perspective suggests that an important part of how management practice gains impact in Routine Dynamics is thus not by designing routines or by prescribing and defining specific understandings of routine performances 'from outside', but by engaging in Routine Dynamics 'from within', as I discuss in Section 29.3.2.

29.3.2 Managers Are Engaging in Routine Dynamics 'from Within'

As the Routine Dynamics research programme shows, organizations are complex, relational configurations of routines and actions, which are continuously enacted, actualized, stabilized, adapted and changed (Becker et al., 2006; Feldman and

Pentland, 2003). To better understand how managerial agency in relation to routines becomes possible, it is important to study managers in their *situated presence in the actual enactment of routines*. Managers can be seen as actors who inform current performances but also inspire and try out spontaneous variations in these ongoing performances, which might be repeated across sites and over time, and subsequently retained (Rerup and Feldman, 2011; Salvato, 2009). For example, such variations can happen by proactively relating routines and external factors (Salvato, 2003); by enacting routines in view of ambiguous or competing pressures (D'Adderio, 2014); or by mobilizing routines for diverse tasks or across different sites (Danner-Schroeder and Geiger, 2016; Turner and Rindova, 2012).

As we learn from Salvato's (2009) study on product innovation processes, management is important in recognizing and taking advantage of different ways in which routines are performed (Salvato, 2009). While 'everyday experimental activities performed by internal and external agents' (Salvato, 2009: 393) lead to diverse performances and adaptations in routine enactment, *managerial action is important to incorporate such adaptations into the organization*, and thus to shape creativity and innovation in the organization. As Salvato shows, this requires mindful micro-activities carried out by individuals in and around the organization, including managers. The intentional experiments re-combine the existing repertoire of routines, hence resulting in increased heterogeneity in the ways they are performed. Timely managerial interventions encode successful experiments into organizational patterns, eventually leading to new performances of routines, as well as new routines.

What we learn from this perspective is the extent to which management can be entangled with Routine Dynamics, allowing scholars to better understand the managerial enactment of how routines are performed as well as how they develop 'from within'. Over time, specific routine patterns are confirmed and stabilized, or rather shifted and changed. As Feldman (2015) argues, the resulting organizational outcomes cannot be deduced from individual intentions or expectations of managers, but emerge from the dynamic interplay of *purposeful, goal-oriented action and purposive actions* (2015: 322–323). She draws on Chia and Holt, who discuss ' ... purposive creation having its center of gravity in itself' (Chia and Holt, 2009: 110), giving rise ' ... to more systemic outcomes that were never intended on the part of the actors themselves' (Chia and Holt, 2009: 111).

In most studies on how management shapes Routine Dynamics, the enactment of routines by managers is primarily addressed as engaging in *experimentation and improvisation* (Salvato, 2009), *creativity and innovation* (Grand, 2016; Salvato, 2003, 2009; Sonenshein, 2016) as well as *change* (Cohendet and Simon, 2016; D'Adderio and Pollock, 2014; Jarzabkowski et al., 2012; Rerup and Feldman, 2011; Zbaracki and Bergen, 2010). Routine Dynamics also emphasizes how experimentation, creation and change are inherently related to the simultaneous enactment of stability and continuity (Feldman, 2000; 2003) and how management can play a role in enacting routine performances to stabilize and protect patterns (Grand, 2016; Salvato, 2003). Both Tsoukas and Chia (2002) and Farjoun (2010) rely on Routine Dynamics studies when they claim that it often requires creativity, improvisation and experimentation to also *accomplish stable patterns of action* in complex situations and changing context.

Management continuously balances enactments and adjustments in routines that *may confirm or alter the pattern* (Farjoun, 2010), deliberately deviating from existing patterns of action by inspiring experimentation and variation, but also protecting and stabilizing proven and successful action patterns. A practice perspective allows scholars to see how this takes place through engaging in Routine Dynamics from 'within' rather than by designing routines 'from outside'. At the same time, such balancing requires managers to systematically reflect and transcend the situated enactment, in relation to how specific routines are performed, as well as to how the organization operates more broadly. How managers are reflecting on Routine Dynamics is further explored in Section 29.3.3.

29.3.3 Managers Are Reflecting on Routine Dynamics

Several studies highlight that *reflective distancing* in relation to situated routine performances is important (Bucher and Langley, 2016; Dittrich et al., 2016). Such reflecting is seen as an essential complement to the situated presence described in Section 29.3.2. Reflecting allows managers to critically observe current performances of routines, or discussing them in view of their current and future appropriateness, or for identifying and enacting alternative courses of thinking and acting (Grand and Bartl, 2019). Recent studies on reflection in relation to Routine Dynamics address different aspects, which inform our understanding of how reflection relates to the managerial enactment of Routine Dynamics. Thereby, these studies also address how reflecting routine performances and enacting Routine Dynamics 'from within' relate.

As Dittrich et al. (2016) show for a start-up company in the pharmaceutical industry, reflective talk is important for changing routines, first by addressing issues in current routine performance, second by exploring alternatives and third by evaluating them from different perspectives. The study builds on an earlier note that Routine Dynamics involves actors 'reflecting on what they are doing, and doing different things (or doing the same things differently) as a result of the reflection' (Feldman, 2000: 625). Dittrich et al. (2016) distinguish *two types of reflective talk*, one when adapting a specific performance, the other when introducing changes to the routine's pattern. The distinction of these two types of reflective talk, as well as their dynamic interplay allows the authors to explain in greater detail how managers explicitly envisage and explore alternatives to current routine performances.

This study is complemented by Bucher and Langley (2016), who describe the dynamic interplay of reflective distancing and experimental routine enactment. They show in a longitudinal case study of two initiatives to change patient processes in hospitals how *interrupting and re-orienting Routine Dynamics* complements the enactment of Routine Dynamics 'from within', through the mobilization of spaces for reflection and experimentation (Bucher and Langley, 2016). The authors see reflection as important when management strives to radically change routines, facing the puzzle that it can be difficult to change established routines or performances of routines when these are bound by pre-existing performances that are recurrently reproduced and well-established. While reflective distancing allows managers to introduce alternative views on current Routine Dynamics, systematic experimentation in protected spaces allows them to explore ways of performing routines differently.

As these studies show, reflecting and enacting Routine Dynamics are intimately related. This confirms the practice perspective on management, describing managerial engagement as 'zooming-in' on situated actions in an organization, while 'zooming-out' on how they relate to organizational practices and emerging outcomes (Nicolini, 2009), '. . . linking the here-and-now of work with wider issues' (Korica et al., 2017: 166, see also Grand, 2016). This connects the description of management practice as distant from mundane organizational work, to *enable critical reflection* (Drucker, 1967), *address non-delegable issues* (Barnard, 1938) or *explore new alternatives* (Simon, 1996), to management as intimately entangled with organizational activities (Mintzberg, 2009). An in-depth understanding of how managers engage in and reflect on Routine Dynamics allows scholars to better understand how '. . . practitioners are ordinarily involved in the relational whole within which they carry out their tasks' (Sandberg and Tsoukas, 2011: 345).

29.3.4 Managers Are Mobilizing Specific Settings to Enact Routine Dynamics

As indicated in Section 29.3.3, the critical reflection of current routine performances, but also the experimental exploration of potential alternatives, can require specific settings, which provide the context necessary for such reflection. Besides enacting Routine Dynamics through situated engagement, managers can *proactively mobilize and shape specific settings*, in order to systematically stabilize or change routines (Bucher and Langley, 2016; Grand and Bartl, 2019). Specifically, managers can mobilize working formats such as workshops or meetings (Hendry and Seidl, 2003; Jarzabkowski and Seidl, 2008), task forces and venturing initiatives (Grand and Bartl, 2019) or specific 'social spaces' (Bucher and Langley, 2016).

In an exemplary way, Bucher and Langley (2016) describe how management creates and mobilizes settings for enacting Routine Dynamics. They discuss different 'spaces' as bounded social settings, which enable reflection and the generation of alternatives, or allow managers for ' ... testing intentional variations' (Bucher and Langley, 2016: 609). The authors show that it is important for managers to protect such settings from the direct exposure to and impact of the ongoing routine performances in the organization, because they can make reflection difficult through their primary orientation towards resolving current tasks.

The authors then address in greater detail the puzzle of recursiveness that comes with this separation: on the one hand, it is important for managers to focus on the distancing from routine actions to enable reflection and experimentation; on the other hand, they have to find ways for connecting such distanced reflection and experimentation back to enacting and changing current routines. Furthermore, we learn from studies on creation and innovation routines that such settings can be *mobilized very situatively*, but they can also be *institutionalized as task forces, creative spaces or laboratories*, which establish their own specific creation and experimentation routines, purposefully enacted to create and explore alternatives (Cohendet and Simon, 2016; Grand, 2016; Salvato, 2003, 2009; Sele and Grand, 2016).

Interestingly, management studies so far primarily focus on managerial work, rather than on the importance of specific settings and spaces for management practice (Tengblad, 2012), thus addressing the organizational embeddedness of management practice. More recent practice-based studies start to emphasize explicitly the importance of specific arenas (Brundin and Melin, 2012) or management platforms (Rüegg-Stürm and Grand, 2020); and research on strategy-as-practice describes for some time the importance of specific types of meetings, workshops, offsites and task forces for strategic management practice (Grand and Bartl, 2019; Jarzabkowski and Seidl, 2008). To consider these settings is a prerequisite for scholars to address the enabling conditions, organizational contexts or 'hinterland' (Law, 2004), which makes the managerial enactment of Routine Dynamics possible.

29.3.5 Managers Are Mobilizing and Enacting Management Routines

A more recent development in Routine Dynamics research builds on the different insights discussed with an explicit focus on what they mean for our understanding of management practice itself and identifies recurrent action patterns performed by multiple managers across multiple situations and sites, as well as over time as *management routines* (Grand, 2016). Studying strategizing routines as specific management routines is one promising direction for this research, which benefits from recent attempts in Strategy-as-Practice research (Golshorki et al., 2015; Vaara and Whittington, 2012) and studies of routines in the context of strategy making (Feldman, 2015; Grand, 2016; Grand and Bartl, 2019; Menuhin and McGee, 2001; Salvato and Rerup, 2011; see Seidl et al. [Chapter 35], in this volume).

In his study on the evolution of strategic management practice in a software company, for instance, Grand (2016) describes how management routines develop as specific organizational routines in the transition from a founder-oriented entrepreneurial management approach to an executive management-based governance model, which requires a coherent collective enactment of Routine Dynamics by the newly established executive management. In this case, the transition is not only characterized by new managerial engagements in Routine Dynamics across multiple situations and sites. Over time, managerial action patterns emerge into specific management routines, which are subsequently mobilized by the executive management to coherently enact Routine Dynamics. The emergence of these management routines is essential to enable aligned decision-making and resource allocation as a newly developed executive management.

Grand (2016) focuses on how management routines emerge from the situated managerial engagement in Routine Dynamics, without a systematic consideration by the managers involved. In a complementary study, Grand and Bartl (2019) describe how executive management is systematically and proactively changing its own repertoire of management routines over several years, in order to make new strategic moves possible. In their analysis of routine enactment and entrepreneurial agility in a large pharma corporation, the authors address an important research puzzle implied in how managers renew and change their own management routines, while at the same time mobilizing these routines in their everyday managerial activities. Building on Routine Dynamics research, the authors find that executive management recurrently enacts its own management routines by mobilizing specific settings, such as working on a policy paper, evaluating major businesses in a task force or experimenting with entrepreneurial initiatives. These settings are mobilized to inform current decision-making and resource allocation, but at the same time they also provide protected spaces for the executive management to experiment with its own ways of managing, which eventually become new or revised management routines.

29.4 Opportunities for Future Research

As this chapter shows, understanding how managers enact Routine Dynamics is an important research area in the Routine Dynamics research programme. At the same time, we can identify several opportunities for future research. On the one hand, we see opportunities in further deepening our understanding of Routine Dynamics and management practice, based on existing studies in the Routine Dynamics research programme. On the other hand, we also see opportunities in more systematically applying insights from a Routine Dynamics perspective to the study of management practice itself, management routines in particular.

A first important opportunity for future research is the more systematic study of *how the management of Routine Dynamics 'from within' and the reflection of Routine Dynamics relate.* Building on studies such as Nicolini (2012), Bucher and Langley (2016) and Dittrich et al. (2016) we might ask questions such as, What happens in the transition between engaging in Routine Dynamics 'from within' and systematically reflecting on Routine Dynamics? How does reflection on Routine Dynamics from a distance and in separate settings distinguish from reflection-in-action? How do zooming-in and zooming-out relate to each other, and which management practices are supportive of one or the other? How do specific management practices enable or protect managerial reflection on and experimentation with Routine Dynamics in this perspective?

A second important opportunity for future research is to systematically explore *how specific settings provide the necessary contexts, enabling conditions or 'hinterland' for the managerial enactment of Routine Dynamics*. Building on studies such as Bucher and Langley (2016), Korica et al. (2017) or Grand and Bartl (2019), we can ask questions such as, How do specific settings and boundary conditions shape routine dynamics and its managerial enactment? How can management practice create, mobilize and change such settings in order to protect, stabilize or advance specific routines, as well as organization-specific repertoires of routines? Can we systematically distinguish different types of settings, which allow managers to critically reflect on Routine Dynamics in specific ways, or to enable and protect systematic experimentation with alternative routines or performances of routines?

A third important area of development is the *study of management routines*: we see an increasing interest in addressing management practice and management routines from a Routine Dynamics perspective, especially also in relation to the Strategy-as-Practice research programme. Building on studies such as Salvato (2003), Salvato and Rerup (2011), Feldman (2015) and Grand (2016), we can ask questions such as, What are the preconditions for management routines to emerge, stabilize or change? How can management practice enact its own repertoire of practices and routines, while engaging in managerial activities? How can specific settings be mobilized which systematically enable and foster the stability and change of management routines?

A fourth important area of development is the *study of different types of managerial engagement* in Routine Dynamics (Korica et al., 2017; Nicolini, 2012). Building on studies such as Thévenot (2006), Feldman (2015), Grand (2016) or Grand and Bartl (2019), we can further differentiate how the managerial enactment of Routine Dynamics depends on the specific contexts and perspectives of engagement in which they take place: How does the managerial enactment of the performances of established routines differ from an engagement for developing new routines? How does the enactment of routines for speed or efficiency differ from enacting routines for variation or experimentation? How does management in Routine Dynamics differ depending on whether incremental or radical change is intended? Answering these questions can benefit from recent *studies of pragmatic engagement regimes* (Grand, 2016; Thévenot, 2006), which Feldman (2015) describes as 'oriented both normatively (to some kind of good) and practically (to some kind of reality)' (2015: 326).

Future research in these four areas will allow scholars to better understand how and why the proactive managerial enactment of Routine Dynamics is possible but also restricted, as well as to what extent management is rather indirect, orchestrating emergent routine patterns. A more systematic understanding of the boundary conditions for management practice to shape and advance organizational value creation and development through engaging in Routine Dynamics will also inform management practice from a Routine Dynamics perspective. At the same time, it will provide important perspectives for management studies, to explicitly address and better understand the organizational embeddedness of managerial activities.

References

Barnard, C. (1938). *The Function of the Executive*. Cambridge, MA: Harvard University Press.

Becker, M. C., Knudsen, T. and March, J. G. (2006). Schumpeter, Winter, and the sources of novelty. *Industrial and Corporate Change*, 15(2), 353–371.

Boltanski, L., and Thévenot, L. (1991). *De la justification. Les économies de la grandeur*. Paris: Gallimard.

Brown, J. S. and Duguid, P. (1991). Organizational learning and communities-of-practice: Toward a unified view of working, learning and innovation. *Organization Science*, 2(1), 40–57.

Brundin, E. and Melin, L. (2012). Managerial practices in family-owned firms: Strategizing actors, their arenas, and their emotions. In S. Tengblad, ed., *The Work of Managers: Towards a Practice Theory of Management*. Oxford: Oxford University Press, pp. 281–300.

Bucher, S., and Langley, A. (2016). The interplay of reflective and experimental spaces in interrupting and reorienting routine dynamics. *Organization Science*, 27(3), 594–613.

Chia, R. and Holt, R. (2009). *Strategy without Design. The Silent Efficacy of Indirect Action*. Cambridge: Cambridge University Press.

Cohendet, P. S. and Simon, L. O. (2016). Always playable: Recombining routines for creative efficiency at Ubisoft Montreal's video game studio. *Organization Science*, 27(3), 614–632.

Cunliffe, A. (2009). *A Very Short, Fairly Interesting and Reasonably Cheap Book about Management*, 2nd edition. London: Sage.

Czarniawska, B. (2008). *A Theory of Organizing*. Cheltenham: Edward Elgar.

D'Adderio, L. (2014). Replication dilemma. *Organization Science*, 25(5), 1325–1350.

D'Adderio, L. and Pollock, N., (2014). Performing modularity: Competing rules, performative struggles and the effect of organizational theories on the organization. *Organization Studies*, 35 (12), 1813–1843.

Danner-Schröder, A. and Geiger, D. (2016). Unravelling the motor of patterning work: Toward an understanding of the microlevel dynamics of standardization and flexibility. *Organization Science*, 27, 633–658.

Dittrich, K., Guérard, S. and Seidl, D. (2016). Talking about routines: The role of reflective talk in routine change. *Organization Science*, 27(3), 678–697.

Drucker, Peter (1967). *The Effective Executive*. New York: Harper & Row.

Farjoun, M. (2010). Beyond dualism: Stability and change as a duality. *Academy of Management Review*, 35(2), 202–225.

Feldman, M. S. (2000). Organizational routines as a source of continuous change. *Organization Science*, 11(6), 611–629.

Feldman, M. S. (2003). A performative perspective on stability and change in organizational routines. *Industrial and Corporate Change*, 12(4), 727–752.

Feldman, M. S. (2015). Theory of routine dynamics and connections to strategy as practice. In D. Golshorki, L. Rouleau, D. Seidl and E. Vaara, eds., *The Cambridge Handbook on Strategy as Practice*, 2nd edition. Cambridge: Cambridge University Press, pp. 317–330.

Feldman, M. S., D'Adderio, L., Dittrich, K. and Jarzabkowski, P. (2019). *Routine Dynamics in Action: Replication and Transformation*. Research in the Sociology of Organizations, Volume 61. Bingley: Emerald Publishing.

Feldman, M. S. and Orlikowski, W. J. (2011). Theorizing practice and practicing theory. *Organization Science*, 22(5), 1240–1253.

Feldman, M. S. and Pentland, B. T. (2003). Reconceptualizing organizational routines as a source of flexibility and change. *Administrative Science Quarterly*, 48(1), 94–118.

Feldman, M. S., Pentland, B. T., D'Adderio, L. and Lazaric, N. (2016). Beyond routines as things: Introduction to the special issue on routine dynamics. *Organization Science*, 27(3), 505–513.

Gherardi, S. (2006). *Organizational Knowledge: The Texture of Workplace Learning*. Oxford: Blackwell Publishing.

Golshorki, D., Rouleau, L., Seidl, D. and Vaara, E. (2015). *The Cambridge Handbook on Strategy as Practice*, Cambridge: Cambridge University Press.

Grand, S. (2016). *Routines, Strategies and Management: Engaging for Recurrent Creation 'At the Edge'*. Cheltenham: Edward Elgar Publishing.

Grand, S. and Bartl, D. (2019). Making new strategic moves possible: How executive management enacts strategizing routines to strengthen entrepreneurial agility. In M. S. Feldman, L. D'Adderio, K. Dittrich and P. Jarzabkowski, eds., *Routine Dynamics in Action: Replication and Transformation*. Research in the Sociology of Organizations, Volume 61. Bingley: Emerald Publishing, pp. 123–152.

Hendry, J. and Seidl D. (2003). The structure and significance of strategic episodes: Social systems theory and the routine practices of strategic change. *Journal of Management Studies*, 37(7), 955–977.

Howard-Grenville, J. A. (2005). The persistence of flexible organizational routines: The role of agency and organizational context. *Organization Science*, 16, 618–636.

Howard-Grenville, J. A. and Rerup, C. (2016). A process perspective on organizational routines. *The SAGE Handbook of Organization Process Studies*. Thousand Oaks, CA: Sage.

Jarzabkowski, P., Lê, J. K. and Feldman, M. S. (2012). Toward a theory of coordinating: Creating coordination mechanisms in practice. *Organization Science*, 23, 907–927.

Jarzabkowski, P. and Seidl, D. (2008). The role of meetings in the social practice of strategy. *Organization Studies*, 29(11), 1391–1426.

Jullien, F. (2005). *Conférence sur l'efficacité*. Paris: Presses Universitaires de France.

Korica, M., Nicolini, D. and Johnson, B. (2017). In search of managerial work: Past, present and future of an analytical category. *International Journal of Management Review*, 19, 151–174.

Latour, Bruno. (2005). *Reassembling the Social: An Introduction to Actor-Network-Theory*. Oxford: Oxford University Press.

Law, J. (2004). *After Method: Mess in Social Science Research*. Abingdon: Routledge.

Menuhin, J. and McGee, J. (2001). Strategizing routines in HSBC (UK). Paper Presented at the DRUID Nelson and Winter Conference, Aalborg, Denmark.

Mintzberg, H. (1971). Managerial work: Analysis from observation. *Management Science*, 18(2), 192–219.

Mintzberg, H. (1994). Rounding out the manager's job. *Sloan Management Review*, 36, 11–26.

Mintzberg, H. (2009). *Managing*. San Francisco: Berrett-Koehler.

Nicolini, D. (2009). Zooming in and out: Studying practices by switching theoretical lenses and trailing connections. *Organization Studies*, 30, 1391–1418.

Nicolini, D. (2012). *Practice Theory, Work and Organization*. Oxford: Oxford University Press.

Nicolini, D. and Monteiro, P. (2017). The practice approach: For a praxeology of organizational and management studies. In A. Langley and H. Tsoukas, eds., *The SAGE Handbook of Process Organization Studies*. London: Sage, pp. 110–126.

Noordegraaf, M. and Stewart, R. (2000). Managerial behavior research in private and public sectors: Distinctiveness, disputes and directions. *Journal of Management Studies*, 37, 427–443.

Parmigiani A. and Howard-Grenville, J. (2011). Routines revisited: Exploring the capabilities and practice perspectives. *Academy of Management Annals*, 5(1), 413–453.

Pentland, B. and Feldman, M. (2008). Designing routines: On the folly of designing artifacts, while hoping for patterns of action. *Information and Organization*, 18, 235–250.

Reckwitz, A. (2002). Toward a theory of social practices: A development in culturalist theorizing. *European Journal of Social Theory*, 5(2), 243–263.

Rerup, C. and Feldman, M. S. (2011). Routines as a source of change in organizational schema: The role of trial-and-error learning. *Academy of Management Journal*, 54, 577–610.

Rüegg-Stürm. J. and Grand, S. (2020). *Managing in a Complex World*. 2nd extended edition. Bern: Haupt.

Salvato, C. (2003). The role of micro-strategies in the engineering of firm evolution. *Journal of Management Studies*, 40(1), 83–108.

Salvato, C. (2009). Capabilities unveiled: The role of ordinary activities in the evolution of product development processes. *Organization Science*, 20(2), 384–409.

Salvato, C. and Rerup, C. (2011). Beyond collective entities: Multilevel research on organizational routines and capabilities. *Journal of Management*, 37(2), 468–490.

Sandberg, J. and Tsoukas, H. (2011). Grasping the logic of practice: Theorizing through practical rationality. *Academy of Management Review*, 36, 338–360.

Schatzki, T. R., Knorr Cetina, K. and von Savigny, E., eds. (2002). *The Practice Turn in Contemporary Theory*. London: Routledge.

Sele, K. and Grand, S. (2016). Unpacking the dynamics of ecologies of routines: Mediators and their generative effects in routine interactions. *Organization Science*, 27(3), 722–738.

Simon, H. A. (1996). *The Sciences of the Artificial*, 3rd edition. Cambridge, MA: MIT Press.

Sonenshein, S. (2016). Routines and creativity: From dualism to duality. *Organization Science*, 27(3), 739–758.

Tengblad, S. (ed.) (2012). *The Work of Managers: Towards a Practice Theory of Management*. Oxford: Oxford University Press.

Thévenot, L. (2001). Pragmatic régimes governing the engagement with the world. In T. R. Schatzki, K. Knorr Cetina and E. von Savigny, eds., *The Practice Turn in Contemporary Theory*. London: Routledge, pp. 56–73.

Thévenot, L. (2006). *L'action au pluriel. Sociologie des régimes d'engagement*. Paris: La Découverte.

Tsoukas, H. and Chia. R. (2002). On organizational becoming: Rethinking organizational change. *Organization Science*, 13(5), 567–582.

Turner, S. F. and Rindova, V. (2012). A balancing act: How organizations pursue consistency in routine functioning in the face of ongoing change. *Organization Science*, 23(1), 24–46.

Vaara, E. and Whittington, R. (2012). Strategy-as-practice: Taking social practices seriously. *Academy of Management Annals*, 6(1), 285–336.

Wenger, E. (1998). *Communities of Practice: Learning, Meaning, and Identity*. Cambridge: Cambridge University Press.

Zbaracki, M. J. and Bergen, M. (2010). When truces collapse: A longitudinal study of price-adjustment routines. *Organization Science*, 21(5), 955–972.

CHAPTER 30

Project-Based Temporary Organizing and Routine Dynamics

EUGENIA CACCIATORI AND ANDREA PRENCIPE

Projects are forms of organizing that have become increasingly common in recent decades. The ad-hoc and temporary nature of projects seemingly poses significant challenges to the patterning of activities into organizational routines. Yet, considerable research in Routine Dynamics has been carried out in project contexts. In this chapter, we show that projects and routines share some common characteristics and that acknowledging the project nature of routines as well as the organizational routine nature of projects offers significant opportunities for the advancement of Routine Dynamics research.

30.1 Introduction

In contexts as varied as consulting, movie making, software development and construction, work is carried out through projects. In these contexts, one of the key challenges of organizing is how to reconstitute often complex organizational processes in each new project (Birnholtz et al., 2007). The ensuing tension between the need to adapt to the unique circumstances of each project and the benefits associated with maintaining some degree of consistency across iterations provides a context that is uniquely suitable for research on themes at the core of the Routine Dynamics perspective, such as the balancing of pattern and variety; the relationships between routines and creativity (or at least customization); and how routines change (Feldman et al., 2016). Indeed, several papers that illuminate critical aspects of the dynamics of routines have been developed in empirical contexts in which projects feature pre-eminently (see Table 30.1 for examples).

Yet, because of their unique and ad-hoc nature, projects are often perceived as in tension with, if not the polar opposites to, routines. For instance, projects that are carried out one-off to change unsatisfactory ways of working can be seen as organizational tools that are alternatives to routines, a sort of rebalancing element in organizing (Obstfeld, 2012). However, many, if not most, projects, from new product development to construction, have a recurring nature in that organizations engage in them repetitively. We focus on this kind of projects in this chapter. We argue that, when projects recur, there is significant scope for the patterning of activities (i.e., making activities recognizable as instantiations of particular routines) and repeatability of those activities. Moreover, the distinction between what is a project and what is a routine becomes blurred. We will argue that acknowledging this blurring, and recognizing the project element in routines as well as the routine element in projects, provides significant opportunities to enhance further the understanding of the key themes at the centre of the current research agenda of Routine Dynamics (Feldman et al., 2016), as well as project-based temporary organizing (Bakker et al., 2016; Burke and Morley, 2016; Cattani et al., 2011).

In what follows, we first define projects and project-based environments. We then discuss how the conceptualization of routines in the Routine Dynamics literature highlights similarities between routines and projects. We then review opportunities to advance Routine Dynamics further.

We are grateful to Katharina Dittrich and Claus Rerup for a very supportive editorial process and for pointing us towards exploring the similarities between routines and projects.

Table 30.1 Examples of Routine Dynamics empirical studies in project-based contexts

Study	Context	Routine	Insights
Berente et al. (2016)	Double project context: Software implementation project in NASA. The space industry is a project-based context (e.g., Mars mission)	Procurement and project management routines	Routines can work as shock absorbers by dynamically adjusting to perturbations. Misalignments are stabilized locally, and this ensures that organizational level objectives can be achieved in the face of external variation in the environment.
Bertels et al. (2016)	Oil and gas industry, in which starting and operating a new extraction site constitutes a project.	Importation of a best practice external routine – the Operational compliance routine, 'which focused on employees' regular use of a new comprehensive database of regulatory compliance obligations and associated specific tasks' (574)	Cultural resources at firm level shape the process of importation so that the emerging routine resembles but is distinct from the original one. This happens through cultural work shaping the artifacts and expectations of the routine even prior to implementation, and then cultural resources being used to protect workaround and maintaining the integrity of the whole routine.
Blanche and Cohendet (2019)	Live performances–where each production represents a project	Transfer of a bundle of interconnected routines (choreographic, musical and design) constituting a ballet to be performed at a different location	The transfer process is guided by implicit metaroutines that are part of the professional culture; the sharing of the ostensive aspect of routine; and the attention to the original choreographer intent. These practices allow the innovation necessary to adapt to the local context while maintaining the artistic integrity of the show.
Cacciatori (2012)	Engineering design – PFI projects	Development of a new bidding routine for integrated procurement of government building in the United Kingdom	Multiple artifacts designed to work as a system to anchor the routine mediate the truce and problem-solving aspects. They connect different communities in problem-solving, while there is substantial activity by specific communities to position their own community artifacts as central to both routine execution and the knowledge accumulation process.
Cohendet and Simon (2016)	Videogame development	Changing the 'stage-gate' product development routine	The alteration of the balance between creativity and efficiency in a routine can be obtained by borrowing elements from other routines and recombining them with elements of the existing routines, with cross-fertilization between the ostensive and performative aspects of different routines.
D'Adderio (2003)	Automotive – NPD	New product development routine	The codification of knowledge into software changes the nature of knowledge and causes changes in routines in ways that are difficult to anticipate and might be counterproductive for cross-functional collaboration by emphasizing heterogeneity and incompatibilities of knowledge bases and practices.
D'Adderio (2008)	Automotive – NPD	Engineering 'freeze' routine during new product development	The relationship between procedures as artifacts and routines evolves across performances (and therefore across projects) through processes of framing (in which the routine is decontextualized and standardized); overflowing (in which elements that were discarded lead to workarounds) and reframing.

Table 30.1 ***(cont.)***

Study	Context	Routine	Insights
Danner-Schröder and Geiger (2016)	Emergency management (where each deployment following a disaster can be seen as an individual project)	Several routines (set-up of the basis of operation, triage, search, rescue . . .)	Participants describe certain routines as stable and others as flexible – while still recognizing a specific pattern for each routine across projects. These differences can be explained by the differences in the role of artifacts, training and modes of knowing in emphasizing workflow in one case or tasks and their possible recombinations in the other.
Deken et al. (2016)	Automotive – Innovation project aimed at developing a new business model	'Toll Gate' and 'Partner selection' routines.	How novel outcomes are reached at the intersection of interdependent routines, balancing the need to generate novel outcomes with the need to manage existing and novel, emerging interdependencies. This requires routines work that flexes existing routines to meet new circumstances, extends routines to new contexts or creates new routines. In turn, this work generates emergent consequences that need to be dealt with, providing the engine for routines dynamics.
Howard-Grenville (2005)	High-tech – Manufacturing process development project	Road-mapping routine	The balance of flexibility and persistence of routines is achieved through human agency (the intentions and orientations of individuals), and the organizational context in which routines are embedded.
Jarzabkowski et al. (2016)	Reinsurance – each reinsurance deal constitutes an individual project, tailored to the risk and the partners involved	Deal appraisal routine	Artifacts play an important role in connecting the deal appraisal routine with individual professional work, collective professional work and work at the industry level involving multiple professionals.
Rerup and Feldman (2011)	Research organization	Recruiting routine	Routines change through processes taking place at the intersection of trial and error processes and interpretive schemata. The processes of trial and error and learning are less homogeneous than previously thought, with different salience and dynamic of trial and error and learning associated with problems and questions.
Salvato (2009)	Design-intensive manufacturing	New product development routine	Individual agency and action is central in both generating variation and embedding it into routines so that it becomes routine change. Variation is produced during the performance of the NPD routine, and managers then play a key role in selecting successful variations and stably embedding them in successive performances.
Salvato and Rerup (2018)	Design-intensive manufacturing	New product development routine	The balance between the conflicting goals of design and efficiency is achieved through human agency in the form of regulatory actions. Regulatory actions emerge in response to problems and direct action towards either of the goals. Regulatory action includes 'splicing' (recombining activities and participants), 'activating' (switching on specific ad hoc actions, such as informal meetings), and 'repressing' (switching off specific actions).

Table 30.1 ***(cont.)***

Study	Context	Routine	Insights
Sele and Grand (2016)	University	Research projects routines	Innovation is the product of interconnected routines, whose generativity (both in terms of outcomes and Routine Dynamics) depends on how actants connecting them are recruited to support action. Actants recruited as mediators simply maintain connections, whereas as intermediaries they modify those connections.
Spee et al. (2016)	Reinsurance – each reinsurance deal constitutes an individual project, tailored to the risk and the partners involved	Deal appraisal routine	Actors achieve balance between flexibility and standardization by shifting the salience of the routines that intersect the focal routine, where each intersection can orient action towards patterns favouring either flexibility or standardization.
Schmidt et al. (2019)	New venture incubator	Prototyping routine	The incubator organization replicates the prototyping routine across all its entrepreneurial ventures. The prototyping routine is embedded in an ecology of routines that accelerate its deployment across ventures by unburdening the core innovation process.

30.2 Projects and Temporary Organizing

30.2.1 Definition

There are multiple definitions of projects in the literature, but most can be summarized around the idea that projects are organizational arrangements set up to achieve a predetermined objective within an assigned time frame (Grabher, 2002b).[1] Thus, two characteristics define a project: a relatively well-defined and specific objective (for instance: launching a specific new product or filming a specific movie); and an 'institutionalized termination' (Lundin and Söderholm, 1995), so that achieving the project's objectives implies the disbanding of the project entity. In practice, there are of course exceptions. For instance, a successful product development team can be kept together over multiple product launches (Maurer, 2010), and some projects have lifespans that might extend into the decades (Davies et al., 2009; Davies et al., 2014; van Marrewijk et al., 2016).

[1] For a review, see Brookes et al. (2017).

While organizations might set up ad-hoc and unique projects to deal with extraordinary circumstances, there are many situations in which organized activity is based around *recurring* projects. For instance, many organizations run a constant stream of new development projects at various lifecycle stages from idea generation to commercialization. Perhaps more significantly, there are entire industries in which the production process itself is carried out through projects, ranging from complex product and systems such as large design and engineering projects (e.g., Davies et al., 2011) to advertising (e.g., Grabher, 2002c) to movie making (e.g., Manning, 2005). We refer to these contexts as project-based, and to organizations that carry out their activities primarily through projects (such as, for instance, consultancies or construction firms) as project-based organizations (see also Gann and Salter, 1998). In this kind of context – where projects are undertaken recurrently – the combination of repetition (e.g., another film project) and diversity (e.g., different actors and a different set of specialized partners) offers significant potential for the advancement of the Routine Dynamics perspective.

30.2.2 Characteristics

The ad-hoc and temporary nature of projects has important implications for the way they operate.

30.2.2.1 The Traditional View of PBO: Discontinuity in Organizing

Much of the early literature on project-based and temporary organizing emphasized the *discontinuity* in organizing associated with the unique and temporary nature of projects. If projects exhibit one-off characteristics, participants confront the difficult task of 'learning from samples of one or fewer' (March et al., 1991) and a 'learning paradox', in which projects are good at generating knowledge but bad at preserving it and building on it (Bakker et al., 2011). Even when they may share some similarities, projects may be characterized by relatively long lifecycles, requiring that similar project activities are executed again only after long time intervals. In addition, the temporary and ad hoc nature of projects means that new individuals and organizations participate in each project and new relationships develop when a new project is started, which can increase barriers to learning from previous experience (Arthur et al., 2001; Bresnen et al., 2004; Gann and Salter, 2000; Hobday, 2000; Scarbrough et al., 2004; Swan et al., 2010). In short, the temporary nature of projects and their unique tasks makes them idiosyncratic social units, creating barriers to learning and replicability of solutions. The implication drawn by this literature was that achieving patterning and repeatability of activities at the project level entails significant complications. Projects, especially long-lasting ones, might well develop their own internal routines and routines might exist in the support activities that organizations run in the background to projects (Gann and Salter, 1998; Gann and Salter, 2000). However, there is not enough continuity in activities and actors to afford effective patterning and repeatability *across* projects. In this sense, each project is seen as organizationally unique.

30.2.2.2 Sources of Continuity in Project-Based Organizing

Subsequent literature provided a counterbalance to the emphasis on uniqueness and discontinuity of the early work, by highlighting that there is more continuity in project environments than initially meets the eye. This literature highlighted that 'no project is an island' (Engwall, 2003) and that organizing in projects is mostly about the tension that emerges 'between the autonomy requirements of project participants [and the project per se] and their embeddedness within organizational and inter-organizational "settings"' (Sydow et al., 2004: 1476). The embeddedness of projects in their context and the continuity this affords can in principle support organizational routines across project iterations.

Two major sources of continuity in project-based and temporary contexts have emerged in the literature, (1) firms or other types of formal organizations participating in the project and (2) the wider institutional context. Firms provide an extensive reservoir of management practices and routines that can be applied to the projects in which they participate (e.g., Grabher, 2004; Ibert, 2004; Stjerne and Svejenova, 2016), particularly when the project is mostly internal (such as in traditional new product development) or when inter-organizational projects take place around a 'hub organization' – organizations that recursively coordinate and integrate the activities of other actors (Starkey et al., 2000). Studies of project-based organizations have highlighted how the general ability to manage projects is an essential capability of firms operating in project environments (Lampel, 2001; Söderlund and Tell, 2009); and that there is a consistent and growing pressure for the standardization of project management tools that an organization uses across projects (Clegg and Courpasson, 2004; Ibert, 2004). Indeed, studies have shown that project-based organizations do develop routines across projects (Brady and Davies, 2004; Davies and Brady, 2000; Davies et al., 2018; Edmondson and Zuzul, 2016; Lampel and Shamsie, 2003; Swan et al., 2016; Tranfield et al., 2003) and that, in fact, the semi-autonomous nature of projects can make it more difficult for firms to change routines across all of their projects (Bresnen et al., 2005).

The second source of continuity is the institutional environment in which firms operate. This has three major components. The first component is industry-wide expectations about how roles are performed within projects, and what the expected sequence of activities for the project is (Bechky, 2006; Bresnen et al., 2005; Grabher, 2002a, 2002c; Windeler and Sydow, 2001). Bechky's (2006) discussion of the film industry provides useful insights. There are clear expectations of what the role of the director entails (e.g., choosing and directing actors, translating the screenplay into images), and these are different from the expectations of, say, what a 'grip' will do (e.g., handle scene lighting, working with the electrical department and the photography director). Second, everyone is familiar with the broad sequence of activities in shooting a scene or making a movie. Third, these widespread expectations provide sufficient stability to make coordination possible but also make room for negotiating practices that allow the tailoring of the role to the specific circumstances of each project. The second component of the institutional environment is the thick social networks that support various aspects of project-based organizing (Grabher, 2002a, 2004). Of particular relevance to the study of routines is that social networks established through collaboration in previous projects may help in sustaining stable routines, either because actors know how the other person works from previous experience, or through word of mouth. Finally, there is often repeated collaboration among firms across a range of projects – a practice increasingly documented in the project-based literature (Ebers and Maurer, 2016; Eccles, 1981; Manning and Sydow, 2011; Schwab and Miner, 2008, 2011), and these arrangements support the development of routines across organizations and projects (Bygballe and Swärd, 2019).

30.3 Routine Dynamics and Projects

As mentioned previously, many studies within the Routine Dynamics perspective feature project-based contexts (see Table 30.1 for an overview of several studies in this area). These studies, read in conjunction with the literature on project-based organizing, provide a foundation to examine the relationship between projects and routines.

First, the Routine Dynamics literature reveals that routines, far from being the dual opposite of projects, share some characteristics with them. In particular, Routine Dynamics emphasizes the nature of routines as 'effortful accomplishment' (Feldman et al., 2016), aimed at carrying out a 'day-to-day operational "task"' (Rerup and Feldman, 2011: 584) such as, for instance, collecting garbage (Turner and Rindova, 2011), changing towels in hotel rooms (Bapuji et al., 2012), hiring (Rerup and Feldman, 2011), patrolling (Glaser, 2017) and shipping products (Dittrich et al., 2016). The name of each of these routines suggests its objective as well as giving some broad criterion for gauging when a routine performance is completed (the decisions of whom to hire has been reached or not for a given pool of candidates; towels have been changed, etc.). Thus, similarly to projects, routines also feature a specific goal and an end-point that makes reasonably clear when a performance of the routine is completed. Further, many routines also share with projects the challenge of relatively long time lags between performances, such as, for instance, routines for managing the accommodation of new students on campus (Feldman, 2000) and hiring (Rerup and Feldman, 2011). An excellent example here is Birnholz and colleagues' (2007) discussion of the annual regeneration of a summer camp that, despite very significant turnover in personnel, manages to maintain a sense of identity and continuity based on re-enacted routines. Explicit goal-orientation has important limitations in explaining action in routines (Dittrich and Seidl, 2018; Feldman, 2016). Yet, one reason why routines are effortful accomplishments rather than mindless repetitions is that actors are aware of the routine's goal and what they need to achieve to complete it, and will, therefore, deal knowledgeably and creatively with current circumstances to achieve that objective – even though this might, in the end, generate new goals for the routine (Dittrich and Seidl, 2018). Thus, it can be argued that an emphasis on the projectual nature of routines is inherent in the Routine Dynamics approach, and it is integral to its core themes. An excellent example of this is the case of emergency management, in particular tasks such as search and rescue, in which the whole routine architecture (artifacts, training and knowledge) is set up to make sure that routines participants can recombine and adapt elements of the routine in the way most suited to the achievement of the task (Danner-Schröder and Geiger, 2016).

Second, the Routine Dynamics perspective understands routines as 'repetitive streams of situated "action", where situated action is embodied and partially "ad hoc"' (Feldman et al., 2016: 506). This approach emphasizes the tension between stability and change inherent in routinized behaviour (e.g., Aroles and McLean, 2016; Birnholtz et al., 2007; Turner and Rindova, 2011) and is similar to the most recent approach to projects, which sees them as negotiating a path between continuity and ad-hoc adaptations to changing circumstances. Indeed, there is a considerable body of Routine Dynamics research carried out in project environments. Examples include technology road-mapping for new product development (Howard-Grenville, 2005), new product development itself (Salvato, 2009; Salvato and Rerup, 2018), software implementation (Berente et al., 2016), video game development (Cohendet and Simon, 2016), emergency management (Danner-Schröder and Geiger, 2016), engineering design (Cacciatori, 2012) and innovation projects (Deken et al., 2016).

The literature on project-based organizing has emphasized that routines can develop either within a project or at the level of the organizations running the project (Bresnen et al., 2005; Gann and Salter, 1998, 2000), particularly when projects are largely internal or in contexts in which a 'hub' organization exists (e.g., Davies et al., 2018). Routine Dynamics research taking place in project contexts has typically examined firm-level routines and their performances across projects. This has provided an ideal setting to explore the situated, ad-hoc nature of action in routines, highlighting the role of agency (both human and non-human) and the nature of routines as effortful accomplishment as performances need to bridge and adapt to discontinuities in projects. This work shows that many of the discontinuities pointed out in the early literature on project-based organizing can be bridged through the knowledgeable and situated action of individuals, actions that coalesce into patterns that are recognizably the 'same' across projects. For instance, Salvato (2009) shows how managerial action is central in evaluating the action variations generated in the performances of NPDs, and then embedding successful variations into successive performances so that they become part of the pattern; Salvato and Rerup (2018) and D'Adderio (2014) show how standardization and flexibility, and attending to different goals, can be maintained through regulatory action in NPDs and actors' sequential attention to different objectives during routines replication projects, respectively; Spee and colleagues (2016) and Sele and Grand (2016) investigate how actors (both human and non-human) juggle the intersection of routines, emphasizing different elements of the routines, to produce either variation and innovation or stability in research projects and reinsurance deal-making, respectively.

Overall, the Routine Dynamics literature in project-contexts has provided a convincing account of how routines that are redeployed across projects are not merely one way in which continuity across projects can be achieved. Rather, routines are themselves core processes through which continuity and adaptation can be achieved in project contexts, as they weave together the various sources of continuity, and human and material agency. For instance, Berente et al. (2016) show how routines act as shock absorbers, making sure that perturbations are resolved locally in order to achieve the overall objectives. Bertels and colleagues (2016) and Cohendet and Simon (2016) show how actors use cultural resources to repair local and global breakdowns, respectively, in a way that ensures that actions still display patterns that are recognizable across performances. Overall then, the need to account for the specific context of each project has helped to bring to the fore the generative tensions between patterns and performances, the role of human and material agency in mediating how these tensions are dealt with and reconciled, thereby affording significant advances in understanding routines as effortful accomplishment achieved by knowledgeable, reflective actors engaged in situated action (Feldman et al., 2016).

30.4 Opportunities for Routine Dynamics

The common elements between projects and routines, as well as the characteristics of project-based organizing, suggest rich opportunities to delve into some of the themes as the centre of the Routine Dynamics research agenda (Feldman et al., 2016).

Temporality. Because of their time-delimited nature, projects afford a unique opportunity to expand the emerging interest in the temporality of routines (Turner and Rindova [Chapter 19], this volume; Turner, 2014; Turner and Rindova, 2018). The body of research on temporality in projects, similarly to the routines literature, emphasizes the role of time orientation (towards the past, present or future) in balancing flexibility and standardization (Ligthart et al., 2016; Stjerne and Svejenova, 2016) and in mediating innovativeness (Lindkvist, 1998). Because projects exist at the intersection of multiple structures (e.g., the firm, the industry and the occupation), they can help in disentangling the role of the temporalities associated with each of these structures on the dynamics of routines, such as, for instance, temporalities associated with career trajectories, the project itself and the participating organizations; and between the clock and event times that each of these levels might employ. This could afford further exploration of the processes that mediate the generative tension between patterns and performances at the intersection of these distinct temporalities. Further, the investigation of time in Routine Dynamics might benefit from bringing to the fore the projectual nature of routines, and looking at routines as processes taking place within defined temporal boundaries. For instance, work in Routine Dynamics highlights the role of urgency (Turner and Fern, 2012), and a focus on routines as projects could help in unpacking how time boundaries interact with intentionality, in particular how timing interplays with means-end rationality (Dittrich and Seidl, 2018). Another promising research avenue that researchers have begun to explore is looking at how temporal boundaries within projects themselves influence the evolution of routines, and the role of transition across phases (Addyman et al., 2020).

The relationality of routines and networks of routines. Recent research has made significant progress in illuminating how different routines interact and intersect. With few exceptions (e.g., Bertels et al., 2016; Blanche and Cohendet, 2019; Jarzabkowski et al., 2016), the focus has been on the interaction of routines within the same organization (e.g., Deken et al., 2016; Sele and Grand, 2016; Spee et al., 2016). Project environments offer the opportunity to extend this understanding to how routines at different levels (e.g., at the level of the group, the organization, the occupation or the industry) and from different sources come to interact and shape action (Rosa, Bulgacov and Kresmer [Chapter 17], this volume). In particular, projects are relatively autonomous entities, and as such tend to develop their own specific routines. And because, as discussed previously, they draw resources from the broader social context in which they operate, projects might import routines from other levels, including occupational groups (Jarzabkowski et al., 2016), and industries (Bertels et al., 2016; Blanche and Cohendet, 2019). This richness has so far been largely left unexplored in Routine Dynamics, and it offers the opportunity to further understanding of the interaction of multiple sources of patterning, some of which are linked to the direct experience of participants with the routine in question in the specific social environment of a given project, while others come from various other forms and levels, including direct experience with how the same routine is enacted in different projects (e.g., developing a concept design for a building), and industry-wide expectations (both written and unwritten) of what the standard pattern is, and what the 'best practice' looks like. Project-based context would, therefore, offer a valuable context to explore the relationships between patterns originating from different levels, in this way furthering several themes that are relevant to Routine Dynamics, such as the development of a multilevel perspective (Salvato and Rerup, 2011); clarifying the relationships between routines and interpretive schemata (Rerup and Feldman, 2011); and between routines and their context (Howard-Grenville, 2005; Howard-Grenville and Lodge [Chapter 16], this volume). At the same time, such analysis could contribute to the literature on project-based organizing, helping to clarify further how projects navigate between autonomy and the need to fit into a broader institutional environment.

Materiality. Project-based contexts also offer unique opportunities to explore the role of artifacts in mediating Routine Dynamics, particularly through socio-material (D'Adderio [Chapter 7], this volume) and actor-network (ANT) perspectives (Sele [Chapter 6], this volume). Indeed, what evidence we have suggests that artifacts are essential in bridging the partial dissolution of social context linked to the termination of projects, and in sustaining the recreation of routines across projects, particularly in contexts where projects are coordinated by hub organizations (Cacciatori et al., 2012). Objects can provide the anchor for the re-enactment of processes even when they are no longer physically present (e.g., the flagpole at Camp Poplar Grove in Birnholtz et al. (2007)). Representations of products and representations of processes can be bundled to support patterning and repeatability across projects (Cacciatori, 2012), with coordination achieved within each project through 'cascades of representations' (Whyte et al., 2016). In the context of emergency management, which is akin to a project context, artifacts with different characteristics (representation of processes vs lists of tasks) help in reproducing routines with different levels of uncertainty (Danner-Schröder and Geiger, 2016). The modular and combinatorial nature of some artifacts, together with libraries of previous instantiations of a specific tool, provides resources that help in the customization of output while maintaining similarity in patterns (Cacciatori, 2008; Grabher, 2004). Further, artifacts appear to be key in connecting the various levels at which routines operate, bridging individual, project, organizational and industry levels (Cacciatori, 2008; Jarzabkowski et al., 2016). While much has been unpacked, much remains to be understood. We propose here two areas of particular interest for the study of how standardization and flexibility can balance. The first relates to the role of configurations of material objects, rather than individual objects. Objects are often linked to each other (Cacciatori et al., 2012; Scarbrough et al., 2015; Whyte et al., 2016), but we know relatively little about how these links are constructed, used and invoked in balancing standardization and flexibility. The second is the complementarity of objects and individual agents. Many objects are associated with specific occupations and professions, and professionals carry with them these objects, often personalized, from project to project. Indeed, over their career professionals build archives of previous solutions developed using a particular tool, and these provide resources they can draw on in new projects (Cacciatori, 2008). Because of the discontinuity of social relations and tacit understanding across projects, project environments constitute an ideal setting to investigate these issues.

Embodiment. The previous discussion also suggests the potential of a focus on the specific characteristics of project-based organizing in furthering the understanding of embodiment in Routine Dynamics. Embodiment, from the role of skills to the role of the body in shaping communication, is a central and yet underdeveloped element of routines (Blanche and Feldman [Chapter 25], this volume). Individuals, through their career trajectories across projects, are, together with artifacts, important sources of continuity in project-based organizing (Arthur et al., 2001; Bechky, 2006; Grabher, 2004, 2005). While routines themselves are sources of connectivity and understanding (Feldman and Rafaeli, 2002), project-based environments offer the opportunity to look at the reverse process – how connectivity and the shared understanding that individuals gain from operating in the same broad milieu can facilitate or hinder patterning across projects in the face of changing membership. Further, a focus on embodiment, possibly using habit as a mediating concept (Simpson and Lorino, 2016; Turner and Cacciatori, 2016), can help to move the discussion beyond cognition, towards a more holistic and embodied view of how patterns are recreated across routines.

30.5 Conclusions

This chapter has reviewed the main characteristics of organizing through projects when these goal-oriented and temporary structures are used in recurrent fashions. Each project is unique and idiosyncratic, while at the same time being embedded in a range of social structures that provide continuity. These characteristics of projects are shared by routines, which have a defined objective as well as a clear beginning and end. We have thus discussed how project contexts, as well as an approach that brings into sharper focus the project nature of routines, can help further understanding in contemporary themes in the Routine Dynamics approach, such as their relationality, their temporal dynamics and the role of artifacts. Additionally, using a routine dynamic perspective, our analysis does point to two inherent dimensions of the nature of projects: the patterned and recognizable nature of projects – i.e., projects are instantiation of previous activities – and their recurrent, repeatable nature. Both dimensions are at the basis of the continuity aspect of projects.

References

Addyman, S., Pryke, S. and Davies, A. (2020). Re-creating organizational routines to transition through the project life cycle: A case study of the reconstruction of london's bank underground station *Project Management Journal,* 51(5), 522–537.

Aroles, J. and McLean, C. (2016). Rethinking stability and change in the study of organizational routines: Difference and repetition in a newspaper-printing factory. *Organization Science*, 27(3), 535–550.

Arthur, M. B., DeFillippi, R. and Jones, C. (2001). Project-based learning as the interplay of career and company non-financial capital. *Management Learning*, 32(1), 99–117.

Bakker, R. M., Cambré, B., Korlaar, L. and Raab, J. (2011). Managing the project learning paradox: A set-theoretic approach toward project knowledge transfer. *International Journal of Project Management*, 29(5), 494–503.

Bakker, R. M., DeFillippi, R. J., Schwab, A. and Sydow, J. (2016). Temporary organizing: Promises, processes, problems. *Organization Studies*, 37(12), 1703–1719.

Bapuji, H., Hora, M. and Saeed, A. M. (2012). Intentions, intermediaries, and interaction: Examining the emergence of routines. *Journal of Management Studies*, 49(8), 1586–1607.

Bechky, B. A. (2006). Gaffers, gofers, and grips: Role-based coordination in temporary organizations. *Organization Science*, 17(1), 3–21.

Berente, N., Lyytinen, K., Yoo, Y. and King, J. L. (2016). Routines as shock absorbers during organizational transformation: Integration, control, and nasa's enterprise information system. *Organization Science*, 27(3), 551–572.

Bertels, S., Howard-Grenville, J. and Pek, S. (2016). Cultural molding, shielding, and shoring at oilco: The role of culture in the integration of routines. *Organization Science*, 27(3), 573–593.

Birnholtz, J. P., Cohen, M. D. and Hoch, S. V. (2007). Organizational character: On the regeneration of camp poplar grove. *Organization Science*, 18(2), 315–332.

Blanche, C. and Cohendet, P. (2019). Remounting a ballet in a different context: A complementary understanding of routines transfer theories. *Routine Dynamics in Action: Replication and Transformation (Research in the Sociology of Organizations, Volume 61)*. Bingley: Emerald Publishing Limited, pp. 11–30.

Brady, T. and Davies, A. (2004). Building project capabilities: From exploratory to exploitative learning. *Organisation Studies*, 25(9), 1601–1621.

Bresnen, M., Goussevskaia, A. and Swan, J. (2004). Embedding new management knowledge in project-based organizations. *Organisation Studies*, 25(9), 1535–1555.

Bresnen, M., Goussevskaia, A. and Swan, J. (2005). Organizational routines, situated learning and processes of change in project-based organizations. *Project Management Journal*, 36(3), 27–41.

Brookes, N., Sage, D., Dainty, A., Locatelli, G. and Whyte, J. (2017). An island of constancy in a sea of change: Rethinking project temporalities with long-term megaprojects. *International Journal of Project Management*, 35(7), 1213–1224.

Burke, C. M. and Morley, M. J. (2016). On temporary organizations: A review, synthesis and research agenda. *Human Relations*, 69(6), 1235–1258.

Bygballe, L. E. and Swärd, A. (2019). Collaborative project delivery models and the role of routines in institutionalizing partnering. *Project Management Journal*, 50(2), 161–176.

Cacciatori, E. (2008). Memory objects in project environments: Storing, retrieving and adapting learning in project-based firms. *Research Policy*, 37(9), 1591–1601.

Cacciatori, E. (2012). Resolving conflict in problem-solving: Systems of artifacts in the development of new routines. *Journal of Management Studies*, 49(8), 1559–1585.

Cacciatori, E., Tamoschus, D. and Grabher, G. (2012). Knowledge transfer across projects: Codification in creative, high-tech and engineering industries. *Management Learning*, 43(3), 309–331.

Cattani, G., Ferriani, S., Frederiksen, L. and Täube, F. (2011). Project-based organizing and strategic management: A long-term research agenda on temporary organizational forms. In *Project-Based Organizing and Strategic Management*. Bingley: Emerald Group Publishing Limited, pp. xv–xxxix.

Clegg, S. R. and Courpasson, D. (2004). Political hybrids: Tocquevillean views on project organizations. *Journal of Management Studies*, 41(4), 525–547.

Cohendet, P. S. and Simon, L. O. (2016). Always playable: Recombining routines for creative efficiency at Ubisoft Montreal's video game studio. *Organization Science*, 27(3), 614–632.

D'Adderio, L. (2003). Configuring software, reconfiguring memories: The influence of integrated systems on the reproduction of knowledge and routines. *Industrial and Corporate Change*, 12 (2), 321–350.

D'Adderio, L. (2008). The performativity of routines: Theorising the influence of artefacts and distributed agencies on routines dynamics. *Research Policy*, 37(5), 769–789.

D'Adderio, L. (2014). The replication dilemma unravelled: How organizations enact multiple goals in routine transfer. *Organization Science*, 25(5), 1325–1350.

Danner-Schröder, A. and Geiger, D. (2016). Unravelling the motor of patterning work: Toward an understanding of the microlevel dynamics of standardization and flexibility. *Organization Science*, 27(3), 633–658.

Davies, A. and Brady, T. (2000). Organisational capabilities and learning in complex product systems: Towards repeatable solutions. *Research Policy*, 29(7–8), 931–953.

Davies, A., Brady, T., Prencipe, A. and Hobday, M. (2011). Innovation in complex products and systems: Implications for project-based organizing. In *Project-Based Organizing and Strategic Management*. Bingley: Emerald Group Publishing Limited, pp. 3–26.

Davies, A., Frederiksen, L., Cacciatori, E. and Hartmann, A. (2018). The long and winding road: Routine creation and replication in multi-site organizations. *Research Policy*, 47(8), 1403–1417.

Davies, A., Gann, D. and Douglas, T. (2009). Innovation in megaprojects: Systems integration at London Heathrow Terminal 5. *California Management Review*, 51(2), 101–125.

Davies, A., MacAulay, S., DeBarro, T. and Thurston, M. (2014). Making innovation happen in a megaproject: London's crossrail suburban railway system. *Project Management Journal*, 45(6), 25–37.

Deken, F., Carlile, P. R., Berends, H. and Lauche, K. (2016). Generating novelty through interdependent routines: A process model of routine work. *Organization Science*, 27(3), 659–677.

Dittrich, K., Guérard, S. and Seidl, D. (2016). Talking about routines: The role of reflective talk in routine change. *Organization Science*, 27(3), 678–697.

Dittrich, K. and Seidl, D. (2018). Emerging intentionality in routine dynamics: A pragmatist view. *Academy of Management Journal*, 61(1), 111–138.

Ebers, M. and Maurer, I. (2016). To continue or not to continue? Drivers of recurrent partnering in temporary organizations. *Organization Studies*, 37(12), 1861–1895.

Eccles, R. G. (1981). The quasifirm in the construction industry. *Journal of Economic Behavior & Organization*, 2(4), 335–357.

Edmondson, A. and Zuzul, T. (2016). Teaming routines in complex innovation projects. In J. Howard-Grenville, C. Rerup, A. Langley and H. Tsoukas, eds., *Organizational Routines: How They Are Created, Maintained, and Changed*. Oxford: Oxford University Press.

Engwall, M. (2003). No project is an island: Linking projects to history and context. *Research Policy*, 32, 789–808.

Feldman, M. S. (2000). Organizational routines as a source of continuous change. *Organization Science*, 11(6), 611–629.

Feldman, M. S. (2016). Routines as process: Past, present, and future. In J. Howard-Grenville, C. Rerup, A. Langley and H. Tsoukas, eds., *Organizational Routines: How They Are Created, Maintained, and Changed*. Oxford: Oxford University Press, pp. 23–46.

Feldman, M. S., Pentland, B. T., D'Adderio, L. and Lazaric, N. (2016). Beyond routines as things:

Introduction to the special issue on routine dynamics. *Organization Science*, 27(3), 505–513.

Feldman, M. S. and Rafaeli, A. (2002). Organizational routines as sources of connections and understandings. *Journal of Management Studies*, 39(3), 309–331.

Gann, D. and Salter, A. (1998). Learning and innovation management in project-based, service enhanced firms. *International Journal of Innovation Management*, 2(4), 431–454.

Gann, D. and Salter, A. (2000). Innovation in project-based, service-enhanced firms: The construction of complex products and systems. *Research Policy*, 29(7–8), 955–972.

Glaser, V. (2017). Design performances: How organizations inscribe artifacts to change routines. *Academy of Management Journal*, 60(6), 2126–2154.

Grabher, G. (2002a). Cool projects, boring institutions: Temporary collaboration in social context. *Regional Studies: Special Issue on Production in Projects: Economic Geographies of Temporary Collaboration*, 36(3), 215–214.

Grabher, G. (2002b). Fragile sector, robust practice: Project ecologies in new media. *Environment and Planning A*, 34(11), 1911–1926.

Grabher, G. (2002c). The project ecology of advertising: Tasks, talents and teams. *Regional Studies: Special Issue on Production in Projects: Economic Geographies of Temporary Collaboration*, 36(3), 245–262.

Grabher, G. (2004). Temporary architectures of learning: Knowledge governance in project ecologies. *Organization Studies*, 25(9), 1491–1514.

Grabher, G. (2005, 6–7 January). Supporting projects, cannibalizing firms? *Personal knowledge networks in creative project ecologies*. Paper presented at the Third KGP Project Meeting. Copenhagen Business School.

Hobday, M. (2000). The project-based organisation: An ideal form for managing complex products and systems? *Research Policy*, 29(7–8), 871–893.

Howard-Grenville, J. A. (2005). The persistence of flexible organizational routines: The role of agency and organizational context. *Organization Science*, 16(6), 618–636.

Ibert, O. (2004). Projects and firms as discordant complements: Organizational learning in the Munich software ecology. *Research Policy*, 33, 1529–1546.

Jarzabkowski, P., Bednarek, R. and Spee, P. (2016). The role of artifacts in establishing connectivity within professional routines: A question of entanglement. In J. Howard-Grenville, C. Rerup and H. Tsoukas, eds., *Organizational Routines: How They Are Created, Maintained, and Changed*. Oxford: Oxford University Press, pp. 117–139.

Lampel, J. (2001). The core competencies of effective project execution: The challenge of diversity. *International Journal of Project Management*, 19(8), 471–483.

Lampel, J. and Shamsie, J. (2003). Capabilities in motion: New organizational forms and the reshaping of the Hollywood movie industry*. *Journal of Management Studies*, 40(8), 2189–2210.

Ligthart, R., Oerlemans, L. and Noorderhaven, N. (2016). In the shadows of time: A case study of flexibility behaviors in an interorganizational project. *Organization Studies*, 37(12), 1721–1743.

Lindkvist, L., Söderlund, J. and Tell, F. (1998). Managing product development projects: On the significance of fountains and deadlines. *Organization Studies*, 19(6), 931–951.

Lundin, R. A. and Söderholm, A. (1995). A theory of the temporary organization. *Scandinavian Journal of Management*, 11(4), 437–455.

Manning, S. (2005). Managing project networks as dynamic organizational forms: Learning from the TV movie industry. *International Journal of Project Management*, 23(5), 410–414.

Manning, S. and Sydow, J. (2011). Projects, paths, and practices: Sustaining and leveraging project-based relationships. *Industrial and Corporate Change*, 20(5), 1369–1402.

March, J., Sproull, L. and Tamuz, M. (1991). Learning from samples of one or fewer. *Organization Science*, 2(1), 1–13.

Maurer, I. (2010). How to build trust in inter-organizational projects: The impact of project staffing and project rewards on the formation of trust, knowledge acquisition and product innovation. *International Journal of Project Management*, 28(7), 629–637.

Obstfeld, D. (2012). Creative projects: A less routine approach toward getting new things done. *Organization Science*, 23(6), 1571–1592.

Rerup, C. and Feldman, M. S. (2011). Routines as a source of change in organizational schemata: The role of trial-and-error learning. *Academy of Management Journal*, 54(3), 577–610.

Salvato, C. (2009). Capabilities unveiled: The role of ordinary activities in the evolution of product development processes. *Organization Science*, 20(2), 384–409.

Salvato, C. and Rerup, C. (2011). Beyond collective entities: Multilevel research on organizational routines and capabilities. *Journal of Management*, 37(2), 468–490.

Salvato, C. and Rerup, C. (2018). Routine regulation: Balancing conflicting goals in organizational routines. *Administrative Science Quarterly*, 63 (1), 170–209.

Scarbrough, H., Panourgias, N. S. and Nandhakumar, J. (2015). Developing a relational view of the organizing role of objects: A study of the innovation process in computer games. *Organization Studies*, 36(2), 197–220.

Scarbrough, H., Swan, J., Laurent, S., Bresnan, M., Edelman, L. and Newell, S. (2004). Project-based learning and the role of learning boundaries. *Organization Studies*, 25(9), 1579–1600.

Schmidt, T., Braun, T. and Sydow, J. (2019). Copying routines for new venture creation: How replication can support entrepreneurial innovation. *Research in Sociology of Organizations*, 61, 55–78.

Schwab, A. and Miner, A. S. (2008). Learning in hybrid-project systems: The effects of project performance on repeated collaboration. *Academy of Management Journal*, 51(6), 1117–1149.

Schwab, A. and Miner, A. S. (2011). Organizational learning implications of partnering flexibility in project-venture settings: A multilevel framework. *Advances in Strategic Management*, 28, 115–145.

Sele, K. and Grand, S. (2016). Unpacking the dynamics of ecologies of routines: Mediators and their generative effects in routine interactions. *Organization Science*, 27(3), 722–738.

Simpson, B. and Lorino, P. (2016). Re-viewing routines through a pragmatist lens. In J. Howard-Grenville, C. Rerup and H. Tsoukas, eds., *Organizational Routines: How They Are Created, Maintained, and Changed*. Oxford: Oxford University Press, pp. 47–70.

Söderlund, J. and Tell, F. (2009). The p-form organization and the dynamics of project competence: Project epochs in asea/abb, 1950–2000. *International Journal of Project Management*, 27(2), 101–112.

Spee, P., Jarzabkowski, P. and Smets, M. (2016). The influence of routine interdependence and skillful accomplishment on the coordination of standardizing and customizing. *Organization Science*, 27 (3), 759–781.

Starkey, K., Barnatt, C. and Tempest, S. (2000). Beyond networks and hierarchies: Latent organizations in the UK television industry. *Organization Science*, 11(3), 299.

Stjerne, I. S. and Svejenova, S. (2016). Connecting temporary and permanent organizing: Tensions and boundary work in sequential film projects. *Organization Studies*, 37(12), 1771–1792.

Swan, J., Robertson, M. and Newell, S. (2016). Dynamic in-capabilities: The paradox of routines in the ecology of complex innovation. In J. Howard-Grenville, C. Rerup and H. Tsoukas, eds., *Organizational Routines: How They Are Created, Maintained, and Changed*. Oxford: Oxford University Press, pp. 203–234.

Swan, J., Scarbrough, H. and Newell, S. (2010). Why don't (or do) organizations learn from projects? *Management Learning*, 41(3), 325–344.

Sydow, J., Lindkvist, L. and DeFillippi, R. (2004). Project-based organizations, embeddedness and repositories of knowledge: Editorial. *Organization Studies*, 25(9), 1475–1489.

Tranfield, D., Young, M., Partington, D., Bessant, J. and Sapsed, J. (2003). Knowledge management routines for innovation projects: Developing a hierarchical process model. *International Journal of Innovation Management*, 7(01), 27–49.

Turner, S. F. (2014). The temporal dimension of routines and their outcomes: Exploring the role of time in the capabilities and practice perspectives. In *Time and Work*, volume 2. Abingdon: Routledge, pp. 125–155.

Turner, S. F. and Cacciatori, E. (2016). The multiplicity of habit: Implications for routines research. In J. Howard-Grenville, C. Rerup and H. Tsoukas, eds., *Organizational Routines: How They Are Created, Maintained, and Changed*. Oxford: Oxford University Press, pp. 71–95.

Turner, S. F. and Fern, M. J. (2012). Examining the stability and variability of routine performances: The effects of experience and context change. *Journal of Management Studies*, 49(8), 1407–1434.

Turner, S. F. and Rindova, V. (2011). A balancing act: How organizations pursue consistency in routine functioning in the face of ongoing change *Organization Science*, 23(1), 24–46.

Turner, S. F. and Rindova, V. P. (2018). Watching the clock: Action timing, patterning, and routine performance. *Academy of Management Journal*, 61(4), 1253–1280.

van Marrewijk, A., Ybema, S., Smits, K., Clegg, S. and Pitsis, T. (2016). Clash of the titans: Temporal organizing and collaborative dynamics in the Panama Canal megaproject. *Organization Studies*, 37(12), 1745–1769.

Whyte, J., Tryggestad, K. and Comi, A. (2016). Visualizing practices in project-based design: Tracing connections through cascades of visual representations. *Engineering Project Organization Journal*, 6(2–4), 115–128.

Windeler, A. and Sydow, J. (2001). Project networks and changing industry practices collaborative content production in the German television industry. *Organization Studies*, 22(6), 1035–1060.

CHAPTER 31 Self-Managed Forms of Organizing and Routine Dynamics

WALDEMAR KREMSER AND JUN XIAO

How to organize work is a topic at the core of Routine Dynamics, and studying novel forms of organizing constitutes a prime occasion for theory development. Though self-managed forms of organizing (SMOs) have held perennial interest by scholars and practitioners alike, contemporary SMOs are larger, and more rule-driven than their earlier counterparts. Our chapter provides a primer on contemporary SMOs and identifies key issues that a Routine Dynamics perspective can offer towards seeing, tracing and understanding contemporary SMOs.

31.1 Introduction

This chapter discusses how a Routine Dynamics approach can contribute to our understanding of self-managed forms of organizing (SMOs). SMOs rely on self-management to coordinate action, and are characterized by the extent to which they *decentralize authority* and foster *continuous coordinating* (M. Y. Lee and Edmondson, 2017; Pearce and Ravlin, 1987; Puranam et al., 2014). Examples are the long-known self-regulating work groups (Cohen and Ledford, 1994; Pearce and Ravlin, 1987), and more contemporary approaches such as Scrum (Schwaber and Beedle, 2002), Holacracy (Robertson, 2015), the Scaled Agile Framework (SAFe; Leffingwell, 2018), Sociocracy (Buck and Villines, 2017) and Teal Organizations (Laloux, 2014).

Existing studies on this topic already indicate that taking a Routine Dynamics perspective seems to be specifically useful for helping us understand key challenges in contemporary SMOs (Dönmez et al., 2016; K. Goh and Pentland, 2019; K. Goh and Rerup, 2018; Kremser and Blagoev, 2021; Lindkvist et al., 2017; Mahringer, 2019). It has proven helpful, among others, to zoom-in on how actors balance competing pressures that are typical for many SMOs (e.g., for stability and change, or creativity and familiarity) during situated performances of interdependent routines. A Routine Dynamics perspective has also shown promise when it comes to tracing situated actions to organizational outcomes, such as agility and innovation – both with the methodological (e.g., path-based analysis of routines) and conceptual tools (e.g., patterning) it has to offer.

Against this backdrop, the purpose of this chapter is to provide a resource for scholars wishing to leverage the Routine Dynamics perspective to study contemporary SMOs. It is structured into three sections. First, we begin with a primer on self-managed forms of organizing. Next, we discuss four key issues in contemporary research on SMOs – accomplishing agility and innovation; engaging in continuous coordinating; transforming into a SMO; and fostering a sense of purpose and satisfaction in individuals – to develop a research programme for Routine Dynamics scholarship. We conclude by summarizing how Routine Dynamics offers novel ways of seeing, tracing and understanding the distributed, complex and dynamic activities that constitute contemporary SMOs.

Both authors contributed equally and are listed in alphabetical order. This work was co-funded by the Erasmus+ programme of the European Union [2019-1-LI01-KA203-000169]: 'BPM and Organizational Theory: An Integrated Reference Curriculum Design'.

31.2 A Primer on Self-Managed Forms of Organizing

SMOs are not new. Starting in the 1950s, members of the famous Tavistock Institute undertook a series of studies in the British coal-mining industry that led to the first systematic studies on self-management (Bucklow, 1966; Trist and Bamforth, 1951). These studies illustrate what we consider to be the two constitutive features of SMOs: *decentralized authority* and *continuous coordinating*. Groups of up to forty coal miners shared the authority for planning all production operations of their shift, and 'management provided supporting services rather than direct supervision' (Bucklow, 1966: 72). At the same time and for the same reasons, coal miners engaged in continuous coordinating efforts. Miners could see what others were doing, and could consequently react by providing assistance, relief and control in a flexible and continuous fashion. 'Seeing what is going on around them, they can decide what they should be doing next, or be seen by others to be defaulting' (Emery, 1980: 25).

Empirical studies demonstrated positive effects of such SMOs on both individual outcomes, such as the reduction of job alienation and an increase in job satisfaction, and collective outcomes, such as group performance and innovativeness (Pearce and Ravlin, 1987). Ensuing scholarship also shed light on the limitations of giving groups the freedom and discretion to organize and structure their work (Langfred, 2000, 2004). For example, self-managed groups might develop restrictive norms that can be overbearing for individual autonomy (Barker, 1993), and might gradually restructure themselves in a way that minimizes collaboration (Langfred, 2000).

With the coming of the software industry – where organizations often work on highly complex tasks in a distributed way – the late 1990s and early 2000s saw further developments of SMOs. Two aspects of contemporary SMOs seem to stand out. First, we increasingly see successful examples of SMO implementations at a larger scale (Rigby et al., 2018). Organizations such as Zappos (Bernstein et al., 2016), ING (Jacobs, Schlatmann and Mahadevan, 2017), Morning Star (Gino and Staats, 2014), Valve (Puranam and Håkonsson, 2015) and Buurtzorg (Gray et al., 2015) have successfully implemented self-managed forms of organizing at the scale of hundreds of employees in dozens of teams. Second, contemporary SMOs tend to rely on specific sets of formal rules to guide organizing processes and practices that align with self-organizing principles. In what follows, we briefly describe two examples of such rule sets: Scrum for team-level SMOs, and SAFe for organizational-level SMOs.

31.2.1 Scrum

Scrum is an example of a contemporary SMO on the team level (see Figure 31.1). This framework relies heavily on formalization and standardization of critical parts of its organizing process in order to facilitate the self-managed adaptation of its roles, routines and artifacts (Schwaber and Sutherland, 2017). At its base, the completion of a Scrum project is organized as an iterative process. Each iteration is known as a Sprint, a set time box generally lasting one month or less, during which team members work together to produce an outcome of usable quality, known as an Increment. Each member of a Scrum team adopts one of three roles: the Product Owner, who is responsible for overall project content and quality, the Scrum Master, who supports process quality, or the Development Team Member, who holds the authority to (re-)organize work *during* each Sprint. Next, Scrum commonly

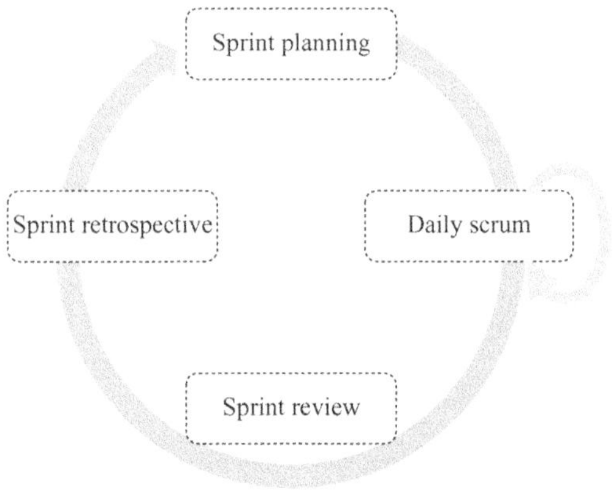

Figure 31.1 A typical Sprint iteration according to the Scrum framework

involves four different meetings which can also be conceptualized as organizing or meta-routines (Dönmez et al., 2016; Mahringer, 2019): (1) The Sprint Planning meeting to establish the main tasks and goals for that Sprint; (2) Daily Scrum meetings, where activities of team members are synchronized and the next 24 hours are being planned; (3) the Sprint Review meeting where at the end of each Sprint progress on the product is evaluated and the team's task list is updated; and (4) the Sprint Retrospective, where the Scrum team evaluates itself and each member makes suggestions on how to optimize the organizing process. In addition to Increments, the Scrum team leverages two important artifacts: the Product Backlog, a list of overall product features that the team ought to deliver, and the Sprint Backlog, a subset of tasks derived from the Product Backlog to be accomplished during a Sprint. Together, these artifacts establish an important connection between the organizing and production activities, or routines, of the Scrum team.

31.2.2 The Scalable Agile Framework (SAFe)

The Scalable Agile Framework (SAFe) – is an example of a contemporary framework for self-management suitable for larger organizations (Leffingwell, 2018). Used by over 70 per cent of US Fortune 100 enterprises (Scaledagileframework.com), SAFe describes how groups of Scrum teams and supporting functions might be organized in a self-managed way. At its baseline, work within organizations is structured along operational or development value streams. For example, a bank might define 'offering customer banking loans' as an operational value stream. Within these value streams, numerous longer-lived Scrum teams collaborate by forming a so-called Agile Release Train to deliver products, services or systems to its customers. As an indication, if a Scrum team consists of 5–9 members, an Agile Release Train can regroup 5–12 Agile teams, or 50–125 members. The Agile Release Train can be conceptualized as a 'team of teams'.

Work at the scale of an Agile Release Train poses additional coordination challenges. In order to organize work both within and among different value streams, SAFe specifies a set of roles, routines and artifacts that are structured to align with and scale those of Scrum. For example, because an Agile Release Train involves coordinated work among several Scrum Teams, a Release Train Engineer operates as a sort of 'Chief Scrum Master'. Just as Scrum teams work in iterations called Sprints (typically 2 weeks long), multiple Scrum teams within an Agile Release Train also work together in iterations called Program Increments (typically 10 weeks long) to deliver pieces of work. And, just as a Scrum team holds different meetings to plan, show and review their work and work processes, multiple Scrum teams of an Agile Release Train regularly meet for the same purposes. Some meetings involve representatives from each team (e.g., Scrum of Scrums), whereas others involve all members of the Agile Release Train (e.g., Program Increment Planning). Because these meetings involve more members and larger-scale objectives, they occur less often than Scrum team meetings. For instance, while the meetings of the Scrum team occur on a daily or bi-weekly basis, meetings at the Agile Release Train level range from a bi-weekly to quarterly basis.

31.3 Key Issues in Self-Managed Forms of Organizing

In this section, we delineate a research programme for Routine Dynamics scholarship on key topics surrounding contemporary SMOs. Using Lee and Edmondson's (2017) meta-analysis of SMOs as a starting point, we reviewed and selected four research areas that hold potential for future Routine Dynamics scholarship. These are: accomplishing agility and innovation, engaging in continuous coordinating, transforming into a SMO and fostering a sense of purpose and satisfaction in individuals. For each topic, we explain the research problem, survey existing studies where a Routine Dynamics perspective has produced first results (see Table 31.1) and highlight pathways for future research.

Table 31.1 Overview of Routine Dynamics research on SMOs

Source	Level of analysis	SMO issue
Dönmez, Grote and Brusoni (2016)	Team	Accomplishing agility and innovation; engaging in continuous coordinating
Goh and Pentland (2019)	Team	Accomplishing agility and innovation
Goh and Rerup (2018, conference proceeding)	Team	Accomplishing agility and innovation
Kremser and Blagoev (2020)	Team	Engaging in continuous coordinating
Lindkvist, Bengtsson, Svensson and Wahlstedt (2017)	Organization	Transforming into a SMO
Mahringer (2019, dissertation)	Team	Accomplishing agility and innovation; engaging in continuous coordinating; fostering a sense of purpose and satisfaction in individuals

31.3.1 Accomplishing Agility and Innovation

Perhaps the most important reason for the increasing interest in SMOs is that they promise to increase the agility of the respective work group, project or organization. This is because the combination of continuous coordinating and decentralized authority is believed to enable faster and more accurate local adaptations of work units (Felin and Powell, 2016). Moreover, SMOs are considered to help unleash creativity and innovation, as decentralizing authority could make self-managed work units more effective in harnessing ideas from individuals and faster in testing them out in practice (M. Y. Lee and Edmondson, 2017).

While there is some research on these issues for autonomous workgroups (Cohen and Ledford, 1994; Pearce and Ravlin, 1987) and agile project management methods (Dybå and Dingsøyr, 2008; G. Lee and Xia, 2010), we know less about larger SMOs and their organizational-level effects. In this area, empirical research is composed mostly of anecdotal evidence on a few prominent cases such as Valve (Felin and Powell, 2016; Foss and Dobrajska, 2015), Zappos (Bernstein et al., 2016) or Morning Star (Gino and Staats, 2014; Hamel, 2011). In addition, research has yet to address *how* outcomes such as agility, innovation and creativity are accomplished in practice and at scale.

31.3.1.1 RD Research: Balancing Competing Pressures to Accomplish Agility and Innovation

We have identified four empirical studies that explicitly take a Routine Dynamics perspective in understanding how outcomes of SMOs are accomplished (see Table 31.1). Dönmez et al. (2016) study Agile software development teams. They find that actors adopt different practices to balance the competing pressure for stability and flexibility. For example, actors engage in different forms of routine 'protection' and make use of temporal triggers in coordinating routines. Zooming in, Goh and Rerup (2018) analyse the role of time and space in balancing the competing pressures for flexibility and efficiency. They find that the temporal regularity of Scrum meetings plays a crucial part in this effort, because it creates a space to reconfigure routine actions. Zooming out, Goh and Pentland (2019) analyse how actions pattern change significantly over the course of a Scrum project, and in so doing elaborate on an important motor of ongoing change in routines: *patterning*. The fundamental openness of many goals in project-level SMOs constitutes a potential driver of such 'patterning work' (Danner-Schröder, 2016). Mahringer (2019) shows that actors explore project goals over time, thereby discovering emerging lacks and needs that, in turn, motivate actors to form new paths and dissolve of old ones.

31.3.1.2 Future Research: Understanding Larger SMOs by Tracing Actions to Outcomes

Our review shows that scholars have so far focused on the team- or project-level of analysis. We see ample room for research that looks at *larger* SMOs' efforts to accomplish organizational outcomes. Routine Dynamics research can help us bridge the micro- and macro-levels of analysis through tracing actions to outcomes. A specifically promising way is to analyse the digital traces that are often created through the performance of IT-enabled self-managed routines. For example, Scrum teams typically rely on software (e.g., JIRA, Axosoft) to monitor routine performances and to create Scrum artifacts, such as the product backlog. The methodological innovations that are currently emerging around path-based analysis of routines (K. T. Goh and Pentland, 2019; Hærem et al., 2015; Maringer and Pentland [Chapter 12], this volume; Pentland, Liu, Kremser and Haerem, 2020) offer an interesting way to trace such actions to outcomes. A path-based analysis of routines keeps the focus on specific performances, while also lending itself to both qualitative (e.g., why and how does the performance of specific paths in the Scrum of Scrums routine accomplish agility?) and quantitative (e.g., do more paths in the Sprint Planning routine lead to more or less innovation?) research on the agility and innovation of larger SMOs.

31.3.2 Engaging in Continuous Coordinating

SMOs can be distinguished from traditional forms of organizing, also with regards to how coordination takes place (Martela, 2019). Traditionally, coordination is chiefly accomplished through governance structures (re-)defined at the top of the hierarchy and implemented during *episodic* interventions, resulting in 'infrequent, discontinuous, and intentional' (Weick and Quinn, 1999: 365) changes in organizational structure. By contrast, SMOs usually require all members of the workgroup, project or organization to engage in *continuous* forms of coordinating. This involves small ongoing adjustments to the organization structure that might cumulate to create substantial change (see Brown and Eisenhardt, 1997; Weick and Quinn, 1999). And, because the nature of contemporary work often involves the accomplishment of complex and distributed tasks, ad-hoc forms of coordinating no longer suffice. Many SMOs have turned instead to 'detailed' and 'elaborate' governance frameworks (M. Y. Lee and Edmondson, 2017) – as illustrated previously with Scrum and SAFe.

More and more SMOs face the additional challenge of sustaining decentralized and continuous coordination as they scale their business. *Scaling* involves the process of synchronizing internal coordination with an organization's increased scale and scope of activities (DeSantola and Gulati, 2017). In this respect, there is little empirical research that addresses how the formal governance frameworks of contemporary SMOs are enacted in practice, which variations we find, why and with what effect. Specifically, scholars have commented on the need to understand how governance frameworks can help multiple self-managing workgroups to coordinate their efforts without having to rely on centralized authority (e.g., Ingvaldsen and Rolfsen, 2012; Rigby et al., 2018).

31.3.2.1 RD Research: Coordinating through Routine Performances

We have identified three empirical studies that explicitly take a Routine Dynamics perspective in exploring continuous coordinating in SMOs (see Table 31.1). First, Mahringer's (2019) study illustrates how organizing routines – such as those involved in the Scrum framework – continuously orchestrate the unfolding of other processes, such as innovation processes. Second, Dönmez et al. (2016) find that multiple self-managed routines can be coordinated through routine links, rather than centralized authority, via two specific mechanisms: triggering signals and information flows. Third, Kremser and Blagoev (2020) look at how role performances intersect with routine performances to explain how actors temporally coordinate multiple routines in the context of an agile consulting project without having to rely on a formal schedule.

31.3.2.2 Future Research: Governance Dynamics and Growing Pains

We have only scratched the surface on the ways routine participants coordinate and govern within and among multiple, self-managed routines. Our review highlights that Routine Dynamics scholars have so far used rather short observation intervals of several weeks or months and put an analytical focus on actors' ongoing and situated efforts to accomplish coordination among multiple, interdependent routines. We know much less about the governance dynamics that characterize SMOs. This could involve empirical research that uses longer observation intervals – multiple iterations rather than a few – and puts the analytical focus on the co-evolution of multiple, interdependent routines and networks or systems of formal governance rules. As such, the reliance on a complex set of formal governance rules in contemporary SMOs provides a great opportunity to study how routines and rules co-evolve in settings where rules are created by routine participants rather than by their superiors (see also Danner-Schröder and Geiger, 2016; M. Y. Lee et al., 2020). By corollary, SMOs also provide an opportunity to better understand how conflicts and truces (Salvato and Rerup, 2018; Zbaracki and Bergen, 2010) develop when authority is distributed.

The *scaling* of continuous coordination efforts represents another challenge that lends itself to be studied from a Routine Dynamics perspective. As SMOs grow, the addition and integration of a large number of different, yet interdependent routines increases the complexity of self-management (see Rosa, Kremser and Bulgacov [Chapter 17], this volume). In this regard, extant work on the morphology of single routines and clusters of interdependent routines (K. T. Goh and Pentland, 2019; Kremser and Schreyögg, 2016; Kremser et al., 2019; Pentland and Feldman, 2007) can help systematically reconstruct the SMO in a way that retains the perspective of the performing actors, all the while securing conceptual clarity and an analytical focus on the practical challenges of scaling. In addition, concepts such as interfaces (Kremser and Schreyögg, 2016) and boundaries (Kremser et al., 2019) direct our analytical attention to issues that arise *among* routines, which will become specifically prevalent at scale, when SMOs need to integrate a large number of different, yet interdependent routines.

31.3.3 Transforming into a Self-Managed Organization

Incumbent firms in industries ranging from healthcare (Bondarouk et al., 2018) to banking (Jacobs et al., 2017) are currently experimenting with the implementation of SMO governance frameworks. No matter in which industry, transforming from a traditional hierarchical organization into an SMO involves organizing challenges that are different from those confronted by SMOs as they grow (see earlier). What makes SMO transformations a special case is that great leadership at the top – usually an important success factor in all major change processes (Stouten, Rousseau and Cremer, 2018) – is essentially antithetical to this type of change. Or, as Gary Hamel put it, 'First, Let's Fire all the Managers!' (Hamel, 2011: 48). This departure from centrally orchestrated organizational change creates characteristic challenges such as the effects of SMO transformations for middle managers who are typically the first losers of such change processes (Dikert et al., 2016). The factors and dynamics that help or hinder transforming into SMOs remain largely underexplored (see also Emery, 1980).

31.3.3.1 RD Research: Integrating Contradictory Learning Processes in Contemporary SMOs

For Routine Dynamics scholars, extant studies on the integration of new routines into established organizations provide a strong baseline for studying organizational transformation (e.g. Bertels et al., 2016; Deken et al., 2016; Edmondson et al., 2001; Kremser and Schreyögg, 2016). When it comes to SMO transformations, we have identified only one Routine Dynamics study (see Table 31.1). Lindkvist et al. (2017) report on the case of Ericsson's Software Development Centre that changed from a traditionally designed organization engaged in large development projects with sometimes over 100 project members, into an agile organization with over 60, much smaller agile teams. Applying a Routine Dynamics perspective, the authors point us to the specific challenge of balancing bottom-up and top-down change efforts. Their analysis highlights the importance of two different trial-and-error-learning processes: (1) an 'offline', pull-directed learning process, taking place away from situated performances of operational routines and (2) an 'online', push-directed learning process more integrated within situated performances. By integrating these two learning processes, Ericsson was able to effectively manage its complex transformation process.

31.3.3.2 Future Research: Multiplicities and Cluster-Level Dynamics in SMO Transformations

We propose two touchpoints for future Routine Dynamics research on SMO transformations. First, the concepts of multiplicity (Feldman et al., 2016) and endogenous change (Feldman and Pentland, 2003) provide a starting point to unpack the process of SMO transformation. Since actors are less able to leverage the integrating power of centralized authority, SMO transformations are likely to be confronted with a multiplicity of different understandings regarding the nature of this transformation in terms of routines. Multiplicity therefore complicates the efforts to effectively influence the 'direction of endogenous change' (Feldman and Pentland, 2003: 115) of new and established routines, and might lead to unintended outcomes. For example, earlier cases have shown that transformations to SMOs might yield less, not more, control for each individual actor (Barker, 1993). Second, transforming into a self-managed organization inevitably involves facing differences between old and new routines. For example, there are conflicting logics between the organizing routines in a Scrum project and more traditional HR or finance routines. We therefore suggest bringing to the fore cluster-level dynamics (Kremser and Schreyögg, 2016), as they specifically concern the integration of new routines into established clusters of routines.

31.3.4 Fostering a Sense of Purpose and Satisfaction in Individuals

The impact of SMOs on individuals represents a key topic for scholars and practitioners for at least two reasons. First, the distribution of decision-making authority makes the commitment, motivation and well-being of each individual employee a top priority for SMOs. When each individual has the authority to change the organization's structure, it might become critical that employees share a high commitment to a common purpose (Adler and Heckscher, 2018). Second, a new generation with different work preferences and a different understanding of what a 'good life' constitutes enters the job market. To gain a competitive edge in the war for talent, firms increasingly adapt to the needs of millennials. This involves providing employees with workplaces that help them find meaning in their work (Hauw and Vos, 2010), and accommodating an increasingly diverse set of needs regarding the balance between work and private life (Rawlins et al., 2011).

Thus, a core puzzle in research on contemporary SMOs is to understand the effect of radical, organization-wide self-management approaches on key individual-level outcomes such as commitment, sharedness of purpose, job satisfaction, well-being and work–life balance. The few studies examining how Agile methods effects individuals (Dybå and Dingsøyr, 2008; Syed-Abdullah et al., 2006) have yielded mixed results. As individuals are called to learn, perform and navigate the elaborate SMO frameworks outlined earlier, Routine Dynamics constitutes a promising perspective to research the situated experiences of individuals in these contexts.

31.3.4.1 RD Research: Emotional Balancing of Competing Pressures

We have identified a single study regarding the situated experiences of individuals in SMOs. Mahringer (2019) shows the importance of emotions in helping routine participants engaged in Scrum software development projects (see Table 31.1). In his ethnographic study, Mahringer (2019) highlights how routine participants regularly exhibited negative emotional reactions, such as anger and confusion, during the performance of Scrum routines. When actors could balance these with positive reactions, this mechanism of *emotional balancing* smoothed team tensions, enabling the performance of multiple, interdependent routines. By noting that emotional components may not be separate from cognitive engagement, but rather underlie them (Grodal et al., 2015), this research advances extant work pointing to emotions as a bridge between routine performances and individual outcomes (see also Baldessarelli [Chapter 26], this volume), such as stress and job satisfaction.

31.3.4.2 Future Research: The Role of Individuals in Self-Managed Routines

There is ample space for future work on the interplay between self-managed routines and individual outcomes. Individuals throughout SMOs are bestowed the power to design, organize, innovate and strategize – actions that are usually consigned to managers. Individual motivation, personality differences and role relations among routine participants can therefore have a greater impact on routine outcomes. Conversely, self-managed routines can affect individual participants in varying ways. Addressing questions regarding the commitment and motivation of specific participants in such contexts thereby calls for a more holistic view of actors, one that surfaces the importance of 'specific actors who perform a routine, and their relationships with other specific participants' (Salvato and Rerup, 2018: 33).

If emotions constitute a first entry point to understanding individual-level dynamics in routines, the notion of roles might constitute a second conceptual point of entry to understand the dynamics of situated performances of self-managing routines and individual outcomes. Kremser and Blagoev (2020) introduce the notion of role-routine ecologies to provide a new way of seeing through the eyes of individual actors. Their study highlights how organizational members juggle work and non-work roles in the accomplishment of interconnected routines (see also Eberhard et al., 2019; Rosales, 2020).

31.4 Conclusion: Seeing, Tracing, and Understanding SMOs

In conclusion, we believe a Routine Dynamics perspective lends itself to exploring the workings of SMOs for three reasons: *seeing*, *tracing* and *understanding*. First, a Routine Dynamics perspective helps us in *seeing* important dynamics and patterns that are characteristic to SMOs. For instance, seeing contemporary SMOs as clusters of interdependent routines (Kremser and Schreyögg, 2016), as routine ecologies (Sele and Grand, 2016) or as role-routine ecologies (Kremser and Blagoev, 2020) can be helpful in describing different aspects of how work is organized under conditions of decentralized authority and continuous coordination. A Routine Dynamics perspective can also help us to better see different degrees of self-management in different 'locations' of the same organization. As Dönmez et al. (2016) point out, each routine can be said to be self-managing *to the extent* to which it is (re-)designed by the routine participants themselves. Future research can develop this line of thought in order to clarify the spectrum within which organizations are implementing self-management principles, and explore how variances in degrees of self-management affect the dynamics of larger patterns or organizational outcomes.

Second, a Routine Dynamics perspective can help us in *tracing* actions to larger patterns or outcomes. Routine Dynamics scholars make process visible by zooming in to the inner workings of routines – such as actions and connections between actions – and link them to the broader context by zooming out to clusters, ecologies, organizations and industries within which they are embedded (Feldman et al., 2016). As practitioners often view SMOs as means to increase project-level or organizational-level agility, and to improve individual level-outcomes such as commitment and job satisfaction (M. Y. Lee and Edmondson, 2017), research is required to clarify how and whether these goals are achieved. Putting action in the foreground allows Routine Dynamics scholars to understand how individual and organizational outcomes are accomplished in practice (K. T. Goh and Pentland, 2019).

Finally, with its epistemological roots in practice theory (see Feldman [Chapter 2], this volume), a Routine Dynamics perspective helps us *understand* how actors deal with tensions and competing pressures over time. Such dynamics are rife in SMOs. For example, actors are requested to be both creative and rule-abiding, and organizations are expected to regularly deliver innovations. These contradictory concepts can be unpacked by focusing on how routines are enacted. Seemingly opposite forces, such as stability and change (D'Adderio, 2014) or creativity and familiarity (Sonenshein, 2016), have already been untangled by Routine Dynamics scholars. A Routine Dynamics view therefore serves scholars wishing to understand such puzzles and paradoxes within SMOs through a focus on effortful and emergent accomplishments.

References

Adler, P. S. and Heckscher, C. (2018). Collaboration as an organization design for shared purpose. In L. Ringel, P. Hiller and C. Zietsma, eds., *Research in the Sociology of Organizations: Vol. 57. Toward Permeable Boundaries Of Organizations?* Bingley: Emerald Publishing Limited, pp. 81–111.

Barker, J. R. (1993). Tightening the iron cage: Concertive control in self-managing teams. *Administrative Science Quarterly*, 38(3), 408. https://doi.org/10.2307/2393374

Bernstein, E., Bunch, J., Canner, N. and Lee, M. (2016). Beyond the Holacracy Hype: The overwrought claims – and actual promise – of the next generation of self-managed teams. *Harvard Business Review*, 94(7/8), 38–49.

Bertels, S., Howard-Grenville, J. A. and Pek, S. (2016). Cultural molding, shielding, and shoring at Oilco: The role of culture in the integration of routines. *Organization Science*, 27(3), 573–593. https://doi.org/10.1287/orsc.2016.1052

Bondarouk, T., Bos-Nehles, A., Renkema, M., Meijerink, J. and Leede, J. de (2018). *Organisational Roadmap towards Teal Organisations* (Vol. 19): Bingley: Emerald Publishing Limited. https://doi.org/10.1108/S1877-6361201819

Brown, S. L. and Eisenhardt, K. M. (1997). The art of continuous change: Linking complexity theory and time-paced evolution in relentlessly shifting organizations. *Administrative Science Quarterly*, 42(1), 1–34. Retrieved from www.jstor.org/stable/2393807

Buck, J. and Villines, S. (2017). *We the People: Sociocracy: Consenting to a Deeper Democracy*, 2nd ed. Washington, DC: Info Press.

Bucklow, M. (1966). A new role for the work group. *Administrative Science Quarterly*, 11(1), 59. https://doi.org/10.2307/2391394

Cohen, S. G. and Ledford, G. E. (1994). The effectiveness of self-managing teams: A quasi-experiment. *Human Relations*, 47(1), 13–43. https://doi.org/10.1177/001872679404700102

D'Adderio, L. (2014). The replication dilemma unravelled: How organizations enact multiple goals in routine transfer. *Organization Science*, 25(5), 1325–1350. https://doi.org/10.1287/orsc.2014.0913

Danner-Schröder, A. (2016). Routine dynamics and routine interruptions: How to create and recreate recognizability of routine patterns. *Managementforschung*, 26(1), 63–96. https://doi.org/10.1365/s41113-016-0003-2

Danner-Schröder, A. and Geiger, D. (2016). Unravelling the motor of patterning work: Toward an understanding of the microlevel dynamics of standardization and flexibility. *Organization Science*. Advance online publication. https://doi.org/10.1287/orsc.2016.1055

Deken, F., Carlile, P. R., Berends, H. and Lauche, K. (2016). Generating novelty through interdependent routines: A process model of routine work. *Organization Science*, 27(3), 659–677. https://doi.org/10.1287/orsc.2016.1051

DeSantola, A. and Gulati, R. (2017). Scaling: Organizing and growth in entrepreneurial ventures. *The Academy of Management Annals*, 11(2), 640–668. https://doi.org/10.5465/annals.2015.0125

Dikert, K., Paasivaara, M. and Lassenius, C. (2016). Challenges and success factors for large-scale agile transformations: A systematic literature review. *Journal of Systems and Software*, 119, 87–108. https://doi.org/10.1016/j.jss.2016.06.013

Dönmez, D., Grote, G. and Brusoni, S. (2016). Routine interdependencies as a source of stability and flexibility: A study of agile software development teams. *Information and Organization*, 26(3), 63–83. https://doi.org/10.1016/j.infoandorg.2016.07.001

Dybå, T. and Dingsøyr, T. (2008). Empirical studies of agile software development: A systematic review. *Information and Software Technology*, 50(9), 833–859. https://doi.org/10.1016/j.infsof.2008.01.006

Eberhard, J., Frost, A. and Rerup, C. (2019). The dark side of routine dynamics: Deceit and the work of Romeo pimps. In M. Feldman, L. D'Adderio, P. Jarzabkowski and K. Dittrich, eds., *Routine Dynamics in Action: Replication and Transformation*. Bingley: Emerald Publishing Limited. *Research in the Sociology of Organizations*, Vol 61, pp. 99–121.

Edmondson, A. C., Bohmer, R. M. and Pisano, G. P. (2001). Disrupted routines: Team learning and new technology implementation in hospitals. *Administrative Science Quarterly*, 46(4), 685–716. https://doi.org/10.2307/3094828

Emery, F. (1980). Designing socio-technical systems for 'greenfield' sites. *Journal of Occupational Behaviour*, 1(1), 19–27. Retrieved from www.jstor.org/stable/3004061

Feldman, M. S. and Pentland, B. T. (2003). Reconceptualizing organizational routines as a source of flexibility and change. *Administrative Science Quarterly*, 48(1), 94–118. https://doi.org/10.2307/3556620

Feldman, M. S., Pentland, B. T., D'Adderio, L. and Lazaric, N. (2016). Beyond routines as things: Introduction to the Special Issue on Routine Dynamics. *Organization Science*, 27(3), 505–513. https://doi.org/10.1287/orsc.2016.1070

Felin, T. and Powell, T. C. (2016). Designing organizations for dynamic capabilities. *California Management Review*, 58(4), 78–96. https://doi.org/10.1525/cmr.2016.58.4.78

Foss, N. J. and Dobrajska, M. (2015). Valve's way: Vayward, visionary, or voguish? *Journal of Organization Design*, 4(2), 12. https://doi.org/10.7146/jod.20162

Gino, F. and Staats, B. R. (2014). *The Morning Star Company: Self-Management at Work* (Harvard Business School Case No. 914-013). Retrieved from https://hbsp.harvard.edu/product/914013-PDF-ENG

Goh, K. T. and Pentland, B. (2019). From actions to paths to patterning: Toward a dynamic theory of patterning in routines. *Academy of Management Journal*, 62(6), 1901–1929. https://doi.org/10.5465/amj.2018.0042

Goh, K. T. and Rerup, C. (2018). The Role of Space and Time in Balancing Conflicting Pressures through Routine Dynamics. *Academy of Management Proceedings*, 1, 14067. https://doi.org/10.5465/AMBPP.2018.172

Gray, B. H., Sarnak, D. O. and Burgers, J. S. (2015). *Home Care by Self-Governing Nursing Teams: The Netherlands' Buurtzorg Model* (The Commonwealth Fund publ. 1818 No. 14).

Grodal, S., Nelson, A. J. and Siino, R. M. (2015). Help-seeking and help-giving as an organizational routine: Continual engagement in innovative work. *Academy of Management Journal*, 58(1), 136–168. https://doi.org/10.5465/amj.2012.0552

Hærem, T., Pentland, B. T. and Miller, K. D. (2015). Task complexity: Extending a core concept. *Academy of Management Review*, 40(3), 446–460. https://doi.org/10.5465/amr.2013.0350

Hamel, G. (2011). First, let's fire all the managers. (cover story). *Harvard Business Review*, 89(12), 48–60. Retrieved from http://search.ebscohost.com/login.aspx?direct=true&db=bth&AN=67484173&site=ehost-live

Hauw, S. de and Vos, A. de (2010). Millennials' career perspective and psychological contract expectations: Does the recession lead to lowered expectations? *Journal of Business and Psychology*, 25(2), 293–302. https://doi.org/10.1007/s10869-010-9162-9

Ingvaldsen, J. A. and Rolfsen, M. (2012). Autonomous work groups and the challenge of inter-group coordination. *Human Relations*, 65(7), 861–881. https://doi.org/10.1177/0018726712448203

Jacobs, P., Schlatmann, B. and Mahadevan, D. (2017). ING's agile transformation. *McKinsey Quarterly, 2017*, 42–51.

Kremser, W. and Blagoev, B. (2020). The Dynamics of Prioritizing: Person-Roles, Routines, and the Emergence of Temporal Coordination in Complex Work Settings. *Administrative Science Quarterly*. https://doi/10.1177/0001839220948483

Kremser, W., Pentland, B. T. and Brunswicker, S. (2019). Interdependence within and between routines: A performative perspective. In M. S. Feldman, L. D'Adderio, K. Dittrich and P. A. Jarzabkowski, eds., *Research in the Sociology of Organizations: Vol. 61. Routine Dynamics in Action: Replication and Transformation*. Bingley: Emerald Publishing Limited, pp. 79–98.

Kremser, W. and Schreyögg, G. (2016). The dynamics of interrelated routines: Introducing the cluster level. *Organization Science*, 27(3), 698–721. https://doi.org/10.1287/orsc.2015.1042

Laloux, F. (2014). *Reinventing Organizations: A Guide to Creating Organizations Inspired by the Next Stage of Human Consciousness*, 1st ed. Brussels: Nelson Parker.

Langfred, C. W. (2000). The paradox of self-management: Individual and group autonomy in work groups. *Journal of Organizational Behavior*, 21(5), 563–585. https://doi.org/10.1002/1099-1379(200008)21:5<563::AID-JOB31>3.0.CO;2-H

Langfred, C. W. (2004). Too much of a good thing? Negative effects of high trust and individual autonomy in self-managing teams. *Academy of Management Journal*, 47(3), 385–399. https://doi.org/10.5465/20159588

Lee, G. and Xia, W. (2010). Toward Agile: An integrated analysis of quantitative and qualitative field data on software development agility. *MIS Quarterly*, 34(1), 87–114.

Lee, M. Y. and Edmondson, A. C. (2017). Self-managing organizations: Exploring the limits of less-hierarchical organizing. *Research in Organizational Behavior*, 37, 35–58. https://doi.org/10.1016/j.riob.2017.10.002

Lee, M. Y., Mazmanian, M. and Perlow, L. (2020). Fostering positive relational dynamics: The power of spaces and interaction scripts. *Academy of Management Journal*, 63(1), 96–123. https://doi.org/10.5465/amj.2016.0685

Leffingwell, D. (2018). *Safe Reference Guide: Scaled Agile Framework for lean Software and Systems Engineering : Safe 4.5. Always Learning*. Boulder, CO: Scaled Agile Inc; Pearson Addison-Wesley.

Lindkvist, L., Bengtsson, M., Svensson, D. M. and Wahlstedt, L. (2017). Replacing old routines: How Ericsson software developers and managers learned to become Agile. *Industrial and Corporate Change*, 26(4), 571–591. https://doi.org/10.1093/icc/dtw038

Lindvall, M., Muthig, D., Dagnino, A., Wallin, C., Stupperich, M., Kiefer, D., … Kahkonen, T. (2004). Agile software development in large organizations. *Computer*, 37(12), 26–34. https://doi.org/10.1109/MC.2004.231

Mahringer, C. (2019). *Exploring Routine Ecologies: A Characterization and Integration of Different Perspectives on Routines* (Dissertation). University of Stuttgart, Stuttgart.

Martela, F. (2019). What makes self-managing organizations novel? Comparing how Weberian bureaucracy, Mintzberg's adhocracy, and self-organizing solve six fundamental problems of organizing. *Journal of Organization Design*, 8 (1), 1–23. https://doi.org/10.1186/s41469-019-0062-9

Pearce, J. A. and Ravlin, E. C. (1987). The design and activation of self-regulating work groups. *Human Relations*, 40(11), 751–782. https://doi.org/10.1177/001872678704001104

Pentland, B. T. and Feldman, M. S. (2007). Narrative networks: Patterns of technology and organization. *Organization Science*, 18(5), 781–795. https://doi.org/10.1287/orsc.1070.0283

Pentland, B. T., Liu, P., Kremser, W. and Haerem, T. (2020). The dynamics of drift in digitized processes. *MIS Quarterly*, 44(1), 19–47. https://doi.org/10.25300/MISQ/2020/14458

Puranam, P., Alexy, O. and Reitzig, M. (2014). What's 'new' about new forms of organizing? *Academy of Management Review*, 39(2), 162–180. https://doi.org/10.5465/amr.2011.0436

Puranam, P. and Håkonsson, D. D. (2015). Valve's way. *Journal of Organization Design*, 4(2), 2–4. https://doi.org/10.7146/jod.20152

Rawlins, C., Indvik, J. and Johnson, P. (2011). Understanding the new generation: What the millennial cohort absolutely, positively must have at work. *IEEE Engineering Management Review*, 39(2), 56–60. https://doi.org/10.1109/EMR.2011.5876176

Rigby, D. K., Sutherland, J. and Noble, A. (2018). Agile at scale. *Harvard Business Review*. (May/June), 88–96.

Robertson, B. J. (2015). *Holacracy: The New Management System for a Rapidly Changing World*, 1st ed. New York: Holt.

Rosales, V. (2020). The interplay of roles and routines: situating, performances and patterning in the emergency department. *Journal of Health Organization and Management, ahead-of-print* (ahead-of-print). https://doi.org/10.1108/JHOM-12-2019-0342

Salvato, C. and Rerup, C. (2018). Routine regulation: Balancing conflicting goals in organizational routines. *Administrative Science Quarterly*, 63(1), 170–209. https://doi.org/10.1177/0001839217707738

Schwaber, K. and Beedle, M. (2002). *Agile Software Development with Scrum. Series in Agile Software Development*. Upper Saddle River, NJ: Prentice Hall.

Schwaber, K. and Sutherland, J. (2017). *The Scrum Guide: The Definitive Guide to Scrum:The Rules of the Game*. Retrieved from www.scrumguides.org/docs/scrumguide/v2017/2017-Scrum-Guide-US.pdf

Sele, K. and Grand, S. (2016). Unpacking the dynamics of ecologies of routines: Mediators and their generative effects in routine interactions. *Organization Science*, 27(3), 722–738. https://doi.org/10.1287/orsc.2015.1031

Sonenshein, S. (2016). Routines and Creativity: From Dualism to Duality. *Organization Science*. Advance online publication. https://doi.org/10.1287/orsc.2016.1044

Stouten, J., Rousseau, D. M. and Cremer, D. de (2018). Successful organizational change: Integrating the management practice and scholarly literatures. *The Academy of Management Annals*, 12(2), 752–788. https://doi.org/10.5465/annals.2016.0095

Syed-Abdullah, S., Holcombe, M. and Gheorge, M. (2006). The impact of an Agile methodology on the well being of development teams. *Empirical Software Engineering*, 11(1), 143–167. https://doi.org/10.1007/s10664-006-5968-5

Trist, E. L. and Bamforth, K. W. (1951). Some social and psychological consequences of the longwall method of coal-getting: An examination of the psychological situation and defences of a work group in relation to the social structure and technological content of the work system. *Human Relations*, 4(1), 3–38. https://doi.org/10.1177/001872675100400101

Weick, K. E. and Quinn, R. E. (1999). Organizational change and development. *Annual Review of Psychology*, 50(1), 361–386. https://doi.org/10.1146/annurev.psych.50.1.361

Zbaracki, M. J. and Bergen, M. (2010). When truces collapse: A longitudinal study of price-adjustment routines. *Organization Science*, 21(5), 955–972. https://doi.org/10.1287/orsc.1090.0513

Unexpected Events and Routine Dynamics

CHAPTER 32

DANIEL GEIGER AND ANJA DANNER-SCHRÖDER

32.1 Introduction

A central tenet of Routine Dynamics studies is that routines are *not* stable and mindless patterns of behaviour that are enacted only in stable and predictable environments (Feldman, 2000; Feldman and Pentland, 2003; Feldman et al., 2016; Salvato and Rerup, 2018). Seeing routines not as things that connect a known response with a specified output, but as 'effortful' (Pentland and Rueter, 1994: 488) and 'emergent' accomplishments (Feldman, 2000: 613) has opened up entirely new ways of understanding how enacting routines enables organizations to deal with novel and unexpected events. Various studies have shown that unexpected events do not necessarily result in a breakdown of routines because (human and non-human) actants are able to deal with these events by flexibly performing routines.

In this chapter, we review the Routine Dynamics literature in terms of its contribution to understanding the management of unexpected events. While the literature on crisis management has already pointed out the importance of routines in managing unexpected events, particularly in the context of high reliability organizations (Bigley and Roberts, 2001; Weick and Sutcliffe, 2007), many studies are still based on the more traditional understanding of routines as stable and mindless. As shown in the following sections, Routine Dynamics allows us to take a second look at some of the established wisdom on the role of routines in managing unexpected events. We have structured our review around four interrelated topics that are all grounded in practice and process theories and have been pointed out as central in the studies of unexpected events. The first part of this review outlines the contribution of Routine Dynamics to our understanding of flexible coordination in the face of the unexpected. This is followed by specific forms and aspects of coordinating flexibly, i.e., sense-making of unexpected events, mindfulness when dealing with unexpected events and improvisation during unexpected events. We conclude this review with suggestions for potential avenues for future research.

32.2 Flexible Coordination and Routines

Managing the unexpected is a common concern of organizations. They face the constant dilemma of stressing the importance of tight structuring, formal coordination and hierarchical decision-making so as not to be overwhelmed in crisis situations with the need to introduce flexibility into their systems in order to be able to react in a timely fashion to the unexpected (Bigley and Roberts, 2001; Faraj and Xiao, 2006). Research on Routine Dynamics is particularly helpful in addressing this paradox because routines are understood as sources of both stability and change (Feldman and Pentland 2003). Following this line of thought, Routine Dynamics studies provide important insights into how organizations can enact flexibility and change in the face of unexpected events. For example, in the study by Danner-Schröder and Geiger (2016) of an organization that provides technical assistance in catastrophes worldwide (particularly after earthquakes), it is shown how a shared understanding of action steps learned by actors during intensive training sessions builds the basis for the flexible enactment of routines. During these training sessions, actors learned how to perform specific routine actions. This knowledge enabled the emergency operators to select and recombine these action steps in novel ways to meet the situation at hand, thus enabling a flexible performance of routines (Danner-Schröder and Geiger, 2016: 652). Similarly, Okhuysen's (2005) study of SWAT teams shows how team members had a repertoire of different action steps that enabled the flexible performance of routines. For example, depending on circumstances, the performance of entering a building can be enacted in multiple ways: by blowing off the roof, entering through the window or using the front door (Okhuysen, 2005: 158).

A study by LeBaron et al. (2016) on the performance of handoff routines in an intensive care unit indicates that while physicians relied on anticipated moves and the expected sequence of how the handoff routine would unfold to ensure a recognizable performance, at the same time, each routine performance could be adapted to the unique needs of each patient. This study shows that the important factor in the ongoing coordination of routines was that actors either decided to conform or deviate from expectations, and that they made this decision visible to other routine participants. The ability to deviate from expectations in the performance of handoff routines provided the physicians with a high degree of freedom for flexible routine performances and allowed them to adapt routine performances to novel and unexpected situations.

In a recent study, Geiger, Danner-Schröder and Kremser (2021) explore how firefighters coordinated routines under temporal uncertainty, i.e., in situations where unexpected events occur frequently. Their study shows that firefighters ensured a reliable performance of routines in chaotic circumstances by sticking to a previously trained temporal sequence (rhythm) in the enactment of single routines. To flexibly adapt to novel situations, firefighters enacted temporal boundaries between routines (the transition between two distinct routines), which enabled them to adjust the performance of subsequent routines according to the specific situation. At these transition points, firefighters energized expectancy frameworks to make sense of the novel situation and to adapt the pace and sequence of subsequent routine performances. Hence, enacting pre-trained rhythms while performing single routines and adapting to specific circumstances by enacting temporal boundaries between routines enabled firefighters to balance the need for reliability and flexibility when facing unexpected events.

Hence, Routine Dynamics studies have revealed how routines are enacted flexibly in the face of unexpected events and how this flexible enactment can introduce flexibility into rather rigid systems, thereby balancing the need for flexibility and stability. While research on Routine Dynamics has provided important insights into how routine participants perform flexibly and reliably in the face of unexpected events, other important topics, such as sense-making, mindfulness and improvisation, which are central in the debate over the management of unexpected events, have not deserved similar attention by Routine Dynamics scholars so far. In the following sections, we outline how Routine Dynamics studies have already contributed to these topics and how related research on routines that builds on similar epistemological grounds has enriched our understanding of how routine participants deal with unexpected events.

32.3 Sense-Making and Routines

One of the central tenets in the debate over how actors deal with unexpected events is the notion of sense-making (Cornelissen et al., 2014; Rerup, 2009; Weick, 1993; Weick and Sutcliffe, 2007). Sense-making is the social process through which 'organizational members interpret their environment in and through interactions with others, constructing accounts that allow them to comprehend the world and act collectively' (Maitlis, 2005: 21). Scholars studying sense-making are concerned with processes of meaning construction and the way people extract cues and interpret events that appear surprising, complex or confusing (Cornelissen, 2012: 118). A large number of studies on sense-making have focused on disruptive episodes as a trigger for sense-making at the expense of more mundane and continuous forms of sense-making (Powell and Rerup, 2017; Sandberg and Tsoukas, 2015). In a comprehensive review of the literature, Maitlis and Christianson (2014: 70) outline three core aspects of sense-making: how events become triggers of sense-making; how intersubjective meaning is constructed; and the role of action in sense-making.

Traditionally, routines and sense-making have been discussed as opposing categories. Unexpected events are meant to interrupt the enactment of routines, thereby instigating a cognitive switch from routine to sense-making processes (Patriotta and Gruber, 2015: 1576). In this perception, routines are the starting point from which processes of sense-making are triggered. Or, as Weick, Sutcliffe and Obstfeld (2005: 411) put it, sense-making starts with noticing and bracketing deviations from routine performances. Here routines are important because they build the baseline for expected behaviour from which deviations become noticeable and hence instigate sense-making processes.

Although research on sense-making and organizational routines has focused on routines as a baseline from which deviations occur in unexpected situations and which lead to retrospective sense-making, research on Routine Dynamics has shifted our focus to in situ sense-making processes. Routine Dynamics studies point out that the performance of routines is not devoid of sense (Feldman and Pentland, 2003: 106). As Feldman and Pentland (2003: 106) argue, the ostensive aspects of routines serve a ' ... retrospective sensemaking function'. The ostensive aspects provide routine participants with a way to describe and understand what they are doing, and hence enable them to make sense of these activities. In a similar vein, in a qualitative study of an emerging research organization, Rerup and Feldman (2011) connect research on organizational interpretative schema and organizational routines. This connection allows them to point out that a change in the organizational schema, i.e., the way people make sense in organizations, is not a one-off singular event, but an ongoing process of trials and errors that is provoked by the effort to enact organizational routines (Rerup and Feldman, 2011: 605). Hence, sense-making is a continual process that cannot be decoupled from the performance of organizational routines. Routine performances create sense, and sense informs routine performances. Building on these insights, Patriotta and Gruber (2015), in their study of how a news organization deals with and makes sense of unexpected events, show how routines were central in creating and performing 'expectancy frameworks'. Expectancy frameworks, which became constituted through routine performances, are seen as important sense-making resources that allowed organizations to navigate transitions between planned and unexpected events (Patriotta and Gruber, 2015: 1586). Hence, these routine performances defined the baseline work expectation in a given setting and set boundaries that enabled organizations to give sense to flows of action. In particular, the ostensive aspects of routines are considered to be a resource for sense-making by providing expectations about the likely unfolding of actions (Patriotta and Gruber, 2015: 1587). Following this study, routines enable sense-making by setting expectancy frameworks and by ensuring synchronicity of actions in the face of unexpected events.

While not explicitly using a Routine Dynamics lens, but taking a closely related practice perspective, Rouleau (2005) was interested in understanding the micro dynamics of sense-making and sense-giving in the context of strategy making, where managers continuously deal with unexpected events. Using routines as a unit of analysis enabled her to study how micro activities are linked to macro actions and outcomes (Rouleau, 2005: 1419). Analysing three distinct routines (building a product and assigning it a symbolic meaning; calling clients; exploring the feel of the market), she shows how the enactment of routines combined sense-making and sense-giving at the micro and macro level through micro-practices (Rouleau, 2005: 1431). These micro-practices were enacted and re-enacted in the routine performances of middle managers, thereby bridging the micro and macro perspectives on sense-making. Rouleau's (2005) study makes the important argument that routine performances do not merely provide the frame against which sense-making takes place. Instead, enacting routines implies enacting sense. Thus, studying routines helps us to improve our understanding of how sense is enacted and how micro actions link to macro perspectives of sense-making.

Hence, as our review points out, Routine Dynamics studies make the convincing case that routines are not just setting baseline expectations against which sense-making happens. Instead, routine performances are sources for making sense of unexpected events and performing routines necessarily involves enacting sense.

32.4 Mindless and Mindful Routine Performance

Compared to the broader category of sense-making, mindfulness as a form of collective sense-making has received more scholarly attention in research on Routine Dynamics. Originating from psychological research, the notion of mindfulness versus unmindful or mindless action has received considerable attention in research on managing unexpected events, particularly in the realm of high reliability organizing. Weick and Sutcliffe (2007) stress that mindfulness is key in operating reliably in adverse settings. They have pointed to a number of antecedents and processes that contribute to mindfulness in organizations: the reluctance to simplify, sensitivity to operations, commitment to resilience, preoccupation with failure and deference to expertise. On the contrary, being mindless is often equated with automated behaviour, or, as Weick et al. (1999: 90) put it, ' ...when fewer cognitive processes are activated less often, the resulting state is one of mindlessness... without awareness that things could be otherwise'. Such mindless behaviour has traditionally been equated with routines (Ashforth and Fried, 1988), and routines are seen as the source of mindless behaviour. From such a perspective, the execution of routines happens automatically, i.e., in a mindless way, whereas a mindful action would be non-routine action.

However, from the perspective of Routine Dynamics, this dualism between mindful and mindless behaviour has received significant criticism (Levinthal and Rerup, 2006). In particular, Levinthal and Rerup's (2006) work has been instrumental in examining the complementarities and tensions of mindful and less-mindful processes by taking a Routine Dynamics perspective. The authors argue that the relationship between the ostensive and performative aspects of routines may be a useful way to understand the relationship between mindful and less-mindful processes in organizations. From this perspective, mindful and less-mindful processes are not distinct, but are, in the sense of a duality, interlinked on the performative and ostensive level (Salvato, 2009; Turner and Rindova, 2012). As per Levinthal and Rerup (2006), Routine Dynamics studies are particularly helpful in understanding how organizations make sense of and act on ambiguous stimuli. Dealing with ambiguous stimuli is a key challenge for organizations that operate in adverse environments where unexpected events are to be expected. Because environments provide stimuli that are far more varied than the existing routines for dealing with these stimuli, the response to the stimuli needs to be flexible and adaptive (Levinthal and Rerup, 2006).

Building on a comparable theoretical foundation, Weick and Sutcliffe (2006: 516) argue that if routines that have been unfolding mindlessly are interrupted by sudden and unexpected events, a void for reflection is created and that this void enables mindful action. In a more recent study, Bucher and Langley (2016) similarly point to the importance of reflective spaces in routine performances that enabled novel and more mindful routine performances. A study by Danner-Schröder (2016) revealed that actors changed the mode of communicating once the performance of a routine was interrupted: Routine participants switched from communicating while performing routines to talking about routines in an effort to overcome the interruption. Here, while performing routines, routine participants immediately switched from a comparatively mindless behaviour to a behaviour that is more mindful. Thus, to stipulate mindful behaviour, it is important that the discrepancy from expected stimuli and the subsequent response patterns become the centre of attention and that this discrepancy not be glossed over and immediately normalized (Weick and Sutcliffe, 2006: 519). Dittrich et al. (2016) developed the concept of reflective talk to unpack how routine performances stipulate reflexiveness and thus become the source of mindfulness. Following this line of thought, Routine Dynamics studies clearly point out that mindfulness and routine performances are not opposing but complementary perspectives (Levinthal and Rerup, 2006).

While Levinthal and Rerup (2006) stress that mindful actions enable flexible routine performances, related studies complement this perspective by arguing that mindful actions are sometimes necessary to protect routine performances from freewheeling and getting out of hand in turbulent settings. The study of emergency response teams by Danner-Schröder and Geiger (2016) indicates that mindful efforts of the members of the teams were required to orient routine performances towards a well-rehearsed standardized performance. This implies that acting mindlessly would have led to deviations from the standardized routine performance, and this would have threatened the safety and reliability of the entire emergency operation. Thus, maintaining the recognition of a stable workflow pattern requires mindful routine performances to avoid freewheeling and chaos.

Thus, this literature review shows that Routine Dynamics studies have significantly helped us in understanding that routines are not to be equated with mindless behaviour. On the contrary, routines are fundamental processes for stipulating mindful behaviours in organizations that are required to respond to unexpected events. Moreover, mindful and mindless behaviour are not dualisms but a duality; both mindful and mindless behaviour is enacted in performing routines.

32.5 Improvisation and Routines

Another aspect that has been identified as central in coping with unexpected events is the capability to improvise. Traditionally, improvisation is framed as an extraordinary and rare event that involves inventing new actions and practices (Cunha et al., 2017: 560). From such a perspective, acts of improvisation are explicitly non-routine, i.e., acts of improvisation are meant to break and overcome routinized behaviour. In this perspective, improvisation implies discarding routines and requires organizational actors to create novel and creative solutions to unforeseeable problems. Accordingly, performing routines would be the opposite of improvisation (Winter, 2003).

However, Routine Dynamics studies have significantly revised this understanding of routines and improvisation as dualisms. Instead, it is a central insight of Routine Dynamics studies that routine performances themselves are '... inherently improvisational' (Feldman and Pentland, 2003: 102). Interestingly, research on improvisation follows Routine Dynamics studies in taking a process lens, and defines improvisation as a process of '... reworking precomposed material and design in relation to unanticipated ideas conceived, shaped, and transformed under the special conditions of performance, thereby adding unique features to every creation' (Berliner, 1994: 241). Sometimes researchers of improvisation use the analogy of jazz to illustrate the peculiar relationship of structure and improvisation; wherein the underlying melody or the script used by musicians is the structure, and the way they leave this structure behind to create something new is improvisation (Cunha et al., 1999; Kamoche et al., 2003). In this analogy, structure is conceptualized as an enabler that musicians creatively 'play' against to obtain new interpretations of the existing script. The presence of this script in the mind of jazz players allows them to improvise and create something new in a flexible way (Kamoche et al., 2003). Cunha et al. (1999) compare this analogy with the metaphor of grammar used by Pentland and Rueter (1994) in their conceptualization of routines. An understanding of routines as grammar enables us to see how different elements of routines can be enacted and recombined in endlessly different ways in acts of improvisation.

This understanding of routines as grammar is used in Bechky and Okhuysen's (2011) study of unexpected events. They compared routine performances of two organizations that expect crises as part of their daily activities: film production crews and police SWAT teams. Although this study does not explicitly refer to Routine Dynamics, it nevertheless provides important insights that are consistent with Routine Dynamics studies by highlighting how routine participants improvise by enacting routines. As a part of their study, they examined how routine performances vary in flexibility, and explored how flexibility is harnessed in dynamic environments to account for changes in routine enactment (Bechky and Okhuysen, 2011: 256). The routine performances of the film production crews exhibited a high degree of flexibility. In contrast, the SWAT teams relied on the exact performance of routines in which they had been trained before (Bechky and Okhuysen, 2011: 259). Contrary to the performance of film crews, SWAT teams enacted improvisation by recombining different sub-elements of routines in novel ways, which allowed them to respond to unexpected situations. By comparing these two settings, the authors show that the visibility of work routines is a common and critical element that enables routine participants to respond to crises. They also show that different types of routine enactments may be used to cope with the unexpected. Due to the significant time pressure and severe danger, SWAT teams choose to reassemble existing routines that can be enacted in novel and improvisational ways without much need for discussion and reflection (Bechky and Okhuysen, 2011: 258). For film crews, the consequences of unexpected events were less dire and the unexpected events felt less urgent. Hence, routine performances could be rearranged more fully, allowing more time for discussion and reflection (Bechky and Okhuysen, 2011: 259). In this context, improvisation entailed a completely different and novel enactment of routines that had not been rehearsed before.

Similarly, Baker et al. (2013) explicitly built on the Routine Dynamics literature to study how mental health care workers responded to the disruption of routine performances by Hurricane Katrina. The authors show how originally non-routine acts of improvisation that had to be enacted to overcome the disruption led to the emergence of entirely new patterns of actions that eventually became the new normal. In a similar vein, the study by Majchrzak et al. (2007: 156) of emergency groups spontaneously formed in response to disasters demonstrated that new routines may even evolve quickly from acts that are originally more improvisational in nature. Hence, considering the insights of Routine Dynamics studies, routines are more than the building blocks of improvisation in the sense of providing a repertoire of action. Instead, routines (patterns of actions) are always improvisational as routine participants respond to novel circumstances by enacting routines.

32.6 Avenues for Future Research

Our review has shown that there are already quite a few studies exploring routine performance in managing unexpected events. We believe that in the areas of crises, disasters, health epidemics and related rare events, where managing unexpected events is of pivotal importance, Routine Dynamics studies still have a lot to offer and can provide important insights.

Routine Dynamics studies can significantly enrich our understanding for addressing such grand challenges in two particular areas: First, by connecting sense-making studies with a temporal perspective, a topic that is gaining increasing attention in Routine Dynamics studies (see Turner and Rindova [Chapter 19], in this volume), and second by examining the dynamics of patterning that might lead organizations to edge into chaos or steer them into path dependence in the aftermath of unexpected events.

Short- and long-term perspectives in making sense of the unexpected: During disasters and situations of crisis, the sense-making efforts of involved participants are quite often focused on the short term (Cornelissen et al., 2014), thereby ignoring the long-term effects of such a short-term perspective (Ravasi et al., 2019). However, managing crises, particularly crises that extend over longer time periods, such as the SARS-CoV-2 pandemic or refugee crises, require connecting long- and short-term perspectives in efforts of sense-making (Danner-Schröder and Müller-Seitz, 2020). Routine Dynamics studies can significantly improve our understanding of how the long- and short-term efforts of sense-making are connected within and through routine performances. From Routine Dynamics studies, we learn that in performing routines, participants are connecting action steps (Feldman and Rafaeli, 2002), thereby enacting patterns of actions. While synchronizing their actions with a short-term focus, routine participants are able to reflect on the long-term patterns that evolve and emanate from these performances (Turner and Rindova, 2018). These insights can help us in studying how people cope with catastrophic and unexpected events such as floods or droughts in the short-term, while being mindful (or not) of the long-term patterns that emanate from actions such as deforestation. Routine Dynamics studies provide fruitful grounds for understanding how short-term sense becomes enacted and how it becomes coupled or decoupled from long-term sense-making patterns that might become the new normal after the immediate crisis has been overcome. As routine performances are the micro-level of what eventually becomes a pattern, Routine Dynamics studies can help us in disentangling different temporalities of sense-making in managing and working through unexpected events. The question of how routines enact new temporal structures of sense-making and/or are entrained to dominant temporal regimes of sense-making is important for understanding the long-term effects of short-term sense-making. Along this line of thought, the question of how short-term mindless actions often have devastating consequences in the long run needs to be examined. This is an important and interesting realm, especially in studies of climate change and its effects (Slawinski and Bansal, 2012). As outlined earlier, Routine Dynamics studies connect mindless and mindful behaviour and thus improve our understanding of the temporally interconnected and entangled nature of crises and disasters.

Tipping points, chaos and path dependence in managing unexpected events: As outlined earlier, Routine Dynamics studies have improved our understanding of how flexibility and stability can be balanced when facing unexpected events. We already know that organizations need to flexibly respond to novel situations and, at the same time, rely on standardized protocols (Spee et al., 2016). Shedding more light on this balancing act seems to be a worthwhile endeavour. Routine Dynamics studies could explore the emergence of specific tipping points that lead to the disruption of patterns and lead organizations to edge into chaos and unconstrained improvisation (Bigley and Roberts, 2001). We already know how routines emerge from patterns of actions and how they are sustained over time, but we lack empirical insights into the phenomena of breaking and dissolving of patterns in the face of crisis and unexpected events. To bridge this gap, Routine Dynamics scholars need to connect insights from patterning dynamics with studies of the potential outcomes of these patterns (Haerem et al., 2015). Studies of improvisation combined with Routine Dynamics have the potential to disentangle these dynamics and identify tipping points that allow organizations to successfully operate on the edge of chaos (Brown and Eisenhardt, 1998).

With organizations running the risk of edging into chaos when dealing with unexpected events, the opposite problem, a lock-in into path-dependent patterns (Sydow et al., 2009), is a significant threat to organizations when dealing with unexpected events. Interestingly, path dependence is often the outcome of flexibility and improvisation in the face of unexpected events (see Sydow [Chapter 36], in this volume). Routine Dynamics studies have the potential to improve our understanding of these dynamics in exploring how improvisational actions create patterns that eventually become sustained, stabilized and difficult to break in the aftermath of crisis and disaster response operations. This also raises questions related to tipping points: At which points do routine patterns become inert and difficult to break? How can we identify such tipping points within routine patterns? How do such tipping points emerge and how can they be avoided? Exploring these dynamics is also important to improving our understanding of how and why systems become inert and difficult to disrupt even when facing unexpected events.

As this review has illustrated, Routine Dynamics studies have already quite fruitfully contributed to our understanding of managing unexpected events. However, the full potential of Routine Dynamics studies has not yet been leveraged. While Routine Dynamics studies are progressing and refining their conceptual toolkit, studies of sense-making and improvisation are likewise taking a processual turn and thus complement Routine Dynamics studies quite fruitfully. Emanating from similar epistemological assumptions, their potential for studying the management of unexpected events from the perspective of routines is huge. The aforementioned research questions might be a catalyst for pushing the research in this direction.

References

Ashforth, B. and Fried, Y. (1988). The mindless of organizational behaviors. *Human Relations*, 41(4), 305–329.

Baker, N. D., Feldman, M. and Lowerson, V. (2013). Working through disaster: Re-establishing mental health care after Hurricane Katrina. *Disaster Medicine and Public Health Preparedness*, 7(3), 222–231.

Baker, T. and Nelson, R. (2005). Creating something from nothing: Resource construction through entrepreneurial bricolage. *Administrative Science Quarterly*, 50(3), 329–366.

Bechky, B. A. and Okhuysen, G. A. (2011). Expecting the unexpected? How SWAT officers and film crews handle suprises. *Academy of Management Journal*, 54(2), 239–262.

Berliner, P. F. (1994). *Thinking in Jazz: The Infinite Art of Improvisation*. Chicago: University of Chicago.

Bigley, G. A. and Roberts, K. H. (2001). The incident command system: High-reliability organizing for complex and volatile task environments. *Academy of Management Journal*, 44(6), 1281–1299.

Brown, S. L. and Eisenhardt, K. M. (1998). *Competing on the Edge: Strategy as Structured Chaos*. Boston: Harvard Business School Press.

Bucher, S. and Langley, A. (2016). The interplay of reflective and experimental spaces in interrupting and reorienting routine dynamics. *Organization Science*, 27(3), 594–613.

Cornelissen, J. P. (2012). Sensemaking under pressure: The influence of professional roles and social accountability on the creation of sense. *Organization Science*, 23(1), 118–137.

Cornelissen, J., Mantere, S. and Vaara, E. (2014). The contraction of meaning: The combined effect of communication, emotions, and materiality on sensemaking in the Stockwell Shooting. *Journal of Management Studies*, 51(5), 699–736.

Cunha, M. P., Cunha, J. V. and Kamoche, K. (1999). Organizational improvisation: What, when, how and why? *International Journal of Management Review*, 1(3), 299–341.

Cunha, M. P., Miner, A. S. and Antonacopoulou, E. (2017). Improvisation processes in organizations. In A. Langley and H. Tsoukas, eds., *SAGE Handbook of Process Organization Studies*. London: Sage, pp. 559–573.

Danner-Schröder, A. (2016). Routine dynamics and routine interruptions: How to create and recreate recognizability of routine patterns. *Managementforschung*, 26(1), 63–96.

Danner-Schröder, A. and Geiger, D. (2016). Unravelling the motor of patterning work: Toward an understanding of the microlevel-dynamics of standardization and flexibility. *Organization Science*, 27(3), 633–658.

Danner-Schröder, A. and Müller-Seitz, G. (2020). Temporal co-dependence between temporary and permanent organizing: Tackling grand challenges in the case of the refugee crisis in Germany. *Research in the Sociology of Organizations*, 67, 179–208.

Dittrich, K., Guérard, S. and Seidl, D. (2016). Talking about routines: The role of reflective talk in routine change. *Organization Science*, 27(3), 678–697.

Faraj, S. and Xiao, Y. (2006). Coordination in fast-response organizations. *Management Science*, 52(8), 1155–1169.

Feldman, M. (2000). Organizational routines as a source of continuous change. *Organization Science*, 11(6), 611–629.

Feldman, M. (2016). Routines as process: Past, present and future. In J. Howard-Grenville, C. Rerup, A. Langley and H. Tsoukas, eds., *Organizational Routines: How They Are Created, Maintained, and Changed: Perspectives on Process Organization Studies*. Oxford: Oxford University Press, pp. 23–46.

Feldman, M. and Pentland, B. (2003). Reconceptualizing organizational routines as a source of flexibility and change. *Administrative Science Quarterly*, 48(1), 94–118.

Feldman, M., Pentland, B., D'Adderio, L. and Lazaric, N. (2016). Beyond routines as things: Introduction to the special issue on routine dynamics. *Organization Science*, 27(3), 505–513.

Feldman, M. S. and Rafaeli, A. (2002). Organizational routines as sources of connections and understandings. *Journal of Management Studies*, 39(3), 309–331.

Geiger, D., Danner-Schröder, A. and Kremser, W. (2021). Getting ahead of time: Performing temporal boundaries to coordinate routines under temporal uncertainty. *Administrative Science Quarterly*, 66(1), 220–264.

Haerem, T., Pentland, B. T. and Miller, K. D. (2015). Task complexity: Extending a core concept.

Academy of Management Review, 40(3), 446–460.

Kamoche, K., Cunha, M. P. and Cunha, J. V. (2003). Towards a theory of organizational improvisation: Looking beyond the Jazz metaphor. *Journal of Management Studies*, 40(8), 2023–2051.

LeBaron, C., Christianson, M. K., Garrett, L. and Ilan, R. (2016). Coordinating flexible performance during everyday work: An ethnomethodological study of handoff routines. *Organization Science*, 27(3), 514–534.

Levinthal, D. and Rerup, C. (2006). Crossing an apparent chasm: Bridging mindful and less-mindful perspectives on organizational learning. *Organization Science*, 17(4), 502–513.

Maitlis, S. (2005). The social process of organizational sensemaking. *Academy of Management Journal*, 48(1), 21–49.

Maitlis, S. and Christianson, M. (2014). Sensemaking in organizations: Taking stock and moving forward. *Academy of Management Annals*, 8(1), 57–125.

Majchrzak, A., Jarvenpaa, S. L. and Hollingshead, A. B. (2007). Coordinating expertise among emergent groups responding to disasters. *Organization Science*, 18(1), 147–161.

Okhuysen, G. (2005). Understanding group behavior: How a police SWAT team creates, changes, and manages group routines. In K. D. Elsbach, ed., *Qualitative Organizational Research*. Greenwich, CT: Information Age, pp. 139–168.

Patriotta, G. and Gruber, D. A. (2015). Newsmaking and sensemaking: Navigating temporal transitions between planned and unexpected events. *Organization Science*, 26(6), 1574–1592.

Pentland, B. T. and Rueter, H. H. (1994). Organizational routines as grammars of action. *Administrative Science Quarterly*, 39(3), 484–510.

Powell, W. W. and Rerup, C. (2017). Opening the black box: Microfoundations of institutions. In R. Greenwood, C. Oliver, T. B. Lawrence and R. E. Meyer, eds., *The Sage Handbook of Organizational Institutionalism*. Thousand Oaks, CA: Sage, pp. 311–337.

Ravasi, D., Rindova, V. and Stigliani, I. (2019). The stuff of legend: History, memory and the temporality of organizational identity construction. *Academy of Management Journal*, 62(5), 1523–1555.

Rerup, C. (2009). Attentional triangulation: Learning from unexpected rare crises. *Organization Science*, 20(5), 876–893.

Rerup, C. and Feldman, M. (2011). Routines as a source of change in organizational schemata: The role of trial-and-error learning. *Academy of Management Journal*, 54(3), 577–610.

Rouleau, L. (2005). Micro-practices of strategic sensemaking and sensegiving: How middle managers interpret and sell change every day. *Journal of Management Studies*, 42(7), 1413–1441.

Salvato, C. (2009). Capabilities unveiled: The role of ordinary activities in the evolution of product development processes. *Organization Science*, 20(2), 384–409.

Salvato, C. and Rerup, C. (2018). Routine regulation: Balancing conflicting goals in organizational routines. *Administrative Science Quarterly*, 63(1), 170–209.

Sandberg, J. and Tsoukas, H. (2015). Making sense of the sensemaking perspective: Its constituents, limitations, and opportunities for further development. *Journal of Organizational Behavior*, 36, S6–S32.

Slawinski, N. and Bansal, P. (2012). A matter of time: The temporal perspectives of organizational responses to climate change. *Organization Studies*, 33(11), 1537–1563.

Spee, P., Jarzabkowski, P. and Smets, M. (2016). The influence of routine interdependence and skillful accomplishment on the coordination of standardizing and customizing. *Organization Science*, 23, 759–781.

Sydow, J., Schreyögg, G. and Koch, J. (2009). Organizational path dependence: Opening the black box. *Academy of Management Review*, 34(4), 689–709.

Turner, S. F. and Rindova, V. (2012). A balancing act: How organizations pursue consistency in routine functioning in the face of ongoing change. *Organization Science*, 23(1), 24–46.

Turner, S. F. and Rindova, V. P. (2018). Watching the clock: Action timing, patterning, and routine performance. *Academy of Management Journal*, 61(4), 1253–1280.

Weick, K. E. (1993). The collapse of sensemaking in organizations: The Mann Gulch Disaster. *Administrative Science Quarterly*, 38(4), 628–652.

Weick, K. E. and Sutcliffe, K. M. (2006). Mindfulness and the quality of organizational attention. *Organization Science*, 17(4), 514–524.

Weick, K. E. and Sutcliffe, K. M. (2007). *Managing the Unexpected - Resilient Performance in an Age of Uncertainty*. San Francisco: John Wiley & Sons, Inc.

Weick, K. E., Sutcliffe, K. M. and Obstfeld, D. (2005). Organizing and the process of sense-making. *Organization Science*, 16(4), 409–421.

Winter, S. G. (2003). Understanding dynamic capabilities. *Strategic Management Journal*, 24(10), 991–995.

PART IV

Related Communities of Thought

CHAPTER 33

Carnegie School Experiential Learning and Routine Dynamics

CLAUS RERUP AND BRYAN SPENCER

33.1 Introduction

This chapter focuses on the relationships and potential opportunities for deepening scholarly exchange between two research communities: The Carnegie School and Routine Dynamics. Although the theoretical connections between Routine Dynamics and Carnegie School experiential learning are substantial (e.g., Feldman, 2000; Rerup and Feldman, 2011; Salvato and Rerup, 2018) these connections are not fully appreciated (Kay, 2018; Koumakhov and Daoud, 2017). The Carnegie School is identified with a series of

> path-breaking books and papers written by Herbert Simon, James G. March, and Richard Cyert. ... In the 1950s and early 1960s, a group of interdisciplinary social scientists at the newly founded Graduate School of Industrial Administration at Carnegie Mellon University set about trying to develop a behavioral approach to understand how individuals and organizations act and make decisions in the real world. They developed a menu of insights that students of organizations now take as foundational ingredients. Concepts such as bounded rationality, satisficing, premises, aspiration levels, and standard operating procedures were developed to describe individuals and organizations acting in the face of the "uncertainties and ambiguities of life" (March and Simon, 1958: 2). The Carnegie School developed a rich, process-oriented understanding of how decision making takes place in organizations, drawing on ideas from cognitive science, economics, psychology, and sociology (Powell and Rerup, 2017: 315).

A noteworthy theme in the Carnegie School tradition is experiential learning (Anderson and Lemken, 2019; Gavetti et al., 2007; Gavetti et al. 2012), which is the change in an individual's or organization's knowledge that occurs as a function of experience (Argote, 2013). Experiential learning consists of three components,

> First, decision makers evaluate performance on a goal relative to a target or aspiration level rather than on an absolute scale. An aspiration level is a threshold between satisfactory performance and non-satisfactory performance .... An organization establishes this threshold by comparing its current performance to its historical performance as well as by a social comparison of its performance to other organizations ... . Second, ... decision makers seek performance outcomes relative to aspirations that are sufficiently good so as to constitute 'success'. When performance is below the aspiration level, the decision maker engages in problemistic search to improve performance ... Third, problemistic search activities are situational because decision makers will first look for local solutions as to what to change before searching more broadly. The search will continue and expand until a solution that satisfies the aspiration level has been identified (Levinthal and Rerup, 2021: 530).

A central aspect of this form of learning is the way in which experience or performance outcomes vis-a-vis goals are encoded into organizational routines, and how organizations use the knowledge stored in routines to accomplish work (Nelson and Winter, 1982). Over time, as experience accumulates though learning, routines develop. For organizations to change as they gain

We gratefully acknowledge insightful feedback on earlier versions of the chapter from Brian Pentland and David Seidl, as well as many helpful suggestions from participants in the Handbook development PDW at the 2019 EGOS Colloquium in Edinburgh. We thank Frankfurt School of Finance and Management for financial support.

experience they need to adapt existing routines or learn new ones.

Given the centrality of experiential learning in the Carnegie School (Argote and Greve, 2007; Greve, 2003), we focus on how this form of learning provides an opportunity for deepening the relationship between the Carnegie School and Routine Dynamics. Experiential learning is central to Routine Dynamics because the flow and progression of routines emerge from experiential learning like processes of taking action, evaluating the results of those actions and, if necessary, making adjustments to future actions (Howard-Grenville and Rerup, 2017: 326). Some studies in Routine Dynamics trace the emergence, stability and change of routines by specifically zooming in on how actors take action, experience problems and make adjustments (Feldman, 2000; Rerup and Feldman, 2011; Salvato and Rerup, 2018). Based on this stream of research, we propose that experiential learning can be seen as a form of 'patterning', which is a central concept in Routine Dynamics (Feldman et al., 2016). The idea behind patterning is that patterns of routines are produced through actions. As noted by Feldman (2016: 38), '[m]utual constitution of performing and patterning, indeed, is necessary for ... the claim that routine dynamics produce both stability and change'. This focus could potentially shine a spotlight on topics within the Carnegie School (e.g., conflict, politics, interpretation, ambiguity, search) that are also important but currently remain largely unexplored within Routine Dynamics. Similarly, the promise of the Carnegie School to serve as micro-foundations in institutional theory (Powell and Rerup, 2017) could potentially improve by conceptualizing experiential learning as a process of patterning. This focus could highlight the role of routine actors, action and artifacts in shaping, maintaining and changing higher level patterns and structures such as institutions (Royer and Daniel, 2019).

The chapter unfolds as follows. First, we present a brief overview of some of the core ideas within each of the two communities. Second, we present the methodology that we used to review the literature on experiential learning and Routine Dynamics. Third, we review the literature and identify opportunities for each community to learn from the other. Research that combines experiential learning and routines draws on the Carnegie School in a superficial way, conceptualizing routines as entities rather than practices and processes. Because only limited research has linked experiential learning and Routine Dynamics, the chapter provides an opportunity for taking stock of what we know and offers an agenda for future work that focuses on how the two communities can use experiential learning to deepen theorizing within Routine Dynamics on interpretation and sensemaking, conflict, political contestation and truces.

33.2 Brief Overview of the Two Communities

The Carnegie School perspective highlights that to do their work members of organizations rely on routines learned from experience (Cyert and March, 1963; Levitt and March, 1988; March and Simon, 1958). Experiential learning occurs by adapting to performance feedback relative to goals, preferences or aspirations (Greve, 2003). Positive feedback leads to repetition of action (i.e., stability), whereas negative feedback initiates search (i.e., change). In this process, a stream of positive feedback establishes a trajectory of learning encoded into routines that provide a model for how to perform specific tasks, whereas a stream of negative feedback establishes a trajectory of learning driven by search for new routines. Building on this work, Nelson and Winter (1982: 14) defined organizational routines as 'regular and predictable behavior patterns of firms'. Feldman and Pentland (2003: 95) extended this work by defining routines as 'repetitive, recognizable patterns of interdependent actions carried out by multiple actors ... at specific times, in specific places'.

As noted in our introduction, experiential learning in the Carnegie School tradition revolves around three elements (Levinthal and Rerup, 2021): (1) goals, (2) problems and (3) actions. The origin of this model is *The Behavioral Theory of the Firm* (Cyert and March, 1963), where a model of simple reinforcement learning is presented. Beyond the presence of actors or decision makers, the model consists of three parts that capture the link between experienced performance and goals as a focal means for generating stability or change in organizations (Greve, 2003). First, actors accomplish work in organizations by participating in routines. They evaluate the performance of specific routines relative to aspirations, targets, preferences or goals. They determine the performance of their actions by matching current outcomes of the routine to historical outcomes as well as by comparing the local performance of the routine to the performance of the same routine in other organizations (Kacperczyk et al., 2015). Actors seek performance outcomes relative to goals that can be considered a 'success'. The actors face a 'problem' when a performance does not meet the goal or is unable to accomplish the task of the routine. Third, to address problems, actors take action to improve the performance of the routine. Scholars working in the Carnegie School tradition label such actions as problemistic search (Posen, Keil, Kim and Meissner, 2018).

As outlined by Feldman et al. in the Preface and Chapter 1 of this volume, the Routine Dynamics perspective can be traced back to the publication of several journal articles (Feldman 2000; Feldman and Pentland, 2003; Pentland and Rueter, 1994). Routine Dynamics is focused on how performances of a routine generate one or more patterns (Goh and Pentland, 2019). Here, we suggest that these patterns can be seen as emerging though a process of experiential learning. In effect, patterning = experiential learning. Consistent with a process perspective, routine outcomes are emergent (i.e., come into being only through specific performances) and generative (i.e., specific actions are capable of producing both stability and change) (Howard-Grenville and Rerup, 2017: 323). Students of Routine Dynamics have long emphasized the relationship between performances (specific actions and performances at specific times at specific places) and patterning (models of and for enacting routines) in constituting routines (Feldman, 2016). For instance, Pentland et al. (2012) emphasized how routines evolve by linking present and future performance to past performance. Similar to performance feedback in experiential learning processes, past performance can be replicated in present and future performances, which can deepen and stabilize the path of routines (Goh and Pentland, 2019). In addition, routine participants can deviate from past performance in present and future performance, which can change or shape a novel path of a routine. Each performance is an 'effortful accomplishment' (Pentland and Rueter, 1994) that can vary and thus move the routine in a direction of either stability or change (Howard-Grenville, 2005). From these principles it follows that experiential learning as well as patterning does not only lead to routine change; learning or patterning can also lead to routine stability (Feldman and Pentland, 2003). As we show later, it is therefore not surprising that 'stability and change' is a core research topic within both experiential learning (Argote and Greve, 2007) and Routine Dynamics (Feldman, 2000).

Given the broad process similarities that we have summarized in this section between Carnegie School experiential learning and patterning within the Routine Dynamics perspective, we were interested in understanding how the two communities have been connected in past research. Put differently, although the Routine Dynamics community focuses on patterning but does not use the term experiential learning, we wanted to understand if 'experiential learning' and the roots from the Carnegie School were incorporated and featured in research on Routine Dynamics.

33.3 Methodology of the Literature Review

In order to identify connections and opportunities for cross-fertilization between the two research communities we conducted a literature review. Specifically, when we use the term 'experiential learning' we refer to the type of organizational learning captured in the Carnegie School tradition. Using Feldman (2000) as a temporal marker, our literature review covered the period from 2000 to November 2019. We searched ISI/Web of Science for articles by using the generic search terms 'routine dynamics' and 'organizational learning'. As explained later, we then coded the articles to identify studies that drew on an experiential learning perspective. This search revealed 197 items. We excluded 38 items that were either written in other languages than English or were unpublished, conference abstracts or inaccessible. We excluded an additional 17 articles because they did not relate to the purpose of this chapter. We ended up with a final list of 142 published works for our analysis (72 per cent of the original sample of 197).

We downloaded all papers to code the content. First, we coded the articles by counting the number of total mentions of routines and learning in each article. This established a rough indicator of the article's relevance to the purpose of the chapter. Second, we established whether the authors used Routine Dynamics or another perspective (e.g., capabilities, organizational economics) to conceptualized routines. Similarly, we traced whether the authors cited Cyert and March (1963) and March and Simon (1958) and whether learning was conceptualized as an experiential process or used another perspective. To be more precise, we used a scale from one to ten to score how deeply each article was embedded within 'Routine Dynamics' and 'experiential learning in the Carnegie tradition'. With respect to Routine Dynamics, a number between one and five signalled that the authors adopted a traditional 'entity' conceptualization of routines, in which the inner workings of routines are black-boxed (Parmigiani and Howard-Grenville, 2011; Salvato and Rerup, 2011), whereas numbers between six and ten indicated that authors took a process or practice perspective on routines, inquiring into their dynamics (see Feldman et al. [Chapter 1], in this volume for detail). We used a similar approach to score how articles were drawing on the experiential learning approach in the Carnegie School.[1]

33.4 Review of Carnegie School Experiential Learning and Routine Dynamics

We created the heat map in Figure 33.1 to visualize the overlap between experiential learning and Routine Dynamics in the 142 articles. The concentration of white in the lower left corner shows that the existing literature has largely conceptualized routines as entities (e.g., capabilities) and conceptualized learning without drawing on the Carnegie School perspective in a substantial way. The darker shades show that some work has combined the Carnegie School and Routine Dynamics perspectives in different ways.

We were especially interested in capturing the work that most clearly linked experiential learning and Routines Dynamics. To do so, we created Figure 33.2, which is a heat map that captures articles that were rated six or above on each of the two scales. The scales in Figure 33.2 start at six and the figure visualizes how embedded the articles are in the experiential learning perspective of the Carnegie School and Routine Dynamics. After several iterations, we arrived at nine papers that were centrally concerned with experiential learning and Routine Dynamics. In the next section, we unpack some of the bridges that were established between experiential learning and Routine Dynamics in the nine papers.

[1] This combined scoring helped us to generate heat maps using ggplot2 in R (Wickham, 2016) and visualize how existing research has linked Routine Dynamics and experiential learning within the Carnegie School tradition. While the scoring and classification of papers is an inherently subjective process, expert grading of data is often used in medical and computer sciences, such as in image labelling, typically for the training of algorithms in order to obtain ground truth about the data (see 'Building the ground truth', 2019 for an overview). We attempted to reduce bias in two primary ways: First, we established the guidelines outlined earlier in which we would score the papers. The second author scored the papers first, in a random sequence. The first author then selected, at random, 10 per cent of the papers, without knowing the scores assigned by the second author. The first author then analyzed the papers in depth based on the scoring guidelines, and assigned a score based on the analysis and the guidelines laid out earlier. The authors then compared results of their scoring and classification, setting a threshold of ± 1 on each score. The results of the remaining 90 per cent of papers were then compared, using the 10 per cent set as a further reference point, to ensure consistency in the scoring process.

Figure 33.1 Heat-map of 142 papers

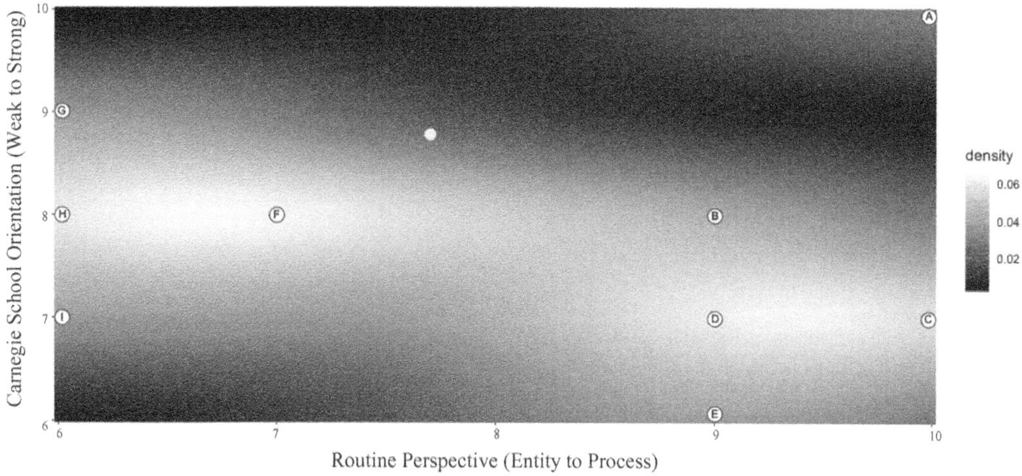

A	Rerup and Feldman (2011)
B	Miller, Pentland and Choi (2012)
C	Pentland and Feldman (2005)
D	Prashantham and Floyd (2012)
E	Mariano and Casey (2016)
F	Levinthal and Marino (2015)
G	Lazaric and Raybaut (2005)
H	Aggarwal, Posen and Maciej (2017)
I	Lyytinen, Rose and Yoo (2010)

Figure 33.2 Heat-map of nine papers

33.4.1 Bridging Experiential Learning and Routine Dynamics

How has experiential learning within the Carnegie School and Routine Dynamics been connected? What are the bridges across the two communities? As summarized in Table 33.1, we coded the nine articles in our sample with a 'paper type' code to indicate whether the paper was conceptual or empirical. Three papers used qualitative data (e.g., interviews, observations, case studies and archival material); two papers were conceptual; and four papers used simulations. We used a 'routine orientation' code to establish whether the paper took a Routine Dynamics perspective, inquiring into the dynamics of various parts constituting the routine, or an entity perspective, in which the inner working of the routine is black-boxed. Six papers used a Routine Dynamics perspective while three papers used an entity perspective, which suggests that both perspectives can be used to study experiential learning within the Carnegie School perspective.

We used a 'Carnegie School orientation' code to indicate how the papers were drawing on the experiential learning logic. Five papers were drawing strongly on experiential learning in the Carnegie School tradition while the remaining four papers were drawing on this logic in a medium to strong way. We applied a 'bridge across' code to indicate how the paper was bridging the two communities. Four papers were building strong micro-level bridges by using

Table 33.1 Overview of nine papers that connect experiential learning and Routine Dynamics

Authors	Paper type	Routine orientation	Carnegie School orientation	Bridge across	Theme 1: Change	Theme 2: Politics and conflict	Theme 3: Cognition
Pentland and Feldman (2005)	Conceptual	Routine Dynamics (strong)	Medium/ strong	Strong, micro-level	Strong	Medium	Weak
Lazaric and Raybaut (2005)	Simulation	Routine as entity	Strong	Weak, abstract, high-level	Strong	Strong	Strong
Lyytinen, Rose and Yoo (2010)	Qualitative	Routine as entity	Medium/ strong	Weak, abstract, high-level	Strong	NA	NA
Rerup and Feldman (2011)	Qualitative	Routine Dynamics (strong)	Strong	Strong, concrete, micro-level	Strong	Medium/ Strong	Strong
Prashantham and Floyd (2012)	Conceptual	Routine dynamics (strong)	Medium	Strong, micro-level	Strong	Medium	Strong
Miller, Pentland and Choi (2012)	Simulation	Routine Dynamics (strong)	Strong	Strong, abstract, high-level	Strong	NA	Strong
Levinthal and Marino (2015)	Simulation	Routine Dynamics (weak)	Strong	Strong, abstract, high-level	Strong	NA	NA
Mariano and Casey (2016)	Qualitative	Routine Dynamics (strong)	Medium	Strong, concrete, micro-level	Strong	NA	Strong
Aggarwal, Posen and Workiewicz (2017)	Simulation	Routine as entity	Strong	Weak, abstract, high-level	Strong	NA	Strong

either conceptual (Pentland and Feldman, 2005; Prashantham and Floyd, 2012) or qualitative techniques (Mariano and Casey, 2016; Rerup and Feldman, 2011). A micro-level bridge was established if the paper was unpacking how routines were tried out when actors were taking action; compared the outcomes of action to goals; and based on the success or failure of the outcomes engaged in either repeating or changing action going forward. One paper established a strong micro bridge at a more abstract level by using simulation techniques (Miller et al., 2012) while another simulation paper established a strong bridge at a more abstract level (Levinthal and Marino, 2015). The remaining three papers all used an entity perspective and built weak and abstract bridges at high levels of abstraction.

An overarching insight from the review is that very limited work has comprehensively and systematically used the experiential learning process to establish a bridge across the two communities. We picked two 'exemplars' (Rerup and Feldman, 2011 and Miller et al., 2012) from the sample to show how past research on Routine Dynamics has created strong micro-bridges between experiential learning and Routine Dynamics.

Exemplar 1: In a longitudinal, inductive study of the relationship between organizational routines and organizational schemata in a new research venture, Learning Lab Denmark (LLD), Rerup and Feldman (2011) unpacked the internal dynamics of hiring, tracing how both the performances and patterning of the hiring routine were linked to higher-level structures such as LLD's interpretive schema and the public university context in which LLD was housed. LLD's goal was to operate as a private-sector organization. When the public university blocked LLD from paying its employees 30–40 per cent more than in public universities, the employees of the Lab took several creative and experimental actions to address this 'problem', so they could continue hiring people at high salaries. The conflict between LLD's private-sector schema/goal and the public university setting was eventually aligned through a lengthy process of trial-and-error learning. By mapping the relationship between goals, problems and actions in Routine Dynamics, Rerup and Feldman (2011) used qualitative data to establish strong micro-level bridges between the two communities. The paper contributes to Routine Dynamics by using trial-and-error learning from the Carnegie School as the glue that aligns the high-level schema or goal of the Lab with the patterning of the hiring routine. The paper contributes to experiential learning by challenging three assumptions about trial-and-error learning that are central to the Carnegie School: (1) errors are largely homogeneous, (2) trials are primarily homogeneous and (3) heterogeneous errors and trials obstruct learning. Overall, the study shows that it is possible to generatively link the two communities, and how each perspective can contribute to the other.

Exemplar 2: In an agent-based simulation study addressing the dynamic interplay between action and memory in organizational routines, Miller et al. (2012) mapped out 'the sequences of actions carried out by ensembles of agents as they handle streams of problems'. While this paper focuses on the link between action, organizational memory and routines, the performances they observe – of agents taking actions to address problems and adapting this performance relative to goals – mirror problemistic search and experiential learning. Further, the work creates connections between cognitive and memory-driven conceptions of routines in the Carnegie School, bringing those elements into Routine Dynamics.

To uncover new bridge building opportunities across the two communities, we applied thematic codes to the content of the nine articles. In what follows, we summarize our findings on the three themes highlighted in Table 33.1.

33.4.2 Theme 1: Change

The dominant theme across the nine articles was change and adaptation in routines, including emergence of new routines in entrepreneurial and established organizations. This finding is not surprising. Experiential learning studies as well as studies of Routine Dynamics often focus on change. In their review of the literature on Routine Dynamics, Howard-Grenville and Rerup (2017: 327) found that the 'most prevalent among the articles was change in routine'.

Typically, studies of Routine Dynamics have focused on micro-level endogenous change in routine (e.g., Feldman et al. 2016), whereas experiential learning studies in the Carnegie tradition have focused on macro-level exogenous change (e.g., Greve, 2003). These patterns also play out in the nine papers. For instance, in several papers there is a strong focus on endogenous routine change (e.g., Pentland and Feldman, 2005) while the focus in other papers is on how technological disruptions in the larger context influence routine and learning dynamics (e.g., Aggarwal et al., 2017). A few papers also focus on how both exogenous and endogenous change drive patterning or learning processes (e.g., Rerup and Feldman, 2011).

There is an opportunity here for establishing stronger bridges across the two communities. Routine Dynamics is a theory of local practice while entity theories of routines which are typically used in quantitative studies of routine change in the Carnegie tradition provide little insight into how routines are enacted, thus creating an 'important challenge for micro research' (Greve, 2008: 199). In quantitative Carnegie studies focused on experiential learning, 'problems' with performing the routine 'cause the actor to do "something" [but the Carnegie literature on experiential learning] does not directly investigate how habits and routines are changed' (Greve, 2008: 192). Routine Dynamics, with its focus on how routine actors enact routines, can supply the micro-processes for unpacking how the detailed dynamics of learning or patterning unfolds. For that to happen, however, the field of Routine Dynamics needs to address some thorny questions (reworked from March et al., 1991: 11).

What conceptual trade-off do we need to make to bring Routine Dynamics to the realm of big-data in large scale empirical research? What is the proper trade-off between incorporating all the nitty-gritty details of Routine Dynamics in a single organization versus across hundreds of organizations? As students develop insights about Routine Dynamics beyond ethnographic research, they balance gains and losses in micro-insights against gains and losses in macro-insights about routines. The metric and the procedures are ill-defined, but to move forward the field of Routine Dynamics needs to develop a position on this issue. Are we open to trade-off weaker conceptualizations of Routine Dynamics for higher-level insights based on quantitative data?

Although previous work bridging the two communities has been limited to qualitative, conceptual and simulation studies, the methodological repertoire could be expanded to include machine learning techniques to analyse large amounts of digital trace data (Lindberg, 2020; Pentland et al., 2020). One way to accomplish this expansion would be to bring the idea of patterning to the fore in research on experiential learning.

33.4.3 Theme 2: Politics and Conflict

In *The Behavioral Theory of the Firm*, multiple actors enact divergent goals which lead to conflict and political contestation (Cyert and March, 1963). To address these conflicts, actors engage in coalition building and conflict resolution. Today, the conflictual aspects of the Carnegie School have moved to the background in experiential learning research (Ganz, 2018; Gavetti et al., 2007; Gavetti et al., 2012). Although recent work on experiential learning (e.g., Levinthal and Rerup, 2021; Rerup and Zbaracki, in press) and Routine Dynamics (Cacciatori, 2012; Cohendet and Simon, 2016; Salvato and Rerup, 2018; Zbaracki and Bergen, 2010) has started to fill this void, much work still needs to be done because conflict and contestation can significantly influence processes of learning and patterning. For instance, the ostensive aspects of routines are multiple (Feldman and Pentland, 2003), but how that multiplicity generates tension, contestation and conflict in the enactment of routines still remains to be fully explored.

In an early simulation study of routines and political conflict, Lazaric and Raybaut (2005) found that two outcomes were possible between groups, truce or conflict. Per Nelson and Winter's (1982) notion of the routine as truce, the stability of a routine can be a resolution to conflict and enhance learning. Lazaric and Raybaut's (2005) found that some organizational designs enhance the dynamics of learning between groups, although these designs are very sensitive to breakdowns in the truce. For instance, an experiential learning process revolves around interpreting and classifying outcomes or experiences as successes or failures relative to aspirations, but if the actors engaged in that process of interpretation support different aspirations, the learning process becomes much more complex. Similarly, if the outcomes or experiences are confusing and ambiguous, actors with different aspirations might research different conclusions about whether a routine needs to change or not. These interpretive processes triggered by disagreements can shape the path of the routine.

In a study of Learning Lab Denmark, Rerup and Feldman (2011) showed how hiring became problematic and conflictual because hiring was intertwined with work and rules enacted at the public university that hosted LLD. In essence, LLD's goal was to hire entrepreneurial people and generally pay them as if they were working in the private sector, but that vision clashed with the public university rules. To accomplish its goal, employees within LLD took creative action to avoid conflicts and to keep the hiring routine going. Over a period of more than a year, the employees of LLD and the University experienced conflict. Eventually, through a process of trial-and-error learning, the various actors reached a truce. This process revealed that problems or errors were multiple and that routine participants responded to these differences in different ways. Errors related to routines generated creative actions or trials that aimed to allow routine participants to accomplish the goal they had articulated for the hiring routine. Errors related to the interpretive schema of LLD generated questions which were broader issues that related to how LLD, as a whole, operated. These questions led to reflections among participants about the culture, identity and overall vision of LLD.

Prashantham and Floyd (2012), in a conceptual paper promoting micro-level explanations of learning in international new ventures, noted that the ostensive aspects of the routine 'incorporate[s] the subjective understanding of diverse participants' (Feldman and Pentland, 2003: 101). Given this diversity, they theorized that the greater the diversity in the ostensive aspects of the routine, the more participants would improvise to keep the routine operational. Building on this idea, it would be valuable to also explore how this diversity might lead to political contestation and efforts of learning to keep the routine operational.

Although politics and conflict is a topic that has only been tangentially covered in the broader literature on Carnegie School experiential learning and Routine Dynamics, we were surprised to discover that this topic appeared in four of the nine papers in our sample. This finding suggests that scholars combining Carnegie School experiential learning and Routine Dynamics can integrate learning, Routine Dynamics and conflict, but that the field would benefit from more systematic integration and theorizing of these ideas. A stronger focus on political contestation and conflict, for instance, could potentially reveal new dimensions of how performing and patterning of routines are emergent and effortful accomplishments; how politics make performing and patterning fall apart or glued together; how the intentions of routine participants are in flux (Dittrich and Seidl, 2018); how coalitions are created and sustained in political processes; how powerful groups either support or block particular performances of routines; and generally more realistically unpack the political struggles that transpire when multiple actors either within a single organization or across multiple organizations are involved in performing and patterning of routines. As noted by Pentland and

Feldman (2005: 808–809), 'Each performance provides an opportunity for members to act out their differences and an opportunity for understanding the routine differently. The [ostensive model of the routine] is always up in the air to some extent, and it can potentially be revisited.' Highlighting the role of political contestation in routine enactments could potentially show how truces dynamics are not just a cognitive activity carried out by senior managers, but a performative process involving many participants (Salvato and Rerup, 2018).

33.4.4 Theme 3: Cognition

Cognition is important to the history of the field of routines (Lazaric [Chapter 18], this volume). March and Simon (1958) argued that decision makers have limited cognitive capability, which is why standardized approaches to tasks – standard operating procedures or routines – provide cognitive efficiency. If a task can be performed semi-automatically in a routinized way, then limited cognitive resources can be directed at other tasks that require more attention. Routine enactment of tasks economizes search and standardizes task resolutions. As a contrast, Feldman and Pentland (2003) developed the idea that routines are flexibly enacted and that the performance of a routine requires reflection and effort. Given this ontological focus, Routine Dynamics moved reflection and action to the foreground and cognition and mindlessness to background of the discourse on routines (Dittrich and Seidl, 2018; Levinthal and Rerup, 2006). Over the past 20 years, Routine Dynamics has been focused on disentangling actions into different types and varieties while the 'actors' doing the acting have remained fairly generic (see Karali [Chapter 27]; Kho and Spee [Chapter 28]; and Tsoukas [Chapter 3], in this volume). Relatively little is known about how the psychological and cognitive make-up of routine participants such as identity, morality, intentions, motivation and other cognitive constructs influence performing and patterning of routines.

Surprisingly, six of the nine papers have a strong focus on cognition. In a study drawing on an agent-based simulation, Miller, Pentland and Choi (2012) investigated the dynamic interplay between action and memory in an organizational routine. Because individual routine participants perform different aspects of a routine, they experience and remember the routine in different ways. How these variations can lead to political contestation and influence the performance of the routine have not been investigated in detail. By investigating how a shared understanding of the routine – memory – might influence the enactment of the routine, the authors find that when organizations go through downsizing, 'large organizations deal poorly with a change in the problem that they face' and 'the greater the reduction in the workforce, the more quickly the organization regains efficiency' (Miller et al., 2012: 2). This study suggests that experiential learning processes – responding to problems – can be fruitfully linked to the more cognitive heritage of the Carnegie School, and that this heritage can be fruitfully linked to the study of Routine Dynamics.

In a longitudinal, qualitative study of a web-based start-up organization, Mariano and Casey (2016) focused on the intention of various routine participants to provide a fuller appreciation of the psychological and cognitive make-up of these actors. They found that how individual actors comprehend and value newly formed routines influence how they take action when performing these routines. For instance, low comprehension and low perceived value of a new routine lead routine actors to avoid and forget the routine, whereas high comprehension and high perceived value of the routine lead actors to commit to the routine and engage in learning. Overall, Mariano and Casey (2016) outline how the intentions of routine participants and a fuller appreciation of the cognitive and psychological make-up of routine actors can shed light on how cognitive mechanisms might regulate the performing and patterning of routines. This focus is important. It suggests that more work is needed to better unpack how the cognitive dynamics of the routine participants are linked to the performative aspects and patterning of Routine Dynamics.

33.5 Future Research Directions

Our review shows that the Carnegie School experiential learning and Routine Dynamics communities are starting to cross-fertilize one another, although, of the 142 articles reviewed, 105 (73.9 per cent) did not use a Routine Dynamics lens. This finding suggests that opportunities abound for further connecting the two traditions. One explanation for the meagre overlap is that most work on experiential learning in the Carnegie School tradition avoids zooming in on specific actors and actions while most work in Routine Dynamics is only starting to embrace ideas related to politics, conflict and cognition. Our review suggests that bridges are being built across the more macro-oriented focus of the Carnegie School and the more micro-oriented focus of Routine Dynamics, however.

The core take-away from the chapter is that experiential learning is central to Routine Dynamics because the flow and progression of routines emerge from experiential learning such as processes of taking action, evaluating the results of those actions and, if necessary, making adjustments to future actions. Some studies in Routine Dynamics trace the emergence, stability and change of routines by specifically zooming in on how actors take action, experience problems and make adjustments (e.g., Feldman, 2000; Rerup and Feldman, 2011; Salvato and Rerup, 2018). Based on this stream of research, we propose that experiential learning can be seen as a form of patterning and vice versa.

To further integrate experiential learning into the process of patterning, we propose using sequence analysis (see Mahringer and Pentland [Chapter 12], this volume) to methodologically map the various steps or sequences of experiential learning: (1) how actors articulate goals or aspirations; (2) take action to accomplish these goals; (3) evaluate the outcomes of those actions; and (4) take action to address eventual problems. This basic sequence can be made more complicated by incorporating (1) how different actors articulate multiple and perhaps conflicting goals (conflict and politics); (2) how outcomes across multiple goals generate ambiguity which makes these outcomes more difficult to interpret and classify (cognition); (3) how ambiguity and interpretive challenges require more mindful and effortful reflection (cognition) and truce building; and (4) how all of these are shaping the patterning of routines. Similarly, the analysis of patterning could be expanded and made more complex by incorporating the 'full' routine participant, including capturing how their psychological and cognitive make-up shape the enactment of specific routines. These shifts in thinking should not be too difficult because both communities share foundational ideas linked to process, performances and patterning. We propose that one way to start the integration is for scholars within both communities to pay more attention to change, conflict, political contestation, truces, interpretation and sense-making.

33.5.1 Cross-Fertilization: Change

Change and stability are core issues within both experiential learning and Routine Dynamics. On the one hand, research in the tradition of experiential learning has mostly focused on how exogenous change drives the search for new routines. On the other hand, research on Routine Dynamics has mostly focused on how endogenous change drives Routine Dynamics. Routines, however, are situated within a larger context (Howard-Grenville and Lodge [Chapter 16], this volume). Future research on Routine Dynamics would benefit from considering how exogenous shocks instigate change in how routines are tried out. Similarly, future research on experiential learning would benefit from better incorporating how routines also change as a result of endogenous processes.

Integrating exogenous and endogenous change processes to advance our understanding of stability and change can contribute to addressing a challenge in the wider organizational theory community – bridging the micro and macro divide (Powell and Rerup, 2017; Salvato and Rerup, 2011). Disentangling exogenous and endogenous change in routines and considering the larger situated context could, for instance, help address puzzles such as the 'paradox of embedded agency' (Seo and Creed, 2002). This paradox highlights a challenge that institutional theorists face: if institutions shape actors and limit their agency, how can those same actors effect change in the institutions meant to control them? (Battilana and D'Aunno, 2009). In looking at this paradox, scholars have previously conceptualized institutions as patterns of change and stability (Zietsma and Lawrence, 2010) – where they explored the interplay of routines and boundaries in managing conflict. In their longitudinal study of harvesting routines in the coastal forest industry, Zietsma and Lawrence (2010) utilized a practice-perspective of routines to understand their role in institutional stability and change (conflict). Despite the practice-inspired approach – the concept of routines is not thoroughly unpacked in their work or those that followed. Future research could utilize a Routine Dynamics perspective to better elucidate the micro-processes that are involved in institutional change and conflict.

33.5.2 Cross-Fertilization: Politics and Conflict

Conflict and political contestation is a foundational issue in organization theory (March, 1962; Simon, 1964). Given the iconic presence of political contestation in social processes it is remarkable that so little work has focused on this topic in Routine Dynamics. The Carnegie School offers solid ground for Routine Dynamics scholars to develop a stronger and empirically supported political and conflictual perspective. Specifically, the Carnegie School can help Routine Dynamics scholars in at least three ways. First, the Carnegie School can bring more attention to goal conflict within organizational routines, including conflict over multiple goals (Levinthal and Rerup, 2021). Second, the Carnegie School can help Routine Dynamics to unpack how problems with accomplishing particular goals or tasks can lead to conflict, and how learning processes can provide theoretical handholds for enacting problem-driven goal conflict. Third, the Carnegie School might also help Routine Dynamics to unpack how adaptations to address problems can lead to, and perhaps deepen, conflict.

Similarly, Routine Dynamics offers solid ground for Carnegie School scholars to develop a more processual and micro-oriented perspective on patterning and how conflicts develop and are managed (Salvato and Rerup, 2018). Specifically, Routine Dynamics can help Carnegie School scholars in at least two ways. First, Routine Dynamics show how problems can motivate actors to engage in various forms of improvisation and trial-and-error learning and take creative action to avoid conflict (Prashantham and Floyd, 2012; Rerup and Feldman, 2011). With a deeper appreciation of how action can be a source for balancing conflict, Carnegie School scholars can focus more on how actors perform rather than avoid conflict. As noted by Feldman (2000: 613–614), routines are

> performed by people who think and feel and care. Their reactions are situated in institutional, organizational and personal contexts. Their actions are motivated by will and intention. They create, resist, engage in conflict, acquiesce to domination. All of these forces influence the enactment of organizational routines and create in them a tremendous potential for changes.

Second, a future research direction for Carnegie School scholars is the study of dynamic truces rather than ossified truces (see D'Addario and Safavi [Chapter 15]). This topic was opened up by Lazaric and Raybaut (2005) and called for by Pentland and Feldman (2005: 809). Within Routine Dynamics, ossified truces have been covered by Zbaracki and Bergen (2010) while dynamic truces have been addressed by Salvato and Rerup (2018). In a dynamic truce routine participants create interpersonal junctures that provide agentic opportunities for working out conflict on an ongoing basis. Salvato and Rerup (2018) identified three types of regulatory actions (splicing, activating and repressing) that routine participants took to manage conflict. However, much more work is needed to further understand truce dynamics, not just Routine Dynamics. For instance, we need to know more about how routine participants can enact a 'stable' truce if their preferences and intentions are unstable (Dittrich and Seidl, 2018).

33.5.3 Cross-Fertilization: Cognition

The enactment of a routine involves interpretation or sense-making of outcomes but Maitlis and Christianson (2014) concluded that there is much to be done in linking sense-making and routines. Specifically, very limited work has explored how routine participants engage in interpreting and classifying outcomes of routines. Similarly, interpretation of outcomes within the Carnegie School perspective on experiential learning is assumed to be automatic and unproblematic (Levinthal and Rerup, 2021).

One explanation for the lack of cross-fertilization may 'stem from a disconnect between long-standing mindsets about routines and the empirical contexts in which sensemaking has frequently been studied. Routines tend to be associated with normal operations, mundane work, and stability, whereas much of the empirical materials of sensemaking studies have been drawn from interruptions to normal operations, particularly crises, rare events, and strategic change initiatives' (Hilligoss, 2020: 3).

Going forward, scholars within both experiential learning and Routine Dynamics would benefit from exploring how interpretation and sensemaking are implicated in processes of experiential learning and patterning.

33.6 Conclusion

This chapter reviewed the potential for cross-fertilization between two research communities: Carnegie School experiential learning and Routine Dynamics. We propose that experiential learning can be seen as a form of 'patterning', and by doing so can address three core areas of interest to both communities: change; politics and conflict; and cognition. Our review of existing literature revealed a strong interest in overlap between the communities, broadly speaking (e.g., that of routines and learning), but that a very limited number of studies have comprehensively and systematically used the experiential learning process to establish a bridge across the two communities. We believe that this can be addressed through creating a shared 'common language' of certain conceptualizations, such as seeing experiential learning as a form of patterning, which then lays the groundwork for expanded methodological opportunities.

References

Aggarwal, V. A., Posen, H. E. and Workiewicz, M. (2017). Adaptive capacity to technological change: A microfoundational approach. *Strategic Management Journal*, 38(6), 1212–1231.

Anderson, M. H. and Lemken, R. K. (2019). An empirical assessment of the influence of March and Simon's organizations: The realized contribution and unfulfilled promise of a masterpiece. *Journal of Management Studies*, 56(8), 1537–1569.

Argote, L. (2013). *Organizational Learning: Creating, Retaining and Transferring Knowledge*, 2nd edition, New York: Springer.

Argote, L. and Greve, H. R. (2007). A behavioral theory of the firm – 40 years and counting: Introduction and impact. *Organization Science*, 18, 337–349.

Battilana, J. and D'Aunno, T. (2009) Institutional work and the paradox of embedded agency. In T. B. Lawrence, R. Suddaby and B. Leca, eds., *Institutional Work: Actors and Agency in Institutional Studies of Organizations*. Cambridge: Cambridge University Press, pp. 31–58.

Cacciatori, E. (2012). Resolving conflict in problem-solving: Systems of artifacts in the development of new routines. *Journal of Management Studies*, 49(8), 1559–1585.

Cohendet, P. S. and Simon, L. O. (2016). Always playable: Recombining routines for creative efficiency at Ubisoft Montreal's video game studio. *Organization Science*, 27(3), 614–632.

Cyert, R. M. and March, J. G. (1963). *A Behavioral Theory of the Firm*. Cambridge, MA: Basil Blackwell.

Dittrich, K. and Seidl, D. 2018. Emerging intentionality in routine dynamics: A pragmatist view. *Academy of Management Journal*, 61(1), 111–138.

Feldman, M. S. (2000). Organizational routines as a source of continuous change. *Organization Science*, 11(6), 611–629.

Feldman, M. S. (2016). Routines as process: Past, present, and future. In J. A. Howard-Grenville, C. Rerup, A. Langley and H. Tsoukas, eds., *Organizational Routines: A Process Perspective. Perspectives on Process Organization Studies*. Oxford: Oxford University Press, pp. 23–46.

Feldman, M. S. and Pentland, B. T. (2003). Reconceptualizing organizational routines as a source of flexibility and change. *Administrative Science Quarterly*, 48(1), 94–118.

Ganz, S. C. (2018). Ignorant decision making and educated inertia: Some political pathologies of organizational learning. *Organization Science*, 29(1), 39–57.

Gavetti, G., Greve, H. R., Levinthal, D. A. and Ocasio, W. (2012). The behavioral theory of the firm: Assessment and prospects. *Academy of Management Annals*, 6, 1–40.

Gavetti, G. Ocasio, W. and Levinthal, D. A. (2007). Neo-Carnegie: The Carnegie School's past, present, and reconstructing for the future. *Organization Science*, 18(3), 523–536.

Goh, K. T. and Pentland, B. T. (2019). From actions to paths to patterning: Toward a dynamic theory of patterning in routines. *Academy of Management Journal*, 62(6), 1901–1929.

Greve, H. R. (2003). *Organizational Learning from Performance Feedback*. Cambridge: Cambridge University Press.

Greve, H. R. (2008). Organizational routines and performance feedback. In M. Becker, ed., *Handbook of Organizational Routines*. Northampton, MA: Elgar, 187–204.

Greve, H. R. and Gaba, V. (2017). Performance feedback in organizations and groups: Common themes. In L. Argote and J. M. Levine, eds., *The Handbook of Group and Organizational Learning*. Oxford: Oxford University Press.

Hilligoss, B. (2020). *Routines and Sensemaking: Strengthening Connections, Extending Theory*. Winner, MOC Best Symposium Award, Academy of Management Conference.

Howard-Grenville, J. (2005). The persistence of flexible organizational routines: The role of agency and organizational context. *Organization Science*, 16(6), 618–636.

Howard-Grenville, J. and Rerup, C. (2017). A process perspective on organizational routines. In A. Langley and H. Tsoukas, eds., *Sage Handbook of Process Organizational Studies*. London: Sage Publications, pp. 323–339.

Kacperczyk, A. Beckman, C. M. and Moliterno, T. P. (2015). Disentangling risk and change: Internal and external comparisons in the Mutual Fund Industry. *Administrative Science Quarterly*, 60, 228–262.

Kay, N. M. (2018). We need to talk: Opposing narratives and conflicting perspectives in the conversation on routines. *Industrial and Corporate Change*, 27(6), 943–956.

Koumakhov, R. and Daoud, A. (2017). Routine and reflexivity: Simonian cognitivism vs practice approach. *Industrial and Corporate Change*, 26, 727–743.

Lazaric, N. and Raybaut, A. (2005). Knowledge, hierarchy and the selection of routines: An interpretative model with group interactions. *Journal of Evolutionary Economics*, 15(4), 393–421.

Levinthal, D. A. and Marino A. (2015). Three facets of organizational adaptation: Selection, variety, and plasticity. *Organization Science*, 26(3), 743–755.

Levinthal, D. A. and Rerup, C. (2006). Crossing an apparent chasm: Bridging mindful and less-mindful perspectives on organizational learning. *Organization Science*, 17(4), 502–513.

Levinthal, D. A. and Rerup, C. (2021). The plural of goal: Learning in a world of ambiguity. *Organization Science*, 32(3), 527–543.

Levitt, B. and March, J. G. (1988). Organizational learning. *Annual Review of Sociology*, 319–340.

Lindberg, A. (2020). Developing theory through integrating human and machine pattern recognition. *Journal of the Association for Information Systems*, 21(1), 7.

Lyytinen, K., Rose, G. and Yoo, Y. (2010). Learning routines and disruptive technological change: Hyper-learning in seven software development organizations during internet adoption. *Information Technology & People*, 23(2), 165–192.

Maitlis, S. and Christianson, M. (2014). Sensemaking in organizations: Taking stock and moving forward. *Academy of Management Annals*, 8, 57–125.

March, J. G. (1962). The business firm as a political coalition. *Journal of Politics*, 24(4), 662–678.

March, J. G. and Simon, H. (1958). *Organizations*. New York: Wiley.

March, J. G., Sproull, L. S. and Tamuz M. (1991). Learning from samples of one or fewer. *Organization Science*, 2(1), 1–13.

Mariano, S. and Casey, A. (2016). The dynamics of organizational routines in a startup: The Ereda model. *European Management Review*, 13(4), 251–274.

Miller, K. D. Pentland, B. T. and Choi, S. (2012). Dynamics of performing and remembering organizational routines. *Journal of Management Studies*, 49(8), 1536–1558.

Nelson, P. R. and Winter, S. (1982). *An Evolutionary Theory of Economic Change*. Cambridge, MA: Harvard University Press.

Parmigiani, A. and Howard-Grenville, J. (2011). Routines revisited: Exploring the capabilities and practice perspectives. *Academy of Management Annals*, 5(1), 413–453.

Pentland, B. T. and Feldman, M. S. (2005). Organizational routines as a unit of analysis. *Industrial and Corporate Change*, 14(5), 793–815.

Pentland, B., T. Feldman, M. S., Becker, M. C. and Liu, P. (2012). Dynamics of organizational routines: A generative model. *Journal of Management Studies*, 49(8), 1484–1508.

Pentland, B.T., Recker, J., Wolf, J. R. and Wyner, G. (2020). Bringing context into the analysis of process with digital trace data. *Journal of the Association for Information Systems*, 21(5), 1214–1236.

Pentland, B. T. and Rueter. H. H. (1994). Organizational routines as grammars of action. *Administrative Science Quarterly*, 39(3), 484–510.

Posen, H. E., Keil, T., Kim, S. and Meissner, F. (2018) Renewing research on problemistic search: A review and research agenda. *Academy of Management Annals*, 12(1), 208–251.

Powell, W. W. and Rerup, C. (2017). Opening the black box: Microfoundations of institutions. In R. Greenwood et al., eds., *The SAGE Handbook of Organizational Institutionalism*, 2nd ed. London: Sage Publications, Chapter 12: 311–337.

Prashantham, S. snd Floyd, S. W. (2012). Routine microprocesses and capability learning in international new ventures. *Journal of International Business Studies*, 43(6), 544–562.

Rerup, C. and Feldman, M. (2011). Routines as a source of change in organizational schemata: The role of trial-and-error learning. *Academy of Management Journal*, 54(3), 577–610.

Rerup, C. and Zbaracki, M. (in press). The politics of learning from rare events. *Organization Science*.

Royer, I. and Daniel, A. (2019). Organizational routines and institutional maintenance: The influence of legal artifacts. *Journal of Management Inquiry*, 28(2), 204–224.

Salvato, C. and Rerup, C. (2011). Beyond collective entities: Multi-level research on organizational routines and capabilities. *Journal of Management*, 37(2), 468–490.

Salvato, C. and Rerup, C. (2018). Routine regulation: Balancing conflicting goals in organizational routines. *Administrative Science Quarterly*, 63(1), 170–209.

Seo, M. G. and Creed, W. E. D. (2002). Institutional contradictions, praxis, and institutional change: A dialectical perspective. *Academy of Management Review*, 27, 222–247.

Simon, H. A. (1964). On the concept of organizational goal. *Administrative Science Quarterly*, 9 (1), 1–22.

Wickham, H. (2016). *ggplot2: Elegant Graphics for Data Analysis*. New York: Springer-Verlag.

Zbaracki, M. J. and Bergen, M. (2010). When truces collapse: A longitudinal study of price-adjustment routines. *Organization Science*, 21 (5), 955–972.

Zietsma, C. and Lawrence, T. B. (2010). Institutional work in the transformation of an organizational field: The interplay of boundary work and practice work. *Administrative Science Quarterly*, 55(2), 189–221.

CHAPTER 34

Dynamic Capabilities and Routine Dynamics

CARLO SALVATO

34.1 Introduction

Explaining how business organizations and their participants address the dynamics of the context in which they operate has been a major focus of recent theorizing in both strategic management and organizational theory. Although concepts and labels coined to understand the phenomenon abound, two of them stand out for the rising attention they attracted and for some striking similarities in their focus – Routine Dynamics (RD) and Dynamic Capabilities (DC). DC scholars investigate how high-level routines, or collections of routines, allow firms to dynamically adapt their resource endowments to shifting competitive conditions (Brown and Eisenhardt, 1997; Teece et al., 1997; Zollo and Winter, 2002). The high-level (or second-order, search, dynamic) routines in which DC are grounded are considered as stable entities that senior managers intentionally create, shape and implement (Helfat et al., 2007) to reliably and systematically alter lower-level (or operational, ordinary, substantive) routines. Scholars in the fast-growing RD field investigate how actors perform organizational routines of any kind. Focus is on the specific actions performed by multiple actors at specific times and places, and on how recognizable, repetitive patterns of interdependent action emerge and change (See Chapter 1 in this volume; Feldman and Pentland, 2003; Feldman et al., 2016; Pentland et al., 2012). Therefore, scholars in both traditions share an interest in routines and in how they, somewhat counterintuitively, engender forms of dynamism.

However, a few sharp differences in how scholars developed DC and RD concepts prevented them from overtly exploring and exploiting the manifest connections between the two fields. Research in DC has tended to happen at the organizational level, understanding DC as collective entities that are intentionally created and maintained by top managers, with limited attention to their internal dynamics (Ambrosini and Bowman, 2009; Ambrosini et al., 2009; Barreto, 2010). Moreover, focus has been on how DC affect firm-level market and financial performance, rather than on organizational participants perform*ing* DC. In contrast, the RD framework has taken individual actions as the unit of observation, with limited attention to how top managers can shape and direct how participants perform routines. Moreover, focus has been on actors perform*ing* routines, rather than on the effects of participants' actions on task performance (Deken and Sele [Chapter 21], in this volume). These differences prevented the DC field benefiting from understanding the possible effects of routine enactments on firm performance, and the RD field from integrating knowledge of how intentional top management intervention enables and constrains how actors perform routines and how effectively a routine task is performed.

The purpose of this chapter is to suggest how the walls that currently separate the two fields can be turned into bridges and how researchers in each camp can walk across those bridges to develop novel and mutually beneficial insights. I will argue that RD may enhance what we know about the sources of dynamism, flexibility and heterogeneity in DC and, thus, how DC can contribute to building and sustaining competitive advantage. From the other side of the bridge, the DC view may expand the understanding of RD by including the role of intentional managerial interventions in shaping the organizational context in which participants enact routines but also in directly shaping routine patterning. Moreover, RD researchers may be prompted by the DC view to more systematically turn their attention towards how RD affects task performance and, eventually, firm competitive and financial performance. In this chapter I will first dig deeper into the similarities and differences between DC and RD, mapping boundaries and connections. Next, I will illustrate how combining insights from the two fields may enhance our understanding of four key questions raised by the dynamics of organizational routines. Finally, I will offer directions for future research grounded in the opportunities for mutual learning across the two fields.

34.2 Routine Dynamics and Dynamic Capabilities: Opposition and Cooperation

When observed from a distance, *Routine Dynamics* and *Dynamic Capabilities* are apparently overlapping approaches. If we assume that an organizational capability is, or is grounded in, a high-level routine or collection of routines (Winter, 2000), the two entities are, at least semantically, very similar. Zooming-in on the two concepts and related literatures, though, profound differences emerge. The two main distinctions refer to ontology and level issues (Table 34.1).

These deep-seated differences, however, do not prevent potential cooperation across the two views.

34.2.1 Different Ontologies

The first main difference between the two views is ontological. DC theory is grounded on the classic view of routines, which rests on a positivist ontology and behavioural or evolutionary theoretical perspectives (Sydow [Chapter 36], in this volume; Schilke et al., 2018). DC refers to entities that objectively exist out there, and can thus be intentionally created, adapted and exploited to produce desired outcomes. In his classic definition, Winter (2000) describes a capability as a routine that 'together with its implementing input flows, confers upon an organization's management a set of decision options for producing significant outputs of a particular type' (2000: 981). Similarly, Zahra, Sapienza and Davidsson (2006) explicitly mention the role of managers in driving the emergence and use of DC,

> The creation and subsequent use of dynamic capabilities correspond to the entrepreneur, the entrepreneurial team, or the firm's senior management's perception of opportunities to productively change existing routines or resource configurations, their willingness to undertake such change, and their ability to implement these changes. This ability is largely determined by the motivation, skills and experiences of the firm's key managers (918).

In contrast to this positivistic approach, the RD view is grounded on a social-constructivist ontology and pragmatist and structuration theoretical perspectives (Sydow [Chapter 36], in this volume). Routines are not objective entities that can be intentionally moulded by actors external to them. They are effortful accomplishments of their individual participants, and they are only stable-for-now. Subsequent enactments steer them in often unanticipated directions, thus altering how participants – and close-enough external observers – view and experience them (Chapter 1 in this volume; Feldman and Pentland, 2003; Feldman et al., 2016).

34.2.2 Different Levels

The second main distinction between DC and RD views refers to the different levels at which they investigate the same or similar empirical phenomena. Different theoretical views may have the same level of theory but different levels of measurement and analysis (Klein et al., 1994). The *level of theory* (also referred to as *unit of analysis*) describes the target (e.g., individual, routine, organization) that a theorist or researcher aims to describe, understand and explain. It is 'the level to which generalizations are made' (Rousseau, 1985: 4). The *level of measurement* describes the actual source of the data – 'the unit to which data are directly attached' (Rousseau, 1985: 4). For instance, a product development routine (level of

Table 34.1 Routine Dynamics and Dynamic Capabilities: Commonalities and differences

Dimensions	Routine Dynamics view	Dynamic Capabilities view
Ontology	Social constructionist	Positivist
Theoretical perspective	Pragmatism – Structuration	Behavioral – Evolutionary
Focal interest	• Understanding how routine participants perform actions that shape/create (and are shaped by/respond to) patterns • Focus on performing and patterning	• Understanding how performance of high-level routines alters (builds, integrates, reconfigures, releases) lower-level routines and resource configurations • Focus on routine performance and pattern-as-entity
Level of theory[1] (focal unit of analysis)	*Routine* (any type of, but mostly ordinary, substantive, first-order) *as pattern* of observed, situated action	*Routine* (search, high-level, second-order), or collection of routines, *as entity*
Level of measurement[2]	Actants (routine participants, artifacts, ideas)	Top managers, routine or collection of routines
Level of analysis[3]	Individual actions (typically in first-order, ordinary routines) performed by actants (routine participants, artifacts, ideas)	Instances of second-order routine performance
Position in multi-level hierarchy	• Routine (pattern) as the *highest* (more *macro*) level of theory. • Main interest is in how individual actions shape and are shaped by action patterns. • Relatively limited interest in what happens *outside* the routine (i.e., in macro-organizational context and in task outcomes and firm performance)	• Routine (entity) as the *lowest* (more *micro*) level of theory. • Main interest is in how routine performance affects task outcomes and firm performance. • Relatively limited interest in what happens *inside* the routine (i.e., in individual actions and in action patterning)

(1) The *Level of theory*, or *(focal) unit of analysis*, is 'the level to which generalizations are made' (Rousseau, 1985: 4), i.e., the target (e.g., individual, group, firm) that a researcher wants to depict, explain and theorize about.
(2) The *Level of measurement* refers to 'the unit to which the data are directly attached' (Rousseau, 1985: 4), i.e., the units from which the data are actually collected.
(3) The *Level of analysis* is the unit to which the data are assigned for empirical analysis. It describes if and how collected data are aggregated at different levels (Klein et al., 1994; Rousseau, 1985).

theory or unit of analysis) can be described by either collecting information (level of measurement) on the specific actions performed by individual routine participants, or by collecting information on the routine as a whole, such as money invested, team size, number of products developed and time-to-market performance over time. The *level of analysis* describes the treatment of the data during data analysis procedures (Klein et al., 1994). For instance, data collected at the individual level may be treated still at the individual level ('John did this … Edith did that'), or aggregated at the routine level ('overall, routine participants did that').

RD and DC scholars would probably agree that they share an interest in the routine as the level of theory (or unit of analysis). As a matter of fact, RD scholars are interested in exploring 'the idea that routines are practices with internal dynamics (Feldman and Pentland, 2003)' (Feldman et al., 2016: 505). This demonstrates that, in the RD field, detailed and longitudinal analysis of routine participants' *actions* is not an end in itself, but is directed at learning more about how participants enact *routines*. DC scholars' focus on routines is probably even more explicit. They are interested in exploring how the high-level routines constitutive of DC are 'directed to the development and adaptation of operating routines' (Zollo and Winter, 2002: 339) and, eventually, to the improvement of firm performance and competitive advantage (Teece and Pisano, 1994; Teece et al., 1997).

This shared interest of the RD and DC views on routines as the level of theory, however, is practised from radically different perspectives. Not surprisingly, ontological differences determine epistemological differences – how routines are known and investigated by scholars in each camp. To RD scholars, the routine has traditionally been the *highest*, or more macro, level of theory. They are interested in what happens at lower levels or *within* the routine. Their focus is on the dynamics that happen within the routine. The level of measurement and analysis are thus the actions performed by individual routine participants at specific times and places, with the aim of understanding how these actions dynamically shape routine patterning and how actors perform the routine over time and over multiple enactments.

In contrast, to DC scholars the routine is the *lowest*, or more micro, level of theory. They are interested in what happens *outside* the routine. Their focus is on the dynamics that routines engender outside, in other organizational entities. The level of measurement and analysis is thus the high-level routine (or collection of routines) itself – in which the dynamic capability as a whole is grounded – with the aim of understanding how it can be intentionally created and shaped by senior managers, and how the DC can adapt operating routines and bundles of resources, i.e., make them more dynamic, and thus potentially improve firm-level performance. This core difference can also be explained by suggesting that RD focus is mainly on *variation* (the actions of individual routine participants are aimed at reproducing the same pattern – or *effortful accomplishment*), while DC focus is mainly on *change* (routine enactments are aimed at producing new or different patterns – *emergent accomplishment*; Cohen, 2007; Feldman et al., 2016).

34.2.3 Potential Cooperation

The aim of this chapter is not to propose a combination of the RD and DC views. It is entirely legitimate that scholars from different traditions and worldviews investigate the same entity from different perspectives and with different methods and purposes. Moreover, ontological differences are so deep-seated that a combination is likely unfeasible (Parmigiani and Howard-Grenville, 2011). However, the insights developed from empirical analysis in each tradition may be mutually beneficial, driving future research in novel and fruitful – although separate – directions. An example is Deken and Sele's (Chapter 21, in this volume) framework for interpreting innovation work with a Routine Dynamics lens. An empirical application is offered by Salvato (2009), who applied a DC approach to studying how a design firm's product development routine evolved over time as a result of improvisations performed by specific routine participants at specific times and places but also as a result of senior managers' involvement in formalizing and replicating those improvisations. The adapted routine, resulting from both participants' improvisation and top management intervention, improved product development outcomes and, eventually, firm performance. In this example, a DC approach allows observers to see how senior managers' interventions frame and substantially alter routine patterns and how routines are performed by their participants. These effects, and their impact on task and firm performance, would otherwise go unnoticed.

In a separate study on the same design firm, Salvato and Rerup (2018) applied a RD approach to studying how improvisations of product development routine participants gradually reshaped routine patterns (with little or no intervention of senior managers), and how these endogenous changes allowed routine enactments to effectively address changes in the firm's competitive environment. In this example, a RD approach demonstrates that routines are sometimes made dynamic by their participants, without any intervention of senior managers on the routine as an entity. Managerial interventions may actually disrupt the effectiveness of ongoing changes from within, lacking detailed understanding of internal Routine Dynamics (Salvato and Rerup, 2011).

Cooperation across the two views should result from their shared interest in routines as the level of theory. This interest is obvious in the RD view. However, the concept of DC is also inherently grounded in organizational routines. An overview of the main definitions shows that not only are DC explicitly grounded in routines, or they even are routines, but also that their conceptualizations may provide several insights into the field of RD (Table 34.2).

Additional insights on how the two fields may cooperate result from reading the empirical results of research in one camp with the conceptual lenses adopted in the other. While DC empirical research has been both quantitative and qualitative, RD studies have been almost exclusively grounded in qualitative research. Therefore, in this chapter I only contrast field studies carried out in the two traditions, disregarding large-n studies in DC and RD.

An analysis of some of the most influential field studies in DC (Table 34.3) shows that research in

Table 34.2 Key definitions of Dynamic Capabilities and connections to organizational routines

Author	Definition	Connections to routines
Teece et al. (1997)	The firm's ability to integrate, build and reconfigure internal and external competences to address rapidly changing environments. Dynamic Capabilities thus reflect an organization's ability to achieve new and innovative forms of competitive advantage given path dependencies and market positions (516).	Managerial and organizational processes, shaped by the firm's asset positions and moulded by its evolutionary and co-evolutionary paths, explain the essence of the firm's Dynamic Capabilities. Managerial and organizational processes are the way things are done in the firm, or what might be referred to as its routines or patterns of current practice and learning (518).
Eisenhardt and Martin (2000)	The firm's processes that use resources – specifically the processes to integrate, reconfigure, gain and release resources – to match or even create market change (1107)	Dynamic Capabilities are the organizational and strategic routines by which firms achieve new resources configurations as markets emerge, collide, split, evolve and die (1107)
Zollo and Winter (2002)	A dynamic capability is a learned and stable pattern of collective activity through which the organization systematically generates and modifies its operating routines in pursuit of improved effectiveness (340)	Search routines – those that seek to bring about desirable changes in the existing set of operating routines for the purpose of enhancing profit in the future – are constitutive of Dynamic Capabilities (341)
Winter (2003)	Dynamic Capabilities are those capabilities that operate to extend, modify or create ordinary (substantive) capabilities (991)	An organizational capability is a high-level routine (or collection of routines) that, together with its implementing input flows, confers on an organization's management a set of decision options for producing significant outputs of a particular type. The points deserving emphasis here are the connotations of 'routine' – behaviour that is learned, highly patterned, repetitious or quasi-repetitious, founded in part in tacit knowledge – and the specificity of objectives (991)
Zahra, Sapienza and Davidsson (2006)	Dynamic Capabilities are the abilities to reconfigure a firm's resources and routines in the manner envisioned and deemed appropriate by its principal decision-maker(s) (918)	Dynamic Capabilities are organizational routines that strengthen with use. The exercise of DC reduces variability in the results, minimizes the costs of repeating these actions and increases managers' confidence in their future use of these routines (928)
Helfat et al. (2007)	A dynamic capability is the capacity of an organization to purposefully create, extend or modify its resource base (4)	A DC consists of patterned and somewhat practiced activity. DC must contain some patterned element (5)
Teece (2007)	DC are capabilities that can be harnessed to continuously create, extend, upgrade, protect and keep relevant the enterprise's unique asset base (1319)	One of the micro-foundations of DC are the distinct processes and procedures that are put in place inside the enterprise to garner new technical information; tap developments in exogenous science; monitor customer needs and competitor activity; and shape new products and processes opportunities (1319, 1323)
Helfat and Winter (2011)	A dynamic capability is one that enables a firm to alter how it currently makes its living, i.e., capabilities that promote economically significant change (1244, 1249)	A (dynamic) capability enables repeated and reliable performance of an activity, in contrast to ad hoc activity that does not reflect practised or patterned behaviour (1244)

Table 34.3 Instances of Routine Dynamics in ten selected DC fieldworks

Study	Situated actions	Knowledgeable and reflective actors	Stable for now. Stability as an accomplishment	Implications for Routine Dynamics
Bingham, Heimeriks, Schijven and Gates (2015)	Relationality and multiplicity among M&A, alliance and divestiture routines were purposefully created at Dow Chemicals by codifying and transferring knowledge across M&A, alliance and disposal routines.	Reflection on cumulated knowledge by actors participating in M&As at Dow prompted the creation of stable patterns in alliance and divestiture routines. Participants in cross-functional M&A, alliance and disposal teams autonomously changed communication patterns.	Dow Chemicals created a dedicated group to codify and transfer knowledge about M&A, alliance and divestiture routines, i.e., to build stable routines.	Knowledge codification efforts create structure that constrains/guides actions performed in routines. Communication *across* routines (meetings, reviews, coaching, training) is essential to create action patterns
Danneels (2002)	The specific technologies developed by five high-tech firms made their production and marketing routines highly path-dependent, preventing access to new markets and technologies.	Existing knowledge (e.g., of specific markets and customer segments) and artifacts (e.g., technology) limit the extent to which participants can dynamically adapt routines (e.g., marketing and product development).	Lacking second-order routines, marketing and product development routines become highly path-dependent and unchanging. Second-order marketing and R&D routines create relationships and network links with new markets and technologies, which allowed participants to change first-order routines.	In order to be dynamic, second-order routines (DC) include network components, in particular, relationships with new markets.
Danneels (2011)	The Smith Corona brand – part of the firm context – negatively affected innovative routine development enactments. The R&D function never developed unique technologies because it was part of manufacturing.	The persistence of inaccurate mental models and cognitions about key resources – which resulted from limited reflection and learning – prevented Smith Corona managers from flexibly adapting product development routines.	Besides routine patterns, the underlying mental models persisted at Smiths Corona, even if inaccurate. Attributional ambiguity favoured the persistence of inaccurate patterns, while constructive conflict would have allowed their adaptation.	Managerial cognition about firm resources is essential to explaining the extent to which routines are flexibly or rigidly enacted. Firm-level resources, such as brand, are a significant component of the material context in which participants enact routines.
Dixon, Meyer and Day (2014)	At the Russian oil company Yukos, how managers performed capabilities was closely related to other processes, such as hiring, training and career development, funding and financial bonuses.	Young managers were hired and trained with the explicit goal of developing search and experimentation in oil exploration and production techniques.	Dynamic capabilities for innovation continuously morphed as a result of senior management interventions, but they were still seen as Yukos' way of doing business.	Senior managers can significantly affect the extent to which routines generate creativity and innovation by acting on hiring, training, providing financial motivation.
Martin (2011)	Within six firms operating in the software industry, participants' actions are	The level of resource autonomy of individual routine participants affected their capacity	Top managers' alteration of groups structures and processes altered established	Group structures, processes and psychosocial characteristics affect

Table 34.3 (*cont.*)

Study	Situated actions	Knowledgeable and reflective actors	Stable for now. Stability as an accomplishment	Implications for Routine Dynamics
	situated in groups structures (composition, incentives, autonomy), group processes (planning, knowledge sharing . . .) and group psychosocial characteristics (conflict, affect, emotion).	and willingness to interact.	patterns of routine interaction.	how participants enact routines. The degree of social equivalence among routine participants (power parity and similar evaluation) influences how effectively (creatively and flexibly) they enact routines.
Prange, Bruyaka and Marmenout (2018)	At DHL, the transition between an acquisition DC and an internal-development DC resulted from participants performing a bundle of seemingly unintentional situated actions.	Change and transition in and between routines at DHL happened even though managers where not conscious of the features of routines and did not intentionally plan changes.	At DHL, the patterns through which routines changed and stabilized differed across life-cycle stages of their development (reactive sequences were observed for routines established in earlier stages of DC development, whereas linear patterns were found when the whole life cycle of the DC was considered)	Besides combinations of routines, research on DC also points to transitions between routines, with one routine succeeding others over time.
Salvato (2009)	Alessi product development capability and its changes over time result from participants performing sequences of related actions. Space and physical artifacts are sometimes essential in shaping routine enactments.	Knowledgeable and reflective routine participants intentionally perform experiments to adapt routine enactments to changing circumstances. Experiments that prove effective are retained by top managers and contribute to creating new patterns.	The apparent stability of Alessi product development routines over 15 years results from constant efforts of participants to incrementally adapt it, and of senior managers to formalize emerging adaptations.	Mapping routines as sequences of actions allows careful tracing of their evolution over time. Senior managers play a key role in shaping routine enactments by formalizing successful experiments performed by participants.
Tippmann, Sharkey, Scott and Mangematin (2014)	At Gamma, a leading ICT multinational corporation, the flexibility of the organizational structure and not storing knowledge in central repositories, triggered knowledge search routines	Elements of Gamma's organizational context significantly affected middle managers' knowledge and reflective behaviour and, therefore, their search actions	At Gamma, routines were continuously morphing due to the efforts of middle managers at routine modification/generation performed by leveraging knowledge architecture competences	The organizational context influences participants' search actions, solution development and routine development.
Tripsas and Gavetti (2000)	At Polaroid, past routines affected how routines for innovation and change were performed, preventing	Knowledgeable and reflective actors (new hires with experience) brought new perspectives to how the	Product development routines and their outcomes were remarkably stable despite intentional	Prior routines and strongly held top management beliefs may dominate routine performance by generating cognitive

Table 34.3 *(cont.)*

Study	Situated actions	Knowledgeable and reflective actors	Stable for now. Stability as an accomplishment	Implications for Routine Dynamics
	creativity and innovation.	product development routine was performed.	attempts at altering their performance	dissonance between senior managers and routine participants, which severely limits Routine Dynamics and task outcomes.
Warner and Wäger (2019)	Dynamic Capabilities for digital transformation in seven German firms undergoing digital transformation resulted from a set of nine lower-level sub-capabilities, which, in turn, were grounded on participants' situated actions.	Developing a digital transformation DC depended on the mind-set of managers involved. Lacking this widespread mind-set, digital transformation did not start or succeed, despite top-down efforts of top managers.	Observed digital transformation DC were continuously morphing because they first resulted in the replacement of the prior business model, followed by changes in the collaborative approach among participants, further followed by a change in organizational culture.	The extent and effects of the dynamics of organizational routines significantly depend on the mind-set of participants. Higher-level routines result from the hierarchical combination of lower-level routines and actions.

this tradition addresses the three core observations that are basic to the RD lens (Feldman et al., 2016): actions are situated; actors are knowledgeable and often reflective; the routine that appears to be stable is only stable-for-now and its stability is an ongoing accomplishment of its participants. The analysis of these DC field studies from a RD perspective thus reveals several potential implications that could be derived from closer collaboration between the two perspectives.

In a similar vein, an analysis of some of the most influential field studies in RD (Table 34.4) shows that research in this tradition addresses the three building blocks of the Dynamic Capabilities lens (Feldman et al., 2016): routines or collections of routines determine a capability, which is a firm-level ability to perform a task; enactments of some 'higher-level' routines result in building, integrating, reconfiguring, releasing resource configurations; this determines economically significant change and effects on a firm's competitive advantage. Therefore, the analysis of these RD field studies from a DC perspective unveils several potential implications that could be derived from closer collaboration between the two views.

Drawing on insights from Tables 34.3 and 34.4, in the next section I will illustrate how the two views jointly contribute to the main four questions in the RD field (Feldman et al., 2016): (1) *How do routines emerge and change? (2) How do collections of interacting routines inhibit and promote stability and change? (3) How do routines inhibit and promote creativity and novelty? (4) How do routines help organizations maintain both pattern and variety?* In turn, these mutual contributions raise interesting avenues for future research, which will be further expanded on in the last section.

34.3 DC and RD Jointly Contribute to Answering the Same Research Questions

34.3.1 How Do Routines Emerge and Change?

Understanding routine emergence and change may significantly benefit from connecting the insights developed in the DC and RD fields. Insights from field studies in DC suggest that intentional efforts by senior managers in codifying and transferring

Table 34.4 Instances of Dynamic Capabilities in ten selected RD fieldworks

Study	Contribution of routines to firm-level capabilities for building, integrating, reconfiguring, releasing resource configurations	Contribution of routines to economically significant change/Competitive advantage	Implications for Dynamic Capabilities
Aroles and McLean (2016)	Organizational participants adapted routines for measuring ink density and assessing the quality of print copies at Crystal Print, a printing factory. This resulted in an adaptation of the standard script that was imposed top-down, to balance efficiency and quality.	Multiple adaptations by routine participants allowed Crystal Print to reduce the cost of printing, by monitoring ink density, and to keep the 'print quality of the copy'.	DC cannot be viewed as mere procedures, simple rules, checklists or standardized artifacts. This limits the possibilities for adaptation in the repetition of DC, i.e., their dynamism. The forces and socio-material or sociotechnical mediations underlying the process of DC repetition must be taken into account.
Berente, Lyytinen, Yoo and King (2016)	Participants gradually adapted procurement and project management routines to absorb tensions created by the implementation of an ERP system at NASA. Routines essentially served as 'shock absorbers' that continuously reconciled local practices with organizational imperatives	The role of routines as 'shock absorbers' brought in stability and achieved integration and control at the organizational level, although sacrificing integration and control at the local level.	Organizational routines may play the role of 'shock absorbers' in processes of DC implementation, by reducing the tensions between the rigidity of the planned solution and the messiness of everyday life. What makes a DC truly dynamic in practice is the adaptability of the routines on which the DC operates.
Bertels, Howard-Grenville and Pek (2016)	Organizational members of a Canadian oil company – which introduced an operational compliance routine that clashed with the existing organizational culture – shaped the routine's artifacts and expectations to adapt it to organizational culture.	The adaptation of the compliance routine by participants allowed the company to become compliant with international operational practices, while the company had previously operated as a scrappy pioneer developing engineering projects in remote environments under tight timelines	The integration of a DC that is a poor fit for the adopting organization, because it clashes with the target firm's culture, involves members' skilful manipulation of both how they perform the routine(s) composing the DC, and how they use cultural strategies of action.
Cohendet and Simon (2016)	At Ubisoft (a videogame development office) the cancellation of a potential blockbuster because of a lack of originality and strategic differentiation prompted the recombination of routines to 'unfreeze' the organization and reboot creativity.	The recombination of existing routines in a new context allowed Ubisoft to recreate its ability to produce successful videogames that were appreciated by customers.	DC do not necessarily emerge by imposing new procedures on an existing hierarchy. The formation of new dynamic routines may also emerge by articulating new procedures through a combination of top-down directions from management, and bottom-up involvement of participants involved in the dynamic routines.
D'Adderio (2014)	An electronics manufacturer dynamically directed the replication of the manufacturing routine of a complex server product in a different location. By involving different 'communities' (groups, teams, functions) and different artifacts (models, rules, procedures, lists), the production routine was first directed towards exact replication (alignment), and later towards improvement and adaptation.	The dynamic and flexible performance of the production routine allowed the electronics manufacturer to adapt it to the specific conditions of the local market in which the routine was transferred.	Firms attempting to transfer a DC in other organizational units must be aware that transfer processes actually undergo an active, emergent and creative process of routine replication. The same DC routine performed through different sets of artifacts and communities may result in the fulfilment of different (even opposing) goals.

Table 34.4 ***(cont.)***

Study	Contribution of routines to firm-level capabilities for building, integrating, reconfiguring, releasing resource configurations	Contribution of routines to economically significant change/Competitive advantage	Implications for Dynamic Capabilities
Dittrich, Guérard and Seidl (2016)	At CellCo – a start-up company in the pharmaceutical industry – talk allowed participants to dynamically reconfigure the shipping routine as they performed it.	Talk among CellCo participants allowed them to adapt the shipping routine by retaining the most effective adaptations that were suggested and tested as the routine was performed.	Talk among people who enact a DC allows them to dynamically adapt the DC from within, and as it is practised, to the shifting needs of markets and customers.
Turner and Rindova (2012)	Routine participants in six waste management organizations actively reconfigured routes to adapt to perturbations	Micro-adaptations of routine performances allowed the organizations to deliver relatively consistent outcomes to customers.	A firm's ability to deliver consistent outcomes amid environmental perturbations results from a combination of planned top-down modifications and endogenous change by employees.
Howard-Grenville (2005)	Participants of the 'road-mapping' routine at a high-tech firm dynamically adapted it to different activities such as materials planning, product development and even 'people development'	The dynamic adaptation of the road-mapping routine to different uses allowed the firm to address its changing environment with a single approach, thus reducing costs and complexity	The level of embeddedness of a routine in the organizational context (technological, coordination and cultural structures) influences how flexibly it is used.
Rerup and Feldman (2011)	Trial-and-error learning aimed at facing the problems emerged in enacting the recruiting routine, determined a reconfiguration of the originally espoused strategic schema.	Changes in schemata engendered by Routine Dynamics allowed Learning Lab Denmark to adapt its strategies to a shifting environmental context.	Organizational routines and the schemata that guide firm strategies are 'co-constituted'. Not only do schemata drive routines performance (as in DC) but routine enactments alter schemata.
Salvato and Rerup (2018)	Product development routines at Alessi behave as DC – embedded mechanisms of 'routine regulation' (activation, repression, alternative splicing) allow participants to reconfigure people, actions and artifacts, aligning them to market needs	'Routine regulation' allowed Alessi to anticipate changes in the market, thus strengthening its competitive advantage over decades.	Mechanisms of 'routine regulation' contribute to making an organizational capability 'dynamic'.

knowledge have a greater role in routine emergence and evolution than RD research suggests. In turn, RD research points to the fact that effective and dynamic routines may spontaneously emerge even lacking higher-level managerial intentionality and the intentional creation of an organizational context conducive of knowledge accumulation and transfer.

Insights from DC. Theoretical as well as empirical studies suggest that DC result from the accumulation of experience, and that more, similar, slowly paced and codified experience is particularly effective in the learning of Dynamic Capabilities (Bingham et al., 2015; Hayward, 2002; Zollo and Winter, 2002; Zollo et al., 2002). Several conceptual and empirical works in the literature on organizational routines have described the spontaneous accumulation and transfer of experience that allows routines to emerge and change (Cyert and March, 1963; Nelson and Winter, 1982). Scholars in DC add an important dimension to this knowledge, which is the intentionality in designing and enacting new or improved routines by structuring learning and knowledge codification and transfer. These dimensions have been partially overlooked by the RD literature, which is less interested in top-down intentionality.

Cumulative experience from multiple enactments of a capability provides participants' knowledge that helps them better understand the causal linkages between actions and outcomes. Codification of experience – the written documentation of knowledge in manuals, rule books and blueprints – impacts the learning of routines underlying DC. In particular, codification helps distil the tacit knowledge that individual routine participants develop across multiple enactments of the routine (Zollo and Winter, 2002). In his study of the design company Alessi, for instance, Salvato (2009) showed how top managers formalized changes to the product development routine resulting from participants' improvisation, when such changes resulted in improvements of the overall effectiveness of routine. The adapted routines were thus included in the firm's product development manual to be replicated. Tippmann et al. (2014) observed that in a leading ICT company, managers adopted a flexible organizational structure and the diffusion of knowledge, which resulted in the generation of knowledge search routines. Similarly, Martin (2011) showed how top managers' alteration of group structures and processes engendered dynamic processes connecting the general managers of different business units in six software companies, which allowed them to adapt company strategies to their dynamic environments.

These insights have also been applied to understand how managers can develop multiple connected DC in parallel. In their field study of Dow Chemicals, Bingham et al. (2015) illustrated how executives intentionally designed a process of concurrent learning and knowledge dissemination to simultaneously develop DC for M&A, alliances and disposals. First, managers 'initiated structure', by setting up a dedicated group to begin knowledge codification and transfer. This group started to codify knowledge from early deals and later made them more granular and systematically updated them. Second, the dedicated group also 'generalized structure', by transferring knowledge from acquisition processes to joint ventures and divestitures and by strengthening communication between the cross-functional teams performing each deal.

Insights from RD. RD empirical research is focused more on routines change than emergence. In contrast with the DC view of dynamic routines as top-down and engineered by top managers, RD research shows that they may spontaneously emerge and change even without higher-level managerial intentionality: 'Each time a routine is enacted is an occasion for variation [...] Variations may be retained (or not) for a variety of reasons, which may or may not be conscious or articulated' (Feldman et al., 2016: 508).

The main reason why routines tend to spontaneously emerge and change in the RD view is that their enactment is situated, which means that it happens in time, space and in given organizational contexts. Therefore, the outcome of enactments is difficult to anticipate and 'participants in a routine may not always be aware of what they are accomplishing or even that they have created a variation' (Feldman et al., 2016: 508). Moreover, variations may be driven by reflectivity, but they are often determined by emotions, for example when alterations are introduced because they are more fun, more familiar or more aesthetically pleasing.

Interestingly, however, empirical research in RD shows that very often routine participants perform changes aimed at making routines more dynamic – more effective, better fitting with connected routines, or providing more opportunities for task performance. In their study of a printing factory, for example, Aroles and McLean (2016) observed that participants enacted multiple adaptations to reduce the cost of printing and to keep the 'print' quality of the copy. At CellCo – a start-up company in the pharmaceutical industry – talk among participants allowed them to adapt the shipping routine by retaining the most effective adaptations that were suggested and tested as the routine was performed (Dittrich et al., 2016). In other studies, the adaptation of routines to a dynamic environment results from a combination of top-down managerial intervention and bottom-up enactments by participants. For instance, Cohendet and Simon (2016) noticed that at Ubisoft – a videogame development office – the formation of new dynamic routines emerged by articulating new procedures through a combination of top-down directions from management, and bottom-up involvement of participants involved in the dynamic routines.

Empirical evidence and theorizing in the RD framework therefore suggest that it might even be possible for a firm to have a DC that was not intentionally designed, because the enacted patterns and the ostensive aspect of the routine may or may not be articulated by its participants or by others. A firm might thus have a DC without knowing, or without being aware of where it resides – in what actions, people and artifacts.

34.3.2 How Do Routines, and Collections of Interacting Routines, Inhibit and Promote Creativity and Novelty?

A second question addressed by both the DC and RD frameworks refers to the role of routines in creativity and novelty (MacLean et al., 2015; Pandza and Thorpe, 2009). Organizational routines are often considered antithetical to creativity because traditional views of routines tended to conflate routines and routineness (Feldman et al., 2016). The DC and RD frameworks provide avenues to explain, for example, how designers, architects and others can consistently produce novel work (Cohendet and Simon, 2016) and how top managers can organize for creativity (Grand, 2016; Salvato, 2003, 2009). However, several questions remain open, and cooperation across the two fields may help answering them.

Insights from DC. DC are grounded in organizational routines, or collections of routines. The classic view of routines (Cyert and March, 1963; Nelson and Winter, 1982) emphasized their path-dependence – the fact that structure and a reproduction regime tend to shape how routines are performed (Sydow [Chapter 36], in this volume). In this view, routines are characterized by structural inertia and institutional persistence, and deviating from pattern is unlikely, although possible. So far, the DC perspective has incorporated this view of routines, with only a few exceptions. As a result, it is still unclear how DC can promote creativity and novelty. DC grounded on this view of their underlying routines may certainly be capable of reliably adapting existing resources but not in a truly novel and creative way, because DC are themselves patterned and learnt from past experience (Salvato and Vassolo, 2018).

Yet DC have been used to explain how firms introduce varying degrees of novelty, including innovative and highly creative actions. What DC bring to the attempts at generating innovation and creativity in organizations is the learning and practice at performing certain tasks (Nelson and Winter, 1982). As Winter (2008: 48) suggests, 'The skilled performer, drawing on years of practice, "makes it look easy".' The learning and practice that grounds high-level routines may in some cases supplant individual creativity as the source of the core change dynamic, while in other cases the stable aspect provided by the routine is only a framework to support and exploit the highly creative individuals who generate the elements of true novelty, such as in R&D departments (Helfat, 1997). In both cases, DC are conducive of innovation and creativity. In his illustration of Intel's DC in creating new semiconductor products, for example, Winter (2008) suggests that the significant novelties introduced by Intel were generated by routines that could thus not be regarded as merely repetitive behaviour.

Within these high-level routines, individual problem-solvers are merely 'interchangeable parts' or 'requisites of the overall system performance' (Winter, 2008: 52). This view of individual actors in routines seems to prevent a connection to RD, in which individual actors are central in determining the core change dynamics. However, as Winter (2008: 53) suggests in relation to Intel's DC, 'it is clear that much more than firm-level capability has been involved, and in particular that there has been a major role for highly structured, continuing interactions among actors of different types'. As in the RD framework, DC scholars also acknowledge a central role of knowledgeable and reflective actors in determining the dynamics conducive of innovation and change in high-level routines. Eisenhardt and Martin (2000), as well as Helfat et al. (2007), explicitly consider DC as purposeful, which indicates a certain degree of intentionality in how DC are performed. In addition, Teece (2012) suggested that, 'In dynamically competitive enterprises, there is also a critical role for the entrepreneurial manager in both transforming the enterprise and shaping the ecosystem through *sui generis* strategic acts that neither stem from routines (or algorithms) nor need give rise to new routines' (2012: 1395).

This discussion suggests that, although DC utilize routines and other organizational processes, they also have an element of agency and intent (Teece 2017, 2018). In their work on how Dynamic Capabilities are created and shaped, Pandza and Thorpe (2009) identified creative search and strategic sense-making as essential components of the managerial agency creating major changes in existing routines. Empirical work further advanced this intuition. For instance, Tippmann et al., (2014) studied how middle managers at a leading ICT multinational corporation played a central role in the enactment of search routines that reliably stimulated the creation of new solutions to modify the operating routines. Similarly, at Polaroid, knowledgeable and reflective actors – new hires with experience – brought new perspectives to how the product development routine was performed (Tripsas and Gavetti, 2000), and at the oil company Yukos, young managers were hired and trained with the explicit goal of innovatively performing search and experimentation processes in oil exploration and production (Dixon et al., 2014).

What DC research further adds to the conversation on routines and creativity is the role of organizational context in facilitating or hindering creative managerial action. For instance, Tippmann et al. (2014) noticed that the decision not to store knowledge in a central knowledge repository, combined with a flexible organizational design, greatly facilitated managerial action aimed at promoting creativity and novelty, while Alessi's top management codification of improvements in the product development routine resulted in more reliable creation of innovative design objects (Salvato, 2009). These insights on the role of the organizational context – which is part of what makes routine performance situated – may advance discussion in the RD view.

Insights from RD. The RD approach may substantially add to the insights developed by DC scholars on how routines may engender creativity and innovation. RD scholars showed that, although action patterning is guided by a reproduction regime, generative moments in which actors introduce substantial alterations to the action pattern are not infrequent and they promote creativity and novelty. Actually, every instance of routine enactment creates opportunities for novelty (Rerup and Feldman, 2011; Zbaracki and Bergen, 2010).

The RD approach is thus focused on deviations from pattern induced by participants' creativity far more than the DC approach (Sele and Grand, 2016; Sonenshein, 2016), while recognizing that endogenous stability is possible (Sydow [Chapter 36], in this volume). As mentioned, at Ubisoft (Cohendet and Simon, 2016), the recombination of existing routines in a new context allowed the firm to recreate its ability to produce innovative and creative videogames. Similarly, at Alessi, routine participants performed regulatory actions that directed the creativity of engineers and designers towards the specific needs of each new product development project (Salvato and Rerup, 2018). In these firms, novelty is a key determinant of competitive advantage and a strategic requirement for firm survival. The RD approach can thus be seen as contributing to the connection between routines and capabilities (Feldman et al., 2016). However, field studies that are squarely focused on routine enactment in highly creative organizations and industries, and an understanding of why and how routine participants can produce truly novel performances while enacting a routine pattern, are still lacking.

34.3.3 How Do Routines Help Organizations Maintain both Pattern and Variety?

DCs and the organizational routines grounding them are paradoxical entities (Peteraf et al., 2013) because they simultaneously involve stability and change, pattern and variety (Feldman and Pentland, 2003). This paradox has profound practical implications because firms need both the stability of routines and the creativity of their participants to systematically reconfigure resources to adapt to change (Helfat et al., 2007). Both DC and RD theories provide elements to partially untangle this paradox, but their insights have not been integrated. DC theory is excessively focused on the path-dependent, structural and stable components to be able to simultaneously explain change and variety. RD theory does a better job at explaining how organizational participants simultaneously maintain pattern and variety. However, it tends to overlook the role of senior managers in intentionally shaping the performance of routines in the desired direction, which is a central strategic management function. Despite this disconnection, both theories developed insights from field studies suggesting opportunities for integration and mutual learning.

Insights from DC. DC theory in its present state cannot adequately explain how actions of individual participants are aggregated into a firm-level ability for systematic resource renewal. Nor can it explain how a dynamic, firm-level routine, once the pattern has emerged, can be perpetuated (the stability element), without also curbing the creativity of its participants, on which the dynamic capacity to adapt is premised (the creativity element). Existing accounts fail to compellingly explain how pattern and variety coexist in DC. Polaroid, for instance, lacked the creativity element when it responded inadequately to the emergence of digital imaging in the 1980s. The firm's capabilities and management structural principles, which were centred on instant photography and the razor-blade model, prevented managers to enact constructive opposition to the outdated business model until an electronic imaging team, composed entirely of new hires, was established after 1990 (Tripsas and Gavetti, 2000). Between 1986 and 1996, Apple lacked the stability element when it failed to assimilate Steve Jobs' creative action into replicable innovation practices, and the company returned to success only after his comeback in 1997 (Heracleous, 2013).

The DC approach is excessively focused on templates, blueprints and routine structure. This focus results from the need to identify stable organizational traits to explain – and to eventually enhance – a firm's ability to systematically adapt to its environment. The limits of an excessive focus on structure and its stability are well exemplified by a quote from Bingham et al.'s (2015) study of Dow Chemicals. Describing how managers enacted recently developed M&A routines, a senior manager noted, 'Each acquisition is completely different. Regretfully, we had a recent acquisition that was too rigidly following the templates. Our group didn't recognize what needed to change on that. I think I have too many people who think if we have a set of guidelines, we have to follow those guidelines' (2015: 1823). Managers at Dow Chemicals addressed this problem by creating more structure. In particular, they developed an additional routine assigning a project management coach to each new deal who 'would pick and choose what would be the appropriate template, the appropriate process or methodology for that particular transaction . . . We work with the business to select what tool is needed' (2015: 1823).

A few studies suggest how combining insights from DC and RD may be a fruitful way to solve the pattern vs. variety paradox. Salvato's (2009) investigation of the product development DC of a design firm over time offers an example. By tracing the specific actions performed by specific participants enacting the routine at specific times and places, Salvato (2009) identified different ways, or clusters, of routine enactments. Out of the ninety observed enactments over several years, thirty-six 'recipe book' processes closely followed the codified ostensive pattern mandated by top managers. Another thirty-four processes showed effortful 'mutations' introduced by knowledgeable and reflective organizational actors with the aim of adapting the routine to novel circumstances. Interestingly, the remaining twenty product development processes incorporated some of the previously enacted 'mutations', which top managers have identified as valuable improvements of the routine and, thus, had codified into an adapted 'recipe book' ostensive pattern.

Insights from RD. While the DC approach addresses how variety may emerge by designing and implementing patterned capabilities, the RD approach takes a somewhat inverse approach by investigating routines as pattern-in-variety (Cohen, 2007). In the RD view, variation is a natural part of routine. While in DC, variation and flexibility somewhat surprisingly emerge from learnt, path-dependent and structured approaches engineered by top managers, RD views pattern as surprisingly emerging from the relentless and situated attempts of participants to adapt task performance to the specific situations at hand. In their longitudinal study of enterprise systems at NASA, for example, Berente, Lyytinen, Yoo and King (2016) investigated the divergence between ostensive and performative aspects of routines and showed that, in practice, standardization was accomplished through local variation by routine participants, more than through standardized work routines and controls. Similarly, D'Adderio (2014) showed that the dynamic and flexible performance of the production routine by its participants allowed an electronics manufacturer to adapt it to the specific conditions of the local market in which the routine was supposed to be transferred. At Crystal Print, a printing factory, organizational participants adapted routines for measuring ink density and assessing the quality of print copies, which resulted in an adaptation of the standard script that was imposed top-down, to balance efficiency and quality (Aroles and McLean, 2016). At NASA, participants gradually adapted procurement and project management routines to absorb tensions created by the implementation of the ERP system, thus turning routines into 'shock absorbers' that continuously reconciled local practices with organizational imperatives (Berente et al., 2016). Future research may combine the insights from DC about how structure and stability engender change and flexibility with the insights from RD about how constant variations by participants allow structure to perform and maintain generativity.

34.4 Future Research Directions

Combinations of insights and approaches from the RD and DC point to some interesting avenues for future research, and methods to address them. Figure 34.1 provides an overview of the connections between the DC and RD approaches, and a synthesis of these possible research areas.

Figure 34.1 suggests that DC are grounded in high/second-order routines (or collections/sequences of interacting routines) that act on (X) lower/first-order ordinary routines (Y) by building, integrating, reconfiguring or releasing them. In turn, ordinary routines determine task outcomes that, together, contribute to overall firm performance. Both dynamic and ordinary routines include a performative and an ostensive dimension. Both are enacted by routine participants ('from within') and shaped by senior managers ('from outside'), within an organizational context including the organizational structure; knowledge codification processes and repositories; rules; best practices; and artifacts. Combining insights from the DC and RD frameworks (Tables 34.3 and 34.4) suggests research directions in at least three areas: routine participants, ecologies of routines and routines performance.

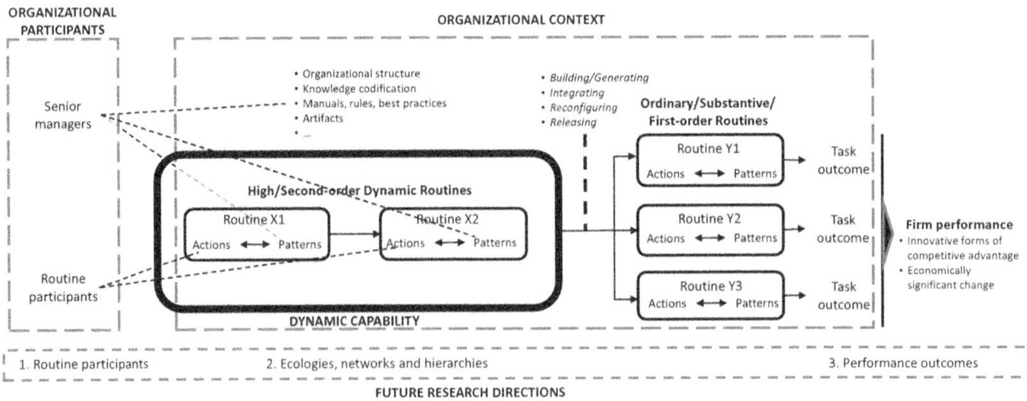

Figure 34.1 Future research directions

34.4.1 Investigating Participants' Intentionality in Designing and Performing Routines

The DC literature provides insights into how senior managers intentionally design high-level routines, while RD provides insights into how routine participants mindfully enact routines and how their actions are shaped by routines. We miss an understanding of how these two different types of intentionality play out and interact in how routines are generated, evolve and determine their outcomes.

Field research displays the importance of the cognitive representations held by senior managers in directing search processes in new learning environments (Helfat and Peteraf, 2015; Hodgkinson and Healey, 2011). Managerial cognition about firm resources is essential to explaining the extent to which routines are flexibly or rigidly enacted (Danneels, 2008, 2011; Salvato, 2003, 2009). Lacking a strong alignment between senior managers' and routine participants' beliefs about the need to promote change through routine enactments, and how such change should be accomplished, the resulting cognitive dissonance will prevent change happening. With few exceptions (e.g., Lazaric, 2008, 2011; Michel, 2014), however, the RD literature explicitly factors out cognition. However, exclusive focus on situated action as the unit of analysis may prevent our understanding of why and how certain networks of routines promote stability or change despite actors' intentions. As Feldman et al. (2016) noticed, exploring the relationality of mind and body in enacting routines would allow us to see new ways in which routine enactments may fail to produce change. The exploration of cognition should be extended beyond the individual routine, to include a broader network including decision-making routines in the executive suite. This leads to the following question: *What types of participants' cognition affect routine performance, and how? (e.g., cognitions about action patterns; relations within and between routines; or artifacts supporting routine enactments).*

Field research on DC shows that lacking strong support from senior managers towards change, existing collections of routines tend to promote stability rather than change. Only a strong cognitive alignment between the beliefs of senior managers and routine participants may allow the latter to promote the flexibility and change required by top managers. A firm's ability to deliver consistent outcomes amid environmental perturbations results from a combination of planned top-down modifications and endogenous change by employees (Turner and Rindova, 2012). The formation of new dynamic routines often emerges by articulating new procedures through a combination of top-down directions from management, and bottom-up involvement of participants involved in the dynamic routines (Cohendet and Simon, 2016). This literature suggests a number of research questions related to the alignment of cognition of different actors participating in DC and ordinary routines. *What type of cognitive alignment between top managers and routine participants is required to allow routine dynamization – alignment about goals, actions or patterns? How are the required forms of alignment developed, and how can they break and prevent routine dynamization?*

Scholars in the RD framework (Feldman et al., 2016) describe the nature of organizational routines as shaped by their relationality (vs. substantialism), that is, by relations between the actions that participants perform to enact them. Every time a person participates, he or she experiences different actions, different action patterns, different relationships and different outcomes. These may, in turn, reshape his or her nature (i.e., knowledge, skills, emotions and motivations). An interesting line of research that may emerge from this insight thus refers to the implications of relationality for routine participants and their subsequent involvement in routine performance. *How are routine participants changed and shaped by their participation in routine enactment? How do routine enactments shape participants' habits and path-dependent knowledge, reflection and cognition, emotions and motivations? Under what circumstances does routine enactment make participants more (or less) motivated to dynamically adapt their actions in subsequent enactments of the same or other routines?*

34.4.2 *Mapping Ecologies, Networks and Hierarchies of Routines*

Conceptual and empirical research in the DC and RD camps convincingly showed that organizational routines at any level (i.e., dynamic or ordinary routines) result from the hierarchical combination of lower-level routines and actions (Kremser and Schreyögg, 2016; Warner and Wäger, 2019). Both DC and RD researchers perform 'cuts' (Feldman et al., 2016) that allow them to zoom-in and zoom-out organizational routines, i.e., to trace boundaries around organizational actions in order to identify routines and how they are connected. Yet how these cuts are performed significantly affects the way we understand routines, actions within routines and routines performance. We miss an understanding of how boundaries traced to identify routines 'as entities' affect routines as enactments, and vice-versa. We also lack knowledge of the 'ecology of organizational routines', which involves an understanding of how participants' actions are connected both at different levels within and outside the organization and over time.

Within organizations, it may hence be interesting to investigate the following questions: *How are routines connected with each other to form sequences and ecologies of routines? To what extent are these connections flexible, thus allowing participants to recombine smaller 'chunks' to flexibly perform different tasks? How are DC connected to the target routines that they are meant to adapt? Is it only through hierarchy, or are less formal, and potentially unintentional, connections also involved?* A promising approach to answering these questions could be, for example, investigating patterns of communication and dialogue across routines through meetings, reviews, coaching and training (Bingham et al., 2015; Salvato and Vassolo, 2018).

Outside organizations, it may be interesting to explore *if DC and ordinary routines include actants and actions located outside the boundaries of the organization, how these external elements are connected to routines performance and how they affect their flexibility and task outcomes.* For instance, Danneels' (2002) study showed that in order to be dynamic, DC include network components, in particular relationships with new markets. Future research may extend these insights by further exploring the external actors, artifacts, actions and knowledge contributing to organizational routine performance. These external elements may make routines more or less flexible and dynamic, thus complementing the explanations of what makes a routine dynamic rather than those offered by the DC and RD perspectives.

Over time, it may be interesting not only to continue exploring how DC affect ordinary routines 'from outside', and how actors shape them 'from within', but also questions such as: *How do routines transition from one form to the other with one routine succeeding others over time?* For instance, a DC may turn into an ordinary one, and vice versa. Mapping routines as sequences of actions allows careful tracing of their evolution over time, as a number of field studies have shown (e.g., Prange, Bruyaka and Marmenout, 2018; Salvato, 2009).

34.4.3 *Understanding Performance Outcomes*

The DC and RD views are interested in different interpretations of 'performance'. Although this is legitimate, the two interpretations capture actual phenomena that affect each other, and that affect (and are affected by) the organizational context in which they happen. We thus miss an understanding of how top-down managerial actions aimed at shaping DC as entities affect how the underlying routines are performed, and we also miss an understanding of how routine enactments affect (facilitate/hamper) desired performance. Moreover, we still know little about how multiple dimensions of the organizational context affect routine performance and the mutual interaction between DC and ordinary routines.

The organizational context influences participants' search actions, solution development and routine development (Tippmann et al., 2014). For example, the level of embeddedness of a routine in the organizational context (technological, coordination and cultural structures) influences how flexibly it is used (Howard-Grenville, 2005). DC cannot be viewed as mere procedures, simple rules, checklists or standardized artifacts. This limits the possibilities for adaptation in the repetition of DC, i.e., their dynamism. It may thus be interesting to further explore *how the forces and the socio-material or sociotechnical mediations underlying the process of DC repetition influence DC effectiveness*, as Aroles and McLean (2016) observed in their study. For example, the same DC routine performed through different sets of artifacts and teams of participants may result in the fulfilment of different (even opposing) goals (D'Adderio, 2014). An interesting avenue to investigate these dynamics could be by *focusing research attention on group structures, processes and psychosocial characteristics, and how they affect how participants enact routines*. For example, as Martin's (2011) study suggested, the degree of social equivalence among routine participants (power parity and similar evaluation) may influence how effectively (creatively and flexibly) they enact routines. Following the lead of Bertels, Howard-Grenville and Pek's (2016) research, it may also be interesting to investigate *how organizational cultures, cultural strategies of action and their skilful manipulation affect how actors perform organizational routines*.

Besides structural components of the organizational context, cognitive elements are also worth exploring. It may thus be interesting to investigate *how differences in the beliefs and mind-sets on top-managers designing DC and managers enacting ordinary routines may generate cognitive dissonance, which may severely limit the effectiveness of DC work and the dynamism of routines* (Tripsas and Gavetti, 2000; Warner and Wäger, 2019).

Finally, routines themselves can be seen as part of the organizational context affecting performance of both DC and ordinary routines. Researchers may thus further explore *what makes some ordinary routines more adaptable and malleable targets of higher-level DC, in line with research that showed the role of target routines as 'shock absorbers' in processes of DC implementation*, by reducing the tensions between the rigidity of the planned solution and the messiness of everyday life (Berente et al., 2016). Besides understanding what makes target routines more suitable to be adapted by DC, scholars may also investigate *the role of some routines as 'regulatory mechanisms' that contribute to making an organizational capability 'dynamic'* (Salvato and Rerup, 2018). Organizational schemata may also play a similar role in driving the effectiveness of DC (Rerup and Feldman, 2011).

34.5 Conclusion

Scholars in the social sciences address phenomena with different theoretical and methodological lenses. The different perspectives and interpretations resulting from this legitimate differentiation of viewpoints provide deeper and more nuanced views of organizations and societies. However, at some point in the investigation path of a given phenomenon, different and even opposing views come closer and scholars from different camps happen to be separated by a thin wall of labels and definitions only. At this stage, it may be fruitful to use the elements that separate to build bridges across camps. The fields of Dynamic Capabilities in strategic management and of Routine Dynamics in organization theory have apparently reached this stage. The goal of this chapter was to map the two camps; identify legitimate differences and visible commonalities; and trace a path across the bridge. Strategic management and organization theory scholars may identify fruitful avenues for mutual learning, while firmly standing on their disciplinary grounds. In particular, DC scholars may benefit from zooming in on managers and the actions they perform when enacting DC and the routines in which they are grounded. In turn, RD scholars may extend their knowledge of actors performing routines if they zoomed out to include the impact of intentional top managers' intervention and of contextual variables on routine patterning.

References

Ambrosini, V. and Bowman, C. (2009). What are dynamic capabilities and are they a useful construct in strategic management? *International Journal of Management Reviews*, 11(1), 29–49.

Ambrosini, V., Bowman, C. and Collier, N. (2009). Dynamic capabilities: An exploration of how firms renew their resource base. *British Journal of Management*, 20, S9–S24.

Aroles, J. and McLean, C. (2016). Rethinking stability and change in the study of organizational routines: Difference and repetition in a newspaper-printing factory. *Organization Science*, 27(3), 535–550.

Barreto, I. (2010). Dynamic capabilities: A review of past research and an agenda for the future. *Journal of Management*, 36(1), 256–280.

Berente, N., Lyytinen, K., Yoo, Y. and King, J. L. (2016). Routines as shock absorbers during organizational transformation: Integration, control, and NASA's enterprise information system. *Organization Science*, 27(3), 551–572.

Bertels, S., Howard-Grenville, J. and Pek, S. (2016). Cultural molding, shielding, and shoring at Oilco: The role of culture in the integration of routines. *Organization Science*, 27(3), 573–593.

Bingham, C. B., Heimeriks, K. H., Schijven, M. and Gates, S. (2015). Concurrent learning: How firms develop multiple dynamic capabilities in parallel. *Strategic Management Journal*, 36(12), 1802–1825.

Brown, S. L. and Eisenhardt, K. M. (1997). The art of continuous change: Linking complexity theory and time-paced evolution in relentlessly shifting organizations. *Administrative Science Quarterly*, 42(1), 1–34.

Cohen, M. D. (2007). Reading Dewey: Reflections on the study of routine. *Organization Studies*, 28(5), 773–786.

Cohendet, P. S. and Simon, L. O. (2016). Always playable: Recombining routines for creative efficiency at Ubisoft Montreal's video game studio. *Organization Science*, 27(3), 614–632.

Cyert, R. M. and March, J. G. (1963). *A Behavioral Theory of the Firm*. Englewood Cliffs, NJ: Prentice-Hall.

D'Adderio, L. (2014). The replication dilemma unravelled: How organizations enact multiple goals in routine transfer. *Organization Science*, 25(5), 1325–1350.

Danneels, E. (2002). The dynamics of product innovation and firm competences. *Strategic Management Journal*, 23(12), 1095–1121.

Danneels, E. (2008). Organizational antecedents of second-order competences. *Strategic Management Journal*, 29(5), 519–543.

Danneels, E. (2011). Trying to become a different type of company: Dynamic capability at Smith Corona. *Strategic Management Journal*, 32(1), 1–31.

Dittrich, K., Guérard, S. and Seidl, D. (2016). Talking about routines: The role of reflective talk in routine change. *Organization Science*, 27(3), 678–697.

Dixon, S., Meyer, K. and Day, M. (2014). Building dynamic capabilities of adaptation and innovation: A study of micro-foundations in a transition economy. *Long Range Planning*, 47(4), 186–205.

Eisenhardt, K. M. and Martin, J. A. (2000). Dynamic capabilities: What are they? *Strategic Management Journal*, 21(10–11), 1105–1121.

Feldman, M. S. and Pentland, B. T. (2003). Reconceptualizing organizational routines as a source of flexibility and change. *Administrative Science Quarterly*, 48(1), 94–118.

Feldman, M. S., Pentland, B. T., D'Adderio, L. and Lazaric, N. (2016). Beyond routines as things: Introduction to the special issue on routine dynamics. *Organization Science*, 27(3), 505–513.

Grand, S. (2016). *Routines, Strategies and Management: Engaging for Recurrent Creation 'At the Edge'*. Cheltenham: Edward Elgar Publishing.

Hayward, M. L. A. (2002). When do firms learn from their acquisition experience? Evidence from 1990–1995. *Strategic Management Journal*, 23 (1), 21–39.

Helfat, C. E. (1997). Know-how and asset complementarity and dynamic capability accumulation: The case of R&D. *Strategic Management Journal*, 18(5), 339–360.

Helfat, C. E., Finkelstein, S., Mitchell, W., Peteraf, M., Singh, H., Teece, D. and Winter, S. G. (2007). *Dynamic Capabilities: Understanding Strategic Change in Organizations*. New York: John Wiley & Sons.

Helfat, C. E. and Peteraf, M. A. (2015). Managerial cognitive capabilities and the microfoundations of dynamic capabilities. *Strategic Management Journal*, 36(6), 831–850.

Helfat, C. E. and Winter, S. G. (2011). Untangling dynamic and operational capabilities: Strategy for the (N) ever-changing world. *Strategic Management Journal*, 32(11), 1243–1250.

Heracleous, L. 2013. Quantum strategy at Apple Inc. *Organizational Dynamics*, 42(2), 92–99.

Hodgkinson, G. P. and Healey, M. P. (2011). Psychological foundations of dynamic capabilities: Reflexion and reflection in strategic management. *Strategic Management Journal*, 32 (13), 1500–1516.

Howard-Grenville, J. (2005). The persistence of flexible organizational routines: The role of agency and organizational context. *Organization Science*, 16(6), 618–636.

Klein, K. J., Dansereau, F. and Hall, R. J. (1994). Levels issues in theory development, data collection, and analysis. *Academy of Management Review*, 19(2), 195–229.

Kremser, W. and Schreyögg, G. (2016). The dynamics of interrelated routines: Introducing the cluster level. *Organization Science*, 27(3), 698–721.

Lazaric, N. (2008). Routines and routinization: An exploration of some micro-cognitive foundations. In M. C. Becker, ed., *Handbook of Organizational Routines*. Cheltenham: Edward Elgar, pp. 205–227.

Lazaric, N. (2011). Organizational routines and cognition: An introduction to empirical and analytical contributions. *Journal of Institutional Economics*, 7(2), 147–156.

MacLean, D., MacIntosh, R. and Seidl, D. (2015). Rethinking dynamic capabilities from a creative action perspective. *Strategic Organization*, 13 (4), 340–352.

Martin, J. A. (2011). Dynamic managerial capabilities and the multibusiness team: The role of episodic teams in executive leadership groups. *Organization Science*, 22(1), 118–140.

Michel, A. A. (2014). The mutual constitution of persons and organizations: An ontological perspective on organizational change. *Organization Science*, 25(4), 1082–1110.

Nelson, R. R. and Winter, S. (1982). *An Evolutionary Theory of Economic Change*. Cambridge, MA: Belknap.

Pandza, K. and Thorpe, R. (2009). Creative search and strategic sense-making: Missing dimensions in the concept of dynamic capabilities. *British Journal of Management*, 20(1), S118–S131.

Parmigiani, A. and Howard-Grenville, J. (2011). Routines revisited: Exploring the capabilities and practice perspectives. *Academy of Management Annals*, 5(1), 413–453.

Pentland, B. T., Feldman, M. S., Becker, M. C. and Liu, P. (2012). Dynamics of organizational routines: A generative model. *Journal of Management Studies*, 49(8), 1484–1508.

Peteraf, M., Di Stefano, G. and Verona, G. (2013). The elephant in the room of dynamic capabilities: Bringing two diverging conversations together. *Strategic Management Journal*, 34(12), 1389–1410.

Prange, C., Bruyaka, O. and Marmenout, K. (2018). Investigating the transformation and transition processes between dynamic capabilities: Evidence from DHL. *Organization Studies*, 39(11), 1547–1573.

Rerup, C. and Feldman, M. S. (2011). Routines as a source of change in organizational schema: The role of trial-and-error learning. *Academy of Management Journal*, 54, 577–610.

Rousseau, D. (1985). Issues of level in organizational research: Multilevel and cross-level perspectives. In L. L. Cummings and B. M. Staw, eds., *Research in Organizational Behavior*. Greenwich, CT: JAI Press, 7, 1–37.

Salvato, C. (2003). The role of micro-strategies in the engineering of firm evolution. *Journal of Management Studies*, 40(1), 83–108.

Salvato, C. (2009). Capabilities unveiled: The role of ordinary activities in the evolution of product development processes. *Organization Science*, 20(2), 384–409.

Salvato, C. and Rerup, C. (2011). Beyond collective entities: Multilevel research on organizational routines and capabilities. *Journal of Management*, 37(2), 468–490.

Salvato, C. and Rerup, C. (2018). Routine regulation: Balancing conflicting goals in organizational routines. *Administrative Science Quarterly*, 63(1), 170–209.

Salvato, C. and Vassolo, R. (2018) The sources of dynamism in dynamic capabilities. *Strategic Management Journal* ('New theory in strategic management' Special Issue), 39(6), 1728–1752.

Schilke, O., Hu, S. and Helfat, C. E. (2018). Quo vadis, dynamic capabilities? A content analytic review of the current state of knowledge and recommendations for future research. *Academy of Management Annals*, 12(1), 390–439.

Sele, K. and Grand, S. (2016). Unpacking the dynamics of ecologies of routines: Mediators and their generative effects in routine interactions. *Organization Science*, 27(3), 722–738.

Sonenshein, S. (2016). Routines and creativity: From dualism to duality. *Organization Science*, 27(3), 739–758.

Teece, D. J. (2007). Explicating dynamic capabilities: The nature and microfoundations of (sustainable) enterprise performance. *Strategic Management Journal*, 28(13), 1319–1350.

Teece, D. J. (2012). Dynamic capabilities: Routines versus entrepreneurial action. *Journal of Management Studies*, 49(8), 1395–1401.

Teece, D. J. (2017). Towards a capability theory of (innovating) firms: Implications for management and policy. *Cambridge Journal of Economics*, 41(3), 693–720.

Teece, D. J. (2018). Dynamic capabilities as (workable) management systems theory. *Journal of Management & Organization*, 24(3), 359–368.

Teece, D. and Pisano, G. (1994). The dynamic capabilities of firms: an introduction. *Industrial and Corporate Change*, 3(3), 537–556.

Teece, D. J., Pisano, G. and Shuen, A. (1997). Dynamic capabilities and strategic management. *Strategic Management Journal*, 18(7), 509–533.

Tippmann. E., Sharkey Scott, P. and Mangematin, V. (2014) Stimulating knowledge search routines and architecture competences: The role of organizational context and middle management. *Long Range Planning*, 47(4), 206–223.

Tripsas, M. and Gavetti, G. (2000). Capabilities, cognition, and inertia: Evidence from digital imaging. *Strategic Management Journal*, 21 (10/11), 1147–1161.

Turner, S. F. and Rindova, V. (2012). A balancing act: How organizations pursue consistency in routine functioning in the face of ongoing change. *Organization Science*, 23(1), 24–46.

Warner, K. S. R. and Wäger, M. (2019). Building dynamic capabilities for digital transformation: An ongoing process of strategic renewal. *Long Range Planning*, 52(3), 326–349.

Winter, S. G. (2000). The satisficing principle in capability learning. *Strategic Management Journal, Special Issue*, 21(10–11), 981–996.

Winter, S. G. (2003). Understanding dynamic capabilities. *Strategic Management Journal*, 24(10), 991–995.

Winter, S. G. (2008). Dynamic capability as a source of change. In A. Ebner and N. Beck, eds., *The Institutions of the Market. Organizations, Social Systems, and Governance*. New York: Oxford University Press, pp. 40–65.

Zahra, S. A., Sapienza, H. J. and Davidsson, P. (2006). Entrepreneurship and dynamic capabilities: A review, model and research agenda. *Journal of Management Studies*, 43(4), 917–955.

Zbaracki, M. J. and Bergen, M. (2010). When truces collapse: A longitudinal study of price-adjustment routines. *Organization Science*, 21(5), 955–972.

Zollo, M. and Winter, S. G. (2002). Deliberate learning and the evolution of dynamic capabilities. *Organization Science*, 13(3), 339–351.

Zollo, M., Reuer, J. J. and Singh, H. (2002). Interorganizational routines and performance in strategic alliances. *Organization Science*, 13(6), 701–713.

CHAPTER 35

Strategy as Practice and Routine Dynamics

DAVID SEIDL, BENJAMIN GROSSMANN-HENSEL AND PAULA JARZABKOWSKI

35.1 Introduction

In this chapter, we compare Routine Dynamics and Strategy as Practice as 'distinct but related theories of organizing' (Feldman, 2015: 317) and ask what they can learn from each other. Routine Dynamics and Strategy as Practice are distinctive communities of thought in organization studies that exhibit a number of striking parallels. Most importantly, both Routine Dynamics and Strategy as Practice scholars identify explicitly with the wider 'practice turn' (Feldman and Orlikowski, 2011; Schatzki et al., 2001) in the social sciences and describe their research as aimed at developing theories of 'routines *as practices*' (Feldman and Orlikowski, 2011: 1245) and 'strategy *as practice*' (Jarzabkowski et al., 2007), respectively. Both streams of research are framed in opposition to traditional approaches in their respective domains, which they criticize for having 'lost sight of the human being' (Jarzabkowski et al., 2007: 6) and for '[separating] the people who are doing the routines from the routine' (Feldman, 2000: 613). In line with that, the Strategy as Practice approach is primarily focused on developing a 'close understanding of the myriad, micro activities that make up strategy and strategizing in practice' (Johnson et al., 2003: 3) and the Routine Dynamics approach 'deliberately puts actions in the foreground and, thus, the unit of observation is situated action' (Feldman et al., 2016: 506).

There is also a striking parallel in the historical trajectories of the two research approaches. Both Routine Dynamics and Strategy as Practice can be traced back to some early publications in the mid-1990s and early 2000s, a time which is often seen as the starting point for the practice turn in organization studies more generally (Feldman and Orlikowski, 2011; Miettinen et al., 2009; Whittington, 2011). In line with other research areas, such as accounting (Ahrens and Chapman, 2006), marketing (Korkman et al., 2010), entrepreneurship (Champenois et al., 2020), learning (Gherardi, 2009) or technology (Orlikowski, 1992), Routine Dynamics and Strategy as Practice started questioning the established views of routines (Feldman, 2000; Pentland and Rueter, 1994) and strategy (Hendry, 2000; Whittington, 1996), respectively; both streams gathered momentum with a number of decisive publications in the mid-2000s, proposing research frameworks and developing a research agenda for Routine Dynamics (Feldman and Pentland, 2003) and Strategy as Practice (Jarzabkowski et al., 2007; Johnson et al., 2003; Whittington, 2006).

In both communities, there is now a substantive body of research: at least 120 papers are explicitly framed as Routine Dynamics (for reviews, see Howard-Grenville and Rerup, 2017; Parmigiani and Howard-Grenville, 2011),[1] and at least 350 papers can be classified as belonging to the Strategy as Practice research stream (for reviews, see Jarzabkowski and Spee, 2009; Vaara and

[1] This number is based on a search of the Web of Science for papers citing the seminal publication Feldman and Pentland (2003) covering the period up to January 2020. Out of these results, only papers identified as being centrally about organizational routines were included. These are the same search criteria as applied by Howard-Grenville and Rerup (2017) in their literature review.

Whittington, 2012).[2] Interestingly, many of the core scholars in the two fields publish in both fields and identify with both communities. This includes authors such as Simon Grand, Katharina Dittrich, Ann Langley, Carlo Salvato and Paul Spee – and also two of the authors of this chapter, who have been involved in Strategy as Practice from the very beginning and have lately also made various contributions to Routine Dynamics (e.g., Dittrich et al., 2016; Spee et al., 2016). At the intersection of the two research streams, there is also one empirical study (Grand and Bartl, 2019) that has combined the Strategy as Practice and Routine Dynamics literature to examine strategizing routines and one conceptual handbook chapter (Feldman, 2015) discussing what Strategy as Practice can learn from Routine Dynamics. All of this highlights the strong affinities between the two research domains.

Given all these obvious parallels and points of connection between the Routine Dynamics and Strategy as Practice communities, the purpose of this chapter is to offer a systematic comparison of the two research streams according to five aspects: *empirical domains, theoretical perspectives, theoretical frameworks, 'levels' of analysis* and *empirical methods*. This will serve as the basis for a discussion of potential areas of cross-fertilization between the two research communities.

35.2 Similarities and Differences between Strategy as Practice and Routine Dynamics

35.2.1 Empirical Domains

In terms of its empirical domain, Routine Dynamics describes itself as 'the study of the internal dynamics of routines', as 'one branch of research on routines that is based in the idea that routines are practices with internal dynamics that contribute to both stability and change in organizations' (Feldman et al., 2016: 505). By comparison, the empirical domain of Strategy as Practice is more loosely defined as the study of the 'social activities, processes and practices that characterize organizational strategy and strategizing' (Golsorkhi et al., 2015: 1). Ultimately, it is concerned with anything that is 'consequential for the strategic outcomes, directions, survival and competitive advantage of the firm' (Jarzabkowski et al., 2007: 8). Related to that, we can find a variety of definitions of the empirical domain: 'managerial activity, how managers "do strategy"' (Whittington, 1996: 732), 'the consequential details of organizational work and practice' (Johnson et al., 2003: 5), 'the actions and interactions of the strategy practitioner' (Jarzabkowski et al., 2007: 6) or 'what actually takes place in strategy formulation, planning and implementation and other activities that deal with the thinking and doing of strategy' (Golsorkhi et al., 2015: 1). As these varying definitions illustrate, the boundaries of Strategy as Practice's empirical research domain are rather diffuse; a relation to strategic activities and the use of practice theories are the only common denominators holding together the different studies under the 'broad umbrella' (Golsorkhi et al., 2015: 1) of Strategy as Practice. In line with that, Langley (2015: 111) characterized Strategy as Practice as 'a sub-field whose empirical focus still remains rather loosely defined'.

Aside from the formal definitions of their empirical domains, we can also examine what concrete phenomena have been investigated by each research community. In Routine Dynamics, most studies have been concerned with activities associated with *operational* routines that often are codified in so-called Standard Operating Procedures. This ranges from studies on the everyday routines of IT software hot lines (Pentland and Rueter, 1994), academic housing (Feldman, 2000) and hiring (Feldman and Pentland, 2003) to the routines of price-adjustments in manufacturing (Zbaracki ans Bergen, 2010), garbage collection (Turner and Rindova, 2012, 2018), environmental compliance (Bertels et al., 2016), physicians' handoffs (LeBaron et al., 2016), patient processes

[2] This number is based on a search of the Web of Science for papers mentioning 'strategy-as-practice' (both with and without hyphens) in the title, keyword, abstract or text covering the period up to January 2020. These are the same search criteria as applied by the 'Strategizing Activities and Practices' Interest Group at the Academy of Management in its review of relevant SAP papers.

(Bucher and Langley, 2016), reinsurance deal appraisals (Spee et al., 2016) or towel changing in hotels (Bapuji et al., 2012, 2019). In addition, there has been a study on *strategic* routines, such as strategic decision-making routines (Grand and Bartl, 2019). In addition, there are an increasing number of studies examining *interaction between multiple (operational or strategic) routines* (see also Rosa et al. [Chapter 17], this volume) such as the ecology of routines underlying a children's summer camp (Birnholtz et al., 2007), the cluster of routines involved in industrial photofinishing (Kremser and Schreyögg, 2016) or the bundle of routines in a research laboratory (Sele and Grand, 2016).

Compared to Routine Dynamics, Strategy as Practice has focused more on discursive rather than non-discursive activities, which is not surprising given that strategy is often conceptualized 'as part of an organizational *discourse* or body of language-based communications' (Hendry, 2000: 957). Examples include the activities of exploring strategic topics (Seidl and Werle, 2018; Werle and Seidl, 2015), strategic planning activities (Kornberger and Clegg, 2011; Vaara et al., 2010), meeting and workshop activities (Healey et al., 2015; Jarzabkowski and Seidl, 2008; Johnson et al., 2010) or strategic decision-making activities (Samra-Fredericks, 2003). Very few studies have also examined more operational activities associated with the enactment and implementation of strategies. In particular, Balogun et al. (2015) provide a detailed analysis of how guided tours within a museum enact the strategy of that museum.

As this brief overview reveals, there are significant overlaps between the respective empirical domains, but there are also differences. This is not surprising given how the two communities emerged, but it should be noted that, at least in principle, each empirical domain could quite readily be examined by the other research community. As the study by Balogun et al. (2015) shows, mundane operative routines, including their non-discursive behaviours, may be studied by Strategy as Practice scholars as part of enacting an organization's strategy. Similarly, Routine Dynamics scholars can fruitfully study strategizing routines, as some of the existing studies demonstrate (Grand and Bartl, 2019); even one-off strategizing activities can be studied by Routine Dynamics scholars to the extent that those activities are typically embedded in practitioners' everyday routines (Samra-Fredericks, 2003: 168).

35.2.2 Theoretical Perspectives

In their conceptual origins and overall perspectives, both Routine Dynamics and Strategy as Practice are firmly rooted in *theories of social practice*. The early Routine Dynamics research drew primarily on the practice theories of Giddens (1984), Bourdieu (1990) and Latour (2005) (see also Feldman [Chapter 2], this volume). As Feldman (2011) wrote, reflecting on her early theoretical influences, 'I found the framework of structuration theory most immediately applicable [. . .]. Bourdieu's relational framework and the concept of habitus were also [. . .] important for thinking about the way people enact routines on a day-to-day basis. Later, I incorporated some of Latour's [. . .] ideas [. . .], or my interpretation of these ideas.' (Feldman and Orlikowski, 2011: 1244). In addition, early Routine Dynamics studies also refer to work in ethnomethodology (Garfinkel, 1967) as well as some non–practice-theoretical perspectives such as the behavioural theory of the firm (Cyert and March, 1963) and evolutionary economics (Nelson and Winter, 1982).

Early Strategy as Practice research, in turn, has 'draw[n] upon a [wide] range of existing [practice] theories' (Jarzabkowski et al., 2007: 19) without focusing on a specific set of theories. Hence, we find studies relying on the theories of Foucault (Knights and Morgan, 1991), Bourdieu (Jarzabkowski, 2004), Giddens (Hendry, 2000) and Sztompka (Jarzabkowski, 2003), in addition to some other theoretical approaches that are not theories of practice in a narrower sense, such as sense-making (Balogun and Johnson, 2004) and Luhmann's systems theory (Hendry and Seidl, 2003). In contrast to the field of Routine Dynamics, these different theoretical resources were not integrated with each other but remained widely scattered across different studies. That is, different studies have drawn on different theories, largely without any attempt at relating the respective concepts to the theoretical concepts employed in other articles. Accordingly, many papers in Strategy as Practice start with the introduction of a particular practice theory, which is then applied to a particular empirical strategy phenomenon.

Over the years, both Routine Dynamics and Strategy as Practice have extended the range of theoretical resources employed. In some cases, additional theoretical perspectives were introduced in order to complement the existing theoretical perspectives, allowing their authors to address aspects that could not be captured within the existing theoretical apparatus or to deepen the analysis of known phenomena. In Routine Dynamics, for example, Cohen introduced Dewey's pragmatist theory, arguing that some of Routine Dynamics' conceptual difficulties can be 'usefully illuminated by Dewey's view' (Cohen, 2007: 773; see also Dionysiou [Chapter 5], this volume); D'Adderio, in turn, mobilized theories of sociomateriality, claiming that '[d]eeper understandings of the role of artifacts can open up new avenues for routines research' (D'Adderio, 2011: 214; see also D'Adderio [Chapter 7], this volume); Dionysiou and Tsoukas introduced symbolic interactionism so as 'to contribute to our deeper understanding of the nature of routines as collective accomplishments' (Dionysiou and Tsoukas, 2013: 201). Similarly, in Strategy as Practice, a wide range of other theories were added to the existing repertoire, including Actor-Network Theory (ANT) and conventionalist theory (Denis et al., 2007), Schatzki's theory of practice bundles (Seidl and Whittington, 2014), Wittgenstein's theory of language games (Mantere, 2013), complexity theory (Campbell-Hunt, 2007), Communication Constitutes Organization (CCO) (Spee and Jarzabkowski, 2011), narrative perspectives (Fenton and Langley, 2011; Brown and Thompson, 2013), institutionalism (Smets et al., 2015) and socio-materiality (Dameron et al., 2015).

In contrast to Routine Dynamics, where studies tend to build on and then extend existing theoretical developments, in Strategy as Practice several papers explicitly challenge the theoretical foundations of Strategy as Practice, proposing new theoretical perspectives to replace the existing ones. In particular, the Heideggerian perspective (Chia and Holt, 2006; Chia and MacKay, 2007; Tsoukas, 2015), the systemic-discursive perspective (Seidl, 2007), poststructuralist analysis (Ezzamel and Willmott, 2010) and Critical Realism (Herepath, 2014) were seen as offering alternatives to the established views. Due to the explicitly pluralistic ethos of the Strategy as Practice community, which we will elaborate later, these conflicting theoretical perspectives have persisted alongside the established theories.

While Routine Dynamics and Strategy as Practice have largely drawn on the same theories, they differ in the way they have dealt with these theories. Strategy as Practice has treated the multiplicity of theories as a kind of repertoire to be mobilized selectively depending on the particular research question at hand (Jarzabkowski et al., 2007: 19). Routine Dynamics scholars, in contrast, have put great effort into integrating the different theoretical concepts into a coherent perspective to guide research. In other words, Routine Dynamics research can be described as research with a distinctive theoretical approach, while Strategy as Practice research is based on a host of related but distinctive theoretical perspectives. As Strategy as Practice scholars have highlighted, 'strategy-as-practice as a field is characterized less by what theory is adopted than by what problem is explained' (Jarzabkowski et al., 2007: 19).

35.2.3 Research Frameworks

Distinctive research frameworks for both Routine Dynamics and Strategy as Practice were developed at an early stage: respectively, a framework describing the interplay between ostensive and performative aspects of routines (see Figure 35.1) and the '3Ps' framework of strategizing (see Figure 35.2). Interestingly, these frameworks, while used only within Routine Dynamics and Strategy as Practice, are rather general and not specific to routines or strategy, respectively. In principle, they could also be used to study phenomena beyond the immediate domain. Hence, the

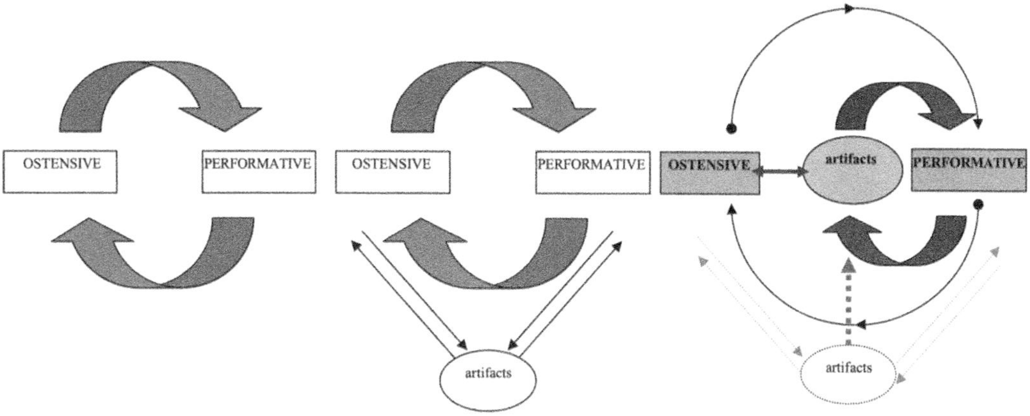

1) Original framework of routine dynamics as interplay between ostensive and performative aspects (Feldman and Pentland, 2003)

2) Relation between ostensive and performative as influenced by artifacts (Feldman and Pentland, 2005)

3) Artifacts at the centre of the interplay of ostensive and performative aspects (D'Adderio, 2008)

Figure 35.1 Successive stages of development of the Routine Dynamics framework (according to D'Adderio, 2011: 224)

Strategy as Practice framework could just as well be applied to research on routines and the Routine Dynamics framework could be applied to research on strategy (Feldman, 2015).

Despite their many similarities, the respective frameworks of Routine Dynamics and Strategy as Practice serve rather different functions. Routine Dynamics initially developed a highly coherent and widely applicable framework for the analysis of organizational routines. In their seminal publication, Feldman and Pentland (2003) presented a framework describing the core mechanism of Routine Dynamics based on the interplay between the *ostensive* aspect of the routine as 'the abstract, generalized idea of the routine or the routine in principle', i.e. a kind of structural aspect, and the *performative* aspect as the 'specific actions, by specific people, in specific times and places [...] the routine in practice' (Feldman and Pentland, 2003: 101). Although not explicitly included in a graphical representation of the framework, this interplay was associated with generativity, improvisation and multiplicity as important aspects of Routine Dynamics.

As Routine Dynamics researchers expanded the scope of the theories employed, the original framework was successively revised and expanded. The first significant extension to the framework concerned the inclusion of *artifacts* as objects capable of action (D'Adderio, 2011) – see Figure 35.1 on the successive stages of development of the initial framework.

A further important modification of the original framework was the reconceptualization of the ostensive aspect in radically processual terms, which led Feldman (2016) to speak of *patterning* as an alternative to the ostensive aspect. With this conceptual modification, Feldman wanted to focus attention on 'the specific actions (doings and sayings) involved in creating patterns or patterning; [...] patterning draws our attention to the work of recognizing and articulating or narrating these patterns'. (Feldman, 2016: 39–40).

Similarly to Routine Dynamics, Strategy as Practice scholars developed a seminal framework to guide Strategy as Practice research at an early stage. Building on the work of Reckwitz (2002), Jarzabkowski (2005) and Whittington (2006), they proposed a framework consisting of three elements, i.e., practices, praxis and practitioners, which came to be known as the '3Ps' framework

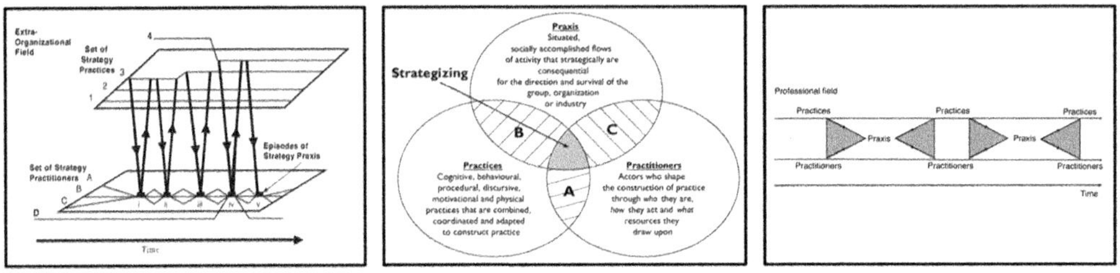

1) Original framework (Whittington, 2006: 621): Practices from the extra-organizational field are enacted by practitioners in concrete episodes of strategy praxis within a focal organization.

2) "3Ps" framework as a map of research areas in Strategy as Practice (Jarzabkowski et al., 2007: 11): Strategizing comprises the nexus between praxis, practices and practitioners. A, B, and C represent stronger foci on one of these interconnections depending upon the research problem to be addressed.

3) "4P" model (Whittington, 2019: 31): Episodes of strategy praxis are infused by practices existing at the level of strategy as profession. Strategy practitioners and their practices belong to and are legitimated by the professional field.

Figure 35.2 Successive stages of development of the strategy as practice framework

(see Figure 35.2). Somewhat analogously to the distinction between the ostensive and performative aspects of the original Routine Dynamics framework, the two concepts of practices and praxis were meant to reflect the structural aspect of strategy work and the actual doing of strategy, respectively. As Whittington wrote, '*practices* will refer to shared routines of behaviour, including traditions, norms and procedures for thinking, acting and using 'things', this last in the broadest sense. By contrast, the Greek word *praxis* refers to actual activity, what people do in practice.' (Whittington 2006: 619). To this interplay between structure and action, Whittington added the practitioners as a third element, highlighting the actors as those 'who both perform this activity and carry its practices' (Whittington, 2006: 619). As Whittington pointed out, the alliteration of the three elements was chosen purposefully to underline the interconnectedness of the three aspects.

The '3 Ps' framework was subsequently further interpreted by Jarzabkowski et al. (2007) as a categorization device for mapping research in the field of Strategy as Practice (see Figure 35.2). Interpreting the '3 Ps' as different elements of strategy work, existing studies were categorized according to the particular element or combination of elements they addressed. In line with the original framework, it was argued that researchers, for pragmatic reasons, would typically foreground one or two elements while 'bracketing' the other elements.

In a further iteration of the Strategy as Practice framework, Whittington added the strategy profession as a missing 'fourth P' (Whittington, 2007: 1580), extending it into the 'the 4P model'. As he wrote, 'the 4P model helps make explicit the trans-organizational dimension that is sometimes neglected in earlier Strategy-as-Practice studies [. . .] Adding the fourth dimension of professional field protects against such insularity: episodes of organizational praxis are typically infused by practices existing at the macro level of Strategy as profession' (Whittington, 2019: 31).

Beyond the content of the frameworks themselves, there are also differences in the role these theoretical frameworks have played in the respective communities. On the one hand, the Routine Dynamics framework, in its various stages of evolution, can be seen as an integral part of Routine Dynamics research. It has served as a theoretical framework guiding the collection and analysis of data. Most Routine Dynamics studies explicitly refer to this framework – even though there are some exceptions, such as Birnholtz et al. (2007) or Salvato (2009). The '3Ps' framework and its extensions, on the other hand, have been far less significant in the Strategy as Practice community. As Langley observed regarding the framework, there is 'no clear consensus concerning its completeness or relevance' (Langley, 2015: 116). Rarely is the framework referred to in Strategy as Practice studies and it is only seldom used to guide data collection and analysis. One reason for that might be that, unlike its counterpart in Routine Dynamics, the Strategy as Practice framework does not describe a theoretical mechanism but merely lists relevant aspects of strategizing aiming to 'sensitize'

(Whittington, 2006: 627) researchers to the relevance of those aspects, while explicitly encouraging them to focus on some aspects while bracketing others (Jarzabkowski et al., 2007). This difference in the roles of the respective frameworks might also explain why Routine Dynamics research appears far more integrated and cumulative than research in Strategy as Practice (Langley, 2015).

35.2.4 'Levels' of Analysis

Another dimension for comparing Routine Dynamics and Strategy as Practice are their respective 'levels' of analysis (for a similar comparison of research communities according to levels of analysis, in this case Routine Dynamics and Dynamic Capabilities, see Salvato [Chapter 34], this volume). We have put levels in inverted commas, since some studies, adopting a flat ontology, reject the idea of there being different levels of reality (micro vs. macro level) and instead speak of 'small' vs. 'large' phenomena (Seidl and Whittington, 2014). However, both distinctions, micro vs. macro and small vs. large, ultimately refer to the same idea of there being different degrees of aggregation (e.g., individual action vs. entire organizations), which is the primary concern for us in this comparison. For pragmatic reasons, we will use the two distinctions, micro-macro and small-large, synonymously here.

Both Routine Dynamics and Strategy as Practice started out with an explicit focus on the 'micro' aspect of organizing. They both positioned themselves against the existing research in their fields by claiming that the 'micro' aspects of specific actions involved in the respective domains, i.e., the domain of routines and strategy, had been neglected by previous researchers. Accordingly, in their seminal papers, Routine Dynamics scholars called for a focus on 'the internal dynamic of routines' (Feldman, 2000: 614) and on examining 'specific actions, by specific people, in specific places and times' (Feldman and Pentland, 2003: 101) as an important part of understanding routines. Likewise, Strategy as Practice claimed its space in strategy research by criticizing that existing research 'typically remained on the macro-level', thereby neglecting how managers '*do* strategy' (Whittington, 1996: 732). They proposed a 'micro perspective' (Johnson et al., 2003), a 'drilling deep, "micro" [. . .] approach' (Jarzabkowski et al., 2007: 6, 14), which would allow for an examination of 'the myriad, micro activities that make up strategy and strategizing in practice' (Johnson et al., 2003: 3).

While both Routine Dynamics and Strategy as Practice explicitly address the 'micro' level of actions, there are some differences in the degree of granularity of the actions considered. Routine Dynamics researchers typically drill down into actions with a greater granularity than Strategy as Practice scholars. For example, in analysing a shipping routine, Dittrich and Seidl (2016) describe the very granular actions that constitute the routine, such as looking for a suitable box, putting shipments in the box, sealing the box, attaching shipment documents to the box, etc. Such a detailed analysis is typically expected of Routine Dynamics studies given that variations in the routines are explained by reference to variations in the actions or in the sequence of the actions. In the case of Strategy as Practice, actions are typically described at a much higher level of granularity. For example, in their analysis of inter-organizational collaborations, Seidl and Werle (2018) describe actions such as selecting new participants for the collaboration, but they do not examine in detail the individual acts constituting this action. Only very few Strategy as Practice studies drill that deep into the actions – see, for example, Samra-Fredericks (2003), who identified individual speech acts of strategists.

Both Routine Dynamics and Strategy as Practice research spans various levels of analysis, but there are some differences between the two communities. Treating the routine as a unit of analysis, Routine Dynamics scholars initially tended to focus primarily on the links between actions within individual routines, while more recent studies have started to link these internal dynamics systematically to the level of routine clusters or even the organizational level. For example, Kremser and Schreyögg (2016) examined how actions involved in individual photofinishing routines were related to dynamics in the cluster of photofinishing routines. Linking to the organizational level, Rerup and Feldman (2011) examined the interplay between micro actions within individual routines and organizational schemata, and Birnholz et al. (2007) examined the interplay between micro actions within routines and the organizational character. In one of the very few studies to go beyond the organizational level, Zbaracki and Bergen (2010) showed the effects of price-adjustment routines on macroeconomic dynamics.

In contrast, and not surprisingly given their empirical focus on strategic activities, the link to higher levels of analysis has been an explicit concern of Strategy as Practice scholars from the very outset. As well as links to the organization level, Strategy as Practice scholars have explicitly called for connections to the societal level. As Jarzabkowski and colleagues wrote, Strategy as Practice research 'emphasizes explicit links between micro- and macro-perspectives on strategy as a social practice' (Jarzabkowski et al., 2007: 6–7). In line with that, Johnson et al. (2007: 18) developed an 'exploded map' spelling out research questions addressing micro, meso and macro levels of analysis (see also Jarzabkowski and Spee's (2009) review, mapping the existing Strategy as Practice literature in terms of different levels of analysis). While many studies have focused on the micro level of actions (e.g., Samra-Fredericks, 2003), others have focused on the relation between the micro and organizational level (Jarzabkowski and Seidl, 2008), and some have examined the relation between micro-action and developments on the societal level (Jarzabkowski and Bednarek, 2018). In fact, there are some studies that are primarily focused on the societal level, such as Whittington (2019), which examined the development of the strategy profession over time. Yet, reflecting on Strategy as Practice research up to 2013, Seidl and Whittington (2014) observed that in spite of all warnings against 'empirical micro-isolationism', most empirical studies remain on the micro level without any explicit concern for developments on the societal level. A focus on the micro and meso level of analysis still seems to be the default mode of inquiry in Strategy as Practice.

35.2.5 Empirical Methods

The final comparison we wish to draw between Routine Dynamics and Strategy as Practice research relates to the spectrum of empirical methods employed. While explicit methodological reflections have been scarce, there are some studies both in Routine Dynamics and Strategy as Practice discussing the suitability of various empirical methods (e.g., Balogun et al., 2003; Johnson et al., 2007; Pentland and Feldman, 2008; Rasche and Chia, 2009). Not surprisingly given the 'need for researchers to be close to the phenomena of study' (Balogun et al., 2003: 198), the main empirical approach in both domains is the *ethnography-based case study*, which relies primarily on direct observation complemented by formal and informal interviews (Dittrich [Chapter 8], this volume; Cunliffe, 2015). More recently, both Routine Dynamics and Strategy as Practice researchers have also started to use video recordings, which sometimes take the form of full-blown *video-ethnographies* (LeBaron and Christianson [Chapter 9], this volume). In Strategy as Practice research in particular, there has also been a rise in studies conducting netnographies, i.e., collecting ethnographic data on the internet (e.g., Luedicke et al., 2017).

As well as various ethnographic methods, there are a host of other methods that have been applied in the two research domains. In Strategy as Practice, in particular, we find many studies primarily based on *interview* data. For example, Mantere and Vaara (2008) conducted interviews in twelve organizations exploring fundamental assumptions about how strategy work in organizations shapes possibilities of participation in the strategy process. As a result of the interest of Strategy as Practice scholars in the way that discourse shapes strategizing, interviews can offer a particularly valuable mode of data gathering. Related to that, there are also many Strategy as Practice studies examining strategy *texts* from the perspective of discourse analysis. For example, Vaara et al. (2010) conducted a close textual analysis of strategic planning documents to reveal the ways in which such texts can shape social reality.

More recently, Strategy as Practice scholars have started to apply *historical methods*. Microhistory, in particular, can elucidate the construction and enactment of strategizing practices in their historical contexts and thus help us understand their historical embeddedness (Ericson et al., 2015; Vaara and Lamberg, 2016). For example, Whittington (2019) applied historical methods to trace the institutionalization and deinstitutionalization of strategy practices over many decades.

In addition to all of these qualitative methods, both Routine Dynamics and Strategy as Practice have applied a range of *quantitative methods*. In particular, in both research areas we find a few, though not many, studies that test hypotheses about strategy practices or routine performances with large-scale survey data or otherwise created databases. For example, in their study on garbage collection routines, Turner and Rindova (2018) tested hypotheses about temporal patterning mechanisms in routines using records of customer reports on missed waste collections and data from a GPS satellite tracking system recording the routes of waste collection vans. Similarly, in their parallel studies on the practice of strategy workshops, van Aaken et al. (2015) and Healey et al. (2015) tested various hypotheses about the effects of different characteristics of strategy workshops. In addition, Strategy as Practice scholars have proposed, yet not applied in empirical studies, a range of other quantitative methods such as computer-aided text analysis to quantify qualitative textual data; network analysis to quantify the relational aspects of strategy practice data; or event study analysis testing the effects of strategy practices (Laamanen et al., 2015).

In Routine Dynamics, in contrast, we find a range of additional quantitative methods applied. One of the methods becoming particularly popular is agent-based modelling to simulate the patterns and effects of observable actions (Pentland et al., 2010, 2011; see also Gao [Chapter 11], this volume). For example, Miller et al. (2012) used agent-based modelling to examine the dynamic interplay between action and memory in routines and Gao et al. (2018) used it to examine the role that cognitive artifacts play in the formation and change of routines. In addition, Routine Dynamics scholars have propagated the use of field experiments in studying Routine Dynamics (see also Bapuji et al. [Chapter 10], this volume). For example, in their study on the towel changing routine in a hotel, Bapuji et al. (2012) manipulated the procedure of exchanging towels to examine the effects of intermediaries on the strengths of routines.

35.3 What Can Routine Dynamics Learn from Strategy as Practice?

Our comparison of Routine Dynamics and Strategy as Practice revealed several differences that also point to opportunities for cross-fertilization. In the next two sections, we will discuss these research opportunities along the five dimensions introduced in the previous section, i.e., empirical domains, theoretical perspectives, research frameworks, 'levels' of analysis and empirical methods (for a summary, see Table 35.1).

In terms of *empirical domains*, there are two areas for potential inspiration. First, Routine Dynamics could follow the lead of Strategy as Practice scholars in paying greater attention to the dynamics of strategic in addition to operative routines. As Grand and Bartl (2019) revealed, strategy work is largely routine-based – and given its far-reaching consequences, including for dynamics such as inter-firm rivalry (Luoma et al., forthcoming), could be of particular interest to Routine Dynamics scholars. In this sense, it offers a particularly promising area for future research. Such research would also be a welcome extension to the Strategy as Practice community given its interest in recurrent practices of strategic change (Hendry and Seidl, 2003). Second, Routine Dynamics could follow Strategy as Practice in its emphasis on communication by further examining the discursive dimensions of routines. Many organizational routines, e.g., meetings, are of a discursive character and could thus be analysed as routinized forms of communication – which is exactly what some studies in Routine Dynamics have recently started to explore (Aggerholm et al., 2016; Dittrich et al., 2016; LeBaron et al., 2016).

Table 35.1 Comparison of Routine Dynamics and Strategy as Practice

	Routine Dynamics	Strategy as Practice	Learnings for Routine Dynamics	Learnings for Strategy as Practice
Research domains	Routines as phenomena	Strategically relevant activities	Cover strategic routines Cover communicative aspects of routines	Cover operative activities Cover non-verbal activities
Theoretical perspectives	Practice theories and related theories (selective adoption of *key ideas and concepts*) Tightly integrated set of theoretical perspectives	Practice theories and related theories (comprehensive adoption of *entire theories*) Loose repertoire of distinct theoretical perspectives	Apply additional perspectives (sense-making, discourse theories, complexity theory, conventionalist theory, institutional theory)	Apply additional perspectives (pragmatism, symbolic interactionism, socio-materiality)
Research frameworks	Distinctive analytical framework outlining the basic mechanism of Routine Dynamics (recursive relation between ostensive and performative aspects and artifacts)	No unifying theoretical framework apart from maps of potential research foci ('3Ps' framework)	Reduce centrality of the framework to increase diversity of perspectives?	Pay more attention to the role of artifacts Adopt the concept of 'patterning'. Increase centrality of shared framework to increase coherence and cumulative research?
Levels of analysis	Tends to focus on the very micro, drilling down to the minute actions constituting routines. Increasing number of studies linking dynamics within routines to cluster level outcomes. Few studies linking to the organizational level	Tends to focus on the level of practices; few studies drilling down to the minute actions constituting practices. Most studies linking practices to organizational level. Increasing number of studies linking practices to societal level	Extend research on the links between micro-and macro levels	Extend research into granular actions
Empirical methods	Emphasis on ethnography Wide range of quantitative methods	Wide range of qualitative methods with an emphasis on ethnography Almost no quantitative methods	Apply additional qualitative methods (discourse analysis, historical methods)	Apply additional quantitative methods (narrative networks, experiments, agent-based simulations)

In terms of *theoretical perspectives*, Strategy as Practice scholars have employed a greater variety of social theories than their colleagues in Routine Dynamics. While some of these theories might be specific to the research questions addressed in Strategy as Practice research, many could also offer fruitful perspectives on Routine Dynamics. One perspective frequently employed in Strategy as Practice and which holds great potential for Routine Dynamics is the sense-making perspective. For example, sense-making could be understood as an important aspect of patterning; that is, routine participants make sense of particular actions by relating them to a pattern of actions. Furthermore, the type of actions people take in performing routines depends on how they make sense of the routine-related cues they encounter. Another important perspective in Strategy as Practice is that of the different communication and discourse theories. While Routine Dynamics research has so far concentrated primarily on non-discursive action, communication and discourse theories could help illuminate the particular role of talk and communication in the dynamics of routines, e.g., in shedding light on how industry-level discourses impact the adoption of operational excellence routines (Bertels et al., 2016). Complexity theory of adaptive systems, in turn, might provide a fruitful perspective for examining how emergent orders in the form of replicating routines arise from social practice (Campbell-Hunt, 2007). In addition, conventionalist theory, with its focus on the ways in which actors cooperate despite divergent values, might be helpful in exploring the underlying mechanisms through which truces in routines are formed and reformed (Kozica et al., 2014). Lastly, institutional theory (see Smets et al., 2012) can provide a link to the field level, drawing attention both to how routines are influenced by institutional context and how routines contribute to the institutional context (elaborated in more detail later). Given that professions play an important role in the enactment of many organizational routines (see Kho and Spee [Chapter 28], this volume), institutional theory could serve as an interesting additional perspective shedding some light on the embeddedness of routines in the context of larger professions.

In terms of *research frameworks*, a comparison with Strategy as Practice might offer Routine Dynamics scholars the opportunity to consider the implications of different types of frameworks on the development of the community. In contrast to the Routine Dynamics framework, the '3 Ps' framework provides more of a map of potential research directions rather than a theoretical model describing causal relations or mechanisms and is thus compatible with any theoretical perspective that addresses any one of the aspects outlined. As a result, the framework has contributed to the proliferation of – even mutually incompatible – theoretical perspectives. At the same time, the lack of any shared framework providing direction to individual research projects has resulted in a literature that is far less integrated than Routine Dynamics research and in which knowledge creation is less cumulative. Reflecting on these advantages and disadvantages might provide valuable insights for Routine Dynamics scholars as they navigate their community into the future. So far, Routine Dynamics has been very successful at being generative while striking a good balance between cohesiveness and pluralism. Yet, as the community moves into the future, a discussion of the role of the framework might prove fruitful: the stronger and tighter the framework, the more coherent and cumulative the research is likely to be (Langley, 2015). In contrast, the looser and less central the framework becomes, the greater the diversity and novelty of perspectives (for a discussion of coherence and pluralism as competing demands of a research community, see Schad et al., 2019). In fact, there are some indications that Routine Dynamics scholars are trying to reduce the centrality of the framework, highlighting that while it 'has provided a foundation for studying routine dynamics', researchers should bear in mind that 'it is but one possible analytic for exploring routines as patterns of action' (Feldman et al., 2016: 506). Relatedly, Feldman (2016: 41) warned against 'succumbing to the pressures of theoretical [...] purity'.

In terms of *'levels' of analysis*, we have also revealed some interesting differences. In particular, Strategy as Practice research has put far more emphasis on linking the micro-level analysis of actions to the field level. While this concern for more macro phenomena is unsurprising given its particular empirical focus, we believe that Routine Dynamics could draw some inspiration from Strategy as Practice in this regard. Doing so would both allow Routine Dynamics scholars to contextualize routines more comprehensively in the institutional level and help elucidate how routines have field-level consequences – such as the effects of organizational routines on so-called grand challenges (George et al., 2016). More generally, given recent advances in Routine Dynamics research that explain outcomes on the level of routine clusters (e.g., Kremser and Schreyögg, 2016; Kremser et al., 2019; Sele and Grand, 2016; Spee et al., 2016; Swan et al., 2016; Turner and Rindova, 2012), routine scholars could learn from Strategy as Practice about potential theoretical lenses (see, e.g., Seidl and Whittington, 2014) and general research approaches for capturing how micro-level actions scale up to organization-level and particularly also field-level phenomena. For example, one might examine how variations in the enactment of routines within a particular organization can scale up to variations in how these routines are enacted across organizations – analogously to how Smets et al. (2012) examined how variations in the enactment of certain legal routines within a law firm led to changes in the way that certain legal issues are handled within the industry more generally. As well as pushing Routine Dynamics scholars to explore more macro-level outcomes, the comparison with Strategy as Practice could help to sensitize Routine Dynamics scholars to the ways in which macro-level phenomena influence micro-level dynamics.

In terms of *empirical methods* applied, our comparison revealed that Routine Dynamics scholars are far more advanced when it comes to the use of quantitative methods. Yet, in terms of qualitative methods they might draw some inspiration from Strategy as Practice, in particular, on the great variety of methods focusing on the discursive aspects of organizational life that might help Routine Dynamics scholars capture how talk and text affect Routine Dynamics. So far, Routine Dynamics research has put the emphasis primarily on examining the 'doings' in routines, neglecting somewhat the role of 'sayings'. There are very few Routine Dynamics studies that have focused directly on the communicative dimension of Routine Dynamics (Aggerholm et al., 2016; Dittrich et al., 2016; LeBaron et al., 2016; Yamauchi and Hiramoto, 2016). Routine Dynamics scholars might also explore the potential of historical methods (Mutch, 2016; Raff and Scranton, 2017; Salvato, 2009; Salvato and Rerup, 2017). To be sure, finding historical data that reveal the fine-grained details of routine performance that are typically required by Routine Dynamics studies is challenging, but if such data are available it would allow for a unique opportunity to 'place that performance in historical context, showing how performance is shaped by factors which are beyond the immediate control or even knowledge of the participants' (Mutch, 2016: 1184).

35.4 What Can Strategy as Practice Learn from Routine Dynamics?

Our comparison of the two research communities has also revealed distinctive opportunities for Strategy as Practice to learn from Routine Dynamics. In terms of the *empirical domain*, there are three areas in particular where Strategy as Practice might draw inspiration from Routine Dynamics. First, Routine Dynamics has demonstrated in a wide range of empirical studies that operative activities develop their own internal dynamics and thus crucially shape organizations as a whole (see, e.g., Birnholtz et al 2007; Rerup and Feldman, 2011). We believe that Strategy as Practice would have much to gain from paying more attention to operative routines, at least to the extent that they might inadvertently affect the long-term direction of the firm (Jarzabkowski et al., 2007: 8). Second, operative routines are the central locus where the tensions between strategic objectives are negotiated in situ. Building on Routine Dynamics's expertise in the study of routine replication and adaptation (e.g., D'Adderio, 2014), Strategy as Practice scholars could look at how strategic tensions become visible on the level of operative routines and incorporate such a perspective in the overarching theorization of the enactment and implementation of strategies. Third, Strategy as Practice can learn about the importance of non-discursive behaviours from Routine Dynamics. Whereas Strategy as Practice has from its inception been focused on strategy as a form of organizational discourse (Hendry, 2000), Routine Dynamics provides an exemplar for analysing non-discursive phenomena in organizational contexts.

In terms of *theoretical perspectives*, there are theoretical resources in Routine Dynamics that could fruitfully be mobilized by Strategy as Practice as well. One particularly promising perspective is the pragmatist tradition, which is prominent in Routine Dynamics research but has received surprisingly little attention from Strategy as Practice researchers. In particular, the different pragmatist theories could help Strategy as Practice scholars to get a deeper understanding of action and agency in strategy work. Based on the Routine Dynamics study by Dittrich and Seidl (2018), Dewey's pragmatist perspective could help Strategy as Practice scholars explore the emerging intentionality of strategists in choosing particular courses of action; or, following Dionysiou and Tsoukas (2013), Mead's theory could help to unpack the micro mechanisms underlying the interactions of organizational members as they strategize. Another potentially fruitful perspective is that of socio-materiality, which has been very prominent in Routine Dynamics (Aroles and McLean, 2015; D'Adderio, 2011; Sele and Grand, 2016). As Lê and Spee observe in their review of the role of materiality in Strategy as Practice, '[a]lthough multiple approaches exist that could shed light on the consequentiality of materiality for strategizing, at present these are not explicitly discussed in the literature' (Lê and Spee, 2015: 582; for exceptions, see Dameron et al., 2015).

When it comes to *research frameworks*, there are some important learnings for Strategy as Practice as well. The Routine Dynamics framework highlights artifacts as a distinctive and integral aspect of Routine Dynamics. Hence, it prompts the Routine Dynamics researcher to pay particular attention to the role of artifacts in shaping the dynamics of routines. Relatedly, incorporating artifacts, and material arrangements more generally, in the '3 Ps' framework could help increase the sensitivity of Strategy as Practice scholars to the distinctive role that these aspects play in strategy work. There are already several studies on artifacts in Strategy as Practice (see particularly the special issue by Dameron et al., 2015, and Lê and Spee, 2015), but these studies are less developed and less sophisticated than comparative studies in Routine Dynamics. Furthermore, Strategy as Practice scholars could draw inspiration from the new concept of 'patterning' in Routine Dynamics research, which radicalizes the processual and constructivist notion of social structures (Goh and Pentland, 2019). Adopting this concept would sensitize Strategy as Practice scholars to the ways in which structural aspects are created in and through social action.

On a more general level, our comparison of the role of the respective frameworks in Routine Dynamics and Strategy as Practice provides valuable insights for Strategy as Practice scholars as they reflect on future directions for their research community. As discussed previously, strengthening the role of the framework would help increase the coherence within Strategy as Practice studies and facilitate cumulative knowledge creation. At the same time, however, this has the potential to reduce diversity and novelty in perspectives.

As well as adopting theoretical perspectives or concepts from Routine Dynamics, Strategy as Practice scholars could also adopt Routine Dynamics itself as an approach to studying strategizing (Grand, 2016). After all, Strategy as Practice research has always highlighted the fact that strategy work is largely composed of routines. For example, in one of the very first Strategy as Practice publications, Whittington emphasized the need to examine 'unheroic work of ordinary strategic practitioners in their day-to-day *routines*' (Whittington, 1996: 734). Similarly, Hendry and Seidl (2003) speak of the 'routines' of strategic change and Feldman highlights that Strategy as Practice researchers could examine the 'ways in which strategies emerge through routines' (Feldman, 2015). Thus, a Routine Dynamics perspective could provide highly valuable insights into how the internal dynamics of routines shape strategy over time.

Regarding *'levels' of analysis*, Strategy as Practice scholarship could learn from Routine Dynamics how to drill deeper into the very micro levels of granular actions making up strategizing work. As Routine Dynamics studies have shown, many higher-level outcomes can be traced back to minute dynamics in actions. Strategy as Practice rarely makes efforts to record minute action and event logs, let alone to subsequently connect them into bundles of narrative patterns. Routine Dynamics, by contrast, not only provides a repeatedly tested set of instruments to conduct micro research but has also come up with various ways to connect the tiny dots such analyses yield (Danner-Schroeder and Geiger, 2016; LeBaron et al., 2016).

Finally, there are several opportunities for cross-fertilization in terms of *empirical methods*. First and foremost, this applies to the wide range of quantitative methods already in use in Routine Dynamics. In particular, Strategy as Practice could learn from Routine Dynamics about how to effectively track minute interaction, for example by developing narrative networks capturing complex sequences of minute strategizing actions. There are also interesting opportunities to use experiments in Strategy as Practice research similar to Bapuji et al.'s (2012) experiments manipulating the setup of towel changing routines. Strategy as Practice scholars could also run experiments on the impact of different settings of strategy workshops on the emergence of new strategic ideas. In addition, agent-based simulations could offer valuable new methods for examining the effects of different types or dynamics of activities that might be difficult to observe in real life (Gao et al., 2014). Analogously to Miller et al. (2012), one could use agent-based modelling to study the role of different forms of memory in the emergence, efficiency and adaptability of different strategizing routines. Given the fact that strategizing activities often have far-reaching consequences, simulations might offer another way to study strategizing phenomena without risking negative real-world consequences.

35.5 Conclusion

In this chapter, we have provided a systematic comparison of the Routine Dynamics and Strategy as Practice communities in terms of their empirical research domains, theoretical perspectives, research frameworks, 'levels' of analysis and empirical methods, and we have discussed a number of areas for fruitful cross-fertilization. A more general question pertains about how Routine Dynamics and Strategy as Practice scholars might navigate the relationship between their two communities in the future. The great degree of overlap and the many similarities between the two communities might lead us to suggest an integration of these communities, thereby increasing their impact and granting the respective scholars better access to a wider range of relevant research insights. Yet, while 'we have much to gain by marrying these compatible approaches' (Feldman, 2015: 327), a *real* marriage of these approaches also has disadvantages, the most important of which would be to reduce the diversity of perspectives available for studying organizations. There are a number of important differences between Routine Dynamics and Strategy as Practice that offer distinctive research opportunities. Integrating the two approaches would most likely lead to a reduction in these variations, thereby diminishing the variety of research insights generated. There is also much to be gained from preserving the distinctiveness of the two approaches, allowing them to develop along their own trajectories. Paradoxically, this might even increase the opportunities for mutual learning, as learning presupposes some form of difference – one can only learn from things that are different. Against this background, the point is not to integrate the two lines of research, but to provide platforms that allow for fruitful exchange between the communities – and the present chapter is an attempt at doing exactly that.

References

Aggerholm, H. K. and Asmuß, B. (2016). When 'good' is not good enough: Power Dynamics and Performative Aspects of Organizational Routines. In J. Howard-Grenville, C. Rerup, A. Langley and H. Tsoukas, eds., *Organizational Routines: How They Are Created, Maintained, and Changed*. Oxford: Oxford University Press, pp. 140–178.

Ahrens, T. and Chapman, C. S. (2006). Doing qualitative field research in management accounting: Positioning data to contribute to theory. *Accounting, Organizations and Society*, 31(8), 819–841.

Aroles, J. and McLean, C. (2015). Becoming, assemblages and intensities: Re-exploring rules and routines. In F.-X. de Vaujany, N. Mitev, G. F. Lanzara and A. Mukherjee, eds., *Materiality, Rules and Regulation: New Trends in Management and Organization Studies*. London: Palgrave Macmillan UK, pp. 177–194.

Balogun, J., Best, K. and Lê, J. (2015). Selling the object of strategy: How frontline workers realize strategy through their daily work. *Organization Studies*, 36(10), 1285–1313.

Balogun, J., Huff, A. S. and Johnson, P. (2003). Three responses to the methodological challenges of studying strategizing. *Journal of Management Studies*, 40(1), 197–224.

Balogun, J. and Johnson, G. (2004). Organizational restructuring and middle manager sensemaking. *Academy of Management Journal*, 47(4), 523–549.

Balogun, J. and Johnson, G. (2005) From intended strategies to unintended outcomes: The impact of change recipient sensemaking. *Organization Studies*, 26(11), 1573–1601.

Bapuji, H., Hora, M. and Saeed, A. M. (2012). Intentions, intermediaries, and interaction: Examining the emergence of routines. *Journal of Management Studies*, 49(8), 1586–1607.

Bapuji, H., Hora, M., Saeed, A. and Turner, S. (2019). How understanding-based redesign influences the pattern of actions and effectiveness of routines. *Journal of Management*, 45(5), 2132–2162.

Becker, M. C. (2005). The concept of routines: Some clarifications. *Cambridge Journal of Economics*, 29(2), 249–262.

Bertels, S., Howard-Grenville, J. and Pek, S. (2016). Cultural molding, shielding, and shoring at Oilco: The role of culture in the integration of routines. *Organization Science*, 27(3), 573–593.

Birnholtz, J. P., Cohen, M. D. and Hoch, S. V. (2007). Organizational character: On the regeneration of Camp Poplar Grove. *Organization Science*, 18(2), 315–332.

Bourdieu, P. (1990). *The Logic of Practice* (Original printing). Stanford, CA: Stanford University Press.

Brown, A. D. and Thompson, E. R. (2013). A narrative approach to strategy-as-practice. *Business History*, 55(7), 1143–1167.

Bucher, S. and Langley, A. (2016). The interplay of reflective and experimental spaces in interrupting and reorienting Routine Dynamics. *Organization Science*, 27(3), 594–613.

Campbell-Hunt, C. (2007). Complexity in practice. *Human Relations*, 60(5), 793–823.

Champenois, C., Lefebvre, V. and Ronteau, S. (2020). Entrepreneurship as practice: Systematic literature review of a nascent field. *Entrepreneurship & Regional Development*, 32 (3–4), 281–312.

Chia, R. and Holt, R. (2006). Strategy as practical coping: A Heideggerian perspective. *Organization Studies*, 27(5), 635–655.

Chia, R. and MacKay, B. (2007). Post-processual challenges for the emerging strategy-as-practice perspective: Discovering strategy in the logic of practice. *Human Relations*, 60(1), 217–242.

Christianson, M. K., Farkas, M. T., Sutcliffe, K. M. and Weick, K. E. (2009). Learning through rare events: Significant interruptions at the Baltimore & Ohio Railroad Museum. *Organization Science*, 20(5), 846–860.

Cohen, M. D. (2007). Reading Dewey: Reflections on the study of routine. *Organization Studies*, 28 (5), 773–786.

Cunliffe, A. L. (2015). Using ethnography in strategy-as-practice research. In D. Golsorkhi, L. Rouleau, D. Seidl and E. Vaara, eds., *Cambridge Handbook of Strategy as Practice*, 2nd ed. Cambridge: Cambridge University Press, pp. 431–446.

Cyert, R. M. and March, J. G. (1963). *A Behavioral Theory of the Firm*. Englewood Cliffs, NJ: Prentice-Hall.

D'Adderio, L. (2008). The performativity of routines: Theorising the influence of artefacts and distributed agencies on routines dynamics. *Research Policy*, 37(5), 769–789.

D'Adderio, L. (2011). Artifacts at the centre of routines: Performing the material turn in routines theory. *Journal of Institutional Economics*, 7(2), 197–230.

D'Adderio, L. (2014). The replication dilemma unravelled: How organizations enact multiple goals in routine transfer. *Organization Science*, 25(5), 1325–1350.

Dameron, S., Lê, J. K. and LeBaron, C. (2015). Materializing strategy and strategizing materials: Why matter matters. *British Journal of Management*, 26, S1–S12.

Danner-Schröder, A. and Geiger, D. (2016). Unravelling the motor of patterning work: Toward an understanding of the microlevel dynamics of standardization and flexibility. *Organization Science*, 27(3), 633–658.

Denis, J.-L., Langley, A. and Rouleau, L. (2007). Strategizing in pluralistic contexts: Rethinking theoretical frames. *Human Relations*, 60(1), 179–215.

Dionysiou, D. and Tsoukas, H. (2013). Understanding the (re) creation of routines from within: A symbolic interactionist perspective. *Academy of Management Review*, 38(2), 181–205.

Dittrich, K., Guérard, S. and Seidl, D. (2016). Talking about routines: The role of reflective talk in routine change. *Organization Science*, 27(3), 678–697.

Dittrich, K. and Seidl, D. (2018). Emerging Intentionality in Routine Dynamics: A Pragmatist View. *Academy of Management Journal*, 61(1), 111–138.

Ericson, M., Melin, L. and Popp, A. (2015). Studying strategy as practice through historical methods. In D. Golsorkhi, L. Rouleau, D. Seidl and E. Vaara, eds., *Cambridge Handbook of Strategy as Practice*, 2nd ed. Cambridge: Cambridge University Press, pp. 506–519.

Ezzamel, M. and Willmott, H. (2010). Strategy and strategizing: A poststructuralist perspective. In J. a. C. Baum and J. Lampel, eds., *Globalization of Strategy Research*, vol. 27. Bingley: Emerald Group Publishing Ltd, pp. 75–109.

Feldman, M. S. (2000). Organizational routines as a source of continuous change. *Organization Science*, 11(6), 611–629.

Feldman, M. S. (2003). A performative perspective on stability and change in organizational routines. *Industrial and Corporate Change*, 12(4), 727–752.

Feldman, M. S. (2015). Theory of routine dynamics and connections to strategy as practice. In D. Golsorkhi, L. Rouleau, D. Seidl and E. Vaara, eds., *Cambridge Handbook of Strategy as Practice*, 2nd ed. Cambridge: Cambridge University Press, pp. 317–330.

Feldman, M. S. (2016). Routines as process: Past, present, and future. In *Organizational Routines: How They Are Created, Maintained, and Changed*. Oxford: Oxford University Press, pp. 23–46.

Feldman, M. S. and Orlikowski, W. (2011). Theorizing practice and practicing theory. *Organization Science*, 22(5), 1240–1253.

Feldman, M. S. and Pentland, B. T. (2003). Reconceptualizing organizational routines as a source of flexibility and change. *Administrative Science Quarterly*, 48(1), 94–118.

Feldman, M. S., Pentland, B. T., D'Adderio, L. and Lazaric, N. (2016). Beyond routines as things: Introduction to the special issue on Routine Dynamics. *Organization Science*, 27(3), 505–513.

Feldman, M. S. and Rafaeli, A. (2002). Organizational routines as sources of connections and understandings. *Journal of Management Studies*, 39(3), 309–331.

Fenton, C. and Langley, A. (2011). Strategy as practice and the narrative turn. *Organization Studies*, 32(9), 1171–1196.

Gao, D., Deng, X. and Bai, B. (2014). The emergence of organizational routines from habitual behaviours of multiple actors: An agent-based simulation study. *Journal of Simulation*, 8(3), 215–230.

Gao, D., Squazzoni, F. and Deng, X. (2018). The role of cognitive artifacts in organizational routine dynamics: An agent-based model. *Computational and Mathematical Organization Theory*, 24(4), 473–499.

Garfinkel, H. (1967). *Studies in Ethnomethodology*. Englewood Cliffs, NJ: Prentice-Hall.

George, G., Howard-Grenville, J., Joshi, A. and Tihanyi, L. (2016). Understanding and tackling societal grand challenges through management research. *Academy of Management Journal*, 59 (6), 1880–1895.

Gherardi, S. (2009). Introduction: The critical power of the 'practice lens'. *Management Learning*, 40(2), 115–128.

Giddens, A. (1984). *The Constitution of Society: Outline of the Theory of Structuration*. Cambridge: Polity Press.

Goh, K. T. and Pentland, B. T. (2019). From actions to paths to patterning: Toward a dynamic theory of patterning in routines. *Academy of Management Journal*, 62(6), 1901–1929.

Golsorkhi, D., Rouleau, L., Seidl, D. and Vaara, E. (2015). Introduction: What is strategy as practice? In *Cambridge Handbook of Strategy as Practice*, 2nd ed. Cambridge: Cambridge University Press, pp. 1–30.

Grand, S. (2016). *Routines, Strategies And Management: Engaging For Recurrent Creation 'At The Edge'*. Cheltenham: Edward Elgar Publishing.

Grand, S. and Bartl, D. (2019). Making new strategic moves possible: How executive management enacts strategizing routines to strengthen entrepreneurial agility. *Routine Dynamics in Action: Replication and Transformation*, 61, 123–151.

Healey, M. P., Hodgkinson, G. P., Whittington, R. and Johnson, G. (2015). Off to plan or out to lunch? Relationships between design characteristics and outcomes of strategy workshops. *British Journal of Management*, 26(3), 507–528.

Hendry, J. (2000). Strategic decision making, discourse, and strategy as social practice. *Journal of Management Studies*, 37(7), 955–978.

Hendry, J. and Seidl, D. (2003). The structure and significance of strategic episodes: Social systems theory and the routine practices of strategic change. *Journal of Management Studies*, 40(1), 175–196.

Herepath, A. (2014). In the loop: A realist approach to structure and agency in the practice of strategy. *Organization Studies*, 35(6), 857–879.

Howard-Grenville, J. A. (2005). The persistence of flexible organizational routines: The role of agency and organizational context. *Organization Science*, 16(6), 618–636.

Howard-Grenville, J. and Rerup, C. (2017). A process perspective on organizational routines. In A. Langley and H. Tsoukas, eds., *The SAGE Handbook of Process Organizational Studies*. London: SAGE, pp. 323–339.

Jarzabkowski, P. (2003). Strategic practices: An activity theory perspective on continuity and change. *Journal of Management Studies*, 40(1), 23–55.

Jarzabkowski, P. (2004). Strategy as practice: Recursiveness, adaptation, and practices-in-use. *Organization Studies*, 25(4), 529–560.

Jarzabkowski, P. (2005). *Strategy as Practice: An Activity-Based Approach*. London: SAGE.

Jarzabkowski, P., Balogun, J. and Seidl, D. (2007). Strategizing: The challenges of a practice perspective. *Human Relations*, 60(1), 5–27.

Jarzabkowski, P. and Bednarek, R. (2018). Toward a social practice theory of relational competing. *Strategic Management Journal*, 39(3), 794–829.

Jarzabkowski, P. and Kaplan, S. (2015). Strategy tools-in-use: A Framework For Understanding 'Technologies Of Rationality' In Practice. *Strategic Management Journal*, 36(4), 537–558.

Jarzabkowski, P., Kaplan, S., Seidl, D. and Whittington, R. (2016). On the risk of studying practices in isolation: Linking what, who, and how in strategy research. *Strategic Organization*, 14(3), 248–259.

Jarzabkowski, P., Le, J. and Balogun, J. (2019). The social practice of coevolving strategy and structure to realize mandated radical change. *Academy of Management Journal*, 62(3), 850–882.

Jarzabkowski, P. A., Lê, J. K. and Feldman, M. S. (2012). Toward a theory of coordinating: Creating coordinating mechanisms in practice. *Organization Science*, 23(4), 907–927.

Jarzabkowski, P. and Seidl, D. (2008). The role of meetings in the social practice of strategy. *Organization Studies*, 29(11), 1391–1426.

Jarzabkowski, P. and Spee, A. P. (2009). Strategy-as-practice: A review and future directions for the field. *International Journal of Management Reviews*, 11(1), 69–95.

Jarzabkowski, P. and Whittington, R. (2008). A strategy-as-practice approach to strategy research and education. *Journal of Management Inquiry*, 17(4), 282–286.

Johnson, G., Langley, A., Melin, L. and Whittington, R. (2007). *Strategy as Practice: Research Directions and Resources*. Cambridge: Cambridge University Press.

Johnson, G., Melin, L. and Whittington, R. (2003). Micro strategy and strategizing: Towards an activity-based view. *Journal of Management Studies*, 40(1), 3–22.

Johnson, G., Prashantham, S., Floyd, S. W. and Bourque, N. (2010). The ritualization of strategy workshops. *Organization Studies*, 31(12), 1589–1618.

Knights, D. and Morgan, G. (1991). Corporate strategy, organizations, and subjectivity: A critique. *Organization Studies*, 12(2), 251–273.

Korkman, O., Storbacka, K. and Harald, B. (2010). Practices as markets: Value co-creation in e-invoicing. *Australasian Marketing Journal*, 18 (4), 236–247.

Kornberger, M. and Clegg, S. (2011). Strategy as performative practice: The case of Sydney 2030. *Strategic Organization*, 9(2), 136–162.

Kozica, A., Kaiser, S. and Friesl, M. (2014). Organizational routines: Conventions as a source of change and stability. *Schmalenbach Business Review*, 66(3), 334–356.

Kremser, W. and Schreyögg, G. (2016). The dynamics of interrelated routines: Introducing the cluster level. *Organization Science*, 27(3), 698–721.

Laamanen, T., Reuter, E., Schimmer, M., Ueberbacher, F. and Guerra, X. W. (2015). Quantitative methods in strategy-as-practice research. In D. Golsorkhi, L. Rouleau, D. Seidl and E. Vaara, eds., *Cambridge Handbook of Strategy as Practice*, 2nd ed. Cambridge: Cambridge University Press, pp. 520–544.

Langley, A. (2015). The ongoing challenge of developing cumulative knowledge about strategy as practice. In D. Golsorkhi and L. Rouleau, eds., *Cambridge Handbook of Strategy as Practice*, 2nd ed. Cambridge: Cambridge University Press, pp. 111–127.

Latour, B. (2005). *Reassembling the Social: An Introduction to Actor- Network-Theory*. Oxford: Oxford University Press.

Lê, J. and Spee, P. (2015). The role of materiality in the practice of strategy. In D. Golsorkhi, D. Seidl, E. Vaara and L. Rouleau, eds., *Cambridge Handbook of Strategy as Practice*, 2nd ed. Cambridge: Cambridge University Press, pp. 582–597.

LeBaron, C., Christianson, M. K., Garrett, L. and Ilan, R. (2016). Coordinating flexible performance during everyday work: An ethnomethodological study of handoff routines. *Organization Science*, 27(3), 514–534.

Luedicke, M. K., Husemann, K. C., Furnari, S. and Ladstaetter, F. (2017). Radically open strategizing: How the premium cola collective takes open strategy to the extreme. *Long Range Planning*, 50(3), 371–384.

Luoma, J., Laamanen, T. and Lamberg, J. A. (forthcoming). Toward a routine-based view of interfirm rivalry. *Strategic Organization*.

Mantere, S. (2013). What is organizational strategy? A language-based view. *Journal of Management Studies*, 50(8), 1408–1426.

Mantere, S. and Vaara, E. (2008). On the problem of participation in strategy: A critical discursive perspective. *Organization Science*, 19(2), 341–358.

Miettinen, R., Samra-Fredericks, D. and Yanow, D. (2009). Re-turn to practice: An introductory essay. *Organization Studies*, 30(12), 1309–1327.

Miller, K. D., Pentland, B. T. and Choi, S. (2012). Dynamics of performing and remembering organizational routines. *Journal of Management Studies*, 49(8), 1536–1558.

Mutch, A. (2016). Bringing history into the study of routines: Contextualizing performance. *Organization Studies*, 37(8), 1171–1188.

Nelson, R. R. and Winter, S. (1982). *An Evolutionary Theory of Economic Change*. Cambridge, MA: Harvard University Press.

Orlikowski, W. J. (1992). The duality of technology: Rethinking the concept of technology in organizations. *Organization Science*, 3(3), 398–427.

Parmigiani, A. and Howard-Grenville, J. (2011). Routines revisited: Exploring the capabilities and practice perspectives. *Academy of Management Annals*, 5, 413–453.

Pentland, B. T. and Feldman, M. S. (2005). Organizational routines as a unit of analysis. *Industrial and Corporate Change*, 14(5), 793–815.

Pentland, B. T. and Feldman, M. S. (2007). Narrative networks: Patterns of technology and organization. *Organization Science*, 18(5), 781–795.

Pentland, B. T. and Feldman, M. S. (2008). Designing routines: On the folly of designing artifacts, while hoping for patterns of action. *Information and Organization*, 18(4), 235–250.

Pentland, B. T., Feldman, M. S., Becker, M. C. and Liu, P. (2012). Dynamics of organizational routines: A generative model. *Journal of Management Studies*, 49(8), 1484–1508.

Pentland, B. T., Hærem, T. and Hillison, D. (2010). Comparing organizational routines as recurrent patterns of action. *Organization Studies*, 31(7), 917–940.

Pentland, B. T., Hærem, T. and Hillison, D. (2011). The (n) ever-changing world: Stability and change in organizational routines. *Organization Science*, 22(6), 1369–1383.

Pentland, B. T. and Rueter, H. H. (1994). Organizational routines as grammars of action. *Administrative Science Quarterly*, 39(3), 484–510.

Raff, D. M. and Scranton, P. (2017). *The Emergence of Routines: Entrepreneurship, Organization, and Business History*. Oxford: Oxford University Press.

Rasche, A. and Chia, R. (2009). Researching strategy practices: A genealogical social theory perspective. *Organization Studies*, 30(7), 713–734.

Reckwitz, A. (2002). Toward a theory of social practices: A development in culturalist theorizing. *European Journal of Social Theory*, 5(2), 243–263.

Rerup, C. and Feldman, M. S. (2011). Routines as a source of change in organizational schemata: The role of trial-and-error learning. *Academy of Management Journal*, 54(3), 577–610.

Salvato, C. (2009). The contribution of event-sequence analysis to the study of organizational routines. In M. C. Becker and N. Lazaric, eds., *Organizational Routines: Advancing Empirical*

Research. Northampton, MA: Edward Elgar Publishing, pp. 68–102.

Salvato, C. and Rerup, C. (2017). Routine regulation: Balancing conflicting goals in organizational routines. *Administrative Science Quarterly*, 63(1), 170–209.

Samra-Fredericks, D. (2003). Strategizing as lived experience and strategists' everyday efforts to shape strategic direction. *Journal of Management Studies*, 40(1), 141–174.

Schad, J., Lewis, M. W. and Smith, W. K. (2019). Quo vadis, paradox? Centripetal and centrifugal forces in theory development. *Strategic Organization*, 17(1), 107–119.

Schatzki, T. R., Knorr Cetina, K. and Savigny, E. von, eds. (2001). *The Practice Turn in Contemporary Theory*. New York: Routledge.

Seidl, D. (2007). General strategy concepts and the ecology of strategy discourses: A systemic-discursive perspective. *Organization Studies*, 28(2), 197–218.

Seidl, D. and Werle, F. (2018). Inter-organizational sensemaking in the face of strategic meta-problems: Requisite variety and dynamics of participation. *Strategic Management Journal*, 39(3), 830–858.

Seidl, D. and Whittington, R. (2014). Enlarging the strategy-as-practice research agenda: Towards taller and flatter ontologies. *Organization Studies*, 35(10), 1407–1421.

Sele, K. and Grand, S. (2016). Unpacking the dynamics of ecologies of routines: Mediators and their generative effects in routine interactions. *Organization Science*, 27(3), 722–738.

Smets, M., Greenwood, R. and Lounsbury, M. (2015). An institutional perspective on strategy as practice. In D. Golsorkhi, L. Rouleau, D. Seidl and E. Vaara, eds., *Cambridge Handbook of Strategy as Practice*, 2nd ed. Cambridge: Cambridge University Press, pp. 283–300.

Smets, M., Morris, T. and Greenwood, R. (2012). From practice to field: A multilevel model of practice-driven institutional change. *Academy of Management Journal*, 55(4), 877–904.

Sonenshein, S. (2016). Routines and creativity: From dualism to duality. *Organization Science*, 27(3), 739–758.

Spee, P., Jarzabkowski, P. and Smets, M. (2016). The influence of routine interdependence and skillful accomplishment on the coordination of standardizing and customizing. *Organization Science*, 27(3), 759–781.

Swan, J., Robertson, M. and Newell, S. (2016). Dynamic in-capabilities: The paradox of routines in the ecology of complex innovation. In J. Howard-Grenville, C. Rerup, A. Langley and H. Tsoukas, eds., *Organizational Routines: How They Are Created, Maintained, and Changed*. Oxford: Oxford University Press, pp. 203–222.

Tsoukas, H. (2015). Making strategy: Meta-theoretical insights from Heideggerian phenomenology. In D. Golsorkhi, L. Rouleau, D. Seidl and E. Vaara, eds., *Cambridge Handbook of Strategy as Practice*, 2nd ed. Cambridge: Cambridge University Press, pp. 58–77.

Turner, S. F. and Rindova, V. (2012). A balancing act: How organizations pursue consistency in routine functioning in the face of ongoing change. *Organization Science*, 23(1), 24–46.

Turner, S. F. and Rindova, V. P. (2018). Watching the clock: Action timing, patterning, and routine performance. *Academy of Management Journal*, 61(4), 1253–1280.

Vaara, E., Kleymann, B. and Seristö, H. (2004). Strategies as discursive constructions: The case of airline alliances. *Journal of Management Studies*, 41(1), 1–35.

Vaara, E. and Lamberg, J.-A. (2016). Taking historical embeddedness seriously: Three historical approaches to advance strategy process and practice research. *Academy of Management Review*, 41(4), 633–657.

Vaara, E., Sorsa, V. and Pälli, P. (2010). On the force potential of strategy texts: A critical discourse analysis of a strategic plan and its power effects in a city organization. *Organization*, 17(6), 685–702.

Vaara, E. and Whittington, R. (2012). Strategy-as-practice: Taking social practices seriously. *The Academy of Management Annals*, 6(1), 285–336.

Van Aaken, D., Kirsch, W. and Seidl, D. (2015). Gesetzmäßigkeiten in der Unternehmensführung?–Unternehmensführung als das Verfügen über Notwendigkeiten. *Die Unternehmung*, 69(1), 54–66.

Werle, F. and Seidl, D. (2015). The layered materiality of strategizing: Epistemic objects and the interplay between material artefacts in the exploration of strategic topics. *British Journal of Management*, 26, S67–S89.

Whittington, R. (1996). Strategy as practice. *Long Range Planning*, 29(5), 731–735.

Whittington, R. (2006). Completing the practice turn in strategy research. *Organization Studies*, 27(5), 613–634.

Whittington, R. (2007). Strategy practice and strategy process: Family differences and the sociological eye. *Organization Studies*, 28(10), 1575–1586.

Whittington, R. (2011). The practice turn in organization research: Towards a disciplined transdisciplinarity. *Accounting, Organizations and Society*, 36(3), 183–186.

Whittington, R. (2015). Giddens, structuration theory and strategy as practice. In D. Golsorkhi, L. Rouleau, D. Seidl and E. Vaara, eds., *Cambridge Handbook of Strategy as Practice*, 2nd ed. Cambridge: Cambridge University Press, pp. 145–164.

Whittington, R. (2019). *Opening Strategy: Professional Strategists and Practice Change, 1960 to Today*. Oxford: Oxford University Press.

Whittington, R., Jarzabkowski, P., Mayer, M., Mounoud, E., Nahapiet, J., et al. (2003). Taking strategy seriously: Responsibility and reform for an important social practice. *Journal of Management Inquiry*, 12(4), 396–409.

Whittington, R., Yakis-Douglas, B. and Ahn, K. (2016). Cheap talk? Strategy presentations as a form of chief executive officer impression management. *Strategic Management Journal*, 37 (12), 2413–2424.

Whittington, R., Yakis-Douglas, B., Ahn, K. and Cailluet, L. (2017). Strategic planners in more turbulent times: The changing job characteristics of strategy professionals, 1960–2003. *Long Range Planning*, 50(1), 108–119.

Yamauchi, Y. and Hiramoto, T. (2016). Reflexivity of routines: An ethnomethodological investigation of initial service encounters at sushi bars in Tokyo. *Organization Studies*, 37(10), 1473–1499.

Zbaracki, M. J. and Bergen, M. (2010). When truces collapse: A longitudinal study of price-adjustment routines. *Organization Science*, 21(5), 955–972.

CHAPTER 36 Path Dependence and Routine Dynamics

JÖRG SYDOW

36.1 Introduction

Path dependence and organizational routines have been twin concepts for a long time, even though their relationship has hardly been scrutinized and has hence remained somewhat unclear. Seminal as well as more recent studies of organizational routines refer to path dependence in order to point to the difficulties of routine change and/or emphasize the contribution of such routines to structural inertia or institutional persistence of an organizational subunit or an entire organization (e.g., Hannan and Freeman, 1977; Nelson and Winter, 1982; compare, Becker, 2004). In turn, studies of organizational path dependence often mention routines as one source of hyper-stability typically associated with the path dependence of such systems (e.g., Koch, 2011; Singh, Mathiassen and Mishra, 2015; Sydow et al., 2009). The unclear relationship between the two concepts results not only from a lack of scrutiny but also from the under-specification of organizational path dependence, which is often simply equated with 'past dependence' (Antonelli, 1999). In addition, the more recent Routine Dynamics perspective (Feldman, 2000, 2016; Feldman and Pentland, 2003; Rerup and Feldman, 2011) requires a new look at the relationship of these two concepts, because routines, from this perspective, are not only a source of organizational stability but also of change.

This chapter contributes to conceptual clarification by systematically comparing and linking the insights from these two research areas: the study of organizational routines, in particular from a Routine Dynamics perspective, and the study of organizational path dependence. It will be shown that both streams of research could benefit from closer collaboration. While several publications have already contributed to linking both areas (e.g. Kremser and Schreyögg, 2016; Pentland and Jung, 2016; Pentland et al., 2012; Schulz, 2008), none of these has done this in any programmatic or systematic way. Based on insights from such earlier work, this chapter will first clarify the meaning of path dependence, starting chronologically from technological path dependence and ending with organizational path dependence. The chapter will then explore the relationship of path dependence and organizational routines, first from the classic view on routines, before turning to the Routine Dynamics view. This systematic analysis will lead to insights about what one stream of research could learn from the other. The chapter will conclude more generally with regard to implications for future research and management practice.

36.2 From Technological to Organizational Path Dependence

Path dependence theory evolved from the study of technology adoption in markets, before the attention shifted from technological to the institutional path dependence of markets. It is only more recently that path-dependent processes within and among organizations have received scholarly attention. Importantly, these shifts with regard to the phenomenon under scrutiny were accompanied by changes in theory and methodology.

36.2.1 Path Dependence of Technologies and Institutions

Economic historian Paul David (1985) was arguably the first who, with his study of the emergence and persistence of the QWERTY keyboard, theorized technological path dependence (elaborated later by Arthur, 1994). He did so with regard to markets, which, despite the demonstrated inferiority of this particular technical solution, seemed unable to come up with a more efficient technology. Without going into the details of this example and the most likely sources of this extremely path-dependent technological development – from the first mechanical and electric typewriters, then word processing systems and personal computers, to today's tablets and handheld devices – several insights have been derived from this ground-breaking study. At the beginning, several technological alternatives or options were available. Then, however, a small event triggered a process that was – and still is – characterized by positive feedback or, in economists' terms, increasing returns to scale. This self-reinforcing mechanism (in the case of QWERTY, for instance, the complementarity of the technological solution with early training efforts and respective learning) stabilized the technological path that has not been challenged until today, although in the near future it may well be shattered by voice recognition. Apart from the investigation of the emergence and persistence of the QWERTY keyboard, many other technologies have been studied with regard to path dependence, including, for instance, video systems, music distribution, photography, train tracks and nuclear power.

Economists and political scientists used the initial ideas and insights of David and Arthur to investigate institutional path dependencies on the level of fields or whole societies. Famously, Nobel Laureate Douglas North (1990) explained the difficulties of transforming rule systems in Eastern Europe after the collapse of the Iron Curtain with reference to ideas from path dependence theory. Kathleen Thelen (1999), to give just one other example, integrated concepts from the theory of path dependence into historical institutionalism. In both cases, the theorizing, which in the case of David and Arthur originally built on chance elements and, starting with a critical juncture, on a rather deterministic understanding of path development, has been somewhat relaxed. Most importantly, strategic/political agency and contingency were injected and the role of the institutional context highlighted (see also, Pierson, 2000).

36.2.2 Path Dependence in and among Organizations

Building on these works, together with Georg Schreyögg and Jochen Koch (2009), I developed the theory of organizational path dependence that is also relevant to better understand the persistence or hyper-stability of inter-organizational relationships (e.g., Burger and Sydow, 2014; Schmidt and Braun 2015). While trying to keep in line with the original ideas and concepts of path dependence developed by economists (and modified by sociologists and political scientists), the theory of organizational path dependence deviates from these earlier accounts in three important ways.

First, instead of relying on uncontrollable chance or unconstrained choice, already the *pre-formation* of an organizational path is conceptualized as imprinted by the past and the context, making some actions/events more likely than others. Second, the actual *formation* phase of an organizational path can be triggered not only by chance events but also by strategic action. What is more, this phase is characterized not only by increasing returns but also by self-reinforcing processes driven by positive feedback more generally. The most important self-reinforcing mechanisms are coordination and complementarity effects as well as single-loop learning and adaptive expectations (see also Dobusch and Schüßler, 2013). Triggered by an event or action, small or big, this phase is increasingly, though not completely, controlled by these social mechanisms that contribute to a certain decoupling of the (inter-) organizational process from the activities and practices of organizational agents. Third, in the *lock-in* phase, it is almost impossible for these agents to leave an organizational path. However, within – as well as among – organizations collaborating in a more or less dense network of relationships, for example, one should not expect the path to be reproduced exactly; rather, the theory of organizational path dependence allows for a corridor of on-path (though not transformative) changes. Admittedly, path dependence, and even a lock-in, is not a problem per se, i.e., under stable, non-changing circumstances. However, in increasingly turbulent environments (Emery and Trist, 1965),

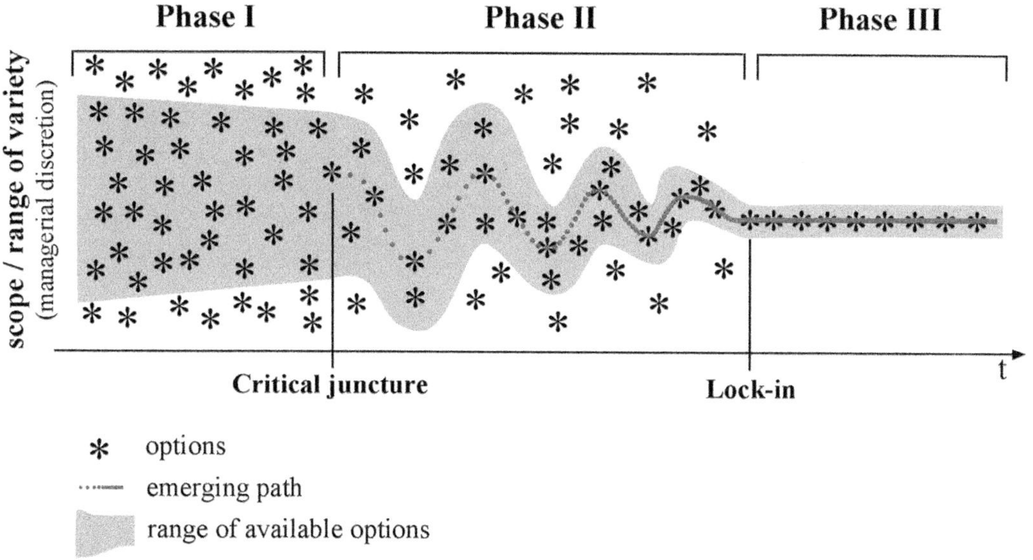

Figure 36.1 Constitution of an organizational path (Sydow et al., 2009: 692)

organizational path dependence is always a problem from a strategic perspective, not only on the level of entire organizations but also of organizational units such as departments or business units (Sydow et al., 2009). The modifications with regard to these three phases (I–III) are depicted in the model of organizational path dependence (see Figure 36.1), which is well-known by now to most management researchers.

36.3 Path Dependence and Organizational Routines

Routines were formerly defined as 'standard operating procedures' (Cyert and March, 1963: 101) that repeatedly had to be enacted and thus guaranteed the much-needed stability of processes in organizations. Organizational change, in consequence, relied significantly on recombining routines, although there is obviously more to an organization than routines. Much later, Feldman and Pentland (2003), when developing their Routine Dynamics view, proposed to consider routines as 'repetitive, recognizable patterns of interdependent actions, carried out by multiple actors' (93).

Organizational scholars pointed early on not only to the importance of routines and routinization for efficiency, reliability, accountability and legitimacy but also to the danger for organizations or organizational subunits to become inert, persistent and, hence, difficult to adapt to changing circumstances (Cyert and March, 1963; Hannan and Freeman, 1977; March and Simon, 1958; Nelson and Winter, 1982). The important role of intra-organizational routines that cause organizations – as well as the role of inter-organizational routines (Zollo et al., 2002) for inter-organizational arrangements – to become inert or persistent[1] is usually based on the classic, competence-based view of routines that gives much credit to March and Simon's notion of standard operating procedures. The relationship of organizational routines and path dependence seems less straightforward, though, from the much more recent Routine Dynamics view that builds on Feldman and Pentland's conception of routines as repetitive,

[1] Interestingly, as assumed by the concept of (dynamics) capabilities, (meta-) routines may sometimes help to overcome such tendencies, as they are an important building block of (organizational, if not dynamic) capabilities (Parmigiani and Howard-Grenville, 2011).

recognizable patterns of interdependent actions (see Parmigiani and Howard-Grenville, 2011, for an excellent review of these two streams of routine research).

36.3.1 The Relationship from the Classic View on Routines

Anchored in behavioural or evolutionary theory, the classic view on organizational routines emphasizes the recurrence of patterns of action, notwithstanding some adaptation of standard operating procedures to situational circumstances, for instance in the face of 'routinely occurring laxity, slippage, rule-breaking, defiance, and even sabotage' (Nelson and Winter, 1982: 108; Parmigiani and Howard-Grenville, 2011: 416–420; see also Kay, 2018: 946–949). Nevertheless, the main focus of the classic view is definitively on stability rather than change, as organizational routines, reflecting a high(er) degree of routinization, are considered to be advantageous for organizational efficiency, reliability, accountability and legitimacy while, at the same time, 'routine rigidity' (Gilbert, 2005) may unfold and cause organizational path dependence.

Levitt and March (1988), for instance, put routines as central in their approach to organizational learning in which they highlight the not only nested but also path-dependent nature of routine-based learning. According to these authors, this form of learning may lead into a competency trap that makes alternative ways of acting and thinking difficult if not impossible,

> A competency trap can occur when favourable performance with an inferior procedure leads an organization to accumulate more experience with it, thus keeping experience with a superior procedure inadequate to make it rewarding to use (Levitt and March, 1988: 322).

Schulz (2008) builds on these insights and analyses how routines themselves are likely to stay on track within an organization. In this context, the author points to 'internal mechanisms of routine reproduction' and circumscribes them as follows,

> Clearly, any such mechanisms need to connect the prior history of the path to its continuation, perhaps via signals and traces left behind, via memories and stories of participants, via structures and artifacts developed on prior passes through the routine, and so on. Action can stay on the normal routine track if there are mechanisms in place that connect current action in some way to prior history. This means that action in routine is path-dependent (Schulz, 2008: 237).

As accurate as this description may be, it does not specify the mechanisms at work. For that very reason Schulz discusses a few lines later, among others, habitualization (on the level of the individual), reciprocal typification (on the interaction level) and institutionalization with a specific focus on value infusion as well as formalization and leadership (on the organizational level). The author also adds competency traps and escalating commitment, two mechanisms that are indeed – like organizational path dependence – characterized by self-reinforcement. As being the underlying reproduction mechanisms that coevolve with the very routines that they help to stabilize, the author identifies the selection of consecutive action, i.e., connecting 'the selection of the next steps to the prior history on the current path and the history of prior paths in ways that reproduce the routine' (Schulz, 2008: 250).

Such a conception of organizational routines, allowing only for a limited degree of variation in idiosyncratic performativity or effortful accomplishment, seems to fit in quite nicely with the theory of organizational path dependence where routines are considered, on the one hand, as being likely to become path-dependent themselves. On the other hand, however, such routines are an important potential source of inertia and persistence for the organization or the inter-organizational arrangement (e.g., Burger and Sydow, 2014; Sydow et al., 2009). In both cases, self-reinforcing mechanisms, not least coordination and complementarity effects, are assumed to cause path dependence. Coordination effects may result from routine interdependencies that, in turn, may well be caused by coordination efforts. Complementarity makes routines 'fit well' into each other and into the context. But the very fit that contributes to efficiency and reliability makes routine change, at least at times, difficult if not impossible. The path-dependent development of routines and their contribution to a whole organization or inter-organizational arrangement becoming path-dependent is particularly likely when the routines are a highly institutionalized result from emergence rather than a deliberate design, and are tightly inscribed in (inter-)organizational structures and practices (Koch, 2011). This embeddedness constitutes a potential seedbed of self-reinforcing mechanisms that characterize the path dependence not only of a single routine but also of an organizational subunit or an entire organization.

Such effects of routinization become particularly prevalent if one considers not only a single routine that has emerged within an organization or an inter-organizational collaboration (Berends and Sydow, 2019) but also a bundle, cluster or network of routines (e.g., Birnholtz, Cohen and Hoch, 2007; Kremser and Schreyögg, 2016; Sele and Grand, 2016). In a study of a European market leader in photofinishing that was confronted in the 1990s with the digitalization challenge, Kremser and Schreyögg (2016) unearthed the restricting dynamics of routine clusters which were based on complementarity effects and respective misfit costs. These dynamics made it difficult, if not impossible, to integrate new routines that worked in the digital world and to fit the interface into existing routines. Closely interrelated and fine-tuned routines, i.e., 'routines clusters', with their programmed interfaces, proved to be particularly inert or persistent. Even newly created routines had to fit the interfaces of established clusters with their own – systemic – dynamics that, as the study makes clear, unfold largely behind the back of the organizational actors. The studied firm only survived the digitalization challenge by setting up a separate organizational subsidiary that specialized in the radically new technology and was located some distance away from the main facility. Today, this subsidiary makes up the core of the firm.

36.3.2 The Relationship from the Routine Dynamics View

The more recent Routine Dynamics view adopts a practice-based approach and is anchored in either pragmatist or structurationist thinking (Feldman and Orlikowski, 2011). This view focuses on how organizational actors produce, reproduce or transform more or less routinized practices. But instead of focusing on any mindless reproduction/repetition, the rapidly increasing research from the Routine Dynamics stream (see Chapter 1, this volume) emphasizes intentional variation by knowledgeable agents (Giddens, 1984) in routine performances. From this perspective, a change of routine behaviour is not only possible, but even likely.

Martha Feldman (2000) initiated this line of research with her seminal study of hiring routines that were not only a source of organizational stability but also of change (see also Feldman and Pentland, 2003). On the one hand, this theorizing highlights the necessity to perform routines in practice (Parmigiani and Howard-Grenville, 2011). On the other hand, however, it corresponds nicely with not only practice-based but also more dialectical approaches that consider stability and change not as opposites but as a duality (Farjoun, 2010; Putnam et al., 2016). As shown by Danneels and colleagues (2018) in the case of Olivetti's transition from mechanical to digital technology, legitimized and powerful agents, supported by allocated resources – considered by the authors as three building blocks of organizational capability – promote inertia and enable change. Routine Dynamics research that adopts a practice-based approach has indeed confirmed time and again that agency, and the artifact agents mobilized in interaction with the help of practices (D'Adderio, 2011; Sele and Grand, 2016), contribute to both the flexibility and stability of routines (Parmigiani and Howard-Grenville, 2011: 435–440). For instance, in a nine-month ethnography of a high-tech manufacturing company, Howard-Grenville (2005) identified the rather flexible performances of a road-mapping routine that nevertheless persisted over time. She identified habitual and imaginative, and less and more powerful agency, respectively, as contributing to persistence and change. On the other hand, however, she found that the routine's organizational embeddedness into technological, coordinative and cultural structures mattered,

> A strongly embedded routine, one that overlaps with many other structures, whose overlap is significant in the sense that a change in the enactment of one type of structure would be consequential of the others, and whose artifacts and expectations are reinforced by those generated by other structures, may be quite difficult to change over time (Howard-Grenville, 2005: 632).

Without mentioning that routines can become path-dependent, the author identifies agent- and embeddedness-related conditions that are likely to produce a 'sticky routine': an actor's primary orientation to the past combined with strong embeddedness, making a flexible performance as well as a change of the routine over time rather unlikely.

In another study, Brian Pentland and colleagues (2012) construct a simulation model that is in line with practice-based approaches and links micro-level actions to macro-level Routine Dynamics in concepts such as not only absorptive capacity and dynamic capabilities but also in a hyper-stability or competency trap. In contrast to Howard-Grenville, the authors mention path dependence – within as well as between routine performances – as a possible outcome. However, they consider variation and selective retention to be 'mechanisms by which recognizable, repetitive patterns form and change over time' (2012: 1485). And these mechanisms are different from those which the theory of organizational path dependence would emphasize. In the light of these two specific mechanisms, the authors focus more on path creation than on path dependence and consider the 'endogenous and less-deliberate possibility of creating paths' (2012: 1499 with reference to Garud, Kumaraswamy and Karnøe, 2010) as being a more likely outcome than ending in a lock-in.

36.3.3 Cross-Fertilization of Path Dependence and Routine Research

Relating this more agency-focused, generative or performative perspective of routines to the emergence of organizational inertia and persistence or 'endogenous stability' (a more adequate formulation from the Routine Dynamics perspective) or even organizational path dependence is much less straight forward than in the case of classic routine research that continues to be advanced (e.g., Suarez and Montes, 2019). For research on Routine Dynamics highlights variation and change, caused not only by idiosyncratic agents but also by the generative, improvisational character inherent to routines (Feldman and Pentland, 2003). Hence, and very much in line with the becoming perspective (Tsoukas and Chia, 2002) or a strong process view (Langley and Touskas, 2010), it is not change but stability that requires explanation. Against this ontological background, organizational path dependence is not a natural or even likely outcome of routinization. Instead, the Routine Dynamics lens requires more than the classic view on routines to name the specific conditions and mechanisms under which path dependence arises – despite the nature of routines to generate change.

However, as the study of Howard-Grenville (2005) demonstrates in an exemplary way, Routine Dynamics research far from neglects endogenous stability either. By contrast, stabilized or sticky routines and, in particular, the collectivities of such routines, which due to their interdependent interactions 'stay on track', are likely to become not only path-dependent themselves but even a potential source of path dependence for organizational subunits or entire organizations. Such a Routine Dynamics view is helpful because organizational path dependence is, in contrast to the classical stance, not considered to be a likely outcome of routinization that deserves no specific explanation. Instead, stability and, in particular, organizational path dependence, which evolve in the face of Routine Dynamics, require not only the working of specific (self-reinforcing) mechanisms but the prevalence of additional conditions. Obvious candidates for the former are the embeddedness in collectivities or clusters of interdependent routines and a tight rather than loose embeddedness in the wider (inter-) organizational context with its structures and practices. Coordination and complementarity effects as well as other self-reinforcing mechanisms are likely to be fed in such context and, in turn, to inscribe organizational path dependence in such context (Koch, 2011). Clearly, both conditions and mechanisms have a greater impact on more aggregate levels of analysis than do single routines.

More recent developments in the theory of organizational path dependence make the conceptual connection between these two lines of research, Routine Dynamics on the one hand and organization path dependence on the other, easier, and a conversation involving the two camps more likely. This is particularly true when scholars of organizational path dependence, not unlike Feldman and Pentland (2003) with regard to Routine Dynamics research, subscribe to a constructivist view and, in particular, to Giddens' (1984) duality of structure and agency that considers structures not only as being a product of agency but also as enabling and, in particular in later phases of the path process, restraining actions. What is more, research on organizational path dependence – or path constitution more broadly – is likely to focus increasingly on (more or less routinized) practices that not only create, maintain, stabilize or extend but also break a technological, institutional or organizational path (e.g.,Aaltonen et al., 2017; Jing and Benner, 2016; Singh et al., 2015; Sydow et al., 2010, 2012).

In any case, the creation and transformation as well as the very reproduction of an organizational path relies from this perspective entirely on organizational agents to enact structures, i.e., rules (of signification and legitimation) and resources (of domination), along the established and more or less action-delimiting path. This theorizing of organizational path dependence acknowledges – again in line with Giddens' (1984) theory of structuration – the possibility or even likelihood of unintended consequences and, thereby, the fact that these (developing behind the back of the agent in a possibly even unacknowledgeable way) may inform the next sequence of action. What is more, these dynamics may accumulate to systemic effects on the level of the organization or an inter-organizational relationship.

As may have already become clear, beyond allowing for historical imprinting, the universal relevance of context in processes of unfolding practices, and the enactment of self-reinforcing mechanisms, distinguishing between different levels of analysis is crucial for a better understanding of when and how routines – even from a dynamic routine perspective – can become path-dependent and possibly lead an organization into a lock-in.[2] In this process of creating, shaping, stabilizing, extending and breaking an organizational path, the role of routines on different levels of analysis may be important. While the central focus of analysis seems to move slowly from single routines to collectivities of routines, the exact link to more macro outcomes, including path dependence on the level of organizational units, entire organizations or inter-organizational arrangements, still needs to be unpacked and requires closer investigation via qualitative as well as quantitative methods, not to mention mixed methods.

In an early contribution, Collinson and Wilson (2006) investigated how two large firms in Japan became inert at times when, in the face of highly turbulent circumstances, organizational flexibility was needed. Based mainly on qualitative interviews, the two authors discovered that not only dense networks of internal and external relationships but also established knowledge-accessing and -sharing routines, typically considered a hallmark of flexibility and innovation, contributed to organizational inertia (which they, however, do not differentiate from organizational path dependence). Like Kremser and Schreyögg (2016), but with a less microscopic view and without any reference to the theory of path dependence, Collinson and Wilson looked at bundles of routines rather than just single ones. It is through these routines that the two firms became inert and were unable to implement new strategies and practices. The respective organizational capabilities that these firms had developed hence only worked well until economic circumstances became turbulent and required novel organizational action in terms of adapted routines, use of

[2] While some practice theories employ a flat ontology, structuration theory sticks with a tall ontology that allows one to distinguish between different levels of analysis (Seidl and Whittington, 2014). The importance of multi-level research on routines and capabilities is widely emphasized (Salvato and Rerup, [2011], for an excellent review).

heuristics and/or even improvisation; three distinct organizational responses to the breakdown of an established routine that put different emphasis on cognitive search and social convergence triggered by increased speed and resource needs, and unanticipated problems and opportunities, respectively (Suarez and Montes, 2019). In contrast to routines, even from a Routine Dynamics perspective, these latter forms of organizational response, i.e., use of heuristics and most of all improvisation, are significantly less likely to become path-dependent.

One extremely important step towards reconciling Routine Dynamics and path dependence research beyond asserting conceptual convergence is thus to conduct empirical studies not only on the level of single routines, but instead on bundles, ecologies, networks or clusters of routines (e.g., Birnholtz et al., 2007; Kremser and Schreyögg, 2016; Sele and Grand, 2016); even more so if such studies take into account the embeddedness of such collectivities of routines in the structures and practices of the wider organizational and inter-organizational context. Such research may show that even collective agency in reflective or experimental spaces, eventually created for adapting existing or developing new routines (Bucher and Langley, 2016), may not suffice to break an organizational path caused, among other things, by certain constellations and interactions of routines embedded in (inter-) organizational contexts. For a better understanding of these stabilizing dynamics, even from a perspective that emphasizes routine change rather than (only) stability, it would be necessary to seriously consider the effects of early imprints in the preformation phase, of multi-layered context, as well as of intentionally and unintentionally enacting at least one self-reinforcing feedback mechanism in the formation phase, on the outcome of staying on or deviating from the course of action in the lock-in phase.

Table 36.1 summarizes the similarities and differences of these two very distinct views on organizational routines and their potential relationship with organizational path dependence.

As several important questions regarding the interplay of organizational routines and path dependence have not yet been well understood, routine research in general and Routine Dynamics research in particular could benefit from a closer look at research on organizational path dependence – and vice versa. For instance, processes of patterning, which are characteristic of any Routine Dynamics (Feldman, 2016), may under specific circumstances develop in a path-dependent way and eventually, as in the case of a bureaucratic cycle (Crozier, 1964), accumulate into a trajectory of routinization that cannot be easily left. Under conditions of organizational path dependence, repetitive action patterns of the past may then not only create recognizability, but – because of coordination, complementarity, learning, adaptive expectation effects and/or similar self-reinforcing processes at work – from a critical juncture onwards help to predict future patterning: the development of routines that keeps aligned to a certain organizational path and, with the latter's structures and practices, contributes to ongoing reproduction by individual and collective agents. From a Routine Dynamics view, the mutual constitution of agency and structure emphasized by Giddens (1984) implies that 'stability and change are different outcomes of the same dynamic, rather than different dynamics' (Feldman and Orlikowski, 2011: 6). While this may be correct, the self-reinforcing dynamic of organizational path dependence is different, adds to this and emphasizes, at least in the longer run and on a higher level of analysis, stability over change, although change remains possible, not only on-path but also in the form of path-breaking change.

Not only would Routine Dynamics research benefit from closer consideration of the dynamics of organizational path dependence but the latter could also benefit from adopting a more dynamic understanding of organizational routines, acknowledging the importance of processes of idiosyncratic variation and systemic patterning. Such an understanding would obviously be more in line with a practice-based, structurationist or constitutive view of path dependence (Sydow et al., 2012) than with one more based on the original works of David and Arthur. Such a view would allow for Routine Dynamics, not only in terms of on-path changes, but for dynamics that, under conditions

Table 36.1 Similarities and differences between research on organizational path dependence and routines

	Path dependence from the classic view	Path dependence from a constructivist view	The classic view on routines	The Routine Dynamics view
Similarities	Focus on recurrent action patterns across time and, more often than not, also space; involving multiple actors, i.e., collective-level concepts; patterning as social ordering; unfolding process comprising potentiality as well as actuality; relying on reproduction, eventually even repetition; allowing for non-linearity; important role of historical imprints; closely related to capabilities and practices			
Differences				
Ontology	Objectivist	Social constructivist	Objectivist	Social constructivist
Theoretical perspective	Evolutionary economics	Complexity or structuration	Behavioural or evolutionary	Pragmatism or practice-based theory
Level of analysis	Technology or institution in market or field	Organization, inter-organizational relationships	Organization, organizational units	Single routines or bundle of routines
Social mechanism	Self-reinforcement via 'increasing returns'	Self-reinforcement via coordination, complementarity and learning effects, though not decoupled from actions/ practices; phase-specific regimes	Action patterning guided by structure and a (re-) production regime	Action patterning, also guided by (re-) production regime, but emphasizing the generative moments
Main methods	Economic history, but also modelling and simulation	Interviews and ethnography	Interviews, archival or survey data	Interviews and, in particular, ethnography
Outcomes	Technological or institutional lock-in, path-breaking only through external shocks	Organizational lock-in, path changes likely, but path breaking unlikely	Structural inertia, institutional persistence; deviating from pattern unlikely though possible	Deviation from pattern always likely, but endogenous stability possible

and mechanisms to be specified, can lead to path-breaking change. Such a view would therefore be sensitive for both path-breaking change by intentional redesign of a routine or even a collectivity of routines as well as path-breaking change via largely unintentional cumulative effects produced through systemic processes by agents enacting an existing routine or combination of routines.

A more precise conceptualization of the interplay of organizational routines and organizational paths may even help to better understand the potentials and pitfalls of meta-routines as well. One example is the alleged overcoming of organizational path dependence with the help of 'dynamic capabilities' (Teece et al., 1997). For, exactly such capabilities, if they really are organizational in character, are necessarily based on routines or meta-routines that – paradoxically – may also become path-dependent (Vergne and Durand, 2011), thereby at times questioning the very ability of dynamic capabilities.

36.4 Concluding Remark

The potential of closer conversation or even collaboration between scholars of Routine Dynamics and organizational path dependence strongly depends on the convergence of the theoretical foundations in a way that – like practice-based theorizing (Feldman and Orlikowski, 2011; Nicolini, 2012) – acknowledges the insights each view can provide for the most important dualities; dualities which – like agency and structure, stability and change, or emergent and designed – characterize 'organization, organizing and the organized in and between societies' (slogan of *Organization Studies*, one of the leading scholarly journals in the field). Practice-based theorizing in general and structuration theory in particular can pave the way to better explore under exactly which conditions and on which levels organizational routines, even from a perspective that emphasizes Routine Dynamics, can become path-dependent and thus become a major, though not necessarily the only, source of organizational persistence.

References

Aaltonen, K., Ahola, T. and Artto, K. (2017). Something old, something new: Path dependence and path creation during the early stage project. *International Journal of Project Management*, 35, 749–762.

Antonelli, C. (1999). The economics of path-dependence in industrial organization. *International Journal of Industrial Organization*, 15, 643–675.

Arthur, W. B., ed. (1994). *Increasing Returns and Path Dependency in the Economy*. Ann Arbor: University of Michigan Press.

Becker, M. (2004). Organizational routines: A review of the literature. *Industrial and Corporate Change*, 13, 643–678.

Berends, H. and Sydow, J. (2019). Introduction: Process views on inter-organizational collaborations. *Research in the Sociology of Organizations*, 64, 1–10.

Birnholtz, J. P., Cohen, M. D. and Hoch, S. V. (2007). Organizational character: On the regeneration of camp polar grove. *Organization Science*, 18(2), 315–332.

Bucher, S. and Langley, A. (2016). The interplay of reflective and experimental spaces in interrupting and reorienting routine dynamics. *Organization Science*, 27(3), 594–613.

Burger, M. and Sydow, J. (2014). How inter-organizational networks can become path-dependent: Bargaining practices in the photonics industry. *Schmalenbach Business Review*, 66(1), 73–99.

Collinson, S. and Wilson, D. C. (2006). Inertia in Japanese organizations: Knowledge management routines and failure to innovate. *Organization Studies*, 27(9), 1359–1387.

Crozier, M. (1964). *The Bureaucratice Pheonomenon*. Chicago: University of Chicago Press.

Cyert, R. M. and March, J. G. (1963). *A Behavioral Theory of the Firm*. Englewood Cliffs, NJ: Prentice-Hall.

D'Adderio, L. (2011). Artifacts at the centre of routines: Performing the material turn in routines theory. *Journal of Institutional Economics*, 7(2), 197–230.

Danneels, E., Verona, G. and Provera, B. (2018). Overcoming the inertia of organizational competence: Olivetti's transition from mechanical to electronic technology. *Industrial and Corporate Change*, 27(3), 595–618.

David, P. A. (1985). Clio and the economics of QWERTY. *American Economic Review*, 75(2), 332–337.

Dobusch, L. and Schüßler, E. (2013). Theorizing path dependence: A review of positive feedback mechanisms in technology markets, regional clusters, and organizations. *Industrial and Corporate Change*, 22(3), 617–647.

Emery, F. E. and Trist, E. L. (1965). The causal texture of organizational environments. *Human Relations*, 18, 21–32.

Farjoun, M. (2010). Beyond dualism: Stability and change as a duality. *Academy of Management Review*, 35(2), 202–225.

Feldman, M. S. (2000). Organizational routines as a source of continuous change. *Organizational Science*, 11, 611–629.

Feldman, M. S. (2004). Resources in emerging structures and processes of change. *Organization Science*, 15(3), 295–309.

Feldman, M. S. (2016). Routines as process: Past, present, and future. In J. Howard-Grenville, C. Rerup, A. Langley and H. Tsoukas, eds., *Organizational Routines: How They Are Created, Maintained, and Changed*. Oxford: Oxford University Press, pp. 23–46.

Feldman, M. S. and Orlikowski, W. J. (2011). Theorizing practice and practicing theory. *Organization Science*, 22(5), 1240–1253.

Feldman, M. S. and Pentland, B. T. (2003). Reconceptualizing organizational routines as a source of flexibility and change. *Administrative Science Quarterly*, 48(1), 94–118.

Garud, R., Kumaraswamy, A. and Karnøe, P. (2010). Path dependence or path creation? *Journal of Management Studies*, 47(4), 760–774.

Giddens, A. (1984). *The Constitution of Society*. Cambridge: Polity.

Gilbert, C. (2005). Unbundling the structure of inertia: Resource versus routine rigidity. *Academy of Management Journal*, 48(5), 741–763.

Hannan, M. T. and Freeman, J. H. (1977). The population ecology of organizations. *American Journal of Sociology*, 82, 929–964.

Howard-Grenville, J. (2005). The persistence of flexible organizational routines: The role of agency and context. *Organization*, 16(6), 618–636.

Jing, R. and Benner, M. (2016). Institutional regime, opportunity space and organizational path constitution: Case studies of the conversion of military firms in China. *Journal of Management Studies*, 53(4), 552–579.

Kay, N. M. (2018). We need to talk: Opposing narratives and conflicting perspectives in the conversation of routines. *Industrial and Corporate Change*, 27(6), 943–956.

Koch, J. (2011). Inscribed strategies: Exploring the organizational nature of strategic lock-in. *Organization Studies*, 32, 337–363.

Kremser, W. and Schreyögg, G. (2016). The dynamics of interrelated routines: Introducing the cluster level. *Organization Science*, 27(3), 698–721.

Langley, A. and Tsoukas, H. (2010). Introducing 'Perspectives on Process Organization Studies'. In T. Hernes and S. Maitlis, eds., *Process, Sensemaking, and Organizing*. Oxford: Oxford University Press, pp. 1–26.

Levitt, M. R. and March, J. G. (1988). Organizational learning. *Annual Review of Sociology*, 14, 319–340.

March, J. G. and Simon, H. A. (1958). *Organizations*. New York: Wiley.

Nelson, R. R. and Winter, S. (1982). *An Evolutionary Theory of Economic Change*. Cambridge, MA: Belknap.

Nicolini, D. (2012). *Practice Theory, Work, and Organization*. Oxford: Oxford University Press.

North, D. C. (1990). *Institutions, Institutional Change and Economic Performance*. Cambridge: Cambridge University Press.

Parmigiani, A. and Howard-Grenville, J. (2011). Routines revisited: Exploring the capabilities and practice perspectives. *Academy of Management Annals*, 5(1), 413–453.

Pentland, B. T., Feldman, M. S., Becker, M. C. and Liu, P. (2012). Dynamics of organizational routines: A generative model. *Journal of Management Studies*, 49(8), 1484–1500.

Pentland, B. T. and Jung, E. J. (2016). Evolutionary and revolutionary change in path-dependent patters of action. In J. Howard-Grenville, C. Rerup, A. Langley and H. Tsoukas, eds., *Organizational Routines: How They Are Created, Maintained, and Changed*. Oxford: Oxford University Press, pp. 96–113.

Pierson, P. (2000). Increasing returns, path dependence, and the study of politics. *American Political Science Review*, 94, 251–267.

Putnam, L. L., Fairhurst, G. T. and Banghart, S. (2016). Contradictions, dialectics and paradoxes in organizations: A constitutive approach. *Academy of Management Annals*, 10(1), 65–171.

Rerup, C. and Feldman, M. S. (2011). Routines as source of change in organizational schemata: The role of trial-and-error learning. *Academy of Management Journal*, 54(3), 577–610.

Salvato, C. and Rerup, C. (2011). Beyond collective entities: Multilevel research on organizational routines and capabilities. *Journal of Management*, 37(2), 468–490.

Schmidt, T. and Braun, T. (2015). When cospecialization leads to rigidity: Path dependence in successful strategic networks. *Schmalenbach Business Review*, 67, 489–515.

Schulz, M. (2008). Staying on track: A voyage to the internal mechanisms of routine reproduction. In M. C. Becker, ed., *Handbook of Organizational Routines*. Cheltenham: Elgar, pp. 228–255.

Seidl, D. and Whittington, R. (2014). Enlarging the strategy-as-practice research agenda: Towards taller and flatter ontologies. *Organization Studies*, 35(10), 1407–1421.

Sele, K. and Grand, S. (2016). Unpacking the dynamics of ecologies of routines: Mediators and their generative effects in routine interaction. *Organization Science*, 27(3), 722–738.

Singh, F., Mathiassen, L. and Mishra, A. (2015). Organizational path constitution in technological innovation: Evidence from rural telehealth. *MIS Quarterly*, 39(3), 643–665.

Suarez, F. F. and Montes, J. S. (2019). An integrative perspective of organizational responses: Routines, heuristics, and improvisations in a mount Everest expedition. *Organization Science*, 30(3), 573–599.

Sydow, J., Lerch, F. and Staber, U. (2010). Planning for path dependence? The case of a network in the Berlin-Brandenburg optics cluster. *Economic Geography*, 86(2), 173–195.

Sydow, J., Schreyögg, G. and Koch, J. (2009). Organizational path dependence: Opening the black box. *Academy of Management Review*, 34(4), 689–709.

Sydow, J., Windeler, A., Schubert, C. and Möllering, G. (2012). Organizing R&D consortia for path creation and extension: The case of semiconductor manufacturing technologies. *Organization Studies*, 33(7), 907–936.

Teece, D. J., Pisano, G. and Shuen, A. (1997). Dynamic capabilities and strategic management. *Strategic Management Journal*, 18(7), 509–533.

Thelen, K. (1999). Historical institutionalism and comparative politics. *Annual Review of Political Science*, 2, 369–404.

Tsoukas, H. and Chia, R. (2002). On organizational becoming: Rethinking organizational change. *Organization Science*, 13(5), 567–582.

Vergne, J. P. and Durand, R. (2011). The path of most persistence: An evolutionary perspective on path dependence and dynamic capabilities. *Organization Studies*, 32(3), 365–382.

Zollo, M., Reuer, J. J. and Singh, H. (2002). Interorganizational routines and performance in strategic alliances. *Organization Science*, 13(6), 701–713.

CHAPTER 37

Business Process Management and Routine Dynamics

BASTIAN WURM, THOMAS GRISOLD, JAN MENDLING AND JAN VOM BROCKE

37.1 Two Islands of Process Research

Routine Dynamics and Business Process Management (BPM) are two academic disciplines that investigate sequences of action for carrying out organizational work. Even though both fields share this phenomenon of interest, they depart from different assumptions, employ different means and target different goals. According to (Pentland et al., 2021), Routine Dynamics and BPM resemble two 'islands', i.e., largely isolated areas of research, with very few scholarly works that attempt to bridge the divide that separates these two communities.

Organizational routines have been described as 'repetitive, recognizable patterns of interdependent organizational actions carried out by multiple actors' (Feldman and Pentland, 2003: 95). Research on Routine Dynamics tries to understand *why and how* routines change. Important to this understanding is the fact that organizational routines are embedded in and are shaped by an interplay of organizational actors and artifacts. As the dynamics of routines are complex, corresponding research uses methods that allow the researcher to immerse in organizational reality and to collect rich data, e.g., by means of ethnography (see Dittrich [Chapter 8], this volume for details). Researchers have explored various aspects to understand Routine Dynamics better, such as intentionality (Dittrich and Seidl, 2018), interdependence (Kremser and Schreyögg, 2016) and patterning of routines (Goh and Pentland, 2019), to name but a few themes of the large spectrum of research on Routine Dynamics.

The research discipline of BPM pursues different ends than typical studies of routines research (Mendling et al., 2021). BPM aims to provide insights that help organizations to *manage* their business processes. BPM is an interdisciplinary research field that has its roots in computer science, management science and information systems (van der Aalst et al., 2003). Given its history, much work in BPM has an emphasis on information systems engineering for designing how work in organizations should be performed. This world-view is reflected in BPM–related contributions that focus on technology, methods and tools for process design and execution (Recker and Mendling, 2016).

In this chapter, we map out the second of these 'islands' of process research, BPM, in more detail. In doing so, we first contrast research on organizational routines with research on business processes. Next, we describe research in the field of BPM by use of the BPM lifecycle (Dumas et al., 2018). This lifecycle is widely used in the BPM community and serves us as an important instrument to explain which management activities exist and how they are idealistically related to each other. Against this background, we then discuss how the fields of Routine Dynamics and BPM can contribute to one another. With this, we intend to lay the groundwork for and inspire future research that strengthens the bridge that connects both fields. Both have their unique views and strengths. A collaboration between them may lead to new study loci, phenomena of interest and methods that help to progress either one of them.

37.2 Interrelating and Contrasting Routines and Business Processes

Organizational routines and business processes are both sequences of actions that are central to executing work within organizations (Dumas et al., 2018; Feldman and Pentland, 2003). Routines and business processes involve multiple actors and are performed recurrently. Despite these shared aspects, there are various characteristics that differentiate research on organizational routines and business processes. On the one hand, the phenomenon as such – sequences of actions to conduct organizational work – is approached from different angles and with different assumptions. Table 37.1 compares typical definitions of both concepts. On the other hand, both communities are concerned with different research agendas. Table 37.2 summarizes knowledge claims, themes and theories. Note that this list does not reflect a rigorous review of the research streams; rather it aims to contrast both communities in terms of common themes and example theories.

The study of Routine Dynamics is grounded in process theory (Tsoukas and Chia, 2002). As such, organizational routines are considered emergent and generative (Howard-Grenville and Rerup, 2017): routines only come into being through specific performances and they can produce both stability and change in terms of the actions of which they are composed. Central is the distinction between the ostensive aspects of a routine (providing models of and for a routine) and a performative aspect (referring to the specific actions taken by specific actors at specific points in time) (Pentland and Feldman, 2005). Since the ostensive aspect guides performances, and performances influence

Table 37.1 Contrasting routines and business processes

	Routine	Business process
Definition	Routine as 'repetitive, recognizable patterns of interdependent organizational actions carried out by multiple actors' (Feldman and Pentland, 2003: 95)	Business process as 'collection of activities that takes one or more kinds of input and creates an output that is of value to the customer' (Hammer and Champy, 1993: 35)
Function	A routine establishes agreement, coordination and a 'truce' between actors (Becker, 2004; Birnholtz, Cohen and Hoch, 2007)	A business process transforms input into output in order to create value, which is measured by certain performance indicators (Dumas et al., 2018; Laguna and Marklund, 2013)

Table 37.2 Contrasting Routine Dynamics and Business Process Management

	Routine Dynamics	Business Process Management
Knowledge claims	Descriptive and Explanatory (Howard-Grenville and Rerup, 2017)	Prescriptive and Predictive (Recker, 2014)
Research themes	• Dynamics of endogenous change (Dittrich, Guérard and Seidl, 2016) and exogenous change (Volkoff, Strong and Elmes, 2007; D'Adderio, 2011) • Micro-dynamics of routines (Berente, Lyytinen, Yoo and King, 2016; Miller, Pentland and Choi, 2012) • Composition and structure of routines (Gaskin, Berente, Lyytinen and Yoo, 2014; Pentland and Rueter, 1994)	• Measuring and monitoring business process work (Dumas et al. 2018; van der Aalst 2011) • Design implications for business processes (Reijers and Mansar, 2005) • Managerial implications of business processes (Altinkemer, Ozcelik and Ozdemir, 2011; vom Brocke and Mendling, 2018)
Example theories	• Process Theory (Dittrich et al., 2016) • Situated Action (Feldman and Pentland, 2003; Feldman, Pentland, D'Adderio and Lazaric, 2016) • Socio-materiality (Leonardi, 2011; Orlikowski and Scott, 2008)	• Algorithms (van der Aalst, 2011) • Petri Nets (van der Aalst, 2002) • Process Modelling (Kummer, Recker and Mendling, 2016) • Contingency Theory (vom Brocke, Zelt and Schmiedel, 2016)

the ostensive aspect, there is a generative dynamic by which routines evolve over time. The resulting dynamics are mostly endogenous and researchers aim to understand why they come into being as well as how they unfold. Thus, Routine Dynamics research is typically descriptive (Gaskin et al., 2014), explanatory (Lindberg et al., 2016) or both (Volkoff et al., 2007).

Hammer and Champy (1993: 35) define a business processes as 'a collection of activities that takes one or more kinds of input and creates an output that is of value to the customer'. This definition emphasizes the value-focused character of business processes, which puts the customer of a process at centre-stage. In more general terms, business processes serve a specific outcome (e.g., a product or service) and BPM comprises concepts and interventions to achieve this in an efficient and effective manner. With the goal to improve operational excellence or reduce costs (van der Aalst, 2013), research on BPM 'has resulted in a plethora of models, methods and tools that support the design, enactment, management and analysis of business processes' (Recker and Mendling, 2016: 55). In line with this, work in BPM is centred around IT artifacts (Beverungen, 2014; Dumas et al., 2018) that are designed to support the execution of business processes. Business processes exist irrespective of their exact performances; they are defined and documented. Further, business processes exhibit certain variation and, with a few notable exceptions (Recker, 2015), this is usually perceived as inhibiting performance. Thus BPM offers tools that aim to reduce variation, e.g., by means of standardization (Wurm et al., 2018), lean management or six sigma (Dumas et al., 2018). More recently, work in BPM has investigated the role of context of business processes and how context needs to be reflected in how business processes are managed (vom Brocke et al., 2016).

Beverungen (2014) conceptualizes the relation of business processes and routines by extending Pentland and Feldman's (2008) framework. According to Beverungen's (2014) analysis, research in BPM deals with the development of artifacts that can be used to control and steer business processes while routines research predominantly investigates how routines are enacted in organizational reality. Thereby, artifacts at the same time constrain and enable actions that resemble the organizational routine (Pentland and Feldman, 2005). In the subsequent section, we describe Business Process Management in more detail.

37.2.1 BPM Lifecycle and State of the Art

Traditionally, BPM research has been interested in designing, analysing, monitoring and improving business process work in organizations (Grover, Teng, Segars and Fiedler, 1998; Kettinger, Teng and Guha, 1997). Researchers have developed approaches and methods focusing on different aspects of BPM. There are a number of frameworks that organize these instruments along stages and managerial dimensions (Dumas et al., 2018; Rosemann and vom Brocke, 2010). In the following, we focus on the BPM-lifecycle (Dumas et al., 2018) to portray business process research. The use of the BPM lifecycle allows us to convey three important messages. First, we use the lifecycle as an instrument to describe how BPM-related tasks contribute to the management of business processes. Second, the lifecycle offers a way to cluster and describe state of the art research in BPM. Third, in the following subsection, we comment on the business process lifecycle from a routines perspective. More specifically, we discuss how the phases of the business process lifecycle can be related to important concepts in the Routine Dynamics literature.

The lifecycle model emphasizes that the management of business processes is not a one-time project, but a continuous effort of multiple stakeholders (Dumas et al., 2018). The BPM lifecycle is depicted in Figure 37.1 with its six phases. The lifecycle starts with *process identification*. In this phase a BPM team identifies the overall set of business processes of an organization to be managed and their boundaries. This effort results in a process architecture that visualizes these most important processes and how they relate to one another. To facilitate the prioritizing of processes and the evaluation of potential interventions, the BPM team defines key performance measures and performance objectives. Standard performance measures are cost, time, quality and flexibility.

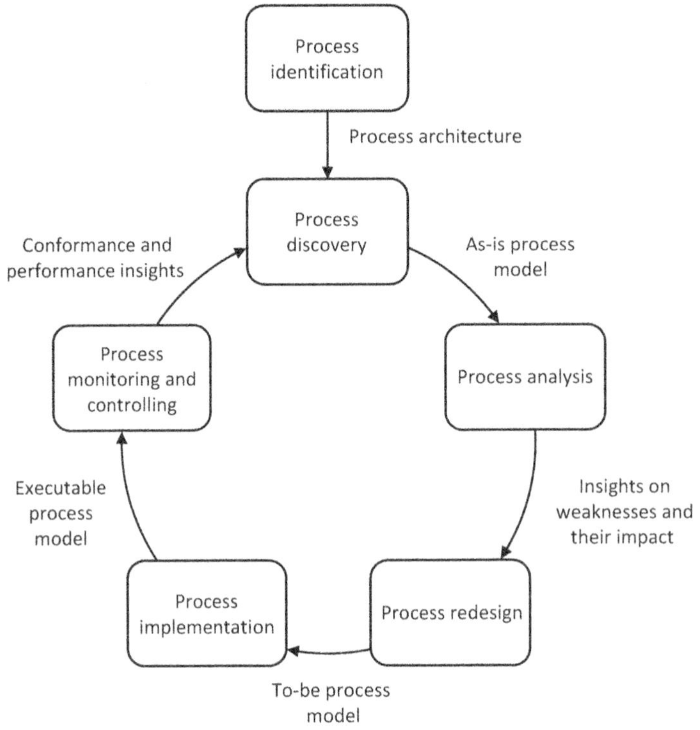

Figure 37.1 The business process management lifecycle (Dumas et al., 2018, p. 23)

Research in this phase of the lifecycle has been mainly concerned with the development of models, methods and systems for process architectures (Gonzalez-Lopez and Bustos, 2019).

In the *process discovery* phase, one specific business process is modelled in order to reach a common understanding among the involved stakeholders about how work is performed. In BPM this is referred to as an *as-is model*, because the model describes the process as it is currently performed. Information on how the process is executed is collected through documents analysis, interviews and observation. As process modelling is the focal task of this phase, corresponding research investigates the suitability of process modelling languages and how different characteristics influence their comprehension. To assess the effectiveness of different manipulations to process models (e.g., introducing different colours (Kummer et al., 2016), symbols (Figl et al., 2013) and representational properties), BPM researchers use experiments. Design and engineering-oriented research in BPM focuses, among others, on process mining (van der Aalst, 2011; van der Aalst et al., 2011). Process mining algorithms automatically discover business processes from event logs recorded in operational information systems. We will discuss the idea and usefulness of process mining in more detail later on in this chapter.

Subsequently, the *process analysis* phase is concerned with the examination of the process by use of the as-is process model in order to identify issues, their root causes and their respective impact (Dumas et al., 2018). Techniques that support this phase can be divided into qualitative and quantitative ones. Qualitative techniques comprise value-added analysis, waste analysis and root-cause analysis, among others. Quantitative analysis techniques build on simulation, flow time analysis and queuing theory (Dumas et al., 2018).

Afterwards, opportunities for process improvement are assessed in the *process redesign* phase. The goal of this phase is the development and design of a *to-be business* process and its corresponding process model. Compared to an as-is process model, a to-be process model visualizes how a process *should be performed* in the future. There are various methods that can be applied for redesigning business processes. The so-called redesign orbit distinguishes between transactional and transformational, inward and outward looking, as well as creative and analytical methods (Dumas et al., 2018). Next to the 'classic' target metrics (cost, time, quality and flexibility), there are emerging approaches that aim at different target outcomes. For example, Wurm, Goel, Bandara and Rosemann (2019) develop design patterns to custom-tailor business processes with regards to specific needs. Note that Wegener and Glaser (Chapter 22), in this volume, explicitly discuss design in Routine Dynamics.

Next, in *process implementation* the to-be process model is put into operation. The implementation is supported by change management on the one hand and the development of IT applications for executing the to-be process on the other hand. BPM research is traditionally more concerned with the second aspect by providing methods and tools that allow the translation of to-be models into software. Process-aware information systems are often used to support process implementation and, later, execution. These include, among others, Enterprise-Resource Planning systems and Business Process Management systems (formally known as workflow systems).

The last phase of the lifecycle is *process monitoring and controlling*. The goal of this phase is to understand how the process is executed and to take corrective measures, if required. Process execution data can be visualized using performance dashboards giving insights into various key metrics and issues of the process (Dumas et al., 2018). Techniques from process mining help to compare the actual process behaviour and prescribed process behaviour as captured by the to-be process model. This is called conformance checking (van der Aalst, 2011). In this way, process monitoring provides information that can be used in process discovery and process analysis, once the lifecycle has to be restarted.

Recker and Mendling (2016) find that most BPM research addresses the phases of process discovery and process implementation. Special attention is directed towards 'models and modeling languages together with techniques for verification, formal analysis and process mining' (Mendling, 2016: 2).

37.2.2 Interpreting BPM through a Routine Dynamics Lens

The business process lifecycle touches on important concepts in the Routine Dynamics literature. Most closely associated with Routine Dynamics are the lifecycle phases of process discovery, process redesign and process monitoring, as they refer to the elicitation of routines and routine redesign, respectively.

The target of process discovery is to understand how the business process is carried out. This covers both the ostensive aspect and the performative aspect of the business process. The ostensive aspect is uncovered by interviewing process participants or holding workshops (Dumas et al., 2018). Since different process participants are likely to have a different ostensive understanding of the business process (Pentland and Feldman, 2005), process analysts help develop a common understanding among the involved actors. At the same time, methods that are based on observation or process mining are action-centric and thus relate to the performative aspect of business processes. Both ways of process discovery complement each other while creating the as-is process model. Process models are an important instrument in BPM for several reasons. First, process models capture how work is carried out (with a focus on either the performative or ostensive aspect). Second, process models shape the ostensive understanding of process participants: Process models serve as a template of how the process should be enacted. Third, process models are important as they serve as input to the subsequent phases of process analysis and process redesign. Hence, the results of the process discovery phase affect problem analysis and redesign considerations.

Existent research in the phases of process analysis, process (re-)design and process implementation provide a large body of knowledge in respect to methods and tools that are suitable to assess routine health, develop improvement scenarios and ease the transition from an old to a new routine design. Likewise, routine (re-)design has developed into one of the core themes in Routine Dynamics (Bucher and Langley, 2016; Dittrich et al., 2016). A key difference between business process redesign and routine redesign is that routine redesign investigates how practitioners make use of use certain methods and artifacts for routine redesign as well as the entailed effects. BPM, in opposition, focuses on developing and evaluating these tools.

Last, process monitoring deals with the performative aspects of the business process. This phase is concerned with closely observing how the business process and important performance indicators develop over time.

37.3 BPM and Routine Dynamics: Potential Overlaps and Opportunities for Future Collaborations

In the previous section, we outlined the field of BPM and used a Routine Dynamics lens to make sense of the business process lifecycle. In the following, we reflect on the connection between Routine Dynamics and BPM. We first discuss what Routine Dynamics can learn from BPM. In turn, we then discuss how Routine Dynamics research can contribute to the management of business processes.

37.3.1 What BPM Can Contribute to Routine Dynamics: Contributions to Computational-Driven Methods

Recent calls to use digital trace-data for theorizing in the social sciences (Berente et al., 2019) have been echoed in the BPM (Wurm, 2018) and the Routine Dynamics community (Feldman et al., 2016; Pentland et al., 2021) alike. Since trace-data occurs naturally (Speer, 2002), it has various advantages. Certain types of actions cannot be captured by and thus remain concealed to researchers that employ ethnography in the traditional sense. Human actors in routines might not be willing to share information on how they carry out specific actions. In an extreme case, routine participants may place wrong tracks to actively distract the researcher and disguise their real actions. Using computational-driven methods, such as process mining, addresses these issues, since all actions that are captured by the employed information systems become discoverable and thus subject to possible theorization.

From a methodological perspective, process mining (van der Aalst et al., 2011), a technique that has been developing in the BPM community, can help to organize, visualize and analyse digital traces collected within process work. In this line of thinking, Grisold, Wurm, Mendling and vom Brocke (2020) argue that process mining offers several features that can support theorizing about process change and Routine Dynamics, in particular. Central to their argument is that process mining algorithms can be used for inductive and deductive theorizing about process dynamics. This idea is captured in Figure 37.2. Digital traces of actions performed by actors can be used to gain an understanding of how a routine is performed (induction); at the same time, elaborate hypotheses and assumptions about how the routine is, was or will be carried out can be empirically examined (deduction). As digital action traces can only convey a limited perspective on the social and organizational dynamics that shape and are shaped by routine performance, gathering contextual insights using qualitative methods is key. This conceptualization of process mining in the theory development process is very similar to our understanding of the more general perspective taken on the use of log-files that is discussed by Mahringer and Pentland in Chapter 12 of this volume.

There are four types of process mining algorithms that are particularly relevant for Routine Dynamics research, (1) Process discovery, (2) conformance checking, (3) variant detection and (4) drift detection. First, *process discovery* serves to reconstruct a routine based on the data stored in the event-log. The outcome of this type of algorithm is a model that represents how the routine is performed. Second, *conformance checking* compares the behaviour of the routine (as captured in the log-file) with an existing process model. Different behavioural measures (Polyvyanyy et al., 2018)

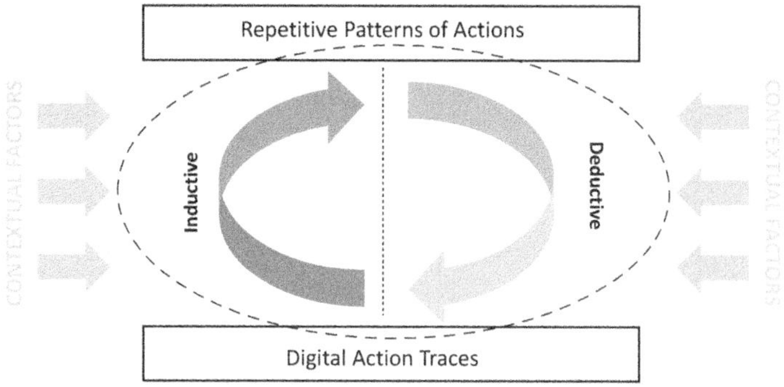

Figure 37.2 Inductive and deductive theorizing with process mining (Grisold et al., 2020: 3)

can be used that illustrate the extent to which actors enact the routine as pre-specified in the model. Third, *variant detection* (Hompes et al., 2015) clusters a routine into different types of enactments. For example, the patient treatment routine within hospitals differs significantly depending on patient age and the condition treated (Hompes et al., 2015). Fourth, *drift detection* (Yeshchenko et al., 2019) can be used to locate changes in the routine. Drifts can take various forms, e.g., change can be sudden when new regulations are set in place or gradual when actors develop their own workarounds over time (Bose et al., 2011).

Process mining algorithms can support theorizing about organizational routines in multiple ways. For example, Howard-Grenville and Rerup (2017) argue for the study of temporality and spatiality of organizational routines. For obvious and pragmatic reasons this is difficult to accomplish following an ethnographic study design. Researchers have only limited time available to collect data. Naturally, ethnographic studies are limited in time and, thus analysis is limited to the respective ethnographic period. Using process mining, routines researchers can collect and analyse routines that span large distances in terms of space and time, given that they are supported by information technology.

Since event logs record a wide range of actions, including those that happen often and those that happen rarely, process mining allows for taking abstract as well as fine-granular views on the process. This resonates with previous calls to zoom in and out (Gaskin et al., 2014) on organizational routines. Thus, researchers can use process mining to gain a basic understanding of how the routine is executed, to subsequently conduct a detailed analysis of aspects that seem interesting and promising for further exploration. In this respect it is important to note that process mining incorporates features that allow for both sequence-based patterning (Goh and Pentland, 2019) and action timing (Turner and Rindova, 2018).

As the digital technologies increasingly penetrate all parts of organizational life and human and material agency are entangled in routine enactment (Leonardi, 2011), research methods can integrate the opportunities provided by digital trace-data. For further elaborations on how digital trace-data can complement existing approaches to the study of Routine Dynamics, we refer the interested reader to Mahringer and Pentland (Chapter 12), this volume. More specific insights into the relation of process mining and organizational routines can be found in Grisold et al. (2020).

37.3.2 What Routine Dynamics Can Contribute to BPM

As argued at an earlier point in this chapter, an important distinction between Routine Dynamics and BPM is that the former tends to be descriptive and explanatory while the latter tends to be predictive and provides prescriptive advice to managers. Following previous claims that the BPM community should merge with and learn from other communities concerned with processes (Recker, 2014), we argue that Routine Dynamics research and a leaning towards a more descriptive stance on business process work may be useful in two respects. First, it allows for transforming business process management into a behavioural science. Second, it can lend a lexicon enabling business process researchers to think of processes in new ways.

37.3.2.1 Progressing BPM as a Behavioural Science

Recker and Mendling (2016) recommend that the BPM discipline can move forward by progressing as a behavioural science. On this view, BPM studies strive to understand and describe key phenomena in terms of why and how actors engage in certain behaviour. Drawing on Routine Dynamics research, BPM studies can take a more dynamic view on business process work. For example, the concept of endogenous change sheds new light on why and how deviances occur. Recent works highlight the need to gain a descriptive understanding of the reasons underlying deviant behaviour (Alter, 2014; Recker, 2015). Approaching this phenomenon from a Routine Dynamics view can reveal mechanisms that give rise to deviant behaviour. For example, the ongoing interplay of ostensive and performative aspects of a routine during deviance might explain how feedback – or the lack of it – contributes to new established understandings of how the routine should be enacted. Additionally, by exploring coordination patterns among actors (Lindberg et al. 2016), it might be possible to explain why and how behavioural patterns develop and shape deviant behaviour. Such an *in-situ view* can be interesting for many other BPM-related phenomena. One specific topic where this could be interesting is business process redesign. Process redesign activities have traditionally been approached from prescriptive (Reijers and Mansar, 2005) and predictive (Altinkemer et al., 2011) perspectives. A Routine Dynamics view could explore and explain process redesign in terms of what happens once new designs are in place (D'Adderio, 2011). This could address the question of how negotiation patterns emerge among actors and why certain design elements are adopted or not, e.g., by means of emerging power-relations of stakeholders (Glaser, 2017).

37.3.2.2 Extending the Lexicon in BPM Research

Routine Dynamics researchers and BPM researchers form distinct epistemic communities, that is, networks of academic experts who generate and verify scientific knowledge (Kuhn, 1970). As argued before, both communities are essentially interested in the same phenomenon – i.e., sequences of actions to achieve organizational work – but they approach this from different perspectives (Mendling et al., 2021). One important implication is that both communities developed their own lexicon to describe, analyse and control knowledge creation (Habermas, 1984). We argue that the lexicon that is used to describe Routine Dynamics can lead BPM researchers to reflect on their underlying assumptions and focus on aspects that have not been considered so far (Recker, 2014).

This point can be illustrated through the distinction between ostensive and performative aspects (Feldman and Pentland, 2003). We argue that the ostensive–performative distinction yields two crucial implications with respect to business process execution. On the one hand, the specific performances, although extensively prescribed, are never the same (Feldman and Pentland, 2003). For example, actors do not necessarily adhere to exact timings. On the other hand, and on a more subtle level, rules and standards cannot be fully prescribed in terms of models or procedures. Regardless of how detailed a process representation is, there is always space for subjective interpretation (D'Adderio, 2011). A central question that arises for BPM researchers is how this ambiguity can be incorporated in management activities or business process representations. Potentially, the ostensive–performative view on business process work can have implications for many stages in the lifecycle. In terms of process redesign, we need to account for the fact that the process as it should be executed (ostensive aspect) may differ from the process as it is executed (performative aspect). In terms of process implementation, we should be aware that one process involves multiple actors and, hence, multiple ostensive aspects (Dittrich et al., 2016); being aware of how ostensive aspects differ across actors may inform learning interventions to facilitate implementation. Finally, in terms of monitoring, the ostensive–performative view can explain why drift occurs in the absence of exogenous factors (Bose et al., 2011). Drawing on routines research, processes can change because goals are not fully specified or because they emerge over time. In that regard, Dittrich et al. (2018) show that actors develop 'ends in view' when they evaluate feedback from their actions (performative aspect) and find ways to improve the routine (ostensive aspect).

In short, being aware of the interplay between performative and ostensive aspects in business process work, BPM researchers can be equipped with a lexicon to explain why and how processes change over time or why they are not enacted in ways they should. This view may be complimentary to recent approaches highlighting that context has an influence on the way business process are executed and thus should be managed (vom Brocke et al., 2016).

37.4 Conclusion and Outlook

In this chapter we introduced BPM and contrasted it to research on Routine Dynamics. While BPM and Routine Dynamics share the phenomenon of interest, there are profound differences between both streams of research with regards to underlying assumptions, research methods and research outcomes that divide both disciplines into 'islands' (Pentland et al., 2021) of research. Irrespective of the differences, we believe there is much to gain for both fields by building a bridge that connects these two academic fields.

Future research can include, but is not limited to, the following. First, routines research can make use of the broad methods pool that BPM provides. Most notably, routines scholars can use process mining to support theorizing about the dynamics in organizational routines (Grisold et al., 2020). Second, at the same time, Routine Dynamics can serve as a reference for progressing BPM as a behavioural science. We believe that these research possibilities will contribute to a more thorough understanding of how work in organizations is carried out and that profits both disciplines alike.

Acknowledgements

This work was co-funded by the Erasmus+ programme of the European Union [2019-1-LI01-KA203-000169]: "BPM and Organizational Theory: An Integrated Reference Curriculum Design".

References

Alter, S. (2014). Theory of workarounds. *Communications of the Association for Information Systems*, 34, 1041–1066.

Altinkemer, K., Ozcelik, Y. and Ozdemir, Z. D. (2011). Productivity and performance effects of business process reengineering: A firm-level analysis. *Journal of Management Information Systems*, 27(4), 129–162.

Becker, M. C. (2004). Organizational routines: A review of the literature. *Industrial and Corporate Change*, 13(4), 643–677.

Berente, N., Lyytinen, K., Yoo, Y. and King, J. L. (2016). Routines as shock absorbers during organizational transformation: Integration, control, and NASA' s Enterprise Information System. *Organization Science*, 27(3), 551–572.

Berente, N., Seidel, S. and Safadi, H. (2019). Data-driven computationally-intensive theory development. *Information Systems Research*, 30(1), iii–viii.

Beverungen, D. (2014). Exploring the interplay of the design and emergence of business processes as organizational routines. *Business & Information Systems Engineering*, 6(4), 191–202.

Birnholtz, J. P., Cohen, M. D. and Hoch, S. V. (2007). Organizational character: On the regeneration of Camp Poplar Grove. *Organization Science*, 18(2), 315–332.

Bose, R. P. J. C., van Der Aalst, W. M. P., Žliobaite, I. and Pechenizkiy, M. (2011). Handling concept drift in process mining. *Lecture Notes in Computer Science (Including Subseries Lecture Notes in Artificial Intelligence and Lecture Notes in Bioinformatics), 6741 LNCS*, 391–405.

Bucher, S. and Langley, A. (2016). The interplay of reflective and experimental spaces in interrupting and reorienting Routine Dynamics. *Organization Science*, 27(3), 594–613.

D'Adderio, L. (2011). Artifacts at the centre of routines: Performing the material turn in routines theory. *Journal of Institutional Economics*, 7(2), 197–230.

Dittrich, K., Guérard, S. and Seidl, D. (2016). Talking about routines: The role of reflective talk in routine change. *Organization Science*, 27(3), 678–697.

Dittrich, K. and Seidl, D. (2018). Emerging intentionality in routine dynamics: A pragmatist view. *Academy of Management Journal*, 61(1), 111–138.

Dumas, M., La Rosa, M., Mendling, J. and Reijers, H. A. (2018). *Fundamentals of Business Process Management*, 2nd ed. Heidelberg: Springer.

Feldman, M. S. and Pentland, B. T. (2003). Reconceptualizing organizational routines as a source of flexibility and change. *Administrative Science Quarterly*, 48(1), 94–118.

Feldman, M. S., Pentland, B. T., D'Adderio, L. and Lazaric, N. (2016). Beyond routines as things: Introduction to the special issue on Routine Dynamics. *Organization Science*, 27(3), 505–513.

Figl, K., Mendling, J. and Strembeck, M. (2013). The influence of notational deficiencies on process model comprehension. *Journal of the Association of Information Systems*, 14(6), 312–338.

Gaskin, J., Berente, N., Lyytinen, K. and Yoo, Y. (2014). Toward generalizable sociomaterial inquiry: A computational approach for zooming in and out of sociomaterial routines. *Management Information Systems Quarterly*, 38(3), 849–871.

Goh, K. T. and Pentland, B.T. (2019). From actions to paths to patterning: Toward a dynamic theory of patterning in routines. *Academy of Management Journal*, 62(6), 1901–1929.

Gonzalez-Lopez, F. and Bustos, G. (2019). Business process architecture design methodologies: A literature review. *Business Process Management Journal*, 25(6), 1317–1334.

Grisold, T., Wurm, B., Mendling, J. and vom Brocke, J. (2020). Using process mining to support theorizing about change in organizations. In *53rd Hawaiian International Conference on System Sciences (HICSS 2020)*.

Grover, V., Teng, J., Segars, A. H. and Fiedler, K. (1998). The influence of information technology diffusion and business process change on perceived productivity: The IS executive's perspective. *Information & Management*, 34(3), 141–159.

Habermas, J. (1984). *The Theory of Communicative Action*. Boston: Beacon Press.

Hammer, M. and Champy, J. (1993). *Reengineering the Corporation: A Manifesto for Business Revolution*. New York: HarperCollins.

Hompes, B. F. A., Buijs, J., van der Aalst, W. M. P., Dixit, P. M. and Buurman, J. (2015). Discovering Deviating cases and process variants using trace clustering. In *27th Benelux Conference on Artificial Intelligence (BNAIC)*.

Howard-Grenville, J. and Rerup, C. (2017). A process perspective on organizational routines. In A. Langley and H. Tsoukas, eds., *The Sage Handbook of Process Organization Studies*. Los Angeles, London, New Delhi, Singapore,Washington DC, Melbourne: Sage, pp. 323–339.

Kettinger, W. J., Teng, J. T. C. and Guha, S. (1997). Business process change: A study of methodologies, techniques, and tools. *MIS Quartely*, 21(1), 55–80.

Kremser, W. and Schreyögg, G. (2016). The dynamics of interrelated routines: Introducing the cluster level. *Organization Science*, 27, 698–721.

Kuhn, T. (1970). *The Structure of Scientific Revolutions*, 2nd ed. Chicago: University of Chicago Press.

Kummer, T. F., Recker, J. and Mendling, J. (2016). Enhancing understandability of process models through cultural-dependent color adjustments. *Decision Support Systems*, 87, 1–12.

Laguna, M. and Marklund, J. (2013). *Business Process Modeling, Simulation and Design*. Boca Raton, FL: CRC Press.

Leonardi, P. M. (2011). When flexible routines meet flexible technologies: Affordance, constraint, and the imbrication of human and material agencies. *MIS Quarterly*, 35(1), 147–167.

Lindberg, A., Berente, N., Gaskin, J. and Lyytinen, K. (2016). Coordinating interdependencies in online communities: A study of an open source software project. *Information Systems Research*, 27(4), 751–772.

Mendling, J. (2016). From scientific process management to process science: Towards an empirical research agenda for Business Process Management. In C. Hochreiner and S. Schulte, (eds.), *8th ZEUS Workshop (ZEUS 2016)*.

Mendling, J., Berente, N., Seidel, S. and Grisold, T. (2021). Pluralism and pragmatism in the information systems field: The case of research on business processes and organizational routines. *The Data Base for Advances in Information Systems*, 52(2), 127–140.

Miller, K. D., Pentland, B. T. and Choi, S. (2012). Dynamics of performing and remembering organizational routines. *Journal of Management Studies*, 49(8), 1536–1558.

Orlikowski, W. J. and Scott, S. V (2008). Sociomateriality: Challenging the separation of technology, work and organizing. *The Academy of Management Annals*, 2(1), 433–474.

Pentland, B. T. and Feldman, M. S. (2005). Organizational routines as a unit of analysis. *Industrial and Corporate Change*, 14(5), 793–815.

Pentland, B. T. and Feldman, M. S. (2008). Designing routines: On the folly of designing artifacts, while hoping for patterns of action. *Information and Organization*, 18(4), 235–250.

Pentland, B. T. and Rueter, H. H. (1994). Organizational routines as grammars of action. *Administrative Science Quarterly*, 39(3), 484–510.

Pentland, B. T., Vaast, E. and Wolf, R. (2021). Theorizing process dynamics with directed graphs: A diachronic analysis of digital trace data. *MIS Quartely*, 45(2), 967–984.

Polyvyanyy, A., Solti, A., Weidlich, M., Di Ciccio, C. and Mendling, J. (2018). Behavioural quotients for precision and recall in process mining. *Technical Report*, (March), 1–19.

Recker, J. (2014). Suggestions for the next wave of BPM research: Strengthening the theoretical core and exploring the protective belt. *Journal of Information Technology Theory and Application*, 15(2), 5–20.

Recker, J. (2015). Evidence-based Business Process Management: Using digital opportunities to drive organizational innovation. In J. vom Brocke and T. Schmiedel, eds., *BPM-Driving Innovation in a Digital World*. Cham: Springer, pp. 129–143.

Recker, J. and Mendling, J. (2016). The state of the art of Business Process Management research as published in the BPM Conference: Recommendations for progressing the field. *Business & Information Systems Engineering*, 58(1), 55–72.

Reijers, H. A. and Mansar, L. S. (2005). Best practices in business process redesign: An overview and qualitative evaluation of successful redesign heuristics. *Omega*, 33(4), 283–306.

Rosemann, M. and vom Brocke, J. (2010). The six core elements of Business Process Management. In J. vom Brocke and M. Rosemann, eds., *Handbook on Business Process Management 1*. Berlin; Heidelberg: Springer, pp. 107–122.

Speer, S. A. (2002). 'Natural' and 'contrived' data: a sustainable distinction? *Discourse Studies*, 4(4), 511–525.

Tsoukas, H. and Chia, R. (2002). On organizational becoming: Rethinking organizational change. *Organization Science*, 13(5), 567–582.

Turner, S. F. and Rindova, V. P. (2018). Watching the clock: Action timing, patterning, and routine performance. *Academy of Management Journal*, 61(4), 1253–1280.

van der Aalst, W. M. P. (2002). Making work flow: On the application of Petri Nets to Business Process Management. In J. Esparza and C. Lakos,eds., *Application and Theory of Petri Nets 2002. ICATPN 2002. Lecture Notes in Computer Science*, Vol. 2360. Berlin, Heidelberg: Springer, pp. 1–22.

van der Aalst, W. M. P. (2011). *Process Mining: Discovery, Conformance and Enhancement of Business Processes*, 2nd ed. Heidelberg: Springer.

van der Aalst, W. M. P. (2013). Business Process Management: A Comprehensive Survey. *ISRN Software Engineering*, 1–37.

van der Aalst, W. M. P., Adriansyah, A., De Medeiros, A. K. A., Arcieri, F., Baier, T., Blickle, T. . . . Wynn, M. (2011). Process mining manifesto. In *Proceedings of the 9th International Conference on Business Process Management (BPM 2011)* (pp. 169–194).

van der Aalst, W. M. P., ter Hofstede, A. H.and Weske, M. (2003). Business Process Management: A Survey. In *International Conference on Business Process Management (BPM 2003)*.

Volkoff, O., Strong, D. M. and Elmes, M. B. (2007). Technological embeddedness and organizational change. *Organization Science*, 18(5), 832–848.

vom Brocke, J. and Mendling, J., eds. (2018). *Business Process Management Cases*. Cham: Springer International Publishing.

vom Brocke, J., Zelt, S. and Schmiedel, T. (2016). On the role of context in Business Process Management. *International Journal of Information Management*, 36(3), 486–495.

Wurm, B. (2018). Patterns of stability and change in business processes. In *Proceedings of the 9th International Workshop on Enterprise Modeling and Information Systems Architectures (EMISA 2018)*, pp. 21–28.

Wurm, B., Goel, K., Bandara, W. and Rosemann, M. (2019). Design patterns for business process individualization. In *17th International Conference on Business Process Management (BPM 2019)*, pp. 370–385.

Wurm, B., Schmiedel, T., Mendling, J. and Fleig, C. (2018). Development of a Measurement Scale for Business Process Standardization. In *26th European Conference on Information Systems (ECIS 2018)*.

Yeshchenko, A., Di Ciccio, C., Mendling, J. and Polyvyanyy, A. (2019). Comprehensive process drift detection with visual analytics. In A. Laender, B. Pernici, E. Lim and J. de Oliveira, eds., *International Conference on Conceptual Modeling (ER 2019). Lecture Notes in Computer Science*, vol. 11788. Cham: Springer, pp. 119–135.

Author Index

Subject Index